DEVIANT BEHAVIOR

DEVIANT BEHAVIOR

Readings in the Sociology of Norm Violations

Edited by

Clifton D. Bryant

Department of Sociology
Virginia Polytechnic Institute and State University
Blacksburg, Virginia

HEMISPHERE PUBLISHING CORPORATION
A member of the Taylor & Francis Group
New York Washington Philadelphia London

This volume is affectionately dedicated to the memory of Edward Sagarin.

The author thanks Xiang Chen and Li Li for their invaluable assistance with the indexing of this volume.

DEVIANT BEHAVIOR: Readings in the Sociology of Norm Violations

1 2 3 4 5 6 7 8 9 0   E B E B   8 9 8 7 6 5 4 3 2 1 0 9

This book was set in Times Roman by Sans Serif, Inc. The editors were Amy Lyles Wilson, Linda Lee Stringer, and Barbara Bodling.
Cover design by Sharon Martin DePass.
Edwards Brothers, Inc. was printer and binder.

Library of Congress Cataloging-in-Publication Data

Deviant behavior : readings in the sociology of norm violations /
edited by Clifton D. Bryant.
p. cm.
Includes index.

1. Deviant Behavior. I. Bryant, Clifton D., 1932- .
HM291.D4847 1989
302.5′42—dc20   89-32932
CIP

ISBN 0-89116-696-3 (cloth)
ISBN 0-89116-779-X (paper)

Contents

PART 3 DEVIANCE: CULTURAL PATTERNS

PART 4 DEVIANCE AS BEHAVIOR

PART 5 DEVIANCE: EXITS AND TRANSFORMATIONS

PART 6 THE FUTURE OF DEVIANCE: PROSPECTS AND PROGNOSIS

Preface

The journal *Deviant Behavior* was founded more than a decade ago. It was to be unique in that it was to be the only extant journal that addressed the topic of social deviance specifically and exclusively. It succeeded in that purpose and remains today the sole professional journal totally devoted to that theme. Over the years various issues have contained articles on a wide variety of deviant behavioral patterns as well as theoretical, methodological, or conceptual issues. The articles have evidently been both insightful and utilitarian to many social scientists inasmuch as many have been cited in numerous books and journals and, according to reports from professional colleagues around the country, have been used for pedagogical purposes in courses such as deviant behavior and criminology, to mention two. It was this latter utility that was the progenesis of this volume.

Because various issues of the journal have contained so many articles that were revealing, intuitive, and imaginatively instructive in illuminating the deviant segment of the human social enterprise, it seemed a shame that they were not more readily available to students for classroom use. Thus, the decision was made to assemble a representative sample of articles into an integrated anthology that would address the major dimensions of social deviance. The resulting anthology was to be something of a showcase volume for the journal, presenting some of its best articles.

This volume contains a comprehensive set of readings that examine the full range of pedogogical concerns in the area of deviant behavior. Additionally, each set of readings is introduced, examined, and connected by appropriate editorial commentary.

The volume begins with an editorial introduction to the concepts of social norms, sanctions, the process of social control, and the deviant violation of social norms. Chapter 2 addresses the form and content of deviance. Deviance research and understanding are the subject of Chapter 3. Chapter 4 examines the social interpretation and reaction to deviance. Chapter 5 explores the cultural patterns of deviance and Chapter 6 the social organization of the deviant world. Chapter 7 addresses the way in which deviants adapt to their particular situations. In Chapter 8, deviance is investigated as different types of social interaction and in Chapter 9 as a social process with an outcome. Chapter 10 focuses on deviance in the workplace to demonstrate how deviance is frequently imbedded in a larger social process—in this case the work setting. Chapter 11 looks at the process of discontinuing or withdrawing from deviance and returning to more conformist behavior. Chapter 12 concludes the book with an editorial assessment of what the future may hold for normative systems, social sanctions, deviant behavior patterns, and the social reaction to deviance.

Although this book is titled *Deviant Behavior,* the subtitle is *Readings in the Sociology of Norm Violation.* The words *norm violation* were specially chosen inasmuch as deviance at its simplest operational level can be defined as the violation of social rules or norms. By focusing on the process of norm violation—regardless of whether such behavioral vagarancies actually constitute crimes, social problems, socially dysfunctional behavior, or a manifestation of aberrant inclinations—any judgmental or idiosyncratic bias is, I hope, avoided. Deviant behavior is, indeed, relative, and in the land of the blind the sighted person is not only king but a deviant as well!

Although there are a number of anthologies on deviant behavior in print and frequently used in sociology courses, I believe this volume has several advantages. All of the readings from the issues of *Deviant Behavior* are relatively new (from the 1980s), are fresh, and, with few exceptions, have not appeared in other anthologies. Some edited volumes have articles that date back decades, and many of the readings in such anthologies have been recycled numerous times. All of the readings in the present volume were selected with an eye toward readability and student appeal. Rather than simply being a collated set of disparate articles, these readings are integrated into a well-structured conceptual framework—articulated and discussed, along with the articles, in the editorial commentaries. Many theoretical postures, methodological approaches, and substantive content are explored in the readings. Various deviance-related issues also are examined. Such a package will, I hope, provide a provocative, insightful, and thoughtful consideration of deviant behavior. I believe that you, too, will find this collection of readings to be both engaging and informative.

This anthology was originally to have been a coedited project. Edward Sagarin, a member of *Deviant Behavior's* Editorial Policy Board since its founding, was to have been my coeditor. We worked together on the idea for, and the structure of, the volume and had formally proposed the notion to Hemisphere Publishing Corporation. Tragically, Dr. Sagarin died suddenly before we could finalize plans for the book. Ed was very enthusiastic about the enterprise, and its thus seems appropriate to dedicate the book to his memory. I have been severely handicapped in writing the editorial exposition in that whatever I have said he could have said better and in a more organized fashion. Dr. Sagarin made a significant contribution to the original conceptual planning of the book. The book's defects and shortcomings are entirely mine, however.

Dr. Dan Dotter of Grambling University carefully reviewed draft chapters of the editorial commentaries and made many helpful suggestions, for which he is sincerely thanked. Ms. Pat Baker worked long and hard, "above and beyond the call of duty," typing original drafts and revised versions of the chapters, preparing articles, and organizing the materials to be sent to the publisher. This process was made more difficult by the fact that I was in Taiwan on a Fulbright grant during the 1987–1988 academic year while she was in the United States, and communication was very much long distance. She is entitled to a large measure of gratitude for her efforts. I also thank Ms. Cindy Crawford and Ms. Machell Schmolitz for typing some of the editorial material. Ms. Sherri L. McGuyer, my summer secretary, handled correspondence concerning the book and also typed some of the editorial material. Finally, my wife, Patty Bryant, is due a special debt of gratitude for her tireless work in typing drafts in the muggy heat of Taipei for transmission back to the United States.

Clifton D. Bryant

Part One

Introducing Deviance

Chapter One

The Social Context

EDITORIAL COMMENTARY

All living creatures live according to "rules" and "laws." The simpler animals behave in accordance with "laws" created and enforced by nature. Their compliance is constituent to their biological nature. They are physiologically "programmed," as it were. Fish, for example, often move in tremendous groupings known as "schools." As they swim in these schools, they move and turn, seemingly in almost perfect unison with every dart and dive synchronized simultaneously among all who make up the school. Compliance with the "traffic rules" is accomplished by means of ultra sensitivity to water pressure and electrochemical signals among the fish, and their programmed biological response.

The animals higher on the phylogenic ladder, such as the mammals, are also genetically programmed to respond to the laws of nature but they have somewhat more behavioral latitude in how they carry out the biological mandates. The exercise of "territoriality," for instance, is characteristic of many species of fish, birds, and animals. In effect, the creatures must compete for a certain amount of space and territory if they and their offspring are to survive. Among mammals (and other species as well) it's the male that defends the area and his mate. This competition for real estate is a survival mechanism, and the territorial instinct and sexual appetite are "profoundly intermeshed" as some writers (Audrey, 1966) have pointed out. In many species, the female is unresponsive to an "unpropertied" male (Audrey, 1966:3). Nature, thus, discourages the reproduction of offspring where there are not sufficient resources to sustain them. Within the framework of this natural instinct the individual animals may sometimes exercise this territorial imperative in a somewhat idiosyncratic fashion. They may be more or less aggressive than other similar animals of the same species in defending their territory and herein lies the mechanism of "selection of the fittest." There are also non-biological dimensions to such behavior in that one wire-haired terrier may be ferociously aggressive in defending his "turf"—his owner's yard and surroundings—while another may be almost passive. The ways in which the respective dogs are raised, their relationship with their owner, and other "social" factors, in addition to differential hormonal considerations, may impact on their behavior. The higher animals, then, may behave somewhat differently on an individual basis in complying with the rules of nature.

Humans, like other animals, also have some biological programming, but much more limited in extent. They experience physiological disequilibrium in the form of the hunger drive and the sex drive, to mention some biological imperatives. How they respond to these biological mandates is socially determined. Everyone becomes hungry, but how, what, and when this hunger is assuaged, is usually a function of the society in which one lives, the culture of that society, and the social beliefs and rules of eating and nutrition that are component to the culture.

HUMANS AND THE SOCIAL ORDER

Beyond the biological drives, and the responses to these drives that are socially shaped, humans have the need to coordinate their behavior if they are to successfully live together in a social group. To this end, they effect rules—or norms of behavior. This can be simply demonstrated by an attempt of two (or more) individuals to occupy a small, potentially unstable boat. They must immediately determine which part of the boat each is to occupy and agree on that placement. Beyond this, they must establish precautionary measures such as not leaning out too far beyond the boat, and certainly not both (or all) doing so at the same time (so as not to capsize), as well as procedures for propelling the boat, such as who will steer, who will row, who will row on one side and who will row on the other, etc. Failure to perfect rules to accomplish these things may well cause the boat to sink, or at least sit still in the water with no purposive direction. In this instance, then, to be successful in sharing the boat and making it go somewhere, there must be rules and agreement to abide by the rules (and, of course, compliance).

Other more complicated social situations require a more complex set of rules. Two or more individuals attempting to live together in a room or an apartment have to quickly establish rules. Who lives in which bedroom? Who sleeps in which bed? At what time is it necessary to turn down the volume of the radio or television at night in order that the other(s) may go to sleep? How are the rent, utilities, food costs, and other expenses to be shared? Who cooks, who washes dishes, who cleans up, and when, how often, etc., etc., etc.? Rules concerning the bathroom may be especially important because of differential time schedules of the occupants. One person may have to leave for work earlier. Here again, to successfully share the apartment, the occupants will have to establish rules, and then agree to abide by the rules (and, of course, comply with the rules).

Where a group of individuals is shipwrecked, and then marooned on a desert island, there will obviously be a need for a prompt institution of a relatively complex set of rules if the group is, indeed, going to enjoy any prospect of survival. The complex rules will probably include a division of labor, some form of group decision making and a means of enforcing those decisions, and the development of a collective goal supported by all. There will also be a need for establishment of appropriate proscriptions and prescriptions for the more routine day-to-day activities as well as guidelines for interpersonal interaction. Only in this way could the group accomplish to provide for the needs of its members and either survive until rescued, or until a means of escape could be devised, constructed and implemented.

In all of these examples, the boat "crew," the roommates, or the castaway group, what would be needed is a preordained organization of behavior— "a social order." Societies, small or large, have the same need or problem. In order to exist and endure—to survive—a social order must be established and enforced.

THE ORIGIN OF A SOCIAL ORDER

A social order, in the form of a set or system of rules or social norms comes about in various ways. Laws and rules may be instituted or declared by fiat on the part of some hereditary rules, king, or chieftain (i.e., "the divine right of kings") or by a charismatic leader, on the basis of being omniscient as well as omnipotent. They may also be issued by persons occupying positions of high hierarchical status on the basis of the authority vested in the position, ("standing" orders or procedures, or "orders of the day" as issued by the Captain of a ship, or the Commanding General of a military base), or their assumed technical expertise (some regulation promulgated by the Director of some federal agency or bureau). Laws, rules, or instructions can even emanate from entities in other worlds—deities, the dead, spirits, or supernatural force, to mention but some. Enactments based on pronouncements, messages, or signs from such entities, of course, need an agent, intermediary, or emissary, such as a religious leader, who has "divine guidance," (a Pope, for example), a medium through whom the dead speak, a witch doctor, oracle, soothsayer, or diviner, who can interpret signs and unnatural events. Moses received the golden tablets directly from God and transported them back down the mountain to instruct the Israelites. Joseph Smith accomplished much the same when he dictated the Book of Mormon directly from the golden plates. Medicine men or witch doctors may have visions that serve as communications from the gods or the dead. Oracles may interpret storms, or earthquakes, or the eruptions of volcanoes as particular mandates of deities or supernatural forces for specific behavioral responses on the part of humans.

Laws and rules may also come from less divine or regal sources. Behavioral instructions in the forms of legislation, statutes, or ordinances, may be issued by a tribal council of elders, a board of aldermen, a school board, a group of city commissioners, a church synod, board of elders, or a regulatory agency. They may emanate from more of a "grassroots" level social entity such as a town meeting of citizens, the vote of a church congregation, a national plebiscite on some issue, a student body referendum, a union balloting, the showing of hands at a neighborhood association meeting, or simply, the consensus of the members of a 2-table bridge group, a small bird-watcher's club, or a slum street gang.

All such rules—be they by-laws, directives, ordinances, laws, codes, or regulations—serve to guide and direct some aspect of social behavior. In effect, they proscribe (prohibit) or prescribe (advocate) certain conduct, and also circumscribe and dictate the circumstances, conditions, contingencies, and contexts of such conduct. The rules are usually linked to some attendant sanctions— punishments and/or rewards to motivate compliance. In a society (or even on a smaller scale such as a community) there are many entities that issue or promulgate rules. Denominational bodies and local churches formulate rules regarding both religious behavior and religious thought in the form of theology (Catholics, for example, are expected to participate in the Sacrament of Reconciliation at regular intervals, and must believe in the Immaculate Conception and the Holy Trinity, as items of faith). States legally require that children attend school until a particular age, school boards issue directives concerning educational policy, and local school administrations create day-to-day rules for the conduct of classes, and the behavior of students. The U.S. government, through its Department of Labor, has developed a complex set of safety rules for the work place, which are administered and monitored by its subsidiary Occupational Health and Safety Administration. Most counties have a health board or health agency which institutes health rules for persons involved in food preparation (appropriate medical tests for cooks, for example), and standards of cleanliness and sanitation for establishments that serve food (periodic checks for insects, rodents, unsanitary conditions in the kitchen, etc.). States, counties, or cities may have fire codes which specify standards of safety in regard to fire hazards, and "Fire Marshalls" to enforce them. Contractors, carpenters, plumbers, and electricians, to name but some craftsmen, are subject to a wide variety of building codes in the construction of a house, or the installation of electrical wiring, appliances, plumbing fixtures, or additions or modifications to an existing structure. The use of certain types of wiring, pipes, electrical outlets, or building materials may be required for safety and aesthetic reasons. Individuals are subject to rules when they drive their automobile (traffic laws and ordinances), are usually required to carry liability insurance on their automobiles, and are subject to a number of rules and requirements in acquiring and using a driver's license. The Federal Aeronautics Administration lays down numerous rules and regulations in regard to qualifying for a pilot's license, the maintenance of airplanes, and the process of flying on an airplane itself. The Federal Communications Commission regulates the acquisition of a license to operate a shortwave radio, and the operation of a radio or television station as well. Farmers, ranchers, and dairymen are all subject to rules and controls imposed by the U.S. Department of Agriculture in connection with raising crops, livestock, and producing milk. Food processors are similarly regulated and controlled. Persons who hunt and fish for sport, or fish and gather shellfish commercially are subject to a number of rules (game and fish laws). The conduct of recreation and sport is subject to many rules, ranging from boating (Coast Guard or various state safety and boating regulations) to playing board games (all played according to historical and traditional rules), to organized sports (which are played not only according to traditional rules, but also governed by league, and conference rules).

Marriage, the family, and the behavior of members of the family are all subject to social rules that include state control of requirements for obtaining a license to marry, the specification of conditions for the dissolution of marriage (divorce laws) to the control of the behavior of husband and wife in a marriage (domestic relations laws). The list of formal rules impinging on social behavior is almost endless and could go on for volumes. Beyond the formal rules are the vast array of informal rules that operate within all sorts of formal and informal groups and settings, and the variety of societal values and attitudes that specify a preference for a particular kind of thought, action, or feeling. According to prevailing societal values, one *should* feel patriotic when the flag passes by, or sad when it is learned that a relative has died. It is *better* to be honest rather than be dishonest, truthful rather than tell a falsehood, and to be altruistic rather than to be selfish. It may be customary for a group of factory workers to stop at a particular bar close to the factory when they get off work and to have a few beers. The worker who might have another preference for place or activity would find himself under considerable pressure to "follow the crowd." The individual discovers that he or she is subject to informal rules that exist within the family, among neighbors, within the church congregation, between friends, among office workers, fellow students, or military servicemen in the same unit, or among fellow participants in a wide variety of leisure activities, to name but some.

In short, the individual lives in a world of rules—a veritable "jungle" of rules—as it were, all supported by sanctions of one kind or another to motivate compliance with the rules. Most rules are assumed to specify behavior that is correct, appropriate, timely, and desirable and, thus, that which is "normal." The rules of normality are, then, what people ought to or should be doing. From these assumptions is derived the term "norm" to generically encompass all of the rules, regulations, laws, statutes, ordinances, and preferences discussed above. The term "norm" would seem to suggest a modal frequency or form of behavior but such is not the case. The social "norms" are ideal statements of specified behavior but, in reality, in many instances only a minority of the members of a society may conform to many norms. Nevertheless, because it is felt that the norms proscribe or prescribe that which is socially desirable (even at an ideal level), the norms are theoretically enforced even if only a small percentage of the public is inclined to so behave. The multitude of norms in a society, plus the attendant motivational mechanisms for compliance, then make up "social order."

THE FORMS OF NORMS AND THE MORAL ORDER

Social norms vary greatly in terms of the types of behavior that they are designed to govern or control. At the level of least social consequence are the norms pertaining to relatively mundane and regular, everyday, conduct. These norms are known as *folkways* (Sumner, 1906). Folkways are rules governing behavior of no great social import or consequences. Such behavior is often grouped into subsystems with distinctive names or labels. Included in such behavior might be the norms pertaining to eating (table manners), the norms governing language usage (correct grammar), or the norms governing appropriate interactional behavior (manners or the "social graces"). We speak of being considerate of others in our interaction such as saying "thanks," or "excuse me," or "I'm pleased to meet you," etc. as politeness or civility. Chivalry refers to the norms of solicitous and helpful behavior toward women, children, and the elderly. Etiquette encompasses the norms such as sending "thank you" notes to acknowledge gifts, sending letters of condolence to acquaintances who have had family members die, or introducing a friend to a person who joins the group. Clothing and personal neatness norms may be subsumed under "good grooming." All of these and thousands of other commonplace behaviors, ranging from covering one's mouth when yawning to conversing softly and minimizing speech while in a library, to being punctual for an appointment, would all quality as folkways. Folkways seldom have severe sanctions, and violators of such norms are generally not severely sanctioned. The folkways are not considered to be of great social consequence because it is believed that even in the face of massive violations of such norms, the existence and continuation of society would not be imperiled. In short, violation of the folkways might make for a less efficient or a more disagreeable society, but does not pose a real threat to the social fabric of life.

Folkways are of two varieties, the interactive folkways, and the technical folkway (Bryant, 1984: 118–124). Interactive folkways refer to "the normative behavior patterns constituent to social interaction such as polite address, appropriate gestures, and conversational propriety." Technical folkways, on the other hand are rules or requirements regarding the selection of certain tools or implements to accomplish a particular task, and the utilization of these tools or implements in a specific fashion or manner. As with social behavior, we are constrained to use designated tools and implements and in a socially indicated manner, as well as specified techniques and procedures. There are sanctions attendant to the technical folkways as well as the interactive folkways. An example of a technical folkway might be the cultural specification for eating with a particular set of implements (chopsticks, perhaps). Beyond the selection of particular implements is the questions of how the implements are to be used. Americans cut meat by holding the fork in the left hand and the knife in the right hand, making the cut and then putting down the knife and transferring the fork from the left hand to the right hand before using it to spear the meat portion and move it to the mouth. The English and other Europeans begin the same way but do not transfer the fork from one have to another. Instead, they simply keep the fork in the left hand after cutting, and move the meat portion to the mouth with the fork in the left hand. Other technical folkways might be the use of a particular "traditional" recipe to cook certain foods, or writing from a specified side of the page to the other (such as here in the U.S. writing from the left to the right). One technical folkway may actually dictate another. Japanese saws are made in such a way that they cut on the pull stroke as opposed to American saws that cut on the push stroke. The Japanese by virtue of being constrained to select that particular type of saw as being the appropriate tool are also mechanically constrained to cut wood with a pull stroke on the saw which in turn produces a fine cut better suited for meticulous joinery work. There are sanctions for violation of technical folkways as well as interactive folkways. A person who attempted to eat the vegetables on his plate with a spoon rather than a fork would likely be laughed at by his table companions. Likewise an individual who made a very traditional food dish using a totally inappropriate recipe would be subject to criticism and ridicule. In some instances, however, the violation of a technical folkway could invoke a formal sanction. Failure to wear the legally prescribed seat belt when driving or riding in the front seat of an automobile, in some states, could mean a fine of $75.00 or more. The violation of some OSHA regulations in the workplace could likewise bring a heavy fine on the owner of the business.

The term *mores* refers to norms that are considered essential to the existence of social life and the continuation of society. Violations of the mores are seen as serious offenses and usually sanctioned severely. Members of society tend to feel very strongly about mores and public compliance with them while, on the other hand, there is usually a low intensity of feeling about the folkways and their violation. Examples of mores would be the prohibition against murder and theft, and the obligation to be loyal to one's country rather than betray it to an enemy nation, and to nurture and protect one's children. If murder and theft were not prohibited and severely sanctioned, individuals would not feel safe leaving their home lest they fall prey to killers and robbers, and social life as we know it would be impossible. Similarly a nation that was betrayed by its citizens could not prevail. Where people routinely mistreated, neglected, brutalized, or abandoned their children, family life could not exist, and children could not grow into healthy, mature, responsible, and productive adults to carry on social life. Understandably, the mores are viewed as essential to society and its members. Aside from prohibitions against murder and theft, perhaps the most socially controlled area of human behavior is sexual behavior. Sexual norms of a wide and complex variety carefully define and circumscribe what is believed to be "proper" and "natural" sexual behavior. Uncontrolled sexual behavior is believed to be especially disruptive to social life. Accordingly, violations of the norms, such as sexual violence, homosexual or other "unnatural" sexual activity, the production or consumption of pornography, or sex with a child are all seen as serious threats (albeit to differing degrees) to social life. Furthermore society harbors strong beliefs that marriage and family stability, and the ability to successfully rear children in the family are all essential to the continuity of social life and that they are only possible where sexual behavior is carefully regulated and controlled. Adultery or incest then would pose a hazard to the stability of marriage and the family.

Where social norms, folkways and mores become formalized to the extent of being enacted as legislation or ordinances and enforced with equally formalized sanctions, we speak of them as *laws*. The enactment of a norm into law is not directly related to the socially perceived seriousness of the violation. One may, for example, see signs in a post office or courthouse in some rural communities admonishing the citizenry not to spit on the walls and indicating that a legal fine may be levied if they do. It may be, however, that some social norms perceived as far more serious, will not be formulated as law, nor will there be a legal sanction.

Where behavior has simply evolved into a normative pattern over a period of time, we may label it as a *custom*. If the custom is widely recognized and if there is either some personal compulsion to continue it, or public encouragement to comply with the norm, it may come to be termed a *tradition*. Social norms and their compliance are not value free. We may view the compliance with some regulatory norm, perhaps such as a city ordinance to only water lawns after 6:00 p.m. for conservation purposes, as essentially a matter of practicality but attach little emotional meaning to the norm or its enforcement. There is, however, often very deep emotional content to many norms, and few norms without some intensity of feeling.

As a case in point, many people tend to drive particular "paths" as they travel about in their community. An individual may come to drive from home to town and back using a particular route. Over a period of time this become the routine route. The choice of the route can be said to have become *habituated*. The individual's wife may have used a different route to drive to town and back home and her route may have also become *habituated*. Both now have come to think of their route as the best, the proper, and the appropriate route to take and may even rationalize the habituated route as the shortest, the quickest, the safest, or whatever. One day the wife rides with the husband to town and he takes his habituated route. The wife becomes distressed because he is not taking the "proper or appropriate" route and criticizes his choice of a route as imprudent. Both husband and wife have developed and emotional involvement in their respective routes. Where many members of a society (or a community) come to attach emotional meaning to a particular habituated pattern of behavior, it is said to have become institutionalized. They feel that the behavior is correct and proper, and perhaps even "normal." That particular behavior becomes valued and those members of society defend it, believe in it, and sometimes try to persuade everyone to support or engage in it to the extent of making it a norm with strong sanctions. It may be that those who bring about the norm are not necessarily in the majority, but are in a position to force their perspectives on others. Antipornography ordinances have often been enacted because of pressure from a limited segment of the population, and the ordinances may tend to reflect the views of those who were responsible for their enactment in terms of what is defined by them as pornographic. Western Missionaries in some folk societies have sought to change the sexual patterns of the native peoples in the belief that their traditional sexual behavior was not "natural" or "proper." Instead, they often attempted to encourage Western sexual patterns in such matters as coital position with particular preference for what the natives laughingly called the "missionary position."

Institutionalization does only come about through the development of ego involvement in a habituated pattern of behavior. In the process of rationalizing certain conduct as preferential or desired, members of a society may attribute ethnocentric, theological, or even magical importance to such behavior. Thus, we may come to view certain behavior as being the "American" way and alternate or contrary behavior as "unAmerican." Similarly, folk or primitive people may say that particular behavior is correct because it is ordained by the gods, or spirits, or other supernatural forces and to violate the norms proscribing such behavior is to invite bad luck or go against the wishes of the gods, etc. Very frequently, certain behavioral norms are rationalized as being consistent with or supported by religious ideology and posture. Thus, compliance with some norms comes to be viewed as the "Christian way" or the "moral way." The norm now takes on religious and moral significance, and assumes a position of right or wrong, with very strong emotional sentiments attached to compliance with the norms and to the sanctions to enforce them.

Sanctions may be formal (imprisonment) or informal (being ridiculed), may be severe (capital punishment) or of minor consequence (a $2.00 parking ticket), may be symbolic (wearing a dunce cap) or real (a jail term), positive (a reward) or negative (a punishment), and applied in this world (trial, conviction, and punishment) or in the next ("burn in hell"). The norms may be enforced in many ways, including educating people in such a way that they are indoctrinated with the norms to the point of internalizing them (socialization). Compliance with the norms is often brought about by the presence of sanctions. Sometimes, compliance with the norms can be "engineered" by such means as removing or minimizing the opportunity structure for violation (sometimes, for example, vehicle traffic is made to go only one way by the expedience of imbedding spikes in the pavement that can be safely rolled over while traveling in the indicated direction, but will puncture tires when travel in the opposite direction is attempted. Finally, continuing pressure for conformity is exerted through a variety of means ranging from public sentiment to moral values and attitudes to the informal influence of pressure groups such as peers, friends, neighbors and fellow workers.

Thus, the complexity of norms extant in a society emanating from many different groups and segments combine to create a *social order*—the existing system of social relations, and the attendant equilibrium of interaction and social behavior. The norms which make up the social order are supported and enforced by a variety of processes and mechanisms which encourage conformity to and identification with the social order, which is known as social control. Inasmuch as the social order is often imbued with ethical, ethnocentric, and even theological content, it becomes a heavily value laden system of rules with a high degree of emotional intensity involved in bringing about compliance with the norms. In this sense, the social order becomes a moral order.

NONCOMPLIANCE AND REJECTION OF THE MORAL ORDER

When and if an individual conforms to the norms, society provides a number of positive labels or identities. At an informal level we may speak of a husband as a good provider, a faithful, industrious wife, a dutiful son or daughter, a studious pupil, tax-paying citizen, hard-working employee, brave soldier, dedicated doctor, pious minister, honest merchant, passionate lover, safe driver, good sportsman, or meticulous craftsman, to name but some. At a formal level, society and the groups that make it up provide numerous positive sanctions for compliance with the norms. Students with the highest grade average are identified as Class Valedictorian and get to give the Commencement Address. Soldiers may receive a Good Conduct Medal. A successful real estate agent may be inducted into the "Million Dollar Club." Outstanding athletes may receive trophies, Olympic gold medals, or become champions. Wives who are good cooks may win a blue ribbon for their jelly at the State Fair. People who find a lost wallet and return it to the original owner may receive a reward. Some men may become "Father of the Year," and workers who demonstrate diligence may receive a bonus. Safe drivers who do not have accidents may get a reduction on their automobile insurance premiums. Professionals who set examples for their peers may be honored by their professional groups with awards or election to office in the professional group. In short, there are many ongoing inducements for compliance with the social norms above and beyond the intrinsic satisfactions of conforming in terms of being an honest citizen, hard-working employee, good husband, and a temperate consumer of food and drink.

For those who fail to comply there are negative labels and negative sanctions. Law breakers are criminals and often punished severely. Errant soldiers are given a Dishonorable Discharge. Elected officials who are guilty of malfeasance may be impeached. Unethical attorneys may be disbarred. Students who misbehave in school could be expelled. Drivers who violate too many traffic laws may lose their license. Children who violate legal norms are labeled as delinquents. Men who patronize prostitutes may be called "whore mongers," and overly promiscuous females may be labeled as "loose women" if not "sluts." Poor academic performers in school may be called dumb or a "dunce," and persons who are less than fastidious in their dress, grooming, and eating behavior may be called "slobs." A person who does not conform to the norms of polite language may be termed vulgar or crude. Persons with sexual tastes that do not conform to the social norms may be viewed as perverts. Beyond all of these derisive terms and labels, there are innumerable negative sanctions, ranging from incarceration and fines to ostracism; from loss of privileges to expulsion from school; and from demerits to having one's pay docked. They extend in severity from execution to having to stay after school.

In spite of all the negative labels and negative sanctions, many persons still do not conform to the social norms. It is this fact that has occupied the intellectual energies of philosophers and theologians as well as psychiatrists and social scientists for centuries. Negative labeling has often failed to work, and many offenders have turned vice into virtue and have even come to revel in the title of bandit, or killer, or "dirty old man." Negative sanctions, no matter how severe, also have frequently failed to deter violations of laws or even noncompliance with relatively minor, inconsequential norms. At one point in English history pickpocketing was a capital offense and offenders were publicly hanged. Spectators at the public hanging of pickpockets often had their pockets picked while watching the spectacle! In spite of all the positive inducements to conform, and the many negative sanctions to discourage violations of the norms, social norms are frequently transgressed, and many members of society are involved in such violations. In fact, it is probably safe to assert that at one time or another and at one level or another almost everyone violates some social norm and theoretically can be labeled as a *deviant*!

THE GENESIS OF DEVIANT BEHAVIOR

At the very simplest level, deviance can be explained on the basis of someone violating a social norm simply because they wish to attain some goal. A child may purloin a cookie from the cookie jar after the mother has forbidden him to do so because he wants to eat the cookie. Willie "The Actor" Sutton, the infamous bank robber, once safely observed that he robbed banks because that's where the money was! Similarly, individuals may view forbidden pornographic photographs simply because they derive carnal gratification from doing so. In short, an overriding hedonistic consideration would seem to be involved in deviant behavior (Riemer, 1981). But, of course, the question is usually much more complex, for how else can we explain the fact of two individuals in a situation of temptation but only one violates the social norm while the other does not.

Historically, there has been a tendency to locate the genesis of deviance internal to the individual. In the distant part, criminals and deviants were sometimes said to be possessed by demons and spirits, or that they harbored evil and sin within themselves. Some were believed to be witches and behaving in cahoots with the Devil (even today, Flip Wilson humorously asserts that "the Devil made me do it!"). A century ago, learned authorities were offering the opinion that physiognomy or the shape and other features of the face, and phrenology or the configuration of the skull might be an indicator of mental faculties and individual character, and especially a criminally prone character. In time, other aspects of anatomy and physiology were invoked as causative agents in deviance, as were heredity and mental deficiencies. Even in more recent periods, the search for biological factors in crime persists. Assorted theories in this regard were offered, including the notion of biological "inferiority," and somatology with the ideal-type models of body type and physique with attendant behavioral characteristics—endormorphs, mesomorphs, and ectomorphs, and brain malfunction. The field of psychiatry offered mental disorders such as insanity and psychopathology, and from the field of genetics came the anomaly of the XYY chromosome syndrome, or the fact of some males having an extra Y chromosome in every cell. Some writers reported an over-representation of XYY males in prison populations, and that some XYY males tended to have criminal histories (For a detailed discussion of these earlier theories of deviance, see McCaghy, 1985: 11-45). Empirical evidence, particularly of contemporary variety, has, however, provided little if any support for any of these diverse theories and notions.

Sociologists, on the other hand, have offered some highly productive, albeit diverse, insights into the etiology of deviant behavior. It almost goes without saying, of course, that some persons violate norms because of impaired cognition or reasoning. An individual who is retarded, sustains brain damage, or is senile, may not even be aware of the existence of the norm, much less the social import and consequences of violating it. Similarly, persons with mental illness are essentially in the same situation. Some persons do have genuine compulsive disorders, such as kleptomaniacs, and cannot resist engaging in the behavior that represents a violation of the norm. There are those who, because of temporary cognitive and/or mental impairment, may engage in deviant acts that they would not otherwise commit. Much deviant behavior can be and is blamed on alcohol and narcotics. Inasmuch as alcohol consumption and narcotic use is voluntary, such an excuse for norm violation seldom has much legal or social legitimation. Under the influence of alcohol or narcotics, individuals may hallucinate or almost totally lose self control, and sometimes commit acts of great social repugnancy.

Sociologists are more prone to look to social factors external to the individual to account for deviant behavior, and the theories attendant to such an orientation are many and varied. Robert K. Merton's (1938) theory of anomie postulated that there are societal norms in terms of goals, and societal norms in terms of appropriate ways of attaining these goals. Individuals may subscribe to the societal goal norms (wealth, fame, success, etc.), but be unable to avail themselves of the normative means of attaining those goals (hard work, education, etc.), and in the face of such a normative gridlock, may have to resort to alternate, and illegitimate means of reaching the socially approved goals, or may otherwise react in a deviant fashion to their dilemma.

It has also been argued that deviant behavior may be functional to society, at least at a latent level (Erikson, 1966). The very presence of deviance better delineates the boundaries of acceptable and conforming behavior. The deviant stands as an example of what not to be. The student forced to sit on a high stool and wear a dunce cap in front of the class, because of his intellectual ineptitude, serves as a model or example of what happens to deviants. The "dunce" is needed for that purpose and, thus, functional. It may well be that the "dunce," the class "cut-up," and the town drunk are tacitly tolerated and, perhaps, even mildly encouraged because of the functional example they serve. Deviance is also functional because the reaction of outrage and indignation to it by members of the community serves to promote social cohesion and, thus, aids in integrating and uniting the community. Finally, deviance may be functional in an economic way. The thief provides cheap "hot" (stolen) merchandise for the less affluent that they could not otherwise afford. The presence of strippers, while perceived as deviant, may attract tourists and, thus, money into a resort area. In both instances, the offenders often rationalize their behavior as helpful to society. Prostitutes not infrequently assert that they help "save" marriages by providing sexual variety to husbands, and help society by affording sexual outlets to person who might otherwise commit sex crimes on innocent females. By rationalizing one's deviant behavior as helpful, one is encouraged to commit such acts.

American society does not have one culture but, rather, many subcultures under a larger, less than unified, cultural umbrella. It has many subcultures because society is made up of many diverse groupings—racial, ethnic, social class, regional, religious, and occupational—to name some. Each subculture may have its own unique normative system. A member of one of these groupings may be conforming to the norms of the respective subculture but be in violation of the norms of other subcultures and of the larger societal cultural umbrella. In this connection the slum dweller who commits an illegal act may not so much be criminally inclined as simply not as prone to view the act as criminal. Abandoned cars in poor areas of New York are quickly stripped of parts. Anyone who lives in New York, however, would probably reveal that many persons, and especially those in low-income levels, do not view taking parts from abandoned cars as stealing. According to their subcultural system, such behavior is simply taking advantage of opportunities that come your way. Studies (Palmer & Bryant, 1985) have shown that in many rural areas, individuals who hunt may not always obey the game laws to the limit. It is traditional for persons in those areas not to do so, because they feel that the game is there for the taking. Deviant behavior, according to the so-called "Chicago School," may occur because of different normative systems in different subcultures and the attendant cultural conflict which results. In this same vein some authors (Sutherland and Cressey, 1970) have spoken of "differential association" or that deviant behavior is often learned from others who have different definitions of what is deviant, and different rationalizations for justifying their behavior. In a society as complex and diverse as the United States, it is not difficult to understand how cultural conflict and differential association might be factors in deviant behavior.

Social scientists who adhere to the so-called "social control/deterrence" school of thought put less emphasis on the structural conditions that may precipitate deviance and look more at why people conform to or violate norms in the "conventional order" (Liska, 1981:89). Simply put, offenders may find norm violations to be attractive and are motivated to do so unless certain controls operate to deter them. These controls may be inner controls which result from the internalization of rules with the attendant satisfactions that go with conformity and the guilt and anxiety that go with nonconformity. The deviant may not have properly internalized the norms. The outer controls are the sanctions—rewards or punishments that surround norms. If a person violates a norm, he or she may lose rewards and be punished. Deviance then is a function of the relative balance between the attractiveness of norm violation and the strength of inner and outer controls.

Some writers have suggested that crime and deviant behavior have a political dimension and argue that the more powerful and the more affluent are in a position to create norms and impose them on others. The less powerful and the less affluent may have other norms that are in conflict with those of the ruling class, but because of their relative powerlessness they are required to conform to the norms of the ruling class. In short, the normative system becomes an instrument of manipulation and oppression of the lower classes. According to such a perspective, lower class behavior may become criminalized or labeled as deviant. The vagrancy laws were a device for getting rid of undesirables (Liska, 1981:184), and white-collar offenders are treated more leniently than are street crime offenders. The laws are selectively enforced. As Liska (1981:191) phrases it, "the general point is clear: what is crime and who is the criminal frequently depend on group interests and political power."

Finally, there are those social scientists who assert that deviance is to some degree socially constructed. Such a view assumes a pluralistic society with numerous sets of norms and values emerging from different interest groups. Certain interest groups prevail and establish their norms as society's norms. Persons who violate those norms then become deviants or criminals because they are so labeled by the prevailing interest group. This labeling is a social process which involves several steps. Because of a variety of factors, social and idiosyncratic, an individual violates a norm (primary deviance) but this fact alone has little impact on the individual and his self-image. The prevailing social order labels him as a deviant and reacts to the label accordingly. The individual then responds to the labeling reaction not infrequently with other kinds of deviant behavior (secondary deviance). This secondary deviance becomes a mode of adaptation to the reaction from others to the original labeling, and in time the individual may develop a new self-concept or identity. As an illustration, a child in a primary grade, because of restlessness, performs poorly on one or more tests. The teacher publicly labels the child as a "slow learner." The other children laugh at him and call him dumb. He responds to this by acting out, misbehavior, and with other antisocial behavior. Others now give him the status of deviant and delinquent and in time, the child assumes that identity as part of his self-concept. According to these writers, the deviance can be traced to the labeling process (see, for example, Dotter and Roebuck, 1988).

What are some of the facilitative or precipitative basic ingredients for norm violation? It would appear that there must be opportunity structure for deviance. The opportunity structure—a position of trust in a firm, for example—may make it easier to commit the offense of theft. Not infrequently, there may be some type of disequilibrium, disruption, or stress that would interfere with the traditional value system of the individual. The need for money to pay for the emergency operation on his daughter may motivate the bookkeeper to steal from his employer, even though he has always previously been scrupulously honest. Often an individual has to learn to be deviant and this sometimes occurs as part of a more conventional learning process. The soldier learns informally in his basic military training experience to "moonlight requisition" or steal that which his unit needs. His socialization is subverted, as it were. There also would have to be some appropriate means of rationalizing the deviant act so as to justify it and, thus, preserve the integrity of the self-image. The traveling salesman may "pad" his expense account because "everyone else is doing it" and the company "expects it." These and other factors and circumstances that contribute to deviant behavior will be explored in the subsequent readings and commentary in this book.

There are a number of other sociological theories which have been advanced to account for deviant behavior, some of which will be mentioned and discussed later in this volume. It has been argued that there may be no single, clear-cut and completely satisfactory explanation for deviance. The violation of social norms may result from multiple factors and an appropriate theory for such behavior may have to employ an integrated or multicausal model. The existing sociological theories of deviance, in various combinations and permutations, may all prove useful. Certainly, the various theoretical schools of thought have provided provocative insights into the deviance process and offer a variety of different approaches and perspectives for further and hopefully more productive examinations and analyses of the phenomena of norm violation.

REFERENCES

Audrey, Robert
1966 The Territorial Imperative: A Personal Inquiry into the Animal Origins of Property and Nations. New York: Dell.

Bryant, Clifton D.
1984 "Odum's Concept of the Technicways: Some Reflections on an Underdeveloped Sociological Notion," Sociological Spectrum, 4:115–143.

Dotter, Daniel L., and Julian B. Roebuck
1988 "The Labeling Approach Reexamined: Interactionism and the Components of Deviance," Deviant Behavior 9:19–32.

Erikson, Kai
1966 Wayward Puritans: A Study in the Sociology of Deviance. New York: Wiley.

Liska, Allen E.
1981 Perspectives on Deviance. Englewood, N.J.: Prentice-Hall.

McCaghy, Charles H.
1985 Deviant Behavior: Crime, Conflict, and Interest Groups (Second Edition). New York: Macmillan Publishing Company.

Merton, Robert K.
1938 "Social Structure and Anomie," American Sociological Review, 3:672–682.

Palmer, C. Eddie, and Cifton D. Bryant
1985 " 'Keepers of the King's Deer': Game Wardens and the Enforcement of Fish and Wildlife Law," pp. 111–137 in Bryant, Clifton D., Donald J. Shoemaker, James K. Skipper, Jr., and William E. Snizek (eds. and contributors), *The Rural Work Force: Nonagricultural occupations in America.* South Hadley (Mass): Bergin and Garvey Publishers, Inc.

Riemer, Jeffrey W.
1981 "Deviance as Fun," Adolescence, XVI: 39–43.
Sumner, William Graham
1906 Folkways. Boston: Ginn.
Sutherland, Edwin, and Donald Cressey
1970 Principles of Criminology. New York: J. B. Lippincott.

Part Two

Deviance: Conceptions and Perceptions

Chapter Two

Form and Content

EDITORIAL COMMENTARY

Deviant behavior, like all social behavior, is seldom haphazard, extemporaneous, random, serendipitous, or unrestrained. Rather, it is often planned or precipitated in a relatively predictable fashion. It is sometimes highly routinized and repetitious. Inasmuch as it usually involves interaction, it is scripted in the sense that others are brought into the routine in an anticipated and reactive manner. Most importantly, it is almost invariable structured in form and purpose.

Even the simplest social behavior has structure and meaning. Bowing, shaking hands, or waving at someone, for example, are usually done in a customary and prescribed manner. They occur or are precipitated in specific socially indicated situations or contexts. The activity itself is done in a highly routinized and predictable fashion (learning to salute properly may take many hours for a military recruit to learn). The behavior by being routinized is intended to convey a particular meaning. Similarly, because it is customary in a given situation such behavior is also intended to elicit a particular kind of predictable response and involvement on the part of others. Such routinization, socially injected meaning, and expectations produce structure. Structured behavior may be planned or it may evolve through trial and error, but it tends to persist because it is effective. Because it is effective, it attains continuity and predictability. Deviant behavior, as social behavior, is no exception. It, too, has structure—social patterning and purpose.

Granted that there are true kleptomaniacs, most persons who steal do so to accomplish some purpose. They may steal for profit (such as bankrobbers), they may steal for patriotic reasons (such as politically committed espionage agents), they may steal for hedonistic reasons (such as the adolescents who "lift" a six pack of beer from a convenience store), or they may steal for thrills (such as the fraternity boys who "swipe" the statue from in front of the rival fraternity house), to name but a few. In most cases the theft is accomplished in a particular fashion. There are limited ways in which a bank can be successfully robbed. Occasionally an amateur attempts to do so in an innovative way and is caught. Similarly, shoplifting may also require a "strategy," as it were. Most deviance, in order to be successful or to accomplish its purpose, does require a strategy or a particular approach. Whether bank robbery, the use of narcotics, rape, armed robbery, plagiarism, fraud, or cheating on tests, there is usually an effective way of accomplishing the desired end. In short, there is a pattern to the activity. Law enforcement officials frequently speak of the "M.O." (modus operendi) or pattern of the crime. So patterned is the mode of many criminal offenses, that the law enforcement officials can often identify the type of offender, if not the actual offender, although they may not know his true identity. Thus, the labeling of the offender may derive from the patterning of this crime—"a second story man," or the "human fly" burglar, or the "oil man" confidence offender, or the "delivery man rapist." Such an "M.O." frequently refers to such characteristics of the offense as the similar time when the crime was committed, the type of business or person that was victimized, the kind of vehicle, or tools, or weapons that were used to facilitate the crime. Also taken into account might be the mannerisms of the offender, the way in which the victims were treated, the type of conversation between offender and victim, or the way in which the offender exited the crime scene to mention some possible components to the pattern.

Students of deviant behavior attempt to learn more about deviance by examining its pattern or structure. They may focus on the deviant, his career in deviance, the factors which precipitate his miscreance, or the self-identity that he develops as a result of this deviant actions. They may focus on the victims of deviance or the customers of deviance. What factors maneuvered them into the deviant situation, or what was their relationship to the deviant actor, or what was their reaction to the event. Researchers may also concern themselves with the structure of deviant behavior systems—gangs, deviant work systems, deviance dispensing units—or deviant subcultures. They may examine the social-psychological dimensions of deviant patterns, focusing on the sociocultural background of the deviant, or the attitudes and values extant in his social network, looking at the deviant with the larger structural or organizational context. Researchers may even explore the patterning of the reaction of society or the group, looking at the process by which the nonconforming actor is adjudged to be a deviant and the consequences which follow.

The initial reading in this section, Joel Best and David F. Luckenbill's "The Social Organization of Deviance," affords an interactional perspective of the structure of deviance. In this instance, the authors view the deviant transaction itself. As they point out, much research on deviance is based on field research, employing observation or interviewing, and usually focuses analytically on deviant careers or deviant behavior systems. Research of a social psychological variety not infrequently explores the "movement through the deviant scene, being labeled and the adoption of the deviant identity." Yet other research efforts may examine the deviant within "a larger organizational and structural context." Such approaches, the authors assert, tend to neglect the character of the deviant act, and disregard the actual performance of deviance. They urge the examination of the social organization of deviant action, and toward this end posit an appropriate classification scheme, "along a dimension of organization complexity."

According to Best and Luckenbill, the deviant transaction—i.e., the pattern of relations between its roles—is characterized by several properties, including the participants orienting themselves toward a specific end that results in gratifications for them, a division of labor, and flexible coordination. Deviant transactions vary along a dimension of organizational complexity. In this regard they identify three major forms of deviant transaction along this continuum; individual deviance, deviant exchange, and deviant exploitation. Such a scheme, they claim, is useful because where several kinds of deviant transactions with different properties occur in behavior systems, they can be distinguished, and because it identifies the underlying similarities in seemingly dissimilar forms of deviance.

In their classification arrangement, the category of Individual Deviance includes both providing illicit services, such as narcotics, abortion, or suicide, to oneself and subscribing to a prohibited version of reality as in religious heresy or schizophrenia. Such disparate forms of deviance only require a single actor (although there may be ties to others, even if part of a social network), they can be isolated for analytic purposes, and they often occur in isolation or a protected setting where the actors can avoid discovery, and/or are not vulnerable to social control efforts.

Deviant Exchange, the second category of deviant transactions, involves two or more persons and includes trades such as homosexual activity or swinging, and sales such as prostitution or drug sales. In the former, the actors provide similar services to the other, and in the latter, one actor sells and the others purchase. In this type of transaction, the principals enter into the arrangement voluntarily out of self-interest seeking goods and services that they cannot provide for themselves. Thus, it is a cooperative activity. Unlike ordinary exchanges, however, its participants are eligible for official sanctions. This necessitates that those involved act with discretion to avoid social control agents, and that they trust one another, since if exploited by the other, there is no recourse to social control agents. Accordingly, the negotiation of trust becomes a seminal concern in the transaction. Trust may be fostered by limiting interaction to acquaintances, friends or relatives, or by offering up their track record for examination. Those involved may seek a sponsor of known integrity, or they may provide something to symbolize their commitment to the transaction, paying in advance, for example.

The final category of transaction, Deviant Exploitation, includes coercion such as murder or robbery, extortion such as kidnapping or racketeering, surreptitious exploitation, such as burglary or pickpocketing, and fraud, such as confidence games or investment fraud. Deviant Exploitation also involves two or more actors, but one participant is the deviant actor and the other is the target or victim. There is, accordingly, a conflict of interest between the two, and such a transaction is not mutually profitable. As a result, this category of transaction is more complex than the other two categories for the deviant actor must control the victim, onlookers or bystanders, and also cope with a possible victim control agent alliance. To do this, the deviant must take additional precautions to those in Exchange Transactions, such as shielding his identity from the victim and relying on special resources, such as speed, stealth, disguises, or weapons. The various categories of Deviant Exploitation are based on the understanding of the victim in terms of two dimensions, awareness of exploitation, and definition of the situation in terms of whether or not the transaction is viewed as exploitation or exchange. In the case of coercion, the victim is aware of it and defines it as exploitation. In extortion, the victim is aware of the transaction, but may view it as exchange—paying a ransom for the safety of a hostage, for example. The victim is usually not aware of Surreptitious Exploitation, such as burglary of an empty building when it occurs and clearly views it as exploitation. In fraud, trickery is often employed, thus deceiving the victim, causing him not to be aware of the exploitation, but instead, leading him to define the transaction as exchange. Indeed, the mark of quality fraud is a victim who really thinks he received full value in the transaction, or even took advantage of the deviant actor.

The authors, having articulated their typology of deviant transactions, then go on to offer several propositions describing the consequences of organizational complexity. They do, however, initially claim that these propositions should be qualified. Such qualifications include indicating that the propositions reflect social control agents' definitions of deviance. Also they are based on field research carried out in the United States over the last 20 years. Finally, their qualifications include the fact that while they focus on the effects of organization, there is no claim that this is the only, or most important, influence on the behavior of deviants and social control agents.

Best and Luckenbill then proceed to suggest that there are effects or consequences of the complexity of the deviant transaction. They assert, for example, that persons involved in the more complex forms of deviant transactions, such as Deviant Exchange and Deviant Exploitation, are more likely to be considered responsible for their deviance than those whose deviance is individual. The more complex the deviant transaction, according to their typology, the more likely the deviance will be defined as serious, the more likely the deviant will be subject to punitive sanctions, and the greater likelihood the deviant will be identified and apprehended by social control agents. Also the more elaborate will be the tactics used by deviants to protect themselves from social control efforts. Finally, it is the contention of the authors that the social control agents are more likely to use "proactive tactics" in dealing with individual deviance and deviant exchange, but they are more likely to use "reactive tactics" against deviant exploitation. Thus, as they view deviant transactions, there are significant social consequences as the level of complexity of the transaction increases.

Deviance, then, is structured along various dimensions, one of which is the organizational complexity of deviant transactions. The authors have offered a typology of such transactions which includes three major categories of transactions, and various specific types of deviance within each of those. In the most complex category, Deviant Exploitation, the elements of victim awareness and definition of the situation are also introduced. Although providing some qualifications for their conclusions, they do suggest that the level or organizational complexity does have important consequences both for deviants and for social control agents. The authors do, however, call for more research to determine if the consequences may be "overridden by other factors," and to "learn whether these relationships hold in other times and places." Such an approach to the structure of behavior, similar to that used in this consideration of deviance, may even have implications for conventional transactions.

Deviance is not without purpose, function, or goal and such function may operate at either manifest or latent level. At a manifest level, deviance may appear to exist primarily to gratify or fulfill the actor engaging in the deviance, i.e., people engage in deviant behavior because they derive something out of it. At a latent level, however, it may serve to accomplish societal purposes by acting as an escape valve for individual frustrations, thus, preventing the possibility of total rejection of the normative system or social rebellion. It may, in effect, channel discontents in a direction that is more easily absorbed or managed by society. The deviant also serves as an example or model of what constitutes nonconformity to those who are more circumscribed in their behavior, thereby effectively establishing borders or boundaries between acceptable and nonacceptable behavior.

Deviance of various kinds has been shown to be functional or beneficial to the individual. Narcotic use or alcohol abuse, for example, has sometimes been used as a means of accomplishing a difficult job or work specialty. The use of such substances has been a psychological of physiological crutch for some individuals with stressful occupational roles. Physicians may use narcotic substances to cope with their demanding regimen. Soldiers may use alcohol or narcotics to allay fear and anxiety in combat, and business executives may rely heavily on alcohol to deal with their career stresses. In some instance, at a community or society level, certain types of deviance have become a kind of economic mainstay, providing employment and generating income, or other economic advantages for the population. Deviance may help people cope with disaffective relationships with others. In some instances, various social benefits may be ascribed to some forms of deviance as a justification for their existence. Prostitutes, for example, may claim that they help marriages by providing sexual variety to frustrated husbands, or keep persons from committing sexual crimes by offering an alternate outlet. Law enforcement officials may tolerate brothels for similar reasons. Much social deviance is seen as having residual benefits in addition to social dysfunction. Thus, deviance of many kinds may be viewed with ambiguity.

Few things in life, including experiences and behavior, are all good or all bad. There are few truly black or white situations. Similarly, even deviant behavior and deviants are not always totally bad or good. Deviance is often gratifying, if not fulfilling, to the offender, and sometimes may even be viewed in a positive light, or perhaps, not in a completely negative light, at least some of the time. Robin Hood and Jesse James were seen as heroes by some. Demonstrators, protestors, and political dissidents may have multitudes of supporters. People may applaud or cheer when they hear of some offenders "beating the rap," as it were, if they were sympathetic to the position and circumstances of the offender. Colonel Oliver North became something of a national hero, in addition to being labeled as a governmental miscreant. Even among children, the "show-off," or class "clown" has a considerable following, even though being, by definition, a deviant. Actors, who portray characters who often "break the rules," and who themselves are frequently "rebels" in real life, are not infrequently enormously popular with the public, who can live vicariously through the character (both on the screen and in real life), and can also vicariously "break the rules" themselves.

In fact, as a nation, Americans have always had an admiration for "mavericks," "rebels," "eccentrics,"—persons who could make their own decisions, break the rules and follow their own dictates or conscience, or march to "the beat of a different drummer," as it were. We like people who are daring, audacious, and such persons have been military leaders, such as General George Custer, General Billy Mitchell, or General George Patton, political leaders, such as Andrew Jackson, or Harry Truman, industrialists and merchants, such as Henry Ford or Clarence Saunders (the originator of the grocery supermarket), actors such as James Dean and Errol Flynn, and musical composers such as John Cage and Spike Jones. Americans have tended to value novelty and innovation, and stubbornness and conviction, and flair and eccentricity, even if deviant in terms of some set of standards. It has been said that the line between genius and insanity is thin, and also that the line between ingenuity and nonconformity (if not rebellion) is also slender.

In the next reading in this chapter, Lesley D. Harman looks at behavior that may sometimes lie in between conformity and deviance in the article, "Acceptable Deviance as Social Control: The Cases of Fashion and Slang." In this article, the author points out that there is nothing absolute about the categories of deviation and conformity, but rather both are "negotiated conditions." According to the author "social behavior rarely exemplifies either ideal type." Rather, much behavior lies somewhere in between in the form of acceptable deviance. This the author defines as "that behavior which deviates enough from the norm such that it is not entirely predictable, yet which conforms enough to the norm to be acceptable as signifying membership."

Acceptable deviance as a category of vagrant behavior becomes necessary, according to Harman, when the individual is confronted with conflicting cultural demands. On the one hand in Western industrialized societies, individuals are encouraged (and, indeed, are told that they have the right) to "express their unique identities," and to manifest individuality and creativity. On the other hand, as the author phrases it, society is "a rule-governed set of individuals interested in a common goal of social order." Thus, the members of society must adopt mutually expectant roles, which include expected behaviors, or rules. In short, individuals must conform to the norms "in order to maintain social order, [and] to maintain the integrity of the group."

The demands of conformity and deviation would then seem to be in conflict. If the individual attempts to be overly "unique" in order to make choices, then he may be labeled as a deviant and a threat to the group for not sharing the basic norms and values. If, on the other hand, the individual is too much of a conformist, then he may be viewed as "overinvolved."

The author asserts that this dilemma is resolved through "a negotiation between the two extreme demands," resulting in a secondary set of norms, which constitutes "acceptable deviance." Such a resolution does not really allow the coexistence of conformity and deviation, but only appears to the a solution to the problem. In reality, so the author contends, acceptable deviance is essentially "a method of social control—a mechanism of ensuring social conformity in the guise of individual freedom."

Acceptable deviance involves some "rule-bending," in that the individual attempts to bend the rules to show "self-expression" and, that he has control over the rules, but not to the point of posing a threat to the social order. The author cites Goffman's distinction between "main" and "side" involvement, and "dominant" and "subordinate" involvement in a social situation. A main involvement "absorbs the major part of an individual's attention and interests," and a side involvement may be engaged in "an abstracted fashion without threatening or confusing simultaneous maintenance of a main involvement." A dominant involvement has priority in the sense of being "the role in which one is expected to be engaged," but the subordinate involvement only serves as a "filler" between one's engagement in dominant involvements.

In regard to acceptable deviance, there does seem to be a legitimized rule-bending procedure. One can bend the rules by engaging in subordinate involvement, as long as one is prepared to engage in dominant involvement when necessary, and as long as main involvement does not become subordinate involvement. Also, if you can show that you know and accept the rules, you will be able to bend the rules by expressing yourself through side and subordinate involvements.

Having laid the theoretical groundwork, Harman moves on to posit the notion of fashion as acceptable deviance. Certain manifestations of behavior "affected by the impulses of conformity and deviation" including "clothing, social conduct, amusements," which are termed "externals" are "meaning-endowed" in that they make a statement about the person affecting them. Such externals "serve the dual functions of self-expression and conformity," and also provide the basis for membership in "*epistemic communities*" or groupings of persons who share a sense of what externals or symbols are "good."

The epistic communities possess a subculture that includes "a set of rules and patterns dictating the symbolic function of externals [that] is known as fashion." Fashion as a norm affects many aspects of social life in that it may prescribe clothing, music, art, language, and even automobiles, to mention some externals. But in prescribing externals, fashion also departs from conventional custom. The author identifies two levels of fashion: the societal level where it is a process, and the individual level where it occurs as a form of interaction.

At the societal level, the concept of fashion assumes a cyclical configuration. If something (a style of clothing, for example) is "in," then something else must be "out." Thus, there is a cyclical and changing perception of what is "in fashion." The cycle of fashion includes three stages: introduction, assimilation, and obsolescence. In the introductory stage, the innovative style is new and, thus, vagrant from the prevailing style. Those who adopt the new style are daring, or pioneers or style setters, as they are sometimes know. The new style serves a differentiating function by setting apart those who have adopted the new style and those who are hesitant to do so or resist it. In time, the new fashion is adopted by more and more members of society to the point that is common and, thus, assimilated into the normative system. At this point, a deviation from the normative fashion may become unacceptable. The fashion now ceases to differentiate between members and nonmembers. The fashion now becomes "old fashioned" and obsolete because of its failure to serve as a symbol of membership, and the cycle may begin again. Fashion then, begins in "novelty" and ends in "obsolescence," both of which represent deviation from the norm.

At the individual level, fashion becomes very significant as a means of "exemplifying self in the face of the conformist force it has at the societal level." The actor is faced with the choice of allegiance to a fashion which is symbolic of membership in an epistemic community, and "a sense of self which seeks to be expressed." The choice may be resolved in different ways by three ideal types of actors. The *outrageous* "live on the fringe of convention, and are the main actors in the societal stage of 'introduction' of a fashion." The *old-fashioned* are persons who did not become involved with the new fashion, and are more identified with the societal stage of obsolescence. The *fashionable*, however, do participate in the new fashion, but within the "safety of the norm," once the fashion has been accepted. Fashion, then, becomes a mechanism through which the individual can acceptably deviate between the two forms of unacceptable deviation—the "outrageous" and the "old-fashioned."

Slang is another such mechanism of acceptable deviation. Slang, as "the privatization and personalization" of meaning in language, has a differentiation function in that a "private language is an effective means of making clear the in-group/out-group distinction." As with fashion, slang provides a means of establishing membership, as well as distinguishing between fashionable and old-fashioned.

A new slang term must be introduced by an individual who, by definition, is daring, innovative, and outrageous. There may be initial awe, discomfort with, and resistance to the new slang term by the group. If the epistemic community finds the slang term to "correspond with the continuous culture of the group," they may determine to adopt it, and the slang then becomes fashionable with the result that the new term differentiates the members of the epistemic community from others. Other persons now become inventive with the term, perhaps combining it with other new slang terms, and using it in individualistic ways as a medium of self-expression. This is acceptable deviance in that it both demonstrates membership, but also attests "to one's ability to innovate within the prescribed rules of convention of the community." The use of such slang terms provides high visibility to the epistemic community. Members of other groups may try to adopt the slang, but lacking the subtle meanings of such terms, may "flounder" in its use, thus exposing themselves as outsiders. Sometimes as these groups become comfortable with the slang, it becomes obsolete and, accordingly, strengthens the boundary between ingroup and outgroup by showing the outgroup to be old-fashioned. When the slang is adopted by a wider and wider population, it ceases to differentiate between members and nonmembers and no longer serves as a criterion for membership.

Fashion and slang represent mechanisms of acceptable deviance that serve to make "the individual feel in control of expression," and also at the societal level, absorb and negate "rebelliousness in that it controls the course of 'change.'" Individuals can access freedom through fashion, and achieve "self expression and self esteem" through the use of slang as privatized language, which also distinguishes group membership. Acceptable deviance *appears* to allow individual deviation, but in reality, it "becomes the *rule* and therefore assures conformity," Acceptable deviance is illusionary. It is "adventurous safety," because it is "institutionalized and therefore a conservative force which acts to ensure continuity." Individuals may seek to be fashionable, but rather than releasing one from the bonds of convention, it simply becomes another form of convention. Acceptable deviance, in the form of fashion and slang, controls uniqueness, by giving "a false sense of freedom while insuring that the 'rules' are followed." It provides a feeling of self-worth and acts as a safety valve by channeling "the self expression impulse," and "sustaining a high degree of uniformity within groups." Through acceptable deviance, according to Harman, there is room for plurality, negotiation between members and nonmembers, and "allows a multiplicity of factors to come into play, based on an underlying assumption that actors seek membership." Deviance then is not without utility, or function, and is sometimes productively employed by society as a means of effecting conformity.

Many assumptions, assessments, or conclusions in life are the product of perspective. As in the venerable example, the bottle with one-half its contents may be viewed as half-empty by the pessimist, but half-full by the optimist. The prevailing conception or perceptions of deviance may be very much a product of perspective. In the next reading in this section, David L.

Dodge explores the existence of what he feels is a biased perspective in his "The Over-Negativized Conceptualization of Deviance: A Programmatic Exploration." Dodge contends that the sociology of deviance tends to overly emphasize the negative in that it tends to focus essentially on "the objectionable, the forbidden, [and] the disvalued and these social phenomena are so designated because they are viewed as offensive, disgusting contemptible, annoying or threatening." Because such social phenomena are so viewed, the reaction is usually negative.

The preponderant concern with negative deviance has been such that positive deviance—the surpassing of conventional expectations—has not been "adequately acknowledged" or "systematically explored," In recent years, the study of deviance has been theoretically broadened to include a variety of influential variables, including sex, power, and the ordinariness of deviance, to name but some. The author suggests that if the "full scope" of deviance is to be examined, then the phenomena of positive deviance must be considered, and that such a consideration may be more important that the exploration of the influence of the previously mentioned variable. Dodge then proceeds to encourage such a perspective, provides reasons for adopting this additional perspective, provides some advantages of doing so, and attempts to stimulate further theoretical and empirical work along this conceptual line. The author does admit that various writers and researchers in the area of deviant behavior have, in fact, noted the existence of positive deviance, and have suggested that it would be equally as profitable to study such vagrancy from the norms as the study of negative deviance.

In way of justification of the reconceptualization of deviant behavior to more emphasize positive deviance, Dodge argues that there is a logical inconsistency in essentially looking only at negative deviance. Deviant behavior, by definition, refers to exceptional behavior—behavior that does not conform to or comply with the social norm. The direction of the nonconformity or exceptionality should be of no consequence. Exceptionality and directionality of behavior should be of equal importance. Positive deviance, therefore should not be ignored. The author further argues that deviance should be a "generic, sensitizing concept" encompassing both positive and negative deviance. Negative deviance can be seen as behavior violating the normative expectations and positive deviance as surpassing the normative expectations.

By introducing the concept of positive deviance into a general consideration of deviant behavior, it must be assumed that, in most instances, a particular form of behavior will fall along a continuum, with three ranges of normative variation. There will be exceptional behavior that falls above the expected (positive deviance), the "normal" range of behavior, and exceptional behavior that falls below the expected (negative deviance). There may well be exceptions to such a behavioral spectrum, but it would obtain in most cases. The author also raises the issue of social response to deviance with special reference to positive deviance. A consideration of this concern raises a variety of questions, such as is deviance of either direction "perceived uniformally by significant others?", or where plural constituencies perceive positive deviance in different ways, how does the actor negotiate an identity, avoid role engulfment, or handle possible problems of secondary deviance?

Dodge suggests that it would be profitable to examine positive deviance rates as they relate to demographic, ecological, or social structural variables. Also he indicates that positive deviance should be examined in terms of existing theories of deviance. In Merton's anomie theory, for example, it is posited that deviance results from the "disjunctures between culturally prescribed goals and socially structured means to attain the goals." Why, the author reasons, could not positive deviance be as much a "normal" adaptive response as negative deviance in such a situation? Finally, he suggests that the numerous "core" definitional statements concerning deviance would hold their relevance if applied to positive deviance. If so, this would be even more compelling evidence for including positive deviance as a legitimate topic in the study of deviant behavior. To make his point, he offers several typical definitional statements for testing.

It has been said, he argues, that the label of deviant "carries with it an ascertainment of morality." Also that it "carries with it a strong essentializing tendency," and "a strong socially isolating tendency." Further, he proffers the assertion that deviancy is both functional and dysfunctional for society, and that the deviant label is always problematic in its assignment. After discussing the application of these statements to positive deviance, he concludes that some, if not all of the definitional statements are, indeed, applicable "with certain modifications."

In summary, Dodge asserts that while theorists of deviance have, in some instances, noted the existence of positive deviance, it has largely been neglected as a seminal topic in the area, with the result that it has not had the systematic examination that it deserves. He concludes that this over-negativized notion of deviance is somewhat analogous to what would have happened in the field of medicine if only illness had been studied to the neglect of wellness or health. The result, he asserts, would have been "preventative medicine would never have developed."

Dodge makes a persuasive argument, but not all agree with his conviction. In the final selection in this chapter, "Positive Deviance: An Oxymoron," Edward Sagarin argues the opposite position.

Sagarin rejects the notion of broadening the concept of deviance to include positive as well as negative deviance. He feels that to do so would "dilute a well defined and widely accepted concept." He applauds the fact that the essay arguing for such a conceptual change was published in the journal from which all of the selections in this volume were obtained, because it would provide an opportunity for scholars of deviance to reject such a suggestion. He begins his counter argument by pointing out that it is important in science to develop classification systems that establish boundary lines. Such classification schemes, he indicates, bring together facts which appear separate but are actually connected in ways that are not always immediately obvious. In fact, the aim and method of modern science is the classification of science in such a fashion that "absolute judgements" can be formed.

The categories, concepts, and cells of such classification schemes do not exist in the world itself, but rather in our minds. In this sense, the classification systems are mental constructs or means of organizing our thoughts. These mental constructs are necessary in "normal everyday thought and communication." Inasmuch as mental constructs and classification systems do not exist in nature, they cannot be inherently wrong, simply superior or inferior to other schemes or systems. Classification schemes are, therefore, arbitrary in that they do not exist in objective reality, and stipulative in that their definition is not given, but rather stipulated "within a language community what these definitions are." In short, we create a reality with our mental constructs.

According to Sagarin, there are certain criteria that are necessary in order to create a concept, place some instances within its boundaries and exclude others, and then formulate a definition based on that construct. The concept or category should possess internal logic, have a usefulness for those who created it, and there should be agreement within a language community.

Having presented the preamble to his exposition, Sagarin moves on to point out that in his experience, an overwhelming majority of social scientists in the field of deviance who had defined it, tended to do so in a negative way. Such individuals, he asserts, represent a wide range of theoretical positions, and were also "persons of the highest reputation in sociology." The writers he reviewed spoke of deviance as "negative, deplorable, devalued, disvalued, disreputable, undesirable, disgusting, frightening, or in some other similar manner." To further make his point, he offers selected quotes from the writings of some of these deviance scholars. He speaks of the desirability of agreement within a scientific community, and contends that because of the general agreement on the definition of deviance, it would likely mean the loss of the concept to sociology if it were effaced by trying to broaden it to include positive deviance. He also demonstrates that the dictionary definition would seem to unquestionably indicate negative characteristics to the term, deviance. Sagarin grants that some writers have spoken of some behavior that is "good" or "functional" to society, and have specifically mentioned, "the genius, the reformer, the religious leaders," with the implication of nondisvalued deviation. Even such writers, however, he asserts, have "second doubts as to the implied definition," and have even put quotes on the words "good" and "deviant." Thus, there is little consensus of persuasion that there is a genuine "positive" deviance.

Sagarin feels that some of the arguments for a positive deviance are, perhaps, based on a confusion of the terms deviation and deviance. To document this alleged confusion, Sagarin resurrects quotes of several writers from the previous argument in behalf of positive deviance and demonstrates that these writers did make a distinction between the two terms. Deviation, reasserts Sagarin, refers to difference in any direction, but the term deviance denotes difference in the negative direction. Deviation, he says, refers "to measure of dispersion from a central tendency," but deviance is the violation "of social norms in ways which prompt punitive and disapproving reactions."

Sagarin contends that to move from deviance to deviation would be to move to a higher level of abstraction and this "would be a great setback in the study of deviant behavior." He also feels that if human behavior exists on a continuum, little would be served by compressing the two skewed ends of the bell curve of frequency into a single entity. In time, he predicts a need for a sociology specializing in one such end and, thus, a new sociology of deviant behavior would occur. He feels that the area of study traditionally called deviance by sociologists is a valuable field of study and has addressed many meaningful questions concerning the genesis of deviance, the individuals who deviate, the reactions of society to deviance, and the implications of deviance for society. He does not see the same value in the study of positive deviance or the meaningful questions to be answered. He particularly extols the value of the study of the social good or social value of deviance, but perceives no problem in the study of the social value of extraordinary individuals, be they musicians, actors, or scientists.

Finally, Sagarin argues that the study of deviance is "an integral part of a larger grouping of sociological concepts." The study of deviance, as now conceptualized is related to many other areas of sociological inquiry, including social control, societal structure, and the differential reaction of society to deviance in various contexts. Through this traditional approach, he says, much has been learned and there is much to be done. To now reconceptualize the field to include positive deviance, would be to, in effect, start over and would result in unlearning what has been learned and undoing what has been done. As he puts it, "Let us concentrate on exciting and important problems."

Deviance then must be viewed as a behavioral configuration with structure and content. It is often routinized, if not institutionalized and, thus predictable in terms of context and outcome. It is patterned in the sense that the actors usually play particular parts in particular ways, to accomplish particular ends, and the process may include specific social mechanisms, devices, and behaviors to accomplish this. It is frequently complex in its construction. Best and Luckenbill, in an innovative perspective of part of the deviance process, propose a research approach that focuses on the actual performance of deviance—the transaction. Toward this end, they provide a typology of deviant transactions and provide appropriate analysis and discussion of their proposal. The level of organizational complexity of the deviant transaction does have social consequences. Their exposition adds additional analytical insight into the nature and implications of social deviance. Deviance also has function and purpose, as has been pointed out in the past. Sometimes, however, it can provide a function in an unanticipated fashion. Harman offers a provocative analysis of two forms of "acceptable deviance"—fashion and slang—and suggests that through these behavioral devices, society is able to effect a particular type of social control without appearing to do so. The individual can seemingly appear to deviate but in actuality is conforming. In this way, the opposing needs of expressing uniqueness but abiding by the rules can be accommodated. Such a mechanism allows a reconciliation of individual freedom and uniformity within groups. Deviance can, indeed, in some instances, be an unusual kind of conformity. In any area of inquiry there is always a basic question, and the basic question in this field is what is deviance? Dodge contends that it is nonconformity to the norm, and the direction of the deviation is of no consequence. Accordingly he suggests that positive deviance has a legitimate place in the field and that it would be profitable to explore this possibility. Sagarin, on the other hand, asserts that deviation from the norm in either direction is not deviance. Instead there is a traditional and correct emphasis on deviance as disvalued nonconformity. Little would be accomplished by changing the conceptualization, he says, and much research accomplishment would be lost if it were necessary to theoretically start over, as it were. Thus, even the basic understandings and constituent conceptualizations of deviance, in terms of structure, function and content, are still contentious and under development. Insight and understanding are always a product of prevailing conceptions and perceptions.

Reading 1

The Social Organization of Deviance

Joel Best
California State University, Fresno
David F. Luckenbill
Northern Illinois University, DeKalb

The social organization of deviance refers to the structure of the deviant transaction, the pattern of relations among its roles. Deviant transactions can be arrayed along a dimension of complexity. Three forms are distinguished: individual deviance can be carried out by a single actor; deviant exchange requires two deviant actors in reciprocal roles; and deviant exploitation needs an offender and a target. Organizational complexity has consequences for deviants and social control agents. As complexity increases, deviants are more likely to be seen as responsible for their actions, those actions are more likely to be defined as serious, the response to deviance is more likely to be punitive, the risks of the deviant's identification and capture become greater, the range of tactics used by deviants expands, and the tactics of social control agents become reactive. The complexity of transactions' organization has implications for the study of deviant and respectable action.

DEVIANT TRANSACTIONS

Field research, employing techniques of observation or interviewing, provides the methodology for dozens of studies of deviants. Regardless of the researcher's theoretical orientation, their data, drawing on the lives of individual deviants, encourage the adoption of concepts that can illustrate features of those lives. Consequently, most treatments of deviance founded on field research use either deviant careers or deviant behavior systems for their analytic foundation. Social psychological examinations focus on deviant careers, movement through the deviant scene, including key events in the deviant's life, such as being labeled and adopting a deviant identity, and the deviant's interpretations of these moments (Goffman, 1963; Lofland, 1969; Matza 1969). Attempting to move beyond the limitations of a social psychological perspective by locating the deviant in a larger organizational and structural context, other researchers describe behavior systems. A deviant behavior system is "an integrated unit, which includes, in addition to the individual [deviant] acts, the codes, the traditions, *esprit de corps,* social relationships among the direct participants, and indirect participation of

An earlier version of this paper was presented at the annual meeting of the Society for the Study of Social Problems, San Francisco, September 1978. We are grateful for comments by Patrick G. Jackson and some anonymous reviewers.

many other persons. It is thus essentially a group way of life" (Sutherland and Cressey, 1974:280; cf. Clinard and Quinney, 1973). These analysts might view safecracking or, more generally, professional theft as behavior systems.

Viewing deviance in terms of careers or behavior systems neglects the character of the deviant act. These concepts can be used to analyze the deviant's background, prospects, perspective, social network, and so forth, in short to locate deviance in its broader context, but at the cost of disregarding the actual performance of deviance. Although dozens of field studies describe deviant acts, there has been relatively little effort to systematically analyze the social organization of deviant action. Generalizing from reports of field studies,[1] we attempt to develop such an analysis in this paper. We classify forms of deviant action along a dimension of organizational complexity and then examine some of the consequences of organizational variation for deviants and social control agency.

The social organization of deviance refers to the structure of the deviant transaction, the pattern of relations between its roles.[2] The unit of analysis is the deviant transaction. A transaction is an activity system in which one or more persons orient themselves toward a specific end.[3] In deviant transactions, at least one participant's action is liable to being defined as deviant; it is subject to the sanctions of social control agents. Like conventional transactions, the deviant transaction is characterized by several properties (cf. Shibutani, 1961: 32–35). First, the participants orient themselves toward a specific end, the achievement of which brings gratifications of some sort to all or some of the participants. To be sure, there may

[1]The logical foundation for generalized theories of this sort can be found in Glaser and Strauss (1967).

[2]Two distinctions should be made. First, the social organization of deviance must be separated from the social organization of deviants, the patterns of relations between deviant actors. Deviants organize in different ways: they may operate alone, in the context of a group, or in coordination with other members of a formal organization. In any case, their organization has relatively little bearing on action in deviant transactions. We discuss the social organization of deviants in a separate paper (Best and Luckenbill, 1980).

Second, in focusing on the deviant transaction, we deliberately ignore other aspects of the deviant's life, such as sociable contacts with other deviants and interaction with social control agents. For the purpose of this discussion, the focus is on the commission of deviant acts, not the experience of being deviant. Committing deviant acts, particularly when the action is known to others, has important, well-documented consequences for the deviant, but these consequences are not addressed in this paper.

[3]The term transaction is used instead of encounter or situation in order to highlight the coordination of behavior between participants. Many, but not all, deviant transactions take the form of face-to-face interaction. The fact of copresence, however, is less important than the relations between the actors' roles; a mugging has some organizational similarities to a computer theft, even though the principals in the latter transaction may never meet. The actors in a transaction may be loners, or they may belong to groups or formal organizations. In some cases, the interests of these larger collectivities are represented by one or more of their members.

be marked variation in the degree to which participants agree on the propriety of the objective and in the types and magnitude of gratifications. Second, transactions have a division of labor, an allocation of tasks among those involved. Achieving a specific end requires that participants coordinate their roles. In some cases, a transaction may involve nothing more than one person performing alone, but other transactions call for two or more persons, each providing a different contribution. Third, transactions involve flexible coordination, "that high degree of adaptability which makes it possible to meet the peculiarities and changes that occur in each situation" (Shibutani, 1961:35).

Deviant transactions vary along a dimension of organizational complexity. Complexity refers to the minimum number of actors required for the transaction and the relationship between the roles they must perform. Some deviant transactions can be accomplished by a single person, but others require two actors. These are minimum requirements; there is no upper limit on the number of people who might be present during a transaction. In transactions featuring several persons, participants may share a common role; but transactions requiring at least two actors involve two distinct roles. The relationship between these roles can range from cooperation to conflict. The more people required for a transaction and the more their roles conflict, the more complex the transaction's organization.

Three major forms of deviant transactions can be arrayed along the dimension of complexity: individual deviance, deviant exchange, and deviant exploitation. Individual deviance requires only one person to accomplish the deviant operation. Deviant exchange demands two actors performing cooperative deviant roles. Deviant exploitation requires two actors in conflict, with one performing a deviant role and the other performing a respectable or quasirespectable role. These basic organizational forms have identifiable subtypes:

1 Individual Deviance
- **A** Self-services (drug addition, suicide)
- **B** Deviant Belief Systems (mental illness, heresy)

2 Deviant Exchange
- **A** Trades (homosexuality, swinging)
- **B** Sales (prostitution, drug sales)

3 Deviant Exploitation
- **A** Coercion (murder, robbery)
- **B** Extortion (kidnapping, racketeering)
- **C** Surreptitious Exploitation (burglary, pickpocketing)
- **D** Fraud (confidence games, investment fraud)

Classifying deviant transactions according to the complexity of organization offers two analytic advantages. First, where behavior systems involve several kinds of deviant transactions, those transactions—which may have different properties—can be distinguished. Thus when addicts use drugs, they engage in individual deviance, but their drug purchases and the thefts to support their habits constitute instances of deviant exchange and deviant exploitation, respectively. Second, the scheme identifies the underlying similarities in seemingly dissimilar forms of deviance, as the examples in the above list suggest. An examination of the different forms of deviant transactions show that each constrains the activities of deviants and social control agents.

VARIETIES OF DEVIANT TRANSACTIONS

Individual Deviance

Individual deviance is an activity defined as deviant that can be accomplished by a single person. The deviant may act in isolation or in the presence of others. The issue is not whether other persons, respectable or deviant, are present but rather whether the individual's action taken alone would merit a deviant label. Two principal forms of individual deviance can be identified. First, there is the provision of illicit services to oneself, as in suicide (Douglas, 1967; Jacobs 1971), self-induced abortion (Less, 1969), the use of illicit drugs (Blumer, 1967; Feldman, 1968; Stoddart, 1974; Winick, 1961), and the excessive use of alcohol (Cahalan and Room, 1974; Spradley, 1970). Second, some actors are considered deviant because they subscribe to a prohibited version of reality, as in cases of schizophrenia (Scheff, 1966; Szasz,1974), forbidden political philosophies (Handler, 1967; Loney, 1973), and religious heresy (Erikson, 1966).[4] These apparently disparate forms of deviance share an important organizational feature: they require only a single deviant actor.

Individual deviants are not without ties to others. They frequently have deviant associates who share their deviance; together, these deviants may form a peer group, such as a skid row bottle gang, or even a formal organization, such as a forbidden political party. Other people may supply the individual deviant with necessary resources; for instance, someone must manufacture and distribute illicit drugs before they can be consumed. Although the individual deviant may be a part of a social network, the act of individual deviance can be isolated for analytic purposes. A single actor, properly prepared and equipped, can commit individual deviance.

[4]Some studies treat certain conditions as deviant. We prefer to view deviance in terms of behavior. The possession of a flawed social identity, however, could be seen as a third form of individual deviance (Goffman, 1963). Examples could include the mentally retarded (Edgerton, 1967), the visibly handicapped (Davis, 1969), and dwarves (Truzzi, 1968).

The fact that the actor's behavior makes the individual eligible for official intervention affects the character of the transaction. So long as the deviant has the capacity for self-control, he or she usually takes precautions to avoid identification and processing by social control agents. Precautions generally center on self-discretion, the control of discrediting information about one's involvement in deviance, often by restricting one's deviance to isolated or protected settings that outsiders do not routinely enter (Goffman, 1963). Thus individual deviance often occurs in isolation, or among other individual deviants, as in some recreational drug use. The control of discrediting information also may be accomplished by cloaking symbols of involvement in deviance as when a drug addict covers needle tracks. Where individual deviants ignore the need for discretion, for instance by carrying out their deviant transactions in public, they are vulnerable to social control efforts (Bittner, 1967; Wiseman, 1970).

Deviant Exchange

Deviant exchange refers to transactions in which two or more persons voluntarily cooperate in the exchange of illicit goods or services. Deviant exchange can take two basic forms. In a trade, the simplest form of exchange, the actors perform comparable roles; each provides a similar service to the other.[5] Examples of deviant trades include homosexual intercourse (Humphreys, 1970; Mileski and Black, 1972; Warren, 1974) and swinging (Bartell, 1971). In a sale, the more complex form of exchange, the actors perform different roles; one or more actors sell a good or service, while one or more others purchase it. Examples of deviant sales include prostitution (Bryan, 1965, 1966; Gray 1973; Hirschi, 1962; Lloyd, 1976), illicit drug dealing (Carey, 1968; Redlinger, 1975), fencing (Klockars, 1974; Walsh, 1977), bookmaking (Hindelang, 1971; Lesieur, 1977), and some forms of bribery (Stoddard, 1968). All of the participants in a deviant exchange are considered deviant.

Exchange, whether deviant or respectable, has certain properties (cf. Blau, 1964; Homans, 1974). The participants voluntarily enter an exchange out of self-interest; they seek goods or services that they cannot provide for themselves. Exchange is a cooperative event. The participants share compatible interest; they operate on the shared assumption that if each party provides the other with rewarding goods or services, the other will reciprocate. Furthermore, exchange is profitable. The participants obtain rewards that are greater than the costs incurred from participation. When the transaction does not yield expected profits, the participants may negotiate for a

[5]Although the actors in a trade perform comparable roles, their parts need not be exactly alike; there may be a division of labor in the transaction. Thus in Humphrey's (1970) language, one tearoom participant acts as the insertor, the other the insertee, but each provides and receives sexual satisfaction, making their roles comparable.

change in the rate at which goods or services are exchanged or withdraw from the operation altogether.

A deviant exchange differs from conventional exchanges in that its participants are eligible for official sanctions. As a consequence, the participants share an additional common interest: they wish to avoid the attention of social control agents. This common interest requires not only that they act with discretion but that they trust one another. Although the shared concern for maintaining discretion offers a potential basis for their alliance, each participant also must be concerned with the other's intentions. This is because a deviant exchange offers opportunities for exploiting one's partner without the exploited member being able to call upon social control agents for assistance. In deviant trades, an actor may worry about being vulnerable to blackmail or to having his or her deviant involvement made public by the other. In deviant sales, customers may worry about receiving less than they are paying for, while sellers may fear robbery or betrayal by their customers. Further, because most deviant sales involve customers who have less experience with deviance than the seller and because social control agents commonly view selling as a more serious offense than buying, the seller has a special responsibility for staging the interaction and managing the customer's responses.[6]

Because the actors must trust each other in the face of potential exploitation, the negotiation of trust becomes a central issue in deviant exchange. Trust may be fostered in several ways. First, participants may limit their operations to acquaintances, friends, or relatives, on the assumption that a partner linked through friendship or kinship can be trusted. Second, they may offer up their track records, informing each other that they have engaged in similar dealings before without ill consequences for their associates. This may involve reference to specific credentials, or it may be achieved through the display of a comfortable, confident demeanor, suggesting familiarity with the exchange situation. Third, participants may use a sponsor of known integrity; they meet through the agency of a sponsor who provides introductions and vouches for the actors. Fourth, participants may provide something symbolizing their commitment to the transaction, establishing a stake in carrying out their part in the exchange. Thus a prostitute may require the customer to commit himself to the purchase of sexual services by paying in advance. The decision to enter into the exchange will depend upon the actor's assessment of the potential advantages and risks from the exchange, as well as his or her assessment of the other's trustworthiness.

[6]Compare the concerns of abortion clients (Lee, 1969) and illegal abortionists (Ball, 1967). Where a deviant good is distributed through several trading levels, a person at an intermediate level may act as a customer in some transactions and as a seller in others, acquiring both sets of concerns (Anonymous, 1969; Redlinger, 1975).

Deviant Exploitation

Like exchange, deviant exploitation involves a minimum of two actors. Exploitation, however, requires only one deviant actor; the other serves as a target or victim.[7] In exploitation, the deviant compels the target to surrender goods or services through stealth, trickery, or physical force. Whereas deviant exchange is characterized by the voluntary cooperation of deviants in pursuit of compatible interests, deviant exploitation involves a conflict of compatible interests, deviant exploitation involves a conflict of interests between the offender and target. Exploitation is not mutually profitable. The payoffs are determined by the deviant, and the payoff structure favors the deviant. The target always loses more by participating in deviant exploitation than by never encountering the deviant.

Because the participants' interest conflict, deviant exploitation is more complex than deviant exchange. Although some exchange transactions are complicated (e.g., distributing a shipment of illicit drugs or operating a numbers game) and some exploitative transactions are straightforward (e.g., a mugging or burglary), exploitation poses special problems for deviants that do not arise in exchange. These problems include managing the target and bystanders and coping with a probable target-social control agent alliance. The resolution of such problems makes the deviant operation more complex. To accomplish the transaction, the deviant must take precautions in addition to those found in exchange, such as shielding his or her identity from the target and bystanders and isolating the operation from the target's potential allies. These precautions typically require special resources, including particular skills, such as speed, stealth, or the skillful manipulation of targets and bystanders, information about the activities of authorities, and special equipment, such as disguises and weapons.

Four distinct forms of deviant exploitation can be identified: coercion, extortion, surreptitious exploitation, and fraud. These are distinguished by the target's understanding of what is taking place. Target understanding varies along two dimensions. First, the target may or may not be aware that exploitation is occurring at the time of the transaction (cf. Glaser and Strauss, 1965). Second, understanding varies in terms of whether the target defines the transaction as an instance of deviant exploitation or some sort of exchange (see Table 1).

Both coercion and extortion occur in a context of open awareness. The target recognizes exploitation for what it is, even while it is occurring, and

[7]In some cases, the person who is forced to surrender goods or services to the deviant may not be the one who bears the loss; for example, it is the bank's money that is stolen, not the teller's. It is therefore possible to distinguish between a victim and a target who acts as the victim's agent. To simplify the discussion, the term "target" will be used to include both of these roles. A target is not necessarily guiltless. For example, con games depend upon the mark's willingness to cheat another person.

TABLE 1 Target's Awareness and Definition of the Situation in Different Forms of Exploitation

Target's awareness	Target's definition of the situation: Exploitation	Exchange
Open	Coercion	Extortion
Closed	Surreptitious exploitation	Fraud

the deviant knows that this is the target's understanding. In coercion, the target surrenders goods or services because the offender uses actual or threatened physical force against the target. Murder (Luckenbill, 1977), forcible rape (Amir, 1971), and armed robbery (Einstadter, 1969; LeJeune, 1977; Luckenbill, 1980) are examples of coercion. In extortion, exploitation occurs under the guise of an exchange (Best, 1982). The deviant threatens to injure a hostage unless the target pays a ransom. The target parts with the ransom of goods or services in return for the hostage's safety. Thus in blackmail the offender agrees not to damage the target's reputation in return for payment (Hepworth, 1975), while in kidnapping the deviant returns a human hostage in exchange fro a ransom (Alix, 1978). Of course, coercion also involves an exchange of sorts; the target of a robbery gives in to avoid death or injury (LeJeune and Alex, 1973). The distinction between coercion and extortion lies in the degree to which the participants define the event as one in which a bargain is being struck. Extortion is more likely to involve overt negotiation between the deviant and the target. Whereas coercive transactions typically take a matter of minutes, the negotiation in extortion can extend over weeks or months. Extortion is less likely it involve a threat to the target's person; the target usually barters to save a reputation, a possession, or another person. Finally, extortion is more likely to become an established relationship, as in cases where a blackmailer or racketeer is paid at regular intervals.

Surreptitious exploitation and fraud occur in a context of closed awareness. Although the target may come to recognize that he or she was exploited, the transaction is over before this realization is made.[8] In surreptitious exploitation, the offender employs stealth to acquire or destroy the target's goods without the target's knowledge. Surreptitious exploitation is clearly exploitative; the target would recognize it as such if he or she knew about the transaction. In some cases, surreptitious exploitation occurs outside the target's presence,. as when an empty building is burglarized (Letkemann, 1973; Shover, 1973), a car is stolen (Savitz, 1959; McCaghy and

[8] In some transactions, awareness may shift from closed to open. Here the target becomes suspicious that the transaction is a deviant one. One form of target management involves reassuring the target that these suspicions are unfounded so that the transaction can proceed.

Giordano, 1977), or a vacant classroom is vandalized (Wade, 1967).[9] In other cases, surreptitious exploitation is accomplished in the target's presence, as in shoplifting (Cameron, 1964) and picking pockets (Maurer, 1964). In fraud, the offender uses trickery leading the target to define the transaction as one in which they will exchange goods or services. Fraud can take different forms. The target may intend to make a legitimate purchase, such as having his or her roof repaired, or the exchange may take the form of a deviant sale, such as buying illicit drugs. In either case, the deviant secretly intends to exploit the relationship by giving the target less that full value in the deal; for example, the roof receives an application of worthless substance, or the drugs are adulterated. In its most artful version, fraud occurs without the target ever realizing that his or her loss was due to exploitation. The forms of fraud range from career crime, such as confidence games (Maurer, 1962), pool hustling (Polsky, 1967), or forgery (Lemert, 1967; Klein and Montague, 1977), through some types of white-collar crime, such as land fraud (Snow, 1978) or investment fraud (Miller, 1965; Soble and Dallos, 1975).

THE SIGNIFICANCE OF THE SOCIAL ORGANIZATION OF DEVIANCE

Individual deviance, deviant exchange, and deviant exploitation are arrayed along the dimension of organizational complexity. Differences in complexity have identifiable consequences for deviants and social control agents. This section advances several propositions describing the effects of organizational complexity. The status of these propositions must be qualified in three ways. First, they reflect social control agents' definitions of deviance. Deviance is behavior that is liable to sanctions by social control agents; the risk of being sanctioned is a central concern for most deviants. Adopting officials' designation of deviance, with its attendant conceptions of responsibility, seriousness, and so on, ignores alternative interpretations. Definitions of deviance are socially constructed; officials and deviants view deviance differently. By adopting the officials' perspective, this analysis reflects some of the underlying assumptions of that point of view. Second, the propositions are derived from reports of field research conducted largely in the United States during the last 20 years. As a consequence, the following discussion refers to a specific time and setting, and its applicability to deviance in other periods or in other societies is an empirical question. Societies differ in their social control ideologies, including their justifica-

[9] Although only the deviant is present during the deviant act, these instances should be considered exploitative, for there is a target who is likely to call on the authorities for aid once the deviance is discovered.

tions for the rules deviants violate and their explanations for deviance, their social control apparatus, the degree to which their reaction to deviance depends on the deviants' position in the community, and so forth. All of these factors have important consequences for deviance and social control. Third, the focus of this discussion is on the effects of organizational complexity, but there is no claim that complexity is the only, or the most important, influence on the behavior of deviants and social control agents. Still, complexity has an effect, and this section attempts to outline some of these consequence.

1. *Persons involved in deviant exchange and deviant exploitation are more likely to be considered responsible for their deviance than those involved in individual deviance.*

In the modern United States, persons involved in individual deviance usually are seen as less than fully responsible for their deviance. The problem drinker, the drug addict, the mentally ill individual, and so forth are believed to engage in deviance because of conditions outside their control Explanations for individual deviance point to various causes, with biological and psychological accounts carrying particular weight. Even when individual deviance appears to involve deliberate action (e.g., suicides or conversion to deviant belief systems), the deviant's action is often attributed to a biological state (such as being under the influence of drugs), an abnormal mental state (such as a compulsion), or beliefs acquired through innocence or foolishness (such as the transmission of deviant belief systems through "brainwashing"). In contrast, persons involved in exchange and exploitation typically are thought to be responsible for their deviance. This is particularly true if they announce or can be presumed to have motives consistent with cultural standards signifying volition, for instance, making money (Cressey, 1962; Biggons and Jones, 1975; Hartung, 1965).

Of course, the relationship between the complexity of the transaction and the imputation of responsibility is not perfect. Deviants involved in exchange and exploitation may be considered, or may plead to have themselves considered, less than fully responsible. Often this is due to their simultaneous involvement in individual deviance. For example, exploitative acts committed by those defined as mentally ill, drug addicts, or compulsive gamblers are viewed as stemming from the conditions causing the individual deviance. Where this condition can be viewed as the direct cause of the exploitative act, for example, an assault committed by a schizophrenic, the deviant is unlikely to be held responsible. However, where the exploitation is only indirectly related, such as thefts by drug addicts, the deviant is viewed as making a calculated choice in response to whatever pressure the individual deviance poses and continues to be held responsible for the exploitation. On occasion, deviants or their spokespersons lobby to redefine some deviants as not responsible for their behavior. Thus early homophile representatives argued that homosexuality is a condition that people occupy rather than a choice that they make, so that one should not be held responsible for one's sexual preference. Such a redefinition places homosexuality, as opposed to homosexual intercourse, into the category of individual deviance.[10]

Just as deviants engaged in complex transactions are sometimes viewed as not responsible for their deviance, individual deviants are sometimes held responsible for their actions. This seems especially common when the individual deviance takes the form of disaffection from a central institution that has the power to control the terms in which deviance is viewed. For example, in Puritan New England, where religion was the community's focal institution and clerics served as moral arbiters, heresy was defined as deliberate, responsible action (Erikson, 1966). Similarly, totalitarian governments, which serve as both central institutions and defining agencies, treat subscription to alternate political ideologies as intentional conduct (Connor, 1972). Imputing responsibility to individual deviants tends to coincide with outside threats to the institution, for example, from rival churches or governments. Although exceptions appear under specifiable circumstances, the relationship between complexity of the transaction and the attribution of the responsibility generally holds.

2. *The more complex the deviant transaction, the more likely the deviance will be defined as serious.*

Social control agents patrol the moral boundaries of communities and protect their members from the offenses of deviants. Individual deviance, deviant exchange, and deviant exploitation violate these boundaries in different ways. Exploitation is viewed as most serious because it inflicts an injury on an unwilling target and because exploitative attacks are unexpected and unpredictable (Conklin, 1975). Further, these transactions directly challenge the ability of social control agents to protect the community's members from predators (cf. Rossi et al., 1974). Inasmuch as participation is voluntary, deviant exchange poses a lesser threat: respectable members of the community may be enticed into participating in these transactions, often as customers in deviant sales. Individual deviance is threatening insofar as it is public, because visible rule breaking challenges the community's assumptions about its moral order. Therefore, the dangers to the community posed by deviance diminish as the transactions become less complex.

The exceptions to this pattern generally reflect stratification within the community. Some areas of the community, such as downtown business

[10]This is the case in which the assignment of responsibility has become a political issue. Although some homophile spokespersons argue that homosexuals do not choose their sexual preference (and, because they are not responsible, should not therefore be blamed for it), others claim that it is a matter of choice and insist that that choice be respected.

districts or upper-middle-class neighborhoods, may be defined as very important, meriting more protection by control agents. Deviant transactions in these sectors may be seen as more threatening than comparable acts in other areas. Control agencies allocate their resources, in part, according to their perceptions of the special need to preserve order in these areas, and deviants in these sectors are more likely to receive the agent's attention than those who engage in deviance elsewhere. Just as agents differentiate between community sectors, they may distinguish between deviants, so that deviant acts committed by some people are considered less serious than similar acts committed by others. Hence, middle-class delinquents may be defined as pranksters rather than vandals, and white-collar crimes are categorized as normal business operations (Chambliss, 1973; Conklin, 1977). In part, this reflects the greater resources of the advantaged. They command private places, so their deviance is less likely to be noticed. If their deviance is discovered, they can call on others, for example, private attorneys, to help cast their activities in favorable terms. Finally, deviance may be viewed as less serious if social control agents or those who set social control policy have a vested interest in the deviant operations. This can involve corruption—bribes paid by deviants to agents—or the authorities' recognition that deviance performs valuable functions. For example, officials may be willing to overlook street-walkers in one part of a city because they fear driving prostitution underground where it cannot be supervised.

3. *The more complex the deviant transaction, the more likely the deviant will be subject to punitive sanctions.*

The methods used by societies to respond to deviance depend upon their resources, culture, and social structure. Before the Industrial Revolution, deviants were typically executed, given corporal punishment, publicly humiliated, or banished, although institutionalization was also employed. In Europe and the United States, the 19th century saw the development of widespread custodial institutions, grounded in various ideologies that explained the causes of deviance and recommended regimens for reform (Foucault, 1965; Hay, 1975; Rothman, 1971; Scull, 1977). In contemporary U.S. society, the legal and medical models are dominant: deviants can be seen either as responsible for their actions—as criminal—or as not responsible—as sick (Aubert and Messinger, 1958; Rothman, 1980; Stoll, 1968). The choice of model is consequential, because crimes are ordinarily punished, while illnesses are treated.[11]

Individual deviance is usually seen as a kind of illness that should be treated. Because there is no second party being intentionally exploited,

[11]Obviously, the use of medical rhetoric should not be taken as proof of a distinctive pattern of practice. Many control programs that provide treatment strongly resemble punitive programs in their concern with custody.

individual deviants are defined as threatening their own personal well-being. The medical model justifies treatment as a method of protecting individual deviants from themselves. Social control is cast in terms of a medical vocabulary; institutions are labeled hospitals, clinics, or centers for detoxification, drug rehabilitation, or methadone treatment; and personnel bear the titles of physician, psychiatrist, nurse, counselor, or aide. The appropriateness of treatment is recognized by the professionals, the legislative and judicial agencies that create and maintain their authority, and the public at large. Surveys show that a large proportion of the U.S. public not only considers mental illness, alcoholism, and drug addiction to be medical-psychiatric problems, but also favors a response of treatment rather than punishment (Dohrenwend and Chin-Shong, 1967; Patterson et al., 1968; Linsky, 1970).

Societal reaction to participants in deviant exchange is mixed and shifting. On the one hand, individuals involved in most forms of exchange are held responsible for their actions and therefore eligible for punishment. This is especially true for sellers in deviant sales, who tend to be held more culpable than their customers. On the other hand, forms of deviant exchange are increasingly viewed as private arrangements that have few, if any, detrimental consequences for others or for the social order. Those who argue that exchanges are "crimes without victims" urge that social control resources be redirected toward dealing with the more serious, exploitative violations (Schur, 1965).[12]

Exploitative transactions are most likely to be viewed as meriting punitive sanctions. Because exploitation attacks the community's members, these are defined as "real crimes," which should be punished (President's Commission, 1968: 159–168; Conklin, 1975). Survey respondents, when asked to indicate the appropriate degrees of punishment for different offenses, generally assign heavier penalties to exploitative deviants than to those involved in individual deviance or exchange (Gibbons, 1969). Public condemnation extends to white-collar or business crimes, particularly when these offenses have a clear exploitative element (Conklin, 1977). In spite of this public sentiment, social control efforts directed at organizational crime are relatively limited, and the sanctions levied against offenders are relatively lenient (Green et al., 1972). This restrained social control activity reflects a reluctance by authorities to interfere with legitimate organizations, as well as the substantial stocks of resources that these organizations can employ to shield illicit practices from targets, create favorable public impressions, and neutralize enforcement efforts.

[12]While the term "crimes without victims" has some analytic uses, it transcends the boundaries of our categories. A drug purchase has the structure of an exchange, but drug use fits the category of individual deviance.

Exceptions to the relationship between the complexity of the deviant transaction and the use of punitive sanctions reflect definitions of the deviant's responsibility or the act's seriousness. Thus medicalization of child abuse means that offenders are treated rather than punished, and as marijuana becomes redefined as relatively harmless, legislatures reduce penalties.

4. *The more complex the deviant transaction, the greater the likelihood the deviant will be identified and apprehended by social control agents.*

The more complex the deviant transaction, the more visible it is to others, and, assuming the authorities will intervene in visible incidents, the more visible the transaction, the greater the likelihood of the deviant's apprehension. Given the capacity for self-discretion, individual deviants can take precautions to make themselves relatively safe from social control efforts. Individual deviants run the greatest risks when they fail to attend to the need for discretion or when their limited resources force them into public view, as when skid row tramps drink in public. So long as their deviance is performed in private, individual deviants are unlikely to be discovered.

Deviant exchange, because it requires at least two actors, is more vulnerable to social control efforts. First, the other parties to the exchange know about one's involvement in deviance, and they may be capable of supplying control agents with enough information to bring about one's identification and capture.[13] However, associates are unlikely to provide the authorities with such information, because they are implicated in the exchange. They are most likely to inform when they are forced to supply such information or when they feel they were exploited in the exchange. Thus pressure from the police may lead an addict to inform about a drug dealer, and a theft by a prostitute may lead a customer to provide vice officers with an anonymous tip. Second, when the participants in exchange meet in public, for example, when the participants in an illicit marketplace are not well known to one another, their risks are greater. Deals conducted in public are more likely to be noticed, and if the existence of the marketplace becomes known to the authorities participants are vulnerable to ambushes and infiltration by control agents.

The existence of the target makes exploitation more visible than individual deviance or exchange. Because targets object to being exploited, the offender must anticipate that after the transaction's completion the target will complain to the authorities and assist them in identifying and apprehending the deviant. Although individual deviance and exchange frequently occur without coming to the attention of control agents, a much higher

[13]If individual deviants perform their transactions in the company of deviant associates, they run similar risks of betrayal.

proportion of exploitative transactions are reported. Because exploitative transactions are viewed as more serious, the authorities are likely to devote more attention to these complaints. The probability of arrest is greater for deviant exploitation, such as rape, robbery, burglary, and forgery, than for deviant exchange, such as drug sales (Peterson and Braiker, 1979:41).

The degree to which deviants involved in exploitation are subject to identification and apprehension varies with the form of exploitation. In coercion, the target typically reports the violation and tries to assist in apprehending the offender. Once they realize that exploitation has occurred, targets of surreptitious exploitation also are likely to report the offense to the authorities. Extortion and fraud, however, have comparatively lower rates of reporting. In extortion, the target may fear that reporting the incident will jeopardize the hostage. In some cases, targets call in officials as soon as they are threatened—particularly when they are confident that the authorities share their concern for the hostage. But in others they delay complaining until the hostage's return, and in still other cases, they never complain because reporting would make their problems worse—blackmail targets cannot complain without explaining to control agents why they are being blackmailed. Targets may not complain of fraud because they do not realize that their loss was due to exploitation (e.g., a target of land fraud never learns that the land is worthless) or because reporting would be personally embarrassing (e.g., the mark in the confidence game must reveal his or her illicit intentions when reporting the loss).

The relationship between the complexity of the transaction and the likelihood of identification and apprehension is also affected by the social organization of deviants—the patterns of relations between deviant actors (Best and Luckenbill, 1980). Although some deviants operate as loners, never associating with other deviants, most deviants belong to a deviant social network and often cooperate with associates in carrying out deviant operations. Deviant associates pose both risks and benefits. Because they know about one's involvement in deviance, associates are capable of betraying the deviant to control agents. This danger accounts for the establishment, in many deviant groups, of codes of conduct that emphasize secrecy and mutual loyalty. One the other hand, deviant groups usually control greater resources than loners, resources than can be used to conceal involvement in deviance and defend members who are apprehended or threatened with sanctioning. Because these resources tend to increase as the organization of deviants become more sophisticated, risks diminish in the more organized groups. Thus loners and gang members are more vulnerable to control efforts than members of teams of professional criminals or organized crime families.

Social control agents' priorities also affect the relationship between risk and complexity. When reformers, the press, or other segments of society mount moral crusades and pressure agents to eradicate particular types of deviance, the deviants' risks increase. Heightened awareness of the part of citizens makes them more likely to report offense, and in response to the pressure agents may give the offense a higher priority and invest more of their resources in the effort.

5. *The more complex the deviant transaction, the more elaborate the tactics used by deviants to protect themselves from social control efforts.*

In any deviant transaction, deviant actors can be expected to try to minimize their chances of being detected, identified, apprehended, and sanctioned. Because the deviant's risks increase with the complexity of the transaction, deviants must employ more elaborate tactics for protection as organizational complexity increases. In individual deviance, the principal defense is self-discretion. The actor's precautions center on controlling information about his or her involvement in deviance by operating in isolated or protected places, concealing evidence of deviant activities, and offering evidence of one's commitment to respectability (Goffman, 1963).

In deviant exchange, discretion is supplemented by additional means of self-protection. Exchange requires associates, who know of and can betray the actor's involvement in deviance. Deviants can usually count on their associates to be discreet, but, as suggested earlier, their discretion can dissolve under certain circumstances, such as pressure from control agents. Therefore, deviants devise supplemental tactics to protect themselves from betrayal and the risks posed by their public dealings. Four tactics can be identified. First, deviants may withhold information regarding their identities from their deviant associates. For example, swingers may operate on a first-name basis and refuse to provide information about their identities, occupations, or places of residence (Bartell, 1971). Second, as noted above, deviants may limit their dealings to associates who are trustworthy. Third, deviants may threaten associates with sanctions, such as physical harm or ostracism, if the associates betray them. Finally, in sales networks, where profits from dealing may be substantial, deviants may insure the safety of their operations by corrupting the authorities to overlook their deviance.

In exploitation, deviants may use all of the protective tactics adopted by those engaged in individual deviance and exchange, including self-discretion, methods of avoiding betrayal by deviant associates, and attempts to corrupt control agents. In addition, deviants engaging in exploitation must manage actual or anticipated resistance from the target. During the transaction, the target must be manipulated so as not to disrupt the operation and jeopardize the offender's safety. In surreptitious exploitation, manipulation involves special techniques, for example, the pickpocket's deft touch, that allow the offender to carry out the transaction without arousing the target's notice. In coercion, the deviant uses other methods to manipulate the target, such as the calculated threat or use of physical force and the management of a capable and credible appearance (Letkemann, 1973; Luckenbill, 1980). In extortion, the deviant typically couples the control over the hostage—which should induce cooperation if the target is concerned for the hostage's well-being—with tactical maneuvers designed to keep the extortionist's identity secret, such as communicating only via notes or phone calls. In fraud, target manipulation is central to the operation, because the deviant deceives the target as to the nature of their transaction. Second, the deviant must cope with the possibility that the target will call on social control agents for assistance. Because exploitative transactions presumably will be reported to the authorities, the offender tries to avoid giving up enough information about his or her identity to be linked to the offense. The concealment of personal identity varies with the form of exploitation. In coercion, the actor may cover up outward appearance, for instance, by wearing a mask; in surreptitious exploitation, the deviant tries to avoid leaving clues behind, for instance, wearing gloves to avoid leaving fingerprints. Extortionists can usually avoid face-to-face contacts with their targets, but they remain concerned with giving off evidence of personal identity; for example, the handwriting on a ransom note can link the deviant to the crime. Because deviants engaged in fraud typically meet and talk to their targets, they must either construct false identities for these encounters or try to keep the target from complaining, for example, by "cooling out the mark" or, ideally, keeping the target from recognizing the fraud for what it is.

The social organization of deviants also affects the deviant's ability to use effective tactics (Best and Luckenbill, 1980). Protective tactics may require resources, such as information about social control activities, enforcers to maintain discipline among deviant associates, or money for corrupting officials. Members of more sophisticated organizational forms are more likely to command these resources. Moreover, experienced deviants can teach newcomers how to recognize and evaluate risks and how to devise tactics to manage them. In short, contact with other deviants helps reduce risks.

6. *Social control agents are more likely to use proactive tactics against individual deviance and deviant exchange, while they are more likely to use reactive tactics against deviant exploitation.*

In order to apprehend and sanction deviants, social control agents must have information about the deviant transaction and the people involved in it (Reiss, 1971; Sanders, 1977). Inasmuch as the source and amount of information available to social control agents vary with the organization of the deviant transaction, agents must adopt tactics suited to the organizational features of the transaction.

Actors engaged in individual deviance and deviant exchange generally carry out their transactions discreetly. This means that social control agents cannot rely on others to report these offenses; agents must uncover them through proactive methods (Reiss, 1971). To be sure, agents do receive some complaints from citizens, particularly about cases involving deviants whose limited resources force them to operate in public places or who lack the capacity to maintain discretion. But these complaints concern only a fraction of all deviant transactions. Social control agencies seeking to eradicate a particular form of individual deviance or deviant exchange must adopt proactive tactics and use their own initiative to cultivate information about the deviants' identities and activities. By employing undercover agents, informants, covert observation, and similar tactics, control agents can penetrate the protected setting that house individual deviance and exchange (Rubinstein, 1973; Schur, 1965; Skolnick, 1966).

In deviant exploitation, control agents usually can expect cooperation from the target, who is likely to report the transaction in hopes of getting revenge, restitution, or other satisfaction. The quality of these reports varies with the form of exploitation. In surreptitious, exploitation and coercion, targets frequently report their loss, usually after the transaction is over and the damage done. Targets of surreptitious exploitation, who generally never see the offender, are less likely to have useful information than targets of coercion, who are attacked face to face (Stinchcombe, 1963). Targets of extortion and fraud are less likely to inform the authorities of their loss. In extortion, targets may fear for the hostage's safety while the transaction is in progress, and once it is completed they may be reluctant to call in the authorities out of embarrassment, either at having cooperated with deviants or at having their personal secrets revealed.[14] Although extortion usually involves no face-to-face contact, targets who report the offense while it is in progress give agents opportunities to disrupt the offenders' plans, for example, by ambushing the ransom delivery. In fraud, targets typically meet the deviants. The failure to complain may be due to ignorance of the exploitative nature of their loss or to embarrassment at being fooled, particularly if the fraud involved an illicit exchange. Whatever the form of exploitation, the fact that targets do report offenses provides agents with valuable assistance. In exploitation, agents rely heavily on reactive tactics (Reiss, 1971). Once they have been called in, agents can interview witnesses, analyze physical evidence, use informants to link offenders to offenses, and so forth, trying to identify, locate, and capture offenders.

[14]In blackmail, social control agents sometimes take special care to protect the target's reputation, for instance, by avoiding public mention of the target's name or the reason for blackmail during prosecution. This tactic is intended to encourage targets to report their exploitation (Hepworth, 1975).

CONCLUSION

Deviant transactions can be arrayed along a dimension of organizational complexity. This paper described three forms of deviant transactions: individual deviance, deviant exchange, and deviant exploitation. The level of complexity has important consequences for deviants and social control agents. As complexity increases, deviants are more likely to be seen as responsible for their actions, those actions are more likely to be defined as serious, the response to deviance is more likely to be punitive, the risks of the deviant's identification and capture become greater, the range of tactics used by deviants to avoid apprehension expands, and social control agents are more likely to employ reactive tactics. These claims must be qualified in two important ways. First, focusing on the consequences of organizational complexity neglects other factors—factors that may have different, even opposing effects. Second, these relationships are derived from a reading of field studies in the contemporary United States. The social organization of deviant transactions has not received the systematic attention awarded the social psychology of deviance. More research is needed, both to determine the circumstances under which the influence of organizational complexity is overridden by other factors and to learn whether these relationships hold in other times and places.

This perspective has implications beyond the study of deviance. The dimension of organizational complexity can be applied to conventional transactions. In the course of respectable life, people frequently engage in individual operations, such as feeding and dressing themselves. In cooperative interactions, people engage in various forms of exchange, from formal purchases to the development and maintenance of friendships. And whenever one party to a transaction acts in his or her own interests at the expense of another—a situation that may occur in the exercise of coercive power or in mundane incidents such as lying—an analogy can be drawn to deviant exploitation. A systematic study of the social organization of conventional transactions may reveal other forms that have no deviant equivalent.

Although there are analogous forms of deviant and respectable transactions, the two should be distinguished because they occupy different positions in the larger institutional order. Deviant transactions, unlike respectable transactions, make one or more participants subject to social control efforts. As a consequence, secrecy about operations and identities forms a central theme in deviant transactions. In addition, deviant transactions are more tenuous than their respectable counterparts. Respectable transactions receive strong institutional support, backed by custom, written codes, and social control agencies. People enter into conventional operations with confidence that the other participants will operate within the confines of respectability. In contrast, deviant transactions do not receive comparable institutional support. Deviants must rely on whatever norms govern conduct between deviant associates as well as their own abilities to carry out operations in the face of opposition by targets or social control agents. Therefore, planning and precautions assume special importance to deviants. Even though its organization may resemble that found in respectable transactions, the fact that an activity is deviant turns the transaction into an occasion for secrecy and precaution.

REFERENCES

Alix, Ernest K.
1978 Ransom Kidnapping in America, 1874–1974. Carbondale: Southern Illinois University Press.

Amir, Menachem
1971 Patterns in Forcible Rape. Chicago: University of Chicago Press.

Anonymous
1969 "On selling marijuana." Pp. 92–102 in E. Goode (ed.), Marijuana. New York: Atherton.

Aubert, Vilhelm, and Sheldon S. Messinger
1958 "The criminal and the sick." Inquiry 1:137–160.

Ball, Donald W.
1967 "An abortion clinic ethnography." Social Problems 14:293–301.

Bartell, Gilbert
1971 Group Sex, New York: New American.

Best, Joel
1982 "Crime as strategic interaction." Urban Life. 11: 107–128.

Best, Joel, and David F. Luckenbill
1980 "The social organization of deviants." Social Problems 28:14–31.

Bittner, Egon
1967 "Police discretion in emergency apprehension of mentally ill persons." Social Problems 14:278–292.

Blau, Peter M.
1964 Exchange and Power in Social Life. New York: Wiley.

Blumer, Herbert
1967 The World of Youthful Drug Use. Berkeley: University of California.

Bryan, James H.
1965 "Apprenticeships in prostitution." Social Problems 12:287–297.
1966 "Occupational ideologies and individual attitudes of call girls." Social Problems 13:441–450.

Cahalan, Don, and Robin Room
1974 Problem Drinking Among American Men. New Brunswick: Rugers Center of Alcohol Studies.

Cameron, Mary Owen
1964 The Booster and the Snitch. New York: Free Press.

Carey, James To.
1968 The College Drug Scene. Englewood Cliffs: Prentice-Hall.

Chambliss, William J.
1973 "The saints and the roughnecks." Society 11:24–31.
Clinard, Marshall B., and Richarg Quinney
1973 Criminal Behavior Systems: A Typology, 2nd ed. New York: Holt, Rinehart, and Winston.
Conklin, John E.
1975 The Impact of Crime. New York: Macmillan.
1977 "Illegal But not Criminal": Business Crime in America. Engelwood Cliffs: Prentice-Hall.
Connor, Walter D.
1972 "The manufacture of deviance." American Sociological Review 37:403-413.
Cressey, Donald R.
1962 "Role theory, differential association, and compulsive crimes." Pp. 443–467 in A. Rose (ed.), Human Behavior and Social Processes. Boston: Houghton Mifflin.
Davis, Fred
1961 "Deviance disavowal." Social Problems 9:120–132.
Dohrenwend, Bruce P., and Edwin Chin-Shong
1967 "Social status and attitudes toward psychological disorder." American Sociological Review 32:417–433.
Douglas, Jack D.
1967 The Social Meanings of Suicide. Princeton: Princeton University Press.
Edgerton, Robert B.
1967 The Cloak of Competence. Berkeley: University of California Press.
Einstadter, Werner J.
1969 "The social organization of armed robbery." Social Problems 17:64-83.
Erikson, Kai T.
1966 Wayward Puritans. New York: Wiley.
Feldman, Harvey W.
1968 "Ideological supports to becoming and remaining a heroin addict." Journal of Health and Social Behavior 9:131–139.
Foucault, Michel
1965 Madness and Civilization. New York: Pantheon.
Gibbons, Don C.
1969 "Crime and punishment." Social forces 47:391–397.
Gibbons, Don C., and Joseph F. Jones
1975 The Study of Deviance. Englewood Cliffs: Prentice-Hall.
Glaser, Barney G., and Anselm L. Strauss
1965 Awareness of Dying. Chicago: Aldine.
1967 The Discovery of Grounded Theory. Chicago: Aldine.
Goffman, Erving
1963 Stigma. Englewood Cliffs: Prentice-Hall.
Gray, Diana
1973 "Turning out." Urban Life and Culture 1:401–425.

Green, Mark J., Beverly C. Moore, Jr., and Bruse Wasserstein
1972 The Closed Enterprise System. New York: Grossman.
Handler, Doug
1968 "Diary of a C.O." Pp. 99–104 in C. McCaghy, J. Skipper, and M. Lefton (eds.), In Their Own Behalf, New York: Appleton-Century-Crofts.
Hartung, Frank
1965 Crime, Law, and Society. Detroit: Wayne State University Press.
Hay, Douglas
1975 "Property, authority and the criminal law." Pp. 17–63 in Hay et al., Albion's Fatal Tree. New York: Pantheon.
Hepworth, Mike
1975 Blackmail. London: Routledge and Kegan Paul.
Hindelang, Michael J.
1971 "Bookies and bookmaking." Crime and Delinquency 17:245–255.
Hirschi, Travis
1962 "The professional prostitute." Berkeley Journal of Sociology 7:33-49.
Homans, George C.
1974 Social Behavior, revised ed. New York: Harcourt Brace Jovanovich.
Humphreys, Laud
1970 Tearoom Trade. Chicago: Aldine.
Jacobs, Jerry
1971 Adolescent Suicide. New York: Wiley.
Klein, John F., and Arthur Montague
1977 Check Forgers. Lexington: Lexington Books.
Klockars, Carl B.
1974 The Professional Fence. New York: Free Press
Lee, Nancy Howell
1969 The Search for an Abortionist. Chicago: University of Chicago Press.
LeJeune, Robert
1977 "The management of a mugging." Urban Life 6:123–148.
LeJeune, Robert, and Nicholas Alex
1973 "On being mugged." Urban Life and Culture 2:259–288.
Lemert, Edwin M.
1967 Human Deviance, Social Problems, and Social Control. Englewood Cliffs: Prentice-Hall.
Lesieur, Henry R.
1977 The Chase. Garden City: Anchor.
Letkemann, Peter
1973 Crime as Work. Engelwood Cliffs: Prenticce-Hall.
Linsky, Arnold S.
1970 "The changing public views of alcoholism." Quarterly Journal of Studies on Alcohol 32:692–704.
Lloyd, Robin
1976 For Money or Love. New York: Ballantine.

Lofland, John
1969 Deviance and Identity. Englewood Cliffs: Prentice-Hall.
Loney, martin
1973 "Social control in Cuba." Pp. 42–60 in I. Taylor and L. Taylor (eds.), Politics and Deviance. Harmondsworth: Penguin.
Luckenbill, David F.
1977 "Criminal homicide as a situated transaction." Social Problems 25:176–186.
1980 "Patterns of force in robbery." Deviant Behavior 1:361–378.
Matza, David
1969 Becoming Deviant. Englewood Cliffs: Prentice-Hall.
Maurer, David W.
1962 The Big Con. New York: New American Library.
1964 Whiz Mob. New Haven: College and University Press.
McCaghy, Charles H., and Peggy C. Giordano
1977 "Auto theft." Criminology 15:367–385.
Mileski, Maureen, and Donald J. Black
1972 "The social organization of homosexuality." Urban Life and Culture 1:131–166.
Miller, Norman C.
1965 The Great Salad Oil Swindle. New York: Howard McCann.
Pattison, E. M., L. A. Bishop, and A. S. Linsky
1968 "Changes in public attitudes on narcotic addiction." American Journal of Psychiatry 125:160–167.
Peterson, Mark A., and Harriet B. Braiker
1979 Doing Crime. Santa Monica: Rand.
Polsky, Ned
1967 Hustlers, Beats, and Others. Chicago: Aldine.
President's Commission on Law Enforcement and the Administration of Justice
1968 The Challenge of Crime in a Free Society. New York: Avon.
Redlinger, Lawrence J.
1975 "Marketing and distributing heroin." Journal of Psychedelic Drugs 7:331–353.
Reiss, Albert J.
1971 Police and the Public. Cambridge: MIT Press.
Rossi, Peter H., et al.
1974 "The seriousness of crimes." American Sociological Review 39:224-237.
Rothman, David J.
1971 The Discovery of the Asylum. Boston: Little, Brown
1980 Conscience and Convenience. Boston: Little, Brown
Rubinstein, Jonathan
1973 City Police. New York: Farrar, Straus and Giroux.
Sanders, William B.
1977 Detective Work. New York: Free Press.

Savitz, Leonard D.
1959 "Automobile theft." Journal of Criminal Law, Criminology and Police Science 50:132–143.
Scheff, Thomas J.
1966 Being Mentally Ill. Chicago: Aldine.
Schur, Edwin M.
1965 Crimes Without Victims. Englewood Cliffs: Prentice-Hall.
Scull, Andrew T.
1977 Decarceration. Englewood Cliffs: Prentice-Hall.
Shibutani, Tamotsu
1961 Society and Personality. Englewood Cliffs: Prentice-Hall.
Shover, Neal
1973 "The social organization of burglary." Social Problems 20:499–514.
Skolnick, Jerome H.
1966 Justice Without Trial. New York: Wiley.
Snow, Robert P.
1978 "The golden fleece." Pp. 133–150 in J. Johnson and J. Douglas (eds.), Crime at the Top. Philadelphia: Lippincott.
Soble, Ronald L. and Robert E. Dallos
1975 The Impossible Dream. New York: Putnam.
Spradley, James P.
1970 You Owe Yourself a Drunk. Boston: Little, Brown.
Stinchcombe, Arthur
1963 "Institutions of privacy in the determination of police administrative practice." American Journal of Sociology 69:150–160.
Stoddard, Ellwyn R.
1968 " 'The informal code' of police deviance." Journal of Criminal Law Criminology and Police Science 59:201–213.
Stoddart, Kenneth
1974 "The facts of life about dope." Urban Life and Culture 3:179–204.
Stoll, Clarice S.
1968 "Images of man and social control." Social Forces 47:119–127.
Sutherland, Edwin H., and Donald R. Cressey
1974 Criminology, 9th ed. Philadelphia: Lippincott.
Szasz, Thomas S.
1974 The Myth of Mental Illness, revised ed. New York: Harper & Row.
Truzzi, Marcello
1968 "Lilliputians in Gulliver's Land." Pp. 197–211 in M. Truzzi (ed.), Sociology and Everyday Life. Englewood Cliffs: Prentice-Hall.
Wade, Andrew
1967 "Social processes in the act of juvenile vandalism." Pp. 94–109 in M. Clinard and R. Quinney (eds.), Criminal Behavior Systems: A Typology. New York: Holt, Rinehart, and Winston.
Walsh, Marilyn E.
1977 The Fence. Westport: Greenwood.

Warren, Carol A. B.
1974 Identity and Community in the Gay World. New York: Wiley.
Winick, Charles
1961 "Physician narcotic addicts." Social Problems 9:174–186.
Wiseman, Jacqueline P.
1970 Stations of the Lost. Englewood Cliffs: Prentice-Hall.

Reading 2

Acceptable Deviance as Social Control: The Cases of Fashion and Slang

Lesley D. Harman
York University, North York, Ontario

The concept of "acceptable deviance" is introduced as a bridge between the ideal types of conformity and deviance. It is argued that as a form of social control it ensures conformity in the guise of individual freedom. The principle has its roots in the work of Goffman ("role distance") and is developed in this paper as a basis for explaining the social control effects of two forms of social action: fashion and slang. In both cases, acceptable deviance exemplifies Sapir's principle of "adventurous safety" by melding the "imitative" and "differentiating" functions discussed by Simmel. Rule-bending is allowed by only within predefined limits of propriety; beyond these boundaries behavior becomes "unacceptably deviant." It is suggested that normality is an achieved status for actors whose expressive capacity is limited by the ability of their audience and others to read their statements. Acceptable deviance regulates such reading and consequently assures conformity.

As theoretical constructs, conformity and deviation have become pivotal, indeed paramount, in the study of social order. It is quite clear that any version of order requires a partner in disorder; the very idea of conformity demands that we have an idea of what deviation could be. Both ideal types exist only by virtue of their opposition: if deviation did not pose a threat to social order, then neither would conformity be problematic (Coser, 1956).

The advent of the labeling perspective to deviance (Becker, 1963; Lemert, 1951; Goffman, 1968; etc.) has led to a realization that there is nothing absolute about these categories, but rather that deviation and conformity are negotiated conditions. This paper is an attempt to contribute to this tradition by further obscuring the line between conformity and deviation. To this end, it will be maintained that social behavior rarely exemplifies either ideal type. Rather, most social actors balance on the tightrope of *acceptable deviance,* which delicately mediates between the two extremes. Acceptable deviance is defined as that behavior which deviates enough from the norm such that it is not entirely predictable, yet which conforms enough to the norm to be acceptable as signifying membership.

The need for such a category becomes evident when the competing demands of conformity and deviation which are placed upon the individual by the liberal democratic ethic of urbanized Western society are recognized. On the one hand, this ideology maintains that individuals have the right and the freedom to express their unique identities. Individuality and creativity are encouraged. On the other hand, however, the existence of society as a rule-governed set of individuals interested in a common goal of social order demands that members share basic conceptions about what it is which makes them a group. This entails a set of roles which members must adopt in relation to each other, and the accompanying set of expected behaviors, or rules. Where there is rule-guided behavior there is social pressure to comply with the rules in order to maintain social order, to maintain the integrity of the group.

So we are faced with a paradox—two social demands which appear to contradict each other: conformity and deviation. Individuals who heed either demand to the exclusion of the other are labeled deviant. If one conforms entirely with the norm, the one is viewed as "over-involved" (Goffman, 1961). That is, one is not able to establish the distance from the norm which is required in order to be recognized as a unique individual capable of making choices. On the other hand, if one deviates entirely from the norm, then one is viewed as posing a threat to the group—as not sharing the basic set of norms and values which would designate one as a member.

How is it possible to satisfy both demands? That is, how is it possible to conform and deviate at the same time? The solution to being perceived as an acceptable member must be arrived at through a negotiation between the two extreme demands, as reached through a secondary set of norms which constitute acceptable deviance. Acceptable deviance will be presented as an apparent solution to the paradox—apparent, because it solves through appearing to solve rather than through allowing the coexistence of conformity and deviation in any concrete sense. Through the example of fashion, it will be suggested that acceptable deviance can and should be seen as a method of social control—a mechanism of ensuring social conformity in the guise of individual freedom.

RULE-BENDING

The concept of acceptable deviance has its roots in the notion of "rule-bending." One may bend rules to the extent that the individual appears to have control over them, but not to the point that s/he poses a threat to the social order. Erving Goffman dealt extensively with social interaction from the implicit premise that rule-bending is a central mechanism. His social actor both needs to be rule-guided (i.e., seeks membership) and needs to bend those rules in order to present self as different (i.e., seeks self-expression). One achieves this, according to Goffman, by controlling one's degree of involvement in the social situation. He distinguishes between "main" and "side" involvements, where a main involvement "absorbs the major part of an individual's attention and interest" and a side involvement may be engaged in "in an abstracted fashion without threatening or confusing simultaneous maintenance of a main involvement" (1963:43). He also differentiates between "dominant" and "subordinate" involvements. A dominant involvement has priority: it is the role in which one is expected to be engaged. A subordinate involvcment, on the other hand, acts as a "filler" between one's engagement in dominant involvements, which "ought to catch only the individual's lesser and unimportant self" (45).

These two dichotomies not only differentiate between degrees of involvement, but assign priority to certain involvements above others, implying two things. First, there seems to exist a legitimatized rule-bending procedure. That is, it is acceptable for an individual to bend the rules of social interaction (by engaging in subordinate involvements) as long as it is clear that one can account for the deviant action (by being prepared to engage in the dominant involvement when it arises), and as long as one's main involvement does not become one's subordinate involvement. The second implication is that social actors know and accept the rules—rules whose making is beyond their control—and that if they demonstrate their commitment to membership then they will be given the leeway to express themselves through side and subordinate involvements.

The principle of acceptable deviance can also be found in Goffman's work on role distance (1961), in which he suggests that actors fear appearing overinvolved in their roles. Overadhering to the rules in as dangerous as breaking them: one risks being seen as antisocial—as identifying one's self entirely with one's role and forgetting one's position as a multifaceted individual. So, in addition to feeling drawn to both following the rules and expressing one's self in one's deviation from those rules, one carefully avoids giving the impression of being overinvolved in whatever one happens to be doing. This avoidance Goffman calls "role distance". As he puts it, "the individual acts to say: 'I do not dispute the direction in which things are going and I will go along with them, but at the same time I want you to know that you haven't fully contained me in the state of affairs.' "(133).

In *Frame Analysis* (1974), Goffman admits that "some deviation from the norm is tolerated. And if effective cover is maintained, a great deal of deviation can be got away with. Indeed, that deviation is an element in almost all fabrications" (346–347). Implicit here is that "breaking frame" creates a new frame, which the previous break structures.

> It follows that if a particular structure of attention is to be maintained, it cannot be maintained intendedly (at least wholly so), since such an intention would introduce a different focus of attention, that of maintaining a particular one. (346)

This reformulation of overinvolvement introduces a subtle dimension of *change* in the norms governing what one may be involved in, bringing us closer to acceptable deviance than Goffman's previous work. The notion that frame can be broken and a reframing, or a change in primary framework, can take place, lends more credence to the collective negotiation of primary framework (that which "provides the first answer to the question 'What is it that's going on here?' " (25).

Posner (1975) suggests yet another indication of acceptable deviance with her notion of the "stigma of excellence." She maintains that individuals who are superior, i.e., who approximate the ideal which is held up by the normative structure, are excluded by normals because they are *too* good. "The identity of being an exceptional individual is truly a 'mixed blessing'. Being superior to others is as problematic and pathological as being inferior. Both sorts of people are marginal to the social system" (141). For Posner, it is the "just right principle" which governs who is stigmatized and who is not.

Merton's (1938) "ritual" mode of adaptation also leads to such an extreme of overinvolvement; his "innovator" may approximate our acceptable deviant as long as s/he does not employ unacceptable (as opposed to merely unconventional) means to reach cultural goals.

Matza's (1964) work on delinquent commitment has revealed a tension in subcultures between public expressions of commitment to the group, and private misgivings about one's role. The ease with which his model may be applied to other subcultures suggests an underlying reality of conflict between group demands and individual desires. When one individual desire is that of acceptability, it would seem that the principle of acceptable deviance is useful in suggesting how that tension is expressed.

FASHION AS ACCEPTABLE DEVIANCE

Conformity and deviation have little overt social function unless they are first and foremost visible: identifiable to others as exemplifying a relation to the rules. Thus, the types of behaviors which are affected by the impulses of conformity and deviation are those which suggest one's membership, and can be read as such. Simmel (1971) isolated just such a realm, which he called "externals." Externals are such things as "clothing, social conduct, amusements" (298) which are meaning-endowed, in that they carry social significance, and therefore make a statement about the one who owns or utilizes them. Material culture and social behavior—even extending to the basic element of language—are used to symbolize self and the relation of self to group. Externals, then, are those symbols which serve the dual functions of self-expression and conformity.

One of the assumptions which is being made regarding acceptable deviance is that individuals desire to be accepted as members. It is important to remember that this involves an element of choice, and therefore that it is to groups which are freely organized on the basis of shared symbols that the idea of acceptable deviance would seem to apply. An appropriate term for these groups was generated by Holzner (1968) when he introduced the notion of *epistemic communities.* Epistemic communities are groups whose membership is contingent upon a common sense of what "good" symbols or externals are. This is exemplified by the group's manifestation of a particular lifestyle, often termed by sociologists as subculture. Because "subculture" often has the unintended connotation of "counterculture," the more neutral term of "epistemic community" will be used. Gans' (1974) concept of "taste community" is also relevant here.

It will be maintained that the "expressive function of externals is limited by the ability of others to read the externals as expressive of certain collectively agreed-upon meanings. The most important of these is group membership. Externals as expressive of group membership both suggest the language in which membership may be expressed (societal rule level) and the individual articulation of self in relation to group, *through* meaning-endowed externals (individual level).

The set of rules and patterns dictating the symbolic function of externals is known as fashion. Fashion is a central mechanism in social organization. It affects most externals—some, such as clothing, automobiles, language, music, and art, more than others. Because it is so pervasive—fashion touches us all, even in a negative sense (e.g., the one who claims to dress totally independently of fashion is her/himself responding to a very powerful force—a force strong enough to elicit a negative response)—and because it is an excellent example of acceptable deviance as it affects the very basis of social behavior, it will be used to illustrate in a general sense the concepts with which we have been dealing.

> Fashion is custom in the guise of departure from custom. Most normal individuals consciously or unconsciously have the itch to break away in some measure from a too literal loyalty to acceptable custom. They are not fundamentally in

> revolt from custom but they wish somehow to legitimize their personal deviation without laying themselves open to the charge of insensitiveness to good taste or good manners. Fashion is the discreet solution of the subtle conflict. The slight changes from the established in dress or other forms of behavior seem for the moment to give the victory to the individual, while the fact that one's fellows revolt in the same direction gives one a feeling of adventurous safety. (Sapir, 1939:140)

There are two levels at which we can speak about fashion: at the societal level, as a process, and at the individual level, as a form of interaction. The societal and individual levels meet in the context of the epistemic community where behavior must incorporate both group and individual demands.

Societal Level of Fashion

The idea of a cycle is implicit in the societal definition of fashion. The very notion that a thing could be "in" makes it necessary that an other be "out"; the very notion that it could be "new" entails an expectation that it will at some point become "old." Fashion, then, is a process which involves changing perceptions of what is "in fashion." There are three stages to the cycle: introduction, assimilation, and obsolescence. Konig (1973) describes the cycle

> At the beginning of a new fashion development we regularly note a distinct hesitation; this period can vary in length: one wants to keep in step with the fashion without being ahead of it. The pioneers are thus always left on their own, if only for a few weeks. After this period of hesitation the wave of fashion spread invariably rises, reaching its crest at increasing speed, only to subside rapidly afterwards. This is the normal picture of development. (180)

At the introductory stage, the fashionable item is new—different from that which has been fashionable before and therefore accepted quite tentatively. It serves a differentiating function in that it is quite clear which members have adopted the new fashion, and which ones meet it with some hesitation. As the new external becomes more common, adopted by more members, it becomes a customary activity, assimilated into the behavior patterns of the group. At this point, fashion becomes the rule, any serious deviations from which may be deemed unacceptable.

When the fashion has become assimilated into the lifestyle of the group, it ceases to be successful at differentiating *between* members, for it is a criterion of membership, and therefore differentiates between members and nonmembers. Due to a push for more innovation, the fashion begins to decline into obsolescense, being gradually replaced as a new fashion is introduced. At this point, the old fashion is indeed "old-fashioned," and is no longer a symbol of membership within the group. The old-fashioned is either rejected and possibly adopted as evidence of membership in another group, or it becomes a permanent part of the originating group's lifestyle, as noted by Blumer (1969). In any case, it ceases to serve a differentiating function within the group.

Erikson (1966) has demonstrated the importance of groups maintaining visible boundaries. Fashion performs this function at the societal level at all of its stages. Introduction of fashion signifies a change in previous group indicators; assimilation speaks to the adoption of the external as a symbol of group membership; and obsolescence disassociates the group from the symbol.

Fashion is truly a cycle in that it has a definite beginning and end. In may ways its beginning and end are similar, for at both stages the fashion may lay no claim to approval by the group. That is, both represent a condition of deviation from the norm (the norm being whatever happens to be "in" fashion at that time). So, as for a circle whose beginning is its end, fashion's origins in novelty predestine its end in obsolescense.

Individual Levels of Fashion

In his definitive work on fashion, Simmel (1971) has isolated two drives which are central in producing fashion: imitation and differentiation.

> Fashion is the imitation of a given example and satisfies the demand for social adaptation; it leads the individual upon the road which all travel, it furnishes a general condition, which resolves the conduct of every individual into a mere example. At the same time it satisfies in no less degree the need of differentiation, the tendency towards dissimilarity, the desire for change and contrast. (298)

At the individual level, fashion becomes important as a way of exemplifying self in the face of the conformist force it has at the societal level. The individual actor is faced on the one hand with a fashion, which is central in proclaiming membership within an epistemic community, and on the other hand with a sense of self which seeks to be expressed. Corresponding to Goffman's categories of overinvolved, noninvolved, and role-distancing, we may generate three ideal types of social actors within the situation of fashion: the outrageous, the old-fashioned and the fashionable.

The *outrageous* live on the fringe of convention, and are the main actors in the societal stage of "introduction" of a fashion. Their lifestyle is one dominated almost exclusively by difference. Innovation is a way of life. Although they sustain revered positions as innovators, the necessity of acceptance by the community limits their innovation to the reorganizing of trends which are already existent. Any acceptable innovation has its seeds in what has been, and is usually merely a reformulation of these in the guise of the new. This fact does not diminish the inherent risk involved in being outrageous. In the fine interplay between self and symbol there is always the possibility that one might misread the social cues and "innovate" in an unacceptable way, i.e., truly deviate. This is what happens when high fashion designers make the mistake of introducing clothing which the public absolutely refuses to accept. A frequently cited case of such a misreading occurred when, in 1970, designers failed at introducing the "midi" skirt after the buying public had been wearing "minis" for several years. Women rejected this attempt to change so radically their clothes, and it was clearly a misjudgment on the part of the designers. A few years later, when the times were more conducive to change, longer skirts were reintroduced and consumers purchased them quite willingly. Thus, in Bell's (1976) words, "the leader must therefore be a follower; he may alter details, but he cannot either arrest or reverse the process" (91).

The outrageous are viewed with a combination of awe and ridicule. They are viewed with awe because they manifest what Sapir identified as a deep desire among us all to break away from the flock and indulge almost exclusively in "self-expression." At the same time, however, there is a sense of ridicule, for they are quite obviously and deliberately different. In Goffman's terms, the outrageous are overinvolved in the new, grounding their membership on the basis of generating the new. The outrageous are unable to distance themselves from their role as creators, because essentially they *are* the externals they create. Their medium of self-expression is the same medium which validates their membership.

The *old-fashioned* are those for whom the relationship with the new is one of total noninvolvement, and they correspond to the societal stage of the "obsolescense" of fashion. The old-fashioned are needed by the community in order to validate the goodness of the new and the necessity of adhering to the fashionable. In this sense, being old-fashioned resembles being unacceptably deviant. The old-fashioned are by necessity denied membership into the group which defines itself according to the fashionable external, for they do not share the same symbol system. It is only in the context of the old-fashioned that the fashionable achieve the desired difference which maintains them as a distinct community.

From the perspective of the "normal" members of the group, the outrageous, who constitute the leaders, and the old-fashioned, who constitute the outsiders, in some sense merge. Neither is satisfied with being fashionable, i.e., "merely" normal, yet both are necessary in order to make fashion possible. The outrageous are necessary in order to introduce the new and validate its acceptability for conformity by members, and the old-fashioned are necessary in order to strengthen community boundaries and provide the community with a sense of difference.

Finally, the *fashionable* are those who, from the safety of the norm, participate in the new once it has become quite acceptable and desirable. The fashionable correspond to the societal stage of the "assimilation" of fashion. It is here that Sapir's notion of "adventurous safety" comes into play. For the fashionable individual, it *is* adventurous to adopt the new fashion. But it is safe adventure, because the new has already become a fashion—it has been introduced by the outrageous and sanctioned by the general membership. To indulge in the new fashion by the time it becomes reasonable for the fashionable to do so is to affirm their membership in the group, as the fashion has become the new criterion for that membership.

To be fashionable is to exemplify acceptable deviance. If so, then it is not enough to simply adopt the fashion. Indeed, one cannot do so without the element of choice which goes in to establishing how the external will become *your* external. As long as one follows the basic guidelines of "style"—which in clothing, for example, are such things as color, cut, hem length—one is conforming to the rule of fashion. Beyond style, it is up to one's individual *taste* to determine how the fashion will work individually. The actor who shows "good taste" is acceptably deviant. Roach and Eicher (1973) comment on this compromise:

> An individual's taste is a measure of his ability to live up to a group standard. We may say that taste operates at a social-psychological level because judgments are applied to an *individual's* pattern of selection from the alternatives open to him, but he is judged on the basis of how well his choices measure up to *group* levels. In other words he is assessed in regard to his ability to differentiate "good" from "bad" as measured against arbitrary standards possessed by the group. (135–136)

Each of the actors that has been developed exemplifies taste to a different degree. The outrageous tends to display the most taste and the least style; however if style is completely absent then there will be no continuity in change, thus dooming the prospects of general acceptance of the new.

The fashionable actor tends to temper his/her taste such that it follows the precedent set by the outrageous—exercising self-expression within the limits set by the outrageous rather than experimenting with totally unsanctioned modes of expression. It follows that the fashionable individual is "safe" in this exercise of taste, because neither then arbiters of convention nor the arbiters of change may threaten one's position as a self-expressive member when the means for that self-expression have been predetermined.

Finally, the old-fashioned actor is forever consigned to having bad taste. In that taste varies with the style, what may be in good taste for one fashion will most likely be defined as in bad taste for the next.

From this brief sketch of fashion at the societal and the individual levels, it appears that "being fashionable" as acceptably deviating mediates between the two forms of unacceptable deviation—being outrageous and being old-fashioned—to become the rule, the socially-prescribed behavior. What appears to be a situation of individual choice in the face of group demands is in fact that condition for membership in the epistemic community for whom the particular external in question is fashionable. That is, there is really very little choice. One is only acceptable if one conforms to the limits of propriety—the acceptable deviations which are bounded quite narrowly at each end by unacceptable deviations.

THE CASE OF SLANG

Language is the most extensively used symbol system in social behavior, and the most subject to interpretation through various factors such as context, intonation, gestures, metaphor, and colloquiality. Language as it acts within the network of these variables is the communicative mode *par excellence.* Slang, as the privatization and personalization of meaning, which mediates between conformity and deviation at the level of language, is of interest as an example of how acceptable deviance affects even the most basic levels of sociability.

Slang works at the level of the epistemic community to achieve a differentiating function: a private language is an effective means of making clear the in-group/out-group distinction. As such, it differentiates between old-fashioned and fashionable. Within the group, slang provides a mechanism for establishing membership and at the same time the role distance required in order that one not appear overinvolved. With this is mind, let us take a look at slang as acceptable deviance.

Within the group, there must be a process of introduction of a new slang term. The actor responsible for this is innovative, risk-taking, outrageous. Individuals aspiring to reconfirm their membership will express mixed delight in encountering the new term. They will be both awed at the outrageous member for using the word, and reluctant to use it themselves until it has become more conventional in the vernacular. In addition, there may also be some question as to what the word means. Thus, the introduction of the term is followed by a period of discomfort in the group, during which members try to adapt their symbol systems to the new usage; to assign a significance to the term, and begin to become comfortable with its use. This is also the period during which the epistemic community chooses whether to adopt or to dismiss the new term. Its meaning and overtones must correspond with the continuous culture of the group in order for it to be accepted, and this is determined early in the initiation period of the new word.

Once a few outrageous members have incorporated the new term into their vocabulary, it becomes increasingly a membership requirement that others do so as well. This is the point at which the slang becomes fashionable, and members outdo themselves to employ the term in their speech, thus demonstrating that they share a symbol system which is different. The existence of their epistemic community becomes grounded in the particular use of the word that has become fashionable, and others are placed as either in-group or out-group members on the basis of their use of the slang. It thus functions to differentiate the community from others.

But it is not enough merely to use the word, which would be sheer conformity. In order to be fashionable, the objective is to be inventive with the word, to make its use interesting, to exhibit taste. It is not merely *that* one uses the word, but *how* one uses it. Slang thus achieves the pinnacle of acceptable deviation when it becomes seen as the medium of self-expression; when its use exemplifies one's taste (individuality) as well as one's style (membership). This inventiveness often takes the form of stringing together a set of slang terms in a way which is different from that in which they have been used before. This is acceptable deviance in that it proclaims membership while attesting to one's ability to innovate within the prescribed rules of convention of the community.

In that language is a key device of between-group interaction, slang is highly visible to other epistemic communities. The mass media often serve to enhance this visibility, especially in advertising, films, and television programmes geared towards the adolescent community, where slang is probably taken the most seriously in its differentiating function. Two peripheral groups which interact to a large extent with adolescents and are therefore exposed to and related to in terms of their language are the family and the mass media (who have to hear and identify the slang before they can feed it back to its users). Parents and mass media members, in their efforts to achieve a stronger communication link with adolescents, may attempt to adopt the latest slang term. This is accompanied by a period of trial-and-error during which the nonmember tries to establish which words are in fact "new" slang and what their contextual meaning is. Schutz (1944) has written about the trial-and-error process of a stranger learning the subtle meanings of group-specific keywords. The floundering entailed itself betrays one's status as an outsider. It is often the case that these outsiders start to feel comfortable with the terms just as they are achieving obsolescence with the group on question. This results in the strengthening of the boundary between in-group and out-group, in that out-group members are old-fashioned in terms of the in-group because they cannot display adequate command of the symbol system which provides the group with its basis for difference.

Slang ceases to serve its differentiating function, and by extension to be a criterion for membership, once it has been adopted by other communities. When a term becomes a component of the larger society's language—a tool of self-expression for Everyperson—then it no longer serves to distinguish members from nonmembers. At this point it will either become an established part of the conventional language, as "ain't" has recently been included in the dictionary of the English language, or it will fade away, perhaps becoming fashionable in other communities (e.g., parents and the mass media) briefly as it makes its way out.

ACCEPTABLE DEVIANCE AS SOCIAL CONTROL

In taking the perspective that norms are negotiated, it is implied that deviating in an acceptable manner preserves autonomy within the limits of cultural propriety. In the case of fashion, externals serve to decorate or extend the self in a way which both attests to the uniqueness of the self and conforms with the criteria of membership.

The function of acceptable deviance at the individual level is that it makes the individual feel in control of expression, and at the societal level, acceptable deviance absorbs and negates rebelliousness in that it controls the course of "change." In the case of fashion, from the point of view of the individual, freedom is accessible through fashion, and from the point of view of the society, change is possible through fashion. In the example of slang, we have found that individuals assert and confirm their membership in the group by using the "privatized language" which sets the group off from others, while at the same time achieving self-expression and self-esteem for their individual, "tasteful" use of the language.

It has been implied by the discussion of acceptable deviance that, rather than allowing for individual deviation as it appears to, acceptable deviance in fact becomes the *rule* and therefore assures conformity. It is clear that there are limits to how far a rule may be bent before it breaks. In a social situation where expected behaviors are clearly defined and shared by those actors involved, then these limits of propriety are also clearly defined. On either end—the overinvolved (conformist) and the noninvolved (deviant)—of the scope of appropriate behavior there is a socially understood degree to which one may stretch definitions of the situation without transgressing the bounds of propriety. But it is also possible to stretch them too far. As we have seen with fashion, the principle of "adventurous safety" predetermines that most individuals will act within the limits, for the limits to acceptable deviation, rather than the institutionalized rule, serve to guide social behavior. Acceptable deviation provides the illusion of solving the dilemma between conformity and deviation—the individual feels free. But what is the nature of that freedom? That freedom is only within the very narrow limits of propriety—limits which still pay allegiance in principle to the rule from which they deviate acceptably.

In that acceptable deviance itself becomes the norm, it does not provide "freedom" at all. From the societal point of view, acceptable deviance is institutionalized and therefore a conservative force which acts to ensure continuity. Acceptable techniques for rule-bending, as Goffman makes clear, change with respect to historical conditions, age, sex, social class, time, and location in any given culture. Thus, how one may go about bending the rules, and what rules one may bend, are just as much culturally defined as the original rules themselves. When the preservation of one's membership requires that one be fashionable, acceptable deviance ceases to release one from the bonds of convention for it merely becomes another form of convention. Similarly, when change at the societal level can only occur when it is responsible to the goals of the culture, it can only ever be conventional change as opposed to real change.

Goffman (1974) alludes to the element of social control in acceptable deviance:

> And at the heart of it? The individual comes to doings as someone of particular biographical identity even while he appears in the trappings of a particular social role. The manner in which the role is performed will allow for some 'expression' of personal identity, of matters that can be attributed to something that is more embracing and enduring than the current role performance and even the role itself . . . There is a relation between persons and role. But the relationship answers to the interactive system—to the frame—in which the role is performed and the self of the performer is glimpsed. Self, then, is not an entity half-concealed behind events, but a changeable formula for managing oneself during them. Just as the current situation prescribes the official guise behind which we will conceal ourselves, so it provides for where and how we will show through, the culture itself prescribing what sort of entity we must believe ourselves to be in order to have something to show through in this manner. (573–574)

We began with the assumption that there can be no deviance without conformity. That is to say, all attempts at unique expression are only unique insofar as they exist in relation to that which is not unique (i.e., that to which people conform). Similarly, conformity depends on the possibility of deviance: if difference did not pose a threat, then there would not be such a concerted effort to stamp it out.

We can now see that individuality is a relative term, one which changes in relation to that which is perceived to be common. In this sense, then, it is also *defined* by what is common. Because of this interrelationship between the rule and the breaking/bending of that rule, it would seem that the notion of individuality that has been presented is an artificial one. There is no sense of absolute individuality. Rather, that which is common dictates that which is to be perceived as unique. It follows that it then *controls* that uniqueness. If an individual can only feel unique when in a sense *not* doing what society deems appropriate, how "free" is that person to choose her/his way?

This is the inevitable outcome of any society which seeks to survive: that members "feel free" to conform and therefore desire to conform. The degree to which the rules can be bent is dependent upon the strength of the society to withstand deviations. The more deviations it allows, the more it gives the appearance of satisfying both demands for conformity and deviation. But nevertheless the basic problematic of social order remains: that there must be rules, and that these rules must be adhered to.

Acceptable deviance, then, functions to provide both individuals and groups with a false sense of freedom, while ensuring that the "rules" are followed. The actor who engages in acceptable deviance, while being ensured that s/he in fact has the liberty to define the situation, is as much a pawn as s/he would be were s/he to follow convention to the letter. Whereas such an actor seems to be expressing "self", that "self" may be seen as a product of the demand to engage in acceptable deviance. Similarly, the epistemic community that perceives itself as changing is engaging in conservative as opposed to real change; it is merely altering the form, not the content; the speech, not the language. The externals change, but they continue to express the same internals.

The mechanism of acceptable deviance is astoundingly successful in promoting among individuals a feeling of self-worth while at the same time sustaining a high degree of uniformity within groups. It is a safety valve because it channels the self-expressive impulse such that is is very much under control. Thus, acceptable deviance poses no threat to the status quo, for it is essentially conservative.

IMPLICATIONS

The notion of acceptable deviance may help to fill in the grey areas which have been noted to exist between conformity and deviation. Clearly, it is not enough to claim that norms are situational and that the process of becoming a deviant is purely a question of attribution of deviant status. Acceptable deviance makes room for plurality, in the sense that different epistemic communities are accorded normative structures which conform to the groups' differentiating characteristics. It makes room for negotiation between members on the one hand, and members and nonmembers on the other. Finally, it begins to provide a context in which rich concepts such as "subordinate involvement," "role distance," and the "just right principle" can be seen to operate.

Most theories of deviance and conformity focus on the one aspect of social life which is seen to govern the attribution of normality. The labeling perspective references exclusionary processes; the conflict perspective invokes macro level agents of imputation; reference group and learning perspectives attend to choice and victimization in one's contacts with others. The introduction of acceptable deviance allows a multiplicity of factors to come into play, based on an underlying assumption that actors seek membership.

Attempts to distinguish between conformity and deviation as discrete categories of human behavior ignore the interplay between self and society in the ongoing negotiation of membership. The principle of acceptable deviance suggests that normality is an achieved status for actors situated in contexts in which their capacity as expressive actors is limited by the ability of their audience and others to read their statements. This ability to read is not a fixed property of group identity but rather an ongoing process of rearticulation and reaffirmation of what it means to be a member.

REFERENCES

Becker, Howard
1963 Outsiders: Studies in the Sociology of Deviance. New York: Free Press.
Bell, Quentin
1976 On Human Finery. London: Hogarth.
Blumer, Herbert
1969 "Fashion: From class differentiation to collective selection." Sociological Quarterly 10: 275–291.
Coser, Lewis
1956 The Functions of Social Conflict. London: Free Press.
Gans, Herbert
1974 Popular Culture and High Culture: An Analysis and Evaluation of Taste. New York: Basic Books.
Goffman, Erving
1961 Encounters: Two Studies in the Sociology of Interaction. New York: Bobbs-Merrill.
1963 Behavior in Public Places: Notes on the Social Organization of Gatherings. New York: Free Press.
1964 Stigma. Englewood Cliffs, New Jersey: Prentice-Hall.
1974 Frame Analysis: An Essay on the Organization of Experience. New York: Harper Colophon Books.

Holzner, Burkart
1968 Reality Construction in Society. Cambridge: Schenkman.
Konig, Rene
1973 A La Mode: On the Social Psychology of Fashion (F. Bradley, trans.). New York: Seabury.
Lemert, Edwin M.
1951 Social Pathology. New York: McGraw-Hill
Matza, David
1964 Delinquency and Drift. New York: Wiley.
Merton, Robert K.
1938 "Social structure and anomie." American Sociological Review 3: 672-682.
Posner, Judith
1975 "The stigma of excellence: On being just right." Sociological Inquiry 46(2): 141–144.
Roach, Mary Ellen, and Joanne B. Eicher
1973 The Visible Self: Perspectives on Dress. Englewood Cliffs, New Jersey: Prentice-Hall.
Sapir, Edward
1939 "Fashion." Encyclopedia of Social Sciences 6: 139–144.
Schutz, Alfred
1944 "The stranger: An Essay in social psychology." American Journal of Sociology 49: 499–507.
Simmel, Georg
1971 "Fashion." Pp. 294–323 in D. Levine (ed.) On Individuality and Social Forms. Chicago: University of Chicago Press.

Reading 3

The Overnegativized Conceptualization of Deviance: A Programmatic Exploration

David L. Dodge
University of Notre Dame

It is the contention of this paper that past and current sociological conceptions of deviance are unduly limited in that they consider only negative conceptualizations of general deviance. The argument is advanced that sociologists are overdue to acknowledge the empirical existence of *posi-*

I am deeply endebted to David M. Klein, J. David Lewis, Walter T. Martin, Michael R. Welch, Andrew J. Weigert and to anonymous referees for their illuminating criticisms and helpful suggestions for organization of major points. Of course, the responsibility for any remaining limitations or problems rests with the author.

tive deviance and to incorporate the positive deviance into a broader, more general study of deviance. Since acknowledging positive deviance would highlight the inadequacy of conceptualizations limited to negative deviance only, guidelines for the beginnings of the solution to this problem are suggested. Suggestions are presented for reworking and reevaluating some of the basic definitional statements of (negative) deviance and some of the elemental aspects of the existing deviance paradigms in order to develop a more general field of study.

The sociology of deviance accents the negative. A thorough survey of the theoretical and empirical works in the sociology of deviance reveals that deviance concerns the objectionable, the forbidden, the disvalued and that these social phenomena are so designated because they are viewed as offensive, disgusting, contemptible, annoying or threatening. Consequently, they excite negative emotions (e.g., hate, fear, anger, annoyance, revulsion) and elicit negative reactions (e.g., punishment, isolation, ostracism, confinement, banishment).

Past and current works in the sociology of deviance have been so overwhelmingly conceptualized in terms of *negative deviance* that another important realm of deviance has yet to be adequately acknowledged and systematically explored, namely, *positive deviance*: those acts, roles/careers, attributes and appearances that are also singled out for special treatment and recognition; those persons and acts that are evaluated as superior because they *surpass* conventional expectations.

The expansion of the field to include the positive dimension of deviance is of no less importance for the study of deviance than the recent introduction of variables that broaden the field's theoretical and empirical parameters, for example: the sex variable (Harris, 1977); power as part of the politics of deviance and the problematics of response to deviance (Liazos, 1972; Schur, 1971:56–69; Thio, 1973, 1978:ch. 4); and the ordinariness or commonness of deviance (Schur, 1979:ch. 2).[1] Indeed, the expansion of the field to include both positive and negative components is potentially a far more important development than the addition of new variables. With the acknowledgment of the positive dimension all past and present conceptualizations of deviance may then be regarded as excluding an important portion of the field. If there is to be an adequate empirically based theory of deviance, the full scope of social deviance must be taken in to account for the social phenomenon under scrutiny is *social deviance*, not merely the study of its negative and positive aspects.

[1]While it is tempting to phrase the positive dimension of deviance in terms of the negative-positive variable, I have refrained from doing so because the thrust of the paper is for the creation of a more adequate theoretical frame of the social phenomenon of deviance and not to simply introduce another possible variable.

Thus, the overall objectives of this paper are fourfold: 1) to encourage the acceptance of a sociological conceptualization of deviance that involves the full empirical expressions of deviance (namely, both negative and positive deviance); 2) to provide sufficient, but not necessarily exhaustive, reasons for the adoption of such a conceptualization; 3) to delineate some of the advantages of such a conceptualization for the study of deviance; and 4) to stimulate future theoretical and empirical work in accordance with this conceptualization.

THE CONCEPT OF POSITIVE DEVIANCE: NOMINAL MOTION

All this is not to say that the notion of positive deviance is unknown or without precedence in the field. In probably the best know text of deviance, a mainstay of the field for at least a quarter of a century, Clinard clearly provides a basis for the consideration of positive deviance:

> Reactions to deviations from social norms can vary in the *directions of approval*, tolerance or disapproval . . . most members of modern societies encourage a certain amount of *nonconformity*, provided it is in an *approved direction*. Deviation which groups approve of may be rewarded by admiration, prestige, money, or other symbols . . . *Approved deviations* may . . . include behavior which is more industrious, ambitious, pious, patriotic, brave or honest *than is called for by the norms of a particular situation*. (1974:15; emphasis added)

Although Clinard does not use the term positive deviance, he is definitely referring to behavior which exceeds normative situational expectations and which clearly does not fall under the label of negative deviance.[2]

No deviance theorist expresses a belief which supports the purposes of this article more than Lemert who, after describing the intent of his deviance textbook as a study of a "*limited part of deviation in human behavior*," goes on to state:

> *variations from social norms in desirable and enviable directions should be explored as profitably as the more frequently studied sociopathic variations.* The behavior of the genius, the motion-picture star, the exceptionally beautiful woman and the reknown athlete should lend itself to the same systematic

[2]While the concept of deviance involves referential phenomena other than behavior, for the purposes of brevity, social behavior will be employed primarily in the following discussions with the understanding that what is presented about behavior may very well apply to roles/careers, attributes and appearances as well.

> analysis as that which is applied to the criminal, the pauper or sex delinquent. (1951:23–24; emphasis added)

The purpose of noting that the notion of positive deviance is not foreign to American Sociology should not give the impression its recognition and acceptance is already a fact.[3] There is no existing body of work that systematically constructs a case for the inclusion of positive deviance, let alone examines the impact such a conceptualization of deviance may have for the sociological study of deviance.[4]

I believe that reasons exist which are sufficiently compelling to warrant the inclusion of the positive deviance dimension in the study of deviance and I will present them below.

ARGUMENTS FOR RECONCEPTUALIZATION: LOGIC, DEFINITION AND IMPLICATIONS

I. Inconsistency in Selection of Referents of Deviance

It is impossible to argue that a logical inconsistency is involved in equating social deviance with only negative deviance. Central to this argument is the appreciation that the very basic concepts and criteria used by sociologists as a basic model in describing social behavior, social control and social normative order are also those used—but not sufficiently in the past—to identify deviance and its referents.

Sociologists generally recognize that social behavior may range from the highly unacceptable to the highly acceptable. What is important here are the criteria of *exceptionality* and *directionality* that imply some *standard* or *norm*. If behavior tends toward one extreme, say the highly acceptable, then it is behavior that is tagged by people as exceptional in a positive direction e.g., Lemert's honorific behavior (1951:24). If however, behavior tends in the opposite direction, failing to meet the expected, it has exceeded situational expectations in a negative direction. The critical point is that both criteria, exceptionality and directionality, are equally important and used by sociologists in describing the full behavior range.

Additionally, sociologists utilize the concept and phenomenon of sanc-

[3]Only a few other theorists refer (but sparingly) to the notion of positive deviance (cf. Thio, 1978:3–8; Wilkins, 1965:45; Scarpitti and McFarlane, 1975:5–6) and these concessions are a marked departure from those who argue that the use of "positive" as a qualifier of "deviance" is a contradiction in terms or that even to refer to "negative deviance" is incorrect because this would constitute a redundancy for deviance is so clearly negative (e.g., Sagarin, 1975:42).

[4]Indeed, Marcello Truzzi laments this state of affairs when, upon reviewing George Becker's historical case study of *The Mad Genius Controversy: A Study in the Sociology of Deviance*, he states his disappointment concerning the opportunity Becker overlooked to begin to introduce the implications of positive deviance for general deviance theory.

tions to elaborate further the full scope of behavior and to introduce the notions of social control and social order. They point out relationships between the perceived degree of acceptability or nonacceptability of behavior and the nature of reactions to it. If the behavior is in some way extraordinary, then reactions to it are usually commensurate in intensity and kind with the degree of the exceptionality and the directionality of the act.[5] Thus, people differentiate behaviors and single out the exceptional for varying levels and types of responses. These responses are identified as sanctions and carry varying positive and negative valences. In turn, these valences elicit and establish the nature and type of social control employed to induce conformity and order (Clinard and Meier, 1979:18–23). Therefore, if a given behavior exceeds only slightly the situational expectations in the positive direction, the appropriate sanction (reaction) to it will be slight, e.g., an approving glance, smile, or some other nonextraordinary conventional sign of approval. If however the behavior exceeded situational expectations strongly in the positive direction, the commensurate positive sanctions would be something outstanding, perhaps involving rituals and ceremonies. Conversely, negative behavior of varying exceptionality would be accompanied by varying types and kinds of negative sanctions.

Thus, empirically, behavior may elicit reactions (sanctions) which designate behavior as expected (conformity), unacceptable (nonconformity), or unexpected but acceptable (*supra* conformity). Exceptional behavior, roles/careers, attributes and appearances are multifarious and ubiquitous throughout social reality. Examples of negative deviants and the behaviors that make them such are cheaters, malingerers, "fags," sinners, murderers, "turncoats," cowards, etc. while examples lying within the scope of positive deviance (*supra* conformity) include saints, "trailblazers," heroes, "triple threats," geniuses, the gifted, "hard-chargers," and the glamorous.

Now if the referents of deviance and deviation are discenable by their departures from conventional expectations and may be viewed as either falling short of conforming adequately or as surpassing these expectations there appears to be no logical reason for sociologists to restrict their attention to one category of exceptional behavior and designate that as deviance while ignoring the other category which also contains instances of exceptional behavior. In other words, if deviance involves the exceptional (i.e.,

[5]It might be noteworthy to underscore the advantage and appropriateness in using the term exceptionality as a criterion for identifying and defining deviance. In accordance with a full delineation of what exceptionality (exception, exceptional, exceptionable) entails, *Webster's New Collegiate Dictionary* (1974:398) reveals that antonymic as well as generic referents are involved. For example, generically exceptionality refers to "a case not conforming to the general rule; forming an unusual instance." However, in terms of the antonyms, on the one hand the negative valence is encountered: "an adverse criticism; to make objection; to take offense; objectionable." On the other hand, positive valences are also encountered: "extraordinary, superior."

where people single out acts and persons for exceptional attention), this logic certainly seems to be applicable to both realms of exceptional behavior. Not to identify both realms as deviance would be an inconsistency in conceptualization, as when sociologists shift their attention from the behavior-control model used to describe social behavior and conformity in terms of norms, sanctions and social control to the concept of deviance which is also identified and described by these same concepts and criteria but now constitutes the behavior-deviance spectrum.[6]

What implications does the domain of positive deviance have for the field of deviance as it currently exists? Two immediate consequences are apparent. First, the substantive scope of the sociology of deviance is greatly enlarged. Secondly, and related to the first consequence, when positive deviance is given equal status with negative deviance, it must be recognized that current conceptualizations cannot be viewed as anything more than special negative conceptualizations of general deviance.

Acknowledging that the current sociology of deviance is a sociology of negative deviance creates a problem of no small stature. However, such an acknowledgment does not imply a rejection of all that has been accomplished heretofore. Nor does a solution simply depend on undertaking studies of positive deviance for this would lead to the same dilemma that currently exists, except a separate sociology of positive deviance would be created. The ideal solution is to develop a *general* theory of deviance that accounts for *both* types, rather than splitting the field by having a special theory of negative deviance and another special theory of positive deviance. This task and its elaboration should be viewed as a point of departure; as an invitation to offset the overnegativized conceptualization of deviance.

II. Assumptions and Definitions: Toward a Reconceptualization

In light of the preceding discussions, two basic assumptions serve as guidelines in defining deviance:

1 The term deviance is a generic, sensitizing concept (Blumer, 1969:147–148; Schur, 1971:26) involving a myriad of specific labels which in

[6]Some sociologists go on to establish a distinction between cultural (ideal) and social (real) norms. Such a distinction should add further credence to the advisability of including positively valued behaviors as referents of deviance for it aids in portraying reality more aptly by distinguishing between "routine" conformity and meritorious performance; e.g., the "creme de la creme" are not rewarded for conforming best to those standards constituting the social norms, but are rewarded for surpassing these, moving toward the ideal. The cultural norms are not imperatives but serve as guides for establishing the socially expected (social norm) and the positive socially unexpected. Thus, positive deviance encourages both conforming and exceptional behavior.

turn are assigned to social phenomena which *differ from* the expectations associated with particular situations.

2 As designating specific referents, these labels are attached to various acts, roles/careers, attributes and appearances considered exceptional by interacting members in a situational context.

Working definition. Deviance may be defined as any act, role/career, attribute or appearance that departs significantly from social situational expectations. Depending on the nature of the exceptionality and the direction of the departure, some deviance is appraised as violating situational expectations and is termed *negative deviance* while other deviance is viewed as *surpassing* social situational expectations and is called *positive deviance.* The degree of exceptionality and direction of departure are determined by observing the expectations and reactions of the members in the situation.

III. An Implication for the Normative Approach

When the concept of positive deviance is introduced into the normative approach to deviance, behaviors are essentially viewed as falling along a continuum which ranges from varying types and degrees of negative deviance through degrees of expected behavior and subsequently degrees of positive deviance. Thus, we have three ranges of behavior. To illustrate and clarify the importance of this implication we shall examine the case of "high academic achievers" as a type of positive deviance.

If we treat grade-point-averages (GPAs) as measuring academic performances and group them accordingly, one cluster represents high academic achievers (positive deviance) and another cluster low academic achievers (negative deviance). The middle cluster or range would be classified as normal academic achievers. In keeping with the ideologies and raison de'etre of the social institution of education, those students who attain exceptional GPAs are viewed by the institution's officials and teachers as "brilliant," extraordinaries, "gifted," who display "emulative" and "honorific" academic performances.[7] Those students at the other extreme are referred to as "dull", "slow," "incompetent," "dumb."

The scope of these performances and roles/careers aptly fits the normative approach to deviance as reconceptualized. Most students usually (but not necessarily) fall within the normal or middle range while the "exceptionals" shade off to the extremes with marked decreases in num-

[7]Note that on academic transcripts it is not unusual to see the grade of A as indicating achievement of superiority which in turn is translated to mean an unusual degree of intellectual ability, while the grade of B refers to a thoroughly acceptable degree of attainment.

bers.[8] Appropriate sanctions in the forms of merit awards, scholarships, as well as remedial rituals and programs, generally accompany the cases in the high and low ranges. Thus, by explicitly introducing the positive dimension of deviance into the normative approach, the behavioral expressions of a norm are viewed as ranging along the full behavior-deviance continuum. Once this has been recognized some interesting conceptual, theoretical, and research challenges arise.

For example, objections might be raised that some forms of behavior do not have expressions that would qualify as positive deviance. Consider the behavior of "killing." If we ignore situationally endorsed forms (e.g., killing the enemy during war, justifiable homicide, etc.) killing would seem to be a behavior that one either commits (violating the norms and therefore constituting "negative" deviance) or does not commit (therefore constituting conformity). The question is, how can one deviate in a positive direction from the form prohibiting killing?

I suggest the norm against killing is actually a special case subsumed under a more general norm, namely one concerning respect/reverence for the lives of others. The full scope of prescriptions and proscriptions for respecting/revering life might be conceptualized as ranging from highly unacceptable behavior (e.g., cold-blooded premeditated murder)through conventional behavior (e.g., not killing anyone and following conventional codes for administering to the well being of others) to highly acceptable, exceptional behavior (e.g., role/career behavior which not only reflects conventional codes for administering to the well-being of others, but additionally demonstrates extraordinary respect/reverence for life as exemplified by a Mother Theresa or an Albert Sweitzer).

Thus, whether or not all behavioral forms have empirical expressions that range the full gamut of the behavior-deviance spectrum proposed is problematic; moreover it is conceptually an intriguing critical theoretical and empirical question requiring examination. Such an examination will force sociologists to consider much more closely their past customary, but limited, way of conceptualizing and using norms; interrelationships among such norms; and the deviance-behavior spectrums that may emerge when people implement those norms in various social situations. The considerations proposed here should have an impact on any attempt to "measure" norms or normative properties in a social situation (cf. Meier, 1981:11–21; Gibbs, 1978).

Additionally, it should be acknowledged that its possible certain organizational structures may be so organized as to inhibit the expression of

[8]While the normative approach has been closely associated with the notion of events being distributed in terms of a statistical "normal" curve this is not a necessary element to which one must subscribe to be a normativist (cf., Meier, 1981:17).

positive deviance. A case in point would be workers who are engaged in piece work production. Theoretically, in keeping with the formal codes by which management has organized the situation, there are no formal standards beyond which the worker can excel and receive extraordinary rewards. The worker can only receive the conventional rewards for each "piece of work" produced or receive punishment for not measuring up to minimal standards. However, such organizational practices do not invalidate the concept of positive deviance; they only add a fruitful avenue of inquiry, namely the exploration of why and under what circumstances there is a repression of meritorious behavior. Of course the obverse is equally interesting: viz., what structures, more than others, are generative of positive deviance? And why?

IV. An Implication for the Reactivist Approach

One of the vital concerns in the reactivist approach to deviance is *the problematics of response*. Not only is it problematic whether a given type of behavior will be labeled deviant (regardless of whether positive or negative deviance is involved) from one time period to the next (e.g., today's sinners are tomorrow's saints), but there is no guarantee the same act will be so labeled in the same time period or even in the same situation (e.g., the "boor" of a conventional group may be the "crazy" of an unconventional group). Different persons and groups, for a variety of reasons, may perceive and evaluate an act differently.

If we bear in mind that labels carry with them certain attitudes, the labels used by the student subculture regarding high academic achievers (e.g., "egg heads," "rate busters," "book worms," "throats," "drags," [(McDill and Coleman, 1963: Wallace, 1964]) indicate subculture members see them negatively as a threat: as those who study all the time; as those who make extra work for others; as those who put others in a "bad light." In fact, if the high academic achiever is male, he is probably "a little feminine," while if the high academic achiever is female "she's probably ugly or fat" (McDill and Coleman, 1963). One can see the mechanisms of stereotyping and putative deviance at work here. Based on these appraisals we can readily surmise that being a high academic achiever is not less socially punishing than being a low academic achiever.

However, being a high academic achiever or a low academic achiever has its rewards also. Within the education institution there are formalized privileges and programs that go along with the role/career of high academic achievers. Such achievers are continually paraded and touted for exceptional recognition and rewards: elite accelerated programs for the gifted; scholarships for college; societally designated merit scholars. Role/career low academic achievers also have their specialized programs: schools for the retarded; remedial programs; the common matriculation alternative of the "shop courses"; graduation by "progress" and "time" rather than merit. Thus, in keeping with our definition and conceptualization of deviance, exceptional children are treated exceptionally regardless of the end of the behavior-deviance spectrum at which they are located, for both reflect exceptional departures from standards. However, once isolated, the nature and intensity of the reactions remain problematic.

Once a behavior is acknowledged by others as deviant, a host of questions arise: Is the deviance perceived uniformally by significant others? If not, how is it perceived, as conventional conformity or the opposite type of deviance? Who constitutes the relevant others? On what grounds or logics do their perceptions and resolutions rest? For example, in the case of high academic achievers, it might be argued that the basis of the *labeling logic* of both the teacher and student subcultures are identical at certain points, but have dissimilar results, (e.g., both the teachers and members of the student subculture seize on how high academic achievers use their "free-time" and the hierarchical priority given to educational attainment). Unlike the teachers, members of the student subculture see the high academic achiever as "studying all the time" and "placing the grade" too high in the priority hierarchy.

Another questions that follows from the preceding concerns might be: What means or mechanisms are used by high academic achievers to deflect negative evaluations of the student subculture? Involvement in systematic deviance as postulated by Lemert? Coupling highly prized status-roles of the student subculture (e.g., those who display "high degrees of athletic prowess"; those who earn "awards of popularity") with that of high academic achievement would seem to be another likely possible means. This question and its response obviously focuses on negotiation, avoidance of role engulfment (Schur, 1971, 1979), disavowal (Garfinkle, 1956) and handling the problems associated with second deviance (Lemert, 1972).[9]

V. Other Normative Considerations

One of the hallmarks of the normative approach to deviance centers on rates and structural variations in deviance. Immediate questions that arise are: Do positive deviance rates vary among structures? If they do, why? What demographic, ecological and social structural variables are useful in accounting for these variations? Are those structural variables useful in accounting for negative deviance (e.g., class, urbanism, geographic mobil-

[9]It is possible to wed the full normative behavior-deviance spectrum with the reactivists' *problematics of response* orientation which produces an heuristic deviance-behavior-control model which should serve as a useful reference point in future studies of constructing typologies of deviance and normative structures. Such a model will capture reality more fully and take into consideration the pools of consensus, dissensus and normative-reaction polarization. Article in progress.

ity, subcultures and contracultures) equally useful in explaining positive deviance rates? In given societies, populations, and subpopulations do the ratios of positive to negative deviance vary? In what manner? Why?

Further developments might involve examining pivotal questions and assumptions raised by the various major theories in the sociology of deviance. Anomie theory, for example, posits that deviances is a product of the excessive stress generated by disjunctures between culturally prescribed goals and socially structured means to attain these goals. Because humans are initially motivated to conform, deviance is a "calculated response" to the stress created by the lack of conventional opportunity structures to legitimate goals and is viewed as a "normal" response to an appraised "normal" situation: namely, socially structured deprivation. Merton's "Social Structure and Anomie" theory (1957:131–160) is the exemplar of the anomie school.

Why should negative deviance be touted as more of a "normal" response to deprivation than positive deviance? History is certainly replete with heroic, legendary figures who overcame socially structured blockages to opportunities and success. Moreover, these figures might readily fall within Merton's innovation and rebellion modes of adaptation. Ford and Carnegie among industrialists; Edison among inventors; Lincoln among American president's Christ and Mohammed among religious founders; Picasso among artists; Martin Luther King and Cesar Chavez among American minority political activists, are but a few of the many historic figures who overcame socially structured adversities and who might readily be considered legitimate occupants of positive deviant categories. While the inclination by design has been to translate Merton's modes of adaptation into negative deviant roles, what would occur to the overall schema if this inclination was to be reversed? What basic social mechanisms and factors would be involved in the development of positive rather than negative modes of adaptation? Could Merton's theory be expanded in light of the positive deviance dimension?

If, as the anomie theorists claim, humans are strongly motivated to conform because they are socialized in light of societal needs which creates an overwhelming desire to "fulfill" the expectations of others, it would appear that positive deviance might be considered as important a consideration as is negative deviance for those members of society "forced" to deviate. Perhaps it might be considered a more logical extension in keeping with the functionalists' model of man, conformity, and social order. Indeed, the intensity of the motivation to excel and succeed, a pivotal point of the anomie logic to deviation, rests on the assumption of societal value consensus and extolling positive deviants to underscore dramatically the fact that "rage to riches," "log cabin to White House" maxims are plausible and possible. The Horatio Alger myths are legends of positive deviants and deviance! It would be very difficult to imagine how and why different societal members from different walks of life would aspire to such lofty heights and aspirations *without* the glorification of concrete examples of positive deviants.

VI. Other Implications for the Reactivist Approach

Thus far we have addressed the question of whether or not those referents which fall within the category of positive deviance bear sufficient similarities with those of negative deviance to be included in the sociological study of deviance. I argue in the affirmative because, like negative deviance referents, those of positive deviance may be singled out as exceptional and receive nonconventional reactions (sanctions). Additionally, deviance can be defined so that the definition would direct social investigators to empirical cases of both negative and positive deviance.

However, there is another way to highlight the logic of acknowledging positive deviance as bona fide social deviance. This is to examine some of the core definitional statements that sociologists have constructed to see if they are applicable to positive deviance and, if necessary, to rephrase them without losing their initial key message. If this can be accomplished, we will have established even more compelling reasons for including positive deviance in the sociological study of deviance.

If the definitional statements selected comprise a critical core of the reactivist approach to negative deviance, an even stronger case will have been established for the programmatic utility of including the positive deviance dimensions in the sociological study of deviance. While a host of different types of positive deviance will be used to further indicate referents of positive deviance, the strategy in covering these definitional statements will be to explore their applicability to positive deviance. In this manner, the emphasis on the similarities between negative and positive deviance will continue to be presented. Since the reactivist approach is presently under scrutiny, the following definitional statements focus on the deviant label.[10]

1. The deviant label carries with it an ascertainment of morality, motivation, and responsibility. Deviant theorists have painstakenly dissected and elaborated the role that ascertainment of morality, motivation, and responsibility plays in the negative labeling process (Becker, 1963:25–39; Simmons, 1969:12–22, 31–38; Katz, 1972, 1975; Schur, 1971: Chs. 3 and 4;

[10]Other fundamental definitional statements derived from the study of negative deviance concerning properties of deviance and on which sociologists agree strongly concerns the universality and relativity of deviance; that deviance is a variable not an attribute, and by definition deviance elicits strong emotional responses. It would seem to me that it takes little imagination and creativity to grasp how readily these definitional statements are applicable to positive deviance, once positive deviance is acknowledged. These and the following definitional statements may be viewed as a set of guidelines for the analysis of deviance (Schur, 1979:6–18) or for identifying the properties of deviance (Scott, 1972:11–32).

Goode, 1978:44–58). Adequate bases for the imputation of *moral inferiority* and culpability are essential elements of the negative deviant label and deviantizing process. Of course the degree of moral inferiority varies by types of deviants and the culpability of the individual must be established, or believed to have been established, if the person is to be viewed as morally depraved. I see no reason why an inverse complementary process would not be involved in the imputation of positive deviance. Of course, the bases for imputation of moral superiority in conjunction with intention and responsibility would be ascertained in this instance.

However, there are some issues that require examination when generalizing to positive deviants. These issues center on the aspects of motivation and intentions. In studying negative deviants a distinction is sometimes made between voluntary and involuntary deviants. The involuntary deviant is viewed as one who did not "intend" to become a deviant, but became a deviant because of factors beyond his or her control. Cases in point would be the ill person, the disabled, the disfigured. In these cases, culpability is waived as a criterion for the assignment of a specific label. However, once in the status roles that the labels designate, the persons are expected to fulfill certain role expectations and it is at this stage that culpability enters the picture of involuntary deviants. For example, the ill person must seek competent help and means to get well, the disfigured and disabled are expected to "handle themselves" in such a manner that their afflictions do not intrude to the point they make interaction with conventional others impossible or too discomforting for conventional persons.

Is the distinction between voluntary and involuntary deviants applicable to positive deviants? If so, what type of positive deviants are considered to be involuntary? Voluntary? What are the role expectations associated with each? Do involuntary positive deviants perceive themselves to be positive deviants? Do the careers and life circumstances of each categorical type differ significantly? These are issues which require further study.

2. The deviant label carries with it a strong essentializing tendency.[11] The person who has been labeled a negative deviant is not viewed as a person who is deviant in one specific aspect of his or her character, but he or she is reconstituted and is ultimately viewed as a general deviant. In other words, the deviant is not morally inferior in one aspect of his or her personality structure, but in all aspects. It is assumed there are no areas of the character which are not morally inferior because of the culpability in the deviant act(s) committed. Of course the essentializing tendency, in most instance, involves a developmental process that occurs over time. In this fashion deviants are created, constructed. Thus, Schur (1971:69-81) elabo-

[11]Considerations concerning involuntary deviants are not explored in the following discussions because of space limitations.

rates "role engulfment," Lemert (1951:55–57; 1972: Ch. 3) delineates the perils of "putative deviance" and the challenge of being a "secondary deviant," Becker (1963:31–39) explores the deviant label as a "master status" and Katz (1972, 1975) elaborates "imputed essences." All are concepts that describe the essentializing nature of the deviantizing process and the deviant label.

Speculatively, positive deviant labels may carry this same tendency. The questions of being morally superior and intending the act(s) *may* be viewed as essential positive labeling tests that must be ascertained before a deviant label is assigned to a person. Thus, the saint and the "saintly acts" flow from a person who may not have just happened to commit the acts, but who may have intended to commit them and who was committed to the principles they reflected, even in the face of adversity (McHugh, 1970).

Who hasn't witnessed the superior, exceptional expectations placed on the person who has surpassed conventional expectations previously in some other situation and was awarded a positive deviant label? Take note of the military heroes that "become" political sages. It is not unusual to see positive deviants in one area of life assigned special talents or capabilities in other areas, when no basis for this assignment exists in empirical reality. While this process constitutes an extension of the putative deviance notion, it also gains credibility from the well known social psychological "halo effect" process (Vander Zanden, 1981:42–43).

How are negative acts of positive deviants evaluated? Often they are not merely excused, but are normalized in light of the essence of the moral superiority of the positive deviant. Consider the gluttonous prima donnas of the opera who once gorged themselves to obesity "for the voice." Schwartz and Skolnick in their study of legal stigma found that physicians who had experienced malpractice suits suffered no extra legal consequences. Their patient clientele did not decrease after malpractice suits. In a few instances, some of them even experienced an increase in number of patients (1964). It may very well be that certain occupations take on the properties of a positive deviant status and carry what small group researchers refer to as "idiosyncrasy credit," but in this case from a communal view (Hollander, 1958).

3. The deviant label carries with it a strong socially isolating tendency. When people feel "something must be done" to a person because of his or her exceptional behavior or appearance, the process of deviantizing may ultimately arrive at a course of action, consistent with the deviant label, that involves confinement. Thus, the criminal is punished by imprisonment; the emotionally disturbed are confined for the purposes of treatment; the delinquent sent to a "youth center" for rehabilitation; the afflicted or crippled to "inhouse" programs for adjustment procedures. It is assumed, correctly or incorrectly, while these people are "out of sight, out of mind" something constructive is being accomplished for the individual and society. But this is beside the point since isolation from conventional society is punitive from the point of view of the deviant, whether punitiveness was intended or not.

However, physical confinement is not the only means of isolation. The deviant label may carry such a stigma that the labeled are prevented from participation in conventional groups and roles so they may fulfill conventional needs by conventional means. Ex-convicts, "dried out" alcoholics, and ex-mental patients are all prime examples of negative deviants (even though they have supposedly paid their dues) who experience social isolation because of the stigma attached to them.

This consequence may be just as applicable to positive deviants as negative deviants. Honorific titles awarded via honorific ceremonies often end up bestowing consequences just as confining and potentially punitive as the consequences of negative labels and degradation ceremonies. The positive deviant is often prevented from participating fully in conventional groups in ordinary ways. "It's vcry lonely at the top!" Because of their high social visibility, they may be denied the very privileges granted routinely to conventional persons who are "in good standing"; denied the kind of freedom regarded as a basic right for conventional people. Examples of tragic consequences include the actress Marilyn Monroe and the was hero Ira Hayes, the American Indian who helped raise the American flag on Iwo Jima in World War II. The former may be an example of a voluntary positive deviant and the latter a case of an involuntary positive deviant. The critical question arises, how do positive deviants successfully cope with this predicament? Obviously these two did not!

Moreover as Scott observes, "formal agencies of social control in our society appear to be better equipped for detecting, apprehending, and confining the deviant than they are to bringing him back from the institution to the center of the community" (1972:16). The same might be said for the honorific agencies, except the latter, (by design) have no intention of bringing the positive deviant back to the conventional center of society because the very quality or essence of positive deviance rests on this demarcation and its permanence! This whole area of the positive deviant and "reverse stigma" or *anastigma* scarcely bears a surface scratch from sociological investigation (for exceptions see Hughes, 1945; Goffman, 1963). Empirically the questions remain, do positive deviants experience the same processes, socialization stages, consequences, etc. as do negative deviants? Moreover, do negative deviants imply neutralization tactics and experience heretofore unknown stages and processes that will become apparent only when all deviants are investigated?

4. Deviance is functional, as well as dysfunctional, for society and the group. The sociology of deviance literature is replete with illustrations of the dysfunctions of negative deviance for society. Additionally, much has been written about the functions of negative deviance for the maintenance of society and the group (Dentler and Erikson, 1959; Coser, 1962; Cohen, 1966).

At first, it would seem quite obvious that society's members promote positive deviants as an example that "it can be done, and done by the rules" to enhance (as well as clarify) a community's common morality and value system; as a demonstration of how to be exceptional as opposed to overconforming (which Cavan [1961] so aptly displays as negative deviance); also as another type of safety value where what is to be exalted is acted out symbolically in honorific ceremonies. Unquestionably, positive deviations and positive deviants serve as antidotes to social disorganization by maintaining trust and the willingness to continue to play approved roles, to strive for a positive "being." Yet, this whole area is open to exploration. The same might be said for the dysfunctions of positive deviance. Positive deviance may lead to conflict, resentment, etc. Modern societies are pluralistic societies and the criteria utilized for identifying positive deviance and deviants may vary considerably across subcultures. Certainly these may be bases for social divisiveness.

5. Assigning the deviant label is always problematic. Just because a particular type of deviance has been labeled in the past does not guarantee it will be so labeled in similar instances in the present or the future. The ever-fluctuating relativity property of social deviance will always be present. However, there are many other factors to consider besides the relativity principle in the deviantizing process. These influences may be grouped under the rubrics of *the problematic of response* and the politics of deviance.

Becker (1963:12–18) lists some of the facts involved in the problematics of response: Who committed the act? When was it committed? Were there any disadvantageous consequences, and if so, how grave and who did they effect? Whose rules were relevant in the situation? Clinard (1975:34–40) lists additional circumstances which enter into the picture when he discusses the factors which affect the "social visibility of deviance." Goode (1978:53) and Rubington and Weinberg (1978:5–7) present propositional synopses of the conditions and factors that enhance the probability of successful labeling in the deviantizing process.

Besides those factors which constitute the problematics of response, the deviantizing process is in a very real sense an interaction situation which includes the "politics of deviance." In other words, power and negotiation enter the interaction situation. Those persons who are about to be labeled, or have been labeled, generally are not passive; they attempt to avoid the label or, if already labeled, to disavow it. If they are powerful enough or employ adequate mechanisms to stay the charge of moral culpability, they may avoid the label (Sykes and Matza; Scott and Lyman; Hewitt and Hall).

If they have been labeled already, they may use all sorts of strategies to escape or disavow the label and its consequences (Rogers and Buffalo, 1974; Goffman, 1963).

I see no reason why some if not all of these comments are not applicable to positive deviance, with certain modifications. I would speculate that there are potential positive deviants, or actual positive deviants, who would seek to disavow statuses of positive deviants for the very reasons and considerations negative deviants would so so: namely, the negative isolating consequences that accompany a deviant label. But what types of positive deviants would seek to do so? For what reason? Under what circumstances? What opportunities to do so are available? What mechanisms of disavowal are used? Are there any parallels to techniques of neutralization (Sykes and Matza, 1957), accounts (Scott and Lyman, 1968), or quasitheories (Hewitt and Hall, 1973)? Of course considerations of avowal of both negative and positive deviance are open to exploration also.

DISCUSSION

This has been a "working" paper; an exploratory paper to provoke and stimulate. I have argued that the sociology of deviance is overnegativized by noting that even though there is some mention of positive deviance in the literature, virtually no work by deviance theorists has addressed this phenomenon. No work has designated critical conceptual inconsistencies that exist between the way sociologists model social behavior, social control and social order and their subsequent selection of the referents for deviance.[12] Nor has any research demonstrated that a definition of deviance can be constructed that broadens its substantive scope greatly without violating the criteria by which deviance is identified. By ferreting out fundamental definitional statements in the deviance literature that were originally formulated with negative deviance in mind, but which show striking similarities between the two broad categories of deviance and illustrate the utility of including positive deviance in the sociological conceptualization of deviance, new insights about answers to "old" questions begin to surface.

In keeping with Lemert's concern about the incompleteness of his own

[12]It might be argued that the normative theorists are more guilty of this fallacy than the reactivist since their explorations and portrayal of the behavior continuum, social control and social order explicitly involves positive and negative valences of sanctions and behavior. Thus, when shifting to the behavior-deviance spectrum, why didn't they continue to carry in toto the essential criteria and logic to identify all forms of deviance? However, it is still odd that the reactivists did not (and have not) "discover" positive deviance and begin to explore it in the same manner as they have negative deviance for surely exceptional reactions, either negative or positive, occurs in reality to all forms of exceptional behavior. Is it possible that reactivist deviance theorists have unwittingly bought, all along, the normative deviance theorists division of behavior prematurely into the two categories of conformity and (negative) deviance?

limited treatment of deviance (1951:23), I believe it is not just the case of learning something about virtuous behavior by treating it as a form of deviance or learning something about virtuous people by treating them as deviants (although this is intended and is surely to occur), but also that we can learn something about deviance by treating it as "virtuous" as well. Explorations of positive deviance should shed light on presently unknown facts and dimensions of negative deviance.

Katz (1972, 1975), another sociologist who has acknowledged the concept of positive deviance (1975:1386) but who has not systematically incorporated it in his treatises on deviance and charisma, examines deviance (inferior moral identities and competencies) and charisma (superior moral identities and competencies) in terms of "imputed essences." Enlarging on Weber's work on charisma and the reactivist conceptualizing of deviance, he views deviance and charisma as "two sides of the one moral coin in which responsibility allocations are transacted" (1975:1384). Katz chides deviance theorists who focus on only acts and rules in identifying deviance and deviants and urges them to conceptualize deviance and charisma in terms of essences—"inherent qualities which may be manifested, reflected, indicated, or represented by, but do not exist in, conduct" (1975:1371). Concerning charisma, he goes on to draw several parallels between its identification and conceptualization and that of negative deviance (1975:1380–1386), some of which lie in the same vein as my comments in the preceding section on deviance identity and its properties.

Katz's work on charisma and deviance is intriguing and provocative. A thorough examination of his contentions and proposals could enlarge the scope of deviance and its conceptualizations along the lines proposed in this paper with charismatics viewed as subcases of positive deviants. Such an endeavor should provide us with glimpses of needed future theoretical and empirical work, and furnish us with possibly fruitful ways of studying charisma and altruism—outcomes which would be unlikely if the sociology of deviance were to remain in its present, negative conceptualizations. Moreover, such an examination portrays the desirable state of affairs where subdisciplinary theory and general sociological theory assist one another. In this instance, the reconceptualization of deviance has some immediate payoffs for the study of some classical issues of social theory—namely, altruism and charisma.

Theorists of deviance have neglected for too long the positive deviance dimension in the historical development of the sociology of deviance. They should pause to consider whether the basic criteria by which they identify deviance singles out phenomena other than negative deviance. In a very real sense, the neglect of positive deviance has produced a consequence somewhat analogous to the results that would have occurred in medicine, if the medical field had based its theories and practice solely on the study of the "ill" and neglected to examine the "well" or healthy: preventative medicine would never have developed.[13]

REFERENCES

Becker, George
1978 The Mad Genius Controversy: A Study in the Sociology of Deviance. Beverly Hills: Sage.

Becker, Howard S.
1963 Outsiders. New York: Free Press.

Blumer, Herbert
1969 "What is wrong with social theory." Pp. 140–153 in Herbert Blumer (ed.) Symbolic Interaction. Englewood Cliffs: Prentice-Hall.

Cavan, Ruth S.
1961 "The concepts of tolerance and contraculture as applied to delinquency." Sociology Quarterly 2:243–258.

Clinard, Marshall B.
974 Sociology of Deviant Behavior, 4th ed. New York: Holt, Rinehart and Winston.

Clinard, Marshall B., and Robert F. Meier
1979 Sociology of Deviant Behavior, 5th ed. New York: Holt, Rinehart and Winston.

Cohen, Albert K.
1966 Deviance and Control. Englewood Cliffs: Prentice-Hall.

Coser, Lewis A.
1962 "Some functions of deviant behavior and normative flexibility." American Journal of Sociology 68:171–179.

Dentler, Robert A., and Kai T. Erikson
1959 "The functions of deviance in groups." Social Problems 7:98–107.

Garfinkle, Harold
1956 "Conditions of successful degradation ceremonies." American Journal of Sociology 61:420–424

Gibbs, Jack P.
1978 "Norms and normative properties." Pp. 140–160 in Edward Sagarin (ed.) Sociology: The Basic Concepts. New York: Holt, Rinehart and Winston.

Goffman, Erving
1963 Stigma: Notes on the Management of Spoiled Identities. Engelwood Cliffs: Prentice-Hall.

Goode, Erich
1978 Deviant Behavior: An Interactionist Approach. Englewood-Cliffs: Prentice-Hall.

[13]If I am right in maintaining that deviance should be studied in all its forms, then questions arise about sociology as an institution. How come the neglect of positive deviance for such a long spell? What historical, political and policy factors influenced the development of the sociology of deviance? Such a sociological inquiry would seem to be in order here. In progress.

Harris Anthony

1977 "Sex and theories of deviance: Toward a functional theory of deviant subscripts." American Sociological Review 42:3–16.

Hewitt, John P., and Peter M. Hall

1973 "Social problems, problematic situations and quasitheories." American Sociological Review 38:367–374.

Hollander, Edwin P.

1958 "Conformity, status and idiosyncrasy credit." Psychological Review 65:117–127.

Hughes, Everett C.

1945 "Dilemmas and contradictions of status." American Journal of Sociology 50:353–359.

Katz, Jack

1972 "Deviance, charisma and rule-defined behavior." Social Problems 20:186–202.

1975 "Essences as moral identities: Verifiability and responsibility in imputations of deviance and charisma." American Journal of Sociology 80:1369-1390.

Liazos, Alexander

1972 "The poverty of the sociology of deviance: Nuts, sluts and 'perverts.' " Social problems 20:120.

Lemert, Edwin M.

1951 Social Pathology: A Systematic Approach to the Theory of Sociopathic Behavior. New York: McGraw-Hill.

1972 Human Deviance, Social Problems, and Social Control. 2nd Edition. Englewood Cliffs: Prentice-Hall.

McDill, Edward L. and James S. Coleman

1963 "High school social status, college plans and interest in academic achievement: A panel analysis." American Sociological Review 28:905–918

McHugh, Peter

1970 "A common-sense conception of deviance." Pp. 61–88 in Jack D. Douglas (ed.), Deviance and Respectability. New York: Basic Books.

Meier, Robert F.

1981 "Norms and the study of deviance: A proposed research strategy." Deviant Behavior 3:1–25.

Merriam-Webster

1974 Webster's New Collegiate Dictionary, Springfield: G&C. Merriam.

Merton, Robert K.

1957 "Social structure and anomie." Pp. 131–160 in Robert K. Merton, Social Theory and Social Structures. Revised Edition. Glencoe: Free Press.

Rogers, J. W., and M. D. Buffalo

1974 "Fighting back: Nine modes of adaptation to a deviant label." Social Problems 22:101–118.

Rubington, Earl, and Martin Weinberg

1978 Deviance: The Interactionist Perspective. Third Edition. New York: Macmillan.

Sagarin, Edward
1975 Deviants and Deviance: An Introduction to the Study of Disvalued People and Behavior. New York: Praeger.
Scarpitti, Frank R., and Paul T. McFarlane (eds.)
1975 Deviance: Action, Reaction, Interaction. Reading: Addison-Wesley.
Schur, Edwin M.
1971 Labeling Deviant Behavior: Its Sociological Implications. New York: Harper & Row.
1979 Interpreting Deviance: A Sociological Introduction. New York: Harper & Row.
Schwartz, Richard D., and Jerome H. Skolnick
1964 "Two studies of legal stigma." Pp. 103–117 in Howard S. Becker (ed.), The Other Side: Perspectives on Deviance. New York: Free Press.
Scott, Marvin B., and Stanford M. Lyman
1968 "Accounts." American Sociological Review 33:46–62.
Scott, Robert A.
1972 "A proposed framework for analyzing deviance as a property of the social order." Pp. 9–35 in Robert A. Scott and Jack D. Douglas (eds.), Theoretical Perspectives on Deviance. New York: Basic Books.
Simmons, J. L.
1969 Deviants. Berkeley: Glendensary.
Sykes, Gresham M. and David Matza
1957 "Techniques of neutralization: A theory of delinquency." American Sociological Review 22:664–670.
Thio, Alex
1973 "Class bias in the sociology of deviance." The American Sociologist 8:1–12.
1978 Deviant Behavior. Boston: Houghton Mifflin.
Truzzi, Marcello
1979 A book review of The Mad Genius Controversy: A Study in the Sociology of Deviance by George Becker. Social Forces 58:962–963.
Vander Zanden, James W.
1975 Sociology: A Systematic Approach. 3rd Edition. New York: Ronald Press
1981 Social Psychology. 2nd Edition. New York: Random House.
Wallace, Walter L.
1964 "Institutional and life-cycle socialization of college freshmen." American Journal of Sociology 70-318.
Wilkins, Leslie T.
1965 Social Deviance. Englewood Cliffs: Prentice-Hall.

Reading 4

Positive Deviance: An Oxymoron

Edward Sagarin
City College of City University of New York

By general agreement among sociologists and other specialists, and by speakers of the English language, deviance refers to rule-breaking and other nonconformity which is viewed in the society in a negative way, and hence reacted to with scorn, hostility, punishment, or an effort to effectuate change. Deviance is a special type of deviation, but the two terms are not interchangeable. The concept of "positive deviance" is and should remain an oxymoron or self-contradicting phrase, because it would obfuscate rather than clarify, would collapse into one group two ends of continua that have nothing in common except that they do not meet in the middle, and would deprive social analysts of the opportunity to determine why and with what consequences people depart from the normative in a manner that elicits dire consequences, as well as why a more conforming public reacts with hostility to some forms of behavior and statuses. The traditional and accepted concept of deviance should be retained, as it links the study of deviant behavior with law, social control, formal and informal sanctions, and the very nature and purpose or need of society itself.

Once again, a small minority of social scientists are trying to broaden, and in so doing dilute, a well defined and widely accepted concept, by including under one rubric what would be termed "positive" as well as "negative" deviance. The latest such effort was made in this journal (Dodge, 1985), and it is highly desirable that it was published, so that it can receive a wide readership, in the hope that it will be intelligently rejected by informed scholars.

THE NEED FOR CATEGORIES

It is extraordinarily important in all discourse, and particularly in the realms of science, to form classification systems, to set the boundary lines, so that one knows the instances that fall inside and those outside a given category, and to construct in general terms a description that indicates the nature of the characteristics that the members of that category share in common and do not share with those outside its area, so that P + non-P = the entire universe. The description, as contrasted with the list of items, is

My thanks to Robert J. Kelly of Brooklyn College and City University of New York, for a critical reading of an earlier draft of this article and for many helpful suggestions.

called a definition, and to the category itself is assigned a label, term, word, phrase, or some other symbol as its identifier.

The great philosopher of science, Henri Poincare (1913:349), described science as "before all a classification, a manner of bringing together facts which appearances separate, though they were bound together by some natural and hidden kinship." A major figure in the history of science, Wilhelm Ostwald (1912:787, vol. 3), stated that "the ordering of facts and their relationships in each individual science is the first and most important function in its development." And the outstanding British scientist and statistician, Karl Pearson (1911:6), wrote that "the classification of facts and the formation of absolute judgments upon the basis of this classification . . . *essentially sum up the aim and method of modern science*" (emphasis in original).

Categories, classes, and concepts do not exist in the world "out there." They are mental constructs; that is, they exist only in our own minds, and in the way we piece together thc real world. Reality itself consists of an infinite and limitless number of ideas, thoughts, acts, reactions, interactions, relationships, and a more finite but nevertheless extraordinarily large number of living organisms, including several billion human beings, living and dead.

The manner in which human beings, their acts, their relationships or their interactions, can be grouped is, if not infinite, then at least so large that no known computer can make all the combinations and permutations. It is thus a necessity, in normal everyday thought and communication, and in science, to form groups, classes, and categories, that are inclusive of some and exclusive of some other humans, infrahumans, acts, relationships, thoughts, and, to use a general word that could embrace all this is found in the universe, things.

The manner in which humans construct such groupings and classifications is not given in the nature of the world, and hence can be subjected to change because a more useful method is proposed. A group or class cannot be inherently wrong, but only inferior or superior to another method of joining together and connecting with one another divergent people, acts, or objects.

Our classifications and the definitions accompanying them are both arbitrary and stipulative. They are arbitrary in the sense that they are not given in the nature of objective reality; they are stipulative because how they are defined is also not given, but is merely how we stipulate within a language community what these definitions are.

This is not meant to imply that we are falling into the morass of a solipsistic approach. The objects, people, things, do exist, and even thoughts and ideas have real though not concrete existence, and their existence is not dependent upon the awareness of any human being, or of humanity as an abstraction. Only the combination that humanity makes of these real things are mental constructs that do not exist in the real world.

In order to form a concept, to place the instances that belong within it inside its boundaries, and to exclude all others from it, and then to formulate a definition based upon that concept, there should be certain criteria. In the philosophy of science, and particularly in philosophical orientations that have focused on language and linguistic analysis, the following appear to be the most significant such criteria, and while there are others, those that follow are suggested as the sine qua non in the formulation and definition of a concept:

1 The category formed should have an internal logic of its own. One can divide the animal kingdom into birds, mammals, reptiles, fish, and other categories, utilizing the Linnean system that has weathered almost two centuries with little improvement. But one can also make meaningful divisions of animals into omnivores, carnivores, and herbivores: and among the carnivores, into vultures and nonvultures ("non" is often a useful method of describing all instances that do not fit into a given category). For purposes of some types of understanding and research, a division may also be made, between males, females, and animals that do not have two different sexes. Biological researchers would find useful categories of animals that have in common their ability to contract a given disease, as distinct from all other animals not having such ability. Animals are divisible into domesticated and all others (or wild and undomesticated); and into those that are held ritually chosen for sacrifice to please the gods. All of these are scientifically valid groups. But unless once can find a logical connection, that does not make for an absurd and unparsimonious category among those placed within a class, the category should be abandoned or revised.

2 The category should not only be internally logical but also, derived directly therefrom, useful for those who have created it. This is not always easy to foresee. But if it has an internal logic, its usefulness is likely to be eventually discovered or created. When the concept of minority groups was first used to describe the ethnically and racially oppressed, it was hardly foreseen that sociologists and social activists would be able to find similarities between the racial/ethnic and other suppressed collectivities to that they would be able to place, within the confines of this concept, such people as women, handicapped, homosexuals, and lepers, among others (see Myrdal, 1944; Hacker, 1951; Sagarin, 1971).

3 There should be a language community that has general agreement on the meaning of a tag or label or word that covers a category. This is an extraordinarily difficult proposition for several reasons: (a) language is fluid, often in a state of change; (b) some words have several different meanings or shades of meanings, that are sufficiently close to be confusing; (c) words are not used in exactly the same way by all the members of a language community, or even of a language subcommunity; (d) definitions of words are contained in dictionaries, some of which are essentially descriptive, reflecting what the members of the language community hear and understand, and the dictionaries describe this in their own terms; whereas other dictionaries are essentially prescriptive, sometimes called elitist by their opponents, and they impose a meaning derived from the most educated, the most learned members of that community; (e) words can be used differently by various subcommunities within the larger language community, and the two subcommunities that here concern us are the public at large and the social scientists as a group of specialists and professionals; and finally (f) an individual or group can set out to deliberately effect a change in the use or meaning of a term or phrase, and seek to convince others of the superiority of a new usage. This last is often a very difficult task, but one that has been pursued with some success by the black, women's, and gay movements, due to general situations prevailing in the 1960s and 1970s. In the physical sciences, it may be far less difficult to bring about a change in definition, as a result of new research, such as the redefinition of the word "element" following the discovery of radium and the work on radioactivity. There is still another consideration, and that is that words or phrases may contain pejorative or favorable connotations, that are more likely to bring confusion than clarity to discourse, whether of an everyday or a scientific nature.

To meet any of the standards given above (internal logic, usefulness, and agreement with a language community), the broadening of the concept of deviance to include the oxymoronic "positive deviance" would be a step backward in the sociological study of an important aspect of modern societies.

USAGE: IN SOCIOLOGY AND IN EVERYDAY DISCOURSE

In the preparation of a previous work, Sagarin (1975) located about forty definitions of deviance in the social science literature, and could find only two instances in which the term (and the closely linked word deviant) were used in anything but a negative way. More than than, whatever choice of words might distinguish the definitions of deviance from one another, the definitions themselves came from persons of the highest reputation in sociology who nonetheless had strong differences in their theoretical approach. Whether labeling, interactionist, functionalist, social control, or other orientation was held by the authority, the definition of deviance encompassed the idea of activities that were viewed in the society as negative, deplorable, devalued, disvalued, disreputable, undesirable, disgusting, frightening, or in some other similar manner. At the risk of repetition, and with apologies for so doing, quoted below are representative, cross-section visions of deviance by authorities in the social sciences:

Ira Reiss (1970): "Deviant behavior, by *general agreement*, refers to behavior that is viewed by a considerable number of people as reprehensible and beyond the tolerance limits." (Emphasis in original.)

Albert Cohen (1966): Deviance is violation of rules, when that violation "excites some disapproval, anger, or indignation."

Marshall Clinard (1968), the sociologist who, with Edwin Lemert, can be considered the father of the field of study (this does not imply that the founding fathers are beyond criticism or improvement, but only that their definitions in founding a field of study can be extremely influential in creating the general agreement mentioned by Reiss): Deviance is "behavior in a disapproved direction, and of sufficient degree [of disapproval] to exceed the tolerance level of the community."

Donald Black and Albert Reiss (1970): Behavior is deviant "if it falls within a class of behavior for which there is a probability of negative sanctions subsequent to its detection."

Talcott Parsons (1951): Deviance is a "motivated tendency for an actor to behave in contravention of one or more institutionalized normative patterns."

Edwin Schur (1971), a proponent of the labeling position: "Human behavior is deviant *to the extent that* it comes to be viewed as involving a *personally discreditable* departure from a group's normative expectations, and it *elicits* interpersonal or collective reactions that serve to 'isolate,' 'treat,' 'correct,' or 'punish' *individuals* engaged in such behavior" (italics in original).

Most of these definitions omit the physically handicapped, and might even be interpreted to omit the mentally handicapped and retarded. Almost all students of deviance have emphasized that there is a negative attitude toward people with physical handicaps, but even if this were not the case, and even if compassion were at least partially replacing rejection, one could hardly say that being a dwarf, crippled, deaf-mute, or in some other way handicapped falls under the rubric of "positive" deviance. That these conditions have been highly stigmatized is well documented and excellently described (see, particularly, Goffman, 1963, and Scott, 1969). Even when people do not define the concept in a manner that would embrace the handicapped, they list the handicapped among those studies. This is true of Edwin Lemert (1951), who in his first major work on deviance studies seven specific groups: the blind, stutterers, political radicals, prostitutes, criminals, alcoholics, and the mentally disordered.

In science, it would be sufficient to show that there is general agreement within a scientific community, and it is unnecessary to resort to common usage, so long as the discourse is within the field and among the practitioners of the science itself. Nevertheless, agreement among themselves or with scientists on the meaning of a word by those who use it in everyday discourse is highly desirable, because it bridges the gap between the scientists and the nonprofessionals and reduces to a minimum the potential for misunderstanding.

The distinguished British philosopher J. L. Austin (1962) coined the word "behabitives" (which, perhaps fortunately, did not become part of the English language), writing that they are "a very miscellaneous group, and have to do with attitudes and *social behavior.* Examples are apologizing, congratulating, commending, condoling, cursing, and challenging." (Emphasis in original.) He might well have added scorning, condemning, putting down, and the numerous other words and phrases that easily come to mind, and there would emerge a clear notion of deviance: it is the behavitive that by scientific and popular consensus describes the action, status, or condition of individuals or groups, not because they are flawed, but because they are seen by others in the society as flawed. Efface this, and one of the clear-cut and significant concepts in sociology is lost.

It is difficult to believe that anyone mingling in the English speaking communities, at least in America and England, is using the term "deviant" in a manner that differs markedly from the definitions of scientists, and particularly to locate anyone using it in a manner applying to all those who differ from the norm or average, whether in a creditable or discreditable direction. *Webster's Third New International Dictionary* (Gove, 1961), the ultimate in descriptive lexicography (that is, it reflects how the language is spoken and written, rather than prescribes how an elite uses it or how it ought to be used), defines the noun deviant as "something that deviates from a norm; esp.: a person who differs markedly in some respect (as intelligence, social adjustment, or sexual behavior) from what is considered normal or acceptable in the group of which he is a member." One might indulge in exegetics to attempt to show that a marked difference from the normal could be positive, but the use of the word "normal" in the phrase "normal or acceptable" clearly demonstrates that the rejection of normal is here abnormal (not supernormal), just as the rejection of acceptable is unacceptable, and that both suggest to the public something wrong, improper, or reprehensible.

The Mavericks

Science seldom achieves unanimity, and those who disagree are often a great value in challenging the taken for granted concepts that periodically require reexamination. In social science, disagreement is even more likely than in the physical sciences. So that such a distinguished person in our field of study as Leslie Wilkins (1964) finds deviance at the outer edges of a frequency curve, and hence some deviant behavior is, he states, " 'good' or functional to society," Wilkins continues: "The genius, the reformer, the religious leaders, and many others are 'deviant' from the norms of society as much as the criminal." Yet, the method of presentation of this notion indicates that Wilkins has some second doubts as to the implied definition, for he places quotes around the words "good" and "deviant," aware that he is using these words in a peculiar manner, that he is unsure as to whether they are the right words, but his does not deny the implication that he is talking about "positive" deviance, or perhaps, positive "deviance."

There is one example in which the concept of positive deviance is put forth, but it is a work on differentness, and not on deviance, although the latter word is appropriated, and it is written by psychologist who show little familiarity with the sociology of deviant behavior. "The person of average intelligence," write Freedman and Doob (1968), "serving as a reporter at a conference of Nobel prizewinners, the person with normal vision at a home for the blind, the man of average height on a basketball court must all fee deviant." Do they feel stigmatized? Disreputable? Despised and rejected? of course not. Just what constitutes the feeling of differentness, how it is communicated to others, when it arises, what comforts or discomforts accompany it, are all of psychological interest, but it only muddles the waters for Freedman and Doob to appropriate the term "deviant" from lexicography, everyday discourse, and another field of social science and use it in this unacceptable, questionable, and easily misunderstood manner. It violates the elementary rules of language usage.

There is a problem, not raised by the mavericks, with the word "deviant," and that is that it has pejorative connotations when used by people in their everyday language, thus possibly giving an impression that people being described by sociologists are disreputable, reprehensible, or bad. It is easy to see how undergraduate students would make this error, but to add the positive to the negative would not clarify the essential point; namely, that deviance is behavior or condition that is considered bad or disreputable in the society, and that it is a proper area of study for sociology to focus on the stigmatized, the outcasts, the rejects. Such a focus does not suggest that the judgments made by large numbers of people have or have not justification

DEVIATION AND DEVIANCE: A CONFUSION OF TERMS

If at this point, it is suspected that someone is beating a dead horse, it is because the veterinarian has arrived, conceded that the animal is dead, and then goes on to act as if it had a breath of life and can and should be saved. But it is not, merely, to continue until we are unforgivably enmeshed in mixed metaphors, that the breath of life is not worth saving; actually, closer examination would illustrate that it is not even there. Thus, the efforts of Dodge (1985) to concede that the negative conceptions of deviance are paramount if not almost unanimous in sociology, and then to excavate a few instances in the opposite direction, at best add nothing new, and at worst are the result of some linguistic misapprehensions. What Dodge has done is to quote from authors who very carefully use the word "deviation" and then read into their work what had not been intended, namely, that they were really talking about deviance. The confusion of words that have somewhat related by nonetheless distinctly different meanings is not uncommon: an example would be disinterested and uninterested. This phenomenon is discussed in Fowler (1965) under such heading as differentiation and slipshod extension.

Thus, Dodge states that Clinard provides a basis for consideration of positive deviance when he (Clinard) writes: "Reactions to deviations from social norms can vary in the *directions of approval,* tolerance of disapproval" (emphasis added by Dodge), and then invokes Lemert as stating that his study is of a "*limited part or deviation*" and that "*variations from social norms in desirable and enviable directions should be explored as profitably as the more frequently studies sociopathic variations*" (emphasis added by Dodge). Then, having found two authorities who carefully use the words deviation and deviance in distinguishable manners, and having himself failed to make that distinction, Dodge quite naturally goes on to use the words as if they were interchangeable: "Now, if the referents of deviance and deviation are . . . " but there is no need to continue reading, because there are two different concepts, and they have overlapping referents but not the same ones.

The error that is made by Dodge is in his confusion between the word "deviation" and the word "deviance" or "deviant". This is a common error, both in everyday language and in science, but there is no question as to the intention of both Clinard and Lemert in choosing deviation in one instance, and deviance and deviant in many others. They understood, and intended the reader to understand, that deviation denotes difference in any direction, and that deviance is difference is the negative direction. Clinard is simply acknowledging this self-evident fact, taking note that deviation is a broader term, and that the sociology of deviance concerns itself with one aspect of this deviation, and not all aspects. In fact, Lemert has stated, in the quoted material, exactly the same idea. No one denies that deviations from the average or usual or ordinary exist. But to so state, and even to say that they are worth studying, does not imply that the study of deviance itself would be enriched by including the positively regarded exceptional persons under its rubric, even with the modifier "positive," as Dodge so wrongly interprets Clinard as stating.

Yes, the horse is dead, and if it continues to be beaten, at least there is no problem of cruelty to animals, but the poor veterinarian cannot quite make the concession. He invokes from the literature theorists who "refer (but sparingly) to the notion of positive deviance," and finds an edited book by Scarpitti and MacFarlane (1975). The book contains many articles on various types of deviance, and despite some introductory words that emphasize positive deviance, there is not a single article in it that would fit that description! The closest one can come to it is the story of a little brat who is a sort of child prodigy, but his deviance is not that he is admired for getting up among six or seven years old and, when asked about the weather, gives a lecture on meteorology. It consists of the fact that, in so doing, he is one of the most obnoxious children ever described in literature. So that the very example cited by Dodge illustrates the colossal failure of the theorists he would invoke to justify his position.

In short, deviance should not be confused with deviation. The latter is a mathematical concept referring to measures of dispersion from a central tendency. It refers to a frequency distribution when the arithmetic mean is used as a measure of a central tendency. Deviance refers to violation of social norms, and as such involves a great deal more than departures from statistical averages. Social norms prescribe behavior, and their importance in deviance theory is reflected in the strength of the reaction to their violations. Social norms, as contrasted with statistical norms, do not necessarily reflect average behavior, or attitudes or dispositions which are more common in a population. They are rather rules and standards concerning what is acceptable within a given cultural ambiance, and as such they provide guidelines for appropriate behavior in particular situations.

The term deviance has little to do with statistical variations per se within a population, except that, should deviant behavior become common, either the norms change or there is a backlash of powerful groups within society to enforce the old norms. To confuse deviance with deviation extends the concept of deviance to those who do not violate social norms in ways which prompt punitive and disapproving reactions, thus obscuring rather than illuminating distinctions among people that demand attention and study.

While negative and positive deviation is a sensible notion in so far as it refers to statistical variations from arithmetic norms, positive deviance does not even have that virtue. Deviance theory is not, as some contend, one-sided, whatever other failings it might have; rather, it focuses its attention on negatively viewed behavior at the expense of an arithmetic deviation as an intellectual choice.

The linguistic error continues with he term "anastigma" to describe "reverse stigma." It is somewhat of a neologism, but not entirely so, for there is a rarely used word "anastigmatic," which means not astigmatic, and the latter refers to having or showing an inability or unwillingness to observe, discriminate, or evaluate closely or in accordance with fact; it is a want of true discrimination of appreciation, especially when resulting from prejudice or deliberate obtuseness (Gove, 1961). To unravel all these negatives and emerge with a semblance of clarity, anastigma would be the observation in accordance with the facts and in a manner free from prejudice. This is not the reverse of stigma, which would be better described as honored and highly evaluated. Sometimes people free from prejudice can be stigmatized, because prejudice is the norm in the society.

SEPARATING LEVELS OF ABSTRACTION

It would be easy to end this piece at this point, but some greater clarity might be brought if there are some short discussions of levels of abstraction, on the one hand, and of behavior on a continuum on the other.

On a higher level of abstraction, one can rightly speak of deviation, as Clinard, Lemert, and Freedman and Doob have done. Then, on a lower level of abstraction, there is a separation: differentness in an approved direction, in a disapproved direction, and perhaps even in a direction toward which most people in the society are indifferent. On the higher level, there is a broader concept consisting of the outer edges of a bell curve, the tags that we give to the two flat edges where a minority of the cases fall are of importance only as identifiers, and require agreement within the language community. This is fine, and if some people want to study the high IQs (not the mad geniuses, because it is the madness that is deviant, not the genius), the piano virtuosi, the 400 baseball hitter, or such inimitable mimes as Chaplin and Marceau, they should be encouraged to do so. Some questions worthy of sociological study might crop up: how frequent do these types of people arise in a society; what psychological problems (if any) are brought about by their becoming celebrities; what nonconformity and even negative deviance and criminality can they display, perhaps flaunt, without discrimination, persecution, and punishment? What is the effect of their exceptionalism on their privacy? But one should always know on what level of abstraction one is working. There is nothing wrong with comparing apples with oranges, if the level of abstraction is fruit, except that two instances of the higher level might be insufficient.

One should always be wary of effacing lower levels of abstraction, because specific problems of overriding interest may be obfuscated. Nonetheless, there is nothing inherently wrong in going to a higher level of abstraction, unless it prevents the best questions from being asked, the best research from being done, and the best answers to be obtained. To go from deviance (which is negative) to deviation (which is within it negative, positive, and other aspects of differentness) would be a great setback in the study of deviant behavior. And, after all, why stop at differentness or deviation? It would be highly desirable to have a theory of human behavior, and much sociology is concerned with explaining human or social behavior as such, encompassing within it the normative and the deviant, the conforming as well as the nonconforming and the overconforming, the conscious and the unconscious, and other.

THE PROBLEM OF THE CONTINUUM

More interesting is that all human behavior exists on a continuum. Every sociologist knows about bell curves, and one can make a curve of intelligence, for example, and find that, if it is defined as synonymous with IQ (which it can be done, by stipulation), there is a point at around 80 or 85 below which dullness begins to get into the range of feeblemindedness, and then the bell skews at the other end, at about 140 or thereabouts, and the person is defined as extremely intelligent, bordering somewhere between brilliance and genius. Examples can be given of the continuum between proper and improper appearance, politeness and rudeness, honesty and cheating, and an almost infinite number of other examples.

The nature of that continuum, where lines of demarcation are drawn, the ability to move to more acceptable points or their possibility of slipping to less acceptable, are worthy of our study. But if the two skewed ends at the bell curve are to be compressed into a single unit, all that will occur is that there will be a need for a sociology specializing in one such end, and we will have a sociology of deviant behavior (negative, of course) all over again, under another name, whether it be stigma or negdev. Any effort to cover both under a single theory may be valiant, but it still would require the theory for the one aspect that those of us interested in deviance in its traditional sense have pursued.

BEING RADICAL BY BEING CONSERVATIVE

The traditional area that sociologists have cut out and called deviance is a valuable field of study, and the effort of a few people to coalesce it into a broader area should not be pursued by serious workers in the profession.

The traditional area addresses such questions as: Why are some types of behavior held in disrepute? Why is some disreputable behavior punishable by law, and other disreputable behavior is nonlegal negative sanctions? How do people manage their lives when they are highly stigmatized? What toll does secret deviance take on the life of a person? Why do people participate in a behavior for which they will, if discovered, face negative sanctions? What are the problems encountered in a society in which values are not widely shared, particularly by divergent racial, ethnic, age or other cohorts, and in which some people have negative attitudes toward behavior that others accept? What are the centers of power that bring about negative reactions on the part of a sector of the populace? What substitutes in cultural and societal action should be offered when a formerly criminal behavior is decriminalized without being socially accepted? What are the social forces that make a once disapproved form of deviance (as nonmarital cohabitation) completely or almost fully normative, so that it largely loses its deviant character?

The traditional area is deeply concerned with the social value, or social good, of deviance, but there is no problem in the examination of the social value of the great violinist or the incomparable actor or the scientist who makes a new breakthrough. The question is whether a reprehensible act unites the good people of a society around socially useful values; whether deviance acts as a safety valve; whether deviance puts the society on notice that there is something wrong with a system and that it needs radical observation and correction. Corruption is a form of deviance, in the most traditional meaning of that term, but Merton (1957) and James Scott (1972) have shown their positive consequences, utilizing particularly Merton's concept of latent functions and perhaps unanticipated consequences. The political machine provided many short-term services: it accelerated the integration of immigrants into the society; it offered more peaceful means for the resolution of factional political conflicts and disputes; it cooled out to some extent class antagonisms; and it afforded opportunities for upward social mobility for groups which otherwise were restrained and oppressed by prevailing social institutions and conventions. Even more important as an example of the view of deviance as having positive functions is found in Durkheim (1951 ed.): "Crime is useful; it provokes reproof and repression, which is of service in the solidarizing of a social group." As an aside, let it be noted that to state that a form of behavior is functional does not imply that the same or a similar function could not be achieved in another manner, causing less difficulty for the society as a whole or for individual members of it.

DEVIANCE WITHIN THE FRAMEWORK OF SOCIOLOGY

As deviance has been traditionally defined, it forms an integral part of a larger grouping of sociological concepts. It is related to social control, society and law, crime, and formal and informal sanctions, and in some instances, it bears a relationship to social problems. This is what sociology is all about: why are societies necessary, how are people kept in line, when and for what reasons are laws passed for that purpose, who obtains and maintains the power to pass laws, why are some violations of the norms punishable by laws while others are officially ignored but unofficially punished, when do social movements arise to change public attitudes and hence to make normative that which has been deviant, or the reverse?

The traditional area of deviance is a conservative approach to the definition that may lead to radical solutions, both sociologically and socially. Let us concentrate on exciting and important problems. There is a great deal to learn, much to be done, but let us not start by undoing the little that has been done and unlearning the minute quantity of fact and theory that has been learned.

REFERENCES

Austin, J. L.
1962 How To Do Things With Words. New York: Oxford.
Black, Donald J., and Albert J. Reiss
1970 "Police control of juveniles." American Sociological Review 35:63-77.
Clinard, Marshall B.
1968 Sociology of Deviant Behavior. New York: Holt,
1974 Rinehart and Winston.
Cohen, Albert K.
1966 Deviance and Control. Englewood Cliffs, J. J.: Prentice-Hall.
Dodge, David L.
1985 "The over-negativized conceptualization of deviance: A programmatic exploration." Deviant Behavior 6:17–37.
Durkheim, Emile
1951 Suicide: A Study in Sociology. New York: Free Press.
Fowler, H. W.
1965 A Dictionary of Modern English Usage. 2nd edition, revised by Sir Ernest Gowers. New York: Oxford.
Freedman, Jonathan L., and Anthony N. Doob
1968 Deviance: The Psychology of Being Different. New York: Academic Press.
Goffman, Erving
1963 Stigma: Notes on the Management of Spoiled Identity. Englewood Cliffs, N.J.: Prentice-Hall
Gove, Philip Babcock, ed.
1961 Webster's Third New International Dictionary. Springfield, Massachusetts: G&C Merriam Co.
Hacker, Helen Mayer
1951 "Women as a minority group." Social Forces 30:60–69. Reprinted in Sagarin, 1971, q.v.
Lemert, Edwin M.
1951 Social Pathology: A Systematic Approach to the Theory of Sociopathic Behavior. New York: McGraw-Hill.
Merton, Robert K.
1957 Social Theory and Social Structure. New York: Free Press.

Myrdal, Gunnar
1944 An American Dream. New York: Harper & Row. Excerpt: "A parallel to the Negro problem." Reprinted in Sagarin, 1971, q.v.
Ostwald, Wilhelm
1912 "The system of the sciences." In the Book of the Rice Institute. Volume 3. Houston, Texas: Rice Institute.
Parsons, Talcott
1951 The Social System. New York: Free Press.
Pearson, Karl
1911 The Grammar of Science. London: Adam and Charles Black.
Poincare, Henri
1913 The Foundations of Science. New York: Science Press.
Reiss, Ira L.
1970 "Premarital sex as deviant behavior: An application of current approaches to deviance." American Sociological Review 35:78–87.
Sagarin, Edward
1975 Deviants and Deviance: An Introduction to the Study of Disvalued People and Behavior. New York: Praegar.
Sagarin, Edward, editor
1971 The Other Minorities: Nonethnic Collectivities Conceptualized as Minority Groups. New York: John Wiley.
Scarpitti, Frank R., and Paul T. McFarlane, eds.
1975 Deviance: Action, Reaction, Interaction. Reading, Massachusetts: Addison-Wesley.
Schur, Edwin H.
1971 Labeling Deviant Behavior: Its Sociological Implications. New York: Harper & Row.
Scott, James C.
1972 Comparative Political Corruption. Englewood Cliffs, N.J.: Prentice-Hall.
Scott, Robert A.
1969 The Making of Blind Men. New York: Russel Sage.
Wilkins, Leslie T.
1964 Social Deviance: Social Police, Action, and Research. London: Tavistock.

Chapter Three

Research and Understanding

EDITORIAL COMMENTARY

Sociology, in many ways, can be thought of as something of a problem solving discipline. The early founders of sociology, such as Saint–Simone and Auguste Comte, developed it as a means of better organizing society and increasing the rate of human progress. There is an implicit, if not explicit, assumption underlying sociological curiosity and investigation that there is something deficient or out of order, as it were, in the realm of human social behavior. Sociologists may study social stratification in order to learn more about inequality and the inequitable distribution of life chances, resources, rewards, privilege, deference, honor, and opportunity, with the notion that, somehow a better understanding of the mechanisms of social inequality will provide insight and impetus for a more equitable social world. Similarly, sociologists may also examine various social institutions such as work, religion, education, or the family, often with an eye toward institutional dysfunction, disaffections, and difficulties. Interest in the family, for example, may revolve around such dysfunctions as marital unhappiness, spouse abuse, or divorce. Many sociology courses focus on the problematic aspects of social life, "Social Problems" being preeminent, of course. Other courses might include "Gerontology," which often addresses the "problems" of the elderly, "Criminology," "Juvenile Delinquency," and "Deviant Behavior." Of the array of subdisciplines that provide the bases for such courses, however, the sociology of deviance may be the least "acceptable," professionally speaking, and the one least likely to be included in the "core" of sociology. There are several reasons for this state of affairs. First, deviant behavior is less defined or circumscribed than the object of study in other sociological subspecialties. In the field of criminology, crime is demarcated in legal as well as social criteria. In the area of marriage and the family there is little question as to the nature of either. In gerontology, old age is usually defined in terms of objective rather than subjective standards. In the instance of deviant behavior, there remains wide ranging controversy and disputatious debate concerning the nature and definition of social deviancy, not to mention its genesis, contributing and facilitative factors and conditions, and social import. Deviancy is a very nebulous concept and, therefore, it lacks the certainty of parameters with which many sociological researchers feel comfortable.

Secondly, the label deviant behavior covers a multitude of sins (no pun intended). At one time or another, behavior ranging from narcotic addiction to being tattooed, from dog beating to incest, and from leering at pictures of nude females to stealing anatomical parts of dead bodies has been termed deviant. The concept of deviant behavior is simply too wide ranging and all inclusive in its coverage with the result that it often proves to be a difficult subfield in which to make generalizations concerning research findings.

Thirdly, deviant behavior is by its very nature, often "esoteric" if not bizarre, and sometimes salacious or even humorous and entertaining in a convoluted fashion. At one period of time, researchers did tend to fixate on the more sensational and colorful varieties of deviant behavior to the point that the field was subject to criticism from some scholars (see Liazos, 1972). Because it is sometimes considered unusual or "weird," some sociologists think it beneath their dignity to specialize in this sub-area. In effect, some feel that to specialize or pursue research on deviant behavior may detract from their image as a "serious" scholar. It is interesting to note that in Far Eastern societies (where "face" and dignity are very important), such as the Republic of China (Taiwan), most sociologists do not consider the study of deviant behavior to be a legitimate topic for sociological research, sociological journals generally will not consider manuscripts dealing with deviancy topics, and while there are sometimes courses on criminology and juvenile delinquency, there are no courses on deviant behavior. There is not even an appropriate translation for the word "deviancy." A special offering of such a course at a major ROC university was titled "Deviation Behavior."[1]

Fourthly, deviancy is a complex and convoluted phenomenon to conceptualize and operationalize. There are difficulties in developing appropriate designs to employ in research efforts. Even with a promising research design, there are many inherent problems involved in carrying out deviancy research. Deviants (or victims for that matter) are not always the most willing research subjects. They may be apprehensive about any publicity that may attend research, they may be fearful about being identified as a deviant and the consequences (being arrested, for example), and they may even be resentful about their privacy being invaded. The setting in which research on deviancy may have to be undertaken may even prove to be problematic. Such settings may prove to be dangerous, disaffective, or difficult into which to obtain entree. In short, deviancy research may be a difficult challenge, especially in terms of obtaining primary data.

Few sub-areas in sociological research have involved as varied a set of research designs, data gathering techniques, data itself, or data analysis as has research on deviant behavior. One of the branches of the ancestral tree of sociological research on deviancy can count among the progenitors, psychiatry, abnormal psychology, and social work. Interests on the part of these disciplines focused on "psychopathology" and the case study was a research mainstay. The jump from psychopathology to social pathology was not a long one. Some early sociological research on deviant behavior also utilized the case study design but focused on the city as a causative factor in social pathology. Perhaps one of the stronger branches of the family research tree, however, were the field studies of social disorganization conducted by sociologists at the University of Chicago, including research on "jack-rollers" (robbing skid-row drunks) (Shaw, 1930), hobos (Anderson, 1923), and the taxi-dance hall (Cressey, 1932). Following the style of earlier social pathology research, the former study was a life-history, intensive case study, but the latter two research efforts were based on urban ethnography, a kind of macro-level case study approach (Orcutt, 1983:37). Many of the early Chicago studies had an almost journalistic quality, perhaps, not surprising, in view of the influences of Robert Park, the Department Head, who had been a newspaper reporter earlier in his career.

Urban ethnography examined the "diversity of urban life" and "depicted deviant activity as an alternate form of organized behavior" (Orcutt, 1983:37). Other approaches to the research study of deviant behavior utilized by the Chicago School included ecological analysis based on "the

[1]The course was one offered and taught by the author while on a Fulbright appointment. The course was considered esoteric, if not "unusual."

organismic model of society and other biological analogies" (Orcutt, 1983:37).

In time, the study of deviant behavior was to move to disengage itself from the larger research concern with "social problems" and emerge as a separate subfield of inquiry with its own unique research agenda and more importantly, with its own theoretical rationale and with its own conceptual inventory, a more proprietous and specialized theoretical underpinning, and methodological approaches that were felt to be more appropriate to the nature of the phenomena under consideration. Merton's anomie theory (1938; 1957) was to have a significant impact on subsequent deviance research, by emphasizing the normative dimension of such behavior. Edwin H. Sutherland (1939; 1947) in contributing his theory of differential association introduced the notion of learning and socialization, as well as cultural conflict to the study of deviant behavior. The perspective of deviant behavior shifted from pathology to normal. As Orcutt (1983:43–44) phrases it:

> Finally, Merton and Sutherland treated deviant behavior as a *sociologically "normal" phenomenon.* With the normative definition of deviance, these theorists were able to conceptualize deviant behavior as a predictable choice made by normal social actors in response to certain kinds of environmental pressures. It was no longer necessary to link deviant behavior to the maladjustment or disorganization of individuals who had lost their ties to organized society. In this new conception, deviants could be just as social, just as well adjusted to their particular social environments as nondeviants.

As the study of deviance further developed and matured, yet other perceptions and foci appeared. Concern with socialization as a mechanism of learning deviant behavior also took into account the influence of subgroups and their unique cultures with goals and values in conflict with the more general culture. Merton's emphasis on social class as a factor in deviant behavior and the resultant "class variations in deviant behavior replaced ecological variations in social disorganization as the central descriptive issue for empirical studies of deviant phenomena" (Orcutt, 1983:46). Subcultural theories, in some instances, were integrated with Merton's anomie scheme. Members of subcultures were simply collectively responding to blocked conventional goals. Because of the numerous subcultures with highly diverse values (and not necessarily consistent with the values of the larger society), deviant behavior was increasingly viewed within a conflict rather than consensus context. Inasmuch as such behavior was often perceived, judged, and evaluated relative to middle class standards and norms, it was frequently labeled as deviant. Scholars came to recognize that such a jaundiced view was, in effect, operationally defining deviance in a prejudicial fashion, inasmuch as such lower class behavior could also be considered as conforming behavior in terms of subcultural values.

Research interest in the field continued to shift in line with these modifications in theoretical orientation. Researchers also began to take interest in the fact that much deviant behavior apparently did not come to the attention of law enforcement agencies, and that certain categories of individuals, such as members of the upper or middle classes, were less likely to be caught, arrested, or convicted of committing deviant acts. The incidence of deviant behavior, however, appeared to be consistent throughout the class structure (Orcutt, 1983:48–49). This observation and the writings of some writers such as Erikson (1962) and Kitsuse (1962) brought forcefully home to the researchers in the field, the significance of labeling or identifying some individuals as deviants with the individuals responding to the label by engaging in deviant activity in a kind of self-fulfilling fashion. Again, the theoretical focus had shifted from the idea of norm violating behavior to the mechanisms by which persons come to be labeled as deviants. The emphasis became more directed at societal reactions to deviance than to the deviant behavior itself. Research trends also moved accordingly. The theoretical controversy continues and the attendant methodological explorations follow suit.

It would appear that the sociological study of deviant behavior has not attained consensus on conceptual clarity or the appropriate theoretical concerns and direction, nor has there been convergence in terms of methodological focus and attack. The theoretical controversy continues and each school of thought has its adherents and apostles, not infrequently vocal and evangelical in seeking ideological converts, and the attendant methodological explorations meander from ideological position to ideological position.

In the first reading in this chapter, "Norms and the Study of Deviance: A Proposed Research Strategy," Robert F. Meier looks at some of the problems attendant to deviance research and makes some suggestions. As observed earlier in this commentary, he too points out that "the study of deviance is afforded low prestige among sociologists." He contends that this state of affairs is based on two factors. First, some decades back, sociology tended to disassociate itself from a social problems orientation and, thus, with "social activism" and the "practical" or the "applied." The second factor, he asserts, is the failure of researchers in the field to show how their "study of deviance bears on basic issues of social organization and social order." Researchers also have not given proper attention to the concepts that are central to this subfield.

Meier points out that much research work in this area has projected the notion of the study of deviance as the study of the "exotic" and the "titillating," in effect, catering to the prurient interests of students. In making this argument, he asserts that researchers are far from unified in even identifying that which is deviant. Using the works of a number of sociologists in the field as illustrations, he shows that these writers have included as examples of deviants, categories of individuals ranging from thieves to midgets and dwarfs, from bums to suicides, and from geniuses to the blind and stutterers. In short, a vast array of types of people that vary in some personal or behavioral characteristic from the presumed normal variety of individual. Scholars have been more likely to list examples or illustrations of deviants than to provide a detailed definition of deviance. There is, as he says, little in the way of "common theoretical or conceptual substance" in these examples. Students of deviance have not "developed principles about basic social process" inherent in the phenomenon. By devoting attention to the major concepts involved in the study of deviance, and especially to the concept of norm, Meier predicts the "dispute may be settled."

The author points out that there are three prevailing, but competing, conceptions of deviance: the *normative* concept that focuses on the violation of a norm; the *reactivist* conception that focuses on societal reaction and attendant labeling; and the *radical* conception that focuses on behavior that violated "fundamental rights." These three conceptualizations of deviance, Meier says, can be reduced to three basic concepts: norm, social control and value. The *reactivist* conceptualization of deviance is not without some defects. In his original exposition outlining this position, Becker (1973) rejected the absolutist notion of "universal standards of morality," and stressed the importance of the reaction to deviance of a social audience. According to Meier, Becker had no intention of producing a "radical" approach to deviance, but did so anyway. There were inadequacies in Becker's definition, as critics were quick to point out. There were also inconsistencies in that Becker spoke of "secret deviance" which, of course, by definition, had no social audience. Meier points out that Becker did not assert that labeling by a social audience creates deviance, but rather that social deviance is not significant until the attendant labeling gives it social meaning. In this, Meier feels, is the failing. Becker neglected the "social nature of norms . . . and the social circumstances surrounding the flexibility of those rules." Meier finds it odd that someone who talked about the "zealous rule makers" or "moral entrepreneurs" would find so little of interest in the "origins and nature of norms" and instead would focus on "logical (though not necessarily empirical) consequences of normative accompaniment, sanctions."

The normative conception of deviance has been somewhat more pervasive. This conception includes theoretical perspectives such as anomie, social disorganization, social learning, and control theory. The normative conception is not without problems, according to Meier. Merton's anomie theory, for example, is "normatively based" but other than his articulation of regulatory norms, and technical, or efficiency norms, Merton gives little other attention to norms. Meier interprets the anomie notion as indicating that nonconformity is the result of the "restraining influence of regulatory (or institutional) norms" being lessened, "thereby increasing the salience of efficiency norms that are not socially condoned." In effect, not only is conformist motivation encouraged, but so, too, are deviant means also "subtly instilled."

Social learning theory, also according to Meier, is not without defect or inconsistence. Akers (1977), one of the exponents of social learning theory, defines norms as "group-supported definitions of expected behavior in specific situations," and deviance as "instances of disapproved behavior considered serious enough to warrant major societal efforts to control them, using strong negative sanctions or treatment coercive techniques." Akers attributes deviance, for example, "to listening and believing the 'wrong' people." The problem as seen by Meier is that it is inappropriate to "explain conduct by norms," and then "turn around and infer the existence of norms via behavioral indicators."

Meier sees norms as extremely important in the definition and possible explanation of deviance, and urges more conceptual clarity. Toward this end, he examines the nature of norms and posits two common conceptualizations: the norm as an *evaluation* of conduct, and the norm as *expected* (or predictable) conduct. Based on these two conceptualizations, he addresses several strategies that have been employed to study norms. These include:

a Inferential strategy. (Norms are detectable or observable only after their violation, by observing sanction patterns.)

b Qualitative. (They do not lend themselves to direct measurement because they are imbedded in social situations and cannot be easily separated as entities outside of the situation.)

c Simply asking members of a social system what persons should or should not do in a given situation. (What people say they ought to do and what they do are not necessarily the same thing, however.)

Meier proposes a somewhat different strategy based on the assumption that norms are "empirical, measurable qualities of persons and conduct." He goes on to argue that norms describe ideal conduct, and are not specific rules. The reaction to deviance is contingent on variations in the act, actor, and situation. Norms are shared evaluations, not individual evaluations of conduct. Norms are quantifiable in that persons can be asked normative questions. Norms are measurable by asking normative questions and "assessing the degree of correspondence of those evaluations," obtained from people in the same social unit.

On the basis of his exposition, Meier offers the proposition that the deviant behavior (norm violation) that will be most strongly condemned is those acts most likely to evoke sanctions. Finally, he posits that infrequent deviant behavior may be infrequent because it is evaluated so strongly, and, therefore, requires special circumstances to overcome the evaluation (or to be able to make use of it). Similarly, evaluation of deviance is the strongest factor in predicting sanctions, or at least preferred sanctions. There is a difference in the sense that the actual application of sanctions for a given type of deviant behavior may take contingent information and events into account.

In summary, Meier concludes that the evaluation of conduct is the essential element in the definition of norm. Such an approach, he argues, permits the use of norms as conceptual units, resolves some of the past conceptual problems, and provides a means of addressing some "traditional and important" questions about deviance. Using this approach, he feels both normativist and reactivist theorists can now work toward the goal of "contributing to the larger issues of sociology."

Beyond the convoluted arguments and debates concerning theoretical and methodological considerations, there are numerous other perils and pitfalls involved in the investigation of deviant social behavior. Deviance is a difficult phenomenon to study for various reasons. It is often among the most emotion laden type of behavior. Individuals may indulge in deviant behavior because of love or lust, anger or compulsion, or depravity or greed, to mention but some of the motivational possibilities. It may well be irrational in intent. The ego of the participants may be significantly involved in the behavior. The participants may seek privacy or confidentiality, or be shamed by their activities. They may be fearful of the consequences of being observed or probed about their behavior. None of these factors lend themselves to objective and dispassionate observation and scrutiny. Their reservation, of course, represents only an initial caveat.

In the reading "Field Research Among Deviants: A Consideration of Some Methodological Recommendations," Robert J. Kelly reviews a range of problems that researchers of deviant behavior may encounter. Kelly suggests that a central concern in carrying out such research is how one is seen by others. It is, as he puts it, "a matter filled with risks and contradictions." A particularly troublesome concern is the problem of maintaining objectivity, and minimizing interviewer-observer effects, and the possible contamination of the phenomenon of observer presence. Overidentification or overly empathizing with the subject population is a possible difficulty. Nevertheless, Kelly feels that most field researchers appear to be satisfied that they have successfully overcome such problems.

For the study of some types of deviance, criminal activity, for example, there are special methodological problems. Criminals obviously do not like to be observed or studied. Even law enforcement groups may not welcome the field study of crime. Because of the secret nature of criminal behavior, social scientists may well have to rely on secondary or tertiary accounts of crime. Accordingly, as Kelly points out, the researchers "cannot independently evaluate their findings in accordance with scientific methods." Where the accounts of crime are derived by governmental agencies, they may be biased or filtered, in that they may "tend to ignore the complicity of the upperworld in sustaining criminal syndicate activity." Kelly does mention some researchers who have successfully attempted to do field work among organized criminals, collecting data using participant-observation techniques.

The author asserts that while it is highly desirable to have information about research techniques when reading reports of field research on crime for possible purposes of replication, such information may be less than explicit, and often elusive, and "highly personal and specific, if not eccentric, to a particular research focus." Some field researchers such as Polsky (1967) have argued that it is possible to do successful research with criminals. The "few advocates of open-air research among deviants, 'street sociologists,' as they are sometimes known" have been criticized because of a lack of methodological rigor in their research, and also because such work does not lend itself to verification and replication. Some like Polsky have, in return, contended that field research cannot effectively employ precise, controlled techniques of observation and insistence on such research protocols may handicap rather than aid the research.

Kelly also takes up the changing role relationship among researchers and subjects. In this regard, he reports that a number of researchers have indicated that their subjects not only provide information, but also are "guides, informal teachers, and occasionally friends." Research and subjects may even exchange information. Such a changing relationship, says Kelly, can have import for the research. The researcher may be transformed into a different person in terms of "interest, tastes, and purpose." This in turn may "affect knowledge production," sometimes making the research more productive, because both researcher and subjects become better sensitized to the needs of the research project.

Kelly reiterates some of Polsky's suggestions for field workers such as getting thoroughly familiar with the frame of reference, interests, and language of the subjects. Also he suggests discarding the usual data gathering devices, such as tape recorders, and trying to better blend into the setting and be a more skilled and astute observer. When entry into the setting has been accomplished, the researcher must clearly separate himself from the criminal activity and avoid pretense concerning the nature and purposes of the investigation. Kelly asserts that developing appropriate rapport may "trigger a snowball effect" in terms of causing a network of informants to appear. Careful and judicious behavior after cultivating rapport may well engender even more and wider rapport.

Because the field worker doing research on crime may actually be exposed to crime does raise some "delicate ethical issues." If the researcher is actually privy to the planning or commission of a crime, he or she might well be guilty of conspiracy or complicity in criminal acts. Most reports from field workers, however, are safely based on verbal accounts of criminal acts.

Accounts of crime or deviance based on verbal accounts are, as Kelly points out, conceptually different from data based on observation, but much of what is sought in field studies can be obtained from these verbal accounts. There is always the problem of determining the validity and reliability of data obtained from interaction, conversation, and casual observation, but the network of informants should provide a means for cross checking information and, in effect, triangulating data to determine its accuracy. The researcher must be alert to the constraints of criminal secrecy, deception, or other types of masked behavior. Again, the informant networks and information and services exchange should serve to help deal with this kind of problem.

If immersal or deep penetration in deviant groups is contingent on the commission of deviant or criminal acts, then they may serve to counterindicate or prevent the type of data gathering techniques previously discussed by the author. Even undercover law enforcement operatives may face such a dilemma. If they have to commit a crime in order to gain admittance to a deviant or criminal organization, or to protect their "cover," they may find this inimical to their purposes and have to extricate themselves from the situation.

Because of the legal and ethical problems inherent in this type of field research, many authorities advise that researchers with doubts or concerns about their involvement should feel morally obligated to remove themselves from the research. Recognizing the difficulties, field researchers in deviance and criminal activities should appreciate that in spite of the candor of informants, and "no matter how skillfully and ingeniously they manipulate the strategies that Polsky and others propose," there are limitations on how productive such research efforts may prove to be.

Because of the theoretical interest in the social reaction to deviant behavior and disvalued characteristics, there have been a number of research efforts to empirically explore the implications of "labeling," as it were. Steffensmeier and Terry (1973), for example, staged episodes of shoplifting observed by customers to determine the reaction. In their study, the shoplifters were differentiated by appearance into either "hippies" or "straight." Data from the research showed that customers were more likely to report the theft if the offender was a "hippie." The research did not resolve the question, however. Another similar study by Hartman and Gelfand (1972), also involving shoplifting and "hippie" or "straight" attire, suggested that the style of dress did not seem to influence whether or not the customer reported the theft.

Social reaction to stigma in terms of prejudice in employment has also been studied experimentally. Larkin and Pine (1979) demonstrated that stereotypical beliefs about the overweight may impact on employment hiring. The next reading in this chapter, Webber and Orcutt's "Employers' Reaction to Racial and Psychiatric Stigmata: A Field Experiment," employs a similar strategy of using an experimental design to explore possible prejudicial reactions to disvalued identity. This study examines the possible impact of racial identity (black vs. white) and deviant status (former mental patient vs. "normal") on differential employment opportunity for job applicants. The authors point out that there had been some design problems in such research. In some of the studies cited in their review of previous research, only job application folders as opposed to actual job applicants had been used. In some instance, the interviewers (simulated employers) had been college students rather than actual employers. In other studies, the students posing as "employment agents" did not submit their material to potential employers in a "pre-selected random order." Webber and Orcutt sought to avoid some of these limitations by using a more ambitious and sophisticated design.

They were interested in the discriminatory implication of two stigmatic factors, psychiatric disability and race. For their study, from a list of 219 employers who hire unskilled workers, they selected a random sample of 80. They employed a research team of confederates consisting of four black students and four white students to provide for differential racial identity. For the psychiatric disability characteristic, the students, in contacting employers, sometimes mentioned that they had been out of work because of hospitalization for mental illness, and in other cases, no mention of hospitalization was made. The student confederates were selected and trained to minimize "the influence of appearance and personal characteristics other than the manipulated variables." Thus, each student confederate contacted 10 employers, alternating the psychiatric status identity, and followed standardized instructions in seeking employment.

After the job interview, the student confederates completed a postcontact information sheet indicating the outcome of the interview in terms of four structured ratings ranging from "will definitely not hire" to "will definitely hire." The students also provided an unstructured rating based on the employer's behavior, his gestures, comments, and concerns. These ratings were later categorized on a ten-point scale. Ten days after the student contact, the employers were formally interviewed and information concerning a number of variables including age and educational attainment was obtained.

In terms of the structured ratings, the black confederates who mentioned a psychiatric record received the lowest score and the white students who mentioned no psychiatric record received the highest. In effect, the black candidates with psychiatric records received the least encouragement from employers and white candidates with no record, the most. In regard to the employers' age and educational level, "older employers generally expressed less favorable reactions to confederates," and "more highly educated employers reacted less favorably to white ex-patients than did employers with lower educational attainment," although the correlations pertaining to educational attainment of employers and their reactions to the various categories of job applicants were generally not statistically significant. In short, whereas the experiment "found some evidence of direct discrimination against job applicants with a record of hospitalization for mental disorder," it failed "to reveal pronounced or consistent liabilities of racial and psychiatric stigmata." The study, however, as a well designed and executed research exercise, did underscore "the utility of field experimentation for examining central implications of the labeling perspective on deviance."

Stigmata may be based on a variety of characteristics. The stigmata and the attendant social stereotypical attitudes and beliefs may have some basis in fact or they may be spurious or totally illusionary. It may be based on major differentiating characteristics or on relatively minor or subtle attributes. Furthermore, stigmatization is often the result of contextual interpretation for seemingly desirable or advantageous qualities or traits, and may, in some circumstances, be translated as objectionable or censurable and the social reaction may, accordingly, be negative.

In the final selection in this section, Jean Huryn looks at gifted students and social reactions to this characteristic. In her "Giftedness as Deviance: A Test of Interaction Theory," the author examines the status of giftedness and the stereotypes and labels that are applied to persons who occupy that status, and she also looks at the interaction between gifted students and others. She seeks to determine if role theory or labeling "best depicts the behavior of gifted students in dealing with this status." Basically, as she explains, role theory would suggest that individuals come to act in a particular manner because of the way in which they perceive themselves based on interaction with others. Labeling, she contends, involves the reaction of others to the individual, and the individual engaging in other deviant behavior as a result. Huryn also investigates the value dimension of giftedness to see how giftedness is valued and by whom.

To examine these questions, she randomly selected sixty students who were identified as gifted and talented by officials in several school systems who had programs for the gifted. Through structured interviews the students were asked about their own attitudes and perceptions about being smart, and about the attitudes and perceptions of others, and society in general, toward them being smart. Various questions probed the students' awareness of stereotypes and labels of giftedness, and the interaction between the students and others, especially peers. Other questions addressed the value dimension of being gifted as perceived by others.

On the basis of an analysis of the interviews, the author found that with few exceptions, most of the students held negative stereotypical perceptions of giftedness. The students, however, spoke of different types of smart people, and tried to make a distinction between the stereotypical types and those that were exceptions to the stereotypes. They were aware of the labels frequently applied to gifted people but most indicated that they did not feel different. They were also aware that in our society, giftedness frequently attracted negative labels.

In regard to the interaction between themselves and others, most of the students interviewed used some form of impression management in way of adjustment to their gifted status. The techniques that they used included such things as denying being in the program, or not offering the information unless asked. Other coping mechanisms mentioned were "playing dumb" and covering the degree of giftedness, pretending not to know the information, not volunteering to answer questions, and asking inappropriate or "pointless" questions.

On the question of the value dimension of giftedness, students reported that some teachers reacted positively to giftedness, but some did not always do so. The subjects did say that parents mostly were very positive about giftedness.

The great majority of the students interviewed indicated that their peers at school held negative evaluations of giftedness. In regard to their own personal evaluation, most of the students saw giftedness as a valued attribute in their own life. Accordingly, they felt that the program was a valuable educational program, and in that sense, they felt the attendant advantages outweighed the negative reaction their gifted status received from peers.

The author concluded that students were aware of the negative label and stereotype of giftedness, especially by school peers, but dealt with this dilemma by acquiring friends who were also in the gifted program, and by using a variety of coping techniques. In this regard, seeking friends with a similar status was, according to the author, more supportive of labeling theory. The gifted students' use of "covering" mechanisms and adapting and managing their behavior to avoid negative sanctions and teasing from peers was more suggestive of role theory. Students would reveal their giftedness to parents and teacher "when and if these persons value giftedness." When dealing with peers, they would revert to deception. Thus, Huryn felt that gifted students use a "chameleonic approach," when moving from one reference group to another. The students were, therefore, able to confront the stigmatizing reaction of giftedness in an adaptive way, "blending to the situational environment in this manner."

Research in the area of deviant behavior is not without its perils and pitfalls. The subject matter is sometimes elusive and the subjects may be evasive, if not uncooperative. Deviance is a complex phenomenon and the appropriate conceptualization of its components has been difficult and laborious, not to mention controversial. These problems and others have often proved to be challenges to effective research. The selections in this chapter have addressed some of these challenges and have offered some illustrations of creative efforts to overcome some of the challenges. Robert F. Meier directed his exposition to the problem of properly conceptualizing deviance and argues for more research emphasis on norms and asserts that the evaluation of conduct is the essential element in norm. The use of norms as central conceptual units will overcome some of the past research problems and the result will make a greater contribution to the larger issues in the discipline. Robert Kelly, in his article, looks at some practical difficulties in field research, and especially the problematic contaminating influence of the presence of the researcher and his possible bias. Reviewing some accounts of past research efforts and how some of these issues were addressed, Kelly concludes that while some field research problems can be mitigated or minimized, there are simply limitations inherent in this type of research that the researcher may have to accept. In their article, Webber and Orcutt demonstrate the design and execution of a field experiment that looks at the possible impact of labeling prejudice on employer preferences in hiring. While their finding did not support the hypothesis of labeling prejudice, it did illustrate an effective research procedure for empirically documenting such stereotypical prejudice. Jean Huryn, in her selection, also detailed a research project. In this instance, gifted students were interviewed about their awareness of stereotypes of giftedness, their interaction with others, and the value dimension of being perceived as gifted by others. The students, she concluded, were aware of negative stereotypes, but saw advantages in such a status that outweighed the stigmata. They dealt with the latter by employing managed and adaptive behavior in a "chameleon" fashion to avoid social sanction. The articles in this chapter have hopefully provided insight into both the perplexity of conducting deviance research as well as the mechanics and outcome of some specific research investigations of deviance.

REFERENCES

Akers, Ronald L.
1968 "Problems in the sociology of deviance: Social definitions and behavior." Social Problems 46:455–465.

Anderson, Nels
1923 The Hobo. Chicago: University of Chicago Press.

Becker, Howard S.
1973 Outsiders: Studies in the Sociology of Deviance, (enlarged edition). New York: Free Press (originally published in 1963).

Cressey, Paul
1932 The Taxi-Dance Hall. Chicago: University of Chicago Press.

Erikson, Kai T.
1962 "Notes on the sociology of deviance." Social Problems 9:307–314.

Hartman, Donald P., Donna M. Gelfand, Brent Page, and Patrice Walder
1972 "Rates of bystander observation and reporting of contrived shoplifting incidents." Criminology 10:247–267.

Kitsuse, John I.
1962 "Societal reaction to deviant behavior: Problems of theory and method." Social Problems 9:247–267.

Larkin, Judith Candib, and Harvey A. Pines
1979 "No fat persons need apply: Experimental studies of the overweight stereotype and hiring preference." Sociology of Work and Occupation 6:312–327.

Liazos, Alexander
1972 "The poverty of the sociology of deviance: Nuts, sluts, and 'perverts.' " Social Problems 20:103–120.

Merton, Robert K.
1957 Social Theory and Social Structure (revised edition). New York: Free Press.
1938 "Social structure and anomie." American Sociological Review 3:672-682.

Orcutt, James D.
1983 Analyzing Deviance. Homewood, Ill.: The Dorsey Press.

Polsky, Ned
1967 Hustlers, Beats and Others. Chicago: Aldine.

Shaw, Clifford R.
1930 The Jack-Roller. Chicago: University of Chicago Press.

Steffensmeier, Darrell J. and Robert M. Terry
1973 "Deviance and respectability: An observational study of reactions to shoplifting." Social Forces 51:417–426.

Sutherland, Edwin H.
1947 Principles of Criminology (4th edition). Philadelphia: Lippincott.
1939 Principles of Criminology (3rd edition). Philadelphia: Lippincott.

Reading 5

Norms and the Study of Deviance: A Proposed Research Strategy

Robert F. Meier
Washington State University, Pullman

The study of deviance seems to have low prestige within sociology and does so at least in part because students of deviance have not shown how the study of deviance bears on wider social processes and conditions. Much of this might possibly be avoided by concentrating on the concepts that are of central concern to the study of deviance, for example, norm. Although norms constitute the central boundary separating normativist and reactivist conceptions of deviance, little conceptual and empirical attention has been devoted to them. The main problem is that norms have not been measured directly (and hence themselves are not studied empirically) but have been inferred from social situations in a post hoc fashion. If norms are conceived properly, however, there exists the possibility for direct measurement. Procedures are proposed to accomplish this task.

In acknowledging intellectual debts incurred in the preparation of his book, *Social Theory and Social Structure,* Robert K. Merton credits Pitirim A. Sorokin with helping him escape "the slum-encouraged provincialism that the primary subject matter of sociology centered on such *peripheral* problems of social life as divorce and juvenile delinquency" (Merton, 1968:xiii, emphasis added). Such a statement would perhaps be easily dismissed as gratuitous were it not contained in as important a volume as this and uttered by one of the most influential sociologists the discipline has yet produced. Yet Merton does not explicate the ways in which the study of delinquency—or indeed any other form of social deviance—is peripheral to understanding larger issues in sociology. It is as though amplification were not required.

Merton is not alone in his thinking. The sociological study of deviance appears to be a specialty that is not highly prized within the discipline. This is surely a curious state of affairs given that many sociologists interested in deviance would presumably subscribe to the view that the study of deviance is absolutely essential for a complete understanding of social life. The problem seems to be that sociologists have not shown why or how this is the case. This paper addresses the problem by making a brief assessment of the sociology of deviance and by proposing a direction for the field. This proposal is not especially novel and can be summarized briefly: students of

This is a revised version of a paper presented at the annual meetings of the American Sociological Association, New York, August 1980. Lee Freese and Jack P. Gibbs were kind enough to provide comments on an earlier draft.

deviance must give more attention to the concepts on which their specialty is based. By doing so, the relationship between deviance and other forms of social behavior can be made clear.

THE STUDY OF DEVIANCE IN SOCIOLOGY

The study of deviance is afforded low prestige among sociologists. Observations to that effect permeate several histories of sociology in general (e.g., Odum, 1951; Hinkle and Hinkle, 1954; Oberschall, 1972), as well as accounts of the development of specialty areas such as criminology (e.g., Wheeler, 1962). One reason for the low esteem conferred upon the study of deviance has to do with sociology's repudiation in the 1920s and 1930s of a social problems orientation and the concomitant rejection of social activism and practical concerns such as social work. And the study of deviance has always been tinged with the "practical" and "applied." Another reason is less historical and relates to the nature and quality of work conducted in the sociology of deviance: students of deviance have not shown how the study of deviance bears on basic issues of social organization and social order. This is a serious charge but one that is documentable, as perhaps Merton himself recognized. Consider the concepts that are of importance to the study of deviance: norm, sanction, social control, motivation, socialization, group process, value, interaction, and power. Although these concepts are central to the study of deviance, they are by no means unique to that specialty—they are commonly invoked in other areas of sociology as well. Deviance theorists have no special claim upon these concepts, but one might well expect that, given their centrality, they would have been given most of their conceptual attention and development within a deviance framework. This is not the case. Deviance theorists, in fact, have avoided a scrupulous examination of these concepts, while at the same time apparently benefiting from their use. The consequences of this neglect have been far reaching.

Instead of attending to the conceptual work necessary in any field, students of deviance have busied themselves with producing a literature that conveys the impression that the study of deviance is a study of the exotic and the titillating; what these sociologists studied actually did seem to reside on the periphery of most social life. Studies of topless waitresses, stripteasers, nudist camps, massage parlors, and frequenters of nude beaches, for example, often failed to explore the meaning of such activities for our understanding of general processes of social behavior. Without at all attempting to do so, this research gives the impression that such work is merely capitalizing on the prurient interests of the most usual consumers for such studies: students.

Moreover, such work suggested strongly that students of deviance had difficulty determining precisely what constituted deviance in the first place. Thus, the concept of deviance (which must be addressed in terms of the concepts listed above) has been more apt to be defined by enumeration than nominally. Davis (1961) would include blacks and career women as deviant. Cohen (1966:1) says his book is about "knavery, skulduggery, cheating, unfairness, crime, sneakiness, malingering, cutting corners, immorality, dishonesty, betrayal, graft, corruption, wickedness, and sin." Gouldner (1968) objects to the empirical literature on deviance and remarks that the focus of study has been limited largely to "the world of the hip, drug addicts, jazz musicians, cab drivers, prostitutes, night people, drifters, grifters, and skidders: the 'cool world.' " Howard Becker (1973) limited study to jazz musicians and marijuana users. A British collection of papers on deviance dealt with drug users, thieves, hooligans, suicides, homosexuals and their blackmailers, and industrial saboteurs (Cohen, 1971). Lemert (1951) illustrated his theoretical position with reference to, among others, the blind and stutterers. Dinitz, Dynes, and Clark (1975) find the following types of persons deviant: midgets, dwarfs, giants, sinners, apostates, heretics, bums, tramps, hippies, and Bohemians. George Becker (1977) finds the "genius" deviant. Finally, Henslin (1972) uses four types of deviants to illustrate research problems in the field: cabbies, suicides, drug users, and abortionees.[1] What unites such lists is anyone's guess, other than the fact that most sociologists have been denied access to the worlds of such "deviants" by personal experience or inclination. So rather than explicating the concept of deviance, most writers have investigated supposed instances of it, even though one would be hard pressed to extract a common theoretical or conceptual substance from these instances.

To the extent that the specialty of social deviance is disvalued, it is probably for these reasons. We have generated a number of facts about deviant acts and actors but have not developed principles about basic social processes. In short, if the study of deviance is disvalued, it is because of how sociologists have (and have not) studied it.

Yet, thinking about concepts central to the study of deviance cannot (and has not) been totally ignored. Indeed, one concept in particular, norm, forms the basis for the major theoretical dispute in the field today. Moreover, it is only through attention to this concept that the dispute may be settled, if at all.

[1]Sagarin (1975:3–5) mentions some of these same lists to illustrate his definition of deviance as disvalued people and behavior. His definition of deviance and my designation of the specialty of the sociology of deviance as disvalued is an ironic coincidence but no more than that. Sagarin's book, however, remains one of the best in the field.

CONCEPTIONS OF DEVIANCE

There are currently three competing conceptions of deviance: the *normative* conception defines deviance as the violation of a rule or norm; the *reactivist* conception defines deviance as the application of a reaction to conduct; and the *radical* conception defines deviance as behavior that violates "fundamental rights." Normative and reactivist conceptions have generally held sway within sociological studies of deviance (albeit in a tenuous balance of differential popularity). The radical conception has been offered as an alternative, and it is reflected in the writings of theorists who propose as legitimate objects of inquiry such acts as violations of human and/or class rights (e.g., Schwendinger and Schwendinger, 1970, 1977).

The major competing conceptions of deviance are reducible, it can be argued, to three concepts: norm, social control, and value, respectively. One would think that these three concepts in particular would have been the object of long and inexhaustible attention; but they have not. The reactivist view, which is often portrayed as antinormative, has paid some attention to social control but only as it applies to deviance and then only narrowly. Normativist theorists employ the same conception of social control but only as it applies to deviance and then only narrowly. Normativist theorists employ the same conception of social control as reactivist—as sanctions—but have not devoted attention to that concept that orients their own work: norm. Radical theorists have used the notion of "value" implicitly but often assume that the values to be used as standards of deviance are well defined, widely agreed upon, and not readily debatable.

Yet attention to such concepts can illuminate the nature of the central theoretical dispute in deviance, that between the normativists and reactivists. In many respects, this dispute hinges on the following question: How useful is the concept of norm for understanding the sociological nature of deviance?

The Reactivist Conception

Few statements in the sociology of deviance have aroused more interest and agitation than Howard S. Becker's *Outsiders* (1973). In that work, Becker argued thoughtfully for a conception of deviance that placed the deviant act within a distinctly social context by exploring the nature of those rules (social control). Rejecting absolutist conceptions that viewed deviance as departures from universal standards of morality, Becker pointed to the importance of a social audience to behavior in interacting with the deviant, an interaction that—depending upon other circumstances—could produce further deviance.

By his own account, Becker was surprised by the reaction his book generated (Debro, 1970). What he took for a relatively simple set of ideas that seemed useful to him in conceptualizing the deviant phenomena examined in that work (the use of marijuana and the "deviant" careers of musicians) were subsequently applied to a wide range of deviant conduct and conditions, from serious criminality to physical disabilities. Clearly, Becker had no intention of producing a "radical" approach to deviance, but that is precisely what he did.

The radical portion of the book was contained in Becker's definition of deviance. "The deviant is one to whom that label has successfully been applied; deviant is behavior that people label" (Becker, 1973:9). Critics of this conception were quick to point to the inadequacies the definition suggested (Gibbs, 1966; Akers, 1968). To make matters even more confusing, Becker (1973:20) appeared to violate his own definition a scant 11 pages later when he identified something called "secret deviance." This was an "improper act" that was committed "yet no one notices it or reacts to it as a violation of the rules." How can this be considered deviant if, as Becker says earlier in the book, a label has not successfully been attached to the behavior? One way out of this apparent quandary was to distinguish deviant acts from deviant actors.[2] That is, while deviant acts are considered undesirable and have a probability, if known, of being sanctioned, deviant actors, because they are deviants, have a vested interest in escaping detection and labeling. Thus, although Becker's definition applies to behavior, the term "secret" is made to apply only to actors who commit acts that are deviant by Becker's definition but are undetected. This explanation, however, is unsatisfying because Becker's definition specifies explicitly that he is talking about deviants not deviance.

Another alternative was to invoke the notion of self-labeling where the deviant defines what was done as deviant, even though the deviant managed to keep others from finding out about it (e.g., Lorber, 1967). This suggests that "secret deviance consists of being vulnerable to the commonly used procedures for discovering deviance of a particular kind, of being in a position where it will be easy to make the definition stick" (Becker, 1973:187). In other words, deviance is a collective phenomenon that results from the reactions of a social audience, either present to the act or imagined to be.

But surely deviance is not a social phenomenon merely because of social control efforts. Such a claim, which has been a favorite target of critics of the reactivist conception, is simply untrue. Police do not define crime, nor do they socially create it (unless, of course, they precipitate it); they do create knowledge of crime, but this is a different matter. Psychiatrists do not generate mental disorders (again, unless they somehow precipi-

[2]Sagarin(1979), for one, advocates this alternative, although for different substantive reasons.

tate the behavior so labeled); they attempt to deal with it once it has occurred and thus create knowledge of mental disorders.

Were Becker arguing against this position, the criticisms just mentioned would have great weight, but he does not. Becker does not indicate that undetected crime is not crime nor that undiagnosed mental disorder is "normal" behavior. What he does say is that the social meaning of deviance is found in the application of a label to an act; the act is not socially significant until the label imputes meaning to it. This, however, suggests a question: how does the audience to an act know when to label and when to ignore it? One possible answer is that audiences label when they observe or otherwise learn about a norm violation. Thus although reactivists consider the labeling process problematic, they evidently do not so consider the labeling process problematic, they evidently do not so consider the basis on which labeling is evoked originally. Becker's sociological "failing," therefore, is not that he draws our attention to the social nature of sanctions and their possible consequences but that he neglects (or rejects) the social nature of norms (or "rules" as reactivists have called them) and the social circumstances surrounding the flexibility of those rules.

This is an odd omission from someone who is credited with coining a term that identifies particularly zealous rule makers, "moral entrepreneurs," or groups of persons who feel sufficiently strong about some behavior that they are willing to campaign actively to persuade others of the deviant nature of the conduct. Becker's interest in the rule-making process, however, does not become linked with the concept of norm but that of sanction as he concentrates on the controlling (or labeling) aspects of entrepreneurial activity. The rule, once made or once others are convinced of its legitimacy, can be applied. This is what interests Becker and what for him defines the conduct as deviant. Thus, what could have become a most penetrating analysis of the origins and nature of norms became instead an exposition about the logical (though not necessarily empirical) consequences of normative accompaniments, sanctions. This was more than a difference in theoretical focus; it was a theoretical challenge of the most basic kind.

The Normative Conception

The pervasiveness of the normative conception of deviance is not difficult to discern. The leading theoretical perspectives in the field have been or are normative: anomie, social disorganization, social learning, and control theory. Even the "theory" of secondary deviation, often erroneously associated exclusively with a reactivist conception of deviance, is normatively based, depending on the theorist; such writers as Edwin Lemert and Thomas Scheff view deviance as violations of norms. (What concerns them beyond this, of course, are the consequences of the application of sanctions once "primary" deviance has occurred.)

Yet, most normative definitions of deviance are not satisfactory (e.g., Gibbs, 1978), largely because of the indifference normativist theorists have displayed toward norms. Consider the following definition: "Deviance constitutes only those deviations from norms which are in a disapproved direction and of sufficient degree to exceed the tolerance limits of a social group such that the deviation elicits, or is likely to elicit if detected, a negative sanction" (Clinard and Meier, 1979:14). This definition employs no less than three concepts—norm, tolerance, and sanction—and their use is ambiguous. What exactly is a norm? What is the referent for tolerance? What kind and intensity of negative sanction is required?

The importance of such concepts goes beyond matters of definition to the content of specific theories of deviance, particularly those that view deviant behavior as one consequence of a particular kind of learning. Norms are central to this perspective because they comprise that which is learned; that is, social learning theory asserts that persons come to acquire something called norms. Norms are thought to be important because they may orient persons' behavior and attitudes. Norms themselves, sociologists often contend, go a long way toward "explaining" behavior.

This is hardly an outrageous view. Most sociologists would agree that much behavior is normative, that persons act in relation to norms much of the time.[3] The dispute centers on what exactly a norm is. Formal definitions are not always helpful. They assert that norms are "situation-specific standards of behavior" (Demerath and Marwell, 1976:37), "specific sets of rules or definitions of proper behavior" (Goode, 1977; 1978:10), or "specific guides to conduct" (Broom and Selznick, 1978:59). Moreover, some definitions are just confusing: "Norms are adjustments which human beings in interaction make to the surrounding environment" (Nisbet, 1970:225).

The identification of norms is far from a trivial issue. It appears to be the major barrier separating normative from reactivist conceptions of deviance. Reactivists have asserted that their conception is more useful because it is *empirical*; that is, one is not forced to consider beforehand which norms are being violated, only the more or less observable sanctions directed toward behavior. As Kitsuse (1972:237–238) put it: "Can the [normative] sociologist specify a priori the social rules or social norms, the behaviors they prescribe or proscribe, the situations in which those norms govern behavior, and the sanctions prescribed as reactions to nonconformance?"

Kitsuse considers the question to be entirely rhetorical inasmuch as an affirmative response would force the reactivist conception to yield considerable theoretical ground. Thus far, Kitsuse and other reactivists have been

[3]This borders on what Blacke and Davis (1964) term the "normative fallacy," or explaining all conduct as normatively based. The fallacy is a conceptual as well as empirical one and can be avoided with attention to the meaning of norms. The fallacy exists and is important only because of this conceptual inattention.

quite secure. They can safely ignore all the attendant conceptual difficulties with norms and proceed to ask questions about sanctions. Of course, there is nothing to preclude normative theorists from adopting the same strategy (i.e., observe sanctions). They could then *infer* the norms whose breach incurred the sanction. This, however, is not a preferable strategy insofar as some norms are probably not inferrable, for example, those that are so wedded into some social situations that participants are often unaware of them. Moreover, inferring the existence and content of norms from sanctions assumes that all norm violations are reacted against, an assumption that is demonstrably incorrect. Yet to address fully Kitsuse's question requires a conceptualization of norms that permits their direct estimation, and normative theorists have not yet conspicuously risen to the task.

Anomie Some of the problems with the normative conception can be illustrated briefly with reference to two widely known normative perspectives. The theory of anomie is normatively based. It is concerned with how social structure produces deviant as well as conformist behavior. In this way, it diverges widely from modern versions of control theory (e.g., Hirschi, 1969) by rejecting the idea that social structure serves as a restraint upon "natural" deviant tendencies, an idea that derives as much from Freud as Durkheim. Merton's deviant (he prefers the term nonconformist) is one who rejects, fails to appreciate, or rebels against norms, those regularities "rooted in the mores of institutions" that reflect "allowable procedures for moving toward" culturally defined goals (Merton, 1968:187). Regulatory norms are distinguished from technical, or efficiency, norms. These latter are "procedures which from the standpoint of particular individuals would be the most efficient in securing desired values," such as through the use of force, fraud, or power (p. 187).

Little more is made of norms in Merton's theory. He states that his stress in on "a society in which there is an exceptionally strong emphasis upon specific goals without a corresponding emphasis upon institutional procedures" (p. 188). Yet it is precisely this focus that precludes attention to that which defines nonconformity in the first place: norms. One might be tempted to find this omission reasonable (and perhaps necessary) given Merton's theoretical interest: he was, after all, interested in describing a social structure that subtly instilled deviant as well as conformist motivation. But Merton's inattention to norms not only fails to facilitate his thesis, it at some point calls it into question. Nonconformity results from a societal imbalance where desired goals, but not acceptable means, are overemphasized. This suggests that the restraining influence of regulatory (or institutional) norms is lessened, thereby increasing the salience of efficiency norms that are not socially condoned. The problem this poses is that this interpretation of Merton's theory bears a strong resemblance to the Freudian and control perspectives Merton rejects. Yet the interpretation of Merton's theory as a "control theory" is at least plausible as long as different kinds of norms, their nature, frequency, content, influence, and so on, are ignored.

Social Learning Akers' (1977) differential association-reinforcement theory of deviance also adopts a normative conception. He defines social norms as "group-supported definitions of expected behavior in specific situations. These normative expectations are definitions of right and wrong, standards of conduct, and rules and regulations" (p. 7). Deviance is "instances of disapproved behavior considered serious enough to warrant major societal efforts to control them, using strong negative sanctions or treatment-coercive techniques" (p. 11).

Norms are important to Akers, not only because they define the field of interest but because they explain behavior as well. Following Sutherland's lead, Akers posits that deviance results from the learning of "definitions" that portray some conduct as desirable, even though deviant. "Definitions are normative meanings which are given to behavior—that is, they define an action as right or not right" (p. 51). This is what is learned; this motivates or makes the criminal willing to violate the law (p. 50). If Merton's deviant acquires deviant motivation from an imbalance in social emphasis whereby goals are stressed more than acceptable means to acquire them, Akers' deviant acquires deviant motivation from listening and believing the "wrong" people. Acceptable means (norms) are not rejected in Akers' theory, they are made irrelevant by defining or interpreting them as inappropriate, inexpedient, or just plain stupid.

Akers' problem, one that is common to normative explanations, is the one Kitsuse identifies. If one explains conduct by norms, one cannot then turn around and infer the existence of norms via behavioral indicators. "[If] heterosexuality is the norm in a social unit because no one commits homosexual acts, then it is circular to argue that no one commits homosexual acts because of the norm" (Gibbs, 1978:145). Normative explanations *require* the identification of norms the violation of which constitutes deviance; it is unsatisfactory to infer norms from conduct and then use the existence of norms to explain that conduct.[4]

THE CONCEPT OF NORM

If the foregoing sounds slightly argumentative, it is because norms occupy a very important role both in the definition and possible explanation of deviance. By avoiding requisite conceptual work, students of deviance have

[4]Akers' formulation has also been criticized for other reasons (see Freese and Sell, 1980:316–320).

opened themselves to charges of sensationalism and irrelevance when faced with broader questions that orient the work of their sociological colleagues. What follows is an attempt to examine the nature of norms and to conceptualize them in a manner that permits norms to occupy the attention of both normativists and reactivists.

There are two common conceptions of norm: norm as an *evaluation* of conduct and norm as *expected* (or predictable) conduct. The former conception recognizes that some conduct (behavior or beliefs) "ought" or "ought not" to occur, either in specific situations (e.g., no smoking in public places) or at any time or place (e.g., no armed robbery, ever). The latter conception points to regularities of conduct that may be based on habit or tradition (e.g., customs). These two conceptions have their roots in classical sociological theory, such as in the writings of Weber, whose types of social action included each of these elements: *wertrational* refers to the type of social action guided through conscious belief in the absolute value of the conduct itself, or conduct purely for its own sake, independent of consequences, and *zweckrational* refers to the use of expectations (or norms of efficiency; see Merton, 1968:186) as "conditions" or "means" for ends that are rationally weighted and pursued. So defined, norms as evaluations of conduct (*wertrational*) may be more typical of Gemeinschaft relations, and norms as expectations (*zweckrational*) more characteristic of Gesselleschaft relations.

Expectations of conduct may be said to refer to the efficient adaptation of means to ends; as such, this meaning of the word norm is essentially economic and associated with the rational pursuit of self-interest, as that condition typified Gesselleschaft relations. Evaluations of conduct, on the other hand, are associated with notions of obligation and legitimacy; "for one who holds an order to be legitimate, living up to its rules becomes, to this extent, a matter of moral obligation" (Parsons, 1937:661). Both the evaluative and expected meanings of norm imply a value element, evaluations in terms of moral obligations, expectations in terms of some end. Neither conception, however, is synonymous with the concept of value.

The expectation meaning of norms has probably been more prevalent in sociology, particularly in the deviance literature, probably because this was the meaning employed by Merton (1938) in his "means-end" theory and because Lemert (1951:27, glossary) initially defined "deviation" in statistical terms as rare or infrequent behavior. Yet the evaluative meaning of norms may have more generality because it makes more explicitly two important features of norms: (1) norms are relative, that is, norms differ from one another according to the degree of condemnation they elicit; and (2) norms are usually linked with sanctions. Persons express their evaluations both individually and collectively and both cognitively and behaviorally. That is, sanctions—or the expressions of evaluations of conduct—may be informal (individual) or formal (collective) and take the form of opinions or stigma (cognitive) or actual rewards and punishments (behavioral).

The more limited utility of the expectation dimension of norms is evident for other reasons as well, not the least of which is that this meaning of norm has led to the most conceptual abuse. Thus, norms as expected conduct have come to be associated with "rules," a term that has been used most frequently in the reactivist conception but that is not confined exclusively to that tradition. Yet, norms are social properties, and there may be nothing uniquely social in the concept of rule. Rules can be formulated individually and imposed upon others (e.g., the "laws" of a monarch or despot). As such, the notion of formal or collective sanctions may have no meaning sociologically, although the consequences on those sanctioned are no less real.

Perhaps because many sociologists would regard the preceding as an "obvious" statement of the properties of norms and sanctions, only two general strategies have arisen to study norms. The first is *inferential* and regards the existence of norms as detectable only in social control efforts. That is, norms are observable only after their violation by observing patterns of sanctions (Scott, 1971; Kitsuse, 1972). The second strategy, which seems like little more than a conditional surrender to the problem, regards norms as *qualitative* properties of social life that are not amenable to either direct measurement or analysis (e.g., Douglas, 1970). Thus, although ethnomethodologists may claim that the object of their study is totally concerned with how persons make sense of everyday situations (through the creation, sharing, and alteration of norms), their approach implies that norms are virtually impossible to study as separate entities independent of social situations, either because they are so deeply wedded to social situations that group members are hardly ever aware of them or because norms are created spontaneously and change as quickly as situations do. In neither of these general strategies are norms thought to be identifiable prior to a violation, and as such most empirical questions have been confined to sanctions (their nature, source, frequency, and consequences).

A third strategy for studying norms has been discussed but dismissed. This strategy is "to ask members of the social systems in question, or otherwise elicit statements from them regarding what persons of particular social statuses should or should not do, think, say, etc., in particular situations" (Kitsuse, 1980:385). Such a strategy is clearly objectionable within a reactivist conception and is so for a number of reasons including the possibility that there may be a distinct gap between what people say and what they do (i.e., if persons say they ought to do one thing but do another, it is questionable that what they say actually guides their behavior). Dismissing this strategy also appears related to the fondness that reactivist theorists have shown the concept of rule. It is not just that "rules were made to be broken," but that rules *are* broken and broken frequently. The concept of norm, to be discussed presently, however, does not require a correspondence between what persons say and what they do; discrepancies are to be expected.

A Proposal

If the concept of norm is to be salvaged (and some would not recommend this, preferring instead to abandon the concept altogether; see Gibbs, 1972), it must be made the object of direct rather than inferential study. This requires that norms be conceptualized differently from how they normally have been in the deviance literature. To say that norms are "rules" or "standards" detracts from such a conceptualization. Traditionally, norms have not been thought to be measurable, quantifiable properties of social life. Here, I proceed from the opposite assumption: norms are not metaphysical attributes of social situations but empirical, measurable qualities of persons and conduct.

1 Types of Conduct Norms describe ideal conduct That is, because norms identify behavior that "ought" or "ought not" to occur, behavior may (and often does) depart from norms. This had led to the observation that the potential for deviance is inherent in all norms (e.g., Blake and Davis, 1964), but this is a common insight and true by definition. The more relevant consideration includes the conditions under which this potential for deviance is realized and the conditions under which norms guide specific conduct.

Because they are ideals, norms are not specific rules to be followed in specific situations; rather, norms are more or less specific depending upon factors associated with the act, actor, and situation (see contingencies below). Again because they are ideals, norms refer not to specific acts but to *types* of acts. Persons may evaluate theft as something one ought not to do in general, but upon closer questioning or a respecification of the circumstances theft may be entirely justified.

It has been usual to view laws as norms (e.g., Black, 1976), but laws are normative only to the extent that they reflect evaluative agreement among citizens to whom they apply. That is, laws are rules, but they may not be norms (see the distinction above). Not all laws generate sentiments of obligation on the part of citizens; in fact, laws are perceived differently in this regard, and this fact alone goes a long way toward accounting for the law violations among some persons but not others. Some citizens obey laws out of feelings of moral obligation, while others obey, when they do, because it is expedient to do so. These latter persons would be likely to have higher violation rates than the former persons.

2 Contingencies The severity with which given acts are evaluated as condemnatory or praiseworthy is modified by contingencies that intervene with the evaluation and concrete characteristics of the act, actor, and situation. Relevant contingencies are potentially innumerable; but there may be a finite set of contingencies that identify acts as instances of norm violations or compliance (e.g., the social position of the actor, the actor's age, the time and place of the act, etc.). If norms can be said to be specific in any reasonable sense, it is because of contingencies that condition the norm's ideal nature; that is, contingencies link specific conduct, specific actors, and specific situation with evaluative ideals.

We know little at present about which contingencies are relevant, and different contingencies may be relevant to different acts. At this point, we can only hope that the number of important contingencies is relatively small so that they can be manipulated in posing normative questions to persons (this issue requires more explanation and is attended to below). In any case, contingencies are important for at least two reasons: (1) they affect the nature of the evaluation itself because the same conduct may be rated as more or less right or wrong depending on contingencies; and (2) they affect the imposition of sanctions as a result of altering the evaluation of conduct and by making certain categories of persons immune from, or more susceptible to, sanctions.

The importance of contingencies also resides in the fact that knowledge of the act alone may not be sufficient for a complete evaluation of it and that an act may be *more or less* condemned or praised depending on which contingencies are stipulated. In this sense, evaluations of conduct are matters of degree; and for this reason, conformity to and deviance from evaluations are matters of degree. Thus, deviance is not an absolute quality of acts but a relative property tempered by certain "conditions" that specify the rightness or wrongness of the act and the likelihood that (and the nature of) sanctions may be applied.

3 Norms are Properties of Groups Norms do not represent individual evaluations of conduct, but shared evaluations. To the extent that at least two persons—the minimum number that can share an evaluation and that can constitute a group—share an evaluation, we can talk of a norm.

Evaluations of conduct that are not shared have been called different things. Some (e.g., Durkheim) call such personal evaluations "attitudes" (see the review in Rokeach, 1980). Individual evaluations of conduct, as defined here, appear to be close to the concept of "value," a term that refers to desired modes of conduct or ideal conditions that transcend situations. Yet norms are not values (Rokeach, 1973). What distinguishes norms from values is that values are relatively enduring properties of action orientation, while norms can and frequently do change. It is this characteristic of norms in particular that reflects their distinctly sociological nature, in that normative change is a social rather than psychological process.

Viewing norms as shared evaluations of conduct (behavior and beliefs) and as matters of degree (depending, among other things, on the number of persons who are the evaluation and the contingencies considered in making the evaluation) is admittedly unhelpful to investigators in identifying *the* norm of a particular group. The idea that one can talk reasonably about, let alone identify, *the* norm is rejected here. There may be several shared evaluations of the same conduct within one group; these evaluations may differ from one another because some contingencies are more important than others for some group members.

4 Norms are Quantifiable Evaluations of conduct are also variables in the statistical sense. They form a distribution for each individual (cf. Goode, 1978:230) that is potentially measurable by asking persons normative questions,[5] that is, individual evaluations can be obtained by asking people to rank a variety of conduct that "ought" or "ought not" to occur. The distribution of evaluation extends from strongly "ought" on one side, to strongly "ought not" on the other. Although it is convenient to talk of this distribution in terms of a statistical "normal curve," this need not typify the distribution. In fact, research may indicate that the distribution is bimodal or some other shape. This is an empirical issue, and it raises several theoretical possibilities. Can one person's distribution (a theologian's) be shaped differently from that of another (an atheist)? Are the distributions of persons who administer sanctions shaped differently from those of persons to whom sanctions are administered (e.g., judges and criminals, priests and penitents, teachers and students, psychiatrists and mental patients, etc.)?

The sizable literature on the perceived seriousness of crimes—though necessarily limited to certain types of acts: crimes—show that evaluations can be obtained by asking persons questions, that these responses can be quantified, and that the quantification so obtained is meaningful to respondents (e.g., Rossi et al., 1974; Hamilton and Rytina, 1980). Evaluations are solicited in the form of responses to normative questions, and these can be counted in a manner that is sensible both to investigators and respondents. Just as some crimes are commonly perceived as "more serious" than others and some as less so, so too are types of acts that are legal, such as observing traditions of etiquette (Goffman, 1963) or not playing by the rules of a structured interaction (Garfinkel, 1967). To date, no one has obtained systematically evaluations of legal conduct, but the procedures developed for

[5]Normative questions are those requiring or requesting a normative response or opinion.

assessing the evaluation of illegal conduct are directly applicable to this problem.

5 Measuring Norms Norms are measurable by asking normative questions of persons and assessing the degree of correspondence of those evaluations with those obtained from other persons in the same social unit. Some may raise the objection that although norms are potentially measurable, they are not so by asking normative questions. Such a procedure assumes some correspondence between the norm and the language used to describe it; it also assumes a semantic correspondence in the language group members would use to describe the norm. These do not appear to be troublesome assumptions. We typically express our evaluations of conduct to others verbally; we say we disapprove of X, approve of Y, or are indifferent to Z. These are normative statements. Although it is true that some persons may be unable to articulate evaluations—particularly with respect to conduct that is subtle and complex or because such persons have difficulty articulating mental states anyway—many kinds of conduct can be expressed in this fashion, and research would conveniently begin with such conduct (e.g., crimes). The assumption that norms are reflected in and measurable from common discourse is not an unreasonable one; we ordinarily *think* about conduct this way, and we *talk* about it with others in this way as well. Ordinary language is not irrelevant to evaluations of conduct, because our evaluations are formed initially in language.[6]

This measurement process could take the following form: (1) normative questions are asked of respondents that stipulate contingencies (e.g., "How strongly ought one not engage in homosexuality if that person is over 21 years of age?"); (2) if two or more persons share the same evaluation, it is a norm; (3) distributions of evaluations are obtained because some acts are rated as more "serious" than others, while other acts are afforded the same degree of "ought" or "ought not"; (4) these distributions are related to one another with a measure of association, such as a correlation coefficient, to determine the degree to which group members agree with one another with a measure of association, such as a correlation coefficient, to determine the degree to which group members agree with one another's evaluations in general; and (5) the degree of overlap (or shared variance) is used as an indicator of group norms or evaluations that are shared more or less with others. Because group norms are matters of degree, a correlation coefficient of 1.0 is not necessary to identify those group norms. It would be difficult, in the absence of even preliminary research, to specify the lower end of the correlation coefficient; that is, there is no rush to decide how strong—.001

[6]In this sense, ethnomethodologists are correct in searching for patterns of order in the common, everyday conversations of people.

or .0001 – the figure must be since the purpose of such research is not to identify *the* norms of groups.

Shared Evaluations and Sanctions

The relationship among norms, violations of norms, and sanctions has always been considered theoretically and empirically troublesome. Indeed, questions about these relationships have occupied a good deal of the attention of reactivists (particularly the conditions under which sanctions are applied) and normativists (particularly the relationship between norms and norm violations). A proposition concerning these matters can be derived from the discussion thus far: Those norm violations that are most strongly condemned (denoting acts most strongly perceived to "ought not" occur) are precisely those that are (1) the most infrequently observed statistically and (2) the most likely to evoke sanctions. This proposition seems to imply that the expectation dimension of norms is more meaningful in accounting for conduct and that the relationship between norm violations and the imposition of sanctions is unambiguous. It is not that simple.

Expected or Frequent Behavior Most writers who define norms as expected behavior confuse the definition with an empirical consequence. Conduct that is relatively infrequent may be so because persons evaluate the conduct so strongly – condemning or praising the extremes on the behavioral scale – and because the behavior is unattainable except under special (rare) circumstances. Just as saving someone's life requires the lifesaver to be present at the right time and place and to have the requisite courage, so too does murder require circumstances that permit either the neutralization of moral evaluations against this conduct (as predicted by control theory) or the acquisition of moral evaluations that permit life taking in the situation found by the murderer and the victim (social learning theory). Most persons are precluded from being lifesavers and murderers through circumstance or ability. But saving lives or taking them does not violate a norm because it is rare; rather, it is rare because of our evaluations of those acts.

There is another argument against the expectation dimension of norms, an empirical one. Evaluations are better able to predict sanctions or at least preferred sanctions. Warr, Meier, and Erickson (1981) analyzed data from respondents that measured their evaluations of types of criminal behavior, their preferred punishments for those crimes, and the perceived frequency with which the respondents thought the crimes were committed. The preferred punishments were then predicted from the respondents' evaluations and from their perceived frequency estimates. The results were unambiguous. Evaluations were able to account for almost *all* (i.e., 97 percent) of the variance in preferred punishments.

Preferred and Applied Sanctions It should be obvious that the evaluative meaning of norms better predicts preferred, *but not applied*, sanctions. That is, it is one thing for persons to evaluate conduct strongly and to assign a severe sanction to violations of norms, but it is quite another thing for those same persons to apply the sanction on evidence of a violation. Persons may *desire* severe sanctions, other things being equal, but they are often willing to settle for less, for a mild sanction, or for none at all depending on the situation. Some people can literally "get away with murder" if they are powerful or clever enough. Thus, although the relationship between knowing evaluations of conduct and predicting preferred sanctions is extremely high, the relationship between evaluations of conduct and applied sanctions is unquestionable more equivocal.

The nature of the contingencies that specify the evaluative ideal are important in determining the probability and severity of sanctions. A mother may strongly condemn burglary in general but request that her burglar son not be punished as strongly as she would ordinarily prefer other burglars punished; persons may be more willing to turn in a strange, barking dog to the police than one that belongs to next door neighbors with whom they get along well; and judges may be more willing to impose a more lenient sentence on offenders who have steady employment, few prospects for recidivism, and a history of meeting social and financial obligations and a more severe sentence on those who fail these "tests."

None of this, of course, says anything about how some contingencies come to be associated with evaluations to increase or decrease the likelihood that a sanction will be applied, nor does it address the nature of that sanction once applied. These are empirical questions and cannot be dealt with here. But it can be pointed out that evaluations of conduct and the contingencies that link specific acts, actors, and situations with those evaluations provide some of the more interesting questions in the sociology of deviance. Thus, the nature, antecedents, and consequences of contingencies should occupy much research attention among students of deviance. Observers have recognized this problem but have tended recently to lump all such contingencies into one: power. Collins (1975), for this reason, suggests that the study of deviance is merely a subset of the more general study of stratification. (Another view is presented by Dadrendorf, 1968, who argues that stratification is a subset of the study of deviance insofar as the origins of social inequality stem from processes of deviance and social control.)

SUMMARY AND CONCLUSIONS

"Evaluations of conduct" is here proposed as the most useful dimension of norm. Such evaluations are measurable, and this means that norms can be studied empirically and directly rather than inferentially. Norms are shared evaluations of conduct; group norms are shared evaluations of conduct that form distributions for persons that overlap with the distribution of others. The probability that sanctions will be applied to conduct and the nature of such sanctions depends on how the conduct is evaluated, and the nature of the contingencies that link evaluative ideals with concrete instances of departures from those ideals.

The conceptualization of norms presented here is not novel, but it does have a number of advantages. First, it permits sociologists to talk about norms as conceptual units, something they are wont to do anyway. Second, it allows us to sidestep many of the conceptual problems that have hampered discussion of norms in the past (e.g., one does not even attempt to discover *the* norm of a group, because what is normative is a matter of degree). Third, this conceptualization presents a method for addressing some traditional and important questions about deviance: for example, (1) What are the origins of shared evaluations? Two competing views, that norms arise in a crescive and in a created manner, are beginning points for this inquiry. (2) What are the relationships among norms, norm violations, and sanctions? (3) What is the stability of norms? How do they change, under what circumstances, and which kinds of shared evaluations are more likely than others to change?

In addition to addressing questions such as these, the proposed conceptualization creates the potential for normativist and reactivist theorists to agree on potentially complementary research strategies. Each can now study deviance—normativists concentrating on the nature and determinants of norms, and the relationship between norms and norm violations and reactivists wrestling with issues relating to norm violations and preferred and applied sanctions—and perhaps be working toward the same ultimate goal: freeing the study of deviance from charges of "provincialism" and possibly contributing to larger issues in sociology.

REFERENCES

Akers, Ronald L.

1968 "Problems in the sociology of deviance: Social definitions and behavior." Social Forces 46:455–456.

1977 Deviant Behavior: A Social Learning Perspective, 2nd e. Belmont, Calif.: Wadsworth.

Becker, George

1977 The Genius as Deviant. Beverly Hills, Calif.: Sage Publications.

Becker, Howard S.

1973 Outsiders: Studies in the Sociology of Deviance, enlarged edition. New York: Free Press. Originally published 1963.

Black, Donald
1976 The Behavior of Law. New York: Academic Press.
Blake, Judith, and Kingsley, Davis
1964 "Norms, values, and sanctions. Pp. 456–484 in Robert E.L. Faris (ed.), Handbook of Modern Sociology. Chicago: Rand-McNally.
Broom, Leonard, and Philip Selznick
1977 Sociology: A Text with Adapted Readings, 6th ed. New York: Harper & Row.
Clinard, Marshall B., and Robert F. Meier
1979 Sociology of Deviant Behavior, 5th ed. New York: Holt, Rinehart and Winston.
Cohen, Albert K.
1966 Deviance and Control. Englewood Cliffs, N.J.: Prentice-Hall
Cohen, Stanley, ed.
1971 Images of Deviance. Baltimore: Penguin.
Collins, Randall
1975 Conflict Sociology. New York: Academic Press.
Dahrendorf, Ralf
1968 Essays in the Theory of Society. Stanford: Stanford University Press.
Davis Fred
1961 "Deviance disavowal: The management of strained interaction by the visibly handicapped." Social Problems 9:120–132.
Debro, Julius
1970 "Dialogue with Howard S. Becker." Issues in Criminology 5:159–179.
Demerath, N.J., III, and Gerald Marwell
1976 Sociology: Perspectives and Applications. New York: Harper & Row.
Dinitz, Simon, Russell Dynes, and Alfred Clarke, eds.
1975 Deviance: Studies in Deviation, Management, and Treatment, 2nd ed. New York: Oxford University Press.
Douglas, Jack D., ed.
1970 Understanding Everyday Life. Chicago. Aldine.
Freese, Lee, and Jane Sell
1980 Theoretical Methods in Sociology. Pittsburg: University of Pittsburg Press.
Garfinkel, Harold
1967 Studies in Ethnomethodology. Englewwod Cliffs, N.J.: Prentice-Hall.
Gibbs, Jack P.
1966 "Conceptions of deviant behavior: The old and the new." Pacific Sociological Review 9:9–14.
1972 "Issues in defining deviant behavior. Pp. 39–68 in Robert A. Scott and Jack D. Douglas (eds.), Theoretical Perspectives in Deviance. New York: Basic Books.
1978 "Norms and normative properties. Pp. 140–160 in Edward Sagarin (ed.), Sociology: The Basic Concepts. New York: Holt, Rinehart and Winston.
Goffman, Erving
1963 Behavior in Public Places. New York: Free Press.

Goode, William J.
1977 Principles of Sociology. New York: McGraw-Hill.
1978 The Celebration of Heroes. Berkeley: University of California Press.
Gouldner, Alvin W.
1968 "The sociologist as partisan: Sociology and the welfare state." The American Sociologist 3:103–116.
Hamilton, V. Lee, and Steve Rytina
1980 "Social consensus on norms of justice: Should the punishment fit the crime?" American Journal of Sociology 85:1117–1144.
Henslin, James M.
1972 "Studying deviance in four settings: Research experiences with cabbies, suicides, drug users, and abortionees." Pp. 35–70 in Jack D. Douglas (ed.), Research on Deviance. New York: Random House.
Hinkle, Roscoe, and Gisela J. Hinkle
1954 The Development of Modern Sociology: Its Nature and Growth in the United States. New York: Random House.
Hirschi, Travis
1969 Causes of Delinquency. Berkeley: University of California Press.
Kitsuse, John I.
1972 "Deviance, deviant behavior, and deviants: Some conceptual problems." Pp. 233-243 in William J. Filstead (ed.), An Introduction to Deviance. Chicago: Markham.
1980 "The 'new conception of deviance' and its critics." In Walter R. Gove (ed.), The Labeling of Deviance: Evaluating a Perspective, 2nd ed. Beverly Hills, Calif.: Sage Publications.
Lemert, Edwin M.
1951 Social Pathology. New York: McGraw-Hill.
1972 Human Deviance, Social Problems, and Social Control, 2nd ed. Englewood Cliffs, N.J.: Prentice-Hall.
Lorber, Judith
1967 "Deviance as performance: The case of illness." Social Problems 14:302–310.
Merton, Robert K.
1938 "Social structure and anomie." American Sociological Review 3:672-682.
1968 Social Theory and Social Structure, enlarged edition. New York: Free Press.
Nisbet, Robert
1970 The Social Bond. New York: Alfred A. Knopf.
Oberschall, Anthony R., ed.
1972 The Establishment of Empirical Sociology. New York: Harper & Row.
Odum, Howard W.
1951 American Sociology: The Story of Sociology in the United States Through 1950. New York: Longmans, Green.
Parsons, Talcott
1937 The Structure of Social Action. New York: McGraw-Hill.

Rokeach, Milton
1973 The Nature of Human Values. New York: Free Press.
1980 "Some unresolved issues in theories of beliefs, attitudes, and values. Pp. 261-304 in H.E. Howe and M.M. Page (eds.) Nebraska Symposium on Motivation, 1979. Lincoln: University of Nebraska Press.
Rossi, Peter H., Emily Waite, Christine E. Bose, and Richard E. Berk
1974 "The seriousness of crimes: Normative structure and individual differences." American Sociological Review 39:224–237.
Sagarin, Edward
1975 Deviants and Deviance: An Introduction to the Study of Disvalued People and Behavior. New York: Praeger.
1979 "Deviance without deviants: The temporary quality of patterned behavior." Deviant Behavior 1:1–13.
Schwendinger, Herman, and Julia Schwendinger
1970 "Defenders of order or guardians of human rights." Issues in Criminology 5:123–157.
1977 "Social class and the definition of crime." Crime and Social Justice 7:4–13.
Scott, John Finley
1971 Internalization of Norms. Englewood Cliffs, N.J.: Prentice-Hall.
Warr, Mark, Robert F. Meier, and Maynard L. Erickson
1981 "Normative Properties and Preferred Punishments." Unpublished paper, Department of Sociology, Washington State University.
Wheeler, Stanton
1962 "The social sources of criminology." Sociological Inquiry 32:139-159.

Reading 6

Field Research among Deviants: A Consideration of Some Methodological Recommendations

Robert J. Kelly
Brooklyn College

Apart from the ethical, moral, and legal problems that beset the study of individuals in their natural settings, investigations of various kinds of criminal conduct engender special difficulties and snares that set limits on the scope of the research effort and the reliability of findings.

Field work depends to a great extent on complicated and continuous concerns, the most central of which is how one is seen by others. It is a matter filled with risks and contradictions.

Constructing and managing fronts, manipulating the impression of self (or selves) in order to gain access, and maintain acceptance with deviant populations under study, have been the subject of much discussion among sociologists.[1] A key element of the debate in the literature focuses on questions of interviewer-observer effects, on issues of objectivity and how observer presence potentially contaminates the phenomenon under study. Despite these and other threats to scientific integrity, most field workers seem to be satisfied that their research accurately depicts the social reality selected for study and that their results are scientifically valid. In writing about his field study of black streetcorner men, Liebow (1967) remarked that "the people I was observing knew that I was observing them, yet they allowed me to participate in their activities and take part in their lives to a degree that continues to surprise me" (p. 253). Gans (1962), in writing about his experiences in an Italian-American lower class ghetto, was more cautious but no less optimistic. For him, the problem endangering the research was the likelihood of overidentification with his subjects, a problem that is especially troublesome when those being studied are deprived, victimized, or oppressed. Empathizing strongly with social underdogs detracts (at least theoretically) from the objectivity of the research, according to Gans. Nevertheless, these problems are not insoluble in his view.

With the study of career criminals and criminal groups, however, the methodological problems are exacerbated and become significant obstacles in the conduct of field work. Regarding organized crime, for example, Cressey (1967) wrote

> The secrecy of participants, the confidentiality of materials collected by investigative agencies, and filters or screens on the perceptive apparatus of informants and investigators pose serious methodological problems for the social scientist. (p. 101)

And in *Theft of the Nation* (1969), he noted that the activities of organized criminals are not accessible to observation by the social scientist. Moreover, even gaining access to law enforcement groups that specialize in organized crime investigations requires, in his words, "connections."

For Cressey and many others, the vaunted secretive nature of criminal syndicate activity precludes the use of many, if not all, of the usual instruments for gathering data. If crime families and syndicates take pains to conceal their activities from law enforcement agents, then it is unlikely that they would disclose sensitive information about their structure to a social

[1]On the front management, see Goffman (1962), Irwin (1972), Ianni (1973), and Polsky (1967). The literature on participant observation among nondeviant populations contains classic statements by Whyte (1943), Levi-Strauss (1968), and Liebow (1967).

scientist or permit him to examine their inner workings. Thus, social scientists must work at several removes from their data.

To a great extent, most of the information available to law enforcement agencies and social scientists derives from two basic sources: the participants themselves and electronic eavesdropping devices (Salerno, 1978). The consequences these methodological hurdles present are ominous. For one, social scientists must rely on secondary and tertiary accounts of organized crime and therefore cannot independently evaluate their findings in accordance with scientific methods. Distortions invariably arise. Second, accounts of organized crime prepared by governmental agencies focus on the criminal act and criminal actor and tend to ignore the complicity of the upperworld in sustaining criminal syndicate activity (Chambliss, 1971; Ianni, 1977). Thus, a bias permeates the bulk of the writing on organized crime from which most social scientists draw their information.

In recent years, some social scientists, notably Ianni (1973, 1974), Chambliss (1971) and Klockars (1974) have attempted field work among organized criminals and have collected data using participant-observation techniques. Chambliss (1975) indicated that a wealth of data about syndicate activity is to be found on the streets, where, incidentally, the absence of sociologists is all too obvious. A review of these studies and others devoted to career criminals and other deviants reveals that much of their methodological inspiration obtains directly or indirectly from the ethnographic work and methodological suggestions of Polsky (1967).

Doubtlessly, most would agree that comprehension of the methodology is a crucial component in establishing the meaningfulness of a work. Although it is most desirable in the interests of replication to have the research apparatus made explicit and available for inspection, too often methodological appendixes in which programmatic statements appear are little more than laudable sentiments disguised in the language of science. As a result, the promise and utility of such documents is greatly diminished, and when they are lucid, their piquancy is principally emotional, permitting the reader merely a peek into the intellectual struggles enveloping the research act. This is not to say that methodological precis and reports are valueless: helpful rules of thumb, details on the tactics and strategy of the research enterprise, and cautions against pitfalls to avoid in the field are abundant. The bulk of these, however, seem so elusive, so highly personal and specific, if not eccentric, to a particular research focus, that they lack as pedagogical and didactic devices sufficient generalizability to be truly helpful.

Polsky's refreshing iconoclasm injected some vitality into the debate on research methods and directly challenged a widespread point of view among law enforcement officials that "those who know won't tell and those who tell don't know." Put another way, Polsky's views clash with the traditional belief that criminals, especially those affiliated with crime syndicates, are not only difficult to identify but are disinclined to provide information about themselves and their illegal activities.

The few advocates of open-air research among deviants, "street sociologists" as they are sometimes known, have been subjected to attack because it is claimed that their work does not lend itself to conventional standards of verification and replication. Research samples, it is argued, are not ordinarily unbiased. The most important criticism, however, is that the collection instrument itself, the field researcher, can scarcely be duplicated objectively. In short, the utilization of precisely defined and controlled techniques of observation cannot be employed in field research. In reply to this, Polsky (1977) argues, quite persuasively, that "precise controlled techniques of observation" are something of a fetish and as a guideline to research quite ambiguous. Even among noncriminal populations, field research, as many widely hailed accounts attest,[2] hardly follows exactly reproducible lines of data collection. The insistence that one strictly adhere to prefield protocols amounts to more of an imposition than an aid.

Another dimension of the participant-observer role frequently ignored in discussions of qualitative research concerns the changing role relationships among researchers and subjects. Ianni, Klockars, and others point out that whatever the initial focus of the research and the role relationships envisioned by the researcher, these are bound to change. According to Klockars (1976), "participant-observation research is never conducted within the bounds of a single role relationship." Informants and subjects are not merely information sources, but often guides, informal teachers, and occasionally friends. Ianni (1972) reported similar results: a bargain emerged between him and his principal informants in which he provided assistance and advice concerning a range of private and public matters about which he had knowledge in exchange for access to subjects.

The implications of these social relationships have important consequences for both the quantity and the quality of knowledge generated in the research setting. Because field research usually involves relatively prolonged periods of contact and interaction with subjects, the characteristics that these relationships take on can affect what is learned about them. In addition, and no less important, interacting with subjects in their natural settings may transform researchers themselves, socializing them to some degree (going native) to the extent that they begin to become, at last, somewhat different people in interests, tastes and purpose. Because the investigators are the data collection instruments, changing role relationships and attitudes occasioned by deeper immersion into the settings may dramatically

[2]See, on this issue, a collection of essays on field experiences (Hammond, 1964).

affect knowledge production. In part, this is what Polsky (1967) is taken to mean when he says that studying the criminal in his natural setting

> (1) allows you to make observations about his lifestyle you ordinarily wouldn't make, (2) causes you to think of important questions about him that ordinarily you wouldn't think of, (3) causes him to think of relevant things to tell you that he otherwise wouldn't think of, and (4) causes him to make explanations of certain events to you that he ordinarily wouldn't make. (pp. 135–136)

Briefly, Polsky's suggestions for the conduct of field work among criminals in their natural settings would apply to any type of observation. In fact, participant observation among deviants is for Polsky merely a special case of general qualitative techniques. The questions Polsky addresses are these:

> How does one determine the culture and social structure of a group without creating complications for the research?
>
> How does one determine and then preserve the "natural setting" that criminals inhabit?
>
> To what extent can research interests be revealed without jeopardizing the study by giving the subjects an orientation by which they provide dramatic presentations of what the researcher wants?

As noted above, the rationale justifying studies of illegal activities and occupations is that such occupations and life-styles can and should be perceived as instances of general occupational theory.

In his essay, "Research Method, Morality, and Criminology," Polsky (1967) enumerates some rules of thumb to guide the field worker in deviant groups and insists that these procedural recipes apply in other research environments as well. Participant observation of criminals, as with participant observation of any others, involves getting thoroughly familiar with their frame of reference, language, and interests. This means close observation without becoming too obtrusive of criminals in their hangouts and play scenes.[3] Blending into the setting by discarding most of the usual research paraphernalia (tape recorders, questionnaires, etc.) may reduce potential information gathering but sharpen observational skills. The researcher who is faced with restrictions on presence and participation and who knows that opportunities to observe particular pieces of action may not occur again may evolve into a more skillful and astute observer.

Once entry has been accomplished, the development, maintenance, and

[3] Whyte (1943) frittered away his time in Cornerville bars until he asked a social worker to introduce him to some slum dwellers. Simply "hanging out" is a necessary but not sufficient condition for the creation of informant networks.

extension of contacts, in short, the sustenance of the research situation, require the clear separation of the researcher from criminal activity and identification and a lack of pretense regarding the purposes of the investigation. It is important that subjects understand that the field worker is neither a law enforcement official nor an informant (in the pejorative sense in which the term is customarily understood in the under-and upperworlds). This problem is not unique to investigations of deviant populations: clearly articulating and preserving the research role so that subjects did not identify him with management was for Blau (1964) a critical stage in his studies on bureaucracy.

Cultivating rapport triggers a snowball effect in which a network of informants is likely to emerge. In work among criminal syndicate members, I found that not until after it was established to everyone's satisfaction that I was not interested in names, places, and specific criminal acts was I introduced to others as someone around whom one could talk freely. In most cases, however, it was clear that unguarded conversations were exceptional despite assurances to the contrary. For the most part, even those with whom I thought I had created implicit trust were often reserved in conversations. On some occasions, thought, as I later discovered, I was actually present during some illegal transaction involving disbursements of cash, distributions of hijacked goods (swag), and large drug (marijuana) deals without realizing what was taking place.

Exposure to crimes raises some delicate ethical issues for the field researcher. In a taped interview, Polsky (1977) indicated that he preferred not to witness criminal acts and informed his subjects accordingly. And nowhere does Ianni say that he observed criminal acts. A careful inspection of Polsky's and Ianni's statements about their field work experience shows that their field work, like that of most others, with the possible exceptions of Chambliss and Klockars, was based largely on verbal accounts of criminal acts. Thus, neither Polsky nor Ianni could be cited for complicity in criminal acts.

As data, verbal accounts are conceptually distinguishable from data based on observation in the pure sense. But in practical terms, as Irwin (1972) points out, "the great bulk of data sought in field studies does appear in conversations" (p. 119). Moreover, participant observation need not necessarily entail actually participating with subjects in their activities in order to be meaningful. Second, the question naturally arises as to techniques and solutions available to determine the reliability of data derived mainly from interactions grounded in unstructured talk and conversations as distinct from organized interviews. Here it seems that a network of informants provides some foundation for cross checking the dependability of information elicited from subjects. Also, extensive contacts with other sources, such as law enforcement agencies and others on the periphery of crime (such as journalists) can be of immense value in determining how well the data agree with verified facts.

In research of organized crime, this problem is intensified. Given the pervasive secrecy cloaking the activities of crime families and their internal codes of silence, the most agonizing problem facing the researcher concerns the validity of the data obtained. How, for instance, does one guard against deception, lying, and other forms of dissimulation? In other words, how can researchers ensure to some degree that they are seeing and hearing what they think they are seeing or hearing? And, what methods might be employed to determine when behavior is being masked? In his research on an Italian-American crime family, Ianni (1972) grapples with these questions: "Why should they bother to attempt to deceive me? It would have been much simpler to have refused to see me" (p.202).

An expanding informant network, immersion in the social surrounds of subjects, and exchanges of services and resources for investigator access and information are all extremely important devices and techniques that can be profitably exploited in field work. Nevertheless, deep penetration of deviant groups, in which crimes are committed and for which entry and acceptance are contingent upon the commission of criminal acts or the willingness to do so, blunts and circumscribes the use of the field research instruments and methods that Polsky recommends. Even law enforcement undercover operations seeking to infiltrate crime families and syndicates have been blocked, mainly because the gatekeeping mechanisms of such organizations choke off entry by requiring that a man commit crimes or be prepared to do so. For the social scientist, access to the higher echelons of crime syndicates, even in relatively nonviolent ones such as gambling and casino operations, would similarly require not only the meticulous cultivation of numerous contacts who could vouch for the investigator, which is in itself a formidable task, but the likelihood of complicity in criminal acts.

Problems of a legal and ethical nature arise as one is exposed to or becomes informed of serious crimes, whether contemplated or actually perpetrated. Wolfgang (1976) suggests that the researcher who has a priori "doubts about a moral obligation to violate the rubrics of confidentiality" should absent himself from involvement in this kind of research (p. 31). Sagarin and Moneymaker (1979) note, in commenting on Wolfgang's advice:

> Not always is this information known, a priori. And excellent as this may be as a guideline for keeping out of trouble, it is hardly of equal standing for doing first-rate research. (p.190)

There are many layers of protective buffers insulating syndicate activists and separating lower level functionaries from core leadership elements. Notwithstanding the engaging candor of informants that one can possibly generate, field workers cannot be expected to approach organized crime research with anything more than a tempered confidence in fruitful results, no matter how skillfully and ingeniously they manipulate the strategies that Polsky and others propose.

REFERENCES

Blau, Peter
1964 Exchange and Power in Social Life. New York: Wiley.

Chambliss, William
1971 "Vice, corruption, bureaucracy and power." Wisconsin Law Review 4:1150–1173.
1975 "On the paucity of original research on organized crime: A footnote to Galliher and Cain." American Sociologist 10:36–39.

Cressey, Donald
1967 "Methodological problems in the study of organized crime as a social problem." Annals of American Academy of Political and Social Science 374:101–112.
1969 Theft of the Nation: The Structure and Operations of Organized Crime in America. New York: Harper & Row.

Gans, Herbert
1962 The Urban Villagers: Group and Class in the Life of Italian-Americans. New York: Free Press.

Goffman, Erving
1962 Asylums: Essays on the Social Situation of Mental Patients and Other Inmates. Chicago: Aldine.

Hammond, Phillip E., Ed.
1964 Sociologists at Work: Essays on the Craft of Social Research. New York: Basic Books.

Ianni, Francis
1972 A Family Business: Kinship and Social Control in Organized Crime. New York: Russell Sage Foundation.
1974 Black Mafia: Ethnic Succession in Organized Crime. New York: Simon and Schuster.
1977 "Ideology and Field Research Theory on Organized Crime." Unpublished paper.

Irwin, John
1972 "Participant observation of criminals." In Jack Douglas (ed.), Research on Deviance. New York: Random House.

Klockars, Carl
1974 The Professional Fence. New York: Free Press.

1976 Field ethics for the life history. Unpublished paper presented to Workshop on Ethnography of Drugs and Crime, Miami, Florida, May 5-7.

Levi-Strauss, Claude
1968 Triste Tropiques. New York: Atheneum.

Liebow, Elliot
1967 Tally's Corner: A Study of Negro Streetcorner Men. Boston: Little, Brown.

Polsky, Ned
1967 Hustlers, Beats and Others. Chicago: Aldine.
1977 Unpublished tape-recorded interview, Feb. 15.

Sagarin, Edward, and James Moneymaker
1979 "The dilemma of researcher immunity." P. 175–193 in Carl B. Klockars and Finnbarr W. O'Connor (eds.), Deviance and Decency: The Ethics of Research with Human Subjects. Beverly Hills: Sage.

Salerno, Ralph
1978 "The structure of organized crime." Testimony before the House of Representatives Committee on Assassinations.

Whyte, William F.
1943 Street Corner Society: The Social Structure of an Italian Slum. Chicago: University of Chicago Press.

Wolfgang, Marvin E.
1976 "Ethical issues of research in criminology." Pp. 25–34 in P. Nejelski (ed.), Social Research in Conflict with Law and Ethics. Cambridge, Mass.: Ballinger.

Reading 7

Employers' Reactions to Racial and Psychiatric Stigmata: A Field Experiment

Avery Webber
Tuskegee Institute, Alabama

James D. Orcutt
Florida State University, Tallahassee

The racial identity (black vs. white) and psychiatric status (ex-patient vs. "normal") of confederates were manipulated in job interviews with a random sample of employers in a medium-sized southern city. Based on ratings derived from confederates' descriptions of these interviews, employers' reactions to applicants with a psychiatric record were significantly more negative than to those with no record of hospitalization.

INTRODUCTION

Writers in the labeling tradition have often compared societal reactions to deviants to the prejudice and discrimination experienced by blacks and other minorities in the United States. Becker (1963), of course, argued that deviant and minority identities can be mutually conceptualized as pejorative "master statuses" that tend to override all other status characteristics an individual might possess. Focusing on a specific deviant identity, Szasz (1961:149) observed that "being cast in the role of mental patient is a form of personal degradation: it is a kind of stigmatization, like being classified as a Negro in Alabama." Above all, labeling theorists (Becker, 1963; Erikson, 1962) have emphasized that occupants of deviant statuses and members of minority groups alike are victims of the "self-fulfilling prophesy" and other discriminatory mechanisms that deny them equal opportunities in employment and in other areas of social life..

This paper reports on a field experiment designed to examine some implications of the deviance/race-relations analogy for the issue of differential employment opportunity. The racial identity (black vs. white) and deviant status (former mental patient vs. "normal") of job applicants were manipulated in the context of employment interviews conducted with a random sample of employers of unskilled labor in a medium-sized southern city. This experimental design provided us with a unique opportunity to determine whether the stigmata of race and/or deviance affect employers' reactions to potential employees.

PREVIOUS RESEARCH

A number of previous investigators have utilized experimental techniques to study the effects of deviant labels or race on employment opportunities while holding constant other potentially confounding variables. Social scientists will be most familiar with a widely reprinted experiment by Schwartz and Skolnick (1962) which used carefully constructed employment folders to manipulate varying degrees of legal stigma. Four groups of 25 employers each were shown folders that differed only with respect to the applicant's court contact, ranging from a "control" folder with no court record to a folder indicating the applicant had been convicted and sentenced for assault. Those employers who saw the "no record" folder were more likely to express an interest in the applicant (36%) than were employers who were led to believe that the applicant had been convicted (4%), with the other two conditions lying between these extremes. However, Schwartz and Skolnick (1962: note 4) suggest that their results "should be treated with appropriate caution" because the student who posed as an "employment agent" did not approach employers in a "pre-selected random order."

In a recent review of research on discrimination in employment interviews, Arvey (1979) touched on a number of experiments that examined effects of various disabilities or handicaps on reactions to applicants. Like Schwartz and Skolnick (1962), most of these studies used resumes to manipulate possibly stigmatizing conditions. However, resume experiments failed to reveal evidence of discrimination against applicants portrayed as having epilepsy, having a "withered arm" or being confined to a wheel chair. On the other hand, when employment agencies were actually visited by an applicant in a wheelchair in an experiment by Johnson and Heal (1976), reactions were clearly more negative than in other agencies where the same applicant appeared without the wheelchair. Commenting on these particular studies, Arvey (1979:760–761) not only noted the advantages of research using actual job applicants rather than resumes or folders, but also a need for studies focusing on disabilities such as "mental illness" that are "perceived more negatively by employers than are other disabilities."

Turning to the question of racial discrimination in job interviews, Arvey (1979:756–757) found only three experiments dealing with this important issue. None of these studies used "live" job applicants and the interviewers were generally college students rather than actual employers. Arvey suggests that these and other methodological limitations may account for the fact that these investigations provide "little evidence . . . that interviewers give more unfavorable evaluations to black job candidates compared with white candidates."

The field experiment presented below responds to several of the problems in previous research by using a relatively large number of carefully trained confederates (eight) who obtained interviews with actual employers. Two factors that Arvey (1979) sees as especially crucial—psychiatric disability and race—are orthogonally manipulated in the experimental design. Furthermore, based on data from post-experimental interviews, we will examine two employer variables, age and education, that have been related to attitudinal rejection of former mental patients (Whatley, 1959; Kaplan, 1972:101–117) as well as to racial prejudice (Myrdal, 1944; Smith 1981a; 1981b). Accordingly, we expect to find that employers' reactions to ex-patients and/or blacks (as opposed to white with no psychiatric record) will be contingent on these two covariates.

METHODOLOGY

Sample

The population for the experiment was employers in the Tallahassee-Leon County, Florida area who generally hire unskilled workers (e.g., food service establishments, car washes, construction contractors). A list of 219 such employers was obtained from the Florida Department of Commerce.

A random sample of 80 employers was selected from this list. Although not by design, all employers contacted by confederates were white.

Research Design

Employers in the sample were randomly assigned in equal numbers to four experimental conditions in a factorial design, racial identity x psychiatric status: Black—Psychiatric Record ($n = 20$); Black—No record ($n = 20$); White—Psychiatric Record ($n = 20$); and White—No Record ($n = 20$). Four black students and four white students were hired as confederates for the racial identity manipulation. Each confederate contacted ten employers, five in each psychiatric status condition. In all conditions of the experiment, the confederates were instructed to ask for the person in charge of hiring.[1] Once in contact with that employer, each confederate followed standardized instructions in asking for a job. In the Psychiatric Record conditions, confederates mentioned that they had been out of work for a while because of hospitalization for mental illness. No mention of hospitalization was made in the No Record conditions.[2]

Measures

The two measures of the dependent variable in this study, employer reaction, were obtained from a postcontact information sheet filled out by confederates immediately after their job interviews. A structured rating was obtained by asking confederates to place the disposition of the interview into one of the following four categories: (1) Will definitely not hire; (2) Will probably not hire; (3) Will probably hire; or (4) Will definitely hire. Second, an unstructured rating was derived from confederates' open-ended descriptions of details about "the employer's behavior in terms of his gestures, comments about a job, his concerns about your finding a job or lack of concern." These open-ended ratings were later categorized according to a ten-point scale by the first author.[3] The categories and frequency distributions for these two ratings are shown in Table 1.

Data on employers' ages and levels of educational attainment (as well

[1]Although one reviewer suggested that this may not, in fact, be the person who actually makes employment decisions, we assume that confederates were typically interviewed by decision-makers in these small firms. Contacts in which this did not occur should, of course, be randomly distributed across conditions

[2]The selection and training of the confederates aimed at minimizing the influence of appearance and personal characteristics other than the manipulated variables. Confederates practiced their applicant roles extensively in simulated and field interviews prior to the experiment. Three-way analyses of variance including a repeated measure factor for the eight confederates yielded no significant confederate effects on the dependent variables. Therefore, the confederate factor is ignored in all analyses reported below.

[3]These ratings were correlated against the independent ratings of six other judges as a reliability check. The reliability coefficients (r) with individual judges ranged from .73 to .92. The first author's ratings correlated very highly ($r = .93$) with the mean ratings of the other six judges on this ten-point unstructured scale.

TABLE 1 Frequency Distribution for Employer Reaction Ratings

Structured rating	Percent (frequency)	Unstructured rating	Percent (frequency)
1 = Will definitely not hire	63.7 (51)	1 = No jobs	45.0 (36)
		2 = No jobs but fill out application	11.2 (9)
		3 = We'll call	8.7 (7)
2 = Will probably not hire	13.7 (11)	4 = Come back (time unspecified)	6.3 (5)
		5 = Come back in a month or so	1.2 (1)
		6 = Come back in a week or so	3.7 (3)
		7 = Come back in a few days	5.0 (4)
3 = Will probably hire	15.0 (12)	8 = Come back (time specified)	6.3 (5)
		9 = Job promised	3.7 (3)
4 = Will definitely hire	7.5 (6)	10 = Confederate hired	8.7 (7)
Total	100.0 (80)	Total	100.0 (80)

as a number of other variables not considered here) were gathered in formal interviews conducted with employers within ten days after the initial job interview. All interviews were conducted by white female students. After three attempts to interview employers, a total of 66 interviews was completed. The age and education of the employer were each coded into five ordinal categories.[4]

[4]The distribution of employers' ages by ten-year intervals was as follows: 20–29, 30.3%; 30–39, 31.8%; 40–49, 22.7%; 50–59, 13.6%; and 60–69, 1.5%. Education was distributed as follows: Some high school, 12.3%; Completed high school, 27.7%; Some college, 29.2%; Completed college, 23.1%; and Some graduate school, 7.7%.

TABLE 2 Means and Standard Deviations for Structured and Unstructured Ratings of Employer Reaction by Experimental Condition

Rating of reaction and Psychiatric record		Race: Black	Race: White	Row mean
Structured rating				
Psychiatric Record	X =	1.40	1.70	1.55
	SD =	(0.82)	(1.08)	
No Psychiatric Record	X =	1.75	1.80	1.77
	SD =	(1.12)	(0.95)	
Column Mean		1.57	1.75	
Unstructured rating				
Psychiatric Record	X =	2.55	3.11	2.83
	SD =	(2.46)	(3.31)	
No Psychiatric Record	X =	4.15	4.35	4.25
	SD =	(3.39)	(3.41)	
Column Mean		3.35	3.73	

RESULTS

Ratings of Employer Reaction

Table 2 presents the means for the structured and unstructured ratings of employer reaction within cells of the experimental design. For both rating scales, a higher mean score indicates a more favorable reaction toward confederates. The means for the structured ratings show only negligible differences across conditions. However, the unstructured ratings in the bottom half of Table 2 indicate that employers tended to react more favorably to confederates with no psychiatric record than to those who admitted to a record of psychiatric hospitalization (note the row mean of 4.25 for No Psychiatric Record versus the row mean of 2.83 for Psychiatric Record). More specifically, confederates in the Black/Record condition received the least encouragement from employers (cell X = 2.55).

Formal tests of differences in the ratings of employer reaction across the experimental design were conducted using two-way analysis of variance (ANOVA). The two-way ANOVA for the structured ratings (not shown here) yielded no significant main or interaction effects of the manipulated variables. A similar test for the unstructured ratings (shown in Table 3) revealed a significant main effect of the Psychiatric Record/No Record factor on employer reaction. This effect, of course, is reflected in the higher row mean for the No Record condition in Table 2. However, neither the main effect of racial status nor the interaction of race X psychiatric status were statistically significant for the unstructured ratings.

TABLE 3 Analysis of Variance for Unstructured Ratings of Employer Reaction

Source of variation	DF	SS	MS	F
Main effects	2	43.42	21.71	2.16
Race (black/white)	1	2.81	2.81	0.28
Record/No Record	1	40.61	40.61	4.05*
Two-way interaction (Race × Record)	1	0.61	0.61	0.61
Explained	76	44.03	14.67	1.46
Residual	76	761.84	10.02	
Total	79	805.88	10.20	

*p<.05

TABLE 4 Zero-Order and Conditional Correlations of Employer's Age and Education with Structured and Unstructured Ratings of Employer Reaction

Correlation and condition	*N*	Structured rating	Unstructured rating
Age correlation	66	-.25*	-.32*
Zero-Order	15	-.15	-.12
Black/Record	15	-.15	-.12
Black/No Record	14	-.28	-.34
White/Record	18	-.34	-.38
White/No Record	19	-.11	-.32
Education correlation			
Zero-Order	65	-.07	-.15
Black/Record	15	-.11	-.01
Black/No Record	14	-.23	-.18
White/Record	17	-.32	-.51*
White/No Record	19	-.09	-.11

*p<.05

Employer Age and Education

The ages and educational attainment of the 66 employers who were contacted for follow-up interviews were correlated with the structured and unstructured ratings of employer reaction. Table 4 reports these correlations for the total follow-up sample (zero-order r) and within cells of the experimental deign (condition r). The overall correlations between age and the two ratings of employer reaction are negative and statistically significant (-.25 and -.32, $p<.05$), indicating that older employers generally expressed less favorable reactions to confederates. Similarly, all of the within cell correlations involving age are negative; however, none of these conditional relations are statistically significant. It is worth noting that the pattern of age correlations across cells of the design is somewhat inconsistent with our expectations. Whereas we expected the contingent effects of employer's age to be most apparent in reactions to the "doubly stigmatized" confederates in the Black/Record cell, these particular correlations are relatively weak in comparison to other cells. However, a general test for age interactions using analysis of covariance indicated that these conditional correlations are not significantly different from one another.[5]

As shown in the bottom half of Table 4, the overall, zero-order correlations of employer's education with the two measures of reaction are negligible. The most surprising finding here is a strong and significant negative correlation between education and the unstructured rating in the White/Record cell (-.51, $p<.05$). Contrary to previous research on attitudes toward former mental patients (e.g., Kaplan, 1972:101–117; Whatley, 1959), this result indicates that more highly educated employers reacted less favorable to white ex-patients than did employers with lower educational attainment. On the other hand, modest positive relationships between education and reaction emerge in the Black/No Record cell. Only weak correlations appear in the two extreme cells of Black/Record and White/No Record. Nonetheless, an overall test for two-way and three-way interactions involving education indicated that these variations in conditional correlations are not significant statistically.[6]

DISCUSSION AND CONCLUSION

While this study found some evidence of direct discrimination against job applicants with a record of hospitalization for mental disorder, the bulk of our results fails to reveal pronounced or consistent liabilities of racial and psychiatric stigmata. The significant main effect of psychiatric record on unstructured ratings amounts, roughly, to a difference between mean responses of "don't call us, we'll call you" toward the ex-patient versus "try again later" toward the non-stigmatized "normal." This subtle distinction would have been more impressive, of course, if it had been backed up by

[5]Using the SPSS MANOVA program (Hull and Nie, 1981), the null hypothesis of equality of slopes across conditions and cells was evaluated by a single test of the three age interactions, Age X Race, Age X Record, and Age X Race X Record. This test failed to reject the null hypothesis for the structured ($F=.461$) and unstructured ($F=.586$) ratings.

[6]The null hypothesis of equality of slopes could not be rejected for either the structured ($F=.974$) or unstructured ($F=1.574$, $p=.21$) ratings of employer reaction.

significant variation in the confederates' structured ratings of employers' reactions. Still, this is an area that clearly deserves further study. The significant effect of our manipulation of ex-patient status is consistent with the observations of other investigators who have examined the stigmatizing impact of psychiatric labeling on employment opportunities (Olshansky et al, 1960; Farina and Felner, 1973; Link, 1982).

In a sense, we are also consistent with previous researchers in finding no effects of applicants' race on employers' reactions. We hardly should describe this outcome as "disappointing," since it suggests that racial discrimination in employment is no more apparent in a "live" interview than it was in earlier resume studies reviewed by Arvey (1979:756–757). Such negative results may have practical significance to the extent that they can be used to dispel unwarranted expectations of discrimination or favoritism which might deter potential minority job applicants (see Link, 1982). However, before we or others embrace the null hypothesis of no racial bias in employment interviews, it is important to bear in mind Arvey's (1979:759) caution about the "paucity of evidence" on this issue. We are particularly concerned about the limitation of our experiment to a population of employers of unskilled labor in a southern city. Theory and research on labor market differentials between the races imply that discrimination might be more apparent in higher status jobs than in the low-wage, "secondary-sector" positions for which our confederates applied (see, for example, Doeringer and Piore, 1971; Kluegel, 1978; Beck et al., 1980; U. S. Commission on Civil Rights, 1982; however, also see Hodson and Kaufman, 1982). That is, blacks may not directly experience discrimination relative to whites when applying for unskilled jobs defined as "black man's work." Research designs that incorporate primary-sector jobs or variations in skill or authority levels are clearly needed in future experimental work on race and employment discrimination.

Rather than focusing on such structural variations in the employment situation, the current study examined certain personal characteristics of employers that were expected to affect their reactions to confederates. Unfortunately, not much can be said about the contingent effects of employer age and education on the basis of these results. Little theoretical importance can be attached to the negative correlations between age and reactions in the absence of a significant and systematic patterning of these relationships across cells of the experimental design. The significant negative relationship between employer's education and reaction to the White/Record confederate runs contrary to our expectations and is difficult to interpret. In fact, given that sixteen within-cell correlations were tested, this one significant result at the .05 level might best be seen as a random fluctuation.

If nothing else, this research reinforces Schwartz and Skolnick's (1962) pioneering demonstration of the utility of field experimentation for examining central implications of the labeling perspective on deviance. Here, we have investigated the empirical grounds for the labeling theorists' venerable analogy between reactions to deviants and discriminatory treatment of blacks. At least in the context of an employment interview, our results suggest that the stigmata of race and psychiatric status are neither as similar nor as interpersonally damaging as this analogy would imply.

REFERENCES

Arvey, Richard D.
1979 "Unfair discrimination in the employment interview." Psychological Bulletin 86:736–765.

Beck, E. M., Patrick M. Horan, and Charles M. Tolbert, II
1980 "Industrial segmentation and labor market discrimination."

Becker, Howard S.
1963 Outsiders: Studies in the Sociology of Deviance. New York: Free Press.

Doeringer, Peter B., and Michael J. Piore
1971 "Internal Labor Markets and Manpower Analysis. Lexington, MA: D. C. Heath.

Erikson, Kai T.
1962 "Notes on the sociology of deviance." Social Problems 9:307–314.

Farina, Amerigo, and Robert D. Felner
1973 "Employment interviewer reactions to former mental patients." Journal of Abnormal Psychology 82:268–272.

Hodson, Randy, and Robert L. Kaufman
1982 "Economic dualism: a critical review." American Sociological Review 47:727–739.

Hull, C. Hadlai, and Norman H. Nie
1981 SPSS Update 7–9. New York: McGraw-Hill.

Johnson, R. and L. W. Heal
1976 "Private employment agency responses to the physically handicapped applicant in a wheelchair." Journal of Applied Rehabilitation Counseling 7:12-21.

Kaplan, Howard B.
1972 The Sociology of Mental Illness. New Haven: College and University Press.

Kluegel, James R.
1978 "Causes and cost of racial exclusion." American Sociological Review 43:285–301.

Link, Bruce
1982 "Mental patient status, work, and income: an examination of the effects of a psychiatric label." American Sociological Review 47:202–215.
Myrdal, Gunnar
1944 An American Dilemma. New York: Harper.
Olshansky, Simon, Samuel Grob, and Marian Ekdahl
1960 "Survey of employed patients discharged from three state mental hospitals during 1951–1953." Mental Hygiene 44:510–521.
Schwartz, Richard D., and Jerome H. Skolnick
1962 "Two studies of legal stigma." Social Problems 10:133–142.
Smith, A. Wade
1981a "Tolerance of school desegregation, 1954–1977." Social Forces 59:1256–1274.
1981b "Racial tolerance as a function of group position." American Sociological Review 46:558–573.
Szasz, Thomas S.
1961 The Myth of Mental Illness. New York: Hoeber-Harper.
U. S. Commission on Civil Rights
1982 Unemployment and Underemployment among Blacks, Hispanics, and Women. Washington, D. C.: U. S. Government Printing Office.
Whatley, Charles D.
1959 "Social attitudes toward discharged mental patients." Social Problems 6:313–320.

Reading 8

Giftedness as Deviance: A Test of Interaction Theories

Jean Scherz Huryn
East Carolina University, Greenville, North Carolina

Perceptions of gifted students concerning their own and others' attitudes toward giftedness were obtained form interviews of 60 students in gifted programs. The research uses these perceptions to examine their awareness of the existence and content of stereotypes and labels toward giftedness; coping mechanisms used by gifted students; and whether giftedness is perceived as valued or devalued by these students based on interaction with peers, teachers, and parents. Interaction theories of deviance (role, labeling) were evaluated to see whether these theories were supported by behavior of gifted students at school. Gifted status was usually associated

The author wishes to thank Buford Rhea for helpful comments on earlier versions of this paper, Susan Hofacre for sharing conception of this research, Lee Matson for transcribing, and Nancy Crouse Smith and Brenda Mills for assistance in interviewing.

with negative stereotypes and labels which limited and shaped peer contacts thus supporting labeling theory. Role theory emphasized activeness of gifted students in using "covering" mechanisms and "passing" to control visibility of deviant status of giftedness. Positive value of giftedness reflected by parents and teachers and negative value of giftedness reflected by peers emphasizes the situational context of deviance and creates a social chameleon effect whereby gifted students display this attribute in interactions where valued and mask where devalued, although giftedness was valued for self.

Deviance is a social construct based on the standards present in a society or social group at any time (Durkheim, 1951). "Nothing is inherently bad or good, but becomes so when defined as such in a process of social interaction." (Scarpetti & McFarlane 1975:5) Two important perspectives using these premises are role theory (Mead, 1934; Goffman, 1959, 1963) and labeling (Tannenbaum, 1938; Lemert, 1951; Becker, 1973). Using these interaction theories, giftedness can be studied as deviance as a social construct that can be either positively or negatively valued.

This research first examines the gifted status by inquiring into awareness by the gifted student of the existence and content of stereotypes and labels applied to smartness. Alexander found that nongifted students felt that "intelligent people dress preppy, wear glasses, talk bout boring things, and . . . prefer to stay inside and study rather than to go outside and play" (1985:139). Are gifted students aware of these stereotypes and what are their reactions to these stereotypes? Secondly, the research examines the interaction between gifted students and others to see whether role theory or labeling more adequately depicts the behavior of gifted students in dealing with this status. In role theory, the individual internalizes his/her self-concept through the process of socialization. One's self is the result of interaction between the person and others which gives the person a mutually accepted role within the group (Mead, 1934). As the self-concept is further clarified, roles emerge which structure the behavior of the individual so that the person acts as one perceives oneself.

Goffman (1963) emphasizes how the deviant person can control this process of interaction. In his work on stigma, Goffman differentiates between those whose "spoiled" identity has already discredited them and those who have a risk of being discredited should their stigmata become known. He discusses the coping mechanism of "covering" used by the former whereby the identified person controls the display of this stigma through impression management. In the latter situation, the identifiable person controls visibility of this stigma through information control.

Labeling theory emphasizes the reactions of others to the deviant and how this reaction leads to further deviance. Tannenbaum (1938) states that the process becomes one of tagging, defining and identifying; the person begins to act as he/she is described. For Lemert (1951), this interaction leads to secondary deviance as the responses of others cut the person off from conventional groups and roles, and further reinforce one's attraction to the deviant role. The person continues into further deviance as a reaction to the labelers and the closing off of alternative behavioral choices.

The third objective of this research is to examine the value dimension of giftedness as perceived by gifted students. Scarpetti and McFarlane (1975) refer to intellectual genius as a positively valued deviance. However, educational researchers (Coleman, 1960; Tannenbaum, 1962; Mitchell, 1974; Morgan, 1981) have found giftedness to be negatively evaluated, especially by school peers. Tannenbaum (1983) felt that attitudes toward giftedness may be curvilinear with IQs up to 150 producing positive social reactions and IQs over this level eliciting more negative reactions, although the number of persons in this higher range is small. Is giftedness positively or negatively valued and by whom?

This research uses perceptions stated by gifted students themselves concerning their own and others' attitudes toward the attribute of giftedness. The paper uses their perceptions to examine the three objectives: awareness and reactions by the gifted student to stereotypes and labels; mechanisms, if any, used by the gifted to deal with these stereotypes and labels; and the value dimension of giftedness (i.e. whether the gifted student feels giftedness is positively or negatively evaluated and sanctioned) based on the reactions received from teachers, parents, and peers. Using giftedness as deviance, the paper examines the applicability of role theory (Mead, 1934; Goffman, 1963) and labeling (Becker, 1973; Lemert, 1951) for understanding positive deviance, provided the status of giftedness is positively valued in our society.

METHOD

Sixty students identified as gifted and talented by their school system were randomly selected from one county and two city school systems in North Carolina. Each of the six schools used in the study had a different program for the gifted. Students were selected by random sampling, but selection of the first 15 students resulted in mostly white females. Therefore, the remaining sample was stratified by sex and race to insure a broader range of perceptions. Sixty-two percent of the resultant sample were females and 68% were white. Three students were Oriental. The students ranged in age from 12 to 18 years and were spread evenly over this age span due to the selection of 10 students from each grade level.

The term gifted refers to any student identified by his/her school as being in the gifted program and on which a yearly IEP (individualized educational program) was completed. Five items were used by the school to identify the child as gifted: grades, IQ, a behavioral checklist, and two teachers' ratings.

A structured interview approximately 30 minutes in length was conducted in a private room at each school. The words "smart" and "gifted" were used as synonymous throughout the interviews. The interviewer asked the student his/her own attitude and his/her perceptions of the attitude of peers, teachers, parents, and society in general toward being smart and toward him/her being identified as gifted.

Four questions dealt with awareness of stereotypes and labels applied to giftedness. If the premises of interaction theory are to be used, the person must be aware of being identified and labeled in the process of interactions.

Four questions concerned this interaction between the student and others, especially peers. Role theory would analyze the student's use of coping mechanisms or limiting information to control the identifying process; labeling would analyze how evaluations by others limit and shape the student's role relationships.

Four questions sought the value dimension of giftedness perceived by the student from teachers, parents, and peers. Is giftedness a positive deviance as suggested by Scarpetti and McFarlane or is it negatively valued as suggested by Tannenbaum and Coleman?

Probes were used to get the students to elaborate. The interviews were tape recorded and comments were also noted on each interview schedule during the session. Tapes were transcribed and used along with the written notes to summarize and exemplify the quantitative findings. In the analysis, peer refers to other students at the school and does not imply the intellectual peer or closest friend of these students.

FINDINGS

Awareness of the Existence and Content of Stereotypes and Labels

In response to the question concerning characteristics associated with being smart, only 11 (18%) mentioned any positive characteristics. Two males stated that gifted students were "good looking." Another male mentioned that smart persons have "stability in their life. They're pretty sure where they're going."

However, most of their perceptions of the stereotypical gifted student were negative, emphasizing characteristics such as opinionated, snobbish, and conceited. A 17 year old stated that a smart person was "able to focus on only one thing or intellectual concept, not very sociable, not very interested in other people's opinions." Another gifted student declared, "not really trying to get along with others, a little obnoxious about being smart." Limiting their interests to books and reading was often mentioned. One student stated "there's your classic smart person that's real shy, always in a book . . . no outside communications or involvement." The most common perception concerned physical characteristics. A female commented "not very attractive, bookish, with glasses." One student related that a gifted friend was visiting a college for scholarship weekend when a student declared "You all look normal. I expected all these walking test tubes."

Students emphasized different types of smart persons similar to the differences found by Tannenbaum (1983). One student described the stereotypical gifted student as "tall and skinny and greasy hair." She continued "If you're talking about really, really smart people, I guess that's the thing . . . but there's some other smart people that, [pause] that are normal." Another female student said, "There's 2 types of smart people: those that have book sense . . . but they're still outgoing and being smart enhances their being popular. And then there are people that are very caught up in their studies . . . and they're not very outgoing . . . they [are] really ridiculed [and] picked on like 'brain,' 'can't do anything.' "

Students continually tried to separate these stereotypic images from what they saw as reality. A 16 year old stated that a smart person was "shy, you know, reads books . . . but at school it's changed a lot . . . people still *think* of smart people being that way but I know a lot of people are smart and popular and outgoing." Another student stated that smart people "usually aren't very attractive, [pause] but you know, that's not true in all cases—its just . . . and image that's been set up . . . its why some people don't like to be called a 'brain.' "

Students were aware of many labels that were applied to the gifted; the most common labels were "brain", "teacher's pet" and "bookworm." A female related "people . . . say 'Oh, there go the goody girls' or . . . 'Oh, you're *so* smart.' " A 17 year old male stated "You get labeled an egghead." When asked if he would like his children to be less smart, as smart, or smarter than himself, he replied, "[I] wouldn't want them to be real smart. [It] sets you apart . . . kind of out of it but not really out of it." However, most gifted students would like their children to be smarter than they are.

Students were asked if being in the gifted program made them feel different from other students. Most (69%) said it did not. A female replied, "No, because I could say I've been labeled . . . as gifted and talented since the second grade." However, 16 (27%) felt that this identification did make them "somewhat" different and 2 felt very different. As one female senior declared, "Let's face it, we are different."

Gifted students were very aware of labels and stereotypes towards giftedness in our society. In their perceptions the stereotypic smart person was aloof, unattractive, boring and self-centered. Some students felt that reality was different. Others felt that there were two types of smart people—those who fit the stereotype and those who don't. The typical labels attached to the gifted status, such as "brain", all had negative connotations to the gifted student.

Interaction between Gifted Students and Others

Almost all students used some form of impression management to deal with their gifted status when interacting with others. When asked if they told other students they were in the gifted program, almost all said they did not unless a person specifically asked. A few would even deny being in the program, thus keeping this "deviant" stigma hidden when possible. "No, no, I wouldn't tell them . . . especially if they're in a lower level. I'd say, 'Well, I'm just a regular person,' " stated a female. Other students would disclose this information, but still held the idea it might discredit them. A male replied "I don't go out and shout, 'I'm in GT' but I'll tell them, I'm not ashamed." The students' remarks supported the concept that giftedness was a "discreditable" stigma (i.e., caused problems only if it became known).

Gifted students used various coping mechanisms within the gifted classroom to "cover" (i.e., they could not pass as a "regular" student in this class but could still cover the degree of giftedness). Most (73%) of the students said they played dumb at one time or another, and some did this quite frequently. A 13 year old replied, "Yes, lots of times . . . so people won't think I'm all that . . . [leaves sentence unfinished]." A 14 year old stated, "some guys [pause] were saying . . . I answer too many times whenever (the teacher) asked a question. I just didn't want to hear any more so I just didn't answer anything for the rest of the period."

One coping mechanism was pretending they did not know the information. A student stated, "somebody'd ask me something and I'd just ell them I didn't know it." A female replied, "By not volunteering in class or [if I have a question] I'll ask it after class."

Asking inappropriate questions was another mechanism. A male replied, "ask a lot of stupid questions and . . . if the teacher asks a question . . . pretend I don't know the answer even if I do." Often clowning and joking was used as a covering. A female stated, "If you could see me for a day, all my friends will say I'm crazy because I like to crack jokes and make people laugh."

Some coped by downplaying their ability such as saying they did badly on a test or pretending they didn't know much. A female recalled, "In Spanish class, I answered something correctly and said 'Well, I got lucky.' " This student also pretended "about 10 times per year" that she did worse on tests than she really did.

When students were asked if they acted differently in GT classes, one student stated that he "didn't really act too different, but I feel more comfortable (in gifted classes). Sometimes, in other classes, I am reluctant to answer unless called on for fear of giving a wrong answer." Earlier this student said "[you] expect smart people to never mess up. When you do, they ride you for it." However, most students (75%) felt they did not act differently in gifted classes except for the pace of work involved.

Teachers occasionally annoyed the student by removing their "cover". A female stated, "Sometimes the teacher will call (out your grade). I hate it when you get the highest one. Everybody looks at you (laughs)." A 14 year old related that in the third grade, a teacher noticed she had read *To Kill a Mockingbird* and told other teachers, which embarrassed this admittedly shy girl because "I don't like to get attention," she declared.

When the students were asked if they had friends who had avoided the label of smart, the majority (54%) said they did. A 17 year old affirmed that friends "don't think its cool to be smart." A 14 year old said his friends "didn't like the stereotype of someone who goes around reading all the time."

Friends used the same coping mechanisms as those previously mentioned. A 17 year old female acknowledged that friends asked "pointless questions, trying to be people they aren't by acting air-headed, pretending like they don't understand." "I know people who . . . try not to do good," responded a 16 year old "if they get 100 on their paper, they act incredulous and regarding someone else's word knowledge, they might say, 'You *knew* that. I didn't', although they really did." "If they answered a really tough question, they'd say 'That was a lucky guess!' when they really knew the answer," recalled another student. "If they make straight A's they don't want everybody to know that . . . And if somebody finds out and starts telling everybody about it, they get upset. They would rather people not know. Or maybe they would like for them to know but not make fun or tease them about it.," a female acknowledged.

Giftedness was the student's master status in school, and "passing" was often not possible. Therefore, the major coping mechanisms were those of "covering." These included not volunteering answers, asking inappropriate questions, asking profound questions after class, pretending lack of knowledge, downplaying one's ability, limiting one's vocabulary, and clowning and joking. Labeling theory emphasizes the reactions of others who identify, tag, label, and role segregate so that the deviant person has little flexibility in managing that role. This did occur; however, the students were actively involved in reacting to these labels, but using impression management to control how these labels were applied to them.

The Value Dimension of Giftedness

Whether giftedness was perceived as valued or devalued in the process of interaction related to whether the student was dealing with adults or peers.

However, in interaction with teachers and parents, giftedness was usually perceived as positively valued. When asked how teachers viewed being smart, students responded that teachers felt they were "good students" whom you "could give more work" and "send on errands as they were more reliable."

However, not all teachers responded positively. Eleven students had encountered a teacher who thought they were "too smart" so that students "acted dumb" or did not ask questions because this would make the teacher dislike them. "We had to act like we were stupid," a 15 year old recalled because the "vocation teacher sees GT students as being egotistical." Therefore, the value of giftedness as assessed by these students, was often a function of the particular context and specific significant other used in their reflections.

Parents, in almost all cases, felt giftedness was a valued attribute. Forty-three percent said their parents were proud to have their child identified as gifted; 27% said parents approved of this identification, and 27% said parents had expected them to be gifted. One student commented that, "Dad had been in gifted classes and expected us kids to be." Another stated that the reaction from parents varied, with the parent who had been in gifted education being supportive and the other parent being somewhat negative toward this identification.

A few students (22%) did feel that peer groups saw the attribute of giftedness as a positively valued status. However, 77% of the gifted felt that groups at school evaluated giftedness as negative. A black female explained that students must be careful when interacting with friends because "they think you got such a big head." A white female responded, "I know a few who don't like people to think they are smart because the way the groups (pause) are set up in school—they think that maybe a group won't like them because they're smart." Another student said, "it might sometimes put me above some of my friends or something, which isn't good." However, her personal evaluation was positive as she continued, "But, I say there's the benefits . . . you need to classify people . . . so they can get the best education they should in any situation."

When asked their personal evaluation, most students (77%) had positive attitudes toward the gifted program, and therefore saw giftedness as a valued attribute for their own lives. Several students said this was an honor and one stated that this made others "look up to you." Only one student answered that she did not like being in the gifted program, stating that it was "kind of different because most of your friends are in a different group and think you've got such a big head because you're so smart." Another female stated "There's nothing wrong with it, I guess, because most of my friends are in it anyway." Most students (69%) had solved this problem of friends, especially in the younger grades, by having as their three or four closest friends other students who were also in the gifted program.

Therefore, most gifted students felt that the gifted program was a valuable opportunity. They would reveal their gifted identity if this allowed them to stay in the program or provided more gifted classes. Some thought negative reactions from peers were due to jealousy because the gifted classes went on more field trips and had more interesting classes. "The work is more interesting", and "wished I had more gifted classes" were often stated. Regular classes were not as challenging. "I learn a lot more because . . . I [don't] get bored," or "School seems to easy," were indicative of this.

Students felt that gifted classes provided a "better education," and "looks good on college admissions." But giftedness was valued only to the degree necessary for adult career goals. "I don't want to center my whole life around study. (You want to) make grades good enough to get in the school you want. (Some smart persons) wear weird clothes, act strange, so brainy, people they hang around with (are weird), " stated a student, exemplifying this idea.

Teachers and parents viewed giftedness positively and give positive sanctions to gifted students. Societal stereotypes were viewed as negative and students gave many examples of negative peer responses, such as sarcasm and teasing. Gifted students had been using various mechanism since grammar school to avoid negative peer responses. At the same time, students saw advantages for themselves in the gifted program. More stimulating classes, more information covered, enhanced academic records, better college choices and improved future career goals were reasons most students used for viewing giftedness as valued, even if the gifted status received negative reactions from peers.

CONCLUSIONS

The existence of stereotypes and labels related to giftedness substantiates it as a deviant status. Gifted students were aware of the stereotypes of a smart person as aloof, unattractive and boring; and the negative label of "brain".However, the students often perceived two types of smart persons—those who fit the stereotype and those who did not.

Students dealt with these stereotypes and labels by selecting friends who were also in the gifted program. In their daily interactions with peers, students tried to "pass" or "cover". They did not reveal their gifted status to "regular" students and used mechanisms, such as pretending ignorance or clowning, to downplay their abilities.

Most of the gifted students felt that peer groups at school devalued giftedness and that most teachers and parents viewed giftedness as positive.

In regard to their own attitude, all but one student was glad to be identified as gifted because this provided better classes, enhanced academic records, and improved career goals.

Students, especially in the younger grades, selected friends who were also identified as gifted thus supporting labeling theory. As the person takes on a deviant identification, their other role contacts were limited and shaped by this identity. Role imprisonment and the formation of a deviant subculture as described by Lemert did occur. On a daily basis however, students dealt with this status by continually adapting their behavior to avoid negative sanctions of teasing and sarcasm. They did not readily reveal their gifted status when interacting with "regular" students so they could "pass" as a regular student. "Covering" mechanisms were used by students in their gifted classes to mask the extent of their giftedness. Thus both labeling and role theory were applicable to the analysis of giftedness as deviance. However, labeling appears more applicable early in the student's career as s/he is first being identified as gifted; whereas role theory is more applicable to understanding how the student deals with this deviant status on a daily basis.

Gifted students were very aware of negative labels and managed their behavior so as to diminish negative reactions from peers. They reduced their vocabulary, concealed their knowledge, asked dumb questions, or clowned so as to "pass" as a "regular" student among the student body or "cover" the fact that they were producing outstanding papers or high test scores. This sensitivity to others' evaluations produces a chameleon-like behavior, allowing them to pass as a "regular gifted" student rather than a brilliant "egghead."

Gifted students often participate in athletics, cheerleading, status clubs, or cliques, even taking part in mischievous pranks to prove their status as "regular" students. Often they change their personalities (vocabulary, knowledge, aspirations) to match that of their peers in these groups, similar to a chameleon which changes its color to blend with its surroundings and conceal its visibility. Likewise, gifted students reveal their giftedness to parents or teachers when and if these persons value giftedness. This concealing and revealing requires a high degree of adaptability and a high level of sensitivity to others' responses. Gifted students who cannot or choose not to adopt this chameleonic behavior, stand out in the school environment becoming those described as "brains" and "eggheads", those "ridiculed" and "picked on."

By using this chameleonic approach, the gifted student moves from one reference group where giftedness is devalued to another where giftedness is valued, concealing ("covering" and "passing") his/her identity and revealing this identity depending on how the situational context values this deviance. Just as the chameleon meets the demands of various environments and keeps it camouflage by changing colors when necessary, so likewise does the social chameleon, regardless of the deviance, adroitly change identities as the situation requires, thereby obscuring visibility of his/her deviant acts or attributes. However, deviant identities are revealed or solidified if the deviant cannot or chooses not to adapt by blending to the situational environment in this manner.

REFERENCES

Alexander, Patricia
1985 "Gifted and Nongifted Students' Perceptions of Intelligence" Gifted Child Quarterly, 29 (3):137–143.

Becker, Howard S.
1973 Outsiders: Studies in the Sociology of Deviance. New York: Free Press.

Coleman, J. S.
1960 "The Adolescent Subculture and Academic Achievement." American Journal of Sociology 65:337–347.

Durkheim, Emile
(1897)
1951 Suicide. J. A. Spaulding and S. Simpson, translators. New York: Free Press.

Goffman, Erving
1959 The Presentation of Self in Everyday Life. Garden City: Doubleday.
1963 Stigma. Englewood Cliffs, N.J.: Prentice-Hall.

Lemert, Edwin M.
1951 Social Pathology. New York: McGraw-Hill.

Mead, George H.
1934 Mind, Self and Society. Chicago: University of Chicago Press.

Mitchell, J. O.
1974 "Attitudes of Adolescents Toward Mental Ability, Academic Effort and Athleticism: Unpublished. Calgary, Alberta, Canada: University of Calgary, Dept. of Sociology

Morgan, H.
1981 Adolescent Attitudes Toward Academic Brilliance in the Suburban High School. Unpublished. Boulder: University of Colorado.

Scarpetti, Frank, and Paul T. McFarlane
1975 Deviance: Action, Reaction, Interaction: Studies in Positive and Negative Deviance. Reading, MA: Addison-Wesley.

Tannenbaum, A. J.
1983 Gifted Children: Psychological and Educational Perspectives. New York: MacMillan.
1962 Adolescents' Attitudes Toward Academic Brilliance. New York: Teachers College Press.

Tannenbaum, Frank
1938 Crime and the Community. New York: Columbia University Press.

Chapter Four

Interpretation and Reaction

EDITORIAL COMMENTARY

The confrontation of social norm and norm violator occurs as much in the eye and mind of the beholder as in the actual context of behavior and interaction. It is the public or the onlooker, generically speaking, who, in effect, socially "processes" deviance. Social norms may be effected by various mechanisms and contrivances but it is the populace, generally speaking, who will have to perceive and interpret the violation of such norms, and what response is appropriate, if in fact, any is called for.

A small segment of the population or, indeed, only a very few persons, likely socially powerful or influential may establish social norms. Etiquette, or the rules of "polite" behavior, for example, has traditionally been articulated by only a small number of individual arbiters of social civility, who have most often been "gentle people," if not members of the upper class. Amy Vanderbilt and Emily Post immediately come to mind. Diplomatic protocol, or the "ceremonial forms and courtesies" that are deemed appropriate, proper, and correct, in the official intercourse between and among heads of state and the representatives of the various nations, may be partly a matter of tradition and partly the creation of a single individual, usually a so-called "Chief of Protocol" for the Department of State or Foreign Affairs of a nation. Many laws and regulations have been enacted at the behest of a small portion of the population. The captains of industry, and the membership of labor unions speaking through their leadership, have both been responsible for the passage of legislation. Affluent citizens, as well as the economically less well off, have on occasion, had vested interests in the enactment of laws and ordinances, and have used their influence to bring about such statutes. Fashion in clothing and dress is dictated by a relatively few individuals who are either strategically placed in the clothing industry or the mass media, or are prominent in the public eye and who command a "following." Public morality as expressed in the form of sexual prescriptions and proscriptions, and legal specifications of pornography and obscenity may be more a product of the idiosyncratic persuasion of an influential few than the consensual belief of the many. A political official, ruler, or potentate may dictate rules and norms by virtue of his bureaucratic authority or his charismatic power. Similarly, a religious leader may also mandate behavior by reason of his office, as in the case of the Pope, or because of divine revelation, as with Joseph Smith, the founder of Mormonism, or Moses. Soothsayers, oracles, prophets, or witch doctors may enjoin or constrain social behavior on the basis of their visions, insights, prognostications, or prescience. Thus, social norms may emerge as the result of a carefully measured and many-staged, reflective, process. They also may evolve out of traditional persuasion, sentiment, and consensus, or may be established by individual fiat by those with the power and/or influence necessary to do so.

Once norms are established, enacted, inaugurated, or created, they must be made operational. It is to the public, or the members of the group, organization, community or society, that the task of activating, implementing, and enforcing norms, usually falls. A school teacher may establish a classroom behavioral rule for the pupils and monitor their conformity. A drill instructor in the military may do the same with a platoon of recruits. So too may an employer constrain workers to adhere to a rule he or she has established, and then insure their compliance. In general, however, it is the members of the collective group or society that must monitor and enforce conformity to norms inasmuch as norms are usually *presumed* to arise out of public sentiment, and be for the public good—of the people, by the people, and for the people, as it were.

As with the creation and enforcement of norms, sometimes it is only a powerful or influential few (or perhaps even one or two) persons who perceive, interpret, evaluate, and judge behavior as conformity or deviant.

But as mentioned above, it is usually the public—the members of society—that "processes" deviance. The public is often involved in the establishment of or strengthening of a norm, and the accompanying sanction that aids in motivating conformity to the norm (i.e., the "public" demand for more stringent drunken driving laws). The public monitors adherence to the norm and may often determine if the norm has, indeed, been violated. The public may also decide on factors of mitigation and extenuation that might tend to neutralize or exacerbate the violation. The public, in effect, is the arbiter that defines the appropriate label for offense and offender. Murder or justifiable homicide; acid humor or insult; crudity or lapse of propriety; sexual perversion or indulgence in catholic sexual repertoire; pornography or cinema verité with redeeming social qualities; attempted rape or overly amorous, romantic enthusiasm; or child abuse or firm and persuasive discipline? The public may determine what sanction, if any, is appropriate, when and how to apply it, and with what degree of severity. Finally, the public will have to make final resolution of the deviant event, and the offender. Will Hester Prynne have to wear the scarlet letter, forever? Will the sinner be forgiven and be reembraced into the fold? Will the convicted offender be rehabilitated and returned to a productive status in society? Will the mentally ill individual, the alcoholic, the addict, or the "pervert" be "cured," and reaccepted as "normal?" May the "Hippie" be permitted to see the error of his aberrant ways and become a "Yuppie"? Was the norm too exacting, the sanction too severe, or the result too dysfunctional? Or does the law need to be modified to be more relevant and instrumental, or should the rule be more rigidly enforced and the sanction strengthened? All of these concerns are component tasks of the members of society in their quest for, and efforts to effect, social order. Of course, as authorities like Howard Becker and Kai Erikson have pointed out, social groups in effect create deviance by establishing norms, defining the violation of these norms as deviant, and then labeling the violators as deviants.

The members of society must first perceive the violation of a social norm if, indeed, deviance is to occur. Like the tree falling in the forest outside of the range of human hearing with the result that no sound is heard, where deviance is not perceived, it cannot socially exist. Humans are remarkable for their selective attention and inattention. The mother that hears her baby crying while others sleep, the peasant family that sleeps over a stable and smells no stench, or the jungle dweller who can see the snake in the underbrush when the visitor from civilization cannot, are all example of such disparate cognition. Culture and the constituent behavior patterns may also program perception in yet other ways. The distinctive language of a culture may provide the people of given society different vistas of the world than those experienced by individuals in another culture, especially in terms of colors, sounds, shapes, and textures, not to mention the assembly of various cultural elements. Cultural conditioning, and the shared experiences of a society's people cause them to have differential ways of viewing reality. What is true in this regard from culture to culture is equally valid from subculture to subculture, and even from status category to status category within a given society such as that of the U.S.

The rich do not see things exactly as the poor. F. Scott Fitzgerald was quite astute in his observation that the rich are different. They are, indeed, different from you (unless you and yours are rich) and I. Because of gender role conditioning and differential treatment and experiences, males and females have disparate perceptions and conceptions of reality and the social context in which they exist. Education surely widens, or even opens new, social vistas, and white Americans and black Americans tend to live in different perceptive worlds. (Some years ago during the "War on Poverty," it was "discovered" that many black youngsters living in northern ghettos erroneously, but perhaps very rationally, based on the evidence they observed, believed that the majority of people in the United States were black!) The rural dweller and the urban citizen, the Southerner and the New Englander, the Chinese-American and the Mexican American, the elderly and the young, all have contrasting perceptions and viewpoints. All of these dimensions (and many others) impact on the public's perception of deviance.

Interestingly, although criminologists had been systematically studying crime in the U.S. for decades, it was 1939 before the public or criminologists "discovered" white-collar crime when it was pointed out to them by Edwin Sutherland, the President of the American Sociological Association in his presidential address (1940). Presumably, because of the tendency to assume that when persons of high social status committed legal transgressions, they were only engaged in shrewd business practices, or perhaps, could simply do no wrong according to the prevalent definition of crime at that time, white-collar offenses were often not perceived as criminal or deviant. As Edward Sagarin (1975) described the situation:

> Edward Sutherland was almost single-handedly responsible (and with great opposition, at that) for attempting to redefine crime in the minds of the American people, so that they would see respectable people as criminals when they violate the law. The concept of white-collar crime was an effort at just such a redefinition.

Today, with full recognition (but still a considerable amount of tolerance) of the existence of white-collar crime, it appears that such criminal activities may well be more costly to society than all of the endeavors of organized crime combined.

Child abuse in the U.S. went almost unrecognized until the 1960s. Battered children who were seen by family physicians or in hospital emergency rooms were considered to have been the victims of household accidents, or in some instances, the result of overly zealous parental discipline. In either case, it was considered to be a family matter, and of no concern to the public. Studies such as the pioneering surveys by the American Humane Association, Brandeis University, and the National Opinion Research Center of the University of Chicago, all in the 1960s sensitized the American public to the existence of child abuse as a widespread form of deviant behavior and a social problem of national proportions (see Pfohl, 1977). After that time, hospitals and clinics began to routinely make X-ray examinations of infants and children who were brought in in a bruised or battered condition. Hospitals and physicians began to report battered children to law enforcement authorities, who in turn developed procedures for investigating and processing such cases as criminal offenses.

In a similar manner, until relatively recently, it was widely believed that incest was extremely rare in our society, and essentially confined to isolated, rural, lower-class families. Spouse abuse was also assumed to be largely a lower-class phenomenon and simply part of the family interactive repertoire. Such behavior was believed not to exist in other contexts even though there were indicators that it did. Because of the way in which it was socially defined, it was not perceived and, thus, did not socially exist. Research has shown quite the opposite. Incest and sexual abuse within the family appears to sometimes occur in families of all social class levels, and is far from rare or isolated. Spouse abuse also has been shown to be a widespread activity that takes place in marriages at every socioeconomic level. As with child abuse, however, the public had to be sensitized to the existence of spouse abuse before full awareness was possible (see Tierney, 1982). The public *now* perceives such deviance where it formerly did not.

Just as the public may fail to perceive deviancy or to define certain norm violating behavior as deviant, so too may members of a society perceive deviancy where none exists. In such cases, the deviant sexual activity is delusional in that it exists exclusively in the mind of the beholder and is, thus, spurious. The absence of an actual behavior, or of genuine guilt, however, may not dilute the social import of even spurious, but believed deviant behavior.

Today's rationality persuades us that the so-called "witches" of seventeenth-century Salem could not possibly be guilty of the crimes of which they were accused, yet the presumption of crime, even though spurious, did in fact lead to their death as punishment. Many persons experience the consequences of deviancy, even if spurious, projected on them by others of suspicious bent. Deviant labeling is very real, socially speaking, even if the process lacks valid foundation. In this regard, prevalent societal stereotypes may well cause a significant proportion of the population to project or attribute various kinds of deviant behavior on a wide array of social status categories, and, indeed, even types of physical appearance (Shoemaker, Smith, and Lowe, 1973), even though there is no evidence to support such attribution. In the instance of marital status, for example, it is widely believed that divorcees are more carnal and lecherous than are married or never married females. Other stereotypical attributions of deviancy might include the belief that all gypsies are thieves, many old men are "degenerate" (see Whiskin, 1968), all politicians are "crooks," male hair stylists are homosexual, all strippers are prostitutes, blacks are more lustful than whites, and many Italians (especially Sicilians) are gangsters. Catholics (and Mormons among others) historically were persecuted in this country because it was widely believed that they indulged in unspeakable acts of deviant behavior (i.e., sexual debauchery among nuns and priests in convents, as well as nefarious Satanic rites and ritualistic infanticide in such settings) (see Chaplin, 1959).

Even where deviance is perceived (and where spurious deviance is not perceived), the public reaction may vary considerably depending on a number of factors. Deviant behavior is not always viewed with the same degree of concern. Different types of deviance will elicit different kinds of public reaction. Murder obviously is viewed as more serious than jaywalking and will result in the application of a more severe sanction. Certain types of sexual deviancy, homosexuality, for example, may be viewed with more repugnance by the public than some types of economic deviance, such as petty theft, even though the former might be "victimless" deviance while the latter would not be. In a given society, there will be a range of toleration for various types of deviant behavior. The range of toleration may also change over time in a society. At one point in history (as recently as the 19th century) in England, homosexuality was sometimes punished by death or long imprisonment. Today, in England it has been legally decriminalized among consenting adults. In the U.S. in the past, homosexuals were persecuted and severely sanctioned, on occasion. Today, homosexuality is widely (although far from universally) accepted as simply an alternate sexual persuasion rather than perversion or deviance. A gay baseball team in San Francisco plays against a police team in one of the city leagues there. A number of openly admitted homosexuals have been elected or appointed to public office, and many prominent Americans in various professions make no attempt to hide their homosexual preference. Gay pride week is openly celebrated in many communities across the country.

In the past, individuals might relatively freely carry handguns, fight gamecocks, engage in duels, hunt any species of game they so desired, engage the services of a prostitute, gamble, purchase and use morphine (and other narcotic substances), exploit child labor, maintain unsafe working conditions in one's own mill or mine, whip their wife, and even in some instances kill an Indian. Today any or all of these activities would cause one to be labeled and treated as criminal for a variety of offenses ranging from murder to cruelty to animals to violation of the Endangered Species Act. In short, at one time, the public had little toleration for some behaviors then labeled as deviant, such as homosexuality, but today would appear to have considerable toleration for such behavior. On the other hand, the public had an almost unlimited toleration for many activities then barely labeled as deviant but today there is little, if any, toleration for behavior of this kind, and violators of the legal norms prohibiting such acts are frequently severely sanctioned.

The degree of toleration or nontoleration for given acts of deviant behavior may be relatively uniform across the membership of society or it may vary differentially depending on the status categories or socioeconomic characteristics of the members of society. The first selection in this chapter, Thomas J. Durant, Jr. and Cecilia Chan's "Social Tolerance for Crime and Justice: An Exploratory Analysis," is an empirical examination of such differential toleration of deviant behavior across social status categories. In this study, the sociodemographic factors that are investigated, as they impact on toleration are sex, race, and student-nonstudent status. The forms of deviant behavior tested for toleration include violent offenses, property offenses, and victimless offenses. Sex, race, and student-nonstudent status would all seem to be significant characteristics in terms of varying cultural conditions and experiences and, thus, differential perceptions of, and toleration of, deviance. The authors hypothesized that there would be different dichotomous toleration within each of the status category sets. It was further hypothesized that males would be more tolerant of all three types of deviant behavior than females, and that blacks would be more tolerant of violent and property crimes than whites, but that whites would be more tolerant of victimless crimes than blacks. The study also included the hypotheses that nonstudents would be more tolerant of violent and property crime than students, but that students would possess more toleration for victimless crime.

The results of the data analysis tended to generally support most of the hypotheses. With only two exceptions it appeared that the majority of all the categories disapproved of all three categories of deviance. The two exceptions were that the majority of whites and the majority of students did not disapprove of victimless crimes. As expected, there was the highest toleration for victimless crime and the lowest toleration for violent offenses, with property offenses ranked in between. Males were somewhat more tolerant toward property crimes and victimless crimes than were females, and blacks were less tolerant of property crimes than whites (many blacks had been victims of property crimes). Students were somewhat more tolerant of property crimes and victimless crimes than nonstudents. The article also further explores the findings in terms of differential toleration of deviance and discusses the implications. Many social, economic, and demographic factors, plus other considerations such as victimization experience, impact on toleration of deviance. Attorneys as well as social scientists are aware of this and often use this knowledge to good effect in jury selection and the manner in which they slant the presentation of their cases. Certainly, differential toleration of various kinds of deviance has considerable significance for societal reaction to deviant behavior, and the social disposition of such nonconformity.

If deviance is perceived, it will elicit a collective reaction based on the relative degree of social toleration or nontoleration which exists in a given social context. Behavioral nonconformity may be perceived as deviance, but so too may physical nonconformity such as deafness, blindness, being "albino," extreme variation in height or weight, deformity, loss of limbs, or any other type of physical disability, handicaps, or infirmity that represents a marked departure from the physical or physiological norm.[1]

In the perception of deviance, the public is extremely prone to make invidious comparisons, often seeking to magnify seemingly insignificant or inconsequential differences in behavior or appearance into categorical departures from the norm and, thus, deviant. Individuals especially sensitive to informal social control may have to assiduously conform to elaborate codes of fashion, including dress and hair styles, least they be labeled as deviant. To be socially accepted by peers, one must "follow the crowd," and slavishly conform to the prevailing standards and codes of dress, hair style, and mannerisms.

So strong is the need to curry approval by the peer group and to be accepted as normal, that some individuals, and especially young females, may go to pathological lengths to maintain what they believe to be the normative standards of slimness so admired in American society. Often holding a much exaggerated or distorted mental image of the normative model of slimness, some females will starve themselves, or go on eating binges followed by regurgitation as a means of holding down their weight and remaining slender. Such an approach to weight control has been identified as a disease syndrome and labeled as anorexia nervosa or bulimia (see

[1]Sometimes, the abnormal becomes the norm and the normal becomes the deviant. As the old saying goes, "In the land of the blind, the sighted man is King." In the science fiction novel, *I am Legend* by Richard Matheson (made into the movie, *The Omega Man* staring Charlton Heston), the author depicts a situation in which an atomic war has left the population partially blind and very susceptible to many diseases. The author has the protagonist, a man who was shielded during the atomic war, emerge unscathed after the attack, with immunity to the germs that are decimating the Earth's population and with intact eyesight. This "unfortunate" individual becomes the deviant because he is "different" from everyone else who seeks to kill him because of his difference.

McLorg and Taub, 1987). In our society, youthful slenderness is an attribute of beauty and desirability, and obesity is abhorred (Larking and Pines, 1979). In the effort to attain or maintain this distorted image of self, the individual may pursue pathological dietary practices to the point of disease and even death.

Just as variations from physical or physiological standards as well as behavioral norms may constitute deviance, so too may vagaries from customary standards in terms of the absence of behavior. Sins of omission may be just as serious as sins of commission. One example of such absence of behavior might be adopting the condition of celibacy and refraining from engaging in sexual intercourse. While mandated for Monks and Nuns, it is not infrequently considered "eccentric" or socially abnormal if encountered in bachelors or "old maids." Impotence, and subsequent inability to engage in sexual intercourse can be a legal grounds for divorce in some states, and represents marital role failure, and a deviation from expectations.

Another interesting case in point is the "failure" to have children. In some societies the normative mandate to produce progeny is religious as well as cultural. In many Christian denominations, there is a strong ideological residue of the Biblical injunction to "be fruitful, multiply and replenish the earth." The Catholic church, of course, proscribes the use of other than "natural" birth control methods. Sexually gratifying coitus that employs contraceptive techniques (and, thus, cannot result in pregnancy) is contrary to church teaching. Similarly, it was only recently that the Vatican ruled that sterilized men can enter into valid marriages. There have also been instances of paraplegic or otherwise impotent males who were not given the sanction of valid marriages in the Catholic church. If the impotent male could not engage in intergenital sexual activity, neither could he produce children.

Sometimes the question of the absence of children in marriage, or the presence of too many may have import for the normative social image of a couple. In his tongue-in-cheek (but devastatingly valid) book, *How to Be a Bishop without Being Religious*, Charles Marrill Smith (1965:24–25) points out that a successful minister with upwardly mobile aspirations must be cautious concerning the number of children that he and his wife have because of the image it may project. If a minister and his wife have no children or too few children, they may appear unusual, or not normal in not serving as a model family—being inadequate at producing children, or appearing not to like children, as it were. On the other hand, having too many children could prove to be socially stigmatizing. This might convey the image of excessive carnality. Instead the minister needs to have the number of children that would lead his congregation to believe that "he really didn't enjoy the procedure essential to this end very much [fathering children]." It is childlessness, however, that is often encountered in U.S. society with consequences for public judgment and reaction.

In the next reading in this chapter, "Perceptions of Informal Sanctioning and the Stigma of Involuntary Childlessness," Charlene E. Miall shows that the fact of having no children may cause a couple to be informally labeled as deviant. Perhaps because the "ideal" American family is invariably pictured as one with children, married couples often experience considerable social pressure to have children even if there are practical reasons to the contrary. The desire of the couple's parents to be grandparents, the need to emulate other couples with children who are friends and acquaintances, and simply recognizing the societal norm to reproduce oneself, may all serve as social pressures on the couple to have children. Social life among young married couples not infrequently includes conversation and activities revolving around children. Not to have children means being an outsider as it were.

As the article points out, previous research has shown that where a couple elects not to have children, they may be viewed as "selfish," "psychologically maladjusted," "sexually inadequate" or "emotionally immature." Similarly, as the author's research findings demonstrate, even if the couple's childlessness is involuntary, there is still a tendency to stigmatize them. The infertility, rather than eliciting social support from friends and family may instead elicit blame, ridicule, status degradation, and informal sanctioning. The cause of the couple's infertility was often viewed by friends as being psychological in origin or the result of sexual incompetence. For the former, couples were offered "cures" such as being told "to relax," not to "try too hard," or to take a holiday rest. In the instance of the latter, the friends provided advice for improving sexual techniques. The female in the dyad is frequently seen as the problem or is assigned the majority of the "blame." The couple may feel alienated and stigmatized, and experience a need to explain or justify their childlessness. Acquaintances may badger them with sexual advice. Infertility is frequently a master status with serious social implications for the social identity of the individual. A childless wife may be conceptualized as an incomplete or unfulfilled female and the male's infertility may be viewed as an "assault on his masculinity." The childless couple, regarded as cultural deviants by friends and family may experience a variety of social sanctions such as sarcasm, ridicule, and undue attention in an attempt to bring about their acquiescence.[2]

The objective reality of deviant behavior is not necessarily the same as that to which the public reacts. Deviance must be perceived and interpreted, and constituent to that interpretation is the symbolic construction of a social reality. In short, that which is, does not necessarily translate into that

[2]The theme of childlessness on the part of a couple and the resultant social pressures to conceive a child or adopt one is a popular and durable one in television family drama shows and soap operas, appearing even in series such as "Dallas."

which is experienced by the public. As a result of cultural orientations or idiosyncratic bias or perceptual distortions, members of a society may construct their own social reality when perceiving and interpreting deviant behavior.

Members of society are not necessarily left to their own devices (or perception) in experiencing reality (including deviant behavior), however, but are instead often aided, facilitated, and directed (in their attention) by the mass media. At the simplest level, a newspaper or television reporter, like a good author, attempts to dramatize a description of an event or situation thereby heightening the experience for the reader, listener, or looker. The reporter also may try and direct the individual's attention to certain aspects or elements of the event or situation. In doing these things, of course, the reporter may intentionally (or unintentionally) slant or distort the event or situation in terms of the reader or viewer's perception. A skilled reporter can help shape the social reality constructed by the individual. Where the mass media embarks on a large-scale, coordinated effort to project the news about an event or situation in a particular light, it can quite readily create a symbolic social reality for the public.

In this sense, the mass media can play a powerful part in creating the social reality of a crime, a disaster, or an episode of deviant behavior for the public. The mass death at Jonestown, Guyana, in 1978 was news of a sensational variety, but as with many news stories, the sensationalism has to be enhanced in order to extract the maximum newsworthiness from the event. In a not surprising fashion, the mass media attempted and succeeded in constructing a symbolic social reality of their own design for the public to experience in order to effectively accomplish their purpose.

In the next reading, Danny L. Jorgensen's "The Social Construction and Interpretation of Deviance: Jonestown and the Mass Media," the author describes and analyzes this process. In regard to the Jonestown tragedy, Jorgensen points out that "official reality of these events . . . [as it was] fashioned and presented by the mass media . . . [resulted in an] interpretation [that] was highly selective and stylized." The Jonestown event received an inordinate amount of media coverage. It contained a wealth of raw material for news and, according to Jorgensen, Jonestown was readily made into a major media event for several reasons. It occurred during a time of "little competition" inasmuch as it was a "slow news period." Cults of one kind or another had a lot of prominence in the media at the time and, thus, the topic was current and relevant. The fact that Jonestown involved death and violence—"blood and gore," as it were—gave it significant commercial value. There was a paucity of accurate first-hand information, particularly at first, but a big demand for news. Jorgensen concludes that this situation contributed to "distortion, bias, and out-and-out deception." Prior to the events that propelled Jonestown into this mainstream of news, it had been viewed in a much different light. The People's Temple was simply categorized as an "alternate religious sect," and its activities had been occasionally reported in the newspapers in a generally favorable fashion. Its leader, Jim Jones, was often "portrayed as a friend of the poor and a promoter of social equality and justice and other humanitarian causes." Jones had even won The Humanitarian of the Year Award in 1976, as presented by the *Los Angeles Herald*.

After the deaths at Jonestown, the People's Temple was frequently labeled as a cult and it was assumed that its members were recruited into its ranks because of socioeconomic deprivation, depravity, or mental pathology. Jones was depicted as sinister, guilty of a variety of misdeeds, and probably insane. From such premises, there is only a short distance to interpretations of perversions, enslavement, criminal activities, mind-control, madness, and mass murder. Reality can have a manufactured veneer to embellish it. According to Jorgensen, "official versions of reality are constructed and imposed on events." News is a social product and such may often be the case with accounts of deviant behavior.

Even when nonconforming behavior is validly perceived as deviant, the public reaction is not necessarily negative. Deviant behavior may not only be tolerated, in some instances it may be approved, applauded, or even encouraged. Thus, a delinquent male teenager who successfully perpetrates some petty theft may be the object of respect or adulation on the part of his peers. His delinquency might even elevate him to leadership of the informal group. The adolescent female who has lost her virginity the night before and confides the fact to her girlfriends may be viewed more as a worldly *femme fatale* than as a fallen woman. Her sexual experience may now make of her something of an authority, advisor, and arbiter of courtship behavior.

There are many instances of deviant as hero. The school "cut-up" or "fool" is often cheered rather than chastised for his nonconformity antics by his fellow students. The rebel or "maverick" has historically frequently been viewed as a hero rather than a zero because of his innovative and persevering orientation. Even criminals—murderers, robbers, and scoundrels—have had their share of accolades and adulation. Robin Hood, fact or fiction, was widely admired by the common folk for his altruistic tendency to rob from the rich and give to the poor. Jesse James, who fought the exploitative corporate vested interest of the railroads by robbing them, lives on in song and folklore as a hero. Vice can easily become virtue in the minds of the public. The public tends to be fickle in its hero worship, however, and it appears that the virtuous labeling of villains may tend to run in historical cycles. In the next selection in this chapter, James K. Skipper, Jr., in his "Nicknames of Notorious American Twentieth-Century Deviants: The Decline of the Folk Hero Syndrome," looks at such a trend or cycle in this century. Skipper asserts the labeling of an individual with an "official" nickname is an indication of folk-hero status. The function of the nickname is to "break down barriers of formality, increase identification, and create a sense of closeness." Using a directory of American nicknames as a data source, Skipper found those persons with nicknames who had engaged in behavior subject to legal prosecution. He found 198 such individuals for the period 1900–1979. Looking at their appearance in speech and literature by time period, Skipper discovered that the number of deviants with public nicknames varied by decade. From 1900, the number rose by decade to a peak in the 1920–1929 period, dropped only slightly in the 1930–1939 decade and declined in subsequent decades. It was the Bootlegger-Racketeer-Gangster type of deviant that appears to predominate during the 1920–1939 decades. Skipper feels that prohibition and the depression were important factors in this trend. Prohibition was not uniformly supported throughout the population, and much of the public openly violated the liquor laws. Prohibition provided opportunities for some individuals to amass great profits by supplying the illegal alcohol. The depression was a period of widespread economic deprivation, and those individuals who "robbed the haves in a have not era," banks and other financial institutions, for example, were made into folk heroes. Many such individuals were of ethnic backgrounds and this identity may well have facilitated the gaining of folk hero status especially among others of ethnic origin. Merton had spoken of the innovator and, indeed, it was only through innovation that many Americans, especially persons of the lower class and ethnic background, were able to achieve success. The Gangster-Racketeer-Bootlegger type deviants achieved success including fame (or infamy) and fortune through innovative, even if illegitimate ways. As Skipper puts it, "These hard times created an atmosphere conducive to admiring, identifying, and glorifying those who beat the system—albeit by illegal means." World War II and the more prosperous subsequent decades caused the number of hero economic deviants to decline. In more recent decades, it is perhaps the political deviants, the protesters and demonstrators that received the public accolades. Such protests against the establishment may come closer to fitting the Mertonian "rebellion" model than the "innovation" model, according to Skipper. Thus, given the right time and circumstances, deviance may be well received by the public, who may even elevate the offenders to folk hero status in the process of admiring and sympathizing with them.

Deviants can be elevated to the status of folk heroes, or they can be leveled with negative identities disproportionate to their offenses. Some deviance may be tolerated to varying degrees, and in other instances deviant behavior may be identified on the basis of invidious comparison of relatively inconsequential variance from the norm. Sometimes, individuals can be accused of deviance when there is no basis whatsoever. This situation is explored in the final article in this section, Lloyd W. Klemke and Gary H.

Tiedeman's "Toward An Understanding of False Accusation: The Pure Case of Deviant Labeling." Expanding an earlier typological category of Becker's, the authors focus on the falsely accused deviant and the social processes by which these "false conceptions of social reality" are generated.

False accusation sometimes occurs at a mass level as well as at an individual. Persons may be falsely accused of a crime they did not commit and be subsequently unjustly convicted and imprisoned (or even executed). In World War II, however, more than 110,000 Japanese-Americans were uprooted from their homes and communities and confined in "relocation camps" because it was feared and assumed that they would be disloyal to the U.S., might aid and abet the enemy, and could possibly become saboteurs or otherwise engage in behavior harmful to the war effort. Other examples of mass false accusation might include individuals from culturally deprived backgrounds being falsely labeled as retarded on the basis of low IQ tests, and school children being labeled as handicapped or retarded and requiring special education when, in fact, they had no such problems. Although the U.S. law enforcement system and the criminal justice and jurisprudence system go to great lengths to guard against punishing the innocent, or falsely labeling individuals, it does occur.

In their examination of the phenomenon of false accusation, the authors posit four ideal type categories of such labeling. The first category is *Pure Error* which is the result of mistakes, accidents, problems with perception, memory, or recognition, and confusion. It might also occur when an individual is falsely stigmatized because of an association or affiliation with deviants. A second category of false accusation is *Intentional Error*. Included here might be perjury for personal gain, police arresting innocent persons because of arrest quotas or initiating incriminating information as a means of enhancing one's situation. Also under this category would be included capricious and vindictive efforts to incriminate and thus harm others. Police might plant evidence as a means of arresting someone they sought to "get." Also false accusation may be used to divert attention from one's own guilt.

The authors also suggest the category of *Legitimized Error*. Here false accusation is based on erroneous assumptions. Deviance may be imputed for reasons that are not valid, such as attributing behavior because of stereotypical beliefs. It could also result from defective indicators such as IQ tests that do not accurately indicate mental retardation, or relying on psychiatric symptoms to diagnose schizophrenia that are not valid.

The final category is *Victim-Based Error*. Here the victim solicits a deviant label, even if false, in order to accomplish some personal goal. The young man who pretends to be mentally ill or a homosexual to avoid being drafted. Corporal Clinger on the M*A*S*H television series, who pretended to be a transvestite in order to try and get out of the Army, would be such an example. Yet other illustrations would be individuals who feign physical handicaps in order to receive welfare, or the individual who confesses to crimes he did not commit in order to receive the publicity he craves.

The authors suggest that a variety of situational contexts may promote or precipitate false accusations. Such contexts include Perceived Threat, Subcultural Heterogeneity, Domain Protectionism, Stereotype Adoption, and Diagnostic Oversimplification. According to Klemke and Tiedeman, false accusors are "likely to possess power, insider status, organizational backing, a profit motive, or legitimacy ('expert' status)." Conversely, those likely to be falsely accused tend to possess "little power, outsider status, no organizational backing, or a lack of legitimacy." The authors conclude that in spite of critics of labeling theory who contend that "one acquires a deviant label primarily because of one's deviant behavior," labeling does occur in the absence of deviant behavior. As they see it, in a complex, bureaucratic society such as our own, "scale and ideology begets expediency, expediency begets simplification, and simplification begets error."

Deviant behavior is not simply a special category of objectively observed activity, but rather involves a process that includes the creation or establishment of norms, the differential perception of the norms, the interpretation of certain behavior (or lack of it) as norm violation, and the subsequent reaction to this interpretation with attendant social import. There is an elaborate subjective dimension to deviant behavior. Even the establishment of norms may be posited on subjectively perceived criteria. Social norms may be as much idiosyncratic, or even irrational, as rational. The violation of norms has to be perceived, and then defined as such inasmuch as such a definition is a function of time, place, and context, and there are also extenuating and mitigating circumstances. Even if the behavior is defined as deviance, the offender is not always considered as deviant, just as sometimes the individual may be labeled as deviant when no deviance occurred.

Deviant behavior is not as much an objective reality as socially constructed reality, with a wide variety of categorical characteristics on the part of the public who react to the violation of norms, determining the type of reality construction and, thus, effecting the relativity of deviance. The absence of certain expected behavior or behavioral outcome can be considered just as deviant as the occurrence of vagrant activity as a norm violation. Even the construction of a social reality which defines and reifies deviant behavior can be embellished or amplified with a facilitated or distorted treatment in the mass media. Relatively mundane occurrences can be transformed into vagrancy of enormous proportions if properly contorted or augmented by the press who, in effect, expedite the creation of a desired type of social reality on the part of the public. Offenders, if defined as deviants, are not necessarily labeled in a negative fashion. The public may instead react to the deviancy in a positive fashion, and make virtue out of vice. The offender may be elevated to the level of hero and his actions deemed worthy of social emulation, no matter how objectively reprehensible. On the other hand, some individuals may acquire an extremely negative label even though they are guilty of no social transgression whatsoever if the accusations of their deviance are false for whatever the reason. Such a situation still involves a social construction of reality but in this instance, the reality is totally inauthentic.

In the final analysis, the social significance of deviant behavior lies not so much in the event itself, as in the perception of the event, the attendant interpretation, and the subsequent response. Deviant behavior is, in effect, what we make of it.

REFERENCES

Chaplin, J. R.
1959 "The 'secrets' of the nunnery." Pp. 13–29 in Rumor, Fear and the Madness of Crowds. New York: Ballantine Books.

Hunt, Morton
1967 The World of the Formerly Married. Greenwich, Connecticut: Fawcett Publications, Inc., esp. pp. 92–117.

Larkin, Judith Candib, and Harvey A. Pines
1979 "No fat persons need apply: Experimental studies of the overweight stereotype and hiring preference." Sociology of Work and Occupations 6:312–327.

McLorg, Penelope A., and Diane E. Taub
1987 "Anorexia nervosa and bulimia: The development of deviant identities." Deviant Behavior 8:177–189.

Pfohl, Stephen J.
1977 "The 'discovery' of child abuse." Social Problems 24:310–315.

Sagarin, Edward
1975 Deviants and Deviance: An Introduction to the Study of Disvalued People and Behavior. New York: Praeger.

Shoemaker, Donald J., Donald R. South, and Jay Lowe
1973 "Facial stereotypes of deviants and judgments of guilt or innocence." Social Forces 51:427–433.

Smith, Charles M.
1965 "Selecting a clerical wife." Pp. 19–28 in How to Become a Bishop Without Being Religious. Garden City, New York: Doubleday.

Sutherland, Edwin H.
1940 "White-collar criminality." American Sociological Review 5:1–12.

Tierney, Kathleen J.
1982 "The battered women movement and the creation of the wife beating problem." Social Problems 29:207–220.

Whiskin, Frederick E.
1968 "Delinquency in the aged." Journal of Geriatric Psychiatry 1:242–252.

Reading 9

Social Tolerance for Crime and Deviance: An Exploratory Analysis

Thomas J. Durant, Jr., and Cecilia Chan
Louisiana State University, Baton Rouge

An exploratory analysis was conducted with the use of a quota sample of 486 college students and nonstudent community residents, in order to determine variation in social tolerance by sex, race, and student-nonstudent status. The study demonstrated that social tolerance can be a theoretically useful concept for studying variations in reactions to criminal and deviant behavior among social groups. Implications of the findings for future research in this area are discussed.

INTRODUCTION

There is some indication that the public has become more apathetic toward the control of crime and deviance[1] in the U.S. society. We believe that this attitude to criminal and deviant behavior may be properly conceptualized as social tolerance. Jessor (1968) defined tolerance of deviation as the degree of personal acceptance or tolerance of transgression. Tolerance of transgression was defined as the degree to which a person expects that such behavior will be followed by punishment or negative sanctions or the degree to which he expects that such behavior is required in order to achieve given goals. Social tolerance is defined here as the degree to which a particular kind of socially or legally defined deviance is permitted to proceed within a given social entity without active intervention of group members or outsiders as individuals or as a group to oppose, suppress, eliminate, or discourage the misconduct.[2]

This study was conducted as an exploratory effort to shed some light on social tolerance of males compared with females, blacks compared with whites, and college students compared with nonstudents, for three broad

[1]Deviance is defined as conduct in violation of the dorminant social norms (Davis, 1970:34–36). Crime is considered a form of deviance involving violations of legal codes or laws.

[2]This definition of social tolerance is a modification of the definition employed by Elmer Johnson (1973:36).

categories of crime, that is, violent crimes, property crimes, and victimless crimes. The major assumpiton that guided this study was that norms, values, definitions of deviant or conforming behavior, and range of tolerance for a given form of deviance vary by sex, race, and student-nonstudent status.[3]

THEORETICAL ORIENTATION

From our viewpoint, social tolerance is a theoretically useful concept for studying individual or community responses to criminal and deviant behavior, as an alternative to focusing on the criminal, the victim, or formal agents of social control. In other words, we believe that by focusing on the public's response (that is, the nondeviant's) to deviance through the use of the concept of social tolerance, greater insight can be gained into the sources of deviance. Feldman (1978) believes that we must not only study the deviant but the community to learn of its standards and to learn who in the community is most important in labeling. That is, we must ask, is it the public at large, official agents of labeling such as police, psychiatrists, or social workers, or members of the deviant's primary group, such as close friends or relatives?

Social tolerance is implied by the societal reaction and labeling perspectives of deviance, as evidenced in the literature (White, 1975; Blumstein, 1974; Orcutt, 1973; and Conklin, 1971). According to Van Vechten (1940), the complex of variables of which the societal reaction is a function can be summed up and expressed in the concept of the tolerance quotient, a quantitative expression of deviation and the willingness of the community to accept or reject it. More recently, Erikson (1962) noted that deviance is a property conferred upon certain forms of behavior by the audiences that directly or indirectly witness them. Kitsuse (1962) also has indicated that it is the response of the conventional and conforming members of society who identify and interpret behavior as deviant that sociologically transforms people into deviants. Following the leads of his predecessor, that is, Frank Tannenbaum, Becker (1963) noted that the deviant is the one to whom that label has been successfully applied, and that deviant behavior is behavior that people so label. We infer from the above perspectives that the nature and degree of labeling is influenced by the level of tolerance for a given form of deviant behavior. It is assumed that there is a certain level of tolerance in the community for a given type of defiance and once this point is passed, labeling is applied (Feldman, 1978). Of course, people's level of tolerance of deviation is influenced by the strength of their norms toward

[3]Student-nonstudent status carries two important distinctions, that is, differences in age and social setting.

that deviation. Each norm can be thought of as having a tolerance limit, which is a function of the definition of a given behavior as deviant by an individual or group and the willingness to tolerate or suppress the behavior (Van Vechten, 1940; Lemert, 1951; Johnson, 1973). According to Sellin (1938), norms have varying degrees of strength, or "resistance potential," and deviaiton from norms can be measured by the degree of severity of the sanction imposed by the individual or the group.

Furthermore, we assume that the concept of social tolerance may be applied to individuals, social groups, or social categories and that the level of tolerance varies among individuals, social groups, or social categories. That social tolerance varies among different groups is implied by several empirical studies. In a study on reactions to mental illness, Yarrow and associates (1955) concluded that level of tolerance may be a function of specific personality needs and vulnerabilities, personal and family value systems, and the social supports and prohibitions regarding behavior. Goode (1978) found that users of marijuana tended to be more tolerant of a wide range of deviant behavior than nonusers. Goode also noted that there were a certain degree of latitude and tolerance and even patterns of accommodation with regard to alcoholism. Moreover, acts that are violently condemned in one setting may be tolerated or even encouraged in another (Goode, 1978).

Our study also assumes that social tolerance differs by such sociodemographic factors as sex, race, and student-nonstudent status. According to Becker (1963), the degree of tolerance, that is, the extent to which people will respond to a given act as deviant, varies over time and space and by social, economic, and demographic characteristics such as age, sex, class, and ethnicity of the deviant as well as the reactor. It is also possible that the intensity, degree, volume, and visibility of the deviation elicit different responses from different groups based on the importance attached to norms covering the deviation (Lemert, 1951). Individuals are not completely molded by the norms of the pertinent culture, and even though they are socialized to conform, many do not (Erikson, 1966). Thus, individuals may act and think differently toward deviance even in the same culture. In addition, groups or persons with different value priorities may differ as to whether a particular kind of deviance is dangerous, harmless, or socially desirable (Davis, 1965). Moreover, values may lead many people to become indignant over certain issues and call for changes (Kitsuse and Spector, 1973). The above evidence suggests that it is indeed feasible to assume that social tolerance for crime and deviance differs by sex, race, and student-nonstudent status.

METHODS

The data used in this study were gathered from students of Louisiana State University in Baton Rouge and the residents of three areas surrounding the university. The data were collected by the use of personal interview technique. A simple quota sample of 322 tudents (1.3% of the total student population) between the ages of 18 and 25 were interviewed at major campus locations, including the student union, the library, classrooms, dormitories, and the park. Likewise, a simple quota sample of 164 nonstudents were selected from one black and two white residential areas in the vicinity of the university (50% of the total hosuehold units of the area). Household blocks were selected randomly and one adult person of age 20 or older from each household, usually the husband or wife, was interviewed. Interviewing began on the selected blocks in a clockwise manner until the desired number of interviews was completed.

Three crime categories were developed from a series of criminal and deviant acts: (1) violent offenses, which included first-degree murder, forcible rape, and armed robbery; (2) property offenses, which included burglary, shoplifting, and theft; and (3) victimless offenses, which included marijuane use, performing an abortion by a physician, and homosexuality. These offenses were categorized with reference to the main target of the crime in a similar fashion to that employed by the Federal Bureau of Investigation (1978). Violent offenses included those of a violent nature committed under the interest of property, and victimless offenses included those without an apparent victim.

In order to determine the definition of an act as deviant, the following request was made: "First, I want to know whether you approve or disapprove of this act (name act) when committed by adults in this community." The fixed choices were: (1) approval and (2) disapproval.

In order to determine the level of approval or disapproval of the defined act, the following was asked: "Secondly, I want to know how much do you approve (disapprove) of this act (name act) when committed by adults in this community. Give your responses on a scale from 1 to 10, where 1 represents the lowest disapproval." This scale was dichotomized into two levels, (1) low and (2) high.

In order to determine the respondents' perceived seriousness of the offense and their opinion of the severity of the punishment for committing the offense, the following questions were asked:

"To what extent do you think this act (name act) is a serious problem for this city and its residents?"

"How severe do you think a person should be punished who commits this act (name act) in this city?"

A 10-point scale for each of the above questions was dichotomized into two levels, (1) low and (2) high.

HYPOTHESES AND RATIONALES

The following hypotheses and rationales were developed to guide the present study:

1 Social tolerance differs between males and females.
- **a** Fewer males than females will disapprove of violent crimes. Thus, males will be more tolerant of violent crimes than females.
- **b** Fewer males than females will disapprove of property crimes. Thus, males will be more tolerant of property crimes than females.
- **c** Fewer males than females will disapprove of victimless crimes. Thus, males will be more tolerant of victimless crimes than females.

2 Social tolerance differs between blacks and whites.
- **a** Fewer blacks than whites will disapprove of violent crimes. Thus, blacks will be more tolerant of violent crimes than whites.
- **b** Fewer blacks than whites will disapprove of property crimes. Thus, blacks will be more tolerant of propety crimes than whites.
- **c** Fewer whites than blacks will disapprove of victimless crimes. Thus, whites will be more tolerant of victimless crimes than blacks.

3 Social tolerance differs between college students and nonstudents.
- **a** Fewer nonstudents than college students will disapprove of violent crimes. Thus, nonstudents will be more tolerant of violent crimes than students.
- **b** Fewer nonstudents than college students will disapprove of property crimes. Thus, nonstudents will be more tolerant of property crimes than college students.
- **c** Fewer college students than nonstudents will disapprove of victimless crimes. thus, college students will be more tolerant of victimless crimes than nonstudents.

Sex is regarded as the most efficient statistical predictor of crime, inasmuch as 95% of all crimes are committed by males. Females are trained to be quiet, gentle, and conforming. Even though successful women are currently viewed in a positive light, they are usually negatively sanctioned if they appear masculine or achieve greater success than men, particularly their husbands (Mason et all, 1976). Many people feel that females are more cautious and guarded in entertaining new ideas (Maccoby, 1966). Others still regard men as the provider or breadwinner. Men are expected to be more active, ambitious, adventurous, and open to new ideas (Stub, 1975). Frequently, their roles lead them into violent, ugly, and competitive experiences, or at least into such situations. On account of these factors and traditional differential socialization practices, we have hypothesized that males will be more tolerant of all three categories of crime than females.

According to statistics, a larger percentage of blacks than whites commit crimes. Because many blacks are poor, property crimes are especially prevalent among them. Traditionally, blacks have been suppressed and discriminated against in areas such as educaiton, occupation, and housing. A larger percentage of blacks than whites are poorly educated, financially deprived, employed in low-status jobs, and in the lower classes. Between 1950 and 1967, the average income of blacks increased but the median income difference between whites and blacks also increased. Unemployment of blacks was three times the national average (Johnson, 1973). Living under such odds and relative deprivation, blacks are more likely than whites to be realistically receptive to violent crimes. Because of idealized beliefs about self-regulation and personal freedom, whites are expected to be more tolerant of victimnless crimes than blacks.

Compared with the public, youth in general and college students in particular are well protected and less likely to get involved in violence (Julian, 1973). The legal system is generally more lenient toward them when they do become involved with the law (Julian, 1973; Reid, 1976). The attitudes and value judgements of college students are likely to differ from those of the general public. College students tend to be romantic, idealistic, and permissive with respect to self-regulation. Contemporary students advocate freedom in behaviors not seen as harmful to others (Julian, 1973). Thus, college students are expected to be less tolerant of violent crimes and property crimes but more tolerant of victimless crimes than nonstudents.

RESULTS

With two exceptions, the results of this study indicated that the majority of the people of all groups expressed disapproval of all three categories of crime. The exceptions were that the majority of whites and students did not disapprove of victimless crimes (Table 1). The percentage scores for students and whites who disapproved of violent crimes and property crimes, respectively, were slightly higher than those for nonstudents and blacks. Contrary to expectation, males showed slightly greater perentage scores for disapproval of violent crimes than females. This small difference should not be taken seriously because the vast majority of males and females disapproved of violent crimes. A possible explanation for these results is that norms against violent crimes are just as strong among females as among males, even though females commit only a small percentage of violent

TABLE 1 Disappproval and Approval of Three Categories of Crime for Three Groups, Showing Percentage Scores[a]

Groups	N	Violent crimes: Disapproval	Violent crimes: Approval	Property crimes: Disapproval	Property crimes: Approval	Victimless crimes: Disapproval	Victimless crimes: Approval
Males	215	94.73	5.27	90.39	9.61	50.47	49.53
Females	269	92.80	7.20	91.80	8.20	56.77	43.23
		$x^2 = 8.76; 1df; p = 0.01$ $D = -0.019$		$x^2 = 1.04; 1df; p = 0.30$ $D = 0.014$		$x^2 = 16.50; 1df; p = 0.002$ $D = 0.063$	
Blacks	99	92.57	7.43	90.50	9.50	64.97	35.03
Whites	372	93.68	6.32	91.40	8.60	46.12	53.88
		$x^2 = 0.61; 1df; p = 0.50$ $D = -0.012$		$x^2 = 0.23; 1df; p = 0.70$ $D = -0.001$		$x^2 = 32.31; 1df; p = 0.001$ $D = -0.140$	
Students	322	99.17	0.83	95.30	4.70	49.60	50.40
Nonstudents	164	82.89	17.11	83.06	16.94	71.40	28.60
		$x^2 = 145.84; 1df; p = 0.001$ $D = -0.163$		$x^2 = 60.19; 1df; p = 0.001$ $D = -0.122$		$x^2 = 60.59; 1df; p = 0.001$ $D = 0.218$	

[a]Percentage scores were computed by dividing the total number of responses for all crimes and for a particular category by the number of responses in each specific category, that is, for disapproval and approval, respectively. Violent crimes included first-degree murder, armed robbery, and forcible rape. Property crimes included burglary, shoplifting, and theft. Victimless crimes included use of marijuana, performing an abortion, and homosexuality.

crimes. It is also very likely that males and females receive very similar, definite, and effective socializaiton toward disapproval of violent crimes.

Of greater importance is the fact that all groups showed much less disapproval of victimless crimes than violent crimes or property crimes. However, the percentage scores for disaproval of victimless crimes were lower for males, whites, and students, respectively, compared with females, blacks, and nonstudents (Table 1). As shown in the table, a significant difference was found between blacks and whites and between students and nonstudents, in terms of reaction to victimless crimes. In both cases, the strength of the relationship, as measured by the *D* coefficient,[4] was moderately strong. Other instances in which a significant difference occurred and in which the relationship was moderately strong were between student-nonstudent status and and violent crimes and between student-nonstudent status and property crimes. Generally, our measures of association support the conclusions reached on the basis of percentage scores, that is, that students approved more of victimless crimes than nonstudents.

Table 2 shows the level of disapproval of each category of crime by sex, race, and student-nonstudent status. The results indicate that all groups reported high disapproval of violent crimes. Although all groups reported high disapproval of property crimes, females showed greater disapproval than males, blacks more than whites, and nonstudents more than students. A significant association was found between property crimes and all three groups; however, the relationship between student-nonstudent status and level of disapproval of property crimes was very weak. The data in Table 2 also reveal a pattern of findings similar to that of Table 1; that is, generally, all groups showed less disapproval of victimless crimes than property crimes and less disapproval of property crimes than violent crimes. Specifically, females, blacks, and nonstudents showed much greater disapproval of victimless crimes, respectively, than males, whites, and students. These results are borne out by our measures of association in Table 2, in which a statistically significant difference was found between sex, race, and student-nonstudent status and level of disapproval of victimless crimes and property crimes. The stronger relationships, however, were found when victimless crimes were interrelated with sex, race, and student-nonstudent status.

Because level of disapproval may vary for each specific type of crime, Table 3 gives a breakdown of disapproval for each of the nine types of crime. The results revealed no significant difference between sex, race, and student-nonstudent status and level of disapproval of first-degree urder, forcible rape, or armed robbery. A significant difference, however, was found between sex, race, and student-nonstudent status and level of disap-

[4]The *D* coefficient, as presented by James A. Davis (1971), is equivalent to Sommer's *d*, a measure of the relationship between a nominal level variable and an ordinal level variable.

TABLE 2 Level of Disapproval[a] of Three Categories of Crime for Three Groups, Showing Percentage Scores

Groups	N	Violent crimes		Property crimes		Victimless crimes	
		Low disapproval	High disapproval	Low disapproval	High disapproval	Low disapproval	High disapproval
Males	215	1.87	98.13	32.31	67.69	69.56	30.44
Females	269	1.23	98.77	18.03	81.97	57.65	42.35
		$x^2 = 0.18; 1df; p = 0.70$ $D = -0.006$		$x^2 = 33.84; 1df; p = 0.001$ $D = 0.143$		$x^2 = 25.55; 1df; p = 0.001$ $D = -0.119$	
Blacks	99	2.22	97.78	15.56	84.44	41.48	58.52
Whites	372	1.27	98.73	26.67	73.33	68.53	31.47
		$x^2 = 4.13; 1df; p = 0.05$ $D = 0.009$		$x^2 = 13.07; 1df; p = 0.001$ $D = -0.111$		$x^2 = 47.89; 1df; p = 0.001$ $D = -0.259$	
Students	322	1.63	98.37	26.34	73.66	72.03	27.97
Nonstudents	164	1.28	98.72	21.15	78.85	46.79	53.21
		$x^2 = 0.10; 1df; p = 0.70$ $D = -0.003$		$x^2 = 4.78; 1df; p = 0.02$ $D = -0.052$		$x^2 = 40.73; 1df; p = 0.001$ $D = -0.252$	

[a]The disapproval score ranged from 1 to 10. Scores of 1 through 5 indicated low disapproval and 6 through 10 high disapproval. The higher the score in the scale for a particular crime, the higher the disapproval.

TABLE 3 Chi-square and D Coefficients for Level of Disapproval of Each Type of Crime by Sex, Race, and Student-Nonstudent Status

	Sex ($N=484$)		Race ($N=471$)		Student-nonstudent status ($N=486$)	
Type of Crime	x^2 1df	*D*	x^2 1df	*D*	x^2 1df	*D*
Violent crimes						
Murder (first-degree)	0.16	0.003	3.82	–0.002	0.08	–0.000
Rape (forcible)	0.49	–0.007	1.11	0.013	0.05	0.002
Robbery (armed)	0.95	–0.015	0.40	–0.004	0.57	–0.012
Property crimes						
Burglary	1.91	–0.033	1.70	–0.012	1.05	–0.026
Shoplifting	163.0[a]	0.180	2.72	–0.091	0.01	–0.004
Theft (petty)	22.14[a]	–0.215	16.63[a]	–0.230	7.02[b]	–0.126
Victimless crimes						
Marijuana use	13.37[a]	–0.164	20.60[a]	–0.252	59.86[a]	–0.359
Performing abortions	6.14[b]	–0.115	31.28[a]	–0.322	18.61[a]	–0.206
Homosexuality	2.75	–0.078	16.68[a]	–0.238	16.03[a]	–0.192

[a]Significant at or beyond the 0.001 level.
[b]Significant at the 0.01 level.

proval of theft, and between sex and level of disapproval of shoplifting. In addition, a significant difference was found between race and student-nonstudent status, and each type of victimless crime. Moreover, a significant difference was found between sex and level of disapproval of marijuana use and performing an abortion. Further comparisons of the specific types of crime are shown in Table 3.

The above findings suggest that if level of disapproval is used as an indicator of social tolerance all groups had low tolerance for violent crimes and property crimes. Males, whites, and students, however, had slightly more tolerance for property crimes than females, blacks, and nonstudents. In addition, males, whites, and students had much greater tolerance for victimless crimes than females, blacks, and nonstudents. The victimless crimes of marijuana use, performing an abortion, and homosexuality were tolerated to a greater extent than other types of crime.

Table 4 shows perceived seriousness of crime by sex, race, and student-nonstudent status. It can be observed in Table 4 that as one goes from violent crimes to property crimes to victimless crimes, the perceived seriousness for all groups declines. Intragroup analyses revealed no great difference in perceived seriousness of violent crimes by sex, race, or student-

TABLE 4 Perceived Seriousness of Three Categories of Crime for Three Groups, Showing Percentage Scores

Groups	N	Violent crimes		Property crimes		Victimless crimes	
		Low seriousness	High seriousness	Low seriousness	High seriousness	Low seriousness	High seriousness
Males	215	21.26	78.74	36.89	63.10	77.72	22.28
Females	269	17.08	82.92	27.32	72.68	68.72	31.28
		$x^2 = 3.46$;1df;$p = 0.05$ $D = -0.047$		$x^2 = 13.53$;1df;$p = 0.001$ $D = 0.080$		$x^2 = 16.72$;1df;$p = 0.001$ $D = -0.095$	
Blacks	99	9.63	90.37	24.07	75.93	52.22	47.78
Whites	372	21.08	78.92	33.63	66.37	77.94	22.06
		$x^2 = 8.77$;1df;$p = 0.01$ $D = -0.092$		$x^2 = 17.02$;1df;$p = 0.001$ $D = 0.111$		$x^2 = 36.75$;1df;$p = 0.001$ $D = -0.179$	
Students	322	17.13	82.87	35.90	64.10	79.14	20.86
Nonstudents	164	23.08	76.92	23.93	76.07	61.32	38.68
		$x^2 = 1.33$;1df;$p = 0.30$ $D = -0.030$		$x^2 = 5.17$;1df;$p = 0.02$ $D = -0.060$		$x^2 = 26.91$;1df;$p = 0.001$ $D = -0.130$	

nonstudent status. The vast majority of all groups perceived violent crimes as being very serious offenses.

Although small differences occurred among the groups, with reference to perceived seriousness of property crimes, the strongest relationship was found between race and property crimes. Accordingly, blacks perceived property crimes as being more serious than did whites. Although strong associations were not manifested, females and nonstudents perceived property crimes as more serious than did males and students, respectively.

The major differences in perceived seriousness of victimless crimes occurred by race and student-nonstudent status. As a whole, a fairly strong association was found between race and student-nonstudent status, respectively, and perceived seriousness of victimless crimes. In terms of direction of the association, whites and students perceived victimless crimes as being less serious than did blacks and nonstudents.

On the basis of the above results, it appears that when perceived seriousness of crime is used as an indicator of social tolerance, males and whites tend to be more tolerant of violent crimes and property crimes than females and blacks. Nonstudents were slightly more tolerant of violent crimes than students, whereas students were more tolerant of property crimes. Males, whites, and students were more tolerant of victimless crimes than females, blacks, and nonstudents, respectively. Of further importance is the fact that the strongest relationships were found between race and perceived seriousness of victimless crimes, between race and perceived seriousness of property crimes, and between student-nonstudent status and perceived seriousness of victimless crimes.

Table 5 shows the severity of punishment assigned by respondents to each category of crime by sex, race, and student-nonstudent status. The data in this table reveal that as one goes from violent crimes to property crimes, to victimless crimes, the severity of punishment assigned declines. There was little difference by sex, race, or student-nonstudent status and severity of punishment assigned to violent crimes. The vast majority of all groups felt that very severe punishment should be assigned for violent crimes. With regard to property crimes, females, blacks, and nonstudents supported stiffer punishment compared with males, whites, and students. However, only in the case of race as related to property crimes, was the strength of the association found to be moderately strong. With reference to victimless crimes, females, blacks, and nonstudents believed that more severe punishment should be applied, compared with males, whites, and students. As shown in Table 5, a significant association and a fairly strong relationship was found between race and victimless crimes and also between student-nonstudent status and victimless crimes.

If severity of punishment is considered an indicator of social tolerance, then males, whites, and students were more tolerant of victimless crimes

TABLE 5 Perceived Severity of Punishment for Three Categories of Crime for Three Groups, Showing Percentage Scores

Groups	*N*	Violent crimes		Property crimes		Victimless crimes	
		Low severity	High severity	Low severity	High severity	Low severity	High severity
Males	215	7.00	93.00	50.00	50.00	76.19	23.81
Females	269	4.92	95.08	37.57	62.43	68.58	31.42
		$x^2 = 4.86; 1df; p = 0.05$ $D = -0.030$		$x^2 = 16.89; 1df; p = 0.001$ $D = -0.093$		$x^2 = 8.89; 1df; p = 0.01$ $D = -0.089$	
Blacks	99	10.37	89.63	32.96	67.04	54.81	45.19
Whites	372	5.00	95.00	46.37	53.63	76.37	23.63
		$x^2 = 10.97; 1df; p = 0.001$ $D = 0.059$		$x^2 = 10.12; 1df; p = 0.001$ $D = -0.175$		$x^2 = 22.55; 1df; p = 0.001$ $D = -0.138$	
Students	322	5.59	94.41	45.57	54.43	79.84	20.16
Nonstudents	164	6.84	93.16	39.32	60.68	57.69	42.31
		$x^2 = 0.35; 1df; p = 0.70$ $D = 0.008$		$x^2 = 3.23; 1df; p = 0.10$ $D = -0.041$		$x^2 = 28.32; 1df; p = 0.001$ $D = -0.124$	

than females, blacks, and nonstudents. Our results suggest that as criminal acts increase in seriousness, the severity of the assigned punishment also increases. Generally, low tolerance was found to be associated with the assignment of severe punishment.

SUMMARY AND CONCLUSIONS

Our exploratory study revealed that for all groups considered, that is, sex, race, and student-nonstudent status, tolerance was highest for victimless crimes and lowest for violent crimes. Property crimes ranked in between but leaned more in the direction of low tolerance. Based on these results, it appears that the greater the disapproval of a criminal or deviant act, the lower the social tolerance. Conversely, low disapproval is correlated with high social tolerance.

Our hypothesis that males would be more tolerant of violent crimes, property crimes, and victimless crimes than females received partial support. Both males and females expressed strong disapproval of violent crimes and property crimes. Males were found to be more tolerant of property crimes than females, however. Males were also found to be more tolerant of victimless crimes than females. This more tolerant reaction of males toward property crimes and victimless crimes may be a reflection of their perceptions of the real world they face and their experiences. It is also possible that even after the advent of women's liberation and sex equality movements, females are still less tolerant of certain property and victimless crimes and toward experimenting with "deviant" innovations.

Our hypothesis that blacks would bve more tolerant of violent crimes and property crimes and that whites would be more tolerant of victimless crimes was supported in part. This study found no difference between blacks and whites with reference to tolerance for violent crimes. Both groups highly disapproved of violent crimes. Contrary to expectation is the fact that blacks showed slightly lower tolerance for property crimes than did whites. This may be explained by the fact that blacks are just as likely, and sometimes more likely, to be victims of property crimes as whites. Many of the blacks included in the study reported that they had been victims of black-on-black property crimes in their neighborhood and complained about the lack of police protection. The rationale here is that high victimization leads to low tolerance for a given crime. As hypothesized, whites showed higher tolerance for victimless crimes than did blacks.

Our hypothesis that nonstudents would be more tolerant of violent and property crimes but less tolerant of victimless crimes than students was partially supported. With few exceptions our study revealed no great difference between students and nonstudents in terms of tolerance for violent and property crimes. Students, however, were found to be slightly more tolerant of property crimes than nonstudents. Students were found to be much more tolerant of victimless crimes than nonstudents. This finding is consistent with the results of a study by the U.S. Department of Justice (1977), which revealed that students were much more tolerant of the use of marijuana than the general public. As suggested earlier, college students may tend to be more idealistic about deviance and value personal liberty and self-regulation. Perhaps they are much more likely to engage in such victimless crimes as smoking marijuana. If these assumptions are correct, it is not surprising that students were found to be more tolerant of victimless crimes, which they see as personal and not harmful to others.

Although our study concluded that social tolerance for some forms of deviance exists to some degree among different groups, our results must be accepted with caution. This study was analytically descriptive, nondefinitive, and exploratory in nature. More theoretically definitive and methodologically rigorous studies must be conducted before stronger conclusions can be made concerning social tolerance.

IMPLICATIONS

The aim of this study was simply to demonstrate in an exploratory fashion that social tolerance can be a theoretically useful concept for studying variations in tolerance of criminal and deviant acts among various social groupings. We feel, however, that the results of our study have several important implications that should be considered by those contemplating research in this area. A major implication of our study is that the higher the tolerance for a given deviant act, the greater the difficulty in controlling this act within a given social entity. Conversely, low tolerance enhances the control of a given deviant act. Future research should focus on factors that influence this relationship within different social entities, including family, church, peer, work, friendship, neighborhood, minority, and protest groups. (For example, see Bryant's anthology (1974) of organizational bases of deviant behavior.) From a practical view, a proper understanding of social tolerance and its relationship to deviant behavior within different social groups may yield valuable information for agencies that face the challenge of correction and control of crime and deviance.

Another implication that can be drawn from our study is that high tolerance for certain criminal or deviant acts may reflect only value differences, anti-establishment attitudes, or the call for social changes by members of certain groups. In the theoretical orientation of Emile Durkheim (1933), high social tolerance by a given social group may be functional for its members and may also serve as a prerequisite for social change. To this extent, deviance is not absolute but defined in sociocultural relativity within group boundaries. Our finding that social tolerance varies by sex, race, and student-nonstudent status in a sense reflects the true picture of the world. People of different nations, societies, or social groups are socialized into different cultures or subcultures. They differ in terms of race, ethnicity, social class, values, and cultural standards. It is not strange then that most people are ethnocentric and incapable of tolerating ideas, attitudes, actions, and behavior different from those familiar to them. Herein lies the potential for comparative group or cultural studies on social tolerance.

If it is true that the public is becoming more tolerant of certain forms of deviance, then it may be true that we are losing a very important means of social control, that is, the informal control of deviance by the public. In a society where high tolerance and apathy of deviance prevail, greater reliance will be placed on formal agents of social control such as the police, and less reliance will be placed on the public as an informal means of norm enforcement. Thus, further research should focus on both attitudinal and behavioral aspects of public tolerance for crime as a part of the crime problem, in addition to the criminal, the victim, and formal agents of social control. In order to determine changes in social tolerance for various criminal and deviant acts, longitudinal research designs must be used. Studies should also show how changes in social tolerance among different groups are linked to such trends as increasing complexity, urbanization, industrialization, formalization, standardization, and impersonalization.

REFERENCES

Becker, Howard S.
1963 Outsiders: Studies in the Sociology of Deviance. New York: Free Press.

Blumstein, Alfred
1974 "Seriousness weights in an index of crime." American Sociological Review 39 (Dec.): 854-64.

Bryant, Clifton D.
1974 Deviant Behavior: Occupational and Organizational Bases. Chicago: Rand McNally.

Conklin, John E.
1971 "Dimensions of community response to the crime problem." Social Problems 18 (Winter): 373-85.

Davis, F. James
1975 "Beliefs, values, power and public definitions of deviance." In F. J. Davis and R. Strivers (Eds.), The Collective Definiiton of Deviance. New York: Free Press.

Davis, James A.
1971 Elementary Survey Analysis. Englewood Cliffs, N.J.: Prentice-Hall.

1970 Social Problems: Enduring Major Issues and Social Change. New York: Free Press.

Durkheim, Emile
1933 The Division of Labor in Society. New York: Macmillan.

Erikson, Kai T.
1966 Wayward Puritans: A Study in the Sociology of Deviance. New York: John Wiley.
1962 "Notes on the sociology of deviance." Social Problems 9 (Spring): 308–14.

Federal Bureau of Investigaiton
1978 Uniform Crime Reports. Washington, D.C.

Feldman, Saul D.
1978 Deciphering Deviance. Boston: Little, Brown and Company.

Goode, Erich
1978 Deviant Behavior: An Interactionist Approach. Englewood Cliffs, N.J.: Prentice-Hall.

Jessor, Richard
1968 "Toward a social psychology of excessive alcohol use: a preliminary report from the tri-ethnic project." In M. Lefton et al. (Eds.), Approaches to Deviance. New York: Appleton-Century Crofts.

Johnson, Elmer H.
1973 Social Problems of Urban Man. Homewood, Ill.: Dorsey Press.

Julian, Joseph
1973 Social Problems. New York: Appleton-Century Crofts.

Kitsuse, John
1962 "Societal reaction to deviant behavior: problems of theory and method." Social Problems 9 (Winter): 247–56.

Kitsuse, John, and M. Spector
1973 "Toward a sociology of social problems: social conditions, value judgements and social problems." Social Problems 20 (4): 407–18.

Lemert, Edwin M.
1951 Social Pathology. New York: McGraw-Hill.

Maccoby, E. E.
1966 The Development of Sex Differences. Palo Alto, Calif.: Stanford University Press.

Mason, Karen, J. Czajka, and S. Arber
1976 "Change in U.S. women's sex-role attitudes, 1964–1974." American Sociological Review 41 (4): 573–96.

Orcutt, James D.
1973 "Societal reaction and the response to deviance in small groups." Social Forces 52 (Sept.):259–67.

Reid, Sue Titus
1976 Crime and Criminology. Hinsdale, Ill.: Dryden Press.

Sellin, Thorsten
1938 Culture Conflict and Crime. Social Research Council Bulletin 41. New York.

Stub, Holger R.
1975 The Sociology of Educaiton: A Sourcebook. Homewood, Ill.: Dorsey Press.
U.S. Department of Justice
1977 Sourcebook of Criminal Justice Statistis. Washington, D.C.
Van Vechten, C.
1940 "The toleration quotient as a device for defining certain social concepts." American Journal of Sociology 46 (July): 35–42.
White, Garland F.
1975 "Public responses to hypothetical crimes: effects of offender and victim status and seriousness of the offense on punitive reaction." Social Forces 53 (March):411–19.
Yarrow, Marian R., et al.
1955 "The psychological meaning of mental illness in the family." Journal of Social Issues 11:12–26.

Reading 10

Perceptions of Informal Sanctioning and the Stigma of Involuntary Childlessness

Charlene E. Miall
McMaster University, Hamilton, Ontario

This study systematically examines the role of informal social response in the emergence of involuntary childlessness or infertility as a stigmatizing attribute. Seventy-one involuntarily childless women provide detailed instances of perceived informal social sanctions related to their infertility. Subjects perceive that normals consider infertility to be caused by psychological or sexual malfunctioning, or by the woman in the dyad. Infertility is also seen by some to act as a master status. Subjects categorize other infertile individuals in terms of stigma and consider male infertility to be more stigmatizing than female infertility. Social sanctions and social control are shown to be relevant to an understanding of the experience of involuntary childlessness.

INTRODUCTION

In the sociological literature on physical disability, much research has focused on the physically disabled as *deviant* because they violate societal norms of physical acceptability. Freidson (1966:73), for example, has characterized disability as a form of deviance because it can be viewed as conduct which violates "sufficiently valued norms" (Davis, 1961; Levitin, 1975;

Lorber, 1967; Smith, 1980). In their review of the literature, Hanks and Poplin (1981:322) have concluded that sociological research on disability generally demonstrates that the physically disabled are *stigmatized* by the rest of society. Indeed, the stigmatized status of the physically disabled has been examined in such diverse areas as amputee rehabilitation (Chaiklin and Warfield, 1977), obesity (Cahnman, 1968), the readjustment of paraplegics (Cogswell, 1977), epilepsy (Schneider and Conrad, 1980), leprosy (Gussow and Tracey, 1975), stuttering (Petrunik and Shearing, 1983), and blindness (Scott, 1969). In addition sociological research on disability as deviant has utilized a social reaction or labeling theory approach to the study of disability (Freidson, 1966; Safilios-Rothschild, 1970; Scott, 1969). This perspective focuses on the role of formal and/or informal response to disability as a key factor in the emergence of a deviant or stigmatized identity.

Despite the preponderance of sociological research on disability as deviant or stigmatizing, little if any use has been made of this research in the study of infertility or involuntary childlessness.[1] Indeed, most research on infertility has been done from a demographic, medical, psychological, social work, or autobiographical perspective. No systematic published work on the interactive or stigmatizing aspects of infertility has been located.

In North American society two major fertility norms predominate. One is that all married couples should reproduce. The other is that all married couples should want to reproduce (Veevers, 1980:3). Indeed, childlessness, whether voluntary or involuntary, has been designated as a form of deviant behavior in that it is statistically unusual and violates prevailing norms of acceptable conduct. Veevers (1980:3-6) has extensively reviewed the literature documenting the existence of *pronatalism*, a term which loosely means "any attitude or policy that is 'pro-birth', that encourages reproduction, that exalts the role of parenthood" (Peck and Senderowitz, 1974:1). Veevers has noted that societal acceptance of the fertility norms of having and wanting children appears to be extremely strong, transcending sex, age, race, religion, ethnicity, and social class divisions (Peel and Carr, 1975; Pohlman, 1969; Rosenblatt et al., 1973; and Van Keep (1971).

In a society that values fertility, childlessness becomes an attribute of the individual which can be discrediting or stigmatizing.[2] Much research has been done which explores the impact of stigmatization of those who are voluntarily childless or childless by choice (Vevvers, 1972; 1980; 1983). Those individuals who are involuntarily childless through subfecundity or infertility have, with a few exceptions, been ignored by sociologists (Hum-

[1]Unless otherwise noted, the terms infertility and involuntary childlessness are used synonymously in this research.

[2]For a detailed discussion of the stigmatic connotations associated with voluntary and involuntary childlessness, see Miall (1984, 1985); Peck and Senderowitz (1974); and Veevers (1972, 1980).

phrey, 1969; Kirk, 1964; Matthews and Martin-Matthews, 1986; Miall, 1983, 1984, 1985). It seems clear however that for most people, involuntary childlessness or infertility is regarded as deficient or abnormal condition (Miall, 1984). Whereas Goffman in his classic work on stigma did not deal specifically with involuntary childlessness as discrediting or stigmatizing, he did quote from another author (Carling, 1962: 23-24) who equated the handicap of a crippled girl with that of women who "felt inferior and different because of . . . inability to bear children" (Goffman, 1963:12).

In his typology of stigma, Goffman (1963:4) differentiates among three kinds of stigma: "First, there are abominations of the body—the various physical deformities. Next there are blemishes of individual character . . . Finally there are tribal stigma of race, nation, and religion." Using Goffman's typology, those who are involuntarily childless could be said to be stigmatized on the basis of abnormal bodily functions; that is, lack of reproductive capability. In terms of the literature on disability as deviance, involuntary childlessness could be defined as "accidental deviance" (Lorber, 1967:303) or "involuntary deviance" (Birenbaum and Sagarin, 1976:35) in that it is usually not motivated, and is associated with "contingencies of inheritance, accidents of infection and trauma" (Freidson, 1966:81).

It is estimated that from 1 in 5 (Burgwyn, 1981; Kraft et al., 1980) to 1 in 10 couples (Mosher, 1982) may be affected by infertility. Within western nations, infertility is usually estimated to occur among 10 to 15% of the population (Benet, 1976; Menning, 1975) although other estimates vary between 5 and 30% of the population (Kraft et al., 1980; McFalls, 1979).[3] In general, infertility appears to be on the increase (Curran, 1980; Mosher, 1982). As noted however, most research on infertility has been done from a demographic, medical, psychological, social work, or autobiographical perspective. No systematic work on the stigmatizing or interactive aspects of infertility has been attempted. Similarly, the selection of samples of infertile individuals for in-depth analysis has often been biased, especially toward the use of such individuals attending clinics (Kipper et al., 1977). Using a sample of 71 involuntarily childless women drawn from the community at large, this research explores the subjective perception of stigma as it is experienced by those who are involuntarily childless in informal interaction with others.[4]

In research which explored the stigmatization of the childless by choice (Veevers, 1979:5), the voluntarily childless were often characterized as "psy-

[3]The lack of consensus on the prevalence of infertility is a consequence of differing definitions of infertility, the varying periods of time over which it is studied, and a failure to differentiate analytically between the voluntarily childless and the involuntarily childless (McFalls, 1979; Rao, 1974).

[4]The decision to limit the sample to women was a consequence of the inability to recruit sufficient numbers of involuntarily childless males.

chologically maladjusted, emotionally immature, immoral, selfish, lonely, unhappy, unfulfilled, sexually inadequate, unhappily married, and prone to divorce." Less is known about the characterizations of the involuntarily childless. Veevers (1979:4-5) has suggested that the infertile may be viewed more sympathetically than the voluntarily childless.[5]

Generally speaking, however, anecdotal or self-help books portray the discovery of infertility as a devastating blow to the individual concerned. Menning (1977) for example, has linked the realization of infertility and the responses made to it to Kubler-Ross's (1969) stages of death and dying. Sorosky et al., (1978:74) have suggested that feelings of shame, guilt, isolation, failure, and loss can accompany the realization of infertility. Pohlman (1970:10) has noted that the infertile may "often feel sexually undemonstrated and imperfect, lacking in adult adequacy, and unnatural."

When consideration is given to psychological research on the infertile, a negative psychological picture is usually presented. Failure to reproduce is often attributed to psychological malfunctioning in women (Pohlman, 1970:10); to the unconscious rejection of sex roles; or to an unconscious fear of pregnancy (Weinstein, 1962:409). Infertility has also been characterized as a psychological insult (Fanshel, 1962:30) and a narcissistic injury to the psyche (Walsh and Lewis, 1969:589). Indeed, infertility has been conceptualized as nature's way of preventing the psychologically inadequate from reproducing:

> As Harlow's disturbed monkeys could neither reproduce nor effectively nurture, that seems true for people too. It is as though to some extent one of nature's failsafe mechanisms is infertility in those who are not psychologically healthy enough to nurture. (Bardwick, 1974:58-59)

Psychological research on the infertile however, has focused on small samples of infertile women already in clinical or psychiatric settings, thus limiting the generalizability of results (Kipper et al., 1977:355-357). Although some forms of infertility may be related to psychological factors, the numbers so afflicted appear small (about 10%) (Weinstein, 1962). Similarly, as infertile individuals are usually studied after their infertility is diagnosed, conclusions about their psychological health *prior* to the discovery of infertility are tenuous at best (Seward et al., 1965:534-535). Still both

[5]From a sociopsychological perspective, the essential component in defining persons as voluntarily or involuntarily childless is not their biological status as fertile or infertile, but their psychic preference to procreate or not to procreate and their ability or inability in present circumstances to do so. For example, although in a marriage only one partner might be diagnosed as physically infertile, both partners would be considered to be involuntarily childless if they had a conscious desire to procreate but were unable to do so.

the anecdotal and psychological research presents a negative picture of the infertile individual. Moreover, the analysis in this kind of research tends to center on individual psychological adjustment to infertility. Indeed, problems with adjustment are often linked to psychological pathology. From a sociological point of view, little attention has been paid to the role of social interaction in the formation of a stigmatized infertile identity. Consideration will now be given to this perspective.

SELF-LABELING, THE STIGMA OF INFERTILITY, AND SOCIAL RESPONSE

In another paper employing the same sample, this author (Miall, 1985) extensively reviewed the literature documenting the relevance of fertility and reproduction for western society in general, and women in particular. The data are clear, social context determines that infertile women will be subject to stigmatization. Indeed, nearly all the respondents in this sample categorized infertility as something negative, as representing some sort of failure or an inability to *work* normally.[6] Over half the respondents indicated that it was difficult to disclose to their families and friends that they were having problems. Often respondents linked the difficulty to personal feelings of failure and shame. Most engaged in secretive behavior as they explored the possibility that they might be infertile. Given that this secret behavior might not be detected, let alone sanctioned, it appeared that the women felt that some negative or devaluing response would be forthcoming if their difficulty became known (Goode, 1981).

This author concluded that the women were *self-labeling* infertility as a discreditable attribute *apart from* a formal or informal devaluing response. Self-labeling strongly indicates the internalization of normative values which discredit infertility.[7] However, a complete appreciation of the evolution of involuntary childlessness as a stigmatizing attribute must include consideration of the patterns of interaction established with others following the revelation of infertility. As noted earlier, little attention has been paid to the role of social interaction in the formation and maintenance of infertility as a stigmatizing attribute. However, individuals who learn they are infertile or involuntarily childless usually do so later in life, after they are married, with presumably well established *ego* or *felt* identities. The ego or felt identity is, according to Goffman (1963:105), "the subjective sense of his own situation and his own continuity and character that an individual

[6]Responses to a series of questions used to determine commitment to motherhood revealed that it had great salience for the identities of the women in this research, a salience which probably contributed to their conceptualization of infertility as stigmatizing.

[7]For a detailed discussion of self-labeling and the stigma of involuntary childlessness, see Miall (1984, 1985).

comes to obtain as a result of his various social experiences." Prior to the realization of involuntary childlessness, the individual probably identifies himself or herself as a *normal*, conforming member of society. It may be therefore, that social reaction to the revelation of infertility plays a part in the establishment of a stigmatized identity. Although stigma may be applied by formal control agents, this paper is concerned with the direct empirical experiences individuals may have had with informal stigmatization.

Using a sample of 71 involuntarily childless women drawn from the community, this paper explores the relevance of perceptions of informal social reaction for the adjustment and self-esteem of these women.[8] The analysis of stigma is extended to include the neglected substantive area of involuntary childlessness and three aspects of the experience of infertility are considered: (1) Actors' real or perceived experiences with others relating to the disclosure or awareness of infertility; (2) actor perceptions of *normal* attitudes about the causes of infertility; and (3) actor perceptions of other infertile individuals.

METHODOLOGY

In the initial stages of this research, an attempt was made to recruit men and women in order to compare their responses to involuntary childlessness. However, it was exceedingly difficult to obtain a sample of men sufficient for this kind of comparison and after two years of concerted effort, the decision was made to limit the study to women. Similarly, it was difficult to recruit women who would participate in this study. Volunteers were recruited through social work agencies, adoptive parent groups, and through research participants who referred the author to others willing to participate. Two characteristics were considered important for the recruitment of respondents: the demonstrations of infertility in the presently contracted marriage, and no biologically related offspring on either side from previous marriages or relationships. Apart from ascertaining through a series of initial questions that volunteers met the requirements of involuntary childlessness as defined above, no attempts were made to screen the respondents. Statistical representativeness, therefore, is not asserted. However, the difficulty involved in obtaining a sample of infertile individuals who would participate is evidence of the secretive processes surrounding infertility.

Volunteers chosen for study were given the option of taking part in an

[8]The decision was made to include fertile women in marriages with documented male infertility as these women also experienced involuntary childlessness. Unless otherwise noted, no discernible differences in response emerged between this group of women (12) and the larger sample of infertile women.

interview or filling in a questionnaire anonymously. The decision to use a questionnaire in addition to interviews was made because in many instances, volunteers refused to be interviewed but offered to fill in a questionnaire. Thus, a pretested, standardized, open-ended interview (Patton, 1980) was conducted with 30 involuntarily childless women and a questionnaire identical to the interview schedule was completed by 41 involuntarily childless women.[9] Questions were based on previous academic research on infertility, over one and a half years of participant observation in an infertility self-help group, discussions with infertile individuals in the community, and popular anecdotal literature in infertility. Interviews lasted from two and one half to four hours. The women in this sample ranged from 25 to 45, were well educated, from middle to upper middle class backgrounds, white, Protestant, with a small subsample of Jews (16).

In the analysis of the data, responses to fixed alternative questions in the interview and in the questionnaire were combined. Given the small sample size and different data gathering techniques, a high degree of precision was not intended. Rather, cumulative frequency responses were used to reflect general trends or recurring regularities in the data.[10] As the viewpoint of the actor was stressed, the discovery of theoretical insights was of prime concern.

INFORMAL RESPONSE AND INFERTILITY AS A STIGMATIZING ATTRIBUTE

In order to examine the role of social reaction in the establishment of a stigmatized identity, respondents were asked if they had experienced informal responses to their infertility which they perceived to be stigmatizing. Specifically, respondents were asked (a) if they felt that responses to their revelation of infertility were supportive or unsupportive; (b) if there were any particular situations which made them, as infertile individuals, uncomfortable; and (c) if there were any particular questions or comments that people has asked or made about their medical condition which made them uncomfortable.

In terms of reactions to the initial disclosure of infertility to others, nearly 51% (36) of the sample said that reactions were supportive although

[9]Separate analysis of the data from the interviews and questionnaires revealed that this sample of respondents was homogeneous in responses made.

[10]No significant differences between the women who took part in an interview or the women who filled in a questionnaire emerged either in responses to fixed-alternative questions or in the themes extracted from open-ended questions. Consequently, although quotes in the text are taken from interview data only, they reflect the sentiments expressed in the written questionnaire responses.

38% (27) said that reactions varied or were unsupportive.[11] In spite of this perception of support, 74% (51) of the respondents agreed that there were situations which made them as infertile women uncomfortable. Similarly, 52% (37) agreed that they had received questions or comments about their medical condition which made them uncomfortable. Indeed, an analysis of open-ended responses to these questions revealed that nearly *all* the respondents in this research were able to provide detailed instances of informal sanctioning where real or perceived negative consequences followed from the announcement or awareness of infertility.

Instances of informal sanctioning ranged in degree of intimacy from encounters with significant others to encounters with acquaintances or strangers. For example, one woman spoke of the real consequences of telling her husband's parents of her infertility:

> Well they were sympathetic about the infertility or so I thought at the time . . . The next day, while my husband was at work, his father and his brother came to see me at home. They sat me down in the kitchen and proceeded to tell me that I must divorce my husband so that he could have children with someone else . . . They were quite firm about it . . . I was so upset by their response that for a time I went to a psychiatrist.

Another spoke of the perceived negative "vibrations" she received from others:

> I was in a group once where a woman was talking about careers for women and so on and someone said that motherhood and having babies was also a worthwhile career. This woman replied, 'Oh well, anyone can do that.' Then there was this awkward silence when everyone realized that I was there. They all knew that we couldn't have children and there was just this sense of not knowing what to say to me; like I was embarrassing all of them just by being there.

According to Garfinkel (1967:205), "any communicative work between persons, whereby the public identity of an actor is transformed into something looked on as lower in the local scheme of social types" is a *status degradation ceremony*. As part of the denunciation, "the denouncer must make the dignity of the suprapersonal values of the tribe salient and accessible to view, and his denunciation must be delivered in their name" (Garfinkel, 1967:210). In this research, several women discussed in detail instances where they were publicly admonished or rebuked by other women

[11]Only 4 said that all reactions were unsupportive and 4 did not respond.

because they had not had biological children. All the women making the derogatory comments had children and the settings where the comments were made invariably contained elements of the celebration of childbearing or children (for example, baby showers). In most cases, the involuntarily childless women felt that they had been personally diminished through the words of others. Thus, as one adoptive mother of two noted:

> A group of my women friends were discussing their birth experiences and I got a bit impatient with it. One of the women told me I wouldn't understand because I had never had a child. I didn't say anything at the time but I was hurt and later angry at her insensitivity. She made me feel like an outsider, inadequate.

Another woman spoke of a similar instance of public *degradation*:

> I was at a shower . . . and I was, I guess, mothering the baby and giving some advice, and someone made the comment, and it hurt, that I was using this child as a substitute. . . . I was feeding it and making comments because I used to work in the nursery with my Mom as a thirteen year old and I was always working in the nursery at church and I think that's what got me. The comment that you don't have any and you can't have any so how do you know what you're talking about.

In these instances, failure to reproduce appeared to the involuntarily childless women to disqualify them as members of an "in-group" of mothers, even though, in most cases these women were adoptive parents. Thus, although some women who are involuntarily childless might consider this status peripheral to their overall status as individuals or mothers, it would appear that "normals" may define them solely on the basis of that attribute (Elliott et al., 1982:287). Indeed Goffman (1963:49-50) has observed that "normals develop conceptions, whether objectively grounded or not, as to the sphere of life-activity for which an individual's particular stigma primarily disqualifies him." Thus, the presence of a stigmatizing attribute can result in the withdrawal of the legitimacy of the bearer of those interacting with him or her (Elliott et al., 1982-281).

On the other hand, it is interesting to note that respondents most likely to agree that involuntary childlessness is stigmatizing were also the respondents most likely to feel that they had experienced stigma of some form or another. This may reflect Goffman's (1963) observation that the stigmatized individual is more alive to the everyday contingencies of interaction than the nonstigmatized. Whether this perception of stigma is empirically grounded however, remains a question for further research.

Although research on infertility has focused on individual maladjustment to infertility as pathological, this research suggests a different emphasis is required. The widespread perception of stigmatizing informal responses to infertility illustrates that a complete understanding of the experience of involuntary childlessness requires some consideration of the role of social sanction and social control. As Meisenhelder (1982:140-141) has observed, personal identity is made up of more than a subjective definition of self. Identity is also constructed on the basis of our perception of the reactions of others. Although the pervasiveness of informal sanctioning and its impact on the self-esteem of the respondents cannot be discussed with authority here, the emergence in this research of a widespread perception of stigmatizing informal responses to infertility adds a new dimension to the image usually presented by the research on infertility.

PERCEPTIONS ABOUT CAUSES OF INFERTILITY

As the intent of this paper was to focus on actor definitions and behaviors, respondents were also asked to document their experiences with others with a view to isolating recurrent themes surrounding the announcement or awareness of infertility. Particular interest focused on actor perceptions of *normal* attitudes about the causes of infertility and recurring themes were extracted from the open-ended responses provided by the respondents.

Apart from responses which were supportive and usually came from family and friends, or responses which focused on the notion of failure and were not widely reported, three main themes emerged: (a) that infertility was psychological in origin regardless of the stated reason given; (b) that infertility was related to sexual incompetence regardless of the stated reason give; and (c) that infertility was caused in the dyad by some problem with the woman. In addition, consideration was given to the notion of infertility acting as a *master status* in terms of how the respondents perceived it.

Infertility as Psychological in Origin

When reporting on their experiences with others, respondents would invariably refer to the oft repeated advice of others to relax. This advice was offered whether or not the respondent had revealed the cause of infertility, and whether or not the cause had been medically established. It seemed almost a truism that failure to conceive or to carry a child to term was a consequence of "trying too hard". In one particularly telling case, a woman had had two widely reported ectopic pregnancies which resulted in the removal of her fallopian tubes. She was asked by a relative if she was sure that that was the cause of her infertility. It was suggested that maybe she just needed to relax. As one woman noted:

> We got a lot of advice about going for a nice holiday, having a rest. I mean the implication is there's something wrong with you . . . You're too uptight, you're too relaxed.

Tied to this notion of psychology interfering with biology was the view of adoption as the *cure* for infertility:

> From different people I got it all, all kinds of reactions. You get it all. My favorite is, 'It's all in your head; go take a vacation and it will be fine' I think the other phrase I got that really drove me crazy was, 'Well you know I had this friend who couldn't and then adopted a child and do you know what? Seven months later she was pregnant'.

On the other hand, there is no systematic evidence for the prevalence of postadoption fertility. Most couples who adopt do so only after extensive treatment for their infertility has failed. Thus Weinstein (1962:409) found that only 10% of his sample of 438 couples had children born to them after adoption. Indeed, 10% postadoption fertility is the figure usually quoted as the norm (Kirk, 1964; Lustig, 1960). It should be noted that, given new medical advances in the treatment of infertility, this figure may now be lower. Specifically, if medical treatment is successful before adoption, the adoption usually will not take place.[12]

Infertility as Sexual Incompetence

The women in this sample also noted with great frequency the tendency of normals to regard them or their husbands as sexually inadequate or incompetent:

> We have one friend who is rather bizarre in his attitudes and he gave us advice on the proper way for union, like you know the two bodies should be in the missionary style or the doggy style or standing on your hear. Or you penetrate more from this angle.

The kind of advice offered by this bizarre friend was reported by a large number of the respondents in this research including one woman who recorded that:

[12]On the other hand, the opposite may be true. While fewer involuntarily childless women will need to adopt as a result of more effective fertility treatment, more involuntarily childless women may be able to bear children after adopting.

> We have friends who practically everytime we see them, he offers to take me upstairs and fix me up. You know, show me how it's done. I don't know what my husband must think about all this.

It is interesting to note that most suggestions for technique improvement reported by female respondents in this study seemed to focus on the male partner. Whereas suggestions focusing on the psychological causes of infertility were most often linked to the female, suggestions for improving sexual technique were most often linked to male performance. This may reflect a more general perception of the sex act as requiring an active, competent male initiator and a passive, compliant, relaxed, female receiver.

Although most suggestions for sexual improvement were apparently done humorously, Birenbaum and Sagarin (1976:61-62) have suggested that sarcasm and ridicule are forms of social control where social control is defined as "an informal interpersonal practice in groups which explicitly strengthens the bonds of social cohesion while it is overtly aimed at persons who may even be beyond the scope of the group's power to control" (Birenbaum and Sagarin, 1976:59) One respondent for example, told of an incident where a couple widely known to be having problems with infertility were exposed to ridicule at a party. Nearly all the people present, according to the respondent, had children:

> I remember being at a party and this particular individual couldn't get his wife pregnant. They'd been trying for five years and they got a gift at the party, a sort of birthday gift and what it was was a dildo, two feet long which he strapped to his waist and he paraded around, and his wife got a target and she wore that and the idea was that he wasn't aiming properly for five years.

As Birenbaum and Sagarin (1976:62) have pointed out, ridicule as a form of humor is "crude and degrading, so that the object gets the point easily". In this instance, the suggestion of sexual incompetence was clearly conveyed. It should be noted however, that humor can serve another purpose. In addition to subjecting the individual to ridicule, or to establishing in-group boundaries, humor can be used to relieve the tension engendered by the presence of the deviant or discredited. By mentioning the unmentionable, by making light of tragedy, humor protects "normals" from the pain or unfairness of stigma. (Birenbaum and Sagarin, 1976: Goffman, 1963).

In terms of trends reported here, it would appear that there is a perceived tendency among normals to assign responsibility for the inability to reproduce to the couples concerned. Infertility does not appear to be considered beyond the control of infertile individuals—they are either too uptight or too incompetent. It may be that this perceived tendency to assign responsibility or blame is reflective of Lerner's (1971) *just world* hypothesis. This hypothesis suggests that the individual who believes that the world is basically just will find a reason to blame other people for the unfortunate events that befall them. In particular, the seeming randomness of a physical condition like infertility is a threat to those who link personal good fortune or misfortune to personal behavior and characteristics. The fear of loss of perceived control may cause "normals" to blame infertile individuals for their condition or to discredit them personally (Gruman and Sloan, 1983:40; Sontag, 1978:29). It is interesting to note, on the other hand, that those who are voluntarily childless may be considered morally suspect precisely because of their perceived control over their childlessness (Veevers, 1980).

Infertility as a Woman's Problem

Generally, there is "the connotation that not getting pregnant constitutes a failure for which the woman might be expected to feel responsible" (Veevers, 1972:577). In all cases in this research sample, women were the first to approach a doctor or clinic for help, an observation that supports the notion that for this sample at least, the initial reproductive failure was perceived as the woman's problem.

To explore this phenomenon further, attention was focused on (a) those women who did not appear to be contributing to the infertility, (b) those who share male-female infertility, and (c) those women with no known medical cause established for their infertility. It became apparent that, in their social circles at least, these women were considered to be responsible for the failure to reproduce. One woman revealed, for example, that her husband's sperm count was nonexistent. She noted however that,

> They always assume it's the woman's fault. That is what is so interesting to me. Everyone always assumes that it's the little lady that can't get it all together. Now you know if you'd just relax, take a vacation. They all think that now that I have two children (adopted), I'll relax and get pregnant.

Interestingly enough, all the respondents whose husbands were responsible for the infertility admitted to readily accepting others' perceptions of them as responsible.[13]

Infertility as a Master Status

The possession of a stigmatizing attribute can have serious consequences for the social identity of its possessor. Goffman (1963:4) for example, defined

[13] For a discussion of this deviance avowal, see Miall (1984, 1985).

stigma as a potentially polluting substance, as "an attribute which is deeply discrediting to its possessor." In terms of physical disability, Gove (1976:60) has noted that "the disabled are typically stigmatized, and their stigma often appears to act as a master status which determines the nature of their interaction with others" (Davis, 1961). Indeed, Scott (1978:285), in his analysis of blindness, has concluded that:

> blindness is a stigma, carrying with it a series of moral imputations about character and personality . . . the fact that blindness is a stigma leads (normal people) to regard blind men as their physical, psychological, moral, and emotional inferiors.

In this paper, interest was focused on whether or not respondents would perceive their infertility as a master status. Most of the respondents were concerned that the awareness of infertility would, to some extent, override their other, more positive attributes. One respondent discussed the implications of being infertile:

> I think it depends on the person. I do believe it lessens you in some people's eyes, makes you different and possible even morally suspect like God is punishing you or something. Somehow infertility lessens your accomplishments for some people.

Another women, employed professionally in a medical setting, expressed her concern about being perceived a infertile by her colleagues:

> I was going to the infertility clinic where I worked. I was also working professionally with these residents. They were rotating through the various services and I would end up having to deal with them on another basis at another time and that was quite a problem. I basically refused to see most of the residents in the infertility clinic for that reason. I didn't want to have to deal with those people professionally afterwards and for them to be connecting the two in their minds.

Presumably the respondent felt that the awareness of her infertility would interfere with others' perceptions of her professional authority and status.

It would appear that in this sample, most of the respondents felt that the awareness of their infertility caused others to view them in a new and damaging light. The analysis of open-ended responses discussed earlier revealed that most respondents felt that normals regard infertile individuals as psychologically impaired or sexually inadequate. These findings reflect

Scott's (1978:285) observations on the psychological and physical inferiority of the blind, and provide support for the notion of infertility as a type of master status.

PERCEPTIONS OF OTHER INFERTILE INDIVIDUALS

In order to gain an awareness of how infertile respondents viewed others sharing the attribute of infertility, respondents were asked (a) whether they behaved or talked differently with other infertile individuals; and (b) whether they would participate in an infertility self-help group if one were available. Nearly two-thirds of the respondents agreed that they felt feelings of openness, rapport, warmth and understanding with other infertile women that they didn't experience with fertile women. In those instances where respondents indicated no differences in feelings or behavior, the reasons ranged from having no contact with other infertile individuals to using meetings with infertile couples to discuss adoption/ that is, rapport stemmed from shared experiences with adoption not infertility.

When asked about participation in an infertility self-help group if one were available, nearly half of this sample said they would participate. As the majority of these women had one or more adopted children, this figure would seem to reflect the salience infertility still had as a discrediting attribute apart from the process of parenting itself.

The analysis of open-ended responses to the two questions discussed above also revealed that the women in this sample tended to categorize themselves and other infertile women in terms of their actual condition and their progress in taking on an infertile identity. For example, respondents categorized and evaluated reasons for infertility such that shared infertility appeared to be regarded as the worst. Further exploration of the values underlying this categorization revealed that shared infertility allowed the marital dyad to share the *guilt* of infertility. In other words, one partner did not have to bear the burden of depriving the other of children and this seemed best for the marital stability of the couple. Unexplained infertility, on the other hand, left the individuals open to charges of psychological or sexual dysfunction. It also removed the possibility of active intervention to correct the infertility. As one respondent observed,

> In our case our infertility is unexplainable so we don't have a reason to present. It is very hard to handle the feelings of failure because we don't have a reason.

Categorization of other infertile women according to the kind of reproductive disability they had appeared to be done with a view to enhancing personal self-esteem in that personal problems of adjustment were played down. For example, one woman who found little rapport with other infertile women expressed the following point of view:

> I'm one of those couples where it's the husband who has the infertility problem. Mostly I've met women who have fertility problems. Thank God I'm not one of them. When I see what they've been through; when I hear the stories. I don't know if eventually one gets reconciled but thank God I missed all that.

Similar sentiments were expressed by other women. For example, one woman who had experienced three miscarriages late in her pregnancies observed that she had less difficulty with baby showers than her friend who had two stillborn births. Another woman who regularly conceived and then miscarried expressed sympathy for women who would never know what it was to be pregnant.

Respondents also tended to categorize others in terms of their personal adjustment to infertility. For example, one respondent noted that participation in self-help groups could be difficult because:

> You run into problems there in that they (other infertile couples) might not be at the same stage and you've got to be very careful about that. You don't want to frighten them off if you've already gone through a stage.

From the analysis of actor responses outlined above, it would appear that infertile women themselves, at least in this sample, create categories of deviance or stigma within their own group. As Goffman (1963:107) has observed, "The stigmatized individual exhibits a tendency to stratify his 'own' according to the degree to which their stigma is apparent and obtrusive." As infertility in itself appears to be a disvalued attribute in the larger society, it is interesting to note the possibility of a hierarchical process which renders infertile women more or less socially disvalued within their own group, a process which reflects the degree to which the stigmatized appear to have internalized the normative viewpoint on infertility.

FEMALE INFERTILITY VERSUS MALE INFERTILITY

As the intent of this research was to focus on actor perceptions, respondents were asked if they felt that society views female infertility differently than male infertility and if so, in what way. This question was intended to reveal the general content of stereotypes of female and male infertility as the respondents perceived it. Concern in this research however, was less with the accurate measurement of degrees of stigma perceived by respondents than it was with the emergence of a general consensus among respondents.

Nearly two-thirds of the respondents felt that society views female infertility differently than male infertility. The analysis of open-ended responses revealed that nearly all the respondents perceiving a difference felt that male infertility was considered more discrediting to masculinity than female infertility was to femininity. As one respondent noted:

> A man's infertility is tied to his virility. Women seem to always be having troubles with their female organs and society is more accepting of these women's problems.

In addition, a recurrent theme in the responses was that in the larger society, male infertility is perceived to be linked to impotence:

> Somehow it's just a medical problem for her but a real assault on his masculinity to the man . . . It's often wrongly thought to be associated with impotence.

Regardless of the empirical accuracy of their perceptions, nearly two-thirds of this sample felt that society regards male infertility more negatively than female infertility. It may be however, that these responses reflect the tendency of these infertile women to create categories of stigma within their own group, in this instance differentiating degrees of stigma on the basis of sex rather than of the basis of the kind of reproductive disorder or personal adjustment to infertility. Research on community sentiments would clarify the accuracy of the respondents' perceptions in this area.

SUMMARY

This sociological work on infertility as a stigmatizing attribute was stimulated by the observation that most studies had been done either from a demographic, medical, psychological, social work, or anecdotal perspective. Little was known about the role of social interaction and the perceptions of the infertile themselves about how they are viewed by other. The apparent relevance of fertility and reproduction for western society in general, and women in particular, suggested that the involuntarily childless might feel stigmatized because of their inability to respond to societal pressures to reproduce. Therefore, this paper was concerned with the direct empirical experiences infertile individuals might have had with informal stigmatization.

The results of this research indicated that nearly all the respondents were able to provide detailed instances of real or perceived negative consequences following from the announcement or awareness of infertility. Respondents perceived that among normals, infertility was felt to be caused by psychological or sexual malfunction, or was caused by some problem with the woman in the marital dyad, and, in many instances, acted as a master status. In terms of their perceptions of other infertile individuals, respondents appeared to engage in a hierarchical process of stigmatization themselves. In particular, respondents felt that male infertility was more stigmatizing than female infertility.

As noted earlier, the women in this sample were, as a rule, well educated and more likely to be found at the upper end of the socioeconomic index. It is difficult therefore to generalize to the larger population of infertile men and women. However, research into stigma and physical disability suggests that high social status enables the physically disabled to resist the deviant label more effectively than low social status (Hanks and Poplin, 1981). It may be therefore, that infertile women in the larger community feel even more stigmatized that the respondents in this sample. It was very difficult, for example, to obtain a sample of women who would participate in this study. The willingness of these female respondents to participate suggests that they were actively engaged in negotiating their status as women and resisting stigmatization. Further research with a broader sampling base is needed to clarify the trends observed in this research.

In addition, the perception of personal debasement or stigmatization by informal control agents does not necessarily indicate that this perceived stigmatization was intended. Similarly, the pervasiveness of informal sanctioning and its consequences for the self-esteem of the individual perceiving it cannot be discussed with authority here. However, the emergence in this research of a widespread perception of stigmatizing informal responses to infertility adds a new dimension to the image usually presented by the research on infertility. As noted earlier, most research on infertility has focused on individual maladjustment to infertility as pathological. However, it may be that individual adjustment to infertility is more reflective of the ability of individuals to resist deviant imputations and to maintain a reasonable level of self-esteem in the face of widespread negative devaluing responses. In any case, this research illustrates that a complete understanding of the experience of involuntary childlessness must include consideration of the role of social sanction and social control in the emergence of a stigmatized identity.

REFERENCES

Bardwick, J.
1974 "Evolution and parenting." Journal of Social Issues 30:39–62.
Benet, Margaret
1976 The Character of Adoption. London: Cox and Wyman.
Birenbaum, A., and E. Sagarin
1976 Norms and Human Behavior. New York: Praeger.
Burgwyn, D.
1981 Marriage Without Children. New York: Harper & Row.
Cahnman, W.
1968 "The stigma of obesity." Sociological Quarterly 9:283–299.
Carling, F.
1962 And Yet We Are Human. London: Chatto and Windus.
Chaiklin, H., and M. Warfield
1977 "Stigma management and amputee rehabilitation." Pp. 103–111 in J. Stubbins (ed.) Social and Psychological Aspects of Disability. Baltimore: University Park Press.
Cogswell, B.
1977 "Self-socialization: Readjustment of paraplegics in the community." Pp. 123–130 in J. Stubbins (ed.) Social and Psychological Aspects of Disability. Baltimore: University Park Press.
Curran, J.
1980 "Economic consequences of pelvic inflammatory disease in the United States." American Journal of Obstetrics and Gynecology 138:848.
Davis, F.
1961 "Deviance disavowal: The management of strained interaction by the visibly handicapped." Social Problems 9:120–132.
Elliott, Gregory C., Herbert L. Ziegler, Barbara M. Altman, and Deborah R. Scott
1982 "Understanding stigma: Dimensions of deviance and coping." Deviant Behavior 3:275–300.
Fanshel, D.
1962 "Approaches to measuring adjustment in adoptive parents." In Quantitative Approaches to Parent Selection. New York: Child Welfare League of America.
Freidson, E.
1966 "Disability as social deviance." ". 71–99 in M. Sussman (ed.) Sociology and Rehabilitation. United States: American Sociology Association.
Garfinkel, H.
1967 "Conditions of successful degradation ceremonies." Pp. 205–212 in J. Manis and B. Meltzer (eds.) Symbolic Interaction, Boston: Allyn and Bacon.
Goffman, Erving
1963 Stigma. Englewood Cliffs, N.J.: Prentice-Hall.
Goode, Erich
1981 "Deviance, norms, and social reaction." Deviant Behavior 3:47–53.

Gove, W.
1976 "Social reaction theory and disability." Pp. 57–71 in G. Albrecht (ed.) The Sociology of Physical Disability and Rehabilitation. Pittsburgh: University of Pittsburgh Press.

Gruman, J., and R. Sloan
1983 "Disease as justice: Perceptions of the victims of physical illness." Basic and Applied Social Psychology 4:39–46.

Gussow, A., and G. Tracey
1975 "Status, ideology and adaptation to stigmatized illness: A study of leprosy." Pp. 112-121 in F. Scarpitti and P. McFarlane (eds.) Deviance: Action, Reaction and Interaction. Reading, Mass.: Addison-Wesley.

Hanks, M., and D. Poplin
1981 "The sociology of physical disability: A review of the literature and some conceptual perspectives." Deviant Behavior 2:309–328.

Hawkins, R., and G. Tiedeman
1975 The Creation of Deviance. Columbus, Oh.: Charles G. Merrill.

Humphrey, M.
1969 The Hostage Seekers. London: Longmans.

Kipper, D., J. Zigler-Shani, D. Serr, and V. Insler
1977 "Psychogenic infertility, neuroticism, and the feminine role: A methodological inquiry." Journal of Psychosomatic Research 21:353–358.

Kirk, David
1964 Shared Fate. Toronto: Collier-Macmillan.

Kraft, A., J. Palombo, D. Mitchell, C. Dean, S. Meyers, A. Wright-Smith
1980 "The psychological dimensions of infertility." American Journal of Orthopsychiatry 50:618–628.

Kubler-Ross, E.
1969 On Death and Dying. New York: Macmillan.

Lerner, M.
1971 "Observer's evaluation of a victim: Justice, guilt, and veridical perception." Journal of Personality and Social Psychology 20:127–135.

Levitin, T.
1975 "Deviants as active participants in the labeling process: The case of the visibly handicapped." Social Problems 22:548–557.

Lorber, Judith
1967 "Deviance as performance: The case of illness." Social Problems 14:302–310.

Lustig, H.
1960 "The infertility problem in adoption." Smith College Studies in Social Work 30:235–251.

McFalls, J.
1979 Psychopathology and Sub-fecundity. New York: Academic Press.

Matthews, R., and A. Martin-Matthews
Forthcoming "Infertility and involuntary childlessness: The transition to nonparenthood." Journal of Marriage and the family.

Meisenhelder, Thomas

1982 "Becoming normal: Certification as a stage in exiting from crime." Deviant Behavior 3:137–153.

Menning, Barbara

1975 "The infertile couple: A plea for advocacy." Child Welfare 54:454–460.

1977 Infertility: A Guide for the Childless Couple. Englewood Cliffs, N.J.: Prentice-Hall.

Miall, Charlene

1983 "Women and involuntary childlessness: The stigma of infertility. A preliminary report." Paper presented at the Canadian Sociology and Anthropology Meetings. Vancouver, June.

1984 "Women and involuntary childlessness: Perceptions of stigma associated with infertility and adoption." Unpublished Ph.D. dissertation. York University, Toronto, Canada.

1985 "The stigma of involuntary childlessness: Implications for self-labeling." Paper in revision stage to Social Problems.

Mosher, W.

1982 "Infertility trends among U.S. couples: 1965–1976." Family Planning Perspectives 14:22–27.

Patton, M.

1980 Qualitative Evaluation Methods. Beverly Hills: Sage.

Peck, D., and J. Senderowitz (eds.)

1974 Pronatalism: The Myth of Mom and Apple Pie. New York: Thomas Y. Crowell.

Peel, J., and G. Carr

1975 Contracetpion and Family Design. Edinburgh: Churchill and Livingstone.

Petrunik, M., and C. Shearing

1983 "Fragile facades: Stuttering and the strategic manipulation of awareness." Social Problems 31:125–138.

Pohlman, E.

1969 The Psychology of Birth Planning. Cambridge, Mass.: Schenkman.

1970 "Childlessness: Intentional and unintentional." Journal of Nervous and Mental Disease 151:2–12.

Rao, S.

1974 "Comparative study of childlessness and never pregnant couples." Journal of Marriage and the Family 36:149–157.

Rosenblatt, P., P. Peterson, J. Portner, M. Cleveland, A. Mykkanen, R. Foster, G. Holm, B. Joel,, H. Keisch, C. Kreuscher, and R. Phillips

1973 "A cross-cultural study of responses to childlessness." Behavioral Science Notes 8:221–231.

Safilios-Rothschild, C.

1970 The Sociology and Social Psychology of Disability and Rehabilitation. New York: Random House.

Schneider, J., and P. Conrad
1980 "In the closet with illness: Epilepsy, stigma potential and information control." Social Problems 28:32–44.
Scott, R.
1969 The Making of Blind Men. New York: Russel Sage Foundation.
1978 "The socialization of the blind." Pp. 284–290 in S. Feldman (ed.) Deciphering Deviance. Toronto: Little, Brown and Company.
Seward, G., P. Wagner, J. Heinrich, S. Bloch, and H. Myerhoff
1965 "The question of psychophysiologic infertility: Some negative answers." Psychosomatic Medicine 27:533–545.
Smith, R.
1980 "Societal reaction and physical disability." Pp. 227–239 in W. Gove (ed.) The Labeling of Deviance, 2nd ed. Beverly Hills, Calif.: Sage.
Sontag, S.
1978 "Illness as metaphor." New York Review of Books, February 23.
Sorosky, A., A. Baran, and R. Pannor
1978 The Adoption Triangle. New York: Anchor Press.
Van Keep, P.
1971 "Ideal family size in five European countries." Journal of Biosocial Science 3:259.
Veevers, Jean
1972 "The violation of fertility mores: Voluntary childlessness as deviant behavior." Pp. 571–592 in C. Boydell, C. Grinstaff and P. Whitehead (eds.) Deviant Behavior and Societal Reaction. Toronto: Holt, Rinehart and Winston.
1979 "Voluntary childnessness: A review of issues and evidence." Marriage and Family Review 2:1–26.
1980 Childless by Choice. Toronto: Butterworth.
1983 "Researching voluntary childlessness: A critical assessment of current strategies and findings." Pp. 75–96 in E. Macklin and R. Rubin (eds.) Contemporary Families and Alternative Lifestyles. Calif.: Sage.
Walsh, E., and F. Lewis
1969 "A study of adoptive mothers in a child guidance clinic." Social Casework 50:587–594.
Weinstein, E.
1962 "Adoption and infertility." American Sociological Review 27:408–412.

Reading 11

The Social Construction and Interpretation of Deviance: Jonestown and the Mass Media

Danny L. Jorgensen
University of South Florida, Tampa

This paper reports on an investigation and analysis of social reactions to the events of November 1978 in Jonestown, Guyana. Critical attention is focused on the manner in which an official reality of these events was fashioned and presented by the mass media. Findings support the contention that the resulting interpretation was highly selective and stylized. Reasons for the symbolic construction of this reality of Jonestown are explored and related to the role played by experts and public officials. These findings are interpreted by way of the sociopolitical process whereby events are labeled and explained as social problems or deviance.

INTRODUCTION

Central to more recent discussions of deviance is the contention that objective conditions, or rule violations, alone do not determine what is socially recognized and defined as deviant (Kitsuse, 1962; Becker, 1963; Erikson, 1963; Blumer, 1971; Spector and Kitsuse, 1977). This view is related, of course, to theoretical perspectives that see social reality as a product of symbolic construction and interpretation (Blumer, 1969; Berger and Luckmann,1966; Garfinkel, 1967; Douglas, 1967; Cicourel, 1974). Investigators have concentrated on so-called subjective factors or, more accurately, social reactions to rule violations as a key to understanding deviance (see Lemert, 1951; Dinitz et al., 1969). The reactions of peers, family, and other people close to the situation and especially the responses of such authorities as legislators, police, courts, and psychiatrists have been the focus of intensive scrutiny (see, for example, Szasz, 1961; Scheff, 1966; Sudnow, 1965; Skolnick, 1966; Blumberg, 1967; Emerson, 1969; Cicourel, 1968; Wiseman, 1970; Spradley, 1970; Quinney, 1970; Rosenhan, 1973).

Currently, there is considerable agreement that the labeling and treatment of social problems, crime, and deviance is a complex political process (see, for instance, Turner, 1969; Douglas, 1971; Graham, 1972; Ross and

An earlier version of this paper was presented to the Southern Sociological Society, Atlanta, Georgia, April 1979.

The author wishes to acknowledge the comments and suggestions of David Altheide, Lawrence Foster, D. Paul Johnson, John M. Johnson on various versions of this paper and the anonymous reviewers of *Deviant Behavior*.

Staines, 1972; Taylor et al., 1973; Quinney, 1974; Sykes, 1974; Mass, 1975; Douglas and Rasmussen, 1977). Although the very concept of "labeling" emphasizes the importance of communication to this sociopolitical process, the reactions of the mass media have been neglected (Ross and Staines, 1972). What information is available to the general public and even to many experts derives from the media. At variance with the popular opinion that the media merely reflect reality is a growing body of literature to suggest that public images of reality are the product of social processes whereby official versions of reality are constructed and imposed on events (Epstein, 1973; Molotch and Lester, 1974, 1975; Altheide, 1976; Schudson, 1978; Altheide and Snow, 1979; Altheide and Johnson, 1980). The media, moreover, stand in dynamic relationship to public officials, experts on social affairs, special interest groups, and the like (Ross and Staines, 1972; Galliher and McCartney, 1977). As part of a larger political process, the media may be viewed as an important institutional basis for social control. The media control access to decision-making information, and they supply certain images and labels. It is frequently on the basis of this information that key actors and organizations within this political arena react to and sanction individuals and groups thought to be problems.[1]

The objective of this paper is to explore the role of the media in defining and interpreting social problems or deviance. The People's Temple and the events of November 1978 in Jonestown, Guyana, will be used for analytic purposes. On the basis of the literature briefly reviewed above, the following questions will be addressed: What was the image of this group and these events as interpreted and presented by the media? What factors determined the presentation of a certain reality of Jonestown over and against other possible interpretations? In what ways were these events interpreted and presented as social problems or deviance? And, what role did experts and public officials play in the emergent interpretation of Jonestown?

THE JONESTOWN EVENTS

The labeling process commonly is initiated when a private event is brought to the attention of the general public or a particular authority (Becker, 1963; Blumer, 1971). Jonestown, as a public issue, began largely as a consequence

[1]Galliher and McCartney (1977:8), for instance, boldly charge:

> Contrary to the myth of an independent and constitutional free press in the United States, the media are part of the larger corporate structure and generally represent that structure's definition of reality, including what is and is not defined as crime and how crime can be controlled.

While there probably is considerable truth to this statement, the actual sources and reasons for distortion require careful analysis.

of reports that certain members of the People's Temple were being abused by other members of the group. Because of these reports, and related to a larger political context and current debate over the issues of cults, mind control, and the like, Representative Leo Ryan of California formed an investigation.[2] The Ryan party—including the congressman, his aide, the press, and Concerned Relatives—arrived in Georgetown, Guyana, on Wednesday, November 15, 1978. After a delay, the party negotiated a visit to the jungle compound of Jonestown.

On Friday and Saturday Ryan and his entourage inspected the commune and interviewed members of the group. The initial investigation revealed little out of the ordinary, but by late Saturday morning dissent surfaced among members about camp conditions. Eventually about 20 members asked for and received permission to leave. Just before departing, however, there was a dispute among some family members about leaving. During a meeting to settle the matter Ryan was attacked but not hurt by Don Sly, a Temple member.

The Ryan party, with 16 Temple members, left the compound by mid-afternoon and arrived at the airfield at Port Kiatuma around 4 p.m. Because there was not enough room on the airplanes for everyone, there was confusion about who would leave or stay and where people would sit on the flights. Just as one plane began to taxi down the runway, the gunmen from Jonestown opened fire on Ryan and the other members of the party. Within minutes 6 people were killed and 11 people were injured. Except for two pilots, who fled to Georgetown without attempting to assist the injured, the survivors spent the night at the airfield.

Following the airfield attack, the gunmen returned to Jonestown and apparently informed Jones of what had transpired. Jones evidently made the decision at this point to call a "white night." Shortly after 5 p.m. preparations were made to commit the previously rehearsed but feigned suicide. With some dissent, members lined up and took or were forced to take poison. It seems most likely that the entire episode in which some 900 people died took less than an hour.

The very nature of this tragedy leaves no room to doubt that the objective conditions of a social problem and deviance existed. Although the absolute horror of this incident is difficult to deal with apart from human emotions and moral outrage, it is an especially valuable case for social scientific consideration. Obviously, it is an important public issue; the objective conditions of deviance are beyond dispute; and, unlike situations in which the mass media devote brief attention to some seemingly strange

[2]Julie C. Wolfe-Petrusky (1979) provides an excellent discussion of the "social construction of the cult problem." This paper also follows a line of argument quite similar to mine. Other discussions of these issues are found in Coser and Coser (1979), Shupe and Bromley (1980), Johnson (1979), Kirsch (1979), and Singer (1979).

behavior or cult, the events in Guyana were the subject of intensive investigating and reporting. How, then, did the media interpret and present Jonestown?

THE MEDIA PERSPECTIVE

News, like deviance, is not somehow given objectively in the nature of things. Instead, news is created socially out of the raw materials of events (Altheide, 1976; Altheide and Snow, 1979). For events to become news human agents must recognize something as worthy of attention, collect information about it, write this information up, edit it, give it form, and present it within the socially defined format of a particular medium. In short, news is a social product involving an ongoing series of complex practical decisions about what it is and how it is made. For any medium these practical problems are not left simply to chance, but rather they are routinely resolved by some set of more or less standardized solutions, or what Altheide and Snow (1979) call "media logic." As a consequence of media logic objective events are placed in perspective or, in the present case, in what Altheide (1976) defines as the "news perspective."

A central contention of this paper is that by way of media logic—the application of the news perspective—the Jonestown occurrences became a media event.[3] So as to examine empirically the manner in which Jonestown was transformed into news and the factors contributing to a particular interpretation of these events, a leading national paper, *The New York Times*, and a principal local paper, *The St. Petersburg Times*, were analyzed, along with other relevant sources of information, such as the several quickly constructed books on this topic.[4] This investigation suggests that the Jonestown story as told by the press involved an inordinate amount of attention, a selective emphasis on some aspects of these happenings, the decontextualization of events, the reduction of complex issues to simple ones, misinformation, and the selective use of expert opinion to support

[3]A media event is the result of complex social interactional processes. Media personnel construct and present certain images, yet they also respond to real and perceived demands for certain kinds of information.

[4]This analysis is based on a systematic examination of content. I collected all stories on the Guyana incidents and related matters from these papers for the period November 19 through November 26, 1978. Thereafter, I depended on what appeared in the local paper. Considering the massive coverage of these events, the material analyzed appears to be representative. I was careful to note identical or basically similar reports in weighting this evidence. Since the *St. Petersburg Times* depends most heavily on the *Los Angeles Times* news service, in addition to the regular wire services, with some material from the *Washington Post*, there was not an undue amount of overlap. An even stronger case might be made on the basis of an analysis of TV reports. Later I had the opportunity to review my analysis in terms of the articles in the *Washington Post*. Although the *Post* is not quoted here, this review confirmed the findings of the previous analysis.

and advance an emergent interpretation of deviance. As a result of these features of the news perspective, combined with the responses of public officials, a sort of "official reality" of Jonestown was created and presented to the public.

Whether something is news and the sense in which it will be reported commonly are problematic from the standpoint of news managers. Although it seems incredible, Charles Krause, a *Washington Post* reporter who survived the airfield attack, indicates that he was uncertain as to how these events would be featured.

> It occurred to me as we drove to the hotel [immediately following a night in the jungle at the airfield] that I still didn't really know whether *The Post* knew all that had happened and I wasn't sure how big a story it all was. Congressmen are a dime a dozen in Washington. They aren't often ambushed in the jungle, but they aren't Senators either. I debated whether I should send a cable explaining all that had happened, suggesting that I thought it was unusual enough to warrant both a news story and a first-person account. Sunday is a slow news day and I thought – or at least hoped – Washington would be sufficiently interested. (Krause et al., 1978:109)

To become a story, then, these events required processing, shaping, and refining, culminating in a marketable product – news. In this example Krause provides several clues as to the factors contributing to this decision. To be news the events had to be recognized as such by an editor, who also decided how the story would be presented (long or short copy, location, number of articles, type of report, and so on). For Krause an important factor was that Sunday is recognized, occupationally, as a slow news day, thereby improving his chances for attention.

While the newsworthiness of Jonestown is beyond question, it is important to note that the amount of attention devoted to these events transformed it into a major event. On the basis of an informal survey, *Christianity Today* (1979:44) reported:

> The major secular media in the United States gave more coverage to the People's Temple tragedy than to any other single religion-related story in recent memory. That includes the election and death of Pope John Paul I and the subsequent election of John Paul II. (quoted in Wolfe-Petrusky, 1979:9)

In answer to the question "why so much coverage?" Wolfe-Petrusky (1979), following Altheide (1976), noticed the important constraint of "commercialism" and the fact that Jonestown occurred during a period of little competition. As a result of these factors – slow news period, the commercial value of blood and gore, and the currency of the cult topic—Jonestown was transformed into a media event.[5]

Media logic is evident especially in terms of the emphasis given to particular aspects of the Jonestown events over and against other possible dimensions and the manner in which these events were featured. During the first several days of news coverage (November 19 and 20), the papers analyzed featured stories about the airfield attack on the Ryan party and the resulting deaths. Background stories on the People's Temple and the country of Guyana also were reported. Needless to say, perhaps, these early, fragmentary reports were riddled with mistakes. Some of the stories about the knifing incident, for example, had Ryan injured, and there were several versions of how he was rescued. The reasons for misinformation are apparent: None of the press was present at the time of the attack, and what information they received came from Ryan, who was killed shortly afterwards.

Newspaper reports also differed on many other details of the airfield attack, such as who and how many people participated, the distance from the compound to the airfield, the role of the Guyanese army and police, which airplanes finally took off and with whom, how and when the survivors were rescued, whether the attack was planned and by whom, and so on. One of the most serious instances of misdirected information is found in a *New York Times* (November 21) story entitled "Anguished Mother Tells How Fear Controlled Cult." This account stated: "Today, Mrs. Johnson said she lives a 'walking nightmare' because she believes her husband, Thomas Kise, Sr., and her youngest son, Thomas Kise, Jr., have been murdered in Jonestown, Guyana by members of the sect." And later in the article: "Her husband Thomas Kise has not been heard from since he was captured by church members as he tried to help their son, Thomas, Jr., escape from Jonestown through the jungle to Venezuela." What most readers of this emotion-provoking piece probably did not know, however, is that Thomas Kise, Sr., led the attack on the Ryan party at the airfield!

There are a number of reasons for misinformation, the selective interest in particular topics, and the inclusion of largely irrelevant stories.[6] As discussed below, the foregoing story on Kise, for instance, fit the emergent

[5]Wolfe-Petrusky (1979:10) summarizes this process nicely:

> The media's need for a "theme" or an "angle" (Altheide, 1976) contributed to a certain definition of the situation being presented to the exclusion of others. The "angle" establishes a broader context for the story, and the "theme" links up the day-to-day coverage. Once these are established, the news is selected and edited to "fit" these definitions.

[6]Because Jonestown became a media event a large number of irrelevant items became news. The November 30 edition of the *St. Petersburg Times* contained a small item in which Ronald Reagan "Says Cult Leader Tended to Attract Democrats," as if the Democratic Party were somehow guilty by association. Or perhaps Reagan meant his comment as a moral

definition of cultic behavior. Additional insight into this problem is provided by Krause et al. (1978:127) in terms of what they call "the farcical and second-hand nature of what often passes for 'news gathering'."

> Unable to reach the Jonestown settlement or even Port Kaituma 150 miles away, the news locusts in Georgetown resorted to the time-honored practice of interviewing one another, collecting stale stories, and embellishing bureaucratic utterances in such a way as to convey the impression that "I am there." One reporter, fortunate enough to fly briefly over the Jones settlement in the jungle, filed a story with the dateline, "Jonestown, Guyana." A major newspaper filled its pages for days with detailed stories on the massacre in Jonestown, though its reporters were stranded in Georgetown where they had to rely on second-hand descriptions of the carnage.

As a result of this commercial demand for reports, competition among news people, and problems related to gathering accurate, firsthand information, many dubious accounts were published.[7]

Another part of media logic is the demand that events appear as fresh as possible. By November 21, partly as a result of this constraint, the focus of news coverage shifted from the attack on the Ryan party to the emergent feature of the discovery of bodies at Jonestown. Related to this angle, minor articles contained information about government warnings, the cult's lawyers, and relatives of those who died. These topics also served as the basis for other minor stories over the next few days. On November 22, headline stories dealt with cult members thought to be missing in the jungle. Several lead stories also made final feature mention of the deaths of Ryan and the newspeople.

Media logic also demands some explanation of events, especially unusual ones, and in this process complex issues are often simplified. Although this issue is discussed in detail below, it is important to note here that by November 22 an explanation of these bizarre events was emerging. This explanation involved three important components: The People's Temple was labeled a *cult*, Jones was held to be *depraved*, and members of the group were defined as *deprived*. The symbolic significance of these labels is evident in the titles of major stories: "Son Depicts Leader of Cult as a

pertinent to what happens to people who engage in so-called liberal or humanitarian causes? In the context of the deprivation explanation of Jonestown (see below) Billy Graham reportedly said that Jones was "possessed by the devil and should not be linked to the church" (*St. Petersburg Times*, February 10, 1979:14).

[7]An almost perfect example of gross distortions of events vis-à-vis the news perspective is the quickly constructed book by Kilduff and Javers (1978). Several interesting examples of distortion are cited by Balch and Taylor (1977). A similar argument about the media serves as the basis for Fox's (1977) discussion of the reality of UFOs.

Fanatic and a Paranoid" (*New York Times*); "Sect Leader's Son: 'I think he became obsessed with power' "(*St. Petersburg Times*); "Explaining the Mass Suicides: Fanaticism and Fear" (*New York Times*); and "Cultists Seen as Victims of Needs" (*St. Petersburg Times*). A number of subsequent accounts supported this early explanation: "Jim Jones was Swallowed by His Own Big Lie" (*St. Petersburg Times*, November 25); and "Lawyer Says the Leader of Cult Had 'lost his reason' " (*New York Times*, November 23).

By November 23 almost exclusive (and, of course, massive) attention was directed to the "mystery" of the missing bodies. Minor articles dealt with the nature of the People's Temple, Jones' biography, and the role of Garry and Lane, the Temple lawyers. Almost as if it had become a novel, the "mystery" continued to be front page news on November 24 and 25. Story after story reported the body counts and then attempted to explain and re-explain the apparent and ongoing discrepancies. By November 26, with the discovery of an approximate total of 910 bodies, the mystery was more or less resolved. It was as if the last major chapter of this unfolding saga had been written. The mystery had been solved, and all that was left were a few loose ends. Consequently, by November 27 the Jonestown affair began dribbling off the front page.

In sum, media logic was employed to produce a certain news perspective on Jonestown. Through massive attention to these occurrences Jonestown was transformed into a major media event. Had the Jonestown events happened during a period in which central attention was directed elsewhere—Iran, Afghanistan, Columbia, the presidential election, etc.—it is doubtful that they would have received this amount or kind of coverage. In the course of becoming a media event selective attention was focused on (a) the murders of Ryan and the newspeople and (b) what became the mystery of the missing bodies. Minor articles were selected and included as they related to the two focal stories. And once Jonestown was identified as an important incident, a host of otherwise irrelevant issues, such as comments from people like Ronald Reagan and Billy Graham, somehow became "news."

While there can be no question about the newsworthiness of the events, the manner in which these occurrences were interpreted, presented, and thereby transformed is highly problematic sociologically. The matter of the bodies, for instance, became big news not merely because of the objective conditions of the situation (a large number of people dying under unusual circumstances) but because of the manner in which the events were reported. The actual mystery was an artifact of the manner in which the factor of time was interpreted by the news industry. The mystery was a product of continuous coverage and the continuous discovery of additional bodies by the authorities. For the authorities, what the media interpreted and featured as a mystery actually was part of the horrible job of searching the compound and accounting for an initially untold number of people. The early body counts were merely part of this investigative process and thereby subject to revision until the number of people supposed to be present was determined and the search was concluded. For the media, however, the investigation was interpreted differently: The initial counts became complete accounts thereby producing a series of discrepancies as new reports were received from the authorities. Each new report, in turn, required revision and explanation as each edition of the paper (or evening news) went to press. This perspective on the events was compounded by the lack of firsthand information. Together these problems resulted in distortion, bias, and out-and-out deception.

The Perception and Explanation of Deviance

Central to the perception and explanation of deviance is a certain news perspective on the People's Temple before versus after the murder/suicide incidents. Prior to these events, the People's Temple was labeled an alternative religious sect involved with timely and important social issues. Its leader, Jim Jones, was portrayed as a friend of the poor and a promoter of social equality and justice and other humanitarian causes. Although this religious group did not possess a national reputation, its activities had been reported by major regional papers. The *New York Times* (September 11, 1976; September 1977), *San Francisco Examiner* (January 1976), *San Francisco Chronicle* (March 1976), and *Fresno Bee* (see Krause et al., 1978:31), for example, all contained stories favorable to Jones and the Temple prior to the incidents. In fact, the *Los Angeles Herald* presented Jones its Humanitarian of the Year award in January 1976!

Part of the reason for this favorable image is that Jones carefully cultivated it.[8] The People's Temple made sizeable contributions to the press, including $4,400 to 12 newspapers for the "defense of a free press" in January 1973 and $300 for the defense of the *Fresno Bee* Four in May 1975. These gifts were in addition to public demonstrations staged by the People's Temple on behalf of the *Fresno Bee* reporters, political support of selected candidates, and an untold number of dollars contributed to political figures. Jones' political power became especially evident when news of an unfavorable story on the Temple to be published in the *New West* (July

[8]Kilduff and Javers (1978:76) notice, for example, that

> Between 1972 and 1977 the only stories that appeared in the press about the People's Temple were reports on the generosity of the church and Jim Jones. Journalists who were admitted to the Geary Boulevard headquarters [in San Francisco] were shown only what the church wanted them to see, nothing more.

It is interesting to note that Jones was arrested in December 1973 on charges of lewd conduct. Although these charges were dismissed because of a dispute over the legality of the arrest, there was no mention of the incident in the press.

1977) became known. In this situation Lt. Governor Dymally of California called Frank Lalli, the publisher, and requested the story be withheld (Krause et al., 1978:53; Kilduff and Javers, 1978:69–78).

Other consequences of this initially favorable labeling of the People's Temple may be cited: While the media occasionally printed negative stories about the Temple and Jones, none of the charges of Concerned Relatives were viewed as especially credible. Dr. Carlton Goodlet, a prominent California physician who observed the People's Temple in Guyana, reported to the *New York Times* (November 23, 1978, page A-17) that: "The deserters from the church had come to me, but they were just a neurotic fringe." Other community leaders, such as the now late San Francisco politician Harvey Milk, observed: "A year had passed and the temple had been investigated by the district attorney, and no one was taking them to court." Referring to "accounts of allegations made by former members of the sect that people inside the movement were being beaten, brainwashed and cheated out of their savings and property by the Rev. Jim Jones," Milk (*New York Times*, November 23, 1978, page A-17) added: "It almost came out that it looked like trial by press."

After the murder/suicide incidents the news perspective shifted radically. The morally charged label "cult" suddenly became an all meaningful designation for the Jonestown group. In this regard Robbins observes:

> Interestingly, the People's Temple was not generally labelled as a "cult" until Jonestown . . . . Whenever there is an "atrocity" linked to any discernable ideological minority, the offending group is immediately labeled a cult and implicitly equated with Hare Krishna and the Unification Church, which are thereby made to shoulder the responsibility for the trespasses of Jim Jones or violent Synanonists. (quoted in Wolf-Petrusky, 1979:7)

Furthermore, this label provided an overall context in which the Jonestown incidents were explained.

Few, if any, of the stories subsequent to the incidents labeled Jones as anything but a madman. This conclusion—that Jones was insane—permitted subsequent reports to enumerate an extensive list of misdeeds by Jones and his followers. Indeed, the complaints of Concerned Relatives, previously held to be incredible, suddenly became biting insights into what was going on all along. This retrospective-reflexive interpretation is illustrated by a feature story entitled "Tales of Violence Have Long Followed the People's Temple" (*St. Petersburg Times*, November 20, 1979). Although the article details a long series of misdeeds by Jones and the Temple, it contains little information that was not available before the murder/suicide incidents. Other story titles also are instructive: "Jim Jones: A Mean Kid in

Town (*St. Petersburg Times*, November 23), and "Unpublished Book by Exfollowers Tells of Jones' Obsession with Sex, Cruelty" (*St. Petersburg Times*, November 30).[9]

Another very important aspect of the news perspective on Jonestown was the use of selected "experts" to support and reinforce the labels used (cult, depraved, deprived) and an explanation of the events. This relationship between the media and experts is, of course, an interactive one: experts use the media for information, and the media use experts to construct and support explanations. Although different experts were interviewed, a more or less standardized "theory" of cults and deviance was applied to Jonestown. Specifically, the deviance of members was explained in terms of some combination of form of socioeconomic *deprivation* and/or psychological *abnormality*.

The first step of this argument is to invoke the label *cult* and assume that marginal movements of this sort arise under social conditions of "disorganization." The second step of the argument is that individuals—as a consequence of social disorganization—are somehow deprived, if not depraved. A few quotations from media sources are instructive:

> Why do so many young people join such oddball sects?
>
> Dr. Leo Rangell of Los Angeles, past president of the American Psychoanalysts Association, believes many are tense, anxious, alienated, disappointed in themselves or their parents, and desperately hungry and groping for love, approval and guidance.
>
> Young, unhappy, unwanted, rootless, unemployed people are particularly vulnerable—easy marks for even the most demented brainwasher. (*Parade*, February 11, 1979:24)

> Martin Marty, professor of religious history at the University of Chicago, attributes the growth of cults to the frustration of rootless people. He is convinced that the seemingly endless choices afforded in modern life frustrate or overwhelm many individuals. He says: "They short-circuit and try to hook their lives to any guiding spirit."
>
> Psychiatrist Marc Galtner, a specialist in research on cults, says . . . that

[9]Although these images were applied by the media to an entire group and its leader, they very much resemble other findings about the labeling process and its stigmatizing consequences. Skolnick and Wadsworth (1966), for instance, discovered that negative labels applied to high-status persons have little of the stigmatizing consequences associated with negative labels applied to low-status persons. In the case of Jones and the Temple it seems that the refutation of negative labels by prominent people and the use of power produced a similar result prior to the murder/suicide events. Other investigators (Cicourel, 1968; Altheide and Johnson, 1980) have demonstrated that once a label has been successfully applied this label then serves as a resource for the purpose of uncovering and documenting the original judgment. Whether the initial label represents a valid judgment is irrelevant for the purpose of understanding the labeling process. The point is that once the label is successfully applied, then all sorts of additional information may be brought to bear without serious question.

> many people join such groups in search for strong, charismatic leaders. He notes that "cults now are picking up the remainder of people who feel their interests have been overlooked."
>
> Sociologists who have studied cults find that many converts are young people, often without strong family ties, who are unsuccessful in dealing with life's problems and are seeking instant solutions suppled by others.
>
> Dr. William J. Winters, a Florida neuropathologist whose daughter was once involved with a large sect, says conversions are most successful when young people are highly disturbed over crises, such as loss of a lover or failure in college. (*U.S. News and World Report*, December 4, 1978:23)
>
> Dr. Lifton (a Yale University psychiatrist and authority on brainwashing) said he believed the increasing rootlessness of American society was spawning new cults, mostly fundamentalist in nature, at a striking rate. (*New York Times*, November 22, 1978:A-11)

Still other examples could be cited.

Whether this perspective on cults and deviance is thought to be viable by contemporary experts may be debated. The ideas themselves, furthermore, could be subjected to an almost endless series of criticisms.[10] Yet this is not the point. What is important is that these views have been emphasized from the news perspective, and apparently people believe them (Gallup, 1979). The pressing social scientific questions thus concern why and how explanations of this sort come to be emphasized by the media.

There are several answers to these questions. The media was confronted with a very unusual situation that demanded some kind of explanation. The cover term *cult* was used to provide a general context for interpreting conduct—an overall definition of the situation. The notions of deprivation and abnormality were applied. These ideas worked in conjunction with the term cult and together they conformed to common sense thinking about deviance. It is important to note that notions at odds with common sense are unlikely to be reported or even to be recognized as explanations from the news perspective. As previously noted, there also is a perceived need to present simple, straightforward explanations. As a consequence of these factors, media personnel construct explanations and select comments from experts to support them. It may be noted, also, that the "expert" need not possess special expertise in the matter at hand. It is sufficient—as the neuropathologist quoted above illustrates—simply to be defined as an "expert."

There are a number of examples of how this process operated. Har-

[10]For a review of this literature see Hine (1974) and Marx and Holzner (1977).

grave (1978:10) presents the following reaction of an anthropologist who was asked to comment on Jonestown:

> I supplied information to give callers what I regarded as important perspective. I pointed out that one person's "cult" is another's religion, and that my own research and study does not lead me to jump to the conclusion that people who join religious movements are somehow psychologically defective, economically deprived, or socially disorganized. I urged caution and explained that I knew little of the particular Jonestown case. I also questioned the obvious focus of the interviewer on the idea of a charismatic leadership controlling a mass of foolish puppets.
>
> All of this was so different from what the callers, interviewers, etc., wished to hear that they simply did not use the material. They had already made up their minds.

Another example derives from a reporter who reviewed a recent book on the "new religions" edited by Jacob Needleman and George Barker. After briefly reviewing the book the reporter concluded that it "will not provide any quick or easy answers for those looking for quick or facile analysis to what happened in Jonestown" (*St. Petersburg Times*, February 10, 1979:14). In other words: This work did not provide the kind of explanation easily integrated into the news perspective. A final example derives from my personal experience in doing a radio program on the Jonestown affair (WSUN Radio). During the program I briefly summarized a situational interpretation of the events. The show continued and after several minutes, the host turned to me and asked: "How might a sociologist explain these events?"

Bureaucratic Responses

Another important part of the media perspective on Jonestown is related to the responses of government officials. Bureaucrats principally responded to criticisms and questions about their role and responsibility in the matter. The press, for instance, asked why the State Department did not warn Ryan of the danger in Jonestown (*New York Times*, November 20) and why the government was ignorant of abuses within the People's Temple (*New York Times*, November 23, 24, 25)? Other questions have been raised about the role of the Guyanese government, letters written by prominent political figures in support of Jones, the role of the U.S. Embassy in Guyana, government removal of the bodies, and so on. Although these responses are interesting in and of themselves, they also supported the interpretation of deviance and perception of the cult problem.

An understanding of bureaucratic responses required an awareness of the intimate relationship between the media and public officials. While this relationship contains both competitive and cooperative elements, the competitive dimension commonly is overplayed. As Ross and Staines (1972:23) correctly observe:

> Media and officialdom . . . usually adopt a cooperative stance. The interests of government are more likely to be enhanced than to be frustrated by media activities. In particular, the media provide politicians with the channels of communication needed to proselytize official images and interpretations of social problems.

While government officials expressed concern for many dimensions of the Jonestown affair, public statements entailed a "cover yourself" strategy.

In spite of State Department responses stating that they warned Ryan of the possible danger in Guyana and the inability of the government to protect his party, there is no doubt that what happened came as a complete surprise to the government. The government ignored the many documented complaints of exmembers and Concerned Relatives, such as the *New West* (July 1977) article, and the 37-item affidavit filed by Deborah Layton Blakey in San Francisco on June 15, 1978 (see Krause et al., 1978:187–194; Kilduff and Javers, 1978:50–91). Instead, the public "cover yourself" statements of government officials were designed to define their responsibilities and then indicate how this responsibility was fulfilled.

The State Department, for instance, took the position that they did investigate complaints even though this was not their responsibility. It further defended its role in the matter by carefully delimiting certain self-defined obligations to the parties concerned.

> The role of the consular service is to assist Americans who are in trouble with foreign governments, not to try to protect Americans from one another.
>
> The consular establishment is not an investigative body and in this case was constrained from interfering with what was considered an American religious organization, protected by American tradition and the First Amendment. (*New York Times*, November 22, page A-11)

The United States Department of Justice employed a similar strategy in representing its responsibilities to the public. In a series of statements, Justice took the position that the right of religious freedoms severely limited what it could and could not do. Their arguments, based on legal judgments about deviance in religious groups, may be summarized as follows:

1 We can only investigate instances of violations of Federal law.

a One such Federal law pertains to kidnapping (18 U.S.C. 1021) but we have tried this and it does not work (Chatwin v. United States 326 U.S. 455). The reason it does not work is that a person cannot be kidnapped if they are exercising free will. "In short, the purpose of the statute is to outlaw interstate kidnapping rather than general transgressions of morality involving the crossing of state lines" (Justice Department reply, quoted in Krause et al., 1978:172).

b Other Federal statutes might apply, like those pertaining to peonage, slavery, and involuntary servitude (13 U.S.C. 1581; 18 U.S.C. 1583 and 1584), but we have tried these and they do not work either (United States v. Gaskin, 320 U.S. 527; United States v. Shackney, 333 F.2d 475 – 2nd Cir., 1964).

2 We also have considered the possibility of new legislation. Although the freedom to believe is absolute (Cantwell v. Connecticut 310 U.S. 296), the freedom to act may be restricted. Such restrictions, however, apply only if there are "grave and immediate dangers to interests which Government may lawfully protect" (Sherbert v. Verner 374 U.S. 396; Church of Scientology v. United States 409 F.2d 1146 – D.C. Cir., 1969 – cert. denied 396 U.S. 963). "Therefore, it appears that the possibility of drafting effective Federal criminal legislation in the area is most unlikely" (quoted in Krause et al., 1978:174).

3 Nevertheless, the FBI has been charged with the responsibility to investigate complaints for the purpose of determining:

a Was the individual actually restrained physically? and

b Was the observer actually present?

4 Finally, we also have pursued these matters on the basis of brainwashing, but this does not work either (People of State of New York v. ISKCON, Inc., et al., Queens County Supreme Court Nos. 2114–76, 2012–76).

5 In sum: "The Department of Justice shares the grief and shock of the families, friends and of the nation arising out of the mass tragedy occurring within the past week in Guyana. It has already and will do everything within its powers to investigate these occurrences so that the perpetrators and participants, wherever located, can be brought to justice. We are making this effort in conjunction with the State Department, consistent with international law and the cooperation of the sovereign state of Guyana. In addition we are assisting other departments and agencies of the United States government in a combined effort to properly identify and return the bodies of the victims and to secure the personal property involved. We are working urgently with the State Department and other agencies to provide for the safe and prompt return of survivors consistent with legitimate investigatory needs" (quoted in Krause et al., 1978:185).

On the basis of then current information, most of which was at least accessible to government authorities, there can be no doubt that sufficient evidence of criminal activities within the People's Temple existed prior to the murder/suicide incidents to merit Federal investigation. There are any number of reasons why the government did not respond, aside from the self-serving arguments presented above. It is of the utmost importance that bureaucratic justifications such as those discussed above be carefully distinguished from the actual reasons for United States government conduct, such as out-and-out incompetence.[11]

DISCUSSION AND CONCLUSION

Labeling and critical perspectives on deviance have focused attention on social reactions to objective conditions as a key determinate of what and how something is defined and treated as deviant. Actual investigation of the labeling process has concentrated on the reaction of particular agents of social control, but it has failed to examine concretely the critical role of the mass media (even though many observers have noted, implicitly and explicitly, the importance of the media). This paper re-emphasized the importance of the media for understanding social reactions to deviance, and drawing on recent studies of media it has articulated specific practices by media personnel contingent upon labeling. These practices, furthermore, were empirically examined by way of the Jonestown affair. This analysis thereby has provided additional knowledge about how labeling operates vis-à-vis the media, and how a certain (official) reality of Jonestown was formulated. While an analysis of this sort cannot provide absolute solutions to the issues discussed, a greater understanding of labeling should be useful for making intelligent policy decisions.

This paper demonstrated that information about Jonestown and the

[11]A beautiful example of bureaucratic conduct is provided by Krause et al. (1978:127). They describe Stephney Kibble, the information deputy as a black U.S. career officer for whom Guyana was to be the crowning assignment in a 30-year career. He planned to retire to a plot that he had providentially purchased years earlier in New Mexico. Dutiful as Kibble was in his role as embassy spokesman, he came under attack from certain quarters in the press on varying grounds, chief among them timidity and incompetence.

Kibble would say nothing that had not been cleared by the Embassy. Even after Kibble had been put in charge of the military press room set up on the lobby floor of the United States Information Agency library, he would volunteer no information. Relentlessly, he would refer newsmen to other sources—Minister of Information Field-Ridley or the American military task force spokesman, Air Force Capt. John J. Moscatelli, a stiff, dark-haired and olive-skinned man with a preference for dark-rimmed glasses and a deep aversion to smiling. Moscatelli would bark out to reporters the numbing catalogue of updated body counts, body bags, bodies flown to Timehri, bodies transferred to aluminum cases, bodies flown to Dover, Delaware. If a reporter persisted in questioning Kibble, he would repeat the drumfire of statistics, moving his finger along the text and numbers as he recited.

resultant public images of these events were the product of a news perspective whereby relevant facts were organized and presented. The news perspective provided a highly selective picture and explanation of these events. Media preoccupation with the "mystery of the missing bodies," for instance, was literally a created story. The emphasis on this and other angles or features vis-à-vis media logic directed public attention away from many other important topics—careful reports of what actually happened at the airfield, what actually happened at the "white night," the actual make-up of the Temple, rival and more complex interpretations of these events, the critical examination of government conduct, and so on. The explanation advanced also produced a simplistic and distorted image of Jonestown and how the People's Temple did or did not relate to public discussion of cults. The statements of social scientists and other supposed experts were selected by way of media logic and presented so as to support the predefined and carefully managed news perspective. There is little doubt that Jones was in some sense demented, but socially marginal authorities certainly have no monopoly on mental instability. Furthermore, notions of deprivation were advanced in the face of considerable evidence to the contrary. The idea that the People's Temple was simply a salvage operation for perverts, drug addicts, prostitutes, and the rest is at best only partly true. This image, moreover, was part of the front created and managed by Jones. Actually, the Temple inner circle included many professional types who hardly fit the deprived or depraved stereotypes. The official reality of Jonestown also supported the impression that this group was representative of contemporary cults. Cults of this sort were presented as a normal and pervasive feature of American life; and the activities inside the People's Temple were presented as routine features of modern cults. Indeed, the very label "cult" conjures up such distorted images as to make it almost worthless as a scientific concept. In fact, most of the images associated with the term cult by the media are largely illusions and gross distortions of the contemporary cult scene.[12]

In comparison with the carefully edited statements of social scientific experts, bureaucratic utterances appeared to be less subject to media distortion. There are several reasons for this situation. On the one hand, government officials, unlike social scientists, are experienced in dealing with the

[12]Based on an intensive study of cultic groups in a large southwestern city I estimate that less than one-tenth of a percent of the U.S. population are involved in groups of this sort. This estimate is an educated guess as to how many people in this city are involved in any way with groups similar to the People's Temple. There is no way of knowing whether this estimate is representative of the country as a whole. However, I suspect this estimate is liberal, and this region of the country supports more cultic groups than most others, the West Coast perhaps excepted (see Jorgensen, 1978; 1979). Most of the cultic groups in which Americans participate are quite different from the People's Temple, who in important ways more closely resemble relatively traditional American sects and denominations (see Jorgensen, 1978; 1979).

mass media. They are thus more likely to anticipate the manner in which such comments will be used. On the other hand, the interrelationship between government officials and the media is founded on ongoing cooperation.

Based on this analysis there is some temptation to conclude that the media as a part of the established institutional order somehow conspired to defraud the public. This may be true in the sense that an interest in being competitive and selling newspapers or programming is a determinate of news. Yet this analysis located the sources of media distortion in the practical day-to-day business of making news. In this sense the images created and presented by the media are the product of practical problems and decision making, not some conspiracy of elites.

On the basis of this paper it should be clear that the complex relationship between media, experts, public officials, and conceivably other interest groups merits continued investigation. The analysis of additional instances of how public images of deviance are constructed should lead to a more comprehensive understanding of the labeling process. Finally, it may be hoped, this knowledge should provide a basis for evaluating and constructing sound public policies. Social scientists may contribute to these policy decisions by pointing out how the media fashion a particular and commonly distorted reality of events, how their comments are used to support simplistic explanations, and the likely consequences of policies based on inaccurate and distorted images. No doubt additional research will reveal other ways that scholars of deviance may contribute to reasonable and humane solutions to these problems.

REFERENCES

Altheide, David L.
1976 Creating Reality: How TV Distorts Events. Beverly Hills: Sage Publications.

Altheide, David L., and John M. Johnson
1980 Bureaucratic Propaganda. Boston: Allyn and Bacon

Altheide, David L., and Robert P. Snow
1979 Media Logic. Beverly Hills: Sage Publications.

Balch, Robert, and David Taylor
1976 "Salvation in a UFO," Psychology Today 10 (Oct.):58–66; 106.
1977 "Seekers and saucers." The American Behavioral Scientist 20:839–860.

Becker, Howard S.
1963 Outsiders. New York: Macmillan.

Berger, Peter L., and Thomas Luckmann
1966 The Social Construction of Reality. Englewood Cliffs, N.J.: Prentice-Hall.

Blumberg, Abraham S.
1967 Criminal Justice. Chicago: Quadrangle.
Blumer, Herbert
1969 Symbolic Interactionism. Englewood Cliffs, N.J.: Prentice-Hall.
1971 "Social problems as collective behavior." Social Problems 18:298–306.
Coser, R. L., and L. Coser
1979 "Jonestown as a perverse utopia: a greedy institution in the jungle." Dissent 26 (Spring):158–163.
Cicourel, Aaron V.
1968 The Social Organization of Juvenile Justice. London: Heinemann.
1974 Cognitive Sociology. New York: Free Press.
Dinitz, Simon, et al.
1969 Deviance. New York: Oxford University Press.
Douglas, Jack D.
1967 The Social Meanings of Suicide. Princeton, N.J.: Princeton University Press.
1971 American Social Order: Social Rules in a Pluralistic Society. New York: Free Press.
Douglas, Jack D., and Paul K. Rasmussen, with Carol Ann Flanagan
1977 The Nude Beach. Beverly Hills: Sage Publications.
Epstein, Edward J.
1973 News from Nowhere: Television and the News. New York: Random House.
Emerson, Robert M.
1969 Judging Delinquents. Chicago: Aldine.
Erikson, Kai T.
1963 "Notes on the sociology of deviance." Pp. 25–29 in E. Rubington and M. S. Weinberg (Eds.), Deviance. New York: Macmillan.
Fox, Phillis
1977 Flying saucers: the media and the social construction of reality." Paper presented at the Pacific Sociological Association Meetings, Sacramento, California.
Galliher, John F., and James L. McCartney
1977 Criminology. Homewood, Ill.: Dorsey Press.
Gallup, George
1979 Religions in America: 1979–80. Princeton, N.J.: Princeton Religious Research Center.
Garfinkel, Harold
1967 Studies in Ethnomethodology. Englewood Cliffs, N.J.: Prentice-Hall.
Graham, James M.
1972 "Amphetamine Politics on Capitol Hill." Transaction 9 (January):14–22, 53.
Hargrave, Barbara
1978 Informing the public: social scientists and reactions to Jonestown." Unpublished paper.

Hine, Virginia H.
1974 "The deprivation and disorganization theories of social movements." Pp. 646–661 in I. I. Zaretsky and M. P. Leone (Eds.), Religious Movements in Contemporary America. Princeton, N.J.: Princeton University Press.

Johnson, D. Paul
1979 Dilemmas of charismatic leadership: the case of the People's Temple. Paper presented to the Southern Sociological Society, Atlanta, Georgia.

Jorgensen, Danny L.
1978 The esoteric community in the Valley of the Sun. Paper presented to the American Sociological Association, San Francisco, California.
1979 Tarot divination in the Valley of the Sun: an existential sociology of the esoteric and occult. Ph.D. dissertation. Columbus, Ohio: Ohio State University.

Kilduff, Marshall, and Ron Javers
1978 The Suicide Cult. New York: Bantam.

Kirsch, Jonathon
1979 "Beyond the law." New West (Dec. 17):105–112.

Kitsuse, John I.
1962 "Societal reactions to deviant behavior." Social Problems 9 (Winter):247–256.

Krause, Charles et al.
1978 Guyana Massacre. New York: Berkeley Books.

Lemert, Edwin
1951 Social Pathology. New York: McGraw-Hill.

Marx, John H., and Burkhart Holzner
1977 "The social construction of strain and ideological models of grievance in contemporary movements." Pacific Sociological Review 20 (July):411–438.

Mass, Armand L.
1975 Social Problems as Social Movements. Philadelphia: J. B. Lippincott.

Molotch, Harvey, and Marilyn Lester
1974 "News as purposive behavior." American Sociological Review 39 (February):101–112.
1975 "Accidental news." American Journal of Sociology 81 (Sept.):235–260.

Quinney, Richard
1970 The Social Reality of Crime. Boston: Little, Brown and Company.
1974 Criminology. Boston: Little, Brown and Company.

Rosenhan, D. L.
1973 "On being sane in insane places." Science 179 (Jan.):250.

Ross, Robert, and Graham L. Staines
1972 "The politics of analyzing social problems." Social Problems 20 (Summer):18–40.

Scheff, Thomas J.
1966 Being Mentally Ill. Chicago: Aldine.

Schudson, Michael
1978 Discovering the News. New York: Basic Books.

Shupe, Anson D., Jr., and David G. Bromley
1980 "Shaping the public response to Jonestown: the People's Temple and the anti-cult movement." In K. Levy (Ed.), Violence and Religious Commitment. Salt Lake: University of Utah Press.
Skolnick, Jerome H.
1966 Justice Without Trial. New York: John Wiley.
Singer, Margaret Thaler
1979 "Coming out of the cults." Psychology Today (Jan.):72–82.
Spector, Malcolm, and John I. Kitsuse
1977 Constructing Social Problems. Menlo Park, Calif.: Cummings.
Spradley, James P.
1970 You Owe Yourself a Drunk. Boston: Little, Brown and Company.
Sudnow, David
1965 "Normal crimes." Pp. 174–185 in E. Rubington and M. S. Weinberg (Eds.), Deviance. New York: Macmillan.
Sykes, Gresham M.
1974 "The rise of critical criminology." Journal of Criminal Law and Criminology 65 (June):206–213.
Szasz, Thomas
1961 The Myth of Mental Illness. New York: Harper & Row.
Taylor, Ian, et al.
1973 The New Criminology. New York: Harper Torchbooks.
Turner, Ralph H.
1969 "The public perception of protest." American Sociological Review 34 (Dec.):815–831.
Wiseman, Jacqueline P.
1970 Stations of the Lost. Englewood Cliffs, N.J.: Prentice-Hall.
Wolfe-Petrusky, Julie
1979 The social construction of the cult problem. Paper presented at the Annual Meeting of the Association for the Scientific Study of Religion, Boston, Mass.

Reading 12

Nicknames of Notorious American Twentieth-Century Deviants: The Decline of the Folk Hero Syndrome

James K. Skipper, Jr.
Virginia Polytechnic Institute and State University,
Blacksburg

This report examines the public use of personal nicknames for notorious American Twentieth Century Deviants. The analysis documents the frequency of nicknames by decade in the twentieth century, the category of the deviant act committed by the person nicknamed, and the connotations of the nicknames. The relationship between the use of nicknames for deviants, and deviants as folk heroes is explored. The data indicate that the public use of personal nicknames for deviants peaks in the 1920s and 1930s and has been declining ever since. This phenomenon parallels the decline in American's belief in the "rags to riches" type of folk hero.

Even from colonial times, American culture has been rich in the production of folk heroes (Brunwald, 1963). Often they have been individuals of ordinary origin and background who have risen by virtue of their own determination, abilities, and talents to considerable fame and/or fortune. Folk heroes have exemplified the "American Dream" that anyone can be successful, if they but try to work hard enough. It has also been noted that American culture has been equally rich in the use of nicknames (Mencken, 1980). Since at least the time of the American revolution, many folk heroes have been accorded nicknames. For example: Henry Lee, "Light Horse Harry," Francis Marion, "The Swamp Fox," Andrew Jackson, "Old Hickory," Abraham Lincoln, "Honest Abe," Thomas Jackson, "Stonewall," William Cody, "Buffalo Bill," Martha Canary, "Calamity Jane," John L. Sullivan, "Boston Strong Boy," George Ruth, "Babe," Louis Armstrong, "Sachmo." It has been argued that one function of nicknames is to break down barriers of formality, increase identification, and create a sense of closeness (Lieb, 1943; Allen, 1956; Harre, 1980; McBride, 1980).

Yet the list of American folk heroes with nicknames includes individuals with such soiled identities that they may be classified as deviants. For instance: Jesse James, "Great Train Robber," William Bonney, "Billy the Kid," Donnie Barker, "Ma," Al Capone, "Scar Face." The thought of deviants as folk heroes may at first appear to be a paradox. Social distance and

Presented at the Mid-South Sociological Association Meetings, October 27, 1983, Birmingham, Alabama. I would like to thank Charles McCaghy, C. Eddie Palmer, Alex Freedman, and Julius Debro for their insightful comments on earlier drafts of this manuscript.

negative connotations are more characteristic of attitudes toward deviant individuals than are feelings of intimacy and personal identification. Deviants are, to use Becker's term, "outsiders" (1969). The main objective of this report is to explore the relationship of nicknames with deviants and deviants as folk heroes.

A nickname is a name not derived from an individual's given names and which is added to, substituted for, or used alternatively with a person's given names. "Legs," "Bugsy," "Machine Gun," and "Happy Hooker" are examples of nicknames which were given to well known American deviants of the twentieth century.

"Nickname" is derived from the Old English *eke name* based on the verb *ecan* meaning to add or augment. Nicknames provide a richer and more explicit denotation than do given names. They often provide thumbnail character sketches or illustrations of aspects of an individual's personality, physical appearance or mannerisms (Morgan et al., 1980). For example, the gangsters Charles Gioe and Jack Guzik were called "Cherry Nose" and "Greasy Thumb" respectively. A nickname may also serve as a capsule history of an individual by selecting and amplifying some particularly significant event in life. For instance Salvatore Luciano earned his nickname "Lucky" from his peer group, when at the age of 16 in New York City he won $244 in one night in a floating crap game. This was a virtual fortune for a slum boy in 1913 (Demaris, 1974).

Although nicknames are a deeply imbedded cultural element in American society (Mencken, 1980), surprisingly little empirical research has been reported in the literature in any discipline. Even the leading onomastic journal *Names* has published only a few articles mentioning American personal nicknames in its over a quarter of a century of existence (Mook, 1967; Lawson, 1973). A survey of research did not uncover any sociological studies of nicknames, let alone one concerned with deviants.

Despite the lack of data, there are some suggestions in the literature to provide cursory guidelines for research. It has been speculated that nicknames are more often used with males than females and are usually accorded during the early school years and then discarded in adult life (Van Buren, 1974; Smith, 1970). Several writers have commented that people feel closer when they use nicknames. Even though they might not be acquainted personally, with one another, nicknames indicate intimacy (Lieb, 1943; Allen, 1956; Harre, 1980). Grosshandler (1978) and others believe that nicknames may have been more prevalent earlier in the century than they are now. Others have pointed out that often times entertainers, professional athletes, politicians, and even underworld figures are made folk heroes and accorded nicknames (Smith, 1970; Van Buren, 1974; Harris, 1979).

Building on these notions, Skipper (1981, 1983) demonstrated that the number of baseball players accorded nicknames varied by decade and has been declining since the 1920s, but especially after 1950. He maintains that this is due to the manner in which major league baseball players are perceived by fans has changed from folk heroes implying intimacy, closeness and personal identification, to entrepreneurs implying impersonality, distance and a low degree of identification. He suggests that this change may parallel the general shift in American society from a gemeinshaft orientation to a gesellshaft type. In addition, his data indicate that the majority of baseball player's nicknames were not carry-overs from childhood.

Following these leads the focus of the research reported here is to shed further light on the use of personal nicknames by examining the public nicknames given to notorious American deviants. The analysis will document the frequency of nicknames by decade in the twentieth century, the category of the deviant act committed by the person nicknamed, and the connotations of the nicknames.

PROCEDURES

As Emrich (1972) has pointed out, nicknames are not remembered much past a person's life time unless fame is achieved. This makes it difficult for the researcher to define a given population let alone a representative sample. The problem, of course, is compounded with the study of deviants since to begin with, the population is limited to deviants who are known to the public or, more precisely to that portion of the public that is likely to record their deviancy. Thus for purposes of research, one is left with deviants whose acts became widely enough known that their nicknames have been recorded and preserved. Unfortunately, this situation is not unique. It is true for most historical analyses of nicknames.[1] For example over time it is not possible to obtain a representative sample of doctors, priests, women, blacks, residents of the state of New York, etc. and discover what percentage were accorded nicknames and what they were. The data simply do not exist.

With this limitation in mind, the nickname of deviants used in this report are derived from the most recent and most complete collection of American nicknames from 1900–1979 available. In 1979 Lawrence Urdang edited *Twentieth Century American Nicknames*. This volume contains 398 pages of nicknames including those of individuals who may be defined as deviants. Urdang lists two criteria for inclusion in his dictionary. First, evidence must be available that the nickname is, or has been widely used in

[1]An exception is the case of major league baseball players. Data has been recorded on every person who played major league baseball since 1871. Even though an individual may have participated in no more than one inning of one game, his nickname is included. This may be a unique data set for historical analysis (Reichler, 1979).

contemporary speech and literature. Second, there must be convincing evidence that a significant number of speakers and writers at one period or another used the nickname without feeling it necessary to explain to whom it referred. He concludes:

> Whenever usage of a nickname becomes that widespread, for however short a period, it must be recorded for future reference. (Urdang, 1979:VIII)

The nicknames listed in such a collection may be termed *official* nicknames. That is, the names by which individuals were known to the public. They are not necessarily the nicknames that were used by friends, relatives, and acquaintances in everyday life. These may be termed *unofficial* nicknames and in most cases have not been recorded for posterity. Mitchell (1982) provides an example with the nicknames used for Al Capone.

> The newspapers called him Scarface, but the soberquet did not safely bear repeating in his presence. It was Mister Capone instead or Big Al; or among trusted lieutenants of his palace guard, "Snorky," a street word connoting a certain princely eloquence. (91)

Experts disagree over what the most useful definition of a deviant or deviant behavior should be. For the purposes of this research a relatively strict definition has been chosen. A deviant is an individual who engages in behavior which was subject to legal prosecution. Using this definition 198 nicknames qualified for inclusion in the analysis.[2]

FINDINGS

As indicated in Table 1, 174 (87.9%) of the 198 nicknames were applied to males, and 24 (12.1%) to females. Thus males predominate. However, it should be noted that the proportion of females accorded nicknames in

[2]There were six nicknames which applied to groups. While they were too few to compare in the general analysis, they are nevertheless worthy of consideration. Five of the six groups were all male. Three were applied to gangster groups: "The Eastmans," a gang of hoodlums led by Monk Eastman in the early 1900s; "Murder Trust," a group of 5 men who murdered Michael Malloy in 1932; and "Murder Incorporated" a group of professional criminals operating in New York City in the 1940s. In the 1920s, the anarchists, Nicola Sacco, and Bartolomeo Vanzetti were referred to as the "Braintree Martyrs." The "Chicago Seven" was accorded to a group of 7 defendants (Jerry Rubin, Abbie Hoffman, Rennie Davis, David Dellinger, Tom Hayden, Lee Weiner, and John Fronines) at a trial for inciting to riot during the democratic National Convention in 1968. The final group, the Harrisburg Seven, also referred to a Viet Nam protest group consisting of 5 men and 2 women who were accused of subversive activities.

comparison to males increases greatly starting in the 1940s decade. During the 1970s half of the 10 nicknamed deviants were female. The actual number of females varies little over the eight decades, the range being two to five.

Most males with nicknames were recorded in the 1920s and 1930s: 103 of the 174. It is also in these two decades that the ratio of men to women is greatest. The number of males with nicknames peaks in the 1920s with 66, and drops dramatically from 47 in the 1930s to just 5 in the 1940s and remains low through the 1970s.

Table 2 indicates the type of deviance by decade for males with nicknames. For the total population 104 (52.3%) were of the gangster-racketeer-bootlegger type. A distant second were murderers 16 (8.3%) followed by gamblers 13 (7.5%) and gang-land bosses 12 (6.6%).[3] Each of the other categories constituted less than three percent of the total. No male sexual deviants appear. The 1920s and 1930s contain by far the most male deviants with nicknames: 66 and 47 respectively. Eighty-two (79.6%) of the gangster-racketeer-bootleggers, 11 of the 12 (91.6%) gang-land bosses, and 8 of the 9 (88.9%) robber-thief-burglar category fell in these decades. Also, 6 of the 16 (37.5%), murderers were accorded nicknames during the 1920s and 1930s. The only major notable exception is gamblers. The first two decades of the century were the most popular for nicknaming gamblers.

As can be seen from Table 3, the pattern for males in Table 2 is not duplicated for females. Sexual deviance (prostitutes, madams, nude entertainers) was the most prominent category, not gangsterism. For the total population, 10 (41.7%) were involved in sexual deviance, followed by political deviance 5 (20.8%) and murder 4 (16.7%). The political category was concentrated in the 1970s, while the sexual deviants received nicknames in all but one of the eight decades, but half were between 1910 and 1929. The murderers did not fit a time pattern.

Table 4 characterizes the nicknames by connotation, that is, to what they refer. "Act of Deviance," is the category with the highest percentage—35.8% for men and 54.2% for women. The nicknames stem directly from the acts of deviance. Examples of this type are: the arsonist Sam Scarlow, "Sam the Torch," the assassin James Earl Ray, "Camouflaged Killer," and the madam Mattie Silks, "Queen of the Denver Red Lights." Obviously these nicknames are acquired after one or more deviant acts have been made known to the public. This means that they do not stem from some childhood or family nickname accorded early in life. This statement cannot be

[3]Gangland bosses are distinguished from the gangster-racketeer-bootlegger category only on the basis of their leadership position. For other purposes they might be included in the same category.

TABLE 1 Number of Public Nicknames of Twentieth Century American Deviants by Sex and Decade

	Decade																	
Sex	1900–1909		1910–1919		1920–1929		1930–1939		1940–1949		1950–1959		1960–1969		1970–1979		Total	
Men	16	9.2%	20	11.5%	66	37.9%	47	27.0%	5	2.9%	11	6.3%	4	2.3%	5	2.9%	174	100%
Women	3	12.5%	5	20.8%	3	12.5%	2	8.3%	2	8.3%	2	8.3%	2	8.3%	5	20.8%	24	99.8%
Total	19	9.6%	25	12.6%	69	34.8%	49	24.7%	7	3.5%	13	6.6%	6	3.0%	10	5.1%	198	99.9%

TABLE 2 Number of Public Nicknames of Twentieth Century American Male Deviants by Category of Deviance and Decade

	Decade																	
Category	1900–1909		1910–1919		1920–1929		1930–1939		1940–1949		1950–1959		1960–1969		1970–1979		Total	
Bootlegger-racketeer-gangster	3	2.9%	12	11.5%	51	49.0%	31	29.8%	4	3.8%	3	2.9%	—		—		104	99.9%
Murderer	1	6.3%	2	12.5%	2	12.5%	4	25.0%	—		4	25.0%	1	6.3%	2	12.5%	16	100.1%
Gambler	7	53.8%	3	23.1%	1	7.7%	2	15.4%	—		—		—		—		13	100.0%
Gangland boss	—		—		8	66.7%	3	25.0%	—		1	8.3%	—		—		12	100.0%
Robber-burglar-thief	—		1	11.1%	3	33.3%	5	55.6%	—		—		—		—		9	100.0%
White collar criminal	1	20.0%	1	20.0%	—		—		—		3	60.0%	—		—		5	100.0%
Western outlaw	3	75.0%	—		1	25.0%	—		—		—		—		—		4	100.0%
Political deviant	—		—		—		—		—		—		1	33.3%	2	66.7%	3	100.0%
Assassin or attempted assassin	—		—		—		—		—		—		2	66.7%	1	33.3%	3	100.0%
Bomber-arsonist	—		1	50.0%	—		1	50.0%	—		—		—		—		2	100.0%
Hobo-vagrant	—		—		—		1	50.0%	1	50.0%	—		—		—		2	100.0%
Informer	1	100.0%	—		—		—		—		—		—		—		1	100.0%
Total	16	9.2%	20	11.5%	66	37.9%	47	27.0%	5	2.9%	11	6.3%	4	2.3%	5	2.9%	174	100.0%

TABLE 3 Number of Public Nicknames of Twentieth Century American Female Deviants by Category of Deviance and Decade

Category	Decade 1900–1909	1910–1919	1920–1929	1930–1939	1940–1949	1950–1959	1960–1969	1970–1979	Total
Sexual deviance	1 10.0%	3 30.0%	2 20.0%	1 10.0%	—	1 10.0%	1 10.0%	1 10.0%	10 100.0%
Political deviance	—	—	—	—	1 20.0%	—	—	4 80.0%	5 100.0%
Murderer	1 25.0%	—	1 25.0%	—	—	1 25.0%	1 25.0%	—	4 100.0%
Gangster	—	2 66.7%	—	1 33.3%	—	—	—	—	3 100.0%
White collar criminal	— 100.0%	—	—	—	—	—	—	—	1 100.0%
Informer	—	—	—	—	1 100.0%	—	—	—	1 100.0%
Total	3 12.5%	5 20.8%	3 12.5%	2 8.3%	2 8.3%	2 8.3%	8.3%	5 20.8%	24 100.0%

TABLE 4 Number of Public Nicknames of Twentieth Century American Deviants by Sex and Connoation of Nickname

Sex	Nickname connotation: Deviant act		Physical character-istics		Behavioral character-istics		Common nick-names		Ethnic reference		Geograph-ical ref-erences		Other people's names		Unique special meaning		Total	
Men	57	32.8%	35	20.1%	30	17.2%	11	6.3%	11	6.3%	6	3.4%	2	1.1%	22	12.6%	174	99.8%
Women	13	54.2%	1	4.2%	3	12.5%	3	12.5%	—		—		3	12.5%	1	4.2%	24	100.1%
Total	70	35.4%	36	18.1%	33	16.7%	14	7.1%	11	5.6%	6	3.1%	5	2.5%	23	11.6%	198	100.1%

made about any of the other categories without evidence of the actual origin of the nickname.

Thirty-five of the men's nicknames (20.1%) referred to physical characteristics such as "Big," "Little," "Slim," "Fatso," "Lefty," "Blackie," "Whitey" and so forth. Only one of the women's (4.2%) did so. This is surprising since almost 42% of the women were involved in sexual deviance.[4] The third most frequent category, men 17.2% and women 12.5% was nicknames that referred to behavioral characteristics, usually an aspect of the deviant's personality or a particular mannerism. Examples were: the murderer Ruth Snyder, "Granite Woman," the gangster Roger Touhy, "Terrible" Touhy, and the racketeer and gang-land boss, Anthony Anatasio, "Tough" Tony.

"Common" nicknames, and those of "Ethnic" and "Location" reference together constituted about 15% of the total. Examples in the common category were "Ma," "Duke," "Buster," "Buddy;" ethnic, "Nig," "Dutch," "Jew," and "Nick the Greek;" location, "Texas," "Minnesota," and "Milwaukee." The final two categories were termed "Other Peoples Names" (2.5%) and "Unique Special Meaning" (11.7%). The former category refers to deviants whose nicknames were not derived from their given names, but in fact were common first names.[5] For instance, the murderer Rose Marie Bjorkland, was nicknamed "Penny," the gambler Christian Bertche, "Barny" and the gangster Paul Carbo, "Frankie." The unique special meaning category is a residual. The nicknames do not fit any other category, are one of a kind, and appear to have a special meaning for one particular individual. Representative of this category were: Louis Webber who was called "Bridgey," the gangster Paul Ricca, "Mops," and the racketeer Enoch Johnson, "Nucky."[6]

DISCUSSION

The data indicate that the number of American deviants accorded public nicknames in the twentieth century varies significantly by decade and are many fewer in the 1970s than in the decades before 1940. The pattern does not follow for women with the dual highs being the 1910–1919, and 1970–1979 decades. Thus, the hypothesis is supported for men but not for

[4]This may be due to the fact that many "popular" nicknames for prostitutes are not considered acceptable to the public ear.

[5]In another context (Skipper, 1980) discovered the same phenomenon with baseball players. In some cases where evidence was available, it was found these nicknames were the first names of close family members—mother, father, brother, uncle and so forth. It is strongly suspected that this may also be the case with deviants.

[6]It is quite likely that the origins of the nicknames are buried in the life history of the individuals well before any acts of deviance were committed and may in fact be carry-overs from nicknames used in childhood.

women. Since many more men than women have been publicly labeled as deviants in the twentieth century, it is not surprising to find that many more of those receiving public nicknames are also males. Although this finding agrees with the hypothesis that more males than females receive nicknames, under the circumstances it can only provide weak support.

Of more importance, however, is the fact that there are as many women with nicknames in the 1970s decade as men! This may have something to do with the increasing equality of women, but it probably has more to do with the type of deviance. Four of the five women given nicknames in the 1970s were political deviants as were two of the five men. The fact that political deviance is the category in the 1970s that accounts for 60 percent of the total nicknames is of significance. It marks a departure from previous decades when nicknames of sexual deviants were more frequent for women, and the gangster-racketeer-bootlegger before the 1950s with men. This theme will be expanded shortly.

There is evidence that some nicknames of the deviants may stem from their childhood. However, the finding that over one-third of the men's and over half of the women's public nicknames are related to the act of deviance undermines the hypothesis, that childhood is the time of acquisition.[7] One suspects that the second and third most frequent types of nicknames, physical and behavioral characteristics were also used as a basis for nicknames in adult life rather than at an earlier age. In any event, these three categories account for approximately 70 percent of the nicknames. It seems reasonable to revise the hypothesis to read. A high percentage of public nicknames stem from a particular act or event in the individual's adult professional life or from a physical or behavioral characteristic noted in adult life.[8]

The most striking finding in this study is the much greater frequency of

[7]A case in point is the nickname "Pretty Boy" given the bank robber Charles Arthur Floyd. Sifakis (1981) explains: "In Sallisaw, Oklahoma, where he grew up, the hill folk were duly impressed by the fact he was never without a pocket comb. They studied his slick-as-axle-grease pompadour and dubbed him 'Pretty Boy' " (339). Floyd despised the nickname and tried to keep it secret. However, it stuck with him and was picked up by the press during his bank robbing days. This is an example of a nickname acquired in childhood, and not appreciated by the deviant but carried into adulthood and made popular by the media. Examples of the opposite side of the coin may also be found. For instance, George Kelly a bank robber and kidnapper of the 1930s was nicknamed "Machine Gun" and popularized by the press. George was not overly imaginative and his career was not progressing as rapidly as his wife Kathryn Shannon felt it could and should. Sifakis reports: "Kathryn began promoting Kelly as a fearless crook who was often 'away robbing banks.' She gave him a shiny machine gun as a present and made him practice shooting walnuts off fence posts. Kathryn, who understood promotion, also passed out cartridge cases in underworld dives, saying, have a souvenir of my husband, 'Machine Gun Kelly' " (340–341).

[8]In the course of analyzing the nicknames, it was discovered that four were given to individuals whose identity was unknown at the time the nickname was accorded! In three cases the nickname is much more familiar than the individuals given name and in the fourth the given name was still unknown at the time it was recorded in the *Dictionary of Twentieth*

male nicknames in the 1920s and 1930s and their sharp decline in the 1940s and thereafter. This needs further discussion and explication. Skipper (1983) found a similar pattern in the frequency of nicknames of baseball players although their peak was a decade before that of deviants, and their greatest decline a decade later. Skipper's explanation was that nicknames imply closeness, intimacy, and personal identification. During the century's first three decades, baseball players were perceived as folk heroes. They exemplified the American rags to riches, humble origins to fame syndrome. Ordinary folk were able to identify with the players using nicknames as was one symbol of that identification. After the 1930s, the belief in the American Dream faded into a greater awareness of social reality and so faded folk heroes, who exemplified the dream. A similar phenomenon may have happened with deviants.

One type of deviant would seem to fit the folk hero image. It is the type Merton has termed an "innovator." According to Merton's anomie theory, anomie results from strains in the social structure which place pressures on individuals propelling them toward unrealistic aspirations. The emphasis placed on financial success in the absence of socially acceptable opportunities creates a conflict between the goal and capacities or means of individuals to attain it. One adaptation common in the lower classes is innovation (Merton, 1957). The innovator being unable to achieve success through legitimate means, literally invents new ones to promote success even though they violate social norms. The gangster-racketeer-bootlegger is the archetype of the innovator (Merton, 1957).

This is exactly the category of male deviants that received nicknames during the 1920s and 1930s. While the data of this research do not provide the social class background on all these men, what is available, indicates that most of them came from lower class origins. In addition 36 (44%) had Italian given names. The contention is that the nature of the social climate made these deviants prime candidates for folk hero status and nicknames.

Century Nicknames. The nickname "Axis Sally" was given to the radio propagandist allegedly working for the Nazi government before her identity as Rita Zucca was known. Albert De Salvo was nicknames "The Boston Strangler" before he was apprehended and identified; the same was true of David Berkowitz—"Son of Sam." In the fourth case the "Skid Row Slasher" of Los Angeles was recorded for posterity in Urdang's dictionary without his identity being known. This is not an isolated case. One of the most infamous deviants of all time was never identified. We know him only by his nickname—"Jack the Ripper." It would seem that the public has a need to afix a name to individuals whose identity is unknown but whose activities become newsworthy and topics of everyday conversation. This is provided when the mass media gives the individual a nickname which is associated with his/her activity. Although this phenomenon is probably most typical with deviants, it may not be unique to them. For instance, the Watergate informer has been nicknamed "Deep Throat." At this writing it is still not known whether "Deep Throat" was a he or a she, or whether the person was involved in the scandal or not. Thus, it is impossible at this time to label the individual deviant or hero, or both.

Two specific events in American history help explain this phenomenon—prohibition and the "great" depression.

Prohibition began in January 1920 and was in effect until December, 1933. The depression began in October 1929 and lasted throughout the 1930s. Prohibiting the manufacture, sale, and transportation of intoxicating beverages was not popular with great segments of the American public and many were eager to break the law. Gangsters and racketeers who supplied them with the illegal booze were treated as heroes and forgiven for many of their other transgressions. As McCaghy put it:

> Prohibition provided not only a new source of profit but also social acceptance. Much of America became lawless as the liquor laws were openly flouted and the gangster attained a respectability he scarcely had dreamed possible. (1980:290)

The depression had a similar affect of catapulting the gangster into hero status, especially those of folk and/or ethnic background who robbed the haves in a have not era. Banks and other financial institutions were especially vulnerable. Widespread unemployment, bank closings, bread lines, tent cities, and foreclosures of mortgages made life difficult for the working classes. These hard times created an atmosphere conducive to admiring, identifying, and glorifying those who beat the system—albeit by illegal means. Perhaps nothing better conveys the folk hero image of gangsters and racketeers during this era than the elaborate funerals they were accorded. The case of Angelo Genna's send off in Chicago is a perfect example.

> Among his mourners were Capone, a state senator, two state representatives, an alderman, and the city sealer. The procession included three hundred cars of people and thirty cars of flowers. The casket was of solid silver and the funeral cost was estimated at $100,000. (McCaghy, 1980:209)

By the beginning of World War II the influence of prohibition was past, and the effects of the depression were being alleviated. It is contended that this was largely responsible for the death of the bootlegger-racketeer-gangster as folk hero, which is reflected in the decline in the use of nicknames for the "innovator" type of deviant. At the same time, however, belief in the folk hero rags to riches complex also declined. It became increasingly clear that Horatio Alger stories were more myth than reality, exception than rule. The changing view began with the first Roosevelt administration and the growing social consciousness concerning the lower classes and minority groups. It resulted in continuing sets of social and welfare legislation to date; designed to protect the rights of minority groups, provide for those who could not provide for themselves and insure educational and occupational opportunities for individuals who would not otherwise be able to secure circumstances favorable to advancement. The death of the belief in the innovator as folk hero was in large part responsible for the decline in the use of public nicknames for deviants.

However, this does not mean that there are no folk heroes left in America with or without nicknames deviant or nondeviant.[9] But, one type of folk hero is probably gone forever. Furthermore, the growing impersonality of modern mass society makes it more difficult to identify with public figures at least to the extent of according them nicknames.

Although today the numbers of deviants with a nickname is small in comparison to those of the 1920s and 1930s, it is significant that in the 1970s 60% of the deviants with public nicknames were in the political category. A closer look indicates that their deviance consisted of protests against the establishment especially the war in Viet Nam. For other purposes an analysis was made of all military personnel accorded nicknames by decade. Only one member of the American military was mentioned in Urdang (1979) as receiving a nickname in the 1970s. It may be that the folk heroes of this era were not those who fought the war, but those who protested the fight itself. In this sense they come closer to the type of adaptation that Merton termed "Rebellion" than "Innovation" (1957).

REFERENCES

Allen, Lee

1956 "Red Lefty a Few Animals," in Charles Einstein (ed.), The Fireside Book of Baseball. New York: Simon and Schuster, 6–10.

[9]There is an alternative explanation for the decline in the use of public nicknames which needs to be considered. It involves both the role of the media and changing social values. Regardless of the origin of the nickname it is in large part through the media that it is made and kept public. As McBride (1980) put it: "But to achieve lasting and widespread value a nickname has to be put into circulation and kept there by writers and broadcasters" (p. 90). There is some evidence that since World War II, and especially since the advent of television newscasting, journalists and broadcasters have been less likely to be flamboyant and to indulge in the hyperbolic. Modern reporting tends to be more detached in an attempt to be objective. Thus the use of nicknames for deviants in everyday life may be as great as ever, but the media are not as likely to publicize them. At any time the police have on file thousands of nicknames of people who have been charged or convicted of crimes (Glionna, 1983). Seldom are these seen in print or heard on radio or TV. This may also be related to change in social values concerning human dignity and civil rights. For instance, ethnic nicknames, sexist ones, and those bringing attention to particular physical features or personality traits are now considered much more offensive than they have been in the past. Therefore, media reporters may not feel it is appropriate to mention such current nicknames of deviants known to the police as: "Fish Head," "Fatty Funk," "Sucker Thumb," "China Man," "King Rat," and "Scaby Woman" (Glionna, 1980).

Becker, Howard
1963 Outsiders: Studies in the Sociology of Deviance. New York: Free Press.
Brunwald, Jan
1968 The Study of American Folklore. New York: W. W. Norton.
Demaris, Ovid
1974 The Lucky Luciano Story. New York: Belmont Tower Books.
Dexter, Emily
1949 "Three Items Related to Personality: Popularity, Nicknames, and Homesickness." The Journal of Social Psychology. 30:155–158.
Emrich, Duncan
1972 Folklore on the American Land. Boston: Little Brown and Co.
Glionna, John
1983 "Many Crooks Caught When Victims Recall Nicknames," Roanoke Times and World News, Nov. 14:A-9.
Harre, Ron
1980 "What's In a Nickname?" Psychology Today. 3 (Jan.):78–79.
Harris, R.
1979 "What's In a Nickname?" Ebony 34 (July):76–82.
Lawson, E.
1973 "Men's First Names, Nicknames and Short Names: A Sematic Differential Analysis." Names, 21:22–27.
Lieb, Frederick
1943 "Dizzy, Lippy, Babe or Cy Give an Image to the Eye," The Sporting News, November 18.
McBride, Joseph
1980 High and Inside. New York: Warner Books.
McCaghy, Charles
1980 Crime in American Society. New York: Macmillan.
Mencken, H. L.
1980 The American Language. 4th Edition. New York: Knopf.
Merton, Robert
1957 Social Theory and Social Structure. Glencoe, Ill.: Free Press.
Mitchell, John
1982 "Al Capone." In America. 1:3:91–97.
Mook, Maurice
1967 "Nicknames Among the Amish," Names, 15:111–118.
Morgan, Jane, O'Neile Christopher and Ron Harre
1980 Nicknames and Their Social Consequences. London: Routledge and Kegan Paul.
Reichler, Joseph
1979 The Baseball Encyclopedia (4th ed.) New York: Macmillan.
Sifakis, Carl
1981 "The Gangsters," in David Wallechinsky and Irving Wallace (eds.), The People's Almanac #3, New York: Bantam Books, 337–344.

Skipper, James K. Jr.
1981 "Analysis of Baseball Nicknames," Baseball Research Journal 10:112–119.

Skipper, James K. Jr.
1983 "Nicknames as a Neglected Element of American Culture: The Example of Baseball Players." Paper presented at the XIII annual Alpha Kappa Delta Research Symposium, Richmond, Virginia, February 17–19, 1983. Forthcoming, Journal of Sport Behavior 6:4, 1984.

Smith, Elsdon
1970 The Story of Our Names. Detroit: Gale Research Co.

Urdang, Laurance
1979 Twentieth Century American Nicknames. New York: Wilson.

Van Buren, H.
1974 "The American Way With Names," in R. Brislin (ed.), Culture Learning: Concepts, Applications and Research. Honolulu: University of Hawaii Press.

Reading 13

Toward an Understanding of False Accusation: The Pure Case of Deviant Labeling

Lloyd W. Klemke

Gary H. Tiedeman
Oregon State University, Corvallis

The phenomenon of the "falsely accused deviant" was introduced by Becker almost two decades ago (Becker, 1963) and has become a *tacit* anchor point for subsequent labeling theory. It has, however, received limited systematic analytic explication. This paper first samples a broad range of research findings affirming the breadth and prevalance of false accusation. A classification scheme identifying four fundamental types of false accusations (pure, intentional, legitimatized, and victim based) is then introduced and illustrated. Finally, several propositions pertaining to the societal and organizational preconditions for the occurrence of false accusation are presented and documented. The roles that (1) perceived threat, (2) subcultural heterogeneity, (3) domain protectionism, (4) stereotype adoption, and (5) diagnostic oversimplification play in the emergence of false accusation are highlighted.

INTRODUCTION

For more than a decade the labeling perspective has been the dominant theoretical perspective in sociology of deviant behavior. Two major themes have been emphasized by the labeling proponents. The first theme suggests that acts come to be considered deviant because some individuals are able to impose their definitions of morality on others. The second theme points to the potential deviance-amplifying effects that may be stimulated by being exposed to the labeling process. In other words, these theorists have sensitized other sociologists interested in deviance to the importance of analyzing how definitions of deviance come into existence, how labels are applied, and the effects of being labeled. Numerous critics have challenged the explanatory power and the empirical validity of the labeling perspective (i.e., Gibbs, Warren and Johnson, 1972). These challenges have tempered the initial claims of the labeling proponents. Thus, the position has evolved that labeling factors are important but that other explanations, such as socialization, status frustration, neutralization, and Marxist conflict, must also be considered for the contributions they can make toward our understanding of deviant behavior.

The central concern of this paper is the phenomenon of the falsely accused deviant. This category was introduced into the deviance literature in Becker's seminal statement of the labeling perspective (Becker, 1963). He developed a classification scheme of types of deviant behavior based on whether one has been a rule-breaker and whether one has been labeled deviant. Thus a person who kills another person and is labeled a murderer is a "pure deviant"; an individual who does not kill and is not labeled is a "conformist"; an individual who kills but is not labeled is a "secret deviant"; and an individual who has not killed but has been labeled as a killer is a "falsely accused deviant." Unfortunately, Becker did not systematically elaborate on this last category but only offered a few examples of its existence. Subsequent deviance literature has also given only passing attention to the falsely accused deviant. This oversight is quite ironic because the falsely accused provides the quintessential example of labeling. Because false accusations are *not* empirically valid, it follows that considerable insight can be derived by examining the conditions and the social processes that are involved in generating these false conceptions of social reality.

Labeling analysts have frequently aimed their research at revealing the foibles, arbitrariness, and discriminatory practices evident in the labeling process. Although there are some interesting studies and many incidental examples of false accusation, there are no efforts to collect and analyze this material. This paper is devoted to systematically analyzing the phenomenon of false accusation. To do this we first review several important studies that illustrate the existing work related to the false accusation topic. Next, we develop a classification scheme of the different types of false accusation. Finally, we develop a set of propositions specifying important conditions that facilitate the emergence of false accusations.

Before proceeding, it seems appropriate to suggest one reason why the fascinating phenomenon of false accusation has received little systematic attention. This is perhaps related to the frustrating problems of documenting that the accusations are indeed false. Thus the analyst could easily fall into the embarrassing position of finding the guilty innocent and thereby become a purveyor of false labeling. Although there is no way of completely avoiding this dilemma, we have attempted to rely on cases where evidence, usually accumulated by a disinterested third party, has established the inaccuracy of the accusation.

ILLUSTRATIVE EXAMPLES OF FALSE ACCUSATION

Media, literary, and social science allusions to the phenomenon of false accusation abound. Endless are the claims of innocence from the ranks of the convicted (Blumberg, 1967). Many spectators, passersby, and members of the press were arrested, brutalized, and killed by social controls agents in the confused emotion-laden disturbances of the 1960s at Kent State, Chicago, Detroit, Newark, and elsewhere (Walker, 1968; Skolnick, 1969; Stark, 1972). More than 110,000 Japanese were placed in "relocation camps" during the post-Pearl Harbor paranoia. The absence of convictions for sabotage, treason, or disloyalty makes this a sobering example of wholesale false labeling (Peterson, 1971:68; Kitano, 1976:86). Several studies that provide significant insights and evidence on the process of becoming falsely accused are now presented.

A fascinating source of insightful material on false accusations is an early publication, *Convicting the Innocent*, by a leading legal authority (Borchard, 1932). Borchard collected 65 cases in which innocent individuals had been accused, prosecuted, and convicted by a jury. The main sources of these errors, according to Borchard, were mistaken identification by witnesses, reliance on circumstantial evidence, perjured testimony, and negligence (overlooking evidence, suppression of evidence, and general overzealousness) by the police and the prosecution.

The most frequent reason contributing to the unwarranted convictions (which was crucial in 29 of the 65 cases) was mistaken identification by witnesses. In one incredible case, 17 victims erroneously identified in sworn testimony that the accused had personally passed them bad checks. Another interesting finding was that in 8 of the 29 homicide cases *no one had been killed!* In most of these cases an individual had unexplainably disappeared. Some circumstantial evidence and, often, perjurious statements pointed out a "suspect." These webs of intrigue and falsehoods ultimately resulted in a homicide conviction of an innocent person. Later events, usually the reappearance of the homicide victim, established the innocence of the convicted person. Other ways that Borchard documented the innocence of the convicted persons were by the subsequent confessions or arrest of the real culprit and by the discovery of new evidence of an irrefutable nature.

Of particular interest for this paper are the conditions and pressures that Borchard identified as instrumental in facilitating the erroneous convictions. Borchard, like other analysts (Wilson, 1968; Schwartz and Jackson, 1976) noted that the police and the prosecutors are acutely sensitive to the organizational reward system that will be triggered by *apprehending suspects* and *obtaining convictions*. If one's professional reputation and career advancement are dependent on one's apprehension or conviction "batting average," there will be temptations to sacrifice accuracy in order to enhance one's record of crimes cleared by an arrest or conviction. Borchard also indicated that many of the erroneous convictions emerged during a period of heightened public opinion. An intensified climate of the public clamoring for arrests and convictions seemed to reduce the legal agents' caution in their handling of suspects. There appeared to be more effort devoted to satisfying the public's desire for retribution than to the rigorous pursuit of justice. Finally, Borchard noted that many of the falsely accused subjects were relatively impotent to effectively contest the charges that had been brought against them. The characteristics that increased their vulnerability to miscarriages of justice included lack of intelligence and possession of prior criminal records.

Several more recent works follow the Borchard model. The Franks (1975) presented 34 criminal cases, and Radin (1964) presented 80 cases from his file of more than 300, in which there was incontrovertible evidence that false labeling had transpired. Like Borchard, they highlighted the importance of errors by witnesses and the intense pressure on prosecutors to obtain convictions. They felt, however, that the legal screening process had become more sensitive to the rights of the accused since Borchard's study. In addition to these central works there is an extensive literature on famous trials in which the guilt or innocence has been a moot point engendering considerable controversy (i.e., Pollak, 1952; Frankfurter, 1961; Kunstler, 1963; Carter, 1969; Becker, 1971).

One of the most significant empirical works on being inaccurately labeled is Mercer's study on the diagnosis of mental retardation (Mercer, 1973). Her analysis led to the conclusion that if low IQ test scores were the only bases for diagnoses of mental retardation many individuals would be inaccurately labeled. When she looked at the social role performance through an "adaptive behavior measure," she found that many of the low IQ test performers were indistinguishable from other adults in the community. Individuals fitting this pattern were called "quasi-retarded." Mercer discovered that Chicanos, blacks, and low-status subjects were must more likely to be falsely labeled retarded by Anglocentric IQ tests. Therefore she recommended that a pluralistic, sociocultural perspective be used to increase the validity of diagnosing mental retardation. This would require that only those individuals who are subnormal on both intelligence tests *and* adaptive behavior measures be regarded as clinically retarded.

An extensive national study of educational diagnosing has been conducted by Craig and co-workers (1978). More than 7,000 children who had been recommended by teachers as requiring special educational resources were subjected to in-depth study. Medical exams, school behavior, developmental histories, and parental responses about home behavior were accumulated to assess the accuracy of the teacher's recommendation. Overall, only about 50% of the children in special programs had been accurately labeled by the teachers. Some specific examples of the erroneous labeling uncovered in this study are as follows: 76% of the children using school resources for mental retardation registered IQ scores of 69 or higher; 95% of the children classified as hearing handicapped showed no hearing handicap when evaluated by audiometric tests; and half of the children identified as visually impaired had normal vision. Although teachers were not very accurate in identifying specific handicaps, they were effective in picking out children who for some reason were not doing well in the classroom. The researchers also noted that students who were poor, black, and male and who exhibited deviant classroom behavior were disproportionately being labeled handicapped inaccurately.

These illustrative examples suggest that false accusations are much more frequent than one would expect and that they constitute a significant social issue and a challenging phenomenon for sociological analysis.

TYPES OF FALSE ACCUSATION

False accusations can be differentiated into several types. The first type of false accusation, *pure error*, is the result of an unintentional blunder. The second type, *intentional error*, is the result of individuals labeling when they know they are wrong. The third type, *legitimatized error*, is the result of individuals invoking criteria that they feel are valid but that are in fact false. The fourth type, *victim-based error*, is distinctly different from the other types. This is because the accused play an integral role in generating their own false accusation.

Pure Error

Pure error constitutes perhaps the simplest type of false accusation. This type of error is a "real accident," unintended and unwarranted. The wrong name is placed in a file, or the contents of two files are accidentally switched. Data punching errors or a programming error lead to inaccurate results from computer-processed diagnostic systems. Police make a drug raid at a *clean* residence because they inaccurately recorded the address or because they reacted on the advice of an anonymous informant. Teachers, seeing students waiting outside the counseling office, assume they are in trouble (Balch and Kelly, 1974). A colleague of ours, doing research in a mental institution, reported being detained on a closed ward after having been suspected (we presume this imputation was unjustified) of being one of the residents.

Other examples of pure error arise when nondeviants are stigmatized because of their affiliation with deviants. Birenbaum has noted that those who are friends or relatives of radicals, homosexuals, criminals, mentally retarded, and so on frequently have to bear what he calls a courtesy stigma (Birenbaum, 1970). Researchers of deviance have likewise been subject to the imputation that because they are studying deviants they must also be deviant (Henslin, 1972). This likelihood is fostered because researchers may seek insider status and therefore dress and present themselves "like one of them."

Borchard (1932) and Frank and Frank (1957) have documented numerous criminal court cases in which eyewitnesses made fallacious identifications while testifying under oath. More recently, Buckhout (1974) summarized his own and other experimental research on eyewitness testimony. In several projects a "crime" was staged in a college classroom. The student witnesses had a poor (13–40%) record in being able to identify the "criminal." Buckhout concluded that eyewitness testimony is remarkably subject to error. A study by Shoemaker and coworkers (1973) revealed that facial stereotypes of criminals were evident when research subjects were asked to assess the guilt of persons in a set of photographs (none of the photograph subjects were criminals). Finally, an extensive review of empirical research (Clifford and Bull, 1978) also concluded that various perceptual, situational, and memory errors frequently undermine the ability of eyewitnesses to identify people accurately. If even eyewitness reports are fallible, one can see a vast potential for pure error to creep into the deviant labeling process.

The difficulty of establishing criminal guilt can also be shown in that 24 percent of the adults prosecuted in the courts were released either through an acquittal or dismissal (Uniform Crime Reports, 1977:214). Some of these cases are bonafide cases of pure error or of intentional errors (which are discussed next). Unfortunately, receiving an acquittal when one has been unfairly prosecuted does *not* erase the police record, the indignity of having been detained and subjected to public degradation ceremonies, or the carryover doubts about one's innocence. Being temporarily, unfairly stigmatized can also lead to long-term stigma and liabilities. Schwartz and

Skolnick (1962) have shown, for example, that an acquittal can significantly reduce one's subsequent employment opportunities.

Some who are arrested and then obtain an acquittal or dismissal are *actually* guilty but escape guilty verdicts because of insufficient evidence, legal loopholes, and so on. Even these cases can, in a sense, be considered to have been falsely accused in that they *technically are innocent* until *proven* guilty. Social reality, however, frequently operates to lend more credibility to the original accusation of guilt than to the inability to validate that guilt legally.

Intentional Error

The intentional error type of false accusation can be discovered not only in Hollywood dramas but in the real world as well. This type emerges when the vested interests of an individual make it attractive to initiate incriminating information or charges that are inaccurate and contrived. One may resort to intentional error to enhance one's prestige and financial position (Traub, 1979). An individual may commit perjury because the "price is right." Borchard (1932) provided several examples in which perjured testimony resulted in erroneous criminal convictions. Police may arrest persons who are *not* currently involved in prostitution but whom they consider "obvious" prostitutes in order to fill their arrest quota for the night (Knapp Commission, 1972). A teacher, hoping to manipulate peer pressure, punishes *all* the students even though only a *few* have disrupted the classroom. An unscrupulous psychiatrist may attach a false diagnostic label to acquire a lucrative client. Political campaigners have an unsavory tradition of planting and circulating false rumors about their opponents (Rosnow and Fine, 1976), Nixon's CREEP and their dirty tricks being the most publicized recent example of deliberate slanderous character assassination.

The counterpart to the motivation to *help oneself* by intentional lies is the motivational thrust that arises when one desires to *get* or *hurt others*. Vindictive and self-enhancement motives often operate simultaneously, as in the planting of slanderous rumors during a political campaign. An example of a situation in which a vindictive motive is more salient would be a teacher deliberately giving a disruptive student a failing grade even though passing work was done. Also relevant here is the case of Mrs. Packard (Packard, 1873). In 1860, she was involuntarily committed to a mental institution by her minister husband because her unorthodox religious views were embarrassing to him. Her case is historically significant because upon obtaining her release, after 3 years in the institution, she successfully lobbied to gain legislation to protect others from being railroaded into an institution.

Even law enforcement personnel unhappy with the ineffectiveness of the legal process may seek illegal advantage to allow them to lock up the bad guys. A vigilante-minded police administrator obtained fingerprints from suspected criminals that had been collected on *previous* cases. He then took these to the scene of a *new* crime and *planted* them there for detectives to discover. At lest 18 innocent persons had been arrested and imprisoned on the strength of this manufactured evidence before his illegal actions were discovered (Lund, 1980).

A third reason why one might resort to deliberate false accusations is for self-protective purposes. Thus one may aspire to divert attention from one's own guilt or involvement by utilizing this tactic (Raper, 1970:37). Was there ever a parent who did not hear reciprocal claims of guilt among their children when a familial infraction had occurred? A mentally disturbed spouse may initiate commitment against a healthy spouse to deflect attention from his or her own mental condition. The Knapp Commission (1972) on police corruption reported the practice of "flaking," that is, planting narcotics on a person arrested with *inadequate* evidence so that one can justify the arrest and maximize the likelihood of obtaining a conviction. There are also reports of police officers carrying an extra pistol to plant on an *unarmed* person that they have killed in "self-defense."

Legitimatized Error

The third type of false accusation is legitimized error. This type occurs when individuals invoke criteria they feel are valid but are in fact false. The criteria may be based on cultural beliefs or on a standardized diagnostic procedure employed by an organization. Many deviant processing organizations employ uncritical screening procedures and standards. Deviance imputation by a relative, teacher, victim, or police officer may be accepted at face value and not be challenged. An IQ test score (Mercer, 1973) or a brief psychological interview (Scheff, 1964) or test score may be all that is utilized or required to place one in a stigmatized category.

Frequently, there is simply no search for contrary evidence once early indicators have promulgated a label (Scheff, 1964). Rosenhan's (1973) now famous "pseudo-patients" study provides an excellent example. False accusations of schizophrenia were uniformly attached immediately upon the subjects' pronouncements that they "heard voices." This "diagnosis" was retained until release from the hospital, despite the subjects' best subsequent efforts to appear fully normal. Furthermore, when release *did* come, it was still not with a written testimony of "normalcy," or even "*return* to normalcy," but of "schizophrenia in remission." Hearing voices, admittedly, could be a symptom compatible with a diagnosis of authentic schizophrenia. If, however, it is the *sole* piece of pertinent evidence and if no efforts are exerted to substantiate and validate the initial diagnosis, it should hardly be surprising that mislabeling could occur and stand unchallenged. These errors are consistent with what Hawkins and Tiedeman (1975:201) called "biography building," in which limited indicators propel a premature label that gathers an inertia that leads to focused searching for only those selective aspects of an individual's biography that confirm and reinforce the initial error.

Mercer (1973) carefully revealed the shortcomings of accepting an IQ test score as a valid indicator of mental retardation for blacks and Spanish-Americans. She stressed that greater accuracy could be obtained by adding a sociocultural adaptive measure that taps how well individuals perform within their own cultural milieu. In like manner, an educator who proffers negative student labels on the basis of a narrow slice of evidence risks making premature, inaccurate conclusions. Any student who does know the material but panics during an exam and receives a low grade can also attest to the frustration of receiving a false accusation based upon a single factor evaluation.

Victim-Based Error

The final type of false accusation, victim-based error, is distinct from the other types in that the person receiving the label has actively and willingly sought to be labeled (Pollack, 1952). A classic example of this type is the prospective military draftee who feigns mental incompetence, mental illness, or homosexual tendencies. A legitimately arrested burglar may "altruistically" confess to burglaries committed by a friend, realizing it will probably not add to his sentence and may keep his friend on the streets. An innocent person arrested for a felony may accept a plea-bargained offer to admit to a lesser offense. This will guarantee him free probationary status rather than risk being brought to trial and being erroneously found guilty and sent to prison. A welfare recipient hearing that those who are blind or mentally ill receive significantly higher payments may use deception to gain eligibility for these higher benefits (Lindsey and Ozawa, 1979:120). Research on *long-term* residents of a mental institution (Braginsky and Braginsky, 1967) revealed that those patients who were led to believe that a "good clinical interview" would result in their release deliberately portrayed themselves as still having problems. Police may receive numerous "confessions" from innocent individuals when crimes like those of the Los Angeles "hillside strangler" receive high publicity. Pollack (1952) cited several cases in which suspects contributed spurious confessions.

Victim-based error is probably the least frequent types of false accusation. The paradoxical nature of victim-based error can be made understandable if it is looked at from an exchange theoretical perspective. Thus individuals may volunteer to be falsely accused when they perceive that the subsequent costs or image losses are less than the anticipated rewards. It is important to emphasize, however, that the benefits obtained by voluntarily becoming falsely accused may be evident only in the eyes of the voluntary victim.

TOWARD AN UNDERSTANDING OF FALSE ACCUSATIONS

The research examples clearly show that false accusations are complex and relatively frequent events. Furthermore, they imply that it is crucial to examine the societal context, the organizational factors, the accusers, and the accused in order to gain an understanding of the conditions most likely to precipitate false accusations. Although the discussion that follows focuses on the societal and organizational levels, it should be emphasized that in many instances this is only an analytical delineation of responsibility. Typically, there is an interaction involved; for example, organizational factors frequently reflect societal values or circumstances, the acts of individual accusers are often a function of their organizational role or context, and so on. We simply propose that the prime focus of responsibility can be analytically isolated. Propositions specifying the conditions most likely to lead to false accusations are developed and supported with illustrative examples and research evidence.

Perceived Threat

Whenever a community (organization or individual) perceives that it has been wronged or is threatened, there are likely to be indiscriminate false accusations against the suspected perpetrator. Rumors and gossip, the most frequent forms of false accusation, proliferate during times of heightened tensions (Rosnow and Fine, 1976). Conditions may become volatile enough to trigger curbside injustice by the police (Stark, 1972), vigilantism (Ronsebaum and Sederberg, 1976), and lynchings by citizens (Raper, 1970), and inquisition, purges, and pogroms by politicians (Conquest, 1968). Many a "reign of terror" can also be aptly described as a "reign of error." Many innocent people who unfortunately happen to be in a suspect location, are relatives of deviants, look like, or are suspected of being sympathetic to "the enemy" may be dealt with as if they *were* "the enemy."

Iranian college students, many of them opposed to the policies and actions of the Ayatollah Khomeini, were recently subjected to visa checks and possible deportation by federal authorities. Meanwhile, *Turkish* and *Iraqi* shopkeepers found their businesses vandalized or boycotted and, in some cases, their lives threatened because they resembled Iranians by name or physical appearance. These incidents parallel the fate of many Chinese-American citizens during the post-Pearl Harbor Japanese paranoia. Likewise, My Lai, McCarthyism, Salem witchcraft hysteria (Erikson, 1966), and Stalin's purges, all provide grim testimony of the tragic excesses of unchecked labeling. In these cases, innumerable innocent parties became the targets of widespread, often officially sanctioned, false accusations as a consequence of collective tensions, fears, and anxieties at a societal level. Although individual actors or organizations formulate and execute such mislabeling, they do so in direct response to broadly dispersed and highly vocal public opinion and thus constitute a supraindividual and supraorganizational point of origin.

An example in which the threat perceived by an organization resulted in a false labeling incident is that of Isidore Zimmerman. Mr. Zimmerman spent 24 years and 8 months in various prisons as a result of wrongful conviction for murder in the first degree. Incredibly, Zimmerman was not even present at the incident (the killing of a police officer during a robbery) but had been convicted *erroneously* of supplying the murder weapon. Originally, he had been sentenced to be executed in the electric chair. Only hours before this sentence was to be carried out, it was commuted to life in prison. The fact that a police officer was the victim appeared to stimulate the legal system to indiscriminate reprisal efforts (Zimmerman, 1973).

Subcultural Heterogeneity

Whenever a society contains a variety of ethnic, social class, and religious subcultures existing in close proximity, there exists a high potential for false accusation. The existence of different norms and values inevitably results in reciprocal misinterpretations and false accusations. In addition, pluralistic societies are often distinguished by differentials in power possessed by the various subcultures. These conditions may, in turn, increase the likelihood that accusations will occur.

Donald Jewell (1952) has written a poignant and jarring depiction of the fate of one Navajo Indian at the hands of the culturally naive personnel of a California state mental hospital. "Bill" (an ironically questionable choice of anonymous pseudonym) was diagnosed as a catatonic schizophrenic and institutionalized for 18 months before Jewell was able to obtain his release. Jewell argues that Bill's inadequate English, in company with his stoical withdrawal, entirely consistent with Navajo cultural posture of passive resistance in the face of threat, resulted in the erroneous diagnosis.

On a more contemporary note, it has been observed that Southeast Asian refugee children, upon entering their new U.S. classrooms, walk to a corner, adopt a squatting position, and refuse to ask questions. Such acts are in keeping with the educational traditions of their native land. Now, however, these children are being branded recalcitrant, troublesome, and lackadaisical by their U.S. instructors, with Pygmalianesque ramifications almost certain to follow.

Research has confirmed that members of one racial group have a difficult time differentiating between members of another racial group (Luce, 1974; Clifford and Bull, 1978). Therefore, the validity of eyewitness testimony becomes less credible when the suspect is of a different race from the victim or from other witnesses. Luce (1974) cited a case in which five white people incorrectly identified a black man as the person who had kidnapped and held them hostage for several hours. These cases and many others like them are based on faulty interpretation and stereotyping that originates at the macrolevel of societal cultural contrast.

Domain Protectionism

Whenever an organization must justify its existence or aspires to expand its domain, false labeling may be stimulated. Highly specialized organizations have come into existence to diagnose, process, punish, and rehabilitate deviants. An insightful article by Currie (1968), titled "Crimes Without Criminals," details the organization and process utilized during the inquisition to find and punish "witches." This zealous campaign served to stifle dissent against the Church and added wealth to the Church from the confiscated property of the "witches."

Most organizations ordinarily seek to perpetuate their own existence. This is true not only of General Motors, RCA, and Dow Chemical but also of prisons, juvenile departments, and mental institutions. In their efforts to ensure continued staffing and funding, people-processing and people-changing organizations are obliged to play the "number-dollar game." They must be able to demonstrate that there are subjects and clients requiring their services (Hasenfeld, 1972; Hawkins and Tiedeman, 1975). This demonstration of effectiveness often requires an annual report that reaches the eyes and ears of the public, pertinent reviewers, and fund allocators. This means, in turn, that increases in the raw number of cases handled can become an organizational priority. Hence, police departments may develop indiscriminate arrest practices, such as drunk or traffic violation quotas, in quest of an impressive annual report. Spradley (1970:124) found that 20 percent of his "urban nomad" respondents claimed to have been arrested on a drunk charge when they had not been drinking at all. His interviewing also indicated that many of the "nomads" had been rearrested the *same day* they had been released from jail. This police department practice appeared to satisfy a secondary organizational need: the acquisition of individuals to fill the many unpaid trustee positions that were necessary to keep the jail operating.

School systems fall prey to the pressures and by-products of organizational aggrandizement when children are too readily placed into various "special education" categories (Kelly, 1976; Craig et al., 1978). Borderline cases may be categorized "downward" when special funds are available for each identified special education student (Goldstein et al., 1975).

The tragic case of Larry, who spent the first 30 years of his life in a private institution for the retarded, is reported by McQueen (1973). In this case the false labeling arose from the unfortunate circumstances surrounding his birth. Larry had been born out of wedlock, posing an embarrassing dilemma for his young mother. An unscrupulous doctor, seeking more financially supported residents for his private institution for the retarded, assumed care of the child. Although he assured the mother that he would seek to have the child adopted, no adoption transpired. Therefore, Larry, classified as retarded, remained a resident until the institution was closed 30 years later. Larry was then committed to the Nevada State Hospital, where McQueen became suspicious and administered several IQ tests to him. These tests revealed that Larry possessed an average IQ of 97.

Thomas Szasz, in *The Myth of Mental Illness* (1961), and Peter Shrag and Diane Divoky, in *The Myth of the Hyperactive Child* (1975), raise basic questions about the validity of the "experts' " conception of problem behavior. Both of these works also agree that acceptance of the "experts" judgments will increase the number of "deviants" and therefore increase security and monetary reward that the "experts" can claim for themselves.

Stereotype Adoption

Whenever people-processing and people-changing organizations adopt societal stereotypes of the most likely targets for their services, there is a strong likelihood that false labeling will ensue. Organizational stereotyping derives, of course, from a multitude of social experiences. Whatever their source, application to the phenomenon of false accusation is clear and straightforward. Long-standing stereotypes can trigger formal false accusation. Heussenstamm (1971) revealed the direct play of such stereotyping in the case of nonlegal factors influencing police behavior. In her study, 15 drivers with exemplary driving records were recruited as experimental confederates. They were sworn to drive in accordance with legal regulations as they went about their regular driving activities. The only modification made was the placement of a "Black Panther" sticker on the rear bumper of each participant's vehicle. The experiment was terminated after 17 days: 33 traffic citations had been received in that time, exhausting the funds that had been accumulated for the payment of fines. Race and sex of drivers did not affect the number of citations received, indicating that the sheer symbolic suggestion of identification with a negatively stereotyped group was sufficient to evoke false labeling.

Several field studies provide additional evidence of police mislabeling attributable to judgments based on stereotypes. Youth selected by police as suspects for field investigations frequently fit their delinquent stereotype (Piliavin and Briar, 1964). Chambliss (1973) noted that police tended to level "trumped up loitering charges" against members of a lower-class group (Roughnecks) while overlooking similar behavior by members of a middle-class group (Saints). After working as a lawyer providing legal defense services, Forer (1970:317) claimed that two-thirds of the defendants, mainly minority background youth, had been falsely accused. As noted elsewhere, Spradley's (1970) skid row informants claimed that a significant portion of arrests for drunkenness occurred when no drinking whatsoever had taken place. Bittner (1967) elaborates on how police employ unjustifiable arrests to expedite their control and protection of skid row residents.

Investigations of the FBI by the Select Committee to Study Governmental Operations with Respect to Intelligence Activities (U.S. Senate, 1976) revealed extensive unwarranted intelligence activity. Files were developed on thousands of U.S. citizens who fit the stereotypes of *suspected* or *potentially* dangerous individuals. In addition to the spying activity, a variety of unsavory tactics (attempts to ruin reputations, careers, and marriages by leaking false information) were unleashed on these unknowing, falsely labeled citizens.

Another significant exploration into the problematic nature of the labeling process is found in Rist's (1973) ethnographic study of a kindergarten classroom in a ghetto school. His observations pointed to the importance of nonacademic criteria (appearance, clothing, smell, family status, and the presence or absence of an intact family) in the teacher's decision as to placing a student in one of several ability groups. Not only was this decision made quickly (by the end of the first week), it was also likely to be a permanent placement. Although Rist did not have incontrovertible evidence that the teacher's judgments were inaccurate, it is clear that he viewed this labeling process as very suspect.

Diagnostic Oversimplification

Whenever agents of control or professionals develop simplified diagnostic procedures (professional stereotypes) for identifying their clientele, false labeling is likely to be prevalent. Specialized occupational training, by definition and design, narrows the scope of one's particular expertise and perceptions. Thus specialists can be expected to see and interpret their clientele in terms of their trained perspective. This is all well and good if the criteria are valid and accurately applied. When such criteria are indiscriminately employed, however, false labeling is inevitable. By way of example, police officers, accustomed to formal and experiential training that highlights disproportionate representation of minority members and males as criminal actors, may come to stereotype black males as willful culprits and white females as innocents. (In the personal experience of one of the authors, the process of teaching sociology in a police academy became a two-way educational experience: white police officers and cadets gradually came to realize that not all blacks and Chicanos were inherently evildoers, while the sociologist's predictable "underdog bias" underwent reshaping as the result of participation in late night, urban squad car patrols.)

Similarly, psychiatrists look for (and find) symptoms of mental illness when others do not by virtue of a specialized training that teaches them to do precisely that. There is abundant evidence in the literature to the effect that psychiatrists overread behavioral and attitudinal cues. Scheff's study of involuntary commitment proceedings (1964) raised considerable suspicion about the accuracy of the screening process leading to psychiatric and judicial commitment decisions. Individuals going through this process were subjected to a brief ritualistic investigation that resulted in a perfunctory decision to commit. Consequently, a considerable number, according to the judgment of Scheff and even by the admission of the examining psychiatrists, were committed who did not meet the legal criteria. Numerous other investigators have looked at the psychiatric diagnostic and commitment process. Temerlin (1968) found that psychiatrists and clinical psychologist were much more likely than a lay jury to classify a mentally healthy case as psychotic or neurotic. Pasamanick et al. 91967) noted that psychiatrists saw more pathology than did nurses even though they were both observing the same cases and using the same rating scale.

An experimental study by Stevens (1978) also verifies that there is a professional propensity to resort to knee-jerk labeling. In her study, samples of parents, teachers, and school psychologists were asked to evaluate three boys for the degree of hyperkinesis each exhibited. The boys were *not hyperkinetic*, and their filmed behavior was selected to be as similar to each other as possible. The social class and the ethnicity of the boys were experimentally varied. When the raters applied the Behavior Rating Scale for Hyperkinesis, they did, however, find evidence of hyperkinesis. Higher hyperkinetic ratings were imputed to the chicano and black boys and the boys identified as "lower class." The teachers and the school psychologist were especially inclined to rate the presumably lower class boys as hyperkinetic.

Scheff (1964) has accumulated evidence that there exists a strong inclination for medical and psychiatric practitioners to invoke a conservative diagnosis. Their professional training and ideology influence practitioners toward making more type II errors (diagnose illness when the patient is healthy) and to avoid making type I errors (failing to diagnose illness when the patient is ill). Given this predisposition, one cannot be too surprised that Rosenhan (1973) found that all of his *normal* research assistants, who had presented themselves to the admissions offices of various state hospitals, were admitted with a diagnosis of schizophrenia.

FALSE ACCUSERS AND THE FALSELY ACCUSED

Labeling perspective writers have stressed that labeling is not a random process. Therefore, it should not be surprising to find that the initiators and targets of false accusation also possess some differentiating characteristics. Because numerous examples have already been cited, we will only briefly summarize and rephrase some patterns evident in the foregoing discussion as they relate to the false accusers and the falsely accused.

The purveyors of false accusations, like the purveyors of valid labels, are likely to possess power, insider status, organizational backing, a profit motive, or legitimacy ("expert" status). Conversely, one's vulnerability to become a target of a false accusation (or of valid labels) is increased if one possesses little power, outsider status, no organizational backing, or a lack of legitimacy. In addition, many of the studies revealed that those with prior deviant labeling (former convicts, troublemakers, and so on) were more vulnerable to becoming recipients of false accusations. Their record predisposes agents of control to seek them out and to be skeptical of their claims of innocence. Thus the value of the labeling perspective is evident in analyzing the false accusers and falsely accused.

SUMMARY

Labeling, which gives its name to an entire school of deviance theory, can be grounded in territory ranging from hard fact to pure fancy. Labeling theory is commonly misconstrued as contending that all deviance is little more than fabrication constructed by officialdom, whereas many of the more viable and durable contributions of the labeling perspective actually pertain to the application of the exacerbation of deviant images emanating from conditions of "true guilt." Our concern here has been the systematic development of a schema for analyzing and understanding the phenomenon of false accusation.

One of the staunchest critics of labeling theory, Gove (1976), asserted that one acquires a deviant label primarily because of one's deviant behavior. We have accumulated evidence that there exists a substantial number of cases in which the labeling occurs in the *absence* of deviant behavior. We are aware of the many limitations of the labeling perspective; however, it should be clear that, at least in the case of understanding false accusation, the labeling perspective is indispensable. The dictum of W. I. Thomas that "situations are real if people define them as real" is powerfully evident in the example of false accusation. The social reality and the human tragedy of being unfairly stigmatized demand that more research, theory, and pragmatic attention should be focused on the topic of false accusation.

Our formative analysis suggests that (1) pure error, (2) intentional error, (3) legitimatized error, and (4) victim-based error constitute the main types of accountings for the appearance of false accusation. These are ideal types in the classic sociological sense and as such imply latitude of degree and of mutual exclusivity. Pure error typically operates independently of other stimuli, for example, while intentional and legitimatized error may exist simultaneously and complementarily.

Pure, intentional and legitimatized forms of error are all reflected within our set of initial propositions designed to spell out dominant societal and organizational conditions facilitative of false accusation. (Victim-based error awaits separate propositional treatment because of its unique feature of culpability on the part of the labelee.) We have put forth a set of propositions that specify social processes and pressures underlying a significant portion of false accusation. These have been identified as (1) perceived threat, (2) subcultural heterogeneity, (3) domain protectionism, (4) stereotype adoption, and (5) diagnostic oversimplification. This listing is not intended to be exhaustive. Indeed, part of our intent is the stimulation of further propositions, theory construction, and empirical testing.

A final observation remains. In a society replete with contending definitions and interpretations of reality, it is not our intention to foster a paranoid, conspiratorial concern over false accusation run amuck but only to heighten attentiveness to the conditions nourishing it whenever, wherever, and however often it *does* appear. For in a society grown increasingly large, increasingly diverse and complex, and increasingly bureaucratic, scale and ideology beget efficiency, efficiency begets expediency, expediency begets simplification, and simplification begets error. Thus do the potentials for false accusation proliferate, and thus does it behoove students of society to understand and analyze the causal influences and their many insidious ramifications.

REFERENCES

Balch, Robert W., and Delos H. Kelly
1974 "Reactions to deviance in a junior high school: Student views of the labeling process." Instructional Psychology 1 (Winter):25–38.

Becker, Howard S.
1963 Outsiders: Studies in the Sociology of Deviance. New York: Free Press.

Becker, Theodore L. (ed.)
1971 Political Trials. Indianapolis: Bobbs-Merrill.

Birenbaum, Arnold
1970 "On managing a courtesy stigma." Journal of Health and Social Behavior 11:196–207.

Bittner, Egon
1967 "The police on skid-row: A study of peace keeping." American Sociological Review 32:699–715.

Blumberg, Abraham S.
1967 "The practice of law as a confidence game: Organizational cooptation of a profession." Law & Society Review 1:15–39.

Borchard, Edwin M.
1932 Convicting the Innocent. Hamden, Conn.: Archon.
Braginsky, Benjamin M., and Dorothea D. Braginsky
1967 "Schizophrenic patients in the psychiatric interview: An experimental study of their effectiveness at manipulation." Journal of Consulting Psychology 31:543–547.
Buckhout, Robert
1974 "Eyewitness testimony." Scientific American (December):23–31.
Carter, Dan T.
1969 Scottsboro: A Tragedy of the American South. Baton Rouge: Louisiana State University Press.
Chambliss, William J.
1973 "The Saints and the Roughnecks." Society (November–December):24–31.
Clifford, Brian R., and Ray Bull
1978 The Psychology of Person Identification. London: Routledge & Kegan Paul.
Conquest, Robert
1968 The Great Terror. London: Macmillan.
Craig, Patricia A., David A. Kaskowitz, and Mary A. Malgoire
1978 Studies of Handicapped Students, Vol. 2. Washington: SRI International.
Currie, Elliott P.
1968 "Crimes without criminals: Witchcraft and its control in Renaissance Europe." Law & Society Review 3:7–32.
Dershowitz, Alan M.
1969 "On preventive detention." Pp. 307–319 in Abraham M. Goldstein and Joseph Goldstein (eds.), Crime, Law, and Society. New York: Free Press.
Duncan, John Allison
1940 The Strangest Cases on Record. Chicago: Reilly & Lee.
Erikson, Kai T.
1966 Wayward Puritans. New York: Wiley.
Forer, Lois G.
1970 No One Will Listen: How the Legal System Brutalizes the Youthful Poor. New York: Grosset & Dunlap.
Frank, J., and B. Frank
1957 Not Guilty. Garden City, N.Y.: Doubleday.
Frankfurter, Felix
1961 The Case of Sacco and Vanzetti. New York: Little, Brown.
Gibbs, Jack
1966 "Conceptions of deviant behavior: The old and the new." Pacific Sociological Review 9:9–14.
Goldstein, Herbert, Claudia Arkell, S. C. Ashcroft, Oliver L. Hurley, and M. Stephen Lilly
1975 "Schools." Pp. 4–61 in Nicholas Hobbs (ed.), Issues in the Classification of Children, Vol. 2. San Francisco: Jossey-Bass.

Gove, Walter
1976 "Deviant behavior, social intervention, and labeling theory." Pp. 219–227 in Lewis A. Coser and Otto N. Larsen (eds.), The Uses of Controversy in Sociology. New York: Free Press.
1975 The Labeling of Deviance: Evaluating a Perspective. New York: Wiley.

Hasenfeld, Yeheskel
1972 "People processing organizations: An exchange approach." American Sociological Review 37:256–263.

Hawkins, Richard, and Gary Tiedeman
1975 The Creation of Deviance: Interpersonal and Organizational Determinants. Columbus, Ohio: Merrill.

Hays, Arthur Garfield
1970 Trial by Prejudice. Westport, Conn.: Negro Universities Press.

Henslin, James M.
1972 "Studying deviance in four settings: Research experiences with cabbies, suicides, drug users, and abortionees." Pp. 35–70 in Jack D. Douglas (ed.), Research on Deviance. New York: Random House.

Heussenstamm, Frances K.
1971 "Bumper stickers and cops." Transaction 8:32–33.

Jewell, Donald P.
1952 "A case of a 'psychotic' Navaho Indian male." Human Organization 11:32–36.

Kelly, Delos H.
1976 "The role of teacher's nominations in the perpetuation of deviant adolescent careers." Education 96:209–217.

Kitano, Harry H.
1976 Japanese-Americans: The Evolution of a Subculture. Englewood Cliffs, N.J.: Prentice-Hall.

Knapp Commission
1973 Report on Police Corruption. New York: Braziller.

Kunstler, William M.
1963 And Justice For All. Dobbs Ferry, N.Y.: Oceana Publications.

Lindsey, Duncan, and Martha N. Ozawa
1979 "Schizophrenia and SSI: Implications and problems." Social Work 24:120–126.

Luce, Terrance S.
1974 "Blacks, whites and yellows: They all look alike to me." Psychology Today (November):105–108.

Lund, Lynn
1980 Presentation at the Rural Jail Seminar. Corvallis, Or.

Mankoff, Milton
1971 "Societal reaction and career deviance: A critical analysis." Sociological Quarterly 12:204–218.

Marx, Gary T.
1974 "Thoughts on a neglected category of social movement participant: The

agent provocateur and the informant." American Journal of Sociology 80:402–442.

Mercer, Jane R.
1973 Labeling the Retarded. Berkeley: University of California Press.

McQueen, Robert
1973 "Larry: Case history of a mistake." Pp. 199–208 in Burton Blatt (ed.), Souls in Extremis: An Anthology of Victims and Victimizers. Boston: Allyn and Bacon.

Packard, E. P. W.
1893 "Madness and marriage." Pp. 53–76 in Thomas Szasz (ed.), The Age of Madness. New York: Anchor Books.

Pasmanick, Benjamin, Frank Scarpitti, and Simon Dinitz
1967 Schizophrenics in the Community. New York: Appleton-Century-Crofts.

Petersen, William
1971 Japanese-Americans: Oppression and Success. New York: Random house.

Piliavin, Irving, and Scott Briar
1964 "Police encounters and juveniles." American Journal of Sociology 70:206–214.

Pollak, Otto
1952 "The errors of justice." Annals of the American Academy of Political and Social Science 284:115–123.

Radin, Edward D.
1964 The Innocents. New York: William Morrow.

Raper, Arthur F.
1970 The Tragedy of Lynching. New York: Dover.

Rist, Ray C.
1973 The Urban School: A Factory of Failure. Cambridge: MIT Press.

Rosenbaum, H. Jon, and Peter C. Sederberg
1976 Vigilante Politics. Philadelphia: University of Pennsylvania Press.

Rosenhan, David L.
1973 "On being sane in insane places." Science (January):250–258.

Rosnow, Ralph L., and Gary Alan Fine
1976 Rumors and Gossip: The Social Psychology of Hearsay. New York: Elsevier.

Scheff, Thomas J.
1964 "The social reaction of deviance: Ascriptive elements in the psychiatric screening of mental patients in a mid-western state." Social Problems 11:401–413.

Schwartz, Herman, and Bruce Jackson
1976 "Prosecutor as public enemy." Harper's Magazine (February): 24–32.

Schwartz, Richard D., and Jerome H. Skolnick
1962 "Two studies of legal stigma." Social Problems 10:133–318.

Shoemaker, Donald J., Donald R. South, and Jay Lowe
1973 "Facial stereotypes of deviants and judgments of guilt or innocence." Social Forces 51:427–433.

Shrag, Peter, and Diane Divoky
1975 The Myth of the Hyperactive Child. New York: Pantheon.
Skolnick, Jerome K.
1966 Justice Without Trial. New York: Wiley.
1969 The Politics of Protest. New York: Clarion.
Spradley, James P.
1970 You Owe Yourself a Drunk: An Ethnography of Urban Nomads. Boston: Little, Brown.
Stark, Rodney
1972 Police Riots. Belmont, Calif.: Wadsworth.
Stevens, Gwendolyn
1978 "Ethnic identification and socio-economic status: Factors which might influence the assessment of behavior. The special case of hyperkinesis." Unpublished paper.
Szasz, Thomas (ed.)
1973 The Age of Madness: The History of Involuntary Hospitalization. New York: Anchor.
Szasz, Thomas
1961 The Myth of Mental Illness. New York: Harper & Row.
Temerlin, Maurice K.
1968 "Suggestion effects in psychiatric diagnosis." Journal of Nervous Disease 147:349-353.
Thorsell, Bernard, and Lloyd W. Klemke
1972 "The labeling process: Reinforcement and deterrent?" Law & Society Review 12:393-403.
Traub, James
1979 "The privacy snatchers: Are information gatherers violating your rights?" Saturday Review (July):16-20.
Uniform Crime Reports
1977 Washington, D.C.: U.S. Government Printing Office.
U.S. Senate, Select Committee to Study Governmental Operations with Respect to Intelligence Activities
1976 Intelligence Activities and the Rights of Americans: Book II. Washington, D.C., U.S. Government Printing Office.
Walker, Daniel
1968 Rights on Conflict: A Report Submitted to the National Commission on the Causes and Prevention of Violence. New York: Bantam.
Warren, Carol A. B., and John M. Johnson
1972 "A critique of labeling theory from the phenomenological perspective." Pp. 69-92 in Robert A. Scott and Jack D. Douglas (eds.), Theoretical Perspectives on Deviance. New York: Basic.
Wilson, James Q.
1968 "The police and the delinquent in two cities." Pp. 9-30 in Stanton Wheeler (ed.), Controlling Delinquents. New York: Wiley.
Zimmerman, Isidore
1973 Punishment Without Crime. New York: Manor.

PART THREE

Deviance: Cultural Patterns

Chapter Five

Becoming Deviant

EDITORIAL COMMENTARY

As discussed in the Introductory Chapter, deviant behavior may sometimes be a function of constitutional factors or physiological predisposition but in most instances, it is likely ascribed or learned. Individuals may learn deviant behavior in a very direct fashion such as by instruction, an older youngster demonstrating to a younger child the mechanics of some mischievous or delinquent act, for example. They may learn it in an indirect fashion by example or observation, or from information they receive, such as a boy who sees his father catch and keep more than the legal limits of fish, or the salesman who begins to "pad" his expense account after hearing that the other salesmen in the company are doing the same. People may also acquire their deviant tendencies in a more generalized manner from the mass media or through experiential inference. In this vein, they may come to believe that the movie image portraying adultery as commonplace is valid and pattern their own sexual behavior accordingly or based on personal impressions, reach the conclusion that most employees take home "samples" from the store, and avail themselves of the same prerogative.

Individuals initially, usually learn of the existence of a particular variety of deviant behavior that may possess some type of attraction for them. They may subsequently learn the techniques of the deviant activity and then have the opportunity structure to engage in such behavior present itself, or they may learn about opportunity structure and then perfect the skills necessary for such behavior. Amateur embezzlers, for example, not infrequently discover the opportunity structure for theft before they develop appropriate techniques for committing such an offense. Similarly, persons may be exposed to, and assimilate, the attitudes and values that support and rationalize deviant behavior before they learn about opportunity structure or techniques. Students, in way of illustration, may acquire cynical attitudes about honesty and diligent study habits before they discover an opportunity to cheat, as a shortcut to good grades, or learn effective ways of cheating.

Persons may learn about deviance within some favorable context and be attracted to it long before the opportunity for full participation in such activities presents itself. Just as teenage females may view women smoking in the movies or television and perceive it as a trait of sophistication, albeit forbidden by parents, before they go away to college and can indulge their status fantasy while they indulge in the nicotine habit, so too may the young corporate employee know of cocaine use and sexual dalliance with "party goers" among the rising business executive set (and be envious), in advance of his or her own opportune chance to give one, or both, a try. Like adolescents who are impatient to lose their virginity, as did their more worldly and "mature," friends, many individuals have to wait for appropriate opportunity structure before engaging in deviant behavior. In other instances, however, some persons may be confronted with opportunity structure for a long period of time before they become aware of it and may then have to delay even longer while they acquire the ability to take advantage of the opportunity, such as the bored young spouse, who finally realizes that the young, divorced next door neighbor finds him or her seductively attractive, but must wait to master the skills of seduction.

While some persons "discover" deviance by themselves, or with minimal direct or indirect suggestions from others, many individuals are more closely instructed or guided into deviant activities. Adolescent boys may be introduced to smoking, and/or drinking, and, perhaps, even pornography by a mentor, usually an older, or at least more adventurous, friend who may carefully coach his "student" in the intricacies of cigarette enjoyment, and the proper mix of alcoholic beverage and soft drink. He may also point out the lurid or sexually explicit passage in the "dirty" novel, carefully explaining the salacious import, just as he may give the less experienced friend his initial lecture in female anatomy while illustrating his remarks with an appropriate picture from an "adult" periodical. Certainly the role of others in assisting the individual in learning to use, and to appreciate, certain kinds of drugs, such as marijuana, has been well documented (see for example, Becker, 1963; Akers et al., 1979; and Winfrey and Griffiths, 1983). As McCaghy (1985:295) describes this assistance, "Friends and relatives provide encouragement, guidance, and a spirit of companionship, making the experience worthwhile."

First time, minor offenders in prison may be "taken under the wing" of an older, more experienced convict who may provide appropriate tutelage for more serious forms of crime and deviance, including both the ability to recognize opportunity structure as well as the knowledge and skills necessary to commit such acts, not to mention the rationalizing ideology. Industrial workers sometimes have to engage in deviant behavior in the interest of maintaining a desired production level. In their classic study, Bensman and Gerver (1963) describe the use of a tool—the tap—employed in the factory, although outlawed by management, as a device to cover up shoddy or defective work. They point out that workers frequently are instructed by the foreman, as well as other workers, on when and how to use the tool. Even some types of sexual deviance may involve an element of introduction, if not instruction. Prostitutes, for example, are generally not able to "naturally" acquire the necessary skills to pursue their trade. Instead, as Bryan (1965) points out, they must be taught a wide variety of technical skills, as well as social skills, "tricks of the trade," hygiene practices, and an appropriate, rationalizing ideology, among other things. Such instruction may come from a "Madame" in a brothel (Heyl, 1977), or from an older, more experienced prostitute. So institutionalized is this instructional process (and particularly in the latter context) that it has a special name—"turned out" (Gray, 1973). Deviant behavior, of whatever variety, would appear to, indeed, be learned behavior, and often with a particular teacher or teachers, guiding the learning, as it were.

The first reading in this chapter, James A. Inciardi's "Little Girls and Sex: A Glimpse at the World of the 'Baby Pro,' " addresses a particularly reprehensible form of learned deviance—child prostitution. Its reprehensibility results as much from the age of the perpetrators as from the nature of the deviant act itself. Our society takes a highly protective posture toward children in the belief that they are extraordinarily vulnerable and, thus, easily victimized. Children are assumed to be completely "innocent" by nature, and without antisocial, carnal, or immoral predisposition. Furthermore, it is also believed that children should be able to enjoy a safe and secure, happy childhood unencumbered by exposure to degeneracy, perversion, or immorality, or by the guilt or shame that might result from involvement in the attendant behaviors, in order to grow into a stable, well-adjusted, mature adult with a positive conception of self and a socially healthy relationship with others. Delinquency on the part of children is, therefore, often viewed as the product of adult example, or encouragement, if not direct instruction, and produces social repugnance and public indignation.

Inciardi's article describes a group of child prostitutes ranging in age from 8 to 12 years of age and details their deviant carnal activities. The extremely young age of these offenders traumatically contradicts the societal stereotypical image of "innocent" children. In these instances, the children were not all ghetto dwellers living in abject poverty, nor were they runaways. They were instead, a mixture of racial and ethic types including whites, blacks, Orientals, and Puerto Ricans, who lived at home with parents or relatives. It was the parents and relatives who introduced the children to prostitution, by serving as role models for a variety of sexually deviant behaviors. In some cases, the parents or relatives were themselves prostitutes, massage parlor masseuses, or pimps. In other instances, the parents were photographers who made pornographic photos and movies. The children often observing such activities, came to accept them as "normal," and were later told to (or offered to) participate. Some of the girls had been taken by relatives to massage parlors where they worked, and subsequently encouraged to provide sexual services to the clientele. In time, they began masturbating or fellating the customers for money, and some later began engaging in sexual intercourse with clients. Some of the girls initiated their sexual career by acting in the porno movies made by parents and moved on to prostitution. A significant proportion of the girls also used narcotics of some variety.

The girls were not forced into prostitution. This appears to be an instance of individuals being exposed to a deviant value system as a prelude to acquiring deviant behaviors. Because of the "overt presence of nudity, sexual promiscuity and prostitution in the home [which] seemed to desensitize them" (p. 75), they were encouraged in this direction. Interestingly, the children knew of the legal implications of their activites, having been instructed by their parents or relatives on the illegal nature of such behavior.

The children, as with other deviants, also acquired rationalizing attitudes, presumably from parents, relatives, or pimps. Such attitudes could be inferred from the derogatory vocabulary they used to describe their "johns" or customers, such as "suckers" or "old farts." They did not use such vocabulary to describe the individuals, including men, who performed with them in the pornographic films.

Inciardi concludes that the children were rather easily guided into pornography and prostitution by parents and/or other relatives, and that their initial motivation was essentially fear of rejection by those parents or relatives. The subsequent economic rewards served to strengthen their motivation. The narcotic usage appears to have been a deviant habit acquired from exposure to their public school drug culture. It is interesting to note that the girls all aspired to conventional vocational careers after they got older, and had even been encouraged to do so by parents. Thus, the children in their naivete, did not perceive the possibility of long term residual psychological or social damage that might accrue from their present sexual activities. These children, in effect, had been victimized by trusted significant others and transformed into sexual deviants by these significant others who were sexual deviants themselves.

Deviance may also result from a more generic induction or socialization process as well as from one-on-one instruction, or from groups of significant others. Often people acquire their deviant patterns as a result of cultural or subcultural exposure and indoctrination. Youngsters in some slum neighborhoods may enter into a pattern of delinquency, crime, and violence because "everyone else" in their age category is doing so, and one must "go along" with the gang as a matter of survival. Just as smoking and/or drinking may be fashionable in some high school subcultures, so too may the use of narcotics. Sexual deviance of different varieties may have a subcultural linkage. A few years back on some college campuses, there was a bisexual movement, and a number of students experimented with homosexuality, as well as heterosexuality, because it was fashionable, and part of the college subculture at the time. As one coed phrased it, "Coming out into the straight world blew my mind. But everybody does bisexuality now. It's really big" (Editors of *Newsweek*, 1974:90). In a similar vain, McCaghy and Skipper (1969) reported that the occupational culture of the stripper tends to promote lesbian behavior among the women in this occupational specialty.

Occupational crime is not infrequently a product of the subculture and the occupational group. Stoddard (1968) has, for example, documented the process by which newcomers to a particular police force were routinely socialized to accept and participate in a variety of deviant and criminal work practices, by members of the force. Such practices had become a constituent part of the subculture, and the newcomers were informally induced and pressured to engage in this type of behavior if they were to be treated as one of the group. Bryant (1979) has pointed out that in the military, many individuals learn to engage in a wide variety of behavior that is deviant and against regulations, but very much a part of military culture. Recruits may learn the skills necessary to perpetrate "Khaki Collar Crime" as they learn the more conventional military skills. The subcultures attendant to some racial, ethnic, nationality, or social class groupings, as well as occupational or avocational groups may all serve as a fertile school for deviant behavior as individuals inculcate the subcultural norms, values, and behavioral patterns. Inasmuch as the norms of many subcultures may be at variance with the norms of the larger culture, deviance at the societal level may also be conformity at the group level. Children or young people may be particularly susceptible to the subcultural influence of family, kinship groups, neighborhood groups, or circle of acquaintances, as the previous article pointed out.

Deviance can also be learned through peer groups association later in life as well as from family contact early in life. The next selection in this chapter, J. Mark Watson's "Outlaw Motorcyclists: An Outgrowth of Lower Class Cultural Concerns," examines the "outlaw lifestyle" of several groups of deviant motorcyclists. Watson studied two local motorcycle groups in middle Tennessee, one regional group from North Carolina, and one national-level group of motorcyclists. Data on these groups were obtained by means of interviews and participant observation.

As with many avocational groups, these motorcyclists developed an elaborate and colorful subculture. Component to this subculture was a distinctive jargon (language) and clothing. The customary clothing included engineer's boots, cut-off jackets with "colors" (club emblems) sewn on the back, dirty jeans, stroker caps with "quasi-military" pins attached, and earrings. Some members carried weapons such as chains, knives, and guns. Other subcultural symbols included tattooing and beards. The most important symbol, however, was their motorcycle—invariably a Harley-Davidson V-twin model. These symbols plus others and a distinctive "outlaw" lifestyle, which included illegal behavior, clearly defined these outlaw "biker" groups and made them highly visible to other bikers. As the author points out, outlaw bikers tend to belong to clubs but even those motorcyclists who do not always affiliate with clubs often tend in some ways to imitate the outlaws and use them as reference groups. The members of the outlaw groups tended to characterize themselves as "outrageous" when compared to other motorcyclists.

Watson observed that the dedication of these motorcyclists to their outlaw lifestyle was similar to the dedication of religious sect, as well as resembling a "lower class variation of bohemian 'drop-out' subculture." Both subcultures were characterized by frequent unemployment, a rejection of many conventional cultural values, and a "disdain for cleanliness [and] orderliness." The subcultures differed in that the bohemian subcultures often espoused humanistic values, while the outlaw bikers tended to emphasize force, violence, male dominance, and even racism and Nazism. The bikers used a variety of drugs but seldom indulged in hallucinogens inasmuch as such substances interfered with their ability to "ride."

The outlaw subculture has a strong antisocial orientation. The bikers view themselves as "outsiders" and feel uncomfortable with middle class culture. They see work as "hostile, weak, and effeminate," and have difficulty relating to the various societal institutions (i.e., they drifted from job to job and many had been married more than once). They tend to be impulsive and are often in conflict with social efforts to control impulsive behavior. They are basically nonconformists and see themselves as "losers," and the most "outrageously" deviant members of the subculture label themselves (literally) as "one percenters." The major themes of outlaw biker culture include "trouble," "toughness," "smartness," "excitement," "fate," and "autonomy." These values, similar to focal concerns of lower class culture, provide a fertile context for deviant and socially dysfunctional behavior.

Like many subcultures, the outlaw biker subculture has a strong system of social control operating at both the formal and informal level. At the formal level, the club rules include a constitution and bylaws and fines are assessed for the violation of rules. At the informal level, rules and norms may be enforced by "self-appointed committees," or "formally designated sergeants at arms or enforcers" who may resort to extraconstitutional means of social control, including confiscation of the offending member's motorcycle, the abuse or assault of his "old lady," and/or violence directed at the member himself. Although such bike clubs may pay lip service to individual freedom and choice, in reality they actually suppress such prerogatives. Once decisions are made, members must follow orders exactly. Failure to conform to the rules and norms will result in recrimination, expulsion, or violence. Thus, the individual has little choice but to conform to the model dictated by the subculture and behave in a deviant fashion. Inasmuch as outlaw biker groups serve as valued role models and reference groups the individual is motivated to want to belong. To become a member in good standing he must demonstrate his dedication, loyalty, and willingness to comply. The subcultural lifestyle offers the pattern to emulate and the extant value system provides the rationalization. The system of social action affords incentive beyond personal inclination. The member is subculturally propelled into deviancy.

Deviant behavior in some instances may be as much a matter of idiosyncratic inclination as that of subcultural participation. Even in such cases, however, the individual inclination and persuasion may have derived from some type of social conditioning, or experiential learning in a social context. In the subsequent article in this chapter, Erich Goode and Joanne Preissler examine an unusual kind of "deviancy" in the form of a specific sexual preference based on individual idiosyncratic taste, and the attendant sexual practices that "run so sharply against the grain of conventional taste and behavior." Goode explores the seemingly convoluted erotic perceptions of men who are sexually attracted to fat women—"fat admirers" or "FAs" as he labels them.

Culture not only dictates behavior, it also dictates thought, tastes, and perception. Values and attitudes are as much a product of culture as are artifacts, social actions, and speech. Culture, for example, delineates and dictates ideal sizes and shapes of automobiles, houses, and women to name but a few entities. Inasmuch as the United States is a youth oriented society, there is much emphasis on vitality and trimness and, thus, thinness. As the author reports, "The current prevailing esthetic standards in this society dictate that women should be thin." Prevailing esthetic standards are different in different societies and in this society the model of female thinness is more slender than in many other societies. Furthermore, the ideal female here has become slimmer through time, today as opposed to the 19th century, for example. The female who departs from this model of slenderness deviates from the social norm of sexual attractiveness as exemplified by Brooke Shields and Cheryl Tiegs. Fat women are deviant not only because they vary from the ideal anatomical shape and weight, but also because they seemingly represent gluttony and self-indulgence, the antitheses of other social norms—those of self-restraint. Obese women are stigmatized women. In past times, women (and sometimes men) who were overweight were categorically denied certain types of jobs—airline stewardess, for example. In other instances fat women simply did not get jobs because the employers sought attractive women and slenderness was one of the components of attractiveness. Nondiscrimination laws today may have eliminated some categorical discrimination, but studies (Larkin and Pines, 1979, for example) have shown that overweight women may be less likely to be hired, even though they may be perceived to be equally competent. The stereotype of the overweight person would appear to include a perception that they are inadequate in terms of personality and motivational criteria. The stigma of obesity may impact on dating and marital chances as well as employment opportunities. So strong is the desire to conform to the cultural model of slenderness as component of attractiveness that some females develop eating disorders such as anorexia nervosa or bulimia in a misdirected effort to remain slender. Such purposeful starvation or binge eating followed by vomiting and/or laxative abuse is pathologically dysfunctional and these eating disorders come to constitute deviant behavior themselves.

Men who are sexually attracted to fat women are, accordingly, also deviant because they depart from accepted standards of erotic tastes and sexual preferences. In the same way that an individual who might find attractiveness in a weed but sees no beauty in a rosebud would be considered weird, the man who is sexually attracted to the curves, bulges, and roundness of fat women is often considered "sick" and his proclivity for obesity, a "festish."

The authors report that past research on this phenomenon suggest that obesity in women may cause many men to view them as *asexual* because the fatness tends to "desexualize" the women, turning them into platonic friends or mother figures. The obesity may also cause them to conceptualize the women as *hypersexual* because the fat transforms them into a "forbidden, excessive, degraded or distorted" sexual creature—"an easy lay, a suitable target for lewdness and degradation." In short, their fatness makes them sexually exploitable because of their "low value on the dating marketplace." Goode and Preissler, however, say the motivation for FAs is somewhat more complex. In this regard, they postulate three dimensions constituent to the pattern of fat admiration, with attendant ideal types of FAs. Included are the "closet" FAs who hide their sexual proclivities versus the "overt" FAs who admit or even flaunt it. Beyond these are the "exclusive" FAs who restrict their sexual activity only to fat women (and may not even be sexually functional otherwise) versus "preferential" FAs who may engage in sex with women of various sizes, but have a distinct preference for fat women. Finally, the authors make the distinction between the "mountain men" FAs who had a genuine attraction for the very fattest women and "middle-of-the-roaders" who desire women that are fatter than the average woman but not necessarily enormous. They simply are attracted to women who are "larger and fuller-figured than the American ideal."

The FAs depart from the standards of beauty in U.S. society in terms of their sexual preference and, according to the authors, demonstrate that "some degree of pluralism exists with regard to criteria for sexual desirability." Many FAs feel socially uncomfortable with their sexual preferences and coming out "of the closet" is critical to the individual's relationship with the fat women he dates, and to his own emotional development. Some fat women come to accept their obesity and that only FAs really are sexually attracted to them. Other women will not accept the self-image of themselves as fat and may even tend to reject the FAs. As with all sexual relationships, there is an element of exchange between fat women and FAs. The fat women are at a disadvantage, however. The fat women complain that the pool of available men for them to date are either "losers" or "exploiters."

The true FA does not find fat women unappealing, but, according to the authors, "the process of sexual exchange, bargaining, and even exploitation, occurred no less frequently than—and possibly even more than—it does between non-FAs and average size women." In short, the FAs with their unique sexual preference display socially deviant taste and are even encouraged to use the fat women's "damaged sense of self-esteem" to their own advantage.

Some deviance is rational, intentional, and purposive, while other behavioral vagrancies are more impulsive or compulsive. The latter modes of deviance are not necessarily inexorable to the point of psychopathology, although in some instances they are. Cases of genuine nymphomania are not unknown in the literature but frequently involve diagnosis of neurotic or psychotic motivation. Similarly, kleptomanic shoplifters, while not numerous, are far from rare. Compulsive participation in deviant activities is more likely the result of habituation and the formation of addictive behavior patterns that are difficult and unpleasant to break. Alcoholics are made, not born (although recently there is some suggestion that a chemical factor in the body may play a part in the addiction). Drinkers may become alcohol abusers over a period of years, developing a psychological and/or physiological dependence on the alcohol, sometimes to the point to social dysfunction, and be unwilling or unable to cease their drinking. Their drinking, in effect, becomes compulsive.

Compulsion does not always have a chemical basis. Many forms of sexual deviance are behaviorally compulsive. Male exhibitionism would appear to often be the result of stress and ambivalence during periods of crisis when the "individual has concerns about his masculinity" (Bryant, 1982:145). Compulsively exposing his genitals serves as "a mechanism for reassurance of masculinity" (Bryant, 1982:145). In his research on "tea-rooms," Humphreys (1970:13) described the homosexual activities that took place in public male restrooms, and reported an individual who claimed to be heterosexual in orientation but who "said he had stopped at this tearoom every evening of the week (except Wednesday, his day off) for years 'for a blow-job.' " Surely, there is an element of compulsion based on habituation in such behavior. Among pedophiles and child molesters there is frequently a history of repeated sexual offenses against children and, thus, "a compulsive element in the pattern of these sex offenders" (Bryant, 1982:323).

It is said that some corporate executives, and other high stress occupational practitioners become "hooked" on their own adrenaline, so to speak, and compulsively pursue a maniacal, and sometimes health threatening, work schedule. Some deviants do much the same. Criminals, like voyeurs, may find an excitement in committing their offenses that is engaging, if not addictive, to the point of compulsion. Some voyeurs, for example, speak of going on a "safari to seek his prey" in referring to their peeping activities (Yalom, 1960:308), and McCaghy, 1985:153) mentions shoplifters who steal for "just plain thrills." Confidence men are alleged to be unable to pass up an opportunity to swindle someone with their spurious and larcenous presentation, even if only for a cup of coffee. Many adulterers, both male and female, may not be able to resist a romantic (and sexual) opportunity. Just as bigamous males often claim that they cannot resist women and marriage, even if illegal, many "lovers" enjoy multiple romantic "conquests," and habitually become involved in new love and sexual affairs, even at the risk of their own marriage, and other serious social consequences.

In the final selection of this chapter, John Rosecrance describes another kind of compulsive deviance, in this instance, gambling on horse racing, or "playing the ponies," as it is more popularly known in the United States. This particular pattern of deviant behavior is unique. Horse race gambling is not illegal in those states that permit racing, at least as long as the betting is done at the track under carefully controlled and supervised conditions (in states where racing is permitted, off-track betting with "bookies" is usually not legal, however). Inasmuch as gambling of some form is legal in many states (after all, state lotteries are gambling), and millions of Americans do gamble, even if only on the stock market or church-sponsored Bingo games, it can hardly be said that gambling in the generic sense is deviant. Many individuals may visit Reno or Las Vegas, or Atlantic City on a vacation or at a convention and place bets in one of the casinos there. They may even lose, and perhaps more than they intended, or anticipated, or could even afford. In doing so, they are not necessarily deviant. Gambling on horse racing is not necessarily deviant, and as the author of the article points out, millions of people go to the horse tracks each year and in a typical year such as 1984, may wager over 8 billion dollars on the "ponies."

Gambling is seldom profitable (except for the house) and gambling on horse racing is no exception. Individuals who gamble habitually and who habitually lose have been labeled as compulsive gamblers and, as such, deviants, as well as constituting a social problem. In this article, Rosecrance looks at such individuals in the form of the "loyal core of patrons who persist at gambling on horses despite the low probability of financial gain." He asserts that habitual or compulsive gambling is not necessarily or totally the function of personality defect or pathology, but rather more the result of "inappropriate betting strategies and poor money management techniques." He further contends that the gambling activities of the majority of horse players are "nonproblematic" in that they "are able to maintain acceptable levels of track participation, while keeping their losses within manageable parameters, by using appropriate gambling techniques." In support of this contention, he explores and analyzes a wide range of race track gambling participation. On the basis of ethnographic data and both focused and general interviews with race track gamblers at several tracks, the author was able to construct a typology of self-identified horse players based on goals, attendance patterns, betting style, reaction to losing streaks, and participation in the conventional job world, and posits five types of regular horse players. The first type, the *Pro* is made of a small percentage of persons (5%) who have proved they can win consistently. They have given up conventional work and for them, handicapping the horses is a full time occupation. They go the track everyday, employ a sophisticated and systematic betting strategy and, if they lose, take it in stride. The second type of player is the *Serious Player* who makes up about 10% of the horse players. This type of gambler has made a serious commitment to earning a living from playing the horses. He either has quit, or intends to quit, his regular job, and goes to the track everyday. Inasmuch as serious players tend to be less emotionally controlled than professionals, they also tend to be less consistent in their betting style and are upset by loosing streaks. Because they are less secure than pros, they may sometimes pursue rash risk taking, and all of these behavioral characteristics do not guarantee, or even necessarily promote success. The next ideal type horse player is the *Bustout*. Only about 5% of the players can be so classified. These individuals seek "action" and, for them, "gambling has become an end itself." They are frequently employed by usually only in low paying menial jobs which they need in order to financially exist. Although they may possess considerable expertise and track knowledge, they use inappropriate betting strategies and poor money management, frequently bet long shots in the hope of winning big. Accordingly, they lose frequently but are resigned to losing and are even fatalistic about it. They have constant financial problems, can only attend the races when they can afford the admission price, and may even have to beg for used racing forms or find discarded ones. They are individuals whose involvement with gambling is compulsive in spite of not being profitable. The fourth type of player suggested by the author is the *Regular*. Persons in this category make up about 45% of all players. They go to the races regularly for recreation and to see friends. They may be flexibly employed but are often retired and have a reliable income. They bet conservatively, frequently on favorite horses, but if they lose they are resigned to it and take their loses in stride. In effect, they are rational players who pay what they see as a modest price for diversion and an avocation and sociability with friends and acquaintances.

The final category mentioned is the *Part-Time Player*. These individuals, representing about 35% of horse players, attend races only on a nonregular basis, usually on weekends or days off. Most have conventional occupations, and they tend to employ relatively conservative betting strategies. A few are dissatisfied with their jobs and would like to become "professional" horse players, but most tend to view their involvement with horse racing as merely "habitual recreation spiced with gambling activity." Those who saw it mostly as recreation took losses in stride, while those who sought to become pros were likely to become upset over losing streaks. These people were not the victims of compulsion.

As the author points out, contrary to popular stereotypes, race track gamblers are not necessarily individuals that are caught up in a compulsive addiction that causes them to be habitual losers. While there is admittedly some financial risk taking in all types of horse race gambling, there is nevertheless quite a variation in betting strategy, financial management, and reactions to losing. Perhaps the vast majority of such gamblers are conservative and/or moderate in their risk taking, and in their expenditure of finances. Even consistent losses may be rationalized as a price for recreation and excitement. For a smaller minority, however, rationality and moderation give way to compulsive, and sometimes financially destructive gambling behavior with socially disruptive consequences and import. Granted that for some, rational gambling strategies permit nonproblematic participation in race track activities, for others, such involvement may mean habitual losses that they cannot afford and the attendant inability to break their habituated and compulsive tendencies. In the absence of any consistent or even occasional pattern of profit, however, it could be argued that long-term, habitual gambling, even at moderate levels of financial loss, and even as a price for recreation or avocation would suggest some deviant behavior is the product of habituation and the subsequent inability to discontinue such activity because of psychological constraint.

REFERENCES

Akers, Ronald L., Marvin D. Krohn, Lonn Lanza-Kaduce, and Marcia Radosevich

1979 "Social learning and deviant behavior: A specific test of a general theory." American Sociological Review 44:636–655.

Becker, Howard S.

1963 Outsiders: Studies in the Sociology of Deviance. New York: The Free Press.

Bensman, Joseph, and Israel Gerver

1963 "Crime and punishment in the factory: The function of deviancy in maintaining the social system." American Sociological Review 22:588–598.

Bryan, James H.

1965 "Apprenticeships in prostitution." Social Problems 12(3):287–297.

Bryant, Clifton D.

1979 Khaki-Collar Crime: Deviant Behavior in the Military Context. New York: The Free Press.

1982 Sexual Deviancy and Social Proscription: The Social Context of Carnal Behavior. New York: Human Sciences Press.

Editors of Newsweek

1974 "Bisexual chic: Anyone goes." Newsweek (May 27):96.

Gray, Giana

1973 "Turning out: A study of teenage prostitution." Urban life and Culture 1(4):401–426.

Heyl, Barbara Sherman

1977 "The madam as teacher: The training of house prostitutes." Social Problems 24(5):545–555.

Humphreys, Laud

1970 Tearoom Trade: Impersonal Sex in Public Places. Chicago: Aldine.

Larking, Judith Candib, and Harvey A. Pines

1979 "No fat persons need apply: Experimental studies of the overweight stereotype and hiring preference." Sociology of Work and Occupations 6(3):312–327.

McCaghy, Charles H.
1969 "Lesbian behavior as an adaptation to the occupation of stripping." Social Problems 17(2):262–270.
1985 Deviant Behavior: Crime, Conflict, and Interest Groups, second edition. New York: Macmillan.
McLorg, Penelope A., and Diane E. Taub
1987 "Anorexia nervosa and bulimia: The development of deviant identities." Deviant Behavior 8:177–189.
Stoddard, Ellwyn
1968 "The informal 'code' of policy deviancy: A group approach to 'blue-coat' crime." Journal of Criminal Law, Criminology and Police Science 59(2):201–204.
Winfree, L. Thomas, Jr. and Curt Taylor Griffiths
1983 "Social learning and adolescent marijuana use: A trend study of deviant behavior in a rural middle school." Rural Sociology 48:219–239.
Yalom, Irvin D.
1960 "Aggression and forbidingness in voyeurism." Archives of General Psychiatry 3:305–319.

Reading 14

Little Girls and Sex: A Glimpse at the World of the "Baby Pro"

James A. Inciardi
University of Delaware, Newark

The literature on child prostitution is limited. There is some historical documentation, but data on contemporary empirical observations is generally unavailable. Moreover, most studies have focused on teenagers rather than on children. Drug abuse was the original concern of this investigation. During the course of the research, nine girls between the ages of 8 and 12 were encountered who admitted involvement in prostitution and/or pornography. They were not runaways. Rather, they had been introduced to their careers by relatives. Their initiation into sex seemed to be motivated by fear of rejection, their drug involvement did not appear to be associated with their sexual activities, and they did not seem to be traumatized by their early association with sex.

The literature on sexual deviance has provided only limited insight into the world of the "baby pro"—the child prostitute. There is considerable historical documentation of the phenomenon as it existed in the Orient and ancient Rome and Greece (Benjamin and Masters, 1965; Pearson, 1972; Sanders, 1970), as well as in nineteenth-century America (Sanders, 1970; Shoemaker, 1977), but empirical observations of contemporary patterns are almost nonexistent. There are reports of the numerous senatorial hearings on child prostitution and pornography which discuss the "evils" of the sexual exploitation of children and the need for legislative reform (Subcommittee to Investigate Juvenile Delinquency, 1978). There are several *pop* sociological monographs which speak of "million dollar babies" who have earned as much as $30,000 per year from engaging in sex for a fee (for example, Harris, 1960). These materials, however, are little more than loosely descriptive, and offer little in terms of the characteristics of child prostitutes, patterns of recruitment and training, the nature of their sexual involvement, and their attitudes toward prostitution. Furthermore, the few empirical investigations of *child* prostitutes have actually been studies of *teenage* girls ages 13 years and above (Gray, 1973; Bracey, 1979), leaving a large gap in the literature descriptive of sex for pay as it exists among truly *little girls*. Within this context, this research note provides some baseline

This research was supported, in part, by PHS Grant #R01 DA01827 from the National Institute on Drug Abuse.

TABLE 1 Total Arrests for Prostitution and Sex Offenses, Ages 12 and Under, 1971-1980

Year	Prostitution	Sex Offenses*
1971	13	1,258
1972	21	1,299
1973	17	1,224
1974	13	1,019
1975	15	1,215
1976	31	1,263
1977	87	1,317
1978	111	1,318
1979	70	1,221
1980	1	177

*"Sex Offenses," in FBI designations, includes statutory rape, and offenses against chastity, morals and common decency.
Source: *Uniform Crime Reports* for the years 1971-1980

data on 9 female child prostitutes, ages 8 through 12, interviewed in New York City and Wilmington, Delaware during 1978–1980.

METHOD

It is understandable that child prostitutes would be difficult to encounter for systematic study. Preteen girls who engage in prostitution do not walk the streets soliciting clients, for the moral outrage over the sexual exploitation of children has made their trade an almost totally underground phenomenon. Furthermore, both the methods of reporting the arrests of children and their processing through the courts make the majority of those that do come to the attention of the criminal justice system unidentifiable as prostitutes. As indicated in Table 1, for example, arrests for both prostitution and other sex offenses appear in the FBI's Uniform Crime Reports, suggesting that child prostitutes do indeed come to the attention of the criminal justice system (although from these FBI data it cannot be determined what proportion of the arrestees are female). Moreover, it is likely that these few cases represent only a small proportion of those actually coming into contact with the police. Typically, a large number of the juveniles arrested who engage in prostitution often become visible to the criminal justice system for some other reason, such as disorderly conduct, loitering, vagrancy, curfew and loitering law violation, or "runaways." As such, while there were 178 persons ages 12 and under arrested during 1980 on charges of prostitution or other sex offenses, there were some 2,637 arrests in these other latter categories. It is likely that a number of these may have been prostitution arrests. Furthermore, in most jurisdictions, arrested juveniles become "status offenders" in the eyes of the courts. As such, even juvenile court data do not reflect the incidence of child prostitutes being processed through the judicial system. All of this suggests that official sources represent a poor base for locating data on child prostitution. The alternative is direct contact with the child prostitute in the street community.

It should be pointed out here that the original purpose of this investigation was not to study child prostitution. Rather, it was an effort designed to study the relationship between the drug use and criminal behavior of active addicts in the street community.

The peculiar life-style, illegal drug-taking and drug-seeking activities, and mobility of active drug users preclude any examination of this group through standard survey methodology. Thus, a sample based on a restricted quota draw was rejected in favor of one derived through the use of a more sociometrically oriented model.

In the field sites, the author had established extensive contacts within the subcultural drug scene. These represented "starting points" for interviewing. During or after each interview, at a time when the rapport between interviewer and respondent was deemed to be at its highest level, each respondent was requested to identify other current users with whom he or she was acquainted. These persons, in turn, were located and interviewed, and the process was repeated until the social network surrounding each respondent was exhausted.

It was during this interviewing process that the first child prostitute was inadvertently encountered. She, in turn, introduced the author to three other drug-using prostitutes of the same age. Intrigued by the possibility of collecting interview data on a yet to be studied cohort of prostitutes, the author shifted the course of the research temporarily, and requested from these respondents introductions to other young prostitutes—drug-using or not. In all, 9 such individuals were contacted—7 in New York City and 2 in Wilmington, Delaware, and all were interviewed "on the street." Given the sensitive nature of the interviews, the settings in which they were undertaken, and the ages of the respondents, only minimal information could be elicited.

FINDINGS

Briefly, the nine child prostitutes ranged in age from 8 to 12 years, with a median age of 11 years. In terms of race/ethnicity, 4 were white-Anglo, one was black, one Puerto Rican, and 3 were Oriental. None of these individuals were engaging in prostitution as a full-time occupation. All were attending elementary school, having completed a median of 6 years of education at the time of interview. None of these children were runaways. Rather, they were living at home with a parent(s) and/or other relatives.

They were introduced to their careers in prostitution by a parent, sister or other relative who was also involved in prostitution or pornography.

More specifically:

Julie, age 11. Born in Oxford, Pennsylvania, Julie is a 7th grade student living with her parents. She was introduced to prostitution at age 9, by her mother, also a prostitute. Julie's first experience involved posing in the nude by herself, and later with other girls her own age. The photographs were taken by her father. Within a few months, she began participating in pornographic films, performing such acts as masturbation, fellatio and cunnilingus with both children and adults. Since age 10, she has worked in a massage parlor, about twice a week, fellating and masturbating older men. She has never engaged in sexual intercourse. She has never used drugs, been arrested, nor did she admit to any criminal activity.

Stephanie, age 9. Stephanie was born in Ponce, Puerto Rico, and is a student in the 5th grade. She lives with her 21-year-old sister who introduced her to massage parlor operations at age 7. Stephanie's sexual activity has been limited to masturbating her sister's clients, both men and women, about once a week. She has never engaged in sexual intercourse. Stephanie smokes marijuana about twice a week, which she has been doing since age 8. On occasion, she sells marijuana to her peers. She is generally high on marijuana when she engages in sex.

Kelly, age 11; Kim, age 12. Kelly and Kim, of Oriental extraction, are sisters. Their parents are pornographers, who introduced them to films at age 7 and 8 respectively. Both have engaged in all varieties of sexual acts, with each other, children and adults of both sexes, and animals. Kelly and Kim also use drugs, a practice they began at age 9. Their drug use occurs several times each week, and has included marijuana, alcohol, minor tranquilizers, organic solvents, and cocaine. Kim, the older of the two sisters, is a part-time prostitute, while Kelly's sexual activity is limited to pornography.

Chris, age 8. Chris, who has done films with Kelly and Kim, is also of oriental extraction. She is an orphaned cousin of the two girls, and lives with them. She did her first pornographic film at age 7. Her primary activity has been oral sex, which she says she enjoys. She has never had sexual intercourse and does not use drugs.

Diana, age 10. Born in Mt. Vernon, New York, Diana lives with her sister and an aunt, both of whom are street prostitutes. They also work in massage parlors. Diana began her career in prostitution at age 8, masturbating some of her sister's clients. By age 9 she was engaging in fellatio and intercourse, occurring at the rate of one or more times a week. Her only drug use is alcohol, but she claims she has never been intoxicated.

Maryann, age 12. Living with an aunt in New York City, Maryann's sexual experiences began at age 5, with sexual intercourse occurring "sometime after that." She has never done "kiddie porn" but has engaged in all varieties of sexual activity, about four times each week. She has never used drugs.

Georgia, age 11. Born in Brooklyn, New York and brought up by her mother and uncle, Georgia began her career with pornography at age 9. Sexual intercourse began at age 10, and since that time she has participated in pornographic films combined with prostitution at the rate of about once each week. She was also in a live sex show with several girls and boys her own age. Her only drug use is occasional marijuana smoking, which she began at age 10.

Laura, age 10. Originally from Chicago, Laura has lived in various cities along the East Coast. She has been a prostitute for two years, and was introduced to it by her teenage brother, who serves as her pimp. Both she and her brother have worked in films and live sex shows. Her drug use is generally marijuana and sometimes codeine, both of which she became involved with "only recently."

The initiation of these girls into prostitution and pornography appeared to be neither forced nor traumatic. Rather, the overt presence of nudity, sexual promiscuity and prostitution in the home seemed to desensitize them. As Julie indicated: "When you see people fucking every since you're little, it seems to be just nuthin." And Diana:

> My sister would take me to work with her [to a massage parlor] sometimes when she couldn't get a baby sitter. I can't remember the first time I saw a dude get on top of her, but it didn't seem to bother her. She said it was fun and felt good too.

After their observations of sexual activity, actual participation began in several ways. Some were just simply told to do it. Kelly and Kim, for example, grew up in a household where pornographic films were produced on an almost regular basis. One day their mother told them it was their turn to take off their clothes and get in front of the camera. Georgia reported a similar experience:

> Mom was doing a film one afternoon and her period was coming real bad and making a mess out of the bed. Then my uncle said "why don't you put the kid in there and have her just give a hand job." I had seen it done often enough so it was no problem.

On the other hand, some of the girls asked to participate. As Chris explained: "Kelly and Kim were on the bed having all the fun and all the attention, so I asked if I could do it too. One day mom said OK." Similarly, Julie commented: "Mom and dad were talking about me doing the films. I told them I'd do it if they'd take me to the beach. . . . It was so easy. All I did was sit in front of the camera with my legs open.

In general, the girls' attitudes towards participating in prostitution and pornography appeared to be rather cavalier and nonchalant. Many viewed it a mechanism for "easy money." Julie stated: "A hand job takes less than two minutes. The old fart is usually already hard when I go in there, and it isn't long before they shoot their load. Twenty bucks for a two-minute *local* [masturbating a male client] isn't a bad deal."

And Laura:

> Giving head isn't the most fun thing I ever did, but it was never scary either. Someone was always there to see that nothing went wrong and so that nobody would hurt me, and then I'd get some nice presents or get taken out somewhere so it was worth it. Now I'm used to it and the spending money is real nice.

DISCUSSION

As indicated earlier, the data collected on these nine young prostitutes are rather sparse. This was due, in part, to the nature of the street-corner interviewing encounters, combined with the fact that all of the informants were both unwilling and unable to fully express themselves. It was apparent during the interviews that all of the girls had been instructed at length by their parents, guardians and peers as to the illegality of their activities, and that there could be severe consequences if their prostitution became known. As one child put it: "My sister said we would all go to jail if people find out about it." Or another stated: "They'd put my mom away, and that would be bad." A second problem was the informants' inability to fully articulate their feelings and experiences. With regard to the topics of drugs or specific sexual activities, most of the girls were able to speak in a rather matter-of-fact and somewhat mature streetwise manner. But when it came to attitudes and feelings, their chronological age and educational level seemed to come forward, leaving them with the same intellectual and perceptual abilities of other children in the 8–12 year cohort. Despite these problems, however, a number of tentative conclusions could be made.

First, it would seem that their early and repeated observations of sexual activity combined with the guidance of a parent or other relative provided them with an easy transition into the worlds of pornography and prostitution. These factors may have insulated them from the trauma that would ordinarily be experienced by other children who became victims of sexual exploitation.

Second, to a noticeable extent, their willingness to participate in sexual activities, both at the outset and as a continuing practice, seemed to be motivated by fear. Not fear in the sense of any physical harm or coercion, but fear of rejection by a parent or guardian. Their involvement was often a way of getting attention from an otherwise ambivalent mother, father, or sister. Many of these children were showered with affection, money, presents, or "a trip to the circus," after many of their sexual encounters. In this behalf, Georgia commented:

> They wanted me to do this [sex] show with a bunch of other kids one afternoon. I didn't mind playing around with the others, but it was in a room with a whole bunch of people watching. I felt kind of funny . . . My mom said that it was just this one time, and after it, she'd take me to Schwartz's [New York City's largest toy department store] and I could pick out anything I wanted.

Third, also apparent were their negative attitudes towards their clients. The *johns* were almost exclusively males, and were typically referred to as "old farts," "suckers," "assholes," "scum bags" and "shit heads." Although this, vocabulary was most likely picked up from their parents and "pimps," they generally spoke of their male clients with some disdain. As Kim stated, for example: "You have to be awfully fucked up to want to be pissed on or screwed by a kid." On the other hand, no such attitudes emerged with respect to the children, *and men*, who performed with them in films. These individuals were viewed as their equals—as others performing a service for a fee.

Fourth, their drug use did not appear to be related to their careers in prostitution and pornography. Rather, they all resided in high drug use areas, and their initiation into marijuana and alcohol use was more a matter of differential association with the public school drug culture. Kelly and Kim, for example, were the heaviest drug users (although not daily users), and had been introduced to substance abuse by a 14-year-old (nonprostitute) schoolmate. A similar type of initiation was clear with several of the other respondents. On the other hand, their drug consumption patterns were made readily possible by the funds earned through sex. This was particularly clear with respect to Kelly and Kim, who would purchase cocaine once or twice a month.

Fifth, and finally, the absurd hypocrisy associated with the way these children had been sexually exploited surfaced when they were asked whether they had intentions of becoming career prostitutes. They all said no, offering as alternatives the same type of professional aspirations that most other children have—to be an actress, a television star, a model, a doctor. Most had been told by their parents—the very same parents that introduced them to sex—that prostitution was no way to earn a living, and that "when they get older," they ought to do something else. Maryann, the oldest, most mature, and the most sexually experienced of the group seemed to have the most realistic attitude toward her activities:

> I know that this is a dirty business and that hookers end up as junkies and street bums. . . . But I also know that as long as I look young I can do OK. . . . Once I grow up I won't be so special anymore.

In conclusion, it is clear that a high degree of coercion, however covert, stimulated the entry of these nine girls into pornography and prostitution and has influenced the development and continuation of their careers. How these experiences will ultimately shape their conceptions of self, development of sex roles and attitudes, and views of the world as adults is open only to speculation.

REFERENCES

Benjamin, Harry, and R. E. L. Masters
1965 Prostitution and Morality. London: Souvenir Press.

Bracey, Dorothy R.
1979 "Baby Pros:" Preliminary Profiles of Juvenile Prostitutes. New York: John Jay Press.

Gray, Diana
1973 "Turning out: a study of teenage prostitution." Urban Life and Culture 1:401–425.

Harris, Sara
1960 They Sell Sex. Greenwich: Fawcett.

Pearson, Michael
1972 The Age of Consent: Victorian Prostitution and Its Enemies. London: David and Charles.

Sanders, Wiley B.
1970 Juvenile Offenders for a Thousand Years. Chapel Hill: University of North Carolina Press.

Shoemaker, Donald J.
1977 "The teeniest trollops: 'baby pros,' 'chickens' and child prostitutes." Pp. 241–53 in Clifton D. Bryant (ed.) Sexual Deviancy Social Context. New York: New Viewpoints.

Subcommittee to Investigate Juvenile Delinquency
1978 Protection of children against sexual exploitation. Washington, D.C.: U.S. Government Printing Office.

Reading 15

Outlaw Motorcyclists: An Outgrowth of Lower Class Cultural Concerns

J. Mark Watson
Tennessee Technological University, Cookeville

The article compares the value system and lifestyle of three groups of deviant motorcyclists in the Tennessee-Kentucky area to the focal concerns of lower class culture described by Walter Miller in his classic study of adolescent gang delinquency. Some striking parallels between the values of the two groups are noted. Some differences in the focal concern are noted, but the differences seem to be due primarily to the age differential between the two groups. Although both groups subscribe to lower class values and share most of the focal concerns described by Miller, the outlaw motorcyclists appear at lest partially the products of downward mobility, which may be a result of subscribing to lower class values and concerns.

INTRODUCTION

Walter Miller's (1958) typology of focal concerns of lower class culture as a generating milieu for gang delinquency is by most standards a classic in explaining gang behavior among juvenile males. Its general heuristic value is here demonstrated by the striking parallel between this value system and that of adult outlaw motorcyclists.

The reader may remember Miller's general schema, which concerned the strain between the value system of youthful lower class males and the dominant, middle-class value system of those in a position to define delinquent behavior. Miller, by describing these values (he used the term "focal concerns"), anticipated conflict theory, without directly pointing out the conflicting values of the middle-class definers of delinquent behavior. Although there have been some disagreements surrounding details of Miller's description of the functioning of adolescent gangs, the basic focal concerns described in the typology have been relatively free of criticism as to their validity in describing the values of young lower class males. Some questions have been raised about the degree to which these values actually are in contrast with those of middle-class adolescents, however (see, for example, Short et al., 1963). Because the typology itself is contained in the discussion of biker values, it will not be discussed separately here.

With apologies to Walter Miller.

METHODOLOGY

The findings of the paper are based on my 3 years of participant observation in the subculture of outlaw motorcyclists. Although I am not a member of any outlaw clubs, I am or have been acquainted with members of officers of various clubs, as well as more loosely organized groups of motorcyclists for 10 years. I am myself a motorcycle enthusiast, which facilitated a natural entry into the biker scene. I both build and ride bikes and gained direct access to local biker groups by frequenting places where bikers congregate to work on their bikes. Building a bike gave me legitimation and access to local biker groups and eventually led to contact with other bikers, including outlaws. Groups observed varied from what could be classified as clubs to loose-knit groups of associated motorcyclists. Four groups were studied in depth. Two small local groups in middle Tennessee were subjects of direct participation. Here they are given the fictional names of the Brothers and the Good Old Boys. In addition, one regional group from North Carolina, given the fictional name of Bar Hoppers, was studied through interviews with club officers and members. One national-level group, one of the largest groups of outlaw motorcyclists, was extensively observed and interviewed, primarily at regional and national events. This group is given the fictional name of the Convicts. Additional information was also gathered by attempting to interview at regional and national events members and officers of a wide range of clubs. This was easily done by simply looking at club "colors" (patches) and seeking out members of clubs that were not already represented in the study. This technique was used primarily to check for the representatives of behavior, values, beliefs, and other characteristics observed in in-depth studies of the four clubs mentioned above. Another source of validation of conclusions was extensive use of biker literature such as magazines and books by or about bikers. These are listed in the bibliography.

Data were collected by means of interviews conducted from January 1977 to March 1980. Interviews were informally administered in the sense that no formal interview schedule was used. Instead, bikers were queried in the context of what would pass for normal conversation. Extensive observations of behavior were made while directly participating in the activities of the groups, everyday events such as hanging out and from building bikes to "runs," (trips), swap meets, and cult events, such as speed week at Daytona Beach, Florida, and the National Motorcycle Drag Championships at Bowling Green, Kentucky. Such events led to contact with bikers from all over the United States, inasmuch as these events attract a national sample of dedicated bikers, including the whole range of types from simple enthusiasts to true outlaws. Notes and impressions were taken at night and/or after the events. Groups and individuals were generally not aware that they were being studied, although I made no attempt to hide my intentions. Some bikers who came to know me were curious about a university professor participating in such activities and accordingly were told that a study was being conducted. This honesty was prompted by fear of being suspected of being a narcotics agent. Such self-revelation was rarely necessary as the author affected the clothing and jargon of bikers and was accepted as such. Frequent invitations to engage in outrageous and illegal behavior (e.g., drug use and purchase of stolen parts) that would not be extended to outsiders were taken as a form of symbolic acceptance. My demeanor and extensive association with lower class gangs in adolescence combined with the type of mechanical skills necessary to build bikes mentioned earlier may have contributed to an ability to blend in. Reactions to self-revelation, when necessary, generally ranged from amazement to amusement. I suspect that, as is true with the general population, most bikers had no idea what a sociologist was, but the presence of a professor in their midst was taken as a sort of legitimation of the group.

Observations and conclusions were cross-checked on an on-going basis with a group of five biker informants whom I knew well, including members of the Brothers, Good Old Boys, and the Convicts who lived in the mid-Tennessee area. Informants were selected on the basis of several criteria. First, informants had to know and be known well enough by me to establish a trusting relationship. This limited informants to local bikers found in my area of residence. As mentioned above, outlaw motorcyclists are not particularly trusting, and this obstacle had to be overcome. Second, informants had to be articulate enough to communicate such concepts as values. Most bikers are not particularly articulate, so this criterion eliminated many members of local groups whom I knew well. Third, informants had to have extensive experience in biker subculture. Consequently, informants were limited to bikers who had traveled and lived in a wide geographic area and had experience wider than that represented by the mid-South region. Consequently, informants were generally older than the typical biker population, varying in age from the early 30s to the mid-40s. Three of the informants were former or current owners of custom motorcycle shops that catered to biker clientele. All were what might be defined as career bikers. Finally, all informants had to possess enough objectivity about the biker lifestyle to be willing to read and comment on the author's conclusions. Many of these conclusions, though valid and objective, one hopes, are not particularly flattering to participants in the outlaw motorcyclists subculture. One informant was lost because of obvious antagonism generated by some conclusions. In addition, conversations with hundreds of unsuspecting bikers were held in order to ascertain the generalizability of observations. The latter technique involved appearing to be ignorant or confused and simply asking for a definition of the situation, for example,

"What's happening?" or, "What are they doing?" or even venturing an evaluation such as, "That's stupid; why do they do that?" all in order to elicit a response from an observer of some act. It must be kept in mind that research conducted with this kind of deviant subculture can be dangerous. Because many outlaws do not welcome scrutiny and carefully avoid those whom they feel may not be trusted, which includes most nonbikers, I remained as unobtrusive as possible. Consequently, the methodology was adapted to the setting. Generally, I felt my presence was accepted. Throughout the study I sensed no change in the cyclist's behavior over time by my presence. This acceptance can be symbolized by my receiving a nickname (Doc) and eventually being defined as an expert in a certain type of obsolete motorcycle (the Harley-Davidson 45-cubic-inch side-valve model). I assumed the role of an inside outsider.

THE BIKER SUBCULTURE

We may locate outlaw bikers in the general spectrum of bikers as the most "outrageous" (their own term, a favorite modifier indicating something distinctively appealing to their own jaded sense of values) on the continuum of bikers, which extends from housewives on mopeds to clubs that actually engage in illegal behavior with a fair degree of frequency, thus the term "outlaws" (Thompson, 1967:9). Outlaws generally adopt certain symbols and lead a lifestyle that is clearly defined and highly visible to other bikers. Symbols include extensive tattooing, beard, dirty jeans, earrings, so-called stroker caps with quasi-military pins attached, engineer's boots, and cut-off jackets with club emblems, called "colors," sewn on the back. Weapons, particularly buck knives and guns of any sort, and chains (motorcycle or other types) are favorite symbols as well (Easyriders, November, 1977:28, 29, 55). By far the most important symbol, however, is the Harley-Davidson V-twin motorcycle.[1] It should be kept in mind that many other motorcyclists affect these symbols, although they are by no means outlaws. Outlaws almost always belong to clubs, whereas many motorcyclists who do not belong to the clubs use them as reference groups and attempt to imitate some aspects of their behavior. These symbols and the basic lifestyle are generalizable to a wide range of bikers and may even be found among British and European bikers, with the exception of the Harley-Davidson motorcycle (Choppers, April 1980:12).

[1]A favorite T-shirt observed at cult events is one saying, "If you ain't a Harley rider, you ain't shit!"

OUTLAW LIFESTYLE

For the outlaw, his lifestyle takes on many of the characteristics of dedication to a religious sect (Watson, 1979). This lifestyle is in many respects a lower class variation of bohemian, "dropout" subcultures. Such similarities include frequent unemployment and disdain for cleanliness, orderliness, and other concerns of conventional culture. For example, I have observed bikes being built and stored in living rooms or kitchens, two nonessential rooms in the subculture. This is apparently a common practice. Parts may be stored in an oil bath in the bathtub, also a nonessential device. The biker and other bohemian subcultures may appear similar on the basis of casual observations, but some outlaw biker values are strikingly different from the beatnik or hippy subcultures of the 1950s and 1960s. Other bohemian subcultures emphasized humanistic values, whereas the outlaw bikers' values emphasize male dominance, violence, force, and racism (Easyriders, October 1977:15). Although individual freedom and choice are also emphasized, the clubs actually suppress individual freedom, while using the value to defend their lifestyle from outsiders. For example, when the Convicts take a club trip called a "run," all members must participate. Those whose bikes are "down" for repairs are fined and must find a ride in a truck with the women. Many club rules require members to follow orders as prescribed by club decisions upon threat of violence and expulsion. Club rules generally include a constitution and bylaws that are surprisingly elaborate and sophisticated for groups of this nature. Many club members express pride in their written regulations. It seems likely that the basic format is borrowed from that developed by the Hell's Angels (Thompson, 1967:72). Most club decisions are made in a democratic way, but minority rights are not respected. Once such a decision is made, it is imperative to all members, with risk of physical retribution for failure to conform. Typical rules include care of colors, which are to never touch the ground or be washed. They are treated essentially as a flag. Other rules mentioned above and below have to do with following group decisions without dissent and such requirements as defending club honor through unanimous participation in avenging affronts to other clubs' members. Club rules may be enforced by self-appointed committees or by formally designated sergeants at arms or enforcers. One informant expressed it this way: "They'll take your bike, your old lady, and stomp the shit out of you if you make 'em look bad." This particular expression related to some prospective "probate" members and their failure to live up to club rules requiring violent reactions to challenges to club honor. The observation came from a retired club member when I queried him about an almost surreal conflict over the wearing of a club symbol by a nonmember.

Use of mind-altering drugs is another area of overlap between biker and bohemian subcultures. Outlaw bikers will take or drink almost anything to alter their consciousness (Easyriders, May 1978:24,25). The groups studied regularly used "uppers," "downers," and marijuana but rarely used hallucinogens. One informant explained that the latter "fuck you up so you can't ride, so we don't use it much." Apparently, one can ride on uppers, downers, or when drunk but not when hallucinating. Curiously enough, the most commonly used drug is alcohol taken in the rather mild form of beer (though in great quantity). Where there are outlaw bikers one will usually find drugs, but one will almost always find beer.

Outsider status, the use of drugs, and the seeking of cheap rent result in frequent overlap between outlaw bikers and other bohemian types, in both territory and interpersonal relations. The bikers usually tolerate the other bohemians, because the latter share an interest in and serve as a source of supply of, or customers for, drugs. Bikers, however, view them with contempt because they are not masculine enough. Hippies, dopers, and fairies are similar types as far as bikers are concerned. Masculinity as a dominant value is expressed in many ways, including toughness and a general concern with looking mean, dirty, and "outrageous." When asked about a peripheral member of a local group, one informant replied, "He's a hippy, but he don't ride. We put up with him because he has good dope. I feel sorry for him because he's just a fucked-up puke."

Some other biker-associated values include racism, concern with Nazism, and in-group superiority. "Righteousness" is achieved through adherence to these values. One celebrity member of the Brothers had been convicted of killing a young black man in a street confrontation. He is reported to have jumped bail and lived with a Nazi couple in South America, where he worked as a ranch hand. This particular member spoke some German and frequently spouted racist and Nazi doctrine. A typical righteous outlaw belongs to a club, rides a American-made motorcycle, is a white male, displays the subculture's symbols, hates most if not all nonwhites and Japanese motorcycles, works irregularly at best, dresses at all times in dirty jeans, cut-off denim jacket, and engineer's boots, drinks beer, takes whichever drugs are available, and treats women as objects of contempt.

OUTLAW BIKER WORLD VIEW AND SELF-CONCEPT

The outlaw biker generally views the world as hostile, weak, and effeminate. Perhaps this view is a realistic reaction to a working-class socialization experience. However, the reaction contains certain elements of a self-fulfilling prophecy. Looking dirty, mean, and generally undesirable may be a way of frightening others into leaving one alone, although, in many senses such an appearance arouses anger, hostility, and related emotions in the observer and results in the persecution that such qualities are intended to protect one from.

Bikers tend to see the world in terms of here and now. They are not especially hostile toward most social institutions such as family, government, and education. Most of the local group members had finished high school and had been employed from time to time, and some had been college students. Some were veterans, and nearly all had been married more than once. Few had been successful in these endeavors, however. They are generally not capable of establishing the temporal commitments necessary for relating to such institutions. For example, marriages and similar relationships rarely last more than a few years, and education requires concentrated effort over a time span that they are generally not willing or in many cases not capable of exerting. Most of them drift from one job to another or have no job at all. Simply keeping up with where the informants were living proved to be a challenge. I frequently had a call from a local biker relating that he was "on his way over" only to find that he did not arrive at all or arrived hours or days later. I have been on runs that were to depart in the early morning and that did not in fact depart until hours later. The biker's sense of time and commitment to it is not only lower class, but more typical or preliterate societies. The result is frequent clashes with bureaucratically organized institutions, such as government and economy, which are oriented toward impulse control, commitment, and punctuality, and failure in organizations that require long-term commitments or interpersonal relations, such as family and education.

A similar view of regulation causes frequent conflicts. Bikers are not basically violent but are impulsive. Regulations that conflict with their impulses are ignored. Attempts to enforce such regulations (generally by law enforcement officers) are viewed not as legal regulation but as unreasonable demands (harassment). Of course, this impulsiveness can be destructive and self-defeating. I have seen bikers destroy engines they spent hundreds of dollars on by simply overreving them. I have also seen doors, jukeboxes, bike gas tanks, and other items destroyed in an impulsive moment—sometimes in rage, sometimes in humor, or out of boredom. Bikers demand freedom to follow these impulses, which often involve behavior defined by the observer as outrageous. Occasionally bikers reinforce this conception by conforming to the stereotype and deliberately shocking more conventional people, especially if they feel their social space is being invaded. An illustrative incidence occurred in 1978 at the National Championship Drag Races, an event for motorcycles in Bowling Green, Kentucky. An area of a local amusement park was designated "for bikers only." The area was clearly marked with large signs. Occasionally local citizens and outraged tourists insisted on driving through to see the scene.

Bikers had begun "partying" and engaging in heavy drinking, drug use, and generally impulsive behavior, including frequent male and female nudity, which occasioned some notice but no shock to other bikers. However, when outsiders drove through, they were deliberately exposed to substantial nudity and what were no doubt interpreted as obscene and disgusting displays by those viewing them. The result was that the city of Bowling Green declined future events of that nature. The races have been held elsewhere in subsequent years.

Outlaw bikers generally view themselves as outsiders. I have on occasion invited local bikers to settings that would place them in contact with members of the middle class. Their frequent response is that they would "not fit in" or would "feel out of place." Basically, they seem to feel that they cannot compete with what sociologists define as the middle class although I have never heard the term used by bikers. Outlaws see themselves as losers, as symbolized by tattoos, patches, and even their humor, which portrays them as ignorant. "One percenter" is a favorite patch, referring to its wearers as the most deviant fraction of the biker fraternity. In effect, the world that they create for themselves is an attempt to suspend the rules of competition that they cannot win by and create a world where one does not compete but simply exists (Montgomery, 1976, 1977.) Pretense and self-importance are ways to loose acceptance quickly in such a situation. One does not compete with or "put down" a fellow biker, for he is a "brother."

It is not that bikers are uniformly hostile toward the outside world; they are indifferent toward, somewhat threatened by, and contemptuous of it.

MILLER'S FOCAL CONCERNS AS EXPRESSED IN OUTLAW BIKER CULTURE

Trouble

Trouble is a major theme of the outlaw biker culture as illustrated by the very use of the term "outlaw." The term refers to one who demonstrates his distinctiveness (righteousness) by engaging in outrageous and even illegal behavior. Trouble seems to serve several purposes in this subculture. First, flirting with trouble is a way of demonstrating masculinity—trouble is a traditionally male prerogative. Trouble also enforces group solidarity through emphasizing the outsider status of the outlaw, a status that can be sustained only by the formation of a counterculture. Given the outlaw biker's world view and impulsiveness, trouble comes without conscious effort. Trouble may come over drug use, stolen bikes or parts, possession of firearms, or something as simple as public drunkenness. Some of the local bikers whom I knew well had prison records for manslaughter (defined as self-defense by the subjects), receiving stolen property, drug possession, statutory rape, and assault on an officer. All saw these sentences as unjust and claimed that the behavior was justifiable or that they were victims of a case of overzealous regulation of everyday activities or deliberate police harassment.

Trouble used to take the form of violence between biker clubs and groups (Easyriders, April 1979:13, 41). Most of this activity was generated by issues of club honor involving the stealing of women or perceived wrongs by members of other clubs. The general motivation for this activity seemed to be an opportunity to demonstrate toughness (see below). The only open conflict that I saw was an incident, mentioned earlier, between the Brothers and the Convicts over the right of the other groups to wear a one percenter badge as part of their club colors. In recent years most groups have abandoned the practice of interclub violence and emphasize instead the conflict between group members and police. An issue that is a current example of this conflict and that therefore serves this unifying purpose is the mandatory helmet laws in many states and the related attempts of the federal Department of Transportation to regulate modification by owners of motorcycles (Supercycle, May 1979:4, 14–15, 66).

Organized reaction to trouble in the sense of attempts to regulate motorcycles and motorcyclists is probably as close to political awareness and class consciousness as bikers come. Outlaw types, however, generally have little to do with these activities, partly because they view them as hopeless and partly because they correctly perceive their support and presence at such activities as unwelcome and poor public relations.

Toughness

In addition to trouble, toughness is at the heart of the biker emphasis on masculinity and outrageousness. To be tough is to experience trouble without showing signs of weakness. Therefore, the objective of trouble is to demonstrate the masculine form of toughness. Bikers have contempt for such comforts as automobiles or even devices that increase biking comfort or safety such as eye protection, helmets, windshields, farings, or even frames with spring rear suspension (a so-called hardtail is the preferred frame). Bikers wear denim or leather, but the sleeves are generally removed to show contempt for the danger of "road rash," abrasions caused by contact with the road surface at speed, which protective material can prevent. Part of toughness is the prohibition against expressing love for women and children in any but a possessive way. Women are viewed with contempt and are regarded as a necessary nuisance (generally referred to as "cunts," "whores," or "sluts"), as are children (rug rats). Curiously, bikers seem to attract an adequate supply of women despite the poor treatment they receive from them in such a situation. One informant expressed his contempt for women this way, "Hell, if I could find a man with a pussy, I wouldn't fuck with women. I don't like 'em. They're nothing but trouble." When asked about the female's motivation for participation in the subculture, one (male) informant stated simply "they're looking for excitement." The women attracted to such a scene are predictably tough and hard-bitten themselves. Not all are unattractive, but most display signs of premature aging typical of lower class and deviant lifestyles. All work to keep up their mate and his motorcycle. I must admit that my interviews with biker women were limited least my intentions be misinterpreted. I could have hired some of them under sexual pretenses, as many may be bought, but ethical and financial considerations precluded this alternative. My general impression is that these women generally come from lower class families in which the status of the female is not remarkably different from that they currently enjoy. Being a biker's "old lady" offers excitement and opportunities to engage in exhibitionist and outlandish behavior that in their view contrasts favorably with the lives of their mothers. Many are mothers of illegitimate children before they resort to bikers and may view themselves as fallen women who have little to lose in terms of respectability. Most seem to have fairly low self-concepts, which are compatible with their status as biker's old ladies.

Of course, the large, heavy motorcycles bikers ride are symbolic of their toughness as well. Not everyone can ride such a machine because of its sheer weight. Many models are "kick start," and require some strength and skill just to start. A certain amount of recklessness is also used to express toughness. To quote Bruce Springsteen: "It's a death trap, a suicide rap" (Springsteen, 1976), and the ability to ride it, wreck it, and survive demonstrates toughness in a very dramatic way. An example of my experience in this regard may be illuminating. Although I had ridden motorcycles for years, I became aware of the local biker group while building my first Harley-Davidson. Full acceptance of this group was not extended until my first and potentially fatal accident, however. Indeed, local bikers who had only vaguely known me offered the gift of parts and assistance in reconstructing my bike and began to refer to me by a new nickname, "Doc." I sensed and was extended a new degree of acceptance after demonstrating my "toughness" by surviving the accident. Toughness, in this sense, is a combination of stupidity and misfortune, and hardly relates to any personal virtue.

Smartness

On this characteristic, biker values seem to diverge from general lower class values as described by Miller. The term "dumb biker" is frequently used as a self-description. Given the choice of avoiding, outsmarting, or confronting an opponent, the biker seems to prefer avoidance or confrontation. Confrontation gives him the opportunity to demonstrate toughness by generating trouble. Avoidance is not highly valued, but no one can survive all the trouble he could generate, and the stakes are frequently the highest – life itself or at least loss of freedom. The appearance of toughness and outlandishness mentioned above make confrontation a relatively infrequent occurrence, as few outsiders will challenge a group of outlaw bikers unless the issue is of great significance. Smartness, then, does not seem to be an emphasized biker value or characteristic. Gambling on outsmarting an opponent is for low stakes such as those faced by the adolescents Miller studied.

Excitement

One of the striking things about the outlaw lifestyle is its extremes. Bikers hang out at chopper (motorcycle) shops, clubhouses, or bars during the day, except when they are in prison or jail, which is not uncommon. Places frequented by bikers are generally located in lower class neighborhoods. A clubhouse, for example is generally a rented house which serves as a headquarters, party location, and place for members to "crash" when they lack more personal accommodations. They are not unlike a lower class version of a fraternity house. Outlaws tend to designate bars as their own. This involves taking over bars to the exclusion of their usual lower or working-class clientele. Such designations are frequently short-lived as the bars may be closed as a public nuisance or the proprietor may go out of business for economic or personal reasons as a result of the takeover. I know of at least one such bar that was burned by local people to rid the neighborhood of the nuisance. Its owner relocated the business some 40 miles away.

Local bikers who worked generally had unskilled and semi-skilled jobs, which are dull in themselves. Examples include laborers, factory workers, construction workers, and hospital orderlies. Many do not work regularly, being supported by their women.[2] In any case, most of their daylight hours are spent in a deadly dull environment, where the most excitement may be a mechanical problem with a bike. Escape from this dull lifestyle is dramatic in its excesses. Drugs, alcohol, and orgiastic parties are one form of escape. Other escapes include the run or simply riding the bikes for which the subculture is named. Frequently both forms of escape are combined, and such events as the Daytona and Sturgis runs are remarkable, comparing favorably to Mardi Gras as orgiastic events. Living on the edge of trouble, appearing outlandish, fierce, and tough, itself yields a form of self-destructive excitement, especially when it can be used to outrage others. Unlike the situation that Miller studied, excitement and trouble rarely seem to center around women, as their status among bikers is even lower than in

[2]Outlaw bikers sometimes support themselves by dealing in drugs, bootleg liquor, and prostitution of their women.

the lower class in general. I have never seen a conflict over a women among bikers and am struck by the casual manner in which they move from one biker to another. The exchange of women seems to be the male's perogative, and women appear to be traded or given away as casually as pocket knives are exchanged among old men. I have on occasion been offered the use of a female for the duration of a run. This offer was always made by the male and was made in the same manner that one might offer the use of tool to a neighbor. (I have never been offered the loan of a bike, however). The low regard for women combined with the traditional biker's emphasis on brotherhood seem to minimize conflicts over women. Those conflicts that do occur over women seem to occur between clubs and are a matter of club honor rather than jealousy or grief over the loss of a relationship.

Fate

Because bikers do not emphasize smartness to the extent that Miller perceived it among the lower class, the role of fate in explaining failure to succeed is somewhat different for them. In Miller's analysis fate was a rationalization used when one was outsmarted. The biker's attitude toward fate goes much deeper and could be described as figuratively and literally fatalistic. The theme of death is central to their literature and art.[3] A biker who becomes economically successful or who is too legitimate is suspect. He is no longer one of them. He has succeeded in the outside and in a sense has sold out. His success alone shows his failure to subscribe to the basic values that they hold. He is similar to a rich Indian—no longer an Indian but a white man with red skin. Members of local groups, the Brothers and the Good Old Boys, came and went. Membership fluctuated. Few members resigned because of personal difficulty. However, many former members were still around. The single characteristic that they all shared was economic success. Although these former members tended to be older than the typical member, many current members were as old or older. Success in small businesses were typical. Some former members had been promoted to lower management positions in local factories and related businesses, apparently were no longer comfortable in their former club roles, and so resigned. Some kept their bikes, others exchanged them for more respectable touring bikes, and others sold their bikes. In any case, although some maintained limited social contact and others participated in occasional weekend runs, their success appeared to make them no longer full participants in group activities and resulted ultimately in their formal resignation from the clubs. Bikers basically see themselves as losers and affect clothing, housing, and other symbols of the embittered and dangerous loser. They

[3]Of the fiction in the entire 1977 issue of *Easyriders*, 40% of the articles concerned themselves with death.

apparently no longer dream the unrealistic adolescent dreams of the "big break." Prison and death are seen as natural concomitants of the biker lifestyle. Fate is the grim reaper that so often appears in biker art.

Autonomy

Autonomy in the form of freedom is central to the outlaw biker expressed philosophy and in this respect closely parallels the lower class themes outlined by Miller. A studied insistence that they be left alone by harassing law enforcement agencies and overregulating bureaucrats is a common theme in biker literature and personal expressions. The motorcycle itself is an individual thing, begrudgingly including an extra seat for an "old lady" or "down" brother. Ironically, the outlaw biker lifestyle is so antisocial vis-à-vis the wider society that it cannot be pursued individually. A lone outlaw knows he is a target, an extremely visible and vulnerable one. Therefore, for purposes of self-protection, the true outlaw belongs to a club and rarely makes a long trip without the company of several brothers.

Outlaw clubs are themselves both authoritarian and democratic. Members may vote on issues or at least select officers,[4] but club policy and rules are absolute and may be enforced with violence (Choppers, March 1978:36–39). Antisocial behavior associated with the outlaw lifestyle itself frequently results in loss of autonomy. Most prisons of any size not only contain a substantial biker population but may contain local (prison) chapters of some of the larger clubs (Life, August 1979:80–81). *Easyriders*, a biker magazine, regularly contains sections for pen pals and other requests from brothers in prison (Easyriders, October 1977:16–19, 70). So, although autonomy in the form of the right to be different is pursued with a vengeance, the ferocity with which it is pursued ensures its frequent loss.

Miller noted an ambivalent attitude among lower class adolescents toward authority: they both resented it and sought situations in which it was forced on them. The structure of outlaw clubs and the frequent incarceration that is a result of their lifestyle would seem to be products of a similar ambivalence. Another loss of autonomy that Miller noted among lower class gangs was a dependence on females that caused dissonance and was responsible for lower class denigration of female status. Outlaws take the whole process a step further, however. Many of their women engage in prostitution, topless waitressing, or menial, traditionally female labor. Some outlaws live off the income of several women and in this sense are dependent on them but only in the sense that a pimp is dependent on his string of girls. From their point of view, the females see themselves as protected by and dependent on the male rather than the other way around.

[4]Officer selection may be based on many processes, some of which would hardly be recognized as democratic by those outside the subculture. Leaders are popularly selected, however. Physical prowess may be the basis of selection, for example.

CONCLUSION

Miller's typology of lower class focal concerns appears to be a valid model for analyzing outlaw biker cultures, just as it was for analyzing some forces behind juvenile gang delinquency. Although there are some differences in values and their expression, the differences are basically those occurring by the transferring of the values from street-wise adolescents to adult males. Both groups could be described as lower class, but my experiences with bikers indicate a working-class family background with downward mobility. A surprising proportion of the bikers interviewed indicated respectable working-class or lower middleclass occupations for their fathers. Examples included postal worker, forestry and lumber contractor, route sales business owner, and real estate agency owner. They are definitely not products of multigenerational poverty. I would classify them as nonrespectable working-class marginals.

The study is presented primarily as an ethnographic description of a difficult and sometimes dangerous subculture to study, which when viewed from the outside appears as a disorganized group of deviants but when studied carefully with some insider's insights is seen to have a coherent and reasonably consistent value system and a lifestyle based on that value system.

REFERENCES

Choppers
1978 "Club profile: Northern Indiana Invaders M/C." (March):36.
Choppers
1980 "Mailbag." (April):12.
Easyriders
1977 "Gun nut report." (February):28, 29, 55.
Easyriders
1977 "Gang wars are a thing of the past." (April):13, 41.
Easyriders
"Man is the ruler of woman." (October):15.
Easyriders
1977 "Jammin in the joint." (October):16–19 (Also "Mail call").
Easyriders
1978 "The straight dope on Quaaludes." (May):24–25.
Gordon, Robert A., Short, Jr., James F. Cartwright, Desmond, and Strodtbeck, Fred
1963 "Values and gang delinquency." American Journal of Sociology 69:109–128.
Life
1979 "Prison without stripes." (1979):80–81.

Miller, Walter B.
1958 "Lower class culture as a generating milieu for gang delinquency." Journal of Social Issues 14:5–19.
Montgomery, Randall
1976 "The outlaw motorcycle subculture." Canadian Journal of Criminology and Corrections 18.
Montgomery, Randall
1979 "The outlaw motorcycle subculture II." Canadian Journal of Crimonology and Corrections 19.
Springsteen, Bruce
1975 "Born to run." Columbia Records.
Supercycle
1979 "On reserve." (May):14–15, 66.
Thompson, Hunter
1967 Hell's Angels: a strange and terrible saga. New York: Random House.
Watson, John M.
1979 "Righteousness on two wheels: bikers as a secular sect." Unpublished paper read at the Southwestern Social Science Association, March 1979.

Reading 16

The Fat Admirer

Erich Goode
State University of New York

Joanne Preissler
National Association to Aid Fat Americans

This paper describes a neglected social phenomenon: men who are erotically and romantically attracted to fat women in part because they are obese. Fifteen formal interviews were held with "fat admirers," as well as numerous informal interviews with many more. In addition, the authors have been participants in a "fat" civil rights organization (the National Association to Aid Fat Americans), which serves as a site for fat admirers and obese women to meet and socialize with one another. At least three dimensions distinguish different types of fat admirers—"closet" versus "overt," "exclusive" versus "preferential," and "mountain men" versus "middle-of-the-roaders. The authors also explore the impact of stigma emanating from conventional society on the sexual life of the fat admirer and the fat woman. Lastly, the role that exchange and social bargaining—following some basic tenets of exchange theory—play in the sexual exploitation of some fat women is elaborated.

There are perhaps millions of men in the United States who have a specific sexual preference, and engage in certain sexual practices, that run so sharply against the grain of conventional taste and behavior that most Americans would either refuse to believe that they exist, or would regard their sexuality as "sick"—a kind of "fetish." Further, the predilections and experiences of these men are so well concealed that they have almost totally escaped serious study or scrutiny by sociologists or psychologists. The men to which we refer have a strong erotic desire for obese women. Within the circles of men with this preference, and among the women who attract the sexual attention of these men, they are referred to as fat admirers (FAs).

To be plain about it, these men prefer their sexual partners to be fat. They do not date fat women in spite of their size, but in part because of it. The vast majority of all men, FAs and non-FAs alike, choose their sexual partners partly—and at first, mainly—because of how pleasing their looks are to them. "It's a matter of chemistry," one man explained to us; "I simply can't start a relationship unless the woman turns me on physically." However, the features of a woman's body that "turn on" the FA are quite different from those that excite his non-FA counterpart. The FA is excited by the softness, the roundness, and the weight of women, their curves and bulges. "After all," one man we interviewed asked rhetorically, "who wants to impale himself on a bag of bones?"

Vestiges of a puritanical morality may be found in American culture. As we cast aside sexual restraints, other sources of guilt remain—indeed, appear even more prominently than was true in the past. Today, self-indulgence is more likely to be equated with an immodest appetite for food than for sex. Gluttony, it seems, is one of the last remaining taboos. After all, if one is now permitted to enjoy sex with multiple partners, even strangers, one must be more concerned with "looking good" when naked—and today, that means being thin. Thin people believe that they have the right to feel more virtuous than fat people: they have resisted the temptation to gluttony to which the overweight have clearly succumbed. Fat people invited, or so the "thin chauvinist" ideology would have it, well-deserved *retribution*: they are derided because they are self-indulgent and lack the willpower of righteous, temperate, upstanding souls. It is entirely possible that this ideological edifice is built on shaky grounds: fat people may very well eat no more than thin people (Wooley and Wooley, 1979). It is even more likely that men and women of average size find fat people esthetically unappealing. And it is here that our story begins.

The current prevailing esthetic standards in this society dictate that women should be thin—standards are considerably thinner here than in other societies of the world, and considerably thinner today than they were in past generations. The trend in the size of the ideal American woman is, perhaps, reflected in the evolution of the models for the "White Rock Girl."

In 1894, she was 5′4″ tall, measured 37-27-38, and weighed 140 pounds; in 1947, she was 5′6″, 35-25-35, and weighed 125; today, she's 5′8″, 35-24-34, and weighs 118 pounds. White Rock's representatives comment on this trend, in a leaflet on "Psyche, Cupid, and White Rock," in the following words: "Over the years, the Psyche image has become longer legged, slim hipped, and streamlined. Today—when purity is so important—she continues to symbolize the constant purity of all White Rock products." (The equation of "slim" with "pure" is a revealing comment on the Puritan attitudes toward the fuller-figured woman that currently prevail.)

The FA's distribution in the population is quite impossible to determine with any accuracy. William Fabrey, founder of the National Association to Aid Fat Americans, a civil rights organization dedicated to the elimination of prejudice and discrimination against fat people, estimates their extent in the male population in this country at 1 in 20, or some two million adult men. (The fact that standards of female beauty with regard to size is subject to historical and cultural relativity is well known—and consequently, FAs are far more common elsewhere than in contemporary America—but should at least be mentioned in passing.) For a variety of reasons, there are relatively few female FAs—women who have a strong erotic desire specifically for fat men. In fact, nearly all of the fat women we interviewed had conventional standards regarding the size of their preferred partners, and desired men with an average or muscular build. In this report, we will concentrate exclusively on the male FA's and the obese women to whom they are attracted.

Considering that the ideal of feminine beauty as represented in the media and in advertising is extremely slender (Brooke Shields and Cheryl Tiegs exemplify these standards), a man's preference for considerably larger women is likely to be met with disbelief and derision. A great deal has been written on the "stigma of obesity" (Cahnman, 1968; Allon, 1979:30–32)—the condemnation that fat people face for being overweight. However, only a small minority of the men we interviewed were themselves fat. One of the issues we wish to deal with in this paper is the role that social stigma plays in the sexual and romantic lives of men who are not fat, but who find themselves irresistably attracted to women who are. In other words, these fat admirers face *stigma by association*.

As to definitions: a commonly accepted measure of "obesity" is 20 percent over the ideal body weight for a given height, age, and sex, according to figures provided by the National Center for Health Statistics. Someone who is 10 to 20 percent over the ideal is simply regarded as "overweight." The women preferred by all of the men we interviewed would be "obese" by this definition. However, I will use the term employed by the men and women I describe—*fat*. Although commonly used derisively by the general public, they themselves found the term "obese" far more derogatory, and preferred the term "fat" as simple, descriptive, and non-pejorative. I will follow that practice.

METHODS

For over two years we have been active members of the National Association to Aid Fat Americans (NAAFA). There are some 1500 members in the national organizations; in addition, there are some 20 local chapters, and the one to which we belong boasts a membership of close to 100. We have attended the organization's "rap" sessions—and even chaired several of them—meetings, social functions, and one of its annual conventions. We are in every way a participant in this organization, and support its aims. Although NAAFA is a "fat" civil rights organization, the overwhelming majority of its members are concerned mainly with, and are by far most likely to attend, its social functions—mainly dances and parties. Roughly 55 to 60 percent of NAAFA's membership is made up of fat women. The 50-pound range within which the median weight of these women would fall is 250 to 300 pounds. About 40 percent of NAAFA's membership is composed of men, roughly three-quarters of which are of average weight. Only a minuscule handful of women of average weight attend NAAFA's functions. The organization's principal function, thus, can be seen as a means for fat women and men who are FAs to socialize with one another.

This report is based on formal interviews conducted with 15 men who are FAs. All have attended NAAFA social functions; all were contacted through informal channels. Four of these interviews were conducted by myself; 11 were conducted by Joanne Preissler. In addition, a great deal of material was gathered through unstructured interviews and participant observation conducted by both Ms. Preissler and myself. A similar report is being prepared on the women in this organization. While the FAs we interviewed are clearly not representative of the group in general, until such a sample has been drawn it will be necessary to rely on information acquired through less systematic means—such as this report.

SEX AND THE OVERWEIGHT WOMAN

In perhaps the only book written by a serious researcher to discuss the fat admirer (almost exclusively, however, from the perspective of the fat women—very few FAs were interviewed), Millman concludes that men treat fat women as either *asexual* or as *hypersexual*, that obesity either "desexualizes" a woman in men's eyes, turning her into a kind of pal or a mother figure, or it exaggerates her sexuality, transforming her into a "forbidden, excessive, degraded, or distorted" sexual being—"an easy lay, a suitable target for lewdness and degradation" (Millman, 1980: 168–169). It should be mentioned that the latter of these two images completely contradicts one current theory that the majority of fat women become overweight in order to escape being defined as a sex object to men in a sexist society (Orbach, 1980). Clearly, either these women are oblivious to the sexual desire they touch off in some men, or the theory is incorrect.

Our interviews reveal a far more complex picture than Millman's simple characterization. Many men do seek maternal nurturance or the sexual exploitation or even the degradation of their partners, regardless of whether or not these women are fat, as Millman herself points out (1980:193). We suspect, however, that the difference between the excessively dreary one that Millman painted and the one we will present here can be traced to a methodological source: Millman interviewed her female informants regarding, among other things, their sexual experiences with men—regardless of whether or not these men were fat admirers. As the interview material with our female informants makes abundantly clear, the relations that fat women have with FAs are quite different from those with men who have either "settled" for them sexually in spite of their obesity, because they "couldn't find anyone else," or sought them out with the intention of exploiting them sexually, believing that they would be a readily available sexual target because of their low value on the dating marketplace. In this study, in contrast to Millman's, we concentrate on the man who specifically prefers the sexual and romantic company of fat women, if given the choice.

Our interviews reveal that, instead of being easily characterized by a simple formula or motivation, FAs are exceedingly varied. We found that there are more or less distinct types of FAs, depending on where they stand in regard to several crucial dimensions or continua. The following seem to us to be most significant.

CLOSET VERSUS OVERT FAs

First, some FAs are overt in their preference; others are what might be called "closet" FAs. An overt FA is willing to be seen in public on a date with a fat woman, to acknowledge his preference to friends and family, and, if he is dating a fat woman on a regular basis, acknowledges that the two are a couple, and that he actually prefers his partner at her current weight. An overt FA can easily imagine being married to a fat woman—indeed, he relishes the idea.

A "closet" FA does not wish to be seen in public with his fat date, and will usually not accompany her to a restaurant or a movie. He does not acknowledge his preference to friends or family, and will minimize the importance of his relationship with fat women if others were to find out about it. Some closet FAs may even "keep a thin girlfriend on the side" as a cover. A common lament by closet cases is: "I love the way you feel in bed, but I can't stand the way you look on the street." It is my impression that the closet admirer is in the clear majority of all FAs.

The closet-overt dimension has at least two elements: one is acknowledging the FA's preference to others, while even more basic than, and prior to, this step is acknowledging it to himself. Some men who find themselves continually attracted to larger women explain their experiences away by means of a number of justifications, including: "I figured she'd be an easy lay," or "I just wanted to see what it felt like," or "Well, she does have a pretty face," or "I like big girls, not fat girls." However, the more often they choose the fat women over the average-size one when they have the choice, the weaker these explanations become, and the more that the man is forced to admit that he is an FA. However, some resist this self-labeling even after extensive experience.

John is 35 years old and a social worker.* His appearance is one of rugged masculinity; he is extremely muscular. He wears tight-fitting clothes that accentuate the bulge of his chest, shoulders, arms, and thighs. He tentatively agreed to be interviewed, depending on whether he liked the questions. He read them over and handed back the interview schedule, refusing to participate in the study. When asked why, he replied that, although he likes big women, he isn't really an FA. He regards those as "sick and dirty." He became cold and defensive, even hostile when questioned. "Look, for me, a fat woman is strictly a sexual thing," he explained; "I haven't got any other interest in them."

John attends social activities, such as dances and parties, at which fat women will appear. He does not approach any of the women, and expects them to approach him. He spends nearly all of his time at these functions with a frozen smile on his face, drinking and staring at the participants. The observer's impression would be that he has a thinly disguised feeling of contempt for these people—fat women and FAs—and that he is laughing at them inside. When asked why he attends these social events, he replied, "Sure, the last couple of things, I showed up, took in all the people, watched all the women and men, had my six-pack, and split, then I go party with my friends." Since he is regarded as so physically desirable, he has dated a few of the women we interviewed, and he is described as an enthusiastic, passionate lover of fat women. He is, however, incapable of admitting it to himself.

A contrary case, an "overt" FA, is represented by Fred, a 40-year-old scientist. Women describe Fred's looks as that of a "cuddly teddy bar." He has always preferred and dated fat women, even in high school and college. He married a large woman about 15 years ago; they had a child and are now

*I have altered some inessential biographical details describing our respondents in order to preserve their anonymity.

divorced. He accepts his preference as part of his natural make-up. When asked about how he felt being an FA, Fred answered, "I feel fine about it. It is normal for me. I have always been attracted to large, soft women, so for me it is just a part of my sexuality." Fred is very overt about his preference. Everyone involved in his life is aware of it. He freely explains to anyone who is interested exactly what turns him on about large women. "Look," Fred explains, "I'm a jiggle junkie. I love to play with unsupported flesh, I love curves and roundness. Nothing compares with the body of a fat woman—their flesh yields to my touch."

When asked if he ever felt uncomfortable about being an FA, Fred replied, "Of course not. A strong part of my identity is the FA part, and I like my image." He admits that being an overt FA does have its difficulties. "The hardest part for any FA are parents. The parental stuff you get is unbelievable. Typical American parents all want their sons to marry the girl next door type. Some finally accept the departure of the FA from this ideal type, and some can't. With time, mine did. Regardless, you cannot live your life to please others. If you're an FA, you might as well fact it—and enjoy it."

EXCLUSIVE VERSUS PREFERENTIAL FAs

A second dimension that distinguishes different types of FAs is the *exclusive-preferential* spectrum. For nearly all our informants, their attraction to fat women was of the "preferential" variety. That is, they dated thin or average-size women, and they dated fat women as well. Some had been involved in long-term relationships with women who were not overweight, and would have preferred that their partners weighed more; some even encouraged them to gain weight. Several said that they discontinued the relationship because their partner's slenderness was a problem for them. We talked to only a few men who said that they had difficulty achieving an erection with an average-size woman, or enjoying sex with one if they were erectilely functional. The men we interviewed, with only a small number of exceptions, had a preference for larger women that ranged from slight to very great, but nearly all of them would choose sex with an average-size attractive woman whom they liked to no sex at all, or a relationship with her to no relationship at all. Only two men with whom we conducted a formal interview said that they had only experienced intercourse with fat women.

Samuel is in his early forties and is a high school teacher. He has a trim, athletic body; most women would find him attractive in appearance. He is of average height and weight. At the age of 19, he attempted intercourse with a prostitute of average size, but, he explained, "I was not fully functional with her." A brief time after that, for a year, he lived with a young woman, also of average weight, with whom he was, again, "not totally sexual functional." After this relationship ended, all of the women he has dated and with whom he has had intercourse have been fat. His former wife's weight fluctuated between 180 and 220 pounds when they were married, and her lack of size was one of the major reasons for their divorce.

Samuel refers to women who weigh between 225 and 250 as "thinner heavy women." With them, he explained, "sometimes I get an erection, but I just can't carry it through to climax. I can't get into it. I keep thinking about how *thin* and *hard* they are." On the other hand, with "much heavier women," those who weigh over 300 pounds, "I have multiple organisms—four or five times in a night." When asked to name a "famous woman or celebrity" who comes close to his physical ideal for a sex partner, his first response was Mama Cass Elliot, "when she was alive." Shelly Winters "comes close," he explained, "but she's a little thin for me." Samuel currently lives with a woman who weighs over 400 pounds; they engage in intercourse "at least twice a day." Almost all of his sexual partners have weighed between 300 and 500 pounds. "I could like thinner women as friends," he told us, "but I would never be sexually functional with them." The physical feature that he likes most about fat women is their softness, their "rolls of flesh." Samuel is, in short, an *exclusive* FA.

As part of this interview, we handed each respondent five different cards with an illustration on each one outlining the body of a woman in one of five different weight categories. Card 1 depicted a woman who would weigh about 150 to 175 pounds, if she was of average height. Card 2 was that of a woman who weighed between 200 and 225 pounds. Card 3 represented a 250 to 275 pound woman. Card 4 portrayed a woman well over 300 pounds. And Card 5's figure was clearly in the over-400 pound range. We asked each respondent to choose which figure he would prefer to make love with. Three of the 15 men we interviewed said that they couldn't choose, that they would enjoy sex with a 150 pound woman as much as with a 400 pound one, and vice versa. Their preference for fat women was only slight, and they enjoyed sex with average-size women almost as much as with fat women.

John was one such "preferential" FA. He is 29 years old and works as a commercial artist. John's looks have been described to us as striking. He is tall, with a slim, lanky, although athletic body. He has a strong-looking face with bright eyes and a cleft chin. Attracting women has never been a problem for him. John's interest ranges from average-size women to those weighing over 400 pounds. He explained: "I like women. I am a very sensual man. I love the feel of a woman's body. I love sex. I love the movement of a woman when she walks. With a big girl, there is a lot of movement; their bodies shake as they move, and that appeals to me. But you can find this in women of all sizes. Some women of average size will walk in a way that I find sexy, too. It's not the weight as much as all the other qualities I look for. It doesn't matter how big she is or isn't. I just like them all." John could be described as a *preferential* FA.

MOUNTAIN MEN VERSUS MIDDLE-OF-THE-ROADERS

Closely related to, but not identical with, the exclusive-preferential spectrum is the *size* of the woman envisioned as the ideal sexual partner by our informants. We found that FAs exhibit considerable diversity in their size preference. Some unequivocally selected Card 5, the over-400 pound woman; we call them *mountain men*. Others picked Card 1 as being most sexually desirable to them; they could be called *middle-of-the-roaders*.

At one end of the spectrum is the man who prefers his sexual partners to be "chubby," "pleasingly plump," or "voluptuous." He prefers and is attracted to women who are larger and fuller-figured than the American ideal, but considerably more petite than is true of the mountain man. The middle-of-the-roader most decidedly likes fat women—but they must be "smaller" fat women, in the under-200 pound size category. Most of these men said that they would prefer being with an average size woman who is shapely to the ones depicted on Cards 4 and 5. Rich is 42, an instructor at a community college in English literature. He is of average height and build. Women consider him attractive. Rick chose Card 1. When asked if there were any "famous women or celebrities" who approximate his physical ideal, he said "Dolly Parton—if she gained about 25 pounds, and her ass was a little bigger." He has had sexual experiences with perhaps a dozen women who would be classified as medically obese; the heaviest weighed about 300 pounds. He has also made love with many more who were merely "overweight," that is, 10 to 20 percent above the medically recommended ideal. He describes his ideal woman as being short, weighing 150 to 160 pounds, with a small waist, a heart-shaped derriere, full legs, fleshy thighs, and large breasts. She could be curvaceous, he explained—soft, round, and definitely on the plump side. Rick is not uncomfortable about being classified as a fat admirer, and he is completely open about his preference, but he is not certain that he is a "true" FA, because he finds himself drawn to the slimmer women at the social gatherings at which many fat women and FAs socialize. One woman we talked to, however, described Rick as "a flaming FA—but at the lowest end of the spectrum."

The most clear-cut case of a mountain man we interviewed was Samuel. Only one man (Fred) rivaled him with respect to the heaviness of the cut-off point determining the woman's physical desirability to him. One of the questions our interview dealt with was the respondent's sexual fantasies. The first one Samuel mentioned was having intercourse with a circus fat lady. He described very large women with a quality that approximated reverence or awe. Samuel is a true mountain man. Fred, like Samuel, is both an "exclusive" FA and a mountain man. The woman Fred lives with weighs over 400 pounds. The sexual fantasy that Fred mentioned first involved living with a woman, caring for her, and encouraging her to eat, feeding her more and more, so that she will become fatter and fatter. Fred and Samuel seem to adhere to the axiom, "the bigger, the better."

The size of the FA's ideal woman physically and whether he is an "exclusive" or a "preferential" FA are related to the range of his size preference. As a general rule, "preferential" FAs have a broader range than those who are exclusive, and mountain men have a broader range than middle-of-the-roaders. However, it is also true that the typical FA's range is considerably broader than the typical non-FA's is. Millman quotes an FA who responds to the charge that he has a "fetish," that he is attracted to women who have a "specific body type" in the following words: "I actually have less specific physical criteria than most men. I'm attracted to women who weigh 170 or 270 or 370. Most men are only attracted to women who weigh between 100 and 135. So who's got more of a fetish?" (Millman, 1980:24).

Note that John, a preferential FA at one end of the spectrum, chose women in a size range of well over 250 pounds, and Samuel had a size preference of 200 pounds—both enormously greater than the man who is attracted to average size women. Even Rick, who preferred smaller fat women, would choose an ideal woman within a size range of about 100 pounds. For him, the size of the woman is secondary. "Some slender women can actually be quite curvaceous," he explained, "while some fat women can have a body that's, like, 42-42-42. Usually, though, the fat women is curvier. So I can be perfectly happy sexually with a woman who weighs 125 or 225, as long as she has a waistline." While FAs can be distinguished from one another by their range of size preference, this range tends to be enormous when compared with that of the non-FA. This factor marks FAs from non-FAs far more than it distinguishes between different types of FAs.

SEXISM AND OBJECTIFICATION

The physical characteristics of women are regarded as more crucial in determining their physical desirability to men in this society than is true of the reverse. Feminists argue that this is a manifestation of a sexist orientation. Women are treated primarily as sex objects; our male-dominated society is more concerned with the appearance of women than their brains or their personalities. With this contention one can only concur. Experimental psychologists have demonstrated that not only is physical appearance extremely crucial in determining how one is treated by others—especially for women—but also that there is a high degree of consensus among evaluators regarding who is beautiful and who is unattractive (Berscheid and Walster, 1974). Standards of beauty in America tend to be monolithic rather than pluralistic; there is considerable uniformity as to what the ideal standards of beauty are. They do not exhibit a wide range; women who do not possess the "right," narrowly defined characteristics are considered unattractive, and tend to be ignored or sexually exploited more than those who are regarded as beautiful by members of the opposite sex. And in contemporary America, these standards include being thin.

We have described a type of male who, like other men, considers physical attributes of women important. In this regard, he is no less "sexist" than the man with more conventional taste in beauty. (We have not dealt with the other aspects of women—such as brains and personality—aside from the physical ones, that attract FAs because, for the most part, they are not significantly different from those that attract non-FAs. Because we have dwelt on the physical aspects does not mean that they are the only ones that count to the FA—just as they are not the only ones that count to the non-FA. Our elaboration of the size factor is simply dictated by the fact that this is the major characteristic that distinguishes the FA from his non-FA counterpart.)

The men that we interviewed are no less fixated on women's looks than the average American man. To the feminist who argues that the FA "depersonalizes" women by selecting them mainly according to their looks—in this case, their body size—one can only reply that the charge is accurate: FAs are no different from the more typical male who makes his selection of partners in large part on the basis of appearance. However, the one crucial difference between the fat admirer and the more typical male is that the FA's criteria for the physical desirability of women create a small crack in the monolithic wall of standards of beauty erected by our culture. However rare FAs are in the male population, they do demonstrate that some degree of pluralism exists with regard to criteria for sexual desirability. In this one respect, the FA does represent a radical departure from the typical American male who harbors negative feelings toward the overweight woman's body—and therefore, toward that woman herself.

STEPPING OUT OF THE CLOSET

Accepting that one is an FA is a crucial step, and determines how a man will treat the fat women he dates, as the contrast between our first two cases reveals. The next step, making a public acknowledgement of his preference, is also crucial in the social and emotional development of the fat admirer. Both of these steps are difficult to make, given the society's stigmatizing attitudes toward obesity and toward the man who chooses and prefers obese women as sexual and romantic partners. All of the men we interviewed (except one) related embarrassing or humiliating experiences they suffered at the hands of society with conventional attitudes—experiences that were instigated by friends, relatives (especially parents)., and even perfect strangers. Consequently, the overt FA must either be an inner-directed, unconventional person, an individualist unconcerned with the opinions of others, or be willing to confront or otherwise deal with taunts he will inevitably face as a consequence of his size preference.

It is not surprising that only a minority of the men we interviewed were completely overt concerning their preference for fat women. One of the major factors making for "stepping out of the closet" is living in a community large enough to support an organization or club (like NAAFA) designed to facilitate the socializing between fat women and FAs. When they first realize their preference, most FAs believe that they are the only men in the world who love fat women. They may be mortified, embarrassed, ashamed. At first, they attempt to explain it away. When they can no longer do so, and must face the full implications of their desires, they may feel that they are psychologically abnormal. The realization that other cultures, or other periods of history, have rhapsodized larger women—as exemplified, for example, in the paintings of Rubens, Ingres, and Renoir—may give the FA an inkling that his taste in women is not bizarre after all. Probably meeting and talking with other men who feel the same way, especially at social gatherings attended by dozens of fat women, and fat admirers eagerly pursuing them, is a major factor in "coming out." (Although it is not necessarily decisive, as our first case reveals.) A typical reaction to such an experience is: "I realized that I wasn't alone, that I wasn't some sort of a freak, but that there are lots of men out there just like me."

THE SELF-ACCEPTING FAT WOMAN'S VIEW

The many studies conducted on weight loss program effectiveness conclude that between 95 and 98 percent are a failure; of all fat people who embark on a weight-loss program, less than 5 percent take off a significant poundage and keep it off 3 to 5 years later (Wing and Jeffery, 1978). Claims of success made by programs attempting to attract potential customers, or books offering yet another diet regimen, are never backed up by systematic, scientific data. They do not mention the failures, or attribute their inability to lose weight to the fact that these enrollees are weak-willed and gluttonous—they just couldn't stick to the diet plan.

However, experts are now questioning the traditional view that fat people are overweight simply because they are compulsive eaters. Two psychologists argue that "there is *no known cause* of obesity and, with the exception of treatments more dangerous than obesity itself, *no known cure*. Overweight people do little if anything out of the ordinary to cause them to be fat, and, once fat, only the most extraordinary behavior will enable them to become and remain thin" (Wooley and Wooley, 1979:69). The more that obesity is studied, the greater the role attributed to hormonal, endocrinal, neurological, and genetic factors—over which the overweight individual has no control (Jung et al., 1979; Rothwell and Stock, 1979; De Luise et al., 1980). As a result of repeated failures to lose weight (all of the women we interviewed had attempted a number of dieting programs), some women, a minority, have come to accept themselves as they are—"big, beautiful women." The minority of women who have come to accept the view that they cannot lose weight, that they will always be heavy, and that this does not preclude their being attractive physically, have radically different experiences with men than the majority of women who cannot lose weight, and look upon their bodies—and, as a consequence, themselves—with strongly negative feelings.

The self-accepting women we interviewed ranked the desirability of their dates or sexual partners according to "how together their heads are" on the issue of their size preference. Ranked at the bottom were non-FAs who "resign themselves" to sex or even a relationship with a fat woman in preference to nothing at all, or the man who approaches a fat woman "because she'd be an easy lay, since she's so desperate." Perhaps most of the men with whom fat women have had sexual experiences fall into these categories (which accounts for the dismal view Millman projects of the sexual experiences that most fat women have). Ranked in the middle is the "closet" FA who acknowledges his size preference to himself, but who won't make a declaration of it to others. "He'll jump my bones in bed," one fat woman explained to us about her current lover, "but he won't take me out in public. At least the sex is great!" At the top of the self-accepting fat woman's hierarchy is the overt fat admirer.

Carol now weighs 375 pounds (a weight at which she attracts only FAs), but once weighed under 200 pounds)—and at that time, attracted non-FAs as well. Men consider her face strikingly beautiful. Carol is an accountant and is in her early thirties. She currently dates an extremely overt FA. She contrasts the FA with the non-FA, and the overt with the closet FA, in the following words:

> Non-FAs are totally humiliated to be out with me in public. They don't want to have to deal with the problems of being with a fat woman. They can't get past the fat thing. It's the difference between having a man who is *proud* of you versus a man who is embarrassed to be with you. The non-FA, they've never made me feel special. It's always as if they're settling for me. They're in a bar, they're drunk, there's not too many women around. There's a *resigned* look on their face. Whereas the real FA will make you feel really desired. With an FA who admits his preference, I feel as if I don't have to make any explanations or excuses for my weight. If I can't fit into a seat in a movie theater, the FA would be supportive or be angry at the theater, that he and I were both being cheated.

Whereas a non-FA, if he would even appear with me in public at all, he'd say, if you don't fit into the seat, why don't you lose weight? If I was with a non-FA, I'd sit in a chair I really didn't fit into and not be able to breathe all evening. It's embarrassing. It's disgusting. With a true FA, he'd ask for another seat. They're sympathetic. They understand. All my relations with non-FAs have been filled with tension. They can't handle it. Non-FAs have never made me feel particularly desired. They make me feel like a one-night stand—even if I wasn't. It wasn't until I dated a few really overt, genuine FAs that it was the very portions of my anatomy that turned most men off that they were most after. Now, with my current lover, it was the first time a man invited my thighs into bed with us. I had almost lost sensation in my thighs. I thought that they were ugly. At first, dating closet FAs, I kept thinking, what's wrong with these men that they want to date me—I didn't really believe that they liked me, or thought that I was attractive. With my lover, I feel less inhibited, more confident, having him accept my whole body and really want me. He's taught me new erogenous zones—they were my humiliation zones before. I never wanted anyone to touch or look at my thighs with closet FAs. They're not as verbally effusive about their preference. They're not as complimentary with me, with any fat woman. I've always felt a little bit *sleazy* with men like that, because I think *they* feel sleazy about the whole thing of dating fat women. It's always left a bad taste in my mouth. I've felt more *used* with closet cases—they were annoyed with themselves for being into my size. Now I don't have to spend the rest of my life apologizing for the way I am. What I call the "flaming" FAs, the "real ones," I feel that they deal with women more as people because the fat is accepted, it's there, it's taken for granted, and so it's less of an issue, paradoxically. It's behind you, so you can go on to the most important things.

Roxanne weighs about 225 pounds. She is 30 years old and takes a great deal of care with her appearance. When she is well dressed and travels to New York City to conduct business, she is attractive enough for men to frequently follow her on the street to pick her up for a date. Roxanne runs a small clothing boutique. She told us that one day she sat down and classified all the men with whom she has had sexual intercourse according to their size preference; 10 were FAs, and 8 were not. She comments on the differences between the FA and the non-FA, or, in her phrase, the FH (fat hater):

I don't want to be with men who aren't FAs any more. I like myself. I love myself. I only want to be around men who like me and love me as I am. I realized that I'm hooked on FAs as much as they're hooked on me. I find that the feelings I have towards them, and myself, are really involved with the fact of their being FAs or not. I can say that I was always uncomfortable and ill at ease with my FH partners. It is amazing when I think of how *completely* different the relationships are with FAs. The main thing is that when I'm with the FH I am *always* uptight over the shape and appearance of my body. I try to

> hide it (nightgowns, sheets, darkness) when I'm with an FH lover I try to knock myself out to please my FH, not because I really want to please him, but because I want to be accepted by him. I have always been tense with an FH and dread being naked in the light with one. They cannot hide their disgust, regardless of how much tact they muster, they cannot hide the fact that they are ignoring your fat body. It is written all over their face. Every FH I know wants to diet me down to *normal* size, so *then* I can be beautiful. Every FH thinks FAs are *sick*. FAs are a whole different ball-game. With an FA, sex is fantastic for me as a *fat* woman. I can disrobe and relax. I just love to watch an FA as I take off my clothes. They light up. They cannot hide their excitement as your body appears before them. An FA enjoys your body so much that I feel that I am presenting them with a priceless gift, they make you feel that good, that beautiful and desired. If an FA is overt, the whole relationship is relaxed, easy and open for depth. The fact of being wanted, exciting, and loved for what you are now, just cannot be compared. Being beautiful to a man is a delight for a woman, especially a fat woman. As long as I am a fat woman, give me a fat admirer. I care for myself, I love myself. I'm 30 years old. I only have time for men who care for me as I am, can love me as I am, can make love with me with delight—as I am.

This does not, however, mean that these self-accepting fat women prefer being fat to being thin or average-size. Nearly every fat woman we interviewed, when asked the question, "If you could take a magic pill and wake up tomorrow weighing 125 pounds—would you do it?", answered in the affirmative. "We live in a thin-oriented society, a thin chauvinist culture," was a common explanation. "It's just easier being thin. I would prefer not having to put up with all the hassles and the humiliation I have to face. It's *inconvenient* being fat. We just don't fit in." However, the self-accepting obese women we interviewed believed that, after repeated failures, it made more sense to accept their current size as inevitable than to try, once again, to lose weight. Along with it, they have accepted themselves as beautiful and desirable women.

THE SELF-REJECTING FAT WOMAN'S VIEW

It should be said that *most* fat women have not reached this kind of self-acceptance regarding their weight. Most feel self-conscious about being overweight—and some even feel disgusted with themselves because of it. They feel that their current size is temporary; "I'm not fat," they will explain, "I'm on a diet." At one extreme, some will put off dating, wearing a bathing suit, buying clothes, or even appearing in public beyond the bare minimum for survival, until they shrink down to an acceptable size. Several women we interviewed discouraged suitors altogether, and one had not been to bed with a man for over ten years; "I just can't take my clothes off in front of a man the way I look now," she told us. A very high proportion of the women we interviewed became divorced as a consequence of gaining weight after bearing children, followed by their husband's sexual rejection of them. Their sexual modesty is therefore not surprising.

More commonly, fat women will date men, but feel uneasy about their sexual interest in them. They will be unable to see themselves as sexually desirable, and will feel extremely anxious with men who adore and are excited by their bodies, feeling that "there must be something wrong with them if they like me the way I look." These men may be attracted to the very physical aspects of them that they hate most. Consequently, self-rejecting fat women find it difficult to enjoy sex with the FA. Many FAs complained to us that most of the women they dated could not deal with the lavish praise they showered upon them. "You *know* I hate my thighs," a man quoted one of his dates as saying. "Keep you hands *off* them!" The 375 pound woman quoted above talked about a long-term lover she dated years ago, before she came to accept herself as a fat woman: "I thought Joey was with me because he was just dumb. Years later, when I got my head together, I finally realized, hey—Joey was an FA!" In many ways, a fat woman's "coming out" *as* a fat woman—that is, her accepting her weight as not only not undesirable, but as one of the many different ways of being physically desirable to some men, and to herself—is as significant as the FA's acceptance of himself as a lover of fat women. Most fat women, as a result of the intensity and the pervasiveness of society's stigma toward the fat person, especially the fat woman, never reach this stage, however.

Eileen weighs 200 pounds. She is married to a very large man—6′6″, 380 pounds. She was married at the age of 17 and weighed only 125 at that time. She has two children and is a full-time homemaker. Eileen is disgusted with the way she looks, and makes critical remarks about fat people, especially women, wherever she sees them. She has a habit of buying expensive dresses which are four sizes too small for her; she hangs them in the closet and never wears them. "Isn't that beautiful," she says, showing an expensive dress to one of us. "It's a size 10. I'm going to wear it to the party next month." To the objection, "But you've got to lose 50 pounds to fit into it," Eileen replies, "I'm on the egg and spinach diet. I can do it." When the date of the party arrives, she is still fat, and she refuses to go to it. She wants as few people to see her at her current weight as is possible.

Eileen does not shop in the stores in her home town where she grew up, but shops in nearby towns, because she is afraid that someone she grew up with will see that she has become fat. She refuses to attend business dinners with her husband, which wives of executives with the firm that he works for are expected to do, because his associates and their wives will see her and think she's fat. She refuses to be seen in public in a bathing suit or shorts that reveal her weight. She won't even walk around the block with her children because neighbors will notice how much she weighs. Eileen leaves the house as little as she possibly can. Almost all of her fantasies revolve around the exciting things she will do when she becomes thin. Eileen has put off living today for an imaginary future. Her obsession with her weight, and the way she has chosen to deal with it, create a major strain in her relationship with her husband, and continually endangers the viability of her marriage. Eileen is acquainted with individuals who are members of NAAFA, but she would never join such an organization.

Fat women like Eileen, who feel negatively about their size find it alarming that FAs are attracted to them, in part, because they are overweight. One of Millman's informants expresses this view in the following words: "Personally, I think a man who would go to a dance looking only for a fat woman is deranged" (1980:21). The reverse of this, the fact that the overwhelming majority of all American men will only look for an average-size woman without being labeled "deranged," indicates the lopsidedness of our society's definition of the size of appropriate partners. While everyone wants a partner "who likes me regardless of my size" (Millman, 1980:21), the fact is, almost no man, FA or non-FA, and very few women, are attracted to a partner regardless of their looks—and size is a major aspect of looks. The negative feelings that most fat women have about their bodies translates into an even stronger negative feeling toward men who are attracted to them because of this undesired physical feature. "There must be something wrong with him if he likes me the way I am," was a common statement made by the women we interviewed. Many FAs, therefore, face stigma not only from conventional society, but from a high proportion of the women they date.

EXCHANGE AND EXPLOITATION

Dating has been analyzed as a kind of exchange or a *bargaining process* (Waller, 1937, 1970:169–180; Edwards, 1969; Laws and Schwartz, 1977:104–116; Harrison and Saeed, 1977). Every individual on the dating "market" commands a certain "price" on that market. Potential dating partners will "rate" one another—reflecting the value or price of the rated individual. They will say, "He's only a 4," or "She's a 10." Exchange theorists argue that there is a fairly high degree of consensus in this rating process. This means that each partner has a given quantum of desirability to "exchange" in a dating transaction.

Conceptualizing dating as a kind of exchange explains: (1) who will date whom, and (2) what the conditions of that dating relationship will be. A 4 might want to date a 10, but does not command a high enough exchange price to do so. The 4 cannot reward the 10 enough to make dating him or her sufficiently worthwhile. This is true for both intrinsic and extrinsic reasons. Highly rated partners are as concerned with eliciting a favorable impression from their peers through the value of their dates as they are in simply enjoying themselves with those dates. Dating an unattractive partner detracts from the overall impression a man or woman makes on others (Bersheid and Walster, 1974:168). As a result, 10s are typically attracted to other 10s, while 4s, unable to attract a 10, will gravitate to other 4s. Of course, attractiveness is not the only commodity that dating partners exchange and bargain with; others include social poise, a good sense of humor, affluence, accomplishments, and so on. (Nonetheless, in our society, men rank women's looks as most important, while women tend to rate men's occupational and economic achievements at the top of the list.) Thus, partners who date tend to be similar in the sum total of their overall level of desirability.

The exchange hypothesis would argue that, so far, a "fair exchange" has been struck: 10s are dating 10s, and 4s are dating 4s. Each partner commands roughly the same "market value," even though, in some characteristics, one may rank higher and the other lower, and vice versa. Does this mean that partners of unequal value never date one another? No, but, according to exchange theorists, it does mean that, where such discrepancies do take place, the chances are, some form of *exploitation* will occur. Where one more desirable partner dates a less desirable partner, the more desirable partner will have less interest in maintaining the relationship than will the less desirable partner. The less desirable partner must "pay" or exchange more to continue the relationship with the more desirable one. The more desirable partner has the upper hand in the relationship, and can extract more rewards from the other partner: "That person is able to dictate the conditions of association whose interest in the continuation of the affair is least" (Waller, 1970:197). In other words, even though simply being with someone less desirable is less rewarding for the more desirable partner, this can sometimes be compensated for by his or partner giving up a much greater volume of rewards. For instance, a woman who is seen as a less desirable partner than a given man may be able to date that man, but only if she yields more readily to him sexually than would a more desirable woman, or be forced to tolerate less sexual exclusivity. A less desirable man may be able to date a more desirable woman, but only if he spends more money on her, tolerates less sexual access, or is extremely indulgent and accepting of her faults (Edwards, 1969; Laws and Schwartz, 1977:104–116).

The validity of these arguments is dependent on an absolutely crucial factor: *the nature of the available competition*. In most dating situations, the sex ratio, and the overall desirability of the entire dating "pool," will be roughly equal. Consequently, partners of roughly equal absolute value will tend to seek out and date one another. But what happens when the sex ratio or the overall desirability of the available men is not equal to that of the available women, or vice versa? In these cases, partners must strike relative, rather than absolute, exchanges, where they seek to date the most desirable partner they can *within a given dating pool*. Dating pools that are unequal in either numbers or desirability take place under certain circumstances—for instance, in isolated mining, logging, or oil-drilling camps, in some age categories, such as the elderly, in certain cities, or in specific socioeconomic strata. Under these circumstances, many partners in the disadvantaged pool—the one with more individuals, or more desirable ones, in it—are only capable of striking a less favorable bargain. They must: (a) date partners who are, in absolute terms, less desirable than they are, (b) involve themselves in a relationship in which they are exploited, (c) if it is possible, date outside the pool of appropriate or customarily available partners, or (d) not date at all.

A commonly expressed lament of divorced women is: "Where are the men worthy of us?" (Robertson, 1978). Beginning in the 30s, the sex ratio becomes increasingly lopsided, with a higher and higher proportion of women in each older decade of life. This is especially true of individuals seeking long-term exclusive relationships. And as the education, the occupational accomplishment, physical attractiveness, and overall desirability of the woman increase, this disproportion is exacerbated, since custom dictates that highly desirable men may date less desirable women—for instance, in a sexually exploitative relationship—but highly desirable women may date only a highly desirable man. (This phenomenon is often referred to as the "Brahman problem.") In addition, likewise dictated by custom, men may date younger women as well as those their own age, while women must date only men their own age or older if they are to avoid social criticism. As a result, the situation facing divorced or never-married women in their 30s and 40s is often one of an insufficient or an inadequate supply of desirable men in their available dating pool. This often results in being pressured into sexually exploitative relationships, combined with periods of not dating at all.

These insights afforded by exchange theory are directly applicable to the sexual and romantic relations between fat women and fat admirers. Since the organization which constituted our research site, the National Association to Aid Fat Americans, serves primarily a socializing function, well over nine out of ten of its members are (or, in a few cases, profess to be) single; the clear majority are divorced. The median age of NAAFA's women is approximately 32, and its men are about two or three years older. Consequently, the same problems that women in general in this social category face are shared by the women we interviewed. Moreover, the sex ratio of NAAFA—approximately three women to every two men—is even more lopsided than it is in the society at large. As a result, if NAAFA constituted a dating pool, and its members only dated within it, then the women in this organization would face a decided dating disadvantage, as predicted by exchange theory. On top of this, FAs are more likely to date average-size women than fat women are to date non-FAs; this becomes increasingly true as the woman's weight increases. Thus, the range of the available selection of the fat admirer's dating partners is far vaster than it is for the fat women we interviewed.

Fat women, perhaps more than the women in the general society, commonly complain that the men that are available for dating (that is, FAs) come in two varieties—"losers" and "exploiters." (See Millman, 1980:22, for a slightly different version of this lament.) Some men are simply socially or personally unacceptable, they claim—unattractive, unintelligent, or simply "creepy." The men that are attractive and intelligent are at a premium. Women tell us that there are so few of them that the competition for their attention at dances and parties is fierce. These men will find themselves approached by a number of women during a given evening who ask them to dance, to accompany them home, or who press notes on which are scribbled their names and telephone numbers into their palms.

One woman said that an FA at a NAAFA dance "is like a kid in a candy store." An FA explained this to us: "Where else can you go and find so many big, beautiful women in one place?"

The sexual lopsidedness, combined with the fact that FAs attend "fat" social activities primarily because the women who go to them are physically attractive to them, creates the temptation for the FA to date women primarily for sexual reasons and, further, to date several fat women at the same time. The charge of sexual exploitation that the fat women in NAAFA commonly make of FAs, then, is not altogether inaccurate. However, it would be erroneous to attribute this to the special personality characteristics of the men who are attracted to fat women. Rather, a more valid explanation as to why sexual exploitation is not uncommon between FAs and fat women can be traced to the structural and dynamic conditions and processes of availability, bargaining, and exchange.

In addition to the external features of exchange on the dating marketplace, we must also consider a subjective aspect of it: the fat woman's self-image. It is difficult to escape the stigma that accompanies being fat in this society. Very few overweight people are able to say, "fat can be beautiful." The women who join an organization like NAAFA typically enter with a wounded self-image. Usually, the neophyte knows very little about it beyond what one new member told us: "I heard there's a club where there are men who like to go out with fat women." She will regard the attentions of these men with a mixture of different feelings: excitement, puzzlement, disbelief, even alarm. It is as if the traditional standards that everyone has been exposed to with regard to the esthetics of weight have been turned upside down. A naive woman with an ego bruised from a lifetime of insults and social isolation may be susceptible to flattery from an articulate, eager FA. One man we interviewed was admonished by a female member of the organization in the following words: "You meet these insecure fat girls who come here [to NAAFA social functions], you take them home, you make them feel good, they fall in love with you, and you never call them again—you're breaking their little hearts. You ought to be ashamed of yourself, mistreating them like that!"

Conventional wisdom would predict that individuals with a low sense of self-esteem would enter into a dating relationship—almost any dating relationship—more readily with someone who shows interest in them than those who feel positively about themselves. As a result, the possibility exists that they would be more available for sexual exploitation. On the other hand, the men we talked to were split down the middle on the issue of whether fat women would be more—or less—eager to enter into a sexual relationship than women of average size. One man, a popular and distinguished looking gentleman in his 40s, expressed the following complaint regarding the impact of the fat woman's lack of self-confidence. (Fat admirers and NAAFA women use the word "thin" to refer to women who are not fat.):

> Fat women are harder to take to bed than thin women because of their lack of self-confidence. They just don't believe that a man really likes them the way they are, and they are self-conscious about being naked in front of a man. Thin women are more sexually aggressive and self-confident. I do worry that fat women I want to date and go to bed with will think that I only want to go out with them because they're going to be "easy"—but that doesn't apply to me at all. There are some guys who do go out with heavy women because they think they'll be "easy." But in my experience, that's a myth.

CONCLUSIONS

A sizeable but unknown proportion of American men can be regarded as "fat admirers"—they are sexually attracted to obese women, in part, because they are fat.

Independent of its medical causes or consequences, being overweight in America today is *stigmatizing*. Obesity is not merely unfashionable—it is considered deviant, a blemish of individual character. Heavy people are ostracized, humiliated, made fun of, and discriminated against for their size. They have been described as the "last minority in America" toward whom prejudice may be expressed with impunity. Children are reluctant to accept a fat child as a friend, adolescents keep a great deal of social distance between themselves and their overweight peers, elite colleges discriminate against fat applicants, and job discrimination toward the obese, which is routine, is usually justified by invoking medical insurance risks or impaired job performance—even when the first reason is suspect and the second, typically irrelevant. The unrelenting rejection on both the organizational and the interpersonal levels generally results in the *internalization* of stigma. Characteristically, fat people come to believe themselves to be an inferior form of humanity, deserving of society's contempt and scorn.

It is possible that in no other area of life is this rejection so powerful and pervasive as in the esthetic and erotic sphere. Numerous commercials advertising weight-loss products to women claim that a thinner figure will induce one's husband to be more affectionate or, if one is unmarried, will attract more romantic interest from a greater number of men. The men we interviewed violate this expectation. While the overwhelming majority of American men—and women—consider fat unsightly, for the FA it is exactly the reverse. Since these men reject dominant esthetic and erotic standards, they are regarded as somewhat deviant by the conventional members of society—and even by some fat women themselves.

For the FA, the stigma of obesity represents "guilt by association"—or, to be more specific, guilt by preference—and to date a fat woman attracts almost as much scorn (in addition to bewilderment) as being fat. Consequently, the majority of FAs remain distinctly covert regarding their preference. Many refuse to escort their dates to a public place, don't admit their preference to friends, and may even keep a thin girlfriend on the side. They are, in short, *closet* FAs. The minority of completely "overt" FAs tend to be unconventional inner-directed individualists.

Fat is, as one observed has written (Orbach, 1980), a "feminist issue." (Orbach's analysis seems to harbor the assumption that fat women are physically unappealing to men—and this is why women become fat: to avoid becoming sex objects to men in a sexist society. None of the men we interviewed found fat women physically unappealing, and none of the women we interviewed sought to avoid the sexual attentions of men.) Women's physical desirability is judged to decline more precipitously for each pound "overweight" than is true for men. It is clear, then, that sexism is inherent in our society's anti-fat prejudices, since women are more strongly and frequently ostracized for being overweight. Standards of what a woman should look like are more exacting—and more weight-oriented—than is true for men. Women are forced to be more concerned—even obsessed—with their body image than men. The stigma of obesity falls more heavily on the shoulders of women. Although some of the women we interviewed came to see themselves as "big, beautiful women," most fat women have internalized this sense of stigma, and see themselves as less worthy human beings overall than their "thin" counterparts do.

In spite of the fact that fat women are extremely physically desirable to the men we interviewed, the process of sexual exchange, bargaining, and even exploitation, occurred no less frequently than—and possibly even more than—it does between non-FAs and average size women. The greatest numbers of divorced and single women in their 30s in general who seek a long-term relationship, and the even greater disparity between the number of fat women and FAs, in part makes this process possible. In addition, many fat women suffer from a damaged sense of self-esteem, and some FAs are not above using this to their advantage.

Since the systematic study of fat admirers has been practically nonexistent, I have chosen to undertake a descriptive, rather than a causal, investigation. Even before we can ask the question, "Why?", we must first establish the nature and the parameters of the phenomenon under study. It would be premature to embark upon an etiological study before we understand just what it is we are investigating. Perhaps later research will establish some of the major factors that lead a minority of men in our society to seek out the sexual and romantic company of obese women.

REFERENCES

Allon, Natalie
1979 Urban Life Styles. Dubuque, Iowa: W. C. Brown.

Bersheid, Ellen, and Elaine Walster
1974 "Physical Attractiveness." Advances in Experimental Psychology 7:157–215.

Cahnman, Werner J.
1968 "The Stigma of Obesity." The Sociological Quarterly 9 (Summer): 283–299.

DeLuise, Mario, George L. Blackburn, and Jeffrey S. Flier
1980 "Reduced Activity of the Red-Cell Sodium Potassium Pump in Human Obesity." The New England Journal of Medicine 303 (October 30): 1017–1022.

Edwards, John N.
1969 "Familial Behavior as Social Exchange." Journal of Marriage and the Family 31 (August):518–526.

Harrison, Albert A., and Laila Saeed
1977 "Let's Make a Deal: An Analysis of Revelations and Stipulations in Lonely Hearts Advertisements." Journal of Personality and Social Psychology 35:257–264.

Jung, R. T., P. S. Shetty, W. P. T. James, and M. A. Barrand
1979 "Reduced Thermogenesis in Obesity." Nature 279 (24 May):322–323.

Laws, Judith Long, and Pepper Schwartz
1977 Sexual Scripts: The Social Construction of Female Sexuality. Hinsdale, Ill.: Dryden Press.

Millman, Marcia
1980 Such a Pretty Face: Being Fat in America. New York: Norton.

Orbach, Susie
1980 Fat is a Feminist Issue: The Anti-Diet Guide to Permanent Weight Loss. New York. Berkley.
Robertson, Nan
1978 "Single Women Over 30: 'Where Are the Men Worthy of Us?' " The New York Times (July 4):A12.
Rothwell, Nancy J., and Michael J. Stock
1979 "A Role for Brown Adipose Tissue in Diet-Induced Thermogenesis." Nature 281 (6 September):31–35.
Waller, Willard
1937 "The Rating and Dating Complex." American Sociological Review 2 (October):727–734.
1970 Willard Waller On the Family, Education and War: Selected Writings. Chicago: University of Chicago Press.
Wing, R. R., and R. W. Jeffery
1978 "Comparison of Methodology and Results of Out-Patient Treatments of Obesity." In George A. Bray (ed.), Recent Advances in Obesity Research. London: Newman.
Wooley, Susan C., and Orland W. Wooley
1979 "Obesity and Woman—I. A Closer Look at the Facts." Women's Studies International Quarterly 2:69–79.

Reading 17

You Can't Tell the Players without a Scorecard: A Typology of Horse Players

John Rosecrance
University of Nevada at Reno

Horse racing, American's number one spectator sport, attracts a loyal core of patrons who persist at gambling on horses despite the low probability of financial gain. Traditional perspectives which view gambling as a social problem and the behavior of its regular participants as deviant have narrowly restricted scientific investigation into a track milieu, and the wide range or behaviors demonstrated by these gamblers have never been placed into a systematic framework. Using data collected from an empirical investigation of several race track settings, I identify a community-designated typology of "horse players." This typology is unique and serves as an initial conceptual model for objective inquiry into behavior of inveterate horse race gamblers.

At race tracks throughout the United States a familiar scene is played out several times during every racing day. When the track announcer warns those in attendance: "Five minutes till posttime! Get your bets in early," a crush of gamblers hurries to place their wages to avoid being shut out. The casual observer sees an aggregate representing a wide range of social groupings, ethnic backgrounds, racial types, clothing styles, and physical characteristics. Even though individual bettors exhibit a singular purposefulness, they do respect one another and demonstrate behavior patterns that permit a diverse number of participants to engage in a common endeavor—trying to win a bet. Regardless of their diversity, the race goers do come together at the betting windows, and sellers hastily punch out tickets until the dramatic announcement: "They're off!"

In 1984, patrons of thoroughbred horse racing wagered over 8 billion dollars at 96 race tracks in North America. The annual attendance at these tracks was in excess of 54 million, making it the number one spectator sport in America. The average daily per capita betting was pegged at 135 dollars and the combined tracks paid over 600 million dollars in taxes to various governmental agencies (Daily Racing Form, 1984 Annual Edition).

Commentators upon the racing scene (Roberston, 1964; Beyer, 1978; Crist, 1981) have identified three broad categories of racing patrons (1) the fan who comes to the track three or four times a year, (2) insiders such as trainers, grooms, jockeys, owners and racing officials, and (3) horse players who attend frequently and wager faithfully. In this study I will systematically delineate behavior patterns of regular horse players. Although this group has been roundly criticized (for losing excessively) by various social observers (Heilbroner, 1957; Wagner, 1972; Wolfe, 1978; Greene, 1982) surprisingly little is known of their behavior patterns. Prior literature on horse racing gambling, although substantial, has not accurately portrayed racing reality from the regular participants' perspective.

Anecdotal reports of race track gamblers abound in the journalistic literature. The foremost writer in the category was Damon Runyon. His colorful (but largely inaccurate) accounts of race track characters, *Guys and Dolls* (1958), have been instrumental in the formation of a misleading stereotype concerning race track patrons. The success of his approach has encouraged other writers to perpetuate the myth of the whacky and colorful race trace habituee. Jim Murray, a long time Los Angeles sports columnist, in the Runyonesque tradition, wrote in *New West* (1980:145), "Shifty Louie—like his friends Sam the Cynic, The Desperado, Lucky Bucky, Tap Out, Cool Eddie, and The Mole—are the kind race tracks depend on." After thirty years of horse playing, it is my experience that while colorful monickers and eccentric behavior can be found in a race trace setting, such phenomena are representative of only a small minority of regular horse players.

Many gambling researchers (Heilbroner, 1957; Kusyszyn, 1977; Crist, 1981) contend that approximately 95 percent of all horse race bettors lose money from the activity. Given the low probability of financial success, investigators have focused upon the problematic aspects of this endeavor (Leisieur, 1977; Skolnick, 1978; Greene, 1982) and have labeled regular gamblers "deviants" who invariably are compulsive losers (Moorehead, 1950; Rosten, 1967; Wagner, 1972). The emphasis upon compulsive gambling and the deviancy of its participants has served to narrowly restrict inquiry into a race track milieu (Newman, 1975).

A social problem's perspective typically portrays regular players as masochists who are unable to control their gambling urges. The following quotation is typical of this viewpoint: "Alcoholics, heroin addicts, even the obese can be saved—but there's no scientific, medical, psychiatric, or practical antidote for a pony player" (Wolfe, 1982:227). Attempts to generalize from reports of troubled gamblers (who represent only a small fraction of the total participants) frequently have led to an inaccurate perception regarding the majority of horse players (Herman, 1976; Rosecrance, 1985a). After conducting an extensive study of national gambling behavior, researchers (Kallick et al., 1979) concluded that compulsive gamblers represent less than 1 percent of the gambling population.

Ethnographic research into the world of horse race gamblers has been meager. Although several researchers have called for studies of gambling in natural settings (Herman, 1967; Scimecca, 1971; Kusyszyn, 1971, 1977; Newman, 1975; Leisieur, 1977; Hayano, 1982), there have been few actual investigations of race tracks.[1] One of the most comprehensive ethnographic studies of a race track environment was conducted by Marvin Scott in 1968. He investigated the full gamut of activities in the social world of horse racing. Using a dramaturgical model, Scott conceptualized the racing patrons as an audience. He divided the audience into two categories (1) occasional and (2) regular. His description of the regular group sensitizes one to the persistence, commitment, and rationality demonstrated by these gamblers. Scott successfully demonstrated that race track behavior is not irrational or serendipitous, but follows discernible, normative patterns. My research builds upon Scott's work by delineating further and placing into a meaningful framework the behavior patterns of the group he identified as

[1]Prior to Scott's classic 1968 work, *The Racing Game*, Zola's (1963) study of an illegal bookie joint and Herman's (1967) study of Hollywood Park Race Track (both journal articles) were the most notable investigations of a horse race gambling setting. Since 1968 there have been only a handful of academic accounts of horse racing environments. Kusyszyn (1971) investigated race track gambling patterns and Case (1984) delineated race track argot. In 1985 I published two works on horse racing (Rosecrance, a and b). The former is a study of off-track gamblers and the latter an investigation of backstretch workers.

regulars. Focusing upon this particular population, I have developed a detailed study of this significant grouping.

While compulsive tendencies and problematic gambling (defined as the losing of relatively excessive amounts of money) are found among regular horse players, these deviant behavior patterns typically are isolated within certain categories of gamblers. The development of deviant gambling generally results from the use of inappropriate betting strategies and poor money management techniques. My research is in essential agreement with Oldman (1978:370) who contends that compulsive gambling is "a consequence not [solely] of personality but of a defective relationship between strategy of play on the one hand and a way of managing one's finances on the other." These findings have import for those seeking to identify and to deal with the consequence of compulsive gambling behavior.

The overall purpose of this study is to demonstrate that race track behavior should be considered from a broad social perspective and not exclusively from a social problem's orientation. The format I have chosen for achieving this goal is to present a community-designated typology of horse players. The typology, based upon 16 months of empirical research conducted in several race track settings, was developed by identifying the types that participants recognize and by exploring the criteria they use in placing themselves and others into various categories (Spradley, 1970; Emerson, 1983). Since the constructed typology is an empirical generalization, individual cases will vary to some degree from the type. However, each pure type can serve as a base line for gauging potential and actual deviations. These nascent categorizations, by providing systematic guidelines, will allow investigators to examine objectively the behavior of horse race gamblers. Hopefully, by providing an ethnographic roadmap, this area of inquiry will appeal to a variety of researchers as well as those studying deviance and compulsive gambling.

METHODS

The main source of data for this study were developed by observing and interviewing race track gamblers at Hollywood Park and Santa Anita race tracks between March 1981 and May 1982. A six week follow-up study was conducted in April and May of 1984. Both of these tracks, located in the Los Angeles area, offer racing Wednesday through Sunday, and average approximately 30,000 in daily attendance and $5 million in daily wagering (Daily Racing Form, 1984 Annual Edition). Officials at each track were notified of the investigation. They were generally cooperative and made no attempt to restrict my activities.

The study focused upon the self-identified horse players in attendance at Hollywood Park and Santa Anita race tracks. Although individual definitions of what constituted a horse player varied, most players mentioned regular attendance, personal commitment, and motivation to persevere despite financial losses as criteria for inclusion. Those who consider themselves horse players take such a designation seriously and generally indicate that their lives had been significantly altered by this activity. The relationship of horse players to those racing groups not being studied needs to be clarified.

There is a group of patrons who attend fairly regularly but who do not consider themselves horse players. Their lack of identification with horse players is directly related to the fact that they do not become actively involved in gambling. Such patrons do not participate in the selection process inherent in horse playing but attend in the company of an acknowledged horse player. Virtually all members of this grouping are women who come with their spouses or boyfriends. The non-participants are most visible during the call of the races when they show little interest in the actual competition, prefering instead to read, knit, talk, or idly sit.[2] A comment of a 43-year-old housewife is representative of this group:

> I'm not into horse racing but my husband comes here every chance he gets. If I want to see him, I'd better come along. Besides, it's better than just staying home.

The occasional fan, frequently in attendance for major races,[3] is an important source of revenue for the race track. However, inveterate race goers do not have much social contact with the infrequent fan. Regular players typically view occasionals as trivial bettors who do not appreciate the seriousness of horse race gambling. The comment of a long-time horse player aptly illustrates this perspective:

> The fuckin' amateurs who waltz in here two or three times a year and expect to handicap a race are a joke. They're living in a different world. They have no idea of what it takes to be a horse player.

[2]In some instances female non-participants act as money allocators in order to control their companion's gambling, e.g., women dole out prearranged amounts of gambling funds and/or lag (keep back) a certain portion of the gambler's winnings.

[3]An example of the occasional fan's interest in major races occurred on Breeder's Cup Day, November 10, 1984, when several important, well-publicized races were held, and more than 64,000 fans swelled Hollywood Park and wagered a record 11.4 million dollars (Daily Racing Form, 1984 Annual Edition).

Horse racing regulars are influenced by the activities of those who are connected with the racing industry such as jockeys, grooms, trainers, owners, and racing officials. However, most of these insiders have little actual contact with regular horse players. Jockeys and grooms are effectively separated from the racing fans by spatial distance as their work area (the backstretch) is off limits to virtually all patrons (Rosecrance, 1985b). While trainers and owners are somewhat more accessible to horse players, various factors limit the possibility of close association. Trainers are constrained to avoid the company of horse players since information regarding the condition of their horses can influence betting patterns (Scott, 1968). The reluctance of trainers to associate with horse players can be illustrated by the following observation:

> As a trainer I steer clear of horse players. All they ever want is information so they can win a bet. They never believe me when I tell them that most of the time I don't know who is going to win. They're just a nuisance.

Horse owners tend to be in upper income brackets and are separated socially and financially from the majority of horse players. The owners view the races from private, box-seating areas that further minimize contact with regular racing patrons. Veteran horse players rarely seek the opinions of owners because of the racing maxim that: "Owners cannot objectively assess the capabilities of their own horses." Racing officials and track administrators have virtually no contact with regular racing patrons. Horse players generally think of racing officials as "white-collar employees who work upstairs in the general offices." Although track officials put on the races, trainers and grooms condition the horses and jockeys ride them, most racing patrons have little association with these individuals. Regular horse players function in their own distinct social world (Strauss, 1978); one that is separate from that of the occasional or insider.

Empirical data was collected through the use of both general and focused interviews. The procedure for determining those patrons to be interviewed was based upon both observation and direct questioning. During the course of a 16 month investigation I attended the race track over 80 times. This period of sustained observation allowed me to recognize patrons who maintained regular attendance. There are no race track norms against inquiring about how often one comes to the track, and questions concerning attendance were permissible and helpful in identifying horse players. While gathering background data in the initial phase of the investigation, I talked with over 240 racing patrons. Subsequently, I conducted 87 focused interviews with self-identified horse players. My wife, a professional educator, interviewed eight female subjects. The kinds of responses that she received were basically similar to those I had received.

Researcher Role and Procedure

I have gambled on horse races for over 30 years and have attended over 75 race tracks in the United States, Canada, Mexico, South America, Puerto Rico, British Virgin Islands, England, and France. In the racing argot, I have "been there" and have "put it on the line." Such sustained participation qualifies me as an established regular in the world of horse race gambling. This type of researcher role has been categorized as an intense form of participant observation (Gold, 1958) or "auto-ethnography"[4] (Hayano, 1979). During the study I was guided by the principles of grounded theory (Glaser and Strauss, 1967) and sought to develop analyses that were generated from the data themselves (Blumer, 1979).

As an insider, I had certain research advantages; ease of entree, similar definitions of the situation, knowledge of the argot, a sense of natural rhythm of events, a longitudinal perspective, and the sensitivity to minimize the reactive effects of interviewing. I had developed a reservoir of tacit knowledge (Baldwin and Baldwin, 1978) that greatly facilitated data collection and analysis. Such knowledge was particularly advantageous since the data collected were mainly qualitative in nature.

The most fundamental dilemmas raised by an insider role involve researcher bias and loss of objectivity. These issues cannot be dismissed easily but by acknowledging their existence I attempted to mitigate their influence. The a priori assumption that a member is an automatic advocate of his or her group frequently is inaccurate. As a long-time horse player, I am fully aware of the problems that can result from this activity. I want to demystify and portray adequately the world of horse race gambling, not to be its champion. Due to familiarity with this milieu, the issue of subjectivity and possible researcher bias was continually confronted. In an attempt to maintain an objective approach, I frequently questioned my personal motivation, distanced myself from the field by taking time off, and solicited the comments of academic colleagues. The early formation of categories and hypotheses allowed me to examine this social world from a new perspective. The once familiar scene took on a new meaning when viewed from an analytical framework.

[4]Auto-ethnography literally means a study of one's own group. Hayano (1982), an anthropologist and poker player, used this method in his study of professional poker players. Other researchers, while not specifically labeling their approach auto-ethnography, have employed their insider status to collect valuable data, often unavailable or incomprehensible to outside researchers. Polsky 91969), a pool player; Pilcher (1972), a longshoreman; Braly (1976), an excon' and Shibutani (1978), a former member of Japanese-American Army unit, all studied groups in which they shared active membership.

In an attempt to interview representative subjects, I divided the race track into five social areas: Grandstand, Infield, Club Horse, Outside Central, and Turf Club.[5] With the exception of the Turf Club, I spent approximately 90 minutes per day interviewing in each area and the time of day at each location varied. The Turf Club is a private area and when access to the Turf Club was gained (through the approval of track management), I spent the entire day in that area.

The timing of an interview was an important consideration. As a rule, the farther from posttime that an interview was started, the better. As post time approached, patrons became increasingly concerned with their gambling decision and concomitantly less interested in the interview. Focused interviews (lasting from 45 minutes to 2 hours) usually followed three sequential stages (1) establishing bona fides, (2) revealing researcher role, and (3) probing.

The natural lead-in to an interview was: "Who do you like in the next race?" Due to track custom, an answer to this query was virtually assured. In the ensuring discussion, I included a few general questions concerning horse racing to insure that the respondent was an acknowledged horse player and to assess the respondent's attendance pattern and betting style. The following excerpt from an actual field interview will clarify this process.

I observed a man about 65 years old, conventionally dressed, studying a *Racing Form*, and sitting in the club house area. He seemed comfortable in this setting and appeared to be a regular racing patron. I sat down, one seat away from the patron, and began the interview.

Researcher: Who do you like in the first?

Patron: (Warily) 'Kind of like the six horse.

Researcher: He's got a shot, but did you check out the five horse? Frankel (a trainer) is dropping him awful cheap. Frankel's shrewd; putting blinks on him, too.

Patron: Yeah, Frankel's dropping him fast, too low; something's fishy. The pig runs second for 20 bills and he's in for 10. (Then about efficacy of training methods.)

Researcher: Do you come here much?

[5]The following is a brief albeit overgeneralized view of the various social areas found at a race track. A similar social ecological pattern has been reported by Herman (1967) and Scott (1968). The Grandstand offers an unreserved seating area and is typically frequented by older patrons and those who attend on a regular basis. Younger patrons, often with children, can be found in the Infield. The Outside Central area contains a mixture and cross-section of all race track types. The Club House, with an additional admission charge, caters to the middle-class patron. The seating is reserved and more comfortable than in the Grandstand. The Turf Club is the domain of the upper class. Membership to the "Club" is kept limited and exclusive by a nomination procedure for new members. The physical surroundings are elegant—chandeliers, leather chairs, and a private elevator add to the ambiance.

Patron: Pretty regularly during the week—skip Saturdays—too crowded.

Researcher: Did you catch that long shot on Wednesday in the feature?

Patron: No! How could anybody play that bum? First time on the turf, carrying 120 pounds. No way. (Then we engaged in a few minutes of banter over the merits of various horses.)

After rapport was sufficiently developed, I identified myself as a researcher in the following manner: "I'm doing research at the university in sociology, studying horse players. Maybe I'll learn something after 25 years playing the horses. OK if I ask you some more questions?" This statement did not deter further discussion since the patron was interested in who I liked in the next race, not in the course of my research.

The last interview segment involved more qualitative questioning; such factors as personal goals, job satisfaction, depth of commitment, and reaction to losing streaks were probed. This form of questioning helped establish the individual's placement in the typological framework.

Researcher: Do you spend much time studying the *Form* (a newspaper used in the horse selection process) at home?

Patron: No. Only at the track. Wife gets pissed off if I always got my head in the *Form*.

Researcher: Yeah. I know what you mean.

Patron: 'Wanted to be a pro when I was younger. Always pissed me off that I was only a part time player. But now I'm real satisfied being a regular.

Researcher: How're you doing this meet?

Patron: 'Bout even. Did good at Hollywood. Last year I really hit 'em good. (Then two or three minutes of discussion over his past winnings and 'almost' big scores.)

Researcher: I've been salty as hell lately. Can't seem to cash a ticket. Any suggestions?

Patron: Are you kidding? You just gotta ride out them tough beats. Shit, it's all part of the game—hard to take though. I know the feeling.

Researcher: Are you retired?

Patron: Yeah. Worked 25 years for Lockheed. Now work out here.

Researcher: You like being retired?

Patron: Sure do. Nice routine coming here every day. Always something to do; something to look forward to.

Researcher: It's been great talking to you. Thanks for helping my research.

Patron: Yeah, sure. You really like that five horse?

Not all interviews go this well. Some racing patrons are unwilling to maintain a conversation regardless of my racing background, while others refuse to talk once my researcher role is revealed. However, the majority of horse players, after they are softened up and a common frame of reference is established, are talkative and willing to be interviewed.

FINDINGS

Horse players typically belong to identifiable subgroups that usually fit into one of five general types. Individuals within the types tend to manifest similar behavior at the race track. These similarities can be effectively placed into categories. This regular patterning led to the development of the following typology (terms used therein will be clarified in the discussion of individual types).

Demographics

The following is a delineation of the salient demographic factors that characterize horse player types (1) source of income, (2) social class, (3) age, and (4) gender. The first three types—pro, serious player, and bustout—all derive or attempt to derive a major share of their income from race track gambling. The remaining types all have outside sources of support and do not rely on race track winnings for their livelihood. The prevailing social class position[6] of the pro is middle to upper middle. Serious players tend to be drawn from the lower middle or working class. Bustouts frequently have been victims of downward social mobility and presently find themselves in the working or lower class. Retired regulars are drawn from all social classes while employed regulars are usually members of the working class. Part-time players can be found in all social classes, but predominantly maintain middle to upper class standing. The vast majority of horse players (of any type) are over 30 years of age. Those in the retired regular group are usually over 60 years old, the bustouts are generally over 45, while the other types are fairly evenly distributed between the ages of 30 and 60. The world of horse players is almost exclusively a male domain. Although some women attend the races regularly, only a few consider themselves horse players. Women have not been attracted to this activity. Even today when women are entering traditionally male dominated areas, they show little interest in the world of horse playing. There are no obvious barriers to distaff participation in this social world. Women are not looked upon as intruders and when they demonstrate racing knowledge, their views are considered as seriously as those of male players. The few self-identified women horse players located during the study (drawn exclusively from the ranks of the

[6] In developing a social class profile, I was guided by the five class scheme developed by Daniel Rossides (1976). Such factors as financial resources, occupational prestige, educational attainment, political influence, and subjective attitudes were used to establish a ranking. The resulting class designation is a rough approximation rather than a definitive grouping.

Typology of Self-Identified Horse Players

Type and percent of total players	Classification Categories: Goals	Attendance	Betting style	Reaction to losing streaks	Participation in conventional job world
Pro 5%	Keep on earning a living	Everyday	Overlay	In stride	Given up
Serious player 10%	Earn a living	Everyday	Not consistent	Upset	Given up or occasional
Bustout 5%	Action	Whenever possible	Prices	Resigned	Casual
Regular 45%	Recreation Friendship	Regularly	Prices Chalk/saving	Resigned	Flexible Retired
Part-time player 35%	Recreation Become a pro	Days off work, most weekends	Chalk/saving	In stride Upset	Straight

*The percentages are estimates based upon research data, discussions with track management, and an analysis of patron surveys (Eyrich, 1974, 1976, 1979).

Types of Race Track Participants Not Included in the Typology

Regular Fans	Occasionals	Insiders
Attend fairly regularly but do not consider themselves horse players	Attend infrequently and do not consider themselves horseplayers	Those connected with the horse racing industry (trainers, jockeys, owners, grooms, track employees).

regular and part-time player) interacted openly with their male counterparts. One possible explanation for the lack of female interest stems from prior gender role modeling. The historical association of any unsavory element with horse race gambling perhaps dissuaded many women from involving themselves in this activity.[7]

The Types

The following is a brief description of the five types of regular horse players.

Pro The professional handicapper is the epitomy of a successful race track gambler. From the horse player's perspective this classification is reserved for the small percentage who have proven that they can win consistently. Pros must be able to demonstrate sustained winnings over an extended period. Most horse players would agree with the observation of one veteran race goer about what it takes to be considered a pro:

> You have to win steady for at least two or three years. Anyone can get on a temporary winning streak. But if you can win fairly consistently for over two years and make enough to support yourself—you deserve to be called a pro.

For the pro, handicapping the horses is a full time occupation. A quote taken from an interview with a pro underscores this concept: "Handicapping is a job—the track is my office. It's a hard, exacting profession and like any good executive I take my work home with me." Pros are usually dressed conservatively, maintain a cool demeanor during the running of a race, and consider it bush (inappropriate) to complain over the outcome.

The characteristics shared by successful handicappers are total attention to their task and possession of an exacting discipline. Professionals employ a calculating betting strategy called overlay betting. Such a strategy involves wagering only on those races where an overlay situation can be identified. An overlay exists when the estimated probability of winning significantly exceeds the expected payoff. If the subjective probability of a horse's winning is three to one, but the actual odds are eight to one, an overlay exists (Rosecrance, 1985a:40–1). This rigidly objective approach to gambling attempts to rule out luck, emotion, hunches, sentimentality, or desperation as factors in wagering decisions. On occasion, this can mean waiting several days to make a serious wager. According to pros such an

[7] While being interviewed an identified female horseplayer indicated: "When I was growing up only men played the horses. They often gambled in bookie joints where no women would dare set foot. It was considered 'unladylike' to bet the ponies. Most of my girlfriends still feel that way. Guess I'm just different."

approach must be maintained throughout the swings in fortune that are an inevitable aspect of sustained gambling. The patience, confidence, and fortitude to maintain an objective, calculating strategy during periods of financial loss is the factor which most clearly separates the pro from other horse players. Only a few are able to withstand periodic losing streaks and emerge in the long run as winning gamblers.

Since pros are not employed by others and earn their livelihood from gambling at the race track, they are under continual pressure to perform their job well. An aspiring pro described this situation:

> It's hard to understand the pressures of full-time handicapping. In most jobs you can settle in, do average work, and draw a regular paycheck. At the track you need to do well all the time. Bottom line—if you screw up, you don't eat. There's no company blue cross, dental plan, or retirement. You're on your own without a safety net. I tell you, that's a shit-load of stress.

Many pros invest a portion of their winnings (usually in conservative, high-income-yielding investments) to mitigate against total dependence upon gambling. In some cases, when sufficient monies have been "squirreled away," handicappers can retire from their profession. The following account, taken from a successful handicapper, will illustrate how goal reorientations can lead to changes in typological categories.

> I was a pro for thirty years. I came to the track everyday to earn my living betting the ponies. More fucking hassle than you'll ever imagine. Finally, I built up enough of a bankroll so I could live pretty good—just from the interest. Nowadays I don't have to worry so much about winning. I can enjoy the races and bullshit with my buddies without sweating the results. In effect I've retired and now consider myself more of a regular than a pro.

Serious player This category is composed of those who have made a definite and demonstratable commitment to earn their livelihood from wagering on horses. The most tangible demonstration of intent is to quit a regular job and begin playing the horses as a full-time endeavor. Race trackers view the decision to commit one's future to the race track as a quantum leap. The individual horse player leaves the relative security and orderliness of a conventional life for the tenuous and problematic existence of a race track gambler.

Unfortunately, the serious player's career commitment does not guarantee success. The ability to win consistently at the races is extremely difficult and can only be proven in the passage of time. During the proving time, or apprenticeship period, the would-be-pro occupies a marginal position. In this study, the majority of those who tried to sustain a livelihood at the race track were unsuccessful. Many serious players eventually gave up their "professional" aspirations, returned to regular jobs, and became part-time or regular players. A few serious players left the race track for good, others lost all and became bustouts, while some continued in a permanent state of marginality, seeking but never attaining full pro status. For those who remained as serious players the process of finding funds to sustain gambling in some cases led to exhausting personal saving accounts, selling possessions, and borrowing from family, friends, business acquaintances or loan companies. The frantic search for gambling funds has been termed "chasing" by Lesieur (1977) in his study of problem gamblers. These deviant behavior patterns are commonly termed compulsive gambling (Kusyszyn, 1979). An important factor in the development of problematic gambling is the horse players' intolerance for losing and subsequent use of inappropriate gambling strategies.

Serious players tend to be less emotionally controlled than professionals, frequently are considered poor losers, and generally do not exhibit a consistent betting strategy. Serious players often can demonstrate a rational purposefulness in the midst of a protracted winning streak. However, when losses mount, they often become insecure and uncertain of their strategy. This can lead to rash risk-taking wherein the need for instant reward precludes all considerations of logic. The phenomenon of an inconsistency in gambling strategy, set off by an upsetting losing streak, can be illustrated by a quote from a serious player:

> I slaved for six months, really busted my ass. Built up my bankroll, slowly, carefull, logically, doing just the right thing. Then I lost for four straight days; big deal, why didn't I shrug it off? No! I couldn't stand the pressure. I had to win. So I bet all the money on one stupid race—the race wasn't even playable! Couldn't wait—no, not me—just had to prove myself; stupid, stupid; guess I'll eat shit all my life.

Bustout This type consists of individuals who exist in a continuing state of poverty. In the racing argot they are "permanent residents of tap city." For this type of patron, gambling has become an end in itself. The goal of this group was described by a down-and-out race goer: "Guys like me need the action—excitement, thrills, whatever, but we gotta stay in play. The action keeps us going." The bustout's attendance pattern often is determined solely by financial considerations. If they have money, they are at the track; if they do not, they are in the process of garnering enough for future attendance. The members of this type are invariably broke. For the most part, they have lost hope that their condition can be measurably improved. Even the possibility of a large track winning will not alter their plights. A sense of fatalism and resignation can be seen in the comments of a typical bustout: "Shit, even if I win big, I'll blow it. I'll fuck it up. Always have, always will. Last year, won 20 big ones on an Exacta—three days later, all gone."

Bustouts frequently are employed in low paying jobs, e.g., dishwasher, car washer, handbill distributor, janitor's helper, washroom attendant. Those who can project a more acceptable image work as desk clerks, stockroom attendants, fast food counter clerks, or lunch counter cooks. These jobs are temporary in nature and can be abandoned easily when the individual has accumulated sufficient funds to sustain regular track attendance. Some receive disability pensions and other forms of government assistance. Bustouts have exhausted credit or loan possibilities and can gamble only with available cash. They are no longer involved in the frantic chase for gambling funds that characterizes the serious player.

This group demonstrates a wide range of survival skills. Bustouts often cannot afford the $2.50 track admission. Instead, they wait outside the gates until after the seventh race when they are admitted free. While awaiting free admittance, they hand money through spaces in the fence to acquaintances who then wager at the windows. Often they pool their money with others to arrive at the price of a two dollar wager. Bustouts do not pay the $1.75 for the *Racing Form* or the 75 cents for a program. Instead they hunt through waste baskets where departing patrons have deposited their *Forms* or programs, and on occasion can be observed wiping saliva, tobacco juice, and beer stains from these papers. They also stand near exits and implore those leaving to give them the *Racing Form*: "You finished with your *Form*, buddy?" "*Form*, please." "Anyone spare a bible?" Sometimes a knowing glance at a departing patron is sufficient communication to command a donation of the *Racing Form*.

Bustouts often have surprisingly high levels of expertise and race track knowledge. Most have been attending the track for decades and have learned the intricacies of handicapping. Their financial undoing seems to result from inappropriate betting strategies and poor money management rather than from lack of knowledge. They frequently employ a price strategy by wagering on longshots, rationalizing they need the high return. One of the most astute figure men, i.e., past-performance analyzer at the local tracks, is a down-and-outer who invariably changes his first selection for a horse of higher odds. When asked why he did not back his original selection, he replied, "With twenty bucks in my pocket I can't bet the chalk. I need a price. Guess I just haven't got the patience or discipline to gradually build it up."

Regular The distinguishing characteristic of regular players is that their employment situation allows them to attend the races during the week.

This type is divided into two groupings: retired and flexibly employed. The retired player is an individual who has retired from an occupation, career, or vocation and is currently receiving an income from that activity. This person's major source of financial support stems either from pensions (including Social Security) or secure investments. Race track winnings, if any, serve to augment their regular income. The majority of those in the retired category have been playing the horses, although not always as regulars, for over 40 years.

Older horse players demonstrate strikingly similar gambling strategies. Their gambling patterns are characterized by a conservative maintaining stance. The gamblers forego the risk of attempting a big score for more predictable, albeit lower payoffs. The possibility of large financial gain is eschewed for the more subdued pleasures of sustained participation and the accompanying social interaction. Such a strategy generally involves betting chalk (favorites) and protecting possible losses by saving (betting more than one horse in one race). This conservative style seems to hold true regardless of the financial status of the older horse player. A 68-year-old horse player who attends the race track on a daily basis, and calls himself a conservative player, described his reasons for such regularity: "It's not really the money. I know I'll never make a big killing, but all my friends come here. If I didn't come to the track I'd be bored stiff."

Retired regulars often believe they are more fortunate than their non-horse playing friends. During interviews the retired patrons frequently commented that their friends had difficulty coping with retirement. The retired group indicated that their non-gambling peers were bored, unhappy and in many cases were just vegetating. Accounts of acquaintances who died six months after retiring were commonplace. Retired horse players disparagingly told of friends who had become Honey Doos—"Honey do this, Honey do that." The authenticity of these claims to superior adjustment could not be verified; however, what seems significant is that the retired group firmly believes that they are true.

Regular race goers view handicapping the horses as a productive endeavor and a logical extension of their working lives. Equating handicapping with productivity facilitates adjustment to retirement. Retired players can enjoy their avocation, free from concerns that they are wasting time. While at the races the players believe they are participating in a meaningful activity. A frequent observation is that playing the horses "keeps the blood pumping." These sentiments were aptly summed up by a middle-aged Los Angeles policeman who stated, "I can't wait to pull the pin so I can come here every day."

The flexibility employed are those who work outside the traditional nine-to-five time frame. Their main source of income is derived from employment, not race track winnings. The kinds of jobs that facilitate attendance during the week include: factory work, gardening, maintenance, sales, construction, bus or taxicab driving, and self-employment. Ethnic (Mexican-American) and racial (blacks) minorities are overrepresented in this category. This group is the most vocal of the various types. They root and cheer their selections during the race and roundly boo the jockeys after the race. The betting strategy of the flexibly employed typically involves long shot or price wagering, and they are avid players of the Pick Six—a form of betting in which the bettor must select six consecutive winners. The difficulty in doing this increases the payoff and a $2.00 winning ticket can return one hundred thousand dollars or more. Santa Anita administration, in a 1980 advertising campaign, related the story of a flexibly employed folk hero. "Then there was Woodrow Wilson Taylor, a Los Angeles maintenance man. Woody came to the track with $4.00 on a single Pick Six ticket. His winnings were $73,942.00."

Most of those in this category seem resigned to losing money and take their losses in stride. A factory employee who worked the graveyard shift (12:00 a.m. to 8:00 a.m.) indicated: "I come here [to the track] for recreation. Shit, I know I'll probably never come out ahead but the track's an exciting, interesting place. It's where I have my fun." Track attendance, for the flexibly employed, provides both a recreational outlet and a vehicle for participation in significant events. Members of this group often view wagering on important races and observing multimillion dollar animals perform as significant happenings in their otherwise routine lives. The horse selection process allows them to demonstrate a rational purposefulness, not always present in their occupational activities. During interviews the flexibly employed were reluctant to discuss their work. This group wanted to discuss the races they had seen, the famous horses they had bet, the time they hit it big, and how they had doped-out that last winter.

Part-time player Although this type includes players who are unable to attend regularly for a variety of reasons (financial, social, psychological), most of its members are employed during the traditional Monday-through-Friday, nine-to-five time frame. They are unable to be at the track during the week but regularly attend on Saturday and Sunday. Members of this type envision that upon retirement they will become regular players. Overall, persons in this group have higher paying, more prestigious jobs than those in other categories. Although certain factory workers qualify for inclusion in this type most members are employed in white collar jobs.

This type is divided on the basis of two factors: job satisfaction and desire to become a full-time handicapper. The majority of this type are fairly content with their present employment and have no plans to become "professional" horse players. The remaining members have a strong desire to become full-time handicappers and generally expressed dissatisfaction with their present jobs. The latter group frequently complained that their work interfered with handicapping and that they never had enough time for careful race analysis. Would-be pros commented that while at work they found themselves flashing (thinking about) on horses.

For those not seeking pro status, race track attendance is a form of habitual recreation spiced with gambling activity. Aspiring pros view attendance as a more serious activity and tensions generated by gambling failure can be problematic. When the recreational part-timers were questioned on how they coped with losing streaks, they commented: "Have a drink and forget it," "Cry a little," and "Just put it out of my mind." The pro seekers were more likely to indicate they brooded, became reclusive or clammed up. These moods often signaled a change to a more aggressive (and more unsuccessful) betting strategy. One part-timer who hoped to become a pro related:

> I followed my usual conservative-saving strategy for five straight losing weeks. Finally I said, 'To Hell with it' and I put three grand on a sure thing. Well, you know the story—nothing's sure in horse racing. Took me six months to get over that fiasco.

The method of distributing winnings is different for those desiring to become pros. Rather than splurge on luxuries as the typical part-time player does, would-be pros horde their winnings, hoping to accumulate sufficient funds to quit their jobs and begin gambling careers. However, as long as part-timers remain employed in career type positions, they have not made a full commitment to earning their livelihood as professional gamblers. Most part-time players never take this quantum leap. One such player mused:

> For years I kidded myself that I actually wanted to become a pro. But I continually found some excuse for not taking the plunge. Jobs, kids, wife, pension, illness—always something made it impossible for me to take the risk. Looks like I never really had the guts.

SUMMARY AND CONCLUSION

In this study I have presented a community-designated typology of self-identified horse players. Although all horse players wager on horse races, their behavior at the track varies according to typological category. While every type participates in some degree of financial risk-taking, their goals, betting strategies, reactions to losing, and job situations vary considerably. The calculating technique of a pro who generates a steady income from gambling participation is far different from the approach of a retired patron who is more interested in maintaining track friendships than in making a big score. The bustout's casual attitude toward employment and willingness to wager a large portion of his resources contrasts with the part-timer's career commitment and conservative betting strategy.

The role of gambling strategies in maintaining nonproblematic participation has been emphasized in this study. The vast majority of players are able to maintain acceptable levels of track participation, while keeping their losses within manageable parameters, by using appropriate gambling techniques. Deviant behavior patterns putatively labeled "compulsive," in most cases, are found among two types of horse players—bustout and serious player. These types have been unable to develop consistent betting strategies or good money management systems. This finding indicates that in order to fully understand compulsive gambling among horse players it is essential to be aware of the participants' gambling methods.

A few horse players exhibit behavior that falls outside typical classification categories. Although some individuals consider themselves players, they do not attend on a regular basis. Frequently such nonattendance is a temporary phenomenon resulting from the press of other life-responsibilities. Horse players have told me that after losing large amounts of money, they had stayed away from the track for periods ranging from two months to three years. During these hiatuses, to straighten out their financial affairs, they still thought of themselves as horse players. One racing patron referred to such a condition as "horse players in remission." Others indicated that on occasion the demands of their jobs precluded regular attendance. I personally experienced this situation when the crush of working on my dissertation significantly reduced my ability to attend the race track. The betting styles of some patrons can vary from others in the same type. Not all employed regulars follow price strategies; some prefer to employ more conservative chalk techniques. On the other hand, some part-time players eschew chalk strategies for riskier price approaches. Notwithstanding these and other minor variations, the typology I have presented provides an accurate portrayal of the reoccurring behavior patterns of self-identified horse players.

The traditional view of horse race gambling as a problem and of regular participation as deviant has narrowly limited scientific inquiry into a race track environment. When the social world of horse players is described in its diversity, a social problem's perspective alone cannot adequately explain a documented behavior patterns. In order to fully comprehend race track behavior academicians must consider broader perspectives. If social science theorists and researchers with varied perspectives and interests examined race track environments they would find a fertile area of inquiry. The horse race industry and its influence on American society can be investigated from a macro level while the dynamics of decision-making could be approached from a micro perspective. The track, with its structured risk taking, is a veritable social laboratory and horse players can be located easily as they voluntarily come together in situations where their behavior can be regularly monitored.

In this paper, I presented a framework that described the behavior patterns of a significant social group—race track gamblers. Their behavior has been examined from an ethnographic rather than solely a social problem's perspective. Building upon the research of Scott (1968), the actions of regular horse players have been placed into a meaningful format. Hopefully, by describing, humanizing, and demystifying race track attendance, my study has established the groundwork for varied research into this important social phenomenon. By developing a community-designated typology, I have provided a scorecard to systematically identify the players involved in this activity.

REFERENCES

Baldwin, John D., and Janice I. Baldwin
1978 "Behaviorism on Verstehen and Erklaren." American Sociological Review 43:335-47.

Beyer, Andrew
1978 My $50,000 Year at the Races. New York: Harcourt, Brace, Jovanovich.

Blumer, Martin
1979 "Concepts in the Analysis of Qualitative Data." Sociological Review 27:651-77.

Braly, Martin
1976 False Starts: A Memoir of San Quentin and Other Prisons. Boston: Little, Brown.

Case, Carole
1984 "Argot Roles in Horseracing." Urban Life 17(2-3):271-88.

Crist, Steven
1981 "The Inside Track at the Races." Fifty Plus 21:82-5.

Daily Racing Form
1984 Annual Review Edition, March 26. Los Angeles: Triangle Publications.

Emerson, Robert
1983 "Ethnography and Understanding Members' Worlds." Pp. 19-35 in Robert Emerson (ed.) Contemporary Field Research. Boston: Little, Brown.

Eyrich, Gerald I.
1974 Santa Anita Patron Survey. Claremont, Calif. Claremont Research Associates.
1976 Santa Anita Patron Survey. Claremont, Calif. Claremont Research Associates.
1979 Santa Anita Mailing List Survey. Claremont, Calif. Claremont Research Associates.

Glaser, Barney, and Anselm Strauss
1967 The Discovery of Grounded Theory. Chicago: Aldine.
Gold, Raymond L.
1958 "Roles in Sociological Field Observations." Social Forces 56:217–23.
Greene, Johnny
1982 "The Gambling Trap." Psychology Today 16(9):50–5.
Hayano, David
1979 "Auto-Ethnography: Paradigms, Problems and Prospects." Human Organization 39:99–104.
1982 Poker Faces. Berkeley: University of California Press.
Heilbroner, Robert
1957 "Are You a Gambler." American Mercury 84:55–60.
Herman, Robert D.
1967 "Gambling as Work: A Sociological Study of the Race Track." Pp. 87–106 in R. Herman (ed.) Gambling. New York: Harper & Row.
1976 Gamblers and Gambling. Lexington, Mass. Lexington Books.
Kallick, Maureen, Daniel Suits, Ted Dielman, and Judith Hybels
1979 A Survey of American Gambling Attitudes and Behavior. Ann Arbor: Institute for Social Research, University of Michigan.
Kusyszyn, Igor
1971 "Locus of Control and Race Track Betting Behavior." Paper presented at the Annual Meeting of the Canadian Psychological Association, St. John's, Newfoundland.
Lesieur, Henry R.
1977 The Chase. Garden City, New York: Anchor.
Morehead, Allan
1950 "The Professional Gambler." Annual American Academy of Political Science 269:81–93.
Murray, Jim
1980 "He Nixed Pick Six Till Pix Clicked." New West 5:145–6.
Newman, Otto
1975 "The Ideology of Social Problems: Gambling, a Case Study." Canadian Review of Sociology and Anthropology 12:540–50.
Oldman, David
1978 "Compulsive Gamblers." Sociological Review 26:349–70.
1977 "How Gambling Saved Me From a Misspent Sabbatical." Journal of Humanistic Psychology 17:19–34.
1979 "Compulsive Gambling: The Problem of Definition." International Journal of the Addictions 13:1095–1101.
Pilcher, William
1972 The Portland Longshoremen. New York: Holt-Rhinehart.
Polsky, Ned
1969 Hustlers, Beats and Others. New York: Anchor.
Robertson, William H. P.
1964 The History of Thoroughbred Racing in America. Englewood Cliffs, N.J.: Prentice-Hall.

Rosecrance, John

1985a The Degenerates of Lake Tahoe: A Study of Persistence in the Social World of Horse Race Gambling. New York: Peter Lang.

1985b "The Invisible Horsemen: The Social World of the Backstretch." Qualitative Sociology 8(3):248-65.

Rossides, Daniel W.

1976 The American Class System. Boston: Houghton-Mifflin.

Rosten, Leo

1967 "The Adoration of the Nag." Pp. 39–52 in Robert D. Herman (ed.) Gambling. New York: Harper & Row.

Runyon, Damon

1958 Modern Library Treasury of Damon Runyon. New York: Modern Library.

Scimecca, Joseph

1971 "A Typology of the Gambler." International Journal of Contemporary Sociology 8:56–70.

Scott, Marvin B.

1968 The Racing Game. Chicago: Aldine.

Shibutani, Tomatsu

1978 The Derelicts of Company K. Berkeley: University of California Press.

Skolnick, Jerome

1978 House of Cards. Boston: Little, Brown.

Spradley, J. P.

1970 You Owe Yourself a Drunk: An Ethnography of Urban Nomads. Boston: Little, Brown.

Strauss, Anselm L.

1978 "A Social World Perspective." Pp. 119–28 in Normal Denzin (ed.) Studies in Symbolic Interaction Volume 1. Greenwich, Connecticut: Jai Press.

Wagner, Walter

1972 To Gamble or Not to Gamble. New York: World Publishing.

Wolfe, Burton

1978 "Race Track Junkie." Oui 7:56–8, 122–6.

Zola, Irving

1963 "Observations on Gambling in a Lower-Class Setting." Social Problems 10:353–61.

Chapter Six

Social Organization of the Deviant World

EDITORIAL COMMENTARY

Much deviance is individual. Many alcohol abusers prefer to drink alone and similarly, narcotic addicts may often enjoy their period of chemical interlude in solitude. Various criminal specialists such as burglars, jewel thieves, contract killers, and embezzlers usually like to work solo, as it were. Individuals who take their own life are almost always alone. Even sexual deviation not infrequently occurs in individual isolation. The lone viewer of x-rated video cassettes or the pornography reader is lost in individual reveries. "Peeping Toms" tend to pursue their voyeuristic activities in a singular fashion, and many rapists assault their victims by themselves. The child molester, the spouse abuser, or the exhibitionist all commit their offenses in a single fashion. Arsonists, automobile thieves, and contract killers tend to operate alone. Of course, persons who are stigmatized by virtue of physical deformity or handicap, or mental incapacity are truly individual deviants.

On the other hand much deviancy is collective and committed in a group fashion. As the old saw put it, "It takes two to tango," and in a similar fashion, some deviant activities may require two or more individuals acting in concert. Various kinds of sexual deviance involving consenting adults such as homosexuality, "swinging," or the adulterous "affair" necessarily call for dyadic participation. Two children may conspire to steal cookies from their mother's cookie jar, or two older children may collectively take the toy away from the younger child. Marijuana users may prefer to "pass the joint around," and cocaine usage may occur in a group fashion. Gang or group rape is not uncommon, and vandalism quite frequently is the work of a group of youngsters. Some deviant behavior may even involve large numbers of individuals, the crowd that turns into a destructive riot or the lynch mob, for example.

Where deviant behavior is a collective activity, it is frequently structured and organized. The social organization of deviance may range all the way from loosely constituted "arrangements," to highly regimented and structured institutionalized systems. In the instance of the former, some deviance is conducted within the context of an habituated practice that involves no planning or coordination and is essentially self-perpetuating. Such patterns are not unlike the practice of "dumb barter" carried on by various primitive peoples. A restaurant diner, for example, orders an 8-ounce steak and the waitress mistakenly brings him a 16-ounce steak. When the diner brings the error to her attention, she permits him to eat the larger steak but only charges him for the smaller one. In gratitude, the diner leaves a particularly large tip. The next time the diner comes to the restaurant, the waitress makes the same "mistake" again, but on purpose, and again receives a large tip. Over time this pattern of undercharging and overtipping becomes habituated and the two participants, diner and waitress, are tacit coconspirators in a system of theft that steals from the restaurant owner. A variation on this system is the department store clerk that gives the customer a "prize" when making a large purchase. The customer buys a shirt and the clerk gives him a "free" pair of socks, although such a premium is not authorized by the store owner. The customer is pleased and comes back to the same clerk on the next trip to the store to make another purchase, and receives another "prize." The clerk enjoys the commission on sales from a regular customer and the customer gets something "extra" for his money. Again, a tacit criminal system steals from the store owner. Such tacit arrangements are essentially, loosely composed, criminal collusion systems. Sometimes such deviant barter systems are more complex. Zurcher (1965:399), for example, describes a complex, informal, illegal barter system driven by the norm of reciprocity, aboard a U.S. Navy ship, and Bryant (1979:91) details a similar elaborate barter system in the U.S. Army that involves the illicit trading of government equipment and supplies in a manner not unlike Malinowski's famous "Kula Ring."

Other types of deviant behavior may occur within the context of some casually structured arrangement or pattern. Laud Humphreys (1970), for example, documented a pattern of homosexual men (and some heterosexual ones) visiting "tearooms" (public restrooms) on an unscheduled basis, in order to be fellated by other homosexual men who themselves went there to engage in such sexual activities. In this case, the pattern which had simply evolved over time was loosely structured but highly predictable. A similar type of loosely structured deviance was reported by Corzine and Kirby (1977) who indicated that in the city where they conducted their research, homosexuals would "cruise" (drive back and forth) various truckstops where some truck drivers who would be seeking sexual encounters with homosexuals tended to stop. The truck drivers were reported to be heterosexuals who were seeking fellatio and other sexual services from the homosexuals as an expedient sexual outlet that was supplemental to that provided by wives or girlfriends. This pattern of meeting and engaging in sexual activities had, like the tearoom arrangement, developed gradually. While loosely disposed, the truckstop centered pattern of collective deviancy did possess some elements of social organization.

Other types of deviant behavior may involve more well defined structuring and, in some cases, the offenders are members of particular types of social organizations. As an illustration, many pickpockets operate in a well rehearsed, team fashion. Bank robbers may also commit their crimes in a team fashion with different members playing different parts. A typical "cast" from such a team might include a "wheel man" (driver) who stays with the car, an armed lookout who stays outside the bank entrance, one man inside the bank who holds a gun on the employees and patrons, and the remaining two individuals who gather up the money from the teller cages and the vault. Einstadter (1969) has studied armed robbery and concluded that such offenders employ a distinctive type of social organization to commit their crimes in an efficient manner. There is planning, deliberation, role assignments, coordination, and strategies. In short, there is an almost military-like precision in the execution of such criminal activities. Many types of deviants engage in such activities as a group. Alcoholic derelicts, or "winos" as they are known, often pool their change, buy a bottle of cheap wine, and share it in a back alley. A year or so ago, the public was shocked by the report of a gang rape in a pool hall in New England where the victim was assaulted on a pool table and the patrons shouted obscene encouragements and applauded the culprits. Juvenile delinquents often commit their offenses in groups, and the production of child "porn" movies usually requires a complete movie making crew.

The social organization of deviancy assumes many forms. In some cases, the social organization may simply involve a complex role set. A prostitute call girl, for example, would appear to operate as a solo practitioner, but as Riege (1969) has indicated, the call girl is really part of an elaborate role set involving various other kinds of practitioners who aid her in the illicit delivery of sexual services. This role set includes trainers, pimps, attorneys, cab drivers, bell hops, and other call girls, to name some. Some deviant activities are organized as a work system such as the counterfeit money "plant," the "moonshine" still, the brothel, the abortion "mill" (in an earlier time when abortions were illegal) as described by Ball (1967), or the massage parlor as analyzed by Bryant and Palmer (1975). Other deviant activities are imbedded in conventional, legal work systems. Examples here might be systematic political corruption in various governmental agencies, some traditional forms of "white-collar crime" in business, or the "strong" (illegally obscene) girlie shows and "flat stores" (crooked games of chance) in some traveling carnivals.

Sometimes, deviant behavior is organized as a game. Feigelman (1974), for example, has described the practice of recreational voyeurism or "peeping" among construction workers. As tall buildings are constructed, the workers have an excellent opportunity to view the dwellers of adjoining buildings. They take special interest in watching the dwellers of adjoining buildings who are undressed or who are engaged in sexual activities. This practice is not so much individual "peeping" as it is collective voyeurism inasmuch as the workers make a game out of it. If one worker views an especially interesting situation in a nearby building, an attractive nude female, for example, he has a "moral" obligation to inform the other workers so they too can "watch the windows." This and other rules converts their voyeuristic behavior with its vicarious sexual satisfaction into a group activity, and a kind of organized game.

The readings in this chapter address some of the varieties of social organization encountered in deviant behavior. Deviant behavior may also be organized within some type of subcultural network. The first article in the chapter, Weinberg and Falk's "The Social Organization of Sadism and Masochism" examines the subculture of such activity and the constituent organizational linkages. As with many forms of deviant behavior, a subculture has developed around sadomasochistic activities. This subculture includes various sexual norms, an argot, and certain values and ideological postures, all of which are shared by the individuals with this particular sexual persuasion. The subculture facilitates the proces of making contacts with other individuals who wish to engage in sadomasochistic activities. Contacts are made in various ways including advertisements in sadomasochistic contact magazines, which are often organized by region. The ads "state the preferences, requirements, and so forth of the placers." Sadomasochist sexual activity relies heavily on fantasy and the magazine ads permit the communication of fantasy. Sometimes sadomasochistic individuals place ads based on their fantasy needs and if partners can be found, then certain theatrical situations complete with appropriate props and costumes can be set up, and the partner can then be invited to participate in the fantasy situation. Many of the ads in the magazines, however, are placed there by prostitutes who specialize in such behavior. By describing certain theatrical situations, the prostitutes hope to attract men who entertain such a fantasy and then charge them for participating in the performance. Sadomasochists may also "advertise" through the use of symbols such as colored handkerchiefs or "strategically located key chains" as a means of possibly making chance contacts.

Different types of formally organized clubs exist within the sadomasochistic subculture. These include discussion or consciousness-raising groups, publishing organizations, sex clubs (similar to gay baths or gay night clubs), and theatrical companies which act out sadomasochistic fantasies, to name some varieties. Such organizations serve to provide opportunities for sexual outlets, they help disseminate information about sadomasochistic techniques, events, films, etc., they aid in developing and communicating justifications and rationalizations for such behavior, thus, letting members feel more normal, and they provide a means for people to segregate and compartmentalize their sadomasochistic behavior and needs from the other parts of their life. All of these types of organizations are linked together within the larger subculture, and afford an elaborate social life for individuals with this sexual inclination. Other forms of deviance such as homosexuality and "swinging" have similar type subcultures, and constituent clubs and groups, and afford a network organizational dimension to the activity.

Deviant behavior and criminal activities may, in some instances, be even more tightly organized. In the next article in this chapter, "Social Groupings in Organized Crime: The Case of La Nuestra Familia," George H. Lewis looks at a Mexican-American criminal group that has a highly organized, hierarchical structure complete with a 16-page, single-spaced constitution. Interestingly, the group originated in the California prison system in the 1960s as a means of Mexican inmates from rural areas protecting themselves from the violence and exploitation of other inmate groups. In time, the influence of the organization spread outside the prison and into Mexican-American neighborhoods in parts of Southern California. The organization has different grades of membership, and different ranks such as Nuestro General, Captains, and Lieutenants. The constitution of the group articulated a wide range of rules and regulations including the steps in building La Nuestra Familia outside of prison. There are also conduct norms, a strict code of honor, and even provision for "semiretirement." Patterned to some degree from La Cosa Nostra and other Mafia-type groups, La Nuestra Familia also bears some resemblance to bureaucratic organizations in both the business and military world. Having originally developed along racial or ethnic lines for physical protection, the tight organizational structure of La Nuestra Familia has permitted it to evolve into a highly functional and efficient criminal group. Other deviant activities are also represented by formal organization, the Ku Klux Klan being a notable example. Prostitutes have a national "professional" organization, Coyote (Call Off Your Old Tired Ethics), and in England and Europe there are some formal organizations (admittedly with small membership) that represent individuals who are pedophiles (persons with a sexual preference for children).

Crime and deviance, in order to be efficient, and/or profitable, and/or competitive, or for protection from the agents and agencies of social control have, on occasion, had to join forces with organizations dedicated to non-deviant goals. Crime and deviance have, in effect, had to coopt conventional organizations, or to infiltrate such organizations and hide in them. In this regard there is a long history (in many countries) of such "unholy" alliances. On occasion, crime or deviant behavior has had to masquerade as religion, or business, or avocation, or even as government. Some groups with deviant sexual inclinations have assumed the identity of cults or religion. Government agencies and sometimes whole governments have been corrupted and subverted to criminal or deviant goals. Other deviant groups have labeled themselves as patriotic or avocational voluntary associations. It is with business, however, that crime and deviance has, perhaps, most often attempted to develop ties. In some instances criminals simply wanted to go "legit" for protection, in other cases the tie with business was a way to expand, to diversify, or to become more efficient. Sometimes the business tie is a way of adding a supplier, new markets, or production and financing resources. Not infrequently, such ties are a means of hiding criminal profits and/or "laundering" money. The last article in this chapter looks at a case of the latter. In their article, "Casinos and Banking: Organized Crime in the Bahamas," Alan Block and Frank Scarpitti examine the complex symbiotic relationship among gambling casinos, offshore banks, and professional criminals. Through a case study of crime and business linkages in the Bahamas, they trace the development of the influence of organized crime there, and how banking and gambling were used as a means of laundering money and providing other needed financial services. Through a variety of linkages with business, banking, and the Bahamian government, organized crime skillfully used many types of organizations for its own purposes and tied these organizations to itself in a larger criminal system.

REFERENCES

Ball, Donald
1967 "An Abortion Clinic Ethnography," *Social Problems*, 14(3),293–300.

Bryant, Clifton D.
1979 *Khaki-Collar Crime: Deviant Behavior in the Military Context*. New York: The Free Press.

Bryant, Clifton D., and C. Eddie Palmer
1975 "Massage Parlors and 'Hand Whores': Some Sociological Observations," *The Journal of Sex Research*, 11(3):227–241.

Corzine, Jay, and Richard Kirby
1977 "Cruising the Truckers: Sexual Encounters in a Highway Rest Area," *Urban Life*, 6(2):171–192.

Einstadter, Werner J.
1969 "The Social Organization of Armed Robbery," *Social Problems*, 17:64–83.

Humphreys, Laud
1970 "Tearoom Trade: Impersonal Sex in Public Places," *Transaction*, 7(3):10–25.

Riege, Mary Gray
1969 "The Call Girl and the Dance Teacher: A Comparative Analysis," *Cornell Journal of Social Relations*, 4(1):58–71.

Zurcher, Louis A., Jr.
1975 "The Sailor Aboard Ship: A Study of Role Behavior in a Total Institution." *Social Forces* 43:389–400.

Reading 18

The Social Organization of Sadism and Masochism

Thomas S. Weinberg and Gerhard Falk
State University of College at Buffalo

Sadism and masochism, traditionally studied as an individual psychopathology, may be more fully understood as a sociological phenomenon. Sadomasochists have developed a subculture characterized by a set of norms, shared ideologies, and a common argot. Contacts among sadomasochists are made through magazine advertisements, participation in clubs and organizations, through exposure to this behavior in other deviant subcultures, and fortuitously.

Sadomasochistic organizations, while differing widely among themselves, serve similar functions for their members: (1) they facilitate sexual and social contacts; (2) they provide members with information about techniques, events, other organizations, films, and so forth; (3) they develop and communicate justifications and apologias enabling people to accept their feelings and behavior as normal; and (4) they enable people to segregate their sadomasochistic needs and behavior from other areas of their lives.

INTRODUCTION

Sadism and masochism, the giving and receiving of pain for erotic gratification, have been largely neglected as areas of sociological study. As two recent papers point out, descriptions of the social aspects of this behavior are virtually nonexistent in the professional literature (Spengler, 1977; Weinberg, 1978). The apparent lack of interest in studying sadomasochistic behavior from a sociological perspective may be attributable to its having been traditionally examined from a psychoanalytic model. The influence of such writers as Krafft-Ebing (1932) and Sigmund Freud (1938) may have been to obscure the social aspects of this behavior by defining it solely in terms of individual pathology. Inasmuch as sociologists have until quite recently ignored sadomasochism, descriptions of its social aspects have been largely left to journalists (e.g., Coburn, 1977; Halpern, 1977; Smith and Cox, 1979a and 1979b). This is unfortunate, because these journalistic observations are neither systematic nor theoretical.

This is a revised version of a paper prepared for presentation at the Annual Meetings of the Society for the Study of Social Problems, September 2–4, 1978 in San Francisco. The authors wish to thank Dr. Edward M. Levine of Loyola University, Chicago, for his critical reading of an earlier draft of the present paper.

In this paper we present, in a preliminary way, some sociological observations drawn from an ongoing research project, which began in December 1977. Our focus is on the ways in which contacts are made among participants in the sadomasochistic (S&M) world, sadomasochistic organizations, and other subcultural supports for and influences upon this behavior. We are primarily concerned with heterosexual sadomasochism, an area that has been less examined than the homosexual S&M world. Although there are some points of contact between these two S&M subcultures, and even though some individuals may participate in both and define their sexuality in a flexible way, the two worlds remain distinct. The homosexual S&M world is much more visible, with many large cities having at least one so-called leather bar. As Spengler (1977) has noted, only homosexual sadomasochists appear to be approachable for study. Heterosexual sadomasochists are extremely reluctant to be interviewed or studied in any way.

METHODS

Given the difficulties in contacting a large sample of sadomasochists,[1] our conclusions must remain tentative. Our data consist of a few formal and informal interviews with men engaging in S&M behavior and with prostitutes, or "dominatrixes", specializing in "female domination." Like Spengler, we found it impossible to question sadomasochistically oriented women who were not involved in prostitution. Our only information about such women comes indirectly through conversations with their husbands, who were themselves involved in sadomasochism. Additional sources of information on the social organization of sadomasochism comes from advertisements, flyers, magazines, and literature produced by sadomasochistic organizations.

Our contacts with respondents were made through answering advertisements placed in S&M contact magazines. We presented ourselves as professional sociologists who were interested in understanding the S&M subculture. Respondents generally wished to remain anonymous; they used pseudonyms and preferred to make contacts on the telephone rather than in person. Other contacts were made fortuitously through people who knew the nature of the study.[2]

[1]Spengler (1977:442) acknowledges this problem when he states, "Extreme difficulties exist in questioning sadomasochists. Heterosexual sadomasochists live undercover; their groups are cut off from the outside world. . . . Anonymity is one of the special norms of sadomasochistic subcultures."

[2]One such chance contact occurred when one of the writers happened to casually mention the study to a former student whom he met one day in the student union. A few hours later, he was surprised by a telephone call from this man, who told him that he had spoken to a friend who might be interested in discussing sadomasochism. About an hour later, the writer received

SOCIOLOGICAL STUDIES OF SADOMASOCHISM

The few studies of sadism and masochism in the sociological literature point out that S&M is a well established subculture characterized by publications, a market economy, and its own argot. Howard S. Becker (1963), for instance, estimated that one catalog devoted to sadomasochistic fetishism, which he had examined, contained between 15 and 20 thousand photographs for sale; and he therefore concluded that the dealer "did a land-office business and had a very sizable clientele" (1963:20–21). Becker further emphasized the importance of some sort of sadomasochistic subculture in developing deviant motivations through providing people with the appropriate conceptual linguistic tools:

> Deviant motivations have a social character even when most of the activity is carried on in a private, secret, and solitary fashion. In such cases, various media of communication may take the place of face-to-face interaction in inducting the individual into the culture. The pornographic pictures I mentioned earlier were described to prospective buyers in a stylized language. Ordinary words were used in a technical shorthand designed to whet specific tastes. . . . One does not acquire a taste for "bondage photos" without having learned what they are and how they may be enjoyed. (Becker, 1963:31)

John Gagnon (1977) notes the existence of clubs for heterosexuals interested in sadomasochism:

> The formalization of the sadomasochistic aspects of the gay community has been paralleled by the creation of "clubs" for heterosexual masochists and sadists. Such sites offer opportunities for people with common sexual preferences to meet. Where once the problems of meeting were solved through word of mouth and through advertisements of various sorts, there is now a more public "velvet underground"in various cities which offers an opportunity for more interaction, and the creation of a local sadomasochistic culture. The city in this case provides for sexual minorities what it provided for literary minorities in the past. (Gagnon, 1977:329)

a call from his student's friend, a young woman who had been a prostitute, dominatrix, and madame in a house of female domination. Over a lengthy lunch the next day, this woman and the writer discussed his work in sadomasochism. She was particularly concerned about his personal reasons for the study (was he really a policeman, or a voyeur, or a sadomasochist attempting to use the research for his own sexual purposes?) and spent the time probing his motivations. Apparently convinced that he had no ulterior motives, understood people in deviant lifestyles, and could be trusted, she became an invaluable resource for contacts and information about the S&M world.

A questionnaire study by Andreas Spengler (1977) of sadomasochistic West German men, however, casts doubt upon the importance of sadomasochistic clubs for making sexual contacts, at least for heterosexual men. He found that these heterosexual men were not so well integrated into a sadomasochistic subculture as were bisexual and homosexual men. Fewer heterosexual men participated in sadomasochistic parties, had an acquaintance with like-minded people, or were successful in receiving responses to advertisements placed in sadomasochistic publications. Prostitution was a more important sadomasochistic outlet for heterosexual men than it was for the other respondents. Spengler explains this finding by noting that there are few (nonprostitute) women who participate in the sadomasochistic subculture. Observations of sadomasochistic clubs and parties by journalists (e.g., Halpern, 1977; Smith and Cox, 1979a), who note a heavy preponderance of men and the presence of professional dominatrixes at these functions tend to support Spengler's findings. Spengler's "unsystematic impression" is that "nearly all the subcultural groups among heterosexual sadomasochists exist in cooperation with prostitutes" (1977:455) and that one of the functions of these heterosexually oriented sadomasochistic subcultures for their members is to maintain the fiction that prostitutes are "really" passionately involved in the sadomasochistic encounter.

Thomas S. Weinberg (1978) emphasizes the importance of sadomasochistic organizations in developing and disseminating apologias, attitudes, and ideologies supportive of sadomasochism that enable their members to justify their sexual desires. He points out the importance of fantasy and theatricality in the sadomasochistic world and examines the ways in which "frameworks" and "keys" delimiting the cuing sadomasochistic episodes are developed through the use of a shared subcultural argot.

Joann S. DeLora and Carol A. B. Warren (1977) believe that there is a general acceptance of "the milder forms of sadistic or masochistic pleasure" in American culture (1977:366), and they note the existence of "sadomasochistic games by couples as part of their love-making rituals" (1977:267). This does not, however, necessarily mean that either sadomasochistic behavior or sadomasochistic subcultures are widespread in this society.

MAKING CONTACTS IN THE SUBCULTURE

There are a number of ways in which sadomasochistic contacts are made. These include placing or responding to advertisements in contact magazines and other publications, finding partners through participation in other subcultural settings such as bars or swingers' clubs or through participation in prostitution. Some contacts occur by chance; others develop through encounters in sadomasochistic organizations (Weinberg, 1978).

Advertisements

The most common means of reaching other S&M devotees appears to be the use of advertisements in sadomasochistic contact magazines. Spengler (1977) found that these ads were the most frequently used way of finding partners and that only 7% of his sample had never placed one. The advertisements contained in contact magazines are usually organized by region, with the advertiser identified only by a code number. The ads state the preferences, requirements, and so forth of their placers. Some of the ads are accompanied by photographs, purportedly of the advertisers.

Placing and Responding to Advertisements Procedures for placing ads and responding to them are similar in all of these magazines. In order to place an ad, one submits a fee ranging from about $5 to $10 and certifies to being over the age of 21. Some publications also require that advertisers subscribe to the publication at an additional cost of $10 or more. In order to respond to an ad, some magazines require that one be a subscriber or a member of a club sponsored by the publisher. Responding to an ad costs $1–$2 per letter. The letters are placed in stamped envelopes with the advertisers' code numbers on them. All of the envelopes are then put into a larger envelop, which also contains the publisher's fee. The publisher then addresses the coded envelopes to the advertisers and thus assures their anonymity. Our experience with this process indicates that the publishers at least do forward the letters if it is at all possible and even go so far as to return undeliverable letters at their own expense. Many of the advertisers also appear to be legitimate. When we sent letters to advertisers in our region, we received responses from some of these people. However, we are still attempting to increase our sample through these informants, an obviously difficult undertaking.

Most of the ads found in S&M contact magazines are supposedly placed by women, the majority of whom are self-described "dominants." The men tend to be "submissives" (Weinberg, 1978). This appears to be the most commonly occurring combination in North American S&M culture. Part of the explanation for the large representation of female advertisers may be that women are usually not charged a fee for advertising, that many of the female advertisers are prostitutes ("Seeks very rich slaves only"; "Photos, used lingerie for sale"; "Correspondence welcome but I expect compensation for my time") and that the purchasers of these magazines are predominantly males seeking dominant females.

According to some of our respondents, they sometimes place ads in the "personals" columns of local newspapers. These ads are disguised as inquiries for "pen pals." Since swingers also use the same kinds of ads ("Modern couple desires couples as pen pals"; "Couple, 30, desires discreet pen pals") it is difficult to ascertain whether an ad is a swingers' advertisement or an

S&M inquiry. Both use similar code words such as "modern" or "discreet" to indicate a sexual interest. Infrequently, an S&M advertiser will include a phrase such as "interested in English culture" to indicate a preference for being whipped.

Advertisements and the Communication of Fantasy Many of the advertisements found in contact magazines illustrate a major aspect of the sadomasochistic subculture; it is, to a large degree, a fantasy world. One cannot fully understand the organization of the S&M scene unless the central importance of the expression of fantasy for its participants is recognized. The subculture serves to segregate the sexual fantasy needs of its members from other aspects of their lives. This is often accomplished by setting up a particular theatrical situation, frequently aided by props and costumes of various kinds, in which the participants don new identities and act out different parts. Popular situations include, for example, the naughty schoolboy who is reprimanded (i.e., verbally degraded) and physically punished by the female school teacher, and the patient who is given an enema by a nurse. The importance of fantasy (and its components of hostility) is apparent in the following ads drawn from contact publications:

1 Blonde Dominatrix dressed in rubber or leather costume. Seeks experienced or novice slaves who believe in Dominant Female Superiority. I'm well qualified in B&D, watersports, humiliation, petticoat training and have equipment built by slaves.

2 Tall, cruel, Creole Beauty seeks Dominant Male partner to assist her in controlling & disciplining her many slaves. Come be my King so we can play King & Queen. Do not answer if you are not sincere and generous. Letter, photo & phone gets you a surprising quick reply. This is for dominants only, have too many slaves now.

3 Beautiful Dominatrix, 24. A true sophisticate of bizarre and unusual. I have a well equipped dungeon in my luxurious home. You will submit to prolonged periods of degradation for my pleasure. Toilet servitude a must. I know what you crave and can fulfill your every need.

4 Very pretty 30 yr old female has fantasies about receiving handspankings on bare behind. I've never allowed myself to act out any of the fantasies. Is there anyone out there who'd like to correspond with me about their fantasies or experiences with spanking?

5 Cruel husband seeking experienced dominant man to assist in training petite, shy, young wife. Eager to watch her transformed from shy, personal, sex slave to slut. Presently serving me and friend in humiliation, verbal abuse, deep throat, GR., golden shower, lewd dancing, nude posing, public display. Prefer man with extensive movie/erotica collection, over 50, obese with a fetish for petite, young girls or hung Black. Also those with aggressive Bi-partners or trained pets.

These ads, as is apparent, contain coded messages. The language of S&M serves to indicate to potential respondents the advertisers' expectations and the sorts of roles and relationships they are looking for. For example, "B&D" (Bondage and Discipline) refers to tying up or restraining a person, along with the possibility of some sort of physical punishment. "Water-sports," refers to urination. "Petticoat training" indicates cross-dressing. "Toilet servitude" (or, sometimes, "toilet training") refers to the handling of feces, being defecated upon, or to coprophagia. The abbreviation "GR" stands for "Greek," an indication that the advertiser is interested in anal intercourse. "Golden shower" is code for being urinated upon, sometimes with the inclusion of urolagnia.

Participation in the sadomasochistic subculture also often develops out of contacts made in other "deviant" sexual scenes, such as the swinging subculture, gay bars, and prostitution. Interestingly, some of the same people who advertise in the S&M contact magazines of one publisher also advertise in the swinging publications of another, using the same picture but with a somewhat different advertisement.

Prostitution and S&M Contacts Prostitution is an important source of sexual contacts of sadomasochistically oriented men (DeLora and Warren, 1977; Spengler, 1977; Weinberg, 1978). Prostitutes have written autobiographical descriptions of their participation in this behavior (Hollander, 1972; Von Cleef, 1974). Many professional dominatrixes advertise not only in sadomasochistic contact publications, but also in sex-oriented publications such as *Screw*. Our interviews with professional prostitutes who specialize in "Houses of Domination" indicate a highly developed skill in S&M. Prostitutes with whom we have spoken pointed out that specializing in sadomasochism is far more lucrative than conventional prostitution.[3] Fees range from $35 to $45 for half an hour, and from $50 to $100 or more for an hour's session. A number of prostitutes advertise "No Straight Sex, S&M and TV (i.e., transvestitism) only" and do not, they claim, have sexual intercourse with their clientele. Apart from the development of special skills and the creation of fantasy scenarios, professional dominatrixes appear to differ little from women engaged in conventional prostitution. Like the more usual forms of prostitution, sadomasochistic specialists practice their trade in houses of prostitution, massage parlors (Evening Tribune, 1980), and as individual entrepreneurs.

[3] Some quotations from the interviews with dominatrixes are reproduced elsewhere (Weinberg, 1978: especially pp. 286–287). The transcript of a fascinating interview with a professional prostitute specializing in S&M appears in Smith and Cox (1979b).

Chance Contacts

Some contacts are made accidentally. One respondent told us, for example, that he was approached and engaged in conversation by a number of men who were attracted by his wife's leather coat and high leather boots, although she had not purposely worn them to advertise her interest in S&M. One way to encourage such approaches, then, is to display symbols commonly accepted in the sadomasochistic subculture. This does not appear to be a very common practice among heterosexual devotees of S&M, apart from their participation in S&M parties, although participants in the homosexual leather scene frequently wear symbols such as colored handkerchiefs or strategically located key chains to advertise their preferences.

Initial Meetings: Determining Compatibility

When contacts are first made among sadomasochists, they follow a format similar to the initial sizing up which occurs among swingers (Bartell, 1971; Palson and Palson, 1972). This is not surprising; some informants have told us that they were introduced to sadomasochism through swinging. Typically, two couples may go out to dinner and spend relatively little time discussing their sexuality. Rather, the purpose of their meeting is to discover, in a nonthreatening situation, whether they are comfortable with each other and socially compatible. One respondent who is a business executive noted that social compatibility is important because sexual activity takes up a relatively small amount of an evening's time and "you have to have something to talk about with the other couple." His group consists of other professionals, such as dentists and attorneys.

Since the S&M scene demands absolute trust and confidence in another person, especially if one may be bound helplessly and gagged, this initial meeting is a critical one. Only after people have built up a certain amount of trust do they proceed to engage in sadomasochistic activities.

Before an actual scene occurs, the participants in it discuss their needs, fantasies, fears, and what they are and are not willing to do. What ultimately occurs during a scene is the outcome of this discussion, in which the original thoughts are somewhat modified, then subjected to bargaining process by which the verbalized desires of the partner are accommodated. This accommodation appears to be necessary because the participants wish to carry their imagination into action by convincing their partner that their wishes are reasonably compatible. Unless there is agreement, there probably will not be mutual gratification. Contrary to the popular notion that the sadist is in command of this situation, S&M devotees often assert that it is the masochist who controls the scene, because it is his or her fantasies that the sadist acts out.

S&M ORGANIZATIONS AND THEIR FUNCTIONS

There are a number of formally organized sadomasochistic clubs and numerous informal groups of sadists and masochists throughout this country. For the purpose of this discussion, we will classify them roughly into the following categories, based upon what seem to be their primary activities: (1) discussion or consciousness-raising groups; (2) publishing organizations; (3) sex clubs; and (4) theatrical companies.[4]

Discussion or Consciousness-Raising Groups

The Till Eulenspiegel Society[5] in New York City describes itself as a "discussion and consciousness-raising group," the objective of which is "to promote better understanding and self-awareness of these (sadomasochistic) drives so that they may be enjoyed as a part of a full sex life, rather than set aside out of fear or guilt." The society explicitly denies being "in any sense a sex club or swingers' organization." During the Eulenspiegel's weekly meetings, members discuss their feelings and behavior and occasionally are given demonstrations and lectures by sadomasochistic experts. Although Eulenspiegel does not appear to propagandize to the larger society nor to lobby for legal change, it does seem to resemble in some of its avowed purposes other minority organizations, such as those studied by Yearwood and Weinberg (1979). Despite the Eulenspiegel Society's denial that it is a sex club, it does, in fact, sponsor parties at which sadomasochistic behavior occurs (Halpern, 1977).

Publishing Organizations

The House of Milan, located in Los Angeles, publishes a number of contact magazines (*Latent Image*, *Aggressive Gals*, *Bitch Goddesses*) that serve to facilitate communication among S&M devotees throughout the country. They also publish magazines for those who enjoy simply reading about female domination, spanking, tranvestitism, rubber fetishes, and so on. This organization gives parties occasionally, which are advertised in its contact publications.

I. Dictor Enterprises in Philadelphia publishes a sadomasochistic contact magazine called *Amazon*. The aim of this magazine, according to its former publisher, Malibu Publications, is to "provide the average person with a publication that reveals S&M/B&D as a normal form of sexual

[4]There are, of course, any number of ways in which these organizations could be classified such as according to whether they are profit or nonprofit enterprises, whether they serve to facilitate sexual contacts and in what specific ways they do this, whether they are politically oriented and so on.

[5]The organization takes its name from a figure in German folklore who is said to have carried heavy loads up mountains because it felt so good when he put these burdens down and thus acknowledged his presumably masochistic tendencies.

activity and alleviates any feelings of guilt and/or perversion arising from long held misconceptions." To this end, the magazine includes not only contact ads, but also a question and answer column written by "a clinical psychologist with long, widely varied experience in sex therapy and family counseling," a section containing news about new publications, other organizations, films of interest to S&M devotees, sources of products, news of upcoming events, and the like, fiction involving sadomasochistic interests and behavior, cartoons, and commercial advertisements for other clubs, films, and sexual devices.

Sex Clubs

Chateau 19 is an "on-premise S&M club" (Smith and Cox, 1979a) in New York City. Its twice weekly sessions are open to the public. For an admission fee ($7.50 for men, $2.50 for women, including two drinks) one is free to participate in any of the night's activities. Smith and Cox (1979a) reported that there was a wide range in the ages of the club's habitues, with most being between the ages of 25 and 35. From their description, Chateau 19 appears to be very similar to other on-premise impersonal sex clubs such as Plato's Retreat in New York City, San Francisco's Sutro Bath House, and gay baths found throughout the country.

Theatrical Companies

Sadomasochistic fantasies have been brought "out of the closet" by an organization known as "The Project." The Project, which calls itself a "research team," was founded in the early 1970s by a New York City radio personality. It has been featured on talk shows on the three major television networks and has been written about in a number of popular culture and sexually oriented newspapers and magazines. Performers in The Project travel throughout the state to churches, colleges, single groups, private parties, and various social organizations, acting out for a fee, fantasies that they have collected through "hundreds of interviews and thousands of letters." The program of one of their productions, called "Another Way to Love," included the following S&M scenarios:[6]

1 " 'The Beauty of Looking Beastly': An authentic psychosexual fairy tale wherein the 'ugliest man in the world' lives his most beautiful moment" (a scene in which a man is publicly humiliated by a beautiful

[6]The writers first became aware of the existence of The Project when one of them saw an advertisement for one of its productions in a Buffalo, New York, homophile publication. He attended the performance, which was held in the Buffalo Gay Community Services Center, in March 1976. The show consisted of a half-dozen scenarios, four of which are described above, performed by a male and a female actor. This was followed by a discussion period, during which the audience could ask the actors questions. In addition to its prerehearsed shows, The

woman who forces him to wear a collar and leash and a mask hiding his face).

2 " 'I'm the Haughtiest Girl in the Whole USA': Wherein a fetishistic 'judge' who specializes in 'justice' for pretty girls convicted of pretty-girl crimes liquifies his toughest prisoner into a splash pool of humiliation by getting to the bottom of her evil" (a scene in which a man dressed as a monk puts a woman into stocks, forcing her to publicly confess her crime of "haughtiness," and then tortures her by tickling her bare feet).

3 " 'Bottoms Up!': A peek into the bedroom of an earnest young wife who endeavors to redesign her color scheme by pestering, plaguing, and provoking her posterior decorator" (a spanking fantasy).

4 " 'Paul(a)': Wherein the fantacist awakens her husband to a galaxy of life changes most profound" (a scene in which a woman, dressed in a translucent black body suit, high heeled boots, and armed with a whip, forces her husband to dress up in a French maid's uniform, complete with female undergarments and a wig).

The list of organizations described above is in no sense exhaustive; however, it does serve to illustrate the variety of more formally developed associations found within the sadomasochistic subculture. Although the purposes of these organizations appear to vary widely, from enterprises designed to make a profit for their owners to those, like Eulenspiegel, that exist to help sadomasochists accept their inclinations, they nevertheless serve similar functions for persons interested in S&M. First, they all provide the possibilities of sexual outlets, either through direct participation as in Chateau 19 or in the parties given by other organizations, through the opportunity to make connections with similarly inclined people by advertising in contact magazines to stimulate sexual fantasies. Second, all of these organizations serve to disseminate information about sadomasochism to their members, enabling them to learn new techniques, develop new interests, and find out about events, news, and so forth relevant to their needs. Third, all of the sadomasochistic organizations develop and communicate, either explicitly or implicitly, justifications and apologias enabling people to accept their feelings and behavior as perfectly normal. Fourth, by providing these special settings, justifications, and the appropriate linguistic tools, they enable

Project also acts out individuals' private fantasies at its own location in New York City. The individual, who pays a fee for this service, does not participate in the performance of his own fantasy, however, but remains strictly an observer. The Project does not appear to have been conceived solely as a profit-making venture for its creator, however. At the conclusion of its two Buffalo performances, the actors made a donation of several hundred dollars to support the activities of the Gay Center. Considering the low cost of admission to the performances ($3 for a Sunday matinee and $3.50 for that evening's show), the fairly small attendance, and travel expenses, The Project does not seem to have made very much money during its visit.

people to segregate their sadomasochistic needs and behavior from other areas of their lives.

CONCLUSIONS

Although sadomasochism has traditionally been studied as an individual psychopathology, in many instances this behavior is a group phenomenon. A variety of sadomasochistic groups and organizations facilitate contacts among members, teach new techniques and behaviors, and serve to normalize individuals' attitudes, interests, and sexual activities. A more comprehensive understanding of sadomasochism requires that it be examined within a broader social context, rather than remain limited to a study of individual case histories. When this is done, some alternative ways of thinking about sadomasochism emerge. For example, S&M may serve recreational as well as sexual needs for its devotees. One journalist (Coburn, 1977:45) speculates that a new sort of S&M "chic" has been developing in this country, and she cites recent popular magazine articles, popular music, billboard advertisements, and so forth, all with S&M motifs as evidence for this speculation. Sadomasochistic themes also appear in recent movies (e.g., "Myra Breckenridge," "The Opening of Misty Beethoven," and "Wholly Moses!" among others) and in novels. Another way of looking at sadomasochism is in terms of economics. Sadomasochistic publications are filled with ads from manufacturers of expensive wearing apparel, devices, equipment, and so forth. There seems to be a lucrative business in magazines, movies, sex clubs, prostitution, and the like, all aimed at a sadomasochistic market.

REFERENCES

Bartell, Gilbert D.
1971 Group Sex. New York: Signet Books.
Becker, Howard S.
1963 Outsiders: Studies in the Sociology of Deviance. New York: Free Press.
Coburn, Judith
1977 "S&M." New Times 8 (Feb. 4):43–50.
DeLora, Joann S., and Carol A. B. Warren
1977 Understanding Sexual Interaction. Boston: Houghton-Mifflin.
Evening Tribune (San Diego)
1980 "Parlor operator sentenced." (Jan. 23):B-6.
Freud, Sigmund
1938 The Basic Writings of Sigmund Freud. (A. A. Brill, trans. and ed.). New York: Modern Library.

Gagnon, John
1977 Human Sexualities. Glenview, Ill.: Scott, Foresman.
Halpern, Bruce
1977 "Spanks for the memory." Screw 420 (March 21):4–7.
Hollander, Xaviera
1972 The Happy Hooker. New York: Dell.
Krafft-Ebing, R. V.
1932 Psychopathia Sexualis. New York: Physicians' and Surgeons' Book Company.
Palson, Charles and Rebecca Palson
1972 "Swinging in wedlock." Transaction/Society 9 (Feb.):28–37.
Smith, Howard and Cathy Cox
1979a "Scenes: S&M in the open." Village Voice 24 (Jan. 15):24.
1979b "Scenes: dialogue with a dominatrix." Village voice 24 (Jan. 29):19–20.
Spengler, Andreas
1977 "Manifest sadomasochism of males: results of an empirical study." Archives of Sexual Behavior 6:441–56.
Von Cleef, Monique
1971 The House of Pain. Secaucus, N.J.: Lyle Stuart.
Weinberg, Thomas S.
1978 "Sadism and masochism: sociological perspectives." Bulletin of the American Academy of Psychiatry and the Law 6:284–95.
Yearwood, Lennox and Thomas S. Weinberg
1979 "Black organizations, gay organizations: sociological parallels." Pp. 301–16 in Martin P. Levine (ed.), Gay Men: The Sociology of Male Homosexuality. New York: Harper.

Reading 19

Social Groupings in Organized Crime: The Case of La Nuestra Familia

George H. Lewis
University of the Pacific, Stockton, California

The paper addresses the question of organization in criminal groups. Organized crime appears to consist of highly organized families loosely linked to one another only by common interests. It is argued that these groups may be an underworld reflection of overworld pluralism and may tend to organize along racial and ethnic lines.

The author wishes to thank the anonymous reviewers, whose comments have greatly strengthened this piece.

Daniel Bell has called organized crime "an American way of life" for the poor but ambitious immigrants to this country who have found themselves caught in urban slums (Bell, 1962:127–150). Others, in agreement with this "functional" view of organized crime, have pointed to an ethnic succession of such (Smith and Alba, 1979:32). In the 1900s the Irish dominated, to be followed by the Jews, the Poles, and then the Italians (Tyler, 1976; Thio, 1968). Authors adopting this perspective and writing concerning the contemporary state of organized crime in the United States seem generally to assume blacks and Puerto Ricans are in the process of developing their own "mafia," and will succeed the Italians when the latter achieve greater success in the conventional upperworld (Haller, 1971–72; Ianni, 1974, 1976). As with much material in the area of crime research, data are difficult to obtain, and a good deal of speculation is based upon a minimum of solid evidence.

This situation has allowed several criminologists working in the 1960s to assert that organized crime in the United States is a tightly knit national organization (Tyler, 1962; Anderson, 1965: 302; Cressey, 1969; Galliher and Cain, 1974:68), a view supported by the President's Commission of 1968. However, the more decentralized and pluralistic picture painted by those who challenged this view seems to be a more acceptable position today. Organized crime, as many criminologists of the 1970s picture it, is a loose, informal confederation of diverse groups of professional criminals operating independently (Albani, 1971). As Ramsey Clark has expressed it.

> As with all crime, we oversimplify our definition of organized crime. There is far more to it than La Cosa Nostra. Our society is much too complex to expect only a single syndicate or type of illegal activity. There is no one massive organization that manages all or even most planned and continuous criminal conduct throughout the country (Clark, 1971:199).

This is, of course, not to deny the fact that La Cosa Nostra is generally believed to be a rather tightly knit national confederation.

This paper is addressed specifically to the question of organization in criminal groups. The general perspective of the author is close to that of Conklin (1973), who conceives of organized crime as consisting of highly organized families loosely linked to one another only by common interests. "Local crime families are highly organized, both on the basis of kinship and, increasingly, on the basis of rational bureaucratic structure. Nationally, links between families exist, especially in times of crisis and conflict. . . . However, the evidence of a monolithic national structure is less compelling" (Conklin, 1973:13). It is argued in this paper that these groups are an underworld reflection of overworld pluralism and tend to organize along lines of racial and ethnic cleavage.

Data in the area of organized crime are slippery and difficult to come by. Thus, a high proportion of what is reported is either highly theoretical and speculative or is based on one or two studies of portions of the East Coast Cosa Nostra grouping (Ianni, 1972; Cressey, 1969). By examining the organization of La Nuestra Familia, a Mexican-American group that originated in California's prison system in the late 1960s, the author intends to add to the literature important descriptive data concerning the form and type of organization such groupings can take. La Nuestra Familia, an unstudied West Coast grouping of relatively recent origin, is quite different from those few organizations about which some data have been collected. Thus, it should be of importance as a case study in organization and criminal behavior.

THE DATA BASE

As Becker has remarked, "Since we stigmatize and punish deviant activities, the people who engage in them care not to be discovered. Their secretiveness takes a variety of organizational forms, and each variation complicates the technical problems of sampling . . . in a special way that requires us to find special solutions" (Becker, 1970:49). This problem, and hints at its solution, has been documented by, among others, Stoddard (1968), Douglas (1972), and Lee (1979).

As is the case with most studies of organized crime, it has proven extremely difficult to obtain data on Mexican-American criminal groups. The one source of information available, *Chicago Prisoners: The Key to San Quentin*, by Davidson (1974), which describes the role of the "Mexican Mafia" in the California prison system, has been refuted by the prisoners themselves, who wrote a critique of the book contending much of it was false and was based on misinformation fed to the researcher, whom they had had no reason to trust. Other than this questionable source, literally nothing has been published that deals at all with La Nuestra Familia. Although there are plenty of "hearsay" reports in California criminal justice circles, no one has really wanted to expose himself or herself to the very real dangers of attempting direct interviews with Familia members. As one prison official remarked: "They [as an organization] may not be as smart as some of the others, but they make up for it in viciousness."

Data collected, then, are of three types: some informal interviews with law enforcement officials who deal with these individuals in the course of their duties (and who did not wish to be formally interviewed "for the record"); analysis of the few newspaper reports that have appeared (Los

Angeles Times, 1974–1979; Stockton Record, 1974–1979); and, most importantly, a content analysis of La Neustra Familia constitution—a protected document that has, nevertheless, been "leaked" through anonymous channels to the author.

As strange as it seems for such information to be written down, the document has been authenticated by several sources in California law and enforcement circles, recent court testimonies, and informal conversations with others in contact with Familia members. Some sixteen handwritten pages in length, the constitution has been used as core information in this paper. Real world behavior of La Nuestra Familia members has been evaluated by means of interviews with officials, news reports, and recent court proceedings involving the group as highly conformative with the prescriptions contained in this document. Thus, although there are always questions as to authenticity of this sort of data, indications are that this is a valid and reliable source of information concerning the social organization of La Nuestra Familia.

ORGANIZED CHICANO CRIME IN CALIFORNIA: A BACKGROUND

To understand the genesis of La Nuestra Familia, one must be aware of another organized crime group, the Mexican Mafia. This group, organized in 1957 at Deuel Vocational Institute near Tracy, California, was formed from a core of urban Mexican-American prison inmates for protection from groups of black and white prisoners, such as the Black Guerrilla Family and the Aryan Brotherhood.

At first, as the strength of this group grew, it concentrated its attacks on other ethnic groups. However, in the 1960s there came an increasing influx of rural Mexican inmates to the state prison system. Many of these individuals were the sons of farm workers who had drifted to urban areas because of the push of new agri-business monopolies and harvesting techniques replacing them in the fields, the pull of urban California, and the rapid spread of hard drugs in this unemployed population. Lacking the street sophistication of those born in the cities, these persons were labeled "Farmers" by the Mexican Mafia. They were brutalized, extorted, assaulted, and murdered until, in 1968, the Farmers organized and began to strike back as La Nuestra Familia.

By 1972, California corrections authorities realized they could not contain the violence in this organized form, so they designated specific prisons as exclusive territory of each gang[1] (Stockton Record, 1978). Deuel Voca-

[1]The newspaper accounts of this were corroborated by conversations with Deuel Vocational Institution employees.

tional Institution became the "capital" of Nuestra Familia, and the two top-ranking members were transferred there from San Quentin.

As the power of La Nuestra Familia grew, it began to extend its influence outside the prison. The constitution states: "The primary purpose or goals of this organization will be for the betterment of its members and the building up of the organization on the outside into a strong and self supporting Familia." Although at present the Mexican Mafia still controls East Los Angeles, La Nuestra Familia is increasingly seen to be in control of organized criminal operations in San Jose, Salinas, Visalia, and Stockton. Official estimates of the present size of the organization range between 400 and 600, with about 150 presently incarcerated at Deuel[2] (Stockton Record, 1979; Los Angeles Times, 1979).

THE FORMAL STRUCTURE OF LA NUESTRA FAMILIA

The structure seems to consist of three characteristics grades of membership organization (Figure 1). In the center are the hardcore soldier members with a central core of officers. At the very center is the Supreme Commander, El Nuestro General. There is then the first captain, up to nine subcaptains, and an unspecified number of lieutenants.

At a second degree of involvement, there are soldiers defined as "loose" members who may not be total participants in organization activities.

At a third grade there are peripheral members, called "fence walkers" or "snakes," who are recognized as being able to "go either way." These persons have never really belonged to the organization, nor are they defined as true members.

The constitution explains the situation with respect to second- and third-level members. "If categories two and three do their duties, we gain strength. If they P.C. (defect) we kill them, and we still gain strength by removing the weak links of our organization."

Absolute loyalty to the organization is stressed. The constitution states that "a Familiano will remain a Familiano member until death or otherwise discharged from the organization. He will always be subject to put the interest of the organization first and always above everything else, in prison or out. An automatic death sentence will be put on a Familiano that turns traitor, coward or deserter."

1. The Nuestro General. This individual is the supreme power in the organization. The constitution states that "his power shall have no limit." He can be removed by death, by impeachment by unanimous verdict of all his captains in writing that he is not working in the best interests of the

[2]The newspaper accounts were corroborated by conversations with San Joaquin County law enforcement officials.

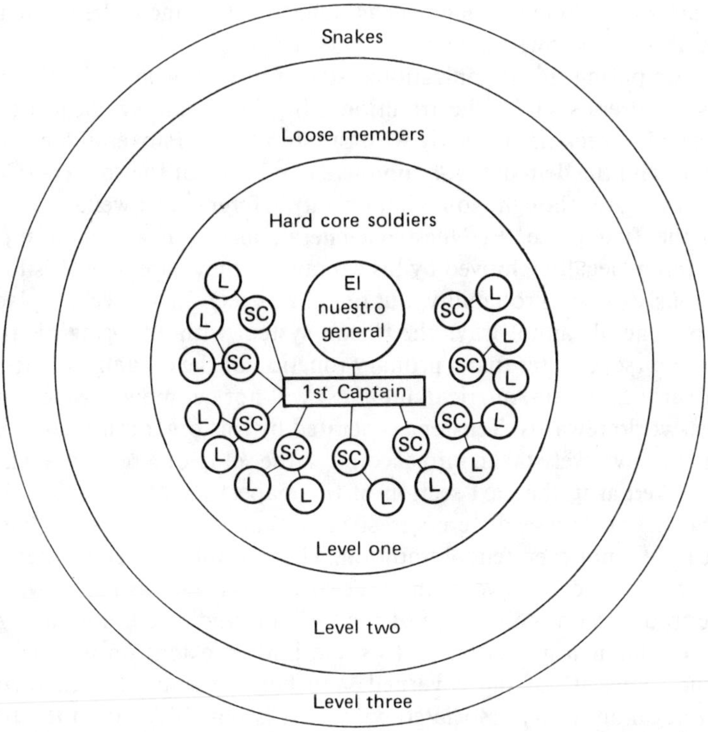

Figure 1 Organizational structure of La Nuestra Familia: SC = secondary captions; L = lieutenants.

Familia, or by having 1 year of less to go in his prison sentence. A Nuestro General cannot rule from outside the prison walls, although he can be transferred from one prison to another. In this case, the headquarters moves with him. Clearly, the constitution leaves it open that *more than one* Familia can be developed, although there is only one known of at present.

2. The Captains. Captains have the responsibility to lead the regiments under their control. They are solely answerable to the Nuestro General, and in "war" no one can question orders set forth by them, although there is recourse in "peace" in appeal to the Nuestro General. If ever the Nuestro General is killed in war, the captains will be automatically stripped of all rank. Captains have the power to appoint their lieutenants.

3. The Lieutenants. Lieutenants are the representatives of the inner core to the soldiers and are responsible for their "schooling, basic needs, and conduct." Their primary responsibilities include building up of the Familia arsenal to a minimum of two weapons per soldier and keeping an updated record of the names and prison numbers (if in prison) of known enemies of La Nuestra Familia that exist or are transferred into territories.

Lieutenants question new members as well, to determine if they have information about unknown enemies.

In comparing this organizational structure with what is known about other structures, such as the traditional Sicilian crime syndicates (Ianni, 1972), one is struck immediately with the similarities in overall hierarchical command and the demands for complete obedience of the soldiers (Carrol, 1974). There are, though, some important differences as well.

In the first place, El Nuestro General, although accorded supreme power, can be legally removed by his captains if they dare to act visibly and unanimously (a rare probability, but one, however). In the second place, El Nuestro General cannot leave the prison system without losing his power. This, of course, ensures that a primary function of the organization (protection of rural Mexican-American inmates) will not get moved aside in favor of street-world rewards. Tensions generated by this organizational arrangement are innovatively taken into account in the setup of street organizations (to be looked at in the next section of this paper).

The first of these differences suggest that the office is not held by "divine right," nor even feudal tradition. There is not the "feudal hierarchy" Cressey believes to be the case in other such organizations (Cressey, 1974), nor the traditional familial base of the Sicilian syndicate (Smith and Alba, 1979:32). This is a model based to some limited extent on power arising from the "consent" of the governed, and has elements of U.S. forms of rational-legal authority associated with it. It is possible, within the formal order, to replace El Nuestro General. There are other checks on his power as well, mainly economic. He may not obtain a sum higher than $10,000 from the organization's bank without requesting and obtaining clearance from the "security department" (made up of captains) at least 5 days before the sum is to be withdrawn. At no time can he remove more than half of the amount in the main bank at one time. These sorts of limitations, written as they are into the constitution, seem to severely constrict the "absolute power" of El Nuestra General, in comparison with his opposite number in more traditionally organized groupings. It is not clear why the model differs in this respect, but one can speculate that it has to do with: the emergence of the organization in a prison setting, where traditional kin ties of early members were not available to build upon; the relatively recent founding of the organization (late 1960s) in a highly rational-legal bureaucratic context; the "we are all brothers and should share decisions as to our fate" sentiments of coalescing ethnic groups of the 1960s; and a lurking distrust of absolute power, again more in keeping with the prevailing climate, and exacerbated by the abuses of power observed in the official prison system. Thus the La Nuestra Familia case adds weight to the suggestions of Lotz and Gillespie (1976), who have examined the utility of applying bureaucratic models to the case of organized crime.

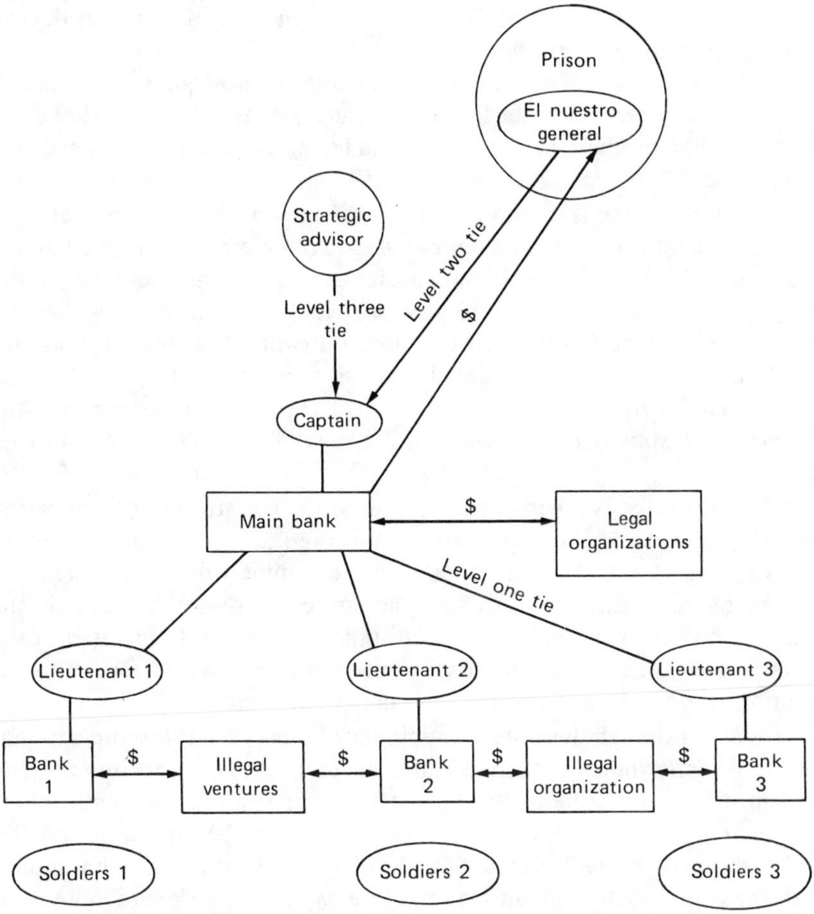

Figure 2 Organizational structure of La Nuestra Familia: street structure.

DEVELOPMENT OF THE ORGANIZATION OUTSIDE PRISON

The constitution states specifically the three steps in building of La Nuestra Familia outside of prison, as presented in Figure 2. The first step is to establish a self-supporting Familia at "regiment" level. Each such Familia will be run by a lieutenant and "shall have a bank with the basis of not less than $1,000 and shall have bought into business either in part or in whole."

The bank, then, becomes the key feature of the outside organization, as Jacobs has noted is the case in other situations involving prison-street linkages (1977). The Familia bank is responsible for all financial matters that occur within its own territory or pertain to its business ventures. "Any familiano who, due to a mission finds himself in need of a lawyer, doctor, or bail, the bank that is supporting the venture will be obligated to furnish him with these items. The Familia bank will buy into legal businesses and have no restrictions about the illegality of such places. All profits that come from a familia business go into the familia bank, and from it are distributed to its various functions," states the constitution.

The second step is to establish a "main" bank with a captain in charge. The main bank functions as a reserve in case of emergencies in the Familia banks and also buys into legitimate businesses. "All businesses being under the jurisdiction of said bank will be kept strictly legal and no illegal activities will be conducted from their premises, nor will they be used for storage of illegal items." The main bank funds all wars declared by the Nuestro General and is the source of the payroll of the Nuestro General and the Regimental Captain. In emergencies, it can confiscate money from lower level banks.

The third step is taken only when and if the Nuestro General in prison feels the outside organization is strong enough to set up and function under its own government. If so, all captains of the Familia will vote to determine who becomes the Strategic Advisor. The Strategic Advisor cannot alter the constitution, but will guide the street authority previously invested in the Nuestra General. In case of imprisonment or other incapacitation, the organization reverts to stage two and awaits developments.

Again, although there are many similarities between this setup and that of the Sicilian syndicate, there are also differences. The most immediately evident difference is the controlling of this unit from prison (until, or if, step three has been implemented). Messages have to be carried both ways, and sometimes this is difficult (though not as difficult as those unfamiliar with the prison system might expect). In any case, this *slows* communication, and the reaction time of the unit to important shifts and changes in its environment. Recognition of this, and the power that does accrue to the captain in charge because of his strategic position in the command chain, has resulted in this innovative stage three, in which (usually) the vote as to who will become Strategic Advisor only confirms what everyone knows is the case anyway, and still leaves the constitution intact as well as short-circuiting any impulses to break away from the larger organization, by coopting the very one on whom the temptation is the greatest, the captain named as Strategic Advisor. It remains to be seen how viable this organizational solution will remain, given expansion of the outside organization and the development of new territories and cash flow that is going on presently in La Nuestra Familia. So far, however, it has acted as an ingenious means of ensuring organizational support of those in the prison system and the channeling of resources to them.

CONDUCT NORMS FOR THE RANK AND FILE

As has been reported with respect to other criminal organizations (Ianni, 1972, 1976; Cressey, 1974), a strict code of honor is articulated and enforced on pain of death. This code is similar to that of any secret organization and even public organizations opposed to existing authority and seeking to overthrow it (President's Commission, 1968) and is very similar to that uncovered by Ianni (1972) in his study of the Lapollo family: primary loyalty is vested in the Familia, rather than individual needs; Familia business is privileged matter and must not be reported or discussed outside the group; each Familiano must act like a man, with honor; lives of members are sacred—the spilling of familiano blood is an act of treason; all arguments are resolved by higher authority, except at the top, where impeachment proceedings may be drawn up.

Rules governing the activities of those on the outside are rigid. Use of narcotics or other habit-forming drugs is forbidden, on pain of death. No heavy drinking is allowed. All members must have a "legal" job, either within the organization's control or outside it. No personal ventures involving money or time can be taken without authorization from the lieutenant in charge.

Upon reaching age 50, with 20 years of service, a man will be given a choice of remaining in active service or going into semi-retirement, working in a branch of the organization with no main connections to illegal activities. There is no such thing as total retirement, once one has been a member of La Nuestra Familia.

CONCLUSION

Although it is obvious a single case study cannot paint the whole picture, several things concerning organized crime as a whole can be inferred from this brief history of the rise of La Nuestra Familia, taken in the light of previous research in the area.

In the first place, the California pattern—developing in the correctional institutions along racial and ethnic lines and growing "in the streets"—seems to lend weight to the interpretation of organized crime as more "pluralistic" (and antagonistic) in organization than the official Mafia version suggests. Work by Ianni (1976) in the East on the styles of black and Puerto Rican organized crime groups as well concludes that a model of distinctly separate, racially and ethnically defined, organized groups is much more reflective of reality. A similar picture seems to be the case in California. The two Mexican-American groups each hold their own territory and are antagonistic to each other. There is evidence as well of the existence of black groups in Los Angeles and Oakland and of families of the more "traditional" Mafia. But what does not seem to be in evidence is any real cooperation among these groups to the extent that they could be seen as subunits of any larger organized criminal group. This interpretation is buttressed by the April 1978 Report of the California Organized Crime Control Commission.

In the second place, organized groups do seem to be "functional" for their members. They arise to fill a need, in this case, physical protection against other organized groups in the urban ghetto systems they found themselves "imprisoned" in.

After having been formed, such groups seem to continue to be important, in that they do offer alternative means to obtain the "coin of the realm" of whatever "realm" the group is attempting to maneuver in. With the La Nuestra Familia, the big payoff today is in the drug trade,[3] and they sem to be successful enough at it in Northern California and the Central Valley to again cast doubt on the traditional model of the monolithic mob in control of all such schemes in this country.

Although La Nuestra Familia constitution states that "as of now the standard answer for a familiano when he is asked by any county, state, or federal authority if he is or if there is any organization known to exist, the answer is no!!!," it is obvious that there is an extremely tightly knit organization in operation. What is more, each member is responsible for knowing all the information contained in the 16-page, single-spaced constitution, and abiding by its provisions—in many instances upon pain of death. That this is no idle threat was dramatically shown in 1977, when three street members attempted to desert. Orders came down from La Nuestro General at Deuel and they were all consequently found executed in the San Joaquin County area (Stockton Record, 1978–79).

What emerges from this look at La Nuestra Familia is a picture of a highly organized group begun and operated in the California penal system. This group has successfully expanded its influence into the streets and is increasingly involved in the standard activities of such organized groupings: selling illegal goods and services, racketeering, large-scale thievery, and infiltrating legitimate businesses. Although only one of several such groupings in the present-day U.S., La Nuestra Familia underscores the fact that organized crime nationwide is both pluralistic in nature and, within each grouping, very well organized.

[3]The end of the Vietnam War broke the Southeast Asian connection on the West Coast, and brown Mexican heroin began to fill the channels by the mid 1970s. This, in turn, was apt to be handled by Mexican-American groups operating across the border and in the U.S. Southwest (Parsons and Gerstein, 1977:30). Such a binational linkage is described in Lupsha and Schlegal (1979).

REFERENCES

Albani, J. L.
1971 American Mafia: Genesis of a Legend. New York: Appleton-Century-Crofts.
Anderson, Robert
1965 "From Mafia to Cosa Nostra," American Journal of Sociology 81:302-310.
Becker, Howard S.
1970 "Practitioners of Vice and Crime." Pp. 31-49 in Robert Habenstein (Ed.), Pathways to Data. Chicago: Aldine.
Bell, Daniel
1961 The End of Ideology. New York: Free Press.
State of California
1978 California Organized Crime Control Commission Report. Sacramento.
Carrol, Leo
1974 Hacks, Blacks and Cons. Lexington, Mass.: Lexington Books.
Clark, Ramsey
1971 Crime in America. New York: Pocket Books.
Conklin, John
1973 "Organized Crime and American Society." In The Crime Establishment. Englewood Cliffs, N.J.: Prentice-Hall.
Cressey, Donald
1953 Other People's Money. New York: Free Press.
1969 Theft of the Nation. New York: Harper & Row.
1974 Sociology of Deviant Behavior, Fourth Edition. New York: Holt, Rinehart and Winston.
Davidson, R. Theodore
1974 Chicano Prisoners: The Key to San Quentin. New York: Holt, Rinehart and Winston.
Douglas, Jack
1972 Research and Deviance. New York: Random House.
Galliher, John, and James Cain
1974 "Citation Support for the Mafia Myth in Criminology Textbooks." The American Sociologist 9:68–74.
Haller, Mark
1971/2 "Organized Crime in Urban Society: Chicago in the Twentieth Century." Journal of Social History 5:21-234.
Ianni, Francis
1972 A Family Business. New York: Russell Sage.
1974 Black Mafia: Ethnic Succession in Organized Crime. New York: Simon & Schuster.
1976 "New Mafia: Black, Hispanic and Italian Styles." In Francis Ianni and Elizabeth Reuss-Ianni (Eds.), The Crime Society. New York: New American Library.
Jacobs, James
1977 Stateville. Chicago: University of Chicago Press.

Lee, Barrett
1979 "Sampling a Deviant Population." Paper read at the Pacific Sociological Association Meetings, Anaheim.
Lindesmith, Alfred
1968 Addiction and Opiates. Chicago: Aldine.
Los Angeles Times
1974–1979 Various issues.
Lotz, G., and T. Gillespie
1976 "Prolegomenon To Research on Organized Crime." Pacific Sociological Association Meetings, Sacramento, California.
Lupsha, Peter, and Kip Schlegel
1979 "Drug Trafficking in the Borderlands: Its Impact on North-South Relations." Paper read to the Latin American Association, Pittsburgh, Penn.
Parsons, Talcott, and Dean Gerstein
1977 "Deviance and Social Change." In Edward Sagarin (Ed.), Deviance and Social Change. Beverly Hills: Sage, pp. 177–213.
President's Commission
1968 The Challenge of Crime in a Free Society. New York: Avon.
Smith, Dwight, and Richard Alba
1979 "Organized Crime and American Life." Society (March-April): 32–38.
Stockton Record
1974–9 Various issues.
Stoddard, E. R.
1968 "The Informal Code of Police Deviancy." Journal of Criminal Law, Criminology and Police Science, 59(2):204, 212.
Thio, A.
1968 Deviant Behavior. Boston: Houghton-Mifflin.
Tyler, Gus
1962 Organized Crime in America. Ann Arbor: University of Michigan Press.
1976 "Sociodynamics of Organized Crime." In Francis Ianni and Elizabeth Reuss-Ianni (Eds.), The Crime Society. New York: New American Library.

Reading 20

Casinos and Banking: Organized Crime in the Bahamas

Alan A. Block
Pennsylvania State University, University Park
Frank R. Scarpitti
University of Delaware, Newark

The symbiotic relationships among gambling casinos, offshore banks and professional criminals are complex. In numerous contemporary cases, professional criminals from the United States and elsewhere are known to utilize both casinos and financial institutions to launder money and to hide large amounts of illicitly acquired money. Long before recent revelations of such activities became known in the Caribbean and the U.S., developers in the Bahamas had started the process of bringing casinos and banks together to serve underworld interests. This paper traces the developments of that process and shows how American organized crime interests penetrated the Bahamas by using gambling and banking to gain a firm foothold.

Within the past few years, both the President's Commission on Organized Crime and the U.S. Senate's Permanent Subcommittee on Investigations have reported on the extensive use of offshore banks and businesses by American criminal interests to launder money and evade taxes (Permanent Subcommittee on Investigations, 1983; President's Commission on Organized Crime, 1984). A recent government report "concludes that the use of so-called 'secret' offshore facilities has become so pervasive that it challenges basic assumptions regarding the ability of federal and state authorities to enforce the laws" (Permanent Subcommittee on Investigations, 1983:1). Such enterprises are established in tax haven countries around the world, but for a number of reasons, those in the Caribbean have grown fastest in recent years and now appear to control billions of dollars of illegally gained and untaxed money. Although the Caribbean's proximity to the United States makes it especially attractive to Americans wanting to hide money, its development as an important stop in the South American drug traffic and the fact that some countries have stringent bank secrecy laws also contribute to its contemporary popularity. In fact, a few Caribbean nations have been so corrupted by illegal foreign dollars that they have virtually offered themselves as crime havens (Permanent Subcommittee on Investigations, 1983:49–95).

Among the Caribbean nations active in hosting offshore enterprises owned by Americans have been the Bahamas. Like all tax havens, the Bahamas are characterized by the essential elements of strict rules of bank secrecy and little or no taxes. Since 1965 bank secrecy has ben based on legislation which prohibits and punishes the disclosure by a bank employee of an account holder's name or financial situation (the 1965 legislation increased the severity of the crime of disclosure). The strict secrecy associated with banks also applies to the activities and ownership of corporations. In addition, there are no income, profit, capital gains, gift, inheritance, estate or withholding taxes in the Bahamas. Although the nation does tax imports and some real property, this has little effect on those who own or use its many banks and corporations. Hence, for a small initial cost and annual fee, one may own a bank or company that can receive and disburse large sums of money in complete secrecy and without the threat of taxation. These advantages, or course, are available to bank depositors as well.

Even though offshore tax havens may provide legitimate investment opportunities for American citizens wishing to avoid taxes, a practice recognized as lawful by U.S. courts, it is the evasion of taxes by using tax haven services that now concerns law enforcement authorities. "Tax evasion . . . involves acts intended to misrepresent or to conceal facts in an effort to escape lawful tax liability" (Workman, 1982:667). Tax havens may be used to hide income or to misrepresent the nature of transactions in order to put the taxpayer in a more favorable tax position. A corollary problem concerns the "laundering" of illegal money gained from strictly criminal activity. This "is the process by which one conceals the existence, illegal source, or illegal application of income, and then disguises that income to make it appear legitimate" (President's Commission on Organized Crime, 1984:1). Offshore tax havens, with their strict secrecy laws, dependence on foreign deposits, and disregard for the sources of overseas cash, provide ideal vehicles for assorted racketeers, drug dealers and financial manipulators to hide "dirty" money while it is being cleaned for further use. For both the tax evader and money launderer, the offshore haven guarantees that any paper trial will be blocked.

The popularity of the Bahamas as an offshore tax haven may be seen in the amount of corporate and bank activity which it hosts. This small island nation of just over 200,000 inhabitants have some 15,000 active companies and 330 chartered banks, or one bank for every 600 residents (Lernoux, 1984:85). The vast majority of these banks are shell of "brass plate" operations consisting of little more than a shared office and an address (Lernoux, 1984:85). Nevertheless, Bahamian banks held over $95 billion of foreign assets in 1978 (Workman, 1982:680) and a 1979 Ford Foundation study estimated that the flow of U.S. criminal and tax evasion money into the Bahamas was $20 billion per year (Blum and Kaplan, 1979).

Even though the accuracy of these figures may be questioned, due largely to the Bahamian government's and banking industry's reluctance to provide reliable data, it seems obvious that the American contribution to these questionable assets constitutes a considerable resource for the Bahamas and a substantial loss in taxes for the United States.

The Bahamas evolved into an offshore haven for tax evaders and money launderers in a very short period of time. The process included receptive public officials, international entrepreneurs and American racketeers entering into formal and informal relationships designed to serve their respective financial positions. A partial examination of the history of the Bahamas reveals the extent of the collusion among political, business and criminal interests to serve their illicit purposes.

The history also demonstrates the important relationships between offshore banks and gambling casinos. In fact, key Bahamian offshore banks were formed by or for individuals deeply involved in Nevada casinos and who subsequently played big roles in developing the first large-scale, modern casinos in the Bahamas. Most likely, the relationship between the casinos and banks emerged in order to hide the casinos' "skim," that portion of casino profits unreported to taxing authorities. The historical material which follows discussed those individuals whose mutual interests embraced both casino gambling and haven banking and who were instrumental in providing organized criminal elements with both an economic bonanza and sanctuary.

THE MAKING OF FREEPORT

The process started on Grand Bahama Island located about 60 miles from the Florida coast. The prime mover on Grand Bahama was an American named Wallace Groves who first came to the Bahamas in the 1930's. Groves' background had been in investment trusts administered through a firm called Equity Corporation which he sold for $750,000. Following this, he became affiliated with a company known as the General Investment Corporation. After these deals were in place, Groves sailed to the Bahamas, started two Bahamian companies (Nassau Securities Ltd. and North American Ltd.), and purchased an island, Little Whale Cay, about 35 miles from Nassau, the capitol of the country. During this first, eventful, trip, Groves met Stafford Sands, a member of the local political elite known as the Bay Street Boys. This elite was composed of certain merchants and attorneys who met on a regular basis after work in a club located on Bay and Charlotte Streets in Nassau. They were invariably white and, by the standards of the Bahamas, wealthy and influential. The Bay Street Boys controlled Bahamian development, both the licit and illicit, until 1967 when the first black Prime Minister was elected (United Kingdom, 1971).

Unfortunately for Groves, in the late fall of 1938 he was indicted on numerous counts of mail fraud and looting the General Investment Corporation of almost one million dollars. Eventually, Groves was convicted and sentenced to two years in prison. He was released in 1944 and returned to the Bahamas. During Groves' time of troubles, his associate, Stafford Sands, was busy arranging a way for casinos to operate legally. Sands successfully sponsored a bill in the Assembly which allowed casinos under certain circumstances. By securing a Certificate of Exemption from the local government, a gambling casino could operate with what amounted to a government license. The bill passed in 1939 and certificates of exemption were granted to two small casinos which had been operating illegally for years.[1]

It was in the 1950s that Groves, Sands, and others to be discussed shortly put their talents together on Grand Bahama Island. They created a new city, Freeport, which soon had a casino and several significant "haven" banks. Stafford Sands, who had become Chairman of the Bahamas Development Board (equivalent to Minister of Tourism) in the 1950's, crafted legislation "to establish a port and an industrial complex" on Grand Bahama Island (United Kingdom, 1971:6). The Hawksbill Creek Act, as the legislation was entitled, was signed on August 4, 1955. The deal called for Groves to organize a company, to be called the Grand Bahama Port Authority Limited, which would undertake to dredge and construct a deep water harbour and turning basin at Hawksbill Creek as a preliminary and an aid for factories and other industrial undertakings to be set up there" (United Kingdom, 1971:6). In return, the government made available thousands of acres of Crown Land to the Port Authority for one pound per acre (equivalent then to around $2.80 an acre). In fact, by 1960 Groves' company had acquired a total of 138,296 acres which was officially "designated as a town (Freeport) in Grand Bahama" (United Kingdom, 1971:6).

The terms of the initial Hawksbill Creek Act allowed "that the whole of Freeport was to be the property of the Port Authority in whom was vested the supreme right to its administration and control" (United Kingdom, 1971:6). An analysis of the legislation by a Royal Commission in 1971 commented on this extraordinary transfer or authority noting that the company had "exclusive responsibility" for traditional governmental services

[1]The two illegal casinos included one opened by American Frank Reid for private membership in 1920. By 1923, Reid's club was joined by another called the Bahamian Club, run by a gambler known as Honest John Kelly. Over the course of the Prohibition Era, the Bahamian Club was managed first by Kelly, then Herbert McGuire, and then purchased by Willard McKenzie and Frank Dineen. Like all Bahamian tourist-supported establishments, it was only open during the three winter months when the wealthy arrived to escape the seasonal rigors. At least one another casino was opened during Prohibition. On a privately owned island close by the Bahamian fishing resort of Bimini, New Yorker Louis Wasey opened a private membership casino called the Cat Cay Club. Authors' interviews conducted in the Bahamas, 1984.

such as education, health, communications, energy "and all other public utilities and services and the performance of all aviation activities." The Commission also wrote that no one was allowed to interfere with the Port Authority's decisions, especially in awarding licenses or otherwise controlling firms doing business in Freeport.

The major shareholders of The Grand Bahama Port Authority in 1959 included Wallace Groves and his wife, Georgette, who individually held a small amount of shares but whose company, Abaco Lumber, held almost one million. Other significant owners were Variant Industries which represented the interests of Charles W. Hayward, an English entrepreneur, and held just over one-half million shares; Charles Allen, whose family's financial interests in New York and Hollywood (especially motion picture companies) were very extensive and who held over a quarter million shares; Arthur Rubloff, a Chicago real estate agent, who had over 70,000 shares; and Charles C. Goldsmith, who owned about 100,000 shares and listed his affiliation in 1959 as the New York Cosmos Bank. Wallace Groves was the company's Director and Charles Hayward and his son, Jack, were other important officers (Grand Bahama Port Authority, 1959). Although Allen and Goldsmith appeared to play no managerial role in the company, they "were well aware that the major partner in the enterprise . . . was . . . a convicted stock manipulator who had served time in federal prison for mail fraud and conspiracy" (McClintick, 1982:89).

Even with his new financiers, Groves' project was barely limping along in 1960. Because the industrial development of Freeport was extremely far off, perhaps far-fetched, Groves and others decided that Freeport could best be developed around tourism. Hence, an amendment to the original Hawksbill Creek Act was enacted which, among other things, allowed the Port Authority to build a "first-class deluxe resort hotel" (United Kingdom, 1971:7). By the time the hotel was completed in 1963, it had the added attraction of a casino, and the Bahamas had become the new Caribbean headquarters of Meyer Lansky's underworld gambling enterprise.

Lansky had operated in the Caribbean for quite some time, of course, running casinos in Cuba with the full cooperation of that country's government. With the overthrow of Battista, however, American organized crime figures and their gambling operations were no longer welcomed and were soon thrown out of the country by Fidel Castro. Even before that actually happened, Lansky was looking around for another site in the Caribbean, a place where tourists from the United States would come for the sun and the gambling, where local officials would be cooperative, and where he could establish a worldwide gambling empire (Messick, 1971:225).

According to Lansky biographer, Hank Messick, the gambling czar moved quickly once he decided to seek additional fortunes in the Bahamas. Early in 1960 he dispatched an associate, Louis Chesler, to the islands to meet with Groves and Sands, presumably to discuss plans by which the Port Authority would be salvaged and gambling established in Freeport (Messick, 1971:228). In order to accomplish the first part of the plan, the Port Authority formed a company called Grand Bahama Development Corporation (known as DEVCO). DEVCO immediately placed Chesler on its Board of Directors, giving him an official position in the Bahamas from which he could supervise the development of casino gambling. Another Lansky associate, Max Orovitz, was also placed on the DEVCO board (Grand Bahama Development Corporation, 1964). But it was Chesler who would protect Lansky's interests and serve as a dominant force in the early development of Bahamian gambling.

Chesler's earliest known contacts with organized crime began in 1942 when he had as partners in several businesses John Pullman and Pullman's brother-in-law, A. C. Cowan (McClintick, 1982:87–93). Pullman, an important associate of Meyer Lansky for a number of decades, had served a prison term for bootlegging in the early 1930's. By the mid-1950s, Pullman had moved to Canada and been granted Canadian citizenship (Charbonneau, 1976). Chesler, also Canadian, had a series of dealings with Lansky and Lansky's associates prior to the formation of DEVCO which are revealing. He hired, for instance, a key Lansky operative, Mike McLaney, as the manager of a Miami Beach dinner club which Chesler owned.

In 1958, Chesler's association with Lansky became more visible through the financial machinations of Maxwell Golhar, another of his partners. Golhar became Chairman of the Board of an enterprise called New Mylamaque Explorations Ltd. A well-known Lansky associate, Sam Garfield, purchased 100,000 shares of New Mylamaque which he divided in the following manner: Edward Levinson, 50,000 shares; Moe Dalitz, former Cleveland racketeer, 25,000; and Allard Roen, 25,000. Roen's shares were then divided further with Ben Siegelbaum receiving 15,000 and Meyer Lansky 10,000. Finally, 50,000 more shares of New Mylamaque were parcelled out, with 10,000 going to Dalitz, 15,000 to Siegelbaum, and 25,000 to Lansky. This same group of investors also provided capital for Miami's new international airport hotel in 1958. Other investors in the hotel (brought in by Lansky and Chesler) were Bryant B. Burton, connected to the Sands and Freemont Hotels in Las Vegas, and Jack Cooper, who owned a highly successful dog track in Miami (New York State Senate, n. d. a.).

With the formation of DEVCO there was only one hurdle left to transform Freeport into a center for casino gambling run by organized crime. That hurdle was acquiring the necessary Certificate of Exemption. The second Certificate ever granted in the Bahamas was offered on March 27, 1963, to a new company called Bahamas Amusement Ltd., which had been formed only the previous week. The Certificate allowed Bahamas Amusement to operate a casino at the Lucayan Beach Hotel in Freeport. In order to secure the Certificate a considerable amount of money had been passed to key members of the government by DEVCO. Stafford Sands acted as the financial intermediary between DEVCO and Sands' political cronies who were hired as "consultants" and paid very handsome fees (United Kingdom, 1967). The original directors of Bahamas Amusement included Chesler, Georgette Groves, and a member of the Hayward family.

Less than a week after the Certificate was granted, there were meetings attended by Meyer Lansky and his brother, Jake, Lou Chesler, Max Orovitz, and others to discuss issues concerning both the hotel and the casino, called the Monte Carlo. A number of important Lansky racketeers were hired to work in the casino, including Dino Cellini, George Saldo, Charles Brudner, Max Courtney, and Frank Ritter. Other subjects discussed at this time included the purchase of casino equipment from Las Vegas and probably the Beverly Hills Club in Newport, Kentucky, and the establishing of a casino training school in London, England (United Kingdom, 1967; Messick, 1971; Block and Klausner, 1985–86). About ten months after the Certificate was granted, the hotel and casino formally opened with the Lansky men firmly entrenched in casino management as well as overseers of all credit arrangements.

BAHAMIAN BANKS

Let us now turn to those banks formed by or for individuals with multimillion dollar investments in Nevada casinos and deeply involved in the Freeport development. John Pullman, mentioned above as a Chesler associate since 1942 and, in effect, an important member of Meyer Lansky's organized crime syndicate, was responsible for putting the banks and casinos together. Pullman, recently identified as a "Canadian organized crime figure" (Pennsylvania Crime Commission, 1980:195), was instrumental in forming two banks (with subsequent numerous off-shoots) created to handle the skim from the Monte Carlo and most likely the Sands and Frontier casinos in Nevada (New York State Senate, n. d. a.).

The bank connected to the Monte Carlo was the International Credit Bank (ICB) which was formed by John Pullman in partnership with a Dr. Tibor Rosenbaum (New York Senate, n. d. c.). The bank was located in Geneva, Switzerland, with branches in the Bahamas. The major shareholder was a trust (international Credit Trust) resident in Vaduz, Liechtenstein. At least part of the Monte Carol skim undoubtedly travelled from the casino to the Bahamian branch of Pullman's ICB, then to Switzerland, and ultimately to the obscurity of Liechtenstein. Other more direct but clumsy avenues for the skim no doubt existed. For instance, a Royal Commission reported that "large quantities of cash up to $60,000, and in one case

$120,000, were being despatched by the Amusements Company to the Marine Midland Grace Trust Co., of New York. They were being parcelled up in Pauli Girl beer cartons" (United Kingdom, 1967:19).

Although formed as a conduit for unreported casino profits, the ICB quickly developed additional interests. One of the early major clients for ICB Geneva, for example, was Investor Overseas Services, the infamous mutual fund operation run by Bernard Cornfeld and later looted by Robert Vesco. The relationships between the fund and the bank became exceptionally close when ICB people were used to smuggle money out of various countries into Switzerland on behalf of mutual fund clients. One of the principal ICB money couriers, Sylvain Ferdman, was identified as an organized crime money mover by Life magazine in 1967. Ferdman performed the same function for another Bahamian bank called Atlas Bank. Actually, Ferdman and Dr. Rosenbaum were two of the directors of Atlas. A close scrutiny of both Atlas and ICB indicates they were virtually identical in ownership, management and function. Furthermore, there is some evidence to suggest that ICB and Atlas, which both had several branches or permutations, were also linked to another bank located in Beirut, Lebanon, which, in turn, appeared to own a major Lebanese casino (Fortune, 1966:93).

The ICB and Atlas banks are two primary examples of the links between organized crime gamblers and the offshore banking industry put together in the Bahamas. Another major example involving much the same cast was the Bank of World Commerce, formed on September 21, 1961, most likely to launder the skim from Nevada casinos (New York State Senate, n. d. c.; Wall Street Journal, 1976). John Pullman was the president and director, while the former Lieutenant Governor of Nevada, Clifford A. Jones, was one of the larger shareholders, holding about 8% of the total. The other directors included Alvin I. Malnik and Philip J. Matthews who owned about 32 per cent of the shares.

Malnik was believed to have been one of Meyer Lansky's closest associates and, when Lansky died in 1982, some speculated that Malnik may have inherited much of Lansky's action (New York State Senate, n. d. a.). In 1980, the Pennsylvania Crime Commission detailed a series of shady transactions involving Caesars World, Inc., which owned casinos in Las Vegas and Atlantic City, and "Alvin I. Malnik and Samuel Cohen, who have ties to Meyer Lansky, a major financial advisor to organized criminals" (Pennsylvania Crime Commission, 1980:252). The Crime Commission also stated that "Vincent Teresa, a former Cosa Nostra capo, said that, in the underworld, dealing with Malnik is the same as dealing with Lansky and that the purpose of Malnik's association with Lansky is to launder illegal cash by investing it in real estate" (Pennsylvania Crime Commission, 1980:252). Other reports cited by the Crime Commission had Malnik with Lansky and members of the Carlo Gambino crime syndicate discussing "the construction and/or ownership of two or three casinos in Florida if a gambling referendum passed. Some $20 million to $25 million was to be invested in the casinos and profits were to be skimmed off the top and channeled back to the investors" (Pennsylvania Crime Commission, 1980:255).

The relationships among Malnik, Pullman, and Matthews (the largest single shareholder in the bank) preceded the formation of the Bank of World Commerce (New York State Senate, n. d. c.). Several years earlier, Malnik and Matthews had been involved with two closely connected firms, including one called Allied Empire, Inc. When the Bank of World Commerce started, Allied Empire showed up as a shareholder and then as the recipient of a large loan from the new bank. Furthermore, Malnik, Matthews and a former racketeer associate of Louis Buchalter (executed by the State of New York in 1944 for murder) had worked together long before the founding of the Bank of World Commerce to purchase a small, "brass plate," Bahamian bank from one of Lou Chesler's associates.

Chesler, Pullman, Lansky, Malnik, Matthews, and other gamblers and racketeers from New York, Miami, Newport, Kentucky, Montreal, Toronto, Las Vegas, and Los Angeles formed both gambling casinos and offshore Bahamian banks, the latter to solve the problem of "washing" the money generated by the former. Stock manipulators like Wallace Groves, allied with well-known financiers from the United States and the United Kingdom, organized crime figures, and, of course, important local politicians, turned Grand Bahama Island into an experimental station for money gathering and laundering. To help the scheme along, the Bahamian government actually relinquished part of its sovereign territory to this mixed group.

SOME CONSEQUENCES

The impact the developers had on the original inhabitants of Grand Bahama Island was hardly beneficial. Prior to the Bahamian government's enacting the Hawksbill Creek Agreement, the island was described by a Royal Commission as nothing more than "a pine barren with less than 5,000 inhabitants" (United Kingdom, 1971:5). After the Agreement and the building of Freeport, most of the island remained a pine barren with the exception of the area around Freeport which the Royal Commission found to be "predominantly non-Bahamian" (United Kingdom, 1971:31). Bahamians made up only 34 per cent of New Providence Island where the capitol, Nassau, is situated. And although some held DEVCO's many construction projects to be a benefactor for Bahamian labor, in fact DEVCO turned to Haiti for a supply of cheap labor whenever it could. Through 1958, the percent of Haitians in Freeport was over four times that of New Providence

Island (United Kingdom, 1971: 31). The Port Authority, of course, contributed to the pattern of exploitation engaged in by its creation, DEVCO. About 30% of the licenses granted by the Port Authority to people wishing to do business in its part of Grand Bahama went to non-Bahamians (United Kingdom, 1971:33).

The combination of Certificates of Exemption, bank secrecy laws, and the Hawksbill Creek Agreement set more than Freeport into motion. It stamped the Bahamas as a center for organized crime activities. Indeed, as we noted earlier, the Bahamas has been recognized as one of the principal transshipment points for drug traffickers moving cocaine and marijuana from South America to the U.S. and Canada (Royal Canadian Mounted Police, 1983:42–46). In one recent narcotics case, the defendants were charged with buying and using "the Darby Islands, a group of five islands in the Bahamas, as a trans-shipment point," and using Bahamian companies including banks and a major Bahamian Trust Company to launder their money (U.S. District Court, 1981). In another case, an officer of the Columbus Trust company, Nassau, has been charged with using the trust company, a Bahamian corporation named Dundee Securities, Barclays Bank International (The Bahamas), and the Southeast First National Bank of Miami in a complicated scheme to wash millions of dollars for a drug syndicate (U.S. District Court, 1980).

The symbiotic relationships among casinos, offshore banks and professional criminals are complex, to say the least. In numerous contemporary cases, professional criminals utilize both casinos and banks to launder money. An IRS Special Agent reporting on a major drug and tax case gave an example of this as he detailed how a financial services corporation served drug racketeers. The "laundering" method included (1) exchanging the smugglers' initial small denomination cash (mostly tens and twenties) for $100 bills in a Las Vegas casino; (2) moving the new "casino" money from the U.S. to offshore banks and depositing it in secret accounts; (3) returning the money to the U.S. "disguised as offshore loans"; and (4) investing the phony loans in businesses through blind trusts and fictitious corporate fronts (U.S. District Court, n. d.).

Even without the use of offshore banks, casinos themselves perform many clandestine banking services for professional criminals. Drug Enforcement Administrator, Gary D. Liming, testified that casinos "exchange small bills for large bills, travellers' checks or money orders; wire transfer money overseas to associate casinos: provide safety deposit boxes; and make loans . . . without being required to report the transactions to the Department of the Treasury" (Judiciary Committee, 1984:8–9). Casinos, therefore, are acting like offshore banks providing anonymity for depositors (players) and various "laundering" options. Consequently, there are enforcement agents who are convinced that certain casinos have been built solely to launder the proceeds of drug transactions.[2]

However, long before the full potential of casinos working either alone or with offshore banks and other shady financial institutions was realized by drug traffickers, developers in the Bahamas had started the process of bringing casinos and banks together. Within less than a decade, the groundwork for organized crime's penetration of the Bahamas was established. Networks of banks, trust companies, holding companies, casinos, hotels, marinas, mutual funds, and so on representing illicit interests all across the U.S. and many other countries were, and most importantly remain, paramount.

REFERENCES

Block, Alan A. and Patricia Klausner

1985–86 "Masters of Paradise Island, part 1: Organized crime, neo-colonialism and the Bahamas." Dialectical Anthropology. Winter.

Blum, Richard and John Kaplan

1979 "Offshore banking: Issues with respect to criminal use." Report submitted to the Ford Foundation.

Charbonneau, Jean-Pierre

1976 The Canadian Connection. Montreal: Optimum.

Fortune

1966 "Business around the globe." 77:93–99.

Grand Bahama Development Corporation

1964 Letter to the Registrar in the Bahama Registry.

Grand Bahama Port Authority

1959 "Annual report." Bahamas Registry.

Judiciary Committee

1984 U.S. House of Representatives. "Statement of Gary D. Liming on casino money laundering." Washington, D.C.: Government Printing Office.

Lernoux, Penny

1984 In Banks We Trust. New York: Anchor/Doubleday.

McClintick, David

1982 Indecent Exposure: A True Story of Hollywood and Wall Street. New York: Dell.

Messick, Hank

1971 Lansky. New York: Putnam.

New York State Senate

n.d. a Select Committee on Crime. Bahamian File: Lansky Folder.

n.d. b Select Committee on Crime. Bahamian File: ICB Folder.

n.d. c Select Committee on Crime. Bahamian File: Bank of World Commerce Folder.

[2]Authors' interview with Special Agent, Department of Labor, June, 1985.

Pennsylvania Crime Commission
1980 A Decade of Organized Crime: 1980 Report. Commonwealth of Pennsylvania.
Permanent Subcommittee on Investigation
1983 Committee on Government Affairs, U.S. Senate. Crime and Secrecy: The Use of Offshore Banks and Companies. Washington, D.C.: Government Printing Office.
President's Commission on Organized Crime
1984 The Cash Connection: Organized Crime, Financial Institutions, and Money Laundering. Interim Report to the President and the Attorney General.
Royal Canadian Mounted Police
1983 National Drug Intelligence Estimate, 1982. Ottawa: Minister of Supply and Services.
U.S. District Court
1980 Western District of Pennsylavnia. Indictment, U.S. versus Thomas E. Long, et al.
1981 Northern District of Georgia, Indictment, U.S. versus Tilton Lamar Chester, Jr., et al.
n.d. Southern District of Mississippi, Affidavit for Search Warrant, U.S. versus Offices and Premises of Red Carpet Inns International, Biloxi, Mississippi.
United Kingdom
1967 Commission of Inquiry into the Operation of the Business of Casinos in Freeport and in Nassau Guardian. Report published in the Nassau Guardian.
1971 Royal Commission Appointed on the Recommendation of the Bahamas Government to Review the Hawksbill Creek Agreement. Report, Volume 1. Her Majesty's Stationary Office.
Wall Street Journal
1976 "Empire builder." December 15.
Workman, Douglas J.
1982 "The use of offshore tax havens for the purpose of criminally evading income taxes." The Journal of Criminal Law and Criminology. 73:675–706.

Chapter Seven

Deviant People: Handling Themselves

EDITORIAL COMMENTARY

Social stigma is an uncomfortable accessory to one's identity.[1] Regardless of how it is acquired, the redefinition that it implies, and the attendant social import, seldom portends well for the bearer. Stigma may derive from a

[1]Various authors of the selections in this volume, and particularly in this chapter, may seem to employ the terms deviance and stigma in an almost interchangeable fashion. We are inclined to use the term stigma to refer to an assigned negative indicator or social mark that is discrediting and tends to contaminate or spoil the total identity or image of the individual. It results from a deviation from the norm whether the norm refer to physical, mental, or behavioral standards. Thus, stigma results from deviation, and members of society react to the stigma. Some authors almost seem to imply that stigma, and especially that based on physical abnormality results in being labeled deviant. If the deformed child is socially stigmatized it is *because* he departs from the norm of what children are supposed to be, anatomically speaking. The deviation causes the disvalued labeling (including the stigma) and the social reaction is to the label (including the stigma). The distinction is perhaps of little consequence (as in the question of how many angels can dance on the head of a pin) but operationally, the usage indicated is preferred.

variety of sources. The "untouchable" in the Hindu society inherits a low caste, stigmatized label from forebearers. In the past the victim of leprosy and, more recently, the AIDS sufferer derived their stigmatized identity from a virus. The club foot or the hunchback came with birth, and the paraplegic or the badly scarred person may have acquired their disfigurement through war or accident. Dark skin, Oriental features, short stature, or even obesity are matters of genes or hormones.

Vagrancies from behavioral exemplars and norms, like deviation from standards of physique, physiological normality, or cultural definitions of beauty and perfection, may also result in stigma. The recluse, the eccentric, the "Hippie," the town drunk, the dedicated cultist, the extreme political radical, the sexual libertine, or the virulently vocal racist all wear their stigma for deviancy by reputation. Some stigmas are formalized but essentially gratuitous, such as the mandatory yellow Star of David for Jews in Nazi Germany. Other formalized stigmas are meted out by the community or society in way of recompense or retribution such as the case of Hester Prynne and her Scarlet Letter, the convict's striped clothing, or the errant military veteran's dishonorable discharge. Some reputational stigmas resulting from deviancy manifest themselves in public labels such as "slut," "whore monger," or "queer." Some stigmas are self-inflicted such as that resulting from extensive tattooing on the body, or a Mohawk haircut with the remaining hair dyed green or purple, as is fashionable in Punk Rock circles. Some stigmas are transitory, the dunce cap for poor student performance, for example, while other stigmas are permanent such as execution for a crime. Stigmas and their consequences change and even disappear over time as the severity of particular types of deviancy is altered in the public mind as witness the fact that at one time divorce was stigmatized as a severely disvalued deviation from traditional marital norms. The behavioral vagrant, be he or she addict, alcoholic, homosexual, suicide attempter, or mentally ill, as well the miscreant, faces the prospect of stigma and its social consequences as a result of the deviant behavior.

The social import of deviancy and the subsequent stigma can be as varied as the array of socially disvalued characteristics and behavior, and the types of stigma. The deviant identity may result in ridicule or recrimination, ostracism or exile, incarceration or hospitalization, discrimination or abuse, punishment or pernicious labeling, or exclusion or relegation to a lower status, to name but a few outcomes. Whatever the outcome, the recipient of the social response must contend with the attributed identity and must attempt to deflect or redefine the stigma and the circumstances from which it arises, ameliorate or mitigate the consequences, and/or manage or manipulate the outcome. This chapter addresses deviancy, stigma, the stigmatized deviants, and the strategies they employ in an attempt to moderate the impact of their deviant identity.

The initial reading in this chapter, "Understanding Stigma: Dimensions of Deviance and Coping," examines the way in which stigma is viewed as a form of deviance that strains the relationship between stigmatized people and normals. Stigma is discrediting and disruptive to interaction because "it calls into questions the ability or willingness of the bearer to satisfy the criteria for legitimacy and thereby sustain the encounter." Deviants are judged as illegitimate for participation in interaction with normals. The authors suggest that trustworthiness is necessary for legitimacy, and deviants lacking the prerequisites for trust, including such criteria as competence, predictability, consistency, and benignancy, do not qualify for such trust. They mention three types of stigmata including physical stigmata (abnormality or defect), mental stigmata (impaired cognitive functioning), and moral stigmata (violations of social norms), and postulate that stigmata may impact on interactions in various ways and to different degrees depending on several characterizing dimensions of the stigma which they discuss in detail. The stigmatized must rely on a variety of strategies to cope with the disrupted interaction and the resulting social situation and, this process may involve a degree of negotiation in regard to the outcome of the deviant's situated identity.

Coping with the label and stigma of deviance may involve a wide array of ploys, mechanisms, and processes. Light-skinned Negroes at one time (and perhaps still do) managed to avoid the social consequences of being black by "passing" (i.e., giving the impression that they were white). Similarly, transvestites, when dressed and wearing the makeup of the opposite sex, may give the appearance of being a member of the opposite gender, and are, thus, also "passing." Male transvestites, when "dressed," are in effect guilty of deviant behavior and derive satisfaction from their sexual transgression, but because they are accepted as females, they manage to avoid the stigma of deviancy.[2] "Passing," whether of the racial or gender variety, is more than simply a cosmetic alteration, but rather may also represent an identity transformation in a more complete sense. In this regard, Edward Sagarin (1975:289) has observed that:

> Although the word "dressed" [referring to a male transvestite wearing female attire] is derived from the fact that one puts on certain apparel, it could be

[2]Sagarin (1975:289) has argued that "for it is clear that there is nothing deviant about being male or being female, or about appearing in male or in female attire. The socially disapproved act resides only in the pretense." While it is true that it is the pretense and deception that is the crux of the offense, I would contend that even the act of "cross dressing" alone would represent deviancy inasmuch as it departs from the cultural norms of appropriate clothing for each gender, and because there is also the implicit, if not explicit, suggestion that such behavior affords the individual some modicum of vicarious carnal, but "unnatural" and therefore, deviant, satisfaction.

extended to the idea of wearing a mask or a costume, even in a figurative sense, and would be useful to indicate situations in which a performer can pick up the mask and then lay it aside.

In effect the deviant becomes a "different person" not only to forestall the social consequences of stigma, but also to bolster his or her own self image. This type of deceptive role playing used as a means of concealing deviancy and avoiding the effects of stigma may be relatively long-term such as in the case of the homosexual who "stays in the closet," as it were, even to the extent of marrying and engaging in an ostensibly heterosexual lifestyle, or it may be cyclical or part of a double-reference group routine. In regard to this latter style of stigma management, Kando (1972) has reported on the pattern of moving back and forth between a previous hometown subculture of family and friends and a newer urban subculture centering around "gay bars, strip joints, and prostitution," engaged in by transsexuals. Jackman, O'Toole, and Geis (1963) have described a similar style of stigma and self-image management in their studies of prostitutes. Some prostitutes, they contend, apparently dichotomize their existence and play two roles, a depersonalized prostitute role with which they tend to disassociate, and a family role with which they could more comfortably identify. This "dual world" mechanism provided a means of coping with stigma and its discomforts. Such alternate role playing can assume strange and wondrous dimensions. Bryant (1972:203), for example, mentions a carnival stripper who was the featured "ecdysiasts" in the girlie show during the carnival season, but was an officer in the P.T.A. in the local school during the winter season. Presumably, the townspeople did not know of this bifurcated identity.

One of the more effective tools for coping and deflecting the social response to deviance is costuming or masking, for our reaction to people is more often based on our assessment of their appearance than their behavior. Wily courtroom attorneys have long known that even if their client is accused of some repugnant offense not infrequently committed by persons of lower socioeconomic status, they can often persuade the jury of their client's innocence by the simple expedient of dressing their client in a fashion more reflective of upper class status. Similarly, many individuals have discovered that they can sometimes avoid arrest if they are appropriately dressed. A law enforcement officer may be less inclined, for example, to arrest a well-dressed "gentleman" on suspicion of driving while intoxicated than he would a "redneck" worker wearing dirty jeans and a T-shirt. Just as prostitutes may sometimes dress in a provocative fashion (i.e., mini-skirt, tight sweater or low-cut blouse, and exaggerated make-up) in order to attract attention and customers, they may also have occasion to dress in a more conventional manner in order not to attract attention and arrest.

White collar offenders and other "respectable" criminals may accomplish to avoid detection, arrest, indictment, or conviction by virtue of their appearance (including dress) and demeanor as much as any other factor.

Costuming or masking can be used in a variety of ways. The short male may resort to shoes with heels higher than normal, or concealed "lifts" inside the shoes, "elevator shoes," as it were, to avoid the stigma of being below average height in a world of tall men. The bald individual may hide his denuded pate beneath a toupee, and Sagarin (1975:290) spoke of the flat-chested female, aware that the American norm of sexual attractiveness includes ample breast measurements, who may wear "falsies" to give the appearance of being larger breasted. She might even seek to have her natural breasts "augmented" in size through plastic surgery. In either case, she seeks to deceive and presents a counterfeit and, thus, deviant appearance. Goffman (1969:19–21) spoke of using one form of deviance to mask another and labeled such an action as a "counter-uncovering move" in distinction to the initial act of masking.

In the next article in this chapter, "Stigmata and Negotiated Outcomes: Management of Appearance by Persons with Physical Disabilities," the authors examine the use of clothing by disabled students as a means of managing their appearance and who, thus, in effect "negotiate the outcome" of social reaction to their stigmatized deviance. Just as perceptions of persons are affected by physical deformities, so too are they affected by clothing cues. Clothing cues, like other misleading symbols, tend to draw attention away from the "stigma symbols" and are "disidentifiers" according to Goffman (1963:122). The students felt that appearance was important in people's responses to one another, and disability could create "attitudinal barriers." They also felt that clothing, as well as other appearance cues such as smiles, hairstyles, and overall neatness can help ameliorate the stigmatizing effects of a physical disability.

Clothing was a means of facilitating normative identification by looking like other people. Accordingly, clothing was employed to achieve the appearance of normalcy using a variety of strategies such as concealing the disability, deflecting attention away from the stigma of the disability, and displaying a social uniqueness to name some. The disabled students were thereby able to have an active part in their own labeling by managing certain aspects of their appearance through the choice of wearing apparel. Their costuming or masking efforts serve to negotiate a more positive public image and aid in neutralizing the social stigma of their disability. It would appear that in some instances, a similar outcome can be negotiated by wearing no clothing. The July 1987 issue of *Playboy* carried a pictorial essay on a young lady who was partially paralyzed as a result of an automobile accident. Even though confined to a wheelchair, this individual sought to demonstrate that being handicapped does not deprive one of sexuality and appeared in a series of seminude photos to prove her point.

The final reading in this chapter, Michael R. Nusbaumer's "Responses to Labeling Attempts: Deviant Drinkers' Pathways of Label Manipulation," posits the notion that persons who are labeled as deviants are active participants in the process of modifying the label. The label recipients seek to reduce stigma and to limit "conforming opportunities inherent in label application." Again, this is an effort at negotiation in terms of the outcome of labeling.

Label manipulation is a widespread process in deviant behavior. Even among school children, the class "cut-up," or mischievous boy, may well be able to manipulate the label to his advantage as a dare-devil and rebel and, thus, hero to his classmates. Many informal leaders among youngsters, even if only with a limited following, may have begun their charismatic career by being labeled as a "bad boy." The high school girl who gets a "reputation" and is labeled accordingly may well use her newly acquired label as "fast" to her advantage inasmuch as it may tend to increase her popularity with boys and, thus, increase her dates. Sometimes the new girl in school (having just moved to town) may well even promote such a label in order to expedite her fame and popularity. Many deviants have been able to turn a label to their advantage and capitalize on it. Many of the bureaucratic miscreants involved in the Watergate scandal and subsequently convicted of a variety of offenses and sent to prison, later became best-selling authors and high paid circuit speakers. One even became something of a folk hero on some college campuses. Many deviants have been able to turn "bad press" into "good press" and explain their behavior in a more favorable light. Carl Chessman, the convicted rapist who ultimately died in the San Quintin gas chamber, spent years fighting and delaying his execution, writing several self-flattering, best-selling books in the meanwhile, and becoming a national celebrity in the process. The robber into Robin Hood metamorphosis is a not uncommon process with many deviant offenders.

Of course, at the most elemental level of label manipulation and negotiated outcome is a simple denial. As many criminally accused politicians have learned—throw dust in the air, deny the offense and stubbornly maintain innocence. Alcohol abusers may vehemently deny that they are alcoholics. Charles McCaghy (1968) has studied child molesters and reported that because of the reprehensibility of their crimes, offenders often "deny the crime," "ascribe their behavior to alcohol," and/or "disassociate themselves from others who molest children." Some offenders do not want to accept the label of child molesting and go to great lengths to avoid such an identity. There is, for example, the case of a defendant in Wisconsin who entered a store and attempted to rape an underage female at knifepoint. Failing in the attempt, he took some money and goods and left. When arrested, he was unwilling to be branded with the label attendant to attempted rape of an underaged female, and instead bargained to plead guilty to the crime of armed robbery, which had a longer prison term as punishment (MacDonald, 1971:302).

Through negotiation, the offender may be able to manipulate the deviant label, either shrugging it off or effectively neutralizing it, or denying the "awkward, embarrassing, or negative aspects" of the resultant social interaction. This latter effort has been termed "deviance disavowal" (Davis, 1961). In some instances, however, label manipulation can work in an opposite direction, with the efforts of the negotiation directed toward accentuating the positive aspects of the stigma. Such machinations have been termed "deviance avowal" (Turner, 1972). Examples here might include "gay is good," gay pride weeks, "black is beautiful," pride in the accomplishments of handicapped persons, the "reformed" drunk, and the "repentant" sinner. Even the biblical parable of the strayed sheep returned to the fold emphasizes that deviance can be made positive. As Sagarin (1975:205) describes it, "stigma [can be] a badge of honor rather than a discrediting discrepancy." Deviant labels can be modified, neutralized, or utilized, and deviants frequently do make such an effort.

Deviant drinkers find the label "alcoholic" uncomfortable and undesirable. In dealing with the negative consequences of such labeling they may attempt one of two strategies. One of these is to deflect and thus avoid the label by trying to demonstrate that they are not a serious alcohol abuser. They will deny to themselves that they have a problem and also engage in deviance disavowal in trying to convince others that their drinking does not seriously interfere with their normal behavior. Failing this they may then turn to deviance avowal inasmuch as this is the "only viable means of reality negotiation." This necessitates medicalizing the deviant drinking and playing a repentant-deviant role. While similar in some respects to the traditional sick role, the repentant-deviant role may offer a more expedited path to social acceptance and make for a less restrictive outcome.

REFERENCES

Bryant, Clifton D. (ed)
1972 The Social Dimensions of Work. Englewood Cliffs, N.J.: Prentice-Hall Inc.

Davis, Fred
1961 "Deviance Disavowal: The Management of Strained Interaction by the Visibly Handicapped." Social Problems, 9:120–132.

Goffman, Erving
1963 Stigma: Notes on the Management of Spoiled Identity. Englewood Cliffs, N.J.: Prentice-Hall Inc.

Jackman, Norman R., Richard O'Toole, and Gilbert Geis
1963 "The Self-Image of the Prostitute," The Sociological Quarterly, 4(2):150–161.

Kando, Thomas
1972 "Passing and Stigma Management: The Case of the Transsexual," The Sociological Quarterly, 13(4):475–483.

MacDonald, M.
1971 Rape: Offenders and Their Victims. Springfield, Ill.: Charles C Thomas.

Sagarin, Edward
1975 Deviants and Deviance: An Introduction to the Study of Disvalued People and Behavior. New York: Praeger.

Turner, Ralph H.
1972 "Deviance Avowal as Neutralization of Commitment." Social Problems, 19:308–321.

Reading 21

Understanding Stigma: Dimensions of Deviance and Coping

Gregory C. Elliott, Herbert L. Ziegler, Barbara M. Altman, and Deborah R. Scott
University of Maryland, College Park

The present paper deals with stigma and its effects on social interaction. The major thesis is that stigma is a form of deviance that leads others to judge individuals as illegitimate for participation in an interaction, because they are incompetent, unpredictable, inconsistent, or a threat to the interaction. Illegitimacy places the stigmatized beyond the protection of a number of implicit social norms that govern any interaction. The disruptive impact of stigma depends on its classification along several dimensions: visibility, pervasiveness, clarity, centrality, relevance, salience, responsibility for acquisition, and removability. Strategies used to cope with stigma can be understood with reference to their focus (biographical identity, situated identity, or performance), target (stigmatized or normals), impact on the social-psychological distance between normals and the stigmatized (assimilative or contrastive), and purpose (concealment, reduction of salience, or redefinition of the situation).

INTRODUCTION

Routine social interaction can proceed because all involved consider themselves and each other legitimate participants. In any interaction, legitimacy is a status that is claimed by an individual but must be conferred by others. The purpose of achieving legitimate status is to come under the protection of a number of implicit social norms that govern any encounter. A person without legitimate status lies outside the boundaries of these social norms and is not entitled to their protection. As a consequence, he or she may find it exceedingly difficult, if not impossible, to realize the goals of any encounter.

In this paper, we discuss the problems that arise when stigma jeopardizes a person's claim to legitimacy. Our thesis is that the bearers of stigma may find even the simplest of social interactions a problem and that these problems stem from the fact that the mere possession of a stigma may be sufficient basis for others to deny one's claim to legitimacy. After discussing the criteria by which legitimacy is determined and the implicit social norms protecting legitimate participants, we distinguish among the various kinds

We thank Edward Z. Dager, John A. Fleishman, Barbara F. Meeker, Morris Rosenberg, and Michael Wagner for their incisive comments on earlier drafts.

of stigmata and discuss the nature of their threats to legitimacy. Finally, we discuss various strategies used to cope with the debilitating effects of stigma. Although much of what we discuss appears in various approaches to deviance found in the literature, the ultimate purpose of this paper is to integrate currently disparate ideas into a coherent perspective on the nature of deviance and its consequences for social interaction.

CRITERIA FOR LEGITIMACY

Several criteria determine the outcomes of social judgments regarding legitimacy. Essentially, they all come down to a judgment that a person is trustworthy: Others must be able to believe that a person can and will sustain the interaction. Trust is defined as the belief that a person will fulfill social obligations, internally or externally imposed. We trust others if they do what they say they will do or what they are supposed to do.

Trust has some necessary prerequisites, and these are the criteria for establishing a claim to legitimacy. The first criterion for legitimate status is competence. A person is a competent participant to the extent that he or she has the requisite abilities or skills to carry on the interaction. Those who are judged incompetent may be excluded from the interaction altogether. For example, people involved in a serious debate on important issues may ignore a severely retarded person who is present because they consider that person incompetent to sustain the conversation. There may occasionally be mistakes in judgment: Victims of cerebral palsy are often thought to be retarded, although the disease does not in fact impair one's cognitive abilities. In any case a judgement of competence is a necessary but not sufficient condition for attaining legitimate status.

Those seeking legitimate status as participants in an interaction must satisfy a second criterion: predictability. A person is predictable if, in the particular setting at hand, others can have reasonably good expectations in a probability sense as to what his or her behavior will be like. In order to plan their own behavior, people need to feel that they understand how others will interpret and react to that behavior; they must believe that the others' behavior will make sense, both as a response to their behavior and as a logical sequence in itself. It is difficult to take the role of the other, if he or she is not predictable. Actors facing an unpredictable other will not be able to orchestrate their own behavior, nor will they know how to interpret the other's behavior. People will tend to avoid the possible chaos that comes with dealing with an unpredictable person. As an illustration, most people find it hard to deal with a psychotic whose conversation is filled with non sequiturs.

Consistency is a third criterion for legitimacy. An actor is consistent if the self presented in a given encounter is not knowingly contradicted in past or future encounters or in the ongoing one. The impression conveyed in the present situation should be a logical outgrowth, or at least not a denial, of identities claimed elsewhere. This form of untrustworthiness is perhaps more serious than the others discussed so far, for there is some intent implied in inconsistency. Incompetent people may not be able to help their plight; some causes of unpredictability are also beyond a person's control. But most people could probably avoid inconsistencies in self-presentation if they really wanted to do so. Mentally stigmatized people provide an exception. Actors themselves are acutely aware of the need for consistency. Goffman (1959:Ch. 3), in his discussion of regions and region behavior, details the efforts people make to ensure consistency across performances. As with the other criteria, others' perception is the decisive factor: It is sufficient to appear trustworthy. As Goffman (1959: Ch. 2) has pointed out, collusion among teams of individuals in a unified effort is often successful in managing a consistent performance, and people can often use a backstage area, in which their behavior gives the lie to their performance, to rest from the rigors of presenting an inconsistent performance.

A final criterion for legitimacy flows from the previous criteria but has its own demands: benignancy. An actor is benign to the extent that the self presented in an encounter does not constitute a threat to others nor to the interaction itself. While incompetent, unpredictable, or inconsistent people can be threatening, it is possible to satisfy all the previous criteria and still threaten an interaction or its participants. Overly aggressive people may find themselves excluded from any gathering until their hostility subsides. The threat need not be physical. Schachter (1951) demonstrated that incorrigible deviants who threatened the solidarity of a group were effectively excluded from a discussion, especially in cohesive groups. It is not necessary actually to disrupt social interaction. An individual can be denied legitimacy simply because of a failure to support the ongoing interaction.

LEGITIMACY AND GROUND RULES

Having attained legitimate status, people come under the protection of a number of implicit social norms that govern any encounter. These norms make possible basic expectations about each other's orientation toward and behavior during the interaction. They serve to accomplish a fundamental desire that underlies all social interaction: Each interaction should be as free as possible of disruptions, discomfort, and embarrassment. Called "ground rules" by Goffman (1971), they ensure that disruptions in the progress of the encounter will be minor. Because there is tacit agreement that these implicit social norms can and will be observed, much of the interaction can be carried out without conscious reflection.

The first such implicit norm is that any participant's legitimate status must not be questioned without good reason. Having gained legitimacy, people should not be continually required to seek reconfirmation of the status. Unless given specific cause, all are expected to accord others the status that they had gained previously, and if need be, all are to give others the benefit of the doubt. In short, this first norm holds that legitimacy cannot be rescinded without cause.

A second ground rule covers threats to legitimacy. If there is any question, those whose legitimacy has become suspect must provide an account which removes the threat to their fully accredited status (Scott and Lyman, 1968). They may offer reasons that excuse the discrediting elements of their self-presentation; they may try to justify these same elements, denying the pejorative quality associated with them; or they may offer evidence that the questioned characteristics are irrelevant to the interaction at hand. Merely offering these accounts is not sufficient, however. Others must accept them, or the interaction will continue to be strained, perhaps even more so. One way of increasing the likelihood that the explanations will be accepted is to offer them before they are needed. Disclaimers (Hewitt and Stokes, 1975), offered in anticipation of a questioned legitimacy, may prevent the issue from arising.

The reactions of others to those whose legitimacy is in question is the focus of the third norm. When the legitimate status of any participant is threatened, the others are expected to accept any proffered account that does not strain credulity. In addition, they are expected to assist the potentially discredited other in preserving his or her status in the interaction, insofar as it is possible to do so (Goffman, 1967:10). Although the others are not necessarily required to go to extraordinary lengths, they are expected to do anything reasonable to save or maintain the offenders face. Otherwise, all will have to deal with the consequences of the discrediting of one or more participants. The nature of the relationship between the discredited and other may determine the lengths to which one is willing to go. Friends may feel a greater responsibility than strangers to help each other out. Those with high social status may feel noblesse oblige and help a lower status other save face, while the reverse is prevented by the status difference (Goffman, 1956). Further, failing to defend the legitimacy of others may subject one to similar attacks at other times, as others abandon this multilateral agreement. Finally, governing these norms is a metanorm. Those involved in a social interaction agree to abide by the above listed norms and not to question their legitimacy in guiding the encounter.[1]

[1]Actually, there is a ground rule that operates prior to the granting of legitimate status. It is assumed that people will make a claim of legitimacy only if they satisfy the criteria discussed above. It is embarrassing for both the claimant and the judges when the claim is denied, and the denial may even result in overt hostility and aggression. Essentially, this prior norm states that the illegitimate actors should know their place and not try to be something they are not.

In sum, satisfying the criteria presented above leads to the granting of legitimate status for an interaction. Legitimacy compels each person to observe the ground rules that protect this status. To the extent that the criteria for legitimacy are not met, voluntarily or involuntarily, violators may be denied legitimate status. Those judged illegitimate are outside the boundary of the ground rules of politeness and consideration characteristic of normal interactions, and, as such, they may be summarily excluded or ignored altogether.

STIGMA AND LEGITIMACY

Erving Goffman (1963:3) has defined stigma as "an attribute that is deeply discrediting," in the sense that the attribute makes the bearer different from others in an undesirable way. Goffman notes that it is not the attribute itself that is the problem. Rather, the stigma emerges from the socially damaged relationship that is implied between the possessor of the attribute and others (called "normals"). More specifically, we assert that the presence of a stigmatizing attribute can jeopardize the granting of legitimacy for an interaction. Stigma has a disruptive influence precisely because it calls into question the ability or the willingness of the bearer to satisfy the criteria for legitimacy and thereby sustain the encounter. In this perspective, possession of stigma can be seen as a particular kind of deviance (Davis, 1961; Freidson, 1965; Haber and Smith, 1971; Levitin, 1975; Glassner and Freedman, 1979).

Stigma is a particularly damaging form of deviance because it violates the criteria for legitimacy. Some discrediting attributes render the bearer incompetent to carry on usual, everyday interactions, as is the case of the severely retarded or handicapped. Other attributes make a person unpredictable; psychotics cannot be counted on to sustain a coherent logical conversation. Certain characteristics involve inconsistency, as when a convicted confidence man attempts to interact with normals. Finally, some attributes constitute a threat either to other participants (e.g., many diseases are contagious) or to the interaction itself (e.g., homosexuality may be seen as threatening the relationships one usually develops in encounters or as demanding an undesired relationship). Whatever the reason, for the stigmatized, their difference renders them illegitimate. Once classified as sufficiently different, stigmatized people are beyond the protection of the ground rules. Others can feel free to ignore these norms in dealing with them. They can question without compunction any claim to legitimacy. Further, it may be that no account can successfully substantiate this claim. Finally, normals need feel no compulsion to help the stigmatized gain legitimate status. In sort, it is no violation of the metanorm to fail to follow these ground rules, because the damaging attributes are prima facie evidence that the stigmatized are illegitimate and therefore do not deserve their protection.

STIGMA AND DISRUPTION

Empirical research has demonstrated that interactions between normal and stigmatized people are indeed strained, both for the normals (Farina and Ring, 1965; Kleck, 1966; Kleck, Ono, and Hastorf, 1966) and the afflicted (Farina, Allen, and Saul, 1968; Farina, Gliha, Boudreau, Allen, and Sherman, 1971; Comer and Piliavin, 1972). Although some studies show that normals are sometimes sympathetic toward the stigmatized (Katz, Farber, Glass, Lucido, and Emswiller, 1978; Katz, Glass, Lucido, and Farber, 1979), their behavior could not be characterized as an interaction between equals.

Unfortunately, these studies offer only a superficial understanding of the phenomenon and show little more than that people are uncomfortable in such interactions. Although they serve as a useful base line of knowledge, much more is needed. Recently, some studies have begun to take a more systematic approach to the effects of stigma. Farina, Holland, and Ring (1966) have investigated the responsibility for acquiring the stigma. They found that those seen as not responsible for the stigma were more easily integrated into an interaction. Hastorf, Wildfogel, and Cassman (1979) found that acknowledging a handicap publicly led to less difficulty in being with a normal person. Snyder, Kleck, Strenta, and Mentzer (1979) showed that normals avoided a stigmatized person more readily if there were alternative explanations for the avoidance.

In general, stigma disrupts an interaction because it threatens the legitimacy of the person possessing it. When legitimacy is questioned, the nature of the interaction changes radically, as the participants are forced to change their focus. Attention and energy that might have been directed toward the product or goal of the interaction must now be focused on the process of the interaction. Those afflicted with stigma must substantiate their claim to legitimacy. In doing so, they must offer evidence that the discrediting attribute does not affect their standing on the criteria for legitimacy in any meaningful way. The burden of proof is on them, however. Normals can refuse to accept their arguments and need not feel obliged to help them gain legitimacy. At the same time, rejecting such claims may be unpleasant to all concerned. Although this fact may in some cases compel the normals begrudgingly to accept the claims, if the differences are great or disturbing enough, normals may overreact and steadfastly refuse to consider the possibility. The exact nature of the disruption and the strategies used to cope with it depend on the nature of the stigma involved.

VARIETIES OF STIGMATA

One can distinguish among three general types of stigmata: physical stigmata, which involve some kind of physical abnormality or defect (paraplegia, disease); mental stigmata, which involve impaired cognitive functioning (retardation, psychosis); and moral stigmata, which involve violations of social norms regulating behavior or beliefs (criminality, deviant sexual preferences). The degree and kind of disruption that each entails is a function of several factors. Locating specific stigmata on these dimensions may help to explain their different impacts on behavior.

Perhaps the most obvious dimension for discriminating among stigmata is the visibility of the stigmatizing attribute. It is simply not possible to hide some kinds of stigmata from the world. Many instances of physical stigmata are very visible (facial scars, paraplegia), although others are not (malformed genitalia). Physical stigmata tend, on the whole, to be visible. Mental stigmata tend to be visible as a consequence of the bearer's behavior. Although a physical stigma can disqualify a person before an encounter begins, the illegitimacy of the mentally stigmatized may come to light only as the interaction proceeds. Moral stigmata, on the other hand, tend to be invisible. People with unpopular attitudes or deviant sexual preferences can reveal these characteristics more at their own discretion.

A visible stigma triggers (perhaps stereotypic) attitudes held by normals, thereby influencing the lines of action taken. As long as the characteristic can be hidden from others, its disruptive influence can be avoided.[2] However, should the deception be revealed, the stigmatized person may find that he or she is in more serious trouble. It is improper to withhold relevant information when making a claim to legitimacy. Further, duplicity revealed can result in being labeled morally stigmatized, as inconsistent or devious. These problems are especially acute when a moral stigma is concealed. Generally considered more reprehensible (see below), moral stigmata are more often hidden by their possessors but are more threatening when revealed. Although there are sanctions for possessing a moral stigma, there may be even greater sanctions for unsuccessfully concealing it.

A second basis for characterizing stigma is its pervasiveness in its bearer's everyday life. Although it is true that the stigmatizing nature of an

[2]Camouflage is no guarantee of success. The bearer's own awareness of the stigma can disrupt his or her behavior. Actors aware of their own defects may take them into account, even if others are not likely to discover them. In addition, they may be wary of somehow revealing the stigma inadvertently during the interaction. Goffman (1959, 1963) has discussed the techniques of self-presentation used by the actor with something to conceal.

attribute depends in part on the context in which it is perceived, it is also true that some attributes seem to discredit the individual in almost all situations. Mental and moral stigmata are more likely to pervade a wide range of social encounters. All interactions with a retarded person will have to deal with the stigma; although there is less rational basis for moral stigmata, such as sexual preference, the emotional reactions they generate are likely to mean greater pervasiveness. Physical stigmata are less likely to be pervasive; a genetic disfigurement may render a person incompetent for some interactions but not for others.

Closely related to pervasiveness is the notion of clarity, the degree of consensus that an attribute is perceived as stigmatizing. The greater the agreement among others that an attribute is discrediting, the more likely that it will affect the encounter. One can distinguish between pervasiveness and clarity by noting that pervasiveness deals with the extent of the problem across situations and clarity deals with the extent of the problem across individuals.

Mental stigmata are likely to be the clearest. Almost everyone would agree that retardation or psychosis would render a person illegitimate. There may also be some shared opinion regarding moral stigmata, although there are more likely to be exceptions here. It depends on the consensus regarding the social norm in question. Most would agree that child molesters are stigmatized people, but there might be disagreement with respect to homosexuals. Finally, physical stigmata are most likely to have variance in the degree to which the attribute is considered stigmatizing. The extent of the consensus may depend on the severity of the affliction. Persons suffering from a massive facial burn or colostomy may evoke greater consensus than those with polio.

A fourth dimension for classifying stigmata is centrality, the degree to which the problematic attribute is seen as reflecting the bearer's real self. Both the stigmatized and those normals involved may make a judgment, which may not coincide, as to whether a stigma is central. A central attribute is inextricably linked to a person's biographical identity and cannot be ignored in making assessments of what the person is like as a human being. Schur (1979:430–431) notes that some attributes may overwhelm judgments made about an actor, achieving the rank of "master status" (Hughes, 1945), in which all perception of the actor is filtered through this attribute. In addition, offending attributes may lead to "role engulfment," in which the self-concept and behavior of the possessor come to be more centered around the deviant role called for by the stigma (Schur, 1979:241–246). It follows that central stigmata should be very disruptive of social interaction. Other attributes are not necessarily self-incriminating. These peripheral characteristics are, in a sense, excess baggage that can be divorced from those essential components of the self, although they may still prevent a claim to full status as a social actor. In this vein, Silverman (1974) found that people were more willing to discriminate among potential roommates on the basis of belief congruence than racial similarity. In other words, differences in belief (which might involve a moral stigma) were more important than differences in race (a physical stigma).

Once again, mental and moral stigmata are likely to be central. Mental retardation is a striking example of a self-defining stigma, and so is sexual deviance. Physical stigmata are more likely to be considered peripheral characteristics. A speech defect may intrude initially on an interaction, but once others have adjusted to it, it need not have any implications about the bearer's character and therefore may not have so great an impact on the encounter.

The relevance of the stigma can influence the interaction. Relevance refers to the extent to which the offending attribute is actually involved in the doing of the encounter itself. Mental stigmata are usually relevant to an interaction. Impaired cognitive functioning means that special care has to be taken in even the simplest of interactions. Moral stigmata are not always relevant, unless the purpose of the interaction is to deal with the violation of social norms. Normals may find the moral stigma salient, in the sense that they cannot ignore the offending attribute, but they may choose not to make it relevant; that is, they may not wish to change the focus of the interaction and address the problematic characteristic directly. Physical stigmata are irrelevant, unless some aspect of the interaction calls for behavior that is prevented by the affliction. For example, paraplegia is a highly visible stigma, but it is not relevant if the purpose of the interaction is to play cards.

Each of the above dimensions is a reflection of an overarching dimension that determines the extent of disruption caused by a stigma. That overarching dimension is salience. Salience refers to the obtrusiveness of an attribute in a situation. It is the extent to which the stigma cannot be ignored (by its bearer or by others) in carrying out the interaction. The salience of a stigma will depend, in part, on its standing with regard to the previously noted dimensions. Stigmata that are highly visible, clear, central, and pervasive are likely to be salient. Yet this is not always the case. For example, paraplegia involves a highly visible stigma, but many people are able to ignore it successfully in interacting with a paraplegic. Similarly, salience is not the same as relevance. In the armed forces, homosexuality is salient but not relevant; paraplegia is both salient and relevant. Further, there may be disagreement in judging the salience of a stigma. Although two people may agree that homosexuality is a stigmatizing characteristic, one observer may be able to overlook the offending attribute, and another may find that it intrudes heavily on the interaction.

The locus of responsibility for acquiring the stigma may influence its disruptive nature. Some attributes are discrediting but are recognized as being involuntarily acquired; in other instances, the possessor can be seen as responsible for acquiring the stigma. (The distinction between ascribed and achieved status is relevant here.) Unless deliberately self-inflicted, most physical stigmata are acquired involuntarily. One can usually point to external causes for those crippled in an accident or deformed at birth and those retarded or driven insane. Similarly, members of racial minorities have no control over the acquisition of their stigmatizing characteristic. Moral stigmata are often different. Criminals may be seen as having freely chosen their deviant lifestyle, rather than as having their lives determined by factors beyond their control. Those believed to have chosen their stigma are likely to be asked to justify their choice, and failure to do so could lead to social sanctions. Those who are not responsible for acquiring their stigma may find that others are more sympathetic to their plight (Farina et al., 1966). In some cases, normals may even go out of their way to ease the stigmatized person's transition to legitimate status.

The last dimension for classifying stigmata is removability. Once acquired, some offending attributes become a permanent part of the individual. The bearers themselves have no power to remove the problem. Such is the case with severe physical and mental handicaps. Although the physically handicapped may try to approximate a normal appearance, using, for example, a prosthetic device, they cannot restore their bodies to a nonhandicapped state. It could also be that others will not allow the stigma to be removed. Once branded as mentally ill, a person may never be able to convince others that he or she should not always be considered as such, even after apparently successful therapy. However, other kinds of stigmata can be removed. Many moral stigmata are considered to be of this kind; unpopular attitudes can be changed, for example. Stigmata that are not removable require the bearer to manage carefully his or her spoiled identity. As is the case with acquisition, those with permanent stigma may find that normals are willing to help them find legitimate status. Those who can remove the stigma will be expected to do so; failure to correct the problem will require some accounting and may destroy the possesor's claim to legitimate status. Many people believe that homosexuals are not responsible for acquiring their sexual preference; they attribute homosexuality to genetic predisposition or socialization. However, some people believe homosexuals can change their situation through therapy or behavior modification. In other words, they believe the stigma is removable. It stands to reason that they would be sympathetic to the homosexual who participates in such programs of change. Anyone who refuses to participate or who emerges unchanged (thereby implying participation in bad faith) is unlikely to receive sympathy or assistance in gaining legitimate status.

With the possible exception of visibility, the above dimensions must be viewed from two perspectives: the stigma bearers and the normals. Each may have a very different understanding of the stigma and its implications for the encounter. For example, although a stigmatized person might consider the offending attribute peripheral, normals may define him or her solely on the basis of that attribute. Unless and until these two perspectives are reconciled, the stigma will continue to be a disruptive influence on the interaction. Indeed, the participants may not realize that there is no shared meaning with regard to the stigma, so that they may not even be able to trace the source of the disruption at first. Each person will be likely to misinterpret the behavior of those who do not share his or her perspective. For the interaction to proceed smoothly, both stigmatized and normals must agree on the nature of the stigma (as determined by the above dimensions) and the manner in which the stigma is to be managed. These issues often mean long, difficult negotiations among the participants.

COPING WITH STIGMA IN AN ENCOUNTER

The situational imperative to determine legitimacy motivates all participants to take part in establishing the situated identity of the stigmatized in the interaction. As mentioned above, this is a process of negotiation. Those afflicted with the discrediting characteristic have the most to gain, for it is their identity that is at stake. They must establish and justify their claim to legitimate status, something normals can usually take for granted. However, normals are also motivated to take part in this negotiation, both to protect the integrity of the interaction (only legitimate people should be allowed to participate) and to avoid more than minimal disruption. Whether they wish to dispute a stigmatized person's claim or facilitate the granting of legitimate status, failure to take part in the negotiation process leaves the outcome in the hands of others.

Once legitimacy is in question, the interaction takes a radically different turn. Because normals cannot count on the stigmatized person to sustain the encounter in an appropriate fashion, every aspect of the interaction is potentially a matter needing clarification. Attention must be paid to those matters of process that are usually taken for granted and both behavior and intentions become subject to reinterpretation and verification. In short, the purposes of the interaction must be temporarily put aside, as the participants engage in face work, and the discredited person can expect to have to offer continuing evidence supporting his or her claim to legitimacy.

Mechanisms used to cope with the stigma and its effects by both the afflicted and the normals are forms of aligning actions (Stokes and Hewitt, 1976), designed to salvage an interaction following a disruption or prevent one from occurring. Investigators have identified a number of coping mechanisms used to minimize the disruption caused by stigma (Goffman, 1963; Schur, 1979, 1980).

The Stigmatized

For the stigmatized, several options are available. Those who can remove the stigma will find that doing so will obviate their problems. When removal is out of the question, disruption can still be avoided if the offending characteristic can be concealed. Concealment may be possible even if the stigma is visible. Self-segregation (Schur, 1979:286–296) is one form of concealment. Stigmatized people may choose to interact only with others who share their affliction or with those who have become "wise" (intimately familiar and comfortable with the stigma; Goffman, 1963:28). By avoiding people who are likely to react badly, the stigmatized can pursue their, perhaps more limited, goals without disruption.

When self-segregation is not practical or productive, the stigmatized may attempt to conceal the stigma by "passing." It may be possible to conceal the stigma entirely and thereby avoid any threat to legitimacy. Moral stigmata are relatively concealable, although sometimes archives or knowing third parties can expose the stigma. Convicted criminals can refuse to divulge their past offenses, but court records are an ever-present source of discrediting. Radicals in a conservative environment can hide their political beliefs but are at the mercy of their confidants. Mental and physical stigmata are more difficult to conceal. The former tend to be visible in the behavior of the possessor, and are more salient and relevant as well. Psychotics have difficulty orienting their behavior toward others and so are less likely to be able to conceal their deviant mental state. Still, some with mild forms of mental stigmata have successfully eluded detection, at least for a time. Many physical stigmata are impossible to conceal, although, as mentioned above, prosthetic devices can help some people approximate normal appearances. Members of a racial minority have occasionally passed as a member of the majority. As with moral stigmata, those who attempt to pass are subject to discrediting by others who share their affliction or who know of it. To aid in passing, deviants can use disidentifiers (Goffman, 1963:93), attributes or elements of one's presenting self that contradict the identity conferred by the stigma. In this manner, homosexuals dress in sex-typed clothing or marry homosexuals of the opposite gender, and short people wear elevator shoes.

An extreme form of disidentification occurs when a stigmatized person attempts to establish some social-psychological distance from others similarly afflicted, especially those who are more thoroughly contaminated by the stigma. One racial minority may claim it is better in some way than another (even within one racial category, distancing occurs: lighter skinned blacks have, in the past, felt superior to their darker skinned counterparts);

a retarded person or psychotic may point out how much less disturbed he or she is than others of their ilk; a common practice in prisons involves establishing a hierarchy among offenders, in which certain kinds of criminals (such as sex offenders against children) are judged worse than others.

When actual concealment is not possible, Goffman (1963:94) notes that it is possible to deflect others' attention from the damaging effects of the stigma by presenting the signs of the stigma as signs of a less deeply discrediting attribute. People who are slightly retarded may prefer that others think that they are hard of hearing or uninterested in the issues at hand rather than uncomprehending. Deflection can also be accomplished if the stigmatized can argue convincingly that they are not responsible for acquiring or maintaining the stigma. If they can portray themselves as unfortunate victims of fate or chance, as noted above, they might be able to avoid the consequences of the stigma.

Stigmata that cannot be concealed will resist attempts at deflection. Some stigmata can be ignored; if the offending characteristic is irrelevant, nonsalient, or peripheral, it need not intrude on the interaction. The stigmatized can claim legitimacy in asking others to pay no attention to the discrediting attribute. If the stigma is salient, central, or relevant, it will require direct confrontation. The ideal solution is normalization (Davis, 1961), in which the attribute loses its stigmatizing properties and no longer threatens legitimacy. Through exposure and negotiation, the identity of the stigmatized is redefined, so that salience is diminished (people get used to the offending characteristic), relevance is reduced (ways of circumventing the stigma's effects are found), or centrality is eliminated (others come to know the "real person" behind the stigma). At some point, the stigmatized breaks through the barriers to legitimacy, (Davis, 1961:127) and normalizes the relationships developed during the interaction. The hope is eventually to institutionalize the normalized relationship. This may entail a sympathetic re-education of the normals, which can often be done with less tensions if the stigmatized deal with the stigma explicitly and with detachment. (The case of John Merrick, the so-called Elephant Man, represents a notably difficult attempt at normalization.) The stigmatized must be careful to avoid what Davis (1961:126) calls fictional acceptance: Sometimes normals will accept a superficial interaction at a "subsistence level of sociability." But the stigmatized may find that it is impossible to proceed to more intimate and meaningful levels of interaction.

Another way to normalize the relationship and gain legitimacy is to compensate for the stigma. This can be done by mastering those areas usually closed off to the stigmatized. Criminal offenders may point to years of good citizenship or involvement with resocialization agencies as evidence that they have learned their lesson. Physically handicapped people may work hard to master activities supposedly rendered impossible by their handicap. Quadriplegics learn to write or type with an instrument held between their teeth or train pets or use machines to help them do what they cannot do themselves; the blind use seeing-eye dogs; the deaf learn to lip read or sign. Those afflicted with mental stigmata may not have this option so readily available. The retarded could learn to use their full potential, but their best may still be woefully inadequate to sustain an interaction.

A second method of compensation is to master areas of behavior that are important to the interaction but for which the stigma is irrelevant. The physically handicapped can take over administrative or socioiemotional roles; the mentally retarded can perform tasks that do not exceed their cognitive abilities. Morally stigmatized people can avoid the occasions of sin that would involve their offending characteristic and concentrate on their more valued personal attributes.

Finally, capitulation may be the only response. As Schur (1979:317–318) has written, when stigma assumes a master status for its bearer, he or she may find the role of discredited person engulfing all others. Giving up, the stigmatized accept the stereotype thrust upon them and the concomitant illegitimate status. They may become nonpersons (Goffman, 1959:151–152) who enjoy interaction with normals only at the normals' discretion. And so it was that blacks learned to shuffle and be obsequious, the retarded played dumb, and the homosexual flaunted his or her sexual preference with outrageous dress or behavior.

Accepting the deviant role need not have only negative consequences, according to Goffman (1963:10–11). In a form of dissonance reduction, the stigmatized may look upon their affliction as a blessing in disguise and marvel at what they have learned about themselves as a function of their stigma. They may reassess the limitations of normals and feel called upon by their example to help the normals enjoy their normality. In a self-serving vein, they can often use the stigma to make secondary gains, as the stigma becomes an excuse for other untoward behavior.

The most extreme reaction in accepting a deviant role occurs when the stigmatized abandon the quest for legitimacy. Failing to convince others, they withdraw from all association with normals into their own circle of fellow afflicted and, perhaps, the "wise." These refugees form a subculture in which the offending attributes are not bases for rejection (although others may be).

Normals

Normals also have strategies to cope with the disruption caused by stigma. For them, the most pressing question is whether or not to grant legitimate status to the stigmatized person. The decision depends, in part, on the classification of the stigma along the various dimensions described above.

This is essentially a question of salience. The more salient the stigma, the less likely one is to accord legitimacy to another.

If the stigma is invisible or concealable, there should be no problem, for the normals are then unaware and the relationship is unaffected. A highly pervasive or especially clear stigma may lead to a rejection; to the extent that there is social support across encounters and other normals for rejection, its probability will be greater. The decision to reject is most likely for a central stigma. When an attribute is seen to be an integral part of a person's self, it cannot be ignored, and normals may not want to make the effort to break through.

An important motivation to exclude the stigmatized person from the interaction is to avoid what Goffman (1963:30) calls a courtesy stigma. Normals may fear that in associating with the afflicted they will find their own legitimate status imperiled, as they pick up the stigma themselves in a kind of guilt by association. Another motivation for a judgment of illegitimacy is to protect oneself from the psychologically threatening aspects of stigma. The stigma can be seen as less threatening if those afflicted are perceived as deserving their fate. As Lerner, Miller, and Holmes (1976) point out, if the afflicted did not somehow deserve their plight, they were victims of chance. In that case, we and those close to us (friends, lovers, future offspring) are potential victims. This threatening thought is sufficient motivation to believe that the stigmatized deserve their suffering. If the identity is sufficiently spoiled, the stigmatized may find themselves in a no-win situation. If they deserve their fate, they may be rejected because they are normally culpable; if they do not, they may be rejected because their presence is too threatening to normals, who will be forced to see themselves as potential victims.

Finally, removability can play a role in the normals' decision. If the stigma is not removable, sympathy may tip the scales in favor of legitimacy, although perhaps at some restricted status. If the possessor is taking steps to remove the stigma, the decision may be postponed, or temporary legitimacy may be granted, to become permanent upon complete removal of the offending attribute. If the stigmatized person will not remove the stigma, legitimacy is almost surely to be denied. Normals are under no obligation to help those who will not help themselves.

There are several ways to carry out a decision to reject a claim to legitimacy. The easiest behavior is often avoidance; normals who can will leave the field and preclude any interaction. When avoidance is not possible, normals may ignore the stigmatized and treat them as if they were nonpersons, carrying on interactions with legitimate participants as if the stigmatized were not present. At best, those who fail to achieve legitimate status may find themselves the object of only occasional and perfunctory attention by normals.

Judgments of illegitimacy can be justified in a number of ways. First, normals may generalize the damaging effects of the stigma to other, usually not discrediting imperfections of the possessor. In a reversal of the halo effect, people may see problematic attributes as clustering together. In this way, the offense spreads beyond the original stigma into areas that might not have otherwise been questioned. Moral stigmata are especially susceptible to generalization. They are based on presumed defects in personality traits, values, or attitudes, and each of us has some implicit personality theory that tells us how personal attributes should be linked in human beings. And so, the dishonest person may also be seen as cowardly, weak, or overly ambitious. It should be noted that even physical and mental stigmata may have implications concerning other potentially damaging characteristics. Second, unrelated minor failings in social behavior that would go unnoticed for a normal person can be seized upon as an expression of the differences between the stigmatized and others. Behaviors that otherwise would have been innocuous now require an account. One possible attribution made by normals is that these other untoward behaviors are explained by the stigma. The stigma becomes the cause for the other failures and evidence that the stigmatized cannot sustain the interaction.

A decision to support the claim to legitimacy can be carried out in several ways. One can ignore the stigma and act as if it were not there. This is difficult if the stigma is salient. In particular, relevant stigmata are very difficult to ignore. The normals themselves may compensate for the stigmatized person and see to it that his or her role in the interaction does not demand impossible behaviors or even do themselves things the stigmatized person would be expected to do. However, normals must beware of patronizing the stigmatized person and thereby themselves straining the interaction. There may be a tendency to treat minor accomplishments as particularly noteworthy, in light of the offending attribute. Mentally retarded and physically handicapped people are often patronized. What is particularly vexing to them is that they may have to put up with it if they wish to keep the support of these normals. By patronizing the stigmatized, normals allow them into the interaction, but they maintain distance. Asking to be treated as an equal is an attempt to eliminate that distance. Normals may be too uncomfortable in an equal interaction and withdraw their support for the stigmatized person.

Others may attempt to become wise and bridge the gap between the worlds of the stigmatized and the normals. If their position in the latter world is secure, they can avoid picking up a courtesy stigma. Normals who are wise can then use their unique position to mediate the negotiation for legitimacy.

Finally, it is even possible to maintain a policy of general denial while making exceptions. Normals may treat the stigmatized person in question as an exception, especially if he or she does not conform fully to the stereotype associated with the stigma. One can then grant legitimacy without setting a precedent that might endanger future interactions.

DIMENSIONS OF COPING WITH STIGMA

In order to distinguish among the various strategies used to cope with stigma, it is useful to consider several dimensions along which the strategies can be classified. Focus refers to that aspect of the person's self addressed by the coping strategy. Any of three aspects can be of concern. The first is the biographical identity, which is the cumulative self, constructed in relation to an individual's life as a whole. It is reflected in one's role set (Merton, 1957) and is the self that one brings to the interaction. Gender, physical form, and ethnic identification are all part of the biographical identity. Second, coping strategies can deal with an individual's situated identity, the self-image relevant to a particular locus of space and time. Negotiations in this case concern role making, in which people choose, create, or modify roles considered appropriate to the encounter (Turner, 1962). The dynamic, interactive flavor of this negotiation is captured in Blumstein's (1975) investigation of identity bargaining. The third aspect of concern is the performance. Coping strategies may address the manner in which the negotiated identity and role are carried out, variously referred to as role playing (Coutu, 1951) and role performance (Turner, 1956). Rather than focus on content, these strategies focus on style.

When a stigmatized person attempts to remove the offending characteristic, this coping strategy is aimed at his or her biographical identity. A similarly focused strategy occurs when people try to change their biographical identity so that the apparently less malleable offending attribute is no longer discrediting. People possessing characteristics considered appropriate only for the opposite gender may go to the extreme of a transsexual operation to bring the biographical identity in line with the problematic personal characteristics. When normals change their understanding of their own roles in being with a stigmatized person, they are focusing on their situated identity. A friend who ends up being a confidant for an emotionally disturbed person finds that his or her situated identity has changed from past interactions. Finally, a stigmatized person who attempts to compensate for his or her problem by exaggerating behaviors that substantiate a claim to legitimacy is coping by working on the performance. Similarly, homosexuals who deliberately exaggerate behaviors stereotypically considered as defining the homosexual are dealing with style to accentuate differences.

The second classification system deals with the target of the coping strategy. A person's aligning action could be directed toward the self or toward the others. Individuals can negotiate their own identity in the encounter or engage in altercasting (Weinstein and Deutschberger, 1963) and attempt to establish identities for others to enact.

Coping strategies can also be distinguished according to their impact on the social-psychological distance among the participants. Some behaviors are intended to be assimilative, to reduce the distance between the stigmatized and normals. Normals who attempt to become wise are trying to reduce the distance between themselves and the deviant. Accentuating similarities and ignoring the stigma also accomplish this purpose. The goal is to include the offender in the circle of legitimate participants. On the other hand, behaviors are sometimes used to increase the distance between the stigmatized and the normals. Such contrastive behaviors may emphasize relevant differences and claim any similarities are irrelevant in order to succeed at this task (cf., Cooper and Jones, 1969). In this way, claims to legitimacy can be more readily denied.

Finally, it is possible to distinguish among coping strategies according to their purpose. There are three general purposes. First, behaviors could be designed to avoid a general public awareness of the discrediting attribute. Actors may try to prevent disclosure or, failing that, focus attention on other characteristics. A second purpose is to reduce the stigma's salience; while acknowledging its existence, one attempts to minimize its impact on the encounter. In establishing the stigma as irrelevant or peripheral, for example, actors can remove obstacles to their claim to legitimate status. Lastly, people may act to bring about a change in the very meaning of the stigma. The purpose is to redefine the situation, to see to it that the stigma and its consequences are seen in a different light. In its most successful operation, there develops a new understanding of the offending attribute, in which it is no longer seen as discrediting.

It should be noted that these purposes are mutually exclusive, in the sense that any given behavior is not likely to serve multiple purposes. Indeed, one can conceive of situations in which these purposes are contradictory. Trying to hide a personal aberration obviates the need to make it less obtrusive or change its meaning. However, this does not rule out the possibility that a person would try to accomplish more than one purpose in a given interaction. If one strategy fails, people may turn to another. For example, upon finding that it is no longer possible to preclude public awareness, people may try to change the stigma's meaning and, failing that, may simply work to minimize the effects of the offending attribute. This does not imply that all actors will sequence their coping strategies or attempt to serve all purposes if they do; the point is that those who find it necessary to cope with a stigma are not locked into strategies serving only a single purpose.

CONCLUSIONS

Past research on stigma has shown that encounters between normals and the stigmatized involve discomfort for both. These results serve as an important starting point for understanding stigma and its effects on an interaction, but more is needed. The present paper is an attempt to provide a more refined conceptualization of stigma and strategies used to cope with the disruption it causes. Viewing stigma as a form of deviance that renders one illegitimate as a participant in interactions with normals helps to explain its impressive impact. Illegitimacy places one outside the protection of the implicit social norms that govern any interaction, and much of the initial phase of an encounter between normals and stigmatized involves negotiation of the stigma bearer's situated identity. Distinguishing among the various kinds of stigmata according to the dimensions discussed above may lead to a better understanding of the variability of their impact of an encounter. Similarly, a greater understanding of the variety of ways in which people cope might be facilitated by reference to the classification scheme proposed above. Fuller use of the perspective presented herein may be a way to refine and advance our understanding of the nature of stigmata that reveals their impressive differences in affecting social interaction.

REFERENCES

Blumstein, Philip W.
1975 "Identity bargaining and self-conception." Social Forces 53:476–485.

Comer, Ronald J., and Jane Allyn Piliavin
1972 "The effects of physical deviance upon face-to-face interaction: The other side." Journal of Personality and Social Psychology 23:33–39.

Cooper, Joel, and Edward E. Jones
1969 "Opinion divergence as a strategy to avoid being miscast." Journal of Personality and Social Psychology 13:23–30.

Coutu, Walter
1951 "Role-playing vs. role-taking: An appeal for clarification." American Sociological Review 16:180–187.

Davis, Fred
1961 "Deviance disavowal: The management of strained interaction by the visibly handicapped." Social Problems 9:120–132.

Farina, Amerigo, Jon G. Allen, and b. Brigid B. Saul
1968 "The role of the stigmatized person in affecting social relationships." Journal of Personality 36:169–182.

Farina, Amerigo, Donald Gliha, Louis A. Boudreau, Jon G. Allen, and Mark Sherman
1971 "Mental illness and the impact of believing others know about it." Journal of Abnormal Psychology 77:1–5.
Farina, Amerigo, Charles H. Holland, and Kenneth Ring
1966 "Role of stigma and interpersonal set in interpersonal interaction." Journal of Abnormal Psychology 71:421–428.
Farina, Amerigo, and Kenneth Ring
1965 "The influence of perceived mental illness on interpersonal relations." Journal of Abnormal Psychology 70:47–51.
Freidson, Eliot
1965 "Disability as social deviance." Pp. 71–99 in Marvin B. Sussman (ed.), Sociology and Rehabilitation. Washington, D.C.: American Sociological Association.
Glassner, Barry, and Jonathan A. Freedman
1979 Clinical Sociology. New York: Longman.
Goffman, Erving
1971 Relations in Public. New York: Harper Colophon.
Goffman, Erving
1967 "On face-work." Pp. 5–45 in Erving Goffman, Interaction Ritual. Garden City, N.Y.: Doubleday Anchor.
1963 Stigma: Notes on the Management of Spoiled Identity. Englewood Cliffs, N.J.: Prentice-Hall.
1959 The Presentation of Self in Everyday Life. Garden City, N.Y.: Doubleday Anchor.
1956 "The nature of deference and demeanor." American Anthropologist 58:473–502.
Haber, Lawrence D., and Richard T. Smith
1971 "Disability and deviance: Normative adaptations of role behavior." American Sociological Review 36:87–97.
Hastorf, Albert H., Jeffrey Wildfogel, and Ted Cassman
1979 "Acknowledgement of handicap as a tactic in social interaction." Journal of Personalty and Social Psychology 37:1790–1797.
Hewitt, John P., and Randall Stokes
1975 "Disclaimers." American Sociological Review 40:1–11.
Hughes, Everett Cherrington
1945 "Dilemmas and contradictions of status." American Journal of Sociology 50:353–359.
Katz, Irwin, Joan Farber, David C. Glass, David Lucido, and Tim Emswiller
1978 "When courtesy offends: Effects of positive and negative behavior by the physically disabled on altruism and anger in normals." Journal of Personality 46:506–518.
Katz, Irwin, David C. Glass, David Lucido, and Joan Farber
1979 "Harm-doing and victim's racial or orthopedic stigma as determinants of helping behavior." Journal of Personality 47:340–364.

Kleck, Robert
1966 "Emotional arousal in interactions with stigmatized persons." Psychological Reports 19:1226.

Kleck, Robert, Hiroshi Ono, and Albert H. Hastorf
1966 "The effects of physical deviance on face-to-face interaction." Human Relations 19:425–436.

Lerner, Melvin J., Dale T. Miller, and John G. Holmes
1976 "Deserving and the emergence of forms of justice." Pp. 134–162 in Leonard Berkowitz (ed.), Advances in Experimental Social Psychology (Vol. 9). New York: Academic Press.

Levitin, Teresa E.
1975 "Deviants as active participants in the labeling process: The visibly handicapped." Social Problems 22:548–557.

Merton, Robert K.
1957 "The role-set: Problems in sociological theory." British Journal of Sociology 8:106–120.

Schachter, Stanley
1951 "Deviance, rejection, and communication." Journal of Abnormal and Social Psychology 46:190–207.

Schur, Edwin
1980 The Politics of Deviance. Englewood Cliffs, N.J.: Prentice-Hall.
1979 Interpreting Deviance. New York: Harper & Row.

Scott, Marvin, B., and Stanford Lyman
1968 "Accounts." American Sociological Review 33:44–62.

Silverman, Bernie I.
1974 "Consequences, racial discrimination, and the principle of belief congruence." Journal of Personality and Social Psychology 29:497–508.

Snyder, Melvin L., Robert E. Kleck, Angelo Stranta, and Steven J. Mentzer
1979 "Avoidance of the handicapped: An attributional ambiguity analysis." Journal of Personality and Social Psychology 37:2297–2306.

Stokes, Randall, and John P. Hewitt
1976 "Aligning actions." American Sociological Review 41:838–849.

Turner, Ralph
1962 "Role-taking: Process versus conformity." Pp. 20–40 in Arnold Rose (ed.), Human Behavior and Social Processes. Boston: Houghton Mifflin.

Turner, Ralph H.
1956 "Role-taking, role standpoint, and reference-group behavior." American Journal of Sociology 61:316–328.

Weinstein, Eugene A., and Paul Deutschberger
1963 "Some dimensions of altercasting." Socioimetry 26:454–466.

Reading 22

Stigmata and Negotiated Outcomes: Management of Appearance by Persons with Physical Disabilities

Susan B. Kaiser, Carla M. Freeman, and Stacy B. Wingate
University of California at Davis

This paper explores the role of clothing in the management of appearances by persons with disabilities. A negotiated outcomes perspective is used to study the clothing choices of disabled persons, rather than viewing them as passive recipients of the labels supplied by perceivers. A two-part study of college students with physical disabilities, including comments from a series of focused group interviews and open-ended responses to a questionnaire with national distribution, resulted in the data presented. The data indicated that most of the students strived to appear as normative as possible through their clothing choices and accordingly used a variety of techniques: "making do" with ingeniously adapted ready-to-wear apparel; using clothes to conceal a disability; deflecting attention from a disability toward more normative but slightly discrediting attributes; compensation through fashionable dress or by emphasizing other social roles and abilities; and social inclusion, i.e., the assertion that all persons vary in physical appearance. Some students employed dress to take advantage of their social uniqueness through such techniques as wearing bright or prominent clothing or by displaying humor. Possible directions for future research on the social interactions of disabled persons, particularly involving the implications of normalizing appearance versus emphasizing social uniqueness, are presented.

A physical disability may be used as a cue to categorize a person as abnormal or different (Davis, 1964) and becomes a source of stigmatization when it is used to discredit an individual in a stereotypical manner (Goffman, 1963). The cultural stereotype that "beauty is good" pervades American culture. At the interpersonal level, persons who are physically attractive in the normative sense are evaluated on the basis of implicit "halo effects" involving clusters of positive personal traits (for reviews of the physical attractiveness literature, see Adams, 1977; Adams, 1982; and Berscheid and Walster, 1974). Conversely, a negative stereotype or stigma is associated with persons who deviate from the norm in physical appearance. Both the

Funding for the study was provided by a Faculty Research Grant from the University of California at Davis. The authors wish to express their appreciation to Joan L. Chandler and Tami Soler for their assistance in the coding of the data, and to the anonymous reviewers who provided constructive and stimulating comments.

physical attractiveness stereotype (Adams and Crane, 1980; Dion and Berscheid, 1974) and the stigma associated with physical disabilities (Popp et al., 1981) appear to be learned at a relatively young age through socialization processes. Additionally, there is some evidence that adults expect able-bodied children to be involved in more intense best-friend relationships than disabled children (Kleck and DeJong, 1981). Stereotypical traits assigned to people with physical disabilities include dependency, sadness, and isolation; in certain contexts these attributions may reduce perceivers' role expectations and lead to restrictions of behavior and opportunities (Altman, 1981).

The extent to which a physical disability is disruptive to interaction is dependent upon contextual factors. Higgins (1980) has noted that disabilities become disruptive when they present a breach in the taken-for-granted social order. A person with a physical disability may be perceived by nondisabled persons, in certain contexts, as threatening to social interaction (Elliott et al., 1982) due, perhaps, to the inconsistency between a physical disability and the perception that the world is a just place where the innocent do not suffer (Katz, 1981; Lerner, 1970). Davis (1964:125) reported an account of a strikingly attractive girl in a wheelchair who frequently elicited such comments as, "How strange that someone so pretty should be in a wheelchair."

Stigmatization does not necessarily lead to the labeling of an individual as deviant, according to Haber and Smith (1971). They point out that stigmatization becomes a social role which may achieve legitimate status in such contexts as the medical and social helping professions. Labeling theorists are more interested in the contexts in which imputations of deviance are made than in the deviance per se (Kitsuse, 1975). The labeling or societal reaction perspective has increasingly emphasized the processes through which persons come to be perceived, defined, and treated as deviant by others. A major criticism of the traditional labeling approach to deviance is that the reaction of those labeled deviant has been overemphasized, while the perceived persons' abilities to affect the imputation of the deviant label have been undermined (Levitin, 1975; Hanks and Poplin, 1981). In other words, the labeled persons have been depicted as passive recipients of the deviant role rather than as impression-managing persons engaged in social transactions. Levitin (1975) has noted that the self-conceptions of a stigmatized individual should be considered in relation to the strategies used to negotiate identities in different social contexts.

The negotiated outcome perspective provides an alternate view of the labeling process in which persons with disabilities actively participate (c.f., Wright, 1960; Levitin, 1975; Hanks and Poplin, 1981). Hanks and Poplin have pointed out that negative evaluations by others may lead to maladjusted, self-perceived deviance only "if disabled individuals are unable to manipulate and to some extent control the labels that are applied to them by nondisabled individuals" (1981:317). The manipulation of appearance symbols affords opportunities for individuals to present other aspects of the self and to communicate visually to others that the disability is not the only aspect of the self. Davis (1964) has argued that by definition, the visibly handicapped person cannot control appearance sufficiently so as to reduce the obtrusiveness of the disability. However, through the manipulation of clothing and accessories, persons with disabilities may emphasize other aspects of self if total concealment of the disability is not possible. This role that appearance plays has frequently been ignored and deserves attention if the role of the disabled person in influencing negotiated outcomes is to be fully understood.

Goffman (1963) has pointed out that just as "stigma symbols" draw a perceiver's attention to a debasing identity, "disidentifiers" are signs which serve to disrupt an otherwise coherent picture, thus casting some doubt on the validity of a disqualifying attribution. Persons with disabilities may strive to present appearances which allow them to take the roles of others more readily. Stone (1962) has argued that appearance is a precursory phase to the ability to identify with others and thus facilitate role-taking.

The perceptions of nondisabled persons when observing disabled individuals are affected by clothing cues as well as physical deformities (Miller, 1982). A study by Feather et al. (1979) indicated that university students in wheelchairs held significantly less favorable attitudes towards clothing than did able-bodied students. Other authors have reported that available clothing in the marketplace does not appear to meet the needs of persons with physical disabilities (Hallenbeck, 1966; Kernaleguen, 1978; Shannon and Reich, 1979). Yet specially designed clothing, as available from some mail-order firms, may not be desirable either, due to distinct normative differences. Cuber (1963) noted that ambivalence often results from the conflict between an individual's attitudes based upon unique needs and experiences, and those based upon cultural norms. Such a case is particularly apparent in specially designed clothing for persons with disabilities. Special features of garments designed for people with disabilities, i.e., the use of Velcro®, large zippers, and other such features in unconventional places, may be sources of stigma which differentiate the disabled from the nondisabled. This clothing may be both positively and negatively received by disabled persons, in that it may be both functional and different from the norm. As Kernaleguen has noted, "Since the handicapped may have different and specific needs, clothing designed to meet these needs can easily become 'special clothing' which emphasizes, rather than minimizes, a handicap" (1978:3).

The purpose of the present research was to explore the self-presentations of persons with disabilities, with respect to personal appearance and clothing as factors in social interactions. The qualitative data reported in this paper are part of a larger study on clothing as a social factor in the lives of persons with disabilities. The present study focused primarily on: 1) the forms of social feedback received by persons with disabilities, in relation to their appearances, and 2) appearance-related responses to physical disabilities. The first focus included social feedback received in everyday encounters with nondisabled persons, and, as the subjects were university students, many of their face-to-face social encounters on a daily basis were fleeting and anonymous, such as during class changes. The second focus of the paper employed a negotiated outcome perspective as applied to the impression management of appearance, considering persons with disabilities as active participants in the labeling process.

METHOD

The data were obtained in two separate phases. The first of these involved twelve focused group interviews with male and female disabled students ($N = 36$) attending six different colleges and universities in Northern California. From one to five people attended each interview. Due to the exploratory nature of the investigation and the limited population, no restrictions were placed on either the age or type of disability of the participants. Thus a broad range of disabilities was represented. The students responded to a series of questions related to the following topics: the forms of social feedback received from nondisabled persons, clothing patterns and preferences, attitudes toward specially designed clothing, and suggestions for names of apparel lines or stores catering specifically to the needs of persons with physical disabilities. The latter suggestions were included in order to determine preferred verbal labels that might be assigned to the nonverbal realm of appearance.

The second phase of the study involved the distribution of a self-administered questionnaire to seventy-two colleges and universities across the United States. At least one college or university from each state was represented. One thousand copies of the questionnaire were distributed to the students through handicapped student offices at each university. Of the 1,000 questionnaires sent to the schools, 960 were actually distributed to legitimate/current addresses. Of these, 327 questionnaires were returned, representing a 34% response rate.[1] Both males (46%) and females (54%) responded to the questionnaires. As in the interviews, many forms of physi-

[1]Although the response rate compares favorably with other mail surveys in which the potential subjects receive only one mailing (c.f., Hansen, 1980; Yu and Cooper, 1983), the possibility of a response bias in the questionnaire data should be considered.

cal disabilities were represented in the sample.[2] The data reported in this paper are derived from the comments in the focused group interviews as well as from the qualitative component of the questionnaire. There were open-ended questions in the questionnaire on the nature of personally owned clothing which may communicate linguistically (e.g., T-shirts with slogans), attitudes with respect to specially designed clothing, and suggestions for names of stores or clothing designs catering to persons with disabilities. Volunteered general comments at the end of the questionnaire are also included in the present paper. (The remainder of the questionnaire dealt with the students' responses to clothing stimuli and attitudinal statements.) As appropriate, some of the students' responses to selected attitudinal statements in the questionnaire are presented as well, because these statements were derived from students' comments in the group interviews. The extent to which there was agreement with these comments is indicated.[3]

The qualitative data were content-analyzed and categorized on the basis of concepts related to visible disabilities and the importance of dress in social perceptions. Previous work by Davis (1964), Goffman (1963), Elliott et al. (1982), Hanks and Poplin (1981), and Kaiser (1983–84) served to provide a framework for the analysis of the data; however, several novel categories of responses to visible disabilities also arose from the data herein. Because the comments obtained from the group interviews and the questionnaires may have varied as a result of the increased anonymity in the questionnaire responses, throughout the presentation of the results an "(I)" will follow those comments obtained from the interviews, and a "(Q)" will follow those derived from the questionnaires.

SOCIAL FEEDBACK

Almost all of the subjects in the focused group interviews felt that clothing and appearance are extremely important in people's responses towards one another when they first meet. And, visible disabilities generally were considered to be conducive to the creation of attitudinal barriers in such cases. Several individuals commented, however, that such effects of disabilities on person perceptions could be at least partially ameliorated by dressing neatly and attractively. There also was some recognition that self-feelings with the regard to appearance are related to social feedback.

[2]The subjects in both phases of the study represented disabilities such as paraplegia, quadriplegia, cerebral palsy, multiple schlerosis, and others. More than half of the respondents used wheelchairs.

[3]Copies of the interview schedules and questionnaires are available upon request from the first author. Additional data derived from the questionnaires are available as well.

> If you are well-dressed and you don't look like you spent three days in the same clothes, then you do tend to get a better response. I've been with people in wheelchairs that look real rumpled and it's not that the clothes aren't good enough . . . It's just that they look unkempt; I'm turned off by that. (I)

> I think that they're more courteous, more social, or smiley if I feel I'm looking nice. I'm more attractive, I'm friendlier, and so they respond differently. (I)

There was almost unanimous agreement in the interviews that when verbal feedback on clothing and appearance is received, it is positive.

> I get a lot of good feedback that makes me feel good. (I)
> I usually get a lot of good comments. (I)

> I get very positive comments about what I wear. (I)

The majority (92%) of the respondents to the questionnaire indicated that they like to receive compliments on their clothes and appearance. Even compliments, however, may be tinged with stigmatization. Some support for the "just world" hypothesis (Lerner, 1970; 1980) was indicated in a response by the wife of a man who had had a stroke that their friends "were astounded that he can look as good as he does or dress as well as he does" (I). Such astonishment seems to suggest that an attractive appearance seems inconsistent with a disability and thus is the source of some ambivalent perceptions.

With regard to fleeting, relatively anonymous encounters during the course of everyday situations such as changing classes, the respondents in wheelchairs frequently commented that people react initially to the wheelchair, rather than the individual in it. Goffman (1963) would refer to a wheelchair as a stigma symbol, due to its salience in social perceptions.

> A lot of times, I think people look at the chair before they look at who's in it. (I)

> I must tell you that the overriding way to characterize them (others' responses) is in relation to my handicap. I suspect that they're noticing my dress . . . second or third. (I)

> People I don't know tend to notice my disability first, and my clothing second. (I) [Sixty percent of the respondents agreed with this statement in the questionnaire.]

> I think the visual impact of a person, sitting in a chair with wheels on it, is so great as to render all other impressions, such as dress or grooming, virtually insignificant. For example, a nude person seen passing down the street in a

> wheelchair will be reported as "a person in a wheelchair without clothes on was seen . . . etc." Rather then, "A person without clothes on was seen in a wheelchair." (Q)

However, many of the students acknowledged that some of the stigmatizing effects of a physical disability can be ameliorated by dressing neatly or fashionably. Ninety-one percent agreed that the first thing people notice is appearance, and clothes are part of that. Thus clothing is not necessarily seen as a source of secondary impressions only. Moreover, 64% of the questionnaire respondents agreed with the following statement: "If I'm attractively dressed, people are more likely to notice me rather than my disability."

A conflict may occur between a) a perceiver's desire to attend to a novel stimulus such as a physical disability or related cue and b) social restraints against staring. This conflict leads to uncomfortable, controlled interactions between disabled and nondisabled persons in face-to-face situations (Kleck et al., 1966; Kleck, 1968; Comer and Piliavin, 1972; Safilios-Rothschild, 1970). Several respondents reported their self-feelings based upon the staring behavior of others. One male student with severe burn scars on one arm indicated a preference for overt verbal attention to a stigma symbol, as opposed to staring:

> On a personal basis, for example, if I wear a T-shirt, I get these eyes that are just staring at my arms . . . I want to tell that person, if you want to sit down we can talk, and I can explain it to you and explain how I got this way. I find it more rewarding when a person will say, "Wow, what happened to you?" Versus somebody who's just looking at you and looking at you. I was in this dance class, and he (a male student) had already seen me for probably three or four weeks, but he was still trying to absorb it. Like trying to look at a picture, and you want to look at it until you finally absorb it. I didn't feel comfortable with that. (I)

Smiles were considered to be a desirable form of nonverbal feedback. Seventy-nine percent of the students responding to the questionnaire indicated that they liked for people they did not know to smile at them. However, one female subject in a wheelchair remarked in an interview that one can never be sure why a person is smiling, so a smile is an ambiguous form of feedback for a person with a visible disability.

MANAGEMENT OF APPEARANCE RELATIVE TO NEGOTIATED OUTCOMES

As a negotiated outcome perspective would suggest, most of the subjects indicated an interest in using dress or other appearance cues (e.g., hairstyles, overall neatness) to present positive impressions to others and thus to supply stimuli to augment or ameliorate the impressions created by a visible disability. The students also seemed to be concerned with their roles in representing the disabled population in general. Eighty-five percent of the questionnaire respondents agreed with the statement, "I want the nondisabled to know that disabled people are concerned with their appearance and clothing."

Only in two instances was there any evidence that individuals were resigned to existing appearances and lacking in motivation to manage the impressions they presented. Such resignation or apathy has been called capitulation (Elliott et al., 1982:291): "Giving up, the stigmatized accept the stereotype thrust upon them and the concomitant illegitimate status." One subject in an interview indicated that he generally wears pajamas and hospital gowns in public despite the fact that he has received negative feedback on the negative image his appearance presents for disabled persons.

> It [appearance] is only important if you take it to extremes . . . hospital gowns, etc. Most of the people I know are attendants. They won't freak out if they see me in a hospital gown. That's what I'm wearing right now because it's the most comfortable thing. . . .When I say dressed up I mean anything more formal than a hospital gown. (I)

It is important to note that this individual was almost completely paralyzed and was unable to sit up in a wheelchair. He was rolled on a flat bed from class to class by an attendant. One factor in his disinterest in dress may have been his inability to see his body, as he was always in a horizontal position. He did express some interest in the appearance and function of the blanket used to cover him.

The only other person whose response to appearance might be characterized as capitulation was also severely disabled and was unable to communicate with the group, due to his cerebral palsy. His attendant gave her interpretation of his self-feelings:

> You don't like the way you look at all . . . [he nods]. He has a great big closet of clothes that he hates. They are a mess . . . He has a condom hookup that isn't very convenient with his clothes. . . .They say he's one of the most disabled people in the country. . . .He had problems with the questions about style and

fashion. I guess he doesn't get around or pay that much attention to it. And maybe he doesn't care. (I)

Facilitation of Normative Identifications

The majority of the students expressed a desire to look like everyone else and considered clothes as a means for such normalization. The idea that deviance is imputed to a disability because other people consider one's appearance to differ from the norm is fundamental to the application of labeling theory to physical disabilities (Davis, 1964; Safilios-Rothschild, 1970). However, Haber and Smith (1971) have argued that stigmatization is not synonymous with deviance. Disability, in their minds, is a social role which is legitimized in some contexts, i.e., in the worlds of the medical profession or social work. In a college setting, such legitimation may not exist, and persons with visible disabilities may need to strive for normalcy.

Davis' concept of deviance disavowal (1964) involves the stigmatized person's attempts to strive for normalcy. If such a person is able to surpass fictional acceptance by others and then to facilitate reciprocal role-taking, then his/her interactions are likely to be more meaningful. This process of "breaking through" (Davis, 1964:128) may be facilitated through normative clothing styles. In both the interviews and the questionnaires, normative styles such as jeans, corduroys, and casual sportswear were preferred for wearing on the campus. The students did not want to appear any more conspicuous than they already were, and some indicated that dress was one area in which they could strive for identification with others. Dress, unlike a visible disability, is a reflection of personal choice.

> They [disabled people] are so different in so many ways. They are in a wheelchair, walk with a cane or a crutch, and when it comes to clothes they want to be like anybody else. (I)

> It is very important to me to dress in fashion, like everyone else. It is sometimes difficult to find clothing that is stylish and still practical for my disability. (Q)

When the students were questioned with respect to possible outlets for the purchase of specially designed clothing for people with disabilities, the importance of normalization with regard to clothing became apparent. Several students expressed strong feelings that the medical profession (the same profession that legitimizes disability as a social role) should not play a part in the distribution of functional clothing, due to the connotations of essential differentness from the norm.

> I'd like to see it away from the medical aspects. Get away from where they sell medical things. The environment—it reminds me of hospitals. . . .I'm going to enjoy shopping, to look at some of the styles of clothing available for disabled people and not to look at braces. They make you sick, whereas if you go to a clothing department you want to buy clothes. It affects you psychologically. (I)
>
> Putting clothing in a medical supply store would not be a good idea. It would alter the way the individual felt about herself. It would be too clinical. It would be nice if the 16-year old girl could go to the store with her friends and pick out clothing like any other teenager. Maybe it would help to lessen the "I'm different" attitude and help instill an "I'm a normal" individual concept. (Q)

Moreover, there were many comments which indicated that the whole idea of special clothing for people with disabilities reinforces the differences between disabled and nondisabled people, and thus should be avoided.

> I like the idea of clothes that fit everyone. I don't like the idea of having a special category. If I need something special, I will ask somebody to do [make] it. But I don't like the idea of having a special store. (I)
>
> Clothes for the disabled. . . .That can be kind of offensive. You want to be as normal as possible, and you don't want to be tripping into some store. . . .The rich, they do the same thing (buy customized clothes), but it's got a different ring. (I)
>
> No disabled labeling—just a brand name. (Q)
>
> Something normal sounding. (Q)
>
> The biggest drawback I've seen with clothing for the disabled is that there is such a heavy reliance on function, style is almost completely ignored. (Q)

With respect to deviance disavowal, or the desire to appear as normative as possible, several appearance-related responses were identified. These responses are discussed in the following sections.

Making do One of the most creative responses to the conflict of function versus style needs with regard to clothing might be referred to as "making do." Goffman (1961) used this phrase to describe the adaptations to clothing made by patients in a mental institution. In the case of persons with disabilities, making do may provide a means for purchasing normative clothing and altering it to suit their own particular physical needs. Many ingenious "make-do's" were reported with a sense of pride by the subjects. In the focused group interviews, the students appeared to enjoy sharing their ideas with one another. For example, one male student dealt with pressure-point problems while seated by having his mother remove the pockets in the back of his blue jeans and sew a patch of sheepskin inside on which to sit. Other make-do's included alterations to shoulders in dresses and shirts for quadriplegic students or alterations to pants to increase their attractiveness in the seated position. One woman who had only one arm wore a prosthesis in the form of an artificial shoulder. She had been provided with a strap to hold the prosthesis, and this strap greatly limited the kinds of clothes she could wear (e.g., high-necked styles and dark colors). She developed the idea of gluing the prosthesis rather than using the straps, and this technique enabled her to wear a greater variety of styles.

Concealment One obvious way of presenting a normative appearance, when possible, is through concealment of the disability. To conceal a source of stigma, according to Elliott et al. (1982) is to engage in "passing" as a normal. Some examples of managing the visual impressions presented through concealment follow:

> I get a different response from people when I wear short sleeves so I very seldom wear short sleeves. It camouflages my disability (missing arm) when I wear long sleeves. (I)
>
> Because of my amputation at the hip, I prefer dresses without a waist or gathering at the bodice of the dress. Dresses that flare out more at the tail are more attractive. (Q)

Similarly, Bregman and Hadley (1976) reported that spinal-cord-injured women reported concealing a catheter leg bag through the use of long skirts or dresses or pants. In many cases, Goffman's notion of "covering" (1963), as opposed to "passing" is likely to apply to the concealment of disabilities by persons with disabilities. Covering involves the concealment of a stigma in order to reduce tension, or to make it easier to withdraw overt attention from the stigma. The individuals are ready to admit possession of the stigma, but do not want it to be the most salient attribute perceived by observers.

Deflection When actual concealment is not possible, a stigmatized person may deflect others' attention from the damaging effects of the stigma by presenting the signs of the stigma as signs of a less deeply discrediting attribute (Goffman, 1963; Elliott et al., 1982). For example, a mentally retarded person may pretend to be hard of hearing rather than have others think he/she does not understand a conversation. Although such a guise would not be applicable to the deflection of attention from a visible handicap, other forms of deflection may be possible. A more applicable form of deflection may be to emphasize another aspect of one's identity which may or may not have positive social connotations. Several respondents to the questionnaire indicated that they wore T-shirts with slogans which would serve such a purpose. Some individuals emphasized their drinking habits through the following slogans: "I don't have cerebral palsy; I'm just drunk," "Ten gallon weekend," and "Moosehead beer." Drinking habits, as opposed to the possession of a physical disability, are elected rather than ascribed behaviors. As such, drinking has ambiguous connotations in American society, but nevertheless serves to deflect attention from the disability. A student may prefer to be known for his/her heavy drinking than for the disability.

A similar example was one student's indication of having a T-shirt saying "Sun your buns." Again, a perceiver might reflect on the questionable taste of a person wearing such a T-shirt, and at least would have an alternate stimulus to attend to in lieu of the disability.

Compensation One way of gaining legitimacy in social encounters is to compensate for a physical disability by expressing mastery in an area usually closed to disabled persons and/or important to a particular situation in which the stigma is irrelevant (Elliott et al., 1982). For instance, other social roles may be emphasized, as a person communicates, "This isn't all of me" (Levitin, 1975). In this way, the disability does not obscure more positive, socially valued aspects of the self. A strong interest in fashion or dress per se may provide a means of compensation. One male in an interview explained that he emphasizes his ethnic status (Mexican-American) and his flair for style through the wearing of white peasant pants, a white vest, huaraches, a Panama hat, and a blue handkerchief around the neck. He stated that at times he has enjoyed wearing this outfit to attract attention. Another subject indicated that she spends a lot on her clothes because she feels that she and others respond toward attractive clothing rather than her disability (quadriplegia). Other students indicated on the questionnaires they had T-shirts emphasizing occupational aspirations ("Social workers do it in the field," "Love a nurse today"), social-political orientations ("No nukes," "Nuclear power—No thanks!" "ERA"), or other aspects of the self ("Joe Cool," "I'm a wild and crazy guy," "Short and sexy").

Social inclusion Another means of disavowing deviance expressed by the students was to include able-bodied persons under the label of disabled, with the assertion that everyone has some form of handicap in certain contexts. In relation to appearance, most people find themselves inappropriately attired for certain situations, for example. And, once attired, persons have little control over the impressions they provide to others. A common comment was that individual differences should be accepted, as they are everywhere.

> I don't consider myself especially handicapped. Everyone has a handicap; some are more obvious than others. No one is perfect. (Q)
>
> You should really send this (the questionnaire) to everyone, because there isn't one person living without some disability. (Q)

One subject suggested that "Rainbow fashions" would be a good label for a clothing line for people with disabilities, because "we all have differences but together we make up the world" (Q). Another individual remarked, while viewing pants with a zipper in the side pants leg during the interview, that if such functional features were incorporated into all pants, for disabled and able-bodied persons alike, then functional clothes would lose their negative connotations.[4]

Displays of Social Uniqueness

Wright (1960) has suggested that disabilities may generate opportunities and positive outcomes as well as grief. Similarly, a review of the literature by Shontz (1977) has provided little support for the assumption that all psychological effects of disability are negative, i.e., disruptive or dissatisfying. There are likely to be situations, at least, in which a physical disability does not lead to a negative outlook on self and society. A physical disability is likely to call attention to a person and make that person memorable in the eyes of perceivers. Although such remembrances may not always be positive, there are likely to be situations in which they are.

People with disabilities, however, do not appear to desire extra attention. Eighty-two percent of the questionnaire respondents disagreed with the statement, "I like the extra attention I get because of my disability." In contrast, there were more varied responses to the statement, "I like to draw attention to myself through my clothes." Thirty-nine percent of the students disagreed with the statement, while 37% agreed with it, and 24% were undecided. Thus clothing per se may be used to call attention to the self, but attention which is considered to be based upon one's disability is less desirable.

Clothing and a visible disability are likely to work together in presenting impressions to observers. Miller (1982) found that the salience of a disability cue leads to dispositional, rather than situational, attributions

[4]The current and innovative style of jogging or tennis shoes with adhesive closures is a good example of the category of social inclusion. This style incorporates both self-help qualities and normative value.

about an individual. That is, a perceiver is likely to believe that a person with a disability is more responsible for the outcome of an event than are situational factors. Miller's research suggested that clothing may lessen the impact of physical impairment on some aspects of impression formation. In his research, the appearance cues of a hearing aid and patterned clothing each increased personal attributions, attributions of leadership, and recall.

Since a person with a visible disability is likely to be noticed he/she may capitalize upon this tendency by further shaping the impression formed through the management of appearance. Some instances of such an attitude were found in the present study, although they were considerably less common than the tendency to emphasize normalcy. A few participants in the focused group interviews indicated that they enjoy the extra attention they receive from others, and they take advantage of this attention by making noticeable clothing choices.

> I like bright colors. I used to think that I didn't like that extra attention, but in the last year I've noticed that I like it. I used to resent all the extra attention I got being in a chair, but I kind-of am finding that I like the extra attention, so I take advantage of it. (I)
>
> Just trying to be sexy. It must be my age. Low cut and things that show off my bustline. (I)

The desire to draw attention to personal appearance was not a common response, and the other subjects in the interview in which the above attendant made her remarks did not seem especially receptive to them. In contrast to the tendency to draw attention to the self, one subject in the same interview said, "I never dress to draw attention to myself." Thus the desire to emphasize social uniqueness is likely to vary across persons and contexts.

Although few disabled persons appeared to draw attention to themselves through clothing, many had suggestions for clothing labels emphasizing social uniqueness in the questionnaire. Following are some of the typical responses: "Special and spirited," "Special and spicy," "Clothes for special people," "Fashion for the positively unique," "My own style," "Innovations and improvisations," and "Pretty 'n progress." It is possible that official labels stressing the social uniqueness of disability may be perceived as legitimizing it as a social role. Of course, there are likely to be drawbacks even to the latter, as one student pointed out: "I'm sorry, a little realistic, I suppose, but I have learned that 'special' anything costs, and what a racket" (Q).

The expression of humor with respect to personal disabilities also was found in some of the students' responses. Humor may serve as a means of tension release in encounters between disabled and able-bodied persons.

During an interview, one male subject in a wheelchair relayed an experience in which his unexpected response to staring disrupted that staring and provided a personal sense of satisfaction. He was in a pizza parlor with his mother when every person in a group at a nearby table stared at him continuously. Finally, he started waving and smiling at them; they were so disconcerted that they got up and moved to a new table where they could not see him.

Other examples of the expression of humor in emphasizing social uniqueness were found in the case of T-shirt messages reported in the questionnaire: "I'm no quad: I'm just tired of walking" and "Guess which part of me is not bionic." Again, such appearance-related responses were not common among the students, but they do suggest that some individuals tend to emphasize humor or social uniqueness through their dress.

Another variant of the emphasis on social uniqueness involved instances in which there was an expression of minority or in-group power. For instance, several students volunteered that there should be more disabled persons in the media, but only if they have done something which deserves to be there. One student indicated that it would be nice to see models with leg braces. There were a number of T-shirt slogans reported which suggest a desire for more recognition from society: "Do it in a wheelchair," "High level quads do it with a 'joy stick,' " and "If I prove I'm better, will you admit I'm equal?"

A slightly different form of social uniqueness emphasized the importance of mainstreaming in society, rather then emphasizing differentness per se. These responses still, however, would be likely to call attention to the person with a physical disability. T-shirt slogans which indicated a desire for mainstreaming included the following: "Rehabilitation publicity," "I'm accessible." And, suggestions for store or clothes names indicated a similar emphasis on the ability to mainstream: "No help needed," "Fashions for free life style," "Free me fashions," "Access Fashion," "Access Wear," "HAIL fashions" (Handicapped Active in Life), and "Freedom fashions." Some comments were made to the effect that nondisabled persons would be more aware of the needs of persons with disabilities if a store catering to their needs were in a mall and were identifiable with respect to its purpose: "It would let them [nondisabled persons] know that handicapped people are concerned with their appearance" (I).

Safilios-Rothschild (1970) has argued that increased visibility of people with disabilities in society is needed if nondisabled persons are to communicate with them in a more meaningful manner:

> Unless modern societies are successful in altering social and affective prejudices in such a way that the disabled are accepted as "people with a disability,"

> in the same way that people with green eyes or blond hair are accepted, we will not have moved very far from the prejudices and discriminatory practices of the Middle Ages. (Safilios-Rothschild, 1970:11)

CONCLUSIONS

People with physical disabilities appear to participate actively in the labeling process through the management of aspects of appearance over which they can exert some control. A negotiated outcome perspective emcompasses such impression management. Like able-bodied persons, individuals with visible disabilities are likely to present the most positive aspects of the self. Positive feedback from others is received by persons with disabilities, particularly with regard to their clothing. Thus all labels applied to such persons are not stigmatizing.

The most commonly preferred form of dress by the students in this study appeared to be styles which were as normative as possible. Clothes reflect personal choice, unlike a physical disability; as such, they may be used to express identification with nondisabled persons and thus to facilitate reciprocal role-taking. A variety of normalizing techniques were displayed by the students in this study: "making do" with ready-to-wear apparel through ingenious adaptations, concealment of the disability, deflection of attention towards other aspects of the self which may be perceived as less discrediting, compensation by emphasizing other social roles and abilities, and social inclusion (i.e., emphasizing that all persons possess disabilities and physical differences). Linguistic forms of communication, in the form of T-shirt slogans, were used by students to emphasize other aspects of the self when these aspects could not be displayed through more abstract symbols of dress.

Although they appeared to be in the distinct minority, some students capitalized on their social uniqueness and the resulting attention by drawing further attention to their clothes. Such a technique may provide observers with other aspects of the self to remember. At the same time, the self-attention of the person with a disability may be focused more upon his/her clothing than on the disability. This prospect for impression management is one aspect of the dilemma which appears to confront persons with visible disabilities. Although most persons with disabilities do not want to attract any further attention to themselves and thus dress in styles which blend in with the norm, the effects of such "normalization" may be to neutralize an aspect of appearance—clothing—that might otherwise be used to decrease the salience of the visible disability and to emphasize other aspects of the self.

The possibilities for the inclusion of dress and other appearance cues in future studies on the social interactions of persons with disabilities are extensive. Appearance manipulations provide a novel focus for such studies; the present data may provide a framework for deriving various forms of dress for such manipulations, in order to determine the impact on perceivers' responses. The categories of impression management defined in these data should be refined through research incorporating other populations of persons with disabilities and a contextual variations.[5] In the meantime, an integration of the present categories with existing literature on physical deviance raises several issues which might be addressed in future research.

First, an expectancy/perceptual bias on the part of a person with a physical disability appears to influence the manner in which he/she interprets others' responses in interactions, specifically by increasing attention to an observer's gaze behavior and tension (Kleck and Strenta, 1980). In conjunction with the present data, one might hypothesize that clothing could provide an alternate stimulus, in lieu of a physical deformity, that might influence both the observed person's expectations and an observer's forming impressions. For example, an observer's gaze behavior might be attributed to the observed person to a dramatic or eye-catching outfit in addition to or instead of a physical disability. Variations in attire (e.g., normative versus socially unique or humorous) might produce diverse foci of attention for both a wearer and a perceiver, as well as provide novel meanings for personal identity.

Second, the self-image of persons with disabilities could be explored in relation to preferred mode of dress. In a study by Landon et al. (1980), abnormal patterns of adjustment on the part of males with cystic fibrosis appeared to be attributable to shortness in height rather than to cystic fibrosis per se. It is conceivable that a stigmatized self-image may be intensified through modes of dress such as those in the category of capitulation or diminished through normative, deflective, or compensatory styles.

Third, the manner in which perceivers explain situational outcomes for persons with disabilities is likely to be altered by clothing style as well as physical disability. Miller (1982) found some support for this idea; further work with a broader range of apparel styles should be undertaken. Due to the importance of social norms in relation to clothing choices, the social norm of kindness toward persons with disabilities (c.f., Strenta and Kleck, 1982) could be incorporated into studies in which other appearance variables are manipulated. For example, normative and compensatory attire may result in a higher degree of kindness from others than more extreme styles (e.g., capitulative or humorous).

Fourth, an examination of social-cognitive processes associated with

[5]For example, a study of disabled persons within a business context might reveal additional appearance-related responses such as protection or defense. The present sample of college students would be more likely than businesspersons to experience a higher sense of freedom in choices of attire.

perceptions of clothing and stigma symbols should consider the importance of social context in relation to emergent meanings, definitions and redefinitions of situations, and attributions (Kaiser, 1983–1984). The joint effects of clothing and stigma symbols may be modified as a result of social interactions and fashion changes. Due to the salience of a wheelchair in person perceptions, as indicated by individuals in this research, this symbol should be considered as a factor in negotiated outcomes. Design researchers might focus upon the development of novel wheelchair styles which, along with apparel styles, emphasize the aesthetic tastes of users. Design prototypes could be used as stimuli along with various apparel styles in order to determine effects on person perceptions.

Finally, the applicability of the present taxonomy for other persons who are stereotyped in a variety of ways in terms of appearance should be explored. Such persons might include physically attractive females in male-dominated business contexts, gays, or obese persons, to name a few. Some of the impression-managing strategies indicated in the present research may apply to individuals who differ from the contextual norm and respond accordingly through the use of appearance symbols so as to negotiate the desired outcomes in social interactions, either by normalizing appearance or by emphasizing uniqueness.

REFERENCES

Adams, Gerald R.
1977 "Physical attractiveness research: Toward a developmental social psychology of beauty." Human Development 20:217–239.

Adams, Gerald R.
1982 "Physical attractiveness." Pp. 253–304 in A. G. Miller (ed.), In the Eye of the Beholder: Contemporary Issues in Stereotyping. New York: Praeger.

Adams, Gerald R., and P. Crane.
1980 "An assumption of parents' and teachers' expectations of preschool children's social preference for attractive or unattractive children and adults." Child Development 51:224–231.

Altman, Barbara M.
1981 "Studies of attitudes toward the handicapped: The need for a new direction." Social Problems 28:321–337.

Berscheid, E., and E. Walster.
1974 "Physical attractiveness." Pp. 157–215 in L. Berkowitz (ed.), Advances in Experimental Social Psychology, Volume 7. New York: Academic Press.

Bregman, Sue, and Robert G. Hadley.
1976 "Sexual adjustment and feminine attractiveness among spinal cord injured women." Archives of Physical and Medical Rehabilitation 57:448–450.

Comer, Ronald J., and Jane A. Piliavin.
1972 "The effects of physical deviance upon face-to-face interaction: The other side." Journal of Personality and Social Psychology 23:33–39.

Cuber, J. F.
1963 Sociology: A Synopsis of Principles. New York: Appleton-Century-Crofts.

Davis, Fred.
1964 "Deviance disavowal: The management of strained interaction by the visibly handicapped." Pp. 119–137 in H. Becker (ed.), The Other Side: Perspectives on Deviance. New York: The Free Press.

Dion, K. K., and E. Berscheid.
1974 "Physical attractiveness and peer perception among children." Sociometry 37:1–12.

Elliott, Gregory C., Herbert L. Ziegler, Barbara M. Altman, and Deborah R. Scott.
1982 "Understanding stigma: Dimensions of deviance and coping." Deviant Behavior 3:275–300.

Feather, Betty L., Betty B. Martin, and Wilbur R. Miller.
1979 "Attitudes toward clothing and self-concept of physically handicapped and able-bodied university men and women." Home Economics research Journal 7:234–240.

Goffman, Erving.
1961 Asylums. Chicago: Aldine.

Goffman, Erving.
1963 Stigma. Englewood Cliffs, N.J.: Prentice Hall.

Haber, Lawrence D., and Richard T. Smith.
1971 "Disability and deviance: Normative adaptations of role behavior." American Sociological Review 36:87–97.

Hallenbeck, Phyllis N.
1966 "Special clothing for the handicapped: Review of research and resources." Rehabilitation LIterature 27:34–40.

Hanks, Michael, and Dennis E. Poplin.
1981 "The sociology of physical disability: A review of literature and some conceptual perspectives." Deviant Behavior 2:309–328.

Hansen, Robert A.
1980 "A self-perception interpretation of the effect of monetary and nonmonetary incentives on mail survey respondent behavior." Journal of Marketing Research 17:77–83.

Higgins, Paul C.
1980 "Societal reaction and the physically disabled: Bringing the impairment back in." Symbolic Interaction 3:139156.

Kaiser, Susan B.
1983–1984 "Toward a contextual social psychology of clothing: A synthesis of symbolic interactionist and cognitive theoretical perspectives." Clothing and Textiles Research Journal 2:1–9.

Katz, Irwin.
1981 Stigma: A Social Psychological Analysis. Hillsdale, N.J.: Lawrence Erlbaum.

Kernaleguen, Anne.
1978 Clothing Designs for the Handicapped. Alberta: University of Alberta Press.

Kitsuse, John I.
1975 "The 'new conception of deviance' and its critics." In W. R. Gove (ed.), The Labelling of Deviance. New York: Wiley.

Kleck, Robert.
1968 "Physical stigma and nonverbal cues emitted in face-to-face interaction." Human Relations 21:19–28.

Kleck, Robert E., and William DeJong.
1981 "Adults' estimates of sociometric status of handicapped and nonhandicapped children." Psychological Reports 49:951–954.

Kleck, Robert, H. Ono, and A. H. Hastorf.
1966 "The effects of physical deviance upon face-to-face interaction." Human Relations 19:425–436.

Kleck, Robert E., and Angelo Strenta.
1980 "Perceptions of the impact of negatively valued physical characteristics on social interaction." Journal of Personality and Social Psychology 39:861–873.

Landon, Christopher, Ronald Rosenfeld, Gregory Northcraft, and Norman Lewiston.
1980 "Self-image of adolescents with cystic fibrosis." Journal of Youth and Adolescence 9:521–528.

Lerner, M. J.
1970 "The desire for justice and reactions to victims." In J. Macauley and L. Berkowitz (eds.), Altruism and Helping Behavior. New York: Academic Press.

Lerner, M. J.
1980 The Belief in a Just World. New York: Plenum Press.

Levitin, T. E.
1975 "Deviants as active participants in the labeling process: The visibly handicapped." Social Problems 22:548–557.

Miller, Franklin G.
1982 "Clothing and physical impairment: Joint effects on person perception." Home Economics Research Journal 10:265–270.

Popp, Rita A., Victoria R. Fu, and Susan E. Warrell.
1981 "Preschool children's recognition and acceptance of three physical disabilities." Child Study Journal 11:99–114.

Safilios-Rothschild, Constantina.
1970 The Sociology and Social Psychology of disability and Rehabilitation. New York: Random House.

Shannon, E., and Naomi Reich.
1979 "Clothing and related needs of physically handicapped persons." Rehabilitation Literature 40:2–6.
Shontz, Franklin C.
1977 "Physical disability and personality: Theory and recent research." Pp. 333–353 in J. Stubbins (ed.), Social and Psychological Aspects of Disability. Baltimore: University Park Press.
Stone, Gregory.
1962 "Appearance and the self." In A. M. Rose (ed.), Human Behavior and Social Processes. Boston: Houghton Mifflin.
Strenta, Angelo, and Robert E. Kleck.
1982 "Perceptions of task feedback: Investigating 'kind' treatment of the handicapped." Personality and Social Psychology Bulletin 8:706711.
Wright, B. A.
1960 Physical Disability: A Psychological Approach. New York: Harper and Row.
Yu, Julie, and Harris Cooper.
1983 "A quantitative review of research design effects on response rates to questionnaires." Journal of Marketing Research 20:36–44.

Reading 23

Responses to Labeling Attempts: Deviant Drinkers' Pathways of Label Manipulation

Michael R. Nusbaumer
Indiana University-Purdue University at Fort Wayne

Recognizing the traditional labeling approach's view of the label recipient as a passive participant in the labeling process, this paper argues that the symbolic interactional roots of this approach indicate this to be an inappropriate formulation. Rather, it is suggested that label recipients are active participants in the process and their major goal is the reduction of stigma and limited conforming opportunities inherent in label application. For the deviant drinker, there are two available pathways of label negotiation. With initial labeling attempts, it is hypothesized that label recipients should attempt to negotiate reality through deviance avowal, whereas with increasing numbers of prior labeling attempts, deviance avowal becomes the only viable means of reality negotiation. Because of the medicalization

An earlier version of this paper was presented at the North Central Sociological Association annual meetings in Detroit, 1982.

of deviant drinking, deviance avowal becomes a means of reducing label-based social costs through occupation of the repentant-deviant role. Given the need to invoke certain aspects of the medically based sick role in order to gain entrance into the repentant-deviant role, it was hypothesized that those attempting to negotiate reality through deviance avowal exhibit attitudes more consistent with the traditional sick role than those attempting to disavow deviance. Although the findings provide general support for these hypotheses, they also indicate inadequacies of the Parsonian sick-role formulations in deference to the more appropriate repentant-deviant role model for deviant drinkers attempting to avow deviance.

Although the societal reaction or labeling approach to deviance has received a great deal of attention over the last two decades, both its supporters and critics continue to recognize that one of its major handicaps to viability is the lack of theoretical specificity and resultant testable hypotheses (Davis, 1972; Gove, 1980; Kitsuse, 1980; Mankoff, 1971; Robins, 1980; Schur, 1980). Nowhere is this problem more evident than in the approach's application to the area of deviant drinking.

The labeling approach to deviant behavior, with its roots in the symbolic interactionism of Cooley (1902), Mead (1934), and Tannenbaum (1938), focuses attention not on the question of why one commits deviant acts but rather on the process of how one becomes defined as deviant, the nature of that definition, and both the society's and the deviant's response to that definition (Schur, 1971).

An issue central to the labeling approach has been the impact and subsequent response of the individual to whom a negative label is being applied. As early as 1938, Tannenbaum noted that "the person becomes the thing he is described as being" (1938:19–20). Later, hedged in more symbolic interactionist terminology, this idea became known as the self-fulfilling prophecy, which stated, that which is defined as real is real in its consequences (Merton, 1957). This view quickly became a central tennant of many labeling theorists (Becker, 1963; Erickson, 1962; Kitsuse, 1962; Lemert, 1951; Scheff, 1966), who suggested that once a label has successfully been applied the label recipient is expected to behave in a manner consistent with the stereotypical characterizations of the particular label. This view has been closely associated with such labeling-based concepts as secondary deviation (Lemert, 1951), master status (Becker, 1963), and role engulfment (Schur, 1971). For the deviant drinker this view dictates that once labeled, deviant drinkers should be expected at least to continue, if not actually to increase, their deviant drinking activity consistent with the label (Roman and Trice, 1968). Indeed, research dealing with deviant drinkers suggests that alcoholic labeling not only reinforces future deviant drinking practices but also limits the label recipient's ability to return to a nondeviant status (Cahn, 1970; Burkett, 1972).

Many, however, would argue that this view represents an inappropriate formulation of the labeling approach and is inconsistent with the interactionist roots of this approach. The self-fulfilling prophecy characterization of the labeling approach portrays an overly deterministic conception of human behavior. The actor in this regard is seen as a passive recipient of the label, one who necessarily conforms to society's role expectations based on that label (Davis, 1972; Gibbs, 1966; Gouldner, 1968; Quadagno and Antonio, 1975).

In contrast, symbolic interaction theory assumes that the individual is an active agent in the interaction process. Rather than simply react to a situation, actors are able to treat themselves as objects, through the development of the self-conception, and thus can weigh the implications of the situation and choose a response to it. As Blumer (1969) writes: "In the face of something which one indicates, one can withhold action toward it, inspect it, judge it, ascertain its meaning, determine its possibilities, and direct one's action with regard to it" (p. 63). In this sense, the individual confronting the application of a deviant label should attempt to negotiate the definition of reality in an effort to bring about the desired outcome (Schur, 1971, 1979; McAuliffe, 1980). Labeling attempts by others should therefore not be seen as the only determinant of the actor's subsequent behavior as the actor's ability to respond to his or her own definition of the situation represents a crucial intervening factor.

For the deviant drinker, the label "alcoholic" is considered undesirable. Goffman (1963) notes the stigmatizing effect of such labels and the general discrediting of the label recipient through the negative reactions of others. The undesirability of such a label is also based, at least in part, on the fact that its successful application would greatly limit one's opportunities. As a result of the stigmatization, the label recipient's opportunities for conforming participation are reduced (Tittle, 1980). Hence, with the limitation of opportunities inherent in the application of the label, one would assume that the potential label recipient would try through the reality-negotiation process to avoid, neutralize, or negate the social pressures associated with the successful application of the label (Turner, 1972).

Because of the need for greater theoretical specificity and the historic identification of the self-fulfilling prophecy as a major component of the labeling approach, this paper attempts to refine the labeling approach's view of the actor's response to label application from a more interactionist based viewpoint, resulting in the establishment and testing of appropriate hypotheses.

The deviant drinker actively attempting to reduce the negative consequences of the labeling process has two modes of response. The first is denial and deviance disavowal: "the attempt to convince others (disavowal) and oneself (denial) that the deviation is not really an impediment to normal existence" (Schur, 1979:296). The actors therefore attempt to argue that they have been inappropriately labeled by others and negotiate reality by defining and presenting themselves as nondeviants. In this case, the drinking behavior that led to the application of the label would be defined as either not in violation of society's drinking norms or at least not indicative of any major drinking problem. This deviance disavowal may often be expressed through techniques of neutralization (Sykes and Matza, 1957) or the making of accounts (Schur, 1979).

For the deviant drinker, as well as other deviants, the deviance disavowal response is most often evidenced in the initial stages of the labeling process (Turner, 1972:315). This response is most likely to occur in the initial stages of the labeling process because the deviant has greater opportunities to explain away the precipitating deviant acts and the generally fewer preceding occurrences of deviant acts. It should be remembered, however, that such disavowal is extremely difficult given the initial labeling attempts, and the attempts on the part of the deviant to drink "normally" in order to prove the inappropriateness of the label may actually lead to increased deviant activity (Roman and Trice, 1968; Turner, 1972). The prerequisite for the disavowal of deviance is the actors' failure or refusal to self-label themselves as deviants. Lemert's differentiation between primary and secondary deviation is crucial here:

> The deviant individuals must react symbolically to their own behavior aberrations and fix them in their sociopsychological patterns. The deviations remain primary deviations or symptomatic and situational as long as they are rationalized or otherwise dealt with as functions of a socially acceptable role. When a person begins to employ his deviant behavior or role based upon it as a means of defense, attack or adjustment to the overt and correct problems created by the consequent reaction to him, his deviation is secondary. (1951:75–76)

Thus, as long as the actors define themselves as normal, as in the early stages of the labeling process, deviance disavowal represents a viable response. As the number of acts of primary deviation increase, however, labeling and stigmatizing efforts also increase. This results in the continued reduction of opportunities to explain or define the deviant acts as part of a socially accepted role by the actor, which would increase the likelihood of secondary deviation.

The medicalization of deviant drinking, as expressed in the definition of alcoholism as a disease, provides the actor with a second mechanism through which reality can be negotiated and the costs associated with the deviant label reduced. Prior to the establishment of the disease definition of alcoholism, deviant drinking was viewed as a wholly volitional act, whereby anyone who maintained aberrant drinking practices was perceived as challenging and voluntarily violating society's drinking norms. In an attempt to maintain the norm boundaries and provide support for society's ability to demand conformity, society's response to such behavior patterns was punishment oriented and allowed little if any negotiation of reality on the part of the drinker. As the disease definition of alcoholism became more widely accepted, however, the deviant drinker was seen as suffering from an illness and was therefore eligible for sick-role occupancy. This access to the sick role allowed deviant drinkers to define their drinking behavior as at least a partially nonvolitional act.[1] Consequently, the deviant drinker is not held responsible for the onset of the illness and therefore cannot be held responsible for alleviating it through will power or simple attitudinal changes. This lack of control over one's illness allows deviants to exhibit deviant behaviors and still maintain allegiance to the normative value structure as long as they fulfill all of the obligations inherent in the sick role (Conrad and Schneider, 1980; MacAndrew, 1969). This explanation also makes the deviant drinker more deserving of help and treatment rather than punishment and ostracism.

Ultimately, the illness model allows for greater reality negotiation on the part of deviant drinkers. They may choose to negotiate reality by openly avowing their deviance through self-labeling and adopting a repentant-deviant role that allows for the conditional acceptance of continued deviant behavior. Successful entrance into the repentant-deviant role is predicated on the following conditions. First, the deviant drinker must fulfill the two major obligations of the sick role: (1) viewing the illness as undesirable and (2) seeking out and cooperating with technically competent help in order to overcome the illness (Parsons, 1951). Second, given that the major treatment goal for deviant drinkers is abstinence, deviant drinkers must express both a desire and an attempt to remain abstinent despite the fact that they may not be able to do so because of the illness' nonvolitional nature. Finally, the deviant drinker is expected to express visibly reformed behavior (at least in regard to nondrinking-related behaviors) in conformity to the norms of the community (Trice and Roman, 1970:541). For the deviant drinker, this repentant-deviant role is translated into the more socially acceptable role of recovering alcoholic.

The reduction of social costs and constraints attainable through this deviance avowal process has become well established for the deviant drinker in numerous discussions of Alcoholics Anonymous (Lofland, 1969; Schur, 1979; Trice and Roman, 1970; Turner, 1972). Additionally, the Alcoholics

[1]Although Parsons' (1951) original formulation of the sick role defined illness behavior as totally nonvolitional, much evidence suggests a general lack of support for the total nonvolitional definition of behavior for the deviant drinker (see, for example, Chalfant and Kurtz, 1971; Haberman and Sheinberg, 1969; Mulford and Miller, 1961; Orcutt and Cairl, 1979).

Anonymous requirement for self-labeling as an alcoholic implicitly supports the importance of self-definition as a reality negotiation mechanism. It should be noted, however, that such avowal opportunities are also accessible through any treatment approach grounded in some form on the disease model of alcoholism.

From this discussion and the recognition of the actor's ability to negotiate reality, one would assume not the simple operation of the self-fulfilling prophecy but rather a more active attempt on the part of the actor to reduce the social costs and constraints of the "alcoholic" label through either disavowal or avowal of deviance. Given this negotiation process, the central question becomes: Are there any factors that serve to differentiate those who will attempt deviance disavowal from those who will attempt deviance avowal as a means of label manipulation?

Noting that attempts at deviance disavowal appear to be a more viable means of reality negotiation in the initial stages of the labeling process and that the greater the number of labeling attempts the less opportunity to define the behavior in relation to a normal social role, we would expect an increasing likelihood of deviance avowal attempts with increasing numbers of labeling attempts. Therefore, the first hypothesis states: The greater the number of previous labeling attempts, the greater the likelihood of attempts to avow (as opposed to disavow) deviance.

Secondly, given the need to occupy the repentant-deviant role in order to reduce the social costs and constraints of the deviant label through deviance avowal, we would expect those attempting deviance avowal to exhibit attitudes more consistent with the sick role than those attempting to disavow deviance. This expectation is based not only on the fact that sick-role attributes more closely fit the community's expectations for appropriate behavior on the part of the recovering alcoholic but also on the fact that the nonvolitional nature of the sick role definition is crucial for reducing the restrictive outcomes of the labeling process through avowal. In addition, those attempting disavowal should tend to reject the sick role and its nonvolitional definition of drinking behavior, which puts responsibility for the control of the behavior in the hands of appropriate professionals and thereby reduces drinkers' ability to make viable accounts of their own drinking practices. If the behavior is defined as outside the control of the drinker, the ability of drinkers to negotiate reality through deviance disavowal is reduced because the lack of personal control over the behavior also negates their ability to invoke personal disavowal mechanisms. The second hypothesis then reads: Those deviant drinkers attempting to avow deviance are more accepting of the sick role for the deviant drinker than those attempting to disavow deviance.

Data were collected on a total of 470 clients who received services at an alcohol detoxification center serving a nine-county catchment area in north-eastern Indiana from April 1980 to January 1981. After eliminating incomplete cases because of early leaves from the center and multiple visits by the same clients during this period, the resultant sample consisted of 412 cases.[2] Whenever possible, basic demographic data were collected on client intake, with additional data being collected as soon as possible after initial detoxification (usually 24–96 hours after intake). As part of the services provided by the detoxification center, clients typically received referrals to various alcohol treatment programs for their drinking problems. Only those clients with referrals were included in the sample.

A follow-up was conducted one week after clients left the detoxification center to see if they had begun any further treatment. This was normally done by contacting the agency to which the client had been referred. In those cases where clients had been referred to Alcoholics Anonymous only, follow-ups were conducted either by noting the clients' attendance at AA meetings held in the center (to which most were referred) or by contacting the clients themselves. Treatment follow-up by the client was considered an indicator of deviance avowal, whereas failure to follow up was viewed as a true indicator of deviance disavowal only for those clients who had received no treatment prior to their current detoxification. Deviance disavowal was operationalized in this manner because of two confounding factors for those clients with previous treatment experiences who did not follow up. First, given the earlier theoretical discussion, we would expect those clients who had experienced previous labeling attempts to be less successful at label negotiation through deviance disavowal because of the decreasing opportunities to provide alternative explanations for the precipitating drinking behavior. Therefore those clients with prior treatment experiences who did not follow up, while possibly attempting deviance disavowal, might also be avowing deviance and simply rejecting the disease definition of alcoholism and treatment based on that model or they might actually be fulfilling the self-fulfilling prophecy as outlined by Roman and Trice (1968). The inability to differentiate between these possible responses in the current data set dictated the use of the above operationalization of deviance disavowal as the most clear-cut and acceptable. Secondly, recognizing the transient nature of a certain portion of the deviant drinking population and their likelihood of numerous treatment experiences (Fagan and Mauss, 1978) suggests the no-follow-up group with multiple treatment experiences may contain a portion of transients who simply left the catch-

[2]Unfortunately, no data were available for those who left the center early. According to center employees, the majority of those who leave prematurely simply use the facilities as a comfortable place to sober up. They appear to have little interest in seeking help for their drinking and leave as soon as possible after sobriety is achieved.

TABLE 1 Comparison of Treatment Follow-Up Rates with Number of Prior Treatment Experiences

	Prior treatment experiences						
Follow-up	0	1	2	3	4	5	6 or more
Yes (%)	14 13.3	16 19.0	13 20.3	8 21.6	6 31.6	6 35.3	32 37.2
No (%)	91 86.7	68 81.0	51 79.7	29 78.4	13 68.4	11 64.7	54 62.8
Total	105	84	64	37	19	17	86

Note. $\chi 2 = 18.59$; degrees of freedom = 6; probability $p \leq .005$.

ment area, thus drawing into serious question their definition as deviance disavowers.[3]

Acceptance of various aspects of the sick role were measured by responses on a five-category Likert-type scale for each of the following statements derived from Parsons' (1951) original work in this area.

1 An alcoholic should be excused from at least some normal responsibilities because of his or her condition (Exemption).
2 If an individual becomes an alcoholic, it is his or her own fault (Fault).
3 An alcoholic is not able to overcome his or her condition by will power alone (Will power).
4 Being an alcoholic is undesirable (Desire).
5 An alcoholic should seek and cooperate with technically competent help to overcome his or her condition (Competent help).

These five items were combined (simply added together after reversing the coding on the Fault item) to give a composite measure of sick-role acceptance.

In Table 1, we find a direct, significant ($p \leq .005$) relationship between the number of prior treatment experiences and the percentage of clients seeking follow-up treatment. Thus the likelihood of deviance avowal as a mechanism of reality negotiation on the part of the label recipients appears to increase with decreasing opportunities for deviance disavowal as evidenced in number of prior treatment experiences. The finding indicating that the most marked change in follow-up rates occurs between three and

[3]In the current sample, the researchers did experience an increasing rate of sample mortality in personal follow-ups with increasing numbers of previous-treatment experiences (these were coded as no follow-up). Similar findings for the agency follow-ups can only be assumed, as data for further analysis are unavailable.

TABLE 2 Comparison of Sick-Role-Based Attitudes between Those Attempting to Avow Deviance and Those Attempting to Disavow Deviance

	Deviance avowers (N = 95)		Deviance disavowers (N = 91)			
Attitude	χ	***SD***	χ	***SD***	***t* Scores**	**Level of significance (two-tailed test)**
Sick role[a]	13,18	1.94	13.81	1.71	-2.37	.02
Exemption	3.88	.89	3.63	.87	2.01	.05
Fault	3.36	.91	3.54	.82	1.42	NS
Will power	2.20	.87	2.60	.94	-3.04	.005
Desire	1.88	.71	2.11	.74	-2.12	.05
Competent help	1.85	.53	1.93	.47	-1.12	NS

Note. Sick-role-based attitudes were scored using a 5-item Likert-type scale (1 = strongly agree to 5 = strongly disagree).

[a]Composite of 5 items.

four prior treatment experiences suggests that after three prior treatment experiences the label recipient's ability to disavow deviance is noticeably reduced and future labeling attempt responses stem more heavily from a secondary deviation basis.

In Table 2, the focus shifts to a test of the second hypothesis. From this hypothesis, the expectation is that those who appear to have attempted to negotiate reality through deviance avowal should accept the sick-role model for the deviant drinker more than those attempting to disavow deviance.

The finding in Table 2 on the composite sick-role score does support the hypothesis ($p \leq .02$); however, findings on the individual sick-role items suggests that such composite scores may represent an oversimplification that does not accurately reflect the true nature of the disease definition of deviant drinking and the reality negotiation process. Significant differences in the expected direction were found in terms of the ability to alleviate the problem by will power alone ($p \leq .005$) and the undesirability of being an alcoholic ($p \leq .05$). The most notable difference, which is found on the will power item, is particularly crucial given the need to define at least certain aspects of deviant drinking behavior as outside of the actor's control.

By indicating less perceived ability to overcome the behavior by will power alone than the disavowers, the deviance avowers are more able to occupy the repentant role and therefore less threatening to societal norm maintenance concerns. In addition, this response allows avowers to seek treatment as an indicator of their desire to change (repent for) their behavior. What is unique, however, is the lack of significant differences on the similarly volition-based fault item. This apparent inconsistency may be more clearly understood by noting the drinker as not being at least partially at fault for their drinking behavior (Chalfant and Kurtz, 1971; Haberman and Sheinberg, 1969; Mulford and Miller, 1961; Orcutt and Cairl, 1979). In order more effectively to fulfill the repentant role, the deviance avower may be more likely to adopt the public's definition of the behavior in an attempt to obtain greater public acceptance without jeopardizing more crucial aspects of the nonvolitional definition of behavior exemplified in the will power item. The significant finding on the desire item is again consistent with the repentant deviant's need to reflect society's normative attitudes regarding the alcoholic label and the requirement to exhibit visible reform through open disapproval of the deviant behavior.

A significant difference was also found on the exemption from normal responsibilities item ($p \leq .05$), but in the opposite direction from the expected. One explanation for this finding hinges on the view that exemption from normal social responsibilities in and of itself serves to limit one's ability to negotiate reality. For those attempting to disavow deviance, the extent to which they view the deviant drinker as unable to meet these responsibilities serves only to strengthen their disavowal position. Similarly, the ability of deviance avowers seeking access to the repentant role to meet normal social responsibilities serves to increase their acceptability into the repentant role. Through meeting these responsibilities, the deviance avowers attempt to establish themselves as being as normal as possible and to make amends for their deviant behavior.

Finally, the lack of a significant difference between the two groups on the competent help item, although not supporting the hypothesis, may simply reflect the nature of self-labeling in the two groups. Although the deviance avowers generally agree that the "alcoholic" should seek out and cooperate with technically competent help, the disavowers, by also indicating agreement with this statement, may actually be attempting to reinforce their disavowal claims by not seeking such help. In other words, they may be indicating that only if they were truly "alcoholics" they too would seek out competent help.

Contrary to much of the literature dealing with labeling, this paper argues that the actor experiencing label application is an active negotiator in the labeling process and attempts to negotiate for the least restrictive outcomes available. For the deviant drinker, this negotiation may take the form of either deviance disavowal or deviance avowal; the latter form of negotiation produces a repentant deviant, one who relies on a disease definition of alcoholism.

It was posited that in the initial stages of the labeling process the actor will attempt to negotiate reality through deviance disavowal but that, with increasing labeling attempts and decreasing opportunities to make accounts for the deviant drinking behavior, the actor will attempt to negotiate reality through deviance avowal. The current findings support this contention, which in turn draws into question the traditional assumption of the operation of a self-fulfilling prophecy. Although these findings are only exploratory, they do indicate that labeling theorists' views concerning the actor's responses to labeling attempts may be in need of further development, with particular emphasis on the recognition of the active part played by the label recipient in an attempt to negotiate labeling outcomes.

These findings also give credence to the traditional Alcoholics Anonymous view that deviant drinkers must first "hit bottom" in regard to their drinking behavior before there is a realistic chance to alter the behavior. This view, however, might more appropriately be operationalized in terms of treatment attempts' being successful only when secondary deviation occurs and the deviant drinker attempts to negotiate reality through deviance avowal; focusing attention on certain stages related to actual drinking practices obscures this fact.

The disease model of alcoholism allows reality negotiation on the part of the actors through access to the repentant-deviant role. It was hypothesized that those attempting to negotiate reality through this mechanism would necessarily have to exhibit attitudes more consistent with the sick role inherent in the disease definition. Despite the fact that the current findings exhibit general support for this view, they also point out the inconsistencies between the traditional sick role and the repentant-deviant role. Those attempting deviance avowal were found to display attitudes more in line with the repentant-deviant role. These findings not only substantiate the inappropriateness of applying the traditional sick-role formulation to deviant drinking but also point out the need to recognize and more fully develop the repentant-deviant role conception. In particular, more attention must be given to the deviant drinker's need to adopt socially acceptable definitions of the deviant behavior, to have socially acceptable expectations for those attempting to overcome their problem, and to make amends for prior behavior in order successfully to reduce restrictive outcomes of the labeling process.

With the general trend toward the medicalization of deviant behavior in a variety of areas (Conrad and Schneider, 1980), these findings indicate that the application of the traditional sick-role formulation may represent an overgeneralization that might more effectively be viewed as a starting point for the more accurate development of disease-based definitions of deviant roles in many areas. In light of the current research, the repentant-deviant role formulation holds promise for further development and application in such areas as crime, mental illness, and drug abuse.

Further, given the societal concern for the social costs of deviant drinking, these findings suggest a need more fully to develop access routes to the repentant-deviant role and to provide greater social acceptance of the "recovering alcoholic" and greater recognition of the value and potential of the repentant role.

These findings also shed important light on the historic success and growth of Alcoholics Anonymous and similar organizations. Their ability to offer access to the repentant-deviant role has provided many label negotiators an opportunity to return to a more socially acceptable role than might otherwise have been possible.

Further explorations are also warranted in terms of the relationship between the medicalization of deviance and the ability to disavow deviance. As pointed out in the current findings, those attempting to disavow deviance may actually be using the disease conception of deviant drinking and its inherent sick-role aspects to actually strengthen their disavowal claims. This appears to occur through a process of accepting the disease definitions and sick-role aspects for the true "alcoholic," thereby supporting their disavowal claims by indicating that these conceptions do not fit themselves.

Unquestionably, the often-cited need for additional work to clarify numerous points is as equally justified here as elsewhere. The repentant-deviant role needs more development, the hypotheses established here need to be tested with other types of deviant behavior, and the labeling approach needs better theoretical grounding and greater specificity. Yet, above all, this paper suggests the need to develop a theoretical approach to its fullest extent before a judgment of its scientific worth is finally rendered.

REFERENCES

Becker, Howard G.
1963 Outsiders: Studies in the Sociology of Deviance. New York: Free Press.

Blumer, Herbert
1962 "Society as symbolic interaction," Pp. 145–154 in Arnold M. Rose (ed.), Human Behavior and Social Processes. New York: Houghton Mifflin.
1969 Symbolic Interactionism. Englewood Cliffs, N.J.: Prentice-Hall.

Burkett, Steven
1972 "Self-other systems and Deviant Career Patterns." Pacific Sociological Review 15:169–181.

Cahn, Sidney
1970 The Treatment of Alcoholics: An Evaluative Study. New York: Oxford University Press.

Chalfant, H. P., and R. A. Kurtz
1971 "Alcoholics and the sick role: Assessments by social workers." Journal of Health and Social Behavior 12:66–72.

Conrad, Peter, and Joseph W. Schneider
1980 Deviance and Medicalization: From Badness to Sickness. St. Louis: Mosby.

Cooley, Charles Horton
1902 Human Nature and the Social Order. New York: Scribner.
Davis, Nanette J.
1972 "Labelling theory in deviance research: A critique and reconsideration." Sociological Quarterly 13:447–475.
Erickson, Kai T.
1962 "Notes on the sociology of deviance." Social Problems 9:307–314.
Fagan, Ronald W., and Armand L. Mauss
1978 "Padding the revolving door: An initial assessment of the Uniform Alcoholism and Intoxication Treatment Act in practice." Social Problems 26:232–247.
Fox, Renee C.
1977 "The medicalization and demedicalization of American society." Daedalus 106(1):9–23.
Gibbs, Jack
1966 "Conceptions of deviant behavior: The old and the new." Pacific Sociological Review 9:9–14.
Goffman, Erving
1963 Stigma: Notes on the Management of Spoiled Identity. Englewood Cliffs, N.J.: Prentice-Hall.
Gouldner, Alvin
1968 "The sociologist as partisan: Sociology and the welfare state." American Sociologist 3:103–116.
Gove, Walter R.
1980 The Labelling of Deviance: Evaluating a Perspective (2nd ed.). Beverly Hills: Sage.
Haberman, P. W., and J. Sheinberg
1969 "Public attitudes toward alcoholism as an illness." American Journal of Public Health 59:1209–1216.
Kitsuse, John I.
1962 "Societal reaction to deviant behavior: Problems of theory and method." Social Problems 9:247–256.
1980 "The 'new conception of deviance' and its critics," Pp. 381–393 in Walter R. Gove (ed.), The Labelling of Deviance: Evaluating a Perspective (2nd ed.). Beverly Hills: Sage.
Lemert, Edwin M.
1951 Social Pathology: A Systematic Approach to the Theory of Sociopathic Behavior. New York: McGraw-Hill.
Lofland, John
1969 Deviance and Identity. Englewood Cliffs, N.J.: Prentice-Hall.
MacAndrew, Craig
1969 "On the notion that certain persons who are given to frequent drunkenness suffer from the disease of alcoholism." In S. C. Plog and R. B. Edgerton (eds.), Changing Perspectives in Mental Illness. New York: Holt.

Mankoff, Milton
1971 "Societal reaction and career deviance: A critical analysis." Sociological Quarterly 12:204–218.

McAuliffe, William E.
1980 "Beyond secondary deviance: Negative labelling and its effects on the heroin addict." Pp. 303–341 in Walter R. Gove (ed.), The Labelling of Deviance: Evaluating a Perspective (2nd ed.). Beverly Hills: Sage.

Mead, George Herbert
1934 Mind, Self and Society. Chicago: University of Chicago Press.

Merton, Robert K.
1957 Social Theory and Social Structure. New York: Free Press.

Mulford, Harold A., and D. E. Miller
1961 "Public definitions of the alcoholic." Quarterly Journal of Studies on Alcohol 23:312–320

Orcutt, James D., and Richard Cairl
1979 "Social definitions of the alcoholic: Reassessing the importance of imputed responsibility." Journal of Health and Social Behavior 20:290–295.

Parsons, Talcott
1951 The Social System. Glencoe, Ill.: Free Press.

Quadagno, Jill, and Robert Antonio
1975 "Labeling theory as an oversocialized conception of man: The care of mental illness." Sociology and Social Research 60:35–45.

Robins, Lee R.
1980 "Alcoholism and Labelling Theory." Pp. 35–47 in Walter R. Gove (ed.), The Labelling of Deviance: Evaluating a Perspective (2nd ed.). Beverly Hills: Sage.

Roman, Paul M., and Harrison M. Trice
1968 "The sick role, labelling theory, and the deviant drinker." International Journal of Social Psychiatry 14:245–251.

Scheff, Thomas J.
1966 Being Mentally Ill. Chicago: Aldine.

Schur, Edwin M.
1971 Labeling Deviant Behavior: Its Sociological Implications. New York: Harper.
1979 Interpreting Deviance: A Sociological Introduction. New York: Harper.
1980 "Comment." Pp. 393–405 in Walter R. Gove (ed.), The Labelling of Deviance: Evaluating a Perspective (2nd ed.). Beverly Hills: Sage.

Sykes, Gresham M., and David Matza
1957 "Techniques of neutralization: A theory of delinquency." American Sociological Review 22:664–670.

Tannenbaum, Frank
1938 Crime and Community. New York: Columbia University Press.

Tittle, Charles R.
1980 "Labelling and crime: An empirical evaluation." Pp. 241-263 in Walter R. Gove (ed.), The Labelling of Deviance: Evaluating a Perspective (2nd ed.). Beverly Hills: Sage.

Trice, Harrison M., and Paul M. Roman
1970 "Delabeling, relabeling and Alcoholics Anonymous." Social Problems 17:538-546.

Turner, Ralph H.
1972 "Deviance avowal as neutralization of commitment." Social Problems 19:308-322.

Part Four

Deviance as Behavior

Chapter Eight

Social Interaction

EDITORIAL COMMENTARY

Deviant behavior is often social interaction. It may involve an actor (or actors) behaving in a particular fashion toward another (or other) actor (or actors) and in turn, eliciting a reaction. In some instances, the process may be relatively habituated or routinized and, thus, essentially scripted and predictable. It can often, however, be quite problematic. Actors sometimes play their accustomed roles differently in given situational contexts, even if the social context is repetitive. Every alteration in role playing and behavior on the part of the actors may be interpreted differently and alternate meanings may be ascribed to the behavior by others in the situation. Circumstances and situations may change and, thus, the context may be altered with an attendant transformation in interpretation and assignment of meaning.

Deviant social interaction is subject to an extremely differential set of definitions. Such definitions, in addition to being a function of time, place, and circumstances, also vary from one segment of society to another, and even from person to person, based on perspective, perception, and interpretive posture. Intervening conditions and events may also impact on perception and interpretation, and consequently on meaning and motivation. Deviant social interaction is accordingly multidimensional and, in effect, often open-ended.

In some instances, one actor may be the deviant and the other actor the victim, such as an armed robber demanding and getting money from a store clerk. In other cases, both actors may be participants in the deviant behavior, (e.g., a businessman on a trip out of town engaging in sexual intercourse with a prostitute). In some situations, a deviant actor may act in concert with another individual or individuals in order to victimize someone. As an illustration, two pickpockets may work together in a team fashion, one distracting the victim's attention with conversation while the other bumps into the victim picking his pocket. Gang rape is another such example.

Deviant behavior may involve a perpetrator and an unwilling victim such as an individual who is held up and robbed at gunpoint. It may also involve a perpetrator and a willing victim (e.g., an adult male who has sexual intercourse with an underage female and is, thus, guilty of statutory rape). The victim might even in some circumstances initiate the deviant behavior, the sexually precocious female child who acts seductively toward an adult man and solicits sex play, for instance.

Some writers (MacDonald, 1971:115–117), for example, have reported child victims of sexual molestation as young as five years of age, who apparently "had initiated the sexual activity." One researcher (Whiskin, 1975:168) told of a "ring" of female children, 7 to 10 years old, "who made a considerable amount of money from older men whom they allowed certain liberties for a fee of 25 cents." The crime of incest, also, not infrequently involves a willing victim (see, for example, Rosenfeld, 1979:406). Where the victim is a relatively mature, adolescent daughter, the girl may even engage in a kind of rivalry with the mother, ultimately playing the role of "wife" to the father to the extent of being a sexual partner. The willing victim, or at least the victim who is contributory to their own victimization, is not confined to sexual deviance. There is a growing research literature on the factor of "victim precipitation" in a wide variety of crimes, sexual and otherwise, ranging from murder (see, for example, Mulvihill and Tumin, 1969:225–226) to rape (Amir, 1970:259–276; 346–347).

The victim of deviance may interact with the offender but not necessarily even be aware that he or she has been victimized. The gullible individual who buys worthless stocks or land from the confidence man may not realize he or she has been swindled, and the child who "plays" with the pedophile adult may not understand that he or she has been molested. Even the woman who was drugged and sexually assaulted might not realize she has been raped.

The response to a deviant act may be an important element in the motivation for the behavior. Some voyeurs, for example, may only derive carnal gratification from their peeping activities if the female "victim" they are watching becomes aware of them, and to this end, may even knock on the window or otherwise try to obtain the attention of the victim (Yalom, 1960:308–319). Similarly, male exhibitionists generally attempt to frighten or shock, or at least interest the women to whom they expose their genitals. Exhibitionism is, among other things, an attempt to assert masculinity and the offender seeks reaffirmation of his maleness in the shocked response of his female victims. Some exhibitionists speak of the act of exposing their genitals as being "exhilarating" (Halleck, 1975:76). This is not the case if there is only a minimal response on the part of the victim. A blasé or "ho-hum" victim response, in effect, takes the exhilaration out of the act. Rapists also may seek a particular kind of reaction in their victims, perhaps wanting the women to struggle, or beg or plead. Strippers and other erotic dancers would seem to enjoy the spirited (and sometimes obscene) response of the audience members to their sexually suggestive performance (Salutin, 1971:18).

The interaction involved in deviant behavior may be highly scripted to the point of genuine redundancy. As Bryant and Palmer (1975) point out the massage parlor is a "quick orgasm establishment" analogous to the fast food restaurant. To accomplish this, the masseuses have to process customers in an expeditious fashion which they do by following a very routinized schedule of activities and interaction. These authors report that the masseuses revealed that in this regard, their motto was "get 'em in, get 'em up, get 'em off, and get 'em out." On the other hand, deviant behavior may also involve interaction that is very spontaneous and original. In this connection it is said that some types of deviant behavior may change, or new forms emerge in response to technological change. Computer crime did not occur obviously until after the invention of the computer. The invention of the Polaroid camera with its instant pictures, as well as the invention of the video recorder and home video camera, have supposedly greatly widened the horizons in the area of sexual deviance. The interaction (particularly verbal interaction), that is constituent to deviant behavior may, in some cases, be quite minimal or perfunctory. Laud Humphreys (1970:13) in his account of "tearoom trade," spoke of spending hours at a time observing homosexual activity in public restrooms. He indicated that with the exception of an occasional phrase uttered by one of the participants in the sexual activity such as "thanks," or "not so hard," the room tended to be silent.

There is often a theatrical or dramaturgical element to deviant behavior interaction. Transvestites will don female apparel and cosmetics and pretend to be a woman while interacting with others. In order to enjoy their sexual fantasies, sadomasochists may have to enlist the aid of others to help them act out their fantasies even to the point of using props, costumes, and a set (Weinberg and Falk, 1980). Successful confidence games will likely require the perpetrator to assume a role and play the part. Seduction likewise may necessitate playing a part, as it were. Luring a victim into a position of more vulnerability may well require some dramaturgical efforts. Much deviant behavior involves deception and calls for theatrical mechanisms. Sometimes, delivering the deviant service may be embellished with dramaturgical flourishes in the same way that chefs in Japanese-style steak houses embellish their cooking performance with acrobatics and other exaggerated behavior. Prostitutes, of course, are frequently called upon to add a dramaturgical dimension to their sexual performance. They may be asked to wear unusual costumes (even dog collars), use special language (often obscenity), engage in bizarre behavior, play dead, or to beat the client or let the client beat them. Sometimes the prostitute may provide the theatrical element on a gratuitous basis. George Stewart (1972:269), for example, studied prostitutes from the perspective of the client and pretended to be a "john." He reported that on his first visit to a brothel, the prostitute that serviced him put on an elaborate contrived performance which included feigned sounds of carnal enjoyment. She even went so far as to compliment his sexual foreplay techniques exclaiming, "Oh wow, you sure have got me hot." Of course, some deviance is pure theater—the obscene, stand-up, blue comic who entertains his audience with pornographic stories and lewd language even though such behavior might transgress the boundaries of community decency or propriety, for example (Salutin, 1973). There have even been reports of lewd puppet shows with a promiscuous Pinocchio (Bryant, 1982:156). The x-rated movie, the obscene stage drama, or children "playing" doctor and nurse in a make-believe fantasy situation are also all illustrations of dramaturgical forms of deviant behavior.

The interaction in deviant behavior may be extremely intense such as in the instance of an individual who violently assaults or rapes a victim who attempts to resist or fight back. On the other hand, the interaction may be relatively subdued, (e.g., the perfunctory transaction of a disreputable, liquor store owner selling a 6-pack of beer to an underaged minor). The interaction may be open or manipulative. It may be exhortive or coercive. It may be ephemeral or enduring. The deviant interaction may be of great social import or it may be relatively inconsequential. Deviant interaction may be furtive or it may be public and even, in some cases, widely advertised.

Finally, deviant interaction, while seemingly pluralistic by definition, may on occasion, like any social interaction, involve only a single actor, who may be socially interactive with spurious others, who are the product of contrived fantasy, or hallucination. The protagonist in the stage play, *Harvey*, who had a giant, invisible rabbit for a constant companion, or the "Son of Sam" mass murderer in New York, who got his instructions from his neighbor's dog, are examples of the latter, and children who invent temporary, "make-believe" playmates are an illustration of the former.

This chapter examines the parameters of deviant social interaction and looks at the contexts and meaning of various configurations of interaction constituent to deviant behavior. The initial selection, Shearon Lowery and Charles Welti's "Sexual Asphyxia: A Neglected Area of Study," addresses a particularly unique form of deviance. Sexual asphyxia represents both deviant sexual behavior and suicide, although the suicide would appear to often be accidental. The victims are almost invariably males. It is a highly convoluted variety of sexual behavior and appears basically to be an attempt to intensify and enhance autoerotic activity. Although there are variations on the practice, the victims usually accomplish to tie themselves up and also put a rope or collar around their neck with which they hang themselves. They sometimes are wearing female clothing or have erotic material at hand. They may even gag themselves.

The hanging or ligature around the neck serves to impede the flow of oxygen to the brain and this produces giddiness and exhilaration. Sometimes the asphyxia is produced by gas or chemical, or even a plastic bag over the head. The asphyxia is supposed to heighten or intensify the sexual pleasure of masturbation. Sometimes the choking alone produces feelings of pleasure, erections or even orgasm. Although the ropes are applied in such a way as to make it possible for the victim to quickly untie himself, sometimes he cannot or perhaps loses consciousness and dies as a result of the hanging, or the loss of blood and oxygen to the brain. It would appear that the victims in general do not seek to commit suicide but die accidentally as a result of their bizarre sexual activities.

The authors suggest that the victims may have engaged in similar behavior since adolescence and in the past have sometimes had partners participate with them in such behavior at least to the extent of helping to protect the victim from mishap. Practitioners in such activities were motivated by isolation and loneliness to seek partners to involve in their perverse behavior, but failing in this effort they pursued it alone and sometimes died in the process. Facing the difficulty of finding more conventional sexual outlets, they turn to autoerotic activity, and in the absence of partners to monitor and participate in their sexual activities they remain solitary practitioners.

Even though this sexually deviant behavior is conducted in a solitary fashion it should perhaps be viewed as interaction from a symbolic standpoint. The individual unsuccessfully seeks a social sexual fantasy and autoerotic sexual fulfillment. Still unable to find others to participate in his sexual activities, he attempts to embellish them with the trappings of a social context—costumes or nudity, self-inflicted bondage, erotic materials, and self-imposed sadistic measures (although they do not necessarily seek the painful "pleasure" of sadomasochism). In some instances, the victims even set up mirrors so that they could view themselves from the perspective of an onlooker. In effect, they were attempting to give a social dimension to a solitary context and animate their sexual fantasies. The autoerotic soliloquy situation is, perhaps, only one step further from the telephone masturbator who calls telephone counseling services and masturbates while talking to the female personnel who answer (Lester, 1973). In this instance, the individual undertakes to transform a solitary masturbatory episode into a socially interactive situation, and attempts to erotically enhance it through the expedient of adding a female outsider's voice, even if her actual presence is not component to the situation and her conversation is not relevant to the sexual activity. The individuals who engaged in sexual asphyxia simply used fantasy and theatrical "props" to provide a social context. They were interacting with themselves, in a soliloquy fashion. They had created a one-man, sexual drama with various roles, and played all of the parts. The drama unfortunately ended in tragedy!

The interaction component to deviant behavior may be largely economic in nature, a mere transaction as it were. Examples might be an addict purchasing narcotics from a dealer, a pregnant female paying a "physician" for an illicit abortion (in an earlier time when abortions were illegal), a customer buying "white lightnin" from a "moonshiner," or an individual seeking sexual services negotiating with a prostitute.

The next article in this chapter, "Buying Sex: The Phenomenology of Being a John" by Holzman and Pines explores the latter, and in this instance from the standpoint of the customer. The authors, in reviewing the literature, found some suggestion that "johns" were individuals whose physical, psychological, or social inadequacies would make it difficult for them to have sexual relations with conventional females. In short, they bought sex because they could not get it otherwise. Researchers that have obtained data directly from johns, however, have concluded that such men are not unusual, and that they generally do not support the stereotypical image of persons with "inadequacies" who found it necessary to purchase sex. The johns in this sample certainly appeared to be average, if not above average, in terms of education, income, and looks.

The authors report that being a john is more a process ("a series of interrelated decisions and acts") than a role ("one who simply exchanges money for sex"). This process begins with the "conception of intent," which included both a desire for sex, and a desire for companionship as well. Beyond this the johns sought to "create" a fulfilling encounter by employing sexual fantasy, and the contemplation of the mystery and risks that might be involved. The john sought the services of a prostitute out of choice, and was, in effect, embarking on an adventure.

Having made the decision to seek a prostitute, the individuals studied entered the second phase of the process, that of the pursuit of the encounter. Here they bathed, shaved, dressed, applied cologne and otherwise tried to make themselves attractive. They then chose conventional social settings such as a bar hoping to meet a prostitute there. Such behavior and the attendant feelings are not unlike those characteristic of courtship. In the next phase, the encounter, the johns met the prostitute, negotiated, and finalized the details of the sexual bargaining. There appeared to be more concern with the personality and interactional skills of the prostitutes than their physical characteristics. The johns were apparently attempting to structure the "objective reality" of the encounter. The final phase, the aftermath, left the johns with a mixture of feelings. Some wanted to leave quickly, some were appalled at what they had done, some were disappointed, but some were satisfied and felt "value had been received." It would appear that the johns had been seeking an experience that contained more than sexual gratification. Toward this end they had contributed to the illusionary dimension of the experience. Like all interaction enhanced by illusion and fantasy, the outcome had not always been totally fulfilling. For some, however, there was the remnant of the illusionary experience that might, given the right circumstances, be "reborn in the conception of intent."

Interaction in deviant behavior may be very much frank and "above board," as it were; buying narcotics from a dealer or sexual services in a brothel as examples. The interaction may have to be subtle, or diplomatic, or even oblique. As an illustration, when an individual visits a massage parlor, masturbatory services are not immediately offered, nor would it be appropriate for the client to request them. Rather in the course of the massage, the masseuse will subtly suggest that other areas of the client's body can also be massaged if he so wishes. As previously mentioned there may also be a need for dramaturgical interaction. But dramaturgy can easily become legerdemain, and the line between legerdemain and conspiratorial deception is, indeed, a thin one.

The next reading in this chapter takes a hard look at professional deception and thus, deviance. Lonn Lanza-Kaduce dissects the phenomenon of unnecessary surgery. The question of surgery is, in many instances, a matter of judgment and election. The surgeon must advise the patient to the best of his ability and experience as to whether surgery is called for. The patient must then act on this advice based on his own priorities and persuasion. Within such a situation, however, is an opportunity structure for manipulative recommendations for gain on the part of the surgeon.

The author informs us that an investigative congressional subcommittee of the U. S. House of Representatives has identified six types of "unnecessary discretionary" operations. These include completely discretionary operations for nonthreatening disorders, operations in which no pathologic tissue is removed, operations that are performed in spite of a matter of difference in judgments and opinion among experts, operations to alleviate endurable symptoms, operations performed in large numbers that may now be considered outdated or discredited, and operations done primarily for the personal gain of the surgeon.

Categories two, five, and six would all suggest the possibility of professional deviance. Monitoring surgical operations is complex and the measurement of professional misconduct is particularly difficult. Nevertheless Lanza-Kaduce, on the basis of a review of the literature, rates studies, epidemiological studies, and second opinion studies, concludes that, "the evidence clearly indicates that unnecessary surgery occurs with regularity." He also asserts that "the proportion of [such surgery] is sizable," that the cost, "in terms of mortality, morbidity, and money is substantial," and that it "may be increasing." The author then goes on to attempt to explain such surgery on the basis of various correlates including training and adult socialization, economic factors, and control mechanisms. Deviance among professionals, it appears, may well be consistent with "a more general and inclusive theory of deviant behavior."

Inasmuch as a confidence man can use fraud and deception to swindle a client, and an appliance, or used car, or home siding salesman can mislead and deceptively induce a customer into an unwise purchase, so too can a surgeon sometimes use deception to convince a patient to undergo unnecessary surgery. The patient, fearful for his health and life, and placing his trust in his surgeon, can be readily maneuvered into submitting to an operation that may only profit the professional. With only a minimum of encouragement from the surgeon, the patients may create their own pessimistic scenario if they fail to have the surgery. The considerable social distance between the surgeon and patient only tends to strengthen and reify the advice of the surgeon, even if only a suggestion of modest indication.

The interaction inherent in deviant behavior can be far more forceful than deceptive or manipulative. The offender can use force and violence or the threat of force or violence to coerce the victim. The admonition, "Your money or your life!" can be a powerful motivating factor, and in this sense, the verbal dimension of interaction can be a persuasive and effective means of coercion. The final reading in the chapter, Holmstrom and Burgess' "Rapists' Talk: Linguistic Strategies to Control the Victim," analyzes this verbal means of coercion. Interviewing 115 female rape victims, the authors identified a variety of major verbal themes, all intended to in some way control or coerce the victim. These themes included: threats, orders, sexual put-downs, racial epithets, or even "soft-sell" ploys such as promises of safe return. Inasmuch as rape is a crime of violence and force, the rapist must play an "exploitation" game. To do this the rapists use "linguistic strategies" both to control and coerce the victim as well as to try and "normalize" the interaction. The themes of conversation increase or augment the power of the offender over the victim. Interaction, in effect, becomes a weapon.

Social interaction can assume many configurations, and deviant interaction may, perhaps, be even more malleable. As noted above, the participants in such interaction may play roles that are concerted and collaborative, or one may have a part that is more active or passive, to some degree, than that of the other or others. Similarly, those involved in such interaction may differentially behave in a fashion ranging from extemporaneous to repetitious, and the pattern of the activity may, accordingly, be highly predictable or serendipitous. The motivation for deviant interaction may vary from hedonistic lust to calculated economic or even political gain and the level of behavioral intensity may also differ considerably, ranging from rapt preoccupation to pathological rage to deliberative and dispassionate detachment or perfunctory indifference. Among the examples offered in the selections in this chapter have been instances of single individual elaborately embellishing the pursuit of solitary pleasure, to the extent of trying to create a pseudo-social context, replete with multiple perspectives, stage "props" and costumes, and a panoply of fantasy in an attempt to create a socially interactive reality. Also illustrated was an elaborately structured and multiple stepped economic transaction involving a client buying sex from a prostitute. Here, too, there was a need to embellish the interaction with illusion and fantasy, and the subjective interpretation of events played an important part in the meaning and social reality of the encounter. In the selection concerning unnecessary surgery, the surgeon in seeming concert with the patient convinces the patient to undergo expensive and possibly dangerous surgery that may more profit the doctor than the patient. Using the patient's own concerns and fears, the surgeon helps the patient construct a social reality that, perhaps, is more threatening than the medical facts indicate. Again, the participants embellish the situation with unwarranted meaning and the surgeon, as the more instrumental of the participants, effectively guides the direction of the interaction and in a deviant fashion brings about an unnecessary and possibly dysfunctional outcome. In the final illustrative reading, the rapist also seeks to embellish the situation, either in some cases using threats and abuse to coerce or frighten the victim and, thus, maximize his control over her, or in other instances, using different linguistic strategies in a attempt to "normalize" or "conventionalize" their behavior. Here, too, is an effort to try and create an alternate social reality, and better shape the direction of the interaction and effect the desired outcome. The offender seeks to structure the reality of the situation. Deviant social interaction, like all social interaction, involves meaning, interpretation, and often the attempted manipulation of the interpretive context. Social reality is what people perceive it to be, and one or both of the participants in interaction may seek to create a social reality that is more congruent with their wants and expectations.

REFERENCES

Amir, Menachem

1970 Patterns of Forcible Rape. Chicago: University of Chicago Press. Especially Chapter 15, "Victim-Precipitated Forcible Rape."

Bryant, Clifton D.

1982 Sexual Deviance and Social Proscription: The Social Context of Carnal Behavior. New York: Human Sciences Press.

Bryant, Clifton D., and C. Eddie Palmer

1975 "Massage parlors and 'hand whores': Some sociological observations." The Journal of Sex Research 11:227–241.

Halleck, S. L.

1975 "Voyeurism and exhibitionism in adolescence." Human Sexuality 9:75–76.

Humphreys, Laud

1970 "Tearoom trade: Impersonal sex in public places." Transaction 7:10–25.

Lester, David

1973 "Telephone counseling and the masturbator: A dilemma." Clinical Social Work Journal 1:257–260.

MacDonald, John M.

1971 Rape: Offenders and Their Victims. Springfield, Illinois: Charles C Thomas.

Mulvihill, Donald J., and Melvin M. Tumin

1969 Crimes of Violence, Staff Report Submitted to the National Commission on the Causes and Prevention of Violence, Vol. II. Washington, D.C.: Government Printing Office.

Rosenfield, Alvin A.

1979 "Endogamic incest and the victim perpetrator model." American Journal of Diseases of Children 133:406.

Salutin, Marilyn

1971 "Stripper morality." Transaction: Social Science and Modern Society 8 (Whole No. 68):12–22.

1973 "The impression management techniques of the burlesque comedian." Sociological Inquiry 43:159–168.

Stewart, George Lee

1972 "On first being a john." Urban Life and Culture 1:255–275.

Weinberg, Thomas S., and Gerhard Falk

1980 "The social organization of sadism and masochism." Deviant Behavior 1:379–393.

Whiskin, Frederick E.

1967 "The geriatric sex offender." Geriatrics 22:168–172.

Yalom, Irving D.

1960 "Aggression and forbidingness in voyeurism." Archives of General Psychiatry 3:305–319.

Reading 24

Sexual Asphyxia: A Neglected Area of Study

Shearon A. Lowery
Florida International University, Miami

Charles V. Wetli
Medical Examiner Office, Dade County, Florida, and
University of Miami School of Medicine

Sexual asphyxia, a solitary autoerotic activity practiced almost exclusively by males, is examined in this paper. The self-induced asphyxia may be either chemical or mechanical, and its purpose is to heighten the sexual pleasure. The practice of sexual asphyxia can result in death; however, many such deaths may erroneously be viewed as suicides or homicides as a result of the lack of knowledge of the practice. Sixteen sexual asphyxial deaths, reported in Dade County (Miami), Florida, are examined in detail. These data confirm that practitioners are overwhelmingly young, white, middle-class, unmarried males. When the practice is fatal among older practitioners, the data show that some complicating factor, such as the use of alcohol or other drugs, may have contributed to the accident. The most frequent method of inducing the asphyxia was simple hanging by rope and in most cases there was no indication nor suspicion of suicidal intent.

The sociological study of sexual deviance has traditionally been limited to the examination and explication of prostitution and homosexuality, although some scholars have also considered premarital and extramarital sexual behavior to be deviant. Even when such a "broad" definition of sexual deviance has been employed, however, other types of sexual behavior such as sadomasochism and bondage have been typically excluded. Consequently, such practices have remained virtually ignored in the literature of sociology. In addition, judging from an examination of that literature, more unusual sexual practices such as sexual asphyxia are apparently unknown to sociologists. Consider, for example, the following case:

> The sheriff's office received a call from the frantic wife stating she had found her husband bound, gagged and murdered. The Police and Medical Investigator rushed to the scene to find a 27-year-old male deceased on the bed. The deceased was clad in brassiere, woman's panties, red negligee and panty hose, all of which the wife identified as hers. He was facedown with his legs flexed at the knees. The ankles were bound with four loops of clothesline, loosely knotted. The clothesline was attached to an elastic strap with metal hooks on both ends. The strap was looped about a dog collar encircling the neck. A bath towel was between the dog collar and the skin of the anterior neck. A handkerchief

> was tied about the shaft and the end of the penis and was stained with seminal fluid. A handkerchief was stuffed in the mouth, and a bandana was tied about the face at mouth level, knotted in the back. A large bathroom mirror had been removed from the door and rested against the dresser where it could be visualized by the deceased. (Lewman, 1978:11)

Although this scene suggests homicide or suicide, the actual manner of death is accidental. This case is in fact a rather typical example of the sexual asphyxia syndrome familiar to medical examiners and to a lesser extent to some police investigators and psychiatrists.

Sexual asphyxia is an autoerotic activity practiced almost exclusively by males. Lethal cases are almost always characterized by an individual male engaged in solitary sexual activity while simultaneously creating a self-induced mechanical or chemical asphyxia. The purpose of the asphyxia is to heighten the sexual pleasure. Cases of lethal sexual asphyxia among females are extremely rare; to our knowledge, only three instances have been reported (Sass, 1974; Danto, 1980; Sullivan and Wray, 1981).

Among males transvestism is frequently concomitant with the practice and there may be erotic literature or mirrors in view of the deceased. Sometimes the deceased's hands are tied behind his back, but close inspection invariably reveals that the victim himself was responsible for this. In addition, it is done in such a way as to permit a quick escape should that be necessary. Finally, the practitioner will have devised some mechanism to impede the flow of oxygen to the brain. This will usually be a ligature (often with a soft material or padding about the neck to prevent abrasion), a plastic bag, or an inhalent (gas, chemical aerosol, etc.). The subjective result is a giddiness and exhilaration; but the objective consequence is asphyxia resulting from mechanical restriction of the airway or chemical replacement of oxygen. If the process continues unabated the individual loses consciousness as a result of the lack of oxygen and the increased retention of carbon dioxide. Death will ensue unless the individual spontaneously breaks away from the asphyxiating device. If that device is a ligature, there is little likelihood of this happening once consciousness has been lost. Instead, the airway becomes further obstructed, as does the venous return from the brain, and finally the arterial blood supply to the brain is disrupted.

The most frequent method used to produce the asphyxia, and the one most discussed, involves ligatures applied to the neck. Ropes, scarves, and the like are tied about the neck in such a manner that they may be manipulated to control the flow of blood and oxygen to the brain. Such choking creates feelings of pleasure and may induce erections and even orgasms in some individuals (Resnik, 1972). Various descriptions of sexual asphyxia appear in literary sources; a particularly graphic passage can be found in DeSade's *Justine*:

> He got upon the stool, the rope around his neck. . . .He got ready and beckoned her to pull away the stool. Hanging by his neck for a while, his tongue lolling way out, his eyes bulging; but soon, beginning to swoon away, he motioned feebly to Justine to set him loose. On being revived he said, "Oh Therese! One has no idea of such sensations, what a feeling! It surpasses anything I know." (p. 101)

In addition, anthropoligists have pointed out that certain ethnic and cultural groups (e.g., Eskimos) are known to choke each other as part of their sexual activity. In such cultures it is common for the children to suspend themselves by the neck during play (Walsh, Stahl, Unger, Lilienstern, and Stephens, 1977).

The limited research that has been done indicates that it is likely that medical authorities underestimate the frequency of death resulting from sexual asphyxia. Some investigators (Sass, 1974; Litman and Swearingen, 1972; Resnik, 1972) have argued that sexual asphyxial practices are relatively common in the United States. Rosenblum and Faber (1979) think that it is reasonable to estimate that at least 250 deaths occur in the United States each year. This estimate is probably very conservative because it is likely that many sexual asphyxial deaths are judged to be either homicide or suicide because of a lack of awareness of the practice in many localities,[1] the sensivity of the sexual aspects of the practice, or the social status of the victims.[2] For example, it is possible that some deaths among youths that have been attributed to glue sniffing could actually have been the result of the practice of sexual asphyxia. More research is necessary before we can adequately address the issue of the reliability of these national estimates; however, it is important that the issues be raised and the subject investigated.

Although it is difficult to estimate the number of annual deaths from this cause it is even more difficult to estimate the number of individuals who engage in this sexual practice (Resnik, 1972; Rosenblum and Faber, 1979). Because we know that those practitioners for whom sexual asphyxia proved to be fatal took elaborate precautions not to die, we must take this factor into account in any attempt to estimate the number of practitioners. Thus,

[1]Werner Simon (1973) has argued that teenage suicides may not have increased as much as it appears. He posits that a number of these tragedies are actually accidental deaths resulting from the practice of sexual asphyxia.

[2]For example, a well-known professional whose death clearly resulted from the practice of sexual asphyxia was reported to have died of a heart attack in his hometown newspaper.

if we accept the view that those who engage in the behavior do not intend to die,[3] it becomes evident that the actual number of practitioners of sexual asphyxia may be considerable. Because of the precautions taken by these individuals, it is likely that the number of fatalities is small compared to the total number of incidents. In fact, researchers of sexual asphyxial practices posit that "such practices are common" (Litman and Swearingen, 1972:11) and certainly not the "oddity or rarity" that many people assume (Enos, 1975:134). But whatever the number of practitioners or the frequency of performance, sexual asphyxia is always potentially lethal and thus deserves careful sociological and psychological examination as well as legal and medical scrutiny.

SOCIAL CHARACTERISTICS OF THE VICTIMS AND THE DEATH SCENE

Almost all of the handful of scientific studies examining sexual asphyxia deal with cases that were discovered because the practitioners were unfortunate enough to die in the process. These postmortem studies do, however, delineate certain patterns. In contrast to most other forms of sexual deviance, sexual asphyxia appears to be an activity confined to middle-and upper-class white males. These males tend to be young; most of the recorded fatalities have occurred among teenage or young adult males who were unmarried at the time of their death. One review of 43 such deaths (Walsh et al., 1977) found the majority of the victims to have been younger than 25; and only 13 were married at the time of death.

Such behavior usually begins in adolescence, when it is a solitary act (Resnik, 1972). However, as the practitioner matures into adulthood the syndrome may become less lethal. This is because he may be able to involve partners in the process to protect him. Such partners are, however, used solely for the purpose of protection of the practitioner and take no part in the act itself. In all other aspects sexual asphyxia remains a solitary act.

The characteristics of the scene of discovery of the victims of sexual asphyxia lead to the conclusion that the practitioner requires solitude and privacy. The body is usually discovered in the victim's residence; many times it is in a bedroom, bathroom, attic, closet, or basement – somewhere that a door might be locked. If the act is performed outdoors, the most frequent setting is a secluded wooded area or an abandoned or little-used structure. There is an obvious need on the part of the participant to avoid any intrusion or interruption during the act (Sass, 1974).

[3]It should be noted, however, that if a practitioner of sexual asphyxia decides to commit suicide, it is probable that he will choose this method. Litman and Swearingen (1972) report such a case.

Danto (1980) reported that the majority of the bodies are found either naked or partially clothed and that there is frequently evidence of transvestism (articles of female clothing such as dresses, brassieres, or panty hose). Moreover, there is usually evidence of penile erection and ejaculation. However, evidence of ejaculation must be carefully evaluated because emission of seminal fluid is a frequent consequence of rigor mortis.

It is estimated that in from one-third to one-half of the cases the hands, body, and feet are bound in some manner. And although some of these binding mechanisms are extremely complex, it can usually be demonstrated that the ligatures and ropes could readily be tied and released by the victim himself. In addition, in some cases the scrotal sac may also be bound with string, thread, rope. Mirrors are frequently present and it is thought that as many as half of the victims may have been viewing themselves in a mirror and/or using erotic materials found near the body. Instances associated with self-inflicted pain or infibulation have also been reported (Sass,1974).

INTERVIEWS WITH LIVING PRACTITIONERS

Among the studies that report aspects of the practice of sexual asphyxia, only one has involved the interviewing of current practitioners. One additional study (Rosenblum and Faber, 1979) reports a psychiatric case history in which a 15-year-old boy has successfully been treated for such practice. This relative absence of firsthand information about social, psychological, and emotional aspects of the practice has not occurred because researchers failed to seek out practitioners. Indeed, Resnik (1972) reported that he had been unable to locate a single living practitioner of sexual asphyxia in the 10 years he had been interested in the subject. Medical researchers Litman and Swearingen (1972), however, were able to locate and interview nine such individuals. In an effort to reach such persons, they had an article ("Whips, Chains and Leather") published in the *Los Angeles Free Press,* and weekly underground newspaper with a circulation of about 90,000. As a result of that article and an advertisement, they received about 30 responses. After screening the respondents, face-to-face interviews were conducted with nine men and three women. Only the men, however, were engaged in the type of behavior that they were trying to study.

All of the subjects of the Litman and Swearingen study were white middle-class males who were characterized as "intelligent, verbal and cooperative." The researchers felt that their volunteer subjects had been motivated to respond to their advertisement by loneliness, a wish to share their interest with others, and a need to find legitimacy for their underground practices. In addition, the researchers felt that for some of them the response was a cry for help.

In general, the sexual orientation of these men was deemed to be homosexual. Even though many of the men had previous heterosexual experiences and several even indicated that they preferred women, Litman and Swearingen classified only two of the men as heterosexual. They also reported a trend toward increasing homosexuality with increasing age. Indeed, the researchers felt that the majority of the subjects hoped that they would find partners by responding to the ad. Finding such a partner is extremely important to them, because such a partner plays a protective role. This desire for partners, moreover, may help to explain the tendency toward homosexualtiy, in that homosexual partners are easier to find for unusual activity than are heterosexual ones. But despite this search for partners, the essence of the practice remains narcissistic. The focus of attention remains on themselves, even when others are participating; the practitioner of sexual asphyxia is preoccupied with his own fantasies and with his own view and sensations of the world.

Three of the subjects were married, and each had difficulty with his wife. The authors felt that this was the result of "basic personality flaws" rather than the result of their peculiar sexual behaviors. Although all of the subjects were aware of pornographic literature, only one-third indicated that they were strongly influenced by it. Moreover, transvestite elements were "surprisingly infrequent" in this group.

Litman and Swearingen saw the defining characteristics of this group of men to be extreme loneliness and isolation. They felt that all of these men were deeply depressed and death oriented: Six of the nine gave histories of serious depression-often accompanied by suicide attempts. They further posit that men used their perversion to fight off the death trend and to defend themselves against suicide. In spite of the researchers' belief that these men were experiencing both psychological and emotional pain, their study revealed no consistent patterns of family pathology or specific traumata in childhood.

CONFLICT IN THE LITERATURE

The death orientation emphasized by Litman and Swearingen is, however, strongly denied by other researchers in the field. Indeed, both Resnik (1972) and Walsh and co-workers (1977) explicitly argue that criteria for inclusion in the sexual asphyxia category should include "no apparent wish to die" and "no well-defined evidence of suicidal intent." Sass (1974:181) states that "death in these cases many times comes as a surprise to those who know the victim, since generally there is no known psychiatric history or sexual disorder." That is, there has been no previous report or indication of psychiatric or sexual disorder.

Walsh and co-workers (1977) argue that there is ample evidence that death is accidental. The victim is often found "incompletely suspended." That is, his feet are still on the ground, or close enough to a chair or stool to allow him to release himself before succumbing. Moreover, there are often indications that the activity has been performed repeatedly—rope marks on the rafters or doors, communications from diaries or friends.

Thus, there is a serious inconsistency in the literature concerning the nature of the practice and its practitioners. Are the victims of sexual asphyxia death oriented? We must remember that the practitioners interviewed by Litman and Swearingen were research volunteers. It is well established in the literature of social and behavioral science that volunteer subjects differ from nonvolunteer subjects on many important psychological variables. Litman and Swearingen point out that their subjects were isolated, lonely, and searching for partners. Perhaps it is true that others who engage in the practice but do not volunteer their existence are not so lonely or isolated and are not searching for partners. They would therefore have no motivation to respond to the newspaper advertisement.

Another indication that the Litman and Swearingen subjects may not be representative of other practitioners lies in the fact that these men were much older than those victims described in the literature. In fact, the youngest was 25, three were in their 30s, and three others in their 50s. Such a difference in age alone could be a significant issue because of the changing life-styles of older practitioners. It is, however, also true that we have no evidence that the known victims of sexual asphyxia are any more or less representative of the population of practitioners.

THE ABSENCE OF A DEVIANT SUBCULTURE

One additional important point should be stressed here: no deviant subculture has grown up around the practice of sexual asphyxia. There is no underlying threat that connects one practitioner with another, and participants do not, however subtly, advertise what they do. The solitary nature of the act means that locating one practitioner, even a deceased one, is not likely to lead us to others among his friends and associates. This is unlike other forms of sexual deviance, such as prostitution and homosexuality, where subcultures are well defined and have been extensively examined in the literature. It is even true of other sexually deviant behaviors such as bondage and sadomasochism that have not been extensively studied by sociologists. People who participate in these subcultures routinely advertise in underground publications for like-minded partners; and browsing any "adult" bookstore leads to the discovery that there is a special B&D (bondage and discipline) section for those who enjoy such practices. Indeed, the coroner of San Francisco, where rates of sexual deviance are high, recently began holding clinics in safe sadomasochistic practices because of concern about the number of homicides related to the activity (Washington Star, March 13, 1981:1).

The additional obstacle that this lack of a subculture presents to the researcher should not, however, preclude systematic and rigorous examination of sexual asphyxia. Even when the researcher is unable to implement "ideal" research design and uses volunteer subjects or must rely on "accidental deaths" that bring practitioners to the attention of local authorities, such studies can be useful so long as their sampling limitations are noted and kept in mind. By using information about those individuals unfortunate enough to die in the process, perhaps the living can learn enough from death investigations to illuminate the scope and dimensions of this potentially lethal sexual practice.

THE DADE COUNTY DATA

It was possible to study a number of cases of lethal sexual asphyxia taken from the files of the Medical Examiner Office of Dade County (Miami), Florida. That office is responsible for the investigation of all deaths within the county that are not obviously the result of natural causes. The purpose of the investigation is to determine the cause, manner, and mechanism of death (see Wright and Wetli, 1981). The scene and circumstances of death are initially evaluated by police agencies and, in cases of apparent lethal sexual asphyxia, by a forensic pathologist as well. Medical and social histories are subsequently obtained by both police and forensic investigators. Finally, a complete autopsy is performed. The data here reported were abstracted from the official reports prepared by these authorities.

Previous medical researchers (e.g., Resnik, 1972; Walsh et al., 1977) have outlined a number of criteria that are believed to indicate that a death may have been the result of the practice of sexual asphyxia. Although each of these indicators may not appear in every case, they collectively define the sexual asphyxia syndrome. These criteria include the following:

1. The act is solitary.
2. There is evidence of sexual activity.
3. There is no well-defined evidence of suicidal intent.
4. The deceased is completely or partially unclothed.
5. Transvestism may be present.
6. There may be evidence of previous episodes.
7. Often the extremities and sometimes the genitals are bound.
8. Erotic materials, especially pictures, are often present.

A detailed examination of the following case from Dade County illustrates the unusual nature of the sexual asphyxia syndrome and provides a concrete example of some of the criteria associated with it.

> A hotel maid discovered a 39-year-old caucasian man hanging by his neck. He was naked, and his feet touched the floor. His hands were looped in a rope behind his back. The ligature consisted of a white nylon rope fashioned as a hangman's noose and threaded through two large eyebolts which had been inserted into the wall. A full-length mirror was positioned in front of and to the side of the victim to permit complete self-viewing. A camera was positioned in front of the victim several feet away, and a remote shutter release device was nearby. A large sheet of dull black paper (approximately six feet wide by ten feet long) was on the floor to one side of the victim, and had apparently fallen from an overhang to which it had been attached with tape. On a nearby table were erotic photographs of women which had been cut out of the latest issue of *Playboy* magazine. On an adjacent chair was an ice bucket partially filled with urine. In the bathroom was a kit for developing 35mm slide film. In the bedroom were some hand tools (pliers, screw driver, etc.) as well as a plaster patching compound.
>
> The film in the camera was removed and subsequently developed. It contained a series of self-taken photographs in which the victim was in various poses. The first revealed the victim clad in a shirt and bath towel imitating female attire. The subsequent pictures revealed a progressive removal of clothing until he was standing naked and holding the noose-end of the rope. The photographs were taken against a dull black background (the paper found on the floor). The penultimate photograph depicted him standing on a low stool and with the ligature mildly constricting the neck. In the final photograph the victim is pictured in nearly the exact position in which he was found at the scene. In none of the photographs was penile erection evident.
>
> A subsequent investigation revealed that this man was a highly competent professional person with a high degree of intelligence. He was married and had two children. At one time he had been in psychotherapy where it was learned that he had marital problems related in part to his spouse's sexual withholding. His wife was aware of the episodes of photo-fantasies. It was learned that she disapproved of them and hence, for more than twelve years, he engaged in this activity outside the home (usually in hotel rooms). The victim's personality was described as narcissistic. He was obsessive-compulsive ("workaholic") and revealed a self-image of being both heroic and sacrificial, qualities which were evident in the self-taken photographs.
>
> It is evident that the self-taken photographs were to subsequently induce sexual stimulation. It must be presumed that, in this sequence of photographs, death intervened before the intended masturbatory activity could take place.

Careful study of Table 1, which displays all of the cases and all of the variables examined in this paper, reveals that each of these cases contains

TABLE 1 Characteristics of Dade County Sexual Asphyxia Victims

Case	Age	Occupation	Marital status	Sexual preference	Place of incident	Method used	Drug/ alcohol	Attire	Erotic materials	Body found by	Psychiatric history
1	12	Student	Never married	Unknown	Residence bedroom	Hanging by belt	Negative alcohol	Transvestism	None	Mother	None; social isolate
2	15	Student	Never married	Unknown	Residence back yard	Hanging by rope	No report	Partially clothed	None	Sister	None; school reports good conduct and scholastic record but "moody and had difficulty adjusting"
3	15	Student (well-to-do)	Never married	Not reported	Residence bathroom	Chemical	Positive barbiturate	Partially clothed	None	Brother	None; good student, church goer; once ran away
4	15	Student	Never married	Not reported	Residence back yard	Hanging by rope	Negative alcohol	Transvestism	None	Parents	None; family and friends said boy was in good spirits
5	17	Student (well-to-do)	Never married	Probable heterosexual	Lot behind residence	Hanging by rope	No report	Nude	Yes	Father	None; good student and good social mixer; Eagle Scout and active in school, sports, and hobby groups

6	19	Student	Never married	Heterosexual	Residence back yard	Hanging by rope	Negative	Nude	None	Religious brother	None; dated girls before becoming celibate Hari-Krishna
7	20	U.S.Army (well-to-do)	Never married	Heterosexual	Densely wooded area	Hanging by rope	Negative	Nude	Yes; fetish literature	Passerby	Shy, with few friends; strong evidence of problems in relationships with females
8	22	College student (well-to-do)	Never married	Heterosexual	Residence garage	Hanging by rope	Negative alcohol	Nude	Yes	Parents	Family refused information; physical indicated victim had been unable to get enough female companionship since a youngster: "sex and females were his life"
9	23	Mail clerk	Never married	Homosexual	Residence rear porch	Hanging by rope	Positive alcohol (.07%)	Transvestism	None	Passerby	Suicide note written five days before death; no note at time of death; friends reported had been in good spirits

TABLE 1 Characteristics of Dade County Sexual Asphyxia Victims

Case	Age	Occupation	Marital status	Sexual preference	Place of incident	Method used	Drug/ alcohol	Attire	Erotic materials	Body found by	Psychiatric history
10	25	Asst. mgr. wholesale liquor	Married	Hetero-sexual	Residence bathroom	Hanging by rope	Negative	Nude	None	Wife	Victim and wife active in erotic bondage and other sexual fantasies
11	25	Electrician	Never married	Hetero-sexual	Residence	Inhaled gas	No report	Partially clothed	Yes	Friend	None
12	28	Fire-fighter	Never married	Hetero-sexual	Residence bedroom	Hanging by rope	No report	Nude	Yes	Police (employer)	Co-workers and employer indicate was "in fairly good spirits"; not depressed at any time before incident
13	32	Travel counselor; musician	Never married	Hetero-sexual	Residence bedroom	Hanging by necktie	Positive alcohol (.10%)	Nude	Yes	Police (friend)	None; friends said had never spoken of suicide
14	32	Boat CPA	Unmarried	Hetero-sexual	Residence bedroom	Neck ligature	Positive Metha-qualone	Transvestism	Yes	Police (mother)	Friends said "somewhat depressed lately"

15	39	Chemist	Married	Hetero-sexual	Hotel	Hanging by rope	Positive alcohol (.08)%)	Nude	Yes	Maid and secuirty	In psychotherapy. Therapist reported victim did so to please wife who was also in therapy. Long series of difficulty with wife, apparently from her withholding sex
16	40	Engineer	Married	Hetero-sexual	Motel	Hanging by clothing	Negative alcohol; positive cocaine/valium	Nude	Sex articles; female clothing	Maid	None; had problems with wife because she sometimes withheld sex

Note: The categories and descriptions contained within this table are based upon the observations of the police and forensic investigations regarding the various physical and social characteristics of the victim. For example, the characterization of the victim as ''well-to-do'' is based on the investigators' impression of the family, neighborhood, and life-style of the victim. It should be noted that the category has no ''absolute'' financial boundaries. In fact, because of the length of time separating the deaths of the victims, such numerical boundaries would be meaningless.

TABLE 2 Sexual Asphyxial Death by Age in Dade County, Florida

Age range	Number	Percent	Cumulative percent
12–19	6	37.5	37.5
20-29	6	37.5	75.0
30–39	3	18.8	93.8
40 plus	1	6.2	100.0
Total	16	100	

elements described in the eight criteria and provide the basis for case identification. All of the 16 deaths discussed here occurred between 1954 and 1980, although 9 of them (56%) have been identified since 1972. All of the deceased subjects were white males, although not all were Americans. One victim was a citizen of Peru who maintained a residence in Dade County.

The distribution of these deaths from sexual asphyxia according to age is displayed in Table 2. The youngest victim was only 12 years old, whereas the oldest was 40. A total of 9 of the 16 were younger than 25 and 2 additional subjects died in their 25th year. Three-fourths of all of the known victims in Dade County between 1954 and 1980 were younger than 30. These data are thus consistent with the age distributions of victims of sexual asphyxia reported by other investigators (Resnik, 1972; Walsh et al., 1977). It is clear that the majority of the victims of lethal sexual asphyxia are adolescent and young adult males. What we do not know, is anything about the age distribution of those for whom the practice is nonlethal.

Judged by the occupations of the victims or the socioeconomic status of their families, the subjects were overwhelmingly members of the middle and upper-middle class. Nearly half were students ($N = 7$) at the time of their death. One additional subject was an enlisted soldier. Thus, half of the subjects were student age. Four of these young victims were reported to be the sons of "well-to-do" families. The occupations of the eight older victims run the white-collar gamut from mail clerk to professional, whereas only two are clearly blue-collar occupations (fireman and electrician).

Of the three victims who were married, two were reported to have had sexual problems with their wives because of the spouse withholding sex. The third married subject was very active in erotic bondage and other sexual fantasies with his wife. She denied, however, any knowledge of the phenomenon of sexual asphyxia and was not aware of her husband ever having performed the act before. The 13 remaining victims were all single; 12 were classified as never married, and the remaining victim was listed as simply "unmarried." Two of the single victims were also reported to have had sexual problems with their girlfriends. In addition, two others were described as "socially isolated," suggesting that they had difficulty interacting with both men and women.

In most of the cases there was no indication or even suspicion of suicidal intent. In only one case had a "suicide" note been left. It had been written five days earlier however, and friends reported that the victim had been "in good spirits" before his death. Moreover, the deceased had written other notes indicating that he had often hanged himself for sexual pleasures. In another case, friends reported that the victim had been "somewhat depressed." However, his neck had been padded and three *Playboy* magazines were opened to various pictures of nude females.

There was definite evidence of repetitive behavior in three of the deaths; and it could not be ruled out in any of the others. In fact, Resnik argues that if the behavior continues it is likely to become more elaborate. That is, fetishism, bondage, and masochism may be introduced to the act—and more precautions taken.

Of these 16 victims of lethal sexual asphyxia, only 1 subject's sexual preference was known to be homosexual. Because of the youth of the victims, this should not be too surprising. The literature is clear in its indication that the tendency toward homosexuality increases with age (Resnik, 1972; Rosenblum and Faber, 1979; Litman and Swearingen, 1972). There was, however, evidence of transvestism in four (25%) of the cases; but this element was confined to neither the older nor the younger victims. In 11 (68.7%) of the cases the victims were either completely or partially nude. Again, these proportions are consistent with the previous literature reporting lethal sexual asphyxia.

The most frequent (81%) method of inducing asphyxia was hanging, usually be a rope. Two of the victims died as the result of using inhalants to induce the asphyxia; only one victim died as the result of compression of the neck with ligature but without hanging.

The fatal incident occurred most often at the victim's residence, usually in a bedroom or bathroom or occasionally in a secluded area of the back yard. Two of the deaths occurred in a hotel or motel, and one took place in an obscure, densely wooded area.

Toxological studies were performed in 12 of the 16 cases, with negative results in half of them. Three victims had intoxicating or near-intoxicating levels of alcohol in their blood (.07%, .10% and .08%). Such levels could likely have had substantial effects on their judgment and, depending on the person's drinking habits and tolerance level, could have contributed to their death. Of the three cases involving other drugs, one had a rather large dose of methaqualone (Qualuude), another had ingested a combination of cocaine and diazepam (Valium), and the third was recorded as simply "positive for barbiturates."

Erotic materials were discovered at the scene of nine of the deaths and were strictly heterosexual in nature, that is, pictures of naked women. Such materials may have been present at other scenes but removed by members of the family or friends before the police arrived, a not uncommon occurrence (Enos, 1973). The data in fact suggest that this probably did occur in some cases. In nine of the cases reported in this article the victim's body was discovered either by a friend or by a member of the family. Of the seven deaths where erotic materials were reportedly not present at the scene, five were discovered by members of the victim's family. It is thus likely that the reported incidence of the presence of erotic materials at the scene of death is conservative.

DISCUSSION

The preceding description of some of the sociological variables in our data associated with lethal sexual asphyxia (in the argot of the bondage underground, terminal sex) leads us to the following conclusions. The data support the observation that, unlike most forms of sexual deviance, sexual asphyxia is practiced by young, white, middle-or upper-middle-class males. It is almost exclusively practiced in the home or some safe place near the home. We do not know the number of practitioners, the frequency with which they perform the act, or the actual distribution of their ages.

Perhaps the young are victims of the practice so frequently because they are, like youth everywhere, often oblivious of the dangers involved in what they do. They are straightforward about it—they simply hang themselves. Moreover, because the act is solitary, when something goes wrong and they lose control, they lose their lives as well.

As practitioners become older, they probably become more cautious; they use more elaborate devices and many search for partners. Perhaps then it is merely adaptive behavior that leads to homosexual liaisons. Such unusual practices are indeed more likely to be accepted or at least tolerated by homosexual partners than by heterosexual ones. Our data indicate that when the practice is fatal among older practitioners some complicating factor such as the use of alcohol or drugs is present that may have impaired their judgment enough to have contributed to the accident costing them their lives.

When we examine the social origin of the act and the actor, it is clear that many of the victims have severe difficulties obtaining sufficient sexual gratifications by other means. They lacked sufficient sexual outlets and generally had difficulty interacting with females. Although some researchers (Resnik, 1972; Rosenblum and Faber, 1979) believe that the act generally becomes more elaborate as the practitioner ages, our data indicate that the introduction of fetishes and transvestism may occur early or late. One plausible explanation for the elements of bondage and sadism that may enter into the practice is that the only source of willing partners the practitioner can find is among members of the bondage community—whether they are heterosexual or homosexual. In order to receive the gratifications of sexual asphyxia with safety, they submit to other forms of sexual deviance, bondage, and so forth. They do not seek the painful pleasures of sadomasochism but rather endure them for the sexual pleasures of sexual asphyxia that they seek. There is a great difference, thus, between the practitioner of sadomasochism and the sexual asphyxiate.

In the end, however, many of these men return to solitary practice or never find willing partners; and when an accident occurs, their search for a satisfactory sexual outlet for their sexual needs becomes terminal. Our data confirm that these deaths were not suicides and that there was no suicidal intent. We caution, however, that the data presented in this paper are limited; in all of the cases we report, the individuals died while practicing sexual asphyxia. This group of practitioners therefore may not be representative of the general population of practitioners of sexual asphyxia. Thus, it is evident that additional research is needed to clarify many of the issues raised in this paper, especially the scope and dimensions of the problem—who practices sexual asphyxia, how often, and how frequently does it result in death.

REFERENCES

Danto, Bruce L.
1980 "A case of female auto-erotic death." American Journal of Forensic Medicine and pathology 1:117–121.
DeSade, Marquis
1964 Justine. New York: Castle Books.
Enos, William F., Jr.
1973 "Commentary." Medical Aspects of Human Sexuality 7(11):184–189.
Lewman, Larry V.
1978 "Case of the month." Office of the Medical Investigator 5:11–13.
Litman, Robert E., and Charles Swearingen
1972 "Bondage and suicide." Archives of General Psychiatry 27:80–85.
1973 "Bondage and suicide." Medical Aspects of Human Sexuality 7(11):164–181.
Resnik, H. L. P.
1972 "Eroticized repetitive hangings: A form of self-destructive behavior." American Journal of Psychotherapy 26:4–21.
Rosenblum, Stephen, and Myron M. Faber
1979 "The adolescent sexual asphyxia syndrome." Journal of the American Academy of Child Psychiatry 19:546–558.
Sass, F. A.
1974 "Sexual asphyxia in the female." Journal of Forensic Sciences 20:181–185.

Simon, Werner
1973 "Commentary." Medical Aspects of Human Sexuality 7(11):189-193.
Sullivan, William B., Jr., and Steve Wray
1981 A Case of Sexual Asphyxia of a Female. Paper presented at the 33rd Annual Meetings of the American Academy of Forensic Sciences, Los Angeles, February.
Walsh, F. M., Charles J. Stahl, H. Thomas Unger, Oscar C. Lilienstern, and Robert G. Stephens
1977 "Autoerotic asphyxial deaths: A medicolegal analysis of forty-three cases." Legal Medicine Annual 1977:157-182.
Wright, Ronald K., and Charles V. Wetli
1981 "A guide to the forensic autopsy—conceptual aspects." Pathology Annual 16:273-288.

Reading 25

Buying Sex: The Phenomenology of Being a John

Harold R. Holzman
Rutgers University, New Brunswick
Sharon Pines
Montgomery County Health Department

The authors obtained data directly from prostitutes' customers on the feelings and perceptions that comprise being a "john." There are four phases involved in being a john: conception of intents, pursuit of the encounter, the encounter, and the aftermath. The image of the john that emerged from this study differed from that typically found in the literature on prostitution.

INTRODUCTION

An extensive literature exists on prostitution. Fictionalized accounts range from the amusing and colorful nostalgia found in William Faulkner's *The Reivers* to the depiction of a troubled, sometimes sordid quest for satisfaction present in John Rechy's *City of Night*. Scientific research runs the gamut from the studies of the physiology of sex that have utilized the services of prostitutes (Masters and Johnson, 1966) to the well-known work of Kinsey and those that followed him.

Somewhere between studies of erectile tissue and accounts of large-

An earlier draft of this paper was presented at the annual meeting of the American Society of Criminology, Philadelphia, 1979.

scale survey research, lie the myriad of books and articles produced by behavioral scientists probing the whos, hows, and whys of prostitution. Alas, in the broad mosaic of knowledge that this research collectively forms there are very few works devoted to the clients of prostitutes—the "johns."

Furthermore, beyond some survey data on frequency and type of contact by men with female prostitutes, most of the information on johns is derived from interviews with prostitutes, not their clients. The reasons for the paucity of data seem to be largely methodological in nature and appear childishly obvious, that is, the assumed difficulty in getting individuals to admit to and discuss sexually marginal if not downright "deviant" behavior. The authors of the present study were struck by the fact that the practitioners themselves were, judging by the existing literature, a very loquacious lot. The hypothesis notwithstanding that discussing the secrets of the profession is certainly not the most intimate request with which these ladies might be confronted, the authors decided that if practitioners talk, clients would too. This was in fact the case.

THE PROBLEM

The objective of the study was to obtain data on the melange of feelings and perceptions that comprise being a john. Because the john has rarely been the actual target of research in the behavioral sciences, the authors believed the potential existed for developing new insights into how men experience buying sex. Attempting to conduct in-depth personal interviews with men on this particular facet of their lives was itself something of a challenge if not actually a methodological departure. Given the nature of the problem, a phenomenological orientation to the research was adopted. Phenomenology focuses on the process by which the individual derives an interpretation of the meaning of events (Berger and Luckmann, 1966; Wagner, 1973). The social actor is the primary unit of analysis and is seen as a subjective being, that is, a rational creature with free will. As such, the social actor is aware of why he or she behaves in a given way and may choose to share these data with the phenomenologist. Clearly, for one seeking data on the social actor's motivations for and perceptions of a specific behavior pattern, phenomenology represents a potentially useful framework for field research.

Images of the John

In *The Honest Politician's Guide to Crime Control*, Norval Morris (1970) discusses prostitution and in the process presents an image of the john:

> Prostitution is an ancient and enduring institution which has survived centuries of attack and condemnation, and there is no doubt that it fulfills a social

> function. It is often asserted that prostitution provides an outlet for sexual impulses which might otherwise be expressed in rape or other kinds of sexual crime. No research has been done in this area but the notion has a certain plausibility. It is undeniable, however, that prostitutes are sought out by some men who, because of a physical deformity, psychological inadequacy, or (in the case of foreigners and immigrants) unfamiliarity with the language and customs, find great difficulty in obtaining sexual partners. The Kinsey report states that prostitutes provide a sexual outlet for many persons who without this would become even more serious social problems than they already are. (p. 21)

Similarly in an article entitled "Prostitution as an Illegal Vocation: A Sociological Overview," Mary Riege Laner (1974) provided a general description of people who buy.

> The basic function of prostitution is to provide a primarily sexual service to people who either fail to meet the requirements of the more legitimate "market" or who exclude themselves from the larger market because they do not feel comfortable in it. The system is very flexible. Almost no one is turned away. (p. 417)

These descriptions are reflective of the rather unsavory image of the john in social scientific literature. It is the image of a person whose physical, psychological, or social inadequacies and personal problems have driven him to engage in sexually deviant conduct with the behavior, visiting a prostitute, being itself defined as sexually deviant regardless of the content of the practitioner-client interaction. Benjamin and Masters (1964:192–193) comment on the prevalence of the belief that johns are psychologically defective or disturbed. This image of the john as psychologically troubled receives support from the work of noted psychotherapist Albert Ellis (1959) and psychiatrists Gibbens and Silberman (1960) that suggests an association between buying sex and personal problems of a psychological genre. By virtue of their respective professional orientations and the particular nature of their respective clienteles, however, these researchers might reasonably be expected to suggest the presence of a correlation between the possession of psychological difficulties and the patronizing of prostitutes.

The image of the john as a person afflicted with social, psychological, or physical problems also receives some support from practitioner-centered research on prostitution. Prostitutes' descriptions of their clientele tend to be somewhat unflattering. Common themes in these accounts include sexual "deviation," drunkness, sexual naivete or inadequacy, gullibility, and marital difficulties (Benjamin and Masters, 1964; Winick and Kinsie, 1971).

Information obtained from practitioners may, however, be somewhat negatively biased. Generally, the position accorded customers in the occupational ideology of prostitutes is not one of respect. Johns are considered "marks" in what is perceived by prostitutes to be a sexually based con game (Bryan, 1965). The john is looked on as a fool who is not only the object of exploitation but is easily exploited as well. Prostitutes are taught different pitches or stories to tell the mark so as to extract more money from him. Similarly, Greenwald (1958) reports that the call girls in his study referred to their clients as "suckers" and consciously manipulated interaction with them to maximize profit. In their study of black prostitutes and pimps, the Milners (1972:38, 116–117, 196) repeatedly present evidence of the image of john as mark, which, judging from reports of other practitioner-centered research, seems to be a standard component of the occupational ideology of prostitutes (Hirschi, 1962; Gray, 1973:420–421; Rasmussen and Kuhn, 1976:479–483).[1] Therefore, it is not surprising that the portrait of the john that emerges from practitioner-centered research is that of a socially and psychologically inadequate human being, one who can never really gain control of the practitioner-client encounter except through violence. The term "trick," a synonym for john often used by black prostitutes, is derived from the belief that prostitutes literally trick a man "by taking money for doing what women should do for free" (Milner and Milner, 1972:38).

Although the negative stereotype of the john may tally with descriptions of their respective clienteles furnished by prostitutes and mental health professionals, it is not supported by data obtained directly from johns through social scientific research specifically designed to study these persons. In research that involved interviews of hundreds of men who had purchased sexual services from women, Winick (1962) failed to find evidence of widespread psychological pathology or other marked patterns of personal difficulty and concluded that the client's relationship to the practitioner was far more complex than traditionally thought.

Noting the common classification of johns as "problematic individuals," Armstrong (1978) studied the customers of a massage parlor where sexual services were sold. Collecting data for the most part on demographic

[1]Rasmussen and Kuhn (1976) studied practitioners who worked in a massage parlor as did several other researchers whose work is cited in this article. The authors of the present study grouped the behavior of massage parlor practitioners with that of prostitute practitioners where the article cited indicates that the massage parlor practitioners were routinely paid to perform sexual services. Furthermore, Bryant and Palmer (1975:238) report that the masseuses whom they studied had developed an "impersonal and unemotional response to sexual intimacies with their clientele" without benefit of the socialization/training process described by Bryan (1965). These data along with other descriptions of the occupational activities of massage parlor practitioners, (e.g., Rasmussen and Kuhn, 1976), suggest that practitioners—regardless of the locus of their activities—stage manage interactions with their customers in essentially similar ways.

characteristics and service requests of customers via a female informant/masseuse, he reported that there appeared nothing particularly unusual about the men studied: "the typical customer was the typical visitor" to the West Coast community where the research took place. Armstrong concluded that "the assumptions that the nature of massage parlors and their customers is somehow known in advance of the data collection process must be uncompromisingly rejected" (p. 125).

Simpson and Schill (1977) conducted a survey of 183 patrons of a massage parlor in Illinois. They stated that their results "refute the allegations of those who warned that parlors attract the young, the perverted and the undesirable" and that "they also fail to support the claims of those who say that parlors are largely frequented by sexually inadequate individuals" (p. 524).

Simpson and Schill describe their typical client as the following:

> a 35-year-old married white male from out of town who has probably given college a try but now is employed in a lower-or middle-class job and goes to church on Sundays. He is likely to be verbally and sexually assertive, reports having had a variety of sexual experiences in the past, has come to the parlor because of lack of sexual partner at this particular time or because of curiosity, will come to orgasm during the local or genital massage, and will find it sexually satisfying. He is likely to have high self-esteem, to consider himself personally and sexually adjusted, to consider his value system as liberal, and to be somewhat sympathetic to the goals of the women's rights movement. (p. 524)

Stein (1974) observed and recorded hundreds of sessions between practitioners and their johns. She did her research with the cooperation of practitioners who allowed her the use of one-way mirrors, peepholes, closets, and other observation posts that permitted her to view and hear events without the knowledge of the customers. Here she describes the johns to whose intimate activities she was privy:

> What struck me more forcefully during those initial encounters was that the women and men involved were all people I might have known in the "straight" world. At first I looked for signs of "abnormality" in the clients. I felt that any man who paid for sex must be some kind of "loser." I was disappointed. I saw a few "losers," of course, but most of the clients were agreeable, reasonably attractive, upper-middle class men, businessmen or professionals. My lawyer, my accountant, my father's business associates, indeed my father, would not have been out of place among them. (p. 10)

Outside of works of fiction, there are few accounts by johns of how they experience the purchase of sexual services. When these accounts can be found, they tend to differ sharply from the images of the transaction that abound in practitioner-centered literature. In such literature, much is made by prostitutes of the seeming necessity to simulate sexual arousal for the benefit of the mark. Here a first-time john—perhaps the most naive of customers—comments on one of those performances.

> Then she said, "oh wow, you sure have got me hot." As if in the grip of great sexual desire she began kissing my neck. "Who does she think she's fooling?" I thought, assuming subjective command of the situation. She kissed her way down my chest and performed an elaborate act of fellatio, lifting her head once to admonish me not to come to orgasm in her mouth. While performing this act she continued to feign, I thought, great passion. My sense of the unreality of the entire situation grew even stronger as she grunted and groaned and snorted. I thought I knew that her arousal was feigned, and her performance had become so absurd-seeming to me that it now had become possible, in my mind, that she knew I knew it was all a fake, and that, in fact, all this was part of "the game," which, by availing myself of her services, I could reasonably be expected to play. A test would have been to say, "you're faking all this, aren't you?" but it would not have been a very good test, for, if she had denied it, I would not have believed her. Another, and it seemed to me likely, response could have been a scornful and angry, "Of course I am, you dumb son-of-a-bitch. This is a whorehouse and I'm getting paid to do this." Scorn for my ignorant stupidity and anger at my violation of protocol. (Stewart, 1972:269–270)

Although this john may have been entertained, he certainly was not conned. Furthermore, practitioners much like bartenders are traditionally supposed to provide customers with a sympathetic audience for a recitation of their troubles. Here, a john of some 20 years' experience suggests that (1) he is routinely required to listen to tales of woe from practitioners, (2) he routinely modifies his behavior to help create or maintain a good rapport with the practitioner, and (3) as was the case with the first-time john quoted above, he fully understands that the practitioner is a paid professional and that the requirements of her occupation govern her conduct.

> She rambled on about the vagaries and trials of her business, and I did nothing more than nod sympathetically from a stretched-out position on the bed. Years of difficulties with lovely girls of simple, direct natures like Sally's had taught me that there is something about my style of conversation which upsets them, something that makes them draw back coolly from my metaphors and turns of phrase as if there were mad, obscene images hidden among them. I generally

> consoled myself by assuming that any form of figurative language must seem a mode of insanity to the semiliterate, but this was poor comfort when, after having burst out with a rich, imaginative paragraph, I found myself being written off simply as another creep. I didn't want one of those quizzical, cold smiles coming from Sally, and so I avoided as much as possible the dangers of language, mumbling only an agreement here and there to punctuate her list of complaints. Then, finally, came a silence, the traditional little interim that always hangs between the amenities of a first-class hooker and the moment of business. She was standing at the foot of the bed, staring down at me, her arms in a determined fold. "Well, what did you have in mind, Jack?" (Richardson, 1970:86)

Clearly, data obtained directly from johns do not seem to support the stereotypical image of the purchaser of sex. Especially in light of the statements by johns presented above, one might conclude that very little is really known about how johns view their interactions with practitioners. Using a phenomenological research orientation, the present study seeks to provide further insights on how persons actually experience the behaviors that involve being a john.

Phenomenology and Reality

It is important to understand how phenomenology views the subjective reality of the individual, for it is on the basis of this reality that free choices are made.

Alfred Schutz, the father of phenomenological sociology, saw the social world as a dialectic between self and society. The individual possesses a subjective reality that is produced by a mixture of pregiven sociocultural environment and experiences (Schutz, 1967). In a quest for knowledge, the individual's subjective reality confronts the objective reality of the world. This ongoing confrontation leads to the individual's formation of cognitive structures, that is, interpretations of reality on which the individual operates. Reality, then, is a social construction (Schutz, 1962; Berger and Luckmann, 1976).

The structure of the shared reality of the social world is held together by the continual exchange of meanings held in common. Phenomenologists hope to penetrate a given reality through their recognition that structures of everyday language represent typifications of common sense thinking, that is, words are themselves elements of a value system that prevails as taken for granted and socially approved. Schutz (1967) observed that slang, with its richness and commonly held meanings, helps the individual to function in a larger social context.

Intersubjectivity was the term that Schutz (1966) used to describe the actual process of communication between social actors; he observed that the activities and creations of one's fellows can be understood by an individual who in turn takes it for granted that others will take his or her actions substantially the way that they are meant.

At once, then, language can be viewed both as a reflection of the individual's thoughts and feelings (expressions of one's subjective reality) and also as typifications of commonly held values that exist in the concrete sociocultural *Lebenswelt* (life-world) that one shares with others in the broad objective reality of everyday life.

In conducting research within a phenomenological framework, one must be aware that each person is a unique subjective being in what Schutz (1962:312) terms a "unique biographical situation."[2] All human beings are possessed of their own very personal reality, which is generated by their personal experiences and in turn shapes their perceptions of the objective reality presented by the larger society (Schutz, 1962:306).

There are however other realities that touch individuals in their everyday life, for example, the worlds of religion, of art, and of science. Hence, there exist what Schutz (1962:294) termed "multiple realities" or "subuniverses" that human beings share. This sharing is accomplished through the use of language, that is, the exchange of meanings held in common. A researcher, then, must study the language of the respondent's answers in an effort to discover the content of a subjective reality, being sensitive to the fact that a word's commonly held meaning is not always identical with the meaning with which a respondent may endow it. In general, a phenomenological analysis attempts to perform two tasks: (1) describe the social actor's interpretation of an event or situation and (2) describe the relationship of the actor's interpretation to what exists beyond that individual in the social world.

Equally important to an awareness of the respondent's subjective reality in phenomenological research is the recognition by social scientists of their own inescapable subjectivity (Bittner, 1973). One may avoid overt

[2]Schutz's recognition of the people as unique subjective beings as well as very much creatures of their sociocultural milieu is evident in the following statement from his essay, "Symbol, Reality, and Society." My actual social environment refers always to a horizon of potential social environments, and we may speak of a transcendent infinity of the social world as we speak of a transcendent infinity of the natural one.

I experience both of these transcendences, that of Nature and that of Society, as being imposed upon me in a double sense: on the one hand, I find myself at any moment of my existence as being within nature and within society; both are permanently coconstitutive elements of my biographical situation and are, therefore, experienced as inescapably belonging to it. On the other hand, they constitute the framework within which alone I have the freedom of my potentialities, and this means they prescribe the scope of all possibilities for defining my situation. In this sense, they are not elements of my situation, but determinations of it. In the first sense, I may—even more, I have to—take them for granted. In the second sense, I have to come to terms with them. But in either sense, I have to understand the natural and social world in spite of their transcendences, in terms of an order of things and events. (1962:330)

bias, but each human being has what Karl Mannheim (1936) called a *Weltanschauung*, or global view—a set of attitudes, values, beliefs that are related to one's social class and to the historical period in which one lives. Although a detailed discussion of the possibility of a value-free social science is beyond the scope of this paper, it is safe to say that phenomenological researchers must almost by definition be sociologists of knowledge, constantly endeavoring to convey the respondent's interpretation of reality and not their own.

METHODOLOGY

Data Collection

The importance that a phenomenological approach places on ascertaining the content of a social actor's subjective experience renders the personal interview the preferred mode of data collection for a study of johns. Similarly, the prostitute must be recognized as part of the johns objective reality with his or her own subjective reality and Weltanschauung. Thus, the prostitute is less than a valuable informant concerning the john's true feelings about prostitution in general and his role in particular. The method of data collection was an in-depth loosely structured interview of approximately 75 minutes. The interview guide used was identical for all respondents. Respondents were repeatedly asked to expand on their answers, this additional information being elicited through the simple expedient of asking "what do you mean by that?" Thus, it was hoped to minimize the amount of subjective interpretation of the respondent's account by the researchers by maximizing information flow at key points in the interview. The taped interviews were studied by the two researchers separately. Each researcher recorded his or her interpretation of the respective respondent's answer to each question. Then the researchers met and quite literally compared notes. The structure and content of the interview was based on the a priori assumption, which will be discussed in detail later, that being a john was a process rather than role. This assumption also guided the analysis of the interviews, which attempted to identify behaviors that would be associated with being a john.

Sampling

At the outset of the research, it was decided that only individuals who had paid for sex $N + 1$ times would be included in the sample. It was reasoned that a person who judged an initial contact with a prostitute to be sufficiently positive to continue beyond this first experience could be defined as a john.[3] In fact, the average respondent has paid for sex in excess of 50 times, the range being from 2 to more than 200 contacts (most respondents reported approximately 50 contacts). The respondents at the upper end of the distribution could not remember exactly how many times they had "been." As the reader might easily imagine, precise record keeping in the area is more the province of the practitioners rather than of the clients.

A sample of 30 johns was obtained through social networks known to exist at the start of the research or subsequently discovered by the authors.[4] In essence, the authors asked friends and acquaintances (1) if they had ever paid for sex and (2) if they knew anybody who had. Individuals who answered affirmatively were asked to interview and, where applicable, to provide introductions to other potential respondents. About two-thirds of those who admitted being johns agreed to interview. Roughly one out of four of the interviewees were willing and able to provide introductions to others. People who denied ever having paid for sex did not usually furnish introductions to people who had.

The authors acknowledge the fact that the sample was almost exclusively composed of white middle-class individuals. However, this bias is endemic to the nonfiction works that seek to describe johns (for example, Greenwald, 1958; Ellis, 1959; Gibbens and Silverman, 1960; Reuben, 1969; Winick and Kinsie, 1971; Hollander, 1972; Gray, 1973; Sheehy, 1973; Stein, 1974; Armstrong, 1978; Bryant and Palmer, 1975; Simpson and Schill, 1977). Thus, this study is consistent with previous research on johns except that here a phenomenological approach was used. Not surprisingly, the

[3]Whether a respondent perceived himself as a john was not considered important in respect to defining the target population. As with other labels associated with social deviance that of john is applied to persons on the basis of their behavior whether they perceive themselves as johns or not (Stewart, 1972:256).

[4]Data for the present study were collected during 1979 and 1980. Interviews were usually conducted during evenings and weekends. With the exception of several johns personally known to the researchers at the start of the study, finding respondents and arranging for interviews was a time-consuming process. It involved attendance at many social gatherings. (Further descriptions of the places where networks were discovered and developed must remain confidential.) Scheduling interviews was at times a difficult task because the researchers had full-time jobs as did most of the respondents. The task was further complicated by the fact that respondents sometimes expressed a definite preference as to where and when they wished to be interviewed.

The fact that data collection was a time-consuming process was influential in the researchers' decision to restrict the number of respondents interviewed for the present study. Initially, 20 persons were interviewed and the data were analyzed. An additional 10 persons who were in networks already under development were interviewed and their responses analyzed. Having completed this development process, it seemed a convenient juncture at which to end the present research. While several other new networks had been identified, their development had not yet begun and would have taken several months to complete. The researchers were anxious to seek the publication of their findings and so proceeded with what they felt was an adequate if not large sample.

image of the white middle-class john that emerged differed from most existing pathology-ridden depictions of the clients of prostitutes.

The potential respondent was asked to submit to an interview with both the authors at which a tape recorder would be used to collect the data. In four instances, the respondent's wishes or logistical problems precluded the use of the tape recorder. Roughly half of the respondents were interviewed by both members of the research team. In half of those instances where one researcher was present, this was due to the respondent's wish rather than logistics. Here, respondents did not mind being recorded but objected to the presence of the male half of the research team. These men were among those recruited by the female researcher, Ms. Pines, at social gatherings and subsequent to the interview did evince an interest in developing a friendship with her. The data provided by these respondents did not differ noticeably from that provided by others.

The authors acknowledge that the fact that Ms. Pines can be viewed as both personable and attractive probably helped obtain respondents. Any bias that this situation may have introduced into the data must be weighed against the reticence that johns are traditionally thought to possess, that is, the data collection problems inherent in such research (cf. Warren and Rasmussen, 1977).

Characteristics of the Sample

Of the 30 individuals interviewed in this study, all were males. All stated a sexual preference for the opposite sex except for one of the males who explicitly stated a sexual preference for partners of the same sex. All of the subjects were white except for one who was black. The ages ranged from 27 to 52 years old, with the majority in their mid-30s. Close to half of the individuals interviewed were currently married.

Educational levels attained by the subjects interviewed were fairly high. All subjects had attained at least a high school diploma; most had completed four years in college. In fact, more than a third of the interviewees pursued academic studies beyond a four-year college degree. Income levels ranged from $8,000 to more than $75,000 a year. The median income was $30,000 a year. Most of those interviewed tended to be reasonably physically attractive. All stated that they had little trouble finding sexual partners who were not prostitutes. The vast majority of the sample stated that they currently had a relationship that involved sex.

The Nature of the Interview: Process versus Role

Being a john was looked on by the authors as a process (a series of interrelated decisions and acts) rather than as a role (one who exchanges money for sex). This influences the methodology used in the interviews. Past research in this area seems to emphasize that the john is a participant in a deviant act. It then seeks not to describe the client's subjective experience but rather to account for his participation in a deviant act. It should not be surprising then that johns are most often portrayed as pathetic or pathological. In his article "The Sociology of Good Times," Alexander Blumenstiel (1973) states that the study of social problems has traditionally applied evilness as opposed to goodness as its basic mode of interpretation. Although one might not wish to adopt Blumenstiel's "good times" orientation to the research at hand, it certainly seemed advisable to escape an orientation based on the need to explain the unwelcome occurrence of deviant acts.

The goal of this research was to describe the subjective experience of buying sex. The same approach might, however, be applied to buying a car or robbing a liquor store. The basic research question was how does the social actor experience the process; the actor is after all a rational creature who feels, reasons, and decides. To focus on the role is to objectify the situation into simply an evil and perhaps unclean act. The term "john" itself is a value-loaded typification—a label that says nothing good about its bearer. Consequently, we asked the respondent to describe under what circumstances thoughts would arise that would eventuate his buying sex. He was then asked to describe that series of acts that would include interaction with a prostitute and also thoughts, feelings, and actions following the actual transaction.

Private Parts

Because the focus of the research was a process that was found in some instances to be of several weeks' duration rather than a short-lived role, for example, insertee, the respondent was not questioned in detail about what sexual dealings actually took place. The existing literature on prostitution is rich in its descriptions of such behavior, and so there seemed no special need to add to it. If a respondent wished to describe behaviors that were directly undertaken to produce orgasm, he was not dissuaded. Few respondents cared to do so. Consequently the tapes yield a dialogue that would be appropriate for motion pictures of a bygone era when fadeouts discreetly suggested the passage of life's sweet mysteries. The authors would commend the more curious reader to works such as those of Dr. David Reuben (1969) and Ms. Xavier Hollander (1972), in which boudoir amusements are described in gloriously unvarnished English.

FINDINGS

Conception of Intent

In exploring the phenomenon of paying for sex, we begin the analysis of the process with the conception of one's intent to engage in the encounter under study. Clearly, the experience of paying for sex begins long before the actual encounter occurs. The conception of one's intent to enter into a transactional encounter in which monetary payment is offered in exchange for sexual services is usually motivated, at least to some degree, by a sexual desire. Fulfillment of one's sexual desire could, however, lead one into an encounter in which monetary payment is not involved. In most instances cited, however, there was a specific intent to fulfill sexual desires through an encounter in which monetary payment was involved. On the basis of the approach used in this study, the authors view the presence of this specific intent as a product of various social experiences from which an individual has formed a subjective interpretation of what the behaviors, individuals, and situations associated with prostitution mean.

In attempting to discover and explore the creation of this intent, the authors deliberately yet carefully probed what meaning the purveyor of sexual services for money (the prostitute) and what meaning such purveyance in and of itself had for those interviewed. Conceptually, prostitution was perceived by all of the subjects as a seemingly acceptable profession, serving a useful function and providing an important service. Despite the overwhelming level of approval for prostitution as an acceptable profession in society, at least half of the individuals interviewed imputed some conventionally negative characteristics and qualities to the actual purveyors of sexual services.

> I guess I have sort of a negative feeling toward a woman who's a prostitute because I think she's cheap, I guess, while I do believe in prostitution—that I think it should exist I don't have high regard for the woman who is the prostitute.
>
> They are driven to it by failure elsewhere—in most cases.
>
> Prostitutes very often hate men . . . a lot are lesbians—they must be.

Despite some of the negative conceptions about prostitutes and the existence of some previous unsatisfactory experiences with them, all of the individuals pursued the encounter with very high expectations of having a positive experience. During the time in which all of the individuals conceived the intent and engaged in the pursuit of the encounter, there was a conscious choice to omit from their awareness a concrete memory of previous unsatisfactory experiences or negative conceptions of the prostitute. Instead, there was a conscious effort to "create" an experience that fulfilled their particular fantasy.

For virtually all of the individuals in the study, the desire for sex was the bottom line of the intention to pay for sex. For slightly more than half of the subjects, this desire for sex was coupled with a desire for companionship. Thus, we have two significant motivators at work. Interestingly enough, however, these two motivators are, according to those interviewed, more often than not at the base of their intent for entering into a nonpaying sexual encounter. So why pay for sex? The conception of the intent to pay for sex was based on different sets of expectations that these individuals associated with what the experience of paying for sex meant to them. Each individual had structured their own subjective sense of what to expect when paying for sex. Each set of structured realities differed to varying degrees from one individual to another.

In the structuring of subjective realities, two common themes prevailed. One of the themes entailed expectations of mystery and excitement. Several of the interviewees spoke of mysterious qualities that they attached to the prostitute and the encounter itself.

> I did have some fantasy about the type of people that would be involved—they would be mysterious, not run-of-the-mill people on the street.
>
> She was going to be very overbearing about it. . . .I thought she would be very mysterious, hardly any talk, just walk in and take over the situation.
>
> I thought that she would have something for sure, like a dildo strapped to her . . . or gloves, a whip. . . .I had envisioned all kinds of neat stuff like she'd turn out the lights and we'd only have one tiny candle and she would take over, maybe incense, or she'd get us all wild with some exotic oil.
>
> [It] adds to it if you meet in a bar. . . .it leads to the mystery.

Some of those interviewed expressed an excitement over that element of risk that they envisage prevailing over such encounters. The unknown quality of what actually happens to them when they pursue such an encounter apparently provides an open space for fantasy that often seems to be flavored with some very real or imagined fear for their safety. For some, this generates a great deal of excitement and anticipation.

> Adventurous . . . you don't know whether you're going to get your brains blown out . . . element of risk . . . the gambling element . . . occasionally people get hurt . . . you never know when someone's going to put a knife to your throat.

For some, the expectation of excitement was based on the myth of the professional—the prostitute was seen as a "pro," someone with exceptional sexual powers, willing to provide special services: "she will probably have all kinds of tricks up her sleeve and something really fantastic will go on."

Another common theme involved an expectation that paying for sex would provide a situation in which the risk of rejection was minimal and one in which sex was guaranteed.

> If I just want to go out and get laid I'm not going to bother going to a bar and buying drinks and dancing with a girl all night because I'm not interested in that . . . you don't want to spend the time looking for it where there is always a maybe—maybe yes or maybe no . . . you almost want a written guarantee.

A number of the individuals interviewed perceived the pursuit of a paid sexual experience as one that was easy—without many of the entanglements and problems that they associated with pursuing a sexual encounter that did not involve monetary payment. It was perceived as a direct way to procure a sexual experience—one that was guaranteed to transpire following minimal effort.

> I can take a woman out to dinner and blow $30–40 and still not be sure that she will sleep with me—at least not that night.
>
> I also like the basic rawness of it . . . the basic honesty of it. There's a lot of honesty in that. You girl, me guy, me have sexual desire, you have the object of my sexual desire, me give you money, you give me what I want, no bullshit, no play, no games . . . it's raw, honesty, and it's good.

Paying for sex was viewed as an alternative to possibly experiencing frustration in response to having to delay gratification or to possibly having to put an enormous effort out even it sex did transpire. Several of the individuals pursued a prostitute for inclusion in a menage à trois, indicating that it would be less difficult than trying to "call around" looking for a willing person and the assumption that "a prostitute would be able to handle it without any problem."

Pursuit of a Paid Sexual Encounter

Once the intent to enter into a paid sexual experience develops, the pursuit of such an encounter may begin at any time. For some it was immediate; for others it took several weeks to arrange the encounter. Regardless of when the pursuit actually began, all of the individuals began immediately on the conception of intent to create with great anticipation a fantasy of what the experience would be like.

Amid fantasies of what is to occur, the pursuit begins with magnified feelings of nervousness, fear, and excitement. It was interesting to note that the tremendous rush of fear and nervousness did not result from a concern or awareness of the legal dangers of paying for sex. None of the persons interviewed mentioned a concern for the possible legal ramifications of the encounter. Instead, many spoke of a concern for their safety.

> So I approached the place . . . stood outside contemplating, shall I, shan't I, do I have enough guts. . . .I saw and watched a couple of guys go in and they didn't get devoured by any white dragons or bumped on their head.

For many, there was generalized fear of entering into strange physical surroundings where they would engage in an intimate encounter with an individual unknown to them. In addition, some of these encounters took place with streetwalkers in areas of town known for their high level of criminal activity. Fear of the unknown and fear of exposure to the criminal element created feelings of vulnerability in many respondents.

During the pursuit, a conscious attempt was made to set up the situation to meet very definite expectations. Clearly, there was an awareness of one's ability to manipulate the objective reality to fit expectations. Each client's subjective reality dictated many of the behaviors and feelings that occurred during the pursuit. In exploring these behaviors and feelings and what they meant for each of the individuals, there emerged a significant finding. In pursuing a paid sexual encounter, most of the individuals experienced feelings and engaged in behaviors that characterize the rituals that are a part of their typical courting experiences.

One of the rituals so often involved in most courting experiences is the desire and attempt to make oneself physically appealing. More than half of those interviewed mentioned an effort to appear physically desirable. This particular need to appear attractive finds expression in the following statement:

> I usually see to it that I have shaved and showered recently. Just before going I usually use aftershave or cologne.

Another courting ritual is that of creating a romantic atmosphere. During the pursuit, most of the individuals were involved in manipulating the environment to be romantic.

> It always adds a little to it if you meet in a bar . . . it adds to the romance of it when the initial contact is made over a drink. I have always found that somewhat better . . . it's an encounter of the first rate . . . it becomes a social event as opposed to a business meeting.

Most of the individuals pursued experiences where there would be a social element—drinking, dancing, or enough time to talk before the actual encounter.

In pursuing the paid encounter, all of the individuals had some sense of what qualities in a person they were looking for. As in the pursuit of a relationship where sexual encounters are not paid for, all of the individuals were looking for a person they found physically appealing.

> undefinable . . . just like any other situation—when you're about to make a friend . . . when you meet a woman.
>
> good looking, good shape, someone who's dressed better—looks sexier—someone who's made the effort to look good.

Many of the individuals spoke of other qualities in addition to physical appeal. Warmth and gentleness were mentioned as qualities to be sought after. Some spoke of wanting some show of interest from the prostitute.

> get some sort of feeling if she's flighty . . . is she putting her attention on you or is she looking at a dozen other guys . . . or is she focusing her attention on you . . . yes, that's important.

Others spoke very directly about evaluating the interaction as it progressed in an attempt to prevent potentially unpleasant experiences. This evaluation often would dictate if an agreement to buy sex was concluded: "if your's having fun with the person, and if you are . . . you put the question to her."

The Encounter

The encounter actually begins when the first moment of contact occurs. More specifically, the encounter is triggered at the time that all parties involved are aware of one another's presence. Thus, the encounter commences some time during the pursuit.

The period between initial visual awareness and verbal interaction varies tremendously. More often than not, this amount of time was dependent on the physical surroundings. Some of the bars and massage parlors or brothels provided a casual atmosphere in which an individual could take as much time as desired before a verbal interaction occurred. In other situations such as when an out-call service is used, verbal interaction generally takes place within seconds of the visual contact.

Unless already confronted by the prostitute, as in an out-call service situation, the verbal exchange was often the pivotal point at which individuals made a determination as to whether the person and situation had at least some of the qualities desired. Certainly this represents a pivotal point because it was the time in which a concrete offer was likely to be made. However, the verbal exchange offered more information for an evaluation of desired qualities such as warmth and gentleness. Of equal importance is the fact that this verbal exchange was often a key element in the pursuer's efforts to endow the situation with a romantic or at least pleasantly social atmosphere instead of a mechanical or cold one.

> The really nice thing about a bar is that you get this communication, and the communication lends to the romance and the intrigue and the whole thing.

This attempt to structure the objective reality to be romantic/social continued for most of the individuals throughout the encounter. There was an attempt to subdue the business end of the encounter in which what and for how much was negotiated. Unless the price was perceived as unreasonable, the duration of this exchange was minimal. In every encounter discussed, the individual paying for sex engaged in social, courting behaviors that were often flavored with varying degrees of romance. According to the subjects in the study, these behaviors represented a conscious attempt to create a positive experience that would fulfill their fantasies, that is, the client via such devices as compliments tries to manipulate the prostitute into complying with his particular vision of a pleasant, satisfactory encounter.

> I always try to establish a good rapport right off the bat—be pleasant . . . the last one . . . I told her she was dressed very nice . . . she had a scar on her nose and I told her she was good looking, and she said, "you don't mind my nose?" And I said, "Oh, don't worry about it, you can't even notice that." . . . And I established a very pleasant relationship with her. . . .It makes the experience for me that much more pleasant . . . it makes it more meaningful . . . when you—slam, bam, thank you ma'am, it would be no more one step ahead or behind masturbation.

There existed a belief that by being pleasant or even quite amorous they could subtly seduce the prostitute into allowing their created illusion to play itself out. Even better, if their tactics worked, the prostitute might exceed mere tolerance of the fantasy—they might become a more energetic (as opposed to passive) participant, albeit still a paid professional.

> my being pleasant to her, she became very pleasant to me . . . we talked all the way up to the room and in the room . . . she made love to me and made me feel very good about it and told me what a good lover I was . . . it increases the illusion, it's got to and it's part of the romance of it.

Clearly, a great deal of energy is invested in the maintenance of the illusion. Regardless of how things were going, most of the individuals continued until the very end to manipulate the situation to fit their expectations. Generally, sexual contact terminated with an orgasm.

The Aftermath

From the time the intent to pay for sex is conceived, one's focus tends to be unidirectional. A fantasy is created, and most of one's energy is directed into the structuring of the situation so that fantasies are fulfilled. Conscious efforts are made to support one's personal illusion; distractions are dismissed when possible or are somehow worked into the fantasy. Soon after sexual contact has terminated, the client's focus broadens—awareness of his surroundings increases. Most of the individuals experienced a sense that the drama was over. All of the individuals emerged from the drama with their own uniquely combined sets of feelings and levels of awareness. Some wanted nothing more than to flee.

> I remember that I was glad to get out of there because I felt very squeamish about the whole situation—the women, the courtyard—I didn't know whether some bandit would break in or what. I felt very relieved when it was all over with.

Others spoke of feeling "appalled at that they had done."

> I felt awful . . . that was just the pits . . . She was so revolting—really, really heavy . . . it was just debasing . . . I just found it to be a very debasing, humiliating experience for me . . . both he [friend] and I, when we came out of there couldn't believe what we had done.

Some mentioned anticlimactic feelings—often a sense of disappointment prevailed immediately following the experience.

> After the act one experiences a pang of feeling as if something is wrong because you just went through something which is not by any way, shape or form personal . . . there's absolutely no communication afterwards. It's over, finished. You are no longer of interest to the girls that you have just been with. And it's a big anticlimax afterwards.

For some, a sense of disappointment and anticlimax was delayed. The more immediate feeling was one of pleasure.

> On reflection, afterwards—come the day afterwards, not the time afterwards because it's a lot of fun and it's exciting and different . . . so you don't think

> about it then. The day afterwards . . . shit, you've dropped $40 or $60 or $20 and you have nothing to show for it. You have no relationship, no communication. You've relieved yourself. . . .Usually the day afterwards you've realized that you're using her as a receptacle and nothing else which is a little cold and leaves you with a sense of anticlimax.

More often than not, it seemed that the aftermath was filled with feelings of disappointment. Either the experience did not live up to the expectation held or if it did, there was often a recognition that in fact it all was just an illusion—the meaning they imputed to the encounter was no more than their own creation. It was clear, however, that in many of the encounters cited, the romantic notions held continued to influence many of the feelings experienced even during the aftermath. In general, even though a satisfactory or even great sexual encounter may have just been experienced, the postclimax phase is often filled with disappointment at the abrupt end of the "relationship." A few of the individuals stated, however, that they usually did not experience the postcoital realization that they were indeed a john, a phallus attached to a dollar bill. One respondent likened his continuing sense of satisfaction and well-being with that of having seen a good movie or having just returned form an expensive vacation; value had been received.

CONCLUSIONS

Definite patterns of behavior emerged in the course of the data analysis. The process of being a john involves four phases: conception of intent, pursuit of the encounter, the encounter, and the aftermath.

The first phase, the conception of intent, begins with the john's conscious decision to seek a paid sexual encounter. This phase may begin weeks before the actual encounter with the practitioner occurs. The johns in this study experienced a set of thoughts and feelings that appeared directly related to the fact that the planned sexual episode involved the services of a prostitute. Almost all of johns interviewed stated that they currently were involved in personal relationships that included sexual activity. They purchased the services of professional "lovers" by choice—not necessity. Furthermore, a forthcoming encounter engenders more than just plans concerning the commission of sexual acts. A sexual fantasy tinged with elements of fear and adventure is created and nurtured. Fear of criminal victimization by the practitioner herself or by denizens of her neighborhood was common. The planned encounter also however assumes a delicious aura of mystery. Although the john is reasonably certain that the meeting with the practitioner can be easily arranged and will result in sexual activity, he is not exactly sure what will occur. He is embarking on an adventure.

The next phase is the pursuit of the encounter. In this phase the john makes arrangements for his meeting with the practitioner. The john chooses a location and time of day for the encounter that are consistent with his personal fantasy. He does not merely "go where the girls are;" rather, he chooses a particular setting, a bar, a street corner, a massage parlor, a hotel room, a bordello, or the practitioner's "trick pad."

One of the most interesting findings of this study is associated with this phase, namely that while in pursuit of a paid sexual encounter johns often experience feelings and engage in behaviors that characterize rituals that are part of their typical courting experience. It was not unusual for johns to state that they attempted to make themselves physically appealing prior to encounters, for instance, they shaved, bathed, dressed fashionable, used cologne. Furthermore, many of those interviewed indicated that they attempted to choose a conventional social setting in which to at least begin the encounter, such as a bar with music and perhaps dancing. Some depicted such a milieu as having a romantic atmosphere and emphasized that this setting provided the opportunity to become acquainted with the practitioner, prior to the start of sexual activities. The john's activities in this second phase of the process quite literally serve to set the stage for the third phase—the encounter.

The encounter phase begins with the start of interaction with the practitioner and ends either with a breakdown in negotiations between the two principals or with the completion of sexual activity if a bargain has been successfully struck. In addition to his eventual participation in sexual relations, this phase sees the john involved in essentially two types of activity: evaluation of the appearance and personality of the practitioner and structuring the objective reality of the encounter.

The evaluation of the practitioner focuses more on her personality than on her physical appearance. Most of the men interviewed were likely to rate a practitioner as physically acceptable if she possessed a "moderate" or "average" degree of attractiveness; few respondents required specific physical attributes, such as large breasts, blond hair, or youthfulness. They tended to look for personal warmth and friendliness. Although these men wanted to pay for sex, it seemed that they did not want to deal with someone whose demeanor constantly reminded them of this fact.

In the opinion of the authors, the finding that johns actually work to structure the objective reality of their encounter with the practitioner is the most important to emerge from the present study. The johns interviewed in this study consciously attempted to influence the behavior of the prostitutes with whom they dealt. Much as more conventional suitors are wont to do, they worked to create a rapport with their date, plying her with compliments and sometimes with alcohol.

This finding has key implications for the study of prostitution. Given johns' efforts to psychologically manipulate prostitutes during the encounter phase, characterizations of johns drawn from practitioner-centered research must be evaluated very carefully. These data may be of limited usefulness because the men under observation might have been masking their true thoughts and feelings. Hence, even Stein's (1974) tape recordings of johns' conversations with practitioners during encounters are suspect in respect to their value for the evaluation of the motives and psychological needs of these men.

The fourth phase of the process of being a john is the aftermath and has as its focus the john's evaluation of the encounter. This phase commences when sexual activities cease and sees the termination of interaction with the practitioner and subsequent evaluation of that interaction. It was not unusual for the men in this study to experience feelings of disappointment. There is the sad realization by some that the encounter has not met their expectations. Others go on their way in better spirits, having enjoyed a satisfying adventure and regretting only that it is over. The aftermath of a particular encounter might influence the john's subsequent behavior with practitioners and so technically might last years.

In examining the findings of this research, one is struck by how much the image of the john derived from a phenomenological study of these persons differs from that generated by practitioner-centered research. As mentioned earlier, the john of behavioral scientific literature is a white middle-class man. So it was with the vast majority of this study's respondents. However, little in the way of the pathological or even marginal behavior usually associated with the role of john was found. Thus, questions arise about the ideological currents and may underlie the traditionally unsavory images of the john and his lady.

It is hoped that, in addition to providing a new perspective on johns, this study has provided evidence of the value of a phenomenological approach to research on a given illegal behavior. The phenomenological approach to the study of the john reveals new insights into behavior often branded as deviant and undesirable, helping one to better understand it. Historically, few criminologists have applied this research methodology to more serious predatory criminality. How is one to understand and perhaps prevent armed robbery if one does not ask armed robbers about the process of being an armed robber. In those relatively rare instances where research on serious criminality has involved an essentially phenomenological methodological approach, such as Lejeune's (1977) study of mugging, and Maida's (1979) and Levi's (1980) work on homicide, valuable new insights have been obtained.

How does the process of "being" a social actor engaged in a recidivistic episode of criminality start; With respect to johns, this was revealed in respondents' statements regarding the aftermath stage of the process. As noted earlier this stage often contained expressions of disappointment. In reaction to these data, the interviewer would routinely inquire if the respondent would entertain the notion of again paying for sex. The initial response was often a grimace coupled with the demure "I don't think so." Within seconds, however, the respondent would smilingly recant this statement saying, "Well, perhaps if she were . . . ." The interviewers realized that in this sequence of statements they were observing the glowing embers of an illusionary experience that although past was again being reborn in the conception of intent – the initial stage in the phenomenology of being a john.

REFERENCES

Armstrong, E.
1978 "Massage parlors and their customers." Archives of Sexual Behavior 7:117.

Benjamin, H., and R. E. L. Masters
1964 Prostitution and Morality. New York: Julian Press.

Berger, P., and T. Luckmann
1976 The Social Construction of Reality. Garden City, N.Y.: Doubleday.

Bittner, E.
1973 "Objectivity and realism in sociology." Pp. 109–125 in G. Psathas (ed.), Phenomenological Sociology. New York: Wiley.

Blumenstiel, A.
1973 "The sociology of good times." Pp. 187–215 in Phenomenological Sociology, edited by George Psathas. New York: Wiley.

Bryan, J.
1965 "Apprenticeships in prostitution." Social Problems 12:287.
1966 "Occupational ideologies of call girls." Social Problems 13:441.

Bryant, C., and C. Palmer
1975 "Massage Parlors and 'hand whores': Some sociological observations." Journal of Sex Research 11:227.

Cicourel, A.
1968 The Social Organization of Juvenile Justice. New York: Wiley.

Douglas, J.
1967 The Social Meanings of Suicide. Princeton, N.J.: Princeton University Press.
1970a "Deviance and respectability: The social construction of moral meanings." Pp. 3–30 in J. Douglas (ed.), Deviance and Respectability. New York: Basic Books.
1970b Observations on Deviance. New York: Random House.
1970c Understanding Everyday Life. Chicago: Aldine.
1972 Research on Deviance. New York: Random House.

Ellis, A.
1959 "Why married men visit prostitutes." Sexology 25:344.

Garfinkel, H.
1967 Studies in Ethnomethodology. Englewood Cliffs, N.J.: Prentice-Hall.
Gibbens, T. C. N., and M. Silberman
1960 "The clients of prostitutes." British Journal of Venereal Disease 36:113.
Goffman, E.
1974 Frame Analysis: An Essay on the Organization of Experience. New York: Harper & Row.
Gray, D.
1973 "Turning out: A study of teenage prostitution." Urban Life and Culture 1:401.
Greenwald, H.
1958 The Call Girl: A Social and Psychoanalytic Study. New York: Ballantine.
Hirschi, T.
1962 "The Professional Prostitute." Berkeley Journal of Sociology 7:33.
Hollander, X.
1972 The Happy Hooker. New York: Dell.
Laner, M. R.
1974 "Prostitution as an illegal vocation: A sociological overview." Pp. 406–418 in C. Bryant (ed.), Deviant Behavior: Occupational and Organizational Bases. Chicago: Rand-McNally.
Lejeune, R.
1977 "The management of a mugging." Urban Life 6:123.
Levi, K.
1980 "Homicide as conflict resolution." Deviant Behavior 1:281–307.
Liazos, A.
1972 "The poverty of the sociology of deviance: Nuts, sluts, and 'perverts.' " Social Problems 20:103.
Madge, J.
1965 The Tools of Social Science. Garden City, N.Y.: Doubleday.
Maida, P.
1979 Murder-for-hire in the Family Setting. Paper presented at the annual meeting of the American Society of Criminology, Philadelphia, November.
Mannheim, K.
1936 Ideology and Utopia. New York: Harcourt, Brace.
Masters, W., and V. Johnson
1966 Human Sexual Response. Boston: Little, Brown.
1970 Human Sexual Inadequacy. Boston: Little, Brown.
Milner, C., and R. Milner
1972 Black Players: The Secret World of Black Pimps. Boston: Little, Brown.

Morris, N.
1970 The Honest Politician's Guide to Crime Control. Chicago: University of Chicago Press.
Polsky, N.
1967 Hustlers, Beats, and Others. Chicago: Aldine.
Psathas, G.
1968 "Ethnomethods and phenomenology." Social Research 35:500.
Rasmussen, P. K., and L. Kuhn
1976 "The new masseuse: Play for pay." Urban Life 5:271.
Reuben, D.
1969 Everything You Always Wanted to Know About Sex. New York: McKay.
Richardson, J.
1970 "A Lively Commerce." Harpers, 82.
Simpson, M., and T. Schill
1977 "Patrons of massage parlors: Some facts and figures." Archives of Sexual Behavior 6:521.
Schutz, A.
1962 Collected Papers (Vol. 1). The Hague: Martinus Nijhoff.
1964 Collected Papers (Vol. 2). The Hague: Martinus Nijhoff.
1966 Collected Papers (Vol. 3). The Hague: Martinus Nijhoff.
1967 The Phenomenology of the Social World. Chicago: Northwestern University Press.
Sheehy, G.
1973 Hustling: Prostitution in Our Wide Open Society. New York: Delacorte.
Stein, M.
1974 Lovers, Friends, Slaves. . . .: The Nine Male Sexual Types. USA: Berkeley.
Stewart, G.
1972 "On first being a john." Urban Life and Culture 3:255.
Wagner, H.
1973 "The scope of Phenomenological Sociology: Considerations and suggestions. Pp. 61–87 in George Psathas (ed.), Phenomenological Sociology. New York: Wiley.
Warren, C. A. B., and P. K. Rasmussen
1977 "Sex and gender in field research." Urban Life 6:349.
Winick, C.
1962 "Prostitutes' clients perceptions of the prostitutes and of themselves." International Journal of Social Psychiatry 8:289.
Winick, C., and P. Kinsie
1971 The Lively Commerce: Prostitution in the U.S. Chicago: Quadrangle Books.

Reading 26

Deviance among Professionals: The Case of Unnecessary Surgery

Lonn Lanza-Kaduce
University of Florida, Gainesville

This paper conceptualizes unnecessary surgery as a form of professional deviance and seeks to conduct a substantial review of the literature on the subject from that perspective. Borrowing from the very nature of professions, one may define deviance among professionals in terms of violating the public service norm. The role that expertise plays in establishing what conduct is deviant is illustrated. The effects of professional autonomy on observing and measuring deviance are explored. Finally, the research findings on unnecessary surgery are summarized. The resulting patterns suggest that applying more traditional theories of deviance to account for the phenomenon may be fruitful.

It is generally acknowledged that deviance among professionals has been inadequately examined. To date, more attention has been given to criminal deviance among white collar groups than to other forms of high-status occupational norm violations. Much of the conduct of concern, however, lies outside the traditional confines of crime (Vold, 1958; Tappan, 1960; Burgess, 1950) and may be better characterized as deviant than illegal. Therefore, this paper modifies Akers' (1977) definition of occupational crime and defines deviance among professionals as those actions of professionals performed in the course of practicing their occupations that violate norms governing professional activities.

Inasmuch as each professional group has its own standards, it is difficult to generalize about deviance across professions. Accordingly, only one kind of deviance in a profession—unnecessary surgery—is reviewed here. The paper examines the conceptualization and definition, observation and measurement, and correlates and possible explanations of unnecessary surgery. The intent is not only to explore unnecessary surgery as an emerging social problem but also to offer insight into studying professional misconduct in general.

I wish to acknowledge the contributions of John R. Stratton, Marcia Radosevich, Ronald L. Akers, and the anonymous reviewers who provided useful criticisms of earlier drafts of this paper.

ISSUES OF CONCEPTUALIZATION AND DEFINITION

The professions have classically been defined in terms of two features: (1) an abstract body of knowledge requiring specialized training (expertise); and (2) a service orientation to the client in particular and the public in general (service ethic) (see Carr-Saunders and Wilson, 1944; Goode, 1960; Wilensky, 1964). Specific professional canons of ethics are concerned with implementing the general service ethic. Consequently, any violation, such as unnecessary surgery, is professionally deviant first because it violates the public service norm. Bosk's (1979) detailed field observation of surgical training graphically illustrates how the moral component overrides technical matters in defining surgical misconduct. Yet the importance of technical competence cannot be discounted. Frequently, it takes the same specialized knowledge to know when a service has been bungled, neglected, or abused as it does to perform competently. The centrality of both the expertise and service components in conceptualizing professional deviance can be seen by examining unnecessary surgery in detail.

Definitional and case findings problem are particularly difficult in the 85% of total operations considered discretionary or elective, that is, those that do not involve emergencies or are not death delaying (see Bunker, 1976). One of the more inclusive approaches to defining and classifying unnecessary discretionary operations is that adopted by a congressional subcommittee in its hearing on the matter (U.S. House of Representatives, Subcommittee on Oversight and Investigations of the Committee on Interstate and Foreign Commerce, hereafter referred to as the House Subcommittee, 1976):

Category I. Completely discretionary operations for asymptomatic nonpathologic, nonthreatening disorders.

Category II. Operations in which no pathologic tissue is removed.

Category III. Operations in which indications are a matter of difference in judgments and opinion among experts.

Category IV. Operations to alleviate endurable or tolerable symptoms.

Category V. Operations formerly performed in large numbers, now considered outdated, obsolete, or discredited.

Category VI. Operations done primarily for the personal gain of the surgeon, wherein the weight of informed opinion would deny any indication to the present.

This categorization provides a heuristic tool with which we can examine unnecessary surgery as a form of professional deviance.

Categories V and VI seem to be obvious instances of professionally deviant practices. Such operations not only violate more specific professional canons that could prompt in-house disciplinary action but also depart from legal standards and may give rise to malpractice suits and perhaps criminal charges if discovered.

Category II also raises a strong suspicion of professional deviance. Operations in this category suggest poor diagnoses and place patients needlessly in peril. A dispute exists, however, about whether the surgical removal of normal tissue can prevent future problems in enough cases ultimately to benefit the patient to justify the relaxation of standards for making certain surgical recommendations. The controversy immediately illustrates the important role of expertise in defining deviance among professionals.

Hysterectomies provide a strategic example of this issue[1] because at least 15% of all hysterectomies are performed when there is no pathology (D'Espo, 1962). Whereas D'Espo was willing to accept prophylactic removal of normal uteri from older women because they were "functionally useless," Cole (Bunker et al., 1976) argued from an actuarial analysis that the added seven months of life for women having normal uteri removed as a prophylactic against future problems were more than offset by morbidity considerations. Physiological complications occur in 30–45% of such cases according to Donahue (Bunker et al., 1976). As Bunker (Bunker et al., 1976) concluded, the removal of normal tissue for prophylactic purposes can be justified only by using a quality-of-life argument inasmuch as these operations do not contribute significantly to overall longevity. Data on whether more people are better off after such surgery do not currently exist. However, in an occupation that uses its expert knowledge and public service to legitimate its self-governing status (see Freidson, 1970a), those who would remove normal tissue need to substantiate the validity of the prophylactic claim.

Even if removal of tissue cannot be shown to have prophylactic utility, it may improve quality of life either by alleviating endurable or tolerable conditions (Category IV) or by making changes in completely asymptomatic, nonpathologic, nonthreatening disorders, as in the case of cosmetic surgery (Category I). The deviance of Category IV procedures again rests on professional expertise establishing whether symptoms are better remedied by forms of treatment other than surgery. Several examples can be offered. A controlled study of surgical versus nonsurgical techniques for treating varicose veins showed that the nonsurgical technique yielded improvement in 8% more of the cases than did surgery after three years,

[1]Appendectomies are also illustrative. Tissue reports indicate that 33% of the appendixes removed are pathologically normal (Howie, 1968; Sparling, 1962). Howie observed a slightly lower expected mortality rate (.004%) for patients of surgeons who more frequently removed normal appendixes because of missing fewer diseased ones. He did not consider morbidity costs or direct or indirect monetary expenses, however. Conversely, Lembeke (1952) found more mortality to be associated with higher appendectomy rates. Neutra (1978) found that greater inclination to remove normal appendixes was not associated with fewer perforated organs, and so surgery had no utility in this regard.

cost less, and had a markedly lower mortality risk even though it had more immediate complications associated with it (Piachaud and Weddell, 1972). Similarly, Neuhauser found the risk of elective herniorrhaphy at age 65 or older to be four times as great as the risk of using nonoperative treatments (Bunker and Wennberg, 1973). Millman (1977) reviewed the evidence regarding coronary bypass surgery and concluded that, although the procedure may relieve chest pain, it also accelerates coronary artery disease. Ultimately, only research can determine whether tolerable conditions can be alleviated as well, or better, by treatments other than surgery. As LoGerfo (1977) commented, however, it is disturbing that many of these studies have not yet been pursued by the profession despite the acknowledged need to do so for years.

The necessity of Category I surgeries (those for asymptomatic disorders) must be decided almost entirely on qualitative criteria. Whether the inevitable risk of mortality[2] and morbidity that accompanies any surgical procedure outweighs esthetic or qualitative benefits derived is a matter of debate. Yet because the patients in these operations do not desire relief from symptoms or pathologies, they themselves are asking for "unneeded" surgery and the surgeons cannot easily be accused of violating a public service norm by performing such procedures. Category I operations may still be questioned, however, to the extent that they interfere with the delivery of more pressing medical services.

The necessity of the remaining category of potentially unnecessary operations (Category III) is by definition controversial. Only research and clinical experience will settle disputes in which indications for surgery are matters of differences in judgments and opinions among experts. Although it is inevitable that some of these procedures will be discredited in time, they can hardly be considered breaches of the service ethic given the current state of knowledge.

The preceding remarks illustrate how viewing unnecessary surgery as a form of professional deviance allows study to move beyond a mere classification scheme and locate a more abstract notion that subsumes diverse practices. The two classic defining characteristics of professions—expertise and public service—are pivotal in identifying deviance among professionals.

PROBLEMS OF OBSERVATION AND MEASUREMENT

It is a third element of professionalism, autonomy, that most affects observation and measurement. Regardless of whether autonomy is the sine qua

[2]The risk of mortality for elective operations is estimated to be .5% (Bunker and Wennberg, 1973).

non of professions (see Hall, 1975; Freidson, 1970a; Moore, 1970) or is merely derived from expertise and public service (see Wilensky, 1964), its acknowledged existence renders compliance to the public service ethic problematic. Because autonomy entails relative freedom from oversight, departures from the public service norm often go unnoticed, or at least underscrutinized, and unsanctioned (see Freidson, 1970a). Accordingly, there are special observation and measurement problems associated with deviance among professionals. This is true for both of the basic approaches to observing and measuring unnecessary surgery—case studies and epidemiology.

Case Studies

The more direct approach to examine professional deviance utilizes case studies; the necessity of surgical procedures ultimately entails professional judgment on a case-by-case basis. The autonomy of professionals and their monopoly of expertise, however, completely undercut such official measures of unnecessary operations as malpractice suits or disciplinary proceedings (see Freidson, 1970a; Millman, 1977). We must find other suitable case study indicators of this professional misconduct.

One indicator is a discrepancy between the initial professional judgment and subsequent review of it. For operations, the diagnoses and surgical recommendations are occasionally reviewed via voluntary or mandatory preoperative consultations (see House Subcommittee, 1976; McCarthy and Widmer, 1974; Grafe et al., 1978), postoperative procedures like tissue committees to assess the pathology of the removed organ or tissue (see D'Espo, 1962; Verda and Platt, 1958), and audits of medical records (Brook, 1974) or insurance claims (Roos et al., 1977a).

From a methodological standpoint, however, there is no good case study vehicle for measuring unnecessary operations. Mandatory consultations are reactive in that the attending physicians come to know of likely review. Grafe et al. (1978) called this a "sentinel effect"—as second-opinion programs become known, surgical rates decline (see also Dyck et al., 1977). Furthermore, among cases that are unconfirmed by second opinions, mandatory consultations are less effective than voluntary ones in predicting eventual surgical intervention (McCarthy and Finkel, 1978; Grafe et al., 1978).

The weakness of relying on voluntary second opinions as a measurement device is that they are sought by only a select subpopulation of patients. Even when second opinions are encouraged by insurance coverage, only 10% of the patients pursue this opinion (McCarthy and Widmer, 1974). According to McCarthy and Finkel (1978) voluntary consultations usually occur when the patient faces major surgery. McCarthy and Widmer (1974) reported that more women voluntarily seek a second opinion. Before the measurement adequacy of voluntary consultations can be determined, it is necessary to elaborate what other variables are associated with the choice to get a second professional opinion so that the estimates can be adjusted to represent better the entire universe of clients.

Postoperative measurement techniques are just as flawed. Tissue committees are reactive in that they prompt a reduction in surgery (Verda and Platt, 1958), and pathology reports cannot make some conceptual distinctions central to the definition of unnecessary surgery.[3] Postoperative record audits may be objected to on several grounds. First, these audits require accurate records and reliable abstracting from records so that the reviewers have the same information as the attending doctors. If doctors know of probable review, they may manipulate the information to their benefit. Observers have often emphasized the uncertainty surrounding medical decisions (Parsons, 1951; Millman, 1977; Bosk, 1979; Freidson, 1970a), and there is some indication that this can be used to insulate the doctor from accountability. Davis (1960) and Millman (1977) observed such "functional uncertainty" in communications with patients and their families. Bosk (1979) claimed that the ritualistic case reviews at mortality and morbidity conferences also allow accounts to be given that purge the record of the normative error associated with misconduct (see also Millman, 1977). A second shortcoming of records audits involves unreliability. The reliability of medical judgments made from records both across time (85% congruent) and across doctors (77% congruent) is not very high (Brook, 1974; see also Rutkow et al., 1979). Abstracting from records by lay people yields even lower consistency (57–65%) according to Demlo et al. (1978).

Epidemiology

The epidemiological approach examines differences in rates of phenomena across subpopulations or subsamples.[4] Comparisons across groupings show

[3]Another measurement of using tissue pathology reports to verify the appropriateness of surgical decisions is linked to the problems of defining unnecessary operations. One should recall that removing normal tissue does not always imply an unsound medical judgment because the observed symptomology may have warranted the procedure. It seems that, even though tissue committees may deter some questionable operations, they do not provide a valid vehicle for measurement.

[4]Surgical rates have been compared across areas both domestically (Wennberg and Gittelsohn, 1973; Lewis, 1969; Massachusetts Department of Public Health, 1971; Vayda and Anderson, 1975) and cross-culturally (Bunker, 1970; Vayda, 1974; Yoshida and Yoshida, 1976; Lichtner and Pflanz, 1971). Epidemiological analysis has also been extended to rate comparisons by type of hospital (Kisch et al., 1969; Peterson and Barsamian as cited in Mackie, 1976; Stockwell as cited in Vayda, 1977), type of insurance coverage (Shapiro, 1967; Anderson and Feldman, 1956), surgical manpower distribution and degree of specialization (Roemer and DuBois, 1969; American College of Surgeons and the American Surgical Association – ASC and ASA – 1975), and the method of organizing practice (Holahan, 1977).

dramatic differences in surgical rates and misconduct is inferred from inflated rates.

The reliability and validity problems presented by the epidemiological method differ somewhat from case study approaches. The information relied on needs not be so detailed and is grouped. Therefore, its reliability is probably better, and any errors that exist are deemphasized by treating the data in aggregate because random fluctuations offset one another. As for surgical rates, those rates derived directly from hospital or doctors' records are probably accurate for most procedures. Even rates gleaned from the claims records of insurance companies and underwriting agencies are reasonably good. LoGerfo and associates (1978) reported that accurate claims information existed on more than 90% of the actual visits made by patients to a prepaid health care project. Roos et al. (1977b) provided further evidence of the reliability of claims data.

The biggest problem for epidemiology lies with the validity of the inference that a disparity in rates among subpopulations results from such deviance as unnecessary surgery. Unfortunately, the reviewed studies did not attempt to assign patients randomly to the subsamples or to control for confounding effects of other variables by adjusting for differences in potential covariates through more sophisticated statistical techniques. Nevertheless, it was commonly assumed that the comparison groups were sufficiently similar to infer that some conditions were associated with inflated surgical rates. Surgical necessity is not thought to vary considerably across subpopulations, so the relative differences in rates were attributed to unnecessary operations. Yet differences may have been due to unavailability or underutilization of professional services by some population segments rather than to professional misconduct. Sufficient controls need to be introduced into rate studies either in designs or by statistical manipulation to eliminate conclusively other possible explanations of rate differences. Until then, only prima facie inferences are warranted about the conditions associated with surgical deviance. Given the shortcomings associated with case study strategies, future research in unnecessary surgery could greatly benefit from adopting a meticulous epidemiological methodology even if the results are limited to examining relative rates of deviance instead of its absolute frequency.

The Extent of Unnecessary Surgery

Despite observation and measurement problems associated with the study of professional misconduct, useful information can be obtained even when the desired precision has not been attained. Our review of the literature provides extensive evidence of deviance across various measurement techniques.

Rate studies indicate that twice as many elective operations are performed per capita in the United States as in England and Wales, whereas the rates for critical, nonelective procedures are very similar across the regions (Bunker, 1970). There is evidence to suggest that some of the unexplained higher incidence of deaths for people under 65 in this country, compared with other industrialized Western nations like Great Britain or Sweden, is a consequence of this difference in surgery rates (Bunker and Wennberg, 1973). They reported a positive statistical association between operation rates and overall death rates.

Epidemiological studies also suggest which operations are most prone to professional misconduct. For example, it has been reported that if the 1969 tonsillectomy practices in Massachusetts continued, 80% of the children born in that state in 1960 would eventually lose their tonsils. Yet the procedure may be justified in only 5–10% of the population according to current medical thinking (Massachusetts Department of Health, 1971). In this country, 90% of tonsillectomies are considered unneeded, with an estimated annual waste of $360 million and more than 60 deaths per year occurring as a result of anesthesia alone (Hiatt, 1975).

Rate studies suggest that the extent of unnecessary hysterectomies is large and growing. Not only are twice as many performed in the United States as in England and Wales (see Bunker, 1970), but the rate here rose 26% between 1968 and 1973 (Bunker et al., 1976; see also Dyck et al., 1977, for Canadian figures).

There are wide differences in surgical procedures having more definitive indications for surgical intervention than tonsillectomies or hysterectomies. These differences are perhaps most readily explained by unnecessary surgery in some areas. From Kansas data Lewis (1969) uncovered twofold differences by region for hernia repairs, threefold differences for hemorrhoidectomies, cholecystectomies, and varicose vein surgery, and even a fourfold difference in appendectomies. As already indicated, these inflated rates translate into more deaths and higher financial costs.

Case studies using tissue pathology reports and operation reports indicate that one third of appendectomies and hysterectomies are of questionable necessity (Rayack, 1967). In a postoperative audit of the Seattle Pre-Paid Hospital Care Project, LoGerfo et al. (1978) found that commonly promulgated indications were met in only 32% of the tonsillectomy and adenoidectomy cases (see also Roos et al., 1977a, for data from Manitoba).

Second opinion study also indicates the degree of unwarranted surgery. One fifth of surgical decisions were unconfirmed when preoperative consultations were mandatory, and one third were unconfirmed when second opinions were voluntary. The proportions of unconfirmed operation cases varied by type of surgery as well as by voluntary versus mandatory consultations as can be seen in Table 1. Orthopedic surgery was least often confirmed by both methods.

TABLE 1 Confirmation for Operations by Surgical Specialty and Type of Consultation (in Percentages)

	Compulsory consultations			Voluntary consultations		
Specialty	Con-firmed	Uncon-firmed	*N*	Con-firmed	Uncon-firmed	*N*
General surgery	86.7	13.3	293	80.2	19.8	242
Gynecology	78.7	21.3	150	59.5	40.5	173
Orthopedics	65.8	34.2	38	57.5	42.5	106
Ear, nose, and throat	89.8	10.2	49	80.2	19.8	86
Urology	70.8	29.2	24	61.4	38.6	57
Opthalmology	78.4	21.6	37	65.0	35.0	40
Others	72.7	27.3	11	78.4	21.6	37
All specialties	82.4	17.6	602	69.6	30.4	754

Note. Adapted from McCarthy and Widmer (1974).

Their follow-up in the Cornell Elective Surgery Second Opinion Program yielded the same pattern of unconfirmed surgical diagnoses except for a higher incidence of unconfirmed diagnoses for otolaryngology cases (Grafe et al., 1978). Paris et al. (1979) found 25% of the surgical recommendations in a voluntary consultation program in New York City to be unconfirmed upon review. The consultants added qualifications to their nonconfirmations in more than 60% of these cases, the most important of which were that surgery was not indicated at that time but might be later, that nonsurgical treatment was indicated, and that more information was needed to make the recommendation. Although the most recent second-opinion study (Gertman et al., 1980) shows that the rate of nonconfirmations is low (8%) and is a consequence of honest disagreement about surgical indicators, the results cannot be used to infer much about unnecessary surgery. Unlike the mix of mandatory and voluntary consultations in the Cornell program, this study was based on Medicaid patients in the Boston area who participated in a statewide mandatory consultation program. Because these doctors had to know that their work would be reassessed, the sentinel effect undoubtedly occurred to an even larger extent than McCarthy and his associates found. Consequently, the 8% nonconfirmation rate is probably a better reliability estimate than an indicator of unnecessary surgery.

Case studies also show that the problem of morbidity needs to be investigated. For example, across 15 operation categories, more than one fifth of the surgical patients in one study died or suffered from moderate morbidity after their operations (Stanford Center for Health Care Research, 1976). Even for more frequent and less complicated procedures like appendectomies or hysterectomies, morbidity or death occurred in 7–8% of the cases. Another study of preventable critical incidents (deaths or life-threatening complications) showed that 88% of the complications across six surgical categories (appendectomies, gall bladder operations, hernia surgery, colon operations, hysterectomies, and prostate surgery) were either surgeon or hospital related with the largest share the result of poor surgical technique or postoperative care (SOSSUS, 1976). Clearly, unnecessarily going under the knife subjects one to a series of additional risks.

Despite definitional and measurement shortcomings, the evidence clearly indicates that unnecessary surgery occurs with regularity. Regardless of the measurement technique used, the proportion of operations of questionable necessity is sizeable, and the cost of this professional misconduct in terms of mortality, morbidity, and money is substantial. Moreover, the amount of unnecessary surgery may be increasing. Whereas standardized surgical rates remained constant from 1931 to 1956 (see Anderson and Feldman, 1956) and from 1956 to 1961 (see Anderson et al., 1963), Bombardier et al. (1977) reported a 14% increase between 1963 and 1970, an increase that continued until 1976 when it leveled off (see Grafe et al., 1978).

EFFORTS AT EXPLANATION: CORRELATES OF UNNECESSARY SURGERY

None of the reviewed studies on unnecessary surgery adopt a clear theoretical orientation; nor does the level of knowledge in this area allow the construction of a coherent, well-formed theory at this time. There are, however, variables concerning professional training, the economics of health care, and certain control efforts that are related to low quality of care and inflated rates of surgery and so are probable correlates of unnecessary surgery. These are summarized as a preliminary step for explanation.

Training and Adult Socialization

Because of their training, it assumed that board-certified specialists are less likely to operate needlessly than are practitioners without specialty certification.[5] A recent review by Hughes (1977), however, failed to find a consistent relationship between board certification of surgeons and overall quality of care. Nevertheless, for some surgical procedures, mortality is slightly lower among certified surgeons (Arnold, 1970). Fine and Morehead (1971) reported that diplomates in surgical specialties made more satisfactory diagnoses for hysterectomies and prostatectomies than did other doctors. Using Canadian data, Roos et al. (1977a) found a weak relationship between

[5]This has significance because approximately 40% of the operations performed in this country are done by general practitioners and noncertified specialists—two thirds of whom have taken but failed specialty certification examinations (see House Subcommittee, 1976).

specialty status and complying with accepted surgical standards for tonsillectomies and adenoidectomies. Small but statistically significant relationships between high standards (and therefore fewer unnecessary operations) also existed for such doctor-related variables as age of physician and place of training. Younger doctors (perhaps more recent graduates) and those trained in Britain, where surgical rates are lower, met surgical indications better.

This suggests that different operating philosophies exist in a systematic way that may be directly reflected in overall operation rates and indirectly related to unnecessary surgery. Exploratory observational studies of both the medical socialization of surgical residents (Knafl and Burkett, 1975) and the decision making of ear, nose, and throat specialists (Bloor, 1976) confirm this. When outcomes for "conservative" as opposed to "radical" operating propensities were compared, radical doctors removed 14% more normal appendixes but had 10% fewer nonoperative cases with subsequent recurrent symptoms than did their conservative counterparts (Donabedian, 1976).

Over and above different operating philosophies, it seems that doctors in the United States widely endorse the efficacy of surgical intervention. Bunker and Brown (1974) found that physicians and their spouses have as high or higher surgical rates for frequently abused procedures than do other professionals and that the rates were 25% to 30% higher than overall national norms. Exaggerated beliefs about the helpfulness of their services probably derives from clinical training where, observers note, idiographic experiences are stressed over general scientific reasoning and knowledge (see Becker et al., 1961; Freidson, 1970a; 1970b; Bosk, 1979). This may also account for why so little of the basic research needed to verify the efficacy of many procedures has been performed.

A final correlate of surgical necessity that pertains to training attends to the type of hospital with which doctors are affiliated. For example, teaching hospitals were associated with fewer unnecessary or questionable appendectomies (Sparling, 1962) and with fewer incorrect diagnoses for pelvic operations (Peterson and Barsamian cited in Mackie, 1976). Freidson (1970a) pointed out that the amount of association among colleagues is highest in teaching hospitals and that the training function requires more formality and supervision (see Bosk's description, 1979), which might account for these findings.[6]

Inasmuch as affiliation with teaching hospitals, conservative operating philosophies, receiving training in England, and perhaps specialization tend

[6]The quality of staff at a teaching hospital and their salary compensation mode may also contribute to the higher standards, but it should be remembered that much surgery is performed by residents rather than by staff surgeons (see Hughes et al., 1974; Bosk, 1979; ASC and ASA, 1975).

to be related to less surgery, it seems likely that different normative milieux exist to which practitioners are selectively exposed. The extensive training period, specialized knowledge, and insulated work situation of professionals argue that the cultural component is important for any theory that would account for deviance among professionals. Millman's (1977) observations of surgical training emphasize how medical professionals employ several collective neutralizing rationales for distancing themselves from their mistakes. The same milieu that ignores, justifies, or minimizes misfeasance is fertile ground for doing the same for malfeasance. Studies of norm violations among other kinds of high status for offenders (see Sutherland, 1949; Clinard, 1952; Cressey, 1953; Geis, 1967) have frequently found neutralizations rationalizations, or vocabularies of adjustment similar to what Millman describes.

Economic Factors

Economic variables in health care delivery were emphasized by Freidson (1970a), and a Marxist account was given by Waitzkin and Waterman (1974). Freidson argued that professional autonomy allows personal or occupational self-interest to conflict with the public interest. He maintained that professional performance (rather than good intentions) is the appropriate measure of how the tension between self-interest and public service is resolved and insisted that the economic terms of work, specifically the methods and sources of compensation, may affect professional behavior. Accordingly, economic organization may either reinforce or undermine compliance to public service standards. Support for Freidson's model comes from investigations of the interrelated areas of social class, insurance coverage, private versus public insurance, and fee-for-service, salary, or prepaid capitation payment schemes.

Anderson and Feldman (1956) found a positive relationship between surgical rates and income level. There was an interaction between income and insurance coverage however. In fact, poor people with insurance coverage showed more surgery than did wealthier people regardless of insurance coverage. The relationship between income and surgery was confirmed for the early 1960s in a recent study by Bombardier et al. (1977); but the effect of income was less strong in 1970 and educational differences observed in 1963 disappeared. Governmental insurance programs like Medicare were thought to account for the diminution in the relationship between class and surgery as Bombardier et al. noted a marked increase in surgeries among the elderly between 1963 and 1970. Significantly, the Bombardier study also found that lower income groups less frequently utilized procedures rated of lowest necessity by physicians than did their wealthier counterparts.

Type of insurance coverage may also relate to surgical utilization and thereby indirectly to unnecessary operations. For example, Medicaid recipients show operation rates more than two times those of the general population, an indication that public underwriting is probably more frequently abused (House Subcommittee, 1976; Forum, 1977). Blue Shield fee-for-service coverage has been found to be associated with surgery rates more than twice those for prepaid group plans (Perrot, 1966; Falk and Senturia, 1961). Bunker (1970) referred to a Columbia University study of medical care in which a prepaid group plan was found to be associated with fewer unjustified operations done by fewer unqualified surgeons than occurred for indemnity Blue Shield insurance plans. Fee-for-service indemnity insurance apparently encourages professional deviance.

Further evidence that fee-for-service remuneration contributes to inflated rates was also found. One government study found that the surgical rate for group practices employing salaried surgeons was half that for practices with surgeons remunerated on a fee-for-service basis (House Subcommittee, 1976). Gaus et al. (1976) reported that patients of salaried physicians show significantly lower hospitalization utilization than do those with doctors having fee-for-service arrangements regardless of whether their doctors were in solo practice, foundation, or group setting. Holahan (1977) found no significant difference between surgical utilization in traditional fee-for-service practice organization methods and a foundation plan in which services were prepaid but on a fee-for-service basis. Fee-for-service payment has been consistently linked to higher surgical rates and prepaid salary or capitation modes to lower rates (Lees and Cooper, 1964; Roemer, 1962; Perrot, 1966; Shapiro, 1967; Falk and Senturia, 1961).[7]

An indirect economic factor is operation work loads. Using 10 hernia equivalents (HEs) as the optimal weekly work load (as reported by Hughes et al., 1972), studies have found that in some areas surgeons in fee-for-service group practices perform only 3.1 HEs weekly (Hughes et al., 1974), whereas chief residents do 8.2 HEs per week (Hughes et al., 1973), and surgeons in a prepaid group practice performed near the optimal work load (Hughes et al., 1974). Fuchs (1969) estimated from aggregate national data that even if all operations were done by surgical specialists, their average work load would be fewer than five operations per week (see also Nickerson et al., 1976). On the average the work load of surgeons is light, and surgeons themselves indicate that they could carry much heavier work loads (ACS and ASA, 1975). The concern is that this inefficient use of surgical skill pressures some physicians to operate in equivocal situations (House Subcommittee, 1976).

[7]Although Wilson and Longmire (1978) could not compare operation rates, they found that salaried physicians (in the military) routinely performed more preoperative tests with no improved outcome and fee-for-service doctors performed appendectomies more quickly with fewer resulting complications. That some quality of care components are positively associated with fee-for-service compensation indicates the complexity of the issue.

Other organizational aspects of the medical profession may also have important economic implications. It may be argued that a surplus or maldistribution of surgeons creates pressures toward operating in questionable cases. Many studies show that areas with more doctors are associated with higher operation rates (Bunker, 1970; Lewis, 1969; Wennberg and Gittelsohn, 1973; ACS and ASA, 1975; House Subcommittee, 1976; for contrary results in Manitoba, see Roos et al., 1977a). Evidence also indicates that there is an oversupply of surgeons and doctors who do surgery. Although the proportion of physicians decreased from 109 per 100,000 people in 1950 to 95 per 100,000 in 1974 (Julian, 1977), the number of surgical specialties increased from 10% of the profession in 1931 to more than 30% in 1968 (Blackstone, 1974). Now about 40% of active physicians (including surgical residents) pursue surgical work as a substantial portion of their practices, and 30% are certified specialists (ASA and ASC, 1975). Recalling the low average work load discussed previously, it is not surprising to learn that surgeons have shorter work weeks than general practitioners, but it is surprising that surgeons also have higher incomes than general practitioners (Blackstone, 1977). One needs not be cynical to see how unnecessary surgery would contribute to obtaining those high incomes given the surgeon surplus and slow practices.

Hospital-related variables are also thought to affect unnecessary services associated with surgery. In fact, 20% to 24% of surgical procedures done in hospitals could be done on an outpatient basis according to testimony before the House subcommittee (1976). But this would mean empty hospital beds, unused operating rooms, less insurance indemnification for patients, and lower income for doctors. In area studies, the number of hospital beds per 1,000 population has been linked to inflated surgical rates even without considering the outpatient possibilities (Wennberg and Gittelsohn, 1973; Lewis, 1969). Hospital size (frequently measured in terms of number of beds) may also affect the kind of care received. For example, in one study smaller hospitals had higher than expected mortality rates resulting from cholecystectomies and larger facilities had lower rates (see Mackie, 1976). Small nonprofit hospitals had slightly more incorrect diagnoses for pelvic surgery than did larger nonprofit hospitals, but proprietary hospitals showed the highest rates (Peterson and Barsamian cited in Mackie, 1976). Kisch et al. (1969) also found significant rate increments for proprietary hospitals but less often for operations based more on intrinsic symptoms (like craniotomies) than for those stemming from extrinsic conditions like appendectomies). It seems that the nature of the hospital in which the surgery is performed may either inhibit or enhance the likelihood of unnecessary surgery.

The evidence just reviewed suggests that there are strong remunerative and utilitarian reasons for departing from the service ethic in the case of unnecessary surgery. There are important differences in surgical rates by fee-for-service versus capitation or salary compensation modes. Insurance coverage, especially governmental underwriting, was linked to inflated rates of surgery as were proprietary hospitals. Other correlates of unnecessary surgery having monetary implications include low surgical work loads, a surplus of doctors who perform surgery, and a maldistribution of practitioners.

Control Mechanisms

One of the major consequences of professional autonomy is the diminished probability that compliance will be secured by the coercion of superior authority (see Freidson, 1970a; 1970b). The two primary informal means of control exercised by fellow practitioner—talking to (Freidson and Rhea, 1963) and personally boycotting (Freidson, 1970a)—apparently have little impact on professional misconduct. Even doctors formally found wanting in malpractice suits suffer little in the way of public stigma (Schwartz and Skolnick, 1970).

Some formal administrative procedures, however, have potent effects on unnecessary surgery. Hospitals that adopt explicit standards of surgical indications show an immediate drop in surgical rates (see Paradise and Bluestone, 1976). Instituting tissue committees to examine the pathology of removed tissue can reduce the number of normal appendixes removed by 60% (Verda and Platt, 1958). Formal peer review (Holahan, 1977) and audits by panels including specialists (Dyck et al., 1977) have been shown to deter questionable operations. Mandatory second consultations have a sentinel effect and reduce the number of unconfirmed diagnoses and surgical recommendations (McCarthy and Widmer, 1974; Grafe et al., 1978).

A more ambitious federally inspired regulatory effort has been less successful. A system of Professional Standards Review Organizations (PSROs) has been erected to review the medical necessity and quality of care prior to federal reimbursement for medical services (see House Subcommittee, 1976). This was designed to deter unnecessary surgery as well as other inappropriate services, especially overlong hospital stays. Some evaluators have claimed that such review is not cost effective (Averill and McMahon, 1977), and others have concluded that there is no evidence that the PSROs reduce inappropriate use of services (Sanazaro, 1977). Brook et al. (1978) in a four-year longitudinal study of one such review organization found that it had little effect except to reduce the number of injections. Because admissions for elective surgery needed only to be approved by a clerk who assigned an expected length of stay for the indicated operation, the review procedure was poorly structured to detect unnecessary surgery. A more extensive nationwide survey of PSROs and the progeny of utilization reviews spawned by the federal guidelines found variability across hospitals in the type of review conducted (Gertman et al., 1979). Again, because nonemergency admissions usually indicated elective surgery, their findings concerning admissions review are most relevant for present purposes. Gertman and his associates reported that review had significant impact, as measured by decline in total Medicare days of care, only among hospitals in which the review rejected admission at least once. Hospitals having no review or never countermanding an admission produced an increase in total Medicare days. Their survey also suggested that in those hospitals in which review significantly affected care, it was cost effective to some extent. Evidently, if PSROs are to reduce inappropriate care (and thereby save money), the implied threat has to be backed up by some concrete action.

Significantly, the preceding indicates that the most effective mechanisms are those in which an errant doctor is more likely to be detected. Noncompliance to practice norms is more certainly determined when the standards are made explicit. A normal pathology report is a concrete indicator that the diagnosis was wrong in the final analysis regardless of the original symptomology. Mandatory second consultations assure review. The expertise of fellow professionals, especially when there is a history of negative reaction, reduces the ambiguity in reviews, and audits when the inexpertise of lay clerks or inaction of professional peers does not. The ineffectiveness of personally boycotting or talking to doctors may also stem from the uncertainty inevitable when such informal control methods are open to interpretations other than professional censure. Why some procedures are effective and others are not may be best explained by differences in the certainty of establishing poor practice. The parallel to classical deterrence theory is obvious.

THE SEARCH FOR MORE GENERAL THEORY

The pattern of findings suggests the applicability of a more general and inclusive theory of deviant behavior to professional misconduct. The importance of beliefs, definitions, and neutralizations, the potency of the economic and reward structures, and the nature of effective punishment and deterrents correspond to central components of social learning or differential association-reinforcement theory (Akers, 1977; Burgess and Akers, 1966). Social learning posits that conforming and deviant behaviors are primarily conditioned by operant learning principles. Deviance requires that definitions unfavorable to norm violation (typifying a strong public service commitment) must be neutralized (as through justifications for operations in questionable cases) or displaced by prodeviance definitions. Definitions and behavior are learned in patterns of differential association with others, and groups comprising colleagues in medical schools, hospitals, and practices are instrumental. Philosophies and beliefs about surgery become important discriminative stimuli for behavior that is a direct function of the amount, frequency, and probability of its being rewarded or punished. How medicine is organized, which involves such matters as fee-for-service payment, surgeon surplus, and poor distribution of doctors, combined with professional autonomy (resulting in a lack of oversight to deter deviance), may erect contingencies that differentially reinforce some for deviating from their service ethic by providing them with a greater balance of reinforcement for misconduct than for good practice. This post hoc marshalling of evidence is consistent with such a social learning explanation. Future research needs to adopt a theoretical framework if deviance among professionals is to be better understood.

REFERENCES

Akers, Ronald L.
1977 Deviant Behavior: A Social Learning Approach. 2nd Ed. Belmont, Calif.: Wadsworth.

American College of Surgeons and the American Surgical Association
1975 Surgery in the United States. ACS and ASA.

Anderson, O. W., and J. J. Feldman
1956 Family Medical Costs and Voluntary Health Insurance: A Nationwide Survey. New York: McGraw-Hill.

Anderson, O. W., Patricia Collette, and Jacob J. Feldman
1963 Changes in Family Medical Care Expenditures and Voluntary Life Insurance. Cambridge, Mass.: Harvard University Press.

Arnold, J. D.
1970 "28,621 cholecystectomies in Ohio." American Journal of Surgery 119:714–717.

Averill, R. F., and L. F. McMahon, Jr.
1977 "A cost benefit analysis of continued stay certification." Medical Care 15:158–173.

Becker, Howard, Blanche Geer, Everrett Hughes, and Anselm Strauss
1961 Boys in White: Student Culture in Medical School. Chicago: University of Chicago Press.

Blackstone, E. A.
1974 "Misallocation of medical resources: the problem of excessive surgery." Public Policy 22:329–352.
1977 "The condition of surgery: an analysis of the American College of Surgeons' and American Surgical Association's report on the status of surgery." Milbank Memorial Fund Quarterly 55:429–453.

Bloor, Michael
1976 "Bishop Berkeley and the adenotonsillectomy enigma: an exploration of variation in the social construction of medical disposals." Sociology 10:43–61.

Bombardier, C., V. R. Fuchs, L. A. Lillard, and K. E. Warner
1977 "Socioeconomic factors affecting the utilization of surgical operations." New England Journal of Medicine 297:699–706.

Bosk, Charles L.
1979 Forgive and Remember: Managing Medical Failure. Chicago: University of Chicago Press.

Brook, Robert H.
1974 "Quality of care assessment: policy relevant issues." Policy Sciences 5:317–41.

Brook, Robert H., Kathleen N. Williams, and John E. Ralph
1978 "Controlling the use and cost of medical sources: the New Mexico Experimental Medical Care Review Organization—a four-year case study." Medical Care (Supplement) 16:1–76.

Bunker, J. P.
1970 "Surgical manpower: a comparison of operations and surgeons in the United States and in England and Wales." New England Journal of Medicine 282:135–44.
1976 "Risks and benefits of surgery." Pp. 2092–2114 in American College of Surgeons and the American Surgical Association, Surgery in the United States 3.

Bunker, J. P., and J. E. Wennberg
1973 "Operation rates, mortality statistics, and the quality of life." New England Journal of Medicine 289:1249–51.

Bunker, J. P., and B. W. Brown, Jr.
1974 "The physician-patient as an informed consumer of surgical services." New England Journal of Medicine 290:1051–55.

Bunker, J. P., V. Donahue, P. Cole, and M. Notmen
1976 "Elective hysterectomy: pro and con." New England Journal of Medicine 295:264–68.

Burgess, E. W.
1950 "Comment of Hartung and concluding comment." American Journal of Sociology 56:33–34.

Burgess, Robert L., and Ronald L. Akers
1966 "A differential association-reinforcement theory of criminal behavior." Social Problems 14:128–47.

Carr-Saunders, A. M., and P. A. Wilson
1964 "Professions." Encyclopedia of the Social Sciences 22:476–80. New York: Macmillan.

Clinard, Marshall B.
1952 The Black Market. New York: Holt.

Cressey, Donald
1953 Other People's Money. Glencoe, Ill.: Free Press.

Davis, Fred
1960 "Uncertainty in medical prognosis, clinical and functional." American Journal of Sociology 66:41–47.

Demlo, L. K., P. M. Campbell, and S. S. Brown
1978 "Reliability of information abstracted from patient's medical records." Medical Care 16:995–1005.

D'Espo, D. A.
1962 "Hysterectomy when the uterus is grossly normal." American Journal of Obstetrics and Gynecology 83:113–21.

Donabedian, Avedis
1976 "A perspective on concepts of health care quality." Pp. 2066–91 in American College of Surgeons and the American Surgical Association, Surgery in the United States 3.

Dyck, Fl J., F. A. Murphy, J. K. Murphy, d. A. Road, M. S. Boyd, E. Osborne, D. deVlieger, B. Korchinski, C. Ripley, A. T. Bromley, and P. B. Innes
1977 "Effect of surveillance on the number of hysterectomies in the province of Saskatchewan." New England Journal of Medicine 296:1326–28.

Falk, S. S., and J. J. Senturia
1961 "The steelworkers survey their health services: a preliminary report." American Journal of Public Health 51:11–17.

Fine, J., and M. A. Morehead
1971 "Study of peer review of in-hospital patient care." New York State Journal of Medicine 71:1963–73.

Forum
1977 "Study finds excessive rate of Medicaid surgery." Forum 1:18.

Freidson, Eliot
1970a Profession of Medicine. New York: Dodd Mead.
1970b Professional Dominance: The Social Structure of Medical Care. Chicago: Aldine.

Freidson, Eliot, and Buford Rhea
1963 "Processes of control in a company of equals." Social Problems 2:119–31.

Fuchs, V. R.
1969 "Improving the delivery of health services." Journal of Bone Joint Surgery 51(a):407–12.

Gaus, C. R., B. S. Cooper, and C. G. Hirschman
1976 "Contrasts in HMO and fee-for-service performance." Social Security Bulletin 39:3–14.

Geis, Gilbert
1967 "White collar crime: the heavy electrical equipment anti-trust cases of 1961." Pp. 139–50 in Marshall B. Clinard and Richard Quinney (eds.), Criminal Behavior Systems: A Typology. New York: Holt.

Gertman, Paul M., Alan C. Monheit, Jennifer J. Anderson, J. Breckenridge Eagle, and Dana Kern Levenson
1979 "Utilization review in the United States: results from a 1976–1977 national survey of hospitals." Medical Care (Supplement) 17:1–48.

Gertman, Paul M., Debra A. Stackpole, Dana Kern Levenson, Barry M. Manuel, Robert J. Brennan, and Gary M. Janko
1980 "Second opinions for elective surgery." New England Journal of Medicine 302:1169–74.

Goode, William J.
1960 "Encroachment, charlatanism, and the emerging profession: psychology, sociology, and medicine." American Sociological Review 25:902–14.

Grafe, William R., Charles K. McSherry, Madelon L. Finkel, and Eugene McCarthy
1978 "The elective surgery second opinion program." Annals of Surgery 188:323–28.

Hall, Richard H.
1975 Occupations and the Social Structure. 2nd Ed. Englewood Cliffs, N.J.: Prentice-Hall.

Hiatt, Howard H.
1975 "Protecting the medical commons: who is responsible?" New England Journal of Medicine 293:235–41.

Holahan, J.
1977 "Foundations for medical care: an empirical investigation of the delivery of health service to a Medicaid population." Inquiry 14:352–68.

Howie, J. G. R.
1968 "The place of appendectomy in the treatment of young adult patients with possible appendicitis." Lancet i:1365–67.

Hughes, E. F. X.
1977 "Board certification and the quality of surgical care: an examination of the issues." Center for Health Services and Policy Research. Northwestern University Working Paper No. 2.

Hughes, E. F. X., J. E. Jacoby, and E. M. Lewit
1972 "Surgical workloads in a community practice." Surgery 71:315–27.

Hughes, E. F. X., E. M. Lewit, and E. H. Rand
1973 "Operative work loads in one hospital's general surgical residency program." New England Journal of Medicine 289:660–66.

Hughes, E. F. X., E. M. Lewit, R. N. Watkins, and R. Handschin
1974 "Utilization of surgical manpower in a prepaid group practice." New England Journal of Medicine 291:759–63.

Julian, Joseph
1977 "Physical and mental health." Pp. 26–77 in Joseph, Social Problems, 2nd ed. Englewood Cliffs, N.J.: Prentice-Hall.

Kisch, A. I., A. T. Moustafa, A. J. Grass, and B. Klein
1969 "An epidemiological approach to the study of the incidence of surgical problems." Medical Care 7:471–80.

Knafl, Kathleen, and Gary Burkett
1975 "Professional socialization in a surgical specialty: acquiring medical judgment." Social Science and Medicine 9:397–404.

Lees, D. S., and M. H. Cooper
1964 "Payment per-item-of-service: the Manchester and Salford experience 1913–28. Medical Care 2:151–56.
Lembeke, P. A.
1952 "Comparative study of appendectomy rates." American Journal of Public Health 42:276–86.
Lewis, C. E.
1969 "Variations in the incidence of surgery." New England Journal of Medicine 281:880–84.
Lichtner, S., and M. Pflanz
1971 "Appendectomy in the Federal Republic of Germany: epidemiology and medical care patterns." Medical Care 9:311–30.
LoGerfo, J. P.
1977 "Variation in surgical rates: fact vs. fantasy." New England Journal of Medicine 297:387–89.
LoGerfo, J. P., I. M. Dynes, F. Frost, and W. C. Richardson
1978 "Tonsillectomies, adenoidectomies, audits: have surgical indications been met?" Medical Care 16:950–55.
Mackie, Anita
1976 "A brief review of selected studies dealing with assessment of the quality of surgical care." Pp. 2105–30 in American College of Surgeons and the American Surgical Association, Surgery in the United States 3.
Massachusetts Department of Public Health
1971 "Tonsillectomy and adenoidectomy in Massachusetts." New England Journal of Medicine 285:1537.
McCarthy, E. G., and G. W. Widmer
1974 "Effects of screening by consultants on recommended elective surgical procedures." New England Journal of Medicine 291:1331–35.
McCarthy, E. G., and M. L. Finkel
1978 "Second opinion elective surgery programs: outcome status over time." Medical Care 16:984–94.
Millman, Marcia
1977 The Unkindest Cut: Life in the Backrooms of Medicine. New York: William Morrow.
Moore, Wilbert E.
1970 The Professions, Roles and Rules. New York: Russell Sage Foundation.
Neutra, Raymond R.
1978 "Appendicitis: decreasing normal removals without increasing perforations." Medical Care 16:956–61.
Nickerson, R. J., T. Colton, O. L. Peterson, B. S. Bloom, and W. W. Hauck, Jr.
1976 "Doctors who perform operations." New England Journal of Medicine 295:921–26, 982–89.
Paradise, J. L., and C. D. Bluestone
1976 "Toward rational indications for tonsil and adenoid surgery." Hospital Practice 11:79–87.

Paris, Martin, Edward Salsberg, and Louise Berenson
1979 "An analysis of nonconfirmation rates." American Medical Association Journal 242:2424–27.

Parsons, Talcott
1951 The Social System. New York: Free Press.

Perrot, G. S.
1966 "Utilization of hospital services." American Journal of Public Health 56:57–64.

Piachaud, D., and J. M. Weddell
1972 "The economics of treating varicose veins." International Journal of Epidemiology 1:287–94.

Rayack, Elton
1967 Professional Power and American Medicine. Cleveland: World Publishing.

Roemer, M. I.
1962 "On paying the doctor and the implications of different methods." Journal of Health and Human Behavior 3:4–14.

Roemer, M. I., and D. M. DuBois
1969 "Medical costs in relation to the organization of ambulatory care." New England Journal of Medicine 280:988–93.

Roos, N. P., L. L. R. Roos, Jr., and P. D. Henteleff
1977a "Elective surgical rates: do high rates mean lower surgical standards?" New England Journal of Medicine 297:360–65.

Roos, N. P., P. D. Hentelleff, and L. Roos, Jr.
1977b "A new audit procedure applied to an old questions: is the frequency of T and A justified?" Medical Care 15:1–18.

Rutkow, Ira M., Alan M. Gittelsohn, and George Zuidema
1979 "Surgical decision-making—the reliability of clinical judgment." Annals of Surgery 190:409–19.

Sanazaro, P. J.
1977 "The PSRO program: start a new chapter." New England Journal of Medicine 296:937–38.

Schwartz, Richard D., and Jerome H. Skolnick
1970 "Two studies of legal stigma." Pp. 568–79 in Richard D. Schwartz and Jerome H. Skolnick (eds.), Society of Legal Order. New York: Basic.

Shapiro, S.
1967 "End result measurements of quality of medical care." Milbank Memorial Fund Quarterly 45:7–30.

SOSSUS Subcommittee on Quality of Surgery
1976 "The critical incident study of surgical deaths and complications." Pp. 2132–44 in American College of Surgeons and the American Surgical Association, Surgery in the United States 3.

Sparling, J. F.
1962 "Measuring medical care quality: a comparative study, part I." Hospitals 36:62–68.

Stanford Center for Health Care Research
1976 "The hospital as a factor in the quality of surgical care." Pp. 2300–39 in American College of Surgeons and the American Surgical Association, Surgery in the United States 3.
Sutherland, Edwin H.
1949 White Collar Crime. New York: Holt.
Tappan, Paul W.
1960 Crime, Justice and Correction. New York: McGraw-Hill.
U.S. House of Representatives, Subcommittee on Oversight and Investigation of the Committee on Interstate and Foreign Commerce
1976 Cost and Quality of Health Care: Unnecessary Surgery. Washington, D.C.: U.S. Government Printing Office.
Vayda, E.
1974 "A comparison of surgical rates in Canada and in England and Wales." New England Journal of Medicine 289:1224–29.
1977 "When is surgery indicated? A book review." Milbank Memorial Fund Quarterly 55:495–504.
Vayda, E., and G. D. Anderson
1975 "Comparison of provincial surgical rates in 1968." Canadian Journal of Surgery 18:18–26.
Verda, D. J., and W. R. Platt
1958 "The tissue committee really gets results." Modern Hospital 91:74–75.
Vold, George B.
1958 Theoretical Criminology. New York: Oxford University Press.
Waitzkin, Howard, and Barbara Waterman
1974 The Exploitation of Illness in Capitalist Society. Indianapolis: Bobbs-Merrill.
Wennberg, J., and A. Gittelsohn
1973 "Small area variation in health care delivery." Science 182:1102–08.
Wilensky, Harold L.
1964 "The professionalization of everyone?" American Journal of Sociology 70:137–58.
Wilson, Samuel, and William P. Longmire, Jr.
1978 "Does method of surgeon payment affect surgical care?" Journal of Surgical Research 24:457–68.
Yoshida, U., and K. Yoshida
1976 "The high rate of appendectomy in Japan." Medical Care 14:950–57.

Reading 27

Rapists' Talk: Linguistic Strategies to Control the Victim

Lynda Lytle Holmstrom and Ann Wolbert Burgess
Boston College, Chestnut Hill, Massachusetts

Rape is a crime of violence and force. The stereotype of the male rapist's attack is that he attains power and control over the victim through strategies based on physical force. The present study shows that not only do rapists use physically based strategies, but also they use a second set of strategies based on language. The sample consists of 115 female adult, adolescent, and child rape victims. Open-ended interviews were used and information was collected on what conversation occurred. In analyzing what rapists reportedly said, 11 major themes emerged: threats, orders, confidence lines, personal inquiries of the victim, personal revelations by the rapist, obscene names and racial epithets, inquiries about the victim's sexual "enjoyment," soft-sell departures, sexual put downs, possession of women, and taking property from another male. What these themes have in common is that they constitute a strategy for exercising power over the victim, either before, during, or after the rape.

Game theory has traditionally been used for analyzing zero-sum conflict situations. More recently game-theoretic frameworks have been generalized to analyze social situations "in which two or more persons or groups are in communication with one another and are engaged in goal-directed action" (Lyman and Scott, 1970:29). One can apply Lyman and Scott's categories of games to rape and see that several games are occurring simultaneously. The primary one is an "exploitation game." Secondarily, there may be a "face game," an "information game" or a "relationship game."

"Exploitation games occur on the brink of power relationships; that is, one actor hopes to obtain 'imperative control' over another but is not absolutely sure he can do so" (Lyman and Scott, 1970:54). Lyman and Scott, as well as the authors of the present paper, utilize the Weberian definition of power; that is, "the probability that one actor within a social relationship will be in a position to carry out his own will despite resistance, regardless of the basis on which this probability rests" (Weber, 1947:152).

The stereotype of the rapist's attack is that he attains power and control over his victim through strategies based on physical force. The present study

Revised version of a paper presented at the 9th World Congress of Sociology, Sociolinguistics Research Committee Program, Uppsala, Sweden, August, 1978.

shows that not only do rapists use physically based strategies, but they use a second set of strategies based on language. These linguistic strategies are the focus in the present paper. An analysis of the victim's linguistic coping strategies has been presented in a prior paper (Burgess and Holmstrom, 1976).

METHOD

This paper reports a subpart of a larger study investigating issues such as what occurs during the rape event, what problems victims experience in the aftermath of rape, and how institutions (police, hospital, court) react to rape victims.

Sample

The sample for this paper consists of the 115 adult, adolescent, and child rape victims that arrived during one year at the emergency wards of a large municipal hospital. The sample is very heterogeneous and crosses the lines of class, race, religion, marital status, employment, and age. This variety is due to police protocol in crime victim cases (the police select which hospital to use) and to the hospital's location. The facility is situated near some of the poorer communities of the city, but colleges and universities also are located in its catchment area for crime-related emergencies.

Data Collection

The study in its entirety relied most heavily on in-depth interviews and participant observation, supplemented by other methods. Hospital staff telephoned us each time a sexual assault victim was admitted. Upon notification, we immediately went to the hospital to gather data—many times late at night or in the early morning hours. Our typical practice was to have both authors present at the initial interview. Frequently one interviewed, while the other took notes that were as verbatim as possible. We did weekly follow-up interviews during the early postrape period and we gathered participant-observation data at the courthouse in cases that went to court.

A detailed report of the methods used has already been published (Holmstrom and Burgess, 1978a:5–29). Perhaps most important for this paper is to note that in interviewing we used flexible, open-ended interview guides and that the same list of general questions was asked of each victim. Early in the interview the victim often gave her own account of what happened. In telling this, the victim often included information on what the rapist said and what she said. In addition, we specifically asked what conversation occurred.

TABLE 1 Rapists' Talk: Linguistic Strategies to Control the Victim Before, During, and After Rape

Threats	75
Orders	68
Confidence line	39
Personal inquiries of victim	28
Personal revelations by rapist	21
Obscene names and racial epithets	20
Victim's sexual "enjoyment"	19
Soft-sell departure (apologies, safe-return, socializing)	19
Sexual put-downs	9
Possession of women	6
Taking property from another male	5

Method: Advantages and Disadvantages

A major methodological advantage is that the sample provides data primarily on *non*convicted rapists—a group seldom subjected to study. Of the 115 cases in the present study, only nine cases resulted in a conviction for rape (adult victim) or for abuse of a female child (victim under 16). The existing research literature on rapists, in contrast, is based primarily on data obtained from institutionalized rapists.

The main methodological drawback is that the data on what rapists say come from victims. The material is secondhand. There does not seem to be any way to get completely out of this difficulty. Rape is not something that researchers can witness firsthand. And only a small percentage of rapists are convicted and thus accessible to researchers. There are some partial ways out of the dilemma. One is to ask victims if the words they are reporting are their own or the same words the rapist used, and then to specifically request that they report the latter. Another is to compare the data on rapists' talk obtained from victims with that obtained from convicted rapists (Chappell and James, 1976). Undoubtedly, the data from victims are more accurate regarding themes of talk (which is what is analyzed in this paper) than they are regarding more technical aspects of language such as precise choice of words or intonation patterns.

FINDINGS

The Occurrence of Rapists' Talk

Rapists' talk is a salient feature of the attack. In analyzing what victims reported that rapists said, 11 major themes emerged (see Table 1). What these themes have in common is that they each constitute a strategy for exercising power over the victim, either before, during, or after the rape.

Rapists' talk is a frequent component of the attack. In 115 reported rape cases, 102 victims stated that the rapist said something to them. In only five cases did the victim report an absence of talk by the rapist. In two of these five the victim was unconscious during the attack—one because she was immediately strangled from behind, the other from intoxication. (In the remaining eight cases, there was no data on the issue.)

Gaining Access: Initial Control of the Victim

The rapist's first goal is a pragmatic one. He must obtain a victim and get her sufficiently under his control so that he can then rape her. Among reported rapes, are two main styles of attack that we have called "blitz" and "confidence" (Burgess and Holmstrom, 1974b:4–11). The blitz rape is a sudden attack in which the rapist confronts the victim out of the blue. There is no preliminary interaction or warning. The emphasis is on physically based strategies. For example, the rapist may grab a woman walking on the street and shove her into a car. His physical action may be reinforced by verbal means. In the confidence rape, the emphasis is on linguistically based strategies. The rapist gains access by winning the confidence of the victim and then betraying it. His "line" may be supplemented by physically maneuvering the victim into a position or place from which it is difficult to escape.

Two main styles of linguistic strategies occur at the point in time when the rapist is trying to obtain a victim. One is that of threats and orders, the other the confidence line.

Threats and Orders The linguistic strategies of threats and orders can occur in either blitz or confidence styles of attack. In the blitz, they support the rapist's quick physical action and may appear very early in the interaction. In the confidence style they do not surface until after the victim's confidence has been attained and betrayed. The switch to threats and orders may happen quickly or it may occur after extensive conversation.

The threats and orders, in either style of attack, typically tell the victim to cooperate or be hurt or killed. Victims reported being told, "If you resist, you're a dead woman," "I'll kill you if you don't do it," "Do what I say or your kids will get it," "If you don't do what I say I'll kill you and lay you next to my [dead] mother," and "Fuck me good or I'll kill you." A 23-year-old virgin who became the victim of a blitz rape reported receiving these threats at the beginning and throughout the event:

> I've raped three other women and killed them and that's what's going to happen to you. (waving knife at her) Undress. If you don't hurry, I'll kill you. If you're not quiet I'll kill you. (poking knife at her nose and eyes) Maybe I'll take off your nose too. I'll cut them out. . . .(after raping her and seeing blood on her thighs) Don't worry, when I get through with you you'll be bloody all over.

> . . .(later) I have a gun. I'll shoot you or anyone who tries to help you. . . .(later) Suck it, suck it. If you don't get it up, I'll kill you.

A 17-year old victim of a confidence rape reported receiving the following threats after she and her date had been lured to an apartment by a confidence line:

> You're going to have to do me a favor. We're doing you a favor giving you a place to stay. (rapist was cleaning his toes with a knife) Look out the window. (victim looked and saw at least 10 males) They're all junkies. All I'd have to do is call them and they'd rape you and rob you and kill you.

Some threats focus on embarrassing the victim. One was told, "What would your mother say if you came home with no clothes?" Another reported, "They said they would tell my family and spread a rumor that I had a bad reputation unless I did it for them. They said, 'Do you want a bad reputation?' " Threats to harm or embarrass help to gain the submission of the victim. They also set the mood of the encounter – that of it being a frightening experience for most victims (Burgess and Holmstrom, 1974a:983).

The Confidence Line The confidence-line strategy can be used with victims known to the rapist or with strangers. If he already knows the victim, his conversation builds on this existing relationship. If the victim is a stranger, he uses a conversation to gain trust. His talk creates an image of normalcy and everyday experience that belies what is to follow.

The confidence rapist has the task of maneuvering the victim to where he wants her or maneuvering himself to where she is (e.g., in the front door of her home). To accomplish these maneuvers, rapists trade on social conventions and everyday activities and expectations. Rapists *offer assistance* ("Do you want a ride [home]?" and "I'll go with you to [find your husband] – I know where he hangs out"); *request assistance* ("Honey, can we use your phone?" and "I need a ride home"); *promise social activities* ("Want to come to my place and talk and listen to the stereo?" "Let's go over [to the building] – we can play pool"); *promise information* ("I want to tell you something," "I have some information about your TV sets [that were stolen yesterday]"); *promise material items such as alcohol or drugs* ("We'll go to the house to get the papers [to roll the marijuana]"); *promise the possibility of employment and discuss business transactions* ("I need someone to do some line drawings"); *request her company while completing a task* ("Why don't you come on up while I put the groceries away?" "Come with me while I get my coat"); *refer to someone she knows or who might be there* ("I want to talk to you . . . about your 'brother's situation,' " "Is your old man home?"); and *trade on social pleasantries and niceties* ("I'm leaving town, I want to say good-by"). Sometimes the rapist's accomplice provides the con line. For example, one victim was persuaded to go to a house by two girls who said, "We know a good place to go—there'll be a party."

A small minority of con lines were elaborate. One victim who knew her assailant reported the following elaborate set-up:

> Jessica was an art student and had met the rapist two weeks earlier at school. He told her he was a commercial artist and that he needed someone to do some line drawings for a job that he was working on. They arranged to meet and go to a studio, but when they arrived there it was closed. There was a note left about a package having been sent to his apartment. They went to the apartment to get the package. He opened it, revealing a pair of pink panties, a white lace robe, and two blue blouses. He said he wanted to show her the work to be done and that the light was better in the bedroom. They went into the bedroom and she sat on the floor and looked at several pictures of fireplaces which is what she would be drawing if she took the job. He then asked her if she had ever done any modeling and she said no. He said that the clothes that he had gotten in the package that morning were things that he was using for a job and if she would model them for him he wouldn't have to go out and hire someone. She refused, but after some further talk she finally agreed to model the clothes. He took several pictures of her in various combinations of the clothes and then left the room. She started to get dressed. He suddenly came back in the room and raped her.

Another victim whose assailants were strangers reported the following lengthy set-up:

> It was about 8:00 p.m. Molly and David, her date, were on the Common. Two men who looked to be in their twenties approached them and asked if they wished to buy some pot. Molly and David said no. The men asked if they wished to smoke some and they again refused. The men, however, continued to talk with them. It was a pleasant and enjoyable conversation. Then one of the men asked what they were doing on the Common. Molly explained that they were waiting for a ride to go to a hotel to sleep. One of the men said they could sleep at his sister's—she had a spare room. Molly thought that was strange of them to say, but David didn't think it was, so they decided to go with the men. All four left to go to "the sister's place." Once in the apartment, the men locked the door. They talked about various things. The men, for example, asked Molly and David if they were a common-law couple. Molly and David decided to go along with that idea and said that they were. One of the men said he wanted to talk with David in another room. He asked David if he minded if he had sex with Molly.

At this point the conversation shifted to the need to repay favors and to the threats, quoted earlier, about junkies being outside the window. The men, joined by a third assailant, raped Molly and forced David to watch (Holmstrom and Burgess, 1978b:6). These assailants, incidentally, had a practice of also bringing neighborhood girls to the apartment and raping them (Burgess and Holmstrom, 1978:64–66).

The con lines of the rapists almost always sounded very ordinary. Their everyday quality is what makes them so effective. They sound credible at the time and do not arouse the victims' suspicions. Even the small percentage of lines that with hindsight look a bit far-fetched seem credible in the context in which they occur. This everyday quality is confirmed by data collected from convicted rapists committed to a maximum security mental institution (Chappell and James, 1976:16, 19). Rapists reported that, to get a victim to open a door, they said they were looking for a friend, needed to use the telephone, were undertaking a survey, making repairs, making a delivery, or making an inspection. To get a victim to go elsewhere the most common ruse was offering her a ride. Other gambits reported were "offers of amusement, assistance, money, food, alcohol, and drugs."

Raping: Sexual Control of the Victim

Contemporary researchers stress the violent nature of rape and see it as expressing power, conquest, aggression, anger, degradation, hatred, and contempt (Bart, 1975; Brownmiller, 1975; Burgess and Holmstrom, 1974a, 1974b; Cohen, Garofalo, Boucher, and Seghorn, 1971; Davis, 1968; Gelles, 1977; Griffin, 1971; Hilberman, 1976; Metzger, 1976; Russell, 1975; Schwendinger and Schwendinger, 1974). Rapists' goals on the social-psychological, motivational level are to demonstrate their power over the victim and to vent their anger at the victim. Sexuality is a component, but not the dominant factor (Groth, Burgess, and Holmstrom, 1977). The rapist's power and anger may be directed at the individual victim, at the male perceived to own her, or at the group she is perceived to represent. Rapists' goals in pair and group rape may also include impressing their fellow rapists. Linguistic strategies are one type of means used to achieve these goals.

Threats Threats may continue throughout the rape. The threats may escalate from those that seem designed primarily to torment and terrify the victim. Following is a case in which the setting, the language, and the actions of the rapist, including the use of props, combined to maximize terror:

> Beth was walking back to her college dorm when a man grabbed her, threatened her with a knife, and forced her into a car. He went out on the highway which scared her. She thought, "This is the end." He took her to the woods and

> raped her there, holding a knife to her all the time. She was convinced as they went into the woods, that he was going to kill her. She kept thinking, "Well, good-by, this was nice being [in this world], but good-by now." Beth also reported, "He kept passing the knife back and forth and saying open your legs. He said he might take the knife and put it up me and cut me up inside. He said he might cut off my tits."

Orders Orders may occur not only before but during the rape. They serve various functions. On the pragmatic level, orders often get the victim to do what the rapist wants. On the symbolic level, orders show both victim and rapist who has the power, who is in control. The rapist tells her to stop the behavior she is engaged in and do instead what he wants her to do.

The two most common types of orders are telling the victim to be quiet or unseen and telling the victim what to do sexually. Rapists tell victims "Shut up," "Be quiet," and "Keep your mouth shut." A quiet victim makes it easier to escape detection, as well as demonstrating who is in charge. Sometimes orders are given to avoid being seen ("Turn the light off," "Have your son go to bed. [victim protests] I *said*, have your son go to bed!" and "Put down the shades"). Sometimes an especially insulting twist is given to the order. A victim for example reported, "He told me not to scream. He said I wasn't justified in screaming."

Rapists order the victim about sexually. Victims reported being told "Blow me," "Fuck me good," "Open your legs," "Rub my dick," "Give us some head," and "Kiss me like you kiss your husband."

Also common are orders to remove clothing ("Well, what are you waiting for—take off your clothes") and to go somewhere ("Sit on the bed. [victim sits on chair] No, I said on the bed").

In a few cases victims were told to go to the bathroom and clean themselves ("Go wash yourself out"). In one unusual case the victim was given orders, after the last assailant had finished, to clean up the room and remake the bed. Thus, as a final act of humiliation, she was ordered to pick up the mess made by her assailants.

The Victim's Sexual "Enjoyment." Whether rapists really believe that their victims enjoy the sex act with them is a controversial issue. Research suggests that one type of rapist acts under the illusion that his sexual prowess is so great that he greatly satisfies an initially protesting victim. Cohen et al. (1971:318) describe this type of rapist, noting that the rapist first repeatedly lives through the scene in fantasy:

> In the fantasy, the woman he attacks first protests and then submits, more resignedly than willingly. During the sexual act, he performs with great skill,

> and she receives such intense pleasure that she falls in love with him and pleads with him to return.

One difference from common adolescent fantasies is that the rapist acts out the fantasy again and again. Geis (1977:29) is more skeptical about the rapist's perception of the victim's enjoyment:

> Perhaps, as reports almost uniformly suggest, offenders believe that their victims like being forcibly raped. The fact that some rapists request testaments of their sexual skills from their victims and that others attempt to make future appointments with them supports this idea. But we believe that for many, perhaps most, rapists there is a clear appreciation that their victims hate what is happening to them and that this is an important element of the behavior.

These two statements are not contradictory if one believes that not all rapists rape for the same reason—that the victim's "enjoyment" is important for some, but not for others.

Inquiries and statements by rapists about the victim's "enjoyment" occurred in our sample. Our interpretation is that at least some of these rapists do believe that the victim wants and enjoys the attack. The rape of a 17-year-old virgin by the man she dated over the summer is a case in point. She reported:

> I think he thought he was doing right. He sounded as though he thought I wanted it. It wasn't that way at all. . . . He even had the nerve to say to me after he did it that I should be glad he did it. . . . Something else that bothered me—when he was all through, I guess he was all through because the pain was gone and he was laying there but still on top of me, he said, "It feels good to you doesn't it?" I just could not stand it and I told him to please just get off of me.

Other victims reported, "He wanted me to say I was enjoying it, I was supposed to moan for him" and, "He said, 'Don't you want me to come in you?' " In another case the rapist inquired repeatedly whether it felt the way it felt when she was with her husband. A few victims reported that the rapist wanted to see them another time. One victim said, "He kept wanting to know if it felt good and I had to say yes to keep him happy. . . .He also wanted to know if he could come and do it again."

Some cases are more difficult to interpret. It is not clear if the rapist is actually inquiring about the victim's enjoyment or whether the rapist knows the victim hates the experience and he is taunting her with comments about enjoyment. In one case, for example, the two rapists kept saying "Now this isn't really bad for you, is it? Aren't you enjoying it?" In context, this question seemed to be a taunt rather than a serious inquiry.

For victims who reply there is the added dimension that they were forced to talk against their will. One victim explained her reaction as follows:

> They asked if I liked it. I had to keep saying I liked it. I went along with it. I hope I didn't give them the idea that women would actually like such a thing, but I had to think of myself. I just wanted to get out of there so I pretended I liked it.

Victims, if they reply, answer in the affirmative. Thus they are coerced into saying they enjoyed what was one of the worst experiences of their lives.

Obscene Names, Dirty Sex, and Racial Epithets Rape is seen as an act of humiliation (Hilberman, 1976:ix). One strategy to humiliate is to hurl insulting names and terms at a person. In the case of rape, these seem to consist primarily of sexual and racial epithets.

The cultural view of females divides them into madonnas and whores (Holmstrom and Burgess, 1978a:177), dutiful housewife-mothers and erotic lovers (Bullough, 1974:49), Virgin Marys and tempting Eves (Chafetz, 1974:39). Russell (1975:25) states, "[A female's] loss of virginity, particularly at a young age, can evoke in males a 'no holds barred' approach. The girl becomes a whore, and only a sucker would treat a whore well. Because a whore is seen as 'bad,' conscience can be suspended." Groth and Cohen (1976:233) note that the dichotomized view of women is especially pronounced among convicted rapists they have studied. In some gang rapes, the fact that the woman submits sexually to all the males (albeit under duress) confirms the offenders' view of her as a whore (Groth, 1978). There is also a cultural ambivalence about sex, with themes that include both its desirability and its dirtiness. With this cultural background, it is not surprising to find that rapists' talk often includes calling victims dirty sexual names.

> The assailant came to the apartment of a family he had known for years. They were friends and the family had helped him at times—gotten him jobs, loaned him a car. The husband was away, but the wife and a teenage son were home. He came in and they chatted a while. He then beat and raped the wife. He said, "I'll treat you like a whore."

Other victims reported being called "bitch," "white pussy," "white tramp," "mother fucker," "half white nigger bitch," "fucking bitch," "black bitch," and "slut." As some of these quotes illustrate, the cultural ambivalence over women and sex becomes intertwined with the cultural ambivalence over race.

Sexual Put-Downs Rapists' talk contributes to the humiliation of the victim by sexual put-downs, as well as by orders and dirty names. The rapist may blame the victim for his lack of sexual satisfaction or taunt the victim with accusations of sexual inadequacy. One victim reported, "He said I wasn't worth it, that he didn't get any pleasure from it." Others reported sexual put-downs and taunts such as "You're very cold," "It won't hurt you" (showing his "dick" to the victim), "Are you a prude?" and "You're gay, you're ruining the country."

Nonsexual put-downs were used in two additional cases. One victim was told, "You're kind of dumb, aren't you?" In a homosexual rape, the male victim was ordered to roll a reefer and the rapist taunted him for his inability to do it properly ("Don't you know how to do anything right?").

Rapists laughed at victims in four cases. At least three of these seem to be put-downs (rather than, for example, laughing for some other reason such as nervousness).

Taking Property Rape is a violent act against the victim. But it can also be perceived as an act against another man's property. The target here is not so much the female victim but the other male to whom she is perceived to belong—traditionally her father or her husband. Clark and Lewis (1977:11b), in their discussion of rape laws, state, "From the beginning, rape was perceived as an offence against property, not as an offence against the person on whom the act was perpetrated." A well-known legal analysis states that one "reason for the man's condemnation of rape may be found in the threat to his status from a decrease in the 'value' of his sexual 'possession which would result from forcible violation" (Yale Law Journal, 1952:73). Research both in the United States and abroad shows that men often have negative reactions to girlfriends or wives that are raped. Some American men are sympathetic to their raped wife or girlfriend; others, however, feel that they, not the woman, was the true victim (Holmstrom and Burgess, 1974). Ibo men often feel ambivalent since another male has shared their "property" (Mere, 1974).

Talk about taking another man's woman or female child occurred in five cases in our sample. There is no reason to assume that taking property as a theme would be restricted to group rape or to interracial rape, although the theme does seem especially prominent in accounts of rape *across group boundaries* (Cleaver, 1968:14–15; Fanon, 1968:254–59; Mere, 1974). In our sample, there were four cases where taking property was a particularly salient theme. These four were all multiple-assailant cases and three were interracial rapes. In two, the rape was carried out in the view of the date or boyfriend of the victim. In the case of Molly, the blacks taunted her white date (who had been presented to them as a partner in a common-law couple):

> The black men started joking and said, "I'm in love with Molly. She belongs to me now. David has lost her." They sang soul songs.

In the other case, the four assailants were white and the victim and her boyfriend were Canadian-Indian. The rapists said to the boyfriend:

> We're going to get some of her. (Holding up her underpants and bra) Know what these are? We're going to fuck your girl.

Cleaver (1968:14–15) talks of the black rape of white victims as an insurrectionary act.

> I became a rapist. To refine my technique and *modus operandi*, I started out by practicing on black girls in the ghetto—in the black ghetto where dark and vicious deeds appear not as aberrations or deviations from the norm, but as part of the sufficiency of the Evil of a day—and when I considered myself smooth enough, I crossed the tracks and sought out white prey. . . .
>
> Rape was an insurrectionary act. It delighted me that I was defying and trampling upon the white man's law, upon his system of values, and that I was defiling his women—and this point, I believe, was the most satisfying to me because I was very resentful over the historical fact of how the white man has used the black woman.

The cases in our sample of explicitly "taking property" suggest that many of the dynamics of insulting a male of another race are similar whether the assailants are black or white. Perhaps one can generalize and interpret many interracial rapes and other rapes that cross group boundaries as statements being made against a class or group of people that the rapists define as adversaries (Holmstrom and Burgess, 1978:249). The power and anger issues are directed not merely at the victim but at the group that is perceived as owning the victim.

Possession as Lover, Wife, or Prostitute Possession of women, as discussed above, is an important issue for many men. In the previous section, the emphasis was on rape as a way to hurt other males by taking their property. The emphasis here is on rape as a way of gaining women for oneself—for one's own use. Having women for themselves was the explicit focus of conversation in six cases. One thing these six cases have in common is that they were all interracial rapes. In each instance, the victim was white and the assailant(s) black. The rapists talked of keeping the victim as lover, wife, or prostitute. The rapist thus would become the lover, husband, or pimp who would control her and control access to her. He would use her for sex and/or money. In one case, the rapist repeatedly referred to the victim as "my woman." In a group rape, one of the four rapists said he wanted to marry the victim and take her back to Africa. In the following case the focus is on prostitution:

> The rape continued through much of the night and it was early morning when the assailants led Molly from the locked apartment. An old black man was walking his dog and one of the assailants said, "Want her for $2?" The man said he was too old for that. One rapist, Clyde, said to Molly, "There could be a lot of money involved here if you would turn tricks for us." Hearing that they were trying to sell her scared her and she managed to start running and duck down an alley and hail a cab.

In contrast, the following case combines lover and prostitute themes.

> He said he wanted me to be his woman. He talked about that over and over. He wanted me to hustle for him on the streets because he was broke. He wanted me to like him. He thought if I stayed there long enough I would. . . . He said he would tie me up and keep me there and that I'd like it. He led me to believe he was going to keep me there. He asked me if I had ever done a trick. I didn't know what he meant and he told me it meant to hustle, to be a prostitute.

In still another case, the victim reported, "[The rapist] said if he ever saw me with another man he would kill me and the man. . . . He kept telling me I'd be all his, no one else's. It would just be me and him." Talk of possession conveys to victims the idea of the rapists' control continuing into the future. For victims, a crucial issue is how long will the control last.

The Information Game: Personal Inquiries "Information games arise whenever one actor wishes to uncover information from another who wishes to conceal it. In one sense information games overlap all others because knowledge of others is a prerequisite to social life, and individuals rarely convey openly the kind or amount of knowledge 'required' by their fellows" (Lyman and Scott, 1970:58).

Rapists engage in information games. Their strategy of asking personal questions increases the victim's vulnerability. They seek details about the victim's biography, living arrangements, habits, and property. The victim does not necessarily provide the information. But even to be asked is upsetting. Furthermore, rapists sometimes do get victims to reveal information they would rather not.

Rapists ask questions that make the victim more accessible to future attack. Rapists, for example, often ask victims for identifying information—their name, telephone number, address. This is information victims do not wish to reveal since they fear the rapist might return. One victim, however, was so distraught that she revealed identifying information:

> He wanted my address. I felt that if I could convince him that I was being honest he would let me go. [What address did you give?] I told him where I lived, but not the right apartment number.

The revelation she made contributed to her sense of still feeling scared after the rape.

Rapists asked victims also about the "goods" that might be taken: sex and money. These inquiries often asked for very private information, that if provided would contribute to a sense of exposure. Inquiries included "How many guys have you had?" "Are you a virgin?" "Have you ever been touched before?" "Have you ever been eaten before?" and "How much money do you have?" One 13-year old victim was asked the following combination of personal data questions:

> Is this the first time you've ever fucked? . . . What's your name? What's your phone number? . . . Do you have any money?

Rapists also ask about the personal habits of the victim in regard to sex, money, and drugs. The information they obtain may later be used to discredit the victim. They asked, for example, "How much money do you make a night [from prostitution]?" and "Do you smoke grass?" In one case the victim admitted to the rapist that she used mescaline.

Presentation of the Self: Personal Revelations As Goffman (1959:4) states, "When an individual appears in the presence of others, there will usually be some reason for him to mobilize his activity so that it will convey an impression to others which it is in his interests to convey." Impressions, he notes, can be created either through verbal or nonverbal communication.

Rapists' talk includes biographical information about themselves. This strategy of biographical revelation helps them gain and maintain control over the victim. Whether the information is "true" is irrelevant. In Goffman's terms, the rapist gives a performance and biographical revelation is one aspect of this performance. From the possible identities rapists could present to be in control they typically present images of "the tough guy," the "dangerous guy," or the "guy deserving of sympathy." The first two impressions play on the victim's fears, the third impression plays on her sympathies.

The "tough" and/or "dangerous" modes included such statements as "He said he was out of jail just a week," "They said they had taken other girls to this place and done it," and "They said they had been in prison, that they were just out." The "sympathy" mode included such statements as "I'm out of work" or "I'm lonely." Some presented multiple identities—for example, a dangerous and a sympathetic (even pathetic) figure. In one case, for example, the 62-year-old victim talked to the rapist in an effort to calm him down and in the course of this lengthy conversation he revealed the following:

> I've stabbed women before, but I don't know if they died. . . .(swabbing her three-quarter inch wound that he had made with a surgeon's scalpel) I stole the scalpel from a hospital where I worked. . . . I worked once at [Central] Hospital and once at [Memorial] Hospital. . . . I know the neighborhood, . . . I was just fired, . . . I don't have many friends because they don't like me doing this.

Another rapist said, "My mother died when I was 11 and I haven't been right since then,"—thus presenting a sympathetic image plus an implication of possible dangerousness.

"Tough" and the "soft-sell" approaches to maintaining power also appear at later stages in the rape event. Either approach may be used to cool the victim out. Either may be used by rapists to influence victims as they decide whether to pursue prosecution of the case.

Whether rapists present "true" information is not the main issue. Nevertheless, it is of interest that in presenting identities some rapists also presented identifying information. Some gave names, and some said where they were from ("I asked them where they went to school and they said [Central] High School," and "He said he was from South Carolina"). In one case, after the rape the rapist walked the girl home, gave her a present, and told her his telephone number and first name. The number and name were sufficient to lead to his identification and arrest; however, the trial verdict was not guilty (Holmstrom and Burgess, 1978a:198). In another case the assailants' strategy also backfired. They bragged to the victim about their prior exploits and the police were able to identify them using that information. One of the assailants was tried and the verdict was guilty of rape.

Raping with Others: Male Camaraderie and the Male Audience

Researchers have stressed that in multiple-assailant rape it is important to look not only at the rapists as individuals but at the group. They have emphasized the group process, especially how the leader is stimulated by the group (Blanchard, 1959:266), that group rape is not merely a series of single rapes (Lucas, undated), that roles and principles of collective behavior are involved (Geis, 1971:101, 113), and that male camaraderie is a focus of the interaction in group rape (Holmstrom and Burgess, 1978b:10–11).

Impression management in pair and group rape is more complicated because of the multiple audiences. In multiple-assailant rape the rapists talk not only to the victim but to each other. The main audience is the other males, the secondary audience is the victim.

The most common theme of conversation among these rapists concerns taking turns. The taking of turns is not just a pragmatic matter, but a focal point for impression management. Rapists tell each other to hurry up because they want their chance to do it. ("The others stood around and watched and yelled that they wanted their turn"). They urged each other to take a turn ("Get some of it too," and "This is good, you should try it").

Comments about what to do to the victim also were made. One can interpret these several ways. A real debate about what to do may be occurring among the assailants. Or the aim may be to impress the other males with how much one can frighten the victim. In one case the victim reported the assailant beat her date with a belt. Then, she said, "He came in with a belt and said he wanted to beat me. One of the others said, 'She'll be so beat you won't be able to knock her.' " In still another case, at least one assailant was taking drugs with a needle. One assailant wanted to inject dope into the victim, but the other assailant said no. They did not do it. In an atypical case, the discussion was whether to rape. One of the robbers said to the robber-rapist, "Why are you bothering with that?"

Identifying names were another component in some conversations. Rapists who were strangers to the victim would sometimes use each other's first names or nicknames. One can interpret such practice as due to carelessness, to a desire to get caught, or, most likely, to a belief that they will not get caught, that one can rape with impunity.

In a few cases, the themes reported were security precautions ("Get her away from here so she can't see the car") and orders to each other ("Take the TV").

Departure: Control over the Victim Squawking

After rape, the rapist must return to the pragmatic goal of departing safely. Having obtained a victim, and raped her, he must now part ways and preferably in a manner that will prevent his arrest. To increase his chances of safe departure, the rapist often engages in what Goffman (1952:455, 462) calls cooling the mark out. He tries to continue to maintain control so that the victim will not raise a squawk. As Goffman notes, there are many procedures for "cooling," including the use or threat of force.

In the present study, rapists' conversation for dealing with the victim after the rape fell into two general types. There was the tough approach and the soft-sell. By definition, the present sample consists of those cases where the rapist's attempt to control disclosure and complaint by the victim was at best only partially successful. All the victims in the study had reported the rape to at least one authority—the hospital—and in some cases also to the police. Threats and soft-sell sympathy appeals did, however, deter some victims in the sample from pursuing prosecution (Holmstrom and Burgess, 1978a:122–23, 152). Many rapes, not located by such a sample, do not get reported at all.

Tough Approach: Threats and Orders Rape is a frightening event for many victims. The terror is reinforced by rapists, orders saying not to tell, not to go to the police. Threats frequently are made to injure or kill the victim if the rape is disclosed to others or reported to authorities. Victims reported that rapists said to them "Don't tell anyone or I'll kill you," and "If you go to the police . . . we'll get you when we get out of prison." Some rapists gave orders to increase the time they would have to leave undetected. ("Lie with your head covered for two minutes.")

Soft-Sell: Apologizing, Safe Return, and Socializing Rapists sometimes depart discussing themes that may appeal more to victims' sympathies. Some rapists apologize. One victim reported:

> I got up and put my clothes on. He asked if I was hungry, if I wanted to eat. He kept apologizing. . . . He said he was sorry I was so upset.

Another rapist combined the tough and soft-sell departures. The woman was asleep in her bed. He stabbed her in the stomach, then put a blanket over her head and kept it there while raping her. He later said:

> You might have to have a stitch in that [wound]. Do you have any bandaids? . . . I feel bad after I do these things. I feel ashamed. I hate to use the knife, but

> I just have to do it. . . . Keep the blanket over your head for twenty minutes. I'm leaving quietly. If you take off the blanket I'll finish you.

Another rapist, after the rape, showed the victim literature about Jesus.

Rapists, when departing, may focus on the victim's safe return home. They may offer to give her a ride or walk her back. They may point her in the correct direction. One said afterward, as if nothing had happened, "I'll see you—you know where [the Avenue] is." A black rapist said to a white victim as he left her, "You'll be all right [walking] on the street—both blacks and whites live here." Some rapists not only talk about a safe return, but take action to repair damage they have inflicted; one swabbed a knife wound, another put ice on the victim's bruises.

Conversation after the rape may also serve to normalize the interaction. Socializing makes it seem like nothing out of the ordinary has happened. In one case, after beating and raping a girlfriend on a Saturday afternoon, the rapist talked and played cards with her. He threatened her and told her if she went to the police he would kill her. He also wanted her to go with him to a party that Saturday night. Such conversation and actions may not normalize the interaction for the victim, but it makes the victim's allegation of rape less credible to outsiders. The account she gives sounds to others more like a social occasion and less like a rape. The case just described went to court. The assailant was found guilty of assault and battery and of unnatural acts, but on the rape charge the court found no probable cause. He received a one-year suspended sentence.

CONCLUSION

Rape is a crime of violence and force. By definition it cannot occur unless the rapist actively plays an exploitation game. For that reason, we have been primarily concerned in this paper with the linguistic strategies of the rapist as related to the power aspect of the interaction. The 11 themes discussed each constitute a linguistic strategy to control the victim either before, during, or after the rape. All interactions, however, contain within them a multiplicity of games. The themes in rapists' talk suggest that many rapists simultaneously exploit and attempt to "normalize" or "conventionalize" their exploitation. Rapists, for example, may seek and reveal personal information, request feedback on the adequacy of their sexual behavior, attempt to increase intimacy with the victim, suggest the desirability of a long-term relationship, or socialize with the victim after the rape. These themes of conversation increase the rapists' power over the victim. But they can also be seen as attempts to normalize what (at least from the victim's point of view) is essentially a nonnormal situation. They can be seen as efforts by the rapist to convince the victim, and perhaps himself as well, that what is happening is not so bad. Thus they constitute attempts by the rapist to transform an illegitimate act into a legitimate one.

ACKNOWLEDGMENTS

We wish to thank David A. Karp for discussions that clarified certain points in the analysis and Severyn J. Bruyn and Barrie Thorne for reading and commenting on the manuscript.

REFERENCES

Bart, Pauline B.

1975 "Rape doesn't end with a kiss." Unpublished manuscript, Department of Psychiatry, Abraham Lincoln School of Medicine, University of Illinois, Chicago. Published in abridged version in Viva June, 1975.

Blanchard, W. H.

1959 "The group process in gang rape." Journal of Social Psychology, 49:259–66.

Brownmiller, Susan

1975 Against Our Will: Men, Women and Rape. New York: Simon and Schuster.

Bullough, Vern L.

1974 The Subordinate Sex: A History of Attitudes Toward Women. Baltimore: Penquin Books. (First published 1973, University of Illinois Press.)

Burgess, Ann Wolbert, and Lynda Lytle Holmstrom

1974a "Rape trauma syndrome." American Journal of Psychiatry, 131 (September):981–86.

1974b Rape: Victims of Crisis. Bowie: Robert J. Brady.

1976 "Coping behavior of the rape victim," American Journal of Psychiatry, 133 (April):413–18.

1978 "Complicating factors in rape: Adolescent case illustrations," in Ann Wolbert Burgess, A. Nicholas Groth, Lynda Lytle Holmstrom, and Suzanne M. Sgroi, Sexual Assault of Children and ADolescents. Lexington, Mass.: D. C. Heath.

Chafetz, Janet Saltzman

1974 Masculine/Feminine or Human: An Overview of the Sociology of Sex Roles. Itasca, Ill.: F. E. Peacock.

Chappell, Duncan, and Jennifer James

1976 "Victim selection and apprehension from the rapist's perspective: a preliminary investigation." Paper presented at the 2nd International Symposium on Victimology. Boston.

Clark, Lorenne M. G., and Debra J. Lewis

1977 Rape: The Price of Coercive Sexuality. Toronto: Women's Press.

Cleaver, Eldridge
1968 Soul on Ice. New York: Dell. First published by McGraw-Hill.
Cohen, Murray L., Ralph Garofalo, Richard Boucher, and Theoharis Seghorn
1971 "The psychology of rapists." Seminars in Psychiatry, 3 (August):307–27.
Davis, Alan J.
1968 "Sexual assaults in the Philadelphia prison system and sheriff's vans." Trans-Action, (Dec.):8–16.
Fanon, Frantz
1968 The Wretched of the Earth. New York: Grove. First published in 1961: Paris, Las damnès de la terre, François Maspero èditeur.
Geis, Gilbert
1971 "Group sexual assaults." Medical Aspects of Human Sexuality, 5 (May):101–113.
1977 "Forcible rape: An introduction," in Duncan Chappell, Robley Geis, and Gilbert Geis (eds.), Forcible Rape: The Crime, the Victim, and the Offender. New York: Columbia University Press.
Gelles, Richard J.
1977 "Power, sex, and violence: the case of marital rape," The Family Coordinator, 26 (Oct.):339–47.
Goffman, Erving
1952 "On cooling the mark out: some aspects of adaptation to failure." Psychiatry, 15 (Nov.):451–63.
1959 The Presentation of Self in Everyday Life. Garden City, N.Y.: Doubleday Anchor.
Griffin, Susan
1971 "Rape: The all-American crime." Ramparts, 10 (Sept.):26–35.
Groth, A. Nicholas
1978 Private communication.
Groth, A. Nicholas, Ann Wolbert Burgess, and Lynda Lytle Holmstrom
1977 "Rape: power, anger, and sexuality." American Journal of Psychiatry, 134 (Nov.):1239–43.
Groth, A. Nicholas, and Murray L. Cohen
1976 "Aggressive sexual offenders: diagnosis and treatment." In Ann Wolbert Burgess and Aaron Lazare (eds.), Community Mental Health: Target Populations, Englewood Cliffs, N.J.: Prentice-Hall.
Hilberman, Elaine
1976 The Rape Victim. Washington, D.C.: American Psychiatric Association.
Holmstrom, Lynda Lytle, and Ann Wolbert Burgess
1974 "Rape: an indicator of woman's family role." Paper presented at the 8th World Congress of Sociology, Toronto. Revised version, "Rape: the husband's and boyfriend's initial reactions," to appear in The Family Coordinator.
1978a The Victim of Rape: Institutional Reactions. New York: Wiley.
1978b "Sexual behavior of assailant and victim during rape." Paper to be presented at the American Sociological Association annual meeting. San Francisco.

Lucas, W. E.
1971 Unpublished communication cited in Gilbert Geis, "Group sexual assaults," Medical Aspects of Human Sexuality, 5 (May):101–113.
Lyman, Stanford M., and Marvin B. Scott
1970 A Sociology of the Absurd, New York: Appleton-Century-Crofts, Meredith.
Mere, Ada A.
1974 Private communication. Unpublished research, Department of Sociology, University of Nigeria, Nsukka, E.C.S., Nigeria.
Metzger, Deena
1976 "It is always the woman who is raped." American Journal of Psychiatry, 133 (April):405–08.
Russell, Diana E. H.
1975 The Politics of Rape: The Victim's Perspective. New York: Stein and Day.
Schwendinger, Julia R., and Herman Schwendinger
1974 "Rape myths: in legal, theoretical, and everyday practice." Crime and Social Justice, 1 (Spring-Summer):18–26.
Weber, Max
1947 The Theory of Social and Economic Organization, A. M. Henderson and Talcott Parsons trans. Glencoe: Free Press. Published previously as Wirtschaft and Gessellschaft.
Yale Law Journal
1952 "Forcible and statutory rape: An exploration of the operation and objectives of the consent standard." Yale Law Journal, 62 (Dec.):55–83.

Chapter Nine

Process and Outcome

EDITORIAL COMMENTARY

Deviance is a behavioral pattern with component steps and stages leading to an end result. It involves actions and reactions on the part of the participants with attendant interpretations and strategies all of which culminate in an outcome, sometimes desired and predictable, and other times, unanticipated and dysfunctional, but unavoidable. The deviance process may be transitory or ephemeral, or it may be of somewhat more exaggerated duration. It may be of brief continuance because of prompt social response with concomitant events that result in closure or conclusion, or it may be prolonged as the consequence of persistence on the part of the actors, or because of community indifference, ennui, or inertia, or even lack of capacity to respond. The social endurance of deviance may even be constituent to a kind of normative "porosity" or ability to absorb without disequilibrium on the part of the community.

Deviant behavior may be the relatively spontaneous act of an individual, who on the spur of the moment and, within the context of an unusual set of opportunistic circumstances, or in the grip of an inordinate impulse, may uncharacteristically violate a social norm. An example here might be the youngster attentively skipping pebbles down the sidewalk, coincidentally noticing a streetlight as an appealing target of opportunity, and motivated by an idiosyncratic urge, throwing the pebble, maliciously breaking the light. Another illustration would be the student, who under social pressure to score well on the test, but not recollecting the correct answers, furtively glancing at the test paper of the student in the next desk and surreptitiously "borrowing" the answers from the neighbor. Both acts have ends or results as well as social consequences.

In the case of the former, the youngster may have been observed in his vandalism, reported to the authorities, and subsequently adjudicated as a delinquent. In the instance of the latter, the "cheater" may have escaped detection and gone on to excel scholastically as a result, or the proctor may have noted the "wandering eyes" of the miscreant student, causing him to fail the course. It is always possible, of course that the student, whose test answers were being "borrowed," may have been aware of the fact and reciprocated, seeking answers for himself from the original deviant, thereby establishing a conspiratorial, dyadic system, with the deviant partnership continuing on in subsequent examinations.

Deviance could also be the yield of elaborate scenarios involving multiple actors, convoluted intentions, complex interaction, unusual circumstances, unforeseen events, and dramatic conclusion with significant social import. Deviance does have an outcome. The alcoholic will ultimately voluntarily give up his drinking and attain a state of sobriety, or he will be placed in a situation where he must abstain from drinking—incarcerated in a jail or asylum, for example—or he may simply drink himself to death. The outcome of the deviance process, of course, may be the establishment of some type of balance or equilibrium in which the deviant behavior continues but at a moderated level, or only in certain circumstances, or perhaps as part of some type of exchange or reciprocal system, which may be the product of negotiation.

Serious deviant processes may arise out of simple acts, and seemingly spontaneous sets of events and circumstances, and portend grave outcomes with complex import. "Russian Roulette" may begin as a game, albeit a dangerous game, and end in tragedy. An unemotional argument may escalate into mayhem and murder. Experimenting with drugs may lead to a life of addiction, and sometimes to criminal offenses to "feed the habit." The serious import of a simple act may be years in occurring as witness the instance of a distinguished jurist nominated for the U.S. Supreme Court, having to withdraw because of admission of some limited use of marijuana some years ago. Recent years have seen the appearance of freeway "snipers," fatigued and frustrated by highway traffic, perhaps burdened by other annoyances, and not infrequently possessed of impaired judgment because of alcohol and drugs, who have sometimes suddenly taken umbrage at a motorist in another vehicle passing them or blowing their horn at them, and in their pique, have picked up a gun and fired at the "offending" driver or occupants of the car. In some instances, although the individual did not actually intend to harm the driver or occupants of the other vehicle, the bullet did in fact hit someone in the other automobile (as was the case with the son of a famous country and western singer who was "accidentally" hit while riding in his parents' car going down the highway, by a bullet fired from another automobile by a truck driver who claimed he did not mean to do so). Such "sniper" drivers may have only intended to frighten persons in another vehicle, but the behavioral process, suddenly precipitated, occurs swiftly, and the outcome is quickly effected. The victim may be seriously injured or killed, the offending deviant may be convicted of a felony and imprisoned, and the subsequent public response may demand preventative or ameliorative measures.

Deviant behavior, even if it violates social norms of the legal or social variety, does not necessarily offend community standards of proprietous sensibilities. On the contrary, the local population may be almost blasé in its toleration, if not acceptance, of some varieties of relatively blatant deviant behavior, *if* it is perceived as relatively innocuous, nonthreatening to the moral order, and/or if it is viewed as functional and, perhaps "necessary." There is an element of truth in the old saw about the community that tolerates the crooked gambling establishment because "it's the only one in town." Many communities may have their "village idiot," "local eccentric" or "town drunk," and take any or all of them in their stride. The "village idiot" may be a retarded youngster, grown to physical manhood, but without adult self control, judgment, or sense of circumspect comportment. This individual may annoy people, make a general nuisance of himself, or engage in a wide variety of proscribed and often offensive behavior, including, in some extreme cases, exposing his genitals or other outrageous activities. Such behavior on the part of others would be severely sanctioned, but in the case of the mentally defective individual, the community may have deemed it cruel and inappropriate for the parents of the retarded child to have had the youngster institutionalized. In a similar fashion, they would likely feel it inhumane to have this individual, even as an adult, incarcerated. Knowing the individual to be not dangerous, not in control of his own faculties, and a product of "God's Will," the townspeople tolerate his vagrant and noncircumspect antics as part of their "Christian Burden."

The community also may have the "local eccentric" in addition to the retarded individual. Knowing the person to perhaps be mentally ill, and the facts of their background, and the circumstances of the mental derangement, the townspeople may be more moved to pity than anger in response to the idiosyncratic, if not offensively deviant behavior of the individual. As in the song, "Delta Dawn," the mentally disturbed spinster may be quietly tolerated in spite of her eccentric behavior as one whose life has simply taken a less fortunate direction. Even the "town drunk" may have his niche in the fabric of community life, in spite of his reprehensible overindulgence in alcohol. Like the stereotypical character in the long-running comedy series, "Mayberry, R.F.D.," the town drunk—pitiful, disreputable, disgusting, but likable—serves as a splendid bad example for children of the community. This is what happens when one loses control to alcohol! For as Kai Erikson has pointed out, the existence and labeling of the deviant serves as a clear demonstration or model of what behavior is disvalued and, thus, maintains boundaries between the deviant and the nondeviant (Erikson, 1962:310).

A community, the local law enforcement apparatus, and the various segment of the population may tolerate a wide variety of deviant enterprises, in the name of functionality and the equilibrium of social life. Until recent decades, for example, many communities across the nation had their own local brothel. These were often small, quite discreet in their activities, and usually administered by some matron of long standing residence. Such brothels were accommodated because they were viewed as preferable to the alternative. Men, young and old, of baser desires, might seek sexual outlets outside of marriage. Better in the local brothel than with the respectable females in the communities! Prostitutes, in a carefully controlled and insulated setting, were functional. In such communities, there were no streetwalkers and no rape. Decent women were protected, as it were. Such community brothels, sometimes in the very midst of a "Bible Belt" locale, often became famous (or infamous) as enduring local institutions, and their passing was often lamented with quite a bit of nostalgia. John Steinbeck, in his fictional *East of Eden*, described a brothel in a small town that included many of the prominent citizens of the community among its patrons. The musical comedy, "The Best Little Whore House in Texas," humorously glorified a "real-life" brothel in a Texas college community. In one Kentucky college community, there was a local brothel of such institutional standing that when the madame decided to retire, she was encouraged to write her memoirs, which she did (see Tabor, 1971). The book enjoyed very brisk sales and the author was written up in a feature article in the *New York Times*, and went on to appear on one of the big late-night, television talk shows. After the brothel was closed, the structure was torn down (part of an urban-renewal program) and some visionary entrepreneur bought all of the bricks from the old house. The bricks were subsequently sold as souvenirs for $10.00 a piece, with an appropriate descriptive sign attached, to individuals who had special memories of the "good old days" at Pauline's, as the establishment was locally known. Pauline, the brothel madame was even invited to give a lecture on her "philosophy" at Vanderbilt University.

Other types of deviant activities may also sometimes be tolerated and accommodated by both community and law enforcement officials for a wide variety of functional and rational considerations. In some parts of the country, "moonshining" or the manufacture of nontax-paid liquor has been a traditional and, in terms of local customs, "honorable," albeit illegal means of making a living or at least supplemental income since the Whiskey Rebellion. In such areas (parts of Tennessee, Kentucky, and West Virginia), for example, there is frequently a depressed economic situation. Local citizens may not be able to afford regular alcoholic beverages and have to resort to "moonshine" because of financial constraints. Thus, the moonshiner serves a social need and may well become something of a craftsman in the process. Because illegal whiskey making often becomes a traditional craft with the necessary skills passed on from father to son, a rich subculture replete with norms and standards concerning quality and other aspects of the illegal activity develops (Gordon, 1974). The community citizenry tolerates and accommodates the practice because it is functional, and traditional. The local law enforcement officials also often tolerate it inasmuch as they may not wish to go against public sentiment or disturb the community equilibrium. Unfortunately, the federal law enforcement agencies, who are not as sensitive to local traditions of lawlessness, tend to vigorously enforce the legal statutes, and accordingly, the "revenuers" (Alcohol Tax Agents), as they are known, ruthlessly pursue the mountaineer whiskey makers with the intent of arresting them and destroying their stills.

Sections of cities, entire towns, and even whole states may accommodate illegal activities. Just as Jesse and Frank James were respected and protected by the citizens in certain rural areas in their home state, various ethnic sections of some cities may well shelter and accommodate gangs and gangsterism. The Mafia or a Chinese tong may be tolerated because they "protect" the community from the "bad elements" and are sometimes good for business. Many a small community in a rural area, especially if on a major highway, may accommodate a blatantly biased, and thus illegal, "speed trap." It brings needed revenues into the town's coffers, does not affect the locals, and only takes money from "outsiders" who can easily afford it (so it is believed), and is, accordingly patently functional.

Mississippi was one of the last states to legalize the sale of alcoholic beverages. For many years, it was illegal, but many of the citizens wished to drink. The state authorized a "Black Market Tax." An entire system of illegal whiskey dealers developed who were in violation of the nonalcohol ordinances, but, who dutifully paid the "Black Market Tax" to the State of Mississippi in order to sell illegal alcohol. The local law enforcement groups would selectively enforce the laws against selling alcohol beverages depending on the community sentiment and bribery arrangements. Once, when it was announced that a prominent wholesaler of illegal alcoholic beverages was retiring in November, the local newspaper carried an editorial appealing to the retiring illegal merchant not to retire until after the Christmas season so as not to discomote the citizenry who would want their regular supply of Yuletide "spirits."

Law enforcement officials may tolerate criminal activities because of personal as well as community considerations. Vice officers are reported to sometimes tolerate some prostitutes in their areas. A vice officer may overlook a prostitute's activities, or drop or reduce charges if he does arrest her, in exchange for information, help in arresting other offenders, sexual services, or in some instances, friendship and emotional support for their problems (Atkinson and Boles, 1977).

Perhaps one of the most prominent areas of accommodation among deviant offenders, the community, and law enforcement authorities is in the area of natural resources. There has been a traditional tendency for many rural dwellers to view natural resources such as water, grass, timber, wild game, and seafood as essentially free for the taking, and to resist attempts to regulate or prohibit the harvesting of such resources. Thus, woodcutters might illegally gather firewood in the national forests, and "poachers" might illegally take game out of season or in excess of limits. According to some studies (Palmer and Bryant, 1985, for example), game wardens who attempt to enforce fish and wildlife regulations frequently encounter quite a mind-set on the part of violators who feel that the wild game is there for the taking and they should not be arrested for doing so, even if out of season. The community might accept such practices as customary and necessary, especially for those of marginal means, and law enforcement officials, such as Forest Rangers and Game Wardens, may have to then determine how strict to be in their enforcement activities. If the offender does not become overly "greedy" and violate the laws to a blatant excess, and especially if the offender "needs" the firewood or game for his family or to be able to make a living, the law enforcement officials may see fit to overlook the transgressions in the interest of humaneness, social equity, community equilibrium, and the nature of local custom. Better ends are often served through the judicious accommodation of deviance than through the insensitive strict enforcement of the letter of the law.

The initial reading in this chapter, Michele Wilson's "Folk Crime: Patterns of Accommodation," details a similar accommodative "arrangement" between deviant offenders, law enforcement officials, and the community. In this instance, the offenders are commercial shellfishermen in a New England maritime community who harvest quahaugs—thick shelled clams. In the interest of the preservation of natural resources, there are legal restrictions on the harvesting of quahaugs, including amount, size, place, and time of day. These restrictions are administered by the enforcement division of the department of natural resources. In the course of their occupational endeavors, the shellfishermen may well violate a variety of these regulations. They do so not out of avarice or evil intent, but because even under the best of circumstances, quahauging is not an easy way to make a living, and they must, accordingly, attempt to maximize their catch and their harvest. They feel, however, that they violate the letter of the law, not the intent. They do not believe that their illegal acts have negative consequences. The author of the article labels such types of offenses as "folk crime." Similarly, a hunter violating the game laws—but not to any blatant degree—would also be a folk crime.

An important dimension of such illegal activity is that of the self-image and the community image of the offender. As the author phrases it, the "law violators are not tainted by a 'shameful differentness.' " They see themselves as honest, law-abiding citizens, who believe in basic decency and good citizenship and they "hold a decent regard for the interests, rights, and welfare of others." They try to avoid being detected in their law violations and often make a game out of such activities. They do not wish to put the wardens on the spot, causing them to arrest the offender or making the wardens mad by being open and flagrant in their violations.

They see themselves as knowledgeable about shellfish and, thus, able to violate the law without harm to the public. They are prohibited, for example, from taking quahaugs from polluted waters. They do, however, dump the shellfish into clean water for a time before selling them, in the belief that the quahaugs will cleanse themselves and pass no threat to the public. The community, in turn, shares a relatively homogeneous culture and there is a tradition of illegal behavior. They view the quahaugers as honest and decent citizens whose offenses have no social consequences, and are not dangerous. The community tolerates and trivializes such offenses. Such behavior is not deviant and is necessary in order to make a decent living.

The enforcers are familiar with the community subculture, its customs and traditions, and the fact that shellfish regulations are traditionally and routinely broken. They also understand that the community does not view such violations as deviant behavior, and that the quahaugers are seen as law abiding and decent citizens. They themselves tend to see such violations of the regulations as no threat to the public or their own professional responsibilities, and do not define such folk crime as a violation of the intent of the law. Although this article addresses quahaugers and regulation violation in New England, studies of other types of commercial fishermen and their own distinctive types of folk crimes in other coastal towns have revealed similar patterns of accommodation by law enforcement officials (see for example Shoemaker and Bryant, 1985). If the quahauger offender is not flagrant in his violations and has a good community reputation, the Wardens will overlook the illegal behavior. By exercising discretion, they reconcile the conflict between full enforcement of the law and maintaining good community relations, along with equitable justice. A social system, replete with norms, is a system of equilibrium. The accommodation of deviant and illegal behavior by both the community and the enforcers is a way of maintaining that equilibrium. The stable system of folk crime, then, is an element in that equilibrium.

Deviant behavior as social process, may result in outcomes other than equitable accommodation as equilibrium. For those skilled in negotiation and bargaining, some type of mutually satisfactory rapproachment based on an exchange transaction may be the consequence of social process, even if deviant. Deviance is seldom without residual benefit for dispenser, receiver, and even the broader public. The stripper who salaciously displays her seminude and erotically contorted anatomy may enjoy the adulation and approbation of the audience. She may also take pride in her ability to elicit the desired reactions from the onlookers, and in her self and public image as an "entertainer." The audience of onlookers obviously enjoys erotic titillation and carnal gratification that the performance affords. Even the public may feel that stripping provides an acceptable and socially safer symbolic carnal alternative or sexual channel to sexual activity, itself. For this reason, deviant behavior in many forms is a function of exchange negotiation. Liquor can be sold and consumed, but only under negotiated controlled conditions. Stripping may be a permitted entertainment form, but anatomy to be exposed must be "metered," as it were, in a negotiated fashion with a particular sized "G-string" and "pasties" of appropriate diameter applied strategically over the breast nipples. Spouses may endure some degree of adulterous behavior as long as parameters are agreed upon and limits set. The purveyor of deviant goods and services could not long endure in the market place if there were no customers for the goods and services. Similarly, much deviant behavior represents an exchange for other deviant behavior. The abusive husband who erratically beats his wife, may be routinely forgiven by his spouse, because in his subsequent guilt and efforts to obtain forgiveness, he may tend to overlook his wife's deviant behavior in the form of slovenly appearance, irresponsible discharge of household responsibilities, or even flirtatious or philanderous behavior with other men. Similarly, the wife may endure her husband's infidelity because of the lavish gifts he provides her when confronted with adultery. Much can be tolerated for that which follows. Thus, deviance may evolve or develop out of negotiation with an exchange process which affords something to both or all.

The next reading in this chapter, David Luckenbill's "Dynamics of the

Deviant Sale," examines the stages in the process by which a male prostitute and his customer consummate the sexual/economic exchange. The dispensing of many illicit goods and services, including narcotics, stolen merchandise, bribery, sex, and criminal abortions, to name but some, all represent deviant behavior and involve a negotiated transaction and an exchange mechanism. This article identifies the principal characteristics of the deviant sale and explores the details of the various stages of the process, and compares the deviant sale with the respectable sale.

Luckenbill bases his analysis on in-depth interviews with 25 male prostitutes of diverse socioeconomic and sociodemographic backgrounds in Chicago. He divides the deviant sexual sale into seven "time-ordered" stages and examines the tasks which are involved in each stage and which the prostitute and customer accomplish together. The prostitute and customer must first make contact, which may be accomplished through an escort service, or through a more casual meeting in the setting of gay bars, gay baths, or other public places in which homosexuals gather. It is usually the customer who locates the prostitute and "cruises" (drives or walks past) the hustler in order to determine availability. The two individuals must now determine suitability in terms of a partner who is trustworthy and not a policeman or potentially exploitative, as well as if the other is a person who will likely make the exchange "rewarding." After appropriate probing and confirming conversation, they will agree to participate and establish that the activity will involve a financial transaction. At this point, the two participants in the negotiation must "come to terms," in the sense of actually agreeing on the specific sexual activity that will be involved and the specific fee to be paid. Conventional sexual services usually command lower fees and more bizarre sexual requests may dictate somewhat higher prices. After agreeing on these concerns, the prostitute and customer must now determine a setting for the sexual activity and then move to it. Both will have a part in choosing the location, inasmuch as they both seek privacy and protection against law enforcement agents or exploitation. After agreeing on a location such as a hotel room, and going there, the two now transfer the money and engage in the sexual activity (usually in that order). Even at this point, both individuals may be wary because of the possibility of the other reneging on providing all of the services, or conversely in paying for the services. After the sexual activities, they will terminate the sale, commenting or not on their reaction, and frequently returning to the original place of encounter. The hustler may even express hopes for future transactions.

Although there are similarities between the respectable sale and deviant sale, there are numerous differences. The former is higher structured and legitimately protected by law while the latter is not, being relatively tenuous. Subjective evaluation is necessary because of the dangerous and problematic nature of the illegitimate interaction and the potential danger for exploitation and harm for both. Because of the nature of the deviant sale, and the official sanctions to which the participants are subject, they both must depend more upon themselves in their negotiations, taking special precautions, and putting more emphasis on trust, precautions, and screening assessments. The relationship of the participants is necessarily guarded, but in order to effect the deviant process and bring about the desired sexual/economic exchange outcome, appropriate negotiation and adaptability to the demands of the situation are necessary.

In the case of the deviant sale, if one individual received the desired sexual services and the other received the agreed upon monetary compensation, then the prior negotiation can be said to have had a mutually satisfactory outcome. In many instances of negotiated deviancy, however, the outcome may not necessarily have been an outcome that is gratifying to both or even to one. The female prostitute who negotiates the sale of sexual services to a customer may be less than pleased when she discovers that the "customer" is in reality, a vice-officer who, in turn, arrests her. Individuals may engage in misleading negotiation, may renege on promises, or even attempt to cheat or swindle the other person. The "cocaine" one purchased after appropriate negotiation may turn out to be nothing more than white flour, and the sexual services one contracted to buy may be somewhat less than satisfactory, if not in fact, totally spurious. However, some individuals, particularly adept at diplomacy, may even be able to socially construct a reality, as it were, and convince others that the outcome is satisfactory, if not equitable, even when this is patently not the case—"cooling out the mark," as Goffman has phrased it.

Failing in equitability, diplomacy, or salesmanship, some individuals may attempt to influence the outcome of the social process by the application of social leverage, including threats, other types of coercion, or even physical violence. The phrase, "arm twisting" can, indeed, be literal, as well as metaphorical. The next article in this chapter, Mary Riege Laner and Jeanine Thompson's "Abuse and Aggression in Courting Couples," examines the use of violence in social process, in this instance, courtship.

Violence between intimates is a sociological observation of long standing, and violent behavior between married spouses and courting couples is component to this generic pattern. Just as in the animal world, some violence between individuals of the opposite sex may be constituent to the establishment of a sexually bonded relationship. Male animals may often resort to violence in establishing sexual dominance over females, and a similar pattern may also occur with humans. As has been observed, human courtship, especially in some societies, involves a kind of negotiated sexual equilibrium with the male attempting to obtain the maximum degree of sexual freedom with the female, and the female, in turn, attempting to withhold as much opportunity for sexual gratification from the male as possible. In this regard, various researchers have reported that sexual aggression and even serious violence in courtship in the U.S. is relatively common and that this aggressive violence is related to an attempt on the part of the males to obtain sexual access to their courting partners as amply cited by Laner and Thompson.

Violence in courtship, and in marriage, is not only linked to sexual interaction. Partners in courtship and marriage as intimates have increased vulnerability to one another and "words and actions may . . . be seen as threats to identity and self-esteem." The tenuous and stressful nature of courtship often exacerbates this vulnerability and increases personal insecurity, and may contribute to conflict. Courtship involves a negotiated interpersonal relationship in terms of regular interaction and emotional involvement, as well as sexual equilibrium. Such negotiation may include threats, coercion, abuse, verbal attack, and violence as means of leverage designed to manipulate the partner's behavior, develop a privileged relationship, or obtain psychological advantage in the relationship. Laner and Thompson, using data obtained from a questionnaire, submitted to 500 students in courtship and marriage classes, sought to examine several hypotheses concerning violence proneness in courtship. They had hypothesized that men and women in more involved premarital relationships would experience higher rates of violence, and the data did indicate that there were higher rates of abuse and aggression in such relationships than in those defined as casual or less involved. Their findings also modestly supported a second hypothesis that there was a greater chance of experiencing violence in courtship if it had been experienced in childhood. The findings did not seem to support the final hypothesis that there would be higher rates of violence in courtship relationships in which at least one partner was of lower socioeconomic level.

It would appear that the interpersonal fragility of the courtship relationship and particularly those of more intense emotional involvement, is sufficiently stressful and anxiety producing as to necessitate bargaining, adjustment, and negotiation. For those with the necessary transactional skills, rapproachment and equilibrium may be possible. Where such skills are lacking, alternate tactics, such as abuse, aggression, or violence may be necessary.

Where violence is employed as a tactic of negotiation, the direction of the deviant process may be cyclical or linear. Studies of wifebeating, for example, indicate that frequently there is an initial relationship involving a dominating, aggressive and often sexually frigid wife, and a shy, subservient, dependent, and unassertive husband (Snell, Rosenwald, and Robey, 1964). Thus, a kind of inappropriate gender equilibrium exists. From time to time, the husband and wife seek a change in role relationships, which occurs when the husband becomes drunk and the alcohol serves as an aid to role alteration. The husband then becomes sexually aggressive, abusive, often violent, and beats his wife. Such a role reversal temporarily helps to release the husband from his anxiety about his ineffectiveness as a man, and in turn provides the wife with some degree of masochistic gratification as well as helping her deal with her own hostility toward her husband, her aggressive posture, and her "controlling, castrating" behavior. Thus, the process achieves a new, albeit deviant, although traditional gender correct relationship equilibrium—for a short time—and then the cycle repeats itself. Sometimes, however, the process is linear, and one or other persons in the dyad may bring the process to conclusion by killing the other.

In the last reading in the chapter, Ken Levi analyzes the transaction between killer and victim in his essay, "Homicide as Conflict Resolution," using Simmel's notion of conflict being "based on divergence within a context of unity," and the conflict process aiming at "overcoming that divergence." The author interviewed a sample of 35 legally defined and self-defined male killers, which included offenders from different types of conflict contexts which were labeled as "antagonistic games," "intimate relations," and "objective interests." The killers from the first type of context were termed "adversaries," those who had killed in the "intimate relations" context were called "lovers" and those from the "objective interests" homicide situation were labeled as "strangers."

Levi examines the interactional conflict between killer and victim, dividing the process into a number of stages. In the "opening move" stage, the victim would behave in an inappropriate fashion (i.e., challenging the killer's symbolic mastery, withdrawing from communication or the relationship, or attempting to block the course of the action). In stage two, the killer would ascribe meaning to the victim's behavior, either interpreting the action as personally demeaning, a possible alienation of affection, or as an impediment (possibly even a dangerous impediment) to his intended course of action. In stage three, the offender has several options, ranging from excusing the violation to retaliation. The killers, at this point, tended not to retaliate, but rather bore their insult in silence, sought additional facts, or either were indifferent or "backed off." In stage four, a "working agreement" to resort to violence was effected, and this was an important component of the homicide process because the victim, in effect, "trapped" the killer into this particular mode of response. In some instances, victims "invaded the established boundaries of the killer's social self," and in a public setting. In other cases, the confrontation involves a proffered test question, which elicited a confirming response. In yet other instances, the victim represents a danger in his or her actions, and the killer experiences an intolerable sense of discomfort and seeks immediate relief. In stage five, the adversary killer resorts to violence to alleviate the discomfort and obtain symbolic mastery over the opponent. In the case of lovers, the killer resorted to homicide in an attempt to "keep" the lover, to save the relationship, or prevent the loved one from leaving. Death effectively prevents the completion of the separation. For the strangers, homicide was a means of "stopping" the victim from doing something to the killer—to bring about an objective state. In the final stage, the aftermath, the adversary killer departed the scene with a sense of "decisive victory," but stranger killers often felt frightened, but "glad to be alive." Lover killers tended to remain on the scene or fled and then returned to it, and felt sorry for their actions, sometimes expressing the wish that they would bring the victim back if they could.

The homicide brought closure to a seemingly otherwise untenable situation. The killer was placed in an uncomfortable predicament, where not unlike a rat in a maze, shocked to action, had to react. The stages of the deviant process which involved interactional feedback from the victim in a cumulative fashion led inexorably to violence and death as a means of reestablishing equilibrium, and effecting an outcome. Deviance, whether simple or convoluted, is a social process with an ultimate result component to the dynamics of the interaction.

REFERENCES

Atkinson, Maxine, and Jacqueline Boles
1977 "Prostitution as an Ecology of Confidence Games: The Scripted Behavior of Prostitutes and Vice Officers." Pp. 219–231 in Clifton D. Bryant (ed.), Sexual Deviancy in Social Context. New York: New Viewpoints.

Erikson, Kai T.
1962 "Notes on the Sociology of Deviance." Social Problems 9 (Spring): 307–314.

Gordon, John L., Jr.
1974 "The Moonshiner: Illegal Craftsman of the Georgia Mountains." Pp. 383–395 in Clifton D. Bryant (ed.), Deviant Behavior: Occupational and Organizational Bases. Chicago: Rand McNally.

Palmer, C. Eddie, and Clifton D. Bryant
1985 "Keepers of the King's Deer: Game Wardens and the Enforcement of Fish and Wildlife Law," Chapter Six (pp. 111–137) in Clifton D. Bryant, Donald J. Shoemaker, James K. Skipper, Jr. and William E. Snizek (eds.), The Rural Work Force: Non-Agricultural Occupations in America. South Hadley. Bergin & Garvey.

Shoemaker, Donald J., and Clifton D. Bryant
1985 "Ecological Law Enforcement and the 'Seafood Police'," Chapter Seven (pp. 139-163) in Clifton D. Bryant, Donald J. Shoemaker, James K. Skipper, Jr., and William E. Snizek (eds.), The Rural Work Force: Non-Agricultural Occupations in America. South Hadley. Bergin & Garvey.

Snell, John E., Richard J. Rosenwald, and Ames Robey
1964 "The Wifebeater's Wife: A Study of Family Interaction," Archives of General Psychiatry 11 (August): 107-113.
Tabor, Pauline
1971 Pauline's: Memoirs of the Madam on Clay Street. Louisville: Touchstone Publishing Company.

Reading 28

Folk Crime: Patterns of Accommodation

Michele Wilson
University of Alabama in Birmingham

Folk crimes, offenses that do not impair the public identity of offenders as respectable, law-abiding citizens, were studied among a group of New England shellfishermen. Through observation, it was discovered that a pattern of mutual accommodation between enforcers and violators distinguishes folk crime from other violations of the same law. The subjective interpretation of the offenses and accommodation as a reaction is based on considerations of rule intent, logical implications of relevant rules, costs and consequences of rule invocation for enforcers, evaluation of violators' motives, perceived consequences of violations, and the imputed identity of violators.

INTRODUCTION

As a system of behavior, folk crime is a criminal activity largely ignored by traditional criminology.[1] Folk crime is not a rarity; on the contrary, crimes of the everyday variety collectively account for the majority of all crimes committed. Yet traditional criminological theory appears incapable of explaining folk crime.

This inability to explain everyday crime and folk crime results from four major inadequacies and biases. First, scholars generally limit themselves to few and unrepresentative offenders (Clark and Tifft, 1966;

I wish to thank Albert K. Cohen, Jerold Heiss, Murray Binderman and John Maiolo for their critical attention to this research. The research was funded in part by a NIMH Fellowship in Deviant Behavior and a University of Connecticut Summer Research Fellowship.

[1]Although folk crime has been discussed in the criminological literature there is not yet consensus about the definition. Ross (1961) uses the term to apply to everyday deviance: it does not impair the identity of the violator and is generally considered relatively harmless. Wood (1974) uses the term to apply to traditional subcultural violations of "folk." This paper hypothesizes that neither of these criteria is necessary. The literature on white-collar crime comes closest to the current attempt.

Hirschi, 1969). Second, the field has not developed a conception of normality corresponding to either the actual distribution of behavior or people's sense of morality (Birenbaum and Sagarin, 1976). Third, theories and studies assume a single normative social order, that is, deviance and conformity as products of socialization into an inflexible system of external and imposed rules (Wilson, 1970). Finally, criminologists utilize unidirectional cause-and-effect models, with one "dependent" variable and one or more "independent" variables, and ignore immediate circumstances and complex interactive "feedback."

A more realistic attempt to deal with criminal behavior requires freedom from traditional and naive assumptions about the nature of crime and criminals. For example, it is productive to view violations as part of a network of directly and indirectly interacting variables whose paths and loops result in a dynamic equilibrium of more or less precarious stability, that is, a system. Sociological methodologies are not well suited to demonstrating the structure and development of such systems exhibited by criminal behavior. [2] Although studies have focused on the patterned features of much criminal behavior (Clinard and Quinney, 1973; Guenther, 1976), systems theory neither asks nor answers the crucial questions: How do the interacting elements actually result in a criminal violation? What rules govern decisions to break or enforce a norm?

THE STUDY

Folk crime presents a particularly interesting criminological problem because it does not fit traditional interests and perspectives. Folk crimes are crimes that do not impair the public identity of offenders as respectable, law-abiding citizens. They are committed repeatedly by offenders who are well known in their communities and who are considered ordinary violators committing ordinary offenses. These law violators are not tainted by a "shameful differentness" (Goffman, 1963). The enforcers and other significant definers of deviance and the violators negotiate the meanings of the violations to the point where these meanings become shared: they have mutually constructed an interpretation of nondeviance indicated by mutual accommodation. It is this lack of symbolic importance of folk crime, the notion that it is not deviant in the real world that needs to be explained. It is not the nature of the offense, but its subjective interpretation and therefore the reaction to it that differentiates folk crime from other crime.

The major elements of the system of folk crime are characteristics of the offenders, of the community, of the enforcers, and the relationships

[2] Examples of stable criminal systems include racketeering, some instances of hijacking, corporate offenses, and folk crimes.

among them, including characteristics of offense behavior and the enforcement process. Because it is argued that these relationships are crucial to an understanding of the nature of folk crime, the data utilized are those that provide a description of the interactions and the social context that generates and sustains the relationships. The major concern is with workaday behavior, with the give and take of social interaction, with the understandings that obtain among the participants, and with the meanings with which they invest the transactions between them. Direct observation and participant observation in particular are the logical methods of choice.

Over a period of five years, the investigator studied commercial shellfishermen known to consistently violate conservation laws in a New England maritime community. These were initially contacted in social, nonthreatening situations where the violators felt free to confide. In addition, numerous boat trips were made to observe methods of operation and to learn more about violations in the "someone told me" and anecdotal form. Patrol, stakeout, and social settings were the environments for observing enforcers-state fish and game wardens-and questioning them about their role.

THEORETICAL CONTEXT

The social sciences endeavor to find predictability and pattern, that is to say system, in the context of the apparent disorder of human behavior. Systems as analytic units of social study provide a framework for the examination of human behavior because they allow us to impose a boundary on the behaviors to be included for study. The major implication of the systems concept is that each element of a system is constrained by, conditioned by, or dependent on all of its elements. A system then is some set of elements in a state of mutual determination. The elements, simultaneously independent and dependent variables, interact in nonrandom or normative ways created by, transmitted within, and enforced by the system. Analytically, a system has both content and structure. Roles as expectations and performances constitute the basis of interaction between the component positions or statuses of the system. Interactants, in their reciprocally influential relationships, are complementary in that their behavior within the system can be continued only if each performs in a manner congruent with others and in the context of the system's purpose. The choreography of performances is possible because of common interpretations of events and circumstances: the interdependence of different behaviors rests on the influence of common understandings. This basis of the organization of a system allows balance and interlocking such that they result in regular events.

The systems approach facilitates the development of typologies by abstracting from concrete data. This technique involves carving out classes of crime and criminal behavior that are thought to be homogeneous. "Such a typology would suggest how persons with certain characteristics and behaviors develop patterns that have a certain probability of becoming defined as criminal and receive a particular reaction from society" (Clinard and Quinney, 1973:13).

On some level, it may be possible to discover that all criminal behavior is of one class, that there is a single model that describes all the systems to which they belong. That is that all of the systems can be derived from or are subtypes of some more general system. But the most profitable procedure is probably to try to identify limited classes of criminal behavior, to try to construct the systems of which they are a part, and then to seek, on another level of abstraction, commonalities among these systems so that they may be understood as subtypes. The working hypothesis of this study was that a promising criterion for distinguishing a system of criminal behavior is the nature of the social reaction, for we may be sure that differences in this respect will make important differences in outcomes.

Using the example of shellfishing violations, basic elements of the system identified as folk crime have been isolated.[3]

Violator Characteristics

1 Violators are otherwise law-abiding citizens and think of themselves as such.

2 Violators generally believe in law enforcement and have respect for legal authorities.

3 Violators are aware that they break the law.

4 Violators believe that they have the right to break the law.

5 Violators believe that their behavior does not violate the intent of the law, that it is congruent with intent.

6 Violators believe that they have special skills and knowledge that enable them to break the law without harm to others.

Community Characteristics

1 The subcommunity is solidary, sharing a relatively homogeneous culture.

2 The subcommunity has a tradition of illegal behavior.

3 The subcommunity offenses are frequent, regular, predictable, and widespread.

4 The subcommunity is aware of offense behavior.

[3]The model has also been tested on moonshining, deer poaching, lobster poaching, and some forms of bunko, such as fortune telling.

5 The community at large sees the subcommunity's traditional offenses as trivial, consistent with the intent of the law, and not dangerous.

Enforcer Characteristics[4]

1 Enforcers have respect for the violators, their way of life, their skills, and their general law-abidingness.
2 Enforcers recognize the traditional nature of offenses.
3 Enforcers do not perceive folk violators or violations as a threat to major occupational goals or to the public.
4 Enforcers' occupational ideology incorporates a concern for the objectives of laws being enforced.
5 Enforcers do not define folk crime as a violation of the intent of the law.
6 Enforcers define folk crime as trivial.

Accommodation Pattern

1 Violators and enforcers develop a pattern of mutual accommodation maintaining the public face of general law-abidingness for violators and conformity with occupational expectations for enforcers.
2 For violators, accommodation involves not flaunting their violations, exercising self-regulation in time and place of offense, not embarrassing enforcers, and remaining within bounds of intent of the law.
3 Accommodation for enforcers is premised on wide discretion in enforcement and involves avoidance of the crime's scene and revealing their presence.[5]

THE VIOLATORS

The primary violators studied are shellfishermen, called quahaugers. Traditionally, quahaugs—thick-shelled clams—are commercially harvested from boats in up to 20 feet of water. The work is physically difficult, comparable to labor in heavy construction and subject to maritime hazards. The work takes place in social isolation, albeit within sight of shore. Making a living by quahauging is somewhat risky and earnings are, at best, marginal. In addition, there are legal restrictions on harvesting quahaugs, including size, place, amount, and time of day. The restrictions, set by state law and statute

[4]These characteristics may not be true for other types of enforcement agencies. Regional or national enforcement personnel may be bound more by policy, may be less in synchronization with the violator, and not be attuned to or in conflict with community standards.

[5]A fourth element in the accommodation pattern, not mentioned in this paper because of the paucity of data, is the adjudication process when invoked trivializes the offenses on the advice of enforcers.

under the advice of the department of natural resources and state health department, are administered by the enforcement division of the department of natural resources.

Those shellfishermen most esteemed within the community embody solid middle-class values and habits although their incomes and manner of making a living do not fit traditionally respected occupational patterns. The average shellfisherman has never had a confrontation with nor been ticketed by a conservation officer. He lives a generally law-abiding life-style-style of hard work and interpersonal restraint. Nevertheless, quahaugers frequently violate the statutes against nighttime harvesting, which in turn facilitates other violations, notably harvesting in restricted or polluted areas and exceeding the legal amount.

The laws are something to be evaded. No quahauger, however, wishes to incur the warden's escalating wrath by repeated and flagrant violation. Therefore quahaugers have developed various coping strategies to avoid detection. A game-like atmosphere surrounds violations. A detected violation has serious consequences but the avoidance-of-detection strategies are a standard topic of jokes. The classic anecdote about strategy involves Leon, a frequent violator, who was detected at night in a polluted area. When he saw that he could not outrun the wardens, he jumped overboard, swam to shore, and reported his boat stolen. Leon not only avoided a fine and possible impoundment of his equipment; he also avoided putting the wardens—who would have had to arrest him—on the spot. Strategies are game-like in another way: outcomes depend on interactions or moves by all participants.

Quahaugers present illegal behavior as appropriate for given situations by viewing their violations as of the letter, not the intent, of the law. They perceive the intent of the relevant laws to focus on safety (reflected in the marking of polluted areas in which shellfishing is illegal) and environmental and resource preservation (reflected in restrictions of quantity). According to these shellfishermen, basic decency and good citizenship mean adhering to the norms of civilized society and holding a decent regard for the interests, rights, and welfare of others. Yet they recognize that the law, as written, prohibits behavior not always harmful when performed by certain people under limited circumstances. The quahauger committing his folk crime assumes the illegal act has no negative consequences, that is, it does not violate the intent of the law. This interpretation of their behavior is reflected in both the evaluative and identity set parts of the self (Heiss, 1976:11). They conceive of themselves as honest and therefore well intentioned. The self as good is constantly reaffirmed in interaction with others.

That they do not wish to violate the law's safety intent is indicated by their dumping of quahaugs for cleaning purposes.[6] The following response by Wall, a young quahauger, is typical: "Shit, we don't want anybody to get sick. But it's o.k. if we make them [the quahaugs] sit for a while. Then nobody gets hurt." When questioned about future resources, the quahaugers reacted with disdain, replying that few would be so stupid as to endanger their own future.

If law exists to protect people from eating contaminated shellfish, then the quahauger's conscience is clear; in his own judgment he abides by this intent. His "sure" knowledge and pride in his own honesty support his view that he is capable of regulating himself. He avoids unrestricted areas that he believes to be polluted, enabling him to demonstrate greater scrupulousness than the letter of the law requires. Law enforcement, he feels, should be restricted to the ignorant and the unscrupulous. Not incidentally, anyone reputed to sell tainted shellfish finds difficulty securing a buyer for his product.

Laws governing quantity are seen as unfair restrictions on commercial fishing because they interfere with gaining a livelihood and give unfair advantage to large-scale commercial trawling operations. Commercial trawlers are thought to damage and disturb the ecology. Time restrictions are thought to exist only to ease enforcement. Laws regulating size are adhered to; no market exists for excessive quantities of undersize shellfish. In sum, commercial quahaugers violate laws by defining the situation in ways conducive to law violation.

THE COMMUNITY

The community, as one major unit of folk crime's behavioral system, supports violations; it tolerates and trivializes offenses. Buttressing the community's responses are its emphases on historical roots of community and residents. Within the community, there exists a strong interest in colonial history that permeates the community and the consciousness of its inhabitants and plays a prominent place in attitudes of residents. This emphasis on history identifies a source of status. Subjectively interpreted, long-time residence, regardless of the contemporary socioeconomic status of an individual or family, brings a certain amount of esteem. The quahaugers have been identified as the descendents of colonial settlers and thus are admired.

Violations are further supported by the community's attitudes about natural resources. The average member of the community is likely to be conservation-minded whereas members of the maritime subculture, in the best of the Judeo-Christian tradition, are more likely to feel that the envi-

[6]Cleaning involves letting the life shellfish sit in unpolluted water for 2–14 days in order to remove harmful bacteria.

ronment is there to be used. This divergence does not create much of a problem for a number of reasons: quahaugers are few in number; violations and their frequency are not that widely publicized; and violations are not seen as a threat to conservation goals because they are committed by well-intentioned, respectable community members.

Social control within a village-type community is based on perceptions of who rather than what. As with all forms of social control it is less a matter of whether a rule is violated; rather, judgments of an act's deviance are related to such factors as time, place, circumstance, actor, and audience—orchestrated into the system of folk crime in such a way that the community judges the behavior to be nondeviant.

THE ENFORCERS

The conservation officers or wardens have a great deal of autonomy. Although schedules are posted for boat or car patrol, for a.m. or p.m. duty, they are frequently ignored. In some units lieutenants make decisions and assignments (conflicting with those coming from headquarters) supposedly justified by tidal considerations and whether opportunities for violations exist. Occasionally, officers received unofficial word about an impending violation or a particular offender "known" to be violating legal intent. Mention of law breaking with impunity is interpreted as authority erosion and exploitation of an enforcement official's good nature. Wardens appear to exercise more discretion than do other law enforcement personnel.

Apparently enforcement officials do not enforce the law simply because it is the law. If they did, folk crime would not occur. Essentially, enforcers are caught in a conflict between the rule of law implying full enforcement and the job demand to maintain order including good community relations and an efficient system of justice. Exercising discretion is one way to reconcile this conflict and allow enforcers to behave in ways consistent with both professional or occupational values and their own social perspective.

Briefly, enforcers trust different segments of the population less according to characteristics having to do with behavioral illegality than with evaluation of the kind of person with whom they interact (Sacks, 1972; Hartjen, 1972). They infer character from behavior (demeanor) and from physical cues. The exercise of discretion is not totally dependent on obvious characteristics such as dress but on the enforcer's interpretation of the meaning of both obvious characteristics and inferred character, especially as indicated by the way in which a suspect relates to the enforcer (Sykes, 1975). Being concerned with position in the status system, most enforcers interpretation of that demeanor, as reflecting respect, are salient determinants of whether to invoke power and arrest or otherwise exercise their authority (Piliavin and Briar, 1964). Given great autonomy and a heavy job load, conservation officers have developed informal practices in the exercise of discretion. This results in not choosing to enforce laws against folk criminals who, in the range of offenders, do not violate the intent of the law. Therefore traditional quahaugers are unlikely to become the object of official action.

For conservation officers, community opinion of violations, violators, and enforcement is important, especially because of flexible policy and little supervision by their organization. Officers realize that little public cooperation and understanding can be anticipated if enforcement policies do not coincide with community views about folk crimes (Quinney, 1970). Socialization for the job occurs in situ rather than in formal teaching situations: norms directing enforcement behavior arise from on-the-job socialization, actual situations, and a mental rehearsing of consequences of enforcement decisions.

Intimacy with folk criminals is another factor in the interpretation of quahaugers' behavior as being within the limits of legal intent. Although intimacy may be too strong a term, maritime officers have frequent contact with commercial fishermen. By being at dockside when catches are brought in and by making spot checks while working, officers come to know each of the commercial quahaugers. Not only are names and faces known, but boats are recognized and quahaugers' reputations for skill, earning capacity, physical strength, and honesty are learned. A "rep" also incorporates, rather accurately, information on illegal shellfishing. Illegal activity by itself may not damage a shellfisherman's good reputation, which is a function of other characteristics, namely, inferences about the quahauger's interpretation of the intent of the law and his lack of a guilty conscience.

The quahaugers' need to earn a respectable living also plays a part in the reaction of those who detect, apprehend, and charge offenders. To the extent that conservation officers empathize with the economic plight of the quahaugers, they tend to overlook violations or at least do not search for them. Given this empathy, enforcers rarely interpret the illegal behavior as reprehensible and do not award it salience in the hierarchy of enforcement priorities.

Officers include the costs of enforcement to the offender in their thinking. If the offender is known to officers as a whole person and his social character is perceived as respectable and decent, the officer is included to weigh the costs of enforcement to the benefit of an offender. The characteristics of both the total situation and the folk criminals maximize the sensitivity of officers.

ACCOMMODATION

Tacit cooperation between both parties—violators and enforcers—facilitates deviance yet permits each party to support the public image of the other. The public face of each group is one of law-abidingness; mutual support enables violators to break the law and encourages wardens to be accomplices in the maintenance of a working social order. Goffman (1969) explains it well:

> The rule regarding . . . unofficial . . . communication is that the sender ought not to act as if he had officially conveyed the message he has hinted at, while the recipients have the right and the obligation to act as if they have not officially received the message contained in the hint. Hinted communication then, is deniable communication; it need not be faced up to. It provides a means by which the person can be warned that his current situation is leading to loss of face, without this warning itself becoming an incident. (p. 278)

The nature of accommodation is governed by rules developing from the mutual definition of the situation. The rules in use of traditional quahaugers who violate the law are following: using their presumed skills and knowledge, they are not to be flagrant—that is, they should not flaunt the fact of their violations and the violations are to be carried out with discretion. The rules in use for the conservation officers are that they will not go out of the way to detect and apprehend the traditional shellfishermen who follow their part of the bargain. A corollary of this is that the wardens will, as much as possible, give some kind of hints about where they might be patrolling. The rules in use between the traditional quahaugers and the wardens comprise the content of the pattern of accommodation.

That the accommodation pattern results from conscious effort, that both sides are aware of its existence, is obvious in the humor of fishermen and wardens. Jokes relate incidents in the "someone" form, indicating that each knows what the other is doing. In their interactions overtime, fishermen and the wardens have developed stable role expectations. Each party has undergone socialization insuring an appropriate performance for the other.

This relativity or *verstehen* does not emphasize enough the mutual definition of the situation as developed through interaction over time. If definitions favorable to law violation were not acceptable beyond the violators' subculture, special effort to rationalize the behavior could be expected. But deviations are reflexive, and there is little effort to alleviate them; reinforcement is available from other concerned parties. In other words, definitions held by violators are shared by others. The autonomy and isolation involved in both occupations make accommodation possible. The motivating factors are occupational and personal.

In short, folk criminals reduce dissonance between the illegality of their behavior and their self-conceptions as law-abiding citizens by distinguishing between the letter and the intent of the law, by making conformity with the latter the criterion of good citizenship, and by moderating and regulating violations to communicate respect for the intent of the law. Furthermore, the violators and their families, because they constitute a large segment of the community, provide consensual validation and support for their self-definitions and their violative behavior. Finally, these definitions are further supported by law enforcement policies and the casual, informal legal procedures of enforcers. Enforcers, in turn, are supported in their behavior by the offenders' deference, their respect for office, their care not to challenge or embarrass, and the generally law-abiding conduct and demeanor. In this manner, the several elements of the system support, maintain, and perpetuate one another. This stable system is order-perpetuating law violation.

CONSTRUCTING THE SYSTEM

Social order exists because rules guide behavior. Yet humans are not passive agents either automatically conforming to or deviating from these rules; rather they apply rules (Garfinkel, 1967). The diversity of rules in any situation further complicates behavior: we may obey the law or other's role expectations, act in a way expressing our personality, act to present a certain self-image, act to confirm our self-concept, follow rules of etiquette, or act to save face for self and others. Choices are made about which behavioral guides will be applied in a particular situation and how they will be expressed. But we do not act alone: we interact with others making similar kinds of decisions. We develop common understanding and coordinate behavior. We cannot blindly adhere to an abstract normative order; because we are forced to reach decisions, any resulting order is a consequence of agreement.

In folk crime, the crucial agreement reached is one of accommodation between violators and enforcers. This mutual accommodation allows criminal behavior to continue. Violators continue in illegal behavior and enforcers do not enforce the law. As such, the accommodation constitutes a system in equilibrium. If accommodation did not exist, there would be no stable system of folk crime.

Why has accommodation become the major rule in use? Various guides, norms, and role expectations are applied by violators and enforcers. Because many rules could be applied in any situation, because rules do not cover all contingencies, and because most rules are sufficiently vague, actors develop principles permitting them to decide which guidelines to follow. If agreement is reached, order is created permitting the work of predictable living to continue.

We examine the interpretive process of enforcers and limit the discussion to why one rule—that of law—is not applied. This is a mutual accommodation; violators are also involved in interpretation and rule application. The perspective of the wardens is used as an illustration of the development or rules in use because as law enforcers their definitions tend to dominate in negotiations.

A Consideration of Rule Intent Wardens perceive the intent of laws governing shellfish harvesting to be general conservation and protection of the public from contaminated shellfish. It is unimportant whether wardens are correctly interpreting intent. Their perception of intent influences how they exercise discretion. In instances of folk crimes, both enforcers and violators interpret intent in a way justifying violation or at least reducing it to minor infraction status.

Logical Implications of Rule(s) Implications of a rule follow at least in part from interpretations of its intent. For instance, if intent is understood to be conservation of future natural resources, officers would not totally eliminate the offenses but would contain them at a level unthreatening to the resource's future. One implication of any rule is that intensity of enforcement is determined in conjunction with other rules. Coexisting rules permit only limited invocation of all rules at any one time. This means that enforcers must exercise discretion to determine priorities.

Costs and Consequences of Rule Invocation for Enforcers Each officer has many projects, many interests, and goals—saving face, meeting occupational responsibilities, maximizing comfort, providing convenience, and ensuring security. When a decision must be made—any decision but certainly an enforcement decision—choice of a course of action will take these considerations into account. Enforcers ask themselves questions such as: How much time will have to be spent in court? Can I finish the paperwork before my shift ends? How will this affect my performance ratings? Will someone try to put in a fix; what are the chances of conviction? Will I lose or gain in my position within the community, with other officers, etc? How will I feel about myself? Many of these questions relate to preferred outcomes of the encounter. Much of decision making results from a compromise decision between maximizing individual desires, such as making life easy, and adhering to occupation role demands, such as enforcing the law and serving the public.

Evaluation of Others' Motives Technically, motive (one's purpose in violating the law) is distinguished from criminal intent and is irrelevant to the determination of mens rea. In fact, both laypeople and criminal justice system functionaries take motive into consideration. Although not bearing on legal culpability, motive bears on moral culpability. Folk criminals are not seen to be morally culpable but as honest, hard-working citizens trying to make a living and in the course of events committing technical violations of the law.[7] Motives of personal gain are not themselves reprehensible so long as violators exercise self-restraint and discipline and contain their violations within limits set by the law's intent. Where motives of personal gain are unchecked by concern for the common good or the wholesome intent of the law, as with traditional criminals, offenders are seen as greedy, selfish, immoral, and worthy of punishment.

Consequences of Violative Behavior The violating behavior is done in a responsible way to ensure conservation intent. It is assumed that shellfishermen would not overharvest and thereby impair their means of making a living. Public safety is not at issue, because the folk criminals "know" the location of polluted water and know how to treat shellfish harvested from contaminated areas. Failure to arrest a folk criminal does not encourage general disrespect for the law because a folk criminal does not flaunt his violation.

Imputation of Personal Identity to Violators Enforcers have general knowledge of the community and specific knowledge of the violators and impute a positive personal identity—law-abiding, hard-working, environmentally knowledgeable—to members of the subculture who have not proven to be untrustworthy. Basically, because there is no negative effect, the wardens do not attribute evil motive or impute a negative personal identity to the violator. Information about violators in other contexts causes a halo effect in enforcer understanding of specific violations. Folk crimes constitute rule violations without being crimes. Thus the rule of law is thought to be inappropriate to guide enforcement behavior.

CONCLUSIONS

That accommodation occurs as part of some violations is crucial to the persistence of illegal behavior. It is this characteristic that differentiates folk crimes from other subjective crime categories. Nonlabeling by official agents of social control becomes, through the process of accommodation, tacit approval of illegal behavior performed by certain people under specific circumstances and thus perpetuates the system of violation.

The accommodation is in part a consequence of the perception of folk crime as qualitatively different from other violations of the same law. Thus one must look elsewhere—beyond life histories or social structure—to explain this form of deviance. Although life history may be important for predisposing individuals to behave and think in certain ways, behavior and thought do not occur in isolation. Rather, behavior is bilateral or interac-

[7]Attribution theory (Wyer and Carlston, 1979; Blum and McHugh, 1971), in which motive and personal identity are imputed in a retrospective manner, indicates the degree to which mutual interaction of independent variables works in real life.

tional; the causes of this behavior system lie in the complex interactions of actors, audience, and social context. The same kinds of interactional processes are involved whether the interaction results in deviance or conformity.

The existence of different subjective categories of the same violation of law points to the importance of a system model for delineating the particular elements involved in any pattern of behavior. That is, the task of determining what actually occurs is facilitated by isolating characteristics that discriminate one recurring event from other similar-appearing, recurring events.

When one looks at folk crime or other rule-violating behavior more representative of the deviance of most individuals than the usual focus of criminology, it is apparent that the actual explanation for behavior lies in the immediate circumstances surrounding the act. In their everyday behavior, humans are forced to make decisions. These decisions are based on interpretations of many factors: self-and-other social identity and resultant predictions of mutual expectations; appropriate presentation of self; general aspects of the definition of the situation; desired outcomes of the interaction. Each decision is reached through application of certain principles to the decision-making process. These rules in use become more important in determining behavior than the rules that are said to comprise the normative system.

REFERENCES

Birenbaum, A., and E. Sagarin
1976 Norms and Human Behavior. New York: Praeger.
Blum, A.F., and P. McHugh
1971 "The social ascription of motives." American Sociological Review 36:98–109.
Clark, J.P. and L.L. Tifft
1966 "Polygraph and interview validation of self-reported deviant behavior." American Sociological Review 31:516–523.
Clinard, M.B., and R. Quinney
1973 Criminal Behavior Systems: A Typology. New York: Holt, Rinehart, and Winston.
Garkinkel, H.
1967 Studies in Ethnomethodology, Englewood Cliffs, N.J.: Prentice Hall.
Goffman, E.
1963 Stigma. Englewood Cliffs, N.J.: Prentice-Hall.
1969 "On face work: An analysis of ritual elements in social interaction." Pp. 262–281 in A. Lindesmith and A. Strauss (eds.), Readings in Social Psychology. New York: Holt, Rinehart, and Winston.

Guenther, A.L.
1976 Criminal Behavior and Social Systems: Contributions of American Sociology. Chicago: Rand McNally.

Hartjen, C.A.
1972 "Police-citizen encounters: Social order in interpersonal interaction." Criminology 10:61–84.

Heiss, J.
1976 Family Roles and Interaction: An Anthology. Chicago: Rand McNally.

Hirschi, T.
1969 Causes of Delinquency. Berkeley: University of California Press.

Piliavin, I., and S. Briar
1964 "Police encounters with juveniles." American Journal of Sociology 70:206–214.

Quinney, R.
1970 The Social Reality of Crime. Boston: Little, Brown.

Ross, L.H.
1961 "Traffic law violation. A folk crime." Social Problems 8:231–241.

Sacks, H.
1972 "Notes on police assessment of moral character." Pp. 280–293 in D. Sudnow (ed.), Studies in Social Interaction. New York: Free Press.

Sykes, R.E.
1975 "A theory of deference exchange in police-civilian encounters." American Journal of Sociology 81:584–600.

Westley, W.A.
1970 Violence and the Police: A Sociological Study of Law, Custom, and Morality. Cambridge, Mass.: MIT Press.

Wilson, T.
1970 "Conceptions of interaction and forms of sociological explanation." American Sociological Review 31:516–523.

Wood, A.L.
1970 "Deviant Behavior and Control Strategies. Lexington, Mass.: Lexington Press.

Wyer, R.S., and D.E. Carlston
1979 Social Cognition, Inference and Attribution. New York: John Wiley.

Reading 29

Dynamics of the Deviant Sale

David F. Luckenbill
University of Illinois, Chicago

This paper examines the dynamics of male prostitution for purposes of identifying some of the principal characteristics of the deviant sale. The deviant sexual sale consists of seven stages, each involving an important task which the prostitute and customer accomplish together: the partners make contact, assess one another's suitability, agree to a sale, come to terms on the conditions of the sale, move to a protected setting, make the exchange, and terminate the affair. The sexual sale is compared with an ideal-typical model of the respectable sale in order to identify the generic features of the deviant sale. The deviant sale is relatively tenuous; the partners must attend to and deal with a wide range of matters that often are glossed over or taken for granted in respectable sales. The sale also is relatively dangerous; deviants face official sanctions and exploitation by their associates. To manage these risks, the partners rely on themselves, operating discreetly and taking special precautions. Some hypotheses on variation in the dynamics of deviant sales are developed.

In labeling theory, a major theme is that deviance is not an inherent feature of behavior, but rather a definition conferred upon behavior. This implies that deviant and respectable behavior are, in large part, analogous; only the attribution of a deviant label sets them apart. This analogy is questionable. When lawmakers declare a category of action "deviant," the declaration can affect the action's dynamics. For example, knowing they are involved in an act that runs some risk of being defined and sanctioned as deviance, actors may take special precautions in performing it. This paper explores the distinctiveness of deviant behavior. Specifically, it focuses on a form of behavior that can be either deviant or respectable—the sale—and examines the ways in which deviant and respectable sales differ and the consequences of these differences for the participants.

In contemporary America, the respectable sale is an institutionalized transaction, a formal, established economic operation (Blau, 1964: 93–97; Hartley, 1979: 28–34). To be sure, respectable sales vary considerably; they differ in scope, hence in amounts of promotion, negotiation, postsale contact, and the like (Kaven, 1971: 16–17). In spite of such variation, the respectable sale is a highly structured transaction. The participants have

I want to thank Harold E. Smith for his help in conducting the interviews. I also want to thank Joel Best, James T. Carey, Weldon T. Johnson, and Douglas Maynard for their instructive comments. This report is based on research supported by the Center for Research on Law and Justice, University of Illinois, Chicago.

little difficulty contacting one another; the customer's wants and the seller's promotion are clear; the sale's terms are fixed or subject to negotiation within established limits; and the order typically can be filled quickly and efficiently. Moreover, the sale is legitimate; norms governing the interaction between the seller and customer have evolved into a body of sales law, violations of which make the offending party eligible for legal sanctions (cf. Stockton, 1981). In the respectable sale, then, the participants perform customary roles regulated by formal rules that are enforced by authorities.

The deviant sale is a transaction in which a customer buys an illicit good or service from a seller (Best and Luckenbill, 1982: 131–56). There has been a fair amount of research on deviant sales, including studies of fencing (Klockars, 1975; Walsh, 1977), drug dealing (Carey, 1968; Moore, 1977: 5–61; Winick and Kinsie, 1971), male prostitution (Pittman, 1971; Reiss, 1961), criminal abortion (Ball, 1967; Manning, 1978), gambling (Hindelang, 1971; Lesieur, 1977), and some forms of bribery (Stoddard, 1968). These studies, however, suffer from one or two drawbacks which preclude a sound understanding of the differences between deviant and respectable sales. First, they fail to delineate the transaction's dynamics. Researchers often focus on specific aspects of the sale, like the customer's acquisition of information about the market and the seller's evaluation of the customer's integrity. They do not examine the dynamics of the entire transaction—the manner in which the participants come together, carry out the exchange, and depart. Second, they fail to articulate the generic features of the deviant sale. Researchers often limit their attention to a particular sale; they do not produce a model transcending specific instances.

This paper seeks to identify some of the principal characteristics of the deviant sale. It delineates the dynamics of a particular deviant sale—male homosexual prostitution.[1] Then it compares this sexual sale with the respectable sale, revealing some basic differences between them and hence some of the distinctive features of the deviant sale. Finally, it employs prostitution as a resource in developing several hypotheses on variation in the dynamics of deviant sales.

[1]There is a growing body of literature on male prostitution. For the most part, researchers have examined the causes of male prostitution, the types of male prostitutes, their sexual identification, and the means for treating them (Allen, 1980; Butts, 1947; Coombs, 1974; Deisher, Eisner, and Sulzbacher, 1969; Ginsburg, 1967; Harris, 1973; Hoffman, 1972; Lloyd, 1976; MacNamara, 1965; Reiss, 1961; Ross, 1959). Researchers have given little attention to the dynamics of the sexual sale. An exception is Reiss (1961); yet his investigation focused only on aspects of the sale, such as how the prostitute and customer meet.

SAMPLE AND METHOD

The data derives from in-depth, relatively open-ended interviews with 25 male prostitutes in Chicago. While this sample probably is not representative, as it does not include any adolescents, it is diverse. The subjects range from 18 to 34 years of age. Two are Hispanic, three are black, and the rest are white. Three have fathers who hold white-collar positions, six have fathers who are unemployed, and the remainder have fathers in blue-collar occupations. Eighteen subjects dropped out of school, but seven completed high school, and three of these finished several years of college. While eight subjects were raised in the Chicago area, the rest grew up elsewhere. Two recently entered the life, nineteen have been involved for at least two years, and six recently quit after careers extending over several years. Whereas nine subjects hustle part-time, sixteen hustle (or hustled) full-time.

The subjects were not incarcerated at the time of interviewing; most were involved in vice. As a consequence, finding and interviewing subjects was difficult. They were leery of outsiders and did not like to spend time talking when they could be hustling. The subjects were contacted through a graduate student whose extensive research contacts with the gay community earned him a reputation as a trustworthy person. He located each subject, and he helped to carry out each interview.[2] The process of contacting and interviewing subjects spanned 26 months.

Each interview covered a variety of issues pertaining to prostitution. Some questions concerned the dynamics of the typical sale—the setting of initial contact, how the hustler and customer meet, the manner in which they agree to the sale, the kinds of problems they face, the ways in which they manage these problems, and so on. Interviews ranged from 45 to 90 minutes, and some subjects were interviewed on more than one occasion. All of the interviews were recorded on tape.

A qualification is in order. Data on the sexual sale flow entirely from prostitutes' observations. Since prostitutes may provide inaccurate descriptions of the sale, one would do well to interview customers about it. Unfortunately, customers were difficult to locate, and persons who admitted to paying for sexual services would not agree to be interviewed. As a consequence, this study relies on prostitutes' observations. They not only described their own orientations toward and roles in the sale, but they also drew on their conversations with customers in describing customers' orientations and roles. Thus, the following analysis employs prostitutes' observations in speaking about the views and activities of both partners.

[2]Only four prostitutes who were approached for an interview refused to participate in the study.

DEVIANT SEXUAL SALES

For analytic purposes, the deviant sexual sale is divided into seven time-ordered stages, each involving an important task which the prostitute and customer accomplish together: (1) the partners make contact; (2) each assesses the other's suitability as a partner; (3) they agree to participate in a sexual sale; (4) they come to terms; (5) they choose and move to an appropriate setting; (6) they perform the exchange; and (7) they terminate the transaction. Each stage will be examined in turn.

Before considering the dynamics of the sale, it should be noted that these transactions often involve strangers. There are several reasons for this. Customers want variety; they look for partners who can provide new, pleasurable experiences. As Jim[3] pointed out:

> Johns [customers] see you out there every day on the same corner, they don't want to deal with you. They're always looking for a new face in town. A new face always makes out . . . If he's a new face, the first couple of days he's going to make money.

This attitude encourages fleeting relationships between strangers. Also, hustlers work in cities with large gay communities, hence large numbers of potential customers, and this makes exchanges between strangers relatively common. Finally, many prostitutes are geographically mobile, making long, stable relationships difficult. In summer, they work the northern cities, like Chicago and New York; in winter, they move south to such cities as Miami, New Orleans, and Los Angeles.

Making Contact

There are numerous settings in which prostitutes and customers make contact, including gay bars, streetcorners, parks, bus stations, gay baths, and pornographic bookstores. Many, if not most, contacts are made in bar and street settings, and these two situations will serve as the basis for this analysis.[4]

In male prostitution, the customer ordinarily seeks out the hustler. This search can be rather difficult, particularly for those who have little experience with prostitutes and little contact with the gay community. Since the deviant sale is subject to social control sanctions, hustlers cannot afford to frequent an area for any length of time or advertise their locations. As a

[3]All names are pseudonyms.

[4]The partners also may meet at the customer's residence, through the mediation of an escort service. The customer locates the service through its advertisements in specialized media or through peers who have used the service. He phones the agency and requests a "date," often specifying the length of time for the affair and the activities he would like to perform with his

consequence, customers need special geographic knowledge to locate hustlers. In general, the customer learns, through his own observations or a peer network, where hustlers work, and he goes there to make contact. Once in the appropriate setting, the customer inspects its inhabitants, trying to identify a hustler. In turn, the prostitute offers cues of his deviant status, so that a customer can recognize him. Thus, street hustlers wear provocative clothing and adopt a stance suggesting sexual prowess. While most passers-by may assume the prostitute is respectable, the knowledgeable customer sees him as a possible partner.

Once a prospective prostitute is located, the customer must determine whether he is available. Availability is determined in a subtle and indirect manner. The customer "cruises" the hustler; he drives or walks by several times or sits at the bar and watches the prostitute. He checks whether the hustler is attached to someone else or occupied by a main involvement. At the same time, the hustler demonstrates his availability. He attempts to appear uninvolved, or he engages in a side involvement, like pitching coins or nursing a drink. He also tries to appear unattached. On the street, he shuns interaction with other hustlers or keeps such contacts short. In the bar, he sits by himself, steering clear of other prostitutes. Rod claimed:

> I'm the kind of person who likes the people to come up to me, instead of having to go to them. If the dude (customer) sees you with somebody, he's going to think you're with him, and he won't come up to you. So I want to be by myself.

In the course of cruising, the customer and hustler make eye contact. The prostitute takes sustained eye contact as a sign of interest; Joe argued, "My eyes may meet with someone and that's generally the signal there. If they look at you long enough, obviously they have a bit of interest." The customer interprets sustained eye contact as a sign of availability.

After deciding the prospective prostitute is available, the customer approaches him and initiates casual conversation. Through conversation, each partner confirms the other's genuine interest in him. The customer

date. Working from a fee schedule, the service quotes the price for the date. If the customer accepts, the agency may ask him a number of questions oriented toward screening troublesome customers. Satisfied that the customer is not working for the police or potentially exploitative, the agency contacts a hustler and asks him to take the job. If the prostitute accepts, the service provides him with the relevant information—the length of the date, the activities to be performed, the time and place of the contact, and so on. The hustler then contacts the customer at his residence.

It is hard to know what proportion of all sexual sales are arranged through escort services. But the subjects of this study argued that most sexual sales are arranged in street and bar settings. This is so, in large part, because most customers cannot afford escort prostitutes. Therefore, this study focuses on sales arranged in streets and bars.

shows his interest by opening the conversation with a sociable query, e.g., "How're you doing," "What's your name," or "Can I buy you a drink," or an observation about the hustler's attractiveness or provocative appearance, e.g., "That looks like a nice tooter you got in there." The prostitute's response is critical. If he ignores the customer, says he is with someone or otherwise indisposed, responds tersely, or takes offense, then he shows disinterest and dashes the customer's hopes. However, if he responds in an attentive, encouraging manner—answering the question and posing another, accepting the drink, and the like—he demonstrates interest and completes the foundation for the subsequent discussion of an exchange.

Assessing Suitability

After making contact, each partner assesses the other's suitability. A suitable partner is one who is trustworthy, who will make the exchange rewarding. The sexual sale carries special risks. One partner can exploit the other—cheating, blackmailing, or injuring him—and the victim cannot turn to the authorities for assistance. Or one can betray the other to the police, or one can be an undercover agent. Given these risks, trust becomes a major concern; each partner wants to be sure that the other is what he claims to be and will abide by the terms of an agreement.

In prostitution, casual conversation provides an opportunity to assess prospective partners and screen those who appear untrustworthy. On the one hand, the customer evaluates the prostitute. He may consider the hustler's temperament, rejecting those judged too aggressive or passive, forward or shy, vulgar or refined, and so forth. He also may ask the prostitute about matters of concern. For example, Mike observed, "A lot of times, they'll come right out and ask you, 'You wouldn't be a policeman, would you?'" On the other hand, the prostitute may use one or more methods to evaluate the customer's suitability. First, the hustler may attend to features of the customer and his behavior that bear on suitability; these cues differ from one prostitute to another, depending on personal experience and preferences. In assessing the customer's capacity to pay, some prostitutes look at his clothing, while others observe the way in which he spends money. To learn whether the customer will be abusive, some hustlers attend to his tone of conversation; Dennis, for instance, considers "very quiet, very timid and shy people" to be safe. Others look at the customer's mental or physical condition; Bob screens the intoxicated because "they're unpredictable." In deciding whether the customer is an undercover agent, prostitutes watch his ease of interaction; Ray said that he can spot an undercover agent by the man's halting, uneasy behavior during conversation. Second, the hustler may ask the customer about matters of concern. For example, hustlers may ask, "What are you into?" If the customer indicates a preference for sadomasochism, many will reject him, as they believe that sadomasochism can lead to abuse. If the customer seems uneasy, the prostitute may ask, "Are you a police officer?" An officer must say so, or the sale involves entrapment. Third, the hustler may act in ways which test the customer's suitability. For instance, Marty tries to kiss a suspicious customer; the response is important—"a cop's not going to let you kiss him."

The prospective partners also can assess one another through a third party who has dealt with the other person. On the street, the hustler or the customer may ask a familiar hustler whether the prospective partner is an informant or undercover agent, whether he has a history of cheating his partners, whether he engages in dangerous sexual activities, and the like. In bars, the bartender ordinarily serves as a third party. In addition to answering specific questions that one partner raises about the other, the bartender performs a broad screening function, refusing to admit hustlers and customers believed to be untrustworthy. As Tom pointed out, "If they thought I was a thief, they wouldn't let me in the bar." Or the bartender may spread the word among the bar's patrons that a particular person is of questionable character.

In male prostitution, trust is problematic. Because the sale carries special risks, and because the partners cannot turn to the authorities for help, each partner seeks to determine whether the other is what he claims to be and will honor an agreement. Once each partner decides the other is suitable, they turn their attention to the sale.

Agreeing to a Sale

Casual conversation provides the base from which the participants can transform their relationship, dropping their pretense of purely sociable interaction and agreeing to a sale. Actually, they make two agreements: they agree to participate in a sexual sale; and they agree on the sale's terms.

The partners first agree to participate in a sale. Either person may bring up the sale. In some cases, the prostitute suggests it. In general, this suggestion is made in oblique terms—"What do you have planned right now," "Would you like some company tonight," or "Why don't we get together?" The customer accepts, stating that he is looking for a good time, would like some company, and so on. In most cases, the customer broaches the sale. The proposal may be direct—"Are you working" or "You looking to make some money?"—or, more often, circuitous—'What's happening tonight," "What are your plans," or "What are you doing now?" The hustler responds favorably—"I'm out for a good time" or "I'm looking to make some money."

Two aspects of this conversation should be noted. First, the partners ordinarily use equivocal language in reaching agreement; their remarks can convey both respectable and deviant intentions. Consider, for example, a typical conversation described by Eddie. The customer asks, "What are you doing right now?" Eddie answers, "I'm looking for somebody that's looking for a good time and wants to spend some money." A "good time" is a euphemism for sex, but it is ambiguous enough to refer to more innocuous activities, like drinking. Similarly, one could "spend some money" for drinks or sex. Equivocal language is a precaution against being arrested for solicitation.

Second, the prostitute must make it clear that they will engage in a sale, not a trade. Misunderstanding is not uncommon, as Eddie indicated:

> I think it's wrong for a hustler to disillusion somebody by leading him on. I seen it happen. A hustler picks up a guy, makes small talk with him, goes ahead and goes to bed with him, then turns around and tells him, "You owe me $40 or $50." And the guy says, "You never mentioned no money." So there's conflict, and a fight.

Equivocal language can lead to misunderstanding. Because the hustler does not explicitly frame the exchange as a sale, it is possible for his partner to interpret it as a trade. The setting where the agreement is made also can lead to misunderstanding. Gay bars, like some street settings, have served traditionally as a sexual marketplace where persons could meet and arrange fleeting sexual trades (Achilles, 1967). Therefore, the hustler must make it clear that he expects payment, not mere sexual satisfaction. But this is not accomplished directly. As Dennis maintained, "You never say you're a hustler. You never say, 'Well, I won't go to bed with you unless you pay me.'" Rather, the hustler makes this point by casually telling the customer that he is trying to make some money, e.g., "I'm trying to get some money for my rent" or, simply, "I'm looking to make some money."

Coming to Terms

After agreeing to a sale, the participants agree on the terms of the sale. Usually, they are concerned with at least two matters: the hustler's sexual services and the customer's payment. Male prostitution displays some feature of the classic bargaining situation (cf. Rubin and Brown, 1975). The partners have somewhat conflicting interests: the customer prefers to pay as little as possible for sex, while the prostitute prefers to maximize earnings with minimal sexual involvement. Still, their interests often are compatible enough for them to reach mutually beneficial terms, where each profits enough to make an exchange worthwhile. They arrive at this solution through discussion and negotiation.

The structure of the discussion varies. In some cases, the prostitute proposes the terms. The customer asks the hustler to state his terms—"How much," "What do you do," or "What are you into?"—and the hustler states his fee and perhaps his services. The customer accepts the terms or makes a counterproposal, asking for a reduced price or other sexual services. In most cases, however, the customer proposes the terms, specifying the price and possibly the services. He may open with a direct offer, e.g., "I'll give you $30 for an hour," or he may propose the terms after asking the hustler how much he wants and being told to make an offer. The prostitute accepts or makes a counterproposal, requesting more money or different services.

In either case, the prostitute normally decides the sales terms. If the hustler finds the customer's proposal or counterproposal agreeable, he accepts. However, if he makes an offer or counteroffer which the customer rejects or counters, the hustler typically will not adjust his terms. Rick, like many hustlers, usually refuses to accept less than his going rate—"I tell them I think I'm worth it." Consequently, the customer either accepts the hustler's terms or withdraws.

The prostitute generally wants the customer to propose the terms for strategic reasons. The customer may offer more than the hustler would be willing to accept. But if the prostitute makes the proposal, the customer may look for a less expensive partner. John observed:

> You are more or less in a bidding market. This man may just be out to get a hustler that night. He may not be particular on who. And you sit there and say $35, and he can go down the bar and get somebody for $25. He's going to get the best deal he can.

Another reason for wanting the customer to propose the sale's terms is to screen undercover officers. If the customer makes the proposal, the hustler can avoid arrest for solicitation.

Prices for sexual services vary, and they depend on the prostitute's experience and preferences and immediate situational conditions. Hustlers have flexible price schedules[5] For example, Joe charges between $20—30 for a brief exchange and $75–100 for an entire night; Don charges $35–45 for a short exchange, $100-200 for an evening. The prostitute's price range is shaped by his personal history, other hustlers, and the market. His first trick typically establishes a lower price limit. In the first trick the hustler is naive; not knowing what to charge, he accepts whatever amount the customer offers. For a time, the newcomer continues to charge what he earned in his first sale. As he associates with other hustlers, he learns what they charge, often for different services and lengths of time. In turn, he raises his

[5]While hustlers seem to vary in their price ranges, Deisher, Eisner, and Sulzbacher (1969) warn that hustlers typically exaggerate their fees as well as their overall income.

lower limit as long as customers are willing to meet it; if he fails to get customers at this price, he will lower it.

The fee in a particular case depends on several conditions, including the services performed, amount of time involved, customer's prosperity and attractiveness, and prostitute's economic circumstances. In general, the more conventional and personally acceptable the service, the lower the fee.[6] Thus, hustlers normally charge less for fellatio than for degradation; Ray argued, "Some guys want you to piss on them, shit on them, stuff like that. Stuff like that to me is gross, and if they want me to do it, they got to pay!" The less time invested in the transaction, the lower the price. The customer who wants the prostitute to spend the night is charged two or three times what a short exchange costs. The greater the perceived prosperity of the customer—shown by his dress, spending patterns, and so on—the higher the price. Bill maintained, "If I meet a guy and he's flashy, automatically the price is doubled." Similarly, Jim said, "If the guy looks like he's got money, obviously you're going to come off with $35 and start at $50." But the hustler may lower his fee for an attractive customer. Marty said that he ordinarily will not accept less than $35; but if an attractive customer can afford only $20, he will take it. Finally, the prostitute's financial need influences the price. After a good day with several sales, the hustler will not accept less than his customary lower limit. But if he needs money, he will take less. Jaime maintained, "I stick to my price 90% of the time, unless I'm hurting, hurting real bad." Similarly, Mike argued:

> I'll start off at $40. A lot of times he'll say, "Well, that's a little too steep. How about $30?" Or, "How about $25?" Depending on whether I've turned another trick yet, or if I'm short, I'll take it.

Moving to a Suitable Setting

After coming to terms, the partners choose a setting for the exchange and move to it. Both participants determine the setting. The prostitute or the customer suggests a place and the other either approves or recommends another place. Settings for sex include the customer's residence as well as hotel rooms, parked cards, gay baths, and viewing rooms in pornographic bookstores. But most hustlers do not use their own residences because of the possible consequences. The hustler's neighbors may discover his illicit involvement and complain, leading to his eviction or even arrest.

Two conditions influence the choice of setting. First, the partners prefer places which afford protection against interference by social control agents and observation by other hustlers. Obviously, the participants do not

[6]Most hustlers find certain sexual services (e.g., sadomasochism and degradation) intolerable, and they usually refuse to perform them.

want to be a public spectacle. Furthermore, the hustler may not want his colleagues to know what sexual activities he performs. Many prostitutes claimed that they do not engage in sexual activities which their colleagues deem unacceptable; among some hustler's for example, it is unacceptable to be the recipient of anal intercourse. As discussed below, hustlers do not always abide by such norms. By performing in private places, the hustler's colleagues cannot know whether he engages in objectionable activities. A second condition shaping the choice of setting is the length of the affair. For a lengthy exchange, the partners often select the customer's residence; for a brief exchange, they select a more proximate setting, such as a hotel room. Once they agree on a suitable setting, they move to it.

Making the Exchange

After they reach the setting, the partners carry out their exchange, transferring the money and engaging in sexual relations. These tasks are problematic, requiring personal regulation.

Consider first the transfer of money. Many prostitutes collect "up front," prior to having sex. For instance, as they are about to undress, Jim asks the customer to set the money on the table or dresser, "so I know it's ok"; as they undress, he casually slips the cash into his pocket. By collecting up front, the hustler is assured that the customer has the money and avoids a later quarrel or fight. However, some hustlers collect after sexual relations. Carlos prefers this practice, as it puts the customer at ease; if Carlos were to collect up front, the customer may fear that he is about to be cheated, paying without receiving sexual services. Still other prostitutes fluctuate between the two methods, depending on the customer. Rick usually collects afterward, but "If they look like they're not going to pay, I'll ask for it up front."

The partners do not always engage in the sexual activities to which they agreed. On the one hand, some prostitutes provide fewer sexual activities than they agreed to perform. For example, Tom terminates the transaction after the customer reaches orgasm, even when he agreed to participate in various sexual activities over the course of an evening. On the other hand, some hustlers provide services in addition to those they agreed to perform. Most prostitutes argued that they refrain from activities which their colleagues disapprove, such as serving as the recipient in anal intercourse, and, when discussing terms, inform customers that they will not engage in such acts. Yet some confessed that they occasionally depart from these terms once they are in bed. Bob and Rich, among others, admitted that they let themselves go, doing what the customer requests and they find pleasant and safe. Thus, where some hustlers, like George, maintain that "You only give what you're paid to give," others deviate, giving more or less than agreed.

In prostitution, the partners can exploit one another. The customer knows that some hustlers are "ripoff hustlers," who cheat, rob, or injure customers, and the hustler knows, usually through personal experience, that some customers refuse to pay and others are abusive, wanting to rob or harm prostitutes. The partners cannot turn to the authorities for protection; they must protect themselves. During sexual relations, the prostitute and customer do not drop their guard and fully relax; each monitors the other, looking for signs of impending exploitation. As David indicated:

> I watch them, eyes on them all the time. It's very frightening sometimes, getting into bed with somebody you don't know. You always have the idea that they might hurt you or something like that. So you have to watch them.

Also, each participant may devise techniques for preventing or coping with exploitation. The hustler uses any of several protective techniques. He may collect up front to avoid being cheated. To prevent abuse, the hustler may avoid sexual positions that leave him open to attack. A major reason many hustlers refuse to engage in bondage is that it makes them vulnerable. Marty argued, "Never put yourself in a situation where you give the customer the automatic advantage over you, the automatic physical advantage. That's letting yourself be tied up or locked." The prostitute may carry a weapon (typically a knife) and, in the event of attack, use it. The hustler who collects after sex must contend with refusals to pay. One response is to cause a "scene" in hopes that the customer will pay so as to avoid drawing attention to his illicit involvement. Rick claimed, "Before I leave the hotel, I'm going to get the money . . . I know if they say, 'No, I ain't going to give you the money,' I'm going to throw a fit and break a few lamps or something." Another technique is to threaten to inform other hustlers and bartenders about the customer's dishonesty; the hustler warns the man that he will be ostracized from the sexual marketplace if he does not pay. As a last resort, the prostitute may use force. Some hustlers carry weapons not only to defend themselves but also to exact payment from difficult customers.

Terminating the Sale

After sexual relations, the participants terminate the sale. This can be rather awkward; it is hard to know what to say or how to express one's thoughts after sex. The partners may indicate their satisfaction or, more likely, remain silent. Generally, the customer returns the hustler to the street, bar, or some other place designated by the hustler. And, assuming the transaction was profitable, the prostitute expresses his hopes for a future relationship with the customer. George noted, "If you're a hustler, you definitely try to make your business as repetitive as possible." While the organization of the marketplace works against repeat business, hustlers prefer steady customers because steadies pose fewer risks. Thus, it is not surprising that prostitutes often give good customers their phone numbers and urge them to call.

DISCUSSION

Comparing the deviant sexual sale with an ideal-typical model of respectable sale, several differences appear, and these suggest some generic features of the deviant sale. The respectable sale is a highly structured transaction. The partners perform established, relatively customary roles that are governed by formal rules. Their interaction is not problematic: the participants recognize that they have come together to engage in a sale and easily adopt their respective roles; the terms of their exchange are fixed or negotiable within established limits; and so forth. In contrast, the deviant sale is not highly structured. Through interaction, the participants establish that one will act as the seller, the second as the customer. Many aspects of the transaction, including the sexual services to be rendered, the price of those services, the time of payment, the place for having sex, and the length of the exchange, are problematic, requiring discussion and negotiation. The partners may not follow their arrangements; they may alter some terms during the event, performing different activities, devoting more or less time to the exchange, and so on.

The respectable sale is legitimate, protected by law; partners who do not fulfill their obligations are subject to official sanctioning. However, the deviant sexual sale is illegitimate. The partners are not only subject to social control sanctions, but they also cannot turn to the authorities when cheated or injured. Because a victimized participant cannot turn to officials for assistance, the other may have few qualms over exploiting him. The illegitimacy of the sexual sale has additional consequences. The deviant market is concealed; prospective partners require special knowledge to make contact. Each partner knows the other may be an undercover agent or someone who will betray him to the authorities. To protect themselves, the partners use equivocal language in agreeing to a sale. They also assess one another's suitability. Each wants assurance that the other is trustworthy—someone who is what he claims to be and will honor the terms of an agreement. Trust is established through personal effort. The partners spend time in casual conversation, not simply to socialize but to evaluate one another, and they may check the other's identity and integrity with a third party. Even when the other appears trustworthy, each partner takes added precautions, like avoiding vulnerable positions and carrying a weapon. Finally, they choose a safe, protected setting for the exchange.

This comparison suggests several features of the deviant sale. First, because it is not highly structured, the deviant sale is relatively tenuous. The partners need to locate the deviant market, reach agreement on a variety of issues, and perhaps revise some terms over the course of the transaction. Second, because the deviant sale is illegitimate, it is relatively dangerous, requiring personal control. The partners are subject to formal sanctioning and, because officials do not enforce deviants' agreements, a greater chance of exploitation. Given these risks, trust and caution are major concerns. These basic features are evident in male prostitution, but they also appear characteristic of such other deviant sales as female prostitution (Prus and Irini, 1980; Winick and Kinsie, 1971), drug dealing (Carey, 1968; Redlinger, 1975), and fencing (Klockars, 1975).

Clearly, deviant sales are not equally tenuous and dangerous and thus do not share the same basic dynamics. Some variance may be accounted for in terms of the partners' experience with the sale. Newcomers are naive; they may spend considerable time discussing terms, take sizable risks, and so forth. Experienced partners have developed a body of knowledge and skill that enables them to carry out the sale with greater ease and fewer risks. Further variance may be explained in terms of the degree to which the seller is related to a larger distributive organization. When the seller is linked to a larger organization, the sale is less tenuous, subject to some outside control. For instance, the sale's terms—the goods and services available, their cost, the setting for the exchange, and so on—are shaped by suppliers and supervisors. The retail drug dealer's goods and prices are influenced by the wholesaler (Moore, 1977: 47–59), the brothel prositute's basic fees are set by the madam (Heyl, 1979), and the numbers runner's operations are directed by those who run the game. Consequently, when the seller is linked to a distributive organization, bargaining between the seller and customer is somewhat limited. But when the seller operates purely as an independent entrepreneur, the sale is largely unbridled. The sale's terms are negotiable within limits established by the partners, and these limits are variable and possibly substantial. Male prostitutes have been regarded as "one of the last remnants of laissez faire" (Harris, 1973: 45). Because hustlers sell services, they need not rely on others for saleable goods, and because they do not have managers (except for those who work in escort agencies), their terms are shaped by personal taste, need, and the like. This study of the sexual sale suggests that additional variance may be explained in terms of the setting of initial contact and prior relationship between the partners. By examining the effects of setting and prior relationship, some hypotheses on variation in the dynamics of deviant sales can be developed.

The setting of initial contact affects the dynamics of the deviant sale. Sexual sales arranged in the streets and bars differ in two ways. First, they differ in length of casual interaction preceding the agreement to a sale. In street hustling, casual interaction often lasts no more than a minute or two;

in bar hustling, it lasts from 15 to 45 minutes. The street setting precludes lengthy interaction; because street contacts are visible to the authorities, the partners want to keep their initial interaction brief. In contrast, the bar is a sociable setting which also shields patrons' contacts from public view. Second, street and bar settings differ in the degree to which the partners can assess each other's suitability. In street hustling, the partners have little time to assess one another and establish trust. In bar hustling, the partners have more time for evaluation and the development of trust. These differences between street hustlers related far more instances of arrest and customer exploitation than bar hustlers. From this analysis, it can be hypothesized that the less public the setting in which the seller and customer make contact, the greater the length of casual interaction between and the more effective the screening of prospective partners, and the lower the risks of arrest and exploitation.

The relationship between the partners also affects the dynamics of the deviant sale. Although most acts of prostitution involve strangers, many hustlers cultivate some regular customers. An exchange between a prostitute and regular customer differs from one between strangers. The partners have little trouble locating each other; they know where to find one another or they have one another's phone number. They dispense with the probing that ordinarily precedes the agreement to a sale. Their casual conversation is genuine, not a means for determining trustworthiness. Often, they do not discuss the terms of the sale, for each knows what the other expects. The hustler is willing to take the customer to his residence. Sexual relations are more relaxed. The prostitute may be willing to perform a wider variety of sexual services. And the hustler generally collects after sexual relations. Many of these differences derive from the problem of trust. In transactions between strangers, trust is tentative. Since the partners do not know one another, they probe to learn about each other and use caution in carrying out the transaction. However, when the partners share a history of mutually rewarding exchanges, trust is not as problematic; the transaction enjoys a measure of certainty and safety. On the basis of this analysis, it can be hypothesized that when the seller and customer are related by a history of profitable transactions, the greater the trust they have in one another and the greater the ease in accomplishing the sale.

CONCLUSION

This study of the deviant sale suggests that deviant and respectable behavior are very different. Deviant behavior is not highly structured and hence is relatively tenuous; deviants must attend to and deal with a wide range of matters that often are glossed over or taken for granted in many respectable activities. In addition, deviant behavior is illegitimate and hence relatively dangerous; deviants are subject to official sanctions and, because they cannot rely on the authorities for protection, a greater chance of exploitation. To manage these risks, deviants must depend on themselves, operating discreetly and taking special precautions. Therefore, declaring an activity deviant is consequential for the activity and its participants, reflected in the differences between deviant and respectable sales.

REFERENCES

Achilles, Nancy
1967 "The Development of the Homosexual Bar as an Institution." Pp. 228-244 in J. Gagnon and W. Simon, Sexual Deviance New York: Harper & Row.

Allen, Donald M.
1980 "Young Male Prostitutes." Archives of Sexual Behavior 9: 399-426.

Ball, Donald
1967 "An Abortion Clinic Ethnography." Social Problems 14: 293-301.

Best, Joel and David F. Luckenbill
1982 "Organizing Deviance. Englewood Cliffs, N.J.: Prentice-Hall.

Blau, Peter M.
1964 Exchange and Power in Social Life. New York: Wiley.

Bryan,James H.
1965 "Apprenticeships in Prostitution." Social Problems 12: 287-97.

Butts, William H.
1947 "Boy Prostitutes of the Metropolis." Journal of Clinical Psychopathology 8: 673-81.

Carey, James T.
1968 The College Drug Scene. Englewood Cliffs, N.J.: Prentice-Hall.

Coombs,Neil R.
1974 "Male Prostitution." American Journal of Orthopsychiatry 44: 782-89.

Deisher, Robert W., Victor Eisner, and Stephan I. Sulzbacher
1969 "The Young Male Prostitute." Pediatrics 43: 936-41.

Ginsburg, Kenneth N.
1967 "The 'Meat Rack.'" American Journal of Psychotherapy 2: 170-85.

Harris, Mervyn
1973 The Dilly Boys. Rockville, Md.: New Perspective.

Hartley, Robert F.
1979 Sales Management. Boston: Houghton Mifflin.

Heyl, Barbara Sherman
1979 The Madam as Entrepreneur. New Brunswick, N.J.: Transaction

Hindelang, Michael J.
1971 "Bookies and Bookmaking." Crime and Delinquency 17: 245-55.

Hoffman, Martin
1972 "The Male Prostitute." Sexual Behavior 2: 16-21.

Kaven, William H.
1971 Managing the Major Sale. New York: American Management Association.
Klockars, Carl B.
1975 The Professional Fence. New York: Free Press.
Lesieur, Henry R.
1977 The Chase. Garden City, N.Y.: Anchor.
Lloyd, Robin
1976 For Money or Love. New York: Vanguard.
MacNamara, Donald E.J.
1965 "Male Prostitution in American Cities." American Journal of Arthopsychiatry 25: 204.
Manning, Peter K.
1978 "Aspects of the Campus Abortion Search." Pp. 85–106 in J. Henslin and E. Sagarin, The Sociology of Sex. New York: Schocken.
Moore, Mark h.
1977 Buy and Bust. Lexington, Mass.: Lexington
Pittman, David J.
1971 "The Male House of Prostitution." Transaction 8: 21–27.
Prus, Robert and Styllianoss Irini
1980 Hookers, Rounders, and Desk Clerks. Toronto: Gage.
Redlinger, Lawrence J.
1975 "Marketing and Distributing Heroin." Journal of Psychedelic Drugs 7: 331–53.
1982 "Informational Uncertainty and the Structure of Illicit Markets." Paper presented at the annual meeting of the American Sociological Association, San Francisco.
Reiss, Albert J., Jr.
1961 "The Social Integration of Peers and Queers." Social Problems 9: 102–20.
Ross, H. Laurence
1959 "The 'Hustler' in Chicago." Journal of Student Research 1: 13–19.
Rubin, Jeffrey Z., and Bert R. Brown
1975 The Social Psychology of Bargaining and Negotiation. New York: Academic Press.
Stockton, John M.
1981 Sales, second edition. St. Paul: West
Stoddard, Ellwyn R.
1968 "'The Informal Code' of Police Deviancy." Journal of Criminal Law, Criminology, and Police Science 59: 201–13.
Walsh, Marilyn E.
1977 The Fence. Westport, Conn. Greenwood.
Winick, Charles, and Paul M. Kinsie
1971 The Lively Commerce. Chicago: Quadrangle.

Reading 30

Abuse and Aggression in Courting Couples

Mary Riege Laner
and Jeanine Thompson
Arizona State University, Tempe

Challenging Gelles' (1972) assertion that violence between intimates is likely to occur only within a family context, more than 60% of a sample of 371 single respondents reported having experienced abusive or aggressive behaviors or having inflicted them during courtship. Theoretical considerations and empirical consistencies derived from the marital violence literature supported hypothesized relationships between more serious courting relationships and violence and between experienced childhood violence and the occurrence of violence in courtship. A hypothesized relationship between social class and violence in courtship was not supported, however. A conflict theory framework and propositions extracted from choice and exchange theory explain these findings. The extent of courtship violence documented here is in all probability an underestimate of its actual occurrence.

A decade ago, research on husband-wife violence was characterized as having received "selective inattention" (see Gelles, 1972). Today, premarital (or courtship) violence is another relatively unstudied phenomenon. Although sexual aggression in courtship has been investigated (see Ehrmann, 1964; Kanin, 1957, 1967a, 1967b; Kirkpatrick and Kanin, 1957), other types of premarital aggression or abuse have not inspired comparable interest. Only one researcher has published on this topic; James Makepeace's groundbreaking paper appeared early in 1981.

Courtship has been called the founding of the family system (Broderick and Smith, 1979). Yet, as Makepeace (1981) points out, "instead of focusing on the premarital period as one of socialization to spousal violence . . . researchers consistently have focused . . . on a link with violence in the family of orientation" (p. 97).[1]

Makepeace's exploratory study estimated the incidence of courtship violence in an opportunity sample of freshman and sophomore college students. Various forms of violence were described, basic social correlates

This is a revised version of a paper presented at the Western Social Science Association Meetings, San Diego, California, April 1981.

[1]Indeed, since the 1960s sparse attention has been paid to any aspect of courtship. It has been virtually excluded from current efforts to develop family theory. Burr, Hill, Nye, and Reiss (1979) include only one indexed reference to courtship. Murstein (1980) has made a point of the reduced interest in mate selection processes during the 1970s.

of premarital violence were identified, and data were obtained on relationship outcomes following violent courtship episodes, among other details. Although his study was descriptive (atheoretical) and although the size of his sample precluded meaningful statistical tests on some of his findings, Makepeace asserts that violent behaviors appear to be a common aspect of premarital heterosexual interaction. He suggests the existence of a major hidden social problem:

> If our results are typical of college students in general, more than one student in five has had direct personal experience in courtship violence. . . . Although the percentages of students who have experienced the more serious forms of violence may seem small, . . . if the 4% incidence of assault with closed fists is typical, then 800 of the students on a 20,000 student campus would have experienced this form of violence (1981:100).

Neither the popular nor the scholarly literature regarding courtship has recognized such a problem, although the competitive nature of courtship, its stresses, and its potential for interpersonal exploitation are well known. Makepeace recommended further research to confirm the extent of abuse and aggression that he found.

The present study was undertaken, in part, to assess the generalizability of Makepeace's findings to a similar sample. In addition, the present study tests hypotheses about premarital violence derived from the theoretical and empirical literature on interspousal conflict.

THEORETICAL CONSIDERATIONS

Theoretically, certain relationships have greater subjective worth than others, varying by their degree of exclusiveness (Sprey, 1979). According to Sprey, the dyadic love relationship is the preeminent intimate bond, and marriage is the dyadic system in which the intimate heterosexual bond is institutionalized. Students of family violence consider marriage a unique and very complex relationship in which the roots of power abuse and violence are to be discovered. Gelles and Straus (1979) identify the purportedly unique characteristics of family life that, they believe, make the family a violence-prone interaction setting (see also Gelles, 1979; Straus and Hotaling, 1980). Their list of characteristics reveals a number of similarities between marriage and courtship, especially at its more meaningful or serious (committed, intimate) levels.

Courting couples of the more serious variety share at least the following characteristics with married pairs, as compared with other dyads: greater time at risk; greater presumed range of activities and interests;

greater intensity of involvement; an implied right to influence one another; sex differences that potentiate conflicts; roles and responsibilities based on sex rather than on interests and competencies; greater privacy seeking (associated with low social control); exclusivity of organization; involvement of personal, social, and perhaps material commitments; stress resulting from developmental changes; and, finally, extensive knowledge of one another's social biographies, which include vulnerabilities, fears, and other aspects of each others' lives that can be used for purposes of attack.[2]

These characteristics of marriage and of serious premarital relationships are not believed to be either the necessary or sufficient conditions for interpersonal violence, however. The major missing link, Gelles (1979) writes, is cultural tolerance for and acceptance of violent behavior; it is primarily within the family that one learns that "it is acceptable (1) to hit people you love, (2) for powerful people to hit less powerful people, (3) to use hitting to achieve some end or goal, and (4) to hit as an end in itself" (p. 15).

Still another factor contributing to the use of aggressive and abusive behaviors between inmates is the sexist nature of society (Gelles, 1979:18–19). Sexism, of course, affects unmarried as well as married couples. In addition, during the slow transition toward more egalitarian relationships between the sexes (Yankelovich, 1981), intimates' vulnerability to one another is probably increased, especially in terms of words and actions that may be seen as threats to identity and to self-esteem (Adams, 1978:78; Edwards and Hoover, 1974:175). Such threats, along with other stresses, act as triggers to violent behavior (Gelles, 1972:188).

Most professionals believe that physical battles grow out of arguments (Martin, 1976:50). The lovers' quarrel is a well-known phenomenon. Moreover, the tenuous nature of the courtship commitment at any stage may contribute to feelings of insecurity, interpersonal vulnerability, and conflict, much as the potential for loss of security may contribute to vulnerability and conflict within married pairs.

Gelles and Straus (1979) have argued that a special theory of family violence is needed, if families are characterized by a set of unique variables or if relationships among variables in the family are different from relationships among variables in other groups (p. 550). However, as has been shown above, courting couples of the more committed, intimate variety have many characteristics in common with married couples. Moreover, the family contains a number of real or potential role relationships that are, for the most part, involuntary at least on one side (e.g., parent-child). Among these role relationships, the marital relationship is unique in that it is chosen, as are

[2]Those characteristics of the family that deal with intergenerational concerns are largely omitted.

courting relationships, and both are bounded, intimate relationships typically between age peers of different sexes. Further, in normative terms, no other family or prefamily relationships are intimate in the same way.

Although there are meaningful structural and functional differences between married and serious courting dyads, it is suggested that a theory of violence between adult intimates, if not a broad "family" violence theory, may be useful in explaining both marital and premarital violence. Further, empirical consistencies found in research on marital violence may be used to predict violence in courtship.

EMPIRICAL CONSIDERATIONS

A review of research on marital violence (Gelles, 1980:878–879) indicates the following empirical consistencies: first, those who have experienced violent and abusive childhoods are more likely to become spouse abusers than are those who have experienced little or no violence in childhood. Second, domestic violence is more likely to be found in lower socioeconomic status families than in higher status families (although it is not confined to lower class homes). Third, family violence is related to social stress.

Some of the stressful aspects of courtship (e.g., vulnerable identities, perceived tenuousness of commitment, and the potential for sexual and social exploitation, among other stresses) have already been noted. The remaining empirical consistencies and theoretical considerations displayed above serve as the bases for a set of hypotheses regarding abuse and aggression in courtship. There hypotheses, and the rationale for each, are presented below.

HYPOTHESES

Relationships defined by unmarried participants as "serious" or "meaningful" are more like marriage in terms of exclusivity, intensity, commitment, and other subjective and objective factors than are relationships defined by participants as "casual" (i.e., less serious, intense or committed). These considerations give rise to the following hypothesis:

1. Relationships defined by participants as "more involved" show higher rates of abusive and aggressive behaviors[3] than relationships defined as "less involved."

The supposition that permissive (i.e., tolerant or accepting) attitudes toward violence directed at loved ones are learned in childhood rather then

[3]Use of the terms "abuse" and "aggression" are based in part on Sprey's (1979) definition of aggression: *(footnote continues on following page)*

during late adolescence or in the early adulthood is the foundation of the following hypothesis:

2. Relationships in which at least one partner had experienced violence in childhood show higher rates of abusive and aggressive behaviors than would relationships in which neither partner had experienced violence in childhood. This hypothesis has two corollaries: (a) abusive and aggressive experiences in courtship do not vary by age or school level among college-age respondents, and (b) abusive and aggressive experiences in courtship do not vary by extent of dating experience among college-age respondents.

3. Relationships in which at least one partner is of lower socioeconomic status show higher rates of violence than relationships in which neither partner is of lower socioeconomic status.

METHOD AND SAMPLE CHARACTERISTICS

A questionnaire was used that included a modified version of the Conflict Tactics Scales, which have been used extensively since 1971 in studies of family violence (see Gelles, 1978; Straus, 1979). A version of the same scales was also used by Makepeace (1981). The questionnaire was distributed to more than 500 students in courtship and marriage classes in the fall of 1980. The task, which was presented as voluntary, along with guarantees of anonymity and confidentiality, was to be completed thoughtfully in private and returned at the next class meeting. (Makepeace's respondents had filled out his questionnaire in the classroom.) The opportunity sample of respondents represented virtually all undergraduate academic fields of study at this large southwestern university.

A lower proportionate response was expected from men than from women on the basis of proportionate responses obtained in marital violence studies (e.g., Gelles, 1972; Straus, Gelles, and Steinmetz, 1980). Questionnaires were returned by 74% of the women and 54% of the men. After

---

> Aggression. . . . relates to the instigation of overt conflict . . . Aggression is assertive behavior aimed directly at certain others. It is an attempt—by whatever means—to get *others* to behave to suit one's own advantage. Furthermore, aggressive conduct occurs at the *expense* of others. . . . Aggression can involve a wide range of behaviors, ranging from the use of force to verbal attacks. (pp. 137–138, emphasis in original)

Although Sprey includes verbal attack as a form of aggression, verbal abuse and threats of violence are distinguished in the present study. The statement "you are ridiculous" is a verbal attack abusive to the target's self-esteem and perhaps identity, at least in intent. "Keep that up and I'll slap you" is a threat of violence.

Gelles has pointed out that the literature on violence is rife with confusing and even contradictory definitions. The definition used here is congruent with the definition developed by Gelles and his associates, although not identical with it. In any case, the terms "violence," "abuse," and "aggression" did not appear in the questionnaire. All forms of abuse and aggression were operationalized in explicit behavioral terms.

TABLE 1 Proportions of Respondents Who Ever Experienced Specific Conflict Tactics in Their Courtship Relationships

Conflict tactics	Respondents in more involved relationships Men %	Women %	Respondents in less involved relationships Men %	Women %
Threatened with violence	18	18.5	2	1
Verbally abused	53	48	16	8
Pushed or shoved	21	25	2	2
Threw object	19	10	2	.5
Slapped, hit with open hand, scratched, grabbed	25	29	3	3
Punched or kicked	10	9	2	1
Pushed down	6	15	—	2
Hit with hard object	3	2	—	—
Choked	4	4.5	—	—
Used knife	2	1	1	—
Used gun	1	1	1	—
Combinations of above	5	4.5	—	1

discarding incomplete responses and questionnaires returned by married students, 371 remained (129 men and 242 women).

The large majority of respondents were white and most were either juniors or seniors. Majorities of both sexes reported having had 6 or fewer "serious" relationships, and comparable pluralities reported having had fewer than 20 "non-serious" or casual dating relationships. More than 60% of both sexes had had at least one courtship experience lasting a year or more. Women ranged in age from 18 to 34 years, and men from 18 to 32 years.

FINDINGS

Table 1 shows the proportions of men and women who experienced abusive and aggressive behaviors in their more involved and less involved premarital relationships. Table 2 shows the proportions of men and women who inflicted abusive or aggressive behaviors on their partners in more involved and less involved relationships. The data displayed in these tables support the first hypothesis: regardless of kind(s) of conflict tactic used, relationships defined as serious and meaningful show higher rates of abuse and aggression than those defined as casual. (The proportions shown in Tables 1 and 2 represent respondents who ever experienced or inflicted any of the conflict tactics, whether frequently, occasionally, or seldom.)

To test the second hypothesis, experiences of childhood violence

TABLE 2 Proportions of Respondents Who Ever Inflicted Specific Conflict Tactics in Their Courtship Relationships

Conflict tactics	Respondents in more involved relationships		Respondents in less involved relationships	
	Men %	Women %	Men %	Women %
Threatened with violence	5	3.5	3	—
Verbally abused	31	29	13	6
Pushed or shoved	10	10	4	1.5
Threw object	7	7	1	1
Slapped, hit with open hand, scratched, grabbed	11	23	2	3
Punched or kicked	4	5.5	—	1
Pushed down	2	.5	—	—
Hit with hard object	—	.5	—	—
Choked	2	—	—	—
Used knife	—	—	—	—
Used gun	1	—	—	—
Combinations of above	—	.5	1	—

(shown in Table 3) were cross tabulated with experiences of violence in courtship. It was found that those who experienced childhood violence were more likely to have also experienced courtship violence (60% of the women and 67% of the men). For both sexes, however, those who had not experienced childhood violence had about an even chance of experiencing abusive or aggressive behaviors in courtship. Restated, it is concluded that violence is more likely to be experienced in courtship if it was experienced in child-

TABLE 3 Proportions of Respondents Who Ever Experienced Specific Conflict Tactics in Childhood

Conflict tactics	Men (%)	Women (%)
Threatened with violence	61	40
Verbally abused	73	63
Spanked on bottom by hand	94	94
Spanked with object	61	52
Slapped on body	64	49
Slapped on face	47	39
Slammed or pushed into wall	21	13
Punched	13	3.5
Hit with hard object	21	7
Choked	4	2
Combinations of the above	20	10
Other types of violence	8	3.5

hood; however, not having experienced violence as a child does not guarantee that one will not experience violence in one's premarital relationships.

Next, experiences of childhood violence were cross tabulated with violence inflicted in courtship. For both sexes, those who had experienced childhood violence were almost as likely to have inflicted violent behaviors on their premarital partners as not; however, those who had no experience of childhood violence were less likely to have done so (33% of the women and 25% of the men). Thus, it is concluded that not having experienced abusive or aggressive behaviors as a child reduces the chance of inflicting such behaviors on a premarital partner but is not a guarantee of nonviolent behavior in these relationships.

The hypothesized association between childhood violence and courtship violence is regarded as modestly supported. However, data were obtained only on respondents' direct experience of abusive and aggressive behaviors as children. The association might be stronger had the extent of respondents' witnessing violent behaviors between their parents also been assessed.

In support of the first corollary prediction, no statistically significant relationships were found between respondents' age or school level and experiencing or inflicting violence in courtship. With regard to the second corollary (predicting no relationship between extent of dating experience and courtship violence), the independent variable was operationalized as number of dates the respondent had had and as length of longest dating relationship. These analyses were carried out only for more involved relationships and only for the first five conflict tactics (those most frequently reported across all respondents).

Number of Dates

Among women, no meaningful differences were found between groups in terms of experienced courtship violence. However, women with the lowest number of dates inflicted more pushing and shoving on partners than did those with the modal number of dates and than those in the category of highest number of dates. Among men, in terms of experienced courtship violence, those with the greatest number of dates reported having been verbally abused, threatened with violence, and pushed or shoved more than others did. In terms of inflicted violence, no meaningful differences were found among men by number of dates. Although the indicated relationships were statistically significant, their correlation coefficients were moderately low. Moreover, of the 20 tests of association examined with regard to number of dates, only 4 were statistically significant.

Length of Longest Relationship

Among women, significantly more of those with longer dating relationships reported experiencing pushing and shoving and also reported having inflicted more slapping, hitting, scratching, and grabbing. Among men, no meaningful differences were found between groups for either experienced or inflicted violence. Here again, although the findings for women were statistically significant, the correlation coefficients were low. Moreover, of these 20 tests of association, only 2 were statistically significant. These findings support the second corollary hypothesis (no association between extent of dating experience and courtship violence).

The final hypothesis predicted an association between lower socioeconomic status and violence in courtship. No relationship was found, however, when father's occupational status was cross tabulated with violent behaviors of their sons and daughters.

Curiously, two statistically significant relationships were noted between mother's occupational status and certain conflict tactics. Men whose mothers were in the highest occupational category more often reported having experienced pushing and shoving, and women whose mothers were in the highest occupational category more often reported having had something thrown at them during courtship. These findings are opposite to the predicted direction and represent only 2 of 40 possible associations tested. It is concluded that the findings do not support the predicted inverse relationship between social class and violence in courtship.

DISCUSSION

In *The Violent Home* Gelles (1972) noted that of 80 married couples studied, only one reported violence prior to the couple's marriage. From this finding, Gelles concluded that premarital violence is not "normative."

> Violence between individuals involved in intimate love relationships is likely *only* when these two individuals are involved in the structural situation of family life with its concomittant stresses and frustrations and surrounded by the inherent complex role relations and role expectations. (1972:136, emphasis in original).

Makepeace's (1981) findings and those of the present study challenge this assertion. Moreover, a recent study comparing unmarried cohabitors with married couples found more violence among cohabitors (Yllo and Straus, 1981).

Table 4 provides a comparison of Makepeace's (1981) data on direct experience of courtship violence among freshman and sophomore college

TABLE 4 Comparisons of Reported Violent Events in Premarital Relationships from the Present Study and Makepeace Study with Reported Intermarital Violent Events from Gelles Study

	Present study sample (n = 371)		Makepeace sample (n = 202)	Gelles sample (n = 80)	
Conflict tactics	Men (%)	Women (%)	Sexes combined (%)	Husbands (%)	Wives (%)
Threatened with violence	20	20	8.4	Not reported	
Verbally abused	59	52	Not reported	Not reported	
Pushed or shoved	22	28	13.9	18	1
Threw object	21	14	Not reported	22	11
Slapped, hit, grabbed, scratched[a]	27	37	12.9	32	20
Punched or kicked[b]	13	13	4.0	25	9
Pushed down	6	15	Not reported	4	0
Hit with hard object[c]	3	2	3.5	3	5
Choked	4	5	1.5	9	0
Assaulted with weapon[d]	4	2	1.0	0	1

Note. Based on present study, Makepeace (1981), and Gelles (1972).
[a]In Makepeace, slapped.
[b]In Makepeace, punched.
[c]In Makepeace, struck with object.
[d]In present study and in Gelles, used knife and used gun combined.

students with data from the present study regarding violent premarital events among junior and senior college students and with Gelles' (1972) findings for marital violence. Inspection of these data indicates that premarital violence may constitute a rehearsal of sorts for later marital violence. Moreover, these data underestimate the extent of courtship violence. For example, reports of conflict tactics that do not appear in Straus' (1979) Conflict Tactics Scales (such as hair pulling, arm twisting, or sexual assault) have been omitted, as have reports of events consisting of combinations of the conflict tactics investigated here. In addition, recalling that 46% of the men and 26% of the women receiving questionaires did not return them, it seems likely that some additional proportion of experienced and inflicted violence in courtship remains undocumented. Of those who did respond, 68% of the women and 64% of the men reported at least one of the conflict tactics occurring in a premarital relationship.

How can Gelles' (1972) finding of little or no premarital violence reported by his married respondents be accounted for? Half of the small sample ($n = 80$) was selected on the basis of known involvement in marital violence. Perhaps these respondents were reluctant to admit having known of one another's violent behaviors prior to marriage. Conversely, it may be that people avoid marriage with those who have been abusive or aggressive toward them during courtship or with those toward whom they have been violent. However, what evidence exists in this regard is in the opposite direction. Makepeace (1981), for example, reports that in his sample,

> Only about half of the relationships "broke off" (55.3%); the other half either were still involved with the other person in the same capacity (15.8%) or had actually become more deeply involved (28.9%) by the time the survey was conducted. (p. 100)

Only longitudinal studies of courting couples, followed for some period into married life (for those who marry), can provide meaningful data on the outcomes of abusive and aggressive courtships.

For the present, the findings of this study are not seen as surprising. Not long ago, a national survey reported that only 66% of college youth believed that using violence to achieve "worthwhile results" was morally wrong (Yankelovich, 1974:91). A major study of singlehood contends that in many ways, people are taught to possess, control, and manipulate those they love; Stein (1976) points out that seeking a mate includes "heavy doses of anxiety, competitiveness, and jealousy" (p. 7). Jealousy, a prime violence-arousing factor, is interwoven with current notions of romantic love (Stein, 1976:60). In fact, according to Walster and Walster (1978), "Romantic passion is often enhanced by unpleasant but arousing states such as anxiety and fear, frustration, jealousy, loneliness, and anger" (p. 80). In intimate relationships, say these authors, "hostility and envy lurk just below the surface, as much a part of love as affection and tenderness" (1978:7).

Earlier, it was recommended that rather than a broad family violence theory, a theory of violence in intimate adult, heterosexual relationships would be useful. Such a theory would presumably fit within a larger conflict theory framework, where conflict is defined as "a struggle over limited resources and/or incompatible goals in which it appears that one person or group will have its way at the expense of the other party or group" (Scanzoni and Scanzoni, 1981:489). As the Scanzonis point out, conflict need not necessarily result in violence but often does among those whose skills in negotiation, bargaining, and cooperation are deficient (see also Goode, 1971) and among those who are unable to perceive other options (Scanzoni and Scanzoni, 1981:490).

Two propositions taken from what Nye (1979:7) calls "partial exchange theory" appear useful in predicting both marital and courtship violence. These propositions, developed to deal with face-to-face interactions and relationships in any dyads are as follows:

1. Humans are rational and, within the limits of the information they

have and their ability to predict the future, they make choices that will bring the greatest rewards at the least cost.

2. It is rewarding to inflict punishments on someone who is perceived as having deliberately hurt oneself.

A third proposition may explain why abusive and aggressive behaviors are not more frequent in such stressful dyadic relationships as marriage and serious courtship. As Nye (1979) puts it in choice and exchange theory terms:

3. If a rewarding activity is seen as preventing one from some other rewarding activities, then one is less likely to desire to plan to engage in that activity (p. 20).

SUMMARY

This study of abusive and aggressive premarital relationships has found that violence is more likely to occur in more involved than in less involved relationships; that having experienced violence in childhood is related to experiencing or inflicting abusive and aggressive acts in courtship; and that among these couples, the expected inverse relationship between socioeconomic status and violence is not supported. The first two findings parallel those reported consistently in the literature on marital violence.

A theory of violence in intimate adult heterosexual relationships has been suggested, resting within a conflict theory framework and using propositions of choice and exchange theory. Because both marital and premarital relationships differ in meaningful ways from other familiar relationships, it seems important to distinguish between intergenerational violence that occurs between relatively helpless victims and more powerful aggressors[4] (as in child abuse or abuse against elderly family members), violence in same-sex pairs (as in sibling violence), and especially between voluntary, privacy-seeking, intimate relationships and those that are involuntary. Those colleagues who are developing family violence theory are especially encouraged to include committed, intimate, premarital relationships in their theory-building efforts.

The study of courtship violence, other than sexual violence, has just begun and warrants far more attention than it has received. At present, we are preparing a paper reporting on the mutuality of abusive and aggressive encounters in courtship, alcohol and drug involvement in violent events, and the "Genovese effect" when others are present during abusive and

[4]It is not implied, for instance, that women may not be more helpless than men, either by virtue of socialization for helplessness or by virtue of relative size and upper-body strength. The purpose of such terms is to point to the intergenerational nature of child abuse (by parents) and abuse of elderly family members (by children) and to the different level of weakness involved in infants and the elderly on the one hand and young adults on the other.

aggressive encounters, and we are presenting data on participants' accounts for violence, both inflicted and experienced.

REFERENCES

Adams, N.

1978 Single Blessedness. New York: Penguin.

Broderick, C., and J. Smith

1979 "The general systems approach to the the family." In W. R. Burr, R. Hill, F. I. Nye, and I. L. Reiss (eds), Contemporary Theories About the Family (Vol. 2). New York: Free Press.

Burr, W. R., R. Hill, F. I. Nye, and I. L. Reiss (Eds.)

1979 Contemporary Theories About the Family (vols. 1–2). New York: Free Press.

Edwards, M., and E. Hoover

1974 The Challenge of Being Single. New York: New American Library (Signet).

Ehrmann, W.

1964 "Marital and nonmarital sexual behavior." In H. T. Christensen (ed.), Handbook of Marriage and the Family. Chicago: Rand-McNally.

Gelles, R. J.

1972 The Violent Home. Beverly Hills: Sage.

1978 "Violence toward children in the United States." American Journal of Orthopsychiatry 48:580–592.

1979 Family Violence. Beverly Hills: Sage.

1980 "Violence in the family: A review of research in the seventies." Journal of Marriage and the Family 42(4):873–885.

Gelles, R. J., and M. A. Straus

1979 "Determinants of violence in the family: Toward a theoretical integration." In W. R. Burr, R. Hill, I. F. Nye, and I. L. Reiss (eds.), Contemporary Theories About the Family (Vol. 1). New York: Free Press.

Goode, W.

1971 "Force and violence in the family." Journal of Marriage and the Family 33:624–636.

Kanin, E. J.

1957 "Male aggression in dating-courtship relations." American Journal of Sociology 63:197–204.

Kanin, E. J.

1967a "Reference groups and sex conduct norm violations." Sociological Quarterly 8:495–504.

1967b "An examination of sexual aggression as a response to sexual frustration." Journal of Marriage and the Family 29:428–433.

Kirkpatrick, C., and E. J. Kanin

1957 "Male sex aggression on a university campus." American Sociological Review 22:52–58.

Martin, D.
1976 Battered Wives. San Francisco: Glide.

Makepeace, J. M.
1981 "Courtship violence among college students." Family Relations 30(1):97–102.

Murstein, B. I.
1980 "Mate selection in the 1970s." Journal of Marriage and the Family 42:777–792.

Nye, F. I.
1979 "Choice, exchange, and the family." In W. R. Burr, R. Hill, F. I. Nye, and I. L. Reiss (eds.), Contemporary Theories About the Family (Vol. 2). New York: Free Press.

Scanzoni, L. D., and J. Scanzoni
1981 Men, Women, and Change: A Sociology of Marriage and Family (2nd ed.). New York: McGraw-Hill.

Sprey, J.
1979 "Conflict theory and the study of marriage and the family." In W. R. Burr, R. Hill, F. I. Nye, and I. L. Reiss (eds.), Contemporary Theories About the Family (Vol. 2). New York: Free Press.

Stein, P. J.
1976 Single. Englewood Cliffs, N.J.: Prentice-Hall (Spectrum).

Strauss, M. A.
1979 "Measuring intrafamily conflict and violence: The Conflict Tactics (CT) Scales." Journal of Marriage and the Family 41(1):75–88.

Straus, M. A., R. J. Gelles, and S. Steinmetz
1980 Behind Closed Doors: Violence in the American Family. New York: Doubleday (Anchor).

Straus, M. A., and G. T. Hotaling (Eds.)
1980 The Social Causes of Husband-Wife Violence. Minneapolis: University of Minnesota Press.

Walster, E., and G. W. Walster
1978 A New Look at Love. Reading, Mass.: Addison-Wesley.

Yankelovich, D.
1974 The New Morality: A Profile of American Youth in the 70s. New York: McGraw-Hill.
1981 "New rules in American life: Searching for self-fulfillment in a world turned upside down." Psychology Today (April):35–37ff.

Yllo, K., and M. A. Straus
1981 "Interpersonal violence among married and cohabiting couples." Family Relations 30(3):34–337.

Reading 31

Homicide as Conflict Resolution

Ken Levi
University of Texas at San Antonio

Homicide research at societal, subcultural, and interaction levels of analysis has not produced a comprehensive model for the killer-victim transaction. But rules for organizing the experience of homicide can be generated from Simmel's definition of conflict as a "resolution of divergent dualisms" (1955:11). A model of homicide as a form of conflict resolution is demonstrated through interviews with a random sample of 35 adjudicated killers. Respondents' definitions of homicide correspond to the conflict resolution model, with their verbal accounts, their sociopsychological orientation to the victim at the point of the killing, their method of killing, and the general dynamics of the killer-victim transaction, all varying as a resolution of a distinctive relationship, either between lovers, adversaries, or strangers. The situational definition casts homicide within the realm of normal behavior and at the same time delineates its distinctive features.

Most studies of homicide have dealt with its static features (Athens, 1974), such as time and location of the offense, type of weapon employed, or race, age, and sex of participants (Bensing and Schroeder, 1960; Boudouris, 1970; Bullock, 1955; Henry and Short, 1954; Wolfgang, 1958). The scant research on dynamic features of homicide has generally focused on subcultural patterns of so-called victim-precipitation, in which victims play a role in provoking their own deaths (Curtis, 1974; Schultz 1967; Silverman, 1974; Von Hentig, 1948). Luckenbill, by contrast, took a more analytic approach by examining the entire "situated transaction" leading to homicide as a dynamic and meaningfully organized process. He described this process as a "Character contest," that is, a confrontation in which at least one but usually both (victim and offender) attempt to establish or save face at the other's expense by standing steady in the face of adversity" (1977:176).

The present article incorporates Luckenbill's findings into a more general conceptual framework: homicide as conflict resolution. Simmel has defined conflict as "designed to resolve divergent dualisms; it is a way of achieving some kind of unity, *even if it be through the annihilation of one of the conflicting parties*" (1955:11). Conflict does not separate, according to Simmel but rather unites those whom "hate, envy, need, desire" had already begun to alienate (1955:13). Not only do people have to "come

The author wishes to thank John Johnson, Lawrence Redlinger, and Daniel Rigney for reviewing and criticizing the manuscript.

together" both figuratively and literally in order to conflict, but they also conflict in order to overcome the differences between them. This is the sense in which they "unite."

While conflict leads to uniting, uniting can also lead to conflict. Simmel gave three illustrations. First, there is the *antagonistic game*, in which the exclusive motivation is the "fascination of fight and victory" over an opponent (1955:34). This formal dualism (winner/loser) "presupposes" unification under the "mutually recognized control of norms and rule" defining the framework of the contest in a "rigorous and impersonal" way (1955:35). The more participants adhere strictly to the norms and rules, the more "extreme and unconditional" the conflict becomes (1955:38). A second type of conflict based on unity that Simmel describes is the "conflict over causes" (1955:38). Here the parties fight over "objective interests." The more single-mindedly they pursue objective interests, the more their conflict is differentiated from personalities or "personal and egoistic considerations" (1955:38). The combatants are then free to fight with a cold-blooded "radicalism and mercilessness" (1955:39). Finally, Simmel described the dynamics of a conflict based on "common qualities" or "common membership," with its most extreme form occurring in "intimate relations" (1955:45). The more participants share with each other as "whole persons," the more their "totalities" are involved in all relationships with their loved one. When one member attempts to leave the relationship, "their separation revolves precisely around the point of their connection" (1955:54), and their connection is all encompassing. The contrast in demands then attains "the highest possible sharpness and accentuation" (1955:54). The desperate lover, clinging to any external proofs of feeling, ultimately explodes with "rage, hatred, contempt, cruelty". And the "most intimate unity" of the combatants can resolve itself into the "destruction of both parties" (1955:55).

To sum up Simmel's argument, conflict is based on divergence within a context of unity, and it is aimed at overcoming that divergence. The more clearly defined the unity, the more clearly defined the divergence, and thus the more focused and unconditional the conflict. The form that the conflict takes varies according to the form of the "unity" on which it is based.

The remainder of this paper extends the implications of Simmel's essay and investigates the applicability of the conflict resolution frame to the inner organization of homicide. In exploring this framework, I shall take a systematic and detailed look at aspects of the homicide transaction that have rarely if ever been investigated. These include overall dynamics of the homicide process, variations within that process, symbolic and existential components of the working agreement (or trap) that precipitate the motive to kill, and the organization of the killer's response in terms of its phenomenological, existential and behavioral components. The investigation into homicide as conflict resolution applies to important issues in homicide research and in the wider literature on conflict.

RESEARCH METHODS

Interview studies in homicide are rare, and they generally focus on a single category of killer, such as female killers (Totman, 1970), killers on psychiatric referral (Tanay, 1972), mass killers (Galvin and MacDonald, 1959) or even "first degree" murders from "middle class" backgrounds "without a history of psychosis" (Duncan et al., 1967). To my knowledge, students of homicide previously have avoided attempts to interview a random sample of typical killers based on a metropolitan-wide offender population.

In the present study a series of tape-recorded, open-ended interviews were conducted with 35 legally defined and self-defined killers. These include 29 men drawn from a stratified random sample of the state prison population, and 6 men drawn from a stratified random sample of the state sanitarium for the mentally ill population. All of the men interviewed were at least 16 years of age and had committed an adjudicated homicide in Wayne County, Michigan (metropolitan Detroit) between 1967 and 1973. Samples were stratified according to race, sex, and disposition of the case.

The inaccuracy of official statistics and therefore of official populations is well known (Douglas, 1967; Douglas, 1977; Quinney, 1970; Sykes, 1978), but the Detroit sample was randomly drawn and stratified according to the official population because it is the broadest population normally available to the homicide researcher. Thus all of the respondents were male, 69% were black, half were less than 35 years of age, all but 3 (sanitarium inmates) were either blue-collar workers or unemployed. This compares favorably to the 95% males and 80% blacks in the population sampled. It also compares with other studies of homicide, in which samples have generally been young, male, blue collar, and, in the United States, black (see Bensing and Schroeder, 1960; Boudouris, 1970; Henry and Short, 1954; Wolfgang, 1958; Wolfgang and Ferracuti, 1967).

Only those who were both legally defined and self-defined as killers were interviewed. While 77 cases were originally drawn from a total population of 582, 9% (5) of the prisoners and 20% (3) of the forensic patients refused to be interviewed. In addition, 50% (29) of the prisoners and 40% (6) of the patients were deemed ineligible, primarily because of claims of innocence. Possible distortions in the sample are therefore manifold. Distortion must also be expected, although these were mitigated by the length, repetitiveness, and intensity of the interviews. (Additional background information was gathered from 12 informal interviews with homicide convicts, outside discussions with 35 chiefs of police in Wayne County, 6 forensic psychiatrists and psychologists, and a comprehensive review of the homicide literature.)

Respondents were generally talkative and friendly during interviews, which lasted from one to five sessions per respondent and covered from 20 to 70 pages of transcript each. Every interview was coded twice: once according to 45 predefined codes and once according to a constant comparative, or inductive, coding procedure that involves the gathering of consistent patterns of response (Glaser and Strauss, 1967).

This is not the place to detail each of the 45 codes. However, they were derived from Simmel and the literature on homicide and were meant to measure the extreme types of conflict resolution that Simmel described. These types include conflict within the context of an antagonistic game, an intimate relation, and an objective interest. For the sake of simplicity these contexts, or forms of unity, are referred to here as adversaries, lovers, and strangers, respectively. Based on the predefined codes, the Detroit sample included 10 adversaries, 9 lovers, and 16 strangers. The 10 adversaries killed people ranging from a rival to a drinking buddy, a sister's boyfriend, an enemy of the killer's gang, the killer's foreman, a policeman who detained the killer on a traffic charge, an adoptive mother, a mother-in-law, a stepfather. The 16 strangers killed people ranging from 5 victims of an armed robbery, 2 people whom the killer met over a game of cards, a neighbor, a friend of the killer's brother, a member of a rival gang, a boarder, a niece's boyfriend, a business partner, the boyfriend of a woman who owned a bar that the killer frequented, and a man on the street. Whether the killer was coded as a lover, an adversary, or a stranger depended entirely on his own stated interest in the victim. Thus people who had known one another for several years but only related for the purpose of transacting business (an objective interest) would be classified as strangers. Once the context of the relationship was established, the events leading to homicide were then measured to determine whether they varied for adversaries, lovers, and strangers, in the way Simmel described.

At the same time, the interview transcripts were inductively coded to determine regular properties of homicide transactions that emerge without the bias of a preconceived model. This double coding procedure was possible because the questions posed during the interview were general and open-ended. Respondents were asked, for example, "What happened?" "How did you feel when that happened?" "What went through your mind?" "What did you do then?" and so forth. The purpose of these questions was to obtain as detailed as possible a picture of all the events leading to homicide, from the Killer's point of view. The inductive coding procedure was useful in two ways. First, it led to the discovery of grounded theory (see, for example, the discussion of the opening move, the trap, and the killer's experience below). Second, the inductive coding procedure enabled an independent test of Simmel, through a comparison of his conflict resolution framework and the killer's own phenomenology.

Inevitable biases in response arose because of the constraints of the prison setting, possible legal repercussions, the distastefulness of the subject itself, and lapse of memory. To counteract these biases, each respondent was (1) paid for the interview, (2) given written guarantees of confidentiality, (3) interviewed in a private room, (4) interviewed intensively and repetitively on several separate occasions about the events of his crime, and most important (5) interviewed about matters that would not tend to further incriminate him, i.e., he was asked about the nature of his motive, not whether he had one. The prevailing attitude among respondents was, "I've told this story over and over again, and I don't care who hears it now."

DYNAMICS OF HOMICIDE

Conflict, according to Lyman and Scott (1970:97), "including deadly engagements," usually occurs in what may be viewed as a game context. Luckenbill also uses the structural form of the game, with its beginning, playing time, and termination, to analyze the encounter leading to homicide. He divides this game of homicide into six stages: the victim's opening move, the offender's interpretation of that move, the offender's retaliation, a "working agreement" to use violence, combat, and the killer's departure from the scene (Luckenbill, 1977). For the sake of comparison, the following section will also be divided into six sequential moves. This will clarify the ways that the present analysis partly incorporates and partly goes beyond Luckenbill.

Inasmuch as this study was not originally conducted with Luckenbill's article in mind, however, some of the data are not exactly parallel to his. The opening move in the present analysis generally occurs days or even years before the final homicide encounter, whereas in Luckenbill the opening move always occurred during the homicide encounter. In addition, stage five—combat—is greatly expanded in the present study; it covers what amounts to an additional three stages, which present the killer's existential and phenomenological view of his own role. Therefore, the scope of the present study is expanded in terms of events prior to the situated transaction ending in murder, as well as events constituting the killer's response. And these departures from Luckenbill's analysis partly reflect the greater ability of the personal interview, versus official records, to render intimate detail.

Stage One: Opening Move

Luckenbill characterizes the opening move as an "event performed by the victim and subsequently defined by the offender as an offense to face" (1977: 179). This characterization is not consistent with the accounts rendered by lovers and strangers in the present study but is consistent with the class of killers that we shall refer to as adversaries.

Adversaries In the antagonistic game, according to Simmel, participants fight for "symbolic mastery" over the opponent (1955: 35). Victims in both Luckenbill's study and in the present study appeared to be playing just such an antagonistic game by challenging the killer's symbolic mastery through verbal insults and/or nonverbal gestures. For example, "I went to the army when I was 18. When I came back out of the army, my wife, she told me she had a baby by this guy, the guy's kid. . . ." (No. 34). This type of event openly damages the would-be killer's presentation of self.

Lovers In intimate relations, according to Simmel, the most "intensive and extensive" conflict occurs when one member attempts to leave the relationship (1955: 48). Just such a withdrawal from the relationship constituted the victim's opening move for the 9 lovers in the Detroit sample. In 2 cases this withdrawal took the form of a coldness in the partner's attitude: "It got to the point where her cold attitude—where it was like living with somebody in the house like a housekeeper" (No. 17). In the remaining cases, the victim seemed to withdraw physically by spending less time with his or her lover: "The time she began to stay was less and less. By the time she'd get to my place, it would be almost six o'clock and maybe she'd stay nine o'clock, ten o'clock and go home that night. She'd go back home and but we didn't go to bed, didn't go to bed at all" (No. 43). The opening move for the Detroit lovers signalled the beginning of a "negative relationship game" (Lyman and Scott, 1975: 35), rather than the "character contest" that Luckenbill saw in all the homicide cases he examined. It was not being faced with a verbal or nonverbal gesture but the withdrawal of any kind of communication that the lovers found disturbing. And what disturbed them about their loved ones' withdrawal was not its offensive or insulting quality but something quite different, as we shall see.

Strangers The pure conflict over causes, according to Simmel, is waged over an impersonal objective (1955:38). In Detroit, strangers experienced three types of opening move. Ten of the sixteen strangers were physically attacked: "We announced that it was a robbery and then said take it easy, to just be calm and nothing would happen. He insisted that he wasn't going to be robbed, so we pushed him back into the car, and when he got in the car, he scuffled. . . . He tried to push me out of the way and grab me" (No. 40). Another four strangers were resisted or ignored, when they asked their victims to do something: "In the process of telling him to hand over the wallet, when he saw the gun, he just panicked, you know, went to pieces; so, he didn't hear anything I said" (No. 13). Another two of the strangers said that the victim verbally challenged or insulted them. Thus, in at least 14 of the 16 cases, the opening move focused the strangers' attention not on a symbolic affront but on what Simmel described as an impersonal objective—in the form of the killer's own physical safety or a block in his course of action.

The opening move suggests that homicide varies according to the way the killer relates to his victim (for example, as a lover, adversary, or stranger). The point to be stressed in Stage One and throughout is that it would be a mistake to try to understand or predict the dynamics of the homicide process solely as a character contest.

Stage Two: Killer's Interpretation

After the opening move, the type of game that ensues depends on the meaning ascribed to the victim's behavior. In all of the cases Luckenbill observed, the offender interpreted the victim's opening move as "personally offensive," in the sense of being "insulting" (Luckenbill, 1977:180). In the Detroit study only the adversaries made this type of interpretation.

Adversaries All 10 of the adversaries interpreted the victim's behavior as personally demeaning, with 6 of them specifically claiming "misuse." "It was just that I knew I had been, *viciously used, misused*. And I knew from prior dealings with my union, they were perfectly legitimate cases that should have been taken care of" (No. 1). This kind of interpretation is consistent with an offense to "face."

Lovers Most of the lovers took a more wait-and-see approach to their victim's opening move of coolness or withdrawal, interpreting it as a possible alienation of affection: "And some days I shouldn't have been thinking about my wife doing something back home—thinking she is going out with somebody" (No. 56). Among the lovers, there were two residual cases. No. 5, whose wife was committed to an asylum, did not claim to attribute her "withdrawal" to disaffection. No. 25, a young man who purported to kill a much loved uncle in self-defense, did not fit the general pattern for lovers and will have to stand as a deviant case. But none of the lovers interpreted the withdrawal as an insult to face.

Strangers Although six of the strangers had opening moves similar to the moves that the victims made in Luckenbill's study, their interpretation of these moves was different. Instead of feeling personally offended, they ranged in their interpretation from viewing the victim's move as an impediment (three cases) to a dangerous impediment (six cases) to a dangerous and unexpected impediment (seven cases) blocking a line of action that they wished to pursue: "Anyway, we go in the store with the *plan* of getting the security guard, and me getting behind the counter. We go in the store, and he announces the holdup, and the security guard seemed to get frantic, . . . and so this throws the whole thing off" (No. 49). All of the strangers claimed to be primarily concerned with the objective aspect of the victim's move. None interpreted the opening move as an offense to face.

Stage Three: Killer's Response:

Luckenbill noted that at this stage the offender has several options in framing his response. He can excuse the violation, leave the scene, leave the victim, or retaliate. In Luckenbill's account, retaliation was always the chosen response. The offender always chose to retaliate in order to "save facc and demonstrate strong moral character" (Luckenbill, 1977:181). In the Detroit study, two-thirds of the killers interviewed chose other options besides retaliation.

Adversaries Half of the adversaries claimed to bear their insult in silence, preferring the tactic of avoidance (Lyman and Scott, 1970: 101) to a strategy of confrontation: "I'm taking care of another man's baby. This is in my mind now. But see, I don't go out of my way to hunt him down or nothing like this here. All I want him to do is just stay on his side. . . . As long as he stayed on his side, and as long as I stayed on my side, cool" (No. 34). The other half of the adversaries did retaliate, either through a verbal challenge (two cases) or a physical attack (three cases).

Lovers Only one of the lovers retaliated against his victim, and this was No. 25, the deviant case who acted in self-defense. A second lover attempted to retaliate against his victim's new boyfriend, and a third lover became hallucinatory, when his wife was placed in an asylum. Instead of retaliating, the remaining six lovers went on a fact-finding mission to determine whether they remained the object of the partner's affections. For example: "I would watch the place sometime" (No. 56). This is certainly not consistent with Luckenbill's statement that "retaliation was always chosen."

Strangers Ten of the sixteen strangers did not retaliate against their victims' opening moves. Four of the ten claimed that they were stunned or indifferent. Six said that they either backed off or ran away: "So, I don't know what got into the guy. We get to arguing then we get to fighting. Like I was backing away from the guy. He come forward to me. I opened the door and I fell out on the ground—my neck against the curb" (No. 44). Six strangers did retaliate. But only one saw his retaliation as an attempt to save face and demonstrate strong moral character. For the rest, retaliation was mainly an impersonal matter, a matter of self-defense: "*I did what was* *necessary.* That's like falling out of the window, I grab the sill. *I don't think the window is against me*" (No. 40).

Stage Four: Working Agreement

According to Luckenbill, the victim's response to the offender's "retaliation" occasions a "working agreement" to resort to violence (1977: 182). This working agreement is an important component of the homicide process because it precipitates the violence. A similar phenomenon has been widely observed in the literature. It ranges from victims who suggest violence either by employing it themselves (Wolfgang, 1958; Wolfgang and Ferracuti, 1967), or "asking for it" (Amir, 1971; Schultz, 1967; Von Hentig, 1948) to victims who suggest violence by blocking other alternatives (Simmel, 1955; Heirich, 1971). In the Detroit sample, something like a working agreement was also perceived, at least by the offender. It took the form of the victim apparently blocking other alternatives and "trapping" the killer into making his violent response. Furthermore, the nature of the blocked alternatives and the nature of the trap were not uniform, but varied according to the killer-victim relationship.

Adversaries According to Goffman, the integrity of the social self is circumscribed by boundaries that are both figurative and territorial (1967: 241). In the Detroit sample, adversary victims appeared to precipitate their own homicides by invading the established boundaries of the killer's social self. In seven of the cases, the invasion was both territorial and figurative: "When I saw him there, I mean when I saw him, man, boom, that's it . . . *because that's my place* you know, that's my place of rest and comfort, that's the place where I sweated, worked hard and after a whole day, come in and lay my head" (No. 34). For the other adversaries, the invasion was only figurative. The victim violated the killer's manhood, or his sister, or his job: "So, he went out and got the general foreman instead of the steward. They went into the office and left me standing there. And they *wrote up my termination*. . . . After I was fired, it was (date), all the hope went out the window then" (No. 1).

An additional feature of the working agreement for adversaries was that for all of them, without exception, this invasion took place in a public setting where one or more third parties were present to observe their humiliation. This is a particularly "fateful" situation (Goffman, 1967: 167), because a record of the actor's character is assured: "If it had been up to me, we would have settled right then and there, and let them know I was a full man. I can't have them around here calling me a coward" (No. 6). Thus the combination of past misuse (for some), plus the serious invasion of self, plus third-party witnesses, appeared to the killer to trap him into making a strong and decisive face-saving gesture.

Lovers Two of the NGRI (Not Guilty of Murder by Reason of Insanity) lovers could not recall the exact events leading to their act of homicide. The other seven, however, all recalled a verbal argument with their victims as the main precipitating event that led them to kill. With one exception (No. 25) the argument contained two crucial patterns: a test question on the part of the killer, and an affirmation on the part of the victim. In the test question, the killer, tired of all the suspicion and uncertainty, asks, in no uncertain terms, whether the victim still cares for him: "So, I said, "You don't want me no more? You had me get my divorce from my wife and everything, and while I was paying $50 a week child support, now I'm paying $85 and everything; *now you don't want me, you got somebody else*?" (No. 35). In the affirmation, the victim replies, also in no uncertain terms:

Killer: "You don't want me no more?"

Victim: "Yeah." (No. 35).

Aside from the test question and affirmation, two related aspects of the argument should be mentioned. First, it is a verbal, face-to-face confrontation; in none of the cases involved did the killer act on the basis of a mere hint or clue, this being characteristic of the lover's tenacity (Simmel, 1955:54). Second, in ending the argument, the victim as much as the killer seems to be attempting to resolve the conflict. Her resonant "yeah" or vigorous shaking of the head in the negative leaves little room for doubt. It evokes a working agreement to violence by ironically closing alternative routes that the killer might pursue in saving his relationship. Thus the lover is trapped but clearly not by any need to save face.

Strangers One armed-robber shot his victim while they struggled in the victim's car. Another man knifed someone who had punched him once, split his lip, and was about to punch again. For the remaining 14 strangers the main precipitating event that lead to homicide was an apparent armed attack launched by the victim against his killer (of course, this is the killer's story). In eight cases the killer felt no doubt that the victim was armed: "He's standing, oh, I guess about 4 or 5 feet from me. . . . All I can see is the blast. I don't even hear the noise no more, you know" (No. 15). In the remaining six cases, the killer suspected that the victim was armed: "So, when his shoulders was moving, I knew that he couldn't be going for nothing but the gun" (No. 51). Whereas adversaries are trapped socially and lovers emotionally, strangers perceive their trap in nonpersonal, objective terms. The armed victim constitutes an objective force.

In addition to this objective force, a second feature of the working agreement for strangers is that they were materially blocked from escape. The blockage took the form of an enclosed area or a physical inability to leave the scene: "And I would have got tagged. The door is way at the end of the hallway, and we're up here in this *little closed area*. And here's this guy charging, coming at me" (No. 3). Thus practically all of the strangers were trapped by a need to save not their face but their hide.

Stage four contradicts Luckenbill's assertion that acts of homicide are invariably precipitated by the need to make a facesaving gesture. On the contrary, strangers, far from standing their ground and making a fateful gesture, typically make every effort to turn and run, even in the presence of third parties before whom they might be expected to feel some shame.

Stage four presents evidence that the precipitant of homicide varies. It varies according to the nature of the victim's relevance to the killer. Adversaries become trapped in the fateful combination of past misuse (for some) plus invasion of established boundaries of the social self, plus the presence of third-party witnesses. Lovers become trapped in the situation of a verbal, face-to-face argument containing an unambiguous test question and clear affirmation. Strangers become trapped by an armed attack combined with a physical block. The function of the trap is to heighten the relevance of one type of unity, with the killer and victim seeming (from the killer's point of view) to focus more and more on a single issue. Both killer and victim seem to move towards an unconditional and clear-cut resolution of that issue. In effect, they enter a zero-sum game which excludes heterogeneous concerns, traps the killer in an untenable situation, and blocks consideration of alternate solutions.

At this point in his article, Luckenbill moved from Stage Four (the working agreement) to Stage Five (combat). The function of the working agreement is to have the killer conceive of violence as a necessary and appropriate response. But as several theorists have noted (see, for example, Douglas, 1977; Goffman, 1974; Simmel, 1955), cognition, per se, is often not sufficient to motivate behavior. Prior studies of homicide, however, have failed to investigate the "feeling" or existential (Douglas, 1977) component providing a bridge from conceptualization to response. "By means of psychological connections these feelings produce forces which are necessary to execute the given task and to paralyze inner countercurrents" (Simmel, 1955:34). Feelings (and the way they are channelled, which we shall discuss in Stage Five) directly motivate the killer's behavior. In the Detroit sample, for instance, *all* of the adversaries felt a sense of humiliation or outrage. "When that guy stopped me and pulled my car over, you know, if he had said, 'You went through a red light; I'm going to give you a ticket,' well, cool. *But you don't pull my door*, the man snatched me out and tell me I'm wrong. What he tell me, *I don't think he tell it to a dog*" (No. 21).

All but one (No. 25) of the lovers felt rejected or lost:

> I was totally, I was so *lost*, like they were putting up a wall between us and I was just so lost. . . . That would describe it, if it was a scene; they would be giants and I would be standing there and they would be talking back and forth real fast, all out of proportion, like somebody speeding up the film, and every now and then little me saying something, and I would be shrinking, getting smaller and smaller, going into nothing. (No. 55)

All of the strangers felt fear or panic:

> He panicked, and when he panicked, I panicked. It's just like a bunch of people in a movie house. If a guy goes wild in there with a knife, everybody is scared, and everybody runs out. His panic jumped right into me. . . . My fear shut me off from everything. (No. 13)

All of these feelings are partly evoked by the trap, and partly by other factors, such as the mood the killer is in at the time, the absence of distractions, and so forth. But the resultant feelings are a crucial feature of the homicide process because they create a sense of discomfort so highly intolerable for the killer that he deems it necessary to seek immediate relief.

Stage Five: Combat

According to Luckenbill, the killer, following the working agreement, proceeds to secure a weapon and engage in lethal combat (1977: 184). The two participants in the game having committed themselves to violence, the killer is bound to make his move. In addition, the availability of a weapon is surely one of the major situational facilitators of violence (Bensing and Schroeder, 1960; Boudouris, 1970; Wolfgang, 1958). The absence of police or other control agents can also reduce the offender's inhibitions (Smelser, 1963). The killer's self-image is another factor that has been linked to his likelihood to respond violently in certain situations (Athens, 1974). The offender's personality type (Guttmacher, 1967; Langner, 1971; McCord et al., 1970), past experience (Douglas, 1967) and present mood (Matza, 1969) can also predispose him to violence. But in addition to all these facilitators (Lofland, 1969) the killer also requires a form for organizing and channelling his "expressive flow" (Bandura, 1973; Douglas, 1977; Goffman, 1974). With few exceptions (Athens, 1974; Luckenbill, 1977), the literature on homicide contains nothing about the organization of the killer's response. Stage Five attempts to fill that gap by describing the killer's feelings, cognitions, and overt behaviors as organized in terms of conflict resolution.

Adversaries According to Simmel, combatants in the antagonistic game act under the "mutually recognized control of norms and rules"; they behave ritualistically with the "severity of a code of honor," and with "the fascination of fight and victory in becoming master over [the] adversary" (1955: 35). Correspondingly, all ten of the Detroit adversaries accounted for their act of homicide as an attempt to obtain a symbolic mastery over their opponent. The following quotation from a 20-year-old white male who killed his 50-year-old white adoptive mother typifies the adversary frame of mind.

> There were always fantasies in my mind of destroying my mother, not killing her, not abusing her, just destroying mother. *I knew that I had to exert my authority*. And so, all the next day I had prepared myself for killing her. I wrote a couple of letters. I had a guy do a charcoal drawing of me [the next day he went to his mother's house for supper]. My biggest concern was that I would back down again from myself, that I would be weak again. So, I just jumped up and walked in on her, you know. She's in the kitchen, and I just grabbed her. She got away from me and ran. Then I grabbed her by the neck. She landed on her back on the floor. And I had her down on the living room floor, and she says, "You can't do this to me, I'm your mother." And I said, *"Well you ain't my mother." And the longer we was looking at each other, the more she realized, you are doing this to me. She knew that I was going to kill her. It's such a hell of a feeling watching the look on someone's face when they know there's nothing they can say, or nothing they can do to prevent themself from dying. And they just look at you. That's what I mean, she resigned herself. So, when she did that, I knew that I had her.* And I got up from her, I got the gun, I turned around and I ran up and I shot her in the head, on the temple, in the eye, in the mouth, and I shot her in the side; *I aimed* up above just where I though the heart would be, and I shot. And then everything just came to a head, I mean not to exist. (No. 30)

The Adversary's Verbal Accounts The adversary commits his killing to resolve the question of symbolic dominance. Five adversaries, including the man quoted above, wanted to exert their authority. Another three wanted to "teach a lesson" to the victim, while the remaining two wanted to "put him in his place." These various accounts are consistent with the desire for symbolic mastery, noted by Luckenbill.

The Adversary's Sensations The adversary's verbal account of his killing, as an attempt to dominate, is consistent with the wider, existential features of his experience. During the killing, he watches the victim, specifically the victim's face and more specifically, the victim's face in an attitude of *submission*. This was the case with 5 of the 10 adversary killers: "It just seemed like he had his mouth open and he just didn't know what to do, he just sat there and looked at me" (No. 46).

Of the remaining five adversaries, two were unable to see their victim's face because the victim was running away from them at the time of the killing (and seeing the victim in fearful retreat is a second way to perceive submission). In the case of the other three adversaries, one was reluctant to describe any of his experiences at the scene, and the other two are deviant cases, in that they do not recall any sense of domination.

The Adversary's Overt Behaviors Aside from their sensations, the adversaries' overt behaviors were also consistent with their verbal accounts. Seven of them expressed their mastery over a submissive victim by inflicting multiple wounds, each wound administered with intent and calculation: "It was all *geometric*, in proportion. I was frightened, you know. But yet, I had forces, I mean, I could reach into any source that I wanted; *I was mentally aware*" (No. 30). Other patterns of behavior were also associated, to some degree, with the adversary's desire to "put his victim down." Seven adversaries chased after their victims and ran them down: "And I chased the guy about six, seven blocks, and I finally got him" (No. 34).

Three sat on top of their victims in the process of killing them. And the man who killed his adoptive mother removed her bra and placed his hand on her bare breast to achieve what he termed her "humiliation." Thus the adversary's verbal accounts, his sensations, and his overt behaviors are all consistent with saving face at the other's expense, the Luckenbill framework.

Lovers According to Simmel, when one partner in an intimate relation attempts to leave the other, this can lead to a conflict in which their "separation revolves around the point of their connection." This type of conflict can become so "intensive and extensive" that the jilted partner, after all attempts to hold the relationship together have failed, explodes with "rage, hate, contempt, and cruelty," destroying his victim and sometimes destroying himself in the process. All but one (No. 25) of the Detroit lovers conforms to Simmel's description to some degree. The following quotation, from an 18-year-old white male who killed his 13-year-old white male companion, illustrates the point

> I felt this was love itself. I never had experienced it, and I thought this was the ultimate, and *I didn't* want this to *leave me*, you know, it might never happen again. *I didn't want to lose this person, lose this moment of my life.* I ended it right there. After all this stuff in my mind building up, I made an unleash of aggressions and hostilities, anger, love, all these feelings, all blown into one little short spurt, which lasted about 30 seconds to one minute, and it was over. I was aware of what was going on, though *it was like my mind and my body was two separate people* and my mind had no control over that body. I just, I had a necktie, and I wrapped it around and tied it and started pulling, that's when I *lost control. I looked at that and even screamed at myself and said stop.* It's *just like a wild animal*—you can beat on them and kick them and every-

> thing, they're not going to stop. He started choking and gasping, and he didn't struggle too much, there wasn't much he could do, and then it was over. The tie broke, and *just like an instinct, you continue.* I had another tie and just continued it. (No. 41)

The Lover's Verbal Accounts Five of the nine Detroit lovers verbally accounted for their act of homicide as an attempt to kill their victims in order to keep them. For example,

> That was my whole life right there. That was everything in the future that was building toward my future; that's what I wanted, that's about the only thing in my life that I could ever recall that I really wanted. Now, it's just like they want to totally forget that I ever existed, like I am no more, and I just couldn't walk away like that, with that feeling. (No. 55)

The remaining three lovers had "no explanation" for what they did. They steadfastly maintained that they "didn't know why" they did it. All three of these people had been adjudicated legally insane, indicating that their behavior was "irrational." However, there may be another explanation for both their lack of a reason and their apparent insanity. Killing someone in order to keep them is the kind of a motive best left unverbalized. It may make very good sense as an impulsive gesture but only if one avoids thinking it through. Thus, the lover's stated motives are very different from the adversary's. The lover wants to save his relationship not to save face.

The Lover's Sensations The lover's sensations are consistent with his verbal accounts. First, he "explodes." This leaves him feeling split in two and enables one half of himself to stand off to the side and watch while the other half inflicts murder with the abandon of a "wild animal." Six of the nine lovers said that they either "exploded" or "blew up" or saw a sudden "flash" before their eyes. "Well, it was just like a *fire cracker* busted, just like something exploded in my mind" (No. 35). Of the remaining three lovers, one was No. 25, and the other two (NGRIs) claimed to have "blanked out" and could not recall exactly what happened during the homicide.

Following the explosion, four of the nine lovers felt a sense of detachment, with half of themselves (the animal half) committing homicide while the other, rational half watched.

> Yeah, it was like my *mind wasn't attached to my body*; it was like, it was like being high; everything was all clouded over and there wasn't no thoughts going through my mind except what I was doing right then. It was strange, I was doing it, but it seemed like it wasn't really me. (No. 55)

The lovers' sensations are highly consistent with Simmel's (1955: 54) description of conflict in intimate relations. The lover, whose "separation revolves around the point of [his] connection," is conceptually being pulled apart. His explosion and subsequent detachment are consistent of reason and thought. Even those lovers who "blanked out" can be seen as having an extreme form of the explosion-detachment experience (they became completely detached). In either case, reason becomes conveniently suspended. Psychiatrists who believe that killing is largely senseless behavior (Tanay, 1972: 815) or simply an outburst of aggression resulting from too much frustration (Dollard et al., 1939), have never systematically explored the context that can make "senseless behavior" seem logical. It is highly convenient for the desperate lover to lose his mind.

The Lover's Overt Behaviors The lover's overt behaviors are also consistent with his verbal accounts. The lover behaves with emotional abandon: "After I shot her, I was *still shooting the gun* and there wasn't nothing in it" (No. 55). He literally behaves like a "wild animal" (No. 41), continuing to inflict wounds without restraint. Five of the nine lovers inflicted multiple wounds upon their victims. Another two could not recall how many wounds they had inflicted. The remaining two inflicted only a single wound, making them deviant cases. But in general the highly emotional accounts, sensations, and behaviors displayed by the lovers are all consistent with an attempt to keep the loved one from leaving (and not to save face).

Strangers According to Simmel, in the conflict over causes, opponents behave "impersonally" on behalf of their "rationally articulated" and "objective conflict interests" (1955:38). The following quote from a black man in his fifties who killed another black man in his fifties shows how the Detroit strangers conform to Simmel's characterization.

> *I didn't think I was going to kill him, but he wouldn't stop.* He just kept following me out on the street, with his knife. But the first time, when I first shot him, see, I was on the sidewalk, and then I got off the sidewalk, see. He still followed me. And when I jumped off that sidewalk, and I done shot the man one time, and he still followed me up, I got to do something then. He's not going to turn around unless I *make him* turn around. *He just, just charged at me like one of these Mexican bulls. And all you can be thinking about, about trying to keep the man off of you, and the reaction of how the guy looked and whatnot like that, you wouldn't have time to be doing that.* I shot him three or four [times]. And like I say, if the man turned around, don't be following me, he'd be living today. (No. 28).

The Stranger's Verbal Accounts All 16 of the strangers accounted for the killing in one of two ways. Fourteen claimed "self-defense." "I was turning around on my knees, and he shot again, and so it went through my right arm, and it came out just above the elbow. He was trying to put me away, and it's natural reflex to try to keep the man from killing me. I guess I fired back at the man" (No. 15). The remaining two strangers claimed that the killing was "accidental" (meaning, "I didn't want to shot the guy but I was in the position where I couldn't do nothing but. . . ." [No. 40]). Whether the stranger claimed self-defense or accident, in either case, "nothing personal" was involved. And in either case the killing is justified as a purely instrumental move: he wants to "stop" the victim from doing something to him.

The Stranger's Sensations The stranger's sensations are consistent with his verbal accounts. He experiences the victim impersonally, as something to be stopped: "I *didn't see him* very well; like I say, he was *just a figure*; (No. 45). All but one of the strangers focused either on their victim's weapon or on their victim's threatening movements. Begging the question, we pressed strangers about taking note of *any* of their victim's personal features—his clothing, his face, his expression. They consistently denied noticing anything at the moment of killing but a flash of oncoming movement: "I never studied the expression on his face. Actually, I panicked, and there is very little I can remember" (No. 13). Whereas the adversary fixates on his victim's face, draws his gratification from that experience, the stranger's apprehension is different. He views his victim, at the moment of the killing, as nothing more than an object.

The Stranger's Overt Behaviors Finally, the stranger's overt behaviors were also consistent with their verbal accounts. They do only what is necessary to obtain their objective (self-defense, money, etc.). Strangers are prone to inflict only a single wound if that suffices to stop the victim's advance. "I see this guy coming at me with this knife; so quite naturally, I had a knife in my pocket and got my knife. So, I stuck, but at the time I didn't know I had killed him. I stabbed him *once*. It was in the heart" (No. 3). Aside from the 9 (out of 16) strangers who inflicted only a single wound, another 4 employed a second pattern of behavior characteristic of strangers. They issued a single shot, paused, then followed with a succession of three or four shots if the victim continued coming on: "When he came out with the weapon, I scrounged for the door. I had pulled my thing out, shot him *one*. He staggered for a minute, he stopped, then he came forward again. *I shot him three times*" (No. 44).

The remaining three cases are deviant cases, in that they inflicted multiple wounds. Thus, the stranger's accounts, sensations, and behaviors were all generally consistent with an attempt to obtain an "objective interest," as opposed to a personal or egoistic consideration," such as saving face (Simmel, 1955:38).

To summarize Stage Five, the avowed aim of almost all of the 35

Detroit respondents is consistent with "resolving a divergent dualism" (Simmel, 1955:13). The killers' verbal accounts, sensations, and overt behaviors all conform to this general interpretation. The lovers killed in order to stay together. The adversaries killed in order to obtain dominance. And the strangers killed in order to obtain decisively an objective interest. Each attempted to overcome opposition and obtain the resolution he desired.

In addition, Simmel predicted that the more extreme the unity, the more extreme the antagonism. Stage Five indicates that at the point of killing (extreme antagonism), killers are not only mindful of their relation to the victim, but are fixated upon that relation to the exclusion of all other matters. The lover acts with total emotional abandon (a wild animal), the adversary with total mastery, and the stranger with total objectivity.

Stage Six: Aftermath

Luckenbill referred to the offender's exiting from the scene as the "termination of the transaction." he cited two essential factors: the "relationship of the offender and the victim and the position of the audience vis-a-vis the offense" (1977:185). In the Detroit study, although we did not question respondents about events after the homicide, many of them volunteered the information anyway, and what they said partially confirms what Luckenbill observed.

Lovers Luckenbill found that when victim and offender were intimately related, the offender typically remained on the scene. Many of the Detroit lovers also remained on the scene or returned to it after a brief departure. Typically, they "felt sorry" for what they had done: "And I'm really *sorry*. If there was anything I could do to bring her back, I would. And every day since that day, it be on my mind, every day since that day" (No. 35).

Strangers Adversaries and strangers both attempted to flee from the scene. But aside from that similarity, the reactions of adversaries and strangers differ notably. Strangers typically felt frightened and glad to be alive.

> I didn't see anything for a second or two, and then finally, I saw blood coming from his head. Well, you know, I didn't want any money then. I wanted to get the hell out of there. So, I ran. I didn't know where I was going; I didn't know where to run to. I run right by my house, right past it. I kept running, running, and running, until I got tired. (No. 13)

Adversaries Adversaries also departed from the scene, but not with any sense of fear: "After, you know, the killing, I felt more of an ease, like you been in hell and all of a sudden they let you out of hell. And walking down the street, it's a feeling like you're on acid" (No. 34). The adversary typically maintains his high. Even in prison, decisive victory over the enemy continues to provide the killer with a feeling of satisfaction.

KILLERS AND NORMALS

Simmel's formula, on the interdependence of unity and antagonism, has lead to the discovery of the general stages in the homicide-transaction, outlined in Table 1.

Just as an adversary relation is not the only type of relation that people can have with each other, so Luckenbill's "character contest" is not the only type of conflict that can lead people to an ultimate resolution of their relationship. Our understanding of the homicide process would be severely limited, if we thought of it as only an attempt to save face. The present article has argued that a conflict resolution framework provides a more fitting scheme of interpretation for the various components of the homicide process including the opening move, the interpretation of that move, the killer's reaction, the working agreement, the killer's sense of threat, and the organization of the killer's response in terms of his verbal accounts, his sensations, and his overt behaviors.

Obviously, not every lover's quarrel, every antagonistic game, or every conflict of interest results in homicide. On the other hand, these are the very situations that people commonly associate with the intent to kill. The present article has lent support to the common view: conflicts that give rise to homicidal intents are similar to everyday conflicts. For this reason, the desire to kill is probably fairly normal.

Given that homicidal situations are similar to normal, conflict situations, then what distinguishes them from each other? The answer, in part, is that homicidal situations contain more facilitators, such as a weapon, concealment from the law, or an appropriate self-image on the part of the offender. But these facilitators are not enough, because there has to be something for them to facilitate in the first place. There has to be a motive to kill, which can be *suggested* by the facilitators, but which is independent of them.

An additional distinction between normal and homicidal situations has to do with the link between unity and antagonism at their extremes. Stage Four, the working agreement, indicates that the desire to kill (extreme antagonism) can be precipitated by the killer's own perception of an extreme unity of interests and understandings between himself and his victim. This perception of unity creates a zero-sum game, which excludes heterogeneous concerns, traps the killer in an untenable situation, and blocks consideration of alternative solutions. The link between the extremes of unity and

TABLE 1 Stages in the Homicide Process for Adversaries, Lovers, and Strangers

	Stages in the Homicide Process					
Killer-victim relation	**I. Opening move**	**II. Killer's interpretation**	**III. Killer's response**	**IV. Working agreement**	**V. Combat**	**VI. Aftermath**
Adversaries	Insults or gestures	Misuse	Possible retaliation	Victim's public territorial invasion; humiliation trap	Ritual dominance	Flee; satisfaction
Lovers	Withdrawal	Alienation of affection	Fact-finding mission	Victim's unambiguous response; rejection trap	Emotional togetherness	Stay; remorse
Strangers	Attack or resistance	Impediment	Possible retreat	Victim's armed attack; panic trap	Impersonal objectifica-tion	Flee; relief

antagonism is also demonstrated in Stage Five (combat). Here, the killer appears to be not only mindful of his relation to the victim, but fixated upon that relation to the exclusion of all other matters. Finally, the link between the extremes of unity and antagonism is evident in the killing itself. In completing the most antagonistic of acts, the killer sees himself as having achieved a decisive, immutable resolution of the victim's role vis-à-vis himself, the offender. This image of a consummately fixed and inflexible relationship—and the processes bringing it about—mark an important distinction between normal versus homicidal situations.

As mentioned before, "lover, adversary, and stranger" are terms derived from Simmelian concepts and are used heuristically in this article in order to specify different types of perceived unity. Other types of unity are, of course, also possible, and the only assertion made here is that whatever the killer perceives the commonality to be between himself and his victim, it will influence many of the variations in homicide.

In closing, it should be emphasized that it is not here implied that every time the sequence of events outlined above occurs, a conflict resolution dynamic was necessarily at play. What remains to be done in future research is to discern precisely when conflict resolution transactions lead to homicide and when they do not.

REFERENCES

Amir, Menachem
1971 Patterns in Forcible Rape. Chicago: University of Chicago Press.
Athens, Lonnie
1974 "The self and the violent criminal act." Urban Life and Culture 3, 1 (April):98–113.
Bandura, Albert
1973 Aggression: A Social Learning Analysis. Englewood Cliffs, N.J.: Prentice-Hall.
Bensing, Robert C., and Oliver J. Schroeder
1960 Homicide in an Urban Community. Springfield, Ill.: Charles C. Thomas.
Boudouris, James
1970 "Trends in homicide, Detroit: 1926–1968." Unpublished manuscript.
Bullock, Henry A.
1955 "Urban homicide in theory and fact." Journal of Criminal Law and Criminology 45 (Jan.–Feb.):565–75.
Curtis, Lynn A.
1974 Criminal Violence. Lexington, Mass.: Lexington Books.
Dollard, James, L. W. Dobb, N. Miller, O. H. Mowrer, and R. R. Sears
1939 Frustration and Aggression. New Haven: Yale University Press.
Douglas, Jack D.
1967 The Social Meanings of Suicide. Princeton: Princeton University Press.

Douglas, Jack D.
1977 Existential Sociology. New York: Cambridge University Press.

Duncan, Glen M., S. H. Frazier, E. M. Litin, A. M. Johnson, and A. J. Barron
1967 "Etiological factors in first degree murder." Pp. 198–209 in M. E. Wolfgang (Ed.), Studies in Homicide. New York: Harper & Row.

Galvin, James, A., and J. M. MacDonald
1967 "A psychiatric study of a mass murderer." In M. E. Wolfgang (Ed.), Studies in Homicide. New York: Harper & Row.

Glaser, Barney G., and A. L. Strauss
1967 The Discovery of Grounded Theory. Chicago: Aldine.

Goffman, Erving
1967 Interaction Ritual. Garden City, New York: Anchor Books.

Goffman, Erving
1974 Frame Analysis. Cambridge: Harvard University Press.

Guttmacher, Manfred
1967 "The normal and the sociopathic murderer." Pp. 114–33 in M. E. Wolfgang (Ed.) Studies in Homicide. New York: Harper & Row.

Heirich, Max
1971 The Spiral of Conflict. Berkeley: University of California Press.

Henry, Andrew F., and J. F. Short
1954 Suicide and homicide. Glencoe, Ill.: Free Press.

Langner, Herman P.
1971 "The making of a murderer." American Journal of Psychiatry 127 (Jan.):950–53.

Lofland, John
1969 Deviance and Identity. Englewood Cliffs, N.J.: Prentice-Hall.

Luckenbill, David
1977 "Criminal homicide as a situated transaction." Social Problems 25 (Dec.): 176–86.

Lyman, Stanford, and M. Scott
1970 "Accounts, deviance and social order." Pp. 92–121 in J. D. Douglas (Ed.), Deviance and Respectability. Scranton, Pa.: Harper & Row.

Lyman, Stanford, and M. Scott
1975 The Drama of Social Reality. New York: Oxford University Press.

Matza, David
1969 Becoming Deviant. Englewood Cliffs, N.J.: Prentice-Hall.

McCord, William J. McCord, and A. Howard
1970 "Familial correlates of aggression in non-delinquent male children." Pp. 41–65 in E. I. Megargee and J. E. Hokanson (Eds.), The Dynamics of Aggression. New York: Harper & Row.

Quinney, Richard
1970 The Social Reality of Crime. Boston: Little, Brown.

Schultz, Leroy G.
1967 "The pre-sentence investigation and victimology." UMKC Law Review 35 (Summer).

Silverman, Robert A.
1974 "Victim typologies: overview, critique, and reformation." Pp. 55–56 in E. Drapkin and E. Viano (Eds.) Victimology. Lexington, Mass.: Lexington Books.
Simmel, Georg
1955 Conflict and the Web of Group Affiliations. K. H. Wolff and R. Bendix (transls.). New York: Free Press.
Smelser, Neil J.
1963 Theory of Collective Behavior. New York: Free Press.
Sykes, Gresham M.
1978 Criminology. New York: Harcourt, Brace, Jovanovich.
Tanay, Emanuel
1972 "Psychiatric aspects of homicide prevention." American Journal of Psychiatry 128:814–17.
Totman, J. M.
1970 "The murderess: a psycho-social history of criminal homicide." Unpublished manuscript.
Von Hentig, Hans
1948 The Criminal and His Victim. New Haven: Yale University Press.
Wolfgang, Marvin E.
1958 Patterns in Criminal Homicide. Philadelphia: University of Philadelphia Press.
Wolfgang, Marvin E., and F. Ferracuti
1967 The Subculture of Violence. London: Tavistock Publications Limited.

Chapter Ten

Deviance in the Workplace

EDITORIAL COMMENTARY

The social context of work is a fertile setting for deviant behavior. A very significant proportion of deviant behavior occurs within, concomitant to, or as a result of, work and occupational specialty. This includes an extraordinarily wide range of deviant behavior, and an equally broad array of occupations and work systems. In some instances the deviance may be of a relatively innocuous variety with only modest social import or it may constitute a criminal offense of an extremely serious variety. Inasmuch as work organization involves both formal and informal normative structure, violations of the work norms attendant to the informal system, such as inappropriate work role performance, product sabotage, "rate-busting," quota restriction, or the use of forbidden procedures—a shortcut technique to cover up mistakes or shoddy workmanship, for example, represent deviant behavior, as well as activities that transgress the norms of the formal structure. Included here might be offenses such as falsifying company records, failing to employ appropriate safety measures, the subversion of required sexual comportment, or fighting on the job to name some. Also included in the latter might be unethical behavior such as "ambulance chasing," professional misconduct, or exploitative or fraudulent practices.

The professions stand among the upper status echelons of occupations. The rigorousness of their training, the extent and depth of their professional knowledge, the intensity of their personal obligation to their art, the degree of their personality involvement, and the essential nature of services they render to society all combine to place them in a unique and superior occupational category. Professionals, along with high-level executive and managerial personnel, and members of certain other high-status vocations constitute a kind of occupational elite. Paramount in almost all work endeavors of such an occupational elite is the necessity for maintaining public faith and trust in the superior qualities of their occupational services. Because of this public faith and trust the elite occupations are allowed a somewhat larger measure of autonomy, a higher degree of occupational self-control, and a wider range of prerogatives than is the case with most other occupational categories. Because members of elite occupations are not expected to violate the norms of their specialty, they are usually not monitored closely. Accordingly, they often do have a significant opportunity structure for norm violations. It is usually a matter of considerable shock to the public when work-related deviance on the part of members of the occupational elite does occur. Such deviance could assume a variety of forms including political corruption, white collar crime, malfeasance in office, inside stock trading, price fixing, criminal collusion and grossly unethical behavior to name some examples.

The first selection in this chapter, H. Kenneth Bechtel, Jr., and Willie Pearson, Jr.'s "Deviant Scientists and Scientific Deviance," addresses a variety of deviance that is both unusual and shocking to the public, that of scientific fraud. The scientist occupies a special niche in the public mind, with an image often stereotypically combining the dedication of a missionary, the sanctity of a priest, and the enthusiasm of a salesman. In the face of such an image, it is especially opprobrious when the public discovers that some scientists have "feet of clay," as it were. The notion of falsifying data, or otherwise perpetrating fraud seems to be, and is, antithetical to the very values of science. In this day and time the stakes are high, however, and some scientific practitioners are apparently motivated to violate their trust and commit fraud.

The authors point out that attempting to document the prevalence of scientific fraud is extremely difficult but that it would "be naive to assume that there are no incidents of scientific fraud that remain undiscovered and/or unreported." They report that some estimates of such unreported fraud run as high as 100,000 but that such estimates are "pure speculation and inherently unverifiable." In this essay, the authors focus on twelve recent cases of scientific fraud, and describe the details of these instances of deceptions. The cases involved manipulating experiments, falsifying data, the destruction of valid data, plagiarism, and the publishing of spurious research results. From these cases, they draw several conclusions.

These deviant offenses tended to be the acts of "loners," and were seen as "primarily defensive in nature, [and] an act to ward off some form of real or perceived threat." The individuals involved reacted to the possible loss of a grant or a position if they did not "produce at expected levels." The offenders tended to rationalize their acts on the basis of the operant "publish or perish" mandate in the scientific community. Elite occupational deviance, such as scientific fraud, does present something of a problem in terms of explaining why "highly educated, talented, respectable persons [choose] to act in an obviously deviant fashion." The authors suggest that Robert Merton's classical theory of anomie may even make a contribution in the way of developing a better understanding of scientific deviance. The scientific enterprise today is no longer a "sportsman-like rivalry between researchers" but rather a "highly competitive enterprise." The researcher who first gets the right results and gets the publication gets the "goodies," so to speak, such as grants, promotions, tenure, etc. Given this situation it is not surprising, perhaps that some individuals take shortcuts or falsify data in order to be the first. Other traditional theories of deviant behavior may also provide valuable insights into the phenomena. It will be necessary to examine more closely the individual dimension of such behavior as well as the structural dimensions of the scientific research context such as the reward system, and the attendant pressure in some instances, to use illegitimate means. The social import of the subversion of science for personal gain is enormous and augurs ill for the human condition.

Inasmuch as specific disaffective routines, pressures, stresses, and problems are constituent to certain kinds of work, it would appear that some occupational structures, and/or work cultures tend to induce, facilitate, and harbor particular kinds of pathological and, thus, deviant behavior such as alcoholism, narcotic addiction or homosexuality. Similarly, the structure and culture of some conventionally legal work and occupational systems seems to be conducive to characteristic forms of illegal activities. Illustrations here might include "white-collar" crime, "blue-coat" crime (Stoddard, 1968), "blue-collar" crime (Horning, 1970), or "khaki-collar" crime (i.e., military crime; see Bryant, 1979), to mention some. Executives may illicitly pad their expense accounts, factory workers may steal tools or materials, policemen may accept bribes and grafts and soldiers may illegally shoot enemy POWs. Such work systems apparently possess singular opportunity structures for crime as well as unique milieus that contribute to the individual motivation for such illicit behavior.

The second reading in this selection examines the characteristic forms of employee theft in one particular work system. Here Richard Hawkins looks at "Employee Theft in the Restaurant Trade: Forms of Ripping Off by Waiters at Work." Based on individual and group interviews, the author was able to construct twelve short vignettes that illustrate the range of theft activity. Some examples of such theft included giving free food to friends, selling restaurant items, short changing customers, and taking other waiters' tip money, to name some. Such theft activity may be directed against the restaurant, its customers, or fellow restaurant employees. The author hypothesized that a larger proportion of waiters will be involved in thefts from the restaurant than when other targets are victimized. He further hypothesized that thefts against customers would represent the next largest proportion of crime and thefts against fellow workers the smallest. Hawkins also hypothesized that the likelihood of employee theft would increase with job dissatisfaction, and finally that workers who can more easily agree with neutralization statements will be more likely to engage in theft.

The author was able to test these hypotheses by submitting a questionnaire to waiters in four "prime rib" restaurants in a large Southwestern city. His analysis of results revealed that, indeed, waiters were more likely to commit theft against the restaurant followed by theft against customer, and with very little theft against other waiters. Hawkins also found that attitudes toward job-related conditions were not related to restaurant theft. In regard to the third hypothesis, it appeared that "neutralization and justification [of theft] are rather rare among the waiters." Thus, it would appear that employee theft in the restaurant is relatively common and varied in form. Such theft would not appear to result from job dissatisfaction and seldom involves rationalization or neutralization efforts. Restaurant employee theft apparently is part of the subcultural pattern and there is a good bit of "theft-talk" in the "shop-talk" at work. Theft and theft-talk would seem to have certain self-actualizing functions for employees. Such theft-talk also helps inform and socialize the newcomer, as well as act as a controlling mechanism "whereby workers set the boundaries of appropriate targets and amounts of theft." Restaurant workers like rookie policemen are socialized to accept theft as a normal component of the job (Stoddard, 1968). Given the opportunity structure of the restaurant, and some degree of toleration for employee theft on the part of management, it is perhaps not surprising that such theft activities play a "critical role" in the restaurant work setting.

Some occupational specialties, while not always defined as illegal, do often transcend the boundaries of propriety and community acceptance, either because of intent or the nature of the service rendered, and can accordingly be classified as deviant. Professional gamblers, or pool "hustlers" with their "professional" overskill and deceptive competition may skirt the edge of legality on occasion. Similarly, there may be a thin line between fortune tellers or soothsayers with their contrived clairvoyance and "future" chicanery, or "quack" healers with their profitable panaceas and nefarious nostrums, and illegal, exploitative confidence games and "grand theft bunko" offenses.

Fraud and deception are relative, not absolute, processes, and the occupation does not exist that does not employ some degree of misrepresentation and deceit, regardless of how minor, in attempting to manipulate the client. The dentist may, for example, minimize the pain and discomfort, not to mention the cost of expensive dental "restoration" when discussing the need for this work with a patient. Some writers have also pointed out that the funeral director may on occasion utilize the psychologically disabled condition of the bereaved family to his or her advantage in "merchandising" funeral services and appurtenances beyond the financial means of the family. Real estate salesmen may neglect to mention that the back of the lot they are attempting to sell stands a foot deep in water after a heavy rain. The stereotype of "Honest John," the used car dealer, who "loses on every sale, but makes it up on volume" is brutal in its indictment of the high pressure sales tactics employed in selling used automobiles. In a similar vein, appliance salesmen admit to a wide array of questionable sales techniques including such hoary standbys as "PM" or "spiff" (push or extra bonus money), "burning" and "switching" (changing the customer's brand preference to a product more profitable to the dealer), and disguising high interest rates by quoting only the amount of monthly payment.

Even in the instances of these less-than-honest occupational practices, however, the practitioners in question are still pursuing a respectable or at least acceptable occupational specialty and are producing or rendering a basically sound service or goods of significant worth. This is not always the case with marginally illegal occupations or other vocations of the deviant fringe. The practitioners of such marginal trades may wear a thin veneer of orthodoxy and respectability and may on occasion operate with all the external trappings of honesty and legality. Their basic aim is, however, profit without regard for the quality or worth of goods or services rendered. Their orientation is basically exploitative. Frequently they operate openly and attempt to merchandise their goods and services as articles of genuine value and function. Unfortunately, the goods and services rendered are often unnecessary, unutilitarian, misrepresented, undependable, dysfunctional to the clientele, or even spurious.

The latter characterizes the nature of the service offered or described in the next reading, "Talk about Visions: Spiritual Readings as Deviant Work." In this selection, John Heeren and Marylee Mason focus on the interactional machinations of spiritual readers or fortune tellers as they deal with clients. Inasmuch as there is no scientific evidence that anyone can tell the future, fortune telling must be viewed as a spurious service. As the authors point out, there are some individuals who do believe they possess clairvoyant powers and certainly there are many persons who believe that others are capable of telling their fortune. In that sense, fortune telling, like some other deviant occupations, often serves a social need. Spiritual readers operate to serve this need and use a variety of dramaturgical and manipulative behaviors to better convince their clientele of their clairvoyance.

This effort is facilitated if the reader and the client share a "common religion," i.e., a set of shared beliefs such as a concern with luck and coincidence, faith in nonrational practices such as astrology or water-witching, or even a belief in magic and the supernatural. The fortune teller relies on three distinct types of conversation including everyday conversation, interview questions, and the "visionary style." Visionary statements may be either of declarative or interrogative variety. The latter is useful in that it is a means of obtaining information from the client. In effect, the spiritual reader leaves gaps in her predictions which the client is encouraged to fill in. By speaking in interrogative form, and using forceful declarations, the reader effectively uses the client as part of the process of convincing him or her of the reader's powers. The reader relies on a dramaturgical performance involving "elaborate ploys, presentational devices, and complex interactive skills" to meet the needs that the client brings to the encounter. In this instance, the practitioner provides a deceptive and, thus, deviant service, and even has the client aid in his or her own deception.

Other such marginally illegal occupations and work systems may offend community standards of decency and decorum, or violate the norms of morality and proprietous comportment. Examples here might include persons in the "erotic" specialities such as burlesque comedians, strippers, go-go dancers, B-girls, actors and actresses in porno films, masseuses in massage parlors, and some members of carnival troops (i.e., persons who operate deceptive or crooked games) to name some. Practitioners of these trades may move back and forth between legal endeavors and illegal activities in the course of plying their occupational specialties. Stripping, for instance, may be legal in a given community, but the law may well establish the normative limits on the degree of nudeness permitted. The law may require that a stripper at least wear a "G-string," and "pasties" (abbreviated coverings over her nipples) as a minimum. In certain circumstances (the last show on Saturday night as an illustration), however, the stripper may, in response to audience enthusiasm and demand, indulge in "flashing" (lowering the G-string from time to time), thereby departing from the more circumspect performance decreed by legal statute and becoming illegal in her occupational behavior.

The marginally illegal occupational practitioners (like some totally illegal pursuits), however, operate to serve certain existing, even if clandestine, social needs but as such do not necessarily enjoy the total and enthusiastic approbation of the community. In the process of rendering the services required, practitioners may operate within a wider latitude of deviant variation than conventionally afforded and tolerated by the normative system. Some individual requirements and wants may themselves, because of their baseness or idiosyncratic bent, lie beyond the pale of normality, convention, or even legality. Such needs are met in the marketplace, for where there is demand there will be supply. The occupational deviant fringe exists to serve this demand and does so usually within a fragile and ephemeral context of legality. Such a work specialty requires considerable dexterity in walking the razor thin edge of legality and community tolerance on the one hand, and criminality and reprehensible nonconformity on the other.

A great many other occupational pursuits are clearly in violation of legal statute even though they provide genuine occupational and career opportunities for the practitioners and are, thus, deviant also. In short, there are illegal vocational pursuits that are, in fact, true occupations. They often have history and rich tradition. They have structure and not infrequently have an elaborate attendant subculture. Individuals are selectively recruited as in conventional occupations. They are subjected to involved socialization processes, sometimes even of a formal nature (Oliver Twist, if you recall, went to thieves' school). Counterfeit money engraving is not an inherited skill, and providing quality fornication requires expertise not acquired through maturation alone. There are operant controls and career contingencies. Illegal practitioners, like members of regular occupations, exhibit craftsmanship values and pride in the product or service they render. Polly Adler, the famous brothel madame, had an allegedly justifiable reputation for what she termed "the quality of my establishment and consideration of my customers." People in deviant occupations develop distinctive work routines, esoteric skills, and occupational ideologies often unique to their calling. They have their career ups and downs, some succeeding and others falling short of "the big time." Like any line of work, theirs may on occasion be disaffective or stressful, if not otherwise dysfunctional. There are also unique hazards, risks, and pathologies attendant to their work. Robbers may be shot during the commission of a crime, and prostitutes may contract AIDS or a venereal disease, for example. In the final analysis, however, where a particular kind of goods or services is demanded (even if contraindicated by law and custom), there will inevitably be those who will supply it—and often with the aplomb and dedication of a professional.

The final article in this chapter, Patricia and Peter Adler's "Criminal Commitment among Drug Dealers," examines the motivation for illegal narcotics sales. The authors gathered data from 65 drug dealers in the Southwest, "through a combination of participant-observation and intensive interviewing." Drug distribution as with other products, requires a network involving the cooperation of a number of people and an elaborate division of labor. Drug dealing was, in effect, a small business community. Such a business enterprise is not without its problems and its challenges, its rewards and hazards, and its satisfactions and disaffections. To cope with the job, as it were, requires a specialized business acumen, and an appropriate commitment to the business. The authors looked at various components of this commitment including normative, economic, social, and egoistic dimensions and drew several conclusions.

In terms of normative considerations, the drug dealers, if they are to operate efficiently and successfully, must rely to some degree on secrecy and security, alliances and trust, a specialized division of labor, and a subscription to the overall norms and values indigenous to the drug trafficking subculture, all elements associated with organized crime. In this sense, they tended to view dealing as a career. From the standpoint of economic commitment, drug dealers are attracted by the large amount of money they can earn, and from the attendant "fringe benefits" such as being self-employed, setting their own hours, etc. From this perspective, crime is a "work situation," with drug dealers bearing "great similarity to legitimate businessmen." Social and egoistic commitment was manifested in their affinity for the hedonistic lifestyle of "the dealing life," the interactional enjoyment derived from associations and relationships with other individuals in the dealing world. Drug dealing is a highly prestigious vocation among drug-using youth and, accordingly, dealers enjoyed high social status and respect in the subculture. Because of their access to drugs, the dealers are desirable sexual partners for some women and, as a result, the dealers are often involved in the hedonistic casual sex scene characteristic of the drug subculture. In the final analysis, drug dealing is a true vocation like other occupational specialities but, in addition to being illegal, it also possesses its own unique motivational dimensions with a constituent multifaceted pattern of job commitment.

REFERENCES

Bryant, Clifton D.
1979 Khaki-Collar Crime: Deviant Behavior in the Military Context. New York: The Free Press.

Horning, Donald N. M.
1970 "Blue-Collar Theft: Conceptions of Property, Attitudes Towards Pilfering, and Work Group Norms in a Modern Industrial Plant," pp. 46–64 in Erwin O. Smigel and H. Laurence Ross (eds.), Crimes Against Bureaucracy. New York: Van Nostrand Reinhold.

Stoddard, Ellwyn R.
1968 "The Informal 'Code' of Police Deviancy: A Group Approach to 'Blue-Coat Crime.' " Journal of Criminal Law, Criminology and Police Science 59 (2).

Reading 32

Deviant Scientists and Scientific Deviance

H. Kenneth Bechtel, Jr., and Willie Pearson, Jr.
Wake Forest University, Winston-Salem

Fraud in the form of the data fabrication/manipulation by scientists, heretofore ignored owing to its presumed nonexistence, is discussed as an area of potential interest for the study of deviant behavior. By way of illustration, twelve recent cases of scientific fraud are described. These examples serve to highlight the question of prevalence as their existence is evidence that deviance in science exists, and belies the argument that the normative structure of science makes such acts unlikely. Primary attention was given to the problem of explaining this atypical form of deviant behavior. Current popular efforts tend to be either individualistic ''bad apple'' explanations, or indictments of the pressures to produce inherent in the structure of modern science. A sociology of scientific deviance is offered by reviewing the potential contributions of anomie, interactionist, and conflict theories. All were found to have a significant application to the study of scientific deviance as a number of questions for further research are suggested.

INTRODUCTION

Increasing reports of misrepresentation and fraud by scientific researchers have provided an interesting and challenging issue for the study of deviant behavior. Traditionally, the analysis of deviance focused primarily on the "nuts, sluts, and perverts" of society, and only recently have eyes been raised to the upper regions of society to examine "elite" deviance. This new found awareness of deviance among the respectable has provided a wealth of information, as well as a basis for critical evaluation of existing theories of deviance (most of which were developed to explain "under-world" deviance). Yet, much of the study of "upper-world" deviance has focused on the institutions of politics, the corporate world, and to a lesser extent the professions of law and medicine. Deviance that involves the actual practice of the scientific craft has been largely ignored, partly owing to its assummed nonexistence, but also because deviance in one's own family is the last to be recognized or acknowledged.

The recent attention given to the incidents of scientific fraud has primarily been confined to the scientific community itself, with a definite split among those involved. On the one hand, there are those who question the

Revised version of a paper presented at the annual meeting of the Southern Sociological Society, Knoxville, April, 1984.

significance of the problem, maintain the principles of scientific purity, and congratulate the ability of science to expose and dispense with the few bad apples. On the other side is a contingent who argue the reported incidents are just the tip of the iceberg, call into question the values and norms of science, and point to the failure of science to deal with a very serious problem. From the sociological perspective, however, the basic issue is not the parameters of the problem per se, but rather the social dimensions of the acts themselves. The creation of norms, their violation, the reaction to those violations, and the response by the violator to the reaction are the principle concerns for the sociological understanding of deviance. Therefore, irrespective of its magnitude, scientific fraud does constitute a deviant act and should be studied as such.

The purpose of this paper is to provide a survey of scientific fraud as an issue of importance for the study of deviant behavior.[1] Primary attention will be given to the issue of prevalence and the problems of determining the extent of the problem, a conceptual development of the issue, an assessment of existing theoretical approaches for providing explanations for scientific fraud, and finally, to provide issues and questions for additional research.

THE QUESTION OF PREVALENCE

Determining the amount of scientific fraud is much like measuring the frequency of crime in society; only those crimes reported and recorded are counted. In this regard, there appears to be few incidents of reported and/or recorded scientific fraud. Broad and Wade (1982), for example, list thirty-four cases of "known or suspected" scientific fraud from the second century BC through 1981; an extremely small number for such a long period of time. But, as with crime statistics, reported incidents are not an accurate reflection of the actual amount of activity; thus it would be naive to assume that there are no incidents of scientific fraud that remain undiscovered and/or unreported. Whether that figure approaches 100,000 as proposed by Broad and Wade is pure speculation and inherently unvarifiable.[2]

[1]For the purpose of this paper, scientific deviance refers exclusively to the practice of fraud (faking scientific experiments and data) in conducting or publishing results of research. One could also include plagiarism, the failure to credit others, abuse of position or power, or unethical practices such as deception (Milgram, Humphries) or crimes against nature (Mengaler). These and other questionable practices of scientists (sexual harassment, misuse of research money) could all be defined and studied as examples of scientific deviance. Nevertheless, we have decided to focus on the issue of fraud for its obvious importance as a major deviation from the norms of scientific procedure, as well as its potential impact (dissemination of faulty data) on the scientific community.

[2]Broad and Wade (1982:87). For a review of this book and a rebuttal of the arguments, see, Bauer (1983).

The primary issue for studying scientific deviance as deviant behavior, however, is not the quantitative dimensions, but rather the qualitative components of the known acts. For the purpose of this paper, twelve recent examples of scientific fraud will be described. These selected cases represent most of the known instances of scientific fraud to have occurred during the past twenty years for which adequate data were available.[3]

One of the first known cases of modern fraud in science occurred in 1974 and centers around the work of William T. Summerlin, a researcher at the prestigious Sloan-Kettering Cancer Center. Summerlin was suspected of faking evidence for his claims that he had solved the problem inherent in transplanting tissues between unrelated subjects without rejection by painting dark patches on white mice to make it appear as if they were bearing healthy skin grafts (Newsweek, 1974: 57–58). Eventually he was charged by a research committee with deliberately falsifying and misrepresenting research results and admitted the fraud, giving as a rationale the heavy workload which had resulted in complete mental exhaustion that had numbed his judgment. (Science News, 1984a:348–349; Time, 1974b:60; 1974c:70; Broad and Wade, 1982:153–157).

About the same time as the Summerlin incident, but not immediately reported, was the case of Zoltan Lucas, a surgeon at Stanford who was accused in 1973 of falsifying data. In 1975, an investigative committee found "probable cause" for further investigation and Lucas was publicly reprimanded four years later by Stanford's president and suspended for twelve weeks. Because Lucas was a tenured member of the faculty, he retained his position, but his research was subject to constant review (New York Times, 1981:31). Lucas confessed to faking citations to research papers of his that did not exist. He explained that his actions were aimed at winning National Institutes of Health (NIH) research grants (Broad and Wade, 1982:230).

In 1974, a case of scientific fraud occurred at the Institute for Parapsychology in Durham, North Carolina. Walter J. Levy, the protege of the renowned J. B. Rhine was charged with faking the results of experiments that purported to demonstrate the ability of rats to influence a pleasure stimulating generator by psycho-kinetic powers. Levy acknowledged that he had, in fact, manipulated the recording machinery so that the data would indicate more than chance results. He immediately terminated his position

[3]Our research plus the list compiled by Broad and Wade (1982) indicate that these twelve cases represent approximately seventy-five percent of the known or suspected cases of fraud among scientists working in western institutions during the twenty-three year period 1960 to 1983. Because the purpose was to give a general description of the deviant activity being discussed, the list was not deemed necessary to be all-inclusive or representative in the strict scientific sense.

at the Institute (Science News, 1974b:100–101; Broad and Wade, 1982:122–123).

Next was the case of Robert J. Gullis, a postdoctoral scientist at the Max Planck Institute for Biochemistry in West Germany. In a published statement, he admitted inventing the results of experiments, giving as an explanation he was so convinced of his ideas that he simply published his hypotheses and made up the data to support them (Science News, 1977:150–151). Later, Gullis also confessed that earlier research, including his PhD dissertation, was also fraudulent resulting in a total of eleven published papers being retracted (Broad and Wade, 1982:151–153).

In 1978, experiments by Jack Shubert and Steven Krogh Derr of Hope College in Holland, Michigan, on the treatment of toxic metal poisoning proved to be fraudulent. Schubert, a known expert on methods of ridding the body of toxic metals, admitted that the experimental results had been invented by Derr, a junior partner in the research. When he was confronted with the charges, Derr refused to deny the allegations and left Hope College to become an instructor at a chiropractic college in Iowa. Although Schubert claimed he was unaware that Derr was faking experiments, questions were raised concerning his reluctance to retract the papers in which the fraudulent results were reported (McGinty, 1979:3–4).

The following year, 1979, the Ivy League was stunned by an incident that involved both Yale and Columbia Universities. The case centers around Vijay Soman, an assistant professor at the Yale School of Medicine, and his alleged plagarism of an article he had been given to review by Philip Felig, vice-chairman of Yale's department of medicine. Felig, believing the incident was one of simple plagiarism dealt with the matter informally within the confines of the scientific community. As the affair began to unravel, however, it became clear that more than a minor case of plagiarism was involved. Two independent audits of Soman's work revealed that, not only had he fudged and fabricated research results, but he had also destroyed large amounts of lab data. The final outcome was Soman's dismissal from the Yale faculty, the retraction of eleven published papers, and Felig's forced resignation as the newly appointed chair of the College of Physicians and Surgeons at Columbia University. Soman's rationale for engaging in the fraudulent activity was the cutthroat pace of research and the "pressure" to quickly publish his findings in order to establish priority. Felig's troubles resulted from his relationship with Soman as his supervisor and co-author of seven of the retracted articles, as well as his "alleged" lack of responsibility in failing to investigate the Soman situation more vigorously (Science, 1980:171–173; Hunt, 1981; Broad and Wade, 1982:162–180).

Shortly after the Soman case, another incident was reported to have occurred at Cornell. Mark Spector, a graduate student at the biochemistry lab was alleged to have doctored research by modifying cell matter to make it look like something it was not. Spector denied the charges, but nevertheless withdrew his dissertation and quit the university (Science, 1981:316; Time, 1981:83; Newsweek, 1981:114; Broad and Wade, 1982:63–69).

In 1980, an incident of scientific fraud was reported in the case of John Long at the prestigious Massachusetts General Hospital. Long had been investigating the ability of chemicals to adhere to the walls of cells afflicted with Hodgkin's disease. The results of these studies eventually were published in an article in the Journal of the National Cancer Institute. However, the findings were false and Long acknowledged faking the results by using cells that were neither human nor contaminated with Hodgkin's disease. His rationale for the fraud was an excessive workload which lead him to engage in irresponsible behavior (New York Times, 1980:22; Broad and Wade, 1982:89–96).

The Ivy League again was shaken by an incident of scientific fraud in 1981. John Darsee, a medical researcher at Harvard's Brigham and Women's Hospital, raised colleagues suspicions with his vast output of data and published articles in the area of drug therapy for heart attack recovery. By secretly observing Darsee, they caught him deliberately faking an experiment and reported the incident to the lab chief, Eugene Braunwald. Braunwald "managed" the matter for six months in response to Darsee's claim that he only had faked the one experiment (Newsweek, 1982:89–91; Science, 1982:478–482). An investigative panel eventually barred Darsee from NIH funding for a period of ten years and was critical of Braunwald's supervision. In his defense, Braunwald claimed Darsee was solely responsible, citing evidence that Darsee had also engaged in fraud while at Emory University before coming to Harvard (Science, 1983:899–1010). In the end, Darsee admitted faking his research which led to the retraction of eight studies he performed at Emory from 1974 to 1979, and nine studies done at Harvard from 1979 to 1981 (Winston-Salem Journal, 1983:8; Broad and Wade, 1982:13–15).

The last three cases also involve the fabrication of research data. In 1981, Arthur H. Hale, an assistant professor of microbiology at Bowman-Gray Medical School, was accused of publishing reports of research based on materials not available to him. Hale denied the allegations though he could not produce lab notes to document the research. He resigned his position but continued to insist on his innocence (Rogers, 1981:1). Also in 1981, M. J. Purvis, a researcher at the University of Bristol, resigned in the wake of an internal investigation after junior colleagues drew attention to irreproducible features in a paper published in the proceedings of the 28th International Congress of Physiological Sciences. Purvis retracted the paper and indicated that the falsification was limited to that one paper. Supported by grants from the Public Health Service and the Wellcome Foundation, colleagues were at a loss to explain why Purvis would engage in such activity

(Nature, 1981:509). In 1982, a report came out of the Mt. Sinai School of Medicine that an established researcher, Joseph Cort, had admitted fabricating data used in journal articles, a federal grant proposal, and an application for a patent on synthetic drugs. Cort's reported rationale for his actions was an effort to save a biochemical company that was financing his research by encouraging continued funding (Chicago Tribune, 1982:10).

Although few in number, these twelve cases provide a point of departure for the sociological study of scientific deviance. As a group, the individuals share a common profile. All were male and white, except for Soman who was from India; not an unexpected finding given the overrepresentation of white males inherent in most prestigious professions. The average age was the middle to late thirties with the youngest and oldest being Spector and Cort at ages 24 and 55 respectively. The act most commonly perpetrated was some form of data manipulation, either the fabrication of nonexistent results or fudging procedures to produce a desired outcome. Also, the institutions in which they were conducting their research are among the most prestigious universities and medical centers in the world. Except for Summerlin, who was placed on leave, and Lucas, who had tenure, all either voluntarily terminated their appointments or were forced to leave the institutions.

THE CONCEPT OF SCIENTIFIC DEVIANCE

The limited number of cases and the sketchy facts surrounding them illustrate the difficulties inherent in the study of "upper-world" deviance. Since much of this type of deviance lacks documentation through sociological research, "we do not know its extent, its nature, its cost to the public, or the scope of the forms in which it appears" (Douglas and Waksler, 1982:348). To begin efforts at unraveling the phenomenon of scientific deviance, the first step is to place it into some type of classification or category of deviant behavior. Based on what we know about the recorded cases of scientific deviance, they appear to fit with what Little (1983) refers as any "illegal or unethical act committed for personal gain by an individual of high social status and respectability in the course of the person's occupation or profession" (Little, 1983:213). Additional conceptual refinement can be provided by applying a classification scheme developed by Best and Luckenbill (1982). In their approach to the study of deviant behavior, "the social organization of deviants refers to the patterns of relationships among deviant actors involved in the pursuit of deviance" (Best and Luckenbill, 1982:24).

In the scheme as developed, the mode that correlates with the act of scientific deviance is that of the "loner." Working alone, the loner's involvement with deviance is seen as primarily defensive in nature, an act to ward off some form of real or perceived threat. This defensive pattern of deviant involvement is especially prevalent among those individuals who have had no prior deviant experience. The deviant route is chosen because they want to be ineffective. Thus, lacking a network of fellow deviants, the loner draws on legitimate resources and training for committing the deviant act. Finally, since loners do not have access to deviant ideology, they usually employ modified versions of respectable rationales as the simplest way of accounting for their actions (Best and Luckenbill, 1982:28–35).

Data on the cases of scientific deviance reported above provide ample support for placing them within these two general categories of deviant behavior. In all twelve cases, the individual was of high social status and respectability within the profession, acted alone, with indications that elaborate efforts were made to conceal the activity. Moreover, it would appear that most of the cases could be interpreted as being defensive in nature; stemming from the perceived threat of losing a grant or a position within the organization if they failed to produce at expected levels. Given their experience and training in scientific techniques, it was a simple task to utilize this expertise in an illegitimate fashion to produce credible results. Finally, the rationales that were most often given were rather mundane, usually some form of the "publish or perish" argument – a legitimate type of response within the scientific community.

EXPLAINING SCIENTIFIC DEVIANCE

With any form of norm violation, there is the desire to explain its occurrence, generally with the ultimate goal of reducing or eliminating the offensive behavior. Given the small number of reported incidents of scientific fraud, there has been limited effort to provide answers to the question of why a scientist would violate essential norms of the profession. The explanations that are available consist primarily of pedestrian responses from within the scientific community or journalistic accounts in the mass media. As a whole, these explanations tend toward either individualistic interpretations or those which focus on the structure of modern science.

The late president of the National Academy of Sciences, Philip Handler, argues that the issue of scientific fraud "need not be a matter of general scientific concern" as it was primarily the result of individuals who were "temporarily deranged" (Raeburn, 1982:C1). This tendency to psychologize the problem was most evident in the Summerlin case. The committee that reported on the incident believed that Summerlin's actions resulted from "self-deception or some other aberration which hindered him from adequately gauging the import and eventual results of his conduct" (Time,

1974:60). This interpretation was reinforced when the president of the Sloan-Kettering Cancer Center, Lewis Thomas, indicated that Summerlin was suffering from a "serious emotional disturbance" and placed him on medical leave with full pay (Time, 1974:60; Science News, 1974:349). Summerlin also got in the act, reporting that he felt much better now that he was under the care of a psychiatrist (Science News, 1974:349). Finally, Eugene Braunwald, Darsee's supervisor and mentor at Harvard reports that he never would have kept him had he known "how seriously disturbed Darsee was" (Begley, 1982:91).

These attempts to explain scientific deviance by attributing it to character or personality flaws of the perpetrators are excellent examples of the "bad person" approach to explaining deviant behavior. Being the least threatening to the status quo, this approach has the added advantage of deflecting attention and potential criticism away from the institutional arrangements in which the deviance occurs—in this case the structure of modern scientific research (Little, 1983:221). Nevertheless, criticism has been forthcoming, much of it from within the scientific community.

The former dean of the Harvard Medical School, Robert H. Ebert (1980:A18), takes issue with the human fraility arguments, claiming that medical schools have "inadvertently fostered a spirit of intense, often fierce competition" with reports of cheating among pre-med students quite common. Altman (1980a:C3), maintains that research today is "big business" with many medical schools being "economically dependent on grants generated by researchers." Power and prestige are now dependent on the ability to generate external funding with younger researchers being "pressured to turn out papers reporting positive results as fast as possible" (Altman, 1980a:C3). Ebert (1980:A18) reinforces this argument by revealing from an insiders view that "promotion in the most prestigious medical schools is based almost entirely on the evaluation of published research." John Fletcher, a specialist in bioethics at the National Institute of Health, adds that the recent cases of scientific fraud "point the finger at the system, not the individual" as the answer to the problem can be found in the publish or perish environment of "intense pressures and rewards given to young individuals doing innovative work" (Raeburn, 1982:C1).

In the debate between those who favor individualistic explanations based on psychological notions of emotional disturbance, and the critics of big science who blame the increased pressures for promotion, tenure, and recognition through publications, one tends to see greater merit in the latter. Intuitively, it is possible to understand how pressure to perform could result in deviant behavior. When scientific journals are "reluctant to accept negative findings, and when careers depend on publications, the temptation to 'improve' the results slightly must be very strong" (St. James-Roberts, 1976:482). Yet, the pressure of the "publish or perish" environment, and the extreme competition for limited funds or recognition, begs the question, why there are not more cases of scientific deviance being reported? It may be that there are thousands of cases that remain known only to the perpetrator because the supposed mechanisms for discovering deception, such as peer review, the referee system, and replication of experiments, are ineffective.[4] When cases are discovered, they may be covered up by a sympathetic lab supervisor, or "managed" by administrators fearful of embarrassment and loss of revenues. On the other hand, the touted self-policing elements of science may be quite effective, so much so that reported cases of scientific fraud represent the extent of scientific deviance. Should this be the case, those who argue for individualist explanations would be standing on firmer ground. Regardless, the issue of scientific deviance needs to be treated more systematically in order to make sense of its individual and structural dimensions.

TOWARDS A SOCIOLOGY OF SCIENTIFIC DEVIANCE

As a form of "elite occupational deviance," fraud in science presents the problem, initially identified by Lemert (1967), of explaining the apparent contradiction of highly educated, talented, respectable persons choosing to act in an obviously deviant fashion. Best and Luckenbill (1982:29), address this inconsistency by arguing that loners "choose deviance because they face situations where respectable courses of action are unattractive." Similarly, deviance in business and the professions is believed to be related to the emphasis placed on individualism, competition, and the stress on winning which often overrides the values of honesty and fairness (Douglas and Waksler, 1982:344). Whether these lines of reasoning are applicable to the issue of scientific deviance is open to question.

Given the general lack of attention to violations of the norms of science in the study of deviant behavior, it is not surprising to discover few if any systematic analyses of this form of deviance in the sociological literature.[5] Nevertheless, there are a number of perspectives that offer interesting possibilities for understanding scientific deviance. One obvious choice is Robert Merton's much maligned theory of anomie. Presumably given its last rites in Clinard's (1964) collection of critical essays, others such as Downs and Rock (1982) believe that anomie theory deserves to be revived. This point is especially relevant with regard to the issue of scientific deviance, as properly clarified, anomie theory has the potential for building a plausible understanding of this form of deviant behavior.

[4]For an excellent discussion and critique of these mechanisms see, for example, Mahoney, 1977; Cole, Cole, and Simon, 1981; Broad and Wade, 1982.

[5]Exceptions include Merton (1973); Weinstein (1979); and Zuckerman (1977).

In its most basic form, anomie theory takes the position that nonconforming behavior is a "symptom of dissociation between culturally prescribed aspirations and socially structured avenues for realizing these aspirations" (Merton, 1968:188). More specifically, when a society's cultural values "extols, virtually above all else," common goals of success for the entire population, while at the same time the social structure "restricts or completely closes access to approved modes of reaching these goals" for certain segments of the population, "deviant behavior ensues" (Merton, 1968:200). Appearing as they did in 1938, these "radical" statements concerning the cause of deviance generated considerable attention and popularity. In time, anomie came under fire from critics who questioned a number of the theory's assumption.

Critics often charge Merton with placing too much emphasis on the cultural goal of monetary success and ignoring other, nonmonetary goals. This evaluation is clearly misplaced given Merton's (1968:211) statement in which he explains choosing monetary success among many alternatives "for purposes of simplifying the problem." The crucial issues is the conflict between goals and the ability to achieve them through legitimate means, "whatever the character of the goals," which leads to anomie (Merton, 1968:220). Freed from this critic-imposed limitation, the concept of anomie could be applied to the area of scientific deviance. While "money" per se is not a primary goal for most scientists, the theory holds "any extreme emphasis upon achievement" which could include striving for personal wealth, winning a national championship in sports, obtaining a large research grant, or gaining promotion and prestige through scientific productivity, "will attenuate conformity to the institutional norms" designed to insure legitimate achievement practices (Merton, 1968:220).

Higgins and Butler (1982:165) speak to this issue when they argue that "anomie may be a useful base for beginning to understand deviance in those organizations and situations where success, achieving goals, or winning is all-important." Clearly, many features of modern science fit this category. For example, funding for the Sloan-Kettering Cancer Center in fiscal 1975 was expected to be near twenty million, an amount for which granting agencies are going to expect results (Culliton, 1974:650). The pressure to produce has been complicated by increased competition for grants. In the 1950s up to seventy percent of the applications for NIH grants were funded, while today that figure has dropped to only thirty percent (Golden, 1981:83).

Science today is no longer a "sportsman-like rivalry between researchers" but rather a highly competitive enterprise where a scientist "publishing a paper first, even if some of the data are not quite accurate" can beat out someone else for a tenured post, promotion, or government grant (Golden, 1981:83). As University of Chicago philosopher Stephen Toulmin states, "you can't change something into a highly paid, highly competitive, highly structured activity without creating occasions for people to do things that they never would do in the earlier, amateur stage" (Golden, 1981:83).

The basic components of anomie provide a good basis for moving towards a sociological analysis of scientific deviance. The case may be made stronger, however, by addressing a second major criticism of Meton's theory. A number of commentators have taken issue with his assumption of value consensus. The critics maintain that the world is pluralistic, composed of diverse reference groups in constant conflict with each other (Sagarin, 1975:110). Thus, as Thio (1983:55) states, "recognition of this 'value pluralism' may reveal the limitation of anomie theory."

At the center of this issue is the supposed difference between "modern" and "traditional" theories of deviance. Traditional theorists, like Merton, tend to stress the "reality of deviant behavior" because they assume the existence of "value consensus" in the society at large. Modern perspectives, such as labeling or conflict theory reject value consensus claiming that in modern, heterogeneous societies, people do not agree on the rules for what is conforming or deviant behavior (Thio, 1983:17). Because of these differing orientations, Thio has proposed that traditional theories are better suited for explaining "high-consensus deviance" such as homicide and rape, while the more subjective modern theories are best suited for interpreting "low-consensus deviance" such as gambling, sexual vices, and government corruption (Thio, 1983:23–24).

The overemphasis on value consensus is a damaging limitation when Merton's theory is applied to societywide deviance; but could be turned into an advantage when applied to scientific deviance. As Thio (1983) argues, traditional theories are better suited to those forms of deviance in which there exists a high degree of societywide value consensus. Taking this point one step further, it may be argued that theories that assume value consensus are also applicable to small, limited subgroups in society were there is a high level of "group-shared consensus" on normative prescriptions. Given the purported level of "value consensus" within the institutional structure of science, it can be argued that when fraud, plagiarism, or other forms of misrepresentation occur, they constitute "high-consensus deviance"; at least within the community of science.[6]

Unleashed from the constraints imposed by it's critics, Merton's theory of anomie deserves serious consideration for developing a sociology of scientific deviance. By placing the primary motivation toward deviance on the frustrations encountered by those who are expected to achieve, even told to achieve, but lack legitimate resources to be successful, anomie may prove

[6]For a discussion of the cultural and normative structure of the scientific community, see, for example, Merton (1973), Cole and Cole (1975), and Gaston (1978).

a useful concept in situations like modern science "where success and goals are very heavily emphasized, even more so than in society at large" (Higgins, and Butler, 1982:165).

Another possible approach is provided by Quinney (1963) in his study of prescription violations by pharmacists. Grounding his analysis of white-collar deviance within the social structure of occupations, Quinney states that prescription violation can be explained according to "structural strain in the occupation" as a result of "differential orientation of the pharmacists" to inconsistent occupational roles. Quinney identified two occupational roles, "business" and "professional," and found that the level of deviance was related to the individual pharmacist's "orientation to a particular role more than another" (Quinney, 1963:184). Specifically, those who identified with the "business" role had higher rates of prescription violation than those who were more oriented to the "professional" role. Given the emergence of "big science" and the increasing linkage between science and the business community, Quinney's model would appear applicable to the issue of scientific deviance. An initial hypothesis could test the possibility that cases of reported fraud are the result of perpetrators being oriented to a "business" role in science as opposed to the more traditional, professional identification. Taking this type of approach would afford the opportunity of learning more about both scientific deviance and the structure of science it reflects (Quinney, 1963:185).

The interactionist perspective offers another possible approach in Lemert's (1967) analysis of the naive check forger. Lemert illustrates a number of similarities with deviant scientists. In his description, the naive forgers are persons "unaquainted with criminal techniques," having "acquired normal attitudes and habits of law observance" making their involvement in deviant activity "out of character" (Lemert, 1967:102). Further similarities can be found in their respective characteristics, as forgers were primarily native white in origin, male, in their late twenties to early thirties, with higher than average levels of education, and were for many years residents of the community in which their crimes were committed (Lemert, 1967:106). Finally, in explaining check forgery, Lemert focuses on their relative "social isolation" which generated a "lowered sensitivity to the 'generalized other' which might otherwise have produced a rejection or inhibition of the criminal alternative of forgery" (Lemert, 1967:106)

Further possibilities for explaining scientific deviance can be found within the conflict perspective. From this view, attention should be directed to the structure of science in a capitalist society and the resulting patterns of power and class relations within the scientific community. Highly suggestive ideas along these lines can be found in a recent paper on fraud in science by Weinstein (1979). Looking at the structure of modern science, Weinstein (1979:642) argues that researchers "not only do not own their laboratory and equipment, but dependency on grants and/or bureaucratic authority alienates them from control of their work," factors that places the present day scientist into the "proletariat". Because competition is the only way to gain access to the "means of research," there is no basis to assume that scientists who have been socialized into a capitalist system will respond to institutionalized competition any differently from people in business (Weinstein, 1979:643).

CONCLUSION

The study of social deviance has come to recognize the existence of deviance within the business, professional, and governing segments of society. Yet, while aggressively publicizing the deviance of other professions, those who study deviance generally have neglected to look in the mirror and consider the possibility of deviance within the scientific community. This paper has attempted to stimulate interest in this direction by outlining some basic conceptual and explanatory parameters. Suggestive in scope, the ideas expressed above have as their goal generation of interest in scientific deviance as a topic worthy of serious investigation. While the possibilities for research in this area are limited only by the creativity of the investigator, certain issues stand out for immediate attention.

The most pressing problem concerns the extent of deviance in science. As indicated, the inherent difficulties in such an investigation are well documented. Nevertheless, the question of prevalence is crucial given the generally excepted argument that science is self-policing, making deviance extremely rare if not nonexistent. The twelve cases described above are testimony that deviance in science does exist; the pressing issue is to determine the degree to which reported incidents represent either the entirety of the problem, or simply the tip of the iceberg. Preliminary work along these lines can be found in a small survey of scientific deviance conducted among the readers of *New Scientist* magazine (St. James-Roberts, 1976b). The sample of 199 respondents, representing seventy-five areas of research, reported 184 individual instances of deviance; forty percent being detected by catching the suspect in the act or from confessions. These results reinforce the argument that scientific deviance is more widespread then the small number of reported cases would indicate. More systematic surveys, therefore, would be important for documenting the magnitude of scientific deviance, as well as delineating any subarea differences, i.e., hard versus soft sciences, and illuminating the range of possible deviant activities.

Turning to the explanatory dimension, the various perspectives on deviance provide a wide range of possible research opportunities. As argued above, the concept of anomie suggests that analysis of the changing organizational and normative aspects of modern science could generate valuable insights into scientific deviance. Of primary interest, would be an examination of the current reward system in science to determine the possibility of a reorientation away from the traditional values of disinterested inquiry, as well as the existence of structural inequities that may work to the disadvantage of some researchers, increasing the pressure to use illegitimate means. Similarly, the structural components of modern science within a capitalist society provide research opportunities for the conflict perspective. An issue that seems suggestive is the effect of "nonscientific" values such as wealth, power and prestige on changing the internal structural arrangements of science. Related to this question, is the impact of increasing interpenetration of science with business and government may have on the structure of science by providing additional opportunities for acquiring power and influence (Weinstein, 1979:649–650).

Also, the interactionist perspective provides a range of possible research issue. Of principle concern would be the situational nature of social interaction which would direct attention towards understanding the emergence of scientific norms and the ways they may be differentially defined and/or applied in given circumstances. Stressing that deviance is the outcome of audience response to particular social acts, interactionist study of scientific deviance would look at the societal reaction to these acts; both by those within the scientific community and those in the general population. Of special interest would be follow-up analysis of "deviant scientists" to determine the impact of response to being so labeled.

Regardless of the direction or outcome of further study on scientific deviance, the results will be beneficial. Assuming the validity of the argument that "deviant behavior is a reflection of social structure" (Quinney, 1963:185), then the study of deviance in science—whether it be faked research, plagiarism, abuse of power and position or fudging/manipulating data—will not only bring additional knowledge and understanding of deviance, but of the institutional arrangements and operations of modern science as well.

REFERENCES

Altman, Lawrence K.

1980a "The doctor's world: How honest is medical research." New York Times, August 5, p.C3.

1980b "Columbia's medical chief resigns: Ex-associates data fraud at issue." New York Times, August 9, Pp.1,8.

Bauer, Henry H.

1983 "Betrayers of the truth: A fraudulent and deceitful title from the journalists of science." 4S Review 1:17–23.

Begley, Sharon
1982a "A case of fraud at Harvard." Newsweek, February 8, Pp.89–91.
1982b "Why scientists cheat." Newsweek, February 8, p.90.
Best, Joel, and David F. Luckenbill
1982 Organizing Deviance. Englewood Cliffs, N.J.: Prentice-Hall.
Broad, William J.
1980 "Imbroglio at Yale (I): Emergence of a fraud." Science, 210:38–41.
1982a "Harvard delays in reporting fraud." Science 215:478–482.
1982b "Researcher denied future U.S. funds." Science 216:1081
Broad, William J., and Nicholas Wade
1982 Betrayers of the Truth. New York: Simon and Schuster.
Browne, Malcolm
1981 "Fakery: It's a pity." New York Times, April 14, p.C3.
Chicago Tribune
1982 "Research scientist admits faking data." December 28, p.10.
Cole, Jonathan R., and Stephen S. Cole
1973 Social Stratification in Science. Chicago: University of Chicago Press.
Cole, Stephen S., Jonathan R. Cole, and Gary A. Simon
1981 "Chance and consensus in peer review" Science 214:881–886.
Culliton, Barbara J.
1974 "The Sloan-Kettering affair: A story without a hero." Science 184:644–650.
1983 "Fraud inquiry spreads blame." Science 219:937.
Dansereau, H. Kirk
1974 "Unethical behavior: Professional deviance." Pp.75–89 in Clifton D. Bryant (ed.), Deviant Behavior: Occupational and Organizational Bases. Chicago: Rand McNally.
Denzin, Norman K.
1970 "Rules of conduct and the study of deviant behavior: Some notes on the social relationship." Pp.120–159 in Jack D. Douglas (ed.), Deviance and Respectability. New York: Basic Books.
Douglas, Jack D., and Frances C. Waksler
1982 The Sociology of Deviance: An Introduction. Boston: Little, Brown.
Downes, David, and Paul Rock
1982 Understanding Deviance. Oxford: Clarendon Press.
Ebert, Robert H.
1980 "A fierce race called medical education." New York Times, July 9, p.A18.
Gaston, Jerry
1978 The Reward System in British and American Science. New York Wiley-Interscience.
Golden, Frederic
1981 "Fudging data for fun and profit." Time. 118:83
Higgins, Paul C. and Richard R. Butler
1982 Understanding Deviance. New York: McGraw-Hill.

Hills, Stuart L.
1980 Demystifying Social Deviance. New York: McGraw-Hill.
Hunt, Morton
1981 "A fraud that shook the world of science." The New York Times Magazine, November 1, p.42.
Knight, Michael
1980 "Doctor at Harvard quit after faking research data." New York Times, June 28, p.22.
Kolata, Gina B.
1981 "Reevaluation of cancer data eagerly awaited." Science 214:316–318.
Lemert, Edwin M.
1967 Human Deviance, Social Problems and Social Control. Englewood Cliffs, N.J.: Prentice-Hall.
Little, Craig B.
1983 Understanding Deviance and Control. Itasca, Illinois: F. E. Peacock.
Mahoney, Michael J.
1977 "Publication prejudices: An experimental study of confirmatory bias in the peer review system" Cognitive Therapy and Research 1:161–175.
McGinty, Lawrence
1979 "Researcher retracts claims on plutonium treatment." New Scientist 84:3–4.
Merton, Robert K.
1968 Social Theory and Social Structure. New York: The Free Press.
1973 The Sociology of Science: Theoretical and Empirical Investigations. Chicago: University of Chicago Press.
Nature
1981 "In Bristol now." Nature 294:509.
Newsweek
1974 "Skin game." April 29, Pp. 57–58.
1981 "A case of fraud in a cancer lab?" September 21, p.114.
New York Times
1981 "Stanford denies cover-up of research fraud." August 23, p.31.
Plummer, Ken
1979 "Misunderstanding labelling perspectives." Pp.85–121 in David Downes and Paul Rock (eds.) Deviant Interpretations. New York: Barnes & Noble.
Quinney, Earl R.
1963 "Occupational structure and criminal behavior: Prescription violation by retail pharmacists." Social Problems 11:179–185.
Raeburn, Paul
1982 "House of science shakes when research is faked." Winston-Salem Journal, January 17, p.C1.
Rogers, Floyd
1981 "Scientist at Bowman Gray resigns." Winston-Salem Journal, November 6, p.1.

Sagarin, Edward
1975 Deviants and Deviance. New York: Praeger.
Science Digest
1977 "An unscientific phenomenon: Fraud grows in laboratories." 81:38–40.
Science News
1974a "False research: The Summerlin scandal." 105:348–349.
1974b "Research found cheating at PSI lab." 106:100–101.
1977 "Researcher admits he faked journal data." 111.
St. James-Roberts, Ian
1976a "Are researchers trustworthy?" New Scientist:481–483.
1976b "Cheating in science." New Scientist:466–469.
Surks, Martin
1980 "Ethnics in research." New York Times, August 12, P.C2.
Thio, Alex
1983 Deviant Behavior. Boston: Houghton Mifflin.
Time
1974a "The S. K. I. affair." 103 (April 29):67.
1974b "The S. K. I. affair (contd.)." 103 (June 3):60.
1974c "The S. K. I. affair (contd.)." 103 (June 10):70.
U.S. News and World Report
1982 "Faked experiment kept quiet." January 24, p.A3.
1983 "Research apologizes for deceits." June 9, P.8.
Zuckerman, Harriet
1977 "Deviant behavior and social control in science." Pp.87–138 in Edward Sagarin (ed.), Deviance and Social Change. Beverly Hills: Sage.

Reading 33

Employee Theft in the Restaurant Trade: Forms of Ripping Off by Waiters at Work

Richard Hawkins
Southern Methodist University, Dallas

The variety of part-time theft techniques used by waiters in the restaurant trade is examined using a self-report methodology. Using twelve hypothetical cases of ripping off in restaurants, three potential theft targets are assessed: the restaurant, customers of the restaurant, and co-workers.

This research was funded by a faculty development grant from Southern Methodist University. The following people played an important role in the project: Elena Argomaniz, Walter Chapin, Fran Hawkins, Dan Lowry and Sean Quinn. My thanks to J. Greg Getz for his critical reading of an earlier draft of the paper.

Predictions about the frequency of involvement of these theft activities are tested using a sample of waiters in four "prime rib" restaurants. Hypotheses dealing with working conditions and the ability to neutralize moral controls against theft are presented to explain which waiters will be involved in employee theft. The theoretical implications of "amateur trading" and pecuniary-based theft are developed in order to show the critical role that theft activities play in the work setting of the restaurant. The findings have implications for the "controlled larceny" solution to the problem of employee theft suggested by some observes.

INTRODUCTION

The work setting in recent years has provided a fertile site for studies of deviant behavior. Bryant (1974:4) suggests that the workplace be examined (a) as a source of problems which result in deviance that carries beyond the job, e.g., work stress and its effect on alcoholism, mental and physical illness, drug abuse, etc., and (b) as a setting where deviant activity can be carried on—often with little fear of formal sanctions. This study of theft activities by service employees, specifically waiters working in restaurants, is an example of this latter approach. This is not an investigation into all forms of employee deviance, which would include both violations of criminal law and activities detrimental to the work organization but not technically illegal, i.e., "those behaviors committed by workers which adversely affect the economic interest of the formal work organization" (Hollinger, 1978:1). Such a broad definition would include theft, and inventory shrinkage, but also work slowdowns (rate-setting), shoddy workmanship, and even sabotage of company equipment which exact an economic loss. Robin (1974:262) uses the narrower term, "occupational crime," to refer to work-based law violations by "normal" persons, a perspective closer to the one taken here.

One reason restaurant theft is of theoretical interest is the possibility of various targets or objects for larceny. Theft in the work setting may be directed against the restaurant, its customers, or fellow restaurant employees. The recognition of different theft areas raises numerous questions. Are customers more likely to be victimized than restaurant management? Do larcenous waiters choose between targets? Are there specialists who use one technique against one target, or are most waiters generalists? In addition to differences by theft target, employee theft can be divided into pecuniary theft and "amateur trading" theft (Henry and Mars, 1978). In the former, the intent and outcome of theft is to make money, i.e., private gain. Amateur trading tends to be dictated by social considerations of exchange: a theft may benefit another, which sets up an obligation to return the favor. These reciprocal arrangements mean that illegal "transactions are only one event in a series" (Henry and Mars, 1978:248). We would expect to find pecuniary theft and amateur trading, here called social theft, to be present in the restaurant trade.

Most of the research on employee theft has focused on retail sales personnel (Dalton, 1959; Ditton, 1977c; Hollinger, 1978; Martin, 1962; Robin, 1969; Zeitlin, 1971), blue collar workers (Clark and Hollinger, 1981; Horning, 1970; Mars, 1974) and hospital employees (Clark and Hollinger, 1981). While there have been numerous studies of restaurant employees, there has been little systematic investigation of theft by workers in what has been termed "the epitome of a service occupation" (Butler and Snizek, 1976:209). William F. Whyte's classic work (1948, 1949) on restaurant workers ignores employee theft. Two studies of cocktail waitresses (Spradley and Mann, 1975; Hearn and Stoll, 1975) suggest that women in this occupation have a common work argot, share a sense of stigma about the job (sexual connotations about the occupation), and often develop a dislike for customers. While some restaurant research hints at employee theft (e.g., Butler and Skipper, 1980, 1981), the topic has not received any systematic attention. If not for a study in England by Gerald Mars (1973), the literature would lead us to believe there was no problem of employee theft in the restaurant industry.

The research by Mars using "retrospective participant observation" is based on one hotel dining room. While he does detail the forms of fiddles commonly used by waiters,[1] he does not develop hypotheses to account for various theft targets, nor does he try to predict which restaurant employees will be involved. The goal of this exploratory study of theft in American restaurants is to assess the forms and frequency of theft involvement by waiters and to test three hypotheses using data obtained by a self-report method.

Hypotheses on Restaurant Theft

Three hypotheses are presented in this section. The first makes a prediction about the theft target of waiters who steal and the frequency of each form of employee theft. The other two hypotheses address the issue of which waiters will engage in employee theft and under what types of conditions.

Donald Horning (1970), in his study of theft by employees in an electronics assembly plant, found a differentiation was made in theft targets.

[1]The terms used by employees for their theft activities may be important in understanding why theft occurs. English waiters used the term "fiddle" to refer to theft from the customers or the restaurant, while "knock off" was reserved for activities such as taking things from the restaurant, e.g., linen or silverware. Our informants, described in the methodology section below, stated that "ripping off" was a general term applied to all theft activities. Hence, the use of the term by waiters in this study is analogous to both "fiddle" and "knock off" in England, (cf. Ditton, 1977b).

Factory goods of uncertain ownership (e.g., scrap metal, discarded assembly parts) were most likely to be the object of theft, followed by company property (e.g., tools, usable materials), with the theft of co-workers' property being a distant third. The last category was clearly defined as theft by plant workers and was seldom engaged in by employees. Following Horning, it is proposed that a hierarchy of theft objects will be found in restaurants.[2] It is hypothesized that a larger proportion of waiters will be involved in thefts from the company. Customer-directed rip-offs should be next in terms of the proportion of waiters involved, and theft from fellow workers should be rare.

This hierarchy of theft target involvement is predicted on the basis of an underlying "affective proximity" of the victim dimension. Victimization of fellow workers should have the lowest proportion of worker involvement. There should be a greater personal identification with the victim and a more direct sense of theft loss. Horning found a strong taboo against stealing from co-workers, and the same result is expected among restaurant workers. The most frequent theft target, on the other hand, should be the restaurant. The work situation of the waiter is important in understanding why the restaurant is a more likely target than the customer. Waiters are largely independent workers who use the restaurant as a place to ply their trade. The fact that very low hourly wages are paid in most restaurants (usually half the minimum hourly wage rate) combined with the expectation that income is derived from tips (Butler and Skipper, 1981) means that waiters may have little identification or commitment to the host restaurant. To the extent a restaurant has a corporate image, ownership of property is less identifiable (cf. Dillon, 1973). Add to this the fact that management-worker friction is likely to occur and that restaurant security arrangements are likely to be perceived by waiters as onerous and bothersome—indicating a basic lack of trust in the employee (Butler and Skipper, 1981:26)—then it follows that most theft should be directed agains the restaurant.

Customer-directed theft should fall between co-worker and restaurant. In this service occupation, waiters and waitresses are in a subordinate relationship to customers, relying upon the tip as a reward for being subservient.

> The tip is traditionally a reward for good and efficient service, but many waiters and waitresses feel that some customers use their tipping power to demand a subservient attitude and special favors. . . . Many blamed the tipping

[2]It is not claimed that restaurant theft has a direct analog to theft activities in a television assembly plant, the setting of Horning's research. There are no customers or tips, and cash is not readily available as a theft target. However, it is hypothesized that a hierarchy of targets exists in both settings, representing an underlying dimension available in both retail and manufacturing sectors.

> system for their inferior position in relation to customers. . . . In America, high-status people do not receive tips for their services, and tipping therefore tends to lower the status of the recipient. (Whyte, 1948:98–99)

The problem is very salient to the waiter or waitress because tips remain their major source of income (cf. Butler and Skipper, 1980). Butler and Snizek (1976) report that the quality of service does little to increase the amount of tip received for service. About the only way the restaurant worker can increase the size of tips is to "push" food and drink to maximize the total bill, thereby enlarging the amount of the tip.

The basic asymmetry in the waiter-diner relationship may produce resentment towards customers, fostering a cynical attitude toward the clientele of restaurants (Butler and Snizek, 1976; Butler and Skipper, 1980; Hearns and Stoll, 1975). However customers, while usually strangers, are physically present and hence identifiable to some extent. The fact that many waiters try to develop "call customers" (persons who will return and ask for a specific waiter) further increases the identification factor. Therefore it is predicted that few waiters will be involved in customer-targeted theft compared to restaurant-directed theft.

Turning now to the question of which waiters will be involved in theft, one set of determinants resides in the actual working conditions and the subjective judgments made about those working conditions. The second hypothesis is that the greater the dissatisfaction with one's job, the more likely that employee theft will occur (e.g., Hollinger and Clark, 1982; Mangione and Quinn, 1975). In restaurant work, the objective conditions conducive to theft might be low pay, low volume of customers, poor tips, poor schedules, or unpopular stations (subsections of restaurant assigned to work). Negative attitudes towards one's work may follow these conditions. Low volume of business and poor tips may produce boredom. Dissatisfaction over working conditions may generate cynical attitudes toward the restaurant management and may reduce commitment to the task of customer service (Hearns and Stoll, 1975). Subjective conditions such as boredom, task dissatisfaction, and poor working conditions have been shown to be associated with theft involvement (Dalton, 1959; Zeitlin, 1971).

Another area of interest is the role of management in the production of employee theft. There are two major ways in which management indirectly contributes to theft by waiters. First, the formal socialization of a new waiter makes the novice aware of the phenomenon of restaurant rip-offs. Training involves showing the worker how to ring appropriate keys on the cash register, to check register tapes, to keep track of and be responsible for dinner and bar tabs. (These tickets or tabs are checked out in serial blocks at the beginning of each shift; used and unused tickets are turned into managers during checkout at the end of each shift.) The novice also receives general instructions on restaurant procedures for checking on sales, e.g., counting steaks and comparing to the number of orders written for steaks. Through this job training, the worker is made cognizant of the restaurant's security system and inadvertantly learns that some ripping off must be going on given the elaborate safeguards. In what Gary Marx (1981) describes as a major irony of social control, attempts at controlling or preventing deviance may precipitate rule violations.

A second way that management contributes to theft is by supporting informal norms which permit certain rule violations and engender a tolerance for certain types of ripping-off activities. For example, a waiter may be told that drinking on the job is not allowed, but he is given a free drink by the bartender toward the end of the shift with the advice: "If you're doing a good job, the manager won't say anything." In these subtle ways, the new worker learns that the manager expects and accepts certain rule violations. The tolerance of some rule violations contributes to the control effectiveness of the manager, whose rule enforcement, like all controllers, depends in part on the good will of subordinates. The manager who enforces petty rules will soon alienate his work staff (Butler and Skipper, 1981:22). Certain rule violations—although not necessarily in the area of ripping off—may be necessary for the worker's efficient task performance; it is then in the best interests of the manager to look the other way.[3] Knowledge that managers are flexible on company rules may allow workers to generalize to theft situations, which makes it more likely that certain forms of ripping off become legitimated.

Some managers may feel that some ripping off is justified by low pay and may be overlooked in good waiters—what Dalton (1959) terms "unofficial rewards." Management may come to realize that control is impossible and basically inefficient: "That is, the cost of an effective security system, plus the cost of achieving equivalent employee stability [lack of turnover] by increasing pay or job quality, is greater than the loss or merchandise due to employee theft" (Zeitlin, 1971:226).

The tolerance by management facilitates expectations of entitlement by workers: certain forms of theft may come to be seen as a legitimate form of remuneration: "It's a part of my wage" (Mars, 1973:202). To the extent these conditions are perceived by workers, they may contribute to a system of neutralizations which justify involvement in employee theft.

Our third hypothesis is that workers who agree with various neutralization statements will be more likely to engage in employee theft than will

[3]See as a parallel example the use of the tap by airline assembly workers (Bensman and Gerver, 1963). At times the company may directly encourage certain customer-based rip-offs to facilitate getting the job done (Ditton, 1977c).

workers who do not support such neutralizations. Following the logic of social control theory (e.g., Hirschi, 1969), it is predicted that workers would have to neutralize the bind of the law, the prohibitions against theft. Those able to neutralize such controls prior to engaging in theft should be more free to steal, other things being equal (Cressey, 1953).

METHOD

Four major approaches have been used to study employee theft. Participant observational studies (e.g., Ditton, 1977c; Henry, 1978; Mars, 1973, 1974) have produced rich details of the process of theft, but findings are limited to one work setting. A second method has been the analysis of official records of action taken against employees who get caught (Martin, 1962; Robin, 1969). Such research is better seen as reflecting societal reaction variables rather than determinants of theft behavior. Low rates of official reactions to employee deviance severely limit this approach. A third method can be seen in Horning's (1970) nondirective interviews of factory workers to get estimates of theft involvement. Dalton (1959) interviewed managers to get their estimates of theft by their employees. The unstructured nature of the questioning of informants limits the generalizability of this approach. A fourth procedure is to use anonymous self-reports of theft involvement (e.g., Clark and Hollinger, 1981; Hollinger, 1978). Self-reports have the following advantages: more than one work setting can be studied; hidden deviance can be recorded; the bias of officially reported deviance is avoided; and a standard set of questions permit a comparable measure of theft involvement across work settings. For these reasons, this research used an anonymous self-report format to study employee theft.

A questionnaire was constructed by using ten veteran waiters and waitresses as informants. These people were interviewed at length, first alone and later in a group setting. Without being informed of the hypotheses or concepts of the study, they were asked to describe types of ripping-off activities encountered in their trade. Based on their descriptions, twelve short vignettes were created to illustrate the range of theft activity (see Appendix). The three theft targets are represented in the twelve examples used in the questionnaire. After the vignettes were completed, the researcher made a judgment about which of the hypothetical rip-off situations fit the amateur trading criteria of theft as opposed to pecuniary theft. The waiter informants supported these judgments.

Four dinner restaurants in a large Southwestern city were selected as the setting for research. These four "prime rib" restaurants were similar in these ways (1) each had a separate dining and bar/lounge area within the restaurant; (2) menu items were similar (expensive meat and fish dishes) and were comparable in prices; (3) waiters could take drink and food orders, although cocktail waitresses worked in the bar area; (4) each restaurant was well known in the city and had been in operation for a number of years; and (5) each was incorporated, with restaurants in other cities. A major difference purposely selected as a criterion for inclusion in the study was the tipping system. Two restaurants utilized a straight tip system and two used a tip pool system. These two tipping systems present different opportunities for ripping off fellow workers.

The names and addresses of all waiters working in each of the four restaurants were obtained from a waiter known to the author in each establishment. (Lists of waiters' addresses and phone numbers are posted in each restaurant and given to each employee to facilitate covering shifts when someone is unable to work. These semipublic lists meant that workers could be contacted without going through the management.) This procedure generated a sample total of eighty-one waiters who were sent a cover letter introducing the study and the questionnaire. Respondents were asked to estimate the number of fellow employees who engaged in each form of ripping off given in the hypothetical vignettes. They were also asked to report their own involvement in each type of theft activity during the past year.

In the cover letter, respondents were given these assurances of anonymity. First, they were told that all waiters in four city restaurants were included in the cover letter in case respondents wanted to check this reassurance with friends working in the other establishments in the sample. Second, the waiters were told that the restaurant management and owners were not involved in the study and that they did not know the study was going on. Furthermore, they were informed that their name and address had been given to the researcher by a waiter in their restaurant. Third, they were told that the results would appear only in statistical summaries and would not be computed for each specific restaurant. This was done to guarantee the anonymity of information for each restaurant.[4] Another assurance was that names and addresses did not appear on the questionnaire, nor did the name of the restaurant. Finally, questionnaires were sent to the waiters' home addresses to enhance the confidential nature of the research.

As a means of trying to improve the response rate, respondents were mailed a dollar as token payment for their participation. This was done on

[4]There are two forms of risk to respondents in the study. First, they may be specifically identified as thieves by management (who might gain access to questionnaires) and be fired or prosecuted. Second, if rates of theft were computed by restaurant, owners who might acquire the data could fire everyone if theft rates were seen as intolerably high for their establishment. Masking the identity of the restaurant prevents this and also protects the researcher. For example, the owner of one restaurant in the study found out about the questionnaire from one of his waiters and contacted me asking for the results of the research for his restaurant. I told him that because specific restaurants were not identified, there data were not available.

the assumption that the cognitive dissonance over the request would help to increase the rate of response (Hackler and Bourgette, 1973). (This may have backfired in that some waiters returned the money, seeing it as inappropriate.) Respondents were also promised a summary of the results as another incentive to cooperate in the study.

Ethical Issues

There is a considerable problem with any self-report form of assessing rates of involvement in deviant behavior. To present an inventory of theft activities to our sample of workers is, in fact, to suggest strategies and even specific tactics of engaging in part-time theft at work. The ethical dilemma is that the method of gathering data—sending specific, detailed vignettes to currently employed waiters—is tantamount to providing them with a manual for ripping off. Respondents unaware of a particular technique might use this knowledge to produce an increase in the absolute theft in the restaurants studied.

This ethical problem was addressed in the following ways: First, the ten restaurant workers used as informants (not included in the final sample) gave assurances that the activities in the vignettes were standard knowledge among most restaurant workers. Even if waiters were not using a particular theft technique, they were likely to know of its existence. The questionnaire would not, therefore, provide workers with any information that they did not already possess. There was still the problem of the newly hired waiter, not yet fully socialized into the ways of ripping off, who might benefit from reading the questionnaire. To avoid this problem, a second protection was built-in to the sampling design. After lists of all waiters currently employed in the four restaurants were obtained, a two-month delay in mailing the questionnaires was imposed. It was assumed that two months would be more than enough time for a new worker to become aware of most forms of restaurant rip-offs. Ditton (1977c) in his research on fiddling by English bread salesman found that the process there took about three weeks. The informants used to generate the vignettes also agreed that a two-month delay was sufficient.

This concession to the ethical problem was achieved at some cost. The delay reduced our final response rate in two ways. As persons were sent the questionnaire to their home addresses, those who had moved during this time period may not have received the questionnaire. Of the eighty-one questionnaires, sent, ten were returned as undeliverable. Another problem with the delay is that waiters may have resigned from the restaurant and consequently did not feel obligated to respond. High turnover rates are a feature of most restaurant work (e.g., Mars, 1973:201).[5] Of the seventy-one waiters who were contacted by mail, forty-one returned the questionnaires for a response rate of 58 percent.

While a higher response rate is desirable, there is no reason to suspect that non-response was correlated with our dependent variable, theft involvement. The reputed openness of rip-off practices in area restaurants implies that fear or reticence to admit theft was not a major factor in nonresponse. This openness was suggested by the informants who helped construct the questionnaire. The findings reported below bear out their contention; as we shall see, the sharing of the knowledge of ripping-off techniques is a salient feature of employee theft in restaurants.

The small sample size ($N = 41$) does limit the scope of our analysis, and caution must be used in generalizing these results to other restaurant employees. While desirable for analysis purposes, large samples of theft in restaurants would require a greater diversity in work settings. In this study, there was an attempt to use only comparable restaurants, given the criteria listed earlier in this section. The use of four restaurants was designed to avoid idiosyncratic results likely to obtain if only one work place is used. (This is a problem with participant observational studies such as the research by Gerald Mars (1973:202) which used one English dining room with a total staff of twenty waiters.) However our attempt to achieve homogeneous work settings reduced the potential pool of waiters in the sample.

One reviewer raised the question of the appropriateness of using self-reports when sample size is under one hundred. Rather than specifying an arbitrary sample size for a research technique, it is better to ask how the technique is used. For example, a common criticism of self report inventories—more often used on juveniles than adults—is that detail is lacking on the deviant acts set down for respondent reaction (Sheley, 1980:57). The use of detailed vignettes should provide a more accurate assessment of theft involvement than would larger sample surveys without specific vignettes.

FINDINGS

Types of Theft Activity

The forms of theft by waiters are as varied as individual ingenuity and restaurant security systems. As it was not possible to assess all forms of theft, certain activities (see Table 1) representing customer, restaurant and fellow workers as victims were presented to respondents. Twelve vignettes

[5]On this issue of employee turnover, waiters in our sample were asked how long they expected to continue working at their present restaurant. Thirty-two percent indicated that they planned to quit within three months.

TABLE 1 Percentage of Waiters Who Knew Fellow Workers to Have Engaged in Theft Activity, and Those Who Reported Involvement in Theft Activity in the Past Twelve Months ($N = 41$)

Theft target and type of theft	Percent knowing others involved	Percent engaging in theft activity
Restaurant theft (social):		
Free food to friends	76	56
Take home restaurant items	68	44
Restaurant theft (pecuniary):		
Fail to ring food items	61	30
Selling restaurant items	44	15
Customer theft (pecuniary):		
Bill padding	66	28
Short change customer	71	23
Add tip to credit card	73	15
Other waiters as victim:		
Take other waiter's tips	15	5
Hold out on tip pool	75*	44*
Infrequent theft:		
No ring, split with cook	15	5
Bring in own wine to sell	0	0
Take money from register	0	0

*N is 16, those employees who worked under a tip pool system.

(see Appendix) were used to assess the relative rates of theft involvement. Two items need to be defined. *Bill padding* is one form of customer-directed theft as illustrated in this vignette:

> Art is waiting on a large party of twelve men, all of whom have been ordering drinks from the bar during dinner. The check is to be presented to the gentleman in charge and he will pay with a credit card. After looking through all the drink tickets, Art decides to inflate the figure of the bar bill, figuring that an extra four or five dollars will not be noticed. Art presents the bill and the man pays it.

Bill padding along with short changing customers and adding tips to credit cards represent customer-directed theft.

The second item, *failure to ring*, is a basic technique for ripping off the restaurant. It involves delivering food items to customers without ringing up the sale on the register. In most cases the customer pays for the items, but the money is diverted to the waiter. Gerald Mars notes that "fail to ring" is the major fiddle in English restaurants, and he provides a detailed description of how waiters engineer this form of theft (Mars, 1973:202–4). This technique is included in three theft activities in Table 1: fail to ring; no ring, split with cook (where there is actual collusion between workers to pull off the theft);[6] and free foods to friends. This vignette illustrates the failure to ring up food for friends, the most frequent form of theft engaged in by the waiters:

> A couple of Greg's friends come in to dinner one night and have Greg wait on them. Greg must ring up the meat order on the register, but he gives them baked potatoes, corn on the cob, and dessert free of charge [items are not rung up]. They pay the meat bill and leave Greg a large tip.

The proportion of waiters who knew co-workers who engaged in the twelve theft activities is given in Table 1. The data show that employee theft is widely known about among waiters. While it is not possible to assess the source of this knowledge (seeing other waiters steal or hearing them talk about past theft activities), the importance of the fact is that it shows theft activity is not secret, but a commonly known phenomenon. The significance of this finding is developed in the discussion below.

The percentage of waiters in the sample who reported committing each type of rip-off activity themselves during the past year shows that our first hypothesis on directness of victimization is supported. The largest proportion of waiters were involved in restaurant-based theft (indirect victim). The proportion who rip-off customers is lower, and very little theft occurred against fellow workers. Blatant theft—stealing money directly from the cash register—was not found in the sample.[7] This is consistent with Hornings (1970) research which also found that direct theft seldom occurs in the workplace.

There was one exception to the directness of victim dimension: a form of co-worker victimization, holding out on tip pools, was a frequent occurrence in the restaurants which had a tip pool system of compensation. Waiters dislike this form of renumeration because it penalizes good waiters (those who consistently receive good tips) and carries poor, less effective waiters. Here there is not a *specific* direct victim in that the loss is spread out among all waiters. This makes holding out *part* of one's tip money an action devoid of connotations of stealing directly from fellow workers (such as taking another waiter's tip money from his table—a rare activity in the

[6]Cooperation between workers is required for employee theft in some occupations, e.g., dockworkers (Mars, 1974), bread salesman (Ditton, 1977c). In this sample, there did not appear to be a collusion requirement for most restaurant rip-offs; splitting with others was relatively rare (see Table 1).

[7]Three forms of theft given at the bottom of Table 1 were very infrequent in this sample of waiters. These three items, all examples of pecuniary theft directed at the restaurant, are omitted from further analysis.

sample). There is also a sense of entitlement which prevents a waiter from seeing holding out as direct theft. He has, after all, earned it.

The distinction between pecuniary theft and socially based theft is also shown in Table 1. Two examples of social theft were used. The theft labeled "free food to friends" involves treating one's associates to a fringe benefit of one's own work. As many of the friends who are treated to free food are restaurant workers in other eating establishments, the opportunity for reciprocity is present. Theft of restaurant items is also termed social in that sets of glasses or silverware are often given as gifts to friends rather than used directly by the waiter. These two examples of socially based theft do have pecuniary aspects. For example, giving free food to friends usually means the waiter profits from a large tip left by the grateful recipients. Restaurant items used as gifts remove the necessity of purchasing such gifts for cash in the legitimate marketplace. However, these two acts are not classified as pecuniary because "the rewards are more social than economic" (Henry, 1978:112).

Since the only target for socially based theft is the restaurant, and given the high involvement of some waiters in pecuniary theft against the restaurant, employee theft represents a sizable source of "inventory shrinkage" for restaurant organizations. One reason for the high proportion of waiters involved in restaurant-directed theft is that these two motives, social and pecuniary, operate side by side. What is disheartening from a management perspective is the fact that these two forms of theft are largely independent (see Table 2).[8] For example, very few waiters who gave "free food to friends" also engaged in "fail to ring" as a pecuniary act, i.e., of the twenty-three waiters who engaged in "free foods to friends," only one-third also used "fail to ring," even though the method of ripping off is identical in both cases. There appear to be two independent reasons for waiters biting the hand that feeds them, illustrating the complexity of the problem of trying to reduce restaurant-directed theft.

When only pecuniary forms of theft are examined, we find that the rates are about the same for restaurant as target and customers as target. One reason that the proportion of waiters involved in customer rip-offs is not lower is that management generally has fewer security measures directed

[8]Table 2 shows that theft activities are not highly correlated. This implies there are multiple reasons for theft involvement. As this is an exploratory study, the intention was to see if certain variables could explain different categories of theft targets and various types of theft, e.g., pecuniary theft versus social theft. For this reason, dependent variables are created in the next section to see if the same hypotheses can predict different types of theft involvement. The fact that the hypotheses have varying success in the endeavor suggests that all possible causal variables have not been uncovered here, i.e., more research needs to be done.

TABLE 2 Correlation Matrix of Employee Theft Activities Using Pearson's Phi Coefficient as a Measure of Association ($N = 41$)

Theft activities	1	2	3	4	5	6	7
1. Free food to friends	1.00	.18	.13	.03	.00	.13	.22
2. Take restaurant items		1.00	.40*	.08	.15	.38*	.18
3. Fail to ring			1.00	.40*	.61*	.47*	.18
4. Sell restaurant items				1.00	.40*	.31	.41
5. Bill padding					1.00	.20	.21
6. Short change customers						1.00	.10
7. Add tip to credit card							1.00

*Significant at or below the .05 level of significance based on corrected chi square.

at preventing customer rip-offs.[9] In other words, the opportunities for ripping off customers may be greater than opportunities to steal from the restaurant. Given the greater security against restaurant theft, even more importance should be attached to the finding that more waiters were involved in restaurant-directed theft compared to the other two possible targets.

The pattern of theft in the four restaurants studied reveals that a majority of waiters were involved in exchange-based, social theft activities, and that a minority (about one-third) were heavily involved in pecuniary theft.[10] Table 2 shows an association between different pecuniary rip-offs, regardless of theft targets. For example, those who "fail to ring" were also more likely to pad a customer's bill or short change a patron—all financially advantageous activities.

Reasons for Employee Theft

In an attempt to test our second and third hypotheses, three dependent variables were generated from the first seven vignettes in Table 1: (1) social restaurant theft—respondents were classified as having engaged in none, one, or both of these activities; (2) pecuniary restaurant theft—involved summing "fail to ring" and "selling restaurant items" (none, one, both); and (3) pecuniary customer rip-offs—these three items were divided into none, one, two or more of these forms of theft. The last five theft items in Table 1

[9]Because four different restaurants were used in the sample, it was not possible to gather information on the direct influence of security system effectiveness and theft. As in indirect means of assessing security system effectiveness, waiters were asked to rate their restaurant as to ease with which ripping off could be done. Respondents' perceptions of ease of ripping off did not correlate with socially-based restaurant theft, but was correlated with pecuniary theft (Gamma = .42 for restaurant theft and .32 for customer theft—as defined in the next section).

[10]Nine waiters (22% of the sample) did not engage in any of the twelve theft activities given as vignettes, although they knew of others who did engage in some of the rip-off methods.

were excluded from the following analysis due to their infrequent occurrence. Our goal in the remainder of the article is to examine some of the possible determinants of restaurant and customer theft.

In this sample, background variables such as education, marital status, and degree of religious involvement did not affect rates of ripping-off participation. Age, found to be correlated with employee theft by Clark et al. (1979)—with younger workers more involved in theft—could not be assessed here. Eighty-eight percent of the waiters in the sample were between 18 and 25 years old. Time on the job, shown by Hearn and Stoll (1975) to be related to cynical attitudes toward restaurant work and customers, did not predict theft involvement. We now turn to work-based factors thought to affect restaurant and customer directed theft.

We predicted in hypothesis 2 that those workers perceiving negative aspects in their work would be more likely to engage in employee theft than those satisfied with their jobs. Features of the work setting were broken down into two major categories: objective job conditions and subjective judgments about one's work. Objective conditions included responses to ordinal items assessing each waiter's perception of volume of business (very good to very poor), level of pay at work (very adequate to very inadequate), and amount of tips at the restaurant (good tips to poor tips). None of the three objective job conditions were associated with any of the three forms of restaurant theft. (Gammas were all below .20 for these nine comparisons).

Likert-type items were used to assess attitudes toward the job, e.g., degree of boredom, attitudes toward one's supervisor, toward the owner, and questions designed to measure injustice, e.g., feelings of being treated unfairly by management, and saying management takes advantage of waiters. These subjective attitudes about one's work did not predict theft involvement when the restaurant was the target. Two factors, negative attitude toward supervisor and feelings of being unfairly treated by management were associated with ripping off the customer (Gammas of .43 and .51 respectively). This displacement effect, or what Butler and Skipper (1981:25–26) term a "spill-over" phenomenon, means that workers unhappy with management are more likely to victimize the customer than the restaurant. This could be because there are more opportunities to rip off customers. As noted above, restaurants are likely to have more security safeguards to protect the firm from theft than its customers.

We conclude that job-related conditions and attitudes were not associated with restaurant-directed theft and only two factors were strongly correlated with customer rip-offs. This failure to find support for hypothesis 2 suggests that job conditions do not directly affect theft behavior. However, dissatisfaction with one's work may operate through the development of neutralization which in turn could affect employee theft.

Our theft hypothesis predicted that failure to develop or support neutralizing statements would prevent theft involvement by waiters. Three types of neutralizing techniques were assessed. One was the use of justification, defined as occurring when "one accepts responsibility for the act in question, but denies the pejorative quality associated with it" (Scott and Lyman, 1968:47). Second, denial of injury, i.e., a person who brings on their own victimization (Sykes and Matza, 1957). These six statements were used to assess a weakening of beliefs (responses to Likert-type questions where "agree" and "strongly agree" were combined):

1 Justification: The management expects some ripping off by its employees (31% agreed).
2 Justification: Most waiters see ripping off as an appropriate method of getting a fair wage (17% agreed).
3 Justification: Ripping off is an acceptable way for me to supplement my low pay (12% agreed).
4 Denial of injury: The management can financially afford to be ripped off by its employees (17% agreed).
5 Deserving victim: Drunk customers deserve to be ripped off (5% agreed).
6 Deserving victim: Persons who frequent this restaurant deserve to be ripped off (5% agreed).

It is apparent from the low percentages of agreement that neutralization and justification are rather rare among the waiters. This is surprising given the high exposure to theft activities of other waiters as well as the heavy self-involvement seen in Table 1.

There is a potential causal order problem here, as with more research on neutralization techniques (e.g., Cressey, 1953; Hirschi, 1969; Sheley, 1980). Reports of past deviant acts are compared to current statements which represent neutralizations. While we cannot resolve this causal order question, it is of less importance because of the low frequency of these attitudes in the sample. However, it could be argued that neutralizing attitudes were important in the past, setting up a pattern of theft which has now become accepted (see Sheley, 1980:55). If such a process were occurring, we would expect new waiters to use neutralization techniques, while waiters on the job a longer time might not. When time on the job was used as a control, the original nonsignificant relationship of neutralization agreement and theft involvement did not change for new waiters (one year or less) and experienced waiters (over one year as a waiter).

In conclusion, hypothesis 3 was not supported. Agreement with neutralization statements was not related to involvement in restaurant theft. It remains to be explained why theft activity can be so high without widespread agreement with neutralizations and justifications.

DISCUSSION

The failure of the neutralization hypothesis raises questions about the role of such beliefs in producing employee theft, questions also raised for other forms of deviance (cf. Minor, 1980; Sheley, 1980). The fact that theft is such an open activity in restaurants may mean that "neutralizations and rationalizations are simply unnecessary" (Minor, 1980:115). As Sheley (1980:15) notes, "neutralization designed to rid an individual of a moral dilemma prior to deviance hardly seems necessary when society or subculture has already accomplished the task." The work subculture of waiters seems to remove the need for neutralizations. There is some evidence that neutralizations are more likely for solitary, secretive acts of deviance such as embezzlement (Cressey, 1953). For example, Hindelang (1970) notes that among youth techniques of neutralization are more likely to account for solitary delinquent offenses where group support is absent. But restaurant theft is not a solitary offense in that most waiters know it is going on and it is openly discussed. This openness of theft activity is seen in these findings: (1) seventy-seven percent of the waiters said they had discussed rip-off methods with co-workers; (b) sixty percent stated they discussed which customers deserved to be ripped off;[11] and (c) eighty percent knew at least one other waiter who had been caught ripping off.[12] This exposure to ripping off was correlated with personal involvement in different types of theft activity (see Table 3).

There are two ways of arguing that techniques of neutralization are irrelevant to socially based restaurant theft. If the motivation for social theft is seen as residing in making and maintaining friendships, or in the carrying out of reciprocal exchange, then it might be argued that there is a built-in neutralization of "appeal to higher loyalties" (Sykes and Matza, 1957). But neutralization must be considered an active process, one consciously engaged in prior to the act to free the actor of any moral qualms (Cressy, 1953). If it is so embedded in socially based theft that it is not verbalized, its active nature seems to be absent. Consequently, the concept

[11]One respondent noted that waiters will try to anticipate which customers will stiff them (leave no tip): "There's a habbit [sic] among waiters at my restaurant to 'size up' customers as they come in as to whether they are 'red-necks' or not. (A red-neck doesn't tip, or if he does, only very little. He also eats a lot of bread, has his steaks well-done, and puts ketsup on them.)"

[12]Respondents indicated that in almost every case the person was fired when caught, but not referred to the police. Five respondents reported they had been caught ripping off in the past. Four of the five reported continuing theft involvement at their current place of employment.

TABLE 3 Exposure to Theft Activities and Amount of Self-Involvement in Theft Talk for Three Types of Employee Theft Using Gamma ($N=41$)

Items	Restaurant Social	Restaurant Pecuniary	Customers Pecuniary
Number of other waiters known by respondents to have been caught: none / one–five / over five ($N=18$ / 17 / 16)	.12	.55	.38
Discuss rip-off methods with co-workers in the restaurant: never / occasionally / often ($N^*=9$ / 24 / 6)	.48	.69	.63
Discuss which customers deserve to be ripped off: never / occasionally / often ($N^*=16$ / 21 / 3)	.52	.76	.56

*N does not total 41 due to nonresponse.

of neutralization from social control theory does little to explain social restaurant theft.

There is a second reason why techniques of neutralization are irrelevant to social theft: the linguistic issue of defining the act. Henry and Mars (1978) suggest that the noneconomic basis of some part-time theft prevents perpetrators from viewing their behavior as stealing. As long as the motivation is exchange, not profit; reciprocity, not gain; altruism, not advantage; "theft" connotations can be avoided. Stealing has a linguistic base in the market-economy and legal systems, but not in the vocabulary of the illegal amateur trader. When the traditional "language of market exchange" (Henry and Mars, 1978:256) is denied, the techniques of neutralizations may be literally uncalled for or inappropriate.

This argument would not explain involvement in more pecuniary theft, activity less open to such linguistic manipulation. Here another sense in which restaurant theft is social must be recognized to account for the failure of the neutralization hypothesis. Theft at work is a source of talk and a ground for communication among workers. It becomes part of the work culture and attendant folklore of the occupation (cf. Horning, 1970). Theft-talk as shop-talk permits the achievement of status in the eyes of co-workers, a form of work-based identity. Discussions of ripping-off techniques result in attributions of experience, competence, and craftiness to waiters. Seen in this way, theft talk becomes a valued activity, increasing group solidarity among waiters (cf. Zeitlin, 1971). In the words of one of

Henry's (1978:97) informants: "There's no point in doing it if you can't tell people about it."

In this sense, all theft activities in restaurants have a social dimension in that group solidarity is achieved. However this does not mean that all theft is social theft. Following the usage of Henry, social theft refers to "amateur trading" activities engaged in primarily without concern for financial gain, i.e., where the intention is purely to do someone a favor. Henry found that the recipient of the favor is often not in the work group, but someone outside it (cf. Henry and Mars, 1978; Henry, 1978).

Theft-talk serves many of the same functions which atrocity stories do in work settings. Atrocity stories are "dramatic events staged between groups of friends and acquaintances that draw on shared understandings about the way of the world. The teller is cast as hero . . . [and through such stories] social structures and parties to them are rendered rational and comprehensible" (Dingwell, 1977; 375). Here such talk informs the newcomer of the work culture and folklore, serving to socialize the novice into the flow of the job. It contributes to a sense of comradery as well as worker morale, viz, theft-talk enriches an otherwise routinized task performance. Worker discussions of ripping off, like theft itself, allows the waiter to "take matters into his own hands, assume responsibility, make decisions and face challenges" (Zeitlin, 1971:24).

Talk about restaurant rip-offs is also controlling mechanism whereby workers set the boundaries of appropriate targets and amounts of theft, what English dockworkers call the "working value of the boat" (Mars, 1974). Within these worker discussions of theft reside both legitimating motives as well as built-in controls to limit theft activity (e.g., Ditton, 1977a:248). In this vein, Stuart Henry (1978) presents a proposal to control worker theft by relying upon the workers and their subcultural expectations.

A recognition of the function of workers' talk and its relation to developing status on the job gives new meaning to Zeitlin's (1971:22) assertion that "a little larceny can do a lot for employee morale." Those seeking to limit employee theft must realize that the subservient nature of service work creates problems of status and that alternative sources of building status on the job would need to be devised to replace the centrality of employee theft and its resultant talk.[13] Only then will an alternative to Zeitlin's (1971) admittedly risky solution of "let them steal" be possible.

[13]If theft-talk is a critical aspect of work identity, future research might focus on the extent to which this talk is accurate. It is possible that workers could make up rip-off stories to satisfy co-workers. Here as elsewhere talk rather than action may be a more frequent occurrence.

REFERENCES

Bensman, Joseph, and Israel Gerver
1963 "Crime and punishment in the factory: the function of deviancy in maintaining the social system." American Sociological Review 28:588–98.

Bryant, Clifton D.
1974 Deviant Behavior: Occupational and Organizational Bases. Chicago: Rand McNally.

Butler, Suellen, and James K. Skipper, Jr.
1980 "Waitressing, vulnerability, and job autonomy." Sociology of Work and Occupations 7:487–502.
1981 "Working for tips: an examination of trust and reciprocity in a secondary relationship of the restaurant organization." Sociological Quarterly 22:15–27.

Butler, Suellen, and William E. Snizek
1976 "The waiter-diner relationship." Sociology of Work and Occupations 3:209–222.

Clark, John P., Richard C. Hollinger, and Leonard F. Smith
1979 Theft by Employees in Work Organizations: A Preliminary Final Report. University of Minnesota: unpublished.

Clark, John P., and Richard C. Hollinger
1981 Theft by Employees in Work Organizations. University of Minnesota: unpublished.

Cressey, Donald R.
1953 Other People's Money. New York: Free Press.

Dalton, Melville
1959 Men Who Manage. New York: Wiley.

Dillon, M. C.
1973 "Why should anyone refrain from stealing?" Ethics 83:338–40.

Dingwall, Robert
1977 "Atrocity stories' and professional relationships." Sociology of Work and Occupations 4:371–396.

Ditton, Jason
1977a "Alibis and aliases: some notes on the 'motives' of fiddling bread salesmen." Sociology 11:223–55.
1977b "Learning to 'fiddle' customers." Sociology of Work and Occupations 4:427–50.
1977c Part-time Crime: An Ethnography of Fiddling and Pilferage. London: Macmillan.

Hackler, James C., and Patricia Bourgette
1973 "Dollars, dissonance, and survey returns." Public Opinion Quarterly 37:276–81.

Hearn, H. L., and Patricia Stoll
1975 "Continuance commitment in low-status occupations: the cocktail waitress." Sociological Quarterly 16:105–14.

Henry, Stuart

1978 The Hidden Economy: The Context and Control of Borderline Crime. London: Martin Robertson.

Henry, Stuart, and Gerald Mars.

1978 "Crime at work: the social construction of amateur property theft." Sociology 12:246–63.

Hindelang, Michael

1970 "The commitment of delinquents to their misdeeds: do delinquents drift?" Social Problems 17:502–509.

Hirschi, Travis

1969 Causes of Delinquency. Berkeley: University of California Press.

Hollinger, Richard C.

1978 "Employee deviance against the formal work organization." Paper presented at the annual meetings of American Society of Criminology.

Hollinger, Richard, and John Clark

1982 "Employee deviance: a response to the perceived quality of the work experience." Work and Occupations 9 (February):97–114.

Horning, Donald N. M.

1970 "Blue-collar theft: conceptions of property, attitudes toward pilfering, and work group norms in a modern industrial plant." In Erwin O. Smigel and H. Laurence Ross (eds.), Crimes Against Bureaucracy. New York: Van Nostrand.

Mangione, Thomas W., and Robert P. Quinn

1975 "Job satisfaction, counterproductive behavior, and drug use at work." Journal of Applied Psychology 60:114–116.

Mars, Gerald

1973 "Hotel pilferage: a case in occupational theft." In Malcolm Warner (ed.). The Sociology of the Workplace. New York: Halsted.

1974 "Dock pilferage." In Paul Rock and Mary McIntosh (eds.), Deviance and Social Control. London: Tavistock.

Martin, J. P.

1963 Offenders as Employees. New York: St. Martin's Press.

Marx, Gary T.

1981 "Ironies of social control: authorities as contributors to deviance through escalation, nonenforcement and covert facilitation." Social Problems 28:221–246.

Minor, W. William

1980 "The neutralization of criminal offense." Criminology 18:103–120.

Robin, Gerald D.

1969 "Employees as offenders." Journal of Research in Crime and Delinquency 6:17–33.

1974 "White-collar crime and employee theft." Crime and Delinquency 20:251–262.

Scott, Marvin B., and Stanford M. Lyman

1968 "Accounts." American Sociological Review 33:46–62.

Sheley, Joseph F.
1980 "Is neutralization necessary for criminal behavior?" Deviant Behavior 2:49–72.
Spradley, James P. and Brenda J. Mann
1975 The Cocktail Waitress. New York: Wiley.
Sykes, Gresham M., and David Matza
1957 "Techniques of neutralization: a theory of delinquency." American Sociological Review 22:6640.
Whyte, William F.
1948 Human Relations in the Restaurant Industry. New York: McGraw-Hill.
1949 "The social structure of the restaurant." American Journal of Sociology 54:302–308.
Zeitlin, Lawrence R.
1971 "A little larceny can do a lot for employee morale." Psychology Today 5:22,24,26,64.

APPENDIX

The following hypothetical situations were created to assess various forms of ripping off which might occur in restaurant work.

Free Food to Friends

A couple of Greg's friends come in to dinner one night and have Greg wait on them. Greg must ring up the meat order on the register, but he gives them baked potatoes, corn on the cob, and dessert free of charge. They pay the meat bill and leave Greg a large tip.

Take Home Restaurant Items

Lennie, after doing his check out and getting ready to go home, will occasionally pick up a restaurant glass and put it in his coat. He has just about finished a service for twelve of glasses from the restaurant. Next, he plans to collect a twelve-place setting of restaurant silverware.

Fail to Ring Food Items

Four customers are seated at one of Ben's tables, two elderly men and their wives. The two men each order the cheapest main course item on the menu and the women order salads. Ben rings up the main course items on the register, but does not ring up the salads. After the meal is finished, Ben presents the bill with the two main course items rung up and the two salads written in by hand and totaled. The two men pay the full amount, plus a tip, and Ben pockets the price of the salads.

Selling Restaurant Items

Three conventioners are asking Carl about the restaurant. They especially like the decor and particularly the drink glasses with the restaurant's inscription on them. They ask Carl if they could buy two glasses and he obliges them for two dollars a glass. Carl keeps the money.

Bill Padding

Art is waiting on a large party of twelve men, all of whom have been ordering drinks from the bar during dinner. The check is to be presented to the gentleman in charge and he will pay with a credit card. After looking through all the drink tickets, Art decides to inflate the figure of the bar bill, figuring that an extra four or five dollars will not be noticed. Art presents the bill and the man pays it.

Short Change Customer

After a particularly difficult time with a group of highly demanding and rude customers, Ian presents the bill expecting little or no tip. After several minutes, one of the customers lays several ten dollar bills on the top of the tab. Ian picks it up and brings it back to the register area to count the money. He finds that the tens are all new and on a bill of $37.50 there are five new ten dollar bills. He figures that the customer was not aware of the fact that the bills stuck together. Ian, feeling that they unknowingly left him ten dollars too much, does not inform them of the mistake. He returns change of $2.50, keeping the ten.

Add Tip to Credit Card

John goes to a table to pick up the customer's Master Charge receipt after they have left the table and finds that they have left him no tip. He looks at the charge and realizes that the customer has only signed it, leaving his copy with the rest and not totaling out the amount. John adds a 15% tip and totals it out, throwing away the customer's copy of the Master Charge form.

Take Other Waiter's Tip Money

Matt's station has been very slow, while the waiter in the next section of tables has been quite busy. There is a tip tray on one of the busy waiter's tables which has been there for some time after a large party departed. Matt is sure the other waiter has not noticed the size of the tip; in passing the table, Matt quickly takes a five off the bottom of the stack of bills on the tip tray, figuring the other waiter will never miss it.

Hold Out on Tip Pool

Ned works in a restaurant which utilizes a tip pool procedure. At the end of the night all the waiters pool their tips and, after the restaurant takes out a certain percentage, the waiters split the remainder between them. Ned receives a $20 tip on a $35 bill. At the end of the night he only turns in $5 of the $20 tip.

No Ring, Split with Cook

Don, a waiter, has gotten to know the head cook quite well. They work out a system whereby Don writes up some of his dinner orders and turns them into the cook without ringing them up on the register. At the end of the night, Don will split the money collected in this way with the cook.

Bring in Own Wine to Sell

Frank has been selling quite a few bottles of Mateús Rose to his customers. He decides to bring in several bottles of his own (which he obtained on sale) and to sell them to the customer at the inflated restaurant price and pocket the difference between what he paid for it and what the restaurant charges.

Take Money from Cash Register

Ken, during a slow point in the evening, notices that one of the cash registers has been left unattended as the cashier was called away to the phone. Looking around and seeing no one, Ken quickly opens the register and takes a few twenties off the stack, pretending to make change.

Reading 34

Talk about Visions: Spiritual Readings as Deviant Work

John Heeren
California State College, San Bernardino
Marylee Mason
Chaffey College, Alta Loma, California

The purpose of this paper is to investigate the linguistic and interactional features of the work done by practitioners of a deviant occupation, spiritual reading. Based on 42 transcriptions of such readings, we uncover the common elements of grammatical form and propositional content and the way readers use setting, self, and talk to make their visionary utterances more forceful. The successful accomplishment of a reading typically requires that the client be an active participant and that reader and client share a "common religion."

As research in the area of deviant behavior has grown, there have been more attempts to differentiate the field. Sexual deviance by itself, for example, has come to be a fairly distinct research focus, as has substance abuse. In still another subarea, the study of deviant occupations, the focus is on those activities that contribute to a person's living but fall outside the law or convention. Although there is a possibility of deviant actions in connection with virtually any type of legitimate work, some occupations involve almost exclusively deviant behavior. Prostitution, contract murder, and racketeering would generally be seen as examples of such criminal callings. Intermediate between those socially acceptable occupations that permit or occasionally encourage deviance and those that are completely enmeshed in it are certain types of work that can be characterized as marginally legal. These are jobs that "neither fully conform nor fully deviate from either legal or community norms" (Easto and Truzzi, 1974:350). Examples include carnival work, medical quackery, and fortunetelling. The last of these—fortunetelling, or more specifically, spiritual reading—is the focus of this paper. Though legally tolerated in many areas, most spiritual readers operate outside the respectability of the community. They are widely regarded as fraudulently offering a service (i.e., knowing the future) that cannot be provided. Moreover, there is a general feeling that they exploit troubled and underprivileged clients who might find genuine help elsewhere.

That there are frauds among the practitioners of fortunetelling is not what makes the occupation deviant. We tend to agree with Bryant (1974:255) that virtually any occupation uses some degree of misrepresentation to manipulate clients or customers. Moreover, the possibilities for exploitation are rife whenever there is differential knowledge, power, or certain other qualities. This is shown in the amount of needless surgery performed, needless lawsuits extended, and needless car repairs done in contemporary U.S. society. Indeed, it may certainly be that exploitation is likely to be endemic where private profit is the driving mechanism of the economy. Salesclerks who are paid on a commission basis are generally known to sell more than those paid hourly wages. If fortunetellers are not alone in the use of fraud and exploitation, neither is it accurate to view them as not providing a significant service to clients. As one commentator (Miller, 1978:73) has suggested, fortunetellers often do offer enough comfort and advice to clients to build a lasting relationship.

However outsiders may regard spiritual readers, this is only part of the picture. It is also necessary to take into consideration the viewpoint of the participants in the deviant behavior—the readers and their clients. Although some readers are no doubt merely frauds (Tatro, 1974), there are without question others who *believe* they can discern a person's character through the palm of the hand and divine the future. How could a reader fail to get a sense of his or her gift when a client returns to report the amazing accuracy of forecasts or the great value of advice previously given? As the occurrence of this type of episode suggests, many clients also believe in the efficacy of spiritual reading and in the extraordinary powers of at least some readers. Beliefs about the human ability to know the future are not only shared by some readers and probably most veteran clients, they are also found widely, though on a "subterranean" level, in various segments of U.S. society. This would explain the popularity of a Jeanne Dixon and the continuing interest in the life of Edgar Cayce. We will show that a set of shared beliefs to be referred to as "common religion" provide the context within which spiritual readings occur. This is similar to an argument made by Levi-Strauss (1967) that the efficacy of the sorcerer's magic is ultimately based on the beliefs and experiences that the shaman shares with his followers.

The perspective to be adopted in this paper derives principally from Matza's (1969) work on deviance. Matza recommended that research take an appreciative stance toward the subjects being studied. This stance implies that one should identify with the participants in the deviance and describe the essential features of their culture. Many such cultural elements could be the focus of one's research. In the area of deviant occupations, the social and technical skills used in the deviant work would be a major point of interest. In this particular paper we intend to concentrate on the interactive processes involved in spiritual readings as they actually appear in the context of communication. This is an ideal focus for such a topic because we can assume that readers will try to conduct themselves in such a way that they appear competent to clients. By the same token, clients themselves must respect certain expectations to treat the encounter seriously, to have an open mind regarding the reader's gifts, and so on.

The existing literature on fortunetelling and related occupations is not extensive. Most prominently, Tatro (1974) has analyzed the features of setting and performance used by fortunetellers to convince clients of the reader's extraordinary powers. In addition to marshaling various religious artifacts, such as statues of Jesus and Mary and "holy water," readers also make use of the verbal devices of "fishing" and "calculated vagueness." Whereas fishing means looking for a client's self-disclosures and restating them as revelations, the second technique involves making several rapid ambiguous statements with the expectation that the client will respond (positively) only to those that fit him or her. Along similar lines, Leland (1971) has characterized numerous rules that fortunetellers should respect in relations with clients. These guidelines cover both what is to be said and how it is to be presented. For example, if the client is a middle-aged man, it is usually safe to say that "they have had a lawsuit or a great dispute as to property which has given them a great deal of trouble" (Leland, 1971;182). According to Leland this should be stated impressively. "Emphasis and sinking the voice are of great assistance in fortune telling. If the subject betrays the least emotion, or admits it, promptly improve the occasion, express sympathy, and 'work it up' " (Leland, 1971:182). Finally, Hyman (1977) compiled a number of recommendations that "cold readers" might use to impress clients with their perceptiveness in personality assessment. These recommendations, which overlap considerably with those of Leland and Tatro, relate to both the content and the presentation of character evaluations.

The problem with these earlier studies is that they have looked only at "rules" for fortunetellers. They put forth some general guidelines that one should respect in taking advantage of customers. Tatro, for instance, apparently had some firsthand knowledge about a group of fortunetellers who felt they had no gift for prophecy or spiritual helping and were merely hoodwinking some gullible segments of the public. Because our analysis focuses on the reader-client interchange as a communicative situation, we are not restricted to studying merely the rules of how readers should behave. Looking at the readings themselves allows us to investigate the process of such interactions. Our analysis is concerned with the way that readers mobilize setting, props, and the like in interactional work. In addition, we are interested in the typical kinds of linguistic forms found in such interactions. The existence of these common linguistic patterns is likely to be more important to the occupation than is the occasionally found ability to dramatically present some standard lines of monologue. In our view, readers are not just mechanically following a set of rules for "conning" an essentially passive clientele. Reader and client together accomplish a spiritual reading.

DATA AND METHODS

The data base for this study consists of two audio recordings from readings with spiritual readers in which one of the present authors acted as client, as well as written field observations of these sessions. The analysis also makes use of 40 transcriptions of readings done between 1972 and 1974 in the southern California area. Although these transcriptions were also made from audio recordings, they are of somewhat more limited usefulness than the two referred to above. This is simply because the original tapes are unavailable, and the transcriptions do not contain extensive comments about paralinguistic and performance elements present in the reading situations. Moreover, it is very difficult to reconstruct the behavior of the client in these situations, whether they were cooperative or nervous or acted as typical clients would.

Some further comments about our sample should be made. All of them were professionals in the sense of earning money for their readings, although several did not support themselves through doing readings. There was considerable variety in the types of readers studied. Tatro (1974:189-190) distinguished four major kinds of fortunetellers—"a night club entertainer, a highly mobile 'big score' operator, an ethnic group member, or an established member of a local community." Virtually every member of our sample would fall into one of Tatro's latter two categories. About one-third of our readers were folk-religious figures serving primarily the lower-class ethnic communities of Mexican-Americans or blacks. The remainder were white and served both regular clients as well as occasional customers from the middle to lower class. None of them presented themselves as "gypsy fortunetellers." Approximately three-fourths of our sample advertised their services in some formal way—classified ads, the yellow pages, and large front-yard signs being the most common means. The other one-fourth depended on word of mouth for their clientele. Almost all operated out of their own homes.

In trying to uncover some of the ways in which spiritual readers resolve the problem of appearing competent in interaction with their clients, two methods of analysis are used. The first of these is a general descriptive ethnography focusing on the presentational aspects of the spiritual reading. This is based largely on Goffman's (1959) "dramaturgical sociology." Specifically, we try to show what a typical encounter with a spiritual reader entails. The second mode of analysis is what is referred to in sociolinguistics as the ethnography of communication. In the last decade or so, social scientists interested in language and speech have developed a useful repertoire of analytic concepts for investigating communication. Included here are such concepts as speech event; speech code, genre, and style; linguistic, paralinguistic and nonverbal forms of communication; and rules of discourse (Hymes, 1972; Bauman and Sherzer, 1974; Labov and Fanshel, 1977). Our intention here is to look at particular linguistic and paralinguistic strategies that spiritual readers employ. The psychic abilities of spiritual readers are not explored in this paper. For present purposes we are bracketing the question of these special powers and simply studying this group with respect to their use of normal interactional skills.

ELEMENTS OF A SPIRITUAL READING

The general definition of the situation in the episodes under study is that they are "spiritual readings." It is expected in a spiritual reading that the client seeks the services of a reader who has some visionary powers quite beyond those humans ordinarily possess. These powers allow the reader—having little or no independent information about the client—to "see" and comment on the client's past, assess the client's personality, foretell the future, and give advice based on all this intuited information. The "insights" that the reader has must be seen as extraordinary. Few, if any, clients would feel that a reader had unusual powers if that reader said such things as, "I see that you had a mother and a father," "You seem like a nice person," or "You will wake up tomorrow morning." The precise form of readers' statements is a major concern of the analysis below. Readers, on the other hand, expect that clients will either have faith in the extraordinary powers of readers in general (preferably in the powers of the specific reader being consulted), or have at least an open mind regarding the unusual psychic abilities of select humans. If a client is openly skeptical or negative about the visionary powers of the reader consulted, the reader is unlikely to devote the same efforts to such a client as to a serious client. In such a situation the reader is likely to accept the client's fee and provide a very minimal reading.

For this definition of the situation to be accepted by both client and reader, common religion is an essential backdrop to the interaction. We derive the concept of common religion from Wilson (1978), who defined it as a layer of religiosity that underlies the official denominations that exist in a society. This common religion pervading society "emanates from below, in the form of folk practices and customs" (Wilson, 1978:26). It is not greatly organized and cannot be "joined." Though neither universal nor unitary across all groups and classes in society, common religion is more widespread than is its official counterpart. Common religion and official churches are distinct enterprises, yet there are continuities and overlaps between the two. Wilson suggested that common religion is organized at various levels. At the lowest level are "efforts to organize the environment, to make a unity of experience which are prompted by the disquiet aroused by anomalies" (Wilson, 1978:31). Included here would be a concern with luck and coincidences as well as beliefs in ESP, UFOs, and folk remedies that contain an element of nonrationality. The second level tends to be more organized and available to be used for practical ends. Here one sees astrology, charms, palmistry, waterwitching, and so on. The third level is more complex and fully elaborated intellectually and includes beliefs in supernatural forces and spirits, systems of ritual magic and witchcraft, and beliefs in God as interpreted by common people. These levels all intertwine with one another as well as with official religion in the world view of individuals.

Spiritual readers—whether they are called palmists, clairvoyants, mediums, or psychics—represent a level of expertise in relation to common religion. Whether through accident, grace, or personal development, they are thought by followers to possess a visionary gift whose very possibility would be denied by the mainstream of our rational society. The clientele of these occult practitioners can be regarded as seekers of various benefits to be gained from the readers' gifts. Beyond simple knowledge or advice about the future, clients come for help with a variety of misfortunes. While death and illness are important instances, a range of social problems involving one's love life, drugs and alcohol, and employment are also included.

Three distinct types of conversation occur within spiritual readings. The first is everyday conversation, which is characterized by sociable chat of the sort most often found between fairly casual acquaintances. This kind of talk runs from comments on the weather to advice regarding healthful foods and to moralizing about various problems that exist in society. The second type of speech involves the use of interview questions. Here the reader asks the client direct questions about the client's biography of personality. Finally, the most distinctive conversation found in a reading is the visionary style. The reader sees or has insights about the client that are announced directly to him or her. For example, "You are going to be receiving some money in the mail." A prominent subvariety of the visionary style is what can be termed "advice-cum-vision." Here the reader recommends a course of action to the client on the basis of some special insight into the client's future. A reader might say, for instance, "You should stay with your present job as I see you eventually being very successful at it." Ideally, both of these varieties of the visionary style are uttered forcefully and assuredly by the reader.

Although these three types of conversation can be analytically distinguished, in practice there is considerable intermingling among them. At times this confounding of conversational styles seems to be explicitly done by readers as a device for facilitating the reading. There were several instances in the data where readers used interview questions as a pretest of a visionary statement to come.

Reader: Was your husband in the service?
Client: Yes.
Reader: I see the service around him. All around him.

These pretests may also be the basis of advice-cum-vision:

Reader: Are you planning on selling something?
Client: Yes.
Reader: Make the sale! Let go! Let go, let go.

What we have been discussing in the immediately preceding paragraphs are the major normative elements of the spiritual reading. We have described the typical roles taken by reader and client and the commonly established definition of the situation. A tacitly shared set of beliefs, a so-called common religion, forms the wider framework within which the interaction occurs. We also analyzed the styles of conversation generally found within the spiritual reading. In the following section we move from a static description of these elements to a dynamic analysis of the spiritual reading in its situational context.

FORCE AND THE SITUATIONAL CONTEXT OF A SPIRITUAL READING

Language philosophers have analyzed the ways in which force is brought out in utterances. Austin (1962) first described performative utterances at length. In making a performative utterance, one not only says something but also carries out an act in the saying. To say, "I promise" is actually to make a promise. Later work in linguistics (e.g., Searle, 1970) has shifted attention to the illocutionary force of utterances. There are a variety of linguistic structures that serve to mark the force of verbal expressions. These illocutionary devices are "symbols used in order to warn the audience as to how an utterance is to be taken" (Furberg, 1963:128). In addition, force may be expressed paralinguistically. For instance, "tone of voice, cadence, emphasis; gestures and ceremonial nonverbal procedures; the circumstances of the utterance and the speaker's status" (Furberg, 1963:207) all affect the force of an utterance. Thus, the meaning of a particular communication and the way it is to be understood (i.e., its force) can be determined only from the context in which it was uttered—by whom, to whom, in what tone of voice, and so on. This notion coincides very nicely with major assumptions used in interpretive forms of sociological analysis (e.g., symbolic interaction and ethnomethodology). Interpretive sociology is also concerned with the elements of performance and setting that accompanying an expression (e.g., Goffman, 1959). With these convergences in mind, we would like to describe selected features of a typical spiritual reading.

The reading to be described was conducted by Sister Davine. She came to the client's attention through a printed handbill placed on an auto windshield in a city nearly 30 miles from her own locale. The sheet read in part:

> Don't confuse her with other readers. She is superior to all other readers. She tells you what you want to know and how to proceed, how to hold your job, why your loved one is acting strange. Why is bad luck following you? Why are

> you so unhappy? If you are suffering from sickness, alcoholism, there is no problem so great she cannot solve it. Come and visit her today and be rid of your problems tomorrow. This gifted woman invites you to her home. She has devoted her life to helping others of all walks of life, regardless of race or religion. She can call your enemies by name and tell you who your friends are and much more.

Elsewhere the bill also mentioned that her powers were God given and that she spoke English and Spanish.

If clients located Sister Davine through such a handbill, they would already have several important expectations of her. For instance, they would be aware that she is concerned with helping find solutions to typical problems in living—work, alcohol, and love life. The statement of these problems itself reveals something about the kind of client Sister Davine typically sees. It is noteworthy that in a society generally oriented to upward mobility, she deals with clients who may be downwardly mobile: "How to hold your job." A second inference a potential customer might draw from the handbill is that there are religious forces that will be mobilized in his or her behalf. Her "powers" or "gifts" are extraordinary and "God given." Finally, the advertisement seems to promise that her knowledge of clients is quite explicit and detailed. Other readers may give very general and universally applicable statements; Sister Davine will "call your enemies by name."

The reading was held in Sister Davine's home in a predominantly white, working-class neighborhood. A well-maintained house, it had a small sign in the window announcing Sister Davine as a spiritual reader. The interior of the house was furnished with swagged French draperies, gold velvet sofa and chairs, and two very ornate crystal chandeliers. One wall was entirely covered with mirrors. Contrary to many such readers' homes, no religious artifacts were in evidence. The inside was much more extravagantly furnished than one would be led to expect from the outside of the house or the neighborhood. In fact, the living area of the house could be characterized as conspicuously fancy. The chandeliers best exemplify this conspicuous display. These crystal fixtures—one 2 feet and the other 4 feet in diameter—were in separate areas of the same room. Because readings were done in this room, it seems reasonable to expect that clients might be rather impressed with Sister Davine's affluence. After all, if she has psychic powers, how can she have failed to use them to some material advantage for herself?

When the client arrived at the appointed time, Sister Davine answered the door. She was a plump woman of Yugoslavian extraction in her mid-to-late 30s. She was wearing a floor-length house-dress. She took several minutes to get the children settled in another part of the house. She and the client then sat on a couch, turning to the side to face each other. After asking if someone had told the client about her, she asked some preliminary questions about going to school, apparently as a result of some books the client was carrying. These questions were intermingled with chatty talk about ripping her dress, getting ready to get in the shower, and so on. She made the transition from this introductory conversation by deciding what type of a reading should be done, palm or cards. Sister Davine did this by bowing her head into her hand, closing her eyes, and "divining" the most appropriate technique. For about 8 seconds she was silent and motionless while she received vibrations about the best method. She then looked up and said (in a low, serious tone of voice), "Palm reading will be better for you today."

Sister Davine began a series of visionary statement in this way:

> Now the very first thing that I see for you, good or bad, I don't want you to get mad. I'm gonna tell you what I see.
>
> The very first thing that shows between you and the good Lord, it shows that you have a very long life ahead of you. You going to live until you be 89 years old.

Each of these statements (paragraphs) and those that followed began in a fairly loud voice and became much softer toward the end. Her speech during this part of the reading was rapid and unhesitating, giving an impression of certainty to her statements. There were no long pauses or questioning rises in her voice that would indicate tentativeness. None of the speech acts contained phrases to signify doubt or lack of certainty as to the truth of her remarks (such as, "I think," "possibly," "maybe"). Each visionary utterance was presented as a statement of fact. This in itself makes them more forceful. In addition to this, there was a rhythmic, almost ritualistic cadence to her speech. This choppy rhythm was more pronounced in the portions of speech of greater volume.

The purpose of the first statement from her reading is to increase the forcefulness of those following it. This first statement is telling the client how to interpret what follows. "This will be the absolute truth, no holding back; good or bad, all will be told, even if it hurts or makes you angry." Within this first speech act, the phrase "I see for you" adds the force to the initial statement. Clearly if the reader had said "I say for you," the statement would have been less forceful, because the visionary powers of the reader would not have been explicitly invoked. The word "see" indicates that the reader is receiving this information from beyond and that it is, therefore, an irrefutable truth. In later speech acts the spiritual reader changes this illocutionary device to "it shows that" and "it shows for you." In a sense, this device is even more forceful than "I see for you." The use of the passive voice minimizes the role of the reader, and gives the impression that the statement is not being interpreted or passed through a middle agent. Instead, it comes directly from beyond.

In a later segment of the reading, Sister Davine turned to using the advice-cum-vision style of talk. The rhythmic speech pattern was supplanted in these statements with a more normal conversational tone. Emphasis was provided by her shaking her fist at key points. Here is an illustration of this section of the reading:

> Well, it shows that there's money coming to you. There's money coming; there's a trip you're going to take. Through your school, what you're trying to do, you *are* gonna make it. But it's gonna take time and a lot of patience.

In this section Sister Davine effectively coupled predictions of the future with advice in such a way that, without being specific about the foreseen future, she was able to give more weight to her advice. In other words, the advice she gave to be patient carried much more significance in her statement of it because of her "foreknowledge." It was not a simple message of uplift. She could "see" that patience would pay off in a very particular way in the future.

The most significant aspect of the spiritual reading is the fact that readers make visionary statements to clients. The force of these statements is contingent on a number of situational elements. The client apprehends a reader's statement in the light of the reader's advertisements in handbills and such. The reader's appearance and the setting of the reading also contributed to the force of the visionary assertions. Finally, as we showed above, there were numerous linguistic and paralinguistic devices that affected the force of Sister Davine's visionary utterances.

THE FORM OF READERS' STATEMENTS

Visionary statements can be treated as speech acts within the context of the spiritual reading. Speech acts are utterances that actually perform some action. In the case of visionary statements we find that they either *assert* something about the biography of the client or foretell his or her future. To understand the meaning of a speech act, it is necessary to investigate separately its grammatical form and its propositional content. Grammatically, visionary acts tend to take one of two forms. The declarative form is simply an assertion about a past, present, or future state of affairs.

Reader: And I want to say to you, yes, I saw a legal action here.

Reader: I want you to know you were born one day to be happy, one day to be lucky. But, so far you've not seen much of either one.

Reader: The very first thing that shows between you and the good Lord, it shows that you have a very long life ahead of you. You're going to live until you be 89 years old.

It is also very common for a visionary statement to take an interrogative form.

Reader: Who is or has had a hand that hurts them? Do you have a sore hand or arm?

Reader: Do you know that someone else is in love with you? A married man.

Because the interrogative conveys that the reader has some special knowledge, the visionary style often couples a declarative with an interrogative form.

Reader: I want to say to you I see you or somebody drinking. Who is it?

Reader: I do see that someone who is very old in your husband's family—85 or 90 years old—is going to die. See, that is the ace of spades there. It's sad, but, after all, when you reach that age you expect to die. Do you know anyone who fits that description?

The considerable use of the interrogative form in visionary speech acts may seem surprising to those who expect only direct declarative prophetic-like statements. When we consider the functions of the interrogative, its prevalence seems much more sensible, for the primary function of the interrogative is to request that the client confirm the reader's assertions about him or her. This is consistent with one of the rules of discourse that Labov and Fanshel (1977) presented. Specifically, the "rule of confirmation" states that when A makes a statement about events known to B, but presumably not known to A, this statement is heard as a request for confirmation (Labov and Fanshel, 1977:100). Thus, the interrogative form makes explicit what is already implied in the reader's making declarative statements about events presumably known only to the client. Ideally, the interaction between reader and client during visionary speech acts should fall into discrete couplets. The reader makes an assertion or forecast about the client; the client confirms the statement and perhaps supplies some relevant detail.

Reader: Your boy is not doing too well at his present school, is he?
Client: No, he is not. He tells me he hates the school.

There appears to be a secondary function served by the interrogative form in visionary speech acts. Ethnomethodologists have pointed out that in everyday conversation participants are expected to fill in meanings when others make ambiguous statements (Mehan and Wood, 1975:101–102). Employing this "et cetera principle" means that one supplies contextual information to make sense of the indexical expressions of others. So it is in spiritual readings. Readers are not expected to spell out precise details of the persons and situations in the client's life. Instead, clients must play an active part by trying to assess the applicability of visionary statements to their lives.

Although it often does not, this should occur ideally without a great deal of effort on the reader's part, as in the following situation.

Reader: I feel that by the vibrations I receive from your fingertips that you are going to be into electronics.

Client: Pardon me, ma'am. I don't see . . . I don't have any . . . Ah! Excuse me. I do see. I'm going to graduate right now in June and one of the first places I'm going to ask about a job is Edison Electric Company. I'd like to see if I can get on out there. That's maybe where the electronics comes in.

Reader: Yes, I just picked the word up; that's all that was given to me. I'm glad you took off on it.

The two functions of the interrogative form overlap in practice and cannot always be easily distinguished. It is common for readers to request confirmation from a client and, not receiving it, follow up with a series of questions or statements aimed at getting the client to fill in sufficient details so that confirmation of the visionary utterance will eventually be granted. In those situations where clients show a resistance to accepting the reader's visions, the reader may become quite directive regarding the client's need to fill in appropriately.

Reader: I want to say to you, did someone get peeved at you for something? Yes?

Client: Probably . . . I can't say . . . someone.

Reader: Yes, they did. You know about it. You know a girl that got mad at you.

Client: Girl?

Reader: Yes, or your roommate. Which was it?

Client: No, he didn't. A. . . .

Reader: Somebody got a little peeved at you—it might have been some time back.

Client: Unless I didn't know about it.

Reader: Yes, you made someone mad at you; probably irritated, you know.

Client: Probably so.

Reader: Yes. You ain't thinking about it, but you better think.

THE CONTENT OF VISIONARY UTTERANCES

As indicated above, the study of the meaning of speech acts requires looking into both the grammatical form and the propositional content of the acts. The latter is the subject of this section. However different the grammatical form of two sentences might be, their propositional content may be the same (Searle, 1971:42–44). Consider these sentences:

1 Are you going to Las Vegas?
2 You are going to Las Vegas

Although the first is a question and the second a declarative statement, both have the same subject, predicate, and object. The variability in the use of these and other propositional elements in visionary utterances is our interest here.

In addition to a number of lesser considerations regarding the content of visionary utterances, there is one major dimension involved in such statements. We refer to the generality or specificity of readers' visions. Clients would prefer to have visionary utterances be as specific as possible, but readers know that the less specific their statements, the less likely *dis*confirmation becomes. Accordingly, a good proportion of the exchanges between client and reader revolve around the specific details of a visionary utterance and the enthusiastic confirmation with which the client responds.

Reader: You are a very intelligent and forceful person who will succeed in whatever you try to do. Let me ask you one question before we continue. You had a last minute change of wardrobe before coming here, didn't you?

Client: Yes, I did.

Reader: You decided to change your slacks before coming here. You originally had on a pair of pants that were darker.

Client: Yes that's amazing.

The generality of readers' visions is important in other respects. It is, of course, quite common to have readers forecast nebulous outcomes for clients. Statements such as the following abound: "You were born to be happy one day." "Your present problems will be resolved." It is also common to find what might be called culture-specific generalities. By this we mean values or viewpoints that would be acceptable to the great majority of people in the United States. Examples here would be: "You like to be your own boss." "You've worked hard for everything you have." One interesting linguistic device involving the use of generalities is the utterance of "paired opposites" by some readers. The financial condition of several clients, for example, was described by different readers as "not rich, not poor." This use of paired opposites gives the illusion of specificty as the reader expects the client to fill in the exact financial position within the large included middle between rich and poor.

One instance of the generality of visionary statements is seen in readers' use of obviously representational images. Words and phrases are used that are not to be understood on the surface level but at the deeper level of symbolic meanings. Obviously, these symbolic meanings are likely to be very nonspecific, requiring once again that the client fill in.

Reader: But your parents have suffered and struggled against bad luck and darkness.

Client: Darkness? What do you mean?

Reader: Well, darkness . . . some kind of sickness, like loss of money, loss of home. Darkness.

Darkness is an almost universal symbol for misfortune and evil. Although the client knew that the denotative meaning of darkness was not intended, she wanted the specific connotative meanings spelled out.

We said above that readers made disconfirmation by clients less likely by limiting the specific details given in a visionary utterance. Another way in which disconfirmation can be made less likely is by referring to events that will occur at some future date. Readers sometimes request confirmation of their forecasts, and clients sometimes specifically disconfirm future projections. For lack of absolute certainty about events to come, however, clients are more likely to accept without challenge statements about the future. Readers seem to recognize this when they add this phrase to a visionary utterance: "If you haven't heard of it, you will."

One final type of visionary utterance of which readers make extensive use is that involving reference to the actions and intentions of people other than the client. In most instances, these utterances cannot be disconfirmed because the events the reader mentions are not known to the client. For example, one reader told a client that, "Someone is working against you." Other readers mentioned that various relatives of the client loved him or her "even though they don't show it." A last example of such visionary utterances makes reference to "secret admirers." Here is one such:

Reader: I got a little bit of news for you, you may not know of. I not only see the man that stands up to you that thinks of you; I see there's another man who also thinks of you. Would you know about the other man or not?

Client: Uh huh!

Reader: Sometimes you feel, honey, they think of you like you are not important. I see, sweety, they both thinking of you, but there are other women in the picture who are thinking of them.

As can be seen here, a statement about a secret admirer cannot be disconfirmed by a client but might be confirmed.

In these last two sections we have been attending to the linguistic patterns that emerge from spiritual readings. We noted that visionary statements take two grammatical forms, the declarative and the interrogative. The latter is of greatest interest by virtue of its use as a device for requesting client confirmation and encouraging the filling in of details by the client. In terms of the content of visionary utterances, the key element was the need for readers to avoid disconfirmation, while they seemingly spoke specifically to the client. Most difficult to disconfirm were statements by readers that were general, that referred to intentional states of people other than the client, and so on.

CONCLUSION

Clients come to spiritual readers with certain expectations. Whether through glowing testimonials from others or some more formal means of promotion, the client may have fairly high expectations of the service the reader will provide. It must be added that most serious clients and readers enter the encounter as coreligionists in terms of certain nonrational or occult beliefs. Clients are commonly seeking some specific service based on these spiritual beliefs. Readers, in turn, utilize certain presentational and linguistic elements to carry out a competent performance. By their immediate affirmations and filling in aloud the details of the reader's vision, clients are rendering a positive judgment about the quality of the reader's work. In this sense it is clear that the success or failure of a spiritual reading depends on reader and client alike. The reader's performance goes for naught if the client does not respond properly.

It seems appropriate to add a final word regarding how spiritual reading compares to similar marginally legal occupations and to more legitimate professions of an advice-giving kind. Consistent with other marginally legal occupations, spiritual reading provides a service to clients. It satisfies a definite social need as Bryant (1974:256) and Miller (1978:73–74) both noted. The problem with most marginally legal occupations is that certain needs, activities, or beliefs have been defined as socially unacceptable by conventional society. To try to satisfy a need to speak with a deceased relative is considered nonrational, as is the attempt to become wealthy through gambling. The latter is economically nonrational, even though taking risks (entrepreneurship) is economically rational action in a capitalist economy. Or again, if one develops specialized skills in football or tennis, he or she may take on heroic qualities and royal wealth. To develop skills in pool or shuffleboard and become a hustler is much less acceptable, if at all. All of this is merely to point up the *overlap* (Matza, 1969) or parallel of marginally legal occupations with more legitimate professions (Miller, 1978).

At the same time, however, we must not neglect the differences between deviant and conventional work. Overall, and with individual exceptions, medical science far surpasses medical quackery in the effective handling of illness. Spiritual comfort and solace are generally more likely to be found through firsthand contact in a church than through the one-way communication of the various religious hucksters utilizing the mass media. And, overall, spiritual readers are less likely to be able to handle clients' problems of living than are competent therapists. Nevertheless, what must be kept in mind is that the effectiveness of a particular (spiritualist or psychiatric) counselor depends heavily on the type of needs and beliefs that the client brings to the encounter.

Perhaps the major contrast between the psychotherapist and the spiritual reader is the greater directiveness of the latter's style. Psychotherapists make much more use of the interview style of talk in order to help the client arrive at certain insights and plan some course of action (Labov and Fanshel, 1977). Because spiritual readers are supposed to have supernatural insights about the client, they do not ask many informational questions. Moreover, they seem much less reluctant on the whole to give clients explicit advice as to what action to take. That spiritual readers make use of elaborate ploys, presentational devices, and complex interactive skills allowed Miller (1978) to liken their work to a confidence game. Indeed, it is important for readers to quickly win the confidence of the client. Clients are paying their own money for the service; it is not reimbursed by medical insurance. Furthermore, clients are likely to expect proof of the reader's talent during the first session. Therapists, by contrast, may tend to lower client expectations by emphasizing the time, effort, and responsibility the client will have to expend. The conditions under which spiritual readers operate go a long way toward explaining the kind of interaction we saw in the spiritual readings.

REFERENCES

Austin, J. L.
1962 How to Do Things with Words. Cambridge, Mass.: Harvard University Press.

Bauman, R., and Sherzer, Jr., eds.
1974 Explorations in the Ethnography of Speaking. Cambridge: Cambridge University Press.

Bryant, C. (ed.)
1974 Deviant Behavior: Occupational and Organizational Bases. Chicago: Rand McNally.

Easto, P., and Truzzi, M.
1974 "The carnival as a marginally legal work activity: a typological approach to work systems." Pp. 336–53 in C. Bryant (ed.), Deviant Behavior: Occupational and Organizational Bases. Chicago: Rand McNally.

Furberg, M.
1963 Locutionary and Illocutionary Acts. Gothenburg: University of Gothenburg.

Goffman, E.
1959 Presentation of Self in Everyday Life. Garden City, New York: Doubleday.

Hyman, R.
1977 " 'Cold reading': how to convince strangers that you know all about them." The Zetetic 2:18–37.

Hymes, D.
1972 "Models of the interaction of language and social life." in J. Gumperz and D. Hymes (eds.), Directions in Sociolinguistics: The Ethnography of Communication. New York: Holt, Rinehart and Winston.

Labov, W., and Fanshel, D.
1977 Therapeutic Discourse: Psychotherapy as Conversation. New York: Academic Press.

Leland, C. G.
1971 Gypsy Sorcery and Fortune-telling. New York: Dover.

Levi-Strauss, C.
1967 Structural Anthropology. Garden City, N.Y.: Doubleday.

Matza, D.
1969 Becoming Deviant. Englewood Cliffs, N.J.: Prentice-Hall.

Mehan, H., and Wood, H.
1975 The Reality of Ethnomethodology. New York: Wiley.

Miller, G.
1978 Odd Jobs: The World of Deviant Work. Englewood Cliffs, N.J.: Prentice-Hall.

Searle, J.
1970 Speech Acts. Cambridge: Cambridge University Press.
Searle, J.
1971 "What is a speech act?" Pp. 39-53 in J. Searle (ed.), The Philosophy of Language. London: Oxford University Press.
Tatro, C.
1974 "Cross my palm with silver." Pp. 286-99 in C. Bryant (ed.), Deviant Behavior. Chicago: Rand McNally.
Wilson, J.
1978 Religion in American Society. Englewood Cliffs, N.J.: Prentice-Hall.

Reading 35

Criminal Commitment Among Drug Dealers

Patricia A. Adler
University of California, San Diego
Peter Adler
University of Tulsa

Conflicting stereotypes have confused the public about the motivations, ideology, and organization underlying soft drug dealing. This field study integrates new and existing images of criminality and commitment to provide insight into the complex and subterranean dealing world.

INTRODUCTION

Popular conceptions of crime, both among sociologists and the general public, have taken varied forms. Overall, the most pervasive image has been the organized crime portrayal, wherein a tightly knit and highly organized central body is seen as controlling a preponderance of major offenses within certain clearly defined territories. Brought to public attention through the well-publicized investigation of the Senate Kefauver Committee (1951) and the series of "Godfather" novels and films, this image is continually reinforced by the news media. Sociological accounts (Ianni, 1972; Wilson, 1975; Bell, 1953; Plate, 1975) have also lent credence to the idea of criminality as characterized by an intense familial commitment, ethnic homogeneity, rigid hierarchical structure, and a lifelong pledge to group

We would like to thank Barry Kinsey and three anonymous reviewers for comments on an earlier draft of this paper.

membership and loyalty beyond the association required by any one particular illegal activity.

A second view of criminal behavior may be called the crime as fun image, wherein deviant commissions are considered to be spurred by a search for excitement and kicks, as in much juvenile delinquency (see Cohen, 1955; Miller, 1958), or by a rebellion from the establishment, as in countercultural crime (see Carey, 1968; Goode, 1969, 1970). Here, while the presence of a supportive peer group is important and pervasive, the organizational commitment binding members is less coercive and more tinged by an emerging personal hedonism.

Analyses fostering a crime as work image (see Letkeman, 1973; Sutherland, 1937) are the least dominant, but these focus on illegal enterprises as aberrant forms of traditional work in legitimate occupations. Attention is paid to the similarities existing between lawful and unlawful activities, and research concentrates on professionalism, technology and its resultant specialization, occupational identity, and the subculture or coterie of colleageal acquaintances. As in noncriminal business, the overriding motivation is ascribed to the desire for financial profit, which sets the prevailing morality and dictates the evolution of organizational forms. Commitment is thus to one's self within a group of others who serve as commercial associates.

Drug dealing, one form of criminal activity, has been conceptualized as either the practice of a massive, hard-core professional organization complete with underworld and political connections or the capricious behavior of daring youths who traffic in intoxicating substances to facilitate their rebellious desire to escape from the traditional morality and life-style through mood alteration. While studies of drug use and abuse are plentiful, little sociological literature addresses the actual merchandising and distribution of illicit drugs (notable exceptions are Atkyns and Hanneman, 1974; Blum, 1973; Blum et al., 1972; Carey, 1968; Goode, 1970; Langer, 1976, 1977; Moore, 1977; Mouledoux, 1972). Yet existing treatments of dealing are overwhelmingly depictions of low to middle-range soft drug trafficking. Little is still known about the highest echelon of drug wholesalers and smugglers. This analysis, though necessarily a short account, attempts to present a more realistic portrait of dealing and dealing community.[1] In particular, emphasis is focused on selected aspects of this enterprise that highlight the nature of commitment among involved individuals to (1) their particular occupation and crime more generally and (2) a fluid and shifting circle of interpersonal affiliates who form their business network.

Although most sociological considerations of commitment have focused on it as an independent variable, a different approach is taken here,

[1]A detailed presentation of this high-level dealing and smuggling subculture can be found in Adler (forthcoming).

analyzing those features of drug dealing that foster diverse types and aspects of commitment among its participants. The concept of commitment is multifaceted, however, and can best be understood by analyzing several of its dimensions. Through a synthesis of the relevant literature, Nieves (1978) has proposed a Total Commitment Index, comprising three components: normative, economic and social. Normative commitment involves the individual's acceptance and internalization (Kelman, 1958) of a group, organization or profession's values and mores. Economic commitment is rooted in the individual's rational cost-benefit analysis of the advantages inherent in pursuing a given line of activity (Homans, 1950; Blau, 1964) and the associated involvements, or side bets (Becker, 1960), which are further tied to remaining associated with this behavior. Social commitment refers to interactional dynamics of the people involved (Sheldon, 1970) and to the individual's self-image (Huntington, 1957), role relationships (Della Cava, 1975), integration into the group (Gouldner, 1960) and identification with the group (Kelman, 1958). To these we add a fourth component, egoistic commitment, which incorporates the degree of personal enjoyment, satisfaction, and fulfillment an individual derives from being involved with a given enterprise.

In this paper, we examine features of drug dealing that pertain to these components of commitment and assess how they interface with the images of criminal behavior that have been outlined.

METHODS

Doing participant-observation work with deviant groups is by its very nature problematic. In fact, the penetration of upper echelon drug-dealing and smuggling circles is a feat constantly being attempted by many federal, state, and local police departments.[2] For this reason, an extensive discussion of the methods used in this research seems warranted.

We started this study largely by accident, not even realizing for some time that it was becoming a study. We had become acquainted with a group of neighbors and began to notice that they exhibited some unusual behavior patterns. People entered and left their houses at all hours, parties sometimes continued for days, and they seemed to have no visible means of financial support. All of these people were fairly young (25–40) and on the basis of their clothing and automobiles, appeared rather wealthy. At first we thought little of this phenomenon and continued to develop our friendship with them, as the limitations of our academic schedules permitted. Based on

[2]For an excellent discussion of how these agencies operate, see Manning, 1980.

previous research experience in the drug field,[3] we began to suspect that drug dealing might be a part of this apparent subculture, but we said nothing. Then one day two new people arrived from out of town who were introduced to us as good friends. During the course of conversation they started talking about a smuggling run that they had just completed for our neighbor, Dave. Dave told them to button their lips, but they thought he was joking, that anybody associating with Dave undoubtedly knew the nature of his business. After revealing the whole story, Dave discussed with us the details of his profession. He said that he knew he could trust us but that it was his practice to say as little as possible about his activity to outsiders. Once his activities were known to us, however, he felt that he might as well be overt with us about his dealing and smuggling, because we were fast becoming good friends. Apparently the fact that we were aware of these activities spread throughout the neighborhood, and others then stopped camouflaging their business activities in front of us.

It was then that we realized what a tremendous data pool we had before us, and we discussed the idea of doing a major study of drug dealing with our few closest friends from the group. Assured of the anonymity and confidentiality of our work, they were happy to be of some help to our professional careers. In fact, they basked in the subsequent interest and attention we gave the details of their lives. But we all agreed that the study should be discreet. Because drug dealers and smugglers are secretive and fearful of prying others, it was decided that we should approach individuals carefully before admitting to be involved in studying them. In some cases our primary contacts approached other dealers and, after vouching for our absolute trustworthiness, convinced their associates to talk to us. In other instances we approached people that we knew to be dealers ourselves, slowly getting to know them and then asking for their cooperation with our project. We gradually widened our circle of contacts over a 7-year period as we became increasingly familiar with the situation and came to be accepted as trustworthy peripheral members of this social milieu. From this vantage point we have been able to observe the activities of many dealers as they passed through stages of increased and decreased involvement with drug dealing.

Data for this study were thus gathered through a combination of participant-observation and intensive interviewing. We observed 65 drug dealers, ranging from very low-level operators to importers, although this paper concentrates on those at the higher levels. With a few exceptions, all of our respondents are white Americans in the 25–40 age group. Addition-

[3]During 1971–1972 we participated in a major study of heroin use that was funded by the Sloan Foundation, where we concentrated on field research into patterns of using and dealing heroin (see Cummins et al., 1972).

ally, this is a predominantly male world; only five persons in our total sample are women. They thus bond together easily into an "old boy" network based on their homogeneity of background, demographic characteristics, and common interests.

Because of the extremely illegal nature of the behavior under study, many delicate methodological problems arose, too numerous to be described in detail here.[4] Several that merit mentioning have been partly or tangentially discussed before, including the problem of divided loyalty between the subculture and the national culture (Carey, 1972); the problem of assuming risks while doing research (Johnson, 1975; Douglas, 1976; Carey, 1972); the problem of breaking the law to study deviant behavior (Whyte, 1943; Polsky, 1967); and the problem of doing research while intoxicated (Wax, 1952). The conflict-ridden and hidden nature of the drug-dealing world also made us feel the need for extreme certainty about the reliability of our data. Therefore, all of our important conclusions are based on independent sources that were carefully verified. Not only did we always use multiple, independent key informants, but all of our key informants were checked out by our own observations and evaluations of the situation, by independent sources, and by hard evidence wherever possible (as described and analyzed in Douglas, 1976).

THE DEALING SCENE

"Southwest Territory," a large area spanning five states, serves as the backdrop for most of the dealing portrayed here. Depending upon their personal style, dealers opt to live and work in the same place or to travel throughout the territory when conducting their business. In a continuously evolving arrangement capable of rapid change, people buy and sell anywhere and contact various associates as deals arise. Taking short business trips is thus a routine practice as dealers fly between colleagues scattered around the territory.

The group under study basically handles two kinds of drugs, marijuana and cocaine. For many years marijuana was the primary commodity, but recent changes in consumption patterns and availability have caused the market to shift, with cocaine the currently desirable substance. Quantities dealt fluctuate enormously so that a single individual may purchase pounds or ounces for resale one day and grams for personal consumption the next. Dealers even buy and sell the same amounts back and forth to each other during different transactions, a phenomenon dispelling the traditional con-

[4]For a complete methodological discussion of this study, the difficulties encountered, and some of the epistemological insights generated, see Adler (forthcoming) methods appendix.

ception of strictly separated levels of dealing populated by distinctly different individuals. Instead of a rigid hierarchical structure, loose and malleable exchanges prevail. Dealers pragmatically put together buyers and sellers, act sometimes as pure intermediaries and other times as real distributors of the drugs, and cut and divide them into smaller units. Discerning their actual level of operation is thus difficult, but most of these people can be considered high-level dealers or smugglers, handling thousands of dollars worth of drugs per transaction (hundreds of pounds of marijuana and ounces of cocaine). Drug dealing is their primary occupation, from which they extract a living income and at which they spend the bulk of their time.[5] They commonly purchase the goods in a foreign country and arrange for air, land, or aquatic importation into the United States. The drugs are then sold and resold among others until quantities have become small enough to be handled by low-level dealers and consumers.

DEALING NETWORKS

Some forms of dealing, particularly straight intermediate transactions where no rearrangement of quantities is necessary, can be easily accomplished by a single person. For other types of transactions, however, especially those involving transportation across an international border, the cooperation of several people is usually required. Here, a division of labor generally prevails, with individuals delegated tasks by a leader according to their role specialization. Successful smugglers act as producers of each drug venture and organize a crew to carry out the plan. Occasionally referred to as "families" by those who have worked together for a long time, such group organization and cooperation ensures that security is maintained and adequate personnel always available when needed. For example, Rob, a smuggler, had a family of approximately seven members, not including himself. Two of these were drivers, and one was a pilot. The dual jobs of pilot and driver were filled by a fourth man. A third pilot functioned in a

[5]As Langer (1977:384) notes in his study of mid-level psychedelics dealers, people who deal drugs are sometimes involved in other businesses. For his group this was a last recourse, followed only when income from dealing could not sustain them. High-level drug dealers and smugglers are more likely to have a side business; the primary purpose of this is to generate the appearance of a legitimate front (legal income), so that IRS difficulties are avoided. Therefore, self-employment, either through individual entrepreneurship or owning one's own business, is highly desirable. Businesses most often favored include those having a high degree of cash flow (i.e., restaurants, theaters, small stores, and coin and gem shops) and the flexibility to set one's own hours (i.e., real estate, mail-order sales, nurseries, entertainment). Usually two sets of books are kept, one to inflate the amount of money actually made (especially for losing businesses) and another to launder drug money through the legal business so that it can be turned into safely spendable income. Whatever the nature and profitability of these side businesses, however, they remain secondary in focus; as with Langer's group, these individual's "pivotal status and self-identification remained that of the dealer."

triple capacity as a smuggler with his own smaller operations and as a customer of Rob's merchandise, besides flying loads for him. The sixth member, an out-of-town "heavy," was Rob's enforcer and "stash house" man (he stored the drugs at his residence). It was also agreed that this person, a large dealer himself, could occasionally sell to Rob's customers when Rob could not supply them. His job was twofold: he lived at the stash house and distributed the marijuana to buyers, and he was available for the threat or execution of violence when Rob deemed this necessary to prevent or respond to frauds, thefts, or delays of payment. Dealing with the legal aspects of business was covered by the final person. His job involved obtaining lawyers and bail bondsmen when needed, laundering Rob's money, and providing a legitimate-looking front.

Other arrangements are more stringently organized. Nick improved security by using his brothers and sisters as buffers between his crew and himself, giving orders and dispersing goods through them:

> When you deal on the scale that I do you have to assume that the police know about your activities. For me, the important thing is to make sure that they can't prove anything against me. That's why I use my sister and brothers in my work—they insulate me against contact with anything illegal. Plus, I can trust them, you know? They're blood.

Nick's distribution network was more sophisticated and wide ranging than Rob's, and his access to masses of "front money" from other reputedly serious criminals enabled him to purchase and periodically replace his heavy equipment (planes, desert trucks, ships) more regularly. As a consequence, his business dealings were more fraught with seriousness and violence. Where Rob might accept getting cheated with anger and regret, Nick always sent someone to hunt down the offender and return the offense. Carrying guns was a regular part of his dealing routine. The intensity and grand scale of his operation made commitment a fundamental necessity among his crew, who worked exclusively for him and were ready to engage in a wider variety of illegal acts when so requested.

Because several states in Southwest Territory border on Mexico, where a steady supply of marijuana and cocaine originates or passes through, this region is the site of a large wholesale drug business. Many people, through their travels, illegal enterprises, and extensive conversing with other dealers and smugglers, have acquired a degree of familiarity with the overlying drug scene and those actively trafficking within it. Although the importance of secrecy serves as a barrier,[6] distancing drug dealers from each other, many are nonetheless brought together by their common age, values, and lifestyle. There thus exists a very loose dealer's community or social system surrounding these discreet individuals. Immediately beyond one's membership in a particular family or crew, one finds a progressive building up of affiliations and networks that form an overlapping social and business sphere, or tribe. Included in a tribe are all those acquaintances who are directly known from casual introductions or partying well enough to acknowledge each other upon sight and exchange a greeting of "hello" or "how's business?" As Barry explained:

> This is a pretty small community and a lot of smugglers live around here. Hell, half of the businesses here are run by dopers, as business fronts, and the other half are supported by dope money. Just the other day I ran into Morgan down at my real estate broker's office. We exchanged looks, gave a casual greeting and moved on. But, you know, it's like a bond of recognition.

Beyond dealers' tribal affiliations is Schutz's (1962) concept of *Umwelt*, a world of relationships that are based not on specific or concrete knowledge but rather on reputation. Without ever having met each other, many dealers know of each other's exploits and feel a shared, sympathetic bond of camaraderie.

THE DEALING ACUMEN

While dealing networks reveal a consistent, regular, and ordered character, there simultaneously exists a vastly disorganized, illogical, and spontaneous side to this trade. The profession is notoriously characterized by a high rate of turnover; of those who enter into the trade, more than half fail in its pursuit. The source of their demise can be external: people may be caught and sent to jail; defrauded and bankrupted; seriously injured and scared away by other dealers; or even killed. More often than not, however, these unfortunate incidents are related to some internal shortcoming: extending trust too freely; comingling dealing with personal money and coming up short; using too much "product" (drugs); dealing over one's head (and not being able to handle such quantity transactions); being unable to cope with the pressure; or acquiring a bad reputation through personal dishonesty or ineptitude. Maintaining a steady, reliable field of connections is made difficult by this state of turnover and flux, as dealers' trafficking capacities can

[6]For a fuller depiction of the vital but often conflictful role of secrecy in the drug world, see Adler and Adler, 1980.

fluctuate mercurially. Most people are either trying to work their way up to a higher volume of business, striving to eke out an existence on the same plane, or sinking down to dealing among shadier and poorer associates. Personifying this dimension is Arnie, a drug entrepreneur continually struggling to stay afloat. He involves himself in any kind of deal that presents itself, even down to serving as middleman for pounds of grass and grams of coke. His aspiration, however, is to work himself up to a steady smuggling practice. He occasionally pulls together a crew of isolated individuals from other organizations or convinces some novice(s) to try something daring, but many of these enterprises have collapsed in failure as planes crashed or foreign connections neglected to materialize. After one breathless adventure, Arnie described his efforts:

> I really had a good shot at it this time, but I don't know, something must be cursing me. I was riding shotgun with the pilot, and we had already picked up the grass in Mexico when something started to go wrong with the plane. He said we've got to take it down, and we had just touched down when I started to smell smoke. I threw open my door, rolled my body away from the plane and a second later the whole thing fireballed. I had to walk and hitch back to the U.S. border and I've been shaking all day. I know I'll bum later about the $6000 I lost, but right now I'm grateful to be alive.

Arnie represents the pragmatic approach to dealing that is so characteristic of today's drug scene. The group idealism of the "turn the world on" ethos (c.f., Carey, 1968; Goode, 1970), popularized during the sixties and early seventies, has been replaced by a hard-driving individualistic orientation.[7] The profit motive fuels the dealing industry, whether profit is extracted in cash or in kind. People entering this occupation's ranks seek not only to gain connections for access to drugs but to learn the rudiments of conducting transactions on the higher scale and international levels. With this knowledge they, like Arnie, can have the specialized business acumen to put together a deal tailored to fit any particular constraints and circumstances. Gone, then, in large measure, is the dominating influence of dealing and other, less specialized criminal syndicates (such as the Brotherhood, the Hell's Angels, and the Mob). In their place is an unorganized mass of amateurs and unconnected professional drug traffickers who are usually trying to expand their business by meeting new connections, recycling profits into larger deals, occasionally stumbling into unsuccessful ventures

[7]At this level of dealing, however, altruism for others has never been an overwhelming motivation. Even at the lower levels, where ounce, pound, and pill dealers enjoyed the ethos of "providing a good high," self-interest was not entirely absent.

as they plunge into unfamiliar areas and associations, and starting anew with their own or someone else's fronted money.[8]

Commitment among this population is vastly different from commitment among members of the former, more steady groups. They have few, if any, long-standing professional ties and experience a frequent shifting of business partners on both buying and selling ends. Rampant dishonesty and the inability to live up to promised responsibilities, whether intentional or not, combine to keep drug dealers most concerned with promoting and protecting themselves against potential incompetents and police informants. Doug outlined his view of interpersonal drug-dealing relationships:

> Yeah, there's no "honor among thieves" in this business, as least not the ones that I seem to come in contact with. You sort of always have to keep an eye out for yourself with everyone, even guys you've been dealing with for awhile. You never know when someone's going to get in desperate straits and rip you off 'cause he needs the cash or set you up to get the cops off his back.

Living surrounded by such danger, dealers often cope by ignoring their potential for destruction and normalizing daily affairs into the financial tasks of an ordinary business. Rationalizations, often in the form of "accounts" (Sykes and Matza, 1957; Lyman and Scott, 1968) abound. Such rationalizations transform illegal acts into highly demanded services that someone must perform. Trust is extended to some new people encountered, usually on the basis of intuitive feelings experienced, since no reliable credit rating system exists. "Paranoia"[9] surfaces occasionally, abetted by the large amounts of drugs that are consumed daily. And yet few seriously think of giving up this line of work until they are adversely forced out of it for legal or continued financial reasons. Most have entered the drug world during their teens and early twenties and been involved seriously for years. Thus, by the time they are 25 to 35, the prime age for smugglers and heavy dealers, they have learned this trade but none other. It is common to hear talk of

[8]Fortunately for dealers, the allure of quick, tax-free money entices many peripheral people, who, while not wanting to deal themselves, are attracted by a 10–20% profit on their money. Thus even after bankrupting themselves, dealers are often able to replenish their stake with front money from friends or business associates.

[9]Although the term paranoia has traditionally been used in clinical settings to describe a specific condition of mental illness, it is used here the way drug dealers employ the term, as part of the street argot. Its meaning there falls in between the psychiatric sense of groundless, irrational fears and Lemert's (1962) usage, where a genuine reason for fear exists. The dealers' use of the term paranoia corresponds to Wedow's (1979), where a factual basis may or may not exist for their being afraid. All drug dealers studied spoke of experiencing varying degrees of paranoia over the course of their work, and they viewed this as an important sixth sense that sometimes warned them when danger was near. They also admitted that unfounded waves of paranoia could be induced through drug use.

putting aside a large profit and exchanging drug dealing for something less risky and wearing, but neither of these outcomes is actually very likely. And because most dealers enter via soft drug use they are unfamiliar with and uninterested in the wider range of criminal activity. Thus, a low level of commitment can be found for many, either to any cadre of associates or to any illegal identity or way of life. The occupation itself, however, holds people intensely, as dealers who are bankrupted or go to prison usually return to try their luck at it again.

THE DEALING LIFE

Another dimension of dealers' commitment to this criminal enterprise is lodged in the way they occupy their time. The style of life pursued by those associated with big-time dealing and smuggling is something special. Dubbed the "fast life" or "flash" by those who crave and scorn it alike, this lifestyle is so carefree that few worry about paying the bills, being tied down, or any sober responsibilities of the dull, workaday world. Those who live the life are children who have grown up to act out their boldest, most wonderful dreams. They are the "glitter crowd," decked out with jewelry and fancy clothes.

In their fast life drug dealers emulate the jet set, with all its travel, spending, and partying. But in contrast to those children of inherited wealth, smugglers have to work for their money. An ever-evolving pattern of work and play characterizes this cyclical life-style, as smugglers take extended periods off from their rigorous work to party, and then return to business once again. Permeating all periods, however, is an attitude of irresponsibility and daring, of living recklessly, wildly, for the moment. Jerry's statement epitomized the *manana* effect:

> It was always tomorrow, tomorrow. You write a check, you think you'll cover it tomorrow. You get some money to pay the rent, but you end up blowing it all on a single night of partying.

Money lies at the base of all this exhilarating madness, more money than most dealers could ever have imagined. Sometimes they cannot resist the temptation to revel in it all. Jana described the feeling of fantasy:

> We were like little children in a big fancy palace playhouse. We'd dump all our money on the living room floor and we'd just laugh and roll in it.

The profits that can be accumulated after even a short period of smuggling can run as high as five figures.[10] Most people do not know how to spend this much, but they soon learn. Gone, then, is the quiet, steady home life of soberly rearing the children, and in its place, the excitement of the pursuit of pleasure. Freedom is exalted and the ability to come and go at will is relished. Jean's attitude typified such impetuousness:

> Now I can do anything I want and not have to worry about someone telling me not to do it. One day I just woke up and said to my little girl, "Honey, pack your clothes. We're going to Hawaii."

Drugs are also an important part of the fast life. Marijuana and hashish are smoked in moderation, and champagne consumed in large quantities, but cocaine is used heavily. As indicated by its soaring rise in popularity, cocaine is the preferred drug of today's beautiful people. Characterized by a subtle effect, cocaine gives users a warm feeling toward those around them and is considered by many to have aphrodisiac effects. Pleasure reigns in this hedonistic world. Cocaine's euphoric effect is highly intensified when drugs are consumed in the quantities that are normal for those who deal most heavily. Typically "coking" themselves up to saturation point, dealers frequently consume more than an ounce a week during periods of heavy partying. The more recent trend toward "freebasing" cocaine, with the product taken backwards one step in the refining process and then smoked, leads to much heavier levels of consumption. Here, an ounce can be used up during a single party session, which may last from 24 to 48 hours. Continued cocaine use leads to an aura of magical omnipotence. The user feels invulnerable, as if nothing bad can happen. In fact, the opposite is sometimes the case. Heavy drug use can have a deleterious effect on important dimensions of dealers' and smugglers' functioning over both long and short periods and cause them to make errors in judgment, neglect important precautions and fail in their commitments to associates. Thus, the tendency to seek immediate gratification is heightened while detachment from the responsibilities of everyday life is accentuated.

Another component of life for many dealers and smugglers pursuing the fast life is the casual sex scene. Although many of these people are married and have children, they may begin taking marital relations for

[10]It is extremely difficult, even for dealers and smugglers themselves, to make estimates of net profits because of the amount of variable expenses that they must absorb (legal fees, transportation, partying drug use, motel and meal bills, operating costs, payment of employees, etc.) and the danger of keeping records. Successful smugglers can earn as much as $50,000 for a single run, while quality high-level dealers can earn $2000–10,000 per deal. Less fortunate entrepreneurs, in contrast, can start out with the most foolproof set-up and lose money. Thus the range in earnings potential is enormous and immeasurable.

granted in their passion to explore urges and desires. Casual attractions, although not the only mode of sexual fulfillment, are a commonly accepted part of life for men and women alike.

The ability to pursue this life-style thus becomes a major factor attracting new people to drug dealing and sustaining those currently involved. Part of the excitement derives from overspending and being forced to arrange new deals to pay the tab. The element of risk and uncertainty holds a mysterious allure for some, especially in the beginning. And once acclimated to the dealing lifestyle and community, many dealers are reluctant to relinquish both the guarantee of a steady source of quality drugs and the patterns of association and friendship resulting from the dealing experience. For many, the locus of commitment may reside more strongly in the mode of living rather than any other occupational or organizational feature of drug dealing, with personal pleasure paramount. Individuals involved thus tolerate the rational and planned business aspects of their existence for the ultimate purpose of living wildly and irrationally.

CONCLUSIONS

Having looked at salient features of the drug-dealing scene, we are ready to reconsider the question of criminal commitment and its relation to one or more of the existing criminal images. In reality, none of the aforementioned hypothetical portraits adequately describes how drug dealers feel about their motivations, ties, and identifications with crime, the occupation of dealing, and their professional associates. Yet a measure of each is evident in the world of upper level drug dealing and smuggling. Elements associated with organized crime must be present for smoothly efficient and successful deals to occur: trust must be extended; alliances formed; a specialized division of labor created; and secrecy and security ensured. Inherent here are elements of both the normative and social dimensions of commitment. With the former, dealers display a subscription to the overall norms and values indigenous in both their social group and the greater drug trafficking profession. They hate police, feel a kinship with other dealers and smugglers, operate under binding principles of honor (at least in the ideal), and treat partners as familially bound. And, true to the Mafia media image, they look on dealing as a career, deriving their self-image and identity from this part of their lives. The organized crime dimension of dealing also enhances the social commitment dealers feel to this enterprise. Through their work they become integrated into a formal (smuggling) or informal (dealing) network of associates where they form role relationships that strengthen their identification with the group. This membership functions as a social side bet, binding them further to continuing illegal activity.

But the organized crime image of behavior and the type of criminal commitment associated with it does not fully describe this dealing subculture. It is partly a crime as work situation, as the affiliations forged for each transaction often fail to endure beyond that temporary scope. People betray their colleagues rather than risk death or imprisonment, as evidenced by the high rate of turned informants, and are concerned primarily about their own well-being and comfort. Income provides the overriding drive and rationale influencing behavior, instead of these being dictated by some central, powerfully controlling coalition. Thus today's illicit drug traffickers bear great similarity to legitimate businessmen. Aspects of the occupation induce an economic dimension of commitment. Dealers are highly attached to the large quantities of money they can make and accord the drug business vast preference for that reason. They also value the fringe benefits of the job: being self-employed; setting their own hours; having the freedom to go as they please; and working in a nonbureaucratic atmosphere (a veritable laissez-faire economy). A number of side bets are also involved here: if they abandon this line of work they lose their acquired knowledge and skills for successful drug dealing, and they lose the clientele (sales) and connections (purchasing) developed and cultivated for buying and selling drugs.

But this second comparison does not provide a complete explanation of drug-dealing behavior and commitment either, as crime as fun elements reveal themselves in most functions of planning and executing deals. The hedonistic life-style pervading high-level dealing echelons that is associated with both the influence of drugs and with personality selection into the trade demonstrates the importance of partying and fun as a simultaneous attraction and reward to participants. These pleasurably decadent features of the dealing scene erode the purely crime as work aspect just as those individual entrepreneurial aspects modify the organized crime portrait. Accompanying the crime as fun image are its associated forms of commitment: social and egoistic. Socially, dealers remain tied to their occupation as a result of the interactional enjoyment generated through their pattens of association and relationships with others in the dealing world. Even more strongly, however, they derive much ego gratification from the power they wield over others by withholding or supplying them with drugs. Dealing and smuggling are highly prestigious occupations among the drug-using youth, and the entertainment and athletic subcultures, and this enhances members' social status. Having good access to high-quality drugs for personal consumption further makes them desirable sexual partners, and so the hedonistic, dealing life-style is filled with pleasurable indulgences dealers are loathe to relinquish.

In this paper we have examined three images of criminality, ranging from the deadly serious to the decadently frivolous, and four associated types of commitment (normative, economic, social, and egoistic). Considered separately, none of these simplified stereotypes accurately depicts either the ambiance, behavioral style, or type of commitment that infuses high-level drug dealing and smuggling. But taken together, each contributes a degree of insight valuable for understanding the full and complex motivational and organizational picture influencing the type of multifaceted commitment inherent in the dealing world.

REFERENCES

Adler, Patricia A.
Forthcoming A Longitudinal Study of Upper Level Drug Dealers and Smugglers in the Southwestern United States. Unpublished Ph.D. dissertation, University of California, San Diego.

Adler, Patricia A., and Peter Adler
1980 "The irony of secrecy in the drug world." Urban Life, 8, 4(Jan.).

Atkyns, R. L., and G. J. Hanneman
1974 "Illicit drug distribution and dealer communication behavior." Journal of Health and Social Behavior, 15 (March).

Becker, Howard
1960 "Notes on the concept of commitment." American Journal of Sociology 66.

Bell, Daniel
1953 "Crime as an American Way of Life." Antioch Review (June).

Blau, Peter
1964 Exchange and Power in Social Life, New York: Wiley.

Blum, R. H., et al.
1972 The Dream Sellers. San Francisco: Jossey-Bass.

Blum, R. H.
1973 Drug Dealers—Taking Action. San Francisco: Jossey-Bass.

Carey, James
1968 The College Drug Scene. Englewood Cliffs: Prentice-Hall.
1972 "Problems of access and risk in observing drug scenes." Pp. 71–92 in Jack D. Douglas (ed.), Research on Deviance. New York: Random House.

Cohen, Albert
1955 Delinquent Boys. Glencoe: Free Press.

Cummins, Marvin, et al.
1972 Report of the Student Task Force on Heroin Use in Metropolitan Saint Louis. St. Louis: Washington University Social Science Institute.

Della Cava, F. A.
1975 "Becoming an ex-priest: The process of leaving a high commitment status." Sociological Inquiry 45.

Douglas, Jack D.
1976 Investigative Social Research. Beverly Hills: Sage.

Goode, Erich
1969 Marijuana. New York: Atherton.
1970 The Marijuana Smokers. New York: Basic.
Gouldner, Helen P.
1960 "Dimensions of organizational commitment." Administrative Science Quarterly, 4.
Homans, George
1950 The Human Group. New York: Harcourt Brace Jovanovich.
Huntington, Mary Jean
1957 "The development of a professional self-image." Pp. 179–188 in Robert Merton, George Reader, and Patricia Kendall (eds.), The Student Physician. Cambridge: Harvard University Press.
Ianni, Frances A.
1972 A Family Business. New York: Russell Sage.
Johnson, John M.
1975 Doing Field Research. New York: The Free Press.
Kelman, H. C.
1958 "Compliance, identification and internalization: Three processes of attitude change." Journal of Conflict Resolution 2.
Langer, John
1976 "Dealing culture: The rationalization of the 'hand-loose' ethic." Australian and New Zealand Journal of Sociology 12.
1977 "Drug entrepreneurs and dealing culture." Social Problems 24 (Feb).
Lemert, Edwin
1962 "Paranoia and the dynamics of exclusion." Sociometry 25.
Letkeman, Peter
1973 Crime as Work. Englewood Cliffs: Prentice-Hall.
Lyman, Stanford, and Marvin Scott
1968 "Accounts." American Sociological Review 33(1).
Manning, Peter K.
1980 Narc's Game. Cambridge: MIT Press.
Miller, Walter B.
1958 "Lower class culture as a generating milieu of gang delinquency." Journal of Social Issues 14.
Moore, Mark H.
1977 Buy and Bust. Lexington, Mass.: Heath.
Mouledoux, J.
1972 "Ideological Aspects of Drug Dealership." Pp. 110–122 in K. Westhues (ed.), Society's Shadow: Studies in the Sociology of Countercultures, Toronto: McGraw-Hill, Ryerson.
Nieves, Alvar L.
1978 "Some further notes on the concept of commitment." Paper presented at the annual meetings of the Pacific Sociological Association, April.
Plate, Thomas
1975 Crime Pays! New York: Simon and Schuster.

Polsky, Ned
1967 "Research method, morality and criminology." Pp. 109–143 in Hustlers, Beats and Others. Chicago: Aldine.
Schutz, Alfred
1962 Collected Papers (Vols. 1, 2). The Hague: Martinus Nijhoff.
Sheldon, Mary
1970 "Investments and involvements as mechanisms producing commitment to the organization." Administrative Science Quarterly 15.
Sutherland, Edwin H.
1937 The Professional Thief. Chicago: University of Chicago Press.
Sykes, Gresham, and David Matza
1957 "Techniques of neutralization: A theory of delinquency." American Sociological Review 22 (Dec.).
Wax, Rosalie
1952 "Reciprocity as a field technique." Human Organization 11.
Wedow, Suzanne
1979 "Feeling paranoid: The organization of an ideology." Urban Life 8, 1 (Apr.).
Whyte, William Foote
1943 Street Corner Society. Chicago: University of Chicago Press.
Wilson, James Q.
1975 Thinking About Crime. New York: Basic.

Part Five

Deviance: Exits and Transformations

Chapter Eleven

Farewell to Deviance

EDITORIAL COMMENTARY

Just as deviants are more likely to be "made" than "born," so too may they often be "unmade" rather than die a deviant. Evidence of the ubiquitous nature of such a conversion or transformation can easily be found in the common adult "confessions" or admissions of indiscretions and deviant episodes during their youth or young adulthood—"sowing wild oats," as it were. Such admissions, not infrequently recalled in the mellow years of maturity, with a certain pleasurable perspective, may range from such inane transgressions as smoking corn silk behind the barn to more sensational disclosures of lechery, debauchery, licentious living, or even criminal activity, such as seducing the sex-starved wife of the basketball coach, "rolling a few queers" as a lark, or shooting out streetlights with a shotgun after a drunken fraternity party. With appropriate ameliorative afterthought, however, such earlier deviant activity often takes on more of the quality of youthful zestful adventure than morally and/or legally vagrant behavior.

After all, the farmer probably never missed the watermelons, it was necessary to sell a little "grass" to the next door dorm occupants in order to afford one's own "nickel bag," and maneuvering the Dean's Volkswagen to the roof of the Chemistry building was only a prank (even though the Dean didn't think so!). Stealing the General's liquor supply was only an inspired instance of "moonlight requisitioning," during World War II, and taking the cuckoo clock from the German Burgher at gunpoint was only a legitimate exercise of the axiom, "to the victim belongs the spoils!" Even the "romantic interlude with a former lover" may have, in reality, been a sordid and illicit sexual affair with the frustrated wife of a business associate. The vantage point of age and the filtering effect of time have a way of giving a mellifluous glow to reminiscences of past deviance. The point is that much deviance is ephemeral in nature and the culprit may often thereafter turn away from such miscreant deeds, and subsequently live a life of more or less, social conformity.

Those of cynical bent may assert that most, if not almost all, individuals have at one time or another, committed deviant and possibly illegal acts. As the biblical injunction intones, "let those without sin cast the first stone." While such affirmations may be difficult to document, there is substantial evidence that many Americans have committed deviant, and often socially serious, acts in their time, and sexual deviance would seem to be especially prominent in many people's past. Alfred C. Kinsey, in his monumental survey of sexual behavior in the United States, for example, reported that 37% of the white male population have had at least one homosexual experience to the point of orgasm at some point in their life between adolescence and old age, and that approximately 50% of the white males have had some homosexual experience that may not have involved an orgasm. In the case of white females, he found that 28% have had some homosexual experience, and that 13% have had a homosexual experience to the point of orgasm. Inasmuch as these percentages are far in excess of the 4% of American white male population, and 2% of the American white female population that he asserted were exclusively homosexual, then it must be concluded that many individuals of both sexes had, perhaps, experimented with homosexual activity at some point in their life but, for whatever the reason, did not go on to adopt a homosexual mode of carnal activity. In short, they engaged in sexually deviant behavior but saw fit to reject such activity on a more lasting or ongoing basis (Kinsey et al., 1948, 1953).

Similarly, in regard to other forms of sexual deviance, many individuals can recall earlier experimentations or short sojourns away from sexual conformity that were temporary and which they likely "outgrew" in time. Examples here might range from having played "doctor and nurse" with other children as a child (Chilman, 1976) or deriving vicarious sexual gratification from "peeping" into the windows of unaware persons who were nude or engaged in sexual behavior, either as an adolescent out roaming the neighborhood at night (Spencer, 1976), or even as a construction worker on commercial building projects or in some other occupational context that provided a suitable vantage point for salacious observation (Feigelman, 1974). Other illustrations might include "streaking," (or "mooning" among the older generation), as a college student (Toolan et al., 1974), visiting prostitutes or massage parlors, brief excursions into bisexuality, as occurred with some female students on various college campuses during the early 1970s (Editors of Newsweek, 1974) and with men who stop off in "tea-rooms" for an erotic respite (Humphreys, 1970), or with truck drivers who seek sexual gratification from homosexual "pickups" in truck stops (Corzine and Kirby, 1977), or perhaps the use of "wrestling" and "armtwisting" as mechanisms of seduction (Kanin, 1967; Laner, 1982), or even sexual escapades with underaged females (thus, statutory rape).

Other than brief (and sometimes not so brief) forays into sexual deviance, individuals may also recollect and bask in the reminiscences of other types of deviant and/or illegal behavior, ranging from cruelty to animals, to escapades of white collar crime, episodes of "real" crime (economic or physical), looting in wartime, the use of narcotics, arson, illegal driving behavior, involvement in social protests and demonstrations (even riots), public drunkeness, and "temporary" automobile theft, to mention but some instances of miscreant and socially reprehensible (but presumably enjoyable) behavior.

A particular context may facilitate or precipitate deviant behavior, which may vanish with the passing of the context. Deviant acts committed component to fraternity hijinx in college are seldom repeated later in life. Similarly, while soldiers may commit unspeakable acts or engage in atrocities in wartime, they are usually not inclined to such behavior as postwar civilians.

Persons who voluntarily leave deviant behavior behind are not necessarily only individuals who sample or experiment with such activities. There are those who are deeply involved with such deviance over a long period of time who still subsequently give it up. Some individuals may simply "walk away" from a life of crime. Heroin is highly addictive, but some addicts are able to voluntarily discontinue the use of the drug on a permanent basis. As Charles H. McCaghy (1985) describes this phenomenon:

> If anything truly "cures" heroin dependence, it is *aging*. Many users simply quit when they reach the mid-thirties. The reason for the relationship between advancing age and termination of heroin use is unclear. Possibly it has less to do with a waning desire for the drug's effects than with a growing

> weariness with the life-style: the continuous risks from financing and finding fixes, concern about overdoses, and the dangers from other junkies and the law. Whatever the reason, it is evident that junkies can and do quit. (p. 285)

McCaghy goes on to say:

> Recent evidence indicates that many addicts permanently stop using heroin even at an *early age*, and still other addicts quit and later use the drug regularly without again becoming dependent. (p. 286)

Thus, even heroin addiction may be temporary and the deviant offenders may be able to leave their addiction and stay "clean," (at least some of the time).

While the incidence of experimentation with narcotic drugs like heroin may be relatively small, this is certainly not the case with other types of drugs. One study of high school seniors in 1982, for example, showed that 59% of those in the sample admitted that they had ever used marijuana/hashish, but only 29% had used it in the previous month. Another 16% had used it in the previous year but not the previous month and another 14% reported that they had not used the drug during the previous year (Johnson et al., 1982). All of which suggests that many adolescents, at one time or another, tried marijuana/hashish but likely did not continue to use it as they grew older.

Some individuals may fondly remember deviant excursions when younger, and even openly talk about it, if not brag. Others may be somewhat more reticent in revealing their past drug sampling, or any other type of trial experiences with deviant behavior. Such revelations can sometimes be costly. It will be recalled that in the search for a new Supreme Court Justice a few years back, one seemingly extremely well-qualified candidate admitted that he tried marijuana on a few occasions in the past but had not used it in recent years. While he received a great deal of sympathy from others, including some members of congress, who had themselves experimented with the drug when younger, nonetheless public sentiment tended to be negative, and within a very short time thereafter, the candidate withdrew his name from consideration for the office.

Because of the possible social costs, some individuals may be quite secretive about deviance in their youth. Many females, even in these sexually liberated times, for example, may be reluctant to reveal their previous sexual activity to boyfriends or fiancés (or husbands, for that matter) lest the subject cause friction and conflict, or make them to be less matrimonially marketable because of lost virginity. The double standard still lives! and virginity, even technical virginity, is still valued among some segments of the population, for moral, social, and psychological reasons! Granted that virginity in U.S. society is not valued to the same degree as it is in some Asian and Middle Eastern societies. Even today in Japan, some brides-to-be may be impelled to obtain a certificate of virginity from a gynecologist to present to their future in-laws, before they can receive their approval for the marriage. Accordingly, some of these girls who are not virgins undergo a simple plastic surgery technique known as "hymen rebirth" in which a new hymen is grafted on. In this way, the girls can remove guilt feelings about past sexual experiences, yet enjoy sex before marriage, without fear of not being able to find husbands later in life (Swift, 1974). Allegedly, a similar surgical procedure exists in Taiwan.

If a woman was reluctant to reveal past voluntary sexual activities, she might also be reticent about disclosing an involuntary sexual experience, such as rape, with the result that only a small percentage of rapes are ever reported to law enforcement authorities. It has been estimated that perhaps no more than 30% of all actual rapes are ever reported. Some estimates suggest that only 10% of all rapes are ever reported (Griffin, 1975). A woman might also be reluctant to reveal the fact that she had owned and used a vibrator before marriage, just as a man might show similar reticence about confessing that he was a regular client of prostitutes and/or patron of massage parlors. Such revelations convey an "inappropriate" social image!

Individuals may give up or drift away from deviance because of boredom, or lack of sufficient gratification, or because it is no longer "appropriate" behavior for a particular age and social status. Such is the case with many "dabblers" in deviance. In other instances, the exit from deviant activities may be more dramatic, if not traumatic. Sometimes people have a "close call," either physically or socially, and may leave their deviant ways rather abruptly! Drunken revelry or too much "grass" ("one toke over the line," as it were) may contribute to an automobile wreck or other accident that might cause the individual to more clearly (and forcibly) see the danger inherent in his social vagrancy and make him decide to give up the deviant behavior that played a part in the accident. Individuals have been known to refrain from (or greatly minimize) drinking or the use of drugs because of a mishap or injury to themself or to others. Similarly, there are social traumas as well. Being arrested or almost being arrested, or otherwise "exposed" for being involved in some type of deviant or criminal activity, even if the involvement was experimental or ephemeral, may be sufficiently anxiety producing to motivate the individual to cease and desist in the illicit activity. Such instances might include the errant husband or wife who "got caught" or almost caught "running around," the amateur criminal who barely escaped apprehension by the police, or the businessman who barely missed public discovery in his first foray into white-collar criminal business practices. Many have given thanks for their "second chance" and "sworn off" the offending conduct, as it were. It should be recalled that the term for prisons, "penitentiary" refers to their function—to make offenders feel "penitent" or remorseful about their crimes. Because the first arrest is usually so socially traumatic, judges are often motivated to give the deviant offender a "second chance" and, thus, the imposition of probation, a suspended sentence, or community service, in lieu of jail time. In many instances, the deviant sees the error of his or her ways, resolves to live a life of social approbation and legal conformity, and is thankful for the second chance and opportunity to leave the deviant behavior behind without further social sanctions. Based on the "second chance" premise, there have been efforts to insure that when deviant acts are committed, the process of remorse can be accelerated, the trauma of discovery and exposure can be exacerbated, and the prospect and experience of social sanction can be magnified, thereby hastening and insuring the offender's exist from deviance. Such approaches sometimes work and sometimes do not. The initial reading in this chapter, John Heeren's and David Shichor's "Mass Media and Delinquency Prevention: The Case of 'Scared Straight,' " provides a descriptive analysis of such an effort.

As the authors point out, in 1979 a documentary called "Scared Straight" was shown on many television stations across the country which attracted much public attention and which won several awards. The film detailed the Juvenile Awareness Project at Rahway State Prison in New Jersey and provided a dramatic look at the program. JAP (as the program was known) attempted to expose youthful offenders to the "harsh realities of prison life" by having them confront a group of long term inmates who verbally assaulted the youths, and dramatically told them of the nature and quality of prison existence, including beatings and rapes by fellow inmates. In theory, the "shock treatment" was designed to cause the youths to be "scared straight" and hopefully motivate them to give up delinquent behavior and live a law abiding and socially conforming life. A subsequent, systematic evaluation of the program by a team of social scientists from Rutgers indicated that the program was "worse than ineffective" and may even have tended "to promote further offenses among those exposed to it." The public, however, appeared to be quite impressed with the approach and both the film and the program enjoyed a considerable public approval, and elicited widespread support from viewers.

The authors examine this paradox and offer some conclusions concerning the apparent inconsistency of the public appeal. In this regard they review research that has explored the connection between the mass media accounts about crime and public views in regard to the crime problem, and offer a hypothetical model of the "natural history" of a social problem including the crime problem. Based on certain elements of this model, they suggest that the public success and popularity of the "Scared Straight" film and its particular rehabilitative approach is based on the film's "resonant assumptions." First they assert the widespread public belief that crime and particularly juvenile crime, is "out of control." Secondly, they contend that the film reinforces the public notion that the prevalent, "liberal" approach to rehabilitating juvenile delinquents—the overly lenient posture with excessive legal protection for defendants ("the slap on the wrist" ideology)—has failed! The prevailing rehabilitative orientation of previous years is, according to the authors, being replaced with a criminal deterrence orientation. The public increasingly is calling for deterrence and the movie "Scared Straight" had such an orientation or goal. The film underscored the emerging public belief that the fear of punishment (or punishment itself) serves as an effective means of deterring persons from committing further criminal offenses. In effect, the public wants juvenile crime to be handled more in the manner of adult crime. As the authors point out, the Juvenile Awareness Project (and the film depicting it) reflects "the revival of the retribution doctrine which predates the rehabilitative notion." In the film the youths are told of the "horrors" of prison life with its hardships, deprivations, beatings, and rapes. In effect, the inmates suffer for their crimes, and the youths mentally suffer imagining what may lie in store for them. This image of suffering criminals satisfies the "public's demand for justice." The law of the jungle assumed to prevail in prison is the retribution which the public seeks. Finally, the film reinforces the public's notion that today's juvenile delinquents are the adult criminals of tomorrow. It is, therefore, very important to intervene early in the lives of juvenile offenders, and that the intervention should be "shocking" and traumatic in order to be effective.

The authors conclude that the film (and the program it depicts) utilizes elements of deterrence, retribution, and rehabilitation and somehow integrates these three seemingly "contradictory approaches" into what was perceived as a logical approach to delinquency. "Scared Straight," say the authors, was successful in the public's eye because it combined "a unique set of five premises into one dramatic package," and because it amplified and exaggerated the reality of prison life, and for that matter, "the extent of criminal involvement of the 17 delinquents shown." The bigger than life picture presented by the film reflected the images that the public held or wanted to hold. The public, in effect, saw it as an idealized exit from deviance.

The Juvenile Awareness Project attempted to force people out of a deviant mode by scaring them with the prospect of what lay ahead if they continued as an offender. Sometimes people may be forced out of deviance in other ways. Alcoholics or alcohol abusers may be told by their physicians that they face death if they continue to drink. The drinkers may be sufficiently concerned about that prospect to discontinue their alcohol consumption. Individuals may be threatened with the loss of job and, thus, major identity, if they do not give up their deviant behavior. Either give up drinking, or drugs, or discontinue their sexual dalliance with a lover (or quit chasing women in general), or desist from whatever deviant or inappropriate business, professional, or political practice, *or* lose their license to practice medicine or dentistry, or be "defrocked" as a priest, or be taken out of the pulpit or cockpit, or be fired or demoted, or be separated from the service, or be given less than an honorable discharge, or be removed from office or impeached, or be expelled from college, or face the loss of positions and reputation! Sometimes the threat comes from an employer, or military superior, or professional association, or licensing board, or Bishop, or constituents, or spouse! Give it (or her or him) up, or give me up, as it were! As the old naval adage goes, "shape up or ship out!" Faced with such a choice, the deviant may elect to curtail, cease, and desist in the proscribed behavior.

The process of curtailing deviance may be abrupt—"going cold turkey"—or it may be gradual—"tapering off," as it were, or "one last one for the road." It may require the help and assistance of a support group. Perhaps the best known of such support groups is alcoholics anonymous. The individual must make the decision to give up alcohol but once he or she has made that decision, members of the support group are available day or night to give advice, counsel, and emotional back-up. The individual is encouraged to attend AA meetings where he or she will listen to others tell their story of alcoholism and sobriety, and then will be given the opportunity to tell their own story. The process involves frequent public self-criticism as a means of reinforcing the goal of sobriety. Individuals are taught that they are not cured or rehabilitated but only "dry" or sober. They are always an alcoholic but hopefully a recovered and sober alcoholic. The actual day of conversion becomes a signal event and many recovered alcoholics have the actual date of their "sobriety" engraved on some object like a key ring that they keep with them to remind them of their transformation. Rather than hide the fact of their former deviance, they wear it on their sleeve, so to speak, as a badge of distinction. They were able to give up alcohol and stay sober! This orientation both aids in neutralizing the deviant label they had acquired but also assists them in maintaining the new status and self image.

There are many kinds of such support groups for previous deviants. There is such a group for gamblers, and one for former mental patients, and today there is even a support group for former sexual deviants of a particular variety. It is called Sex Addicts Anonymous. The next reading in this section examines another kind of deviance and another kind of support group for such deviants. Marc S. O'Brien and William B. Bankston, in their "The Moral Career of the Reformed Compulsive Eater: A Study of Conversion to Charismatic Conformity," examine the stigma of obesity and the way in which it is managed through participation in a "self-help" weight control group.

Obesity, at first glance, might seem to be an unusual manifestation of deviance, similar to being short or tall or thin or redheaded. In U.S. society, however, even though obesity may result from hormone, glandular, or other physiological origin, it is usually viewed as the end product of gluttony and overeating. The fat person, it is assumed, lacked the necessary self-control to resist the temptation of overindulgence. Lack of self-control is, therefore, a weakness and overeating, by extension, a vice. Obesity is the resulting stigma. In Western culture, and particularly in the U.S., youthfulness, and, thus, thinness and vitality is the cultural ideal, and the mass media communicates, exaggerates, and reinforces this ideal. The appearance of being overweight departs from the normative expectation of reflecting the cultural ideal, and is, therefore, a deviant appearance. As a result of obesity, the individual confronts unacceptance, criticism, discrimination, lack of opportunity, and in some instances, even persecution.

Obesity, like all stigmas, may be incorporated into the social identity of the individual and into their self-identity as well. As the authors point out, an individual who has had a deviant identity forced on them must somehow contrive to manage the identity in order to account for it. They may attempt to deny or disavow their deviant status, or try and neutralize (by claiming it is biologically determined and, thus, beyond their control), or they may turn to a support group "which encourages a return to a strict conformity to the norms of community as well as creating a stereotype which is socially acceptable" (Trice and Roman, 1975:268).

This group stresses the notion that being overweight is a "spiritual" problem and that if overweight people will admit this, God will reward them. Weight loss is to be accomplished through a conversion process, "and maintained through ritualized behavior that is implicitly and explicitly of a religious nature." For the group, there is no category of "ex-overeaters," only abstaining overeaters. The group conceptualizes the individual as weak and unable to control his or her overeating behavior without the help and support of the group. In this sense, Overeaters Anonymous is not dissimilar to Alcoholics Anonymous. Not all members of the organization were ideologically integrated to the same degree, and the authors of the study were able to identify several categories of members.

At the core were a set of members that O'Brien and Bankston labeled "Devout Adherents." These were the most dedicated of the members who were also the most intensively involved in group processes. They provided the leadership and impetus to the activities of the organization. They typically had been a member for two years or more, had often lost as much as 100 pounds, and as the authors put it, "this type exemplifies the presence of divine intervention into their lives."

Another category of member in the authors' typology was the "Social Club." These individuals were usually middle-aged females who had developed their weight problem later in life than the Devout Adherents. They tended to use the open forum discussions of the organization to talk about "minor" domestic problems. They were not as successful as the Devout Adherents at weight loss and tended to be "back-sliders." They were, in effect, verbal converts, who supported the goals of the organization in word more than deed. They were quite functional to the organization, however, in that their failure to lose much weight and their subsequent repentance tended to strengthen the solidarity of Devout Adherents and their commitment to the ideology of the organization, as well as serve as an example of failure.

The Devout Adherents experienced a true identity transformation that influenced their view of the world and their place in it. The Social Club members did not enjoy the same conversion and moral career. As with any genuine conversion experience, there were predisposing conditions and situational contingencies. The Devout Adherents had experienced prolonged tension as a result of being "fat." They were unhappy with their social identity, had negative experiences when they sought medical help for their condition, and were "characterized by a tendency to impose a religious meaning on their deviant status." In way of situational contingencies, the Devout Adherents had experienced a major "turning point" in their first contact with the organization, and had perceived an opportunity for a "new line" of action. They were especially pleased by the development of "close affective ties" with the other members and the opportunity for intensive and significant interaction with them. They were able to interpret this opportunity for new direction as an "alternate life style," and imposed a religious and charismatic meaning to this turning point. They were, in effect, delivered into a new symbolic existence. As a result of their conversion, they experienced a new "symbolic universe," a new master status, and a "new vocabulary of motive." Most importantly, they now had a new sense of "charismatic self-control."

Some deviants "drift" out of their unorthodox behavior, but the subjects in this study experienced a shift to a new identity and a new moral self through a process of conversion to conformity. The old behavior is "purged" and a new conventionalized identity is attained through conversion to charismatic conformity with the help of conversion agents who are ex-members of the deviant category within the context of a voluntary organization.

The departure from deviancy may be relatively simple and without public fanfare—the individual merely gives it up and proceeds in a more conventional fashion. But inasmuch as deviance is socially perceived and socially interpreted as such, the exit from deviance may also necessitate social admission, if not entail a public forum. The Catholic confessional, for example, permits the errant individual who is repentant to disclose his deviance to a priest, who can prescribe appropriate penitence which will allow him to exit the deviant status. Communist dissenters must undertake self-criticism of their actions; members of self-help groups, like Alcoholics Anonymous, must publicly admit their alcoholism; and miscreants often are required to openly apologize to their peers or members of their group (General George Patton was ordered to do so for his offense of slapping a sick soldier!). One of the more prominent illustrations of public withdrawal from deviance is the open admission of sin and repentance in the religious context. Although widespread in all Protestant denominations, it is particularly seminal to many fundamentalist denominations. The Preacher gives his sermon (not infrequently of the "hell fire and brimstone" variety) and calls for sinners to "see the light" and repent. One or more members of the listening congregation are inspired and come forward to openly confess their sins, and usually profess their acceptance of Christ and the doctrine of forgiveness. In some church gatherings, this can be particularly dramatic and traumatic. The repentant sinner may loudly admit all sorts of past indiscretions (sometimes quite shocking to the congregation), and is often quite emotional in doing so. The public confession is an emotional catharsis—a purging and "cleansing" of the conscience, as it were. Not infrequently, other members of the congregation will also become emotional in way of sympathy, and sometimes will be motivated themselves to confess sins and accept or reaccept Christ and salvation. Preachers may be judged on their ability to elicit such responses from congregation members, and in some denominations, the summer "Revival" services are designed to do exactly that—precipitate an emotional purging and public confession of sin, and reaffirmation of faith—a massive revival of religious belief and commitment to Christian conformity. Such occasions may cause the preacher to retell the biblical parable of the "lost sheep" and the lesson that the one lost sheep returned to the fold is of greater significance than the 99 that did not stray. Both repentant major sinners as well as those guilty of more minor transgressions may then proudly assume the status of "Born Again" Christians—for the process of the egress from deviance and the public announcement of such an exit along with the new acceptance of conformity is a reflection of a symbolic death and spiritual rebirth. In the movie "Sergeant York" made many years ago and starring Gary Cooper, the protagonist, Alvin York, is a blatant deviant and sinner, who because of a traumatic event, comes into church, startling the congregation with a confession of sin and an acceptance of Christ, salvation, and Christian conformity. Once committed to such an ideological posture, York is reluctant to take up arms against the Germans in World War II, but as the movie portrays, is ultimately able to reconcile his new commitment with doing violence against an enemy of the United States, and goes on to become a war hero.

The assumption of the deviant label may require some type of public ceremony and approbation. The transformation must occur within a social context. Examples here might range from the child being made to sit in the corner for being "naughty," to the miscreant student being forced to sit on a stool and wear the "dunce cap," to the public dunking of village "scolds" in pre-Colonial New England, to Hester Prynne's wearing of the scarlet "A" (or the Jews being forced to wear the yellow Star of David in Nazi Germany), to the branding of offenders, to the public dismissal of a disgraced soldier, replete with fife and drums playing the "Rogue's March," the ripping off of rank and insignia, and the breaking in half of the sword or other symbols of rank and status. The civilian legal trial of today serves such a function as does the impeachment of politicians or the Courts Martial (or Board) for military personnel. In an earlier time, "tarring and feathering" accomplished the same purpose in a informal and violent fashion, as did the practice in France, immediately after World War II, of publicly shaming women who had been involved in romantic and/or sexual liaisons with German soldiers or officers, of shaving their heads, and forcing them to leave town completely naked. Such public transformations have been termed "status degradation ceremonies" by Harold Garfinkel (1956). According to Garfinkel, such ceremonies serve to transfer the identity of the actor "into something looked on as lower in the local scheme of social types." It is, in effect, the antithesis or opposite of ceremonies of "investiture and elevation," and brings about the construction of a new social reality with the actor being "reconstituted" into a totally new identity.

There are also public ceremonies for the transformation of deviants back into conventional identities. When Captain Dreyfus of the French army was finally exonerated of the crimes of which he had been falsely accused, tried, convicted, and imprisoned on Devil's Island, he was formally reinstated in the military and his commission returned in a public ceremony, marking the occasion. The former sinner can be baptized and/or accepted into the Church, the convicted offender can receive a pardon, or the mentally ill individual can be adjudicated as sane. In the subsequent reading in this section, Thomas analyzes this process in his "Becoming Normal: Certification as a Stage in Exiting From Crime," as he explores the "social verification of the individual's 'reform.' " This social recognition of exiting from crime and adopting conventionality, which he terms, certification, represents a legitimation of conformity.

On the basis of a number of in-depth interviews with male prison inmates with histories of property crime, the author conceptualized such subjects as having a dual identity—a personal identity in terms of how they defined themselves, and a social identity which "is the self imputed to the individual by others." The two identities may be in conflict with each other. According to the author, many of the respondents had personal identities that were "shakily" noncriminal. They viewed themselves as having already exited from crime. On the other hand, the respondents felt that others saw them still as criminals. They perceived that others thought of them as not to be trusted, and expected them to behave in a deviant fashion. As Meisenhelder puts it, "At best, the exiting ex-felon felt that others saw him as a deviant feigning conventionality." Certification was then a means of reconciling these disparate identities. It was a mechanism for constructing or creating a noncriminal social identity.

Certification is not resocialization (which the subjects do not perceive as being needed) but rather "more of a process of self-presentation than of socialization." In effect, conforming members of society must verify that the ex-deviant is normal and, thus, others will treat him accordingly.

Various programs and organizations such as church involvement or participation in the rehabilitation programs of various social service or criminal justice organizations may serve as certification agencies. Some ex-offenders may see such programs as designed to effect some change in the personal identity of those involved. Inasmuch as the ex-offenders possessed a personal noncriminal image, they did not see the need for change and had to "deceitfully manipulate" their involvement in the program in a dramaturgical presentation of reform.

The physical places or setting where an ex-offender is observed to spend time is a significant factor in certification. Ex-offenders tried to avoid deviant settings, such as pool halls, taverns, or even loitering, and instead tried to present themselves in more conventional settings, such as places of employment, or "normal" places of leisure, such as churches, civic associations and other recognized settings for the constructive use of leisure time.

Conventional settings are, of course, likely to be peopled by conventional, noncriminal individuals, and these come to serve as certifying others. Examples here would be family, kinsmen, nonfamilial work associates, and carefully selected friends and leisure associates. Thus, by contacts and the cultivation of relationships with normal people, the ex-criminal can project a social image of noncriminality. By accepting the individual, these conventional acquaintances certify that he can be considered a conventional conforming member of society.

In summary, the author demonstrates that the ex-offender's personal image of noncriminal is not sufficient to totally exit from crime. The individual needs social verification and social legitimation. He needs a social image of noncriminality to match the personal image. To accomplish this, he involves himself in programs sponsored by certifying agencies, locates himself prominently in certifying settings of work and leisure, and associates with certifying others in the form of family, kinsmen, and conventional friends and associates. More and more people come to categorize him as a "conventional societal member." Thus, having been certified as noncriminal, the personal and social images are congruent, and the "informal process of reality construction that results in the acceptance of the ex-felon as one who can be trusted" is complete. But, as the author points out, certification is a process and thus changeable. Remission is possible!

The conversion process back and forth from normal to deviant and vice versa is not always so obvious in terms of which of the persons is the "normal" and which is the "deviant." Transsexuals who have surgery to alter their gender—sexual or gender "reassignment" as it is known—say that they previously felt as if they were males locked inside female bodies or the other way around, as the case may be. In effect, from their standpoint, the previous gender was "counterfeit," and they often experienced considerable "gender discomfort." After surgery, when they were cosmetically altered to resemble the opposite sex, however, the individuals tend to think of themselves as normal and enjoy a more personally comfortable life with their new gender. Society often tends to think of them as deviant or freaks after surgery, and they may experience persecution, discrimination, loss of job, even arrest, and social condemnation or repulsions, especially from friends, family members, or ex-spouses, as well as members of society (Bryant, 1982).

Similarly, some women undergo a change from the normal to a new, unique, religious status quite distinctive and different from their former status when they convert to a nun. The reconversion or role passage back to the secular life can be equally dramatic and traumatic as a conversion and quest for normalcy. The "rediscovery of gender," and the reassumption of the old status can take on disparate social meanings. For some non-Catholics, the nun, living "outside the mainstream of secular female culture," might represent a deviant status (SanGiovanni, 1983). For some Catholics, however, the role passage of nun back to secular existence might also be seen as something of a deviant act. Individuals and society do not always hold perfectly congruent images of deviant versus normal statuses.

The final selection in this chapter, Edward Sagarin's "Deviance Without Deviants: The Temporal Quality of Patterned Behavior," provides yet another perspective to the question of exits from deviance. Sagarin takes up the semantic and philosophical distinction between activity and identity. He rejects the practice of necessarily attaching the identity of deviant to someone as a result of their having engaged in a deviant activity. Identity, he argues, suggests permanence, while activity, he asserts, indicates "voluntarism, responsibility, and the labile nature of human conduct." By attaching such an identity to an individual who engages in the activity in question, the individual is reduced "from [a] whole being to a specific status." Beyond this, the status is a negative one and, accordingly, is a disvalued one. The identity then becomes a "master status, dominating how one is seen in other aspects of life, and how one sees oneself in relation to other activities." There is, thus, confusion between the individual and the activity with the result that the "identity tends to take on an aspect of continuity, and to lose its sense of potential transience and temporarity." Sagarin proposes to shift attention to the deviant action rather than the deviant actor.

In the space of daily life, the individual engages in many activities and occupies many statuses, some of which are ascribed while others are transient, essentially only existing while the individual is engaged in some activity. The individual is a driver only when he is driving a vehicle, for example. Status, then, according to Sagarin, may refer to what one is doing while doing it, and also "what one does with sufficient regularity to have it known that one does it." By labeling one as a deviant, however, the status may refer to what one did at one time, even though he no longer does it. By identifying an individual with a status of the latter variety, the person is reduced to "a partial and unfavorably evaluated aspect of their humanity," and dehumanized in the process.

The individual is in reality a collection of statuses and in some instances, the other positive status may tend to dilute or obscure the negative deviant status. The nature of the activity that led to the deviant activity could, however, be sufficiently reprehensible as to overpower or effect all of the other positive statuses. Sagarin asserts that if one accepts the notion that some persons who commit deviant acts continue to do so even when they know that in doing so, they will suffer more pain and unhappiness than the pleasure derived from the activity, then it must be assumed that such individuals experience a "sense of doom," or resignation to the fact that there is no escape from the pattern and that they are predestined to engage in that deviant behavior. In effect, "self-labeling, when accompanied by a belief in destiny, is a self-fulfilling prophecy." Society's tendency to provide a total negative identity to persons who engage in deviant acts may also predispose them to accept the immutability of their behavior. This process is exacerbated by the fact that disvalued status may involve beliefs, feelings, or behavior (and combinations of these), and deviant "behaviors usually preceded by the inner need, urge, desire, or demand." As Sagarin then sees it, the problem of the deviant identity arises from the fact of "the implicit connotation that some statuses constitute essence or *isness*, rather than behavior or feeling." He, therefore, argues that students of deviance should simply explore deviance without deviants. Such a perspective would "stress the non-permanence of human behavior, the potential of all persons to go in all directions, the responsibility of individuals for the direction in which they seek to move." Rather than deviants, the individuals should be viewed simply as persons who "do acts or have feelings that are disvalued in society."

Deviance comes and goes, as it were, and deviants become and unbecome. They engage in the disvalued behavior and then frequently disengage. Unless they die prematurely and abruptly, few go to their grave as unrepentant sinners or as motivated deviants. Dabbling in deviance would appear to be part of the socialization process. One learns what is socially proscribed and what is prescribed often by trial and exploration, and having sampled that which is disvalued, often moves on to a more circumscribed lifestyle. The amateurish experimentation with deviant behavior in youth may even come to be viewed as youthful zest and exuberance later in life, and not infrequently with a kind of mellow aftertaste, and savored in reminiscences. Most youths, however, outgrow their miscreant propensities and embrace a life of, more or less, conformity and circumspectness. In later years they may openly disclose their deviant experience, or they may elect to keep it "buried in the past."

Even deviants of more seasoned years, and of a more determined and decisive bent who take up more condemned patterns of behavior, including narcotic addiction, sexual perversion, or criminal activities, may also accomplish to exit from their deviant mode voluntarily and seek social approbation. This exit, however, may be hastened by some type of traumatic incident—a wreck, public exposure, arrest and near conviction—or other type of "close call." Even punishment—fines or incarceration may also, in some instances accelerate the permanent exit from deviance.

The Juvenile Awareness Project at one prison, and the television documentary detailing it, was a contrived context that sought to motivate young offenders to exit and mend their ways, as it were. Experts concluded that it was somewhat less than successful at this enterprise, but it was well received by the public who applauded the approach, and reinforced their belief that crime "was out of control," "liberal" rehabilitation efforts had failed, criminal deterrence was called for, and the "horrors" of prison life reflected appropriate retributive justice. The youthful offenders should probably take heed.

Sometimes, a support group like alcohol anonymous may aid and facilitate the exit from deviance. Overeaters anonymous was such an organization. It sought more than rational volition to overcome fattening eating habits and the resultant deviant stigma of obesity. This group defined the deviant eating mode as a "spiritual problem," and sought to have the neophytes experience a religious conversion, "purge" the old behavior as part of an emotional cartharsis, and undergo a true identity transformation to charismatic conformity. The true believer—the Devout Believer—in this case emerged with a new control over their eating habits, a new "symbolic" universe, and a new master status of more normal variety as an abstaining overeater.

The exit from deviancy may call for public acknowledgment and/or ceremony. The sinner must be publicly returned to the fold, and the errant alcoholic must openly admit his alcoholic addiction and transgression. Even the prison inmate, after having served his time, and paid his debt, and after readmission to the "straight" world, must somehow legitimate his exit from crime and return to legal and social conformity. This requires reconciling the ex-offender's personal noncriminal identity, and the social identity which often was still tainted with the residue of deviance. Social certification was required to accomplish this, and entailed appropriate involvement in rehabilitation programs, spending time in conventional settings, and associating with conventional persons such as family, work associates and selected friends. The "certifying" programs, settings, and others all served to convey an image of conventionality and conformity, and to legitimate a new social identity congruent with the personal identity.

There may even be the possibility of exiting deviance via a semantic vehicle, inasmuch as some claim that deviance and deviants are not the same. To attach the tag of deviant on someone who has simply engaged in deviance in the past is to reduce the individual who is really a collection of statuses to a specific, disvalued status and to dehumanize him. To do so is to effectively lock them into an ideological posture of resignation and acceptance of immutability—a self-fulfilling prophecy, as it were. Researchers should study deviance and not deviants, and in doing so would stress the nonpermanence of human behavior and allow the deviant to exit his status and simply exist as a person who does things or has feelings that are disvalued in society.

Whatever the mechanisms or devices, deviants may depart from their disvalued behavior just as they entered into it, volitionally coerced, or as a result of engulfing circumstances and context.

REFERENCES

Bryant, Clifton D.

1982 Sexual Deviancy and Social Proscription: The Social Context of Carnal Behavior. New York: Human Sciences Press.

Chilman, Catherine S.

1978 Adolescent Sexuality in a Changing American Society: Social and Psychological Perspectives. Washington, D.C.: U.S. Government Printing Office, p. 93.

Corzine, Jay and Richard Kirby

1977 "Cruising the Truckers: Sexual Encounters in a Highway Rest Area," Urban Life, 6(2), pp. 171–192.

Editors of Newsweek

1974 "Bisexual Chic: Anyone Goes," Newsweek, May 27, p. 90.

Feigelman, William

1974 "Peeping: The Pattern of Voyeurism Among Construction Workers," Urban Life and Culture, 3(1), pp. 35–49.

Garfinkel, Harold

1956 "Conditions of Successful Degradation Ceremonies," The American Journal of Sociology, 6, pp. 420–424.

Griffin, Susan

1975 "Rape: The All-American Crime," in Leroy G. Schultz (ed.), Rape Victomology. Springfield, Ill.: Charles C Thomas Publishing, p. 20.

Humphreys, Laud

1970 "Tearoom Trade: Impersonal Sex in Public Places," Transaction, 7(3), pp. 10–25.

Johnston, Lloyd D., Jerald G. Bachman, and Patrick M. O'Malley

1982 Student Drug Use, Attitudes, and Belief: National Trends 1975–1982. Washington, D.C.: National Institute of Drug Abuse, p. 19.

Kanin, Eugene J.

1967 "An Examination of Sexual Aggression as a Response to Sexual Frustration," Journal of Marriage and the Family, 29(3), pp. 428–433 and;

Kinsey, Alfred C., Wardell B. Pomeroy, and Clyde E. Martin

1948 Sexual Behavior in the Human Male. Philadelphia: W. B. Saunders, pp. 650–651.

Kinsey, Alfred C., Wardell B. Pomeroy, Clyde E. Martin, and Paul H. Gebhard.

1953 Sexual Behavior in the Human Female. Philadelphia: W. B. Saunders, pp. 474–475.

Laner, Mary Reige

1982 "Abuse and Aggression in Courting Couples," Deviant Behavior, 3(2) pp. 42–62.

McCaghy, Charles H.

1985 Deviant Behavior: Crime, Conflict, and Interest Groups, Second Edition. New York: Macmillan, p. 285.

SanGiovanni, Lucinda

1983 "Rediscovering Gender: The Emergent Role Passage of Ex-Nuns," in Howard Robboy and Candace Clark (eds.), Social Interaction: Readings in Sociology (Second Edition). New York: St. Martin's Press, pp. 541–552.

Smith, Spencer, R.

1976 "Voyeurism: A Review of Literature," Archives of Sexual Behavior, 5(6), pp. 585–609.

Swift, Pamela
1974 "Keeping Up—With Youth: Chastity Reborn," Parade. October 27, p. 15.

Toolan, James M., Murray Elkins, Paul D'Encarnacao, et al.
1974 "The Significance of Streaking," Medical Aspects of Human Sexuality, 8(7), pp. 152–165.

Trice, H. and P. Roman
1975 "Delabeling, Relabeling and Alcoholics Anonymous." Pp. 268–275 in F. Scarpitti and P. McFarlane (ed.), Deviance: Action, Reaction, Interaction. Reading, Mass.: Addison-Wesley, 1975 (as quoted in the O'Brien and Banksten article, "The Moral Career of the Reformed Compulsive Eater: A Study of Conversion to Charismatic Conformity." Reading 37 in this volume).

Reading 36

Mass Media and Delinquency Prevention: the Case of "Scared Straight"

John Heeren
David Shichor
California State College, San Bernardino

This paper focuses on the Oscar winning television documentary "Scared Straight." This documentary describes the Juvenile Awareness Project (JAP) at Rahway State Prison in New Jersey, which attempts to deter juvenile delinquency by briefly exposing young offenders to the harsh realities of prison life. The paper analyzes the possible reasons for the popularity of this show and the JAP. It is suggested that factors such as the public perception of increasing crime rates, declining support for rehabilitation, and a dramatic promise of a new, synthetic solution for delinquency were among the major reasons for the success of the television documentary.

INTRODUCTION

Early in 1979 about 200 independent television stations in major cities across the United States broadcast a documentary film called "Scared Straight." The film focused on the Juvenile Awareness Project[1] at Rahway State Prison in New Jersey as a noteworthy attempt to reduce youth crime and delinquency. The project, organized by a group of inmates known as The Lifers, subjects juveniles to a close-up look at, and discussion of, the harsh reality of prison life. This is quite different from the treatment-oriented measures—warnings, diversion, restitution, probation—most delinquents initially incur. The opening narration of "Scared Straight" frames the JAP by discussing the problem of increasing juvenile crime and the failure of established solutions. The body of the film is a documentary segment in which seventeen "hard-core" delinquents are subjected to "shock therapy." They are verbally assaulted by the Rahway Lifers as a means of deterring future offenses. Concluding scenes show the "scared" delinquents professing their intent to avoid criminal behavior, and reports on a three-month follow-up in which only one youth had reoffended. In the intervening months, events have not been so kind to the program. Its first formal evaluations by Rutgers social scientists found the project to be worse than

[1]The program is variously referred to as the Juvenile Awareness Project, Juvenile Awareness: Project Help, and Juvenile Awareness: Project Self-Help. We shall use the first of these names and the acronym, JAP, throughout this paper.

ineffective; it actually seemed to promote further offenses among those exposed to it.[2] Furthermore, the JAP tour was subsequently curtailed and the warden criticized for his considerable involvement in it.

This paper is an attempt to understand the popular appeal of "Scared Straight" in terms of the public's perception of the seriousness of the problem of juvenile delinquency and the JAP as a potential solution. Mass media of communication are likely to have played some role in creating public awareness of youthful criminals. Accordingly, we expect that it is possible to understand the success of "Scared Straight!" by looking at its images of delinquents and the assumptions about prevention it embodies.

Mass Media and Social Problems

In recent years a strong interest has developed about the interaction between the mass media and criminological concerns. One of the major issues here has to do with the relationship of mass media portrayals of crime to public perceptions about crime. An early investigation of this issue (Davis, 1952) offered "some support to the hypothesis that public opinion reflects trends in the amount of crime news rather than in actual crime rates." This relationship was more clearly substantiated in a series of papers by Gerbner and his associates (Gerbner, et al., 1977; Gerbner, et al., 1978; Gerbner, et al., 1979). They found in general that heavy viewers of television were much more likely to see reality as fearful and violent, and this distorted image essentially mirrored that in the medium. Though this "cultivation analysis" has been sharply criticized and unconfirmed by further analysis and research (Hirsch, 1980; Hughes, 1980; Doob and Macdonald, 1979), Gerbner, et al. (1980) have further refined their formulations and carried out more sophisticated analyses which support their hypothesis. Research by Jaehnig, et al. (1981:95) also suggests that "people's fear of crime seems

[2]The systematic evaluation of the program by Finckenauer in a comparison between an experimental group of juveniles participating in the JAP and a control group found:

> no difference between the groups of their attitude
> toward law,
> no difference between groups on their attitude
> toward justice
> no difference between the groups on their attitude
> toward the concept of 'policemen'
> no significant variance between groups in their attitude
> toward punishment
> no effect upon . . . self perception (National Center on Institutions and Alternatives, n.d.:12)

In fact,

> A significantly higher proportion of the juveniles who did not attend the project did better in terms of avoiding subsequent offenses than did the group that attended. The failure rate among the control group was only 11 percent: among the experimental group, 41 percent. (Finckenauer, 1979:6)

to be associated more closely with newspaper emphasis on violent crime than with the actual frequency of occurrence of such crime as measured by the FBI Uniform Crime Reports."

On the other hand some research has found little or no evidence for the notion that public opinion about crime or other social problems is significantly shaped by mass media. Although few details of his research are given, Roshier (1973) reports that public perceptions of crime approximated the official picture much more than the media-distorted image. Similarly, Hubbard, et al. (1975) found that citizen ratings of the relative prevalence of ten types of social problems reflected the "actual" occurrence of these problems as they appeared in the records of various agencies. Moreover, while the research did not use the pattern of media usage as a variable, the investigators saw no relationship between citizen rankings of problems and the media emphasis given them. Most recently, Sacco's (1982) research showed no relationship between patterns of media consumption and perceptions of crime.

In spite of contradictory findings, the numerous studies of the media effects on perceptions of crime have not been unproductive. Few would now maintain that media presentations of crime directly create unmitigated images in the public mind. Furthermore, recent studies have been able to clarify some issues and point the way to new research questions. Hubbard, et al. (1975:31), for instance, note that their research on the prevalence of certain social problems says nothing about their relative importance. They concede that "the media may play a role in shaping conceptions of importance" of social problems. Also of significance is that, even though both Hubbard, et al. (1975) and Sacco (1982) find little support for media influence of public perceptions of crime, they are willing to admit that the media probably play a major role in the emergence or initial identification of a social problem. This position indicates the importance of considering the degree of development of public concern over a problem in estimating the role of the media in shaping opinion.

It may be useful, then, to regard a social problem, such as crime, as having a "natural history." A recent reformulation of the natural history perspective on social problems has been presented by Spector and Kitsuse (1977). They suggest that the evolution of a social problem be conceived as occurring in four stages:

1 Group(s) attempt to alert the public to the existence of some troublesome condition;
2 These group(s) are recognized by officials as having raised a legitimate issue—this recognition possibly leading to investigation or other action;
3 Reappearance of claims and demands by original group(s) or new ones that the problem is not being adequately handled; and

4 Rejection of official response to new claims and demands; attempt to establish alternative or parallel programs to handle problems.

The last two stages above represent a kind of "second generation" of a social problem, where earlier attempts at solution are seen as failures and new approaches are demanded.

With respect to juvenile delinquency, benevolent groups such as the "child savers" alerted the public to the problems of lower class urban youth and launched a large-scale attempt to deal with the problem of delinquency, which culminated in the late 19th century with the establishment of juvenile courts (Platt, 1969). That era of reform had the effect of implementing the rehabilitation model for handling delinquency. This "child savers" movement argued that juvenile offenders get involved in delinquency as a result of adverse individual and social conditions, and there is a need to save them by placing them in "positive" moral and material surroundings. Even "predelinquents," who had not yet committed a crime, needed early intervention to save them from delinquency (Pisciotta, 1982). The idea of prevention became prominent and the formal proceedings of the court were given a diagnostic purpose (Schlossman, 1977).

Representing the second stage of the natural history, this rehabilitative model was premised on very specific ideas about children. The latter were seen as more innocent and uncalculating than adults and deserving of special care. More malleable than an adult, a child's behavior pattern could be improved by helpful intervention. The earlier the intervention, the better for the child and society (Empey, 1982).

These premises led clearly to the espousal of the rehabilitation ideal which suggested that delinquents: "could be restored to conditions of health and social repute by scientifically designed programs of care and treatment" (Empey, 1982:304). Rehabilitation, then, is optimistic about the prospects for personal change.

Over the past several years, there has been a "second generation" of the problem of delinquency. That is, significant groups in the United States are claiming that the problem is not being adequately handled. In addition to the public perception that youth crime is on the rise, there is a widespread sense that the rehabilitative model of the juvenile court has failed (Castillo, 1981). One series of polls found that for crime in general support for harsher sanctions in the United States rose from 48.9% in 1965 to 84.9% in 1978 (Stinchcombe, et al., 1980). As for the juvenile courts, a New York Times/CBS News Poll found that 68% of a national sample supported jury trials for 13 year old juveniles accused of committing a violent crime rather than a trial by a judge—since judges were seen as too lenient (Castillo, 1981).

It is our contention that the success of "Scared Straight!" can be understood in terms of the underlying premises which it embodies. The film's success in terms of popular appeal seems beyond dispute. The Los Angeles showing brought 2000 overwhelmingly supportive letters from viewers. In New York, "Scared Straight" attained a 39% share of the viewing audience. It won an Oscar, an Emmy, and a host of other awards (Finckenauer, 1982:98–99). The popularity of the film is the result of its premises resonating strongly with public opinion, which demands, as mentioned, greater punitiveness toward juveniles. However, the movie maintains some well-established elements from earlier approaches to correctional policy. Let us examine the film's resonant assumptions in more detail.

1. In the first place, there is the widespread public belief that crime is out of control. This belief is supported by the rising crime rates reported by the Uniform Crime Report (1980) and the mass media (Van Dijk, 1979; Schneider, 1979; Sherizen, 1978; Dominick, 1978). From these messages, the public is likely to conclude that drastic solutions are called for in "the battle against crime."

The alarm over rising juvenile crime would seem to parallel that over crime in general. There was not only concern in the mid-to late-1970s about specific juvenile offenses, such as drug use (Hindelang, et al., 1977:310–11) and theft (Hindelang, et al., 1981: 214), but the public seemed increasingly conscious of gangs. The 1978 HUD Survey on the Quality of Community Life found that 39.9% nationwide felt that teen-age gangs were a problem in their locality. This figure was 60.7% in urban areas (Hindelang, et al., 1981: 177). Beyond these poll data, we might expect that the public—and, even more so, television station managers or owners who decided to broadcast "Scared Straight"—were sensitized to juvenile crime by increasing news reports of such from about the mid-1970s. The watershed of this reportage might be the Time (1977) cover story on "The Youth Crime Plague" in mid-1977. This article reported that half of all serious crimes were committed by juveniles and that juvenile crime was growing twice as fast as adult crime.

2. The second premise embodied by the film is the failure of the liberal ideal of rehabilitating offenders. The public tends to blame the courts and correctional institutions for the crime problem (Graber, 1980). Judges are seen as allowing excessive legal protections for defendants, while correctional institutions are viewed as recycling offenders without regard for whether they have reformed. These changes in the public's view also embrace the juvenile justice system. The view is that rehabilitation with juveniles does not work either and many hardcore young offenders get away with a "slap on their wrist." A Gallup poll in 1976 found that 41% of a national sample thought that the juvenile courts do a poor job in handling juvenile delinquents (Parisi, et al., 1979:325). The Time (1977) article mentioned above pointed the finger at what they called "Kiddie Court's leni-

ency" as a major cause of rising delinquency. This likely reinforced the already extant public perception of the failure of juvenile court. This attitude is even expressed by Senator Kennedy (considered to be a "liberal"): "There has been a notorious lack of rehabilitation and an equally notorious increase in arbitrariness," and later he comments on the juvenile court: "We know that the ability of such courts to rehabilitate the violent juvenile or predict future criminal behavior must be viewed with increasing suspicion" (Kennedy, 1978, II, 7).

These ideas led to the conclusion that the efforts at rehabilitation had failed. As is known, the traditional rehabilitation model is associated with various methods of therapy and seeks "not just a change in behavior, but a change of heart that leads to the change in behavior" (Nettler, 1978:50). This model was held especially relevant in the case of juveniles, by assuming that the juveniles' attitudes toward society will change as a consequence of rehabilitation, and these changes will affect actual behavior as well.

3. The popular assent held for many decades by the rehabilitation model has recently been replaced by support for the deterrence of criminals. Deterrence is defined as "a function of the declaration of some harm, loss, deprivation, or pain that will follow noncompliance with commands" (Zimring and Hawkins, 1973:91). In simpler terms deterrence can be seen as the meting out of punishment in order to deter the offender from further involvement in criminal behavior (specific deterrence) and to deter others who know about the punishment from committing crimes (general deterrence). Clearly, JAP was intended to be a delinquency prevention program aimed at achieving specific deterrence. The movie, "Scared Straight!" was mainly oriented toward specific deterrence, but, as a media event, it became a general deterrence vehicle.[3]

An L.A. Times poll (Endicott, 1981:1) found that while only 20% of a national sample mentioned rehabilitation as a reason for punishing criminals, almost twice that number (38%) mentioned deterrence. This is a sharp change from previous decades (cf. Erskine, 1974:498–99). With respect to delinquency, the popularity of deterrence (as well as incapacitation) has meant that the public wants juvenile crime to be handled more like adult offenses. The New York Times/CBS News Poll found considerable support for this in connection with violent juvenile crime (Castillo, 1981).

One of the basic premises of both specific and general deterrence is that offenders are making a rational choice when they get involved in delinquent or criminal behavior. Therefore, the logic goes, the possibility of getting punished will influence their decision about whether to indulge in lawbreak-

[3]This is the position taken by Finckenauer (1982). He sees the JAP as representing the deterrence doctrine in the form of aversive behavior modification. We feel this is too narrow an interpretation of the content of "Scared Straight." See below.

ing behavior. To what degree this premise is correct is not known. It seems that it is built more on assumptions than on hard evidence. In fact, there are those who point out that many people, especially juveniles, just do not believe that they are going to be apprehended if they commit a crime (Silberman, 1978; Finckenauer, 1982). Unfortunately, the low clearance rate of crimes (the number of crimes which are cleared by an arrest) would support this belief. Even though there is a lack of reliable evidence to support deterrence as an effective means of social control, its popularity is widespread in the public and among certain social scientists as well (see, for instance, Nagin, 1978; Blumstein, Cohen, and Nagin, 1978; Wilson, 1975).

4. The JAP also represents the revival of the retribution doctrine which predates the rehabilitative notion. The retributive ideal demands that the person who causes personal or social harm will receive what he deserves, i.e., severe punishment. Morris (1974:75) states in this vein: "The link between established crime and deserved suffering . . . is a central precept of everyone's sense of justice." The fact that in the film the inmates are describing vividly the horrors of the prison and their suffering in it, fulfills to a degree the public's demand for justice. While the juveniles are the main focus of the film, viewers cannot help but see the brutal punishment to which the adult criminals are subjected.[4] Again, while only 20% in the L.A. Times poll mentioned rehabilitation as a reason for punishing criminals, 30% mentioned vengeance as a reason (Endicott, 1981).

Retribution is also significant in that it reinforces the sentiments of conformists. This is consistent with Durkheim's (1933) reasoning about the social functions of punishment in reaffirming the values and norms of the public. Toby (1971:106–107) puts it succinctly: "The social significance of punishing offenders is that deviance is thereby defined as unsuccessful in the eyes of conformists, thus making the inhibition or repression of their own deviant impulses seem worth while." In emphasizing the hardships which law violators experience, "Scared Straight" serves to reinforce conformist behavior among the audience.

Fitting this mold is the secular version of "hellfire and brimstone" to which the juveniles participating in this program are subject. To those tempted by lives of crime, prison is portrayed as a way of life beyond civilization, where physical aggression prevails. The state no longer even tries to guarantee the security of inmates. They become subjected to the law of the jungle. This is justified by looking at them as "outlaws." They become the "enemy." Since we have been unable to ensure the conformity of delinquents through adequate socialization or positive rewards, the JAP holds forth the ancient prospect of brutal punishment.

[4]This retributive notion is mentioned by Cavender (1981), who claims that the film satisfies the audience by showing the negative effects *on juveniles* during the program.

5. The last premise of "Scared Straight" which found a responsive chord among a national audience has to do with an implied image of delinquents. Specifically, these youthful offenders are seen as the adult criminals of the future. Thus, it becomes very important to intervene early in these young lives to prevent them from developing a commitment to a life of crime. Peter Falk's narration in the film describes the delinquents as "prison-bound" and cites the JAP as "saving many kids from a life of crime." In addition, a brochure (Finckenauer, 1982:95) which accompanied the film noted the following:

> Fact: Virtually all adult criminals were juvenile offenders.
>
> IF ONLY THEY COULD HAVE BEEN STOPPED THEN!

Although we have not been able to locate any poll data regarding this premise of early intervention, it is noteworthy that it is quite explicit in Time's (1977) discussion of possible "cures" for youth crime.

What is most interesting about this premise is that it has its origins, and is most closely associated, with the ideology of rehabilitation. As noted earlier, rehabilitation assumed that youths were more malleable then adults and that early intervention was called for. Since juveniles were regarded as not strongly committed to criminal activity, a brief, shocking intervention (such as, exposure to the JAP) could be effective. Exponents of rehabilitation saw long-term exposure to adult criminals as likely to be harmful to delinquents (Empey, 1982; Platt, 1969). This notion is still shared by a large portion of the public; for instance, the New York Times/CBS News Poll showed that 93% of those polled felt a 13 year old convicted of a violent crime should be imprisoned separately from adults. Thus, the JAP is quite consistent with these kinds of rehabilitative assumptions.[5] Further confirmation of this coincidence of assumptions is seen in the fact that the JAP was often used on "predelinquent" populations (e.g., Kleiman, 1979).

CONCLUSION

In concluding, we would argue, then, that the film, "Scared Straight," evinces assumptions from three apparently contradictory approaches to delinquency. Deterrence would appear to be the dominant model being espoused by the JAP, but the film also offered its audience a serving of

[5]It is worthwhile to mention that research in the area of delinquency points out that even if all adult criminals were once juvenile offenders, this does not mean that all, or even most, delinquents will become adult criminals. Moreover, labeling theorists (e.g., Schur, 1973) feel that intervention is what makes the transition to adult criminality more likely.

retribution and a significant portion of rehabilitative assumptions. With respect to the latter, it is interesting to note that while the traditional approach to rehabilitation is rejected as a failure, the film utilizes the premise that youthful criminals are corrigible and require early intervention to put them on "the right track." Empey (1978) sees retribution, rehabilitation and deterrence as representing different stages in the evolution of policy toward delinquency over the last century. However, he notes that the appearance of a new approach to delinquency never totally replaces the older approaches. Instead, older approaches come to be institutionalized and continue to exert some influence even after a new solution has emerged.

With regard to the media issues discussed at the outset of this paper, "Scared Straight" presents two notable features. First, its success is largely due to its combining a unique set of five premises into one dramatic package. These premises are seen as consistent with certain assumptions popular with the public at large. A second consideration has to do with the film's effects. It is our view that an important consequence of "Scared Straight" was to *amplify* or exaggerate the reality on which it supposedly reports. Wilkins (1965) shows how this amplification works in connection with the system feedback processes for crime rates. Media presentations can do essentially the same thing by their selection, magnification, and slanting of reality (Altheide, 1974). In this sense, "Scared Straight" amplified the extent of criminal involvement of the 17 delinquents shown. At worst, most of this "hard core" group had committed mere status offenses (Finckenauer, 1982). In addition, of course, the film amplified the supposed effectiveness of the JAP (Finckenauer, 1982). And, finally, "Scared Straight" amplified the dramatic brutality of prison life. While rapes and beatings certainly occur, boredom is often the major problem which prisoners confront. While the media success of "Scared Straight" mirrors the public perceptions discussed in this paper, it also tends to foster the creation of others.

REFERENCES

Altheide, David

1974 Creating Reality: How TV News Distorts Events. Beverly Hills: Sage.

Blumstein, Alfred, Jacqueline Cohen, and Daniel Nagin (eds.)

1978 Deterrence and Incapacitation: Estimating the Effects of Criminal Sanctions of Crime Rates. Washington, D.C.: National Academy of Sciences.

Castillo, Angel

1981 "Juvenile offenders in court: the debate over treatment." New York Times, July 24, I:5.

Cavender, Gray

1981 " 'Scared Straight': ideology and the media." Journal of Criminal Justice 9:431–38.

David, F. James

1952 "Crime news in Colorado newspapers." American Journal of Sociology LVII (January):325–30.

Dominick, Joseph R.

1978 "Crime and law enforcement in the mass media," in C. Winnick, Deviance and Mass Media. Beverly Hills: Sage.

Doob, Anthony and Glen E. Macdonald

1979 "Television viewing and victimization: is the relationship causal?" Journal of Personality and Social Psychology (37) 2:170–79.

Durkheim, Emile

1933 The Division of Labor in Society. New York: Macmillan.

Empey, LaMar T.

1982 American Delinquency: Its Meaning and Construction. Homewood, Ill.: The Dorsey Press.

Endicott, William

1981 "Discontent over crime focused on judiciary." Los Angeles Times, Feb. 2:1.

Erskine, Hazel

1974 "The polls: control of crime and violence." Public Opinion Quarterly 38(3):490–502.

Finckenauer, James O.

1982 Scared Straight! and the Panacea Phenomenon. Englewood Cliffs, N.J.: Prentice-Hall.

1979 "Scared crooked." Psychology Today 13(3):6–11.

Gerbner, George, Larry Gross, M. F. Eleey, Marilyn Jackson-Beech, Suzanne Jeffries-Fox, and Nancy Signorielli

1977 "TV violence profile no. 8: the highlights." Journal of Communication 27(2):171–80.

Gerbner, George, Larry Gross, Michael Morgan, and Nancy Signorielli

1980 "The 'mainstreaming' of America: violence profile, no. 11." Journal of Communication 30(3):10–29.

Gerbner, George, Larry Gross, Nancy Signorielli, Michael Morgan, and Marilyn Jackson-Beech

1979 "The demonstration of power: violence profile, no. 10." Journal of Communication 29(3):177–96.

Gerbner, George, Larry Gross, Marilyn Jackson-Beech, Suzanne Jeffries-Fox, and Nancy Signorielli

1978 "Cultural indicators: violence profile, no. 9." Journal of Communication 28(3):176–207.

Graber, Doris

1980 Crime News and the Public. New York: Praeger.

Hindelang, Michael J., Michael R. Gottfredson, Christopher S. Dunn, and Nicolette Parisi (eds.)

1977 Sourcebook of Criminal Justice Statistics—1976. Washington, D.C.: U.S. Government Printing Office.

Hindeland, Michael J., Michael R. Gottfredson, Timothy J. Flanigan (eds.)

1981 Sourcebook of Criminal Justice Statistics—1980. Washington, D.C.: U.S. Government Printing Office.

Hirsch, Paul M.

1980 "The 'scary world' of the nonviewer and other anomalies." Communication Research (7)4:403–56.

Hubbard, Jefferey C., Melvin L. DeFleur and Lois B. DeFleur

1975 "Mass media influences on public conceptions of social problems." Social Problems (23)1:22–34.

Hughes, Michael

1980 "The fruits of cultivation analysis: a reexamination of some effects of television watching." Public Opinion Quarterly 44(3):287–302.

Jaehnig, Walter B., David H. Weaver, and Frederick Fico

1981 "Reporting crime and fearing crime in three communities." Journal of Communication 31(1):88–96.

Kennedy, Edward M.

1978 "Speech at the Annual Conference of the International Association of Chiefs of Police." New York. Quoted in Los Angeles Times, Nov. 17, Section II:7.

Kleiman, Dena

1979 "Fifth graders go to jail for a short, harsh lesson in life." New York Times, April 15:30.

Morris, Norval

1974 The Future of Imprisonment. Chicago: University of Chicago Press.

Nagin, Daniel

1978 "General deterrence: a review of the empirical evidence," in A. Blumstein, J. Cohen, and D. Nagin (eds.) Deterrence and Incapacitation: Estimating the Effects of Criminal Sanctions on Crime Rates. Washington, D.C.: National Academy of Sciences.

National Center on Institutions and Alternatives

n.d. Scared Straight: A Second Look. Washington, D.C.

Nettler, Swynn

1982 Explaining Crime. New York: McGraw-Hill.

Parisi, Nicolette, Michael R. Gottfredson, Michael J. Hindelang, and Timothy J. Flanagan (eds.)

1979 Source book of Criminal Justice Statistics—1976. Washington, D.C.: U.S. Government Printing Office.

Pisciotta, Alexander W.

1982 "Saving the children: the promise and practice of parens patriae, 1838–98." Crime and Delinquency (July):410–25.

Platt, Anthony M.
1969 The Childsavers: The Invention of Delinquency. Chicago: The University of Chicago Press.
Roshier, Bob
1973 "The selection of crime news by the press," in S. Cohen and J. Young (eds.) The Manufacture of News. Beverly Hills: Sage.
Sacco, Vincent F.
1982 "The effects of media on perceptions of crime." Pacific Sociological Review 25(4):475–93.
Schlosshman, Steven L.
1977 Love and the American Delinquent. Chicago: The University of Chicago Press.
Schneider, Hans Joachim
1979 "The influence of mass communication media on public opinion on crime and criminal justice," in Council of Europe: Public Opinion On Crime and Criminal Justice. Strasbourg: Council of Europe.
Schur, Edwin M.
1973 Radical Non-Intervention: Rethinking the Delinquency Problem. Englewood Cliffs, N.J.: Prentice-Hall.
Sherizen, Sanford
1978 "Social creation of crime news: all the news fitted to print," in C. Winick. Deviance and Mass Media. Beverly Hills: Sage.
Silberman, Charles E.
1978 Criminal violence, Criminal Justice. New York: Random House.
Spector, Malcolm, and John I. Kitsuse
1977 Constructing Social Problems. Menlo Park, Calif.: Cummings.
Stinchcombe, Arthur L., Rebecca Adams, Carol A. Heimer, Kim Lane Schepelle, Tom W. Smith, and D. Garth Taylor
1980 Crime and Punishment – Changing Attitudes in America. San Francisco: Jossey-Bass.
Time
1977 "The youth crime plague." (110) July 11:18–28.
Toby, Jackson
1971 "Is punishment necessary?" in E. Stanley Grupp (ed.) Theories of Punishment. Bloomington: Indiana University Press.
Van Dijk, Jan J. M.
1979 "The extent of public information and the nature of public attitudes towards crime," in Council of Europe: Public Opinion On Crime and Criminal Justice. Strasbourg: Council of Europe.
Wilkins, Leslie T.
1965 Social Deviance. London: Tavistock.
Wilson, James Q.
1975 Thinking About Crime. New York: Vintage.
Zimring, Franklin E., and Gordon J. Hawkins
1973 Deterrence: The Legal Threat in Crime Control. Chicago: The University of Chicago Press.

Reading 37

The Moral Career of the Reformed Compulsive Eater: A Study of Conversion to Charismatic Conformity

Marc S. O'Brien
William B. Bankston
Louisiana State University, Baton Rouge

This paper reports the findings of an intensive study of participants in a "self-help" weight control group. The objective of the study was to investigate the development of deviant identity among the obese and the process by which the group of reformed deviants effected changes in the eating behavior of its members. Participant observation and interviews revealed successful members experience radical conversion and that these converts to conformity (self-controlled eating) shared common biographical characteristics, i.e., moral careers. Theoretical implications of such conversions from deviance to conformity are then discussed.

OBESITY AS STIGMA

This paper examines the process by which the stigma of obesity is managed through participation in a radical weight control group. The type of group studied here is termed "radical" because its program involves the creation and maintenance of dramatic shifts in the world view and self-identity of its participants. It is also radical in the sense that traditional methods of weight-control, e.g., dieting and medical treatment, are not emphasized and, in fact, are given negative evaluation. Rather, for the group we have studied, weight reduction is defined as a form and consequence of "spiritual rebirth."

To understand the nature of commitment to such a group, it is first necessary to conceptualize obesity as a form of deviance. It may be treated as such in that obesity in Western culture is viewed as morally reprehensible (Cahnman, 1968). Overweight persons cannot hide their stigma, and their character is descredited because appearance is a departure from normative expectations. As Goffman (1963:7) notes with respect to stigma generally: "Shame becomes a central possibility, arising from the individual's perceptions of one of his own attributes as being a defileing thing to possess, and one he can readily see himself as not possessing." The glutton is, where leanness is a cultural ideal, one who lacks the will to resist the temptation of overindulgence. Thus, the obese are held accountable for their plight as their systematic avoidance by others suggest: "Children revile them on the streets, persons of average size refuse to date, dine, or dance with them, and many businesses, government, and professional associations refuse to employ them (Lyman, 1978: 218)". The fat person is a discredited person often facing an unaccepting social world—obesity, in effect, spoils one's social identity (cf. Goffman, 1963:19). The common derogatory labels associated with it easily demonstrate this point, e.g., lard-ass, jug-butt, porky, fatso, blubber-butt, fat-ass, pig, etc.

A basic quality of stigmatizing traits is their potential for incorporation in the identity and, therefore, in the self-evaluation process. The attribution of such labels to actors and behaving towards those actors in terms of the moral meanings implicit in such labels may well result in the transformation of public identity and self-concept in a direction consistent with the imputed deviant attributes (Pfuhl, 1980:245). Once a deviant identity has been assumed by and/or forced upon an individual, the problem of managing it arises. Because obesity is a stigma observable to all, fat persons are confronted continually with employing tactics that account for their deviance. Often they may disavow their deviant status (cf. Davis, 1961) by denying the condition is abnormal or by using accounts that neutralize the negative moral meanings associated with their obesity, e.g., by suggesting their problem is biologically determined and, thus, beyond their control (cf. Scott and Lyman, 1968). However, where such stigma managing techniques fail, and so do the various "individual treatment" methods they imply, then we often see stigmatized persons such as these turn to a "mutual aid organization which encourages a return to strict conformity to the norms of community as well as creating a stereotype which is socially acceptable" (Trice and Roman, 1975:268). It is this process that our research investigates.

Our study focused upon participants in an Over-Eaters Anonymous group. We were interested in determining the developmental sequence of the identity of these overweight persons in an effort to understand the process by which such a group may conventionalize the deviant behavior of its participants. Goffman (1963:9) has suggested stigmatized identities may be maintained even in the absence of the stigma, i.e.: "When repair is possible, what often results is not the acquisition of fully normal status, but a transformation of self from someone with a particular blemish into someone with a record of having corrected a particular blemish." Previous research indicates "self-help" groups may encourage the retention of negative social labels and use the application of such labels to convert members to conventional behavior (Warren, 1974; Laslett and Warren, 1978; Trice and Roman, 1975; Sagarin, 1975). Our research extends this interest to include the analysis of the content of deviant careers that make some susceptible to such identity transformations.

METHODOLOGY

Information on the group and its members was gathered in two ways. First, participant observation of the group's weekly meetings was carried out for a period of six months, during 1981 and 1982. The researcher was a full participant, joined the group in the same manner as the members, and engaged in group discussion and ritual. The group members were, however, aware of the researcher role as well.

A second method of data collection used was in-depth, open-ended interviews through which biographical material and individual perceptions were obtained. The interviews ranged in length from roughly forty-five minutes to nearly three hours, the average being about ninety minutes. A total of 14 depth-interviews were conducted, this representing over half of the 24 regular participants. The analysis to follow is drawn from both these sources.

THE WEIGHT CONTROL GROUP AS A CONVERTING AGENT

Group Philosophy: Overeating as Sin

Participation in the group readily revealed that weight loss was attained through affecting the self-identity of the member in the form of a conversion experience and maintained through ritualized behavior that is implicitly and explicitly of a religious nature. The philosophy of the group is that being overweight is primarily a "spiritual" problem. Everywhere the idea abounds that God will reward those who admit this truth and the group is perceived as a mediator between the member and a higher power. The definition of a situation that emerges in group interaction is that there is no category of "ex-overeaters," there are only abstaining overeaters, and without continued group support relapse is probable. Participation in the group in this way fosters an uncomplimentary view of self. The perception of the individual as weak and incapable of controlling his/her behavior without the help of the group is promoted. This view must be accepted by an actor if commitment, integration, and conversion is to be achieved. Not all participants do this.

A Typology of Participants: Devout Adherents and Their Supporting Cast

Though group ideology stresses the "equality" of the members, our observations revealed considerable differential allocation and acceptance of the meanings and moral implications of obesity. The most highly visible, committed, and successful members we have labeled "Devout Adherents." This type is composed of those most dedicated to the principles of the group. They were the most intensively involved in group processes, filling leadership roles, organizing group activities, and leading discussions. They claim to have experienced the spiritual strength promised by the group's philosophy. The Devout Adherent has typically been a member for more than two years. The success of this type is obvious, many having lost well over one hundred pounds. Never do these participants question or criticize any aspect of the philosophy or program, either publicly or privately. To the group as whole, this type exemplifies the presence of divine intervention into their lives.

Another segment of the group is what we have labeled the "Social Club" members. These members are typically middle-aged females and tended to have developed their weight problem later in life than Devout Adherents. The open forum discussion of the group meetings is tailored to the liking of these participants, who often use the occasion to discuss "minor" domestic problems. The members are not as successful with weight-loss and experience much "back-sliding." It appears the intrinsic reward of group interaction is the principal bond that maintains their participation. The Social Club members are basically *verbal converts* in Lofland's terms (1966:32) in that they proclaim their allegiance and praise the group's goals, but commit little time and effort outside of the group meeting. The group does not appear to be a significant source of self evaluation. Devout Adherents, on the other hand, are *total converts* as they "exhibit their commitment through deeds as well as words" (Lofland, 1966:33).

The Social Club members, however, do serve an important function in the maintenance of success among Devout Adherents, and thus the continuance of the group. They, in a sense, are permanent "back-sliders," not nearly as successful as Devout Adherents, yet at the same time professing the validity of the group's philosophy. Failure is interpreted as a consequence of their character, not the premises upon which the group is founded. They are, thus, "repentant deviants" (cf. Gusfield, 1967), who pose no challenge to the legitimacy of the group's norms and beliefs. Because of this, their failure strengthens the solidarity of Devout Adherents. The deviance (failure) of Social Club members is channeled and organized in a manner that produces positive consequences for the group (cf. Dentler and Erikson, 1959). The failure *and* repentant attitude of the Social Club member provides an ever-present source of boundary-maintenance for the group. The identity and commitment of the Devout Adherent is enhanced by the favorable subjective comparison with the Social Club member. In this case, deviant behavior is managed and solidarity increased without exclusion of the deviant, but rather through tolerance of the behavior. Devout Adherents often verbalized to the researcher that those whom we have labeled Social Club members lacked sincerity as compared to their own. A group that seeks to transform deviant life-styles is likely to meet with rather high rates of failure. It may be that effective converting groups must develop a moral division of labor that enables some to enter the role of charismatic leadership and, thus, reform, while others remain contaminated by their deviant status, but necessarily tolerated (Warren, 1980).

THE MORAL CAREER OF THE DEVOUT ADHERENT

The process of commitment to the group was essentially a process of identity transformation. Our observations of the Devout Adherents suggest this transformation may be understood best as moral career, i.e., as a "sequence of changes . . . in the person's self and his framework of imagery for judging himself and others" (Goffman, 1961:127–128). The committed member's identity transformation is, in essence, a conversion experience in which the stigma of obesity is transformed into the new pervasive identity (cf. Travisano, 1970) of "abstaining compulsive overeater." This label is not simply an image of self worn at meetings but is a way of living, of viewing the world and one's place in it for Devout Adherents. This transformation of deviant identity appears not to be a random occurrence in the lives of obese persons but rather involves a developmental process similar to that described by Lofland (1966) in the biographies of converts to a radical religious cult.

Predisposing Conditions in the Careers of Reformed Compulsive Eaters

Lofland (1966) suggested two types of conditions need by included in a model of conversion, predisposing conditions and situational contingencies. Predisposing attributes characterize the overeaters prior to contact with the group and are created or develop through interaction with the group.

Characteristic of the Devout Adherents and predisposing them to a profound influence from contact with the group was the prolonged experience of tension (cf. Lofland, 1966) associated with the attribute "fat." The true converts had long perceived themselves as being isolated because of their physical repugnance and the socially unacceptable nature of their obesity. This is exemplified in the following statement by one Devout Adherent who had been a committed member for two years:

> I was overweight as a child and I have been that way almost ever since. I think my father was sexually attracted to me and wanted me to be big—that way I wasn't pretty. I remember when I was in the eighth grade, I was so fat I couldn't cross my legs. But I didn't think about it too much, because Mom and Dad always said I was healthy and that was all I ever thought about it, even when the other girls teased me because I was too fat and slow to play jump rope. Everything was alright until the other girls started dating and no one would

> ever ask me out. Nobody had to tell me why, it was because I was a pig and boys don't like pigs. I finally lost some weight and that's when I realized that fat people are sick. But I started eating too much again right after I got out of school. I was married and nothing was going right—that's when it happens, you eat when everything else is bad because food makes you feel good.

This tension seems to be typically associated with a negative evaluation of their physical beauty, especially feminine beauty, explaining the high ratio of women to men (4 to 1) in the group. The following was an attitude exhibited by most: "Fat women are cows. Nobody will date you, men just aren't interested. You can't buy any attractive clothes or anything. Who wants to be seen with a clumsy ox. There's nothing attractive about getting stuck in a chair."

In the dispositional phase of their career, the frustration with their social identity had lead all Devout Adherents to contact with medical practitioners. Such contact may serve to limit the potential for charismatic conversion from obesity, especially if there is some degree of success, but for these converts, the experience had been unanimously negative, and they remained hostile to the medical approach. One noted:

> Pills, pills, pills, that's all he ever gave me. I started going to a doctor when I was thirteen. He started prescribing medication for my weight immediately. For over twelve years I took every kind of "speed" imaginable. I could never quite reach a weight that made me feel good about myself. I was high all the time though. Finally I realized that I was becoming dependent on the medication—I was eating it like candy. I realized this was no way to solve my problems. I was killing myself, or rather my doctor was killing me and I had all that I could take.

The prolonged tension, though necessary, is not sufficient for creating a potential convert from compulsive overeating. Alternatives are possible—maybe more probable. The stigma may simply be endured; alcoholism or drug addiction may result. But those who were to eventually become Devout Adherents shared another predispositional trait (cf. Lofland, 1966). Specifically, their pregroup career was characterized by a tendency to impose a religious meaning on their deviant status. The following descriptions were typical of the Devout Adherents:

> My whole life revolved around the refrigerator. The therapist kept telling me that I wasn't crazy, but I knew I was because it's crazy for someone to hide food. Normal people don't do that. I began to realize that I was out of touch with God; that's why I was going insane and my whole life was going to hell. I

> didn't have the faith anymore. I prayed all night one night for God's help and sure enough, a couple of days later I heard about this group.
>
> I realized that I was insane and that I was trying to destroy myself but I didn't care anymore. I was driving down the street one night and I decided I had had enough, it wasn't worth it. I ran my car straight into a canal because I wanted to die and be done with it. However, being my normal self I screwed that up too because I didn't get hurt but I totalled my car. That night when I was at home in bed I realized what I had to do. I put my faith in the Lord and asked Him to guide me. I still have troubles, but I have held my faith ever since.

This particular characteristic was correlated with religious background and further differentiated Devout Adherents from the less committed Social Club members. The respondents were predominately Protestant, but the Protestant/Catholic ratio was about equal that of the community in which the group was located. Nine were Protestants and five were Catholics. Eight of the Protestants were Devout Adherents and only one was Catholic. The Catholics were far more likely to be Social Club members. It would seem that Catholic background is not as likely to produce a set of religious meanings congruent with the "born again" conversion philosophy of the group. In other words, Catholicism does not appear to *predispose* its adherents in a way similar to Protestantism.

Situational Contingencies in Becoming a Devout Adherent

As conceptualized by Lofand (1966) situational contingencies are conditioned by predisposed attitudes or meaning held by converts. This pattern was apparent among the reformed overeaters. All Devout Adherents had experienced major "turning points" in association with their first contact with the group. Turning points are events which offer a perceived opportunity for a "new line" of action (cf. Lofland, 1966; Bankston, et al., 1981: 288). Typically, the predisposing characteristics of the converts lead them to define the situation in such a way as to make their first contact with the group to be perceived as an alternate life-style. For example, one related the following: "I'll never forget, the first night I was here I knew I was home. All these people with the same problems I had. I knew I wasn't alone anymore and I thanked God for my deliverance." Sometimes the experience of initial contact was mediated by closely preceding events such as the following, which the converts recalled as having special significance:

> I'll never forget, I was getting undressed and he looked at me and told me to put my clothes back on. At first I didn't understand, but he just told me that I dressed in a way that hid my weight too well and he couldn't become sexually

> aroused now that he saw how fat I was. I cried until six o'clock the next morning.

After the turning point of contact with the group all Devout Adherents experienced a phase of development of close affective ties with other members and settled into a pattern of intensive interaction. These likewise are crucial contingencies in conversion, for the outcome is the development of a modified world view or "symbolic universe" (cf. Berger and Luckman, 1967). The Devout Adherent, much like the total converts studied by Lofland (1966) developed or incorporated a system of meanings through which everyday life and everyday events become interpreted in a manner reinforcing the world view of the group. Devout Adherents are constantly notifying each other of the appearance of a "cosmic force" in their everyday lives:

> Like the other day, I went to the store for a pack of cigarettes and on my way out I saw a box of doughnuts. I really wanted those doughnuts, but I reached in my back pocket to get my wallet, when I realized that I had inadvertantly left it at home. I just laughed and thanked the Lord for watching over me.

The outcome of the career of these converts was that of a new master status (cf. Becker, 1963) and a new vocabulary of motive (cf. Mills, 1970; Foote, 1970). The new identity contained, symbolically, much of the stigma of the old, but the reorganized vocabulary of motive produced a sense of charismatic self-control.

CONCLUSION: THEORETICAL IMPLICATIONS OF CHARISMATIC CONFORMITY

The stigma of obesity as Cahnman (1968) notes is a vicious circle which leads to further discrimination and further withdrawal. So it is with many forms of deviance. It is with these forms that self-help groups such as that studied here seem to emerge (cf. Trice and Roman, 1975; Laslett and Warren, 1978). These groups function to restore an acceptable identity, but not through purging the self of the experience of stigma. The group we have studied, in fact, promoted the retention of a stigmatized identity. The effect, however, is clearly not that predicted by the theory of secondary deviance.

Deviant identities may be transformed in a number of ways. Disengagement from deviance may occur because of "drift," e.g., aging often produces a slowly changing definition of self and behavior (cf. Bankston, et al., 1981: 282). One may drift out of a deviant lifestyle as well as into one. The *conversion* to conformity experienced by our subjects is the opposite of drift. It involved a dramatic shift of identity through what Warren (1980: 62) has conceptualized as a "purification" process which "involves the death or cleansing of the old moral self and the substitution of a new moral self." It is our suggestion that this is a dialectical process of self in which a new moral identity is constructed in opposition to the old. This can be a sudden occurrence for the "material" of the transformed self exists dialetically in the old – it is its reflection. The new conventionalized identity is maintained by symbolic reference to the old. In this dialetical manner, an old stigma (e.g., "overeater") is an essential part of this new self, while the behavior of the old is purged through the expression of its dialectical opposite, i.e., *charismatic* conformity (e.g., "abstaining").

Such conversion experiences are not common among deviants. Only certain interactional contexts may produce them. Warren (1974: 307–308) argues the context with the most potential for creating such change is one where the converting agents are ex-members of the deviant category, and where contacts occur within a voluntary association. Coercive associations such as prisons are alienating, and are thus associated with the emergence of secondary deviance. Our research has suggested another dimension – that of the moral career of the potential convert. Like other forms of conversion, charismatic conformity may be effected only in selves with certain dispositions and in the presence of specific contingencies. It is for this reason that all exposed to the converting group are not similarly affected. Further investigation of similar forms of conventionalizing self-change with different contents will be of considerable theoretical value. The sociology of deviance may profit as much theoretically through the investigation of the process of becoming "normal" as through study of the process of becoming deviant.

REFERENCES

Bankston, W. B., H. H. Floyd, Jr., and C. J. Forsyth
1981 "Toward a general model of the process of radical conversion." Qualitative Sociology 4 (Winter):279–297.

Becker, H. S.
1963 Outsiders. New York: Free Press.

Berger, P. L. and T. Luckman
1967 The Social Construction of Reality. Garden City, New York: Double Anchor.

Cahnman, W. J.
1968 "The stigma of obesity." Sociological Quarterly 9 (Summer):282–299.

Davis, F.
1961 "Deviance disavowal." Social Problems 9 (Fall):120–132.
Dentler, R. A., and K. T. Erikson
1959 "The functions of deviance in groups." Social Problems 7 (Fall):98–107.
Foote, N.
1970 "Identification as a basis for the theory of motivation." Pp. 480–489 in G. Stone and H. Farberman (eds.) Social Psychology Through Symbolic Interaction. Waltham, Mass.: Xerox.
Goffman, E.
1961 Asylums. New York: Doubleday.
1963 Stigma. Englewood Cliffs, N.J.: Prentice-Hall.
Gusfield, J.
1967 "Moral passage." Social Problems 15 (Fall):175–188.
Laslett, B., and C. A. B. Warren
1978 "Losing weight: the organizational promotion of behavior change." Pp. 119–128 in J. Manis and B. Meltzer (eds.), Symbolic Interaction, Third Edition. Boston: Allyn and Bacon.
Lofland, J.
1966 Doomsday Cult. Englewood Cliffs, N.J.: Prentice-Hall.
Lyman, S.
1978 The Seven Deadly Sins. New York: St. Martin's Press.
Mills, C. W.
1970 "Situated actions and vocabularies of motive." Pp. 472–480 in G. Stone and H. Farberman (eds.), Social Psychology Through Symbolic Interaction. Waltham, Mass.: Xerox.
Pfuhl, E.
1980 The Deviance Process. New York: D. Van Nostrand.
Sagarin, E.
1975 "The rise of voluntary associations: in S. Dinitz, R. Dines, and A. C. Clark (eds.), Deviance: Studies in Definition Management and Treatment. New York: Oxford Press (second edition).
Scott, R. A., and S. Lyman
1968 "Accounts." American Sociological Review 33 (February):46–62.
Travisano, R.
1970 "Alternation and conversion as qualitatively different transformations." Pp. 594–606 in G. Stone and H. Farberman (eds.), Social Psychology Through Symbolic Interaction. Waltham, Mass.: Xerox.
Trice, H., and P. Roman
1975 "Delabeling, Relabeling and Alcoholics Anonymous." Pp. 268–275 in F. Scarpitti and P. McFarlane (eds.), Deviance: Action, Reaction, Interaction. Reading, Mass.: Addison-Wesley.
Warren, C. A. B.
1974 "The use of stigmatizing labels in destigmatizing human behavior." Sociology and Social Research 58 (April):303–311.
1980 "Destigmatization of identity: From deviant to charismatic." Qualitative Sociology 3 (Spring):59–72.

Reading 38

Becoming Normal: Certification as a Stage in Exiting from Crime

Thomas Meisenhelder
California State College, San Bernardino

Certification is the final stage in exiting from a career in crime. This paper presents the major elements in the process of certification as revealed by an analysis of a set of life-history interviews. This look at the process of certification uncovers that, like deviance, conventionality is a social phenomenon constructing from both social action and societal reaction.

INTRODUCTION

The final aspect of the process of exiting from a career in crime can be termed "certification," which is briefly described as follows:

> The formal completion of a successful exiting project requires a symbolic component, certification. This final phase in exiting was required in order for the individual fully to achieve a social identity as a noncriminal. Certification is simply the social verification of the individual's "reform." Some recognized member(s) of the conventional community must publicly announce and certify that the offender has changed and that he is now to be considered essentially noncriminal. (Meisenhelder, 1977:329)

This paper presents an expanded analysis of this final stage in the process of criminal change.[1]

The instigation of an exiting project by a criminal offender depends on the individual's decision to attempt to "go straight." This decision seems to be at least in part based on the individual's personal identity as a noncriminal. However, change within criminal careers also includes the social recognition (as perceived by ex-offenders themselves) of their abandonment of criminal activity. Thus change is not complete when individuals fully commit themselves to conventionality, rather, commitment must be supple-

[1]As a process of social interaction, certification undoubtedly develops as a series of general steps or phases. Thus, as one *Deviant Behavior* reviewer has commented, it would be beneficial to be able to present a thorough "phase analysis" of the process of certification. I am sure this is possible and it should be done. However, the data collected in this study seemed more open to a somewhat static analytical framework. Therefore I have concentrated on uncovering the primary elements within the process rather than explicitly treating the stages of the process of certification. Still, in order to avoid a complete neglect of processural description, several case histories are presented in the text.

mented by the social recognition of their reform. The process by which exiting from crime is conceived of as socially recognized is called certification. By certification, individuals convince themselves that they have convinced others to view them as conventional members of the community. They perceive by the reactions of others that they are defined as being largely conventional. They begin to feel trusted; that is, they feel that their contemporaries are likely to see them as normal and noncriminal. They no longer feel suspect (Matza, 1969:195). Certification, then, completes the exiting, or change, process by solidifying the self-concept of the ex-offender.

It is important to note that along with the impression of conventionality certification often produces an increased probability of noncriminal patterns of behavior. A social identity as noncriminal may regenerate and support the changed felon's commitment to conventionality. This may be so for several reasons. First, certification produces an integrated conception of the self as normal, and this congruence of self may facilitate the abandonment of crime (see Lofland, 1969:281). In addition, certification through the testimony of others often parallels the formation of strong interpersonal ties between the ex-offender and conventional others. These social bonds provide the changed criminal with meaningful reasons for staying "straight" (Meisenhelder, 1977).

In sum, certification is a process of social interaction through which the ex-offender's social identity is changed to one of noncriminality. Certification signals the end of exiting as a stage in the individual's biography. In the following pages this outline is filled out by a detailed description of how certification is experienced by the offenders themselves.

METHODS

The research reported here has been conducted within a frame of reference that Matza (1969) has referred to as the "appreciative stance." Simply put, this point of view requires that the sociologist strive to grasp the experiential life-world of his or her subjects. In this case the stance of appreciation directs the researcher to attempt to understand the role of the process of certification within the larger exiting project and criminal career of the offender.

In line with this approach the data presented in this paper were collected during tape-recorded interview conversations with 25 male prison inmates (see Meisenhelder, 1977). These data originally formed part of a larger study of the stages in the development of criminal careers. Thus, as a whole, each interview was guided toward uncovering the phases of involvement in crime in the life history of the respondent. The interviews were ordered chronologically according to the respondent's cycle or cycles of criminal activity. They were conducted in two institutions (one in the eastern and one in the western United States), and they were largely unstructured or nonstandardized in format. At both research sites potential respondents were selected from the total inmate population through a review of inmate files. Inmates were chosen if they manifested offense histories composed entirely or largely of property crimes. Then each of the 48 selected inmates was briefly introduced to the general project, assured of its confidentiality, and asked to volunteer to be interviewed. It should be noted that participation in the study offered no advantage to the respondents, and they were all clearly aware of the purely academic interests and position of the researcher.

All the interviewing was conducted by the author in a vacant office of the prison administrative building. The length of the interviews ranged from 1 to 3 hours, and the average interview was about 2 hours in length. Approximately 50 hours of tape recordings were produced by these sessions, which were completed during two 3-month periods approximately 1 year apart. Each recorded interview was fully transcribed prior to analysis of the data. The interviews were analyzed in order to reveal the patterned similarities (if any) shared across respondents as they reflected on their exiting experiences. During this analysis, the interviews were listened to and read several times in order to identify elements that respondents shared as they described the process of becoming certified as a noncriminal. The findings presented below are a result of that analysis and represent the most common and most significant aspects of the process of certification as the respondents described it.[2]

THE SOCIAL AND PERSONAL CONTEXT OF CERTIFICATION

The social self is a central notion in modern sociology. In order to understand the process of certification, the self must be thought of as a dual identity. That is, each person is conscious of himself or herself in terms of both a social and a personal identity.[3] The self is both socially imputed and personally constructed.

Personal identity refers to the manner in which the individual defines

[2]The use of incarcerated respondents in a study such as this is of course controversial. However, all these men have, in their own minds, experienced a significant, though temporary, exit from crime. A more important question stems from the ethnomethodologist's notion of accounting. It must remain, at least for the time being, an open question whether certification is an event or the offender's way of accounting for a crime-free period in his biography.

[3]For a similar discussion of the self, see Laing, Phillipson, and Lee (1966) and Hawkins and Tiedeman (1975).

his or her self. The concept concerns the judgmental, emotional, and cognitive categories into which the individual places himself or herself. Prior to certification, the typical respondent's personal identity was shakily noncriminal. He had constructed and committed himself to a personal identity as basically a conventional member of society. The men realized that they had been "in trouble"; yet they did not conclude from this aspect of their lives that they were criminal types of persons. These feelings are revealed in the following statement taken from the interviews:

> Contrary to what you, they might think, I ain't no hard-down criminal. I just consider myself as an average person. But there is one difference, I got into some troubles, I've been to the joint.

Indeed the plan to exit from crime is in large part founded on this sense of the self as noncriminal.

> I try to be straight. If the people give me half a chance, I'll take it. I'm just like any other person, looking for stuff like settling down, having me an old lady, couple of kids.

Our sense of self entails more than a subjective definition of ourselves. Identity is also constructed on the basis of received evidence; that is, our self is socially imputed to us through our perception of the reactions of others. An awareness of social reactions results in a social identity, which may be defined as the self imputed to the individual by others (See Hawkins and Tiedeman, 1975:243). Laing and his co-workers (1966) refer to this as "my view of your view of me" (p. 6). Social identity is my perception of what type of person the other thinks I am.

Logically, then, one's sense of personal identity may conflict with one's perception of his or her social identity. As discussed earlier, the ex-felon felt that he was basically conventional, but he realized that many other people saw him as a criminal type. The respondents related that they sensed that many people "on the street" believed that they were simply, once and for all, criminals. Others are perceived by the ex-offender as seeing him as less than normal and not to be trusted. They believed that others expect them to behave and live in a fundamentally deviant fashion. These sentiments are evident in the following interview excerpt:

> You no longer considered as being a man. Now that I've committed a crime, I got incarcerated, I don't get no respect. You just a plain criminal in their eyes. People in the streets are down on you all the time.

At best, the exiting ex-felon felt that others saw him as a deviant feigning conventionality (see also Matza, 1969:174).

Thus, the exiting ex-criminal experiences disagreement between his personal identity and other people's definition of his self. His social identity remains that of a criminal while his personal identity is noncriminal. Certification is essentially a process of constructing a conventional, or noncriminal, social identity for and by the ex-offender. Just as negative reactions may result in a criminal social identity, certification as an adjudication of conventionality labels the changing ex-offender as noncriminal.

CERTIFICATION

Certification is the final social verification of the ex-offender's substantial reform. It can be described as a set of communicative actions through which the ex-offender impresses others with the conventionality of his motives, values, and personality (see Brim and Wheeler, 1966:42).[4] In certification, some recognized members of the conventional community publicly announce and verify that the ex-felon need no longer be considered a criminal but rather should now be treated as a normal member of the social group.

In order to impress others with their successful reform and to achieve certification, the respondents employed some adept forms of self-presentation and impression management. For instance, although they believed that change is an activity conceived and achieved by the individual, they were well aware that it must be finally verified through the testimony of others. In their own words, although all the men believed that "you rehabilitate yourself," they also knew that "you got to appear normal. . . . It keeps them off your back," and "you have to, I had to, find someone to change me. To make me look good."

Further, the men related that the certification process involved the manipulation of the image of oneself held by others rather than any "real" personal or personality change (see Becker, 1964:42). Certification, then, can be seen as a specific instance of the general process that Goffman (1959) has described as the presentation of self. It too involves procedures, strategies, and tools that are used to present oneself as a particular sort of person. Here, the ex-offender must present his social audience with verbal and

[4]In reference to Brim and Wheeler's work, and others on resocialization, it must be noted that these men do not think of themselves as having been resocialized. Neither do they think of themselves as in need of such a process. Although the general culture and much of the criminal justice system seems to attribute criminal behavior to the criminal's subjective deviance (motives and values), the men themselves explain their pasts through more rational and practical contingencies. In other words, certification is more a process of self-presentation than of resocialization.

behavioral evidence of his normality. This evidence most typically includes others or a presentational team (Goffman, 1959:104) and social settings (Goffman, 1959:22). That is, by appearing with conventional others and in conventional places the exiting felon is able to demonstrate his change from crime. Likewise, by appearing with him others can testify to the individual's noncriminality and socially certify that he may be trusted to behave in a normal fashion. The phenomenological logic of certification seems to be that if one's close associates seem reasonably normal and if they further seem to define one as trustworthy, others should and will do likewise. In short, as Schutz (1962) has noted, others assume that they would see things as one's associates do if they were in their place. If he achieves certification and the construction of a noncriminal social identity, the individual no longer feels stigmatized. He has a chance to become anonymously conventional. He is now, for all practical purposes, typically conventional, and he has successfully (if temporarily) exited from crime.

In the following pages, a closer analysis of the certification process is presented. This analysis is ordered according to the most frequently mentioned tools of certification: other persons, physical settings or places, and formal agencies of correctional reform.

Certification Agencies

Certification may be achieved through participation in the rehabilitation programs of various social service and criminal justice agencies. Lofland (1969:288) has noted that these agencies provide the public with a reasonable accounting of their clients' criminality and subsequent reform. That is, they justify seeing the ex-offender as noncriminal.

However, it is easy to exaggerate the actual importance of these agencies to the ex-offender. The interviews reported here indicate that only a very few of the respondents used these agencies to demonstrate their reform. Further, most of these men used the programs in a manner far removed from their stated purposes.

> I tried the church thing, I'm not really religious, but I was gonna try it out. I'm gonna make people think that, like, I trying to change, which I was in my own way.
>
> Sure there are programs to help you, but it's, most people get into them account of it looks good. They see that you're in the program, they don't know that you ain't getting nothing out of it. They think you are changed.

As these comments suggest, formal agencies are often used purely as techniques of self-presentation.

From the point of view of the ex-offender, an important shortcoming of these agencies is that they are most often designed to effect some change in the personal identity of their clients. To the contrary, the exiting ex-offender already possesses a conventional personal identity and merely wants to use the program as ceremonial evidence for others in order to construct a similar social identity. Thus the ex-felon is forced to deceitfully manipulate his involvement in the program in order to demonstrate his commitment to change and in order to publicly announce and account for his presumed reform. The exiting experiences of "Ron," described below, illustrate the role of rehabilitation agencies in the certification process.

Ron Ron is a middle-aged black male who has lived most of his years in the southwest and in California. As a youth he became involved in petty theft and some semiorganized shoplifting. As a result he has a fairly long juvenile arrest record that includes one substantial incarceration. As an adult Ron graduated into a career of property offenses, particularly in theft and burglary. He experienced one significant period of exiting that lasted about 14 months.

A prison-administered self-improvement course was a significant factor in Ron's exiting experiences. He clearly felt that this program both convinced him that he alone was responsible for his actions *and* changed his image for others: "You're trying to determine a new image so to speak, whether knowingly or unknowingly." Ron changed his image in the minds of others through his everyday behavior and through his participation and acceptance of the self-improvement course. While attending the program, which he did twice, Ron began to construct a new social identity. Besides altering his style of adjustment to prison toward that of a "square john" (Irwin, 1970) and beginning to associate with other model prisoners, Ron methodically catered to the image he presented to his environment. As he himself put it:

> I was very methodic about it, I didn't break no rules. And a lot of the people I had known objected to how I began to react to situations. I knew what I was doing.

Ron's case provides us with an example of an individual consciously using an agency program to achieve certification. By his participation in the self-improvement course Ron loudly announced to his social environment at the time that he was a changed man. Admittedly a weak and partial case, Ron's is the exception rather than the rule among the respondents. More often certification was achieved through the informal testimony of conventional others and conventional places.

Certifying Settings

Certification of change may also occur via the physical places where the ex-offender can be observed to spend his time. As he continually appears in conventional surroundings, others may begin to define the person as non-criminal. As Lofland (1969) has suggested, "an Actor's places serve to communicate a part of what he 'is'" (p. 238).

It seems that in the everyday world one's appearance in deviant places leads to the imputation of personal deviance, and one's appearance in conventional places indicates that one is normal or conventional. Thus, as revealed in the comments below, many of the respondents consciously attempted to avoid deviant surroundings and to put themselves in more normal social settings.

> Some places get you in trouble just by your being there. . . . The wrong place at the wrong time.
>
> I always made it my business to try and get away from bad places. Places where I shouldn't be. I try to be more skeptical about where I would be.

A setting of primary import for certification is the person's place of employment. Appearance in a legitimate occupational setting for 8 hours a day, 5 days a week, is one of the most effective techniques of self-presentation available to the exiting ex-offender. The men interviewed were clearly cognizant of this fact. One respondent related that a conventional job made people accept him because

> They know what your job consists of, know what you is supposed to do. They think you is all cut and dry.

As Weber (1958) realized long ago, our culture seems to equate work with moral worth, and the changing offender's appearance in a conventional work setting strongly implies that he is worthy of trust. In short, he becomes as familiar as his job. Of course, work also gives the ex-offender practical economic aid and resources as he attempts to disengage from crime. But, beyond these practicalities, the work place also may lead others to impute conventionality to the ex-felon.

Places of leisure are also available as ways to achieve a certified non-criminal social identity. Being visible in churches, civic associations, and other socially recognized sites for the constructive use of leisure time can help the individual to become verified as having reformed. On the other hand, the exiting offender must not be seen frequenting pool halls, certain taverns, or other settings characterized by conventional others as the site of loitering, wasting time, and looking for trouble. Places such as these lead to the imputation of deviant and criminal social identity. As one respondent phrased it these kinds of places make "people look hard on you" or, even more to the point, "Pool halls and stuff, they's frustrating and full of trouble. And you looks bad there." Finally, as implied by the above, conventional places of leisure aid the exiting ex-offender in a more practical way as a result of the fact that they are less likely to present the individual with the temptation to return to crime.

In sum, physical settings assist in the achievement of certification by providing evidence that leads others to label the ex-offender as noncriminal. That is, they can announce and verify the conventionality of those that work and play within them. The case of "Bob" highlights the role of places in the process of certification.

Bob Bob is a middle-aged white male whose most frequent offense is passing and writing bad checks. He began his career in crime late in life (at the age of 30), and since then he has been incarcerated twice for passing bad checks. From 1965 to 1969, Bob "turned over a new leaf and went straight." In discussing these years of his life Bob continually pointed to the significance of his social and physical surroundings as a tool for achieving certification.

Bob stressed the negative impact of parole, for instance, as a symbolic place that is by definition reserved for criminals. Parole then involves the social imputation of criminality to the parolee. As Bob himself put it:

> Parole . . . is not beneficial to that man whatever. They (parole agents) come around, they'll sneak around, they peep on him. In some cases harass a man and cause him to do things he wouldn't normally do. If people, if they find out you're on parole they don't want to be around you. Parole doesn't help a man.

For these reasons Bob (and many other parolees) must actually skip parole in order to achieve certification as a noncriminal.[5]

After "running from parole," Bob achieved certification through his appearance in more conventional environments. He intentionally avoided known "bad" places where he might find the opportunity to "get into trouble" and where he surely would find the social imputation of deviance. Instead he began to associate with a more or less conventional group of people and to frequent conventional places. He "got involves with work."

[5]Parole may be considered an agency, but the reference to it by the respondents continually reflected its status as a place for felons rather than an agency for reforming exconvicts.

Beyond its mere economic effects, Bob's job was a place wherein he would be likely to be seen by others as normal and noncriminal.

> I was a cook in this restaurant in a small town. I enjoyed my work and the people I met were friendly. They saw me as a good cook, that's all.

Thus, through his appearance in the restaurant, Bob was able to achieve some degree of certification as a conventional person. His new associates and acquaintances did not know of his criminal past or present (he had skipped parole) and seeing him everyday "at work," they simply assumed that he was just like any other person in the community. That is, they imputed to Bob a normal social identity.

To further the process of certification Bob also acquired a car and a stable residence. Again these aspects of his daily life provided Bob with conventional surroundings. Driving his car to and from work, spending his nonwork time at his home, Bob became an accepted member of the community. It is extremely important to note the correctional paradox explicit in Bob's case. All these sources of certification might have been denied Bob if he had remained under parole supervision. However, by fleeing his parole (and thus violating the law) he was able to leave a deviant symbolic environment and adopt a new set of social places in the conventional world. As he acquired a new community, a conventional job, a car, and a home Bob was defined as normal. He had achieved certification. But, ironically, in order to accomplish all this, Bob was forced to violate the law once more. Finally, the parole violation caught up with Bob, and he was returned to prison.

Bob's case is an example of the flow of the process of certification when it is primarily assisted by the individual's appearance in conventional settings. Equally important to certification are the people whom one finds in such environments.

Certifying Others

Places are, of course, peopled by others as well as by the ex-offender. Most social settings are normatively defined as the proper locations for particular types of persons and activities. For instance, the post office is a place thought to be inhabited primarily by post office employees and their customers. The respondents indicated in the interviews that they felt that the people with whom they associated were extremely important for their eventual certification.

The single most important group of others for the changing ex-offender is his family. A conventional family, newly formed or renewed, provided the individual with a significant group of close associates that could overtly testify to his noncriminality and trustworthiness. The importance of the family for exiting from crime was continually mentioned during the interviews. For example,

> They made me feel that I was doing right. I looked good while I was with them, living at home. And I stayed out of it for two years, with my family.
>
> I got tired of the life, so I went back home. There I had a place to stay and people accepted me for myself. I was doing my best.

A family gives the changing ex-offender both a place that is recognized as conventional and others who announce to the public world that the family member has changed and is now to be considered noncriminal.

> It's very important, it keeps society from looking down on you. If you married and got kids, they think: "Well, he's rehabilitated. He's married and settled down, not wild anymore." Some people use it as a front, for others like me it ain't no cover-up.

Of course, kin also present the ex-felon with much practical assistance, including job opportunities, financial loans, and simply "a place to start off from." Emotionally, families provide individuals with a sense of belonging, of being at home in the conventional world. Within his family the ex-felon is able to at least partially overcome his feelings of strangeness as he confronts the conventional world. By caring for him his kin create relational ties that are most important during the trials of exiting. These ties in turn represent an investment in conformity that works to keep the ex-offender "straight." The family, then, is defined as one of the primary rewards of settling down (Meisenhelder, 1977).

> The last nine months of my life, being with my wife and my son and doing the things that normal people do is actually, seriously, have been the most important months of my life.

Besides these very important contributions to exiting, the family also provides the changing ex-offender with an effective means of self-presentation in order to achieve certification. Through his presence within a conventional family group, the individual announces that he is normal. At home and at ease in this most fundamental of social institutions, the ex-offender is seen by nonfamilial others as one to whom normality and respectability may be reasonably imputed (see Ball, 1970). The ex-felon's family members testify that he can be trusted and that he is not a dangerous person.

Nonfamilial associates also help to certify the individual's reform. Many of the respondents indicated the importance of carefully selecting one's friends and companions. Bad associates lead to the social imputation of personal deviance. On the other hand, conventional associates create an impression of conventionality. Recognizing this common practice, many of the respondents attempted to steer clear of "bad crowds."

> I quit hanging around with bad crowds, that helped me. Police and folks didn't look at me the way they used to. If you hang around with a bad crowd, they would follow you more.

> I always made it my business to try and get away from those kind of people. I wouldn't come in contact with those that look bad whatsoever.

By avoiding bad persons and by cultivating relationships with conventional people at work and at home, the changing offender presents himself as a noncriminal. By their acceptance of him, conventional acquaintances certify that the ex-felon can be considered a conforming member of the community.

Scott Scott is a middle-aged white male whose varied career in crime includes theft, automobile theft, and check passing. Prior to his most successful change he was deeply involved in "checks." Scott experienced a 3-year disengagement from crime that ended with incarceration for auto theft and parole violation. His change experience provides a nice example of certification through others.

Scott decided to "get out of the life" because he was tired of "being on the run," a frequently noted hazard of check writing as an occupation. Passing checks forces the criminal into a very mobile existence, and Scott grew tired of this type of existence:

> This was a time when I just got exhausted and said, "This ain't worth it." I just up and quit, tore up my check book.

He then went to a small town where he was "not known at all" and attempted to establish a normal life. In the process of doing so, Scott was able to get a job at a service station, and, importantly, he established a meaningful relationship with a woman and her child. He related this experience:

> I met a girl there that I became very interested in, her and her child. I decided to stay there, settle down with her. I was interested in her. She was something that I wanted to hold on to.

After he settled down in this family and became known in the area, Scott says that he began to feel accepted by the local community. People who knew him only as the new mate of "June" began to show that they trusted him with their friendship and with more material signs of acceptance. One such person loaned Scott a considerable sum of cash, and Scott's reaction to this event reveals that, to him, it was a meaningful sign of admission to the conventional world:

> He entrusted me with that money. I could have just took that money and gone, I didn't. And by doing that it let me know *I was accepted for what I was.*

In short, by being seen around the community with his new girlfriend, a lifelong resident, Scott too received trust and acceptance from his new neighbors. Further, his own perception of these reactions from others led him to believe that he was no longer judged to be a criminal. The reactions of others, then, certified Scott's change. This is reflected in the comments below,

> I met some pretty nice people in that town. My wife's friends and all, and they went out of their way to make me feel at home. That was a place, a nice place to live, nice people. If I hadn't been violated, I'd still be working and living there.

Obviously, Scott felt that he succeeded in becoming an accepted member of a conventional community. His own recognition of the trusting reactions of others led him to believe in his own change and further pushed him along the path of exiting from crime. Here certification was clearly the result of relationships with conventional others.

SUMMARY

In the preceding sections of the paper, the process of certification was reviewed by holding the tools or means of achieving certification analytically separate. In actuality, of course, some combination of places, others, and to a lesser extent agencies is evident in the total process. The ex-offender's continuing presence in conventional places and with conventional others forms an imputational process similar to that which Lofland

(1969) has termed an "informal elevation ceremony" (p. 227). Such ceremonies made up of the behavioral evidence that testifies to the conventionality of the ex-felon lead more and more people to categorize him as a conventional societal member. Having been seen with a "good job," a "fine family," and "respectable friends," the individual is presumed to be someone who can be trusted, someone,

> who is normal, who upholds social order and is deserving of order-maintaining and sustaining gestures of worth-acknowledgement from like-minded persons in society. (Ball, 1970:339)

At this point, then, exiting is at least temporarily complete. The actor's self is consistently conventional, and he has developed a pattern of behavior and a style of life that, for the time being, are noncriminal.

Thus, certification is the final contingency in the abandonment of criminal behavior. Now the individual's social and personal identities join into a consistent sense of the self as noncriminal. The actor sees himself as normal and feels that others see him in the same fashion. However, it must be noted that certification is a process and as such is changeable and impermanent. Remission remains a possibility:

> Its a habit, like smoking. I thought I had it beat that one time. I was doing pretty good; got into a job that I loved doing, had a family, people began to accept me for myself, staying out of trouble. I thought I had it beat. I stayed out for one year and three months. Had a divorce, lost my job, easiest thing for me to do was go back to my old habits. What I knew best, what I knew how to do.

CONCLUSIONS

Deviance is a social phenomenon involving both the deviant and his or her contemporaries. As Becker (1963) has declared, "deviant behavior is behavior that people so label" (p. 9). Likewise, conventionality is a social phenomenon that involves societal reactions. This paper has explored certification as the process by which people label ex-offenders as normal. It is an informal process of reality construction that results in the acceptance of the ex-felon as one who can be trusted. Certification revolves around the dual self of the actor and the use of others, places, agencies, and activities as means of self-presentation. These results in a sense confirm Davis' (1961) earlier conclusions concerning "deviance disavowal" among the visibly handicapped by revealing a similar process in the career of criminals. Certification is a way in which the stigmatized ex-offender attempts to resist a societal imputation of essential deviance and to deny that he is anything but a conventional person. The ex-felon, too, may be granted "fictional acceptance" at the onset of social encounters (Davis, 1961:126). He also uses settings, activities, and particularly others to encourage the other to identify with him through role-taking and thereby legitimate the ex-offender's noncriminal identity. Finally, like the visibly handicapped person (Davis, 1961:130–131), the ex-felon must sustain these normal relationships over some extended period. These parallels in the cases of two very different (ascribed versus achieved, for instance) kinds of deviant statuses and their normalization seem to lend support to the generalizability of the labeling position's emphasis on the interactional nature of social deviance. Any social reality is bounded by horizons of more or less open possibility. Through the process of certification, the individual has relegated criminality to the fringes of his life-world, but it does exist there as well as in his personal biography. Thus, criminal behavior remains, as it does for us all, a possibility.

REFERENCES

Ball, Donald W.
1970 "The problematics of respectability." Pp. 326–371 in Jack Douglas (ed.), Deviance and Respectability. New York: Basic Books.

Becker, Howard
1963 Outsiders. New York: Free Press.
1964 "Personal change in adult life." Sociometry 27:40–53.

Berger, Peter, and Thomas Luckmann
1968 The Social Construction of Reality. Garden City: Doubleday.

Brim, Orville, and Stanton Wheeler
1966 Socialization After Childhood. New York: Wiley.

Davis, Fred
1961 "Deviance disavowal." Social Problems 9:120–132.

Goffman, Erving
1959 The Presentation of Self in Everyday Life. Garden City: Doubleday.

Hawkins, Richard, and Gary Tiedeman
1975 The Creation of Deviance. Columbus: Charles Merrill.

Irwin, John
1970 The Felon. Englewood Cliffs: Prentice-Hall.

Laing, R. D., H. Phillipson, and A. R. Lee
1966 Interpersonal Perception. New York: Harper & Row.

Lofland, John
1969 Deviance and Identity. Englewood Cliffs: Prentice-Hall.

Matza, David
1969 Becoming Deviant. Englewood Cliffs: Prentice-Hall.

Meisenhelder, Thomas
1977 "An exploratory study of exiting from criminal careers." Criminology 15:319–334.
Schutz, Alfred
1962 Collected Papers I. The Hague: Nijhoff.
Weber, Max
1958 The Protestant Ethic and The Spirit of Capitalism. New York: Scribner's.

Reading 39

Deviance without Deviants: The Temporal Quality of Patterned Behavior

Edward Sagarin
City College of City University of New York

Social scientists oriented toward labeling have argued that there are unfortunate consequences, in the form of self-fulfilling prophesies or secondary deviance, of placing people into a deviant category and giving them the label associated with that grouping. This paper proposes that such a process of categorization is inaccurate because it transforms activity into identity. Identity suggests permanence, whereas activity suggests voluntarism, responsibility, and the labile nature of human conduct. Deviance without deviants would stress the impermanence of patterns of behavior, even though they be patterns, and the potential of all persons to go in all directions.

As one who has written a book called *Deviants and Deviance* (Sagarin, 1975), which title was meant to imply that these are two separate but clearly interrelated phenomena, the people on the one hand, the behavior on the other, I now find myself increasingly veering toward the position that the concept of deviants should be abandoned in favor of that of deviance. This

This is one of a series of working papers that the author has been writing on deviance and the confusion between doing and being. The others include: "The tyranny of isness." Pp. 144–154 in Deviants and Deviance: An Introduction to the Study of Disvalued People and Behavior. New York: Praeger-Holt, 1975; "The high personal cost of wearing a label." Psychology Today. 9:25-31, March 1976; "Doing, being, and the tyranny of the label." et cetera. 34:71–77, March 1977; and several unpublished papers: "Judicial power and the tyranny of the label," "The tyranny of isness: A limited theory of deviance and its specific application to sexuality." A paper on transsexualism, briefly touching on the problem of being and doing but mainly concerned with other related issues, written by myself, appears in C. Winick, (ed.), Deviance and the Mass media. Beverly Hills, Calif.: Sage Publications, 1979.

position, in some ways not unlike that of the labeling people with whom I am otherwise in sharp disagreement, is based on the proposition that there are unfortunate consequences, both in social science and for social policy, when people are called deviants, or for that matter when they are called by the labels that could constitute a sort of subgroup, on a lower level of abstraction: prostitutes, transvestites, transsexuals, burglars, rapists, murderers, retardates, or whatever other category is under discussion.

Would it be meaningful and helpful, one might ask, to put forth, on this lower level of abstraction, the notion of drug addiction without drug addicts? What could possibly be meant by such a formulation? A colleague writes to me: "If a man has a heroin habit, if he has had his daily dose of heroin for a year or more, if he has psychological and physiological dependence, if he constantly requires greater amounts in order to satisfy his cravings, if he starts to feel severe withdrawal symptoms when he does not obtain his fix—in short, if he has an addiction, then surely he is an addict. In fact, is not the term *addict* when used here both accurate and necessary for proper communication about him? Is it not useful in order to alert the individual himself and all those around him of certain information that is summarized by the single word, *addict*?"

I suggest that in this instance it is neither useful nor necessary, although not as harmful as in other cases, and that the accuracy is not quite as self-evident as the correspondent would have it. In place of speaking of the drug addict, we (social scientists and public at large) should be talking of people who take drugs, have a craving for drugs, have a dependency on drugs, or whatever accurate description can capture the actions and patterns of the individual. When it is said that he takes drugs, rather than that he is an addict, several sharp distinctions are implied: that this is a matter of doing and not being, that although he takes drugs he does many other things, and that if he fits into a preconceived or even an empirically validated mental image, it is the image of action (the taking) rather than of a class of people (the addicts). In this vision, there is addiction, but there are no addicts.

Now, from this, let us generalize: there are no deviants, there are only people who pursue a line of conduct, or who have inner desires to pursue that line of conduct, which is deviant by definition of what constitutes deviance; that is, it is stigmatized by society, reacted to in a negative manner, and is disvalued and held in low repute. Unlike the labeling group, that seeks to shift the attention from the actor to the condemnatory and stigmatizing public or audience, I propose to shift it from the deviant actor to the deviant action, but only within certain limits that I shall examine here. Again in contrast to the labeling orientation, that makes this shift to exculpate the deviant actor, I find that the shift as proposed here places upon the deviant actor greater responsibility for his behavior.

There are several major problems that are confronted when the language, and hence the conceptualization that both reflects and influences the language, veers attention from the conduct to the performer. These include but are not limited to the following:

1 The individuals are reduced from whole beings to a specific status, which is a dehumanizing process in the sense that they are not seen as whole human beings, but as a status that stands for the entire person.

2 In the study of deviance, the specific status that is singled out is by definition a negative one, and since it replaces the full person with one status, it throws an aura of disrepute or disvaluation around the individual as a whole.[1]

3 The reference to the specific status as synonymous with the individual tends to make that into a master status, dominating how one is seen in other aspects of life, and how one sees oneself in relation to other activities.[2]

4 The status becomes confused with an identity in the way that an activity cannot, and as such the identity tends to take on an aspect of continuity, and to lose its sense of potential transience and temporarity.

THE INDIVIDUAL AS MANY STATUSES AND ONE

People conduct themselves in innumerable different ways, during the daily round of activities, and during a period of years. Most of these activities are probably mutually supportive, or at least compatible with one another, and they can be handled over the same period of time without difficulty. "Over the same period of time" does not necessarily mean simultaneously: one cannot simultaneously, in the sense of exactly at the same moment, be an ice skater and an airline pilot, but these and numerous other activities can be carried on at different times over the same period of time, without necessarily involving the person in status conflicts.

In a single day, a young man may go to school, ride an automobile, walk along the street, earn some money on the job, buy something that his mother asked him to pick up for her while in a downtown area, bring it home to her, and then go out to meet his girlfriend. To name the statuses explicit and implicit in this short but extremely abbreviated description of one day in the life of one person would only skim the surface, yet many are

[1]This is inherent in the definition of deviance as used by most sociologists. For deviant behavior, rather than deviance as a state, I find the definition of Schur (1971) very useful: "Human behavior is deviant *to the extent that* it comes to be viewed as involving a *personally discreditable* departure from a group's normative expectations, *and* it *elicits* interpersonal or collective reactions that serve to 'isolate,' 'treat,' 'correct,' or 'punish' *individuals* engaged in such behavior" (emphasis in original).

[2]The concept of the madster status comes from Everett C. Hughes, (1945). It was applied to deviance by Howard S. Becker, (1963, pp. 33–34).

there: he is a male, student, autoist, pedestrian, worker, customer, son, boyfriend. Implicitly, he may be described by race and national origin, by citizenship, residence, age, religion, political belief or affiliation, hobbies, fanaticisms, enthusiasms, dislikes, and sexual orientation. Thus, if we were to examine this person, we might add such other statuses as white, Irish-American, youth, Catholic, liberal, chess player, Yankee fan, jazz enthusiast, antiwar fighter, and heterosexual.

Some of these are ascribed statuses over which he has no control: white, male, Irish-American, and if one chooses to use religion as related to birth rather than to belief, Catholic. Others are statuses that are transient in the sense that they cease to exist when one is not performing them: pedestrian and autoist. Others will outlive their day as a status and be discarded, willingly or otherwise: student and youth. Some statuses are less easy to categorize into types or classes, and depend upon the given situation, the context, the tacitly understood meanings. If the youth plays chess with some degree of frequency, interest, and skill, it would be accurate to say that he has the status of and can be described as a chess player, even when he is not in the act of playing a game (unlike the pedestrian, who ceases to be that when he is not engaged in walking, crossing the street, or standing still waiting for a light to change). But here an ambiguity arises, illustrated if one points to two men. The first is sitting, staring at a chess board, face to face with his opponent. You ask who he is, and an obvious answer would be: He is a chess player. But what that means is that chess playing is what he is doing, not what he is or "is being." Another man is sitting at a bar, drinking beer, talking to some friends, and you pose the same question and are given the same answer. But the meaning is different. The two answers refer to activity rather than being, but the first refers to the action at a specific moment, the second to the action that takes place with sufficient regularity, frequency, enjoyment, and skill to gain the descriptive terminology.

Thus, status seems to have at least two different meanings, in addition to the classic division into ascribed and achieved: it refers to what one is doing while doing it, and it also refers to what one does with sufficient regularity to have it known that one does it. However, in the case of deviance, the complexities grow, as do the ambiguities, and the term thief, for instance, may refer not only to what one is doing at a given time (an unlikely usage), what one does with some regularity, but also what one has done at any one time, even though this is not a pattern and the doing has been abandoned.

Inasmuch as all of these are real statuses, it can become misleading, under certain conditions, and have negative connotations for life chances, under the same or other conditions, when the individual is equated with the status. On the contrary, the status replacing the entire person may enhance that individual, as when one speaks of a person as a youth or a physician.

Under other conditions, and this is particularly true of deviance, the synechdoche resulting from the substitution of the partial (status) for the whole (person), serves to reduce human beings into one partial and unfavorably evaluated aspect of their humanity. Although people are not dehumanized by being called white, male, or professor, someone is clearly reduced to a portion of self by being called a black or a woman, in the sense that it tends to engulf the entire person into one aspect of that individual's being. Furthermore, these terms are often used descriptively in an irrelevant manner that does not refer specifically to activities in the capacity of being black or woman, but rather to conceal all else about a person. So long as one went to a dentist, a woman dentist, or a black dentist, but never to a white dentist or a male dentist because these were implicit within the term "dentist," woman and black were synechdoches in which a part stood for the entirety, effacing or concealing the remainder. When this happens to an individual who is a Yankee fan or a student, it can have little ill effect, except under the most unusual circumstances. If it happens to him because he is an atheist, an ex-convict, a drug addict, or a homosexual, the depersonalization takes place by reducing him to a negatively viewed status.

Yet, these are not "pure" examples, and I am avoiding pure ones in order not to simplify but to grasp the diversity and complexity of the issues. Atheist in a highly secular society is often not branded with extreme negativism; it might depend on whether the individual is very militant, is obtrusive, and argues that religious institutions are not only based on wrong dogma, but are very bad for society as well. The label of ex-convict is stigmatizing by and large, but the man who made good after having fallen might be a hero for having risen so high; also, he might have been a political prisoner, who comes out of prison proud of his record. The drug addict may be seen with a great deal of sympathy because of the way that he can handle this aspect of his life, or the stigma may be reduced by his baring his breast to youth and warning them of their dire fate if they follow in his footsteps. The homosexual label may be one whose negative connotations are rejected by the involved individuals and significant others around them; these persons may point a finger or thumb the nose at society in an accusatory manner for having had fingers pointed at them.

THE WHOLE PERSON AS COPOUT

It might seem from this that the shift of emphasis from one status to the person as a collection of innumerable statuses would give a more accurate image of the individual. On the other hand, it can be used to conceal a deviant activity of such enormity that it deserves central place in the evaluation of that person by members of society. These are instances in which the activity is sufficiently significant in evaluating the life of the performer that, to focus on the numerous normative behaviors that he indulges in, on the innumerable ordinary statuses that he has, would be only a ruse to lead people away from seeing the life as it is.

Thus, it is not quite convincing when people point out that an organized crime figure is also a good parent, a fine provider, a polite customer at a store, a careful driver, a generous contributor to charities, a faithful member of a parish or a congregation, and spends a predominant amount of time in pursuits no different than that of the most law-abiding citizen. It is partialling the person to have him known as, and known only as, an organized crime figure, but when this is put into full context with his other activities and statuses, he still emerges as someone who is a menace to society. The concept of how he spends "most of his time" is likewise misleading, for if one spends five minutes during an entire year committing a murder or ordering that it be done, this cannot be measured as only one/one hundred thousandth of one's time. Surely the same can be said of one who commits rape and other serious activities, the extreme antisocial nature of which is not in dispute.

DEVIANT STATUS AS IDENTITY AND CONTINUITY

The question has often been raised, and it is done most brilliantly in a book by Mordechai Rotenberg (1978), as to why people persist in activities that are not gratifying to them and that indubitably hurt their life chances.

In the utilitarian view, and particularly that of the Benthamites, there is a pleasure-pain calculus going on, the brain of the participant making a rapid, sometimes incorrect (and later on the Freudians would add, no doubt largely unconscious) advance calculation of the potential gain as against the potential hurt to self, the chances of each alternative turning into reality, and the actor would commit the forbidden act when the scales seemed to work out in favor of anticipated pleasure as against anticipated pain (gain as against self-hurt) (Geis, 1972). The pleasure-pain theory has been argued by criminologists for over a century, and it would serve no purpose in this paper to review that argument, except to say that it does not satisfactorily answer the questions that it poses. For one thing, the utilitarian vision of the human being is that of an incredibly rational person. For another, it omits from consideration the degree that exists in the society, and that has been internalized within the individual, of a feeling of social cohesion or alienation, respect or disrespect for law and for authority, and other factors.[3] Finally, it appears that some persons will receive pleasure from knowing that they have hurt others, and some are pained by the same realization: for example, the rapist brutally beats a victim, and another rapist apologizes after concluding the forcible rape. What evolves is a complex picture of the human actor in which the pleasure-pain calculus loses most of its significance and explanatory power.

Learning theorists take the concept of the pleasure-pain calculus, and add to it a new dimension: reinforcement or aversion through the pleasure obtained or the pain suffered, rather than a calculation of the probability of what will be gained or suffered in the future.[4] People are reinforced in patterns that give them pleasure, and there is a negative reinforcement (or aversion) when the activity gives them pain. The peculiar thing about this approach is that it can explain normative behavior so much better than criminal or deviant behavior. Punished children do not invariably abandon the activities that had led to the punishment; sometimes, in fact, they continue them, escalating them in seriousness and frequency, as an expression of anger and defiance. The person comes out of prison and goes back to his old ways, despite the suffering that the prison has caused him, and while this may sometimes be traced to lack of job opportunities, there are other instances in which prison has not been aversive.

Many, although not all, alcoholics, drug addicts, pedophiles, homosexuals, tell of their sufferings, and yet they return to repeat their pain-producing behavior. Some people go through several marriages, or even more couplings without benefit of clergy or state, making the same mistakes, suffering the same unhappiness, and learning theory notwithstanding, they appear to have learned nothing from their experiences.

To call these and other people "psychic masochists" who receive their pleasure from suffering pain is to answer nothing, and in fact serves primarily to make the learning theory into a catch-all that does little more than make a tautological statement: the repeated behavior must have given pleasure (for otherwise it would not have been repeated), and hence pleasure is the cause of the repetition.

Rotenberg joins a number of individuals who believe that some continuity in a deviant life pattern may be traceable to the sense of resignation that one feels, the sense of doom, the belief that escape from a pattern is blocked. On some prisoners, one will find the tattoo: "Born to lose." In a skillful manner that deserves the attention of all persons interested in the intricacies of human behavior, Rotenberg contends that the "born to lose"

[3]Some of these factors are prominent in the well-known theory of differential association (Sutherland and Cressey, 1966).

[4]The best elucidation and defense of learning theory as applied to deviance is found in Akers (1973).

syndrome can be traced to the Calvinism that imbued the Protestant ethic. Calvinism promulgated the thesis that people were chosen or damned from the moment of birth, and that if damned, nothing that they might do would overcome the emotional and mental difficulties, the self-defeating behavioral patterns. Such people are made to feel that they must walk eternally in the dark shadows on the periphery of the good society, and that they will be rescued from this fate only by death that snatches them and carries them off to an eternal hell. If doomed, one is unlikely to have faith in an ability to change, and without faith in that ability, one is unlikely to make the effort. Labeled by others, placed in a category from which escape hatches are absent, the individual comes to accept the label and with it renounces any effort to achieve success in reaching another category.

Although brilliantly conceived, the Rotenberg thesis on the Protestant ethic does not quite hold up under cross-cultural analysis (and here Rotenberg may take umbrage by the knowledge that he is being placed in the same company with an illustrious predecessor Max Weber). The idea of doom has certainly been as strong in the largely Catholic as in the largely Protestant countries, and if the United States is singled out as the ideal land where the Calvinist ethic came closest to being incorporated into the spirit of the people, particularly among the early colonists and in the first years after the establishment of the Republic, it is also true that America was the land where psychotherapy took strongest hold, and more people made an effort to change their life patterns by seeking all types of counseling and assistance. If France and Italy lacked the Calvinist influence and the Protestant ethic, they also lacked any large and serious psychotherapy movements. If efforts to change were made at all in those countries, it was in the hope that it would be achieved through a miracle, and Calvinism left little room for such a miracle, because nothing could be done to overcome damnation.

But what Rotenberg has pinpointed, and although not the first he is one of the outstanding in the insights that he brings to the task, is that self-labeling, when accompanied by a belief in destiny, is a self-fulfilling prophecy. The failure comes about by reason of the belief in the failure. The source of this belief may indeed be in religion (although it is shared by people of all religions, an indicator of the well-known proposition that the Protestant ethic extends far beyond Protestant boundaries), but this belief in failure may have other sources. It may come from the belief, whether true or false, that the deviance is inborn, is an inherent part of the self, genetic, biological, and hence inescapable. I should like to suggest that it both comes from, and results in, linguistic confusion with regard to statuses.

ANOTHER COMPLICATION: BEHAVIOR AND FEELING

Earlier, mention was made of a few disvalued (hence deviant) statuses: atheist, ex-convict, drug addict, homosexual. Now, a new complicating element arises, namely that these can involve beliefs, feelings, or behavior, and they can involve combinations of two or three of the triad.[5] Atheism is a belief, and may or may not be translated into behavior; if not, it remains secret (for behavior includes linguistic), but would not qualify for description as secret deviance, in the sense that undetected arson would. One can make a decision as to whether or not to translate one's beliefs into activities, but if not transformed, they remain nothing but a state of mind, and take no psychological or other toll of the person who fears that a life of masks will fall apart as hitherto secret aspects are disclosed. The ex-convict on one level is a biographical fact of life, part of one's history, and thus, under the principle of the moving finger, the status is immutable. No one would seriously contend that a man can cease being an ex-convict, but only that he can conceal it or make it known, that it might be made known though he sought to conceal it, or that he can cease the course of action that led to his becoming a convict in the first instance (unless he was a completely innocent person, falsely accused and falsely convicted). The drug addict involves purely behavior, but no matter how free an individual was when he voluntarily began to take drugs, the concept of biological addiction is one that denies the full freedom of choice, setting limits upon it. In the last of the four examples, homosexuality, one is dealing with an intertwining of feelings and behavior. While it is beyond serious dispute that to engage in homosexual or heterosexual behavior is conduct that an individual can decide to do or not to do, the same decision-making process is not present in the inner feelings. Inasmuch as these feelings may be the primary force leading to the behavior, one can no longer say, as assuredly as one does in discussing the autoist, the student, or the thief, that these are statuses that have reference to doing, and not being. Homosexuality, heterosexuality, and an entire group of other sexual patterns (transvestism, transsexualism, pedophilia, and so one could continue) are behaviors usually preceded by the inner need, urge, desire, or demand. If a person has such an inner urge, then the translation of the status into an identity, or the doing into a being, might appear to be accurate, although such a transformation would still be undesirable insofar as it reduces a person to a fraction of himself.

It is here that Rotenberg's thesis (with or without the relationship of the spirit of failure to the Protestant ethic, whatever you may prefer) is valuable. It is obvious that, when one does something, one can decide to cease

[5]The word "feelings" summarizes all that comes from within, urge, arousal, inner demand; I borrow the word from Bell and Weinberg (1978).

doing it, although carrying out such a decision is by no means simple. The fact that others come to expect and suspect the same action, that alternative roads are closed, may make the decision to cease a difficult one, but it is still a free choice to be made. However, when the feeling or desire appears to come from within, and the behavior is merely its acting out, then only a decision that the feeling is destiny, is immutable, whether it be the road of the elect to heaven or of the damned to hell, would transform, in the mind of the subject and of significant others, such a status (the status of one who has such feelings) into being, essence, or identity.

Deviants are then faced with a dilemma of their own making. If they claim that the feelings arose spontaneously and are beyond their control, they then relinquish any semblance of free choice, admit to being a captive of an unconsciousness that may or may not be to their liking, and their defenses of identity become *ex post facto* justifications. If they claim that the feelings are those that they wish to have and would have chosen had there been a free choice, they must take responsibility for and explain the rationale of making a choice contrary to the advantages offered by an alternate path. It may be argued that the same is true of those who feelings lead them into normative directions; absent any indication of an instinct toward consenting adult heterosexual relationships, the same argument holds that it is more meaningful to speak of a person who has heterosexual feelings and does heterosexual things, rather than of being a heterosexual. The differences should not be overlooked, in that a false labeling of an individual as being heterosexual does not have the same effects as the corresponding error in terming a person a pedophile or a transvestite, for example.

The sense of helplessness and hopelessness surrounding people locked into certain deviant identities may well be derived from, or fortified by, the implicit connotation that some statuses constitute essence or *is*ness, rather than behavior or feeling. Those who *do* should be studied, but should be conceptualized as actors. Deviance without deviants would stress the non-permanence of human behavior, the potential of all persons to go in all directions, the responsibility of individuals for the directions in which they seek to move. Those persons would still be subject to study, and in certain instances, to formal or informal social control. They would not be conceptualized as deviants, but as persons who, among other things, do acts or have feelings that are disvalued in the society.

REFERENCES

Akers, Ronald L.
1973 Deviant Behavior: A Social Learning Approach. Belmont, Calif.: Wadsworth.

Becker, Howard S.
1963 Outsiders: Studies in the Sociology of Deviance. New York: Free Press.

Bell, Alan P., and Martin S. Weinberg
1978 Homosexualities: A Study of Diversity among Men and Women. New York: Simon and Schuster.

Geis, Gilbert
1972 "Jeremy Bentham (1748–1832)." Pp. 51–58 in Hermann Mannheim (ed.), Pioneers in Criminology, 2nd ed. Montclair, N.J.: Patterson Smith.

Hughes, Everett C.
1945 "Dilemmas and contradictions of status." American Journal of Sociology 50: 353–359.

Rotenberg, Mordechai
1978 Damnation and Deviance: The Protestant Ethic and the Spirit of Failure. New York: Free Press.

Sagarin, Edward
1975 Deviants and Deviance. New York: Praeger.

Schur, Edwin M.
1971 Labeling Deviant Behavior: Its Sociological Implications. New York: Harper & Row.

Sutherland, Edwin H., and Donald R. Cressey
1966 Principles of Criminology, 7th ed. Philadelphia: Lippincott.

Part Six

The Future of Deviance: Prospects and Prognosis

Chapter Twelve

Deviance over the Horizon

There is a certain predictability about deviance that almost equals that of death and taxes! Deviance is, operationally speaking, rule-breaking, and as long as there are social rules, there will likely be instances of rule-breaking. A deviance-free society is a most unlikely conceptualization inasmuch as it would necessarily involve one of two scenarios. The first scenario would entail an absence of rules—norms and laws—with complete freedom of behavioral prerogative. Such a society would be anarchistic and chaotic, with nightmarish economic, political, and social implications. Social life in this type of context would be reduced to little more than a struggle for individual or small group survival as illustrated in a very small way by social conditions during the "Dark Ages."

In the second scenario, there is a total observance of all rules. Such a view would also include a mechanistic-type world with a robotic-like population, a society of human automatons, as it were, with all members moving and behaving in perfect synchronization and in a completely harmonious and scripted fashion. This type of society would lack spontaneity and individualism and would, accordingly, be without direction or leadership. It would lack ingenuity and innovativeness and would, therefore, be without progress. And it would lack purpose and will and would, thus, lack motivation and momentum. Both scenarios are highly improbable, if not impossible in their inherent unworkability. The prediction of the persistence of deviant behavior in the future is, therefore, relatively easy and reliable.

THE IMMEDIATE PAST POINTS TO THE FUTURE: OLD WINE IN NEW BOTTLES

The nature of deviance in the future, however, may vary somewhat from today. On the basis of past events, contemporary occurrences, possible future exigencies, and ongoing social predilections, certain future trends and tendencies in regard to deviant behavior are, perhaps, also predictable. First, the social awareness and perception of deviant behavior will be subject to change. New forms of deviance and crime will be "discovered." For a variety of reasons, some types of norm violations may go unnoticed or ignored for long periods of time, even centuries. Business fraud has been the object of social proscription since the time of Hammurabi, but business crime or crime in the office was essentially overlooked or disregarded until Edwin H. Sutherland, in his Presidential address to the American Sociological Society in 1939 brought "white-collar crime" to the attention of social scientists (1940). Today, of course, such criminal activities are household words, and much social concern and energy is directed at white-collar crime in terms of its understanding, and its control and prevention.

After social scientists (and subsequently the public) were sensitized to the existence of white-collar crime, the way was paved for the "discovery" of other types of previously unnoticed or unnoted crime, all of which had existed in various degrees and contexts throughout much of history. Sociologists subsequently identified "blue-collar crime" (Horning, 1970), "blue-coat crime" (Stoddard, 1968; see also Westley, 1953; Petersen, 1971), and "khaki-collar crime" (Bryant, 1979). Although piracy and other sea-related, criminal patterns predate civilization, it was only in recent years that some sociologists have identified ocean-connected or "briney crime" (Bryant and Shoemaker, 1975; Adler, 1987) as a separate and unique configuration of deviant or illegal activity. A number of other "new" or "neglected" patterns of crime have also been "discovered" or newly conceptualized, including rural crime (Carter, et al., 1982) and "zoological crime" (Bryant and Palmer, 1976), to mention two. In the instance of the former, the much increased incidence of criminal offenses occurring in geographic areas hitherto thought to be essentially crime-free led to a highly vocal calling of attention to this phenomenon by a number of sociologists. In the case of the latter, new public and governmental concern with ecology, the environment, and imperiled flora and fauna, not to mention a new public concern with the care and treatment of animals, gave rise to a wide variety of laws and regulations that addressed animals (and plants and other natural resources, as well) in some way. Many traditional patterns of human behavior toward animals were now prohibited and, thus, illegal acts. The cumulative impact of such new legislation resulted in an essentially new form of crime.

Other instances of newly "discovered" crime and deviance might include child "battering." Until a few years back, the notion of severely beating a child resulting in serious injury or death was almost unthinkable, and the public was generally unaware of how widespread was such a phenomenon. Children with injuries were frequently brought to hospitals and clinics, but usually there was the parental explanation that the injury resulted from an accident. In the 1960s some hospitals began to routinely X-ray children brought in for such injuries and it was revealed that many of these injured children had sustained previous injuries—sometimes numerous injuries—in the past as evidenced by broken and fractured bones that had healed or from internal scar tissue. This led to research that provided a fuller picture of the extent and seriousness of the problem (DeFrancis, 1963; see also Helfer and Kempe, 1968). The public became aware of the "battered child syndrome" and the subsequent concern and outrage brought about national efforts to better monitor the cause of childhood injuries and, hopefully, reduce the incidence of "battered" children (for a detailed account of the emergent social awareness of this type of deviant behavior, see Taylor, 1971).

Similarly, other types of related deviance were late to be recognized, in terms of their full extent, by social scientists and the public. The sexual abuse of children (see Pfohl, 1977) and spouse abuse (Gelles, 1974) especially as they occurred across the population spectrum are notable examples. Another illustration is that of incest, which prior to recent decades, was widely thought to be confined to isolated, degenerate rural families in the Ozarks or Appalachia. It was simply believed that such things did not occur in "nice" families. Once it was demonstrated that these types of deviant behavior did occur in families of all social classes, there was considerably more acceptance of assertions that they were, in fact, relatively widespread and not infrequent occurrences, although some of the claims of the actual incidence were not well documented, and may have been exaggerated in the interest of sensationalism (see for example, Butler, 1978; Forward and Buck, 1978). Nevertheless, once sensitized to the existence of childhood sexual abuse, and spouse abuse, the public came to recognize the seriousness of the problem and treat it accordingly. Some forms of crime, while considered serious by the public, took on special significance when publicized by advocacy groups. A case in point is rape, and especially rape by nonstrangers, which was forcefully presented by various feminist groups (Rose, 1977).

Some forms of crime and deviance, such as white-collar crime or wife beating, simply were not noticed or given appropriate attention because they were "hidden" or otherwise unobtrusive, others because they were not considered widespread or serious enough to represent a problem, and yet others because they were not really considered deviant. The toleration represented a kind of selective inattention based on the principle of "out of sight, out of mind." Thus, when attention was persuasively focused on them, they were "discovered" as "new" varieties of norm violation, or considered to be far more serious than had been previously thought.

The deviance "discoveries" of the past few decades strongly suggest a probable direction of scholarly interest in the future. Undoubtedly there will be similar new "discoveries" as students of deviance sift and examine the vagaries of human social behavior and accomplish to assemble their finding within new conceptual frameworks. With the development and perfection of new conceptual configurations, all scientific disciplines are capable of new perceptual horizons. It is possible to see many new things when new ways of looking are utilized. The years ahead will likely witness sharpened perceptions and different focuses on the part of social scientists with the resultant cognizance of hitherto unrecognized configurations of deviant behavior, and the identification of previously unnoted cause and effect linkages attending that deviance.

NEW AWARENESS, ALTERED PRIORITIES, AND FUTURE MANDATES

In regard to some kinds of "new" deviant behavior, it has been more a question of dramatic changes in public values and attitudes. One example is smoking. For centuries, smoking was considered to be an innocent, hedonistic activity. It was redolent of sophistication, adult maturity, and masculinity (and after the invention of the extra-long cigarette, liberated femininity), and was an acknowledged "crutch" or "prop" for poise. While taboo for children (it would "stunt their growth"), it was tacitly tolerated in adolescents, and seen as having only minimal physical health implications for adults, which were offset by presumed mental and social health benefits. After the Surgeon General's report, there was widespread recognition of the serious health threat that smoking represented and smoking began to take on more of the character of a socially disvalued activity. Many persons gave up smoking and those who continued were viewed at best as weak or "addicted," or not perceptive enough to recognize the true hazard and potential harm to which they were subjecting themselves. In time, the dangers of passive smoking were recognized and nonsmokers increasingly went on the offensive. Restrictions on smoking were demanded, and such rules were inaugurated in some areas, in certain contexts. Such demands have escalated with more and more restrictions on smoking in terms of where and when it is prohibited, and even, in some instances, with mandated requirements (or at least *very* strong encouragement) for certain categories of persons to cease and desist smoking, members of some organizations and military personnel, for example. Smoking has, in many ways, become a kind of deviant behavior (Markle and Troyer, 1979; see also Austin and Garner, 1980). There is little doubt that antismoking sentiment will continue to grow in the future, to the extent that cigarette manufacturing may be legislated out of existence, smoking may come to be seen as antisocial behavior equivalent to violence or crime in severity, and smoking may even be outlawed in all contexts. But of course, those addicted to cigarettes may continue to smoke in secrecy, inasmuch as tobacco can easily be grown, and a clandestine and criminal industry may grow up to supply an illicit demand. Where there is likely to be the fire of desire, there will also likely be smoke from smoking.

THE CYCLICAL NATURE OF DEVIANCE

In some instances, there has been a kind of cyclical or "faddish" quality to public attention and reaction to certain kinds of deviant behavior. One example might be that of narcotic addiction (Bryant, 1971:345–346). Prior to World War I, narcotic addiction in this country was quite widespread. Such narcotics as morphine, opium and marijuana were freely available and a significant number of persons used them on a regular basis. Many Chinese immigrants used opium as part of their cultural patterns. Many veterans of the Civil War relied on morphine to relieve the residual pain of old battle wounds or primitive surgery for those wounds that left them with lingering and often intense discomfort. Narcotics eased pain in the absence of competent medical care. Narcotics were used liberally for medicinal purposes during the Spanish American war and the wounded veterans of that conflict also used morphine to deal with their post-war discomfort. Morphine addiction became known as the "soldiers' disease." "Patent" medicines used by much of the population, and especially women, for chronic ailments were heavily laced with narcotics. The Harrison Act, passed in 1914, made narcotic addiction a criminal matter. At that point the addiction rate in this country had reached an all-time high of 1 in 400 persons. Yet, public concern with, and reaction to, narcotic addiction was not as severe as today. After the passage of the Harrison Act, the addiction rate fell steadily, reaching an all-time low of 1 in 10,000 population by the end of World War

II. The illegal distribution of narcotics continued to flourish, however. The illegal manufacture of drugs persisted. The illegal importation of drugs grew. Thefts of narcotics from hospitals, pharmacies, and even police evidence rooms began to occur. By the 1960's, the rate of addiction had risen to 1 in 4,000. Much of the drug supply came from South America, the Middle East, and Southeast Asia. Enforcement of the Harrison Act shortened the supply and drove up the price. Illegal traffic in drugs became enormously profitable and many addicts turned to crime to obtain money for their drugs. The rate of addiction today is significantly lower than 70 years ago, but today narcotic usage involves virtually all segments of the population, including even young children. The variety of drugs available is much greater than in the past and many of the narcotics being illegally sold are incredibly powerful and dangerous, and are capable of permanent brain damage, unbalancing the marginal psychotic, and even damage to the chromosomes. Public outrage is mounting and the "war on drugs" has become a major political issue in the presidential campaign. Society will no doubt take drastic steps to control narcotic use and we may likely see the decriminalization or legalization of some drugs, such as marijuana, in order to ameliorate the criminal distribution aspect of that drug use, and all that attends it. Other narcotics may be medicalized and made available to addicts under carefully controlled circumstances monitored by physicians, as a means of negating the criminal dimensions of the sale of those drugs. In the instance of other drugs, however, public attitudes will likely become even more adamant to the point that a maximum national effort, drawing on all law enforcement resources, including the military, will be mounted in an effort to eliminate the manufacture, importation, distribution, sale, and use of such drugs. Sanctions for the violation of drug laws will likely be made much more severe, and traditional legal and judicial restraints may be loosened considerably in order to obtain convictions. Just as with the forced internment of Japanese Americans in World War II, if the American public becomes sufficiently aroused, historical concerns for civil rights may be temporarily discarded.

It is, perhaps, in the area of sexual deviancy, that the evidence of cyclical or "faddish" public concern and reaction is most prominent. Several examples may suffice. In the not too distant past, prostitution was morally condemned and legally proscribed. It was, however, socially tolerated to some degree, at least tacitly. While morally repugnant, prostitution was seen as having residual, socially redeeming functionality. It was widely believed that "male lust" required a sexual outlet, and that in the absence of prostitution, sex crimes like rape, and depravity forced on "decent" women, would result. Prostitution, then, was seen as a necessary sexual escape valve, protecting the unmarried females of virtue and even, in some instances, the married woman from the excessive sexual demands of her husband. Even many small towns had their "clandestine" but also well known "cathouse" for the use of local males. Some such brothels were venerable masculine institutions in their communities and often attained regional and even national fame (or infamy, depending on one's point of view). The hit musical "The Best Little Whore House in Texas" (also made into a movie) was such an establishment. Most large cities housed a full array of prostitution facilities ranging from street "cribs" to elaborate brothels of genteel architecture and stunning decor. Shifts in theology, morality, medical epidemiology and social values may combine to bring about changes in public sentiment and formal sanctions. In the decades after World War I, tacit toleration for prostitution in small towns, and even in large cities in some parts of the country gave way to social indignation concerning prostitution, with a resulting legal "crackdown" and the removal of the offending brothels. Prostitution tended to persist, however, in many large cities, specifically in resort areas, and in towns near large military bases.

With the various waves of female emancipation and liberation, and the general trend toward sexual freedom and public enlightenment that occurred in the 1960s and 1970s, there was more of a tendency toward toleration of all things sexual, even prostitution. Prostitution tended to flourish in newer guises that were more unobtrusive than brothels, such as call girls, or in camouflaged contexts such as massage parlors. Employing the services of a prostitute, while technically illegal, came to be widely viewed as a "victimless crime" and something that should cause little social concern. In time, the physical saturation of massage parlors and similar establishments in many cities, plus the increasingly prominent presence of call girls and less discreet prostitutes in public places, such as hotels and bars, elicited a new wave of public censure and social retribution. In many communities, massage parlors were closed and prostitutes who were visibly plying their trade were arrested or chased out of town.

NEW EXIGENCIES AND THE NORMATIVE ORDER

The appearance of AIDS, with its deathly implications, has significantly altered the public perspective of prostitution. Given the epidemiological potential for prostitutes spreading the disease in an exponential fashion, it is highly unlikely that society will entertain any toleration of prostitution in the future. Prostitutes may well be treated quite harshly as will likely their customers. Society will not be able to permit prostitution because of the enormous health hazard that it will constitute, although law enforcement efforts may well concentrate more on the clientele of prostitutes than the prostitutes. If customers are routinely arrested and hauled into court and prosecuted, this will likely prove to be a very effective deterrent for prostitution.

Almost all forms of sexual deviance have elicited a cyclical type of societal reactions. Throughout history, there have been cyclical periods of sexual repression and very strong attempts to control sexual expression along with severe sanctions for violations of sexual proscriptions. Such times have not infrequently been followed by periods when there was a much more relaxed, permissive, and tolerant societal posture toward sexual activity, even to the extent of near carnal license in some instances. In the nineteenth century in England and America there was the strongest type of social proscription against homosexual behavior, and there were severe sanctions, including long imprisonment and execution. In the first one-half of the twentieth century, there was still a social repugnance of homosexuality, but formal sanctions were often somewhat less severe—court fines or jail terms of modest length, although informally, homosexuals were subjected to harassment, derision, discrimination, ostracism, and sometimes violence. In recent decades, however, public repulsion and condemnation of homosexuality had softened to the point that homosexuality was decriminalized or legalized in many states, and it was less stigmatic as evidenced by the fact that many persons openly admitted their homosexual inclination, including celebrities and even some persons running for public office. Homosexuality was openly labeled as simply an alternate sexual persuasion, and in some states and communities laws were passed prohibiting discrimination against or harassment of homosexuals, with relatively severe penalties. The clock had come full circle, as it were. The pendulum of public perception may be beginning to move in a reverse direction, however. The specter of AIDS and the possibility, if not probability, of a deathly epidemic involving millions of people is beginning to reshape public sentiment toward homosexuality. Initially the spread of AIDS appeared to be largely the result of homosexual activity. Subsequently, heterosexual behavior and intravenous injections of narcotics have also been identified as factors in the spread of AIDS. As the AIDS problem becomes more serious and more widespread, and society becomes more threatened, there is every reason to believe that social disapproval of homosexuality will drastically increase, with a concomitant effort to control or prohibit such sexual behavior and severe sanctions to enforce these efforts. If AIDS cannot be effectively addressed medically, then society may react toward homosexuals with great repression and abhorrence, if not malevolence. But, of course, homosexuality, like prostitution, may be diminished by voluntary withdrawal of those who engage in it as much as by coercion. Fear of AIDS may simply cause many individuals of homosexual persuasion to try and lead a monogamous homosexual life with a carefully selected partner, or to elect a celibate life.

In that sense, heterosexuals may be faced with a similar dilemma. In the late 19th century and into the first two decades of the 20th century, the "Victorian" ethic prevailed and sexual activity was sternly proscribed outside of marriage and highly circumscribed within marriage. In the 1920s there was some loosening of the sexual mores and more of a tendency toward sexual experimentation, and an increase in the incidence of sexual activity before marriage and outside of marriage. During the next few decades the movement in the direction of sexual permissiveness continued and involved an ever wider segment of the American population. By the late 1960s and the 1970s the so-called "sexual revolution" had blossomed across America with sexual liberation for almost everyone. The prevailing sentiment was "if it feels good, do it." Premarital sexual activity was extremely widespread, even among younger adolescents. Married couples sought advice from books and sexual experts for new directions in their sexual life. According to some polls and surveys, extramarital sexual activity became relatively common. Both young unmarried adults and divorced persons often sought a hedonistic lifestyle in the "swinging singles" culture, and sexual variations and behavior hitherto thought scandalous, degenerate, perverted, or even unimaginable, were incorporated into the sexual inventory of American culture and the sexual repertoire of many Americans. Pornography and sexually suggestive material became commonplace in the media. The traditional sexual norms became relaxed to the point that even the most taboo sexual behavior was viewed empathetically, if not with some degree of toleration. "Swingers" held national conventions, x-rated video tapes were available at the nearest video tape store, and "dial-a-porn" was as close as the telephone receiver. Experts began to counsel "humanistic treatment" (Giarretto, 1978), for incest offenders, and father-daughter incest became topics of prime-time entertainment with, in some instances, nonsocially disastrous outcomes.

As with other forms of sexual deviance, however, the cycle may be moving in a different direction. Some of the sexual excesses of the past two decades are diminishing. The sexually liberating lifestyle has proved to be disappointing, disillusioning, and dysfunctional for many. The excitement of sexual freedom is, perhaps, giving way to sexual ennui. Most importantly, the prospect of AIDS is causing an enormous amount of apprehension, concern, and fear. Sales of condoms are booming, young people are seeking advice on "safe sex," the promiscuous are becoming more selective, individuals are asking for an accounting of previous sexual history from prospective sexual partners, the "swinging singles" are moderating their lifestyles, and many young people are beginning to view an early marriage and a monogamous marriage thereafter as the only alternative, other than celibacy, available to be completely safe from AIDS.

In the future, there is every likelihood that the swing away from the sexually liberated value system of recent times will continue. Individuals will likely seek a more prudent and circumspect sexual lifestyle, both before and in marriage, because they may come to find it more emotionally rewarding, because it will offer a safeguard against AIDS, and because it may have a tremendously increased social support in terms of prevailing values and attitudes. Society, of course, will have a vested interest in tightening the control of sexual behavior, because of the generalized fear of AIDS.

THE DETECTION OF DEVIANCE

In centuries past, "mysterious" events, odd behavior, and singular circumstances might point conclusively to witchcraft and thereby implicate witches. In the 19th century, among the Zulus, the detection of deviance was the responsibility of the witch doctor. Periodically, the members of a village would be assembled and the witch doctor would closely inspect each person as he passed by them. He would "smell" evil in some, who would subsequently be put to death. Sometimes, at a "smelling out," as these ceremonies were known, hundreds of deviants were detected and dealt with. Even today in many folk societies (and in some industrial societies) answers to difficult questions are sought through the ancient process of divination—using bones, or tea leaves, or divination blocks, or even the entrails of a chicken. Among the questions that can be answered are inquiries concerning the future, one's fate, critical decisions, and matters of evil, malevolence, curses, hexes, crime and deviance. The guilty cannot escape detection, and the truth always reveals itself, at least as perceived by the diviner and the onlookers!

In the United States today we, of course, rely on a wide variety of highly sophisticated means of detecting crime and deviance, identifying the offender, and obtaining appropriate sanctions for the guilty. We detect speeding with radar devices, drunk driving with "breatholators" and blood tests, narcotic use with urinalysis, rape and similar sex crimes with blood and semen analysis, murder with autopsy, tax evasion with a computer, conspiracy with a wiretap, employee theft with a polygraph, and other types of crime and proscribed behavior with an array of equally technological advances, procedures and devices. We also use unsophisticated devices, such as trained dogs to detect smuggled narcotics, and terrorists' explosives. Detection by such means also usually provides the evidence necessary for arrest, indictment, and conviction.

In the future, the use of such sophisticated means to detect deviance will undoubtedly spread and intensify. Because of complex questions of law involving self-incrimination, invasion of privacy, and other aspects of civil rights, there will likely be vocal opposition, including protests, court cases, and perhaps even violence. There is little doubt, however, that the efficacy of such means will decide the issue in favor of their use. Unpopular or not, crime and deviance detection in the future will rely heavily on much improved existing techniques and procedures and other high technology yet to be developed. Computers, data banks, telecommunications, and various biometric monitoring devices will all play an ever greater instrumental role in crime detection and the apprehension and conviction of offenders. Even today, computers are being used to monitor employees' work behavior and urinalysis for drug use is already routine in some work situations. Computer monitoring and closed circuit surveillance, now relatively common, will probably become almost ubiquitous. Data banks such as the National Automotive Paint File will become increasingly used. This data bank permits the identification of hit-and-run vehicles "by comparing the composition of a paint sample from the suspect's vehicle with known automobile paints" in the file (Stephens, 1987:21). Technology will likely provide many other effective means of detecting crime and deviance. Routine breath, urine, and even blood analysis may become required in many situations in the future to monitor disease as well as deviance.

Technologies used to detect crime and deviance also serve to deter norm violations. Electronic detector devices in stores do tend to prevent or deter shoplifting, just as radar detectors cause many drivers to slow their speed, and burglar alarm systems tend to discourage break-ins. Already the technology exists to make most homes secure from burglary (Atlas, 1988) and in the future, this technology may well be included in homes in the way that air-conditioning and dishwashers are now.

Although there will be objections to the various kinds of intrusive technologies used to monitor and detect crime and deviance, they will prevail because they are effective! It has been generally recognized that current strategies of corrections and rehabilitation have been somewhat less than successful. With the jails and prisons already overcrowded to the point of sometimes having to release inmates prematurely in order to make room for incoming offenders, the public seeks an anticrime strategy that works and intrusive monitoring and surveillance does tend to prevent, deter, or at least minimize some kinds of crime and deviance. In time, members of society will come to accept or tolerate such intrusive efforts in the same way that they now accept and tolerate metal detection devices and baggage searches at airports—because it is a practical necessity!

Along with the high tech monitoring and surveillance, we will, unfortunately, see law enforcement authorities rely even more on entrapment or near entrapment as a strategy for making arrests and getting indictments and convictions. Today, of course, in some areas of criminal offenses, entrapment is a much used law enforcement tool. One prominent example is that of vice squad activities. In many cities, male vice squad officers pose as "johns" and importune women they think to be prostitutes. If a suspected prostitute "takes the bait," the vice officer may go so far as to accompany her to a hotel room, undress, and prepare to engage in sexual behavior. At this point the vice officer arrests the woman. Female vice officers play a similar game pretending to be prostitutes and soliciting customers. The male customers who may not have been actively seeking a prostitute may be tempted by this ruse, respond to the offer and then be arrested. Such techniques have been ruled acceptable by the courts.

It has been reported that agents of some governmental agencies sometimes attempt to illegally purchase a firearm from gun dealers, sometimes using convoluted dramaturgical routines, and then arrest the dealer if he agrees to sell the firearm. They also run a plethora of ads in firearm periodicals offering a wide variety of merchandise that is legal on the surface of it, but potentially illegal. They will, for example, offer gun parts that could be used to somehow modify a legal firearm into a configuration that is illegal. A particular type of trigger and sear mechanism may be legal by itself, but if installed in certain firearms, it might convert them into a gun capable of full-automatic fire, and therefore illegal. The usual approach is to run the ad and hopefully sell some of the gun parts or other merchandise. After a period of time, the agents may then raid the premises of some of the individuals who bought the parts in the hopes of finding a firearm that has been modified or altered in such a way that it is illegal.

Recently a particularly chilling account of entrapment was reported (Becker, 1988). The U.S. Postal Service and Customs, as part of an investigation of child pornography, arrested a dealer and obtained a customer list from him. They sent fake letters to persons on the list offering child pornography material. One customer placed an order and the law enforcement agents waited for him to pick up the package. The agents subsequently obtained a search warrant, seized pornographic material from his home and arrested him. They charged him with knowingly receiving pornographic material through the mail. He was tried and ultimately fined $10,000 and only bad health saved him from prison. He was sentenced to 200 hours of community service in addition to the fine. He could have received 10 years in prison and a $250,000 fine. He was a 66-year old, retired factory worker of limited education. More than 100 across the country were arrested and indicted in this scheme. Because entrapment seems to work so well, it will undoubtedly be used with greatly increased frequency in the future.

Technology has always been closely linked to crime and deviant behavior. The invention of the automobile precipitated at least one major pattern of crime—car theft! Of course, the automobile also facilitated all sorts of criminal activities, from bootlegging to kidnapping. The automobile made it easier and quicker to escape from the scene of a crime, to transport stolen merchandise, and to elude law enforcement officials. Conversely, the automobile aided law enforcement officials by making it easier to pursue offenders, easier to patrol and monitor an area, and quicker to reach the scene of a crime being committed. The invention of the computer paved the way for computer crime, and air piracy only began to occur after international airline travel became relatively commonplace.

Deviants have made good use of technology ranging from firearms to transportation devices to radios. The Polaroid camera and now the camcorder have made possible instant pornography in way of quick feedback for some kinds of sexual deviants. The photocopier has founded a whole counterfeiting and publishing piracy industry, and, of course, the telephone has long been a key implement in all sorts of swindles and confidence games, not to mention the obscene phone call and the telephone masturbator (Bryant, 1982). Even the early magneto telephone provided an expeditious means to poach fish. The poacher could put wires from a magneto into the water and "telephone" (shock) the fish so they would float to the top and be easily retrieved. Likely, the ingenious deviant and criminal offender of the future will make use of technological progress as effectively as will law enforcement officials. Some writers have predicted that in the future, the computer will make fraud the "Crime of Choice" (Albanes, 1988).

THE WHO AND WHY OF DEVIANCE IN THE FUTURE

Some new categories of deviants and victims may be more prominent in the future. Youth gangs, always a problem, are now posing a massive social problem in some areas. Deteriorating cities, widespread youth unemployment, and new immigrant groups who may be perceived as a threat to more established minority groups may all be factors contributing to youth gang phenomena.

There have always been childhood delinquents, but recent years have seen children of extremely young ages committing serious crimes (there was even a preteen bank robber) including crimes of violence. Narcotic use and alcohol abuse among even grade school children are not uncommon, and there are substantial numbers of sexually active children in their preteens. The high divorce rate, the resulting large numbers of one-parent families, and more families with both parents working all combine to leave the child alone and unsupervised at home. In such a setting, the likelihood of involvement in delinquent and deviant acts is much increased, and these trends are likely going to continue if not increase in the future. The same circumstances are leading to increased criminal victimization of children. It is estimated that one in five victims of rape in the U.S. is under 12 (Egger, 1985). Because of tensions in the home, abuse, or a poverty situation, many children run away, and a significant number are subsequently sexually exploited in child pornography enterprises, or become prostitutes. They may willingly become prostitutes, or in some cases, be abducted and forced into prostitution. In the future, children will continue to be a major category of crime and deviance victim, and perhaps a major category of offender as well. The unbroken cycle of poverty, the absence of one or more parents in the home, and the obvious contrast of life as portrayed by the media and the real life that they encounter every day, will continue to produce deviants and delinquents. Already some children are earning large amounts of money assisting in narcotic distribution. They may well serve as role models for other children.

In the future, there will be a significant increase in both the number and percentage of elderly persons in the population. Even though the elderly have not proved to be a crime prone group in the past, there is an increasing incidence of property crime by elderly offenders (Egger, 1985). Some old people, frustrated by their economic circumstances may well turn increasingly to theft, and other economic crime as a means of financing their living costs and enjoying a modicum of luxury in their life style. Inasmuch as they are often victims of both property and personal crime, many elderly persons today are banding together in crime prevention or "crime-watch" programs. Just as some victimized homosexual groups have resorted to vigilante action, so, too, may elderly citizens, if sufficiently frustrated by their victimization.

College campuses are increasingly becoming the locus of crime. There has always been deviance and crime on college campuses, of course, but generally of relatively minor consequences. These have included minor theft, vandalism, drunkenness, drunk driving, plagiarism, premarital sexual intercourse, and cheating on tests, to name but some. Today's crime on college campuses often includes grand theft, robbery and assault, rape, and even murder (Burgess, 1988). Only about 20% of campus crimes are perpetrated by nonstudents. This would suggest both that the college population is more crime and deviance prone than in the past, and that there is a greater temptation to commit such acts than in the past. In regard to the former, the "democratization" of the student body has produced a college population that more closely resembles the population at large. No longer only upper class "ladies and gentlemen," the student body consists of individuals of all walks of life. Social control is not as tight as was once the case and opportunity structure for crime and deviance is much enhanced from times past. Much high tech equipment is there for the stealing and brings high prices in the stolen goods market, or can be kept for personal use—electric typewriters and computers, for example. Females are not as restricted in their movement or closely monitored as in the past and are more vulnerable to assault and rape. College represents a big economic and social investment and students may be willing to break rules, if not laws, in order to stay in and graduate, by buying term papers, stealing tests, buying grade changes, or "hacking" into confidential computer banks. Narcotics sales bring big profits, and even robbery may net large yields. There is no doubt that in the future all of these trends will continue and the situation will be much exacerbated. The college student body of tomorrow will be much more victimized as will be the colleges themselves, and the same student body will have an inordinate share of offenders.

Society is seeing a surge of spontaneous deviance. Some drivers, frustrated by traffic and congestion, have shot persons in other cars. Arguments and trivial disputes that lead to violence and even death are not infrequent. There have been cases of individuals, perhaps driven by pressures to mental illness, who have literally exploded in violence, sometimes taking hostages or committing mass murder. Other citizens who have been previously victimized by criminals, are sometimes acting as one-person, vigilante efforts and initiating violence on would-be offenders. Frustrated individuals who felt themselves losers in divorce and child custody suits have resorted to abduction, violence, even murder and suicide. It should also be recalled that court decisions, legislation and some public sentiment have all contributed to the emptying of the mental hospitals. All of these kinds of behavior suggest a massive sense of frustration and loss of control. Helplessness and frustration may easily lead to loss of toleration, which in turn may result in a wide variety of antisocial deviance ranging from child battering to the murder of random persons on the street. Certainly the conditions which fuel such frustration may well be exacerbated in the future with the attendant deviant reaction and violence. Mass society may well lead inexorably to anomie.

THE RISE OF ANTISOCIAL ORDER DEVIANCE

Perhaps symptomatic of a larger social malaise is the disturbing appearance and increasing incidence of militancy among the malcontented or "private disobedience" as some authors have termed it (Scheel, 1986). Examples of such deviance might include the antiabortionist picketing, harassing, or even bombing an abortion clinic, or an environmentalist disrupting a deer hunt or driving spikes into trees that would ruin a chainsaw or injure a logger attempting to cut down the tree. Other instances of such behavior might be fired or otherwise disgruntled computer operator employees sabotaging the information stored in the computer by causing the computer program to self-destruct, or an unemployed factory worker attempting to sabotage the work plant or product it produces in his last few days on the job.

Such acts, perhaps, more represent antisocial order behavior than antisocial behavior. The individual is attempting to retaliate against the existing order of things that he perceives as the cause of his problems or hostile to his own self interests. This type of behavior, it is asserted, grows out of frustration and resentment, and many social and economic conditions have contributed to it. There is, and will be even more, competition for jobs and careers among the baby boomers. Technological change and foreign competition is causing great job dislocation and unemployment in the industrial sector. The increased cost of housing is depriving many people of the American dream of ever owning a home. Privacy in the workplace is being invaded by polygraph testing, mandatory urinalysis, computer monitoring of job behavior, and biometric security devices. Many new jobs are semi-skilled or in the service sector and pay less than traditional skilled jobs. New waves of immigrants from Asia, South and Central America, and Africa are taking many jobs traditionally held by blacks and other minority groups in this country. The increasing number of elderly persons are becoming more militant because of economic difficulties and perceived inequities in obtaining access to many areas of American life. The social and economic gap between management and professional level employees and blue-collar workers is becoming greater, as is the general gap between haves and have-nots. All of these trends and events of things and others as well are creating cleavages and fractures in the social structure, as well as frustrations and hostilities among those who feel themselves disadvantaged. The clash between diverse subcultural value systems, and ideological differences of opposing advocacy groups would seem to be growing more harsh. All of these conditions and trends are likely to be exacerbated in the future with a probably much increased frequency of private disobedience of widening variety. Deviant behavior then will more and more represent a type of protest and will, thus, have a "political" dimension to it.

In a similar vein, we are beginning to see more of an international flavor to protest or antisocial order deviance. Immigrant groups in the U.S. today not infrequently break the law by engaging in illegal demonstrations and violence against various foreign embassies and diplomats, as well as segments of the U.S. government and some industrial entities. (It should be recalled that several decades ago, members of a Puerto Rican "freedom" group stormed the White House in an attempt to kill President Truman, and did succeed in killing a guard). Some American terrorists groups, like the Weathermen, have had ties with foreign terrorist groups, and various American ethnic and nationality groups have actively engaged in gun-running to antigovernment groups in other nations. The South African controversy has even surfaced in upheaval and violence on some college campuses. Many antinuclear, and environmental protestors have international ties. There have been threats of international terrorism here in the U.S.

Just as business and industry has become multinational, so, too, has some forms of deviance. In the future, we will unquestionably see an increase and intensification of internationally linked, antisocial order deviance, especially in the form of political terrorism (Jenking, 1987). But we shall also see other forms of deviance, but still internationally linked, such as drug related crime, illegal immigration, weapon and technology smuggling, and money "laundering," spread and increase. We may also see the appearance of genuine new and chilling forms of internationally linked deviance, such as illegal body and body organ acquisition and smuggling schemes take advantage of new biotechnology breakthroughs. With even more improvements in mass communications and rapid global transportation in the future, more and more will crime and deviance not be circumscribed by national boundaries.

THE CONTINUING SEARCH FOR CAUSATION AND CURE

Throughout history many explanations for crime and deviance have been offered. Such explanations have run the gamut of possible causations ranging from possession by demons and spirits to evil and sin, to Flip Wilson's assertion that "the Devil made me do it!" A century ago, learned authorities were offering the opinion that physiognomy or the shape and other features of the face, and phrenology or the configuration of the skull might be an indicator of mental faculties and individual character, and especially a criminally prone character. In time, other aspects of anatomy and physiology were invoked as causative agents in deviance, as were heredity and mental deficiencies. Even in more recent periods, the search for biological factors in crime persists. Assorted theories in this regard were offered, including the notion of biological "inferiority," somatology with the ideal-type models of body type and physique with attendant behavioral characteristics—endormorphs, mesormorphs, and ectomorphs—and brain malfunction. The field of psychiatry offered mental disorders such as insanity and psychopathology and from the field of genetics came the anomaly of the XYY chromosome syndrome, or the fact of a male having an extra Y chromosome in every cell. Empirical evidence, particularly of contemporary variety, has not tended to support any of these diverse theories and notions.

In the future, the search for biological and genetic factors will certainly persist and new findings will provide new support for those of physiological conviction. Quite recently, for example, researchers at the University of California-San Francisco announced that they had discovered a difference between blood cells reproduced from the cells of alcoholics and those reproduced from cells of nonalcoholics, thus tending "to confirm epidemiologic evidence of an inherited aspect to alcohol dependency" (Associated Press,

1988). Laboratory and experimental work goes on now and will likely continue in the future seeking biological links to many types of crime and deviance. The emerging discipline of sociobiology, already attracting a wide following, will grown in advocacy and no doubt offer new insights in to the linkages between biology and behavior.

Other new and decidedly different, nonsocial science approaches to the explanation of crime and deviance will emerge. There is already a recognized influence of weather and climate on behavior. Law enforcement officials already take an interest in this connection and this area of behavioral influence could easily become a far more significant focus in the future (Lab and Hirschel, 1987). Already the Uniform Crime Reports provide a breakdown of crime rates by month and season of the year. Many other factors, such as temperature, humidity, precipitation, and length of daylight, not to mention moon phase, as they relate to behavior, may be more systematically examined in the future. Information in this area could impact on the deployment of law enforcement resources and personnel, closer attention to sociobiological influences of climatological conditions, and conceivably even efforts at weather control as crime control measures.

Considerable interest is now being given to possible biomedical factors in the causation of crime and deviance. There have been assertions that some deviant behavior may result from nutritional disorders, such as too much sugar or toxic additives in foods, as well as other problems such as vitamin deficiencies or an imbalance of peptides (Stephens, 1987). (It should be recalled that John Hinckley, the would-be assassin of President Reagan, was said to have been the victim of too much junk food). Such a line of thinking will probably have an impact on the treatment of crime and deviance as well. Already nausea-creating drugs are being used to treat alcohol abusers, and Depo-Provera, a drug that inhibits the sex drive, is being used to treat sex offenders. In the future, vitamin megadose therapy or peptide implements to release serotonin and lower levels of aggression may be commonplace treatments for some criminals and deviants (Montgomery and MacDougall, 1986). Researchers in the biophysical and medical fields will no doubt continue their search for biological causes of deviance in the hopes that such behavior can be addressed like disease—with a pill, a potion, or a shot—but their goal will likely be elusive. The public will likely watch and applaud the efforts, however.

The learned theologians of Medieval times engaged in disputatious debate concerning such matters as the number of angels who could dance on the head of a pin. In the recent decades of the 20th century, sociologists and other social scientists have similarly engaged in lively debates in regard to the explanation of deviance. Whole schools of thought have developed in support of the various ideological positions and every segment of every premise concerning sociology of norm violation has been exhaustively dissected and examined. The respective arguments and evidence of the various theoretical schools—structural/functional, social disorganization, social control, conflict, ethnomethodological, and labeling, among others—provide the intellectual substance for the subdiscipline.

No clear and complete sociological consensus has emerged, but there is agreement that deviance is a function of definitional conception and, thus, relative. There is further agreement that most deviant behavior is based directly or indirectly on socially causative factors, and can be functional as well as dysfunctional. Finally, there is accord that there is great social significance in the process that determines who, why and under what circumstances individuals are labeled as deviants, and what is the outcome.

In the final analysis the problem of achieving balance between public need and private prerogative, in an increasingly heterogenous society, may become so great that new ways of conceptualizing the normative order may be necessary. As one writer has asserted, there will be a need for a "middle ground" because "in a rapidly changing world, societal values will continuously be in flux, and lawmakers will have a difficult time keeping current laws in harmony with changing mores" (Stephens, 1987:20). In short as this author sees it, crime (and presumably most deviance) will come to be viewed as essentially a "conflict in values among competing interests" and "due process" may have to give way to "equity" as a means of sustaining social order.

REFERENCES

Albanese, Jay S.
1988 "Tomorrow's Thieves," The Futurist 22(5):24–28.

Alder,
1985 Outlaws of the Ocean. New York: Hearst Marine Books.

Associated Press
1988 "Study Backs Hereditary Links to Alcoholism," Roanoke Times & World News, (Thursday, Sept. 15), p. A4.

Atlas, Randall
1988 "Secure Homes: The Future of Anti-Crime Technology," The Futurist 22(2):25–28.

Austin, W. Timothy, and Samuel W. Garner
1980 "Light Up or Butt Out: An Assessment of Antismoking Laws in the United States," Deviant Behavior 1(3–4):395–410.

Bryant, Clifton D.
1979 Khaki-Collar Crime: Deviant Behavior in the Military Context. New York: The Free Press.

Bryant, Clifton D., and C. Eddie Palmer
1976 "Zoological Crime: A Typological Overview of Animal Related Laws and

Deviant Behavior." Paper read at the annual meeting of the Southwestern Social Science Association.

Bryant, Clifton D., and Donald J. Shoemaker
1975 "Briney Crime: An Overview of Marine and Maritime Deviancy and Delinquency." Paper read at the annual meeting of the Southwestern Social Science Society held in Atlanta, Georgia, April 9–12.

Bryant, Clifton D. (ed.)
1971 Social Problems Today: Dilemmas and Dissensus. Philadelphia: J. B. Lippincott.

Burgess, Mike
1988 "Wave of Violent Crime Sweeping Universities," U. The National College Newspaper, Vol. 1 (April), pp. 1–6.

Butler, Sandra
1978 Conspiracy of Silence: The Trauma of Incest. San Francisco: New Glide.

Carter, Timothy J., G. Howard Phillips, Joseph F. Donnermeyer, and Todd N. Wurschmidt (eds.)
1982 Rural Crime: Integrating Research and Prevention. Totowa (N.J.): Allanheld, Osmun & Co.

DeFrancis, Vincent
1963 Child Abuse: Preview of a Nationwide Survey. Denver: American Humane Society, Children's Division.

Eggar, Steven A.
1986 "The New Predators: Crime Enters the Future," The Futurist 19(2):15–18.

Forward, Susan, and Craig Buck
1978 Betrayal of Innocence: Incest and Its Devastation. Los Angeles: J. P. Tarcher.

Gelles, Richard J.
1974 The Violent Home: A Study of Physical Aggressions Between Husbands and Wives. Beverly Hills: Sage.

Helfer, Ray E., and Henry C. Kempe (eds.)
1968 The Battered Child. Chicago: The University of Chicago Press.

Horning, Donald N. M.
1970 "Blue-Collar Theft: Conceptions of Property, Attitudes Toward Pilfering, and Work Group Norms in a Modern Industrial Plant," Pp. 46–64 in Erwin O. Smigel and H. Lawrence Ross, eds., Crimes Against Bureaucracy. New York: Van Nostrand Reinhold.

Jenkins, Brian Michael
1987 "The Future Course of International Terrorism," The Futurist 21(4):8–14.

Lab, Steven P., and J. David Hirschel
1987 "Predicting Crime from the Weather," The Futurist 21(2):30–33.

Markle, Gerald E., Ronald J. Troyer
1979 "Smoke Gets in Your Eyes: Cigarette Smoking as Deviant Behavior," Social Problems 26(5):611–625.

Mizell, Terrance A., and Howard Robboy
1980 "Tender Feet and High Stepping: Soaring in the Tennessee Walking Horse Industry," Deviant Behavior 1(2):217–229.

Montgomery, Reid H., and Ellis C. McDougall
1988 "Curing Criminals: The High Tech Prison of Tomorrow," The Futurist 22(5):36–37.

Peterson, David M.
1971 "Informal Norms and Police Practice: The Case of the Quota System." Sociology and Social Research 55 (April):354–62.

Pfohl, Stephen J.
1977 "The Discovery of Child Abuse." Social Problems, 24(3):310–323.

Rose, Vicki McNickle
1977 "Rape as a Social Problem: A Byproduct of the Feminist Movement," Social Problems 25(1):75–89.

Rose, Vicki McNickle
1977 "The Effects of Rape," Social Problems 25(6):24–35.

Scheel, Randall L.
1986 "Private Disobedience: The New Militancy." The Futurist 20(3):16–18.

Stephens, Gene
1987 "Crime and Punishment: Forces Shaping the Future," The Futurist 21(1):18–26.

Stoddard, Ellwyn
1968 "The Informal 'Code' of Police Deviance: A Group Approach to 'Blue-Coat' Crime." Journal of Criminal Law, Criminology, Police Science 59 (June): 210–13.

Sutherland, Edwin H.
1940 "White-collar Criminality." American Sociological Review 5 (Feburary): 1–12.

Taylor, Craig
1971 "The 'Battered Child': Individual Victim of Family Brutality," pp. 210–216 in Clifton D. Bryant, ed., Social Problems Today: Dilemmas and Dissensus. Philadelphia: J. B. Lippincott.

Westley, William A.
1953 "Violence and the Police." American Journal of Sociology 59 (July):34–41.

Subject Index

Name Index